1 MONTH OF FREE READING

at

www.ForgottenBooks.com

By purchasing this book you are eligible for one month membership to ForgottenBooks.com, giving you unlimited access to our entire collection of over 700,000 titles via our web site and mobile apps.

To claim your free month visit:
www.forgottenbooks.com/free819029

ISBN 978-0-483-66647-4
PIBN 10819029

THE

NEW CHURCH REPOSITORY,

AND

MONTHLY REVIEW.

DEVOTED TO THE EXPOSITION

OF THE

PHILOSOPHY AND THEOLOGY

TAUGHT IN THE WRITINGS OF

EMANUEL SWEDENBORG.

CONDUCTED BY

GEORGE BUSH, A. M.

VOL. I.

NEW-YORK:

PUBLISHED BY JOHN ALLEN, 139 NASSAU STREET.

LONDON: J. S. HODSON AND W. NEWBERY.

1848.

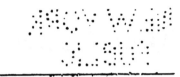

J. P. PRALL, Printer, 12 Spruce St., N. Y.

INDEX.

ORIGINAL PAPERS, &c.

BOOKS NOTICED.

POETRY.

THE

NEW CHURCH REPOSITORY

AND

MONTHLY REVIEW.

Vol. 1.　　　　　JANUARY, 1848.　　　　　No. 1.

EDITOR'S ADDRESS.

THE proposed publication of a periodical devoted to the interests of any department of the Christian Church seems naturally to call for a statement of the grounds and reasons of the undertaking.

The purpose in the present case has originated in a conviction, shared by many intelligent New Churchmen, that the present aspects of the cause which they have so deeply at heart demand a new organ of communication with themselves and with the world. This conviction is not uttered in disparagement of any work of the kind hitherto or at present existing as a stated vehicle of New Church sentiments and views. Several such have already been established and the issue continued for a longer or shorter time, but at the present moment a single journal only of this character exists in our country. We refer to the "New Jerusalem Magazine," published at Boston. This work has ever been judiciously conducted, and its original plan adhered to with so much unity of execution as to entitle it to the praise of a discreet and well sustained consistency from the outset. It has been the repository of numerous essays of permanent value as elucidations of the truths and principles of the New Church, and still continues to perform an important service in the sphere which it occupies. But its circulation has ever been limited, though its use, we are persuaded, is not to be measured by the extent of its subscription-list, as the proprietors have adopted a liberal policy in regard to its diffusion.

The progress of the Church, or of the principles which constitute the Church, have developed new exigencies, and however well adapted the Boston Magazine might have been to the circumstances in which it originated, it cannot, we think, be doubted that, at this day, there exists the necessity for a Periodical of wider scope and more varied character to meet the demands of the times. A few years since an acquaintance with Swedenborg's writings was almost wholly confined to New Church societies, and the sole incitement, which New Church writers felt, to literary effort, lay in the wants of this restricted circle. To elucidate the received doctrines of the Church, and to make them still more level to the ordinary understanding; to exhibit the doctrine of life in all its bearings upon the individual conscience, and to enforce the practical obligation of its precepts—these seemed almost the only functions which New Church pens were called upon to perform. The benefits which we ourselves and the Church at large have thus derived from the labors of men who are honored wherever they are known, we cordially acknowledge. Such services will always be in requisition in the Church, and we should be sorry not to contemplate a special provision for them in the plan of our Journal.

But other labors than these are now also called for—labors that shall respond to the moral demands made by those who have no present ecclesiastical sympathy with the Church, but only the sympathy that stands in the desire to learn, and a degree of preparation to acknowledge, the same exalted truths. The writings of Swedenborg are beginning to be widely diffused without the limits of New Church societies, and scarcely a week passes but we see in the popular journals proof of the deepening hold they are taking of the public attention. A manifest *curiosity* concerning them is aroused—a curiosity so marked and ominous as recently to have elicited two several works from distinguished Old Church theologians with a view to its extinction. The name of Swedenborg is no longer an offence to the popular ear—lectures expository of his philosophy and his theology meet almost every where numerous and respectful auditories—growing assemblages wait upon the services of our sanctuaries without the fear of exposing themselves to the peril of a contagious insanity—while tracts and other publications designed to set forth the doctrines of the New Jerusalem are with multitudes eagerly sought for. Without being unduly elated or made over-sanguine by these encouraging signs, we still cannot but feel that this altered state of the public mind calls for a corresponding change in New Church effort, and invites a publication adapted especially to *inquiring* spirits, one which shall aim to satisfy their thirst of further knowledge, and smooth their pathway to the courts of heavenly Truth.

A chief incitement to our undertaking is undoubtedly to be found in the extraordinary advance which is making in the sphere of the Sciences—an advance which, by necessitating a corresponding elevation of religious faith, seems likely ere long to exhaust the Old Church

THE

NEW CHURCH REPOSITORY

AND

MONTHLY REVIEW.

Vol. 1.   **JANUARY, 1848.**   **No. 1.**

EDITOR'S ADDRESS.

THE proposed publication of a periodical devoted to the interests of any department of the Christian Church seems naturally to call for a statement of the grounds and reasons of the undertaking.

The purpose in the present case has originated in a conviction, shared by many intelligent New Churchmen, that the present aspects of the cause which they have so deeply at heart demand a new organ of communication with themselves and with the world. This conviction is not uttered in disparagement of any work of the kind hitherto or at present existing as a stated vehicle of New Church sentiments and views. Several such have already been established and the issue continued for a longer or shorter time, but at the present moment a single journal only of this character exists in our country. We refer to the "New Jerusalem Magazine," published at Boston. This work has ever been judiciously conducted, and its original plan adhered to with so much unity of execution as to entitle it to the praise of a discreet and well sustained consistency from the outset. It has been the repository of numerous essays of permanent value as elucidations of the truths and principles of the New Church, and still continues to perform an important service in the sphere which it occupies. But its circulation has ever been limited, though its use, we are persuaded, is not to be measured by the extent of its subscription-list, as the proprietors have adopted a liberal policy in regard to its diffusion.

The progress of the Church, or of the principles which constitute the Church, have developed new exigencies, and however well adapted

so long as variant views of doctrine are entertained by minds equally intent upon the attainment of truth, we know no sound reason for refusing a hearing to both sides of debateable topics, provided ever that the disputants shun a resort to harsh personalities and indecorous crimination of motive. The Editor will in no case deem himself responsible for the sentiments advanced by correspondents, although it is to be expected that the tenor of all communications will be in accordance with the general plan and scope of the work. If the positions of any writer are assailed, he is to be supposed competent to defend them, and upon him will it rest.

A prominent department of the Journal will be given to Reviews, more or less extensive, of such issues of the press as shall be especially entitled to the attention of New Churchmen. In the conduct of this department we shall aim to divest ourselves of all that prejudice or favoritism which would prevent the exercise of an impartial censor ship of the various works that may come under our notice.

We deem it also expedient that some portion of our pages should be devoted to the exegesis or critical explanation of the Sacred Text, especially with a view to discover how far a light may be cast upon the spiritual sense by a careful study of the literal. In the accomplishment of this object we shall of necessity have recourse to the inspired originals, and as occasion may offer shall propound amended versions of passages deemed to be erroneously rendered.

The plan we contemplate will necessarily involve the consideration of the prominent theological dogmas of the Old Church, whether Papal or Protestant, and the attempt to hold up their apprehended errors and fallacies in contrast with the celestial certainties that mark the system of the New Jerusalem as unfolded in the writings of its appointed herald. But in doing this we shall aim to preserve the spirit of meekness and the laws of candor, and to abstain from all distortion and caricature in the exhibition of religious doctrines which, however erroneous in our view, are still held with honest conviction and regarded with devout reverence by their adherents. Opportunity however will be freely given to all those who shall, in a Christian spirit, be disposed to question or canvass any of the leading doctrines of the New Church, or to array against them, on the ground of reason or Scripture, the coun ter tenets of the prevailing theology. In such cases we shall of course reserve to ourselves the right of reply, as our sole object in the proffer is to elicit truth by the attrition of argument.

In the more miscellaneous province of the Journal we shall make it an object to chronicle all the important events of the passing times that may have a bearing on the fortunes or interests of the Church—to notice the movement of ecclesiastical bodies in the connection—to record such documents and reports as may subserve the future history of the Church—and to incorporate such information in Science, Lite-

of all cordial and rational allegiance to its spiritual authorities. The varied walks of physical science are daily unfolding such marvels of order and goodness in the natural creation, as to beget an irresistible conviction of the prevalence of a like order and goodness in the spiritual creation, while the irrepressible yearnings of the philosophic mind incessantly sigh for access to that sphere of *causes* which has hitherto been precluded it. The Old Church does next to nothing to enlighten or guide this nascent sentiment: she even denies the spiritual creation to be a proper object of thought or knowledge, and consequently frowns upon every attempt to communicate its sublime lore to her children. Has the Divine Providence then left this urgent want uncared for? Is it for Faith simply to believe in and to guess at a spiritual world without the rational intelligence of its verities, or any clear perception of the law which connects the natural with the spiritual, and thus sanctifies Science by wedding it with Religion? Every enlightened New Churchman will unhesitatingly answer, No, because he is firmly persuaded that the interior sense of Scripture, as unfolded by its science of correspondences, proclaims an order in the spiritual creation unspeakably more grand and impressive than any sensible order can be, and that nothing more is requisite to the perception of the harmony which reigns between the spheres of nature and spirit, than a mind studious of truth from the love of its underlying good. Disclaiming, however, for ourselves any peculiar ability to connect the higher facts of science with the spiritual truths of which they are representative, we profess simply to stand in the forecourt of the magnificent temple of knowledge which is now opening to the human intellect, and though not unvisited by occasional gleams of the central effulgence, yet we by no means boast of any complete illumination. It is as disciples rather than as teachers that we present ourselves—disciples of truth in every sphere, because we believe it to be in all alike one and divine. But it shall be our endeavor, with all our strength, whether great or little, to annul the divorce which has taken place between science and religion, by displaying the rational correspondence which unites the truth of both. In order to do this worthily we should doubtless need an ampler space than we can now promise ourselves, but always to do it as well as our means allow, will be a leading object of our Journal.

The grand purpose of our projected enterprise is to furnish a repository of all the most valuable exposition, discussion, and information which can be concentrated in its pages. Without surrendering the right of judgment as to the suitableness of the matter presented to the general aim and objects of the work, we would still fain impress upon it a character of freedom and liberality. The interchange of opposite opinions, when conducted in the spirit of charity, can scarcely be termed controversy, *at least in the offensive* sense of the term, and so long as variant views of doctrine are entertained by minds equally intent upon the attainment of truth, we know no sound reason for refusing a hearing to both sides of debateable topics, provided ever that the disputants shun a resort to harsh personalities and indecorous crimination of motive. The Editor will in no case deem himself responsible for the sentiments advanced by correspondents, although it is to be expected that the tenor of all communications will be in accordance with the general plan and scope of the work. If the positions of any writer are assailed, he is to be supposed competent to defend them, and upon him will it rest.

A prominent department of the Journal will be given to Reviews, more or less extensive, of such issues of the press as shall be especially entitled to the attention of New Churchmen. In the conduct of this department we shall aim to divest ourselves of all that prejudice or favoritism which would prevent the exercise of an impartial censorship of the various works that may come under our notice.

We deem it also expedient that some portion of our pages should be devoted to the exegesis or critical explanation of the Sacred Text, especially with a view to discover how far a light may be cast upon the spiritual sense by a careful study of the literal. In the accomplishment of this object we shall of necessity have recourse to the inspired originals, and as occasion may offer shall propound amended versions of passages deemed to be erroneously rendered.

The plan we contemplate will necessarily involve the consideration of the prominent theological dogmas of the Old Church, whether Papal or Protestant, and the attempt to hold up their apprehended errors and fallacies in contrast with the celestial certainties that mark the system of the New Jerusalem as unfolded in the writings of its appointed herald. But in doing this we shall aim to preserve the spirit of meekness and the laws of candor, and to abstain from all distortion and caricature in the exhibition of religious doctrines which, however erroneous in our view, are still held with honest conviction and regarded with devout reverence by their adherents. Opportunity however will be freely given to all those who shall, in a Christian spirit, be disposed to question or canvass any of the leading doctrines of the New Church, or to array against them, on the ground of reason or Scripture, the counter tenets of the prevailing theology. In such cases we shall of course reserve to ourselves the right of reply, as our sole object in the proffer is to elicit truth by the attrition of argument.

In the more miscellaneous province of the Journal we shall make it an object to chronicle all the important events of the passing times that may have a bearing on the fortunes or interests of the Church—to notice the movement of ecclesiastical bodies in the connection—to record such documents and reports as may subserve the future history of the Church—and to incorporate such information in Science, Literature, and Art, as may tend to confirm and illustrate the principles that distinguish the system we profess to have received.

Such is a general outline or programme of the work which we propose to issue. Various other items will doubtless enter the details, which will be suggested by experience whenever the undertaking has got fairly under way. It is impossible to anticipate in the outset all the aspects which the work may assume in its progress. But the *ideal* of the enterprise, we flatter ourselves, will meet the general views of the friends of the New Church, and if we may venture to count upon the available talent which we know to exist among the members of the church, we shall have little hesitation in promising to our readers and patrons a publication in some degree worthy of the cause it is designed to represent, and of the countenance we invoke for it.

It is obvious that the *materiel* of such a work as we here announce can only be supplied by the joint contributions of those who may be at once both qualified and disposed to enlist in its support. These, for the present, must be free-will offerings, as the resources of the publication, being but scanty in the outset, do not enable us to hold out the prospect of pecuniary recompence. It will still be our object, however. to stimulate aid by this incentive whenever the proceeds of the work will warrant it. Meantime, we have no doubt that there is abundant ability in the Church to sustain our labors, if that ability is but coupled with such a degree of interest in the undertaking as we may reasonably presume upon from those who have given in their adhesion to truths of the New Church. We are, therefore, emboldened to appeal to all those who *can* co-operate with our enterprise, freely and fraternally to do it. We venture to commend it to their auspices as an enterprise entitled to an interest proportioned to that which they feel in the grand system itself to which they have become devoted. If their present views are dear to them, and if they are intrinsically calculated to be equally precious to others, why should they not be deeply stirred to their dissemination? To minds of different orders, and of different habitudes of thought, the philosophical or theological principles of the Church will naturally present themselves under different aspects, while still a substantial unity reigns throughout, and this diversity of view may be easily made to redound to the spiritual benefit of others. We earnestly invoke, therefore, in behalf of the sacred cause to which we are pledged, under the most solemn assurance that it is the TRUTH OF GOD, the sympathy and succor of our brethren in the faith, in order to an effective presentation of the grand system of doctrine and life vouchsafed to the world in these latter days. As it is the felicity of the New Church to possess a revelation of the grand doctrines of the Word so clear as to preclude all debate respecting *fundamentals*, there is nothing, we conceive, in the minor points of difference, here and there occurring among *receivers, which ought to* operate as a bar to a united expres sion of sentiment upon the cardinal topics ; and it is these especially that we wish to propound to the consideration of all seriously reflecting minds. As we have every confidence that the grand positions we have been led to assume will stand the strictest test both of Scripture and reason—that every tenet we have embraced is defensible on the ground of logical argument, as well as responsive to the voice of our higher moral intuitions—we deem it proper to plant around them every legitimate form of munition, and while we do not aim to make our movement directly aggressive against the errors of the prevailing faith, yet as in spiritual things the negation of evil is the presence of good, so the confutation of falsity is the establishment of truth, and truth established is the invasion of darkness by the approach of light. Virtually then our labors may be considered as aggressive, and in this we can hardly doubt that we are fulfilling the counsels of the Divine Providence in regard to the mission of the Church of the New Jerusalem, which can only become the "crown of all other Churches" by the dispersion of their evils and falses and the appropriation of their goods and truths. In this work it is surely an honor and a blessedness to be engaged, a full conviction of which would leave little to be effected by our own solicitations, however urgent.

ORIGINAL PAPERS.

ARTICLE I.

THE SACRED SCRIPTURE.—No. 1.[*]

"I envy," says that great philosopher, Sir Humphrey Davy, "no quality of the mind or intellect in others; not genius, power, wit, or fancy. But if I could choose what would be most delightful, and I believe most useful to me, I should prefer a firm religious belief to every other blessing. For it makes life a discipline of goodness, creates new hopes when all earthly hopes vanish, and throws over the decay and destruction of existence, the most gorgeous of all lights; awakens life even in death, and from corruption and decay calls up beauty and divinity; makes an instrument of torture and of shame the ladder of ascent to paradise; and, far above all combinations of earthly hopes, calls up the most delightful visions of palms and amaranths, the gardens of the blest, the security of everlasting joys, where the sensualist and the sceptic view only gloom, decay, annihilation, and despair."

"*A firm religious belief.*"—Who that is wise would *not* prefer this to every other blessing? And on what can a *firm* religious belief rest, but on THE WORD OF GOD? And how can it rest on this foundation—calmly, peacefully, and *firmly*—unless we are firmly convinced that the written Word is divine—is God's Word and not man's—and that we rightly understand its meaning? So far as we are in doubt on either of these points, just so far must our religious faith waver. Are there no doubts on these points?—doubts not only in the minds of the irreligious, but in the minds of professedly religious men?

I read some time ago an article upon the Sacred Scripture in one of the ablest religious periodicals of our country,[†] in which the writer, himself a clergyman in external connection with the Old Church, has the following remarks:

"No one, who is accustomed to regard with much attention

---

[*] The present article is part of a Lecture introductory to a series of Lectures on the Sacred Scripture, delivered some time since in this city. The sequel will appear in our next number.

[†] The Christian Examiner for Jan. 1844.

the history and tendency of religious opinions, can fail of being convinced, that the question [concerning the inspiration of the Scriptures] is soon to become the most absorbing question of Christian Theology. The minds of men are in that position in reference to this subject, which cannot long be maintained. They must move one way or the other. They must attain to some sort of consistency, either by believing less, or by believing more. The authority of the Scriptures, and especially those of the Old Testament, must either become higher and stronger, or be reduced almost to nothing. It is vain to imagine that with the present secret or open scepticism, or at least vague and unsettled notions, with which they are regarded, even by many who are defenders of a special revelation, they can be read and taught in our churches, schools, and families, as books *sui generis*, so as to command much of real reverence for themselves."

"For ourselves," continues this writer, "we are at no loss in deciding as to which direction opinions will ultimately tend. We are satisfied that the Scriptures are to open out their revelations with new light and beauty upon the human mind."

It is obvious that this writer had caught some gleams of the truth. It is most undoubtedly true, as he says, that the question concerning the Sacred Scripture or Word of God, involving that of its supreme divinity, the nature and extent of its inspiration, the laws of its composition, the principle according to which its true meaning is to be elicited, *is* soon to become *the* question in Christian Theology. For IT IS THE QUESTION of questions. And it is not only true, as this writer affirms, that the minds of men cannot long maintain their present position in reference to the Scripture—that they must move either one way or the other—but it is true that they are already moving, some in one direction and some in another. One class—and this by far the largest it is to be feared—are coming to believe less and less, and another class to believe more and more.

The fact, we think, is too palpable to be denied, that reverence for the Sacred Scripture as the Word of God, has been rapidly diminishing for the last half century throughout our country and throughout the professed Christian world. True it is that men continue to *call* the Bible the Word of God as formerly, and to read it in their families and in their churches. And this is something—far better than the total neglect of it. But how few comparatively will you find, who attach to this title the meaning which it naturally conveys, or which was formerly attached to it! What proportion of the people in almost any Christian community approach the Bible as devoutly now, and study its pages as diligently, and listen to its teachings as reverently, and plant their footsteps as trustingly on this ROCK OF AGES, as did the Christians in the early age of the Church ? Is the authority of the Scripture as controling and absolute as it once was ? When men read it, or hear it read, do they hear there the voice of the living God as they once heard it? Is there the same undoubting and prevailing faith in its divine inspiration, and consequently in its complete infallibility, that there once was? Is there not on the contrary abundant reason for believing, that there exists in the bosom of the great body of the professed Christian Church a vast amount of latent infidelity? Are there not a great many persons who have doubts—serious and honest doubts, which perhaps they seldom if ever express—whether the Scripture be divinely inspired, and whether therefore it be the Word of God in any strict or proper sense?

We think there cannot be much difference of opinion upon any of these points among candid, reflecting, and observing men.*

And if, as we think must be admitted by all, the Sacred Scripture is gradually losing its authority, and falling into disrepute with a large and continually increasing class of minds—if honest doubters respecting its divine inspiration are every year multiplying, and scepticism waxing bolder and bolder—it is indeed a calamity of all others the most to be deplored. I know of no calamity that can befal an individual, a community, or a state—I can imagine none—so dreadful as a loss of reverence for the Holy Scripture, or of faith in the infallibility of its teachings. For a loss of this cannot fail to be accompanied or followed by a loss of reverence for God and his laws—a loss of pure religion and virtue—a loss of heavenly desires, heavenly hopes, heavenly aims, and heavenly graces—a loss of that

---

* Since the above paragraphs were first written, a singular book has been published, entitled "The Principles of Nature, her Divine Revelations, and a Voice to Mankind, by and through Andrew Jackson Davis, the Poughkeepsie Seer and Clairvoyant."

This book denies in the boldest and most positive manner every thing like *inspiration* in the Scripture, and treats the Bible in the same manner, and with as little reverence or respect, as it is treated in Paine's "Age of Reason." And not only does it pronounce the Bible altogether *uninspired*, but declares "that the elements and qualities contained in the Bible are *positively impure.*" Yet this book—avowedly infidel as it is respecting the divinity and inspiration of the Scripture—has met with a rapid and almost unprecedented sale. Many who have read it, have openly declared their belief in the truth of its teachings concerning the Scripture as well as concerning other things; and even some professing Christians, and ministers of the Gospel, have sought to promulgate the doctrines of this book by public Lectures and otherwise, and have manifested a zeal worthy of a better cause. Are not these facts full of mournful significance ? Must not men's reverence for the Scripture as the Word of God be feeble and ill-founded indeed, when it can be thus easily and suddenly uprooted and destroyed ?

righteousness which alone can exalt an individual or a nation. Hence it is the constant endeavor of the Divine Providence to keep men in some degree of acknowledgment and reverence of the written Word; for however unintelligent and blind that reverence be, it is still better than none, since while it remains, the Word is a Divine Medium of consociation with the angels and of conjunction with the Lord.

Several causes may be enumerated of that irreverent and sceptical tendency of men's minds with regard to the Scripture, to which we have adverted. To say nothing of the opposition of the mind of the natural man to the mind or will of God, which is one fruitful cause, we may mention in the first place the exceedingly loose and low views of the nature and extent of inspiration, which have been gaining currency for the last few centuries among Christian teachers and theologians themselves. It is matter of history, to which we shall have occasion to allude hereafter, that since the time of the Reformation there has been a gradual downward progress of opinion in the Church respecting the inspiration of the Scripture, until at last it has reached a point so low, that it is extremely difficult in many cases to draw the line between it and no inspiration whatever. When a kind of inspiration comes to be generally attributed to the Scripture, which differs so little from that which is admitted to belong to all other books, that it is difficult for the learned to distinguish between them, is it to be expected that the Scripture can long command for itself a reverence much superior to that which is felt for other books? Men cannot reverence the Scripture as the Word of God, while they are allowed, and even *taught,* to believe that many human errors, prejudices, passions, and infirmities, are mingled with it.

Another cause of the existing and increasing disregard for the Scripture is, the great number of sects into which the Christian Church is divided, and the innumerable volumes of commentaries on the Word, which have been published, and which are known to contain not only different, but often conflicting and opposite, views of the same text. It is natural (is it not?) that men should by degrees lose their reverence for that about which there is so little agreement and so much dispute, as there has been and is about the Scripture, even among those who have studied it most, and who might, therefore, be considered the most competent to decide upon its meaning.

Another natural and very fruitful cause of the downward progress of men's minds in regard to the Scripture so observable at the present time, is to be found in the many irrational and absurd doctrines, which are confidently put forth from the pulpit and the press as the doctrines of the Bible. And it is commonly supposed that they *are* really taught in the Bible. Yet some of these doctrines are not only unreasonable and unphilosophical, but such as require of men a complete surrender—nay, an absolute crucifixon or annihilation of their reason, before they can be received.

Theologians themselves have long been aware of the want of accord between the doctrines of their creeds, and man's sober reason. Hence it has long been, and still continues to be, the fashion with many religious teachers to depreciate human reason in matters of religion, thinking thereby to exalt the wisdom of God. This is the way in which they have sought to oppose the introduction and progress of every new truth in philosophy or religion : this is the way that the religious error which now darkens the sky and blackens the face of the moral world, has crept in and been propagated from age to age in the church. It is by undervaluing human reason ; by teaching men to trample on their understanding, to reject all reason and common sense in religious matters, as " the wisdom of this world," which is in opposition to the wisdom of God ; and to yield a blind and unquestioning assent, not to the Word of God, but to the false and foolish construction which unauthorized and fallible men have put upon the Word. This is the way that Romanism has managed for so long a time so rivet its fetters and maintain its grasp on human minds, by discarding the exercise of reason, and denying the right of private judgment in the things of religion. And this is the way that Protestantism has contrived to gain the assent of such multitudes to dogmas that are scarcely less irrational than transubstantiation, purgatory, the canonization and invocation of dead men. And this is the way that *all false* doctrines must, and will, seek to retain their hold on the minds of men,—by denying and discarding the use of reason in matters of faith.

But the cause of true religion never has been, and never can be, advanced by this blind surrender of our understanding to our faith. And when a man's religious doctrines are such, that they cannot stand before a sound and enlightened reason —that they shrink from a too close inspection by reason's eye— you may set it down as good evidence that his doctrines are not true. No : God is a reasonable Being. He does nothing that is unreasonable ; He teaches nothing that is unreasonable, and He requires no one to believe that which is unreasonable, and every intelligent and reflecting man knows this. Our Reason is from Him, and is one of His noblest gifts. And those who rail at the use of reason in matters of faith, should know that they thereby do but a poor service for God or religion.

What wonder, therefore, in this age of free thought and searching inquiry, that men should doubt whether doctrines, which demand an absolute surrender of their reason, could ever have emanated from the God of Truth! And believing that such doctrines are really taught in the Bible, what wonder that they should have secret doubts whether the Bible be indeed the Book of God!

Another cause of the growing scepticism in regard to the divinity of the Word, may be found in the modern prevailing and generally-admitted principles of sacred hermeneutics or science of biblical interpretation. It is taught in all our theological seminaries, and by clergymen of the old church generally, that the Bible is composed like any other book, and consequently is to be interpreted in the same manner as any other book, i. e. in the same manner as if it were a merely human production; that there is but one sense to Scripture, and this the sense which the writers themselves intended, and which was understood by those whom they originally addressed.* This one sense, such as the Jews themselves understood, is, of course, the lowest, most external, or literal sense.

Thus the Bible has come to be regarded and spoken of by professing Christians generally as altogether human in the style of its composition, and therefore as a book to be interpreted like any other human composition. Anything like a

---

* Prof. Stuart says: "There is one simple principle that should run through all preaching and all expositions; which is, that *the mind of the scriptural writer* should be given as it was originally expressed by his *language*. The *meaning* of any book is simply what the writer had in his own mind and intended to express. This being given the work of interpretation is done."—*Hints on Prophecy*, p. 42.

Again, this author says: "If now we could in all respects place ourselves in the condition of those who were originally addressed by the sacred writers, we should then understand at once nearly every thing [why not *every* thing?] in the Scriptures without any difficulty; just as easily as we now understand religious instructions from our pulpits."—*Ib.* p. 45.

Thus also, Prof. McLellan, in his "Manual of Sacred Interpretation," designed for the special use of Theological Students, lays down several *Maxims*, which he would have to be the guide of every one who enters upon the task of biblical exegesis. Among them are the following:

MAXIM I. "*The object of Interpretation is to give the precise thoughts which the sacred writer intended to express*. No other meaning is to be sought, but that which lies in the words themselves, as he employed them." But may he not have employed words of which he himself did not understand the meaning? Daniel at least affirms that this was the case with him. "I came near unto one of them that stood by, and asked him the truth (*i. e.* the true meaning) of all this. So he told me, and made me to know the interpretation of the things." "And it came to pass when I, even I Daniel, had seen the vision and sought for the meaning, then, behold, etc."

divine style as characterizing or belonging to the Scripture, is virtually denied on all hands: consequently anything like an internal or spiritual sense—a sense, be it remembered, which was *uniformly* admitted by the fathers of the Christian church —and which is to be developed by any divine rule of exegesis, is utterly rejected.

Now as the rational faculty of man is continually becoming more and more unfolded, and freedom of thought on all subjects is beginning to be everywhere asserted, and men discover many things in the Bible, which, according to their plain, obvious, literal import, appear unreasonable, many things trivial and unimportant, many things attributed to the Divine Being entirely contrary to an enlightened idea of His character and attributes, some things asserted which appear plainly to contradict other things,—when men, I say, in the exercise of their free thought and sober reason, discover all this in the Scripture, and when at the same time they find all escape from these difficulties absolutely precluded by what are called *the settled principles of Biblical interpretation,* and the established theological maxim that there is but one *sense* to the Scripture, and this the apparent and obvious one, *is* it much to be wondered at that doubts should arise in many minds respecting the divine origin of the Scripture? When reasoning and reflecting men, in the full and free exercise of their rational powers— which alike with the Scripture are the gift of God—learn from the Bible that our earth was clothed with living verdure before the natural sun was created,—nay, that light existed, and was separated from the darkness too, before the sun, moon, or stars were made,—when they learn that the first human pair in their earliest prime—before they were a week old—unwarned of

---

MAXIM II. "*Scripture is to be interpreted in the same method which we employ in discovering the meaning of any other book.* It was indited to men; it speaks to men in the language of men; and was to be understood by those to whom, in ancient times, it was addressed, as they understood any other communication. The design of God in giving it was to communicate certain ideas—in order to which he must speak to us, *just as do others.* * * * In reading Scripture, therefore, we are to use the same appliances and aids employed in other cases. Inspiration gives it no special privileges."

MAXIM III. "*The sense of Scripture is* (*in general*) ONE: *in other words, we are not to assign many meanings to a passage.* * * * Without affirming that there are no secondary senses in Scripture, we believe that (the phrase being properly understood) there are very few. Generally, the meaning is, as in other books, *one;* and that lies near the surface. Who ever heard of a man in common conversation attaching different signification to the words he used—unless indeed he was playing a game at riddles, or *double* entendres ?'"

Such are the principles of sacred hermeneutics in vogue in our Theological Schools. What are they but a virtual denial of any divine element in the Word—of any sense or significance beyond the *intention* of the several writers? Let any man of intelligence ask himself what work these principles would make with many of the Psalms of David, and with many of the oracles of the Prophets.

the approach of their subtle foe, and ignorant of the consequences of yielding to him, were permitted to be tempted and led astray by the lowest and meanest creature in the animal kingdom, thereby involving all the future and unborn generations of men in their own crime of disobedience,—when they read of robberies, wars, and inhuman massacres, committed by the express command of Jehovah God,—when they find the worst of human passions, anger, hatred, jealousy, and revenge, attributed to the Divine Being Himself,—when they read of the journeyings and encampments of the children of Israel in the wilderness, the particular account of their sacrifices, of the different animals offered and the mode of offering them, of the dress of particular persons, as of Aaron and his sons, the minute description of the tabernacle, its hangings, its cloths of service, its rings of gold, its spoons and bowls, its candlestick with its branches, bowls, knops and flowers,—when men in the free exercise of their rationality read all this, and many other things of a like nature in the Bible, and when at the same time they find themselves shut up to the bare cortex of the letter by the authority of the professed expounders of the Bible—not allowed to go beyond the one, plain, obvious, and literal sense of what is recorded, *is* it much to be wondered at that doubts should arise in their minds whether this was really dictated by the Holy Spirit, and whether the Bible be indeed the Word of God? Is it strange, that men should ask themselves the question, If there be no higher meaning to this than that which the Jews themselves understood, and which is apparent in the sense of the letter, how is it inspired? Wherein lies its divinity and its sanctity? What need was there of any especial and peculiar operation of the Holy Spirit upon the minds of the writers to enable them to record such things?

"It is universally confessed," says Swedenborg, "that the Word is from God, is divinely inspired, and of consequence holy; but still it has remained a secret to this day in what part of the Word its divinity resides, inasmuch as in the letter it appears like a common writing, composed in a strange style, neither so sublime nor so elegant as that which distinguishes the best secular compositions. Hence it is, that whosoever worships nature instead of God, or in preference to God, or in consequence of such worship makes himself and his own *proprium* the centre and fountain of his thoughts, instead of deriving them out of heaven from the Lord, may easily fall into error concerning the Word, and into contempt for it, and say within himself whilst he reads it, What is the meaning of this passage? What is the meaning of that? Is it possible this should be divine? Is it possible that God, whose wisdom is infinite, should speak in this manner? Where is its sanctity, or whence can it be derived, but from superstition and credulity?

" Lest therefore, mankind should remain any longer in doubt concerning the divinity of the Word, it has pleased the Lord to reveal to me its internal sense, which in its essence is spiritual, and which is, to the external sense, which is natural, what the soul is to the body. This internal sense is the spirit which gives life to the letter; wherefore this sense will evince the divinity and sanctity of the Word, and may convince even the natural man, if he has a disposition to be convinced."—*D. S. S.* 1, 4.

We have thus glanced at some of the principal and more obvious causes of the sceptical tendencies of our age, and of that growing irreverence of the Word of God which is so manifest and so much to be deplored. These causes are constant and unremitting in their operation; and as we need not expect that the progress of that scepticism and irreverence which we deplore, can ever be checked, except by removing them, or by setting in operation different and countervailing causes,—by presenting to the minds of men considerations in regard to the Scripture, of sufficient weight to produce different effects from those which we know have been produced by causes that still exist. We need not expect that men will abandon their doubts respecting the divine origin of the Scripture, until they see reasons for abandoning them. They will not have different feelings towards the Scripture, until they have different views of its inspiration, its divinity, and *its meaning.* They will not revere it as the Word of God, until they are *rationally convinced that it is such.*

The mass of men in christendom were once willing to receive their theology, as they did their philosophy, upon authority—the authority of a few individuals. They were content to receive what the minister, the church, the prayer-book, or the catechism taught, without asking or caring to know the reasons for it. They were told that the Bible was divine and holy, and must be reverenced as the Word of God: they believed and obeyed. And there is something which we cannot help admiring in this simple faith, as there is in the faith of little children. But, however much we may lament it, the fact is indisputable, that the world, or a considerable portion of it at least, has passed beyond this simple, believing, child-like state. It has arrived at years of manhood, when it instinctively withholds its assent from the mere dicta of priests or prophets, unless it is shown the reason why. It can never return to its childhood, nor to childhood's simple faith, except in the way that a man becomes a child again. *It can never again* have a blind faith. No: henceforward men will have a faith which answers the severest demands of an enlightened reason, or they will have no faith. And it is in vain to talk of the divinity and sanctity of the Scripture, or to urge upon men their obligation to believe, love, and reverence it as the Word of God, unless we show them in a manner to satisfy their sober reason, that it is altogether divine and holy—the veritable voice of God to man. It is useless to ask or to expect a blind reverence for the Scripture at this severely questioning age of the world. The time is rapidly approaching, when men will have an *intelligent* reverence for the Bible, or they will have no reverence. The world in its manhood must be treated as we treat men, not as we treat children.

I doubt not but a large number of persons may be found in almost every Christian community, who have doubts—honest doubts—respecting the divine origin of Scripture, which, perhaps, they *dare* not or *do* not express, and which they would rejoice to have removed. I doubt not but there are many, who, in their hearts, are on the very verge of denying and rejecting the Scripture as the Word of God—an awful precipice indeed!—but who would be sincerely glad to be saved from such a denial and rejection by evidence which would satisfy the demands of their reason. I doubt not but there are many others, who love and reverence the Scripture, but who would heartily rejoice to be enabled to see in clearer vision how it is inspired, and wherein its divinity and sanctity reside; persons who believe that they have but little knowledge of its true meaning, and who long to understand it better: who believe it to be the Fountain of life to the soul; who in their hearts acknowledge that "the well is deep," but feel that they have nothing to draw with. It is these classes of persons whose attention is respectfully invited to the considerations which I shall have to offer in the course of lectures to which this is the Introduction. I shall aim to exhibit, with as much clearness and force as I may be able, those exalted views of the Divine Word which I have derived from the writings of Emanuel Swedenborg; views which have done me good, and which I think will do good to all who can receive them; views which ask to be received on no other ground than that of their intrinsic truth and rationality; views which commend themselves to my understanding and my heart—which for me, have raised the Scripture from the dead, and breathed into it the breath of life, and presented it transfigured—full of glory—before my eyes. To those who have any genuine love of the truth, or who desire to be convinced that the Scripture is altogether divine and holy, the message that I may bear will be glad tidings of great joy. But I cannot promise that it will be either useful or acceptable to others. The mind must be in an honest, ingenuous, truth-seeking state, in order to estimate evidence fairly, and to arrive at just conclusions.

We have said that the doctrine concerning the Sacred Scripture which it is our purpose to unfold and explain in these Lectures, is that taught in the writings of Emamuel Swedenborg. And Swedenborg professes to have arrived at it, not by any ordinary process of study and research, but through an extraordinary, divine illumination. The doctrine comes to us therefore, professedly, as a Revelation from Heaven. Now the claim of being a Revelator which Swedenborg sets up, is a very high claim, and one which we do not expect men very readily to acknowledge; one which no man *ought* to acknowledge upon insufficient or slight evidence. And one of the first objections to his claim, which arises in the minds of most men, is that which usually expresses itself in this interrogative form: " Is the Bible a Revelation from God, and can *another* Revelation be needed to enable us righty to understand the Bible ?" A very natural and fair question, to the consideration of which our next Lecture will be devoted.

ARTICLE II.

A PLEA

IN BEHALF OF SWEDENBORG'S CLAIM TO INTERCOURSE WITH THE SPIRITUAL WORLD.

COMPILED FROM HIS LIFE, LETTERS, AND WORKS.

THE great and paramount fact to be established in regard to Swedenborg is *the reality of his intercourse with the spiritual world.* While it is admitted and contended that his theological doctrines are, in themselves considered, in the highest degree rational and scriptural, it is still affirmed with equal confidence, that they are entirely beyond the reach of unassisted reason : that although their truth may be seen and recognized when distinctly announced, yet that the annunciation could never have been made by one who was left to the exercise solely of his native powers, however heightened by the most elaborate cultivation or invigorated by long continued use. If this shall be construed as an implication that the Christian Church has been hitherto in darkness as to the true sense of the Scriptures, we admit the charge, so far as their *interior spiritual purport* is concerned ; and to the question, why the true explanation should have been so long delayed, we reply, for the same reason that the Lord's Second Coming and the establishment of the New Jerusalem was prophetically deferred to a late age of the world, for with these events we hold that Swedenborg's mission is indissolubly connected. It was on this ground that he was enabled to make his Revelations. Our conviction then, on the score of his doctrines, rests upon the fact that they are built upon the very inmost laws of being—upon the principles of *ontology* itself—a region which has never been penetrated by the unaided intellect of man, and which is, by common consent, placed beyond the reach of its researches. Take for instance the simple point of the love-element which he makes to be the ground work, the substratum, of all existence, and the parent of thought, and seeing how it stands related in his system to the whole fabric of our being, we shall find that nearly every great doctrine of Revelation receives its construction from the light thrown upon it by this fundamental fact in our interior moral economy. Apart from it neither the true idea of the Divine Trinity, of Redemption, of Regeneration, of Justification, of Salvation, of Heaven and Hell, can be adequately understood. But this knowledge of the central law of our being, this grand discovery of love as the *esse* of our nature, and of thought as its *existere*, manifestation, or form, could never have been

achieved but by means of a superhuman insight into the most hidden
arcana of the created universe, and an absolutely angelic perception
of the properties of its uncreated Author. In other words, it required
an illumination which was equivalent to a positive intromission of the
revealer's spirit into the world of spirits, in order to make known the
essential constitution of the human mind. So far then as the verities
of all revealed doctrines depend upon the essential laws of our spiritual
being, so far was the necessity indispensable of precisely that prerogative of supernatural enlightenment to which Swedenborg lays claim.
It is consequently altogether vain to think of separating the doctrines
from the disclosures, and of admitting the truth of the one while at
the same time denying the reality of the other. When the doctrines
are clearly understood it will be seen to be absolutely impossible that
he should ever have been able to announce them in this world, except
upon the assumption that he was taught their veritable grounds in the
other. They are the legitimate issue of the translation of his spirit
into the spiritual sphere. That such a translation is intrinsically
possible, must be conceded by every one who reposes faith in the scriptural oracles, in which we have numerous instances of its occurrence.
But the admission of its *possibility* in any case advances us far towards
the admission of its *probability* in the case of Swedenborg. The only
question that then remains is the question of the *reasons* which may be
assigned for a belief in the fact, and of the *nature of the evidence* by
which the claim is to be substantiated, and this we shall consider more
at length in the sequel.

We have spoken of this interior illumination as "supernatural," notwithstanding we are aware that this term may be said to be impro-
perly applied to phenomena of this kind, especially as Swedenborg
himself, in his second letter to the Landgrave of Hesse Darmstadt
(*Doc. concern. Swed.* p. 169), says in respect to his disclosures to the
Queen of Sweden (*Doc.* p. 92), that "it is entirely true, but it should
not be regarded as a miracle; it is but one of those *memorabilia,* of the
same kind as those concerning Luther, Melancthon, Calvin and others.
All these *memorabilia* are but testimonies that I have been introduced
by the Lord into the spiritual world, as to my spirit, and that I converse with spirits and angels." From this we are at liberty to infer
that the opening of the spiritual senses, which is but another name for
intromission into the spiritual world, is in strictness a *natural* process,
or, in other words, does not imply an absolute infraction of the laws of
spiritual order. The truth is, man is constituted, by his very creation,
an inhabitant at once of the spiritual and the natural world, and though
his association with spirits is not ordinarily a matter of *consciousness,*
yet it may become so under the peculiar circumstances without any
violation of the laws of his being, any more than such laws are vio-

lated by the fact of his regeneration, which is in effect the opening of
the spiritual degree of the mind, or the actualizing of an inherent po-
tentiality of his nature, resulting normally from his shunning evils
as sins, and thus putting himself into an attitude for receiving the
divine influx, upon which regeneration depends. All this, however,
does not, in ordinary cases, amount to such a degree of spiritualiza-
tion, as to confer upon its subjects the power of *conscious* intercourse
with the inhabitants of the world unseen, though it doubtless approximates it in proportion to the measure of regeneration actually attained.
But in the case of Swedenborg we suppose such a vast advance beyond the ordinary elevation of the renewed mind—such an harmonious
development of the whole man, physical, intellectual, and moral, that
he passed, by a kind of natural transition, into the state of open or
conscious intercourse with the spiritual world. It was thus in fact a
virtual anticipation, during his mortal life, of that unfolding of the interior faculties which awaits, sooner or later, every regenerate soul
after death in the progress of his life in heaven. The theory of this
translation is well expounded by Mr. Clissold. "Being, from his
earliest years, of an humble and pious disposition; a spiritual mind
having been formed within him; his natural mind, which, by the
Divine blessing, had been sufficiently guided into the true principles
of science and philosophy, was capable of being brought into such a
correspondence with the laws of the heavenly kingdom, that there
could be an influx from the latter into the former, and hence, an intercourse between one and the other. This is the state in which, as
Swedenborg shows, man was created to live. This was his first and
natural state; his present darkness being his last and unnatural state;
his spirit being as truly designed to commune with heaven within, as
his body with the natural world without. Thus, when the Word of
God has filled the internal man with spiritual truths, when the natural
mind is filled with natural truths, and when, by the process of regeneration, the natural is brought into correspondence with the spiritual,
the whole man becomes regenerated, the image and likeness of God,
a heaven in its least form, a temple of Divine light and love; and he is
a living fulfilment of that prophecy of old 'Behold! the tabernacle of
God is with men; and he will dwell with them; and they shall be his
people; and God himself shall be with them, and be their God."—
(*Letter to Abp. of Dublin*, p. 196).

Why, then, it may be asked, do we denominate the process in Swedenborg's case "supernatural," a term so commonly regarded as tantamount to *miraculous*, which he himself expressly disclaims? Our
reply is, that we deem it due to a just estimate of the mission with
which he was entrusted, to hold it up as implying a *special designation*,
on the part of the Lord himself, of Swedenborg to the office of herald

or proclaimer of the New Dispensation of the Heavenly Jerusalem, and of expounder of the sublime mysteries of Heaven and Hell, and the laws and phenomena of the other life. To this work we conceive him to have had an *express vocation*, as truly as had John the Baptist to his function of harbinger of the first advent. And we employ the term "supernatural" with a view to counteract an opposite impression; for the idea that such a state as that into which Swedenborg was brought is *merely* natural and normal, will be very apt, in many minds, to draw after it another, viz: that there was nothing special in his case; that it was simply a superior kind of *clairvoyance;* and that consequently no peculiar authority or sanctity can be supposed to attach to his revelations, inasmuch as they might have occurred to any one else who should have chanced to be as happily moulded and *balanced* in his constitutional temperament. Just so far as the phenomena in his case can be resolved into *idiosyncrasy*, the claim to a special mission is vacated, and his alleged revelations sink to the level of mere natural utterances, the result of a peculiar condition or *crasis* of the natural man. Now it is this view of his case which we wish to preclude, and by the epithet "supernatural," applied to his illumination, we would indicate that character of it which is to be referred to the divine selection and extraordinary endowment of the man for the work to which he was called. In view of what he has accomplished it must, we think, be admitted, that there was *something* by which he was pre-eminently distinguished above all other men who have laid claim to or manifested similar powers of insight into spiritual arcana; *something* which marks him out as a *chosen instrument* for the proclamation of an order of truths incomparably transcending anything which had previously been communicated to the world. It is then not so much to the simple fact of the opening of his spiritual senses that we apply the term "supernatural," as to the whole train of providential circumstances leading to it; the circumstances of his parentage and birth; the influences that acted on his childhood; the course of his education and his subsequent pursuits; the development of his genius in the line of scientific and philosophical research; his immense attainments in every sphere of knowledge; his strong proclivity to psychological inquiry; and all directed by an unseen control to an issue the most momentous to the interests of the world—it is in this that we recognize the decisive evidence of a *special divine appointment*, and this we term "supernatural," in order that we may not confound the endowments of a prophet with the gifts, however splendid, of a sage.

Our position then is, that Swedenborg has revealed truths which he never could have revealed, but for the high prerogative of intercourse with the spiritual world. That there is such a world—the abode of spirits and angels—is universally believed by all Christians. But that it is separated by an impenetrable veil or impassable gulf from the present world; that all intercourse with it is barred, banned, and precluded to men sojourning in the flesh, is held with equal assurance by the mass of mankind. As a natural consequence, nothing is regarded at first blush as more incredible and preposterous than the claim to such intercourse. Although it is impossible to specify any declaration of the Most High forbidding the expectancy of farther light from this source—although no decision of the reason can be cited, pronouncing that that which has once occurred may not occur again—yet, so deep rooted and inveterate is the persuasion that all professed revelations from the inner sphere are the product of mental hallucination, that it is no matter of wonder to find Swedenborg's alleged disclosures turned away from as the mere idle creations of a diseased brain, and fit only to be entertained by those who are themselves laboring under a similar infirmity. Even the display of miraculous testimony in their behalf would, we are convinced, be powerless to countervail the current incredulity that prevails on this score. The antecedent improbability of new disclosures would, in the estimate of thousands, be so strong as to nullify the evidence of the reality of any miracle, however great, which might be wrought in their support. The Bible, it is said, is the last, the only revelation from God to man, and nothing supplemental to it is to be listened to for a moment, as that which followed would be a virtual impeachment of the completeness of that which preceded.

On what then can reliance be placed for the success of the appeal made by this system to the calm consideration of the Christian world? To one who has become at all acquainted with the writings of Swedenborg, it is clear that he was himself fully aware of the reception with which his claims would meet at the hands of the great body of Christendom, and that, as miracles would avail nothing towards securing their acknowledgment, the evidence that would avail must be sought in the intrinsic character of the revelations themselves and in the reasons alleged for their bestowment. Of these reasons, the chief of all is to be found in the prophetic announcement of the Lord's Second Advent at the period assigned by Swedenborg, and the connected establishment of the New Jerusalem Church, which forms so prominent a theme in the predictions of the Apocalypse. It is confidently affirmed by him and all his adherents, that that coming, which is entirely spiritual, or a coming in the glory of the internal sense of the Word, is to be viewed in most intimate and indissoluble relation to the formation of the Church known to prophecy as the Church of the New Jerusalem, announced by John. This assumption sets before us a grave question of Scriptural interpretation, in respect to the true nature, time, and object of our Lord's second Advent, and not the least progress can be made towards the overthrow of his pretensions till the fallacy of his interpretation of prophecy, in regard to this event, is exposed. But this has never yet been attempted. The assailants of Swedenborg unanimously refuse to encounter his defenders on the ground which the latter continually declare to be the fundamental ground, although *they* have never shrunk from entering the controversial lists, even in regard to the secondary and subordinate details of the system. It may, we think, be fairly questioned whether the world has ever witnessed an assault upon a body of religious opinions so unfairly conducted as that made upon the system of Swedenborg. On every other controverted subject the disputants feel themselves bound in honor and justice to grapple with the fundamental principles involved in the topics in debate. They see and acknowledge the propriety of dealing with premises, and not simply with conclusions. They aim to overthrow the edifice of error by undermining its foundations. But in the case of Swedenborg, opponents with one consent, decline to wage their war with anything but conclusions. Deaf to all our protests against the manifest injustice of such a course—heedless of all entreaty that they should candidly weigh the arguments adduced in favor of our central positions—they incessantly spend their strength in the attempt to *show up* the minor fallacies of our belief, and to turn into ridicule those features of the scheme which contravene their own prepossessions. Yet, as the very same things which appear ridiculous to them must also, in the outset of our inquiries, be supposed to have appeared ridiculous to us, it would seem that a fair-minded opponent would bestow some attention upon the course of reasoning which has so completely changed our views in regard to them, and converted to our minds the apparently monstrous and absurd into the supremely rational and consistent. Why should not this process, as a part of the experience of sensible men, be at least an object of curiosity, even if followed by a sentiment of contempt or pity? One would think that even as a study in the department of curious mental phenomena, it would press itself upon the reflection of intelligent minds. But no hint or inkling of any such prompting ever meets us. Nothing seems ever to divert attention for a moment from the *monstrosities of the visions*, and the daring *presumption* of asserted intercourse with spirits. Unavailingly do we implore a moment's calm for considering whether the thing *may* not be possible to Omnipotence, and if so, whether it *may* not be certified by evidence that shall approve itself as sound and unimpeachable to the more rigid requisitions of reason. That our evidence is actually such, we do not at present affirm; but we demand a hearing for it. Our faith is built upon evidence, and we cannot but protest against the condemnation of our faith while no heed is given to the grounds on which it rests. We have most explicitly declared that, if the *reasons* on which we accept any one of the visions can be shown to be unsound, we will relinquish the whole. The basis of our faith is in the conscious psychological verity of the principles affirmed by Swedenborg. These are to us so palpably undeniable, that we could as soon question the fact of our existence as to think of calling them into doubt; and admitting the principles, we are compelled by a logical necessity to admit the results. As then, his disclosures respecting the state of spirits in the other life rest upon the laws of spirit of which we are conscious in the present life, we are not only forced to regard these disclosures as true in themselves, but true to the exclusion of any other possible view. We cannot even *conceive*, on rational grounds, that the facts in respect to the future life, should be different from what he has represented them. If this high affirmation should be called in question, it will at least devolve upon the dissentient to acquaint himself thoroughly with the arguments and considerations which underlie it, and when this is done, we have a strong assurance that he will cease to be a dissentient. We anticipate no controversy with those who have come to *understand* the true grounds and reasons of the faith we repose in Swedenborg's revelations, and controversy with others scarcely deserves the name. Objections from such a source are a mere idle beating of the air.

In what follows, we propose to make Swedenborg the pleader of his own cause. From the entire range of his works we have collected and woven together an extended array of passages in which he sets forth some of the leading items of his experience in an asserted intercourse with the spiritual world of twenty-seven years continuance. It is, indeed, but a mere fragment of the whole body of his relations, but it embraces a very considerable portion of the *personal* allusions which bear upon the main fact of the high privilege accorded him. From these the reader is to judge of the credibility of his statements. They furnish the data on which he is called to pronounce whether his utterances savor of the ravings of a deluded visionary, or of the wisdom of an illuminated seer. A calm decision is earnestly sought of the question whether, supposing such intercourse to be possible and real, there is any thing contained in the revelations inconsistent with our most rational ideas of the state which he professes to describe. Granting that many of the intimations are new and surprising, are they any more so than we should fairly anticipate, even had an angel from heaven appeared commissioned by the Lord himself to make the disclosure? If then, on the whole, he seems to our candid intelligence to utter the words of truth and soberness, on the subject of his *mission*, can we successfully ward off the claims made upon our serious entertainment of the purport of his *message*?

P. S. As our readers may not be familiar with the works cited, of which we have given the abbreviated titles, we here exhibit the titles in full:—A. C. *Arcana Cœlestia*—T. C. R. *True Christian Religion*—A. E. *Apocalypse Explained*—E. U. *Earths in the Universe*—Inter. *Intercourse of Soul and Body*—S. D. *Spiritual Diary*—D. P. *Divine Providence*—H. & H *Heaven & Hell*—D. L. & W. *Divine Love and Wisdom.*

§ I.

SWEDENBORG'S MISSION VIEWED IN RELATION TO THE LORD'S SECOND ADVENT.

1. *The Second Coming of the Lord not personal but spiritual.*—"The opinion at this day prevailing in the churches is, that the Lord, when he shall come to the last judgment, will appear in the clouds of heaven, with angels and the sound of trumpets, and will gather together all who dwell upon the earth, and also those who are deceased, and will separate the evil from the good, as a shepherd separates the goats from the sheep ; and that then He will cast the evil or the goats into hell, and raise up the good or the sheep into heaven ; and that then also He will create a new visible heaven and a new habitable earth, and upon this send down a city, which will be called the New Jerusalem, the structure of which will be according to the description in Revelation xxi. ; namely, of jasper and gold, and the foundations of its wall of every precious stone, and its height, breadth, and length equal, each of twelve thousand furlongs ; and that all the elect, both those who are living, and those that have died since the beginning of the world, will be gathered together into this city ; and that they will then return into their bodies, and enjoy eternal bliss in that magnificent city, as in their heaven. This opinion concerning the coming of the Lord, and concerning the last judgment, is at this day reigning in Christian churches.

"Concerning the state of souls after death, these things, in general and in particular, are at this day believed ; that human souls after death are spirits, of which they cherish an idea as of a breath of wind ; and that, because they are such, they are reserved until the day of the last judgment, either in the middle of the earth, where their place is, or in the *Limbo* of the fathers. But in these things they differ : some suppose that they are ethereal or aerial forms, and that thus they are like ghosts and spectres, and that some of them dwell in the air, some in the woods, and some in the waters ; but some suppose that the souls of the deceased are transferred to the planets or to the stars, and there abodes are given to them ; and some that, *after thousands of* years, they return into

bodies. But most suppose that they are reserved to the time
when all the firmament, together with the terraqueous globe,
will be destroyed, which will be effected by fire, either bursting forth from the centre of the earth, or cast down from
heaven, like a universal lightning; and that then the sepulchres will be opened, and the souls which had been reserved,
clothed again with their bodies, and transferred into that holy
city Jerusalem, and thus, upon another earth, they will dwell
together in purified bodies, some below there, and some above,
because the height of the city is to be twelve thousand furlongs, as its length and breadth (Rev. xxi. 16).

"When any of the clergy or laity are asked whether they
firmly believe all those things, as that the antediluvians, together with Adam and Eve, and the postdiluvians, together
with Noah and his sons, and also Abraham, Isaac, and Jacob,
together with all the prophets and apostles, as well as the
souls of other men, are still reserved in the middle of the earth,
or are flying about in the ether or air; and also whether they
believe that souls will be clothed again with their bodies, and
become united with them, which yet are carcasses eaten up
by worms, mice, and fishes, and those of the Egyptians, as
mummies, eaten up by men, and some merely skeletons burnt
up by the sun, and reduced to powder; and likewise whether
they believe that the stars of heaven will then fall upon the
earth, which yet is smaller than one of them; are not such
things paradoxes, which reason itself dissipates, as it does
things that are contradictory? But to these things some answer nothing; some, that those are matters of faith, under
obedience to which we keep the understanding; some, that
not only these things, but many more that are above reason,
are of the divine omnipotence; and when they name faith
and omnipotence, reason is banished, and then sound reason
either disappears and becomes as nothing, or becomes like a
spectre, and is called insanity. They add, 'Are not those
things according to the Word? Who will not think and
speak from that?'

"That the Word in the letter is written by appearances and
correspondences, and that, therefore, there is in every part of
it a spiritual sense, in which the truth is in its light, and the
sense of the letter in the shade, was shown in the chapter concerning the SACRED SCRIPTURE. Lest, therefore, the man of
the New Church, like the man of the old church, should wan-
der in the shade, in which the sense of the letter of the Word
is, especially concerning heaven and hell, and concerning his
life after death, and here concerning the coming of the Lord,
it has pleased the Lord to open the sight of my spirit, and

thus to let me into the spiritual world, and not only to give
me to speak with spirits and angels, and with relations and
friends, but with kings and princes, who have departed from
the natural world, but also to see the stupendous things of
heaven, and the miserable things of hell; and thus that man
does not live in some unknown place of the earth, nor fly
about blind and dumb in the air, or in empty space; but that
he lives as a man in a substantial body, in a much more perfect state, if he comes among the blessed, than before, when
he lived in the material body.   Therefore, lest man should
become more deeply grounded in the opinion concerning the
destruction of the visible heaven and habitable earth, and
thus concerning the spiritual world, from ignorance, which is
the source of naturalism, and then, at the same time, atheism,
which, at this day, among the learned, has begun to take root
in the interior rational mind, should, like a mortification in
the flesh, spread itself around more widely, even into his external mind, from which he speaks, it has been enjoined upon me
by the Lord, to promulgate some of the things seen and heard,
both concerning HEAVEN AND HELL, and concerning the LAST
JUDGMENT, and also to explain the APOCALYPSE, where the coming of the Lord, and the former heaven, and the new heaven
and the holy Jerusalem, are treated of; from which, when
read and understood, any one may see what is meant there
by the coming of the Lord, and by the new heaven, and by
the new Jerusalem."[a]

2. *That by the Lord's spiritual Coming is meant a Coming
in the internal, essential, and spiritual sense of the divine Word,
which is from Him and is Himself.*—" It is read in many places
that the Lord is to come in the clouds of heaven.   But hitherto
no one has known what was meant by the clouds of heaven:
they have believed that He would appear in them in person.
But that, by the ·clouds of heaven, is meant the Word in the
sense of the letter, and by glory and virtue, in which also He
is then to come (Matt. xxiv. 30), is meant the spiritual sense of
the Word, has been hitherto concealed, because no one has
ever yet even conjectured, that there is in the Word any spiritual sense, such as it is in itself.   Now, because the spiritual
sense of the Word has been opened to me by the Lord, and
it has been given to me to be together with angels and spirits
in their world, as one of them, it has been discovered, that by
the clouds of heaven is meant the Word in the natural sense,

---

[a] T. C. R. 768–771.

and by glory, the Word in the spiritual sense, and by virtue, the power of the Lord by means of the Word."[b]

"That the Lord is the Word, is evident from these words in John: 'In the beginning was the Word, and the Word was with God, and God was the Word; and the Word became flesh' (i. 1, 14). That the Word there is the divine truth, is because Christians have divine truth from no other source than from the Word, which is a fountain from which all the churches named from Christ draw living waters in their fulness, although as in a cloud in which its natural sense is, but in glory and virtue, in which its spiritual and celestial sense is. That there are three senses in the Word,—natural, spiritual and celestial, —one within another, was shown in the chapter concerning the Sacred Scripture, and in the chapter concerning the Decalogue or Catechism. Thence it is manifest, that by the Word, in John, is meant the Divine Truth. John also testifies the same in his first epistle: 'We know that the Son of God hath come and given us understanding that we may know the True, and we are in the True, in his Son Jesus Christ' (v. 20). And therefore the Lord so often said, 'Verily [Amen] I say unto you;' for *amen* in the Hebrew language is truth; and that He is the Amen, may be seen Rev. iii. 14; and the Truth, John xiv. 6. When, also, the learned of this age are asked what they understand by the Word in John i. 1, they say, that they understand the Word in its supereminence; and what else is the Word in its supereminence, than divine truth? Hence it is manifest, that the Lord is also now to appear in the Word. The reason that He is not to appear in person, is because, since his ascension into heaven, He is in the glorified Human; and in this He cannot appear to any man, unless He first open the eyes of his spirit; and these cannot be opened in any one who is in evils, and thence in falses; thus not in any of the goats which he sets at the left hand. Wherefore, when He manifested Himself to the disciples, He first opened their eyes; for it is read, 'And their eyes were opened, and they knew Him; but He became invisible to them' (Luke xxiv. 31). The case was similar with the women at the sepulchre after the resurrection; wherefore they at that time also saw angels sitting in the sepulchre and speaking with them, whom no man can see with the material eye. That neither did the apostles, before the Lord's resurrection, see the Lord in the glorified Human, with the eyes of the body, but in the spirit (which appears, after awaking, as if it were in sleep), is evident from his transfiguration before Peter, James, and John, in that 'their eyes

---

[b] T. C. R. 776.

were heavy with sleep' (Luke ix. 32).   Wherefore, it is a vain
thing to believe that the Lord is to appear in the clouds of
heaven in person ; but He is to appear in the Word which is
from Him, thus is Himself."[c]

3. *That this Coming is effected, in the first instance, through
the instrumentality of a man divinely qualified and endowed for
this sacred office.*—"Since the Lord cannot manifest Himself in
person, as has been shown just above, and yet He has foretold
that He would come and establish a New Church, which is the
New Jerusalem, it follows that He is to do it by means of a
man, who is able not only to receive the doctrines of this
church with his understanding, but also to publish them by the
press.   That the Lord has manifested Himself before me, his
servant, and sent me on this office, and that, after this, He
opened the sight of my spirit, and thus let me into the spiritual world, and gave me to see the heavens and the hells, and
also to speak with angels and spirits, and this now continually
for many years, I testify in truth ; and also that, from the first
day of that call, I have not received anything which pertains
to the doctrines of that church from any angel, but from the
Lord alone, while I read the Word."[d]

"In your gracious letter, you ask, how I attained to be in
society with angels and spirits, and whether that privilege can
be communicated from one person to another.   Deign, then, to
receive favorably this answer.   The Lord our Saviour had
foretold that He would come again into the world, and that
He would establish there a New Church.   He has given this
prediction in the Apocalypse, xxi. and xxii., and also in several
places in the Evangelists.   But as he cannot come again into
the world in person, it was necessary that He should do it by
means of a man, who should not only receive the doctrine of
this New Church in his understanding, but also publish it by
printing ; and as the Lord had prepared me for this office from
my infancy, He has manifested himself before me, His servant,
and sent me to fill it.   This took place in the year 1743.   He
afterwards opened the sight of my spirit, and thus introduced
me into the spiritual world, and granted me to see the heavens
and many of their wonders, and also the hells, and to speak
with angels and spirits, and this continually for twenty-seven
years.   I declare in all truth that such is the fact.   This favor
of the Lord, in regard to me, has only taken place for the
sake of the New Church which I have mentioned above, the
doctrine of which is contained in my writings.   The gift of

---

conversing with spirits and angels cannot be transmitted from
one person to another, unless the Lord himself opens the spiritual sight of that person.   It is sometimes permitted to a spirit
to enter into a man, and to communicate to him some truth;
but it is not granted to the man to speak mouth to mouth with
the spirit.   It is even a very dangerous thing, because the
spirit enters into the affection of man's self-love, which does
not agree with the affection of heavenly love."[e]

"With regard to what passed in the earlier part of my life:
from my fourth to my tenth year, my thoughts were constantly
engrossed by reflecting upon God, on salvation, and on the spiritual affections of man.   I often revealed things in my discourse which filled my parents with astonishment, and made
them declare at times, that *certainly the angels spoke through
my mouth.*   From my sixth to my twelfth year, it was my
greatest delight to converse with the clergy concerning faith;
to whom I often observed, that charity or love was the life of
faith, and that this vivifying charity or love *was no other than
the love of one's neighbor.*   That God vouchsafes this faith to
every one; but that it is adopted by those only who practise
that charity.   I knew of no other faith or belief at that time,
than that God is the Creator and Preserver of Nature.   That
He endues man with understanding, good inclinations, and
other gifts thence derived.   I knew nothing at that time of this
systematic or dogmatic kind of faith, that God the Father
imputes the righteousness or merits of the Son to whomsoever, and at such times as He wills, even unto the impenitent.
And had I heard of such kind of faith, it would have been then,
as now, perfectly unintelligible to me."[f]

"I was prohibited reading dogmatic and systematic theology,
before heaven was opened to me, by reason, that, unfounded
opinions and inventions might thereby easily have insinuated
themselves, which with difficulty could afterwards have been
extirpated, wherefore, when heaven was opened to me, it was
necessary first to learn the Hebrew language, as well as the
correspondences of which the whole Bible is composed, which
led me to read the Word of God over many times; and inasmuch as the Word of God is the source, whence all theology
must be derived, I was thereby enabled to receive instructions
from the Lord, who is the Word."[g]

"I have been called to a holy office by the Lord himself, who
most graciously manifested himself in person to me, his servant, in the year 1743; when he opened my sight to the view

---

[e] Let. to Landg. of Hesse (Doc. p. 138.)   [f] Let. vii. to Dr. Beyer (Doc. p. 129).
[g] Let. iv. to Dr. Beyer (Doc. p. 125).

of the spiritual world, and granted me the privilege of conversing with spirits and angels, which I enjoy to this day. From that time I began to print and publish various *arcana* that have been seen by me, or revealed to me ; as respecting heaven and hell, the state of man after death, the true worship of God, the spiritual sense of the Word ; with many other most important matters conducive to salvation and true wisdom. The only reason of my latter journeys to foreign countries, has been the desire of being useful, by making known the arcana entrusted to me."[h]

"It is asked, *why from a philosopher I have been chosen to this office ?* Unto which I give for answer : to the end that the spiritual knowledge, which is revealed at this day, might be reasonably learned, and naturally understood ; because spiritual truths answer unto natural ones, inasmuch as these originate and flow from them, and serve as a foundation for the former. That what is spiritual is similar unto, and corresponds with what is human and natural, or belonging to the terrestrial world, may be seen in the treatise *On Heaven and Hell*, 87–115. I was, on this account, by the Lord, first introduced into the natural sciences, and thus prepared from the year 1710–1744, when heaven was opened unto me.[*] Every one is morally educated and spiritually regenerated by the Lord, by being led from what is natural to what is spiritual. Moreover, the Lord has given unto me a love of spiritual truth, that is to say, not with any view to honor or profit,

---

[h] Let. to Hart. (Doc. p. 38).

[*] From an unpublished manuscript by Oetinger, containing his autobiography, Dr. Tafel has given a number of extracts, from one of which we insert the following :—

" Swedenborg (says Oetinger, in another place) is, in my estimation, the forerunner of a new era. That, in the kingdom of Jesus Christ upon earth, the faithful will have a faculty, by which they will be able to hold communion, and converse with those who are in the marriage of the Lamb, cannot be doubted. This gift, or this office, by which others, who cannot see and hear, may be instructed in the things of heaven, ought not to be doubted or denied in respect to Swedenborg, because the facts evincing Swedenborg's communication with the world of spirits, are denied by nobody in Stockholm, and this fact proves that Swedenborg's assertion is true, when he says, that he has communication with the world of spirits. Hence it may be seen, why God has, at this time, permitted such a man as Swedenborg to arise, and why he was educated by his father, a most venerable bishop, and of noble rank, so carefully, in innocence and in scientific learning ; all these preparations, under Providence, tended to fit him to pass through the most important events, which no other man has had to experience. As Swedenborg is the instrument of restoring the lost communion with the invisible world, that pure and unspotted life, in which we see he was trained and educated, was necessary. The first promise that Jesus gave to His disciples, was, ' That they should see heaven open' (John i.) ; and this, we might reasonably expect, would be the first thing announced at His second coming. God may have appeared to Swedenborg in a way which we may not fully understand, but he is certainly a phenomenon, such as the world never saw before."—*Doc. Conc. Swed. p.* 150.

but merely for the sake of truth itself: for every one who loves truth, merely for the sake of truth, sees it from the Lord, the Lord being the 'way and the truth' (John xiv. 6). But he who professes the love of truth for the sake of honor or gain, sees truth from his own self-hood, and to see from one's self, is to see falsity. Falses confirmed shut the church, but truths, rationally confirmed, open it. What man can otherwise comprehend spiritual things, which enter into the understanding? The doctrinal notion received in the Protestant Church, viz., that in theological matters, reason shall be held captive under obedience to faith, locks up the church; what can open it but an understanding enlightened by the Lord?"[i]

4. *A more particular statement of the reasons of Swedenborg's illumination.*—"Men are enlightened variously, every one according to the quality of his affection and consequent intelligence: those who are in the spiritual affection of truth, aré elevated into the light of heaven, so as to perceive distinctly what comes from the Lord, and what from the angels; what comes from the Lord is written [or given in my writings], and what from the angels is not written. Moreover it has been given me to discourse with the angels as man with man, and likewise to see the things which are in the heavens, and which are in the hells: the reason was, because the end of the present church approaches, and the beginning of a new one is at hand, which will be the New Jerusalem, to which it is to be revealed, that the Lord rules the universe, both heaven and the world; that there is a heaven and a hell, and what is the quality of each; that men live also as men after death, in heaven those who had been led of the Lord, in hell those who have been led of themselves; that the Word is the Divine [Principle] itself of the Lord in the earth; also that the last judgment is passed lest man should expect it in this world to eternity; besides many other things which are effects of the light now arising after darkness."[j]

"It has been given me to be in company with angels, and also to speak with those who are in hell, and this now for several years, sometimes continually from morning to evening; and thus to be informed concerning heaven and concerning hell; and this in order that the man of the church may not continue any longer in his erroneous faith concerning resurrection at the day of judgment, and concerning the state of the soul in the mean time, as also concerning angels, and concerning the devil; which faith, because it is a belief of what is

---

false, involves darkness, and with those who think on those things from their own intelligence, induces doubt, and at length denial. For they say in heart, How can so great a heaven, with so many constellations, and with the sun and the moon, be destroyed and dissipated? And how can the stars then fall from heaven to the earth, when yet they are larger than the earth? And how can bodies eaten by worms, consumed by corruption, and scattered to all the winds, be gathered together again to their soul? Where is the soul in the mean time, and what is it when without the sense which it had in the body? Besides many similar things, which, because they are incomprehensible, cannot become objects of faith, and with many destroy faith concerning the life of the soul after death, and concerning heaven and hell, and with these the other things which are of the faith of the church. That they have destroyed it, is evident from those who say, Who has ever come from heaven to us, and told that it is so? What is hell? Is there any? What is this, that man is to be tormented with fire to eternity? What is the day of judgment? Has it not been expected in vain for ages? Besides other things, which imply a denial of all. Lest therefore those who think such things, as many do, who from their worldly wisdom are called erudite and learned, should any longer trouble and seduce the simple in faith and heart, and induce infernal darkness respecting God, respecting heaven, respecting eternal life, and respecting other things which depend on them, the interiors which are of my spirit have been opened by the Lord, and thus it has been given me to speak with all whom I have ever been acquainted with in the life of the body, after their decease; with some for days, with some for months, and with some for a year; and also with others so many that I should say too few if I should say an hundred thousand; many of whom were in the heavens, and many in the hells. I have also spoken with some two days after their decease, and have told them that preparations were now being made for their interment. To which they said, that they did well to reject that which had served them for a body and its functions in the world; and they wished me to say, that they were not dead, but that they live equally men now as before, and that they had only migrated from one world into another, and that they are not aware of having lost any thing, since they are in a body and its sensuals as before, and also in understanding and in will as before, and that they have similar thoughts and affections, similar sensations, and similar desires, to those which they had in the world. Most of those who were recently dead, when they saw themselves living men as before, and in a similar state (for after death every one's state of life

is at first such as it had been in the world, but that is successively changed with him, either into heaven or into hell), were
affected with new joy at being alive, and said that they had
not believed this: but they wondered very much that they
should have lived in such ignorance and blindness concerning
the state of their life after death; and especially that the man
of the church should be in such ignorance and blindness, when
yet he, above all others in the whole world, can be in the light
concerning those things.   Then they first saw the cause of that
blindness and ignorance, which is, that external things, which
relate to the world and to the body, occupied and filled their
minds to such a degree, that they could not be elevated into the
light of heaven, and view the things of the church beyond the
doctrinals; for from corporeal and worldly things, when they
are loved so much as they are at this day, there flows in mere
darkness, when men go farther."[k]

"I this year published the work entitled *The Revelations Revealed*, which was promised in the treatise *On the Last Judgment*, and from all which writings it may be plainly seen that
I converse with angels.   Every person may see, that by the
New Jerusalem is meant a new church or congregation, the
doctrines or articles of whose faith cannot shine in their true
splendor, and give light to others, without the divine aid, because they are only figuratively described in the Revelations,
that is to say, according to *correspondence;* and the true doctrine of it cannot be published to the world, but by such as to
whom the needful revelation is made.   I can sacredly and solemnly declare, that the Lord Himself has been seen of me,
and that He has sent me to do what I do, and for such purpose
has He opened and enlightened the interior part of my soul,
which is my spirit, so that I can see what is in the spiritual
world, and those that are therein; and this privilege has now
been continued to me for twenty-two years.   But in the present state of infidelity, can the most solemn oath make such a
thing credible, or to be believed by any?   Yet such as have
received true Christian light and understanding, will be convinced of the truth contained in my writings, which are particularly evident in the book of the *Revelations Revealed*.
Who, indeed, has hitherto known anything of consideration of
the true spiritual sense and meaning of the Word of God, the
spiritual world, or of heaven and hell; the nature of the life
of man, and the state of souls after the decease of the body?
Is it to be supposed that these and other things of a like consequence are to be eternally hidden from Christians?   That
many very important particulars relating to them are at this

k H. & H. 312.

day revealed for the first time, is done in regard to the New Jerusalem, and for the sake of the New Church, because the members thereof are endowed with a capacity to apprehend them, which others might also have, were it not for their weak unbelief of the possibility of such things being made known to any, and by them to the world. These writings of mine do not come under the term of prediction, but of revelations."[1]

"The Lord is preparing at this time a new heaven of such as believe in Him, and acknowledge Him to be the true God of heaven and earth, and also look to Him in their lives, which is to shun evil and do good ; because from that heaven shall the New Jerusalem, mentioned in Rev. xxi. 2, descend. I daily see spirits and angels, from ten to twenty thousand, descending and ascending, who are set in order. By degrees as that heaven is formed, the New Church begins and increases. The universities in Christendom are now first instructed, from whence will come ministers ; because the new heaven has no influence over the old clergy, who conceive themselves too well skilled in the doctrine of justification by faith alone."[m]

"Unless the Lord defended man every moment, yea, even the smallest part of every moment, he would instantly perish, for such mortal hatred exists in the world of spirits against these things of love and faith towards the Lord, as cannot possibly be described. That this is the case I can declare with a certainty, inasmuch as I have now for some years, though also in the body, been with spirits in another life, and surrounded with evil spirits, yea the worst, and sometimes by thousands of them, to whom it was permitted to pour forth their venom, and infest me by every way in which they could, yet they could not hurt the least hair, I was so protected by the Lord. From so many years' experience I became thoroughly instructed concerning the world of spirits, of what quality it is, and also concerning the combat which they who are regenerated cannot otherwise than sustain, that they may attain the felicity of eternal life."[n]

5. *The testimony of miracles not to be expected in confirmation of such a mission as that of Swedenborg.*—"To the interrogation, *whether there is occasion for any sign, that I am sent by the Lord, to do what I do?* I answer, that at this day no signs or miracles will be given, because they compel only an external belief, but do not convince the internal. What did the miracles avail in Egypt, or among the Jewish nation, who, nevertheless, crucified the Lord? So, if the Lord were to appear now in the sky, attended with angels and trum-

---

[1] *Let. l. to Oeting.* (Doc. p. 152).   [m] *Let.* iv. to Dr. Beyer (Doc. p. 125).
[n] *A. C.* 59.

pets, it would have no other effect than it had then.   The sign, given at this day, will be an *illustration*, and thence a *knowledge* and *reception of the truths of the New Church ;* some *speaking illustration* of certain persons may likewise take place ; this works more effectually than miracles.   *Yet one token may perhaps still be given.*"o

"It cannot be denied but that miracles induce faith, and strongly persuade that that is true which he who does the miracles says and teaches ; and that this in the commencement so occupies the external of man's thought, that it as it were binds and enchants : but man is thereby deprived of his two faculties, which are called rationality and liberty, so that he cannot act from freedom according to reason, and then the Lord cannot flow in through the internal into the external of his thought, except only to leave to man to confirm that thing from his rationality which was made of his faith by the miracle. The state of man's thought is such, that by the internal of thought he sees a thing in the external of his thought, as in a certain mirror ; for, as was said above, man can see his thought, which cannot be given except from interior thought.

"From these things it may be evident, that faith induced by miracles is not faith, but persuasion ; for there is not any rational in it, still less any spiritual ; for it is only an external without an internal : it is the like with all that man does from that persuasive faith, whether he acknowledges God, or worships Him at home or in temples, or does kindnesses : when a miracle alone induces man to acknowledgment, worship, and piety, he acts from the natural man, and not from the spiritual ; for a miracle infuses faith through an external way, and not through an internal way ; thus from the world, and not from heaven ; and the Lord does not enter through any other way with man but through the internal way, which is through the Word, doctrine and preachings from it : and because miracles shut this way, therefore at this day no miracles are done."p

"Instead of miracles, there has taken place at this present day an open manifestation of the Lord Himself, an intromission into the spiritual world, and with it illumination by immediate light from the Lord, in whatever relates to the interior things of the church, but principally an opening of the spiritual sense of the Word, in which the Lord is present, in His own Divine Light.   These revelations are not miracles, because every man as to his spirit is in the spiritual world without separation from his body in the natural world.   As to myself, indeed, my presence in the spiritual world is attended with a certain separation, but only as to the intellectual part of my mind, not as to the will part.   This manifestation of the

o Let. iii. to Oeting. (Doc. p. 153).   p Div. Prov. 130, 133.

Lord, and His intromission into the spiritual world, is more excellent than all miracles; but it has not been granted to any one since the creation of the world as it has been to me. The men of the golden age, indeed, conversed with angels; but it was not granted to them to be in any other light than what is natural. To me, however, it has been granted to be in both spiritual and natural light at the same time; and hereby I have been privileged to see the wonderful things of heaven; to be in company with angels just as I am with men; and at the same time, to pursue truths in the light of truth, and thus to perceive and be gifted with them, consequently, to be led of the Lord."[q]

" I hope that my new work, entitled *True Christian Religion,* is now in your hands, and that the two copies, which I sent at the same time to the Landgrave, have reached him. I desire to have your judgment upon the subjects there treated of, because I know that, being enlightened by the Lord, you will there see in light, more than others, the truths which are there manifested in accordance with the Word. I send to-day my reply to the letter which his Highness, your Prince, has recently sent to me; and by his orders, I speak to him of the conversations which I have had with two personages in the spiritual world. But these conversations, as well as that between the queen of Sweden and his brother when he was living, which was made known to me by him in the spiritual world, ought by no means to be regarded as miracles; they are only testimonies that I have been introduced by the Lord into the spiritual world, and that I have been in association with angels and spirits, in order that the church, which until now had remained in ignorance concerning that world, may know that heaven and hell exist in reality, and that man lives after death, a man, as before; and that thus there might be no more doubt as to his immortality. Deign, I pray you, to satisfy his Highness, that these are not miracles, but only testimonies that I converse with angels and spirits.

" You may see in the work above mentioned that there are no more miracles, at this time; and the reason why. It is, that they who do not believe because they see no miracles, might easily, by them, be led into fanaticism. I have seen two volumes, in quarto, of miracles wrought by the Abbe Deacon Paris, which are nothing but falsehoods, being partly fantastic and partly magical; and it is the same with the other miracles of the Roman Catholics. Examine, I pray you, what I have said on the subject of miracles in that work. At this day, faith will be established and confirmed in the New Church,

---

q Hob. Life of Swed. p. 42.

only by the Word itself and by the truths it reveals; truths which appear in light to the reader of my last work, which is itself an indication that the Lord is present and enlightens him.   For every truth contained in the Word shines in heaven, and comes down from thence into this world to those who love truth because it is truth."[r]

6. *His anticipation of the manner in which his relations would be received.*—" I foresee that many, who read my Relations will believe that they are inventions of the imagination ; but I assert in truth, that they are not inventions, but were truly seen and heard ; not seen and heard in any state of the mind buried in sleep, but in a state of full wakefulness.   For it has pleased the Lord to manifest Himself to me, and to send me to teach those things which will be of his New Church, which is meant by the New Jerusalem in the Revelation ; for which end He has opened the interiors of my mind or spirit, by which it has been given me to be in the spiritual world with angels, and at the same time in the natural world with men, and this now for twenty-seven years.   Who in the Christian world would have known any thing concerning Heaven and Hell, unless it had pleased the Lord to open in some one the sight of his spirit, and to show and teach?   That such things as are described in the Relations, appear in the heavens, is manifestly evident from the like things, which were seen by John, and described in the Revelation, as also which were seen and described in the Word of the Old Testament by the Prophets.   From these and many other things in the Word, it is evident that the things which exist in the spiritual world have appeared to many, before and since the coming of the Lord: what wonder that they should also now, when the church is commencing, and the New Jerusalem coming down out of heaven?"[s]

"I have conversed with many after their decease, with whom I was acquainted during their life in the body; and such conversation has been of long continuance, sometimes for months, sometimes for a whole year ; and with as clear and distinct a voice, but internal, as with friends in the world. The subject of our discourse has sometimes turned on the state of man after death; and they have greatly wondered that no one in the life of the body, knows, or believes, that he is to live in such a manner after the life of the body ; when nevertheless it is a continuation of life, and that of such a nature, that the deceased passes from an obscure life into a clear and distinct one ; and they who are in faith towards the Lord, into a life

---

r Let. to Venat (Doc. p. 169.)   s T. C. R. 851.

more and more clear and distinct. They have desired me to acquaint their friends on earth that they were alive, and to write to them an account of their states, as I have often told them many things respecting their friends : but my reply was, that if I should speak to them or write to them, they would not believe, but would call my information mere fancy, and would ridicule it, asking for signs or miracles before they should believe ; and thus I should be exposed to their derision : and that the things here declared are true, few perhaps will believe, for men deny in their hearts the existence of spirits ; and they who do not deny such existence, are yet very unwilling to hear that any one can converse with spirits. Such a faith respecting spirits did not at all prevail in ancient times, but does at this day, when men wish by reasoning of the brain to explore what spirits are, whom, by definitions and suppositions, they deprive of every sense ; and the more learned they wish to be, the more they do this."[t]

"I know that few will believe it possible for any one to see the things which exist in the other life, and· thence to give an account of the state of souls after death ; because few believe in a resurrection ; and of the learned fewer than of the simple. They affirm indeed with the lips, that they shall rise again, because it is according to the doctrine of faith ; but still they deny it in heart. Nay, some even openly avow, that if any one should rise from the dead, and they should see, and hear, and touch him, they would then believe. But if this were to take place, it must be done for each one, and after all, not a single person who in heart denies, would be thus persuaded, but a thousand objections would flow in, which would confirm him in his negative conclusion. Some profess to believe that they shall rise again, but at the day of the last judgment ; and the notion they have conceived of that day is, that then all things appertaining to the visible world are to be destroyed : but, because that day has been expected in vain for so many ages, they still have doubts. Hence it may appear what sort of persons there are at this day in the Christian world. The Sadducees, spoken of in Matt. ch. xxii. 23, openly denied a resurrection : yet they did better than those at this day, who profess not to deny, because it is an article of faith, and yet deny in their hearts ; so that their profession is contrary to their belief, and their belief to their profession. Lest, therefore, mankind should any longer confirm themselves in that false opinion, it has been granted me, by the divine mercy of the Lord, whilst I am in this world in the body, to be in the spirit in the other life (for man is a spirit clothed with body),

---

t A. C. 443.

and there to discourse with souls that have risen again not long after their decease, and, indeed, with almost all those whom I knew when they lived in the body, but who have since died; as, also, now for some years, to converse daily with spirits and angels, and to see there stupendous sights, such as never entered into the idea of any person; and this without the least fallacy. As many persons say, that they would believe, if any one should come to them from the other life, it will now be seen, whether they will be persuaded against the hardness of their hearts."[u]

(Concluded in our next.)

ARTICLE III.

DEGREES, CONTINUOUS AND DISCRETE.

SWEDENBORG early saw the importance of a thorough knowledge of degrees, as laying the foundation to all those grand superstructures which he subsequently reared. Even before he entered upon his theological career, he gave significant indications that the grand object of his pursuit—a knowledge of the human soul—could not be attained without certain new doctrines, among which was that of Degrees. He saw this holding out to him the key that should unlock many a mystery and admit him to the secret chambers of the soul. He early determined, at whatever pains, to possess himself of this key; for he already saw that this alone would open to him the portals that lead to the soul, " who, sitting like a queen in her throne of state, the body, dispenses laws and governs all things by her good pleasure, but yet by order and by truth." " I propose," says he in the Prologue to the Animal Kingdom, " to give an introduction to Rational Psychology, consisting of certain new doctrines, through the assistance of which we may be conducted, from the material organism of the Body, to a knowledge of the Soul, which is immaterial: these are the Doctrine of Forms; the Doctrine of Order and Degrees; also, the Doctrine of Series and Society; the Doctrine of Influx; the Doctrine of Correspondence and Representation: lastly, the Doctrine of Modification."

It appears from this, that Swedenborg, even at this stage in his career, looked upon the doctrine of Degrees as essential to a right understanding of the connexion between the soul and

---

[u] C. A. Pref. to Gen. xvi.

the body. This will appear still more evident as we advance ; for it will be seen that the soul sustains the relation to the body of cause and effect, between which there is a discrete degree. Indeed spirit is distinguished from matter, and in the complex, the spiritual world from the material, only by discrete degrees, the one being a world of causes and the other of effects resulting from those causes.

These grand conclusions Swedenborg *as a philosopher* never reached, but *as a theologian* he fully grasped and put them forth in beautiful order and harmony. In his philosophical works are found the latent germs, which, in his theological works, are matured into a plentiful harvest. He had a faint conception of what was necessary to complete his stupendous system of mind and matter, as originating from, and dependent upon, the Great First Cause ; but he had not himself yet risen into that degree, or plane of the mind, from which causes are discerned, and where, to use his own words, " we may properly for the first time commence, or rather return, from principles, and put them forth, as of sufficient authority, by a clear and intelligible definition." It was not until Swedenborg had been led to the top of the spiritual Pisgah, beneath which lay outspread in beauty the land which he so earnestly sought to explore, that he was able not only to trace the journey from Egypt into Canaan, but to indicate the nature and quality of the Promised Land itself; or, to drop the figure, it was not until he had himself passed from the natural and scientific, into the spiritual degree of the mind, that he was able to point out those distinct states of life, through which he had passed, and the peculiarities of each. During the whole of his scientific and philosophical career, he labored under a most serious disadvantage, of which he seems, at times, painfully aware. He strove with a diligence and zeal truly astonishing to penetrate to a knowledge of the cause of all things, and to open to the rational mind the relations existing between the world of causes and that of effects. He brought to the task all the energies of his powerful mind, furnished with the varied learning of his time, to which he made most important additions. " We must," says he, in speaking of the preparation necessary to gain a knowledge of the soul, " make ourselves thoroughly masters of all the sciences, doctrines, and arts,—nay, from those already known, we must generate and discover others ; for by these means the work is constructed, and the mind led directly to the summit." Swedenborg did all this. As a scholar, a philosopher, and a naturalist, he had not his equal ; for though many a star of the first magnitude shone in the firmament of letters in his time, his was in the zenith, and the brightest of them all. But possessed of such a prodigious fund of knowledge, and a

Herculean mind to dispose it into order and harmony, he failed to attain the goal for which he was striving upon that plane. It was not there. It was above and beyond the reach of the philosopher or the naturalist. It lay within the spiritual confines of the mind. As a philosopher, therefore, or before he rose from the scientific into the spiritual degree of the mind,—for in this consisted the opening of his spiritual vision,—he failed to gain a knowledge of the soul, or to develope the laws of spirit as operating upon, and resulting in, matter. The eye which could gaze undimmed upon the noon-day light of natural truth, was dazzled and darkened when it turned to contemplate the nature of the Divine. Though the objects were distinct and well defined upon the natural plane of vision, all was dark and uncertain above. There is within the mind which possesses, as Swedenborg's did, " an innate love of truth, an eager desire of exploring it, and a delight in finding it," a heavenly region, lit up by the light which ever flows down from the spiritual sun ; but this timeless and spaceless region, where are the substances of things, the mind which thinks and reasons under the conditions of time and space cannot penetrate. The mental eye looks forth into the fathomless void, till it is pained and exhausted, but it catches no glimpse of that world where spirits walk in robes of light. The stars are not seen by the light of the sun, but by that emanating from themselves. So neither could Swedenborg, with all his superior endowments, explore the world of causes by the light of science. It must be revealed, and it was finally revealed to him, by the light which emanates from that world, or rather from Him who is the source of spiritual light and life. As a philosopher, he never arrived at the grand conclusion that,

> " The mind is its own place, and in itself
> Can make a heaven of hell, a hell of heaven."

In his " Outlines of a Philosophical Argument on the Infinite," Swedenborg does not rise above the common darkness that overspread the mind of philosophers and divines in his age. He reasoned as a master, but not with satisfactory results. He, in common with others, came at last to the cheerless conclusion that the Divine cannot be known. Hear his confession :—" As the mind, in the course of philosophizing, peers into and courses over finite nature, its parts and its whole, it cannot but at last arrive at the utterly unknown and inexplicable, *i. e.* at the infinite, and the essence of the finite ; and as the infinite is identical with the non-finite, the mind there stops,—there finds an insurmountable and impenetrable difficulty, and remains involved in its gordian knot."—P. 6.

Yes, truly ; and there it must ever remain, so long as it

cumbers its flight with the conditions of nature; but Swedenborg found no difficulty in untying the gordian knot when his mind was elevated above the natural into the spiritual plane.

Farther on in the work above referred to, Swedenborg declares the melancholy results to which this philosophizing concerning the Infinite and Divine too often leads. "At last, when he (the philosopher) sees all these impenetrable mazes, when he has had such repeated experience of their difficulties, and has found that they all combine to form one and the same unfathomable problem, viz. this, that by all the reasons of the case no infinite can possibly exist, because it does not exist for any rational, natural, or geometrical analysis,—after this result, he secretly concludes that the divine essence is probably not infinite but indefinite, and the least and the greatest in all things: and as he sees in the greatest too a natural and geometrical condition, or an analogue of the least in quantity, space, and time, he guesses that the Divine is the prime being of nature; and consequently *that nature and God are in a manner one and the same.*"—Pp. 11, 12.

Such is the downright pantheism to which all philosophizing concerning the Infinite and Divine leads, without a knowledge of those discrete degrees or spheres through which the creative life descends from God into nature. Aside from these degrees, God is viewed upon the same plane with nature,—a God of time and space,—and the inevitable conclusion is "that nature and God are in a manner one and the same." Upon this dreary shore, which bounds the ocean of natural truth, the noble mind of Swedenborg, like thousands of others, would have made shipwreck, had he not subsequently possessed himself of the chart and compass of Continuous and Discrete Degrees. Of the nature and distinction of these degrees we shall now speak more directly, or rather let Swedenborg speak for himself.

In his work on Heaven and Hell, he says:—

"There are degrees of two kinds; there are continuous degrees, and degrees not continuous. Continuous degrees are as the degrees of the decrease of light from flame even to obscurity; or as the degrees of the decrease of sight, from those things which are in light to those which are in the shade; or as the degrees of the purity of the atmosphere, from its lowest to its highest; distances determine these degrees. But degrees not continuous, but discrete, are discriminated as prior and posterior, as cause and effect, as what produces and what is produced. He who examines will see, that in all and each of the things in the universal world, whatever they are, there are such degrees of production and composition; namely, that from one is another, and from the other a third, and so on. He who does not procure to himself a perception of these degrees, *cannot possibly know the distinctions of the heavens,* and the distinctions of the interior and exterior faculties of men; nor the distinction between the spiritual world and the natural world; nor the distinction between the spirit of man and his body; and thence he cannot understand what and whence correspondences and representatives are, nor what influx is."—N. 38.

And again, in the Divine Love and Wisdom, Swedenborg remarks:—

"THAT DEGREES ARE OF TWO KINDS, DEGREES OF ALTITUDE AND DEGREES OF LATITUDE.—The knowledge of degrees is as it were the key to open the causes of things, and enter into them: without it scarcely anything of cause can be known; for without it, the objects and subjects of both worlds appear so general as to seem to have nothing in them but what is seen with the eye.—Moreover, without a knowledge of these degrees, nothing can be known of the difference of the interior faculties of the mind in men; or, therefore, of their state as to reformation and regeneration; or of the difference of the exterior faculties, which are of the body, as well of angels as of men; and nothing at all of the difference between spiritual and natural, nor therefore of correspondence: yea, or of any difference of life between men and beasts, or of the difference between the most perfect and the imperfect beasts; or of the differences between the forms of the vegetable kingdom, and between the materials which compose the mineral kingdom. Whence it may appear, that those who are ignorant of these degrees, cannot from any judgment see causes; they only see effects, and judge of causes from them, which is done for the most part by an induction of causes continuous with effects; when nevertheless causes do not produce effects by continuity, but discretely, for a cause is one thing, and an effect another; there is a difference as between prior and posterior, or as between the thing forming and the thing formed."—N. 184, 185.

From the foregoing extracts, which contain a summary description of the two kinds of degrees, it will be seen that a vast field is laid open to our investigation, which Swedenborg was the first to explore. Let us accompany him a little way, and note the most prominent objects which present themselves to our view. In these extracts he has instanced several things, to a right understanding of which he declares a knowledge of discrete degrees to be essential. These are the distinctions between the heavens;—between the spiritual world and the natural;—between the spirit and the body;—the interior and exterior faculties;—the life of man and that of beasts; and the difference between the spiritual and natural life, which involves also the doctrine of influx and correspondence. We cannot, of course, in the limits assigned us, treat of these various and profound topics at length, but only allude to them by way of illustrating and applying our subject.

The nature of continuous degrees is easily comprehended. They embrace all kind of increments and decrements from light to darkness, heat to cold, rarer to denser, softer to harder, thicker to thinner, lower to higher, and their opposites. But discrete degrees hold the relation to each other of end, cause, and effect; of producer and produced; of that which precedes and that which follows. They discriminate between the orders of life, and the modes of existence. They show us by what laws the Great First Cause operates upon or into spirit, and through that into matter; and while they connect these as cause and effect, they by no means confound them with each other.

For the sake of illustrating the nature of these two kinds of degrees more distinctly, let us take the three elements, earth, water, and air. It will readily be seen that these are different in kind and quality. The one rests upon the other from the highest to the lowest. They flow forth in regular order from the sun; for the heat and light of the sun, which are the primary agents concerned in natural production, emanate from him by means of the atmospheres, and terminate in the different elements in a serial connexion. The connexion existing between these elements is that of discrete degrees, the one resting upon and terminating in the other, so that the last, or the earth, is the basis and continent of the other two. But in each of these there are continuous degrees. Take, for instance, deep waters, and they decrease from denser to rarer as you ascend from the bottom to the surface. This affords an illustration of continuous degrees, of increase or decrease by regular gradations. But when you have reached the surface of the water you pass into the atmosphere, and this is the transition from a lower to a higher discrete degree. Again, in ascending through the atmosphere, you pass through degrees of continuity from denser to rarer, till you reach the purer ether, which may be considered another discrete degree.

The three kingdoms of nature, animal, vegetable, and mineral, may be instanced as affording another illustration of continuous and discrete degrees. Everything that is common to the mineral kingdom, yet different from other things belonging to the same, differs by continuous degrees. That kingdom is a degree, or order of existence, by itself, and as such, is discriminated from the others; this constitutes it a discrete degree. But it is made up of strata of rocks and earth, which may be considered as forming its continuous degrees. Upon the mineral kingdom rests and subsists the vegetable, and these two are separated by a discrete degree. The same may be said of the animal kingdom as dependent on the vegetable, and constituting a distinct and higher order of life. But these two have their orders and forms more or less perfect within themselves. The proper definitions of continuous degrees, is the perfecting, or filling up, of a discrete and distinct plane or order of being. But discrete degrees involve the distinction between this plane or order, and another which is prior or posterior, and to which it sustains the relation of precedent or sequent. The stones in the foundation, or the bricks in the walls, of an edifice, make up those separate parts; but they are distinct from each other in form and design. The foundation, the walls, and the roof are distinguished by discrete degrees, the one springing from and resting upon the other. The trunk, the branches, and the leaves of a tree; the bud, the blossom, and the fruit; the seed, the pulp, and the rind of the fruit itself,—the orange for instance,—are discriminated and connected by discrete degrees. They are diverse in nature and quality, and the precedents act as proximate causes to the sequents.

But let us pass from inanimate to animated existence, and trace the distinction of our two kinds of degrees in the orders of life. The first object that attracts our attention is the worm at our feet. Mark it well. See how it advances by slow and laborious steps. It is confined to the earth, and all its habits are grovelling. This is its first stage or degree of life. Observe it when a few days have passed. It is now torpid and motionless. It is inclosed in a living tomb, awaiting its resurrection to another and a higher life. This is its chrysalis state, and is a degree of life wholly distinct from the former. But look again! It has burst its prison and come forth! It leaves the earth, and flits through the air, a gay and gaudy thing, feasting upon the essences and aroma of flowers! Mark how distinct were those three grades of life through which it passed, and how one was developed from the other, and you have a very good idea of discrete degrees.

Or shall we touch upon man, the crowning work of the Creator, made in his image and likeness? Look at the different conditions under which he exists before birth, in the world, and after death. How diverse; and yet each the precedent and proximate cause of the other. These are distinguished by discrete degrees; man's advancement and gradual maturing in each of these states take place by continuous degrees, from the infant to the angel.

We might, were we disposed, trace the three discrete degrees throughout the physical system; for " all things which exist in the world," says Swedenborg, " of which trine dimension is predicated, or which are called compound, consist of degrees of altitude or discrete degrees." If we take the blood, we find that it consists of the *animal spirits*, (perhaps our modern mesmerizers would prefer the term, *magnetic* fluid,) the *white blood*, and the *red blood*, each flowing into and producing the other, so that the blood contains these three degrees one with the other. The same may be said of the muscles; for each consists of very minute fibres, which, fasciculated, constitute those larger ones, called moving fibres, and bundles of these produce the compound called a muscle. Likewise the nerves are formed from very minute nervous fibres, which are collected into filaments, and from many of these filaments the nerve is produced. The same degrees are seen between the blood, flesh, and bones; the three kinds of skin which are laid one upon another, and in fact in every organ and compartment of the physical system.

But why do these discrete degrees exist in all things of the body? We answer unhesitatingly, because they exist in the mind by which the body is elaborated, and of which it is a type. That the mind or soul is the real man, with all his sensations, faculties, and functions, being an organized substance and in the human form, is one of the highest postulates in the psychology of Swedenborg; and the grand principle which underlies his physiology is, that the soul elaborates for itself a body to connect it with the material world, all its faculties and functions being ultimated in corresponding material organs. There is, therefore, a plenary correspondence between the soul and body, one being the cause, the other the effect, and therefore discriminated by discrete degrees. Matter is thus the ultimate of mind, and materiality of spirituality. But the mind is not independent. It is only a proximate cause of the body. It is itself an emanation from the First Great Cause, in whose image and likeness it was created, who is essential humanity, in the human form, and embodies the grand triplicate distinction of essentials, the Divine Love, the Divine Wisdom, and the Divine Proceeding, or creative energy, called Father, Son, and Holy Spirit. Thus God, the soul, and the body sustain the relation of cause and effect in a connected series, by which the divine life descends through discrete degrees from its fountain into nature. These three degrees are treated in the three sciences of physiology, psychology, and theology, terms expressive of three planes, or degrees of life.

"These three sciences," says Mr. Clissold, "however, may all be considered as treating concerning life. Theology, of life as it is in God; for God is Life itself. Psychology, of life as it is in the soul, or rather the spirit; for the functions of the spirit constitute its life. Physiology, of life as it is in the body. Thus physiology treats of outward or natural life; psychology, of inward or spiritual life; theology, of inmost or Divine Life."*

---

* Introductory Lecture addressed to the members of the Swedenborg Associa tion, December 7th, 1846.

We cannot here help expressing our consciousness of holding in our hands the key that unlocks the whole mystery of creation,—reveals the Creator every where in his creation, without compounding him with it; exhibits the connexion between the spiritual world and the natural, or the soul and the body, opens to our view the universal law of correspondence, of the relation of mind to matter, of spiritual to natural things; develops the true nature of the Word as containing truths adapted to the three states or degrees of life; and stamps the system of Swedenborg with a character all its own. All this is opened to us by a knowledge of discrete degrees, or the discriminated planes of life, which flow into and produce one another in a descending series.

We may now understand Swedenborg when he says, " Without a knowledge of these degrees, nothing can be known of the difference of the interior faculties in the mind of men ;—or of the difference of the exterior faculties, which are of the body, as well of angels as of men ; and nothing at all of the difference between spiritual and natural (things), or therefore of correspondence." We have seen how life, from the inmost Divine Life, flows into and produces the mind, and hence the spiritual world (for that world is the empire of mind) ; and thence into the body through the mind, or in the complex, into the natural world from the spiritual ; and thus the spiritual world is the immediate receptacle of creative life, and the natural world the remote or ultimate receptacle. Hence the spiritual exists within the natural, and the Divine within both, as the perpetual Fountain of Life in all things. But these are discriminated by discrete degrees, else the system of Swedenborg would be pantheism. Were the Divine Life infused through nature upon the same plane, it must be identical with it, and this was the system of Spinoza and a host of other pantheists. But the system of Swedenborg differs *toto celo* from these by distinguishing between the degrees of life from the highest to the lowest. He never degrades the Creator, while he truly exalts creation as a continual efflux from Him, showing how the Infinite Life becomes finited in the very act of flowing into and being received upon the discriminated planes or degrees in the human mind (both in the natural body and out), until it is ultimated in the material forms of nature. This is the only ground of correspondence, which is no other than the necessary and inherent relation of cause and effect, of mind and matter. That relation can exist only between discriminated degrees *in the mind;* for this alone, as made up of the will and understanding, can be considered a receptacle of the Divine Love and Wisdom, which are *the primary* agents of creation ; and it is in the mind therefore as a recipient of these agents, that we must look for the distinction between the natural and spiritual worlds, they being, with all their objects, alike outbirths from the mind, the one from its spiritual or interior, the other from its natural or exterior, degree.

This brings us to speak of the distinctions of the heavens, as existing in the different planes or degrees of the mind, into which the Divine Life is received, and upon which, as a theatre, all the apparently external objects are produced.

"He who does not procure to himself a perception of these (discrete) degrees," says Swedenborg, "cannot possibly know the distinctions of the heavens;" but having procured a perception of the nature of these degrees, as existing in the human mind, we can see the rationality of the distinction of the three heavens,—the celestial, the spiritual, and the natural,—that they consist in the reception of the divine influx of life into the different planes or degrees of the mind. He who is in a natural state, that is, whose thoughts, affections, and perceptions are of a comparatively low and natural order, may be said to inhabit the natural degree or plane of the mind; and this determines the heaven which, as an angel, he will occupy. He can only, such is his capacity, receive the divine life into this natural degree. And as his moral stature does not rise above that degree, he remains a natural spirit,—an inhabitant of the lower or natural heaven, which is composed of those who are in a like state and of a like capacity. This is the spirit's selfhood or proprium, and he can never rise above it, because he can never go out of himself. Hence in such a state of life as he had confirmed himself in while in the body, in the same he remains in the future life. If he had loved and pursued the things of time and sense in this life, to the neglect of spiritual and divine things, and yet had not confirmed his mind against them by evils of life, he continues in the same general state hereafter, that is, he has low and natural views of spiritual things, and, as he dwells in his own mind, he is in the natural heaven; for the natural degree only had been opened and cultivated in this world. He passes into the spiritual heaven at death, if in this world he had opened and cultivated the spiritual degree and faculties of his mind. "It is known in the world," says Swedenborg, "that there is both a natural and a spiritual, or an external and an internal man; but it is not known that the natural man becomes spiritual by the opening of any superior degree in him, and that such opening is effected by a spiritual life, which is a life according to the divine commandments; and that without such a life, a man continues natural."—(*D. L. & W.* n. 248.) The natural and spiritual degree in the mind constitute the natural and spiritual heavens, as the celestial degree, or a state of love, constitutes the third or celestial heaven. But let us explore these degrees of the mind with Swedenborg for our guide, for he is familiar with the whole field.

"The human mind," says he, "which consists of will and understanding, by creation, and thence by birth, is of three degrees, so that a man has a natural mind, a spiritual mind, and a celestial mind." "When a man is born, he first comes into the natural degree, and this increases in him by continuity, according to his knowledge and the understanding he acquires by it, to the highest point of understanding called rationality. Nevertheless the second, or spiritual degree, is not hereby opened. This degree is opened by the love of uses derived from intellectual things, that is, by the spiritual love of uses, which is love towards the neighbor. This degree likewise may increase by degrees of continuity to its summit, and it increases by the knowledges of truth and good, or by spiritual truths. Nevertheless the third or celestial degree, is not opened by these, but by the celestial love of uses, which is love towards the Lord. These three degrees are thus successively opened in man.

"So long as a man is living in the world, he knows nothing of the opening of these degrees in him, because he is then in the natural or ultimate degree, and thinks, wills, speaks, and acts from it; and the spiritual degree, which is interior, does not communicate with the natural degree by continuity, but by correspondences, and communication by correspondence is not felt. Nevertheless, when he puts off the natural degree, which is the case when he dies, he comes into the degree which was opened in him in the world; if the spiritual degree was opened, into the spiritual degree, and if the celestial degree was opened, into the celestial degree."—*D. L. & W.* n. 237, 238.

Let it here be distinctly kept in view, that the degree of the mind which, by the life of the individual, was *unconsciously* opened in this world, and *consciously* opened at death, determines the heaven, or if he be evil, the hell, in which he will spend his future; for the different heavens, as well as the different hells, depend on the degrees in the mind of man. The progress or extension of the mind upon any one of these discrete degrees, is effected by continuity, or continuous degrees, by the acquisition of those knowledges and truths which are peculiar to that plane or degree. But these do not open the superior degree. That is effected only by the dominant love or life of the subject; so that the three heavens are wholly distinct, and connected only by correspondence, or as cause and effect; and the angels of either heaven may progress, by continuous degrees, *ad infinitum*, without rising into a superior heaven or degree. Love to the Lord alone, who is above all, attracts them upward, and assimilates them to Him, as the attraction of the sun determines the positions of the planets in the system.

We cease to wonder that the Christian world make no distinction in the measure of future happiness or misery, but suppose the soul at death is ushered into absolute bliss or wo, when we reflect that there has been no knowledge of the real nature of the mind, as composed of three distinct degrees or capacities for receiving the divine life, and hence of the distinctions of the heavens as dependent upon them. But as we have already exceeded our limits, we will close this whole subject in the concise language of Swedenborg:

"That the nature and quality of discrete degrees, and the difference between them and continuous degrees, may be still better comprehended, let us take the angelic heavens for example. There are three heavens, and these distinct by degrees of altitude, so that one heaven is under another; and they do not communicate with each other but by influx, which proceeds from the Lord through the heavens in their order to the lowest, and not *vice versa*. But each heaven is distinct by itself, not by degrees of altitude. but by degrees of latitude: those who are in the midst, or in the centre, are in the light of wisdom, and those who are in the circumference to the boundaries, are in the shade of mission; thus wisdom decreases to ignorance as light decreases to shade, which is done by continuity. It is the same with men: *the interiors of their minds are distinguished into as many degrees as the angelic heavens, and one of these degrees is above another;* wherefore the interiors of their minds are distinguished by discrete degrees, or degrees of altitude: hence, a man may be in the lowest degree, or in the higher, or in the highest. according to the degree of his wisdom; and when he is only in the lowest degree, the superior degree is shut, and this is opened as he receives wisdom from the Lord. There are also in man, as in heaven, degrees of continuity or of latitude. *A man is similar to the heavens, because as to the interiors of his mind, he is a heaven in its least form, so far as he is in love and wisdom from the Lord."—D. L. & W.* n. 186.

T. D. S.

ARTICLE IV.

LETTERS TO A TRINITARIAN.

LETTER I.

THE ANGEL JEHOVAH.

DEAR SIR,

In our frequent conversations upon the distinguishing features of Swedenborg's Theology, you have more than once intimated your objections to his doctrine of the Divine Trinity as being really subversive of the true tenet, while yet holding forth a show of sustaining and confirming it. The position so distinctly and emphatically announced throughout his writings that the Jesus of the New Testament is the Jehovah of the Old, and that in Him is concentrated the only Trinity we are taught to recognise in either, strikes you as so inconsistent with what you have been led to believe in regard to the Tripersonal distinction, in which Christ holds the second rank, that you are prompted to an instant rejection of the entire scheme, and scruple not to affirm that if reduced to the alternative of giving up either the personal Trinity or the absolute Unity, you should feel compelled to resign the latter. This is doubtless more than most Trinitarians would be willing to say, notwithstanding their firm assurance that a threefold distinction of *persons* is unequivocally taught in the pages of Revelation. They have never yet, I believe, intimated that they considered the doctrine of the Tripersonality *more clearly* taught by the sacred writers than that of the Unipersonality. Your views on this head are probably peculiar to yourself. But in what I propose to offer on the general subject I shall take no advantage of this ultraism of position. I shall address you and aim to reason with you as occupying simply the ordinary Trinitarian ground—that is, as admitting that Jesus Christ is in some sense possessed of divine attributes, while at the same time he is, as divine, the second *person* of the adorable Trinity, in which character he assumed our nature, and accomplished the work of redemption on our behalf.

In the ensuing series of letters I propose to canvass the general theme of the Supreme Deity of our Lord and Saviour, Jesus Christ, with a special reference to the established views of Trinitarians on that subject, and by a course of argument founded upon the Old Testament Scriptures. In the prosecution of my purpose, I have the satisfaction of knowing that we shall agree as to the authority appealed to. In a controversy *with a Unitarian I fear I could not promise myself this advan-*

tage, as I perceive in the leading writers of that class a striking backwardness, to say the least, to abide by the testimony of the Old Testament in respect to the central doctrine of our Lord's divinity.   They evidently regard this portion of the scriptures as a mass of ancient historical documents, venerable indeed by age, but embodying merely the statements and sentiments of fallible men, who have chronicled facts and given utterance to poetry, prophecy, and parable under the promptings of a certain religious fervor, which at the same time falls immeasurably short of any thing that can be properly called *an infallible divine inspiration*.   With the advocates of this opinion it would of course be impossible to enter upon such a discussion as I now propose, without a long preliminary debate upon the claims of the Old Testament Scriptures to a character of equal authority, as a standard of doctrine, with that of the New.   But all this, in the present instance, I am happily spared.   I require no concession on this head but such as you are prepared at once to make.   I shall, however, venture to hope that if the eye of any candid Unitarian shall fall upon these pages, he will be somewhat arrested and impressed by an array of evidence drawn from this source, on the main position, of which perhaps he was but little aware, and the force of which I trust may not be diminished to his mind by any air of novelty in the form of its presentation.   I trust, too, that he will at least be ready to admit that on the ground which we assume, of the inspired character of the Law and the Prophets, our grand conclusion is one that is not easily resisted.   For the proof of our postulate, we refer him to the various writers on the canon who have treated it in all its bearings.

To one who has been so familiar as I have long known you to be with the original languages of the Scriptures, it must often have occurred as a query what could be really intended by the remarkable phrase *Malak Yehovah*, or, *Angel of the Lord*, so frequently met with in the Pentateuch and the subsequent books.   Who was the true personage intended by that appellation?   Was it the veritable Jehovah himself who was thus indicated, and if so, whence or why the denomination?   If it were a created angel, what relation does he sustain to Jehovah, and on what ground does he speak in His name and claim for himself His attributes?   This is a feature of the sacred record too prominent not to have attracted the notice of commentators in all ages, and yet scarcely any one, I think, can fail to have been struck with the vague and vacillating air of their expositions.   It has formed a problem that has defied their solution.   Yet nothing is *of more* importance than to ascer-

tain the grounds of this denomination. If it has any bearing
at all on the grand question at issue, it is of an import the
most momentous, as its relations are ramified, to a vast extent,
over the whole compass of revelation; and, if I mistake not,
it will appear that no adequate view can be obtained from the
New Testament of the true character of Christ which involves
an omission of the testimony gathered from the earlier Jewish
oracles. No other satisfactory clew, I am persuaded, can be
obtained to the leading titles applied to our Lord by the Evangelists and Apostles. But the evidence of this remains to be
adduced.

The first instance of the occurrence of the phraseology adverted to is Gen. xvi. 7: "And the angel of the Lord found
her (Hagar) by a fountain of water in the wilderness." After
questioning and commanding her, " the angel of the Lord said
unto her, I will multiply thy seed exceedingly, that it shall not
be numbered for multitude." It is then said of Hagar that
" she called the name of the Lord (Jehovah) that spake unto
her, Thou God seest me." From this it is clear that, whatever
be the grounds of it, an identity of some kind is here asserted
between Jehovah and the angel of Jehovah, so far as community of appellation can go to establish it. I propose in the
sequel to offer from Swedenborg the true, and, as I believe,
the only true, solution of this remarkable form of phraseology;
but my object at present is to exhibit distinctly the usage as
a basis for the final induction. In order to this I shall make
the array of passages somewhat copious.

Gen. xxii. 10–12, 15–18.—" And Abraham stretched forth his hand,
and took the knife to slay his son. And the angel of the Lord called
unto him out of heaven, and said, Abraham, Abraham. And he
said, Here am I. And he said, Lay not thine hand upon the lad,
neither do thou any thing unto him: for now I know that thou fearest
God, seeing thou hast not withheld thy son, thine only son, from me.
. . . And the angel of the Lord called unto Abraham out of heaven
the second time, and said, By myself have I sworn, saith the Lord, for
because thou hast done this thing, and hast not withheld thy son, thine
only son: That in blessing I will bless thee, and in multiplying I will
multiply thy seed as the stars of the heaven, and as the sand which is
upon the sea-shore; and thy seed shall possess the gate of his enemies: and in thy seed shall all the nations of the earth be blessed;
because thou hast obeyed my voice."

Here also it is obvious that the angel predicates of himself
what can only strictly pertain to the supreme Jehovah. This
is abundantly confirmed by Paul (Heb. vi. 13, 14), "For when
God made promise to Abraham, because he could swear by no
greater, he sware by himself, saying, Surely blessing I will
bless thee, and multiplying I will multiply thee." If the an-

gel sware by himself, and *could* swear by no greater, there must surely be some sense in which the angel is Jehovah. He is besides expressly called "God" by the Apostle.

Num. xxii. 21-27. "And Balaam rose up in the morning, and saddled his ass, and went with the princes of Moab. And God's anger was kindled because he went: and the angel of the Lord stood in the way for an adversary against him. Now he was riding upon his ass, and his two servants were with him. And the ass saw the angel of the Lord standing in the way, and his sword drawn in his hand: and the ass turned aside out of the way, and went into the field: and Balaam smote the ass, to turn her into the way. But the angel of the Lord stood in a path of the vineyards, a wall being on this side, and a wall on that side. And when the ass saw the angel of the Lord, she thrust herself unto the wall, and crushed Balaam's foot against the wall: and he smote her again. And the angel of the Lord went further, and stood in a narrow place, where was no way to turn either to the right hand or to the left. And when the ass saw the angel of the Lord, she fell down under Balaam: and Balaam's anger was kindled, and he smote the ass with a staff."

This angel is mentioned repeatedly in the subsequent verses, and in ver. 32–35 it is said—

"And the angel of the Lord said unto him, Wherefore hast thou smitten thine ass these three times? Behold, I went out to withstand thee, because thy way is perverse before me: and the ass saw me, and turned from me these three times: unless she had turned from me, surely now also I had slain thee, and saved her alive. And Balaam said unto the angel of the Lord, I have sinned; for I knew not that thou stoodest in the way against me: now therefore, if it displease thee, I will get me back again. And the angel of the Lord said unto Balaam, Go with the men: but only the word that I shall speak unto thee, that thou shalt speak."

It is then the angel of the Lord who speaks to Balaam, and dictates what he is to say to Balak. Yet it is clear that he regarded him as the Lord himself, for he says to the king of Moab, "The word that God putteth in my mouth, that shall I speak." Moreover, it is expressly said (ch. xxiii. 5), "And the Lord put a word in Balaam's mouth, and said, Return unto Balak, and thus shalt thou speak." So, also, ver. 16, "And the Lord met Balaam, and put a word in his mouth, and said," &c. The evidence, therefore, would seem to be decisive, that the titles, "angel of the Lord" and "Lord," are here used in common.

Judg. ii. 1. "And an angel (or, the angel) of the Lord came up from Gilgal to Bochim, and said, I made you to go up out of Egypt, and have brought you unto the land which I sware unto your fathers; and I said, I will never break my covenant with you. And ye shall make no league with the inhabitants of this land; ye shall throw down their altars: but ye have not obeyed my voice: why have ye done this?

Wherefore I also said, I will not drive them out from before you ; but they shall be as thorns in your sides, and their gods shall be a snare unto you."

On this passage I give an extract from my "Notes on Judges :"

" Who but Jehovah himself could or would adopt such language as this ? It was not a creature that brought the Israelites out of Egypt : but Jehovah. It was not a creature that made a covenant with them : but Jehovah. It was not a creature to whom they were accountable for their disobedience, and whose displeasure they had so much reason to dread ; but Jehovah. As to the circumstance of his being said to 'come up' from Gilgal, which is supposed to militate against this interpretation, it rather confirms it ; for it was in Gilgal, near to Jericho, that this same divine person had appeared to Joshua as an armed warrior. That *he* was Jehovah cannot be doubted, because he suffered Joshua to worship him, and even commanded him to put off his shoes from his feet, inasmuch as the ground on which he stood was, by reason of *his* presence, rendered holy. In his conversation with Joshua he had called himself the ' Captain of the Lord's host,' and therefore there was a particular propriety in his appearing now to the people, to inquire, Why they had not carried his orders into effect ? and to threaten them that he would fight for them no longer. Besides, at Gilgal the people had renewed the ordinance of circumcision and the passover, in which they had consecrated themselves to God afresh, and engaged to serve him as his redeemed people. In coming therefore as from Gilgal, the Angel upbraided them with their base ingratitude, reminded them of their solemn engagements, and humbled them the more for their violation of them."

Judg. v. 23. " Curse ye Meroz, said the angel of the Lord, curse ye bitterly the inhabitants thereof, because they came not to the help of the Lord, to the help of the Lord against the mighty."

There can be no doubt from the connexion that the term here points to the same personage as is indicated above. It was Jehovah who commanded the curse. A created angel would not have assumed such a prerogative in his own name.

Judges v. 11–16.—And there came an angel of the Lord, and sat under an oak which was in Ophrah, that pertained unto Joash the Abi-ezrite : and his son Gideon threshed wheat by the wine-press to hide it from the Midianites. And the angel of the Lord appeared unto him, and said unto him, The Lord is with thee, thou mighty man of valor. And Gideon said unto him, O my Lord, if the Lord be with us, why then is all this befallen us ? and where be all his miracles which our fathers told us of, saying, Did not the Lord bring us up from Egypt ? but now the Lord hath forsaken us, and delivered us into the hands of the Midianites. And the Lord looked upon him, and said, Go in this thy might, and thou shalt save Israel from the hand of the Midianites : have not I sent thee ? And he said unto him, O my Lord, wherewith shall I save Israel? behold my family is poor in Manasseh, and I am the least in my father's house. And the Lord said unto him, Surely I will be with thee, and thou shalt smite the Midianites as one man."

The language employed leaves no room for doubt, as to our main position. The " angel," called also, verse 20, " the angel of God," is distinctly said to have been the " Lord." So also, verse 21–24, the same character is clearly recognized.

"And when Gideon perceived that he was an angel of the Lord, Gideon said, Alas, O Lord God! for because I have seen an angel of the Lord face to face. And the Lord said unto him, Peace be unto thee : fear not : thou shalt not die. Then Gideon built an altar there unto the Lord, and called it Jehovah-Shalom : unto this day it is yet in Ophrah of the Abi-ezrites."

The more appropriate rendering would be, " When Gideon perceived that he was *the* angel of the Lord." The form of the expression in the original is precisely the same here and elsewhere, and there is no ground for the wavering of our version between " *an* angel" and " *the* angel."

In Judges xiii. 8–23, we have an account of a remarkable interview between "the Angel of the Lord" and Manoah and his wife, the parents of Samson. In the outset of the narrative he is termed "a man of God," a designation which he himself acknowledges, v. 11, but this is dropped in the sequel, and that of "angel" alone employed. After reciting his answer to their interrogatories the story proceeds :—

" And Manoah said unto the angel of the Lord, I pray thee, let us detain thee, until we shall have made ready a kid for thee. And the angel of the Lord said unto Manoah, Though thou detain me, I will not eat of thy bread : and if thou wilt offer a burnt-offering, thou must offer it unto the Lord. For Manoah knew not that he was an angel of the Lord. And Manoah said unto the angel of the Lord, What is thy name, that when thy sayings come to pass, we may do thee honor? And the angel of the Lord said unto him, Why askest thou thus after my name, seeing it *is* secret? So Manoah took a kid, with a meat-offering, and offered it upon a rock unto the Lord ; and *the angel* did wondrously, and Manoah and his wife looked on. For it came to pass, when the flame went up toward heaven from off the altar, that the angel of the Lord ascended in the flame of the altar, and Manoah and his wife looked on it and fell on their faces to the ground. But the angel of the Lord did no more appear to Manoah and to his wife. Then Manoah knew that he was an angel of the Lord. And Manoah said unto his wife, We shall surely die, because we have seen God."

I again refer to my Commentary on this passage :—

" Why askest thou thus after my name, seeing it is secret?" This has at first blush the air of a rebuke for putting such a question ; but comparing it with what follows we imagine it is such in appearance only. A rebuke supposes something criminal or censurable in him who is the subject of it. But what offence could attach to a respectful and reverential question of this kind ? Why was the mere *secresy* of the name a reason for its not being asked ? Was it not in fact for this very reason that he *did* ask it? We admit, indeed, that if Manoah had been *previously* informed that the name was *ineffable*—that it was designed to be kept a profound secret—he would have been guilty of high presumption in demanding it. But we see no evidence of this in any part of the sacred text, and conclude therefore that the angel made use of this interrogative form of speech merely in order to introduce in the most suitable and impressive manner the declaration that follows constituting the real *point* of his reply. 'It is secret;'—or rather as in the margin, 'It is wonderful,' for so the original (פלא *pelai,*) properly implies, and so is it expressly rendered, Is. ix. 6, 'His name shall be called *Wonderful* (פלא *pela*);' i. e. his nature, his character shall *be* wonderful; properly implying that kind of wonder which is the natural effect of *miracles*, of *marvellous and superhuman works*. In *apparently* declining therefore to reveal his name he does in fact make known one of his most august and glorious titles, one which went far towards conveying an idea of the divine attributes of his nature, and one which was therefore eminently appropriate to the drift of Manoah's question. The implication probably is, 'You have scarcely any real occasion to inquire as to my name (nature); it is obvious from the words, promises, and actions already witnessed and yet further to be displayed, that *I am*, and am therefore *to be called, Pela, the Admirable One, the great Worker of wonders, the Master of Miracles.*' The original (פלאי *pelai*) has the *form* of a proper name, but the *force* of an appellative. Whether he fully understood its entire import is perhaps to be doubted; but whether he did or not, the declaration is to us, considered in one point of view, immensely important; for by assuming a title which unquestionably belongs to the promised Messiah, he identifies himself with that divine personage, and consequently puts it beyond a doubt who it is that is meant by the term 'Angel' or 'Angel of the Lord,' so frequently occurring in the Old Testament Scriptures, in connection with miraculous appearances and revelations."

In ver. 19 it is said that "Manoah took a kid, with a meat-offering, and offered it upon a rock unto the Lord, and *the angel* did wondrously." As the words "the angel" are supplied by the translators, not being found in the original, and as "Lord" is the next immediately preceding subject, it might as properly be rendered, "and *he* (the Lord) did wondrously." The Heb. term for "did wondrously" is מפליא *maphlia*, from the same root with פלא *pela*, occurring above. The term, therefore, corresponds with the name which he had before attributed to himself. Being *wonderful*, he put forth a *wonderful* manifestation.

I shall pursue the subject in another number. The results will be seen to be very important.

G. B.

SELECTIONS.

EXTRACTS FROM SWEDENBORG'S SPIRITUAL DIARY.

NOW FIRST TRANSLATED FROM THE ORIGINAL LATIN.

Concerning Taste.

3998. I spake with spirits concerning the sense of taste, which they do not perceive, but are merely conscious of something from which they know how a substance tastes to a man. They said that it was a species of odor, which they could not describe. It was perceived that taste and smell very nearly agree, as in the case of certain sapid bodies which are almost similar when perceived by the smell. This is especially clear, as was said, from the fact that brutes perceive by the smell those kinds of food which are suitable for them, the quality of which they learn by the smell before tasting of them. Thus it is not the taste, but the smell which indicates the quality of their food; they therefore eat no other than such as is adapted to their nature, and which are wholesome. It is otherwise with man, who is governed by taste in his eating, and provided the taste be agreeable cares little whether his food be wholesome or not.

Concerning Life.

4096. (It may be observed) that there ought to be to man and spirit one life, which is true life, to wit, that of love, and thence of the knowledges of faith, and thus of things confirming. Such a life is truly angelic, and such was at first the life of the Most Ancient Church; but when (their pure) loves were successively turned into cupidities and thence into falsities, there arose the direful persuasions of the Antediluvians; thus the life of persuasions. After the flood the life was severed. and thence became two lives, namely, one of cupidities, which remained, being hereditarily transmitted with increase, while (the other) the life of faith, was made a life by itself and separate; for there may be given a life of faith, yea, of the knowledges of faith, which was the life of the Church after the flood; and at length, as they were ignorant of external rites, they were inaugurated into that life, and then into the precepts of the law, which they had not previously known. Wherefore there is also given at this day a life of faith without love, which, however, cannot enter heaven, unless the Lord shall previously have conjoined it with the life of love.

That there is no external Worship except from internal Principles.

4099. I spake with spirits as to the gestures and external signs which are prompted by affections, that they are as it were their bodies; as for instance, humility of heart prompts kneeling and other acts, and deep pity, tears. Thus interior principles have in them an exterior (language of) worship prompting to the frequenting of churches, and so forth. Wherefore one who places worship in externals only is a hypocrite, feigning gestures and reverential acts similar to those that flow from internals. Even preachers may by habit acquire such devout airs and be able to move the feelings of others, when yet it is all mere outside show. Thus the worship in externals is of no account except as flowing from internal promptings.

Concerning the Speech of Spirits.

4102. The spirits round about me, whoever they were, kept up a conversation respecting some matter known to me during the whole night, so that there was a kind of unceasing chat, embracing ratiocinations. The effect was to awaken me repeatedly from sleep, and their speech flowed into certain representations made in dreams. They then said to me that they were in continued conversation and they brought forth such a multitude of arguments and reasonings on the subject as was incredible. I perceived that there was with them such an indefinite series of reasonings on one topic as would exceed all belief. It was perceived also and said that evil spirits frame various shadowy things which do not truly relate to the subject in hand, and these they connect with numerous other shadows and phantasies of the subject, and which can only be taken as the imagery of dreams just spoken of; and so on.· On other occasions, they seem to converse together altogether as men, for they do not reflect that it is through ideas. With me, however, the intercourse was wholly like that of one man with another.

Concerning the Posterity of Jacob, and the Church.

4103. It was insinuated that when at length they became so immersed in falsities, that nothing but the false occupied their minds, which happened in the time of Jacob, that then they were vastated, as *they* are wont to be in the other life who are in the life of the persuasions of the false, so that they knew nothing of true worship and then knowledge was first insinuated into their minds. This was done from their being in such ignorance and such a confused mental obscurity, that they neither knew moral nor civil law, nor that they were forbidden to commit adultery, to kill, or to steal. They could not be made to know this either by miracles or by prophets, because such was the life of their cupidities derived from Jacob.

NOTICES OF BOOKS.

1.—*Eman. Swedenborgi Adversaria in Libros Veteris Testamenti è Chiro-grapho ejus in Bibliotheca Regiæ Academiæ Holmiensis asservato nunc primum edidit, Dr.* Jo. Fr. Im. Tafel. *Partis primæ Volumen primum, continens Explicationem Geneseos, cap. I. ad cap.* XXIX. *vers.* 50, *seu inde N.* 1–680. Tubingæ *et* Londini, 1847; *8vo.* pp. 457.

This first volume of Swedenborg's Adversaria, or Notes, on the Old Testament books, has recently made its appearance. It is published by Dr. Tafel, from the author's manuscript, which was kindly loaned for the purpose by the Curators of the Royal Academy Library of Stockholm. Parts second, third, and fourth, carry-ing on the work from Leviticus through the historical books to Chronicles, and embracing also Isaiah and Jeremiah, had been previously published. It is now, we believe, complete, with the exception of the part containing the remainder of Genesis and the whole of Exodus, which, it is supposed, will make two or three volumes more.

The Adversaria differs from the Arcana, according to the English correspondent of the N. J. Magazine, in this, that while " the latter gives the spiritual sense of the Sacred Books, the former gives a philosophical and scientific sense, in harmony as well with the letter as with the spiritual sense." The result of our own exam-ination hardly responds to the impression produced by this statement. The Ad-versaria is indeed more confined to the letter than the Arcana, but as far as it goes ·it *lies in the same direction,* and we find in it the germs of many of the lessons of spiritual wisdom so beautifully expanded in the Arcana.

We regard the work as, on the whole, less intrinsically valuable than the Diary. It derives its principal importance from affording evidence of the progressive char-acter of Swedenborg's illumination. It dates from the very commencement of the opening of his spiritual senses, and it is quite clear, from a multitude of passages, that his mind emerged very gradually from the dogmatic falsities of the Lutheran Church, in which he had been nurtured. He evidently had not yet be-come emancipated from the fetters of the *tri-personal theory* of the Trinity, and he undoubtedly regarded the first three chapters of Genesis as the record of literal historical facts. These with numerous other items evince that his perceptions of truth were at the time comparatively obscure, and therefore it is important to bear in mind that this posthumous publication does not stand upon the same level of authority with those which he himself gave to the world at a subsequent period of his experience.

The following extract is peculiarly interesting from its having been written only eight months after the opening of his interior senses.

475. " Of what quality the kingdom of God is to be may be known from the Scriptures of the Divine Word, for in its inmost sense is contained only that which has respect to the Kingdom of the Messiah. The simple fact that there is a King-dom of God, is all that comes to the view of the mass of men; but the quality of it is perceived when the higher way to the mind is opened, for there are in every man two ways to his intellectual mind; the one from the world through his external

senses, the other immediately from heaven through his more exalted mind, which is specifically termed the soul. This way is to be called the superior or interior, the other the inferior or exterior. The superior way, or that through the soul, is utterly unknown to the human race, for ever since the fall of Adam it has been closed to all those who, while living on the earth, were not admitted into the Kingdom of God ; it was opened to those only who were introduced into it, as were many in the primitive times, who conversed with the Messiah Himself, as Abraham, Isaac, and others, so frequently mentioned in the Divine Word. Now if the quality of this Kingdom of God were described, it would exceed all human belief, especially with those who have known only a worldly kingdom, or the world, and blinded by the love of this and of self are wise only through the external senses. Such persons, when told that there is another way that may be opened to heaven, than that through the senses called external, would reject it as a mere fable ; for which reason the superior way leading directly to heaven cannot be opened in such until those worldly and selfish loves are dispersed, and the exclusive love of the Messiah and of His Kingdom succeeds in their place. This way could never hitherto be opened by any one who is in Heaven, except by the Messiah alone, and to him only whom he designs to intromit to himself or into his kingdom : then for the first time the quality of his kingdom can be apprehended. To speak of it in few words, it is such that it involves the privilege of hearing and conversing with those in Heaven, yea, with celestial spirits, with holy men long since deceased, yea, even with Abraham, Isaac, and Jacob ; and through them mediately, or, if so infinite a favor is bestowed, (without them) immediately with the Messiah himself, and even of seeing Him. The speech in that case is altogether such as is the speech of men with their fellow-men on earth, but flowing from heaven, from on high, from every side, and is heard afar off, near by, yea, internally, and yet as perceptibly as if it were the speech of the mouth, but still in such a way as not to be heard or perceived by those standing near, nor even by those in the same society, whether composed of few or many : thus every one hears (himself addressed) in his own proper dialect. The sight also is similar to common sight, but yet so that unless one is admitted into the interior heaven, he sees only representatives, especially when the eyes are closed and he is moreover in a certain intermediate state between waking and sleeping ; he then sees (these representative objects) as clearly as we see with our eyes at mid-day. Besides hearing, seeing, and speech, the presence of objects is made known, not obscurely but manifestly by the touch. What the quality of the Kingdom of God is, therefore, is evidently perceived by the senses above-mentioned ; yet still no one would believe that such immense felicities (as pertain to it) were possible But lest these things should be rejected among fables, I can sacredly testify that I have been introduced by the Messiah Himself, the Saviour of the world, Jesus of Nazareth, into that Kingdom, and there have spoken with the celestial genii, spirits, the dead who have arisen, yea, with those who declared themselves to be Abraham, Isaac, Jacob, Esau, Rebecca, Moses, Aaron, and the Apostles, particularly Paul and James, and that now almost continually for the space of eight months, except during the time occupied by a journey from London to Sweden ; as also continually while writing the things now given to the public. Nay, these very persons, or their angels, have suggested, in many cases, the very words employed. Hence my readers may be able to know that there is a Kingdom of God, and from what is said here and elsewhere in continuation, of what quality it is. This only it is here granted to add, that I am, in a certain manner, intromitted into heaven not only with the mind, but, as it were, with the whole body or the bodily sense, and that too while wholly awake,—a fact which must necessarily appear to every one too wonderful not to be called in question ; but as I have seen, have heard, and ascertained by the senses of the body the truth of what I relate, I cannot forbear, from permission granted me, to affirm and testify the same.

"As to the things, however, which I have written concerning myself, I cannot as yet so confidently affirm them as to call God solemnly to witness to their truth ; for I am not so absolutely assured on the subject as to assert that every single word of the description tallies precisely with the reality, wherefore, with the divine permission, these matters will be reserved subject to future revision, when all doubts may perhaps be wholly removed from my mind."

2.—*The Work claiming to be the Constitutions of the Holy Apostles, including the Canons; Whiston's Version, revised from the Greek; with a Prize Essay, at the University of Bonn, on their Origin and Contents; translated from the German, by* IRAH CHASE, D. D. New York, D. Appleton, 1848, 8vo. pp. 496.

An intrinsic value attaches to everything that goes to throw light upon the subject of Christian Archæology. The "Constitutions of the Apostles" is obviously of this character. Though the proof fails of its being the genuine work of the apostles, yet it is clearly of very great antiquity, probably as high as the third or fourth century, but of uncertain authorship and doubtless ascribed to the apostles in order to give it greater currency. The work consists of a large body of "instructions" relative to church polity, church ceremonials, and christian duty. As a record of opinion and usage in the Christian Church at that distant day the book is worthy the attention of every student of ecclesiastical history. To a New Churchman it derives its value chiefly from the evidence it affords of the early foothold obtained in the Church by many of the leading errors against which the doctrines of the New Jerusalem array themselves. The germ of the Babylonian heresies is plainly visible throughout, especially in the high claims made in behalf of the episcopal dignity, of penances, festivals, &c. From the basis laid in the "Constitutions" it is easy to see how the fabric of the Papacy should at length have towered up to heaven.

The Prize Essay appended to the main work is a voluminous discussion of all the literature connected with the subject, and filled with choice gleanings from the field of church History. To us indeed the lore of the fathers is of very small account; it is a kind of *exuviæ* cast off and cast out, but which we occasionally like to contemplate as a curiosity. We are therefore glad to have such works made accessible to us in English, that they may serve an occasional turn in our resort to antiquity, if for nothing else yet to remind ourselves how far we have travelled away from it.

MISCELLANY.

THE JEWS.—The letter of the French correspondent of the N. J. Magazine, published in the Jan. No., contains a series of remarks upon the prophetical destiny of this people, which are well entitled to profound consideration. After referring to certain passages in Swedenborg, in which he affirms that the Jews have been preserved nationally distinct solely for the sake of the Word, as guardians of its external integrity and sanctity, the writer proceeds to observe, that as this end has been thus far fully obtained, and as the establishment of the New Church is in itself a pledge of the future conservation of the Word in an incorrupt state, this function of the Jewish nation will be hereafter in effect vacated, and they will enter upon a process of *fusion*, the result of which will be to merge them indiscriminately in the great mass of the civilized and christian world. This process, the writer suggests, has in fact already commenced, the evidence of which is to be seen in the relaxation and gradual setting aside of the distinguishing features of their religion, such as circumcision, the passover, the seventh day Sabbath, the prohibited meats, and intra-national marriages. Indeed, a Reformatory Society has been instituted in Germany, making public profession of the three following principles,—1st. That the Law of Moses is susceptible of development and progress; 2d. That the Talmud has no binding authority either in principle or practice; 3d. That the coming of the Messiah to conduct the

Israelites into Palestine is neither waited for nor desired by them. This is cutting the very sinews of Judaism. But this is not all; measures are now being taken in different countries to remove from the Jews the civil disabilities under which they have hitherto labored, and for admitting them to all the privileges of citizenship under the governments of the countries where they reside. Who can doubt in view of all these ominous facts, that the result predicted by the writer before us, and so clearly inferrible from the language of Swedenborg, is indeed about to be realized; and that the Jews as a nation will eventually disappear from the face of the earth? If they are therefore ever to be converted, in any number, to vital christianity, it will not be apt to be *as* Jews, but as Christians, multitudes of whom are only such in name.

EXTRACT OF A RECENT LETTER FROM LONDON.—"Will you tell *** that I should like well just now if he would drop in at 25 Church Row for a three hours chat: I should introduce him afresh to Swedenborg. In plain words, I have received this week from Stockholm three most valuable MSS. by that venerable man, viz., the Continuation of the Animal Kingdom, the Treatise on Generation, and that on the Human Faculties. These MSS. exceed in interest and importance any that I have yet seen: especially that on Generation, which will make about 500 pages, 8vo., and will form, I am certain, the most attractive treatise ever yet published on the Human Body. It is a subject to which I had paid some attention in the old way, but how far Swedenborg has distanced competition in his treatment of it, is difficult for me to express. What is wonderful, his *observations* beat those of the most *knowing* physiologists quite as much as do his *inductions*. This, then, on Generation is a most masterly work, and ought to belong to the world as soon as possible. Besides this there are a score of small treatises on different organs, which are gems of thought; and one, on the Female Breast, worthy of the exquisite subject, which the father and the baby both love so well. I have already half turned it (from the MS.) into English, and shall *perhaps* send it to *** for a present. Furthermore, there are very elaborate inductions on the senses of Smell, Hearing, and Sight. Now can you, just for your love of me, stimulate *** to endeavor to procure support for the publication of these works? Here, in London, we are quite drained by what has been done already, and unless other places interested can come forward, the MSS. must go back to Stockholm unprinted. They will, however, be of great use to me in the preparation of my Lectures: but this is a poor consummation for the labors of a Swedenborg."

NOBLE'S LECTURES ON THE TRUE CHRISTIAN RELIGION.—We are happy to announce that this valuable work is about to be reprinted and offered to the public in this country. It will be immediately put to press and brought out in handsome style, and yet sold at a price much reduced from that of the English edition.—DE GUAY'S "Letters to a Man of the World," will be ready for publication in the Spring. They will include an additional series by the author on "The Word." For laying open the spiritual philosophy of Swedenborg no work superior to this can be put by New Churchmen into the hands of their friends.

THE

NEW CHURCH REPOSITORY

AND

MONTHLY REVIEW.

| Vol. 1. | FEBRUARY, 1848. | No. 2. |

ORIGINAL PAPERS.

ARTICLE I.

THE DRUIDISM OF ANCIENT BRITAIN:

ITS DOCTRINES, RITES, CORRESPONDENCES, ETC., AS DISCOVERED IN AN-
CIENT BRITISH MANUSCRIPTS, REVIEWED AND COMPARED WITH THOSE
OF THE ANCIENT CHURCH.

THE man who is in the internal perception of the truths of
the New Dispensation, sees and feels in these truths all that is
necessary to satisfy him of their Divine origin. Other evidence than the truths themselves he needs not to convince him
of their descent from the Lord, any more than the man who
sees and feels the influence of the natural sun, needs other
evidence than the rays of heat and light which fall upon him
to convince him that they are emanations from the sun. But
the interior reception of these heaven-descended truths creates
in man an ardent desire to see others brought to the enjoyment
of the same light and blessedness which he experiences; therefore, though he needs not for himself any external evidence of
the truth, the interest he feels in the spiritual welfare of his
fellow-men makes truly welcome to him the new discoveries
in science and the history of ancient nations which are confirmatory of the truths of the New Jerusalem. Evidences
from these sources, confirmatory of the Heavenly Doctrines,
are becoming numerous, and will necessarily become more and
more so as we become more thoroughly acquainted with the
history of the earth and its inhabitants. The science of Phre-

nology, as it becomes better known, increasingly confirms the New Church philosophy of the human brain, with respect to its organization and uses, as revealed to us in the science of correspondence. Mesmerism, though generally an evil, because contrary to divine order, and therefore only permitted to prevent a greater evil, demonstrates the existence of the spiritual world, its proximity to the natural, the relation of one to the other, their mutual dependence upon each other, and the elevation of spirit, even while connected with the body, above the influence of space and time. Geology refutes the fallacious opinion entertained in the prevailing church, founded upon the literal sense of the Word, respecting the creation of the world, and infallibly shows that the only rational interpretation which can be given of the first two chapters of Genesis is that which is found in the writings of Swedenborg. And the history of Egypt, indelibly recorded in the mystic hieroglyphics of the ancient monuments of the land of Mizraim, now partially brought to light through the labors of Champollion and others, makes it evident that the Bible narration of the deluge, and of the descent of mankind from Noah, is not literally true; the history of this nation being traced in their monuments to a period many centuries anterior to the date of the flood, and found to be at that period in the most flourishing condition, and highly advanced in the arts and sciences; thereby confirming the statements made in the writings of Swedenborg, in regard to Egypt in particular, and the ancient church in general. Another fact, which in some measure evidently tends to confirm the statements of Swedenborg concerning the ancient church, is, that some years ago, in Wales, where the name of Swedenborg is almost unknown to the present day, ancient manuscripts of British Druidism have been brought to light, which contain doctrines and correspondences most strikingly resembling those of the ancient church, said by Swedenborg to have spread itself over a vast territory, and among many nations around and remote from the land of Canaan. Of the authenticity of these manuscripts not the least doubt is entertained; but they are universally received through the Principality, and in England by those acquainted with the British language, the language in which they are written, as the genuine productions of the ancient Druids. Indeed their contents prove them to be the production of an age anterior to the introduction of Christianity into Wales, but which possessed far more elevated and consistent views of the Divine Being and His government than those possessed by the prevailing church of the present day. The reason why these manuscripts have remained to so late a period unknown to the world, is thus given by the Rev. D. James, of Almondbury, a clergyman of the Church of England in his "Manual of British Druidism:"

"The ever-memorable Reformation from Popery in the sixteenth century, commenced a new era in the history of European literature. It produced a great thirst for knowledge throughout the continent and the British Isles, and was followed by a general search for ancient records on every subject of interest. Most nations seemed emulous of bringing to light their respective stores, in order to enrich the common stock; and the Press teemed with publications of various merits, on every topic connected with history, science, and religion. Druidism was not forgotten. Many learned men in England and on the Continent applied their time and talents to the study of it; but unfortunately they did not know where any fresh or undiscovered memorials of it lay. They seem to have forgotten that a people still existed in a corner of Britain, who could boast of a lineal and uninterrupted descent from those very Britons of old, among whom Druidism had originated and reigned for ages, in its greatest splendor and purity; and who also spoke that very language in which the Druids themselves had once performed their solemnities, and instructed the people, and taught the young. As these remarkable circumstances did not occur to them, of course their attention was not directed to these quarters: but they went in pursuit of Druidism in every direction except where it was to be found: like the pious women of Galilee, in a mistake, they sought the body in an empty tomb. And the result was such as might have been expected. Their productions on the subject were vague and unsatisfactory, and worse than useless, because so calculated to mislead. For truth, they substituted hypothesis; for facts, conjectures: so that, instead of filling up with a judicious hand the outline which had been drawn and left imperfect by the ancients, they effaced almost every vestige of its native simplicity and innocence, and exhibited to the world a picture so highly colored with human blood in the Vandal style, that Druidism has been looked upon by most, ever since, as a monster too hideous to be mentioned, except in terms of abhorrence and disgust. All this time, a vast treasure of original records on the subject lay undisturbed in various parts of the Principality, covered with the dust of ages, and suffering wofully from the ravages of time. The ancient Druids and Bards had committed their traditions to writing, at the time they were in danger of being lost through the invasion and persecution of the Romans. These were afterwards transcribed from time to time, by different hands, as appears from notes subjoined to the copies still extant. But the language in which these records had been preserved, being the ancient British, rendered their contents inaccessible to most except the natives themselves; and they apparently were all asleep. However, at length some of them were roused from their lethargy by the constant misrepresentations that issued from the Press, and began to explore these fast-decaying remains of Druidic lore, with a view to vindicate the general character and religion of their remote ancestors. These manuscripts have since been given to the public, in three octavo volumes, under the title of 'Myfyrian Archaiology.' They were carefully transcribed by the late Owen Jones of London, a native of Denbighshire, and eventually published at his sole expense."

These volumes were published in London in the year 1801, under the supervision of three editors, Owen Jones, Edward Williams, and William Owen. In their "General Advertisement," prefixed to the work, these gentlemen speak as follows:—" With a view of preventing the Welsh Archaiology from being depreciated, the editors are anxious of giving a brief and general account of the collection, which is now added in this form to the scanty store of archaiological literature. There still happily remains a great number of ancient manuscripts in the Welsh tongue; some of them brought together into the valuable depositories of public-spirited gentlemen, who are liberally solicitous of preserving such treasures for posterity; and many manuscripts are fortunately saved by attentive individuals. These books are venerable monuments of enlightened periods of literature amongst the Britons, while scenes of barbarity were acted over Europe, and darkened the light of our island: a literature whose origin was not borrowed, but matured at home, under that extraordinary system, the Bardic Institution; concerning which, under the name of Druidism, much has been written, much understood, and of which the world yet knows but little. From a consciousness that time was rapidly diminishing the number of our most curious manuscripts, the conductors of the present undertaking were induced to take the necessary measures for preserving the contents of those remaining, by printing a few copies to supply the demand of the collectors of British History and Antiquities. Towards accomplishing such a design, they lately increased a collection, which they had been several years accumulating for themselves, by purchasing many manuscripts, and by procuring transcripts of others: and the editors made application also to gentlemen possessed of rich treasures of this kind, for the use of their writings. Our old manuscripts have for ages been locked up in the libraries of some of the first families in Wales, first in rank, first in fortune, and what on the present occasion is worth notice, first of birth and descent. These libraries have not for several centuries been disturbed by change of proprietors." The editors furnish the following list of persons in whose libraries the principal collections of manuscripts have been preserved:

In North Wales.—Sir W. W. Wynne, at Wynnestay. Sir Thos. Mostyn, at Gloddaith. Griffith H. Vaughan, Esq., at Hengwrt. Paul Panton, Esq., at Plas Gwyn. —— Leo, Esq., at Llanerch. Griffith Roberts, M. D., at Dolgellau. Mr. Rice Jones, at Blaenau, near Dolgellau. Rev. Richd. Davies, at Bangor. Davydd Thomas, y Bardd. Thomas Edward, y Bardd.

In South Wales.—Thomas Jones, Esq., at Havod. Herbert Hurst, Esq., at Ceubalva, near Llandaf. David Thomas, Esq., at Trev Groes, near Cowbridge. —— Turbenville, Esq., at Llanaran. Rev. Josiah Rees, at Gelli Grou. Henry Williams, Esq., at Cruc Hywel. Mr. Edward Williams, the Bard, at Flimston.

In London.—The Collection, at the British Museum. The Welsh School, at Grays In Lane. Mr. Owen Jones, Thames street. Mr. Edward Jones, at St. James' Palace.

In Oxford.—The Collection of Jesus' College. The Rev. Mr. Price, at the Bodleian Library. The Earl of Macclesfield, near Oxford.

The following gentlemen are mentioned as having furnished them with valuable manuscripts, and assisted them in the work by their advice, encouragement, and good offices in conducting it :—

George Chalmers, Esq.; Sharon Turner, Esq.; Rev. John Whitaker; Rev. William Coxe; Rev. Edward Davies, of Olveston, Gloucestershire; Rev. Richard Davies, of Bangor; Rev. Mr. Williams, of Treffos, Anglesey; Rev. Walter Davies, of Meivod, Montgomeryshire; Rev. Peter Williams, of Llan Rug, Caernarvonshire; Rev. Mr. Herbert, of Dolgellau; Rev. Mr. Evans, of Brechva, Caermarthenshire; Mr. Edward Jones, Green street, Grosvenor square, London; Dr. Griffith Roberts, Dolgellau; Mr. Rice Jones, the aged bard of Blaenau: Mr. Hugh Maurice, Tooley street, London; Davydd Thomas, y Bardd; Thomas Edward, y Bardd.

In a preface of 24 pages, octavo, the Editors give a particular account of these manuscripts, and give evident proofs of their authenticity; but our limited space will not allow us to enter into these particulars; nor indeed is it necessary, as the above names of some of the most responsible and influential gentlemen, both clergymen and laymen, in Great Britain, are a sufficient warrant that there is no imposition practised upon the public by the claims of these documents. Indeed, the works themselves bear internal evidence that they are not productions of modern date. Those portions of them handed down from the Druidical age are in the form of triads, triplets, and aphorisms, the character of which will be seen in our quotations from the works. Previous to the publication of these manuscripts, about the year 1792, a short sketch of "Bardism," which had been from the commencement a component part of Druidism, and was still a surviving branch of it, was given to the public by William Owen, Esq., F.S.A., the celebrated Welsh Philologist and Lexicographer. Two years after, appeared another short Epitome of the Druidic System.

accompanied by extracts from the original documents, from the pen of Edward Williams, the venerable Bard of Glamorgan, a person of acknowledged worth, and lineally descended from the ancient sages of the Isle of Britain. In 1836 the Rev. D. James published his "Manual of British Druidism," in which he gives a full and lucid description of the religion, morals, customs, &c. of the Ancient Druids in the Isle of Britain. We mention these works, that the reader may, if he choose, have recourse to these English documents, translated by men who were strangers to the doctrines of Swedenborg, and compare them with what we shall advance upon the subject.

Swedenborg informs us that the internal doctrines of the ancient churches were in substance the same as those taught by the Lord to the Christian church, but that the ancients derived their knowledge of these doctrines from the science of correspondence. He writes thus : " They who were of the ancient church were not internal men (like those of the most ancient church), but external ; wherefore the Lord could not flow by internal way, but by an external, and teach what was good, and this first by things which represented and signified, whence arose the representative church. The Christian church in its essence is the same, as to internal form, with the representative church."—(*A. C.* 4489.) "It is known that the Lord opened the internal things of His kingdom and His church, but still those internal things were known to the ancients : but they were led to them by the external things which were representative."—(*A. C.* 4904.) The knowledge which the Druids possessed of the Lord and His kingdom, according to Swedenborg, was derived through the medium of representatives ; for to suppose otherwise would be to suppose that they were internal celestial men, and therefore in a far more elevated state than the men of the ancient church spoken of in the Word.

We will now glance at the doctrines which the Druids taught concerning the Lord, or the Divine Being.

The following are among the names by which the Deity was known to them. They are collected from their writings by Wm. Owen, Esq., F.S.A.

" Celi ;—*The Invisible One.* The most ancient church. and the ancient church worshiped an invisible God."—(*T. C. R.* 786.) " Jor ;—*The Eternal.* Duw ;—commonly translated *God,* more properly, *He who wills.*"—(*Dr. W. Richards.*) " Rheen ;—*The All Pervading Spirit.* , Peryf ;—*The Author of Existence.* Dofydd ;—*The Governor.* Deon ;—*The Distributor.* Yr Hen Ddihenidd ;—*The Eternally Ancient One,* or, *the Ancient of Days.*" "The Ancient of Days is the Lord from eternity." "By the Ancient of Days is signified the Lord as to the Divine good, or the Divine love, who is called the Ancient of Days from the most ancient time, when the celestial church existed."—(*Ap. Ex.* 195, 504.)

The following aphorism of the ancient Druids, conveys an idea respecting the nature of the Divine Being, which can be appreciated by those only who are in the truths of the New Church:

"Nid Dim ond Duw ; Nid Duw ond Dim."

There is no essential substance but God ; God is not but what is essential substance. Here we find the same doctrine taught respecting the Divine nature as that taught in the writings of Emanuel Swedenborg. "Truth Divine is the veriest essential, and is the only substantial, by which all things are."—(*A. C.* 8861.) "The Divine Love and the Divine Wisdom are substance and form in themselves, consequently the self-subsisting and sole-subsisting Being." "Nothing whatever in the created universe is a substance and form in itself, nor life in itself, nor love and wisdom in itself; yea, neither is a man a man in himself; but all is from God, who is man, wisdom and love, and form and substance, in himself: that which is in itself is uncreate and infinite ; but what is from thence, as having nothing about it which is in itself, is created and finite, and this represents the image of Him from whom it is and exists."—(*D. L. & W.* 44, 52.)

The following theological triads will show more fully the Druids' knowledge of the character and perfections of the invisible God whom they worshiped,—the God whom we now worship in the person of the Lord Jesus Christ. We give the triads with parallel passages from the writings of Swedenborg:

(DRUIDS.)

1. "There are three primary UNITIES, and more than one of each cannot exist: one God ; one Truth ; and one point of Liberty, the point where all opposites equiponderate."

(SWEDENBORG.)

"The Divine Spirit is the Divine Truth, proceeding from the one only God, in whom there is a Divine Trinity."—(*U. T.* 139.) "Without there be an equilibrium of all things nothing can exist, because there is neither action nor reaction without it ; for equilibrium is the balance of two forces, of which one acts, and the other reacts. Man is in freedom by virtue of the equilibrium between heaven and hell, which is an equilibrium between the good which is from heaven, and the evil which is from hell, and consequently it is a spiritual equilibrium, which in its essence is freedom."—(*H. & H.* 589, 597.)

(DRUIDS.)

2. "Three things of which God necessarily consists: the greatest Life; the greatest Knowledge; and the greatest Power; and of what is greatest there can be no more than one of anything."

(SWEDENBORG.)

"God alone, consequently the Lord, is love itself, because he is life itself."—(*D. L. & W.* 4.) "We say of the Divine Love, that it is infinite, and of the Divine Wisdom, that it is infinite, and in like manner of the Divine Power." "The Divine Esse and Existere in itself cannot produce another Divine that is Esse and Existere in itself; consequently there cannot be another God of the same essence."—(*U. T.* 36, 23.)

(DRUIDS.)

3. "Three things it is impossible God should not be: whatever perfect Goodness should be; whatever perfect Goodness would desire to be; and whatever perfect Goodness is able to perform."

(SWEDENBORG.)

"God is Love itself, and Wisdom itself, and these two constitute his essence." "God is infinite, because he is and exists in himself, and all things in the universe are and exist from him."—(*U. T.* 37, 28.)

(DRUIDS.)

4. "Three things evince what God has done, and will do: infinite Love; infinite Wisdom; and infinite Power; for there is nothing of power, of knowledge, or of will, that these attributes want in order to perform."

5. "The three grand attributes of God: infinite plenitude of life; infinite knowledge; and infinite power."

(SWEDENBORG.)

"In the Lord there are three things which are the Lord: the Divine of Love, the Divine of Wisdom, and the Divine of Use."—(*D. L. & W.* 296.) "Omnipotence, omniscience, and omnipresence, are properties of the Divine Wisdom derived from the Divine Love."—(*U. T.* 50.)

(DRUIDS.)

6. "Three things it is impossible God should not perform:

what is most beneficial; what is most wanted; and what is most beautiful, of all things."

(SWEDENBORG.)

"The Divine Love and the Divine Wisdom cannot but be and exist in other beings or existences created from itself."   "All things created by the Lord are uses; and they are uses in the order, degree, and respect in which they have relation to man, and by man to the Lord their Creator."—(*D. L. & W.* 47, 327.)

(DRUIDS.)

7.   "Three things that none but God can do: to endure the eternities of the circle of Infinity; to participate of every state of existence without changing, and to reform and renovate every thing without causing the loss of it."

(SWEDENBORG.)

"What is infinite in itself and eternal in itself is the same as what is divine."   "There is no proportion between infinite and finite; finite is not capable of infinite."—(*D. P.* 48, 54.) "The Divine fills all spaces of the universe without space. The Divine is in all time without time.   The Divine in the greatest and least things is the same."—(*D. L. & W.* 69, 73, 77.) "Redemption was a work purely divine, consequently it could only be effected by an omnipotent God."—(*U. T.* 124.)

(DRUIDS.)

8.   "Three causes have produced rational beings: Divine Love possessed of perfect knowledge; Divine Wisdom knowing all possible means; and Divine Power possessed by the joint will of Divine Love and Divine Wisdom."

(SWEDENBORG.)

"God, by reason of His being Love itself and Wisdom itself, is also Life itself, which is Life in itself.   The essence of love is to love others out of itself, to desire to be one with them, and from itself to make them happy.   Love and wisdom in God make one.   These properties of the Divine Love were the cause of the creation of the universe, and are also the cause of its preservation."—(*U. T.* 39, 41, 46.)

(DRUIDS.)

9.   "The three regulations of God towards giving existence to every thing; to annihilate the power of evil; to assist all that is good; and to make discrimination manifest, that it may be known what should and what should not be."

(SWEDENBORG.)

" The wicked continually lead themselves into evils, but the Lord continually withdraws them from evils. The operation of Divine Providence in saving a man begins at his birth, continues to the end of his life, and afterwards to eternity. It is a law of the Divine Providence, that a man should be led and taught from the Lord out of heaven by the Word."—*D. P.* 295, 382, 154.

The above triads show that the views which the Jews entertained of the Divine character, are far more elevated, and much better agree with the truths of the New Church, than those now entertained in the prevailing Church.

We subjoin the following paragraph, from the pen of Wm. Owen, Esq., which contains a synopsis of the doctrines of Divine Providence as taught by the Druids in their triads and aphorisms:

" God is benevolence in all His laws of nature ; for He has so ordered that the arrival of every being at a state of bliss is by all possible means accelerated. Thus the vortex of universal warfare in which the whole creation is involved, contributes to forward the victim of its rage to a higher state of existence. Even the malignancy of man is rendered subservient to the general and ultimate end of Divine Providence, which is to bring all animated reasonable beings to happiness."

This is to be understood as virtually a commentary on the last of the preceding triads. It announces what is to be regarded as the aim, the *conatus,* of the Divine Providence acting in consistency with the free will of man, and not the actual attainment of happiness by every individual of the race ; for the Druidical doctrines, as will hereafter appear, distinctly recognise the existence of a hell as well as of a heaven. Viewed in this light, it will be seen that the sentiments above cited are in strict accordance with the tenor of Swedenborg's teachings on the same subject.   T. W.

(To be continued)

ARTICLE II.

A PLEA

IN BEHALF OF SWEDENBORG'S CLAIM TO INTERCOURSE WITH THE SPIRITUAL WORLD.

(*Concluded from our last.*)

~~~~~~~~~~~~~~~

§ II.

SWEDENBORG'S STATE OF SPIRITUAL ILLUMINATION PSYCHOLOGICALLY CONSIDERED.

1. *Man was originally created capable of conversing with Spirits and Angels.*—" Inasmuch as, by the Divine Mercy of the Lord, it has been granted me to know the internal sense of the Word, in which are contained the deepest arcana, such as have never heretofore come to the knowledge of any one, nor can come, unless it be known how things are in another life, for most things which are in the internal sense of the Word regard, describe, and involve those things; it is allowed me to lay open the things which I have heard and seen, now for several years, in which it has been given to be in the fellowship of spirits and angels.

" I am aware that many will say, that no one can ever speak with spirits and angels while he lives in the body; and many, that it is a phantasy; others that I relate such things, that I may gain credit; others otherwise; but I do not regard these things, for I have seen, have heard, have felt.

" Man was so created by the Lord, that during his life in the body, he might have a capacity of conversing with spirits and angels, as also was done in the most ancient times; for he is one with them, being a spirit clothed with a body; but because in process of time mankind so immersed themselves in bodily and worldly things that they paid little regard to any thing else, therefore the way was closed; yet as soon as the bodily things, in which he is immersed, recede, the way is opened, and he is among spirits, and associates his life with them."[w]

---

[w] A. C. 67, 68, 69.

"That man is a spirit as to his interiors, has been given me to know by much experience, which, if I should adduce all of it, would, so to speak, fill volumes. I have spoken with spirits as a spirit, and I have spoken with them as a man in the body; and when I spoke with them as a spirit, they knew no otherwise than that I myself was a spirit, and also in a human form as they were: my interiors thus appeared before them, since, when I spoke as a spirit, my material body did not appear.

"That man as to his interiors is a spirit, may be evident from this, that after the body is separated, which takes place when he dies, still man lives afterwards as before. That I might be confirmed in this, it has been given me to speak with almost all whom I had ever known in the life of the body; with some for hours, with some for weeks and months, and with some for years, and this principally in order that I might be confirmed, and that I might testify.

"To the above it is proper to add, that every man, even while he lives in the body, is, as to his spirit, in society with spirits, although he does not know it; a good man is by them in an angelic society, and an evil man in an infernal society; and that he comes also into the same society after death: this has been frequently said and shown to those who after death have come among spirits. A man does not indeed appear in that society as a spirit, when he lives in the world, because he then thinks naturally; but those who think abstractedly from the body, because then in the spirit, sometimes appear in their own society; and when they appear, they are easily distinguished from the spirits who are there, for they go about in a state of meditation, are silent, and do not look at others; they are as if they did not see them, and as soon as any spirit speaks to them, they vanish."[x]

"When my interior sight was first opened, and spirits and angels saw, through my eyes, the world and the objects contained in it, they were so astonished, that they called it a miracle of miracles, and were affected with a new joy, that a communication was thus given of earth with heaven, and of heaven with earth: this delight, however, only lasted for a few months: the thing afterwards grew familiar to them, and now occasions no surprise. I have been informed, that, with other men, spirits and angels do not see the least of any thing in this world, but only perceive the thoughts and affections of those with whom they are. Hence it may appear, that man was so created, that, during his life on earth amongst men, he might at the same time also live in heaven amongst angels,

---

x H. & H. 436, 437, 438.

and vice versa, so that heaven and earth might be together,
and might form a one, men knowing what is in heaven, and
angels what is in the world; and that when men departed
this life, they might pass thus from the Lord's kingdom on
earth into the Lord's kingdom in the heavens, not as into
another, but into the same, in which they were during their
life in the body. But as man became so corporeal, he closed
heaven to himself."⁷

2. *This privilege may even now be enjoyed, but not except upon
certain conditions.*—"They who are in heaven can discourse
and converse with angels and spirits, who are not only from
the earths in this solar system, but also from other earths in
the universe out of this system; and not only with the spirits
and angels there, but also with the inhabitants themselves,
only however with those whose interiors are open, so that they
can hear such as speak from heaven: the same is the case
with man, during his abode in the world, to whom it has been
given of the Lord to discourse with spirits and angels; for
man is a spirit as to his interiors, the body which he carries
about in the world only serving him for the performing functions in this natural or terrestrial sphere, which is the ultimate
of all spheres. But it is given to no one to discourse as a
spirit with angels and spirits, unless he be such that he can
consociate with angels as to faith and love; nor can he so
consociate, unless he have faith and love to the Lord, for man
is joined to the Lord by faith and love to him, that is by truths
of doctrine and good principles of life derived from him; and
when he is joined to the Lord, he is secure from the assaults
of evil spirits from hell: with others the interiors cannot be so
far opened, since they are not in the world. This is the reason
why there are few at this day, to whom it is given to speak
and converse with angels; a manifest proof. whereof is, that
the existence of spirits and angels is scarce believed at this
day, much less that they are attendant on every man, and that
by them man has connection with heaven, and by heaven with
the Lord; still less is it believed, that man when he dies as to
the body, lives a spirit, even in a human form as before."ˢ

"Inasmuch as there are many at this day in the church who
have no faith concerning a life after death, and scarce any
concerning heaven, or concerning the Lord as being the God
of heaven and earth, therefore the interiors appertaining to my
spirit are open by the Lord, so that I am enabled, during my
abode in the body, to have commerce with the angels in hea-

---

y A. C. 1880.   ₂ E. U. 123

ven; and not only to discourse with them, but also to see the
astonishing things of their kingdom, and to describe the same,
in order to check from henceforth the cavils of those who urge,
' Did ever any one come from heaven and assure us that such
a place exists, and acquaint us with what is doing there ?'
Nevertheless I am aware, that they who in heart have heretofore denied a heaven and a hell, and a life after death, will
even still continue in the obstinacy of unbelief and denial ;.
for it is easier to make a raven white, than to make those
believe, who have once in heart rejected faith; the reason is,
because such persons always think about matters of faith
from a negative principle, and not from an affirmative. May
the things, however, which have been hitherto declared, and
which we have further to declare, concerning angels and spirits, be for the use of those few who are principled in faith !' "[a]

3. *What is to be understood by one's being in the Spirit, &c.*
"Since by the *spirit* of man is meant his mind, therefore, by
being in the spirit, which is sometimes said in the Word, is
meant a state of the mind separate from the body ; and because, in that state, the prophets saw such things as exist in
the spiritual world, therefore that is called the *vision of God.*
Their state then was such as that of spirits themselves is, and
angels in that world. In that state, the spirit of man, like his
mind as to sight. may be transported from place to place, the
body remaining in its own. This is the state in which I have
now been for twenty-six years, with this difference, that I have
been in the spirit and at the same time in the body, and only
several times out of the body."[b]
" ' I was in the spirit'—That hereby is signified a spiritual
state in which revelation is made, appears from the signification of being in the spirit, as denoting the being brought into
that state, in which spirits and angels are, which is a spiritual
state. Into this state man is brought when he is introduced
into the state of his spirit, for every man is a spirit as to his
interiors. When man is in this state, the things which exist in
the spiritual world appear to him as clearly as the objects in
the natural world : but the objects then seen by him, because
they are from a spiritual origin, are in themselves spiritual,
and such things as are of celestial wisdom are presented to
him as it were in natural images. Thus divine things are
presented in visible forms before the eyes of spirits and angels ;
hence it is that all things which are seen in heaven, are representatives and significatives, as were also the things seen by

---

[a] R. U. 124..   [b] T. C. R. 157.

John, which are treated of in the Apocalypse. Whilst man is in the body, he does not see the things that are in heaven, unless the sight of his spirit is opened, but when. this sight is opened, he sees them; thus John saw the things which are described in the Apocalypse, and in like manner also the prophets saw, who are therefore called *Seers*, and are said to have had their *eyes opened;* thus also angels were seen in ancient times, and thus also the Lord was seen by the disciples after his resurrection. This sight is the sight of the spiritual man; and because in such case all things seen appear representatively, therefore it was opened in John. He who does not know anything of this sight, believes that angels, when they were seen by men, assumed a human form, and that when they vanished out of sight, they laid it aside ; this, however, was not the case, but angels then appeared in their own form, not before the sight of the bodily eyes, but before the sight of the spirit, which sight was then opened; this is evident from the Lord being seen by the disciples after his resurrection, when he himself showed them that he was a man in a perfect human form (Luke xxiv. 39; John xx. 20–28) ; and nevertheless he became invisible; for when they saw him, the eyes of their spirits were opened, but when he became invisible they were closed. That man has such a sight, is manifest to me from much experience, for all the things which I have seen in the heavens were seen by that sight, and on those occasions I was in a like state of wakefulness as when they were not seen; but that sight is seldom opened to any one by the Lord at this day, and that for many reasons."c

4. *How Swedenborg's state, in this intercourse with spirits, differed from that of other men.*—" Unlike what happens in regard to other men, spirits have been with me as they were in the world, for with me they have been not only as men as to their mind and memory, but also as to sense, so that they would even suppose themselves to be, as it were, in the world, or to have returned into the world. They were able to lead me, to see through my eyes, to hear through my ears, others speaking, yea, to speak with them in return in their own speech, had permission been given, and to write to them in their own style ; but these things were not permitted, neither to touch others through my hands. With other persons the case is different, for my state is so ordered by the Lord, that I can be possessed by spirits, and yet without injury, very much like those who are obsessed, though *they* lose all command of themselves, whereas

---

c A. E. 54.

I was perfectly myself throughout; and this has been the case for several years, even from the first of my enjoying this intercourse; I have been as I was before, without the least observable difference."ₐ

"It is to be known, that they who are in the other life, cannot see anything which is in the world through the eyes of any man; the reason why they could see through my eyes was, because I am in the spirit with them, and at the same time in the body with those who are in the world. And it is further to be known, that I did not see those with whom I discoursed in the other life, with the eyes of my body, but with the eyes of my spirit, and still as clearly, and sometimes more clearly than with the eyes of my body, for, by the divine mercy of the Lord, the things which are of my spirit have been opened."•

"Before my mind was (spiritually) opened so that I could converse with spirits and thus be persuaded (of spiritual things) by lively experience, there were, for many years, such peculiar indications in my case, that I now wonder that I did not sooner come into the conviction of the Lord's ruling men through the medium of spirits. I not only had dreams for a number of years informing me upon the subjects of which I was then writing; but there were also changes of state during the time that I was engaged in writing, and a certain extraordinary light shed upon what was written. I had afterwards numerous visions when my eyes were closed, and a kind of miraculous light was granted me; the influx of spirits was also as manifestly perceived as any bodily sensation; and infestations and temptations occurred in many cases and in various ways through the agency of spirits. Afterwards evil spirits held in so much aversion what was written, that I was horribly beset by them. Then there appeared fiery lights, and voices were heard in the early morning hours, besides many other things, till at length a certain spirit spake to me in a few words, causing me great astonishment that he perceived my thoughts, and still more at finding my interior senses so opened that I could speak with spirits; and equally astonished was the spirit abovementioned at the same fact. From all this it may be inferred with how great difficulty man is brought to believe that the Lord rules by means of spirits, and to recede from the opinion that he lives his life from himself independent of spirits. I perceived also, after the space of some months, when I spake with spirits, that if I were remitted into my former state, I could easily have slid into the belief that the whole was mere phantasy."ᶠ

---

d S. D. 3983.   • A. C. 4622.   f S. D. 2951.

5. *How spirits are present to each other.*—"The divine omnipresence may be illustrated by the wonderful presence of angels and spirits in the spiritual world. In that world, because there is no space, but only an appearance of space, an angel or spirit may, in a moment, become present to another, provided he comes into a similar affection of love, and thence thought, for these two make the appearance of space. That such is the presence of all there, was manifest to me from this, that I could see Africans and Indians there very near me, although they are so many miles distant upon earth; nay, that I could be present to those who are in other planets of this system, and also to those who are in the planets in other systems, out of this solar system. By virtue of this presence, not of place, but of the appearance of place, I have conversed with apostles, deceased popes, emperors and kings; with the founders of the present church, Luther, Calvin and Melancthon, and with others from distant countries. Since such is the presence of angels and spirits, what limits can be set to the Divine presence in the universe, which is infinite! The reason that angels and spirits have such presence, is, because every affection of love, and thence every thought of the understanding, is in space without space, and in time without time; for any one can think of a brother, relation, or friend in the Indies, and then have him, as it were, present to him; in like manner, he may be affected with their love by recollection. By these things, because they are familiar to every one, the divine omnipresence may, in some measure, be illustrated."⁸

"Since angels and spirits are affections which are of love and thoughts thence, therefore neither are they in space and time, but only in the appearance of them: the appearance of space and time is to them according to the states of the affections and thence of the thoughts: wherefore, when any one thinks about another from affection, with the intention that he wishes to see him, or to speak with him, he is set forthwith present. Hence it is, that spirits are present with every man, who are in like affection with him; evil spirits with him who is in the affection of evil, and good spirits with him who is in the affection of like good: and they are so present, as when one is included in society: space and time make nothing towards presence, for the reason that affection and thought thence are not in space and time; and spirits and angels are affections and thence thoughts. That it is so, has been given me to know from a living experience of many years; and also from this, that I have spoken with many after death, as well with those

---

⁸ T. C. R. 64.

who were in Europe and its various kingdoms, as with those
who were in Asia and Africa and their various kingdoms; and
they were all near me; wherefore, if there had been space and
time to them, journeying and the time of journeying would
have intervened. Yea, every man knows this from what is
implanted in himself or in his mind; which became evident
to me by this, that no one thought of any distance or space,
when I related what I have spoken with any one deceased in
Asia, Africa, or Europe; as, for example, with Calvin, Luther,
Melancthon, or with any king, officer, or priest, in a distant
country; and it did not at all fall into their thoughts, how one
could speak with those who lived there, and how they could
come to and be present with him, when yet lands and seas intervene: from this it has also been manifest to me, that no one
thinks from space and time, when he thinks of those who are
in the spiritual world."[h]

" The spirits who are thought of by others (as those who
have been in any degree acquainted together during the life of
the body), are present in a moment, when it is granted by the
Lord, and so very near that they can hear and touch each
other, or at any little distance, notwithstanding they may have
been thousands of miles distant, yea, even at the stars; the
reason is, because distance of place does not operate in the
other life."[i]

"In the spiritual world, they appear present with whom another desires to speak, provided the person has had any idea of
them, from seeing them in the world, especially if this has been
the case with both. Hence it is, that friends meet together
there, and also wives and husbands; the reason is, because the
internal sight, which is the understanding, in a spirit, acts as
one with the external sight or sight of the eye; and as spaces
in the spiritual world are not as spaces in the natural world,
what any one desires to see in that world is near, and what is
not desired is far off. From this circumstance it is that aspect
signifies presence."[j]

6. *Swedenborg made a medium of vision to spirits in the
spiritual world.*—" As to what pertains in general to spirits
and angels, all of whom are the souls of men living after the
death of the body, they have much more exquisite senses than
men, viz., sight, hearing, smell, and touch, but not taste. Spirits however are not able, and angels still less, by their sight,
that is, by the sight of the spirit, to see any objects in the
world; for the light of the world, or that of the sun, is to them

---

h D. P. 50.   i A. C. 1274.   j A. E. 25.

as thick darkness. So man, by his sight, that is, by the sight of the body, is not able to see any objects of the other life; for the light of heaven, or the heavenly light of the Lord, is to him as thick darkness. Still, however, spirits and angels, when it pleases the Lord, can see the objects of the world through the eyes of men; but this is only granted by the Lord, when he gives to man to discourse with spirits and angels, and to be in company with them. It has thus been granted them to see through my eyes the objects of this world, and to see them as distinctly as myself, and also to hear men discoursing with me. It has several times happened, that some have seen through me, to their great amazement, the friends whom they knew when in the life of the body, as present as formerly. Some have seen their husbands and children, and have desired that I would tell them that they were present, and saw them, and that I would tell them concerning their state in the other life. This, however, I was forbidden to do, and for this, among other reasons; because they would have said that I was insane, or would have thought that it was the invention of a delirious imagination: for I was well aware, that although with their lips they allowed it, yet they did not in heart believe in the existence of spirits, and the resurrection of the dead."[k]

"The spirits who were with me saw through my eyes the objects of this world, as perfectly as I; but some of them, who were still in the fallacies of the senses, supposed that they saw them through their own eyes; but it was shown them that it was not so, for when my eyes were shut they saw nothing in this atmospherical world. The case is similar with man: it is not the eye which sees, but his spirit through the eye. The same may also appear from dreams, in which sometimes man sees as in open day. But this is not all: the case is similar with this interior sight, or that of the spirit. This does not see of itself, but from a vision still more interior, or that of its rational: yea neither does this see of itself, but there is a sight still more interior, which is that of the internal man: but not even does this see of itself: but it is the Lord, through the internal man, who alone sees, because he alone lives; and he gives to man that he may see, and that it may appear as if he saw from himself."[l]

7. *That he was also in several respects brought into a like state with them.*—"That spirits have a pulse and respiration as well as men in the body, cannot be shown otherwise than by

<hr>

[k] A. C. 1880.   [l] A. C. 1954.

spirits and angels themselves, when permission is given to converse with them.   This permission has been given to me. When questioned concerning this matter, they said that they are as much men as men in the world, and that they also have a body, but a spiritual one, and that they also feel the pulsa- tion of the heart in the chest, and of the artery at the wrist, like men in the natural world : on this subject I have ques- tioned many, and they all said alike.   That a man's spirit re- spires in his body, has been given me to know from my own experience.   The angels were once allowed to guide my re- spiration and diminish it at pleasure, and at length to stop it, until the respiration of my spirit only remained, which I then sensibly perceived.   That the like was then done to me when I was instructed of the state of dying persons, may be seen in the work on *Heaven and Hell*, n. 449.   I have some- times also been reduced to the respiration of my spirit alone, which I then sensibly perceived to be in concord with the com- mon respiration of heaven.   Many times also I have been in a similar state with the angels, and likewise elevated to them into heaven, and then in the spirit out of the body, and spake with them with a respiration in like manner as in the world. These and other living proofs convinced me, that a man's spi- rit respires not only in his body, but also after he has left the body ; and that the respiration of the spirit is so secret, that it is not perceived by a man, and that it flows into the manifest respiration of the body, as cause into effect, and as thought into the lungs, and by the lungs into speech.   Hence also it is. evident, that the conjunction of the spirit and body in a man, is by means of the correspondence of the cardiac and pulmon- ary motion of both."[m]

"Angels speak one with another just as men in the world, and also on various subjects, as on domestic affairs, on affairs of civil society, on the affairs of moral life, and on the affairs of spiritual life: nor is there any other difference than that they converse more intelligently than men, because more inte- riorly from thought.   It has been granted me often to be in company with them, and to speak with them as a friend with a friend, and sometimes as a stranger with a stranger ; and then, because I was in a similar state with them, I knew no otherwise than that I was speaking with men on earth."[n]

"There were shown to me certain species of respirations, concerning which much conversation also was had, as, for in- stance, that there is conjoined with the usual respiration an external one, which is common to the world of spirits ; then

---

[m] D. L. & W. 391.   [n] H. & H. 234.

shade into light, because he passes from the things of the world to the things of heaven, and from the things of the body to the things of the spirit ; but, what is surprising, although they can understand these things, still they think the contrary, namely, that the state of life in the body is comparatively clear, and the state of life, when the body is put off, is obscure. Secondly, they may know, if they would but use their reason, that the life which man has formed to himself in the world, follows him, in other words, that he has a life of the same nature after death ; for they may know, that no one can put off the life which he has formed to himself from infancy, unless he dies absolutely, and that this life cannot be instantaneously trans-muted into another, still less into an opposite life. For exam-ple : he who has formed to himself a life of deceit, and has found in deceit the delight of his life, cannot put off the life of deceit, but is also in that life after death'. So, too, they who have lived in self-love, and thereby in hatred and revenge against those who have not submitted to them, or in other sim-ilar evils, continue in the same after the life of the body, for those evils are the things which they love, and which consti-tute the delights of their life, consequently the very life itself ; and so in other cases. Thirdly, a man may know from him-self, that when he passes into another life, he leaves many things behind, such as cares respecting food, clothing, habita-tion, and the acquirement of money and wealth, for in another life there are no such cares ; also cares respecting promotion to dignities, which so much engage man's thoughts during his life in the body ; and that these are succeeded by other things, which have no relation to the kingdom of this world. Hence, Fourthly, it may be known, that he whose thoughts have been employed solely about such earthly things, so as to be totally occupied therein, and to make such things alone the delight of his life, is not fit to be among those whose delight it is to think of heavenly things, or things relating to heaven. Hence also it may be known, Fifthly, that when these external things of the body and the world are removed, man is such as he was inwardly, namely, thinks and wills such things. In this case, if the thoughts inwardly had been deceitful, engaged in artful machinations, aspiring to dignities, to gain, to reputation, for the sake of worldly or corporeal things, or if they had been influenced by hatred, revenge, and other similar evils, he will necessarily after death think the same things, consequently he will think infernal things, however with a view to the above ends he might have concealed his thoughts before men, and in an external form have appeared upright, and induced others to believe that the above evils never had engaged his attention.

with men the light of heaven flows-in into the light of the
world, and thereby into such things as either extinguish, or reject, or darken, and thereby make dim the light of heaven ; the
cares of the world and of the body are such things, especially
those which flow from the loves of self and of the world;
hence it is that the things which are of angelic wisdom are for
the most part unutterable, and also incomprehensible.   Nevertheless man comes into such wisdom after the rejection of the
body, that is, after death, but only that man who had received
the life of faith and charity from the Lord in the world ; for
the faculty of receiving angelic wisdom is in the good of faith
and charity.   That the things are ineffable, which the angels
see and think in the light of heaven, hath been also given
to know from much experience, for when I have been elevated
into that light, I have seemed to myself to understand all those
things which the angels there spake, but when I have been let
down from thence into the light of the external or natural man,
and in this light was willing to recollect the things which I
had there heard, I could not express them by terms, and not
even comprehend them by ideas of thought, except in a few
instances, and these few also in obscurity ; from which considerations it is evident, that the things which are seen and
heard in heaven, are such as the eye hath not seen, nor the ear
heard."ᴾ

9. *With whom Swedenborg conversed in the Spiritual World.*
"That worldly blessing is nothing in respect to heavenly
blessing which is eternal, the Lord thus teacheth in Matthew,
' What doth it profit a man if he shall gain the whole world,
and lose his own soul' (xvi. 26) : nevertheless the man, who is in
worldly and terrestrial things, doth not apprehend this word,
for worldly and terrestrial things suffocate and produce this
effect, that it is not even believed that there is eternal life ; but
I can avouch that man, as soon as he dies, is in another life,
and lives a spirit amongst spirits ; and that on this occasion he
appears to himself and to all others in that life, altogether as
a man in the world, endowed with every sense internal and external ; consequently the death of the body is only the casting
off such things as had served for use and employment in the
world, and moreover that death itself is the continuation of
life, but in another world, which is unseen before the eyes of the
terrestrial body, but is there conspicuous in a light which a thousand times exceeds the mid-day light of the world ; inasmuch
as I know this from living experience of so many years, which

P A. C. 9094.

is still continued, therefore-I avouch it; I discourse still and have discoursed with almost all whom I have known in the world, and who are dead; with some after two or three days from their decease; most of them were exceedingly indignant, that they did not believe any thing of a life which was to remain after death: with some of them I have discoursed not for a day, but for months and years; and it hath also been given to see their states of life in succession or progress either to hell or to heaven: wherefore whosoever wishes to be happy to eternity, let him know and believe that he is to live after death; let him think this and remember it, for it is a truth: let him also know that the Word is the only doctrine which teaches how a man ought to live in the world, that he may be happy to eternity."q

"It being permitted me to declare what I have heard and seen for several years, it is first to be told how the case is with man, when he is resuscitated, or how he passes from the life of the body into the life of eternity: and that I might know that men live after death, it has been granted me to speak and converse with many who were known to me during their life in the body, and this not for a day and a week, but for months, and almost years, speaking and conversing with them as in the world: these very much wondered that they themselves, during the life in the body, had been, and that others, and the greater part, still are in such unbelief, that they think they shall not live after death, when yet hardly a few days intervene, after the decease of the body, before they are in another life; for it is a continuation of life.".r

"The queen expressed her satisfaction at seeing him, and asked him whether it was true that he could converse with the deceased? He answered, Yes. She inquired further, Whether it was a science that could be communicated to and by others? No. What is it then? A gift of the Lord. Can you, then, speak with every one deceased, or only with certain persons? He answered, I cannot converse with all, but with such as I have known in this world; with all royal and princely persons, with all renowned heroes, or great and learned men, whom I have known, either personally, or from their actions or writings; consequently, with all, of whom I could form an idea; for it may be supposed that a person whom I never knew, nor of whom I could form any idea, I neither could nor would wish to speak with. The queen then asked him, Whether he would undertake a commission to her lately deceased brother? He answered, With all my heart. On this he followed the queen,

---

q A. C. 8933.   r A. C. 70.

with the king and Count Scheffer, to a window in the apartment, where the queen gave him his commission, to which he promised to bring her an answer.   After this he was invited to the royal table, where they put a thousand questions to him, which he answered truly.   Some time afterwards, Count Scheffer paid him another visit, and asked him whether he would accompany him to court again, to which he consented.   The queen on seeing him, said, Do not forget my commission.   He answered, It is already done.   And when he delivered her his message, she was extremely surprised, and became suddenly indisposed ; and, after some recollection, she said, This no mortal could have told me !   On my inquiring whether any person had heard what the queen had said when she gave him the commission, he.answered, I do not know ; yet she did not speak so low but that the king and Count Scheffer, if they had attended to it, might have heard it.   This may be depended upon, as the late venerable man himself related it to me."[*]

"I have spoken one whole year with Paul, and also of what is mentioned in the Epistle to the Romans, iii. 28.   I have spoken three times with John ; once with Moses ; and I suppose a hundred times with Luther, who owned to me that, contrary to the warning of an angel, he had received the doctrine of salvation by faith alone, merely with the intent that he might make an entire separation from popery.   But with the angels I have conversed these twenty-two years past, and daily continue so to do ; with them the Lord has given me association, though there was no occasion to mention all this in my writings.   Who would have believed, and who would not have said, Show some token that I may believe ? and this every one would have said who did not see the like."[†]

10. *What may be known concerning the Future Life.*—"The things they might have known for themselves, if only, as was said, they had been willing to use their reason, are the following.   FIRSTLY, that when man is divested of the body, he enjoys much greater powers of understanding than during his life in the body, from the cause that whilst he is in the body corporeal and worldly things engage his thoughts, and these induce obscurity ; whereas when he is divested of the body, such things do not interrupt, but he is like those persons who are in interior thought by an abstraction of the mind from the outward things of sense.   Hence they might know that the state after death is much clearer and brighter than the state before death, and that when a man dies, he passes comparatively from

---

[*] Let. of Gen. Tuxen (Doc. p 150).   [†] Let. iii. to Oeting. (Doc. p. 154).

cool reflection (in which many things are to be met with as hitherto unknown,) it is easy enough to conclude, that I could not come to such knowledge but by a real vision, and by conversing with those who are in the spiritual world. If any doubt shall still remain, I am ready to testify with the most solemn oath that can be offered in this matter, that I have said nothing but essential and real truth, without any mixture of deception. This knowledge is given to me from our Saviour, not from any particular merit of mine, but for the great concern of all Christians' salvation and happiness; and as such, how can any venture to assert it as false? That these things may appear such as many have had no conception of, and of consequence, that they cannot easily credit, has nothing remarkable in it, for scarce anything is known respecting them."[y]

REMARKS.

In view of the preceding array of testimonies to the truth of Swedenborg's claims, a question of great moment inevitably comes up :— On what grounds are these claims rejected? In what point precisely is concentrated the essence of the incredibility alleged? Is any portion of the above statements open to the charge of being either irrational or absurd? Suppose that either Ezekiel, Daniel, or John had given the same account of their own psychological state, when made the medium of divine communications, would it not have been deemed satisfactory? Granting the intrinsic possibility of such a preternatural illumination in any case, do not the circumstances in respect to Swedenborg fulfil the requisite conditions? Is not the evidence afforded just such as we feel *ought* to be given, in case the asserted translation of spirit actually took place? Could the phenomena be more appropriate? But the prophetic trance is surely possible, because it has repeatedly occurred, and the inspired character of the biblical books is a standing testimony of the fact! Again, then, we ask, wherein do Swedenborg's pretensions fail of their due authentication? If it be said that the doctrines promulgated by him in that state are in themselves anti-scriptural and false, and that this fact stamps the alleged extacy as a delusion, why will not his impugners condescend to argue this point on its own merits? We are prepared to meet them in the open arena of debate, making the inspired volume the grand tribunal of appeal. But we regret to say, that to this proposal they universally and pertinaciously refuse to accede. The simple fact that any alleged sys-

---

[y] Let. to the King (Doc. p. 72).

That these external appearances or pretences of uprightness, are also taken away in another life, may likewise be known from the fact, that external things are put off from the body, and are no more of any use ; hence every one may conclude from himself, how man will then appear in the sight of angels. The SIXTH thing which may also be known, is, that heaven, or the Lord by and through heaven, is continually operating, and flowing in with good and truth, and that if there be not in men something recipient of good and truth, as a ground or plane, in the interior man which lives after the death of the body, the influent good and truth cannot be received, and that man on this account, during his life in the world, ought to be solicitous to procure to himself interiorly such a plane. This cannot be procured but by thinking good towards the neighbor, and by willing what is good from him, and thence doing good to him, and thereby acquiring to himself the delight of life in such things. This plane is acquired by charity towards the neighbor, that is, by mutual love, and it is this plane which is called conscience. Into this plane good and truth from the Lord can flow, and be received therein, but not where there is no charity, and consequently no conscience. In this latter case the influent good and truth is transfluent, and is changed into what is evil and false. The SEVENTH thing which man may know from himself, is, that love to God and love towards his neighbor are what make man to be man, distinct from brute animals, and that those loves constitute heavenly life or heaven, and their opposites infernal life or hell. But the reason why man does not know the above things is, because he is not willing to know them, for he lives an opposite life ; also, because he does not believe that there is a life after death ; and further, because he has received principles of faith, and none of charity, and hence believe according to the doctrinals which generally prevail, that in case there is a life after death, he may be saved by virtue of faith, without any regard to his manner of life, and this, if he should receive faith even at his dying hour."[u]

11. *Swedenborg's assurance of the vast difficulty that men would have in crediting his reports of the other life.*—" I am aware that the things which have been heretofore said, will not be believed by those who are immersed in corporeal, terrestrial, and worldly things, that is, by such of them as hold those things for an end, for these have no apprehension of other things than those which are dissipated by death. I am aware also, that neither will they believe, who have thought and in-

---

[u] A. C. 3957.

quired much about the soul, and have not at the same time comprehended that the soul is man's spirit, and that his spirit is his very man which lives in the body. For these cannot conceive any other notion about the soul, than that it is something cogitative, or flamy, or ethereal, which only acts into the organic forms of the body, and not into the purer forms which are of its spirit into the body, and thus such that it is dissipated with the body; and this is especially the case with those who have confirmed themselves in such notions by views puffed up by the persuasion of their own superior wisdom."[v]

"How difficult it is to induce mankind to believe in the existence of spirits and angels, and particularly in its being possible for any one to speak with them, was made apparent to me from the following instance. There were certain spirits, who, during their life in the body, had been among the more learned, and who were then known to me (for I have conversed with almost all with whom I was acquainted during their life in the body, with some for several weeks, with others for the space of a year, altogether as if they had been alive in the body). These spirits were once reduced to a state of thought similar to what they had been in during their abode in the world, which is easily effected in the other life. It was then insinuated to them, whether or not they believed it to be possible for man to converse with spirits? They then in that state said, that it is a phantasy to believe any such thing: and this they continued to assert. Hence it was given me to know, how difficult it is to persuade mankind, that any discourse can take place between men and spirits, by reason of their not believing in the existence of spirits, still less that themselves are to come amongst spirits after death; at which also these same spirits were then greatly surprised. Yet these were men of the more learned class, and who had spoken much in public concerning the other life, and concerning heaven and angels; so that there was reason to suppose that this was perfectly well known to them scientifically, especially from the Word, where it frequently occurs."[w]

. "I have conversed with spirits, and on their inquiry, explained to them how the particulars I have written in regard to them seem to be received by men, when I am about to publish them; because bad spirits insinuated into me a belief that no one would receive them, but that every one on the contrary would reject them. I entertain myself at present with this subject in company with spirits when walking in the street, and it has been granted me to perceive that there are

---

[v] A. C. 4622.   [w] A .C. 1636.

five kinds of reception of my writings, or rather, if you please, five sorts of readers. *The first* is formed of those who reject them entirely, because they are in another persuasion, and also those that at the same time receive no faith. These reject them, as such things cannot be received by them, inasmuch as they do not enter into their mind. *The second* kind of reception is of those who receive them as scientifics, and as objects of mere curiosity. *The third* sort are those that receive them intellectually, so that they find the subject agreeable enough, but whenever it requires an application to regulate the conduct of their lives, they remain where they were before. *The fourth* kind consists of those who receive the matter in a persuasive manner, so that the subject penetrates even in a degree to the amendment of their lives, which leads them sometimes towards uses. *The fifth* kind consists of all those who receive it with delight, and confirm it in a life agreeable thereto."[x]

"I have already informed your majesty, and beseech you to recall it to mind, that the Lord our Saviour manifested himself to me in a sensible personal appearance; that He has commanded me to write what has been already done, and what I have still to do: that He was afterwards graciously pleased to endow me with the privilege of conversing with angels and spirits, and to be in fellowship with them. I have already declared this more than once to your majesty, in the presence of all the royal family, when they were graciously pleased to invite me to their table with five senators, and several other persons; this was the only subject discoursed of during the repast. Of this I also spoke afterwards to several other senators; and more openly to their excellencies Count de Tessin, Count Bonde, and Count Höpken, who are still alive, and were satisfied with the truth of it. I have declared the same in England, Holland, Germany, Denmark, and at Paris, to kings, princes, and other particular persons, as well as to those in this kingdom. If the common report is believed, the chancellor has declared, that what I have been reciting are untruths, although the very truth. To say they cannot believe and give credit to such things, therein I forgive them, for it is not in my power to place others in the same state in which God has placed me, so as to be able to convince them by their own eyes and ears, of the truth of those deeds and things I publicly have made known. I have no ability to capacitate them to converse with angels and spirits, neither to work miracles to dispose or force their understandings to comprehend what I say. When my writings are read with attention and

---

[x] S. D. 2955.

selves as impregnable to their most enlightened reason. They challenge the most unsparing scrutiny of the truth of these *principles*,
whether psychological or exegetical. · It is impossible that any one
should have a stronger conviction in regard to any particular feature
of the system that it is *false*, than they have in regard to the system as
a whole that it is *true*. Nothing, therefore, of the nature of an objection has with them the weight of a feather, till what they affirm to be
intrinsically *true* is shown to be *untrue*.

But another evasion is still in reserve—"If the evidence of Swedenborg's truth is so convincing to his disciples, why is it not produced
and set blazing before the eyes of others? We ask for it, and it is
never forthcoming." That is possible, and yet his adherents be excul-
pate in the premises. They can only point to it where it is to be found,
and where *they* have found it—in the body of the writings. It is by the
perusal of these that they have acquired their conviction of their truth
as a whole, and the refutation of their faith must of necessity require
a careful study of the documents in which it is embodied, and an elaborate investigation of their character on the score of the asserted
principles. This, however, we are constrained to repeat, is a course
which our opponents invariably shun. They do not trouble themselves
to master the system *as a whole*. Yet this is an indispensable requisite
for one who would deal controversially with our faith. It is in view
of the system *as a whole* that we have embraced it, and it is only by its
being shown fallacious *as a whole* that we can ever renounce it. Let
then this acquaintance with the writings in question be candidly and
patiently formed, and we shall acknowledge a competency on the part
of assailants to meet our assumptions in the fair field of debate. But
if this be done, the debate, we believe, will seldom *come off*. Our conviction is very strong, that whoever sits down in a proper spirit to the
inquiry as an adversary, will rise from it as a disciple. Let him that
doubts make the trial.   G. B.

tem of religious doctrines differs from the established belief, is accounted sufficient to condemn it at once, notwithstanding their advocates
are usually very emphatic in asserting the superior rational and logical
consistency of their scheme of theology, and are far from being reserved in their challenges of argumentative refutation.   But for the
most part, they will not argue with Swedenborg or his adherents.
The different sects will readily engage in wordy warfare with each
other—the Arminian will encounter the Calvinist, and the Calvinist the
Arminian,—the disciples of the Old School in all the churches will earnestly " try conclusions" with those of the New,—but neither the one nor
the other will deign to meet the New Churchman in debate on the fundamental principles which underlie *all* their controversies, and in comparison with the importance of which their endless logomachies on
minor points sink into absolute insignificance.   Against such an adversary, however, they seem to have agreed, by common consent, that the
proper weapons to be employed are ridicule and abuse, instead of reason and logic.

We have no hesitation in affirming, that there is, to a candid mind,
a certain indescribable air of truth diffused over the preceding extracts ; and the same character we declare predicable of the entire system.   Now this agreement of the disclosures with the mind's native
intuitions, is a fact to be accounted for.   As the spontaneous conviction of their truth cannot be easily resisted, how is this truth consistent
with the presence of a mass of utter falsities ?   Does the same fountain send forth at the same time bitter waters and sweet ?   Undoubtedly
there are many things strange and startling in the body of the
revelations, and calculated to create a *prima facie* against them.   But
the objections from this source have been actually overcome in the
minds of multitudes of men of high intelligence and cool judgment,
by the force of countervailing evidence in their favor, and is not some
consideration due to the grounds of their decision ?   It is gratuitous to
assert that they were insensible to the difficulties which meet every
reader at the threshold of the system.   They could not but feel them
in all their force, yet these difficulties gave way before the overwhelming pressure of confirmation from a hundred sources.   And in all this
they strenuously maintain that the mental process through which they
have passed cannot be impeached of precipitation or infirmity.   They
wish the world to be assured, that they profess to have yielded to the
most sound and legitimate evidence of truth.   They declare themselves
unable even to conceive of stronger grounds of belief than they find
in the internal evidence of what Swedenborg has taught respecting the
nature of man, the nature of God, the import of the Word, and the
conditions of future existence.   They clearly perceive that all his
statements on these heads rest upon *principles* which assure them-

Each of these causes of the present position of men's minds in regard to the Scripture, were dwelt upon at some length in the last lecture.

Now granting the Bible to be really the Word of God, and considering the doubts which have arisen and are continually arising in the minds of men in regard to it—considering the neglect and disrepute into which it has long been falling with a large class of minds, might we not reasonably conclude that God would, in some manner, interpose to arrest this swelling tide of scepticism—this downward progress of men's minds in regard to His Word? Might we not reasonably conclude that He would display the beauty, glory, and perfection of His Word, in such a manner as to remove the doubts of honest doubters, and to satisfy the severest demands of enlightened reason in regard to its divinity and its sanctity? And how could he do this except by something like a further revelation? And this is claimed for Swedenborg. It is claimed for him that he has made a revelation which removes the difficulties in regard to the Bible, that have hitherto embarrassed the minds of men, and that he has exhibited the Word in such a light as shows it to be altogether worthy of its divine author. The doctrine concerning the Sacred Scripture as held and taught by the New Church, is not that which Swedenborg *found out* by ordinary study and research, but that which was revealed to him by the Lord. It comes to us, therefore, professedly as a revelation.

But a grave objection meets us in the very outset, "Is the Bible a Revelation from God, and have we need of another revelation to teach us what the Bible means? Does not the very term *Revelation* imply that something is here made known to men, which they did not know before? With what propriety, therefore, can the Bible be called a *revelation*, if we must have another revelation to enable us to understand it? If a revelation, in order to be such, must *reveal* something previously unknown, the very claim set up by Swedenborg in relation to this subject, is of itself sufficient to stamp him as a deluded visionary, and his teachings as the dreams of an enthusiast or a madman." Thus Professor Woods, in his recent "Lectures on Swedenborgianism," asks, "Is it credible, that the revelation which God made under the former and the latter economy, absolutely required another revelation from heaven, to disclose its true meaning?" This is one of the first objections which it is common to hear made, and we, therefore, shall attempt to meet and answer it on the threshold.

And in the first place we say that there are some things—that there are *many* things—revealed in the Bible, which, as

ARTICLE III.

THE SACRED SCRIPTURE.—No. II.

In the previous portion of the present essay some remarks were made upon the sceptical tendencies of our times in regard to the inspiration and divinity of the Sacred Scripture. It was stated that the Bible was obviously falling into neglect and disrepute with a large and continually increasing class of minds;—that it is much less revered and studied by the men in Christendom now, than it once was:—and that large multitudes are to be found who have secret and honest doubts whether it be the Word of God in the strict and proper sense of that expression.

We also enumerated several of the more obvious causes of the irreverent and sceptical tendency of men's minds in regard to the Scripture, which is so apparent and so much to be delored. Among these causes were mentioned—

(1.) The loose and low views of the nature and extent of inspiration which have been gaining currency for the last few centuries among christian teachers and theologians themselves;—views which render it exceedingly difficult to define the difference between the inspiration of the Bible and that of any other book.

(2.) The great number of sects into which the Christian Church has been divided, and the almost countless volumes of commentaries on the Scripture which have been published, and which are known to contain different and often opposite views of the same text.

(3.) The many irrational and absurd doctrines which have been, and are still, confidently put forth from the pulpit and the press as the doctrines of the Bible; and the consequent disposition among religious teachers to undervalue and discard the use of reason in matters of religion.

(4.) The established theological maxim of the modern church, that the Bible has but *one* sense, and this the apparent, obvious, literal sense; according to which maxim much of the Bible is seen to be unintelligible, some of it unreasonable, some of it trivial, and wholly unworthy the character of the Being claimed as its author.

they have been hitherto understood, could not have been known unless they had been revealed. Although these things, many of them, have been but imperfectly apprehended, still they have done unspeakable good. Imperfectly, therefore, as the Bible has hitherto been understood, on account of its own perfection, and the relative imperfection of man, it is proper to call it a revelation. It is by no means essential to the true idea of a revelation, that what is revealed shall be perfectly understood in all its parts by the men to whom it is at first vouchsafed. It may be of such a nature that only a little of it will be understood at first, and this quite imperfectly; that it will be better understood at a subsequent period, and better still at a period still later. Thus it may be so constructed that its true and full import shall gradually and successively unfold, keeping pace all the while with the gradual and progressive development of the human intellect, and the improvement of the human heart. The Jews, at the time of the Lord's first advent, had the Old Testament Scriptures; and we think it not improper, therefore, to say that they had a revelation from God. But we have the Lord's own declaration that they did not rightly understand this revelation. " Ye do err," He says, "not knowing the Scriptures." And we are assured that one object of this advent was to impart unto men a better knowledge of the Scriptures. "I am not come," He says, "to destroy the law or the prophets, but to fulfil," or *to fill out,* i. e. by explaining and illustrating its true meaning by words and actions.

A revelation, therefore, is none the less such, and none the less entitled to the name, because there are different degrees in which it may be understood; or because more and more of its true import may be unfolded at different epochs of the world's history, adapted to the progressive advancement of the human race. Indeed if we reflect deeply upon the subject, we shall see that it is this very characteristic which allies the revelation to the works of God, and which ought, therefore, to stamp it as of divine origin.

" It is no objection," says Dr. Woods,[*] " to the inspiration of the Scriptures, *that the real and full meaning of some passages was not known at the time they were written, or even that it remains unknown to the present time.* In this respect, the same is true of the Scriptures as of the natural world. There are many things in the creation, the nature and design of which lay concealed for thousands of years, and many which are, even at the present day, but imperfectly understood, or not understood at all.

---

[*] Lect. on Insp. of Script., p. 33.

Notwithstanding this, it is true that God created them, and preserves them; and it is doubtless true, that they are designed for some important end, and that they will ultimately accomplish that end. So, as to those things in Scripture which are not well understood; it may be that they will ultimately be understood, and that some special and additional good may result from them in consequence of their having been so long involved in obscurity. Even during the time they are not understood, they may be of use in promoting among good men a humble sense of their limited knowledge, and in exciting them to diligent endeavors after higher acquisitions. And there is nothing inconsistent with the infinite wisdom of God in the supposition, that he should, by *subsequent revelations*, as well as by the course of his providence, and the well directed labors of his servants, explain that which was before left designedly obscure. This would evidently be analogous to the method of divine instruction in other cases."

We are happy to be able to avail ourselves of such excellent authority as this. And it is the more to our purpose, because of its emanating from that particular section of the Old Church, which, more than almost any other, is accustomed to urge the objection against Swedenborg's revelations to which we have referred. It makes our objectors themselves answer. in a good degree, their own objection.

The question whether a heaven-taught, divinely-illumined expounder of the Sacred Oracles is needed, and therefore likely to be sent, depends upon whether the Scripture has been, is, or is likely to be, correctly understood without such an expositor. And this question, or two-thirds of it at least, depends upon another which is purely a question of fact. *Have* expositors been agreed as to the meaning of large portions of the Bible? Let the present state and past history of Biblical exegesis answer this question. It is a known fact, proved from history, that the members of the Church—Christian teachers—Professors of Theology—have not, since the earliest age of the Church, been generally agreed as to the nature, kind, or extent of inspiration which belongs to the Scripture, nor even as to the books which are to be reckoned in the Sacred Canon as inspired books. It is a known fact that there are many things in the Bible—large portions of Holy Writ—of the meaning of which the most learned in Theology are free to confess themselves ignorant. It is known that there are still larger portions, which christian teachers *profess* to understand, but about which there is, and has ever been, a wide difference of opinion among them. It is known that there is scarcely a single doctrine taught in the Bible, about which the Church has been generally agreed. And a disagreement about those which are regarded as *the cardinal doctrines* of the Bible, has been not less wide than upon minor points. It is known that doctrines which some regard as fundamental, and which they think they see clearly taught in the Bible, are utterly denied and rejected by other equally learned and pious men ; and the latter appeal as confidently to the Scripture in support of their denial, as do the former in support of their belief, of the doctrine. Hence the great number of fragments into which the Christian Church has been broken, and the almost countless volumes of Commentaries which have been written to explain the Bible. Professor Stuart says: " It would hardly be possible to calculate, without great pains and much expense of time, how many Commentaries on the Bible have been printed and circulated in the Protestant religious community, since the operations of the British and Foreign Bible Society first commenced."— (*Bib. Repos.*, Jan. 1833, p. 132.)

It is true that these commentaries do not differ from each other on all points, nor give a different meaning to every text. But it is equally true that there is scarcely a single point on which any one of them will be found to agree with all the rest ; and frequently there will be found to exist a violent conflict between the meaning of the same text as elicited by these different writers, all of whom may be very honest well-meaning men.

But some, perhaps, may think that we have stated the case a little too strongly ; that there is not really so much confusion, ignorance, doubt, and disagreement among commentators and christians generally in regard to the meaning of Scripture, as our language would seem to import. It may be said that we have spoken with the feelings of a man who desires to make out a case, and who, therefore, gives utterance to more than facts would warrant. Very well. We will not ask our readers to take our word on a point like this. They shall hear the confession of those whom they will not suspect of any disposition to state the case too strongly—the confession of Biblical scholars and commentators themselves.

" If the interpretation of the Scripture were easy and obvious," says Bishop Marsh, in his Lectures on that subject, " there would be little or no diversity in the explanations which different commentators have given of the same passage. But if we compare the Greek with the Latin commentators, we shall frequently find such a variety of interpretation, as would appear almost impossible to be extracted from the same text.

If we compare the Jewish commentators either with the Greek or with the Latin, we shall find as great a variety, though a variety of a different kind. If we compare our English commentators with any of the preceding, we shall find no diminution in the variety of interpretation. Nor do we find uniformity among commentators of the same language, or even among commentators of the same church. It is true that in all things relating to *doctrine* and *discipline*, the Church of Rome preserved, during several ages, an uniformity of interpretation by the commentary which was called the *Glossa Ordinaria*. But when the revival of learning had opened new sources of intelligence, and the Reformation had restored the right of unfettered exposition, the *Glossa Ordinaria* was exchanged for *new* systems of interpretation, from Luther and Melancthon, from Calvin and Beza, from Grotius and Spanheim."—(*Lect. on Interp. of Sac. Scrip.*, p. 271.)

Again, this learned writer says: "There is not the slightest historical evidence that the apostles transmitted to posterity any rule but what is recorded in the New Testament. The fathers, therefore, are on precisely the same footing with respect to the authority of their interpretations, as the commentators of the present age. Nor, in fact, are they uniform in their interpretations even in regard to doctrine, notwithstanding the agreement alleged by the Church of Rome; the same commentators may be selected, both ancient and modern, who agree on particular points."—(*Ibid.* p. 274.)

Mr. Birks, another English commentator, in his *Elements of Prophecy* says with reference to the Apocalypse:

"The present state of Apocalyptic interpretation is one. among many features in the actual condition of the Church. which should lead the Christian to humiliation and sorrow. That holy prophecy, which was given for the guidance of believers to the end of time with such a peculiar solemnity and so repeated a blessing, still remains to most Christians, a watchword of silent contempt, a signal for controversy, or a field for conjecture. Few, comparatively, seem to have gained for themselves an assured conviction even on the main outlines of its meaning."—(*Apud Clissold, Apoc. Int.*, Vol. 2, p. 316.)

A third commentator, Mr. Maitland, in his *Second Inquiry*. remarks:

"When we reflect on the number and talents of the men who have attempted to illustrate the visions of St. John, and the great discordance of opinions, it would seem as if there must be something radically wrong, some fatal error, at the very foundation of all their systems of explanation, which is one great cause of the mistakes and confusion that appear to pervade them all. What this is deserves to be maturely considered."—(*Ibid,* p. 317.)

Another distinguished commentator, Mr. Faber, in his *Sacred Calendar,* says:

"If, in the case of numerous predictions, history, conclusive as the argument hath till lately been deemed, affords no valid evidence of their accomplishment; it is but too plain, that no future supposed coincidence, though it may be strenuously urged by the expositors of the day, will ever be allowed to demonstrate their then fulfilment. The principles of our present Futurists are of universal and never dying application. What they now urge as objections, may always be urged as objections; and thus a succession of Futurists, and their natural offspring a succession of sceptics, may go on to the day of judgment, handing down the cabala of their sect, and ever denying that prophecy has received its accomplishment."—(*Ibid,* p. 817.)

It is a very convenient and a very common way of getting rid of the difficulties inherent in the prevailing systems of interpretation, to say, when the systems fail to explain a prophecy, that the prophecy is yet *unfulfilled.* An ingenious device by which ignorance seeks to conceal itself; for in this way the *onus* of interpretation is transferred from the interpreter to future history. Hence one expositor, (Jurieu), gravely and frankly says respecting a certain prophecy: " And understanding nothing of it, I put it among those things that are to come, according to the usual custom of them who interpret prophecies; who say of every thing which they understand not, that it is not yet come to pass."—(*Accomplt. of Script. Proph.,* Part II., p. 97. *Apud Clissold,* vol. I., p. 341.

These are a few, and but a few, of the confessions of learned commentators themselves, respecting the confusion, doubt, and disagreement that exist among them with regard to the import of the Apocalypse generally. And were we to descend to particular texts, and quote you the explanation of them given by different authors, the darkness and utter chaos which exist would appear still more palpable. But we have not time for this. We will, however, give a single instance by way of illustration.

Take, for example, the opening of "the six seals," mentioned in Rev. 6th chapter. The *general* opinion among commentators has been, and is, that this prophecy has received its fulfilment; but there are those who maintain that it is yet *unfulfilled.* One class of expositors say, that the judgments mentioned in the seals fell upon the Jewish people, and were accomplished in the destruction of their city and temple. An-other class suppose the opening of the seals to be the judg-ments upon the Pagan Roman empire,—to be prophecies of the conflict between Christianity and Paganism, which ended in the establishment of the former under the Emperor Con-stantine, to which result they conceive the sixth seal applies. Among the writers who support this view, are Bishop Newton, Mede, Lowman, Doddridge, Holmes, Hale, and others of less note. And even these are not agreed as to the particular events in the history of the Pagan Roman empire, intended by the several seals. One expositor will tell you of a particular Roman emperor as designed by one seal, whom another sup-poses to be designed by the following or the preceding seal. Mr. Faber agrees with the writers just mentioned as to the period and event with which the seals terminate, but has a view peculiarly his own with respect to the first four seals. Mr. Ir-ving, who has written at great length upon the Apocalypse, supposes these seals to *commence* with the very event with which the writers just mentioned suppose them to *end*, viz. the establishment of Christianity under Constantine. He, there-fore, makes them refer to an entirely different order of events.

Another class of expositors—Mr. Cunningham and Archdea-con Woodhouse among them—suppose these seals to be alto-gether spiritual or rather ecclesiastical; and the events which they think denoted by them are, first, the progress of the gospel from the time of its first announcement; second, the dissensions which arose in the church in the fourth century between the Arians and Donatists; third, the dark ages of Pa-pacy : fourth, the establishment of the Inquisition, and the perse-cutions of the Albigenses and Waldenses; fifth, the dawn of the Reformation; sixth, the French Revolution, including, however, certain other events yet to be accomplished. The learned Dr. Keith agrees in some points with this class of com-mentators, but thinks the second seal refers to Mahometanism, the fourth, to Infidelity, the fifth, to the persecution which is to follow. and the sixth, to the last great catastrophe which shall decide the fate of the world and the triumph of the church.

Mr. Burgh, seeing the disagreement among commentators in respect to the meaning of these seals, and the difficulty of de-termining what *past* events they refer to, seeks the very con-venient and easy mode of escaping all difficulty by referring them to events yet future. He says, in his *Exposition of the Book of Revelation—*

" There is no one point, perhaps, in the whole range of Scriptural exposition, on which there exists so universal an agreement as on this

—that all these seals have been opened, and are fulfilled; and what then? If they be fulfilled, they ought to give a certain sound, and there ought to be no difference of opinion as to what events fulfilled them; and yet it is strange that there is not, on the other hand, in the whole Scriptures, a passage upon which there exists more diversity of opinion! The fact is, if I were to attempt to detail the different opinions —were I even to sketch in outline, the variety of fulfilments which have been assigned to these six prophetical seals—it would occupy much more time than we have to devote to the whole of the chapter." (*Cliss. Ap. Int.*, vol. I. p. 42.)

These are only a *few* of the discordant views respecting these six seals, maintained by different commentators—commentators, too, of acknowledged credit and standing in the Christian Church. And so might we go through this whole book of the Revelation, and upon almost every text cite as great a variety of conflicting opinions held by those whose business and profession it is to explain for us the meaning of the Scripture.

But some may say—"We admit that the Apocalypse is a very dark and mysterious book—extremely difficult to understand. We admit that there is not, and has not been, much certainty or agreement among commentators with regard to its meaning; and we regard their expositions as but little better than fanciful theories or vague conjectures. But it cannot be said that there is the same uncertainty and disagreement about other parts of the Bible, especially the New Testament. Here all is plain and easily understood, and expositors are generally agreed as to its meaning."

It is true that there is not here the same amount of confusion and contradiction that we find respecting the Apocalypse. But is there none? Is there felt any thing like *certainty* in regard to its meaning? Is there, or has there been, a very general agreement about it? even about the meaning of texts, which appear quite plain and simple? You shall have the answer to these questions in the words of one who is abundantly qualified to decide, and whose testimony on a point like this no one will dispute: we refer to Prof. Tholuck of the University of Halle, in Germany.

"It is a matter of experience," says this learned author, "that there is no greater source of disquiet to the young theological student, than the endless variety of opinions in respect to the doctrines of faith and the interpretation of Scripture which are presented to him in the history of the church, and in the courses of exegetical lectures. Even laymen, when aware of the want of accord among theologians in this latter respect, are often not a little disturbed; and it has been a case of actual occurrence, that one and another have been ready to take refuge from this disquietude in the Pope; where, as they suppose, the solution of all difficulties is to be found. They know not, or do not remember, the discrepances of Catholic interpreters, not merely with one another, but even with themselves ; how Augustine, for instance, in four different passages of his works, has given four different expositions of one text, while no Pope has ever yet decided which is the correct one.

"But who is there who would not, at the first glance, be justly disquieted, and even despair of any certain way to the understanding of the Scriptures, when on a single passage not less than TWO HUNDRED AND FORTY-THREE expositions are placed before us ? as is done by Weigand in his work on Gal. iii. 20.* To these the author subjoins the two hundred and forty-fourth, which also has since been eclipsed by later attempts. It were well worth while thoroughly to weigh the causes of so enormous a discrepancy of opinion in the interpretation of the Holy Scriptures—a discrepancy of which the whole range of classic literature no where affords so portentous an example."—(*Bib. Repos. Oct.* 1833, p. 684, 685.)

This same author then proceeds to give some examples of the different expositions of the first verses of the Sermon on the Mount ; and he cites not less than twelve different interpretations which have been given to the very short and simple text, "Blessed are the poor in spirit !" The Roman Catholic interpreters understanding the Greek word πτωχοι (*ptokoi*) as referring to *external* or *natural* poverty, have founded upon the passage the doctrine of voluntary indigence. And even the Reformers, Luther, Zwingle, and Melancthon, supposed that external poverty was here referred to, although Luther contends strongly against the merits of a voluntary poverty. Others think that both *internal* and *external* poverty is referred to, and that the meaning is "Blessed are those who beg [i. e. in the natural sense], provided they feel their poverty." Others maintain that internal poverty, poverty of the *spirit*, is what is referred to ; and among these, some understand it to mean, "Blessed are they who have few earthly desires,"—others, "Blessed are they whose minds are open to the truth ;" others, "Blessed are the humble ;" others, "Blessed are the modest ;" others, "Blessed are they who acknowledge that they are ignorant of divine doctrine ;" and others, "Blessed are they who are destitute of talent and learning,"—according to which latter exposition, the kingdom of heaven must needs be shut against all scholars.

A similar diversity of opinion with regard to the meaning of the other beatitudes, is spoken of by Professor Tholuck as existing among biblical expositors. Thus, in the text, "Blessed are the meek, for they shall inherit the earth," some, he tells us, suppose that *the earth* here refers to a heavenly inheritance,

---

* " Now a mediator is not of one ; but God is one."

—others, that it refers to the land of Canaan,—others, to an abundance of the good things of this world,—others, to the goods of this world and of the next also. "The humble sufferers," says Bengel (and Calvin agrees with him), "receive at last the earth as their inheritance; and in the mean time, they triumph even upon earth in their humility and depression." Others think the promise refers to the favor and friendship of mankind generally; and a commentator of no less note and authority than the distinguished Le Clerc explains it to mean, "Blessed are the gentle, who for their gentleness will be approved by the powerful, and not compelled to till the earth, like others of a more warlike disposition ! !"

What say our objectors now? That the Bible is understood? That the New Testament is understood? That most of it is so plain and simple as to preclude the possibility of doubt or disagreement? The commentators tell a very different story. They exhibit a great diversity of opinion in regard to the meaning of even the simplest texts. This much, therefore, is certain: that they cannot all be right; but may they not all be wrong?—wrong in the rule which they bring to the interpretation of the Bible, and consequently wrong in the meaning which that rule elicits? May there not be, to cite the language of one of these very commentators, "something radically wrong, some fatal error, at the very foundation of all their systems of explanation, which is one great cause of the mistakes and confusion that appear to pervade them all?"

We have exhibited a few facts in respect to the past and present state of biblical interpretation, showing the utter confusion, uncertainty, and disagreement which exist in the prevailing church with regard to the true import of Scripture. We have allowed expositors—and not those of small learning or mean authority, either—to speak for themselves on this subject; and were it necessary, we might produce volumes of just such facts and confessions as we have here presented: facts which no man will pretend to call in question. for we can refer to volume, chapter, and page.

In view of the facts adduced, what becomes of the oft-repeated objection to Swedenborg, that he claims to have received a revelation which is to explain for us the meaning of the revelation given of God many centuries ago. *Has* the former revelation been thoroughly understood? Has there been any *tolerable* certainty or agreement among Christians as to its real meaning? The answer of undeniable facts is, No. Tribes of expositors have risen up in succession, and whole libraries of commentaries have been written to tell us what this revelation means; and what do we find them all but a chaos of contradiction? What do these commentaries as a whole show us more plainly than the fact, that the writers have not themselves understood the book which they attempted to explain? that to their eyes there has been a thick cloud round about this mount of God? In view of such a fact, what might we reasonably expect, but that a merciful God, in His own good time, would rend this cloud asunder?—would dissipate the darkness that surrounds His church, and reveal to the longing eyes of men the divine beauty and glory of His Word? We have seen how much an interpreter of the Divine Oracles is needed; an interpreter not blind or short-sighted, but with vision clear and far-reaching; an interpreter, not self-taught, but heaven-taught; an interpreter, teaching us not in his own name, but in the name of the Lord, and "with wisdom from On High;" an interpreter furnished with such credentials of his heavenly mission as approve themselves to enlightened reason: such is the interpreter which the Church needs; and what might we expect, but that God, in the plenitude of His mercy, would send us such an one? Such an one, prepared and illumined by the Spirit of God, has been sent in the person of Emanuel Swedenborg: sent in answer to many a longing, trusting, waiting soul: sent in answer to many a fervent prayer, which has gone up from out the silent depths of many a humble, pious heart: sent to make the crooked straight, and the rough places plain; and to reveal more clearly in the Divine Word the wisdom and the glory of the LORD.

B. F. B.

LETTERS TO A TRINITARIAN.

LETTER II.

THE ANGEL JEHOVAH.

DEAR SIR,

In my former letter, the evidence was somewhat largely presented of the fact of a remarkable usage by the sacred writers in regard to the term *Angel*, in connections where, at the same time, the real personage intended is obviously Jehovah himself, as the predicates apply to him rather than to any created being. In what is affirmed of the Angel, there is a clear implication of attributes and prerogatives which the mind is compelled to assign to the Lord of Angels alone. This is pre-eminently the case in a passage which was not cited in my former communication: I allude to the divine appearance to Moses at the burning bush.

Exod. iii. 1–6.—"Now Moses kept the flock of Jethro his father-in-law, the priest of Midian: and he led the flock to the back side of the desert, and came to the mountain of God, even to Horeb. And the angel of the Lord appeared unto him in a flame of fire out of the midst of a bush; and he looked, and behold, the bush burned with fire, and the bush was not consumed. And Moses said, I will now turn aside, and see this great sight, why the bush is not burnt. And when the Lord saw that he turned aside to see, God called unto him out of the midst of the bush, and said, Moses, Moses! And he said, Here am I. And he said, Draw not nigh hither: put off thy shoes from off thy feet; for the place whereon thou standest is holy ground. Moreover he said, I am the God of thy father, the God of Abraham, the God of Isaac, and the God of Jacob. And Moses hid his face, for he was afraid to look upon God."

Throughout the entire narrative, it is plain that it is Jehovah himself who speaks in the person of the angel, for he says, v. 6, "I am the God of thy father, the God of Abraham, the God of Isaac, and the God of Jacob;" and Moses is said to have hidden his face, because "he was afraid to look upon God." Again, when Moses inquired what answer he should return to his people, when they demanded of him in whose name he came to them—

"God said unto Moses, I AM THAT I AM: And he said, Thus shalt thou say unto the children of Israel, I AM hath sent me unto you.

And God said moreover unto Moses, Thus shalt thou say unto the children of Israel, The Lord God of your fathers, the God of Abraham, the God of Isaac, and the God of Jacob, hath sent me unto you : this is my name for ever, and this is my memorial unto all generations."

This, be it observed, is spoken by Him who is called in the outset the "angel of the Lord," for the same original term translated "appeared" is applied to each. We have seen, v. 2, that the angel is said to have "appeared" to Moses, and in v. 16 it is said—

"Go and gather the elders of Israel together, and say unto them, The Lord God of your fathers, the God of Abraham, of Isaac, and of Jacob, *appeared* unto me, saying, I have surely visited you, and seen that which is done to you in Egypt."

Nothing can be more unequivocal than this. The angel that made himself manifest in the burning bush is expressly declared to be "the Lord God of Abraham, of Isaac, and of Jacob," and if this title do not designate the supreme Jehovah, we may well despair of finding any such title in the entire compass of Revelation. The momentous inferences that follow from this, will appear in due time ; but at present I would offer a remark upon the nature of the *appearance* here predicated of the Personage spoken of, and the remark will hold good in general of the divine and angelic *theophanies* or *manifestations* so frequently mentioned in the Scriptures. The phraseology doubtless implies a *visibility* of some kind, and judging from the simple letter, we should probably suppose that the function merely of the natural or outward eye was involved in the *seeing* affirmed of the spectator. If the Lord *appeared* to Moses or the patriarchs, the spontaneous impression would be, that they *saw* him, and that they saw him just as they would have seen any other object that came within the range of their ocular vision. But our Saviour declares in language that would seem incapable of mistake, that "no man hath seen God at any time ;" and the Most High himself is equally explicit in his reply to Moses on a subsequent occasion, " there shall no man see me, and live." You are moreover well aware of the prevalent belief among the Jews, that the sight of the Divine Being would be followed by the instant extinction of life. Here, then, we have a problem to be solved, in the apparent conflict of two classes of texts, one of which affirms the visibility of Jehovah, and the other denies it. How shall we reconcile them ? Does Moses utter the truth when he affirms of himself, of Aaron, of Nadab, and Abihu, and the seventy elders, that " they *saw* the God of Israel ?" Does Isaiah declare the truth when he says, " Woe is me, for mine eyes have seen the King, the Lord of hosts?" And is it equally true, on the other hand, that "the blessed and only Potentate, the King of kings, and Lord of lords," is He "whom no man hath seen or can see," as the apostle Paul unequivocally affirms? Surely some explanation is needed which shall relieve these passages of the air of direct contrariety in their literal teachings. Whence is it to be sought? Are we not inevitably shut up to the conclusion that the *kind* of seeing is not the same in the case in which it is denied, as in that in which it is affirmed? Is not the predicated *seeing* in the one case that of the outward eye, and in the other that of the inward? How is it possible that spiritual objects can be perceived by any other than a spiritual eye? An angel is a spirit, and a spiritual organ only can behold a spiritual being. Of this, however. the beholder may not himself be conscious, as the outward and inward vision act in unity. When the servant of Elisha saw the mountain covered by horses and chariots of fire, it was not surely by the natural eye that he perceived them, for it is said that the Lord "opened his eyes" for the purpose, and no one can imagine that his outward eyes were previously closed. Yet I know of no reason to suppose that he was himself aware of seeing the spectacle by any other than the natural organs of vision. Still there was the opening of an inward eye, and the necessity for this which existed in his case, exists in every similar case. No object can be seen by the material eye which does not reflect the rays of the sun's light. But a spirit, being immaterial, cannot reflect these rays, and cannot therefore be seen by the operation of the ordinary laws of optics. It requires the couching, as it were, of the inward eyes of the spirit, in order to produce this effect. When the women entered the vacated sepulchre of our Lord, on the morning of his resurrection, they at first saw nothing. A moment after, two angels in white stood before them. Why did they not see them on their first entrance? Obviously for the reason, that their internal organs of vision were yet sealed. As soon as the spiritual eye had its film removed, the spectacle of the angels appeared. So in the case of the risen Saviour himself, and so in *every* case of angelic or divine apparition. The external human eye is not competent to the perception of spiritual beings or spiritual objects.

If it be said that it may still be *made* competent by a miraculous act of divine power, our reply is, that omnipotence evermore abides by the laws of its own order. That which is contrary to order, is, for that reason, for ever impossible to the Deity, for he will not deny himself. However a miracle may appear to us to contravene the established order of the universe, it will nevertheless always defy the intelligence of man to show that such a work does not accord with some such law, though for the present it may be beyond our power to detect and define it.   What are denominated the laws of the physical world are ever the result of the influx of *causes* from the spiritual world ; and as our knowledge of these *causes* is but limited, we are not competent to trace, in all cases, the connection between them and their effects in ultimates.   The true philosophy of the matter I believe to be unfolded in the following extracts from Swedenborg :

" All the miracles and works of the Lord, when he was in the world, signified divine, celestial, and spiritual things, that is, such things as pertain to heaven and the church, and this because they were divine and what is divine *always operates in ultimates, from first principles, and so in fulness.   Ultimates are such things as appear before the eyes in the world.*"—*A. E.* 475.

" How signs would persuade to believe, shall be briefly explained : those miraculous signs, as that they should cast out demons, speak with new tongues, take up serpents, that if they drank any deadly thing it should not hurt them, and that they should restore the sick by the laying on of hands, were in their essence and in their origin spiritual, from which those things flowed and came forth as effects; for they were correspondences, which derive their all from the spiritual world by influx from the Lord : as that they should cast out demons in the name of the Lord, derived all its effects from this circumstance, that the name of the Lord spiritually understood is the all of doctrine out of the Word from the Lord, and that demons are falses of every kind, which are so cast out, that is, removed, by doctrine out of the Word from the Lord ; that they should speak with new tongues, derives its effect from this, that new tongues denote doctrinals for the new church; that they should take up serpents was, because serpents signify the hells as to malice, and so that they should be safe from the infestation thereof ; that they should not be hurt if they drank the deadly thing, denoted that the malice of the hells should not infest them ; and their restoring the infirm by laying on of hands, signified, that by communication and conjunction with heaven, thus with the Lord, they should restore to health from spiritual diseases, which are called iniquities and sins, the laying on of the hands of the disciples corresponding to communication and conjunction with the Lord, and so as to the removal of iniquities by His divine power."—*A. E.* 706.

" Inasmuch as diseases represented the iniquities and evils of spiritual life, therefore by the diseases which the Lord healed, is signified liberation from the various kinds of evil and the false, which infested the Church and the human race, and which would have induced spiritual death ; for divine miracles are distinguished from other miracles by this, that they involve and have respect to states of the Church and the heavenly kingdom; on this account the Lord's miracles consisted principally in the healing of diseases."—*A. C.* 8364.

This, you will observe, is spoken of divine miracles, which are phenomena exhibited in *ultimates,* or material agencies,

but flowing from spiritual causes acting in an orderly manner
in the spiritual world.   It appears, however, that this law of
spiritual causation may be so perverted by evil spirits as to
give rise to what are properly termed *magical* miracles, which
are a species of simulations of the divine.   The distinction is
thus clearly drawn by Swedenborg.

" As to what concerns miracles, it is to be known, that divine miracles differ from magical miracles, as heaven from hell : divine miracles
proceed from divine truth, and go forward according to order; the
effects in ultimates are miracles, when it pleases the Lord that they
should be presented in that form ; hence it is that all divine miracles
represent states of the Lord's kingdom in the heavens, and of the
Lord's kingdom in the earths, or of the church ; this is the internal form
of divine miracles.   So is the case with all the miracles in Egypt, and
also with the rest that are mentioned in the Word : all the miracles
also, which the Lord himself wrought when He was in the world, signified the approaching state of the church ; as the opening of the eyes
of the blind, the ears of the deaf, the tongues of the dumb, the lame
walking, the maimed and also the lepers being healed, signified, that
such as are represented by the blind, the deaf, the dumb, the lame, the
maimed, the leprous, would receive the gospel, and be spiritually
healed, and this by the coming of the Lord into the world : such are
divine miracles in their internal form.   But magical miracles involve
nothing at all, being wrought by the evil to acquire to themselves
power over others ; and they appear in the external form like to divine miracles.   The reason why they appear like, is, because they
flow from order, and order appears like in the ultimates where miracles are presented : as for example, the divine truth proceeding from
the Lord has in it all power, hence it is, that there is also power in
truths in the ultimates of order : therefore the evil acquire to themselves power by truths, and gain dominion over others.   From these
things it is evident that magical miracles, although in the external form
they appear like unto divine miracles, nevertheless have inwardly in
them a contrary end, namely, of destroying those things which are of
the church, whereas divine miracles have inwardly in them the end of
building up those things which are of the church.   The case herein is
like that of two beautiful women, one of whom from whoredom is
wholly and altogether filthy, but the other from chastity or from genuine conjugial love is wholly and altogether pure ; their external forms
are alike, but the internal differ as heaven and hell."—*A. C.* 7337.

From this you will be able to judge of the grounds on which
we hold that a genuine divine miracle never involves the infraction of the principles of order, and consequently reject entirely
the theory which supposes that a spiritual being can be seen
with the natural eye.   The hypothesis of the opening of a spiritual eye labors under no such difficulty, as the potency of such
a mode of vision is inherent in every man by the very law of
his creation.   Wherever an effect, therefore, of this nature
can be ascribed to a cause which acts in accordance with the
general order of the world of causes, we do not hesitate to

give such a cause the preference over another that implies a
violation of that order, for although we may not always be
able to determine what *is* according to order, yet, we have in
a thousand cases, no hesitation to declare what *is not* according to it; and the present is one. We assume, without reserve, the position, that in no recorded instance of divine or
angelic *theophany* was the appearance made to the outward
eye; it was invariably to an interior or spiritual vision, the
power of which was preternaturally developed for the occasion. If this be disputed we feel at liberty to demand that the
grounds be distinctly exhibited on which the contrary position
is taken, and that some rational solution shall be proposed of
the manner in which the phenomenon is held to have occurred.
If Abraham, Hagar, Moses, Balaam, Gideon, and Manoah, saw
the angel Jehovah, who is also expressly called Jehovah himself, *how* did they see him? Had he, for the time being, a body
of flesh and blood? Was it a temporary incarnation of the
Deity? If so, how does this consist with the declaration that
"no man hath seen God at any time?" We protest against
all evasive dealing in the matter. Let the opponent of our
views come manfully to the point, and if he rejects the solution proposed, let him unequivocally state his own. On subjects of this serious nature a candid disputant will not bring
the charge of error without sustaining it by the presentation
of the opposite truth. This we have an indefeasible right to
claim at the hands of opponents.

Regarding it then as a point established that the *appearances*
of the angel mentioned were in no case made to the outward
organ of vision, I proceed to the consideration of the legitimate inferences yielded by the general subject. A solution is to
be sought of the grounds on which the titles "Jehovah" and
"Angel of Jehovah" are interchangeably employed in the sacred record—a fact of which no possible doubt can remain
after the abundant testimony I have adduced. This solution
I give in the language of Swedenborg. That he professes to
have come to the knowledge of the truth on this head in consequence of a special illumination, is certain. At the same
time, this *is* not the point to which your assent is, in the outset, demanded. I leave you at full liberty to enjoy your own
opinion on this score. The question submitted to your decision is, whether what he affirms does not approve itself as intrinsically true, independent of the medium through which he
declares it to have been received. Upon this you are competent to pronounce. If you find it to stand the test of your severest judgment, and yet is such a view of the subject as was
never before announced to the world, and such as cannot well

be accounted for on any other supposition than that of its being the product of a special divine enlightenment, I do not see that you can refuse to admit his claim as so far made good. But of this I leave you to judge. I wish nothing to be forced upon you but what forces itself.

I would here remark that the *usus loquendi* of the Scriptures discloses, in several instances, a phraseology in regard to human agents, in the relation of principals and subordinates, which throws an illustrative light upon the diction we are now considering. A person employed or delegated in a *vice* capacity sometimes speaks in the name and character of his principal just as if he were himself present. In a word, he *personates* him whose message he bears or whose interests he represents. Thus when Abigail returned an answer to David's messengers (1 Sam. xxv. 39–41), she evidently spake as if David had been personally present. She sees him, as it were, with her mind's eye. "And David sent and communed with Abigail, to take her to him to wife. And when the servants of David were come to Abigail to Carmel, they spake unto her, saying, David sent us unto thee, to take thee to him to wife. And she arose, and bowed herself on her face to the earth and said, Behold, let thy handmaid be a servant to wash the feet of the servants of my lord." Thus also it will appear by comparing Matt. viii. 5–13 with Luke vii. 6–8, that it was not the centurion himself who came to Christ, but his friends, and yet we read that "Jesus said unto the centurion, Go thy way and as thou hast believed, so be it done unto thee." Thus, too, by consulting Matt. xx. 20, in connection with Mark x. 35, it will be seen that it was the mother of James and John, and not those disciples themselves, who presented the petition to Christ. So again in certain cases where men have uttered messages from the Most High they have spoken as if He were speaking in them. Thus, Deut. xxxi. 23, "And he (Moses) gave Joshua the son of Nun, a charge and said, Be strong and of a good courage ; for thou shalt bring the children of Israel into the land which I sware unto them : and I will be with thee." Moses here seems to lose himself in the Divine Prompter of his words. In like manner the Lord says to Jeremiah, "Behold, I have put my words in thy mouth, I have this day set thee over the nations and over the kingdoms, to root out, and to pull down, and to destroy, and to throw down, and to build, and to plant."

From all this it is clear that the usage in question is not without parallels, and the various instances adduced may be viewed as examples of the well known exegetical adage—, "Qui facit per alium facit per se." (He who acts by another acts by himself). From the pre-eminence, however, of the subject in the present case, the peculiarity of diction is itself pre-eminent, of which all minor instances are mere shadows, and from which they probably derive their origin. Now as to the explication we give the following from Swedenborg as a key to the mystery of the divino-angelic theophanies:

"The angel of Jehovah is sometimes mentioned in the Word, and every where, when in a good sense, represents and signifies some es. sential appertaining to the Lord, and proceeding from him; but what is represented and signified, may appear from the series. There were angels who were sent to men, and who also spake by the prophets, but what they spake was not from the angels, but by them: for their state then was, that they knew no otherwise than that they were Je. hovah, that is, the Lord: nevertheless, when they had done speaking, they presently returned into their former state, and spake as from themselves. This was the case with the angels who spake the Word of the Lord; which has been given me to know by much experience of a similar kind at this day in the other life; concerning which, by the divine mercy of the Lord, we shall speak hereafter. This is the reason that the angels were sometimes called Jehovah; as was evidently the case with the angel who appeared to Moses in the bush, of whom it is thus written, 'The angel of Jehovah appeared unto him in a flame of fire out of the midst of the bush.—And when Jehovah saw that he turned aside to see, God called unto him out of the midst of the bush. —God said unto Moses, I am that I am.—And God said moreover unto Moses, Thus shalt thou say unto the children of Israel, Jehovah God of your fathers hath sent me unto you' (Exod. iii. 2, 4, 14, 15); from which words it is evident, that it was an angel who appeared to Moses as a flame in the bush, and that he spake as Jehovah, because the Lord, or Jehovah spake by him. For, in order that man may be spoken to by vocal expressions, which are articulate sounds, in the ultimates of nature, the Lord uses the ministry of angels, by filling them with the divine, and by laying asleep what is of their own proprium, so that they know no otherwise than that they are Jehovah: thus the divine of Jehovah, which is in the supremes, descends into the lowest of na. ture, in which man is as to sight and hearing. Hence it may appear how the angels spake by the prophets, viz. that the Lord himself spake, although by angels, and that the angels did not speak at all from themselves. That the Word is from the Lord, appears from many passages; as in Matthew: 'That it might be fulfilled which was spoken of the Lord by the prophet, saying, Behold, a virgin shall bear in the womb, and shall bring forth a son' (i. 22. 23): besides other passages. Because the Lord speaks by angels when he speaks with man, it is hence that he is throughout the Word called an angel; and then by an angel is signified, as was said, some essential appertaining to the Lord, and proceeding from the Lord."

G. B.

(*To be continued.*)

ARTICLE V.

——

POETRY AND ANALOGY.

ALL traditions of remote antiquity agree in ascribing to man at one time a higher degree of purity and intellectual elevation than he has since attained to. They all agree with respect to his degradation or fall, which the sacred Scriptures ratify by incontestable authority. To man, in that golden age of innocence, what are now to us arcana of nature were things plainly discernible. He saw into the life of things, and was in the intelligence of all the uses of nature. His only food was the fruits of the field and of the trees, spontaneously afforded, while his affections and thoughts were constantly nourished by the harmonies of creation. The tree of life supplied him from all its branches every variety of beautiful and truthful nutriment. His highest intellectual pleasures were in scanning the works of creation, and in contemplating his own image in the universe: the warmest delight of his heart was in adoration of its beneficent Creator; while the only language he could utter was the melody of feeling ultimating itself in rythmical and expressive cadences,—in

" Thoughts that voluntary move harmonious numbers."

Such was the origin of Poetry and Music,—or rather their first manifestation from the heart of man: for harmony is the very form of divine order, and music is the mode of its audible perception—a means by which man may recognise within himself the essential beauty of his microcosm, and discern its correspondence with the great world and with the universe,— by which he gives utterance to his more heavenly perceptions of analogy, and fills his soul with love, and gratitude, and joy.

Poetry, then, in its essence, is no longer poetry as we commonly understand it, but prophecy: for the whole phenomenal universe affords the bass notes of one immense instrument, whose higher chords are in the heart-strings of humanity. The whisper of the breeze, and the roll of the thunder—gentle emotion and awful sublimity—what are they, in the outward and in the inward world, but resulting effects and energies, the offspring of a spiritual and natural marriage? The highest capacity of man is to contain the future in the present, the highest faculty, to discern it; the highest privilege, to be a medium of their connexion. When this privilege was granted, in the ages of antiquity, prophecy found utterance in a language at once spiritual and natural, nay, in a language whose inmost essence was divine; a language adapted to an indefinite development of the human mind, and still infinitely beyond its possible attainment; a language whose inmost is the soul of the spiritual sun, whose outmost is the letter of God's Word. Such is the only genuine poetry, which is divine truth in ultimates.

In after ages, poets, instead of being Seers capable of divine inspiration, were only men of superior affections and energies, who in their better or higher moments had glimpses of the inner life, which is only revealed by analogy, and who struggled to express their undefined conceptions of the marriage of the mind to the universe; who labored and toiled with an overwhelming sense of the good and the beautiful, which always seemed to be near, but which always eluded their pursuit: in short, poets, not of inspiration—for the celestial and spiritual degrees of life were closed,—but of genius, who, longing and striving after what they could not acquire, called it the unattainable—the ideal.

Yet the principles of life which remained were still operative in their degree; but their effects were only approximations and assimilations to what would result from the full comprehension of man's capacity. From being a capable recipient, man degenerated to an imitation. Hence absolute analogy could no longer be apprehended by him. Its reality, however, was felt, though not perceived, and served as the basis of rhetorical analogy. Had it not been for the absolute, the arbitrary could not have been possible: poets were, therefore, only imitators of real actions by the use of representatives, or correspondences altogether arbitrary, except such as were traditionary from more ancient times. Such was their mythology, or science of myths, an imitation and perversion, for the most part, of the science of correspondence, which was according to the very order of creation in the true degrees of life, which mythology became the cause of all their polytheism, for poets were the first legislators. Since the analogy that absolutely exists between the external world of nature and the internal world of affection and thought, must necessarily force itself on the natural mind of man, because the external and the internal are co-operative,—therefore, as man has progressed, it has discovered, and always must discover, itself in intellectual expressions and in human actions. In proportion as the affections of man are warmed, or his passions inflamed,—in proportion as his mind is elevated, from whatever cause, above the dead level of every day experience,—in that degree will his language be figurative, metaphorical: for in such states of excitement, elevation, or enthusiasm, he is for the time transported beyond conventional ultimates, and speaks a language remotely allied to correspondence ; for he speaks from interior perception, with all the illustration of which his unregenerated mind is capable, from an impulse within, and from a spiritual natural dictate.

In support of this conclusion, we will adduce the following passage from Dr. Campbell's Philosophy of Rhetoric, in order to show, that some who have studied the subject of rhetorical language, without probably having even read a line of Swedenborg's, have unavoidably been led to believe that there is a real connection between metaphorical language and the mind of man. "Having discussed," says the author, "what was proposed here concerning tropes, I shall conclude with observing, that in this discussion there hath been occasion, as it were incidentally, to discover, that they are so far from being the inventions of *Art*, that, on the contrary, they result from the original and essential principles of the human mind : that, accordingly, they are the same, *upon the main*, in all nations, barbarous and civilized ; that the simplest and most ancient tongues do most abound with them." "But as to tracing those figures to the springs in human nature from which they flow, extremely little hath yet been attempted." Yet he says, "the sole business of art in this subject is, to range the several tropes and figures into classes, to distinguish them by names, and *to trace the principles in the mind which gave them birth*." It must follow, that only in proportion as we are successful in investigating these essential principles, shall we be able to lay a solid foundation for poetic criticism.

That man is in some way connected with the external world of nature, is a fact which to some extent forces itself on his attention : for he could not live without the atmospheric air, and many other necessary things, which, by means of nature, are constantly provided for him ; but he does not so readily perceive that he is also *vitally* connected with the animal, vegetable, and mineral kingdoms of nature : though it is not difficult to understand this, he neither has discovered nor perceived the connecting link between them—a link which contains some quality common to them all, though possessed in very different degrees. Now, the common measure or connecting link between the various recipients of life, is, the effort to co-operate with each other in order to perform their several uses. This effort to co-operate is *life*.

As there is only one real life, which is Life Itself, or the Divine, every created thing having life is only a recipient of this, through successive mediums, while the life of every recipient is according to the quality of the recipient. Man was made in the image and likeness of God, that he might be a medium to manifest the divine triunity; and as every thing in nature was made with reference to this end, therefore man is, as was wisely said of old *the measure of all things,*—his mind being the ratio between his soul and all created things.

Though man, in a certain sense, was created *last* among the things of nature, yet no other form or receptacle of life was truly vivified till man appeared: so that, really and truly, there could have been no outbirth of phenomenal life, till life assumed humanity, as there could be no spiritual life, till life itself assumed humanity. We know that man gave *names* to every living thing, and by names are signified *qualities.* It is through the mind of man, as a medium, or common measure, that all phenomena of the external world exist, and it is by means of the life of his mind that he acts on nature, and is reciprocally affected by it. Hence the three kingdoms of nature, in all their species, represent the varieties of affection and thought in man. By an effort to co-operate with higher mediums of life, the uses of the mineral, the vegetable, and the animal kingdoms, ascend through man, upward through higher mediums of life and use, to the very fountain of life and use, which is the Creator. In this effort, the mineral sustains the vegetable, the vegetable and the mineral the animal, while man is not only sustained in his natural life by them, but derives as a resulting effect from them, and from the spiritual life that flows downward, interior delights and refreshment according to his state of activity and reception. Because the uses of the lower kingdoms of nature are derived through the mind of man, therefore, in their return to their great orginal, man receives those uses back again into his affections and thoughts, to which they correspond, and transmits them in forms of transfigured beauty, radiant with human affection, so that the angels may receive them, and transmit them in still new forms of spiritual and celestial beauty, to the very Throne of beauty and use Itself. This is the meaning of that golden chain of which the old poets sang, connecting all things, held by the great First Cause : and thus we may understand, to some extent, the circle of life and uses, which is at once the most comprehensive and the most beautiful of all intellectual objects. We would here notice that the connexion between spiritual and natural things was not wholly unknown to Milton, who, however, only ventures to suggest it by the mouth of an angel:

> " What if Earth
> Be but the shadow of Heaven, and things therein
> Each to the other like, more than on earth is thought?"

In every particular of nature, man may see something resembling himself, while in universal nature he may see himself entire, as in a mirror.   Though he do not see it intellectually, he may perceive it in his affections, in proportion to the true order of his life.   This is the cause of that love of nature which every one with a soul alive to its sweet influences is known to feel and to cherish.   To a well ordered mind, however, it is not so much itself that is seen in nature, as the God of nature, in whose image it is immediately created.   Yet in proportion as we are *at one* with him, or in harmonious correspondence with him, will our own image be truly reflected, and our affections and thoughts delighted: for the uses of the natural world are in their degree perfect: while the uses of man's life become so, only in proportion as all discordant evils are removed from the soul's centre.   Only in the light of the New Church dispensation does the world cease to be "a riddle and a mystery."   R. D.

COINCIDENCES.

" ALL sensation and all perception, which appears so various, refers itself to one common and universal sense, namely, the touch ; the varieties, as the taste, the smell, the hearing, and the sight, are nothing but the genera thereof, arising from the internal sensation, that is, from the perception."—*A. C.* 3528.

"External objects are represented to the mind in a great measure by the senses.   Seeing is a *touch* upon the expansion of the optic nerve, called the retina, by a focus of the rays of light.   Smelling, the *contact* of odoriferous particles with the olfactory nerve.   Tasting is the *feel* of sapid bodies in the palate and the tongue.   Hearing, the *impression* of a sonorous wave or undulation of the air upon the auditory nerve."— *Collier's Essays upon the Progress of the Vital Principle, from the Vegetable to the Animal Kingdom and the Soul of Man,* p. 201.

SELECTIONS.

EXTRACTS FROM SWEDENBORG'S SPIRITUAL DIARY.

NOW FIRST TRANSLATED FROM THE ORIGINAL LATIN.

Concerning Love.

4104. It was perceived that to him, who, in the life of the body, loves his neighbor as himself, it is given in the other life to love his neighbor better than himself, for the goods of love are then indefinitely increased. Such is the life of the body, that one cannot go beyond the point of loving his neighbor as himself, because he is in corporeals, but with those who have passed out of this life, the love is more pure and becomes at length angelic; and this is to love others more than one's self.

That the Love is the Life.

4105. In conversing with spirits respecting love, it was said that the love is the life and that without love there is no life, and because spirits are of contrary natures, so there are contrary loves, as the love of self and the world, whence arise corresponding delights; and that as nothing could vegetate without the vernal and summer heat, so nothing could live in the spiritual world without love. Hence it was made manifest that true love is the alone life, and that there is no other life than that of love.

Concerning a civil State.

4107. There are those in the other life who live in a so called civil state, which is pleasant and agreeable, and in which I was for some time. Living in their own agreeable and pleasant sphere, they fear no one, and when any spirit not good approaches they speak civilly with him as one who is too good to say or do aught that is amiss. Such a spirit is there himself also reduced into a civil state, and either demeans himself as good, or departs, for the mind or disposition of the one affects the other. They never, in that state, say that any one is bad; though it still is not a state of dissimulation, but of sincerity, for they speak from civil promptings, and it is the state of those who, in the world, have lived happily and well in the conjugial relation, and have loved children.

4108. Others who were civil upon coming among them could not remain there, because they were put in pain, as I heard from certain ones, that they could not be there, as civil things affected them unpleasantly, just as they did in the world, and thus they showed themselves evil. They were very averse to that kind of companionship. In like manner in the world when any one has a good opinion of a bad man, he (the latter) cannot well refrain from appearing accordingly : wherefore as their interiors are fully disclosed in the other life, they are pained and thus separate. They are prompted to act out their evil, but dare not.

Concerning things in the other Life.

. 4109. It was observed and insinuated, that whatever a man had done in the life of the body, this returns in the other life, for there are perpetual changes of states, through which spirits are led, so that there is no state which had existed in the life of the body, but it then returns ; thus the hatreds and other things, which one had not only done, but thought; nay, everything of the kind which had occurred from infancy to the extreme limit of life, even the very persons against whom he had cherished enmity either open or concealed, are instantaneously present, so lamentable are the states into which they are driven. But, what is peculiarly observable, all the evil deeds and thoughts of the evil return to the very life, but with the good and those who were in faith it is not so ; all their states of good, of friendship. and of love return with the highest delight and happiness. Experience, in this respect, testifies that evil does not reign with me.

4110. These states return often, and because they are many, as, for instance, in which the man had cherished open or latent enmities, pretended friendships, and so on, with much variety, as also numerous other evils, the indulgence of worldly and selfish love, the commission of adulteries, &c. all these not only return, but are manifested before spirits and angels, with shame and grief. He thus undergoes not one kind of punishment, but many. and as often as it occurs, and his character is exposed, he suffers a punishment conformed to his evil and iniquity ; but still one general kind of punishment, and consequently one hell remains for him, which is that of his ruling evil and iniquity.

Concerning actual Evil.

4113. I have perceived that so long as evil is in the thought only, it does not so (frequently) recur ; but that so soon as it becomes actual. it passes into the will, when both the thought and the will, thus, the whole man, conspire (to the evil). Anything may be extirpated from the thought before it enters the will, but when it is in the will it is not easily extirpated, for it then also occupies the thought.

Concerning the Omnipresence of the Lord.

4016. Those who think in ultimates, and from ultimates, cannot comprehend how the Lord can be omnipresent. But in order to this being made in some degree intelligible, it is to be known that in the other life there is neither space nor time, thus that all are as present to each other as if in the nearest proximity. even though they should really be in the extremity of the universe. It may also somewhat appear from this, that the soul of man, or his intimate (most interior) principle, may possess a kind of omnipresence by being everywhere throughout the contracted limits of his body; and so govern all the internal organs, and all the thoughts, and whatever belongs to the man, how manifold soever they may be, that everything shall fitly cohere, and also by its omnipresence provide for all and singular its parts, without which kind of providence the whole would be dissolved and dissipated in a moment. This principle (the soul) acts from an end, and because it is the intimate of man, the Lord alone provides by means of it.

4017. That distances are phantasies, and that they are ideas, was evinced in a great variety of ways; for when I saw or perceived any one depart, or to be at a distance, or when I represented him to myself as in some other place, or when I spake with certain spirits that were elsewhere, myself knowing the place, or when a certain one was separated from me to the bounds of the universe, then the distance was perceived according to an idea formed from sight or from thought, and thus apprehended by him or by me; for they are present in a moment. Place, therefore, is none at all; where the idea is, there the spirit is, for the spirit is not separated from the idea; without the idea the spirit would not be, as it is his life: therefore where the life is, there is the spirit. Distance in purer things amounts to nothing; still less is it anything in more intimate, and least of all in the most intimate, thus absolutely nothing with the Lord; wherefore He is omnipresent, and sees and orders each single thing.

Concerning Faith and Good Works.

4021. Among those who contend that faith without good works is saving, I spake with one, asking him if it was not true that a saving faith cannot be given without love, which he affirmed; afterwards, I inquired whether love could be given without good works, on which he hesitated, because he thought of works separate from love, and because he knew that if he should have given all his goods to the poor, and yet had not love, it would amount to nothing: this he comprehended, and thence the inference, that a saving faith is of love, and that love without good works cannot exist,—as also, that faith without good works is no faith at all, as being a mere speculative (*intuitive*) faith, or a faith supposed to exist without good works and even without love. He seemed willing to admit that love was of faith, but not that faith was of love.

4022. It was said to him that heaven consists of love, and that it thence derives from the Lord all the knowledges of faith that are necessary to it, and in which knowledges the celestials are. On the other hand, they who are only in faith without love, and thus without good works, are in no knowledge at all; they do not even know that there is an internal man, as I perceived in regard to this spirit that he was ignorant of it. The same remark may be confirmed from the case of one who is in false and spurious love, that he is thereby persuaded and thus confirmed in many falses which flow from this spurious love or cupidity. It was further said to him that they are much better who do good works from a conscience received from this—that the Lord has commanded that we give to the poor and do good; for those who act from a conscience thus formed, do not place merit in their works, and thus such are admitted to heaven, while those who confirm themselves in the belief that faith without good works is saving, they cannot be admitted into heaven, for they know not what love is, which is yet the all in all of faith.

4023. I discoursed still further with him, as he said that if the matter were rightly explained it would be found that he held the truth. I replied that it was indeed true that it was faith that saved, but that as the quality of the faith was, so was the salvation; if the faith was false and spurious, it could not save, but only the faith which is true, which carries with it the knowledges of faith, and consequently love. It was moreover said that the pontificals affirm that faith saves, but what kind of a faith? to wit, that men should believe everything that the Pope has uttered and ordained, as being of the true church,—as also that they should believe everything which their priests teach them, upon whom they depend for their faith.

Concerning Love.

4046. That love is the fundamental principle from which and by which heaven exists and subsists, is evident from the circumstance that there must be such harmony and unanimity, and hence so universal a consociation, that the whole heaven, the whole world of spirits —that is, the whole human race from its first creation—should form a ONE, as all and every particular in man, in whom there are indefinite things, forms one body, and thus constitutes one man; in which body, if any thing were to prefer itself to any other thing, and not to love another thing better than itself, it could not subsist. He who is in genuine love has an idea of the common good, and of the universal human race, in respect to which every individual man should be as nothing, as is known; wherefore, unless a man regards himself as associated with his fellow, and esteems himself as nothing in respect to the common good, and love his neighbor better than himself, he can by no means be in the unanimous body. (heaven), but he necessarily expels himself from it so much as he removes himself from that love.

Concerning the Holy Spirit.

4048. It was perceived that men could clearly enough comprehend that there is no Holy Spirit (as a third person in the Trinity), especially from this—that the Holy Spirit proceeds from the Lord, by which is signified that the Holy of the Spirit is (the Holy) of the Lord, and this is implied in its *proceeding;* for what else proceeds from any one than what is of him (or of his essence), besides that the Lord openly declared this, and demonstrated it by His breathing (upon the disciples, and saying to them), that they should receive the Holy Ghost, and that it was from Him. From the Lord proceed the truths and the knowledges of faith, which are of Him and to Him, because from Him. The knowledges of faith, goodnesses, and truths are holy things, nor do they pertain to any one but the Lord, for the Lord is faith, and the all of all faith; these are the things which proceed from the Lord, and when this proceeding is through angels and spirits, they know not that they speak, and thus they may be called the Holy Spirit, because it is the Lord, who proceeds through them as organs and mediums.

How Punishments are incurred.

4055. It was perceived that whenever a spirit rushes or attempts to rush beyond those things which he has acquired to himself by actuality in his life-time, namely, into greater evils, that he then immediately incurs punishment, lest by actuality he should acquire still more evil in the other life. This was also observed with regard to the dragon, that punishment immediately ensues when he tends to advance beyond the due limits.

NOTICES OF BOOKS.

A REPORT *made to the Seventh Annual Meeting of the Central Convention, held in the City of Philadelphia, in October, 1847, on the Question of the Trine in the Ministry.* BY REV. THOMAS WILKS. (*Printed by order of the Convention.*)

This Report, though inserted in the Journal of Proceedings of the Convention, is printed also in a separate pamphlet, with a view to wider diffusion. A counter report, it seems, was expected from the Rev. Mr. De Charms, President of the Ecclesiastical Council, which, from some misunderstanding, does not appear, though promised to be given hereafter to the public through another channel. We should have been glad to see the two in juxtaposition, that we might have had the whole argument before us. The pamphlet of Mr. Wilks is evidently the result of a very careful study of the Word and of the writings of Swedenborg, in reference to the general subject of the constitution of the New Church Ministry. The position which it controverts is that assumed by the Convention at a former meeting, viz. " the existence of three distinct offices in the Ministry, to be filled by three distinct officers, the lower subordinate to the higher." This position Mr. W. submits to a very rigid examen, and urges against it, (1) The fact that the words of our Lord in his commission to the twelve and the seventy, imply no kind of precedency of one over another, but an entire parity of rank and authority ; (2) That the priesthood of the Jewish Church, which is thought by some to be the designed model of that of the New Church, was wholly abrogated along with the other rituals of that dispensation, and that though Swedenborg often employs the word *priest* in speaking of the ministry, yet this was in accommodation merely to prevalent usage, and that its true import in such cases is that of *teacher, preacher, or pastor ;* (3) That the argument drawn from the analogy of human governments established for the preservation of order in the world, does not avail to the countenancing of a system of subordination of inferior to superior officers, because Swedenborg says nothing respecting the subordination of civil governors to each other, and because the genius of civil and ecclesiastical institutions is entirely different, the one being designed to control men by compulsion or the restraint of outward laws, with suitable penalties, while the other aims to make men a law to themselves, and to govern by the force of moral suasion. Priests, i. e. ministers, are to *teach* men the way to heaven, and to *lead* them by means of truth to the good of life, without claiming to themselves any power over their souls. (4) That the passage in the Coronis which is mainly relied upon as teaching the trinal distinction of grades in the ministry, if interpreted according to the strictness of the letter, inevitably goes to establish the hierarchy of the Jewish, Roman, and English Churches, and consequently if this trine be established in the New Church, it must be after the same model. But in point of fact, the order actually adopted, though temporarily, by the Convention, does not agree with the platform laid down in this passage, inasmuch as it disclaims the *primus* or head which Swedenborg's language recognises. The true meaning of the language is then affirmed to be, simply, that as there will naturally be (erit) a trine in civil governments, so there will naturally be in the Church (not the New Church) *in its present form,* a similar trine; for, in every order, and in every thing, there will be a trine, and nothing can exist without it. But that it was far from Swedenborg's intention to teach the necessity of such an external order in the New Church ministry, as is set forth by the letter of the above extract, is evident from a variety of considerations ; as first, that it is, at the present day, impracticable; second, that if it were essential, it would have been explicitly declared in the writings of the Church ; third, that Swedenborg teaches, in the general scope of his writings, that the perfection of the external order of a government, whether civil or ecclesiastical, is in exact ratio to the internal corruption of that government, for the reason that internal evils require more stringent external restraints to keep them in check ; fourth, that to suppose that Swedenborg teaches, in the Coronis, the necessity of the above external order in the New Church ministry, is to suppose that he these teaches a doctrine contrary to the Word of God, and contrary to the tenor of his own writings explanatory of that Word.

Such is the drift of the argument in the pamphlet before us, which is certainly conducted with great ability; and when the opposing views are given to the public, we shall be happy to present an equally explicit summary of them to our readers.

MISCELLANY.

INTELLIGENCE FROM GERMANY.—Our readers have been previously informed that our indefatigable friend, Dr. Tafel, of Tubingen, has been put in possession, through the Royal Academy of Sciences at Stockholm, of the manuscripts of Swedenborg, called the Adversaria on Genesis and Exodus. These MSS., the first volume of which, consisting of 500 pages, has been printed and received for sale in this country, will constitute about three additional thick octavo volumes to the works of Swedenborg. The substance of these Adversaria, which consists of a running commentary on the text, is deeply interesting to the learned inquirer who desires to trace the progress of Swedenborg's spiritual illumination.—*Intel. Repos. for Jan.*, 1848.

The No. of the Intellectual Repository quoted above, at the close of a review of the continuation of the work on the Economy of the Animal Kingdom, gives the following additional particulars respecting the MSS. mentioned in our last as lately received in England from Sweden:—

"By way of appendix to this review, and in order to call attention prominently, we may here state that Mr. Wilkinson has received for the Swedenborg Association some valuable documents from the Royal Academy of Sciences at Stockholm. From time to time we shall give extracts from, and accounts of, these manuscripts in our pages. At present it is sufficient to observe, that they consist of *the continuation of the Animal Kingdom*, comprising full and interesting Treatises on the senses of SMELL, HEARING, and SIGHT, with an Epilogue on SENSATION GENERALLY; also of the TREATISE ON GENERATION, quite complete, and written out for the press. This work may justly be considered the most interesting of these physiological manuscripts, being on a subject of which there is no rational knowledge in the medical world, although Swedenborg treats it with the same prodigious analytic power that he has brought to bear upon the lungs and the other structures, and the locks of the mysterious organs yield easily and beautifully to the key of truth and order. There is no doubt that if the work were published, it would in a short time be one of the most popular of medical books, and carry the name and fame of Swedenborg with it, wherever these arcana of the human body are studied.

"The third work received is *The Treatise on the Loves and Faculties of the Human Mind;* a work also of the most interesting kind, and which may be appreciated by any reader. For the most part the subjects are shortly treated, which gives great variety to this Treatise.

"We have no time to say more at present, but will conclude with a short extract which arrested our attention in the *Continuation of the Animal Kingdom* :—

"'It would seem,' says Swedenborg, 'that there may possibly be more than five senses; particularly if we consider all the varieties of substances which present themselves to us from the macrocosm; besides which, objects are seen by some people more distinctly than by others. One organ, excepting the internal organs or the brain, receives the varieties of but one sense, or degree. Wherefore the organ is perfect which attends to its own senses; but two senses may exist in one and the same organ. Moreover, I. There may be an organ which enjoys the perception of the lesser distinctions of substances floating in water, as is the case with the human organs. II. There may be a sense that. apperceives the lesser discriminations of effluvia in the air; and perhaps also those that float in the ether: this dogs have in smell. * * * III. There may be a sense to perceive the minutest effluvia in the purer ether, IV. as well as the very modification of that ether, which runs in vortical forms, rendering animals magnetic, and making them know their quarters. V. It is our rational mind, or the fact that we are creatures of reason, that causes our sensations to be so blunt, as both psychology and reason itself demonstrate. VI. These considerations show, that there may be communications or messages of sympathy by virtue of the mere influence of the purer ether; this is the case in the state after death, when every one knows the other's thoughts; but not so in this state.'

"To this we will add, that in a highly interesting chapter *On the State of the Soul after the Death of the Body,* in the work ON THE HUMAN FACULTIES (where Swedenborg canvasses physiologicallyand psychologically many questions respecting the process of death, the state of the soul before it is fully emancipated from the intricate meshes of the body, &c., &c., &c.), there is the following; which shows that Swedenborg was not unaware of some of those remarkable passages in human nature and history which have been brought out prominently in this age, by Mesmerism.

" ' To say nothing,' says he, ' of those manifest sympathies which are acknowledged even in this lower world, and which are too numerous to record, *so great is the sympathy, and, as it were, magnetism in human kind, that communications often take place [between individuals] at a distance of many miles; which, however, are rejected as idle tales by some persons;* ALTHOUGH EXPERIENCE SHOWS THEIR TRUTH.* Nor, do I wish to mention, that the ghosts of some after death and burial have distinctly appeared; which could never have been (granting for the once that it was,) unless the animal spirits were mutually conjoined, and inseparably united with each other in the bonds of fellowship.' " * * * *

MASSACHUSETTS ASSOCIATION OF THE NEW JERUSALEM.—At the January meeting of this Association, in Boston, the following resolutions were offered:—

" *Resolved,* That the following language of Swedenborg has at this time a peculiar interest:

" ' At this day no miracles are wrought, for miracles . . . . would compel man to believe, and the things which compel, take away freedom, when yet all the reformation and regeneration of man is effected in his freedom.' A. C. 5606. ' Hence it is, that no miracles are wrought at this day. That they are also hurtful may hence be manifest; . . . . when the ideas derived from miracles are dissipated, there is effected a conjunction of what is false with what is true, thus profanation. Hence it is evident how hurtful miracles are at this day in the church, in which the internals of worship are discovered.' A. C. 7290.

" *Resolved,* That if preternatural evidence of an external character is to become an instrument for the spread of the church, the example of Swedenborg, the character of the doctrines of the New Church, the relation of this Church to all which have preceded it, and other considerations of moment, lead us to the belief that evidence of this kind will continue to occupy a very subordinate position: and that it cannot usefully or without danger be made prominent."

These resolutions gave rise to an animated discussion, in which many persons took part. None dissented from them; but as there seemed to be a general desire to consider further the interesting topics which the resolutions suggested, they were, on motion of Mr. Parsons, referred to the next meeting of the Association.

---

* The italics and small capitals are not Swedenborg's.

THE

NEW CHURCH REPOSITORY

AND

MONTHLY REVIEW.

| Vol. 1. | MARCH, 1848. | No. 3. |

ORIGINAL PAPERS.

ARTICLE I.

THE DRUIDISM OF ANCIENT BRITAIN:

ITS DOCTRINES, RITES, CORRESPONDENCES, ETC., AS DISCOVERED IN AN-
CIENT BRITISH MANUSCRIPTS, REVIEWED AND COMPARED WITH THOSE
OF THE ANCIENT CHURCH.

(*Continued.*)

In our preceding article, we showed at some length, by parallel passages from the Druids and Swedenborg, the striking
coincidence which exists between the Druidical Theology concerning the Divine nature and character, and those of the New
Dispensation, which, says Swedenborg, were the doctrines
taught in the ancient church. Between these elevated and truly
beautiful views of the Divine Being and those entertained in
the prevailing church upon the same subject, there is a very great
dissimilarity. Christian writers, in speaking of the Divine attributes, distinguished them into the natural or essential, and
the moral, as if the moral character of God were not essential
to his nature, but simply a quality assumed by him in consequence of the fall of man. Thus Dr. Dick, in his "Christian
Philosophy:" "By the natural or essential attributes of God,
we understand such perfections as the following :—His eternity, omnipresence, infinite knowledge, infinite wisdom, omnipotence, and boundless beneficence. These are the characters and
attributes of Diety, which, we must suppose, form the chief sub-

jects of contemplation to angels, and to all other pure intelligences—and in investigating the displays of which the sons of Adam would have been chiefly employed, had they continued in primeval innocence. These attributes form the ground work of all those gracious relations in which the God of salvation stands to his redeemed people in the economy of redemption. The Christian Revelation introduces the Diety to us under new relations, corresponding to the degraded state into which we have fallen. It is superadded to our natural relations to God, and takes it for granted, that these natural relations must for ever subsist." "It is, doubtless, owing to the want of clear and impressive conceptions of the essential character of Jehovah, and of the first truths of religion, that the bulk of mankind are so little impressed and influenced by the leading doctrines and duties connected with the plan of the gospel salvation."—*Christ. Philos.* p. 25, 26, 29.

Now it is obvious from the language of this writer, that, in his mind, what are called moral attributes, Divine love, Divine mercy, Divine justice, &c., are not essential to the Deity, otherwise than as it became necessary that he should assume them in consequence of the fall of man; for, in his opinion, if man had not fallen, nothing of these attributes would have been seen by men or angels in all the manifestations of the Deity. The sentiment here expressed by Dr. Dick is the sentiment entertained by all orthodox divines, and is universally held forth by them in their writings, and from their pulpits. But how different the doctrine taught by the Druids; according to them, the Divine power or omnipotence, is of the joint will of the Divine love and the Divine wisdom, by which all things are produced; so that in every manifestation of the Deity, his love, and wisdom, and power are unitedly seen, and necessarily in these his justice and his mercy.

With regard to what constitutes the Divine nature, the first Christian Church professes to know absolutely nothing. Dr. S. Clarke, one of the most distinguished divines of his age for his learning and the natural powers of his mind, in speaking upon this subject, says, "What the substance or essence of that Being, which is self-existent, or necessarily existing, is, we have no idea, neither is at all possible for us to comprehend it. The self-existent Being, must be a most simple, unchangeable, incorruptible Being; without parts, figure, motions, divisibility, or any other such properties as we find in matter. For all these things do plainly and necessarily imply finiteness in their very notion, and are utterly inconsistent with complete infinity."—*Dr. Clarke on the Being and Attributes of God.*

Another popular divine, whose book is in almost every one's possession, says, "As the Divine Being possesses a nature far beyond the comprehension of any of his creatures, of course that nature is inexplicable. All our knowledge of invisible objects is obtained by analogy; that is, by the resemblance which they bear to visible objects; but as there is in nature no exact resemblance of the nature of God, an attempt to explain the divine nature is absurd and impracticable. All similitudes, therefore, which are used in attempting to explain it must be rejected."—*Buck's Theo. Dict.*

Such are the sentiments of Christian divines upon a subject which is the foundation of all true knowledge,—a subject, the knowledge of which is absolutely necessary to the right understanding of the first principles of the gospel. But we turn from the writings of these divines to the teachings of the Druids, and, in addition to what we have already seen, learn further their views of the divine nature, concerning which Christian Theologians confess themselves to know nothing, and to look into which they consider absurd and impracticable.

In our translation of the triads, we have not been able, in every instance, to give the full import of the original, for the reason that we cannot find terms by which the exact shade of meaning can be perfectly conveyed.

The work from which we make the following selection, is entitled " Triodd Dœthineb," *Triads of Wisdom.* Of the manner in which these triads were handed down by the Druids, from generation to generation we shall speak hereafter. At present we proceed to exhibit a series of these triads, relating to Divine and moral themes, in which the leading sentiments will be seen at once by the intelligent reader of Swedenborg to be in accordance with the spirit of his teachings on the same subjects. We shall therefore dispense, in what follows, with the adduction of parallels from his works.

TRIADS.

1. The three fundamentals of underived Existence, that is to say, the three essentials of God : Love, Essential Knowledge, and Power; Being and Existence are by virtue of the union of these three.

Another triad says, The three things which are the original cause of all things : Wisdom, Love, and Power.

2. The three essentials of the Being of God : Substance, Life, and Action ; by the proceeding forth from these (yn dreigledig o han) are all (derived) substance, life, and action ; that is to say, all things are of God and his Institutes.

3. The three essentials of Life : Essential Heat (*Gni*), the Existere of Knowledge* (*Gwybodoldeb*), and Action.

---

* See Triad No. 13, in which it is said, that truth, knowledge, and light, are one

We have rendered *Gni, essential heat,* for the want of a better term. The literal signification of the word is, the all-pervading essence, or principle, the obstruction of which shakes and rends, and by which are caused earthquakes and thunder. "Earthquakes take place in the spiritual world," says Swedenborg, "by the coming of the influx of the divine principle, which removes the obstruction, arising from the corrupt state of the church, and thus in removing the evil changes the state of the church."—*Ap. Expl.* 400. "In the spiritual world there are heard thunders: the light of truth from God appeareth as lightning, the good itself as thunder, and the truths thence derived as variations of sound. The reason why good is heard there as thunder, is, because good which is of the affection, or of the love of man, likewise which is of the will, doth not speak, but only sound; but truth, which is of the understanding, and thence of the thought of man, articulates that sound into expressions."—*Ap. Expl.* 821.

By the word GNI *is evidently meant this divine principle of good,* or love, as will appear, first, by comparing this triad with others which speak of the divine nature, where it is invariably represented as being love; and secondly, from the fact, shown in the preceding article from Swedenborg, that all the knowledge which the Druids professed of spiritual things, was derived through the science of correspondence. "The divine good of the Lord is esse itself, and his divine truth is the life thence derived."—*A. C.* 3619. "The vital principle of man is from spiritual fire and heat, and this is love."—*A. C.* 4906.

4. There are three Infinitudes, and in these is necessarily t all of being: Immensity, Eternity, and God; and these three, unaffected by space and time, are necessarily every where and in all time.

5. There are three things which the infinite has not: beginning, end, and middle.

6. The three primitive things of derived existence: material, quality or state, and action.

7. The three primitive things of knowledge: sense, understanding, and will.

8. The three primitive things of power: impulse, effort, and order.

9. The three grand powers of the soul: affection, understanding, and will—(the conjunction of the understanding and the affection).

10. The three grand operations of the mind man: to think, to choose, and to perform.

11. Three things which result from the proper exercise of the powers of the mind: knowledges, power, and an internal state of good.

12. There are three things which are necessary to just knowledge, nor can there be righteous knowledge where they are not: truth, order, and peace; these three will produce righteousness, and thence knowledges in lieu of subtle fallacies.

13. Three things which are but one: truth, knowledge, and light.

14. The three guides of the understanding: the just, the beautiful, and the beneficial.

15. Three things that flow from the same origin: truth, justice, and mercy; these three proceed from one love, which is the love of wisdom.

16. The three primary principles of wisdom: obedience to the laws of God, concern for the welfare of mankind, and suffering with fortitude all the accidents of life.

17. The three branches of wisdom: the wisdom which relates to God, the wisdom which relates to mankind, and the wisdom which relates to one's self.

18. The three knowledges which appertain to wisdom: the knowledge of God, the knowledge of mankind, and the knowledge of one's own heart.

19. The three efforts of wisdom: to understand nature by light which is of the Divine, to see truth by searching into it, and to exercise love and peace.

20. There are three things with which wisdom cannot exist: covetousness, licentiousness, and pride.

21. Three things which are essential to wisdom: liberality of mind, temperance, and beneficence.

22. Three elements of wisdom: prudence, justice, and peace —the fruit of benevolence.

23. Three things evince wisdom: to resist the false whenever it presents itself, to love and practise the truth, and to avoid every thing which demands secrecy and concealment.

24. The three great ends of knowledge: duty, utility, and décorum.

25. The three branches of man's duty: to strive for an assimilation of character to the Deity, to benefit his fellow-man, and to improve his knowledges.

26. The three laws of man's actions: what he forbids in another, what he requires from another, and what he cares not how it is done by another.

27. The three grand characteristics of goodness: to speak the truth at all times fearless of consequences, to love every good, and to suffer with fortitude for the sake of truth and good.

28. Three things rightly understood will give peace: the tendencies of nature, the claims of justice, and the voice of truth.

29. The three principles of happiness: the knowledge of truth, the performance of good, and patience under sufferings.

30. Three things corrupt the world: pride, superfluity, and indolence.

31. Three men who love neither their country, nor God: he who loves his belly, he who loves riches, and he who loves bodily ease.

32. There are three things for which God will not love him who delights to look at them: contention, a monster, and the pomp of pride.

33. There are three species of lies: verbal lies, the lies of silence, and the lies of false appearances; each inducing us to believe what we should not.

34. The three laughs of a fool: at the good, at the bad, and at he knows not what.

35. Three things which are odious in a man: licentiousness, deceit, and malice; things which in the end will destroy him.

36. Three things which are detestable in man: to be a liar, to be revengeful, and to be coveteous.

37. Three infernal qualities in man: pride, envy, and violence.

38. Three things he who dislikes which should not be loved by another: the odor of clover, the flavor of milk, and the song of birds.

In this triad, we have beautifully represented by correspondence the principles of regeneration, and in this sense only can the triad be understood: otherwise why should it be an established maxim of the church, that man should not be loved for his dislike of these things?

"The tender herb denotes that which first springs forth in the regeneration."—*A. C.* 29.

"Milk denotes the celestial spiritual principle, and to suckle denotes the implantation of that principle."—*A. C.* 2643. "Birds denote things rational and intellectual, and song the harmony consequent upon regeneration."—*A. C.* 40, 420.

39. There are three men that all should look upon with affection: he who looks with affection upon the face and beauty of the earth, he who is delighted with the contemplation of the arcana of science, and he who looks lovingly on little infants.

40. Three things in man, in which will be found the most of

God: that in which is the least of self, that in which God is mostly loved, and that in which he is most sought.

41. Three injunctions which God has laid upon man : to strive for the possession of all commendable knowledges, to do all the good he can, and to beget children in lawful wedlock ; for by these three the world is preserved in order.

42. There are three persons whom every Briton, being a landed proprietor, must keep and support : a married wife, a man in arms, if he do not bear arms himself, and a family tutor.

43. There are three things with which every man should acquaint himself : the customs and manners of his country and tribe, the laws of wisdom, and a calling by which he may maintain himself.

44. Three things which support the world : love, diligence, and just laws.

45. The three chief duties of man, which should be aimed at in all he does : to procure, by innocent and just means, a worldly competency ; to seek, to the best of his knowledge and strength, the good of his country and tribe ; and, according to his ability, to observe the institutes of God and of man wherever he may be, while he remains in the world.

The reader will perceive that the doctrines of the above triads differ but little, if any, from the doctrines of the New Church ; the difference, where there is any, being in the modes of expression rather than in the idea expressed. The doctrines which are here taught concerning God and the soul or spirit of man, be it remembered, were altogether unknown in the Christian Church until revealed by Swedenborg. The trine which the Druids represent as existing in God, they also represent as existing in man ; for they say that God is divine love, divine wisdom, and divine power emanating from the two former, and that the human soul is affection, understanding, and act, which last is from the conjunction of his understanding and affection ; thus they taught, as Swedenborg from the Word now teaches, that man was created in the image and likeness of God. But they did not teach, according to the doctrine of the prevailing church, that God, by the exertion of his omnipotence, created the world, and consequently man, from nothing ; but they taught, agreeably to the doctrine of the New Jerusalem, that all things are of the Divine essence, or substance, by the proceeding forth from him, who is essential substance, and life in itself,—substance and life, because he is love itself and wisdom itself. In perfect agreement with their views of the character of Deity are also the doctrines of life which they taught ; the good, which by Swedenborg is called charity, and the love of the neighbor, being by them evidently set forth as the first principle of the church, and the practice of it enforced as the all-important duty of man, and indispensable to happiness.

We learn from Swedenborg that the conjugial relation is most sacred and holy in its character, because the origin of conjugial love is from the marriage of good and truth; and that this relation was regarded as sacred by the men of the ancient church. What the views of the Druids were upon this subject may be seen from two or three of the above triads; but as some writers have unjustly represented them as living in promiscuous concubinage, without the least sense of decency or propriety, we will allow them to speak more fully upon the subject, that the reader may form his opinion respecting them from the testimony of their own laws. The following triads are from the laws of Dyfnwal Moelmud—of the signification of which name we shall have to speak hereafter, when we come to speak of the science of correspondence among the Druids.

1. There are three causes of welcome progression: co-proximation, alliance by marriage, and defence.

2. There are three happy progressions: bards announcing peace, a meeting in harvest-time, and a marriage.

3. There are three progressions for mutual support: the chief of the tribe, a married person, and he that is employed by the country and district.

4. There are three kinds of private possession belonging to every man, whether he be a foreigner or a Cymbrian (Briton): a wife, children, and moveable property.

5. There are three kinds of private possession belonging to every man which must not be shared with another, nor be given in payment for a fine: a wife, children, and paraphernalia. The paraphernalia denote clothes, arms, and the implements of the privileged arts; for without these a man is deprived of his just station in society; and it is not right for the law to unman a citizen, or to prevent him from practising the arts.

6. There are three legal injuries to a man: to murder him, to have illicit intercourse with his wife, and to violate the protection he may have given.

7. There are three removals which have no return: first, a woman by marriage, for she quits the privilege of her family, and obtains that of her husband according to the authority and will of the law. She can no more assume the privilege of her family, neither will the law knowingly revoke what it has once determined.

8. There are three indispensables of a voter; that he be a free-born Briton without defect in pedigree, and without meanness in dignity;—that he be an efficient man; and that he be the head of a family, having a wife and children by marriage. Without these a man will not be recognized in law as the head of a family, and with these he will not decide against privilege and justice, but will vote conscientiously on their account.

9. There are three kinds of vassals who do not obtain the dignity and privilege of free-born Britons until the ninth in descent: the first is an illegitimate child that is legally denied by his father; or in another manner according to law, because he was not born in honorable and organized wedlock; or in another manner still, because he was begotten in opposition to the law and the privilege of the country and tribe.

A similar law was given to the sons of Israel. "A bastard shall not enter into the congregation of the Lord; even to his tenth generation shall he not enter into the congregation of the Lord."—*Deut.* xxiii. 2. "Those things which are of the state of faith are signified by this, that a bastard might not come into the congregation of Jehovah to the tenth generation."—*A. C.* 6239. Nine and ten have frequently the same signification. Three signifies all, and as nine is the square of three, it necessarily has the same signification. Likewise ten frequently denotes the same thing; hence the decalogue, comprising the whole of the law, and the ten virgins significative of the whole church, or the kingdom of heaven. To be deprived of the privileges of the congregation or nation, to the ninth or tenth generation, therefore, denotes that while a man remains in a state of evil, or a state in which truths are adulterated, he cannot enter into the kingdom of heaven. The coincidence between these two laws is remarkable, and evidently tends to confirm the idea that the Britons had a knowledge of the science of correspondence.

10. There are three reasons for vassalage as it respects disorderly persons, who are neither recognized by the law nor by the citizens: first, to prevent treachery by strangers and their confederates; secondly, to prevent foreigners to obtain the land of free-born Britons; and thirdly, to prevent celibacy by getting children promiscuously and illegally through illicit commerce with abandoned women.

These laws make it sufficiently clear that the Druids looked upon the marriage relation of one man and one woman as most sacred and holy; and that the violation of it was by them considered to be a far greater evil than it is now generally believed to be in Christian countries.

In strict accordance with the elevated views which the Druids had of God and his government, and of the nature and duties of man, were the ideas they entertained of a future state. But having already given so many of their triads, we must, for the sake of brevity, present their views upon this subject in as short a compass as we can—giving their thoughts, as near as possible, in their own language, selected and arranged according to the present style of composition.

HEAVEN.

THE STATE OF THE GOOD. If during human life, or the state of probation, the soul attaches itself to good, it passes in the instant of death into a higher state of existence, where good necessarily prevails; for in all states of existence above humanity, good preponderates, and therein all beings are necessarily good: hence, they can never fall, but are still advancing higher and higher in the scale of happiness and perfection, till they arrive at their final destination, where every being, in his allotted place, will be completely happy to all eternity, without the possibility of ever falling into evil; and, knowing that he could not possibly be equally happy in any other station, will never have any desire to quit that wherein he is. Liberty, however, will still remain in the exertions of love and benevolence; for love is the principle which rules everything in those states of existence which are above humanity.

ETERNITY.

No finite beings can possibly bear the infinite tedium of Eternity. They will be relieved from it by continual renovations at proper periods, by passing into new states of existence, which will not, like death, be dreaded, but be eagerly wished for and approached with joy. Every state will impart its peculiar knowledge, for consciousness and memory will forever remain; or there could be no such thing as endless life.

Let the reader compare this with what Swedenborg says, in his Treatise on Heaven and Hell, in the section "Concerning changes of state with the angels in heaven." That no other changes of state than those mentioned by him are meant by the Druids, is obvious from the sentiment of the preceding paragraph, where it is said, that the good advance higher and higher in the scale of happiness and perfection, till they arrive at their final destination, where they will be completely happy to all eternity.

HELL.

THE STATE OF THE EVIL. Rewards and punishments are so secured by the eternal laws of creation, that they take place necessarily and unavoidably. Pride is the utmost degree of human depravity: it supplies the motive for perpetrating every kind of wickedness: it is that passion by which man assumes more than the laws of nature allow him. By this assumption man attaches himself to evil in such a degree that his soul falls at death into the lowest deep (*i Annwn*). Man, by attaching himself to evil, becomes, in the passions of his soul, depraved and brutalized; and at death he falls into such a state as corresponds with the malignity acquired.

The meaning of the *Annwn* exactly corresponds with the apparent locality of hell in the spiritual world as described by Swedenborg;—that which is deep beneath the feet, as it were, in the centre of darkness. In the works of the British bards, hell is represented as a place abounding with quagmires, and frost, and snow, and infested by every variety of noxious and loathsome animals. One of the cantos of an ancient Druidic poem entitled "A Panegyric to Lludd the Great," ends with these words: "Before the covering stone, I tremble in the presence of the Sovereign of boundless dominion, lest I sink, adhesive, to the quagmire of that multitude which peoples the depths of hell."

It is generally thought the Druids believed in the transmigration of the soul; but this opinion is founded upon the many passages in the writings of the bards, and in one class of the triads, which are not in the least understood, where the affections and thoughts are represented as beasts and birds, and where, according to correspondence, internal changes of state are described. To a person acquainted with the science of correspondence, this affords no other evidence than that the Druids understood the science, and that they clothed their ideas in its language. This fact we think we shall be able to show in a future number.

(*To be continued.*)

ARTICLE II.

WHAT IS TRUTH?—SWEDENBORG'S POINT OF VIEW.

To vindicate, in some slight measure from the charge of having committed their faith to unsubstantial fancies and idle dreams, that small band in our community who have attached themselves to the doctrines of the New Church, will be the object of some of our further endeavors; and if, in the course of our inquiries, we shall be led to hold language and to maintain opinions differing widely from those long advocated and ably defended by some with whom we are connected in many ties of esteem and affection, and to whom it is still our delight to render honor, we trust it will not be attributed to a mere love of novelty in opinion, nor to any decline of a feeling of true reverence in ourselves,—but rather to a transfer of that sentiment to what we cannot but deem its legitimate object, a higher teaching of Divine Truth.

As when the two poles of a galvanic battery are introduced into some chemical solution, an immediate commotion ensues, the various elements of which it is composed developing into action dormant affinities, and seeking for themselves new combinations,—some arranging themselves around one pole, some clinging to the other—some depositing themselves in salts at the bottom, and others, rendered relatively imponderable, creeping rapidly into the air,—so, often, will our clusters of ideas, and trains of thought, and modes of teaching, hasten to re-arrange themselves in reference to some new Truth introduced into the field of our mental vision, or some new point of view obtained from which the old truths are re-examined.

The system of Swedenborg, containing as it does a series of doctrines concerning the most recondite truths, must necessarily exercise such an influence over the minds of those who receive it ; throwing the broad mantle of its new developments over every region of human thought. As it deals in many cases with new ideas, it needs a new terminology. As the new terminology must for the most part be constructed out of old words, the old words often need new definitions. To those who would understand the system, either for the purpose of an intelligent reception, or for a candid rejection, it is requisite that they possess themselves of its definitions, and the aspects it proposes to take.

"Truth," says Dean Swift, " is that which is."

"Truth," says Archbishop Whately, in his system of Logic, "in the strict logical sense, applies to propositions, and to nothing else; and consists in the conformity of the declaration made to the actual state of the case; agreeably to Aristotle's definition of a true proposition—vera est, quæ *quod res est* dicit."

" Truth," says Professor Tappan, in his Primordial Logic, " is an antithetical idea; its opposite is falsehood. Truth in itself is identical with the highest form of reality—with absolute and necessary reality—and it is the parent of all other reality, the reality of actual objective being. The ideas and the necessary and universal conceptions which immediately spring out of them, are the essential body of truth: actual being is the exterior embodiment of truth. Hence truth is that in which the reason ultimately, necessarily, and securely reposes."

Without presuming to call in question the entire sufficiency of any of the above definitions for the purposes for which they were enunciated, it nevertheless falls directly within the province of our present undertaking to exhibit briefly the one which, though nowhere stated in words, we conceive the system of Swedenborg tacitly proceeds upon.

Truth is so fundamental and pervading a term in all discussions relating to the higher classes of subjects, that the mode in which it is defined may oftentimes exercise an important influence over our manner of treating distant and subordinate branches of a subject; and our failure at the outset to comprehend an author's view of it might, in many cases, throw considerable confusion over subsequent stages of our inquiry.

The universe presents itself to the human intellect under two distinct phases, the external and the internal,—the world of outward fact and being, and the world of inward thought and feeling,—or, as they are usually called, the objective and subjective; or, as some have been pleased to express it, the *me,* and the *not me.* The objective universe is a series of facts, some of them developed in time and space, others developed in time only. The subjective universe presents itself as a series of ideas.* Anything which takes place in the outward world is called a *phenomenon.* Anything which takes place in the inward world has been called a *noumenon,* and sometimes a *metaphenomenon.*

Of the objective universe, truth is not predicable, but actuality only; it simply *exists.* Nor is it applicable to ideas merely—they may be erroneous: but it is the result of a subjective correlation between an idea and a fact; that is, of an exact agreement between the *noumenon* and a *phenomenon;* between a thought and that which is the object of thought. Truth is predicable only of ideas thus correlated. Now this

---

* Used in the general sense as including conceptions, &c.

correlation may be of two kinds : first, relative—second, absolute. As the correlations are of two kinds, so truth requires
two definitions : first, relative—second, absolute.

Relative truth only is predicable of any ideas which float
across the field of a finite consciousness, and is what Swedenborg distinguishes as *apparent truth.* Absolute truth is predicable only of the ideas which revolve in the divine consciousness, and may be defined to be that idea which God forms of a
thing, and is what Swedenborg calls *real truth.*

The ideas of the finite subject are relative because they are
derivative. The idea is a transcript of the fact, and arises from
or is caused by it. The ideas of the Infinite Subject are absolute,
because they are causative. The idea exists before the fact ;
the fact is a transcript of the idea, and arises from or is caused by it.

We pass out into the phenomenal world, and take cognizance
of an object ; a tree, for instance. We describe it—its height,
figure, color ; we are not satisfied—we examine its leaves,
trunk, seeds, flowers. We make drawings of it. At each stage
of the process our descriptions are correct, and relative truth
may be predicable of them. But they are incomplete. Political economy comes in, and inquires what uses commerce may
make of that tree, its fruits, its roots, its bark. Botany explains
its relationship to other individuals of its class, assigns it a
place, and gives it a name. Not satisfied with this, physiology
interrogates it, penetrates within the rind, and developes a new
" photosphere" of ideas clustering around. It has interior fluids, circulations, secretions, a complicated system of spiral vessels, through which motion reigns, as their normal condition.
And then, not content with asking questions, chemistry steps
in to know what kind of new matter enters into the composition of these ; and the result is, that it only finds the old matters in a new form. It nevertheless notes patiently the new
combinations therein presented. Thus does every object in
nature grow under the eye of science, and become a centre,
around which circle after circle of new conceptions are found
to cluster, as we extend the " sweep" of our telescope.

The acknowledged body of Truth, under the title of " Positive Philosophy" is constantly invading higher ground, and
has already pushed its out-posts to the confines of the spiritual
world ; seeking to add to its harmony the " music" of another
" sphere." So also do the series of ideas expand in circle above
circle before the eye of the Reason. Thus too all relative
Truth is progressive ; correct, but incomplete. The nearness
of its approaches to the Divine Ideas must be the measure of
its value. Towards them it took up its march on the first

morning of its existence. Reach them it never can—the spiritual asymtote of the universe.

Agreeably to this definition of absolute Truth we legitimate Swedenborg's teaching in relation to space and time in the other life. All who have read his writings must have observed, and many have been staggered at it, that he frequently asserts that spaces and times in the spiritual world are only appearances, but do not exist in reality.

"The spirits who are thought of by others (as those who have been in any degree acquainted together during the life of the body) are present in a moment, when it is granted by the Lord, and so very near that they can hear and touch each other, or at any little distance, notwithstanding they might have been thousands of miles distant, yea, even at the stars; the reason is, because distance of place does not operate in the other life."—*A. C.* 1274.

"Since angels and spirits are affections which are of love, and thoughts thence, therefore neither are they in space and time, but only in the appearance of them: the appearance of space and time is to them according to the states of the affections and thence of the thoughts; wherefore, when any one thinks about another from affection, with the intention that he wishes to see him, or, to speak with him, he is set forthwith present.

"All progressions in the spiritual world are made by changes of the state of the interiors, so that progressions are nothing else than changes of state : thus also I have been conducted by the Lord into the heavens, and likewise to the earths in the universe, and this as to the spirit, while the body remained in the same place. Thus all the angels move; hence to them there are no distances, and if there are not distances, neither are there spaces, but instead of them states and their changes."—*H. H.* 192.

Our ideas of space and time have excited a great deal of discussion in the speculative world, and almost every important work on Philosophy has a considerable space allotted to them. It is not worth while for us at present to attempt to determine whether they be " cognitions a priori" or " the results of experience," but it will be sufficient to quote Mr. Whewell's[*] closing remark on the subject, as showing the philosophic conclusion of the matter. He says " they are the essential conditions of knowledge residing within the mind." They are almost universally held by philosophers to be two fundamental ideas, which lie at the foundation of all thought—the "receptivities" into which all the matter of our knowledge is introduced in order to resolve its form. It might appear from this, that Swedenborg is at issue with Philosophy on this point. Such however is not the case, for some philosophers, as Fichte, and his German followers, in carrying out Kant, have arrived at the notion that space is only an appearance, and those who do not agree with him, do not carry their inquiries to the point at

---

[*] Philos. of the Inductive Sciences.

which they would conflict with Swedenborg. They retire within themselves, dive down into consciousness, and the first thing they find there is the "*me :*" and the next thing is a space beyond the *me*, by which it is bounded, in which it is not. Hence our idea of space—which, according to our belief, is only one of the modes in which we perceive our own finiteness; that we are not infinite.

Now ceasing to pursue the study of psychological astronomy from the earth of our own consciousness as its centre, let us endeavor to carry this experiment to the operations of the Divine mind, and ask ourselves if, when the Infinite consciousness reflects itself upon its own operations, there is any such experience of a space by which it is bounded, and in which it is not? We cannot conceive of any space lying without the bounds of the Divine consciousness; in fact, we clearly see it to be impossible. But space is not predicable of consciousness, as lying within it. Then of course our ideas of space are not true in the absolute sense, but are only representatives of apparent truth.

So with our idea of time. We reflect upon the operations of our own minds. We think, and we recal the thought instantly, and look again at it; we are conscious of our first emotion and of our apperception of it; hence of two ideas, and hence of succession, and arrive at once of our idea of time. We remember the past which we have experienced; we look forward to the future which we have not experienced. But let us again revert to the operations of the Divine Mind, and ask, whether to it the things which are past, and the things which are future, are not *present*, and as much present as when, to our conceptions, they were actually transpiring. Moreover, will the Divine Mind find itself under the necessity of resolving first one idea and then another, in succession? Do not, rather, all ideas lie reflected upon the field of the Divine consciousness, equally, and at the same time?

Thus we arrive at the conclusion that our idea of time is only another mode in which the perception of our own finiteness forces itself upon us; we find that we cannot take in the universe of thought at a single glance, but are obliged to occupy ourselves, first with one sand, then with another.

In every inquiry, then, after truth in the lower sphere, the question which arises cannot be the one so universally put, of a mathematical *yes* or *no;* one view right, the other wrong; but all views must be treated as approaches, more or less near, to the absolute realities of the case. Now the system of Swedenborg professes to take its view of all subjects which fall within human contemplation, as they appear to an immortal spirit after he has passed into the heavenly regions. Taking up his position, so to speak, in the celestial heaven, he looks down upon men, and human affairs, and material nature, as all their vast and varied topography appears unmasked in the full blaze of the risen sun of eternity, instead of the detached and fragmentary parcels, the indistinct outlines of whose bulky forms, loomed around him in the mists of his spiritual morning. He regards the soul of man as being in its own nature essentially immortal, and consequently knowing no maturity. His life on earth is only the embryo state of his spiritual existence; and all his doctrines and teachings in their logical bearings, constantly maintain a reference to this view. So in relation to the Divine economy of the scheme of salvation; God is treated of as the father of all the spirits in the universe of worlds, and the inhabitants of our earth are looked upon as one body among a vast multitude.

The Christian Church, is not regarded as confined in its geographical limits to the fraction of a single planet, but as including in its comprehensiveness all the planetary atoms of space, exhibiting to the eye of Christian charity the great Head of the Church as marshalling a whole universe of souls towards the mansions of eternal rest, instead of representing him as leading only an "elected" few along the straight and narrow path. The human mind has become so accustomed to the contemplation of objects as they first present themselves, and in their outward and most apparent relations only, that it is not surprising that such views should at first be generally regarded with a feeling somewhat akin to aversion. Those who have been at all in the habit of casting their eyes philosophically over the history of opinion, would not have found it difficult to have predicted, that a system coming before the world, with its starting point in heaven, would necessarily encounter a very slow and difficultly acquired reception.

The utter hopelessness which some have felt in ever being able to convey their views, and explain their stand-point to sceptical unbelief, has induced them to shut themselves up more closely in the phraseology of Swedenborg; and thus render what from the first needed translation, still more incomprehensible. It is not surprising that intelligent minds taking up his system hastily, stumbling upon it from the outside, and seeing all its objects in inversion, should lay down his works with the idea of his insanity.

But what a monitor the Almighty has placed at the door of all the knowledge of the race, if we would but heed it. The image on the retina of the eye is an inverted picture of the object seen. Thus everywhere and without intermission reminding us that our first impressions are always to be reconsidered, before taking them home to the reason.

If we will take into the mind in its full force as an axiom to make deductions from, and not merely as a proposition externally assented to, the doctrine, that all our views are the more or less valuable as they approach towards, or recede from, the ideas of the Divine mind, we shall find that it will essentially modify our method of handling all the questions of Theology and the Philosophy of Science. We shall feel less anxiety to impose our peculiar views upon others as the ultimatum of truth, or as complete descriptions of it; and shall have more hesitation in consigning those who differ from us to the category of error. This definition of truth involves in it also, by direct implication, a definition of error. Absolute, and unmitigated error is a monstrosity which never existed. All the forms of belief which we call errors, are only such from not having advanced so far along the path of a higher teaching as ourselves are supposed to occupy, but were each in its time a nearer approach than the form which immediately preceded it.

To those who, to their own satisfaction, have arrived at what they call a fixed system of truth, have learned all they wish to know of spiritual and Divine things, and are at logical ease in Zion, our addresses would without doubt be unavailing; our appeal is to another, and we trust a larger class; that wide spread and uncounted multitude scattered up and down the highways and by-ways of Christendom, among all sects and in every communion, members of Christ's mystical body: who are patiently waiting or hopefully looking for the second coming of their Lord, and the latter day glory of his Church; many of whom no doubt resting too implicitly in the sense of the letter have been led to expect a personal coming in the literal clouds of heaven.

For the sincere lover of, and humble inquirer after, the truth, the system of Swedenborg will be found to possess peculiar charms; and, as patiently pursued, will develope to him peculiar advantages; accomplishing pre-eminently for the mental vision what the Rosse telescope has performed for the physical eye; carrying it far away, out across the illimitable spaces, resolving its nebulæ into clusters of stars, and showing systems of shining worlds, which to ordinary observers, lay drawn together in the indefinitely receding perspective, like the particles of a morning mist.   W. B. H.

ARTICLE III.

LETTERS TO A TRINITARIAN.

LETTER III.

THE DIVINE HUMANITY

DEAR SIR,

In order to a just appreciation of the extract given in my last from Swedenborg and of numerous others to follow, it will be requisite to present more distinctly his leading doctrine of the Divine nature, in which the attributes of Love and Wisdom are made to comprehend the sum of all the perfections usually ascribed to Jehovah. As Heat and Light may be said to comprise all the properties of the sun, so the Divine Love and the Divine Wisdom embrace within themselves all the moral and intellectual attributes which the mind conceives of as inhering in the infinite and uncreated source of all being. What are ordinarily termed Holiness, Justice, Mercy, Benevolence, &c., are merely the different modifications or phases of Love. Omniscience, Omnipresence, and Omnipotence, refer themselves to the operation of Wisdom, for which we may substitute Truth, just as we may speak of Good or Goodness in the place of Love, for Good is the correlate of Love, as Truth is of Wisdom. This holds as well in regard to man as to God, since man, in the grand constituents of his nature, is an image of God. Assuming these then as the paramount attributes of Jehovah, we shall have little difficulty in admitting that the Divine Love is to the Divine Wisdom what the *Esse* of any thing is to its *Existere*, or the *substance* to the *form;* for thought in all intelligent beings is the *form* of Affection. But the *Esse* of all existence is its Life ; the Divine Life, therefore, is the Divine Love, and all human life is, in the last analysis, identical with love. That the truth of this proposition may not strike you at once, is very possible ; yet I am persuaded that it will eventually force itself upon your conviction. How otherwise will you account for the effect produced even upon the physical system by the shock of disappointment falling upon a dominant and all-absorbing love? What an utter prostration of all the faculties and functions of the body oftentimes ensues. But the life of the body is in the life of the spirit, and the spirit is the seat of love, or rather its very essence is love.

In assuming that Love is the *Esse* of all being, whether Divine, angelic, or human, we necessarily preclude the idea that it is a *quality* pertaining to some unknown substance or substratum, as sweetness is the quality of sugar. It is itself the primary substance and substratum. As in regard to Heat, it is impossible for the mind, in its researches into the nature of this element, to reach the conception of a primordial substance of which it is a quality, or to say that Heat proceeds *from something hot*, so in respect to Love, we must at length inevitably rest in the conclusion, that there is nothing that *lies back of it*—nothing of which it is to be predicated as a quality. It is fundamental and primary in every idea of intelligent being. In God it is underived, self-subsisting, and eternal. In angels and men it is derived by incessant influx from its infinite source. And as the love is the life of every thing that lives, life itself is not creatable, because Love is not. Throughout the universe of dependent being, whether angelic, human, animal, or vegetable, there is no *created life*. It is perpetual influx, from the self-existing fountain of life in the Deity, into adapted receptive organs. In Him we live, move, and have our being.

Such, then, if our position be sound, is God—infinite Love and infinite Wisdom, or, what is equivalent, infinite Goodness and infinite Truth. In this character he is to be viewed as subsisting from eternity, and it is a character predicable strictly of *one* being, in whom no distinction can exist that will admit of being expressed by a term indicative of a divided personality. Love and Wisdom, or Affection and Intellect, or Will and Understanding, enter essentially into the very elemental conception of an intelligent person, whether create or uncreate, and the duality involved in the idea of these principles offers no more disturbance to the impression of absolute unity of being, than does the fact of man's possession of Love and Intellect interfere with the conviction of his being still but one person and not two. As easily could we imagine that the unity of the sun was destroyed by reason of its two-fold emanation of light and heat, as that the Divine Love and Wisdom could be the basis of a bi-personal distinction. If now we add to this the idea of *action, operation, proceeding energy*, we complete our conception of a personal agent without at the same time mentally *trichotomizing* him into three. There is indeed a triplicity of aspects in which he is presented to the mind, and one too founded upon a real threefold distinction, in the constituent principles of his nature, but not one that can, with any propriety, be laid as the foundation of a *tri-personal* distinction. The terms Father, Son, and Holy Ghost, denote not three *persons*, but three *essentials of one person*.

All this, I think, is somewhat easy of apprehension, and what many Trinitarians would perhaps admit, so long as their thoughts remain centred in the contemplation of the abstract and absolute Godhead, apart from all reference to Christ as "God manifested in the flesh." But no sooner does the idea of the Lord's incarnation form itself in the mind, than a vague conception of some mysterious Trinity of *persons* ensues, to the *second* of which the assumption of our nature is attributed. But the view already given of the necessary and essential unity of the Divine Being, we hold to be absolutely imperative on our belief and to be utterly exclusive of any theory of the Godhead which involves the idea of three *persons* subsisting from eternity. Whatever be the true character of Christ as the Redeemer of men—whatever the Divinity predicated of Him—it *must* be such as to consist entirely with the unity above asserted. This lies at the foundation of every correct view of the nature of the Deity, as truly as the axioms lie at the foundation of every course of mathematical reasoning. The denial of it is the denial of a first principle, which does violence to intuition. Nor can this conviction be shaken by the most multitudinous array of Scriptural passages *apparently* declaring the contrary, for so overwhelming is the evidence from inspiration and reason on this head, that we *know* the position cannot be contravened by any thing in holy writ when *rightly understood*. While, therefore, we readily concede and strenuously maintain the fact of a threefold distinction in the Divine nature, indicated in its reference to the economy of redemption by the terms Father, Son, and Holy Ghost, we at the same time reject, with equal assurance, that form of the doctrine which makes the second *person* of the sacred three, in contradistinction from the other two, to have come into the conditions of humanity. The true doctrine we hold to be, that the one, undivided, and absolute Jehovah took upon him our nature and accomplished redemption on our behalf. This we affirm to be, upon the authority of Revelation, not only true in itself, but *the* great and paramount truth of the Christian system without the real recognition of which there is no genuine faith in the God of the Scriptures. This I shall hope to show still more distinctly in the sequel.

The ground I have thus far assumed will necessarily govern the tenor of the whole discussion upon which I have entered. The ultimate scope at which I aim is to determine the true character of Christ's work in the scheme of human redemption, and this can never be done without first discovering his true character in himself, and the relation which he sustains to the Supreme Deity. The knowledge of what Christ was prior to the incarnation is indispensably requisite to a knowledge of what he was and did *in* his incarnation. That he was from eternity divine, you have no hesitation to admit. But if he was divine he was God, and if God, the supreme God ; for the terms are of identical import. Again, the supreme God is Jehovah, and God incarnate is Jehovah incarnate, which necessitates *with you* the admission, that Jesus and Jehovah are one and the same. The Unitarian of course denies this, because he denies the competency of the Old Testament to determine the point for Christians, who are shut up, in their view, exclusively to the teachings of the New Testament in relation to every thing touching the person and work of the Saviour. I would not, however, imply by this that the view of Christ for which I am contending is not sustained in the writings of the Evangelists and Apostles. On the contrary, I am fully persuaded, and shall hope to show, that the testimony of the two Covenants is perfectly univocal on this head, and that the Unitarian must be cast before his own tribunal ; but, as I remarked in the outset, I propose to found my argument primarily on the Old Testament Scriptures, by which the language of the New on this subject is throughout controlled.

Maintaining, then, on adequate grounds, that Jesus Christ prior to his incarnation was the veritable and only Jehovah, it remains to be ascertained, if possible, what view can be gained of his nature which will make it conceivable that in this character he should have assumed the earthly humanity of the sons of men. This is the grand problem to be solved. This is the master mystery, the unfolding of which discloses the true economy of redemption and converts faith into knowledge. And here it is that we are constrained to avow our grateful thanks to the God of all grace for the illumination vouchsafed to his servant Swedenborg, in consequence of which a flood of light has been thrown upon the deepest arcana pertaining to the Divine Being and the universe of creatures. We, who have studied the purport of these sublime revelations and compared them with the fairest deductions of our own minds, can scarcely desire any information on the subjects treated of which has not been granted. Still I am well aware that what is from this source authority with me, on the themes in question, cannot be supposed to be authority with you in your present state of mind, and I shall therefore endeavor to present the matter in such a light that the conclusions reached may stand before you independent of any estimate you may have formed of Swedenborg as a professed messenger from Heaven. Indeed, it is because we perceive that what he has announced is intrinsically true in itself that we so firmly believe he was commissioned to announce it. Our credence is given to the truthfulness of the messenger from our conviction of the truth of the message; while at the same time we refuse to admit that the intelligence which thus recognises the truth of the message was competent to have reached it apart from the medium of the messenger. Human reason may put the seal of its sanction on a multitude of truths which it could never have discovered by its own powers.

That "God is a spirit" is one of the most emphatic declarations of holy writ, and equally clear is its teaching that man was made in the image of God. It is reasonable, therefore, to look for the leading points of this similitude in the spiritual nature of man. On the same grounds we are authorised to suppose that the divine image will be more clearly recognised in the disembodied than in the embodied man, especially when a *moral* conformity to his divine prototype exists. The essential constituents of humanity are more in the spirit than in the body, inasmuch as the body is an effect of which the spirit is the proximate cause. Yet as every effect is potentially *in* its cause, we infer that there is that in the human spirit which is normally represented in the human body; the body is the exponent of the spirit, as far as that which is natural and material can effigy that which is spiritual; in a word, that the body *corresponds* to the spirit, which is but another form of saying, that the body is what it is from the influx of the elaborating spirit into it. The hidden potencies of the spirit develope themselves in sensible manifestation in the structure and functions of the corporeal fabric. I am unable to see why it is not a fair deduction from this, that if man is created in the image of God, and what we term his essential humanity,—made visible to the senses in his bodily frame—is virtually and elementally comprised in his spiritual entity, that this very humanity is a part of the divine image—that is, that there is a sense in which the true human principle pertains to the divine exemplar after which man was formed. Indeed, how can it be otherwise? Does not man derive his distinctive nature from the possession of Understanding and Affection? Are not these the very principles and attributes which constitute him man? Take these away and what of humanity is left to your conception? If you say, the body, still there would be no human body if there were no human spirit to form it, and what possible idea can you have of a human spirit to which Will or Affection and Understanding were wanting? But the Will and the Understanding in man are the finite counterparts to the infinite Love and Wisdom of his Maker. It is in these faculties that the image of God is reflected, and yet these are the very groundwork of his humanity. How then is it possible to avoid the conclusion that there is in God a Divine Humanity? That these terms may, at first blush, strike you as utterly incompatible with each other, is very possible, but the sequel, I trust, will dispel the air of paradox which invests the position. That your conception on this head may also be embarrassed by the consideration of *form* is by no means unlikely, but I beg you, nevertheless, to ponder well the proposition and see whether it can be by any possibility avoided. If it do not involve an essential truth, pray what *is* the truth in regard to the inspired declaration that man was made in the image of God? Does not image imply resemblance? If a child is said to be an image of his father, do we not necessarily convey the idea of that in the child which reflects the father, as the impression on wax reflects the seal that stamped it? If you say that this is merely external, relating only to the aspect of the father, I entreat you to carry your thoughts a little further, and inquire whether the external similitude is not due to an internal cause, or in other words, whether the soul of the child, derived from the father, has not moulded the countenance to the paternal image? If so, it can by no means be maintained that the likeness is merely external. The outer man is evermore the creation of the inner man, and the father, in his distinguishing attributes, is reproduced in the child. Shall we hesitate to say, then, that man is man because God is Man? The relation is that of a type to an archetype—of a copy to a pattern. *Man could not possibly be an image of God, were not God an exemplar of man.*

But God, you say, is infinite, and man is finite. How can the finite represent the infinite? But this is a question which you are as much concerned to answer as I am. We are both estopped in our interrogation by the unequivocal averment that man *was* made in the Divine image. You have to determine the sense in which this holds as well as myself. My position, however, involves no difficulty; the difficulty pressing on yours is, I conceive, insuperable. But of this more as we proceed.

As to the fact of God's existing in the human form, one thing may with all confidence be asserted. Love and Wisdom cannot subsist, or be conceived of, apart from a subject in whom they inhere. "No intelligent person," says Swedenborg, "can deny in himself that in God are love and wisdom, mercy and clemency, and good and truth itself, for they are from Him; and as he cannot deny that these things are in God, neither can he deny that God is man; for none of these things can exist abstractedly from man; man is their subject, and to separate them from their subject is to say that they do not exist. Think of wisdom, and suppose it out of a man; is it any thing? Can you conceive of it as something ethereal and flaming? You cannot, unless possibly as in those principles, and if in them, it must then be wisdom in a form such as man has." Indeed the idea of Love and Wisdom existing out of a personal subject is as absurd as to suppose that the heart and lungs can exist and act apart from a body which they actuate. Can any thing more completely baffle all rational conception?

We are shut up, therefore, as we believe to the inevitable conclusion that God is Very Man—the Infinite Man—comprising within Himself all the distinguishing attributes of our human nature, and thus affording an adequate ground for man to be made in his veritable image. But as we have already seen that Christ is God, therefore the infinite humanity of Jehovah must be the humanity of Jesus, or in other words, our Lord Jesus Christ must have possessed from eternity a Divine Human principle, and this admitted it is comparatively easy to conceive that this Divine Human may have clothed itself with the ultimates of our *human* Humanity, so to speak, in order to come down to our level and to reach us by its vivifying influx of spiritual life. For the same reason, we can more readily apprehend the grand truth which we are endeavoring to establish, that the manifestations of Jehovah were made to the fathers from the earliest periods under a human form, for this was the appropriate form, inasmuch as the Lord, from his very nature, exists in that form. Of this I shall hope to adduce still more abundant proof in the progress of the discussion.

G. B.

(*To be Continued.*)

EXTRACT.

"I will relate what must needs seem wonderful: every man, in the idea of his spirit, sees God as a man, even he who in the idea of his body sees Him like a cloud, a mist, air, or ether, even he who has denied that God is a man: man is in the idea of his spirit when he thinks abstractedly, and in the idea of his body when he thinks not abstractedly. That every man in the idea of his spirit sees God as a man, has been made evident to me from men after death, who are then in the ideas of spirit; for men after death become spirits, in which case, it is impossible for them to think of God otherwise than as of a man."—*A. E.* 1115.

ARTICLE IV.

THE CALCULUS.

PHILOSOPHY has ever been in want of a Calculus, wherewith to solve the problems continually pressing themselves upon the attention.   Long has she looked abroad for a clear and deep light to illumine the world of causes—long has she waited for a hand to rend away the snares perpetually entangling her feet while threading the world of effects.   Her votaries have been fortunate if they have escaped disappointment—if they have not perished amidst the mazes around her path.   When they have sought light she has turned them off with fatuous and dreamy forms; when they have sought substance she has fed them on shadows; when they have asked for actual substantial organizations she has replied with empty metaphysical entities.   When the theologian has approached her temple, the oracle has given equivocal responses; and when it has been thought to wed her to Theology no sooner have they looked each other fairly in the face than their respective attendants have discovered an incompatibility, and hastened to file a bill of divorce in the Court of Conscience, even before the nuptial covenant was signed.   So long has an unnatural celibacy existed, that an innumerable brood of illegitimate heirs seek to inherit estates mouldering in ruins, and overgrown with brambles.

But is Philosophy ever to be deprived of a Calculus?   Are evasive responses ever to resound in her temple?   Are she and Theology never to cease a calamitous war?   These questionings come up on every side—many are the human understandings, seeing the necessity; and many the human hearts feeling the want, of a speedy and favorable answer. Too long have they moved amidst turbid waters and sweeping floods— too long has the great heart of Humanity groaned for an at-one-ment—too long waited for that day-dawn, when it shall pulsate harmoniously with the animations of its brain.

The recent translation of the scientific and philosophical works of Emanuel Swedenborg into English, under the auspices of the London Swedenborg Association, instituted for that purpose, is highly significant of the wants of the present era. What those wants are, every one is well aware, who has studied the science and philosophy of the present day with the expectation of resting his mind upon a comprehensive and integral system, which would at once furnish a Calculus potent to

resolve the phenomena continually arising; and to assign
with spontaneous ease, each analytical and synthetical pro
duct a place therein.

The question arises, whether the attempt has been success
fully made by Swedenborg? To allege that the attempt has
been made by him with complete success, would doubtless
be considered premature until the merits of those extraordir
ary works have been thoroughly canvassed, by all the legiti
mate appliances known to the present philosophy. Yet we
hazard the prophecy, that when that canvass shall have been
fairly made, it will be found that Swedenborg discovered th
UNIVERSAL CALCULUS; and applied it with signal success to th
highest problems that can engage the human intellect—and
such is the ease with which it penetrates the most hidden se
crets—measures forces, however strong or occult—delineate
forms, however complex or latent—developes principles, how
ever comprehensive or arcane; and arranges them all into an
order so surpassingly beautiful—into a system of which MAN
is at once the exemplar and complex; that it declares itself to
be the organon of an universal philosophy; a die, which will
coin the appropriate symbols of a Mathematical Philosophy of
Universals.

This Calculus, so potent in the hands of Swedenborg, is no
where stated or given in his works, in the form of an integra
formula; but its application therein is everywhere seen. I
was his intention to have thus stated it, after he had applied
it to all branches of human research—after its utility had
been tested in every work and labor—after it had wrought·it
destiny, then to have brought it forth distinctly, clothed only in its
native simplicity, and standing forth as itself its only monument
But this was never done, and doubtless many will regret it
yet might he not have truly supposed, that it would be better
that it should be seen and studied while performing its good
uses, while busied in those offices for which he had called it
forth from its secret chambers?—for we can learn more of the
structure and use of a piece of mechanism at a single glance
when it is in operation, than we can by studying its motionless model for days.

This Calculus consists of certain Doctrines, denominated as
follows:—The Doctrine of Forms: of Order and Degrees: of
Series and Society: of Influx: of Correspondence and Repre
sentation: of Modification.

These doctrines are generalizations drawn from an integral
survey of all the sciences. They are universal in their appli·
cation. Not confined, like the Newtonian doctrine of gravita
tion, to the Mundane systems; these they pervade, and then

transcending them, apply themselves to all superior spheres. No other than a transcendant genius could have elicited them. This may be thought an extravagant claim, yet we hesitate not to make it; because we have good evidence that their application is as extensive as we have asserted. The means by which, and the end for which, these doctrines were discovered will be learned from the following statement by the author:

"The end I propose to myself is a knowledge of the soul, since this study will constitute the crown of my studies. This, then, my labors intend, and thither they aim. For the soul resides and acts in the principles, not of the body only but of the universal world; inasmuch as it is the supreme essence, form, substance, and force of the microcosms; and appoints, establishes, and governs the order thereof, of itself and by its own nature, consequently it is in the sphere of truths. For these reasons, the soul has engaged the profound attention of nearly all human minds, ever since the infancy of philosophy; and still holds them in suspense, division, and perplexity. But as yet, her mode of being and her nature are almost absolutely unknown; and such is the general state of doubt and hesitation as to preclude all distinct thinking. This has given rise to so many obscure guesses on the subject—it has caused so many clouds to collect round it, that all hope of discovery is nearly at an end. In order, therefore, to follow up the investigation, and to solve the difficulty, I have chosen to approach by the analytic way; and I think I am the first who has taken this course professedly.

"To accomplish this grand end, I enter the circus, designing to consider and examine thoroughly the whole world or microcosm which the soul inhabits: for I think it is in vain to seek her any where but in her own kingdom. Tell me where else can she be found, than in that system to which she is adjoined and enjoined, and where she is represented and momentarily exhibits herself to contemplation? The body is her image, resemblance, and type; she is the model, the ideal, the head, that is, the soul, of the body. Thus she is represented in the body, as in a mirror. I am, therefore, resolved to examine carefully the whole anatomy of her body, from the heel to the head, and from part to part; and for the sake of a closer approach, to examine her very brain, where she has disposed her first organs; lastly, the fibres also, and the other purer organic forms, and the forces and modes thence resulting.

"But since it is impossible to climb or leap from the organic, physical, and material world—I mean, the body—immediately to the soul, of which neither matter, nor any of the adjuncts of matter are predicable (for spirit is above the comprehensible modes of nature, and in that region where the signification of physical things perish); hence it was necessary to lay down new ways by which I might be led to her, and thus gain access to her palace—in other words, to discover, disengage, and bring forth, by the most intense application and study, certain new doctrines for my guidance, which are (as my plan shows) the doctrine of forms, of order, and degrees, of series and society, of communication and influx, of correspondence and representation, and of modification; these it is my intention to present in a single volume under the title of *An Introduction to Rational Psychology.* When this task is accomplished, I am then admitted, as it were, by common consent to the soul, who, sitting like a queen in her throne of state—the body—dispenses laws, and governs all things by her good pleasure, but yet by order and by truth. This will be the crown of my toils, when I shall have completed my course in this most spacious arena. But in the olden time, before any racer could merit the crown, he was commanded to run seven times round the goal, which also I have determined here to do."—*A. K.* n. 15, 18.

But the crowning use designed by Swedenborg in these works is thus stated:

"But these pages of mine are written with a view to those only, who never believe anything but what they can receive with the intellect; consequently, who boldly invalidate, and are fain to deny the existence of all supereminent things, sublimer than themselves, as the soul itself, and what follows therefrom—its life, immortality, heaven, &c. &c. These things perhaps, since such persons do not perceive them, they reject, classing them among empty phrases, *Entia rationis,* phantoms, trifles, fables, conceits, and self-delusions, and consequently they honor and worship nature, the world and themselves; in other respects, they compare themselves to brutes, and think that they shall die in the same manner as brutes, and their souls exhale and evaporate; thus they rush fearlessly into wickedness. For these persons only I am anxious; and as I said before, for them I indite, and to them I dedicate my work. For when I shall have demonstrated truths themselves by the analytic method, I hope that those debasing shadows or material clouds, which darken the sacred temple of the mind, will be dispersed; and thus at last, under the favor of God, who is the sun of Wisdom, that an access will be opened, and a way laid down to faith. My ardent desire and zeal for this end is what urges and animates me."—*A. R.* n. 22.

It will be seen that these doctrines are not ideal abstractions, resting upon either a hypothetical, or a metaphysical basis.

They are founded upon an universal experience, such as was known to the learned world at the time they were eliminated. Not one, but all sciences, gave their suffrages to these doctrines. A more limited franchise might have subjected their legitimacy to suspicion. The seeker after truth may take hold of them with absolute confidence; he may carry them with him in all his explorations, they will not fail to indicate the true meridian.

The method of their deduction cannot be unacceptable to the negative philosophy of the present day, which takes no *prima facia* evidence, stamps every thing with a negative until it leaps forth naked to the touch; until the scribe and rule have measured it. The spirit of this sceptical philosophy is finely illustrated by the pertinacity with which it has contended, inch by inch, against the doctrine of an ethereal medium pervading the interplanetary spaces. Although the undulatory theory of light, founded upon the supposition of such a medium, has answered all the objections of the optician; although the astronomer has watched comets navigating this medium with laboring oars, still a timid philosophy dare go no further than pronounce it "almost certain." To a superficial observer, one whose vision spans scarcely half the horizon, these doctrines, from their breadth and scope, from the almost infinite distance between their limits, will seem to want flexibility and application; will appear to conflict with well established facts and principles; hence the necessity that they should be seen in their practical aspect, that they should be studied in use, by use, and from use; in use, in the works of our author; by use, in applying them to all investigations; and from use, in contemplating the fruitful harvest they have already gathered to the granaries of philosophy. However profound these doctrines, however artistic, however attractive to a speculative mind, their value must be measured by their good uses. This is the only standard which a true philosophy will recognize.

Swedenborg having thus matured his Calculus, and certified himself that it was both legitimate and competent to the end, proceeded to apply it in that field of arduous research where his success was unrivalled.

His method in the "Animal Kingdom" was this: If the lungs, or any other part of the animal economy, were to be studied —in the first instance, he collected the experience of the best authors, such as Heister, Winslow, Malpighi, Morgagni, and Swammerdam.

This experience was, in the next place, subjected to a severe

and searching analysis : each fact, as it emerged from the cru-
cible, and each phenomenon, as it appeared, was taken up by
the Calculus, and passed through each of its doctrines as a di-
gesting, assimilating, measuring, sensating, or motory organ ;
its form was delineated, its degree ascertained, and its position
determined ; it was placed in its series, and assimilated to its
fellows ; its correspondence was indicated, and its representative office defined ; its communications and inflowings were
discovered, and its susceptibility to modification and its power
to modify, determined.   Thus each phenomenon successively
was passed through this ordeal, whereby its cause and function, effect and use, were completely elicited.

All these products this same Calculus, as an organific power,
then arranges in their order and degree ; their proper series,
and homogeneous society : so that, each in its own degree, as
a cause or effect, end or use, corresponds to and represents its
subordinate and co-ordinate fellow, in a lower or higher, interior or exterior degree ; so, likewise, that there is between all
a mutual and reciprocal influx of aliments and forces ; and a
reciprocal and harmonious modification affecting each, each
sustaining the whole, and the whole comprehending and embracing each.   Thus there stands forth a beautiful unity ; a
living, moving, tangible synthesis.

The lungs or other organs thus differentiated, all three parts,
forms, and forces equilibrated and equated, raised to higher
powers, reduced to lower roots, and finally integrated by this
potent Calculus, yield up all their secret functions, disclose all
their transcendent geometry and mechanism, and standing forth
wholly discovered, display at once their cause and their end.

At last, by way of confirming all this, each particular and
all universal predicates are tested by particular and universal
experience.   If this final test be successful, all doubt vanishes,
and the whole is stamped with the signet of Truth.

These doctrines may be considered as a bridge and an equilibrium between the two essential forces of the human mind,
—between the internal and external, the prior and posterior,
the spiritual and the natural, cause and effect.   They are at
once the soul, body, and synthesis of the Cartesian and Bacon-
ian systems.   They afford a common ground for experience and
theory ; they offer a veritable passage from the known to the
unknown—from the visible to the invisible.   They offer to Materialism a tangible spirituality ; to Scepticism a rational faith ;
to Transcendentalism a light and support in its dizzy career ; and
to Pantheism a GOD IN THE HUMAN FORM.   Between philosophy
and theology, they offer a covenant of perpetual peace.   Here
they can adjust their long standing differences, and unite to

solve the problem of human destiny, and insure it a happy issue.

These doctrines may find a useful application in spheres in which we all move and are interested. Reformers of all classes, whether seeking to restore the dilapidations of present structures, or to remodel things upon a new basis, may here take lessons to their profit. The politician may discover principles which will give him invaluable assistance in constructing his machinery in such a manner that its parts will be so subordinated and co-ordinated and harmoniously blended, that human passions, smitten with a love for order, will yield up their violence and intrigue, conscious that by so doing, they are serving, under an order happily instituted, their own personal interests in the best possible manner. The social reformer may find a formula by which to shape his external organization and the soul to animate it.

To the New Churchman, these doctrines commend themselves with peculiar force. To him, desiring to see the spiritual, social, and political elements combined into an harmoneous organization, representing in all its parts those heavenly spheres, where Love, Wisdom, and Use, are life, thought, and work,— to him, who, wearied with fruitless efforts to find among the theologies of the age, a life for his soul; in its philosophy, a light to his understanding; in its ethics, a strength to his hands; in short, to him who feels a want, and strives to attain, not only a personal redemption, but a plenary redemption of humanity,—these doctrines, pervaded by a celestial love, rationally organised, and acting in freedom, are the only hope and satisfaction.

Their value will be measured by their utility—by the good uses they bring to each and all. That they are not a merely ideal formula, meet only for contemplation, but are suited to uses prolific of good, is attested by the results they have heretofore achieved and still are achieving in spheres where they are working with a silent yet efficient power,—unsought, yet present, unseen, yet felt.

When the fall of an apple suggested to Newton the law of gravitation, perhaps he little thought at that time that the simple formula deduced therefrom would map out the heavens, trace out their stupendous mechanism, and project them into the intellectual plane of man. So, neither, did Swedenborg, when his Calculus was elicited from the sciences, imagine that it was a celestial power in a spiritual form, ultimated in and planted upon the natural universe; until he saw the heavens opened, and beheld therein the Divine Origin, the infinite beauty and plenitude of what he had discovered, flowing into and represented by the lowest spheres of the creation.

We have not proposed to discuss in this article the doctrines of this Calculus in detail; we have given a few general reflections, hoping thereby to awaken attention and invite investigation, so that others might be led to examine these writings of Swedenborg, and by their aid, like ourselves, plant their hopes and faith upon the Divine Word and Works.

W. H. B.
Lockport, N. Y.

ARTICLE V.

REASON AND AUTHORITY—WHICH IS TO GUIDE US?

"LANDIS ON THE RESURRECTION."*

Not for the purpose of attempting to overthrow the popular doctrine of the resurrection of the material body, nor for undertaking, in contradiction thereto, to establish the doctrine of the elimination of the spiritual body at death, do we place the title of this work at the head of our article; but with the intention of saying a few things which we do not happen to have seen said, in relation to the application of "Reason and Philosophy" to theological opinions. The standard to which we would appeal, and on which we would rely, is that of the individual reason; or, as the asserters of authority term it, ultra individualism.

To a person born and educated in one of our protestant communities, who had early heard that the starting-point of the Reformation was the assertion of the right of private judgment, and who, by his associations and his course of reading, should have been brought, for the most part, in contact with certain habits of thought and modes of expression current among us—such a proposition would not seem to require any proof, and scarcely the formal assertion of it: as he would be

---

* The Doctrine of the Resurrection of the Body asserted and defended; in answer to the exceptions recently presented by Rev. Geo. Bush, Professor of Hebrew, New York University. By Robert W. Landis. Philadelphia, 1846. 12mo. pp. 379.

under the impression that we are now living in its actual reception.

On the other hand, to a person similarly born and educated, who should have become conversant only with certain other classes of views and habits of teaching, current to a still greater extent among us, such a proposition, asserted in its unrestricted sense, would wear a dangerous aspect; and, if not tending to downright infidelity, would be regarded at least as savoring very strongly of unevangelical rationalism. The actual opinion of protestant Christendom is in a state of compromise between these two.

Since the time of the Reformation there has been a gradual lapse in the direction of freedom. Good people, fearing the general license of opinion which the movement seemed to threaten, have been constrained to set up landmarks assuming different degrees of authority, at various distances from Rome. These, in their day, and to the extent of their respective spheres, have exercised a conservative influence, and operated as a sort of drag-chain upon the general wheel. This, too, was a period which was to be passed through, and has had its uses: for it is more common, as well as more safe, that when the great current of opinion changes the level of its bed, it should accomplish this through the milder process of a series of rapids, than risk the shock of a precipitous fall. These standards, confessions of faith, " articles of belief," decisions of assemblies and synods, still echo from hill-top to tower, throughout the protestant lands, the prolonged reverberation of those vatican thunders of which we have heard so much. Many pious men, tired of the eddies and whirlpools which confuse the surface, with a strong yearning for a fixity of faith, and fearing to enter the pass towards which they saw things were tending, have started to their feet, gathered up their garments, and set their faces towards Rome.

Finding by how large a company they were attended, they have supposed the general movement to be in the same direction, without stopping to inquire whether theirs was anything more than the superficial reaction, that more clearly indicates the irresistible momentum with which the profounder depths are hastening in the opposite direction. Those who have stood at the foot of Niagara have observed that for many rods below the cataract the waters on the surface set strongly backward towards the fall. Nevertheless, they, and we, are all well convinced of the overwhelming pressure with which the vast under-current is sweeping to the " whirlpool."

It is held by many, and feared by others, that the rejection of authority involves, in its progressive development, the gradual frittering away of article after article of the Christian faith, and that individual authority, after having amused itself for a while by tearing the body of unity into fragments, will finally plunge us into the "night of atheism."

We cannot help thinking, however, that this is a generalization which has been registered too soon. A state of positive belief is the normal condition of the human mind; and it is always unsafe to rest in conclusions drawn while contemplating merely the necessary inchoateness of a formative period.

For ourselves, believing as we do that the Lord Jesus Christ is in all history reconciling the world unto himself, we are contented to wait until Protestantism, having exhausted its protests and its denials, shall have rounded the point it has been three centuries in making;—after having come fully to the comprehension of the idea it stárted by declaring for, shall have entered upon the earlier stages of its positive constructiveness, and the general "consensus" of Individualism begin to come in. This is not to be brought about, however, by a denial of the validity of the instrument by which it is to be accomplished; but, on the contrary, by a manly and unshrinking adherence to the logical results of the Protestant position. Our assertion of the right of private judgment has thus far been only a half way assertion; and at this time there is a general disposition among Protestant theological writers to repose on the discoveries of the past, and to represent the reason as something calculated to lead men to fallacious results. They are rather expounders of former men's opinions than firm asserters of their own. It is because we have found in Mr. Landis' work a more definite assertion and application of this opinion than we have elsewhere recently met with, that we have selected one of his chapters for the foundation of our remarks.

Mr. Landis' object is to show that " *Professor Bush's argument from Reason cannot be safely relied on;*" and after several paragraphs, in which, as we conceive, he fails to exhibit any very clear exposition of the actual question, he proceeds ;—

"Hence, the appropriate position of reason is at the feet of revelation; and hence, when the deductions of our reason plainly conflict with clearly ascertained testimony of God's word, the duty of the Christian is not (as Professor Bush pretends), to take God's declaration 'as type, figure, allegory, metaphor, symbol, accommodation, anthropomorphism—ANY THING RATHER THAN THE DECLARATION OF ABSOLUTE VERITY' (see *Anastasis,* Preface p. xi.), but remembering how easy it is, with all his care, and assistance from logic and philosophy, to reason himself into error and falsehood, and to employ reason itself in their defence, he will rather suspect that his deductions are wrong, even though his premises appear impregnable; or he will suspect that there is some imperceptible error in the construction of his argument, or some flaw in his logic which he has not been able to discover."—P. 52.

And again, he says,

"After all, God may be wrong and our reason may be right; for to this conclusion the principles of such men as Professor Bush (notwithstanding a few unavailing and most inconsistent disclaimers), must inevitably lead."—P. 53.

We are at a loss to discover how any progress is ever to be made in the disposal of a subject, if we are to be for ever dodging around the point, instead of addressing our attention directly to it; if we are to waste our energies in "diffusely arguing every question on which men are long ago unanimous." That "the appropriate position of reason is at the feet of Revelation" no one has any inclination to doubt. But what *is* the Revelation? That is the question at issue. Roman Catholics, Unitarians, Swedenborgians, all are, and always have been, agreed that the Word of God is infallible authority. There has never been any question raised on that point. But what is the sense of the Word of God? The whole question always has been one of interpretation merely. Of what value then is it to be continually asserting that the "Bible is the only rule of Faith?" The Bible settles nothing until it is interpreted. But waiving the further discussion of the point in this place, let us pass to the consideration of some of the "facts" to which Mr. Landis "appeals" in order to "place in its proper light" the "egregious error" of relying upon the argument from Reason.

"The doctrine of the infinite divisibility of matter is susceptible of fuller and more perfect demonstration than the hypothesis upon which Professor Bush rests his argument: for it rests upon a chain of actual mathematical demonstration. The acutest and mightiest intellects have bowed before the argument, and have conceded that its conclusions are irresistible. May it not then be taken as a fair and honest *ipse dixit* of reason and science? Even Professor Bush will admit that it may. According then to this mathematical demonstration a line of an inch in length has an infinite number of parts. Now, Professor Bush himself will admit that it must of necessity take some portion of time to pass any portion of space. Hence, as this line of an inch long, has an infinite number of parts. it requires an infinite number of portions of time for a moving point to pass by this infinite number of parts. But an infinite number of portions of time is an eternity! Consequently it must require a whole eternity to move an inch!

"Now, human ingenuity has never been able to detect a flaw in this argument. The premises appear to be perfectly sound, and the conclusion perfectly legitimate. And thus reason and mathematical science (the most certain of all sciences), conduct us irresistibly to a conclusion which no man in his senses could believe."—P. 54.

We are not surprised that men who, armed with the best logic they can command, arrive at no better conclusions than the above, should begin to entertain doubts of the competency of their reason, and to withhold their confidence from its results. If they find it impossible to repose on it themselves, assuredly they will not expect us to bow implicitly before its dictum, or hold it in extremely high reverence. We cannot for a moment bring ourselves to believe that the great Masters of Logic ever supposed the argument which our author has adduced, to be really irresolvable; but probably only regarded it as an ingenious puzzle of words. It is in fact nothing more; for the moment we rise beyond the verbal formula, to the matter which gives force to the formula, it ceases to be an argument altogether, and becomes a sheer absurdity. To those who suppose it to be the province of logic to deal with words merely, it may present an irrefutable series; but to one who regards the system of terms as only the varying signs by which conceptions are indicated, and who is aware that true logic deals with the sequences of ideas only, such an argument offers no puzzle whatever. The defect lies in the assertion of the following proposition; "Now Professor Bush himself will admit that it must of necessity take some portion of time to pass any portion of space," and in the inference which is immediately drawn from it; "hence as this line of an inch long, has an infinite number of parts, it requires an infinite number of portions of time for a moving point to pass by this infinite number of parts." The argument derives whatever force it may seem to have, from the supposed analogy between a "portion of time" and a "portion of space." The very first step, however, taken in the argument destroys the force of such analogy, if it before existed; for, first, the smallest portion of matter with which we are acquainted, is taken, and then *infinitely subdivided;* and, secondly, the smallest portion of time with which we are acquainted is taken, without any subdivision. Now, did there exist the assumed equipollency between the smallest portion of time, and the smallest portion of space, that equipollency would be destroyed by the infinitesmal subdivision of the one, and not of the other.

There is, however, no such analogy existing as the argument supposes; for succession in time is by no means equivalent to extension in space. The inference is sustained by a double use of the term "portion:" and it is only necessary to assert the proposition with a due regard to scientific accuracy in the application of the terms, that the whole enigma may unravel itself.

"It takes a *second* of time to pass an *atom* of matter." Not by any means. Every one sees at once that the assertion is false; for in a second of time an infinite number of these atoms may be passed. It does indeed require some portion of time to develope any motion whatever; but the same portion of time which suffices to pass the first atom of matter, will also suffice to pass an indefinitely large number of them. In order to furnish the grounds necessary to sustain the inference, it is requisite that the proposition should be able with truth to assert that it took a second of time to pass each particular atom of matter; "matter in extension" being "the exact representation of space." This it cannot do, and consequently the inference is a *non sequitur*. The fallacy is the same in kind with the others adduced in this chapter, and which it is unnecessary to follow. To this remark there is one exception; it is the subject refered to in the following passage—

"Equally conclusive is the demonstration which proves the world to be merely ideal. The opinion of the ablest judges seems to be, as Dr. Reid himself admits, that the arguments which sustain this position neither have been nor can be answered. And yet no man in his senses can believe the conclusion to which those arguments lead. And Dr. Reid himself could only rebut these arguments (not really refute them,) by maintaining that the great masters of reason, Des Cartes, Malebranche, Locke, Berkley, and Hume, had wholly misunderstood the dicta of science and reason. And if this be so, surely we may ask, What are the dicta of reason and philosophy? How are we to ascertain what they are? And who will give us a fair representation of them?"—P. 55.

We have neither the time nor the inclination to go into an analysis, a defence, or a refutation of Idealism. We must, however, entirely dissent from Mr. Landis' view, that the errors of Berkley cannot be refuted, or that they have not been. That Dr. Reid did not succeed in overthrowing some things which Berkley taught, is very true; for Dr. Reid committed some errors himself, and many of the supposed errors of Berkley have turned out to be truths. We thought that it had now come to be very generally conceded that the blunders which Berkley committed had been pointed out and refuted, and those doctrines of his which have not been refuted, though considered erroneous at that time, had passed into the category of correct philosophy. There are no such unanswerable arguments, by which absurdities are proven as our author supposes. Either the assumption is false, the inference a *non sequitur*, or the conclusion is reliable, and must be taken as true. The opposite supposition would throw all Science into confusion, and open the door to a scepticism more fatal than would the admission of Idealism in its worst form.

The reputation which Mr. Landis enjoys as a theologian and

a scholar, among that class of Christians for whom he professedly speaks, would be a sufficient reason for our paying attention to the line of his argument : but in addition to this, we
believe that he has brought together within the compass of
a single chapter, a very fair expression of the general sentiments of the orthodox theologians on these points, and a tolerably correct exhibition of what may be denominated, the
logical attitude of the old Church in relation to them. We
shall therefore give him the advantage of speaking for himself
in a few paragraphs further. ·

"Now suppose, for illustration, that the Bible contained the first enunciation of the axiom, that two lines which continually approach, must
meet, or intersect one another (a truth which so soon as announced, the
common sense of every man admits to be self-evident), and that some
learned, prying philosopher like Professor Bush, should have, in the
course of his inquiries, discovered the demonstration of the asymptote.
He then, laying down the proposition that " no two truths in the universe can be inconsistent, or clash with each other," proceeds to display his actually *mathematical demonstration*, and to exhibit his right
line, and his curve, and convinces every one who can understand the
language of mathematical science that this right line may continually
approach nearer the curve to all eternity and yet can never meet it.
No flaw can be discovered in the argument, no *non sequitur* in the conclusion. And then, with the full assurance that no two truths in the
universe can possibly clash with each other, this learned philosopher
proceeds to show that the announcements of revelation and those of
science can be reconciled. He first starts with the proposition that the
knowledge of Revelation is progressive ; and then lays down his principles of accommodation, and finally so explains the Bible announcement as to make it utter the very reverse of what it did before.
    " Would such a course be warrantable ? and would it be too much to
say to that philosopher, ' Sir, you are proceeding too fast, and your
principles are unsound. It is true that two truths cannot be inconsistent with each other ; but truth itself, and your view of truth may be
very different things.' Professor Bush, I have no doubt, would address this philosopher in some such language as this. And would it
be too much to say to Professor Bush, who has pursued a course somewhat similar, ' Sir, your procedure in this matter is very unreasonable
and unphilosophical. The proposition which you advance respecting the incorporation of a part of the human body with
other substances *may* be strictly demonstrable: and yet the announcement of Revelation respecting the resurrection of the same body that
dies may be literally true. Your mind can take in but a single point of
the vast plain which lies before you. That plain, sir, is so
extensive (as you would know if you could see the whole of it,)
that it fills up the space between the point which your eye is fixed
upon, and that point, the existence of which God has announced to
man. In other words, both of these propositions may be true, and
we should see them to be so, had God made the subject fully known to
us in all its parts."—P. 55.

Waiving for a while the evident absurdity of supposing the Bible to contain an assertion contradictory to a geometrical demonstration, let us suppose for the moment that the Bible did contain such an announcement. What would be the course of every reasonable man in relation to it? Would he give up the truth of the demonstration? Would science give up its conclusions? Not at all. No one is at a loss to answer such a question: the letter of Scripture would have to give way, and we should be obliged to infer, that we had mistaken the interpretation of the passage. Whenever any declaration of Scripture comes in direct or implied antagonism to the results of mathematical or physical science, then will the literal interpretation of that passage be held in abeyance, and "reason and philosophy" will impose a new one. The "dicta of reason and philosophy" which so many affect to despise, are the "dicta" which govern the opinions of men; and, by the grace of God, will continue to govern them. The New Church takes her stand on the doctrine of universal theological or ecclesiastical suffrage; she throws open the franchise of the priesthood to all. Asserting it not simply as the right, but as the duty, of all, to exercise their reason in matters of faith. If we are going to have a theology resting on a firm basis—if we are ever to have a teaching which shall command the general assent—it must not be by denying the competency of the reason to decide on such teaching; but, on the contrary, it is to be arrived at only by stoutly asserting it as the only authority which is to decide. Pragel peaks and Balkan ridges are not to be passed by denying to the human foot the power to tread them; nor will those who doubt their capacity to do so be the ones most likely to accomplish the task. Mysteries belong to ignorance only—knowledge eschews them. The reason during its past history and its infant state has reposed on authority, as the child, in its first attempts to walk, on the chairs and tables. But it takes the eye of no prophet to see that the human mind has well nigh passed through the *go-cart* period, and is beginning to gird itself as a strong man to run a race. As navigation in its earlier attempts skirted only the shore, and feared the unknown waters beyond, now, by the appliances of science, ventures boldly out into the ocean, and ferries its men, and delivers its cargoes, unawed by the tempest, unswamped by the billow—so can the reason, by an appliance of the instruments which Providence has thrown in its way, and its own action developed, put boldly forth on the sea of opinion. To know is the great law of the human understanding: to know itself and to know the universe. God himself has implanted the impulse; God himself has spread out the attractions for it. To an untramelled intellect it would appear as irrational to deny the right of the reason to inquire into every problem of the universe, as to deny to the physical eye the right to roam over any prospect which might be spread out before it, on reaching some celebrated height.

Those who plant themselves on the letter of Scripture in opposition to the advancement of science, only place themselves and their system in a position to be gradually rolled away into the category of ancient superstitions. The perceptions of the reason are as legitimate as are the perceptions of the physical eye; both may be deceived; both can, and do, by continued action, correct early errors. The human reason is the most universal solvent in nature, and is destined in its progressive enlargement so solve the mysteries of the universe.

W. B. H.

SELECTIONS.

EXTRACTS FROM SWEDENBORG'S SPIRITUAL DIARY.

NOW FIRST TRANSLATED FROM THE ORIGINAL LATIN.

' *Concerning Cupidities.*

4057. I wondered that the deceitful, sirens, adulterers, and the wicked, were possessed of such knowledge and skill in infusing and doing evil. I could not but marvel both at the nature and degree of their adroitness in this respect, when I was yet aware that in the life of the body they knew nothing of the kind; as, for instance, that the deceitful should flow in with the utmost subtlety into all things of thought and affection, and pervert them, which is done by sirens and adulterers. They are acquainted with such magical arts as are never known in the world; and yet when they come into the other life they are in them, just as if in the life of the body they had practised such arts and deceits. But it was perceived that he who is in any cupidity whatever, and in its delight, and consequently in its insane love, no matter what the accompaniments are which pertain to such an insane love, he knows them all. All evil spirits of this class, besides many others, conspire and inbreathe their evils, and when such is the quality of any one, he knows no otherwise than that he is fully versed in them; the life of cupidity involves this in it, for whoever is in cupidity or in-same love, he is in the knowledge of all such arts, even while the prompting is from others.   Wherefore, as much as one is in the life of cupidities, so much is he in the science of those things which belong to cupidities, and thence in the other life are such deceits and such malignities.

4058. The same thing appears clearly also from the love of goodness and truth. As much as any one is in love from the Lord, so much is he in knowledges, which knowledges come from the Lord alone, as well immediately as through heaven.

4059. That affections have with them all (appropriate) science, may abundantly appear from animals—as much those that are evil cupidities, as which are (good) affections, and especially from birds, which know all and singular the things pertaining to their affections, of which much might be said; as, for instance, that they know how to bring forth and nourish their young, how to obtain food for themselves, how to foresee and provide for themselves against a coming winter, how to construct their nests, how to live with their mates, and what forms of government to adopt,—all which they know better than man with all his sciences. Man would have no need to establish such artificial systems of science, and to learn them, nor to write so many books respecting the training of infants and children, if he had been in the love of true faith.   But since he is only in cupidities, and has merely persuaded himself of certain things of faith separate from love, he therefore knows nothing except through sciences orally taught or delivered through the medium of books, because such things as follow love are (now) to be learned.

Concerning Providence.

4060. Certain spirits, holding me in a kind of obscurity, objected that ideas arise from the objects of sight, and not the objects of sight from ideas,—thus that the life of the Lord does not flow in directly, but is excited by visible objects occurring in a vast variety of ways. Of this I have spoken before, but it was (now) answered them by thought, and perceived, that this was very much like saying that the innumerable applications of the lungs to the several muscles and their fibres, according to all the intention and will of the thought, together with the muscles and motive fibres, flowed into the ideas of the thought and will, instead of the reverse; when, in fact, not a single compound action can take place but by means of innumerable applications of the lungs prompted by ideas, and bringing into play an equally countless number of muscular fibres, all of which are disposed according to the influx of the will alone, and that too in such boundless diversity of manner that one fibre seems to act altogether differently from another.   Since these things are so, and such incomprehensible facts occur even in the lowest plane of nature, how can sceptical reasonings avail concerning the influx of the life of the Lord into ideas, and thence into objects, as though a different law prevails here; besides various other inferences that are liable to be drawn.

Concerning the Memory of Spirits.

4001. If spirits enjoyed corporeal memory, no spirit could be with man, consequently he would die; for there cannot be two memories acting in conjunction, unless, indeed, spirits should take away man's memory and think from their own, when they would both speak together, as in the case of obsession. Besides, it is not allowed to any spirit to teach man, nor consequently to lead him, except from cupidity; but the Lord alone wills to teach man and lead him, which could never be done if ought of corporeal memory pertained to a spirit.

Concerning Providence and Influx.

4002. I have been infested by (the suggestions of) spirits as to the question, how an influx of the Lord's life into all and singular the things of man, can be given, especially when one considers the variety of things which must occupy his thoughts, as, for instance, that he must reflect as to the diversified objects which he sees; as to the conversations of numbers on a multitude of topics, now on this, and now on that, and now on a hundred others; how such and such persons can come together and not others; then, how such particular discourses should arise among them and not others; then, as to the consequences of one determination of a man, from which flow others in successive series; besides a multitude of other things that concern the influx and providence of Lord—in all which I was held by spirits to a point of utter weariness, and yet from which I could not free myself. It was shown me by representation of what quality, or nature, such things are, viz. by a chamber of a greyish (or dusky) color, not swept out, where earthen vessels and other furniture were in disorder.

4003. But it is enough to know that the Lord's life flows into the heavenly societies, which are innumerable with all variety, according to the varieties of love; that is, it is received variously by all. In the interior world of spirits, also, it is variously received from heaven, according to societies. So also in the lower world (of spirits), where ideas are still variously received, according to the state of the recipients; with men it is received still more variously, according to their corporeal memories; so that these influxes can never be understood as they are in their origin, which appears from this, that they may be turned into contraries, or other obliquities, according to a man's persuasions, or the state of his memory at the time, and then according to the vessels which apply themselves in that state, as also according to cupidities and their states; for there are states of persuasions and states of cupidities.

4004. That all this is so appears likewise from the fact, that it can never be known in ultimates how things are in interiors, much less in intimates, causing angelic ideas to be represented by animals and such like things, in the world of spirits; the ideas of evil spirits by circumflexions of the body, and other things of the sort which there appear.

4005. Especially is this evinced by the circumstance, that angelic ideas can fall into innumerable diverse ideas, both in the lower (spiritual) world and with man; as for instance that the representatives of good alone with the angels can fall into all the innumerable forms of man's good, whether into his worship, into sweet things, into fat things, thus into countless particulars, according to his states, yea, into things contrary and intermediate. Wherefore it can never be known from the objects of the external memory and from the objects of sight, what is the nature of things in the more intimate, much less in the most intimate (principles).

4006. Moreover, angelic ideas are not only representatives which are thus indefinitely varied as they emanate, but they even become parables which with man are capable of being varied in innumerable modes; for from one parabolic idea there shall follow innumerable things that are analogous and applicable to it,

4007. as originating from one principle: just as so many various things are afterwards produced from a (single) seed, which were never (except potentially) in the seed; and so on.

4008. It morever appears that the providence of the Lord is in all the most singular or particular things. This may be evinced solely from what are deemed matters of fortune, as in games, and such things as appear altogether fortuitous; as, for instance, in a lottery, and other things that may be noticed; such contingencies pertaining to the lowest department of nature can never be explained as to their source; and if this holds in things of this kind, what shall be said of all and singular other things, which entirely baffle research as being the contingencies of Providence?

4009. Since then these things of the lowest nature cannot be explored, how can those which are of interior nature, from which the former proceed, and how those of a still more interior character, and how, above all, those of the most intimate nature, where the process is not so inconstant, but uniform? for the most indefinitely variable results exist in degrees in the lowest things which yet flow from the most unvarying constancy in the intimate principles; besides many other things.

4010. From what has been said we are at liberty to conclude, that

it is better to be ignorant of all these matters, and simply to believe
that the life of the Lord flows into all and singular things, and that His
providence governs all and singular things, than to suffer one's self to
be absorbed in such speculations. It is better, I say, to be ignorant; for
if men covet this kind of knowledge, they must necessarily launch out
into a boundless field; just as in my own case, when I wished to know
in what manner the actions of the muscles were ordered in their representative relation to the ideas of the thoughts, and how the endeavors and forces of the will conspired to the effect, I spent many laborious years in investigating the appliances of the lungs in each of their
functions, then those of the muscles, of the motive fibres, of the nervous fibres, together with the connection and disposition of all the parts,
how actions resulted from the fluxion of the brains, as in the case of
the tendinous fibres drawing backwards, obliquely, or into a gyre, and
so on, when yet, after all, the action was dependent on other laws, all
which thoroughly to explore were the labor of many years, and still
scarcely even the most general things could be known. Wherefore it
is better simply to know that the will flows in (and actuates the body);
far more is this expedient in those things to which pertain the influx
of the Lord's life, and of his providence.—These things were thought
with spirits, through spirits, from the angels.

Farther concerning Influx.

4013. Actions do not flow into ideas, consequently not into the will
and the thought, but thought and will flow into actions; in like manner
also angelic ideas flow through the ideas of spirits into the thoughts of
man. But to know how this influx takes place is to desire to know
how the fibres exist in their first principles, then how they act in the
brain, where they are like a jelly, and then lastly to trace the operation
through their inextricable fluxions into the muscles, to say nothing of
the various and countless motions which precede any single action.
Every idea is in like manner a certain general something which may
be compared to an action.

4014. But how the gestures of one may flow in through the eyes of
others, from which they judge of a man's character; how the countenance of another makes him known; and especially how the speech
of one flows into the ideas of another,—all this, it is clear, is effected
by the removals or abstractions of lower things, or by their extinction,
so that they may become nothing, as otherwise the perception does
not take place. The sounds, or material accompaniments whence flow
the proximate ideas, are forthwith rejected or removed, then these
ideas are rejected, whence arise the interior ideas respecting a man's
end, and in many other things which thus flow from the speech of an-

other. Without these removals, nothing of the kind can be perceived;
but let them be made, and then the interior idea of another is communicated, and is set forth nakedly manifest and separate from all extraneous appendages.

4015. Inasmuch as there may be such removals of lower things, it
hence appears how the case is with man, that there must be a death
of corporeal things, even of the corporeal memory, that the spirit may
be developed. The ideas also which are appropriate to lower spirits
must undergo a kind of death, in order that one may be in interior ideas,
or the ideas of angelic spirits. It hence appears, too, how these ideas
must be removed in order to one's becoming an angel, when communication is immediate; and finally, how lower ideas are nevertheless
represented; besides other things.—All this is said in the presence of
spirits who have pondered upon the subject.

NOTICES OF BOOKS.

1.—*An Historical and Critical View of the Speculative Philosophy of Europe
in the Nineteenth Century.* By J. D. MORELL, A. M. (*Complete in One
Volume*). NEW YORK: ROBERT CARTER, 1848, 8vo. pp. 748.

Systems of Philosophy, so called, whether Moral or Intellectual, are judged by
New Churchmen, by a standard peculiarly their own, and the verdict pronounced
without hesitation according to their agreement or disagreement with certain funda.
mental principles that, to their minds, have all the force of axioms. The starting
point with them of every train of investigation relating to the laws or phenomena
of mind is the paramount fact of the distinction between Affection and Intellect;
answering to the like distinction of Love and Wisdom in the Divine nature. This
distinction, which is one of a *discrete* degree, we are constrained to regard as the
only adequate key to the mysteries of our nature, psychologically viewed, and any
system of mental philosophy which ignores its appliance must necessarily involve itself in perpetual mazes of uncertainty. So long as Understanding and Will
(*voluntas*) are treated as the mere co-efficients of the same unknown quantity in the
algebra of our being, so long will all mental science be a mental puzzle, and the doctrine of *final causes, or ends*, which, as flowing from the affections, ought ever to be
pre-eminent in our inquries, be thrown disparagingly into the background. On the
contrary, let this distinction be clearly laid down in the outset, and a luminous
development at once ensues of all the grand phenomena of the soul. When it is
clearly perceived that Love is the substantial element—the *esse*—of being, and
Thought its form or *existere*, the labyrinth of the human mind is easily threaded
without the aid of any Ariadne's ball. As this great law of our interior economy has
been hitherto unknown to philosophy, its boasted results pale in the eyes of the

men of the New Church before the brighter light which has opened upon his vision, and he is prone to say of them all as one philosopher confutes another,— "Let the dead bury their dead." The voice in his ear is, "Friend, come up higher."

We would not be understood by this to pass a slighting sentence on all the labors of the past in this department, or to intimate that the school of Swedenborg is a little Goshen of illumineeism, while nothing but mental and moral darkness enwraps the surrounding Egypt. We conceive, indeed, that so far as our state of good qualifies us for the recipiency of truth, we have a clearer perception than others of the laws of its influx, and a more open access to its knowledges : but we are not restrained from availing ourselves of every treasure hitherto accumulated, or from awarding the due meed of praise to those who have contributed their quotas to the general mass. Especially are we prompted to be grateful for being put in possession of such a work as that of Mr. Morell, containing as it does a comprehensive *resumé* of nearly all that has been accomplished by the speculative philosophy of the last age. In no other work, as we believe, in our language, will the reader meet with so ample a survey, and so candid an estimate, of the various systems and schools which have represented the progress of metaphysical inquiry during the past and present century. Without attempting to give a summary even of its table of contents, we can only say, that it is a work replete with interesting details respecting the thousand-fold phases of opinion that have waxed and waned among the *savans* of mental science in England, France, and Germany.

To a New Churchman, its value is greatly enhanced by the fact, that the author has not shrunk from giving to Swedenborg a prominent niche in his philosophical temple. It is the first work, we believe, of any character, that has done this. The testimony to his genius is frank, noble, and generous, while at the same time it is evident that he is unprepared to view his philosophy from the stand-point of his theology. Though conceding to him the highest merits in the earlier periods of his career, yet he tacitly deplores the fatuity that came over its later stages, in which, as he intimates, "he lost himself in the visions of his own inmost soul." Rather he *found* himself in these visions, and by the sublime disclosures embodied in them he has taught all others how to make the same discovery in regard to themselves. Well would it have been for a multitude of the great names recorded in this volume had they been *blessed* with a similar *misfortune*. We can hardly refrain from looking upon them as a kind of intellectual " babes in the wood," who would at least have had reason to be grateful to any guidance that should have conducted them forth from their wanderings into the highways and cleared fields of truth.

Mr. Morell's testimony to Swedenborg has been transferred to the recently published volume of " Documents, &c.," and is there accompanied by a series of critical remarks, which will tend in great measure to neutralise the effect of his uttered misconceptions.

2.—Review *of the Rev. E. B. Elliott's Horæ Apocalypticæ, or Commentary on the Apocalypse, Critical and Historical.* By D. N. LORD. Philadelphia : W. S. Young, 1848. 8vo. pp. 41.

This pamphlet is well entitled to attention, not only for its caustic exposure of the fallacies of perhaps the most distinguished work on the Apocalypse to which the present century has given birth, but still more for its boldly broaching principles in regard to the interpretation of the symbolic language of prophecy, which are in vain sought for out of the limits of the New Church. We do not mean by this that the present is a New Church work, for it is within our personal knowledge that both the pamphlet before us and a larger work on the whole of the Apocalypse by Mr. Lord, were written without the slightest reference to Swedenborg, and in fact without any acquaintance with the peculiar laws of exposition laid down by him, and so amply illustrated in his own voluminous commentary on this book. Our author will, therefore, doubtless, be himself as much surprised as any of our readers at the remarkable coincidences, on the score of *principle*, to which we propose briefly to advert, between his interpretation and that of Swedenborg, in regard to a few of the prominent features of the Apocalypse. The respected author will allow us to express the hope that he may not, in popular phrase, "get out of conceit" with his own interpretations on finding them, in their sounder portions, approximating so closely to those which were long before given by one whom he has probably, with the rest of the Christian world, regarded only in the light of a pseudo-seer, a wild and visionary pretender to divine revelations. If he should still retain such an impression of the man *on the whole*, we trust he will find some other proof of its correctness than his emphatic confirmation of the leading results of his own apocalyptic studies

We would, however, previously say in respect to the pamphlet, and to the volume just mentioned, that a prominent object in both is to show, that not only Mr. Elliott, but nearly, if not quite, every other writer on the Apocalypse, has entered upon his task of professed exposition without ever attempting to settle, upon definite principles, the exegetical laws that are to govern the interpretation of symbols. They have invariably *assumed* and *postulated* the import of these symbols, and thus neglecting to lay a solid foundation in the outset the superstructures reared have been mere castles of cards, which could not but topple down before the faintest breath of critical wind. For the most part, these various commentaries have gone on the gratuitous assumption that a given order of *symbolic* agencies represents an order of *real* agencies of the same species; thus, that a mounted conquering warrior shadows forth a *military* chieftain or a succession of them—that a symbolic king denotes a literal king,—and the symbolic martyrs *other* real martyrs; and so in a multitude of similar instances. Now all this, according to Mr. Lord, who has devoted years to the patient investigation of prophecy, is not only the sheerest hypothesis, but is directly at variance with the true law of symbolization, which requires that the real should be of a different order from the representing agency. On the contrary theory, he maintains that the grossest absurdities will inevitably follow. " If a victorious warrior be a representative of bodies, or successions of conquering warriors,—if a civil magistrate be a symbol of a combination or series of civil magistrates of a similar character;—then must an animal also be taken as a precursor of a herd, and succession of similar animals ; and monster shapes like the locusts and horsemen of the fifth and sixth trumpets, and the seven-headed and two-horned wild beasts be regarded as foreshowing, on the theatre of the world, of races of similar monsters. Otherwise there can be no uniform law of symbolization, and thence no certainty of interpretation." The true relation between the sign and the thing signified, and consequently the true ground of symbolization, is, not, he contends, similarity of nature, but analogy and certain general resemblances.

by which objects of one species may be employed to represent those of another; as, for instance, a series of tyrannical rulers may be represented by a ferocious wild beast, from the similarity of their actings. So, also, civil and military rulers may symbolize ecclesiastical rulers, from certain common attributes of their several agencies. This principle, applied as a test to Mr. Elliott's work, makes sad havoc of his most brilliant discoveries in the field of the Apocalypse, as it shows conclusively that he is not only at war with the facts of history, but at war with himself. He is perpetually acting the *felo de se* upon his own assumptions, and seems to see everything more clearly than the conflict between his premises and his conclusions.

Whether our author, however, has himself reached the grand fundamental law of symbolic interpretation, we see great reason to doubt; but that in the solution of several of the Seals, he has approximated in a remarkable manner towards it will be evident from what follows. And we cannot but look upon the fact as the effect of a special influx from the spiritual sphere which, in accordance with the intimations of Swedenborg, is continually pressing down with more and more intensity upon the general mind of Christendom. We trust Mr. Lord will pursue his investigations in a spirit free to the admission of all legitimate results.

On the opening of the first seal, the prophet " looked, and lo, a white horse, and he that sat on him having a bow, and a crown was given to him, and he went forth conquering and to conquer." Upon this our author remarks :

MR. LORD.—" As the symbol is drawn from the civil and military customs of the empire, we are to look, in order to find the persons denoted by it, not to the same, but to some resembling department of life. And where shall we find any such analogous community as the symbol requires, except in the religious world? —any such conquerors, except in the faithful ministers of the Christian church? —or any such conquests, except in the conversion of worshippers from idols to God?" " The symbol conqueror, like other symbols of men in the prophecy, is the representative, not of an individual merely, but of the pure teachers of Christianity at large, who went forth, from the period of the vision, and fulfilled their office conformably to the word of God, assailing with the arrows of truth the hostile armies of idolatry, and subjecting them to the sceptre of Christ."—*Expos. of Apoc.*, p. 6.

SWEDENBORG.—" That hereby is signified the understanding of truth from the Word, appears from the signification of a horse as denoting the intellectual principle; and from the signification of white, as being predicated of truth. It is said that a white horse was seen when the Lamb opened the first seal, and a red horse when he opened the second, a black horse when he opened the third, and a pale horse when he opened the fourth; and inasmuch as a horse signifies the intellectual principle, specifically as to the Word, it may hence be manifest that the understanding of truth from the Word, and its quality with those who constitute the church, are here described by horses. Whether it be said that the understanding of truth is described, or that they who are principled therein are described, amounts to the same thing; for men, spirits, and angels, are the subjects in which truth dwells. Hence it may be known what is described in this chapter, and in the next following, in the internal or spiritual sense, namely, the understanding of the Word."—*Apoc. Expl.*, 355.

Mr. Lord will probably find himself at a loss to admit that a horse denotes the intellectual principle; but there must be a congruity in the whole imagery, and if the rider is symbolical, the horse must be also, denoting something that is appropriate to the general scope. But for proof that a horse has this import, we appeal to the Old Testament usage, from which the symbols of the Apocalypse are to be explained, Hab. iii. 15, 18 : " Was the Lord displeased against the rivers

Was thine anger against the rivers ? Was thy wrath against the sea, that thou
didst *ride upon thine horses* and thy chariots of salvation ? Thou didst walk through
the sea with *thine horses*, through the heap of great waters." "Who," says Swedenborg, " does not see that by the horses mentioned in this passage are not understood horses ? for it is said of Jehovah, that he rode upon his horses, that he walked through the sea with his horses, and his chariots are called chariots of salvation.
These things are so expressed, because riding upon horses signifies that Jehovah,
that is, the Lord, is in the understanding of the Word in its spiritual sense." If
this be not the meaning, what sense is to be affixed to the words ? If it be said
that it is a bold metaphor, still a metaphor has a meaning, and there must be something predicable of the Lord which is properly represented by such a figure. What
is it ? Again, Zech. xii. 4 : " In that day, saith the Lord, I will smite *every horse*
with astonishment and his rider with madness ; and I will open mine eyes upon the
house of Judah, and will smite *every horse* of the people with blindness." Is this
the announcement of a literal fact ? Does the Lord utter predictions against horses ?
It is clearly a judgment denounced against *men*, and not against *brute beasts*, and
it is a judgment against something in men which is susceptible of an effect termed
blindness, by which is doubtless meant *mental blindness*. Let Swedenborg explain :
" That by a horse is here signified the understanding of truth with the members of the
church, is evident : for otherwise, to what purpose could it be said that the horse
should be smitten with astonishment, and every horse of the people with blindness ?"
So, also, the august personage called " The Word of God" riding upon a white
horse, and followed by the armies of heaven upon white horses, denotes the spiritual presence of the Lord in a clear understanding of his Word, that is, of himself,
for " his name is called the Word of God." (See Swedenborg's treatise entitled
" The White Horse.") A vast array of passages might be cited in support of this
interpretation, but we pass on to the second seal :—" And there went out another
horse that was red. And power was given him that sat thereon to take peace from
the earth, and that they should kill one another ; and there was given unto him a
great sword."

Mr. Lord.—" For the counterpart to the military and political agents in this
symbol, we are, as in the former instance, to look to the religious world. As the
symbolized agents are not of the same class as the symbol, but of an analogous
species, they are not an order that literally take a sword and gain their victories by
force, but that conquer by persuasion and authority, and whose dominion therefore is religious, not military and political. And they are of the Christian Church,
as there has been no other religious teachers since the date of the visions, that have
not relied chiefly or wholly on mere force for the propagation of their doctrines."
" To slay one another with the sword being to destroy by violence,—as the counterpart of the natural life is the spiritual,—to destroy each other's spiritual life by violence is to sentence to an exclusion from salvation by what is deemed an authoritative act ; and in a still higher sense to compel one another by the power of their
office to embrace an apostate religion, by which they naturally and necessarily
perish. What class then of teachers and rulers is there in the church in whose
agency these peculiarities meet, a usurpation of powers which Christ has not authorized, an interception thereby of religious peace from the earth, and finally a
compulsion of men to apostacy in order to confirm and perpetuate that usurpation ?" " In the exercise of the stupendous powers thus usurped, they (the ec-
clesiastics), took peace from the earth by animosities, rivalries, contests and endeavors to conquer and destroy each other officially."—*Expos. of Apoc.* p. 75, 76,
82.

SWEDENBORG.—" 'And there went out another horse, that was red,'—That hereby is signified the understanding of the Word destroyed as to good, appears from the signification of a horse as denoting the intellectual principle, and from the signification of ruddy or red as denoting the quality of a thing as to good." " 'To take peace from the earth.' Hereby is signified the Word thence not understood, whence arise dissensions in the Church. The reason why it is here said that power was given to him that sat on the red horse to take peace from the earth is, because peace signifies the pacific principle of the mind, and the tranquil principle of the disposition originating in the conjunction of truth and good; hence to take peace from the earth signifies an unpacific and untranquil state in consequence of the disjunction of those principles, whence arise intestine divisions." " 'That they should kill one another.' That hereby is signified the falsification or extinction of truths appears from the signification of killing, as denoting to extinguish truths; for by killing in the Word is signified to kill spiritually, or to kill the spiritual principle of man, or his soul, which is to extinguish truths."—*Apoc. Expl.* 365, 366.

On the opening of the third seal, " Lo, a black horse; and he that sat on him had a pair of balances in his hand. And I heard a voice in the midst of the four beasts say, A measure of wheat for a penny, and three measures of barley for a penny; and see thou hurt not the oil and the wine."

MR. LORD.—" What agency of the ministers of the spiritual kingdom can this misrule represent? What is it in those whose office it is to feed the flock of God, to subject it to a famine analogous to that to which the population of the empire was reduced by tyrannous and wanton exaction? To withdraw from them the supports of spiritual life; that knowledge of God, of themselves, as needing redemption, and of the method of salvation to which they are entitled, and which are requisite to a vigorous piety; to obstruct them in its cultivation, and render their endeavors after sanctification fruitless. This perversion of their office was the most conspicuous characteristic of the agency of the ministers of the church, from the close of the second century to the second quarter of the fourth."—*Expos. of Apoc.*, p. 110.

SWEDENBORG.—" 'And behold a black horse'—That hereby is signified the understanding of the Word perished as to truth, appears from the signification of a horse, as denoting the understanding; and from the signification of black, as denoting what is not true; thus by a black horse is signified the understanding perished as to truth. The reason why black signifies what is not true, is, because white signifies what is true; the reason of which is, because white derives its origin from the brightness of light, and light signifies truth; and the reason why black is predicated of what is not true, and signifies the same, is, because it derives its origin from darkness, or from a privation of light, and darkness, inasmuch as it exists from the privation of light, signifies ignorance of truth. That a black horse here signifies the understanding of the Word perished as to truth, is moreover evident from the signification of the red horse treated of above, as denoting the same perished as to good. In the church, also, in process of time good first perishes, and afterwards truth, and at length in the place of good succeeds evil, and in place of truth what is false."—" 'Had a pair of balances in his hand'—That hereby is signified the estimation of truth from the Word in that state of the church, appears from the signification of him that sat on the horse as denoting the Word; and from the signification of the balances in his hand, as denoting the estimation of truth thence derived."—" 'A measure of wheat for a penny, and three measures of barley for a penny'—That hereby is signified, that the genuine good of the church was of no account with them, as also the genuine truth, appears from the signification of measure, as denoting the quality of estimation."—" This piece of money, being the smallest of all, is used to denote the least price, and in the present case it denotes as it were no price or estimation; the reason is, because by the red horse spoken of above, is signified the understanding of the Word perished as to good, and by the black horse, the same perished as to truth; and when the understanding of the Word as to good and truth is perished, then the genuine good and genuine truth of the church is estimated as it were at nothing, or as of no account."—*Apoc. Expl.*, 372–374.

It would be easy to extend the parallels between the respective interpretations under review; but sufficient has been adduced to show that Mr. Lord, upon purely independent grounds, has made a wonderful advance towards the principles recognised by the New Church, as lying at the foundation of all correct development of the true sense of the Apocalypse. He has seen with a depth of insight not evinced by any other English or American writer, the frontal fallacy of all former expositions of this book; and he has struck upon a new axiom of hermeneutics in dealing with the symbolic visions, and one which in his own commentary has led to very important results. But he will allow us to intimate that he has but just entered upon the vista that his fortunate researches have opened before him. He will feel impelled to go forward, and he cannot well advance in the direction in which he has set out without nearing more and more the grand goal which we trust he may reach—the discovery that *the laws of symbolization are the laws of creation.* Every natural object throughout the whole domain from which prophecy draws its imagery is the effect of a spiritual cause—the embodiment of a spiritual essence—with which it *corresponds.* There could be no such thing as the existence of a natural horse if there were not a spiritual horse as its archetype; and a spiritual horse is the fixed and normal representative of a certain intellectual state among the inhabitants of the spiritual world. The ascertainment of the relation there subsisting between the sign and the thing signified, is the clue to its symbolical purport, as used in the Scriptures, for they are constructed on the principle of *corresponding representatives.* The key in this particular case is thus given by Swedenborg in speaking of the symbol of the horse:—" That the horse here mentioned does not literally signify a horse, but refers to some of the things treated of in this chapter, may evidently appear from this circumstance, that the horses were seen when the seals were opened, and it is said that they went out, for horses could not go out from the book, but the meaning obviously is, that those things were manifested which are signified by horses."

What is here said of horses applies to all other animals which enter into the prophetic machinery. " All things which appear in the spiritual world are representative of things spiritual, which are exhibited in forms such as exist in the world; hence there appear beasts of the earth of every kind, and birds of heaven, also houses and chambers in them, with various decorations, likewise gardens and paradises full of trees bearing fruits and flowers—all from a spiritual origin, and representative of spiritual things." " Inasmuch as the affections of the natural man are signified by beasts, therefore those affections, when they are presented visible in the spiritual world in the correspondent forms of animals, appear altogether as forms of various beasts; thus as lambs, sheep, she-goats, kids, he-goats, heifers, oxen, cows: also as camels, mules, horses, asses; and also as bears, tigers, leopards, lions; likewise as dogs and serpents of various kinds; but such things are only appearances of the affections of the spirits who are present, and when they appear, it is also known there not only that they thence exist, but also from whom they are derived; but as soon as the affections cease, the appearances cease also. From these considerations also it may be manifest, whence it is that beasts are so often mentioned in the Word."

We have here the assertion of the grand law of symbolization, as far as this order of scriptural hieroglyphics is concerned, and the *principle* which lies at its foundation covers the whole ground of the inspired Word. *Natural terms are expressive of spiritual ideas.* The truth of the principle can only be denied by denying the reality of Swedenborg's revelations of the facts and phenomena of the spiritual world; and he that assumes this, we will venture to say, has little idea of the herculean task which he undertakes. He has then to account for the stupendous problem involved in Swedenborg's case. He has to give some adequate solution of the fact that such a sublime conception should ever have entered his mind—that he should ever have propounded so magnificent a theory, connecting, in indissoluble bonds, the great laws of the universe with the internal structure of the written Word. It is of very little avail for one to say that he does not see the evidence of the truth of the theory. Does he see the evidence of its falsity? Can he possibly rest in any other theory? Does science, does philosophy, does intuition, reclaim against the developments which Swedenborg has made of the spiritual nature of man, upon which all his disclosures of the other life are built? Let the matter be brought to the most rigid ordeal of reason, and then let it be seen if the verdict does not confirm every position upon which his system plants itself.

MISCELLANY.

CALVIN AND HIS PREACHING.

The following sketch is taken from Dr. J. Augustine Smith's "Monograph on the Moral Sense: consisting of two discourses delivered in the chapel of N. Y. City University, on the 5th and 12th March, 1847." The authority cited for the statement respecting Calvin's sermons, is the "Histoire Litteraire de Geneve, par Jean Senebier, a Geneve, 1786, pp. 257-8.

"From fictitious scenes, intended to enforce particular, and, as we have seen, most erroneous views, or, designed to do nothing, we now pass to sad realities—where bad reasoning was followed by its legitimate and most woful consequences. And, of these unfortunate dialecticians, the celebrated John Calvin must, I fear, stand as the representative. Nor have those, who assume his name, the slightest cause for offence. They do not acknowledge him for saint or idol, and have, therefore, no right to object that he is dealt with according to his deserts, where the intention is to do good, and where a strong hope, at least, exists that good will ensue.

"Before I come, however, to the facts, and the inferences those facts may authorize, candor requires the acknowledgment, that the Reformer of Geneva lived an austere life of excessive literary labor, devoted to the investigation and promulgation of what he conscientiously believed to be truth. His health was indifferent, nor, in all probability, was his temper very mild, even at the outset, and it was, in addition, soured and embittered by persecutions suffered, and, what was far worse for him, inflicted. And, furthermore, it were utterly unpardonable in those of us particularly who philosophise as we list and pour forth results from our reflexions, fraught, as we think, with truth, not most gratefully to feel the obligations we owe to many who took the name of Calvin. Defects, and grievous defects, they doubtless had, and these it was sufficiently easy for Mr. Hume to ridicule, and for Sir Walter Scott to expose—the one, in conformity with his general character, the other, to indite a telling tale. But if the isle, which produced these distinguished writers, had not given birth to men cast in a far different mould, the Stuarts had never been expelled, nor, for us, had the glorious Reformation ever been effected.

"If pushed to the wall, indeed, we are obliged to acknowledge, that the reformers of the 16th and 17th centuries neither foresaw, nor intended, all the results of which we boast. But if, in the tenderest relation of life, we are advised

> " Be to her faults a *little* blind,
>   Be to her virtues *very* kind,"

we may not lose sight, indeed, of the truth, but, surely, we may dwell as much as we can, and as long as we can, with safety, upon the fairer side of the picture.

"But these very considerations render Calvin the fitter for the purpose I have in view. He was the most prominent man of one of the most important eras the world has ever seen—a man of great vigor of intellect—considerable acquirement, and, as was before remarked, ardently and constantly engaged in the diffusion of what he undoubtedly conceived to be the truth. Now, if bad reasoning could induce such a man to fall into the grievous errors and crimes which marked the life of the Genevese Reformer, what might not be apprehended, and what, in fact, did happen to minds less gifted, and less furnished? Is the moralist, therefore, to be blamed, who exposes the defects of that deplorable logic, in the only mode it is permitted him to expose them, by exhibiting, in all their breadth and depth, the lamentable consequences of Calvin's deceptive dialectics? I should think not. Let us see then what those consequences were.

"It appears that, in about the twenty years he ruled Geneva, Calvin preached nearly two thousand sermons. Of these, some twenty have been printed, while, of the remainder, the texts only have been preserved. And, of a truth, with two, and only two barely possible, exceptions, these texts are remarkable. They are as follows :

OLD TESTAMENT.		NEW TESTAMENT.		
Genesis	123	Acts		189
Deuteronomy	200	St. Paul, 1st Corinth.		110
Job	59	Do.	2d do.	66
Psalms	94	Do.	Galatians	43
Isaiah	343	Do.	Thessalon.	46
Jeremiah	91	Do.	1st Timothy	55
Lamentations	25	Do.	2d do.	31
Ezekiel	174	Do.	Titus	48
Daniel	47			
Ezra	65			588
Joel	17			1337
Amos	43			
Obadiah	5			1925
Jonah	6			
Micah	28			
Zephaniah	17			
	1337			

Nineteen hundred and twenty-five sermons, and not one of them from either of the Gospels !!

" Now, what may be the effect produced upon the minds of others, by this strange enumeration, is more than I can say ; but, when first brought to my knowledge, the emotion it excited was one of unmixed amazement. I had not supposed it possible, although, when connected with the reli- gious sentiment, false conclusions might, as indeed I well knew they did, pervert and deaden the moral sense, yet that they could, in addition, as in the case of Calvin, so thoroughly chill all the kindlier feelings of our nature. It had not entered my imagination, that any man, viewing with reverence the Gospels, could preach, upon an average, very near ly two sermons every Sunday, for twenty years, without having even his fancy sufficiently brightened, or his sensibilities sufficiently roused, or his heart sufficiently warmed towards his fellow-creatures, by the exalted morality everywhere diffused, and by the gushing affection, bursting from almost every page written by the four Evangelists, with- out being coerced, during the whole of that protracted period, to be- stow at least one single solitary discourse upon Matthew, Mark, Luke or John."—*Monog. on Mor. Sense, p. 53-57.*

THE LONDON ATHENÆUM AND SWEDENBORG.—In the course of a very long and elaborate review of Davis' Revelations, the paper above mentioned contains the following :—

" Time will roll on,—and the Revelations of Andrew Jackson Davis will be put on their proper shelf in that curious museum which men call human nature. One man, we foresee, will be treated with injustice—we mean Emanuel Swedenborg. Davis and he will be classed together. Against this we protest. We have read enough of Swedenborg to justify us to ourselves in declaring that *we would rather*

it may be presumed that a new lustre will be shed around his name, somewhat as the fame of Socrates is enhanced by that of Plato. The master will naturally be measured by the guage of the pupil.—Mons. Le Boys des Guays, editor of "La Nouvelle Jerusalem," is still proceeding with the translation into French of the "Arcana Celestia." The version has reached Chap. xxiv. (No. 3141). The last No. of his Periodical contains an article on the "Religous Rites of the Ancient Gauls compared with the Biblical Symbols," in which the writer alludes to the Druidical System in a manner strikingly analogous to that of our correspondent T. W. Another article by the late Ed. Richer is entitled "Spiritual Medicine," in which the physical effects of mental exaltation are largely considered. This article will well bear being transferred to our pages if we should find room for it.—Dr. Tafel has translated into German from the English the following Tracts, published by one of the N. C. Societies in England :—" The Apostolic Doctrine of Reconciliation of Mediation, of Expiation, and of Imputation ;" "Of Repentance ;" "Of Justification by Faith ;" "Is it true that we cannot keep the Commandments ?"—The "London Printing Society" has recently issued a new and beautiful stereotype edition of the "*True Christian Religion*," in one volume, containing a most copious index of subjects, and also (what has never appeared in any previous edition) the index of "Memorable Relations," drawn out by Swedenborg himself. This index is rather a digest, presenting the cream and substance of the special instruction contained in the several "Relations." It has in addition to this an index of the numerous texts of Scripture explained or referred to in the volume. The same Society has also published new editions of the latter volumes of the "*Arcana Celestia*," carefully collated with the original and much improved in the style of expression. — The Rev. Thomas Worcester, of Boston, was lately appointed chairman of a series of meetings of the clergy of different denominations, convened for the purpose of taking into consideration the opportunities existing in that city for the indulgence of licentious passions. During the course of the sittings, more than seventy clergymen belonging to the various Protestant sects were in attendance, and it was resolved to prepare an Address on the subject to the citizens of Boston. This Address, which appears in the Christian Register, understood to have been drawn up by the chairman, is a document of great ability, urging the claims of the subject in a most impressive and fervent vein of appeal.

The Rev. Dr. Pond has published a long letter in the Portland Christian Mirror in reference to Mr. Cabell's "Reply," in which he denies that any one of his objections to Swedenborg's Theology or Philosophy is fairly answered, and brings heavy charges against the work on the score of vituperation, misrepresentation, &c. He opens his rejoinder by saying, that Mr. C. has "entirely mistaken the *design* of my review, as set forth in my preface. I said expressly :—' This work is not to be regarded as strictly of a *controversial* character. My purpose has been rather to *exhibit* Swedenborg's than to *refute* him. If the former of these objects can be well accomplished, the latter, I have supposed, would no longer be necessary.' In pursuance of the purpose here expressed, I had no occasion to go into a consideration of the explanations and defences of Swedenborg which have been put forth by his followers ; and if Mr. C. had understood the matter, his frequent and severe censures of what he deems my omissions in this respect might all have been spared."

This must needs appear strange to one who has read the Dr.'s book. Not only is its very staple made up of formal "objections" to Swedenborg's system, but after stating that "if he can be shown to have taught much that is unworthy of God, untrue, not in accordance with reason, Scripture, and fact, then he could not have received his instructions from the Lord, and his credit as a supernatural teacher, a revealer of heavenly things, is destroyed"—he goes on to say, "No Swedenborgian can object to our *arguing* the question on this ground; and such in general is *the line of argument* which I propose to pursue in the following pages," pp. 40, 50. How far does this come short of a professed and formal *refutation* of Swedenborg? And how can the Dr. say that he had "no occasion to go into a consideration of the explanations and defences of Swedenborg which have been put forth by his followers," when he is referring to them all along in the course of his work? But supposing this were not his intention, where is the justice of holding up the offensive features of a system of Christian doctrines in total disregard of the "explanations and defences" which are propounded by its disciples? Would Dr. P. think this fair dealing on the part of one who should aim to hold up the system of Calvinism in an odious light to the world? Would he deem it possible to justify a presentation of the subject which took no account of the *fundamental principles* on which the whole was built? And if he saw this done by a process, in repeated instances, of gross perversion, caricature, and ridicule, would he not feel that such conduct ought to be *severely rebuked?* Would he not feel assured also that he was warranted by apostolic example in the use of stern and emphatic language? We do not plead for intemperate, unchristian, or indecorous abuse of an opponent; but we would suggest that Dr. P. should make the case his own—should conceive his real views to have been grievously misrepresented, and set in a light that he knew would convey the most false impressions, and that too when the means of getting at the truth were abundantly in the writer's reach; and then let him say whether the stern reproof of this procedure ought to subject him to the charge of railing abuse. We do not mean by this that Mr. Cabell may not in some cases have overstepped the limits of Christian courtesy, but we do mean that Dr. P. is not the man justly to complain of this treatment. If Mr. C. is rightly required to enter the confessional of conscience, Dr. P. is bound to accompany him; and if he should be at a loss to recall his "*peccavi's,*" we will venture to remind him of a few. On p. 44 of his "Review" he says, "Swedenborg taught that the regenerate, in this life, might fall away." For proof he refers to "Div. Prov." § 279. On turning to this passage, the only warrant we find for the charge is, that Swedenborg asserts it "as an error of the present age to suppose that evils are separated, and even cast out, when they are remitted." He affirms, on the contrary, that they still remain adherent to the man's nature, but are, in his phrase, "removed from the middle to the sides," thus as it were from the central light of self-inspection to the comparative shade of the circumference. Consequently he remarks, "because evils are not separated, but only removed, that is, put away to the sides, and a man may be transferred from the middle to the circumference, it may also happen, that he can return to his evils which he thought rejected." Is not this true? Did it not happen to David and to Peter? and is it not a fact familiar to all Christian experience, that the spiritual enemies which a man thought slain revive and trouble him afresh? There is evidently no implication of a *permanent* return to evil, but of those occasional *tempo-*

rary relapses usually understood by the term *backsliding*.—Again, Dr. P. says, p. 72, that by " the great red dragon spoken of, Rev. xii. 3, Swedenborg understands the *Reformed Churches* who hold the doctrine of the Trinity and of justification by faith. By the woman in travail is signified the *New Church*. The man child denotes *Swedenborg's Works*, particularly ' The Doctrine of the New Jerusalem, published in London in 1758, also *the Doctrines Concerning the Lord*, concerning *the Sacred Scriptures*, and concerning a *Life according to the Commandments of the Decalogue* published in Amsterdam in 1763.' The child's being ' caught up unto God and to his throne' denotes the protection of these works ' to *the end* of the former church, and *the beginning* of the new.' But the New Church is already in existence, and has brought forth her man-child—*Swedenborg's Works*, as above. Yet these works are to be protected *till the beginning of the New Church! !* The former church ended, and the new one commenced, according to Swedenborg, in the year 1757, the date of the last judgment. The man-child was born, i. e. the works referred to were published, partly in 1758 and partly in 1763. Yet these works are to be protected by God, *till the end of the former church, and the beginning of the new ! !*" Now we must freely declare, that a more direct and downright caricature of an author's meaning has never come under our notice. He first begins by confounding Swedenborg's works with the doctrines which they contain, making the one the subject of the prophecy instead of the other, and upon this most baseless assumption goes on to convict him of a glaring inconsistency on the score of chronology ! We give the passage from Swedenborg:—" Since by the woman who brought forth, is signified the New Church, it is plain that by the male child is signified the doctrine of that church. The doctrine here meant, is *The Doctrine of the New Jerusalem*, published in London, 1758 ; as also *The Doctrine concerning the Lord*, concerning *The Sacred Scripture*, and concerning *A Life according to the Commandments of the Decalogue*, published in Amsterdam ; for by doctrine are understood all the truths of doctrine, doctrine being the complex of them. When these doctrines were written, the dragonists stood around me, and endeavored, with all their fury, to devour or extinguish them ; this strange circumstance it was permitted me to relate, because, of a truth, it so happened. The dragonists who stood around me were from all parts of the reformed Christian world."—*A. R.* 543.

Again, he says—" ' And her child was caught up unto God and his throne,' signifies, the protection of the doctrine by the Lord, because it is for the doctrine of the New Church, and its being guarded by the angels of heaven. By these words is signified the protection of the doctrine by the Lord, because it is said that the dragon stood before the woman who was ready to be delivered, to devour her child as soon as it was born ; and by a child, and a male child, is signified the doctrine of the New Church. Being guarded by the angels, is also signified, because it is said, that it was caught up unto God, and to his throne ; and by a throne is signified the angelic heaven."—*A. R.* 545.

Now we would ask if there can be a greater perversion than to represent Swedenborg as teaching that the birth of the man-child was the publication of his own works, partly in 1758, and partly in 1763, which latter date, by the way, the Dr. has introduced here as *a part of the quotation from Swedenborg*, when in fact it does not occur there, and is *surreptitiously* introduced in order to serve a purpose. We can easily conceive cases in which a procedure like this, however trifling in itself, would receive no lighter name than that of *moral forgery*. But look at the truth in regard to this charge of inconsistency and self-contradiction. Swedenborg says that the New Church is symbolized by the woman—that the woman's fleeing into the wilderness denotes that that church should at first be confined to a few—by her having a place prepared for her by God, and being there nourished for a certain period, denoted that God would provide for the church, and that the period of 1260 days is a period extending to the end of the former church and the beginning of the new one, without any minute or definite specification of time, which is a feature wholly unknown to Swedenborg's interpretation of prophecy. He says indeed that the last judgment took place in 1757, which was in one sense the commencement of the New Church, just as Christ's personal presence was in one sense the commencement of his kingdom on earth, but that this church was still to be of gradual establishment, and admitting the lapse of a long period before it should reach its culminating point; for the new heaven, constituting its internal, was first to be settled. Accordingly he says, in the "True Christian Religion," 784, that "in proportion as this new heaven increases, in the same proportion the New Jerusalem, that is, the New Church, comes down from that heaven; so that this cannot be effected in a moment, but in proportion as the falses of the former church are removed." So also in his letter to Dr. Beyer, dated 1767, he writes, in answer to the question, *How soon the New Church is to be expected*—"The Lord is preparing at this time a new heaven of such as believe in him, &c., and by degrees as that heaven is formed, the New Church likewise begins and increases." And again, in 1769 :—" I am now much inquired of respecting the New Church, when it will take place?—to which I answer : by degrees, as the doctrine of justification and imputation is extirpated. It is known, that the Christian Church did not take place immediately after the ascension of Christ, but increased successively, which is also understood by these words in the Revelations: 'And the woman flew into the desert, into her place, where she is nourished a time, times, and half a time, from the face of the serpent.' "

If then the very *beginning* of the New Church is gradual, for the same reason the *end* of the old church is also gradual. The decline of the one goes on *pari passu* with the increase of the other; and as this is the evident import of the passages cited from the Apocalypse Revealed, there is not the least shadow of ground for Dr. P.'s *manufactured* charge of inconsistency. The rise of the New Church does not necessarily synchronise with the date of Swedenborg's writings, nor does he deal in any exact specifications of time in expounding the Apocalypse. He professes to give the *spiritual* sense of that book, and that is the sense in which it is understood by the angels, who are raised above all the conditions of time and space. The data upon which this charge is founded are now all before the reader, and he will put his own construction upon the promptings which dictated it. That a more groundless charge could not well be framed, is clear; and sorry we are to say that this is not the only one of similar stamp occurring in his volume. But we have no room at present to dwell upon them. Dr. P. will see, however, from this, that if the Romans wondered at the Gracchi complaining of sedition, we have some cause to marvel at his protest against abuse. If Swedenborg were now alive and residing under the shadow of the Bangor Seminary we cannot but think that he would feel as holy an indignation as Dr. P. now expresses, in view of the injustice done to his sentiments and teachings by the published work of his neighbor. Why then should

Dr. P. complain of a treatment at the hands of Mr. Cabell, of which Swedenborg might as properly complain at his hands? We do not say that he has no ground for complaint; we simply express surprise at his making it. Take, for instance, the following sentence in his "Review" in respect to what Swedenborg says of the Grand Man of heaven. "To my own apprehension the whole account is supremely ridiculous; being destitute alike of sense and decency, and worthy only of contempt." Now as we believe in the truth of this sublime *arcanum*—as we regard it as one of the most magnificent facts of the spiritual universe—as we see it to follow by the most inevitable sequence from the very constitution of our being, Dr. P. can hardly fail to perceive how seriously such a sentence reflects upon our understandings, as readily assenting to what he terms a "supremely ridiculous" and "contemptible" fancy. If he had deigned to take into account the *reasons* of our belief on this score—if we could see that he had bestowed any attention upon the *principles* which we affirm to necessitate just such a result in the other world, and had attempted to show their fallacy, we could perhaps have better borne the reproach thus thrown on our intelligence. But it doubtless tasks our philosophy to receive calmly a judgment which virtually pronounces us simpletons, without so much as an attempt to prove it. But we forbear.

We find a number of things that "move our special wonder" in the letter which has called forth these remarks, but few that do it more than the following: "He (Mr. C.) admits, for example, that the planet Saturn is farthest distant from the Sun;" which Dr. P. had urged against Swedenborg. But the reader will see that this is a strange kind of *admission* as it stands in Mr. C.'s Reply: "According to the present English translation, Swedenborg speaks in a certain connexion of the planet Saturn as being *farthest distant* from the Sun. To this others have replied, that the original (*longissime* distat ab sole) may be lawfully rendered "*very far* distant." Or, if the present version is retained, any one, who was not determined to find fault, would know that he meant nothing more than that it was the *farthest of those which were then discovered*, or of which he had been speaking." Dr. P. is of course welcome to all the aid his cause can derive from *such* admissions.

In the course of his letter he intimates the intention of soon issuing a second edition of "Swedenborgianism Reviewed," in which he shall not only renew all his former objections, but reinforce them with several fresh ones. "In particular," says he, "I shall urge against the system of Swedenborg, that it is a refined *materialism*. The present world is *material*. And yet it is an emanation, according to Swedenborg, from the very *substance of God*. It was made in fact from his *substance*. What then *is the substance of God?* And what, according to Swedenborg, is the *human soul?* It is no other than the *nervous or spirituous fluid*. "This fluid is *the spirit and soul* of its body." "We may take it for certain that if this fluid and the soul agree with each other in their predicates, *the fluid must be accepted as the soul*."—(*Econ. of the An. King.* vol. ii. pp. 233, 238.) And what say the expounders of Swedenborg on this subject? "The distinction between mind and matter," says Mr. Clissold, "lies *not in essence but in form*." Mr. Dawson represents it as "one of the great uses of Swedenborg's writings, that they help to break down the mischievous man-made distinction *between spirit and matter*." And Mr. Wilkinson says: "We regard body and soul together as *distinctly* and *inseparably one*." Either Dr. Pond or his printer is not a little at fault in the above reference to the "Economy of the Animal Kingdom." We have turned to the volume and page indicated, and find no such language, though it probably occurs elsewhere in his philosophical works, which, by the way, are not the basis of the theological belief of his adherents. The position, however, is undoubtedly sound in the sense which Swedenborg intended, viz, that of the soul or the *psyche* as the formative organific principle of the body. Dr. P., ought to know that Swedenborg teaches—what we defy him to deny—that the human soul is an organized receptacle of the Divine love and wisdom, which he terms a *spirituous fluid*, rather from the inability of language to express the true idea than from its intrinsic fitness for the purpose, and accordingly Coleridge, while greatly admiring his reasoning, has objected to this use of the term as inadequate. If Dr. P., will suggest a better we will acknowledge our obligations. But let him not forget that if he makes man an entity capable of subsisting by himself he makes him a God. If he is an organ of life, the organism must consist of something. The reference to Mr. Clissold is also a mistake. Not he, but Mr. Wilkinson, wrote the Introduction to the " Economy ;" and here Dr. P. would have done as well to quote the whole sentence; " The distinction between the mind and matter lies not in essence but in form : for all things have but one essence, viz, the love and wisdom of the Creator." This will answer the Dr.'s question propounded above, " What is the substance of God ?" Swedenborg teaches that God as love and wisdom is self-subsisting substance, and that from this, through graduated series, is derived every created substance, of which the human soul is one. But to infer, because man's psychical organism involves the nervous or spirituous fluid as an element, that therefore the *substance of God* is primarily such a fluid, is as absurd as to say that because the light and heat of the sun, by means of atmospheres, form mineral and vegetable substances, therefore the body of the sun itself consists of such substances. But Dr. P., no doubt supposes that God created the universe *out of nothing*—an hypothesis which the New Churchman leaves him to cherish with all the devotion he sees fit to bestow upon it. He would, however, have done less injustice to Mr. Wilkinson, if he had adverted to the fact, that in the very paragraph from which the above sentence is quoted he is all along expressly aiming to vindicate Swedenborg from the charge of materialism, and closes with these words :—" So long as we maintain the definition of matter given by Swedenborg, viz. chemical form as distinguished from organic, he must maintain that the mind is bodily (*i.e.* possessed of form), *but assuredly not material.*" So again as to Mr. Dawson, who is not an acknowledged " expounder" of Swedenborg, nor, as far as we know, an avowed receiver of his doctrines, but whose statements nevertheless, are put sadly out of joint by the manner in which they are here presented to the reader. The passage is as follows :—" *This was one of the great uses of his writings ; they help to break down the mischievous, man-made distinction between spirit and matter.* Not that he believed them to be alike. The world had had its attempt to degrade spirit into matter only, but after this there would probably come a knowledge which would show the point of reconcilement; that after all, there was not that distinction between them which we had been taught; but that we must resort to the doctrine of degrees taught by Swedenborg, who says that the spirit flows outwards from its source and in all subsequent manifestations, the farther it gets from its original source, the nearer it approaches to materiality. Then, if this be the case, the old doctrine will be correct, that matter is but the garment in which the spirit cloaks itself. No one believes that the laws of the soul are the very same as those which regulate the body." For ourselves we see nothing in this very wide of the mark. If Dr. P. scents a rank materialistic odor in it, we hope he will enable us to detect it. Indeed, we confess to great curiosity to see the proofs developed by which Swedenborg is to be made out an apostle of *materialism*, as he has generally been assailed from the opposite point of the compass, as strangely *spiritualising* every thing. On one feature of Dr. P.'s work we feel constrained to animadvert with a very pointed distinctness. He makes it a prominent objection to Swedenborg that he frequently and palpably *misrepresents* the doctrines of others, especially of the Reformed Churches. Thus, for example, " he almost invariably represents Trinitarians as believing in *three Gods*, or in other words of being *Tritheists*."— This is undoubtedly correct, and his " disciples" or " followers," as they often are termed, have no disposition to shield him from the charge, for it is a charge which has been reiterated again and again by his followers. But both he and they are perfectly aware that Trinitarians deny its truth. We know very well that they claim to hold a Trinity of persons in entire consistency with a Unity of essence, and it is here that the issue is made between us. We affirm with equal confidence that the two tenets are utterly and hopelessly incompatible with each other—that whether upon philosophical or exegetical grounds the one is absolutely destructive of the other—in a word, that tripersonalism is, by logical necessity, inevitable tritheism, however earnest and sonorous the disclaimers of its advocates. But upon this ground we are never met except by the argument *ab ignorantia*. " We *know* that God is one person in some sense ; we *believe* that he is three persons in some other sense, but *how* this can be, is an inscrutable mystery which we presume not to fathom." Now this tenet we maintain to be, not a mystery but a contradiction, and that the plea of mystery is resorted to as a cover to the contradiction. We hesitate not to affirm that any process of reasoning or interpretation which brings out the result, that the Father, Son, and Holy Spirit are three Divine persons, that is, each of them God, and yet that God is but one, is a contradiction. If put in mathematical form it would be ; $A=1$, $B=1$, $C=1$, yet $A+B+C$ is not equal to $1+1+1$, but to 1. Now when we declare this to be a solecism or a sophism, we are charged with *misrepresentation ;* but nothing can be more unfair. We do not say that Trinitarians *avow* a belief in three Gods, for this would be a misrepresentation ; but we say that logically their belief involves this ; and the charge of a logical consequence, made in good faith, is not properly liable to the counter-charge of misrepresentation. Whenever Dr. P., or any of Swedenborg's opponents, will come manfully up to the *fundamental principles* of the system, and show wherein its *psychology* is unsound, we shall feel that we have a tangible subject of controversy : and so also of the *theology*. But so long as the policy is to take the prevailing views of orthodoxy for granted, and to horrify the public mind by exhibiting Swedenborg as opposed to them—which he undoubtedly is, and, as we believe, for the best of reasons—the end will unquestionably be answered of exciting a prodigous prejudice against him, while at the same time the absolute truth remains as immovable as the pillars of the earth, and the inward peace of its disciples is " as a river."

THE

NEW CHURCH REPOSITORY

AND

MONTHLY REVIEW.

| Vol. 1. | APRIL, 1848. | No. 4. |

ORIGINAL PAPERS.

ARTICLE I.

THE DRUIDISM OF ANCIENT BRITAIN:

ITS DOCTRINES, RITES, CORRESPONDENCES, ETC., AS DISCOVERED IN AN-
CIENT BRITISH MANUSCRIPTS, REVIEWED AND COMPARED WITH THOSE
OF THE ANCIENT CHURCH.

(*Continued.*)

In every system of religion, especially in the Representative
Church, the priest, as the minister of God, and the teacher and
leader of the people, necessarily occupies a conspicuous place;
and a knowledge of the laws and institutes of the priesthood
is indispensable to the knowledge of the religion, of which that
priesthood forms a part. We shall therefore in this number
attempt a brief description of the priests and teachers of the
Druidic System.

We learn from Swedenborg, in his explanation of Gen. x.
that the different branches of the ancient church differed from
each other in many particulars of their doctrinals and rituals,
though there was a general resemblance between them, and
that the representatives of the Jewish church, afterwards instituted, in like manner differed from all these; the representatives of the ancient church were the external correspondences
of the internal state of the men of that church, while the representatives of the Jewish church under the exclusive government of the priests were the correspondences of the celestial

kingdom, though the church had no internal but what was evil. This general resemblance, we think, will be readily traced, and the correspondence of the spiritual church distinctly seen, in the Druidical priesthood. At what remote period of antiquity this church was established in Britian it is not possible to ascertain ; but we shall hereafter show that it was established at a period long anterior to the institution of the Jewish religion in the land of Canaan, at a period when the ancient church flourished in that region in comparative purity, and when men lived in charity with each other. The order of civil and ecclesiastical government at that time in Britain was doubtless most simple, as may be learnt from statements made in several triads respecting the primitive state of the nation, and the successive steps taken age after age in the establishment of the order which ultimately prevailed. The ecclesiastical order of government thus ultimately established, embraced three functionaries or classes of men, who were unitedly called " the Bards of the Isle of Britain." Their orders and duties are thus described in the laws of Dyfnwal Moelmud.

" There are three orders of the profession of Bardism : First, The Chief Bard, or the Bard of full Privilege, who has acquired his degree and privilege though discipline under a master duly authorized, being a Conventional Bard. His office is to preserve the memory of all arcana and knowledges, whilst he shall continue in his office of Bard regularly instituted, and also to preserve every record and memorial of the country and tribe respecting marriages, pedigrees, arms, inheritance, and rights of the country and nation of the Cymbry.

" Second, the Ovate, whose degree is acquired in right of his possessing natural poetic genius, or praise-worthy knowledges, which he shall prove by the correctness of his answers when examined before a customary and honorable congress of Bards ; or where there is no such congress, by a lawful session granted by the tribe of the Lord of the district ; or by twelve of the judges of his court ; or by the twelve jurors of the court in the customary manner. The Ovate is not to be interrogated respecting any regular discipline through which he may have passed, nor respecting any thing else, except his proficiency and accuracy in knowledges. This is so regulated for the maintenance of knowledges, lest there should be a deficiency of regular teachers, and thus knowledges, and the art of memory, and wisdom, through the deficiency of regular instruction should be lost ; and also for the further improvement of the arts and sciences, by the addition of every new discovery approved by the judgment of the masters and wise men, and confirmed as such by them; and also lest the advantage arising from the powers of natural genius and invention should be repressed.

"Third, the Druid-Bard; who must be a Bard regularly initiated and graduated, of approved wisdom and knowledges, and of language to make known judgment and reason founded upon knowledges. He is raised to his office according to the privilege granted by reason and the regular court of the tribe, being elected by ballot, and his election warranted by the vote of the Convention. His duty is to teach and make known the knowledges of wisdom and godliness, in the convention of the Bards, in the palace, in the place of worship, and in every family in which he has full privilege.

"Each of these three has a just and lawful claim to five free acres of land in right of his profession, exclusive of what he is entitled to as a free-born Briton: for the right by possession, does not abrogate that by nature, nor the natural right the professional."—*Triads of Social State.*

The Chief Bard, besides the duties mentioned in the above triad, also was governor or the ruling order, and was by virtue of his office called the Presiding Bard.

"The three orders of primitive Bards: the Presiding Bard, or Primitive Bard positive, according to the rights, voice, and usage of the Bardic Convention, whose office is to superintend and regulate; the Ovate, according to poetical genius, exertion, and contingency, whose function is to act from the impulse of poetical inspiration;* and the Druid according to reason, nature, and necessity of things, whose office is to instruct."—*Institutional Triads.*

The Druid-Bard, though mentioned last in both these triads, was nevertheless the most honorable of the three, being elected to his office from amongst the Presiding or Chief Bards. Also from among the Druidicial order was elected the Chief Priest of the nation, or the Arch Druid, who in his person united the priestly and kingly offices, according to the order of the Melchizidek of the ancient church. With the exception of those already mentioned, we read of no distinction among the Druidical order of priesthood, nor of the subordination of one class to another. They were distinguished, not as superior and subordinate inferior, but according to the peculiar function of each, the most honorable among them being, not the ruling

---

* The Ovate is elsewhere mentioned as being the physician of the tribe; he studied the productions of nature with the view to ascertain their medicinal qualities; among these productions the misletoe was considered to be of the highest value, being designated "Healer of all."

priest, but the teacher in the Convention of Bards, in the palace, in the place of worship, and in the private family.

The character of these men, as teachers and governors, will appear from the following institutional triads.

1. " The three ultimate objects of bardism : to reform morals and customs; to secure peace; and to praise all that is good and excellent.

2. " The three joys of the bards of the Isle of Britain : the increase of. knowledges; the reformation of manners ; and the triumph of peace over devastation and pillage.

3. " The three splendid honors of the bards of the Isle of Britain : the triumph of learning over ignorance ; the triumph of reason over irrationality ; and the triumph of peace over depredation and plunder.

4. " The three attributes (or necessary and congenial duties) of the bards of the Isle of Britain : to manifest truth, and diffuse the knowledges of it ; to perpetuate the praise of all that is good and excellent ; and to make peace prevail over disorder and violence.

5. " The three necessary, but reluctant duties, of the bards of the Isle of Britain : secrecy for the sake of peace and public good ;* invective lamentation required by justice ; and the unsheathing of the sword against lawlessness and depredation.

6. " There are three avoidant injunctions on a bard : to avoid sloth, because he is a man given to investigation ; to avoid contention, because he is a man given to peace ; and to avoid folly, because he is a man of discretion and reason."

Have Christian ministers and magistrates higher ends and purer motives than the Druids had ? We trow not. A few other triads from the laws of Dyfnwal Moelmud will give us an idea of the character of their government.

1. " There are three native rights belonging to every free-born Briton, whether male or female. First, *The gift and free use of five acres of free land, by privilege of his descent from a native Cymrian ;* and the descendants of the foreigner and stranger shall obtain the same upon the fourth in descent by honorable marriages, because such then enjoy a state of liberty. Second, The privilege of carrying defensive arms and armorial bearings, which are not allowed to any one except a free-born Briton of unquestionable nobility. And, Third, *The privilege*

---

* This may appear to conflict with one of the triads in the preceding article; but it must be remembered that every family, every society, every government, has its secrets, or private affairs, which it would be unwise to reveal to all the world. Besides, secrecy is here represented to be a reluctant duty.

of a vote under the protection of the chief of the tribe, which a male attains when he has a beard, and a female when she marries."

Let the reader compare this triad with the law given to Israel concerning their inheritance of the land of Canaan.

"Unto these shall the land be divided for an inheritance according to the number of names. To the many thou shalt give the more inheritance, and to few the less inheritance : to every one shall his inheritance be given according to those that were numbered of him. Notwithstanding, the land shall be divided by lot : according to the names of the tribes of the fathers they shall inherit. According to the lot shall the possession thereof be divided between many and few. And the Lord spake unto Moses, saying, The daughters of Zelophehad speak right : thou shalt surely give them a possession of an inheritance among their father's brethren ; and thou shalt cause the inheritance of their father to pass unto them."—*Num.* xxvi. 53–56, xxvii. 7.

"If thy brother be waxen poor, and hath sold away some of his possession, and if any of his kin come to redeem it, then shall he redeem that which his brother hath sold. And if any man have none to redeem it, and himself be able to redeem it, then let him count the years of the sale thereof, and restore the overplus unto the man to whom he sold it ; that he may return unto his possession. But if he be not able to restore it to him, then that which is sold shall remain in the hand of him that hath bought it until the year of jubilee : and in the jubilee it shall go out, and he shall return unto his possession."—*Lev.* xxv. 25.

By this law, a certain amount of landed property was inalienably secured to every family in Israel ; and the same thing was secured to every free-born Briton, whether male or female, by the Druidical law.

2. "There are three privileged conventions that have a right to the homage of all who apply for protection, employment, or honor, or the benefit which results from art and the sciences, according the privilege and equality of these conventions respectively :

"First, The convention of the bards of the Isle of Britain, which requires the respectful homage of every person that seeks the advantages arising from the art and science of bardism, and of all who are under the protection of that convention, according to the regulations of its offices and privileges.

"Second, The convention of the king or lord of the district, with his jurors, judges, and barons,—that is, every Briton who is a landed proprietor, thus assembled for the purpose of forming a court and deciding on legal causes.

"Third, A convention assembled for INDEPENDENCE, which is a collective assembly of the country and its dependencies : *and to this the two others owe homage and the preservation of their privileges.* For though the convention of the bards is the most ancient in dignity, and from which proceed all knowledges, yet the convention of the collective power of the country and its dependencies *takes* PRECEDENCE *by right of* POWER *and necessity,* for the regulation and establishment of justice, privilege, and protection, in the country, and the neighboring country, and the annexed and separate territories in alliance. *Without this general constitutional assembly, the other two could possess neither privilege nor power :* for this general court of legislation possesses three glorious qualifications—that is to say, it consists of the *wisdom, the power, and the will* of country and dependency, clan and clan united, to make, amend, and confirm law and union. *This general convention controls all other right of determination, power, law, or authority, so that none is equal to it.*

3. "There are three things which must not be done but by the consent of the country, the neighboring country, and in particular the nation : abrogating the king's law ; dethroning the sovereign ; *and teaching new doctrines, and new regulations in the convention of the bards.* For these things (that is, the teaching of new doctrines, &c.) must not be done until the country and tribe understand their nature, tendency, and regular order, according to judgment formed by the instructions of authorised learned and wise men, who are regularly inducted teachers in the efficient convention of the bards of the Isle of Britain. All doctrines which are contrary to reason are vain, and no good can result from them ; nor is there law, nor order, nor art, nor any kind of reason to be derived from knowledges, however plausible they may appear, which by illustration and learning cannot be shown to be true. From truth illustrated and seen, teachers and wise men of acknowledged learning have found in them judgment, and knowledges, and authority, according to the privileged regulations of the country and nation."—*Triads of Social State.*

These triads give abundant proof that they were framed by good and wise men, whose object was to promote the public good, rather than their own aggrandizement. In no country, in the present day, do we find a more elevated form of republican government than that established in Britain in the days of the Druids ; when every free-born Briton, both male and female, by right of birth, enjoyed a small estate, and had a vote in the councils of the nation, the voice of the people being the highest authority in the land.

. "The Cymbric acre," observes Mr. James, "was nearly equivalent to two English acres, statute measure, being 160 square perches of 20 feet each; so that each free man and woman, by right of birth, had between nine and ten acres of ground, which in those primitive times, when men had few artificial wants, were a little estate."

Such privileges Christian England, though first among the nations of Europe, never knew; nor is it likely she will ever know them, nor anything equivalent to them, until the influence of the New Dispensation is properly felt, both by the governors and the governed of the land. It is the power of Divine Truth only, descending from God out of heaven, and reigning in the hearts of men, that will establish order, and charity, and peace, and prosperity among the nations of the earth, when each one will enjoy the rights and privileges which Divine Providence designs that man should enjoy. The laws and government of the Druids clearly show that the power of this truth was not unfelt by them, nor by the people whose ministers and governors they were.

The Druids had their stated seasons for worship and religious adoration, at which time the people were called together by the sound of the horn or trumpet, according to the instruction afterwards given to the sons of Israel: "And the Lord spake unto Moses, saying, Make the two trumpets of silver, that thou mayest use them for the calling of the assembly. And when thou shalt blow with them, all the assembly shall assemble themselves to thee at the door of the tabernacle of the congregation," &c.—*Num.* x. 1–10.

TRIADS.

1. "There are three horns (or trumpets) for mutual progression: the horn of harvest, the horn of war, and the horn for religious adoration." Parallel with this is the Mosaic institute: "If ye go to war in your land against the enemy that oppresseth you, then ye shall blow an alarm with the trumpets. Also in the days of your gladness, and in your solemn days, and in the beginning of your months, ye shall blow with the trumpets."

2. "There are three causes for the good wishes of the country: the horn of march, a shout in the court, and the silence of religious adoration.

3. "There are three mutual friendly progressions: an assembly of the country and parents, organizing the laws and administering justice to the neighboring country; bards teaching

knowledges where they meet in convention ; and the mutual greetings of a tribe that meets for religious adoration upon the solemn festivals.

4. "There are three things common in the country : wars, legal disputes, and religious adoration ; and information of these shall be sent to every free-born Briton,—therefore they are called the three common occasions for meeting.

5. "There are three common rights of the neighboring country and the bordering country : a large river, a high road, and a place of meeting for religious adoration ; and these are under the protection of God and his peace so long as those who frequent them do not unsheath their arms against those whom they meet. He that offends in this respect, whether he be a citizen or a stranger, shall be visited with a fine of murder, upon application to the lord of the district."

6. "There are three places in which it is not allowed a man to appear with naked arms : the first is in a meeting of religious adoration, according to the privilege of the bards of the Isle of Britain, under the protection of God and his peace ; the second is in the national court of judicature, and the court of the country and lord of the district ; and the third is a guest where he is entertained under the protection of God and the king."

From the above triads we learn the following particulars. The Druids had their meetings for religious worship and solemn festivals ; the people were called together upon those occasions by the blowing of the horn ; they observed silence whilst they were engaged in religious adoration ; their public worship and places of adoration were open to strangers and the neighboring inhabitants, and protection was afforded by the laws of the land to all who met on such occasions. And we learn from the triads which speak of the orders and duties of the bards, that the people in these meetings received religious instructions from the priests. The character of this instruction we learn from the triads which speak of the object and glory of bardism, which was, to dispel ignorance—prevent disorder, plunder, and violence—diffuse knowledge—promote learning —make truth manifest—reform manners and customs—secure the triumph and establishment of peace, and praise all that is good and excellent.

The Druids were emphatically sincere lovers of truth, liberty, justice, order, and peace. One of their grand maxims was—

"The Truth in opposition to the World."

Another was—

" In the Face of the Sun, and in the Eye of Light."

Agreeably to the sentiment of this last motto, they held all their public meetings or conventions in open temples, concerning which we shall speak hereafter : thereby representing in their act that they received all their knowledges and wisdom from God, represented by the sun, to whom all their thoughts and deeds were known, and that the light and heat they received from him they sought to impart to all others, as by them expressed in the doctrines of their triads.

As ministers of religion, governors, and men of science, they wore appropriate robes, each order having its appropriate color, corresponding with and representing his particular function. These dresses are beautifully described by Mr. James in his treatise, and we cannot do better than transcribe from him, omitting, however, some of his remarks, and giving our own views of their correspondence.

COSTUME OF THE BARDO-DRUIDIC ORDERS.

1. " *Of the Druid-Bard.*—His dress was pure white. Taliesin* calls the dress of this order 'the proud white garment which separated the elders from the youth.' But several French authors assert that the white garment of the continental Druids had a purple border.

" *A Druid in full costume.*—On his head, a garland or crown of oak leaves ; in his right hand the crescent, or the first quarter of the moon, to signify that the time of the festival had arrived ; around his neck, a string of white glass beads, called Glain ; short hair, long beard, and a linen robe of pure white flowing down from the shoulders to the ancles, differing in shape from the surplices which are now worn by the ministers of religion, in that one side folded over the other in front and was fastened by a loop and button at the shoulder like a cassock ; the sleeves were also open on the upper side along the arm as far as the shoulder, disclosing at once the tunic or white jacket worn underneath, which had tight sleeves with cuffs turned up at the wrists, and cut in points. The crescent was of pure gold.

2. " *The Chief or Privileged Bard.*—The distinguishing dress of this order was the uni-colored robe of sky-blue. Thus Cynddelw in his ode on the death of Cadwallon, calls these bards 'wearers of long blue robes.' And since the sky without a cloud appears serene, and exhibits to an advantage its vivid blue, this color was the best that could have been chosen as

---

* Taliesin was a Druid-bard, and wrote many poems.

an emblem of peace, of which the bards were professedly the advocates and heralds.

"*A Bard in full costume.*—In addition to the robe we have just described, the privileged bard, on all occasions that he officiated, wore a cowl or hood of the same color, as a graduated badge or literary ornament. This custom was borrowed from the British bards by the Druids of Gaul, and from them by the Romans. Whence this cowl, on its being made use of at Rome obtained the name of 'Bardo-cucullus,' or the bard's hood, which was adopted by the monks, and is still worn by the Capuchin friars. But the dress of the bards differed a little in shape as well as in color from that of the Druid-order. It seems to have been more open in front, and with narrower sleeves, lest they should be in the way when the bard had occasion to play on the harp. Around his neck was a string of blue glass beads, called, as before, the Glain. His hair was short and his beard was long, similar to the Druid or priest.

"The original British harp was strung with hair, and consisted probably of the same number of strings as the ribs of the human body, viz. twelve. And such harps were used at first by scholars so late as the tenth century, as appears by the laws of Howel the Good, who directed a fee to be paid to the master of the art when the minstrel left off playing on them.

3. "*The Ovate.*—The dress of this order was green, the symbol of nature, the mysteries of which the Ovate was considered more particularly to study, as the physician of the tribe. He studied astronomy, the revolution of the seasons, and the use of letters, but, above all, the productions of nature, with a view to ascertain their medicinal qualities. Taliesin, in one of his poems, makes an Ovate to say, 'With my robe of light green, possessing a place in the assembly.' He also had a cucullus or hood attached to his robe. and a string of green glass beads around his neck, and a staff with a golden top in his hand, which measured about five feet six inches—a badge of his being an honorary member of the Bardo-Druidic institution. His beard was also long, and his hair short. With the people it was otherwise. Their hair was allowed to grow like that of Absalom, and their beard was kept close, except on the upper lip.

"*The National Druid in his Judicial Habit.*—He was clothed in a stole of virgin white, over a closer robe of the same that was fastened by a girdle on which appeared the crystal stone, which was incased in gold. Hence Taliesin says, 'O thou with pure gold upon thy clasp.' Round his neck was the breastplate of judgment, in the form of a crescent with a full moon or circle fixed to each point, so as to present an even superficies to the spectators. Below the breastplate appeared the string of white glass beads set in gold. Encircling his temples was a wreath of oak leaves, and a tiara of pure gold in the form of a crescent placed behind it, the narrow points of which were concealed behind the ears, whilst the broad or middle part presented a bold front over the crown of the head. On the middle finger of the left hand was a ring, and a chain ring on the next to it, while the hand itself rested on the Peithynin or Elucidator, supported by an altar of stone. This Elucidator consisted of several staves called faith-sticks or lots, on which the judicial maxims were cut, and which being put into a frame were turned at pleasure, so that each staff or bar, when formed with three flat sides, represented a triplet; when squared or made with four flat sides, a stanza. The frame itself was an oblong with right angles.

" The appearance of the National Priest in his judicial robes was splendid and imposing; inferior certainly to the Jewish High Priest, but not altogether dissimilar in the distant view of him."

Before we examine the representatives and correspondences of the Druidic vestments, we shall first inquire into the meaning of the names by which the different orders were designated. The word translated Druids, is, in the original Derwyddon, a compound of Derw, an oak, and Gwyddon, wise men. The Druids worshiped in oak groves, which fact must be taken into consideration in seeking for the correspondence of their name. The signification of oak groves is thus given by Swedenborg : "Oak groves represent and signify perceptions, but such as are human from scientifics, and from the first rationals thence deduced. What perception is at this day, is a thing most unknown, because at this day no one is in the perception, in which the ancients were, and particularly the most ancient ; the latter of whom from perception knew whether a thing was good, and consequently whether it was true. Such perception was lost when man was no longer in celestial ideas ; and instead thereof conscience succeeded, which is a species of perception. The perception of conscience, however, is not from the good which flows in, but from the truth, which, according to the holy of man's worship, is implanted in the rational from infancy, and is afterwards confirmed." (*A. C.* 2144.) Since, therefore, oak groves signify perceptions from scientifics, and from the first rational thence deduced, and since the perception of conscience is from truth implanted in the rational from infancy, and afterwards confirmed, the perception of conscience in the rational, which is deduced from the truth or scientifics of the natural, must necessarily be the perception which is signified by the oak groves. Derwyddon, therefore, denotes wise men who are in such perception. Such a man, the Druid, who was the teacher of the people, is described to be. "From truth illustrated and seen, teachers and wise men of acknowledged learning, have found in them judgment, and knowledges, and authority, according to the privileged regulations of the country and nation." Concerning those who were called wise men among the ancients, Swedenborg says, "Inasmuch as the ancients were in representatives and significatives of the Lord's kingdom, in which kingdom is nothing but celestial and spiritual love, they had also *doctrinals*, which treated solely *concerning love to God and charity towards the neighbor*, from which doctrinals they were also *called wise*." (*A. C.* 3419.) Such doctrinals the Druids had, and loved, and taught, and practised. "The Wise signify those who teach the Word." (*Ap. Ex.* 1179.) Bardd (translated Bard) literally means, one that illustrates, or master of wisdom. (*Wm. Owen.*) A priest, a philosopher. (*Dr. W. Richards.*) Ofydd (translated Ovate) a scientific person, a natural philosopher. (*Titus Lewis.*) The term Bard was common to the three orders, each one being distinguished by its appropriate prefix; the Ovate Bard, the Presiding or Privileged Bard, and the Druid Bard; these names being expressive of the distinctive function of each. "Each of the orders had a peculiarity of estimation. Thus the Privileged (or Presiding) Bard was peculiarly the ruling order—the Druid Bard, the religious functionary—and the Ovate Bard, the literary or scientific order." (*Wm. Owen.*)

The robes worn by these priests, or men of wisdom, were of fine linen. "Linen signifies the truth of spiritual love. Fine twined linen, signifies truth from a celestial origin, or the intellectual quality of the spiritual man, or which is an angel in the Lord's spiritual kingdom." (*A. C.* 9873, 9596.)

The Druid or teaching-priest was robed in pure white. "White is predicated of truths, by reason that it derives its origin from the light of the sun." (*A. R.* 167.) The Druids say that truth and light are one.

The ruling-priest was robed in blue. "Kings signify the truths of the Word, and rulers the good thereof." (*Ap. Ex.* 811.) Hence ruling priests correspond to the goods of the church. "Blue is twofold, from what is red or flaming, and from what is white or lucid: that which is from red is the celestial love of truth, or the external of the good of the celestial kingdom: but that which is from white or lucid is the spiritual love of good, or the internal good of the spiritual kingdom." (*A. C.* 9870.) Sky blue evidently corresponds to the latter.

The Ovate, or scientific priest was robed in green. "Green ignifies the scientific and sensual principle." (*A. C.* 7691.)

On the head of the chief Druid was a garland of oak leaves, and a tiara of pure gold. "The leaves of the oak denote scientifics and knowledges of truth." (*Ap. Ex.* 504.) A crown of stars denotes intelligences; a similar signification, though inferior in its character, is evidently represented by the garland of leaves. "A crown on the head signifies wisdom, and a golden crown wisdom proceeding from love."(*A. R.* 189, 235.) This crown being in the form of a moon, denotes the wisdom of the spiritual church, which is signified by the moon. The leaves of the oak and the crown of gold, were evidently significative of the knowledges of the law, and the wisdom which decided according to that law. The breastplate of judgment had not the stones which were in Aaron's breastplate; but in lieu the crystal stone was fastened to the girdle, incased in gold; thus representing truth shining forth from good, for the stone represented transparent truth, and the gold and the girdle from which it shone, the good of love which unites or conjoins, and thus preserves the church in order. The necklace of white glass beads set in gold, signified the conjunction of interior principles with exterior, and that consequently all judgment was by virtue of divine truth from the Lord. "Necklace is significative of the conjunction of interior things with exterior." (*A. C.* 5320.) We cannot enter into an explanation of the Elucidator, until we have first given an explanation of the faith-sticks of which it was first composed, which will be done hereafter. Taking into consideration the difference which existed between the two dispensations, there is certainly a remarkable agreement between the representatives of the Druidic Priesthood and those of the Jewish Church.

(*To be continued.*)

EXTRACT.

" The doctrines of the Most Ancient Church consisted solely in the explanation of the significative or enigmatical representations of terrestrial objects; thus they taught that mountains, morning, and the east, signified celestial things and the Lord; and trees of different kinds, with their fruits, denoted man, and what is celestial in him; and so in other instances. Such were the doctrinals collected from the significatives of the Most Ancient Church, which also imparted a typical character to their writings; and as in these representatives they admired and seemed to themselves even to behold what was divine and celestial, and also because of their antiquity, worship grounded in them was begun and permitted. This was the origin of their worshiping upon mountains, in groves, and in the midst of trees, and of their erecting statues in the open air; until at length they built altars, and offered burnt-offerings, which afterwards became the principal characteristics of all worship."—*A. C.* 920.

ARTICLE II.

THE LAWS OF CREATION.

SPIRITUALLY AND NATURALLY CONSIDERED.

No. I.

By the habitual use of terms to which we attach little or no definite meaning, we become insensible to the palpable absurdity which they frequently involve. Perhaps we have been accustomed from our childhood to hear them reiterated from the sacred desk, clothed with the authority of religion, and have let them pass as things not to be too closely scrutinized by the eye of reason. We have heard them so long as Bible language, that we really begin to believe that they are somewhere to be found in it. There is a story told of a good prelate who had written his sermon from the text, "In the midst of life we are in death;" not doubting but that he could turn to the chapter and verse in the Bible where it might be found. But what was his surprise when a brother clergyman, happening into his study, called his mind to the fact that he had taken his text, not from the Bible, but from the burial service of the Church!

So it is that we are too apt to take things for granted without testing them either by common sense or rationality. The most absurd dogma needs only be asserted as a religious fact for a few ages, to be so recognized by everybody of sound faith; and to call it in question, after being consecrated by the dust of some generations, is to write yourself down Infidel, in the estimation of the defenders of the faith once delivered to the saints.

Of this class of admitted propositions which never have and never can be demonstrated, is the tenet, *that God created the universe out of nothing.* This is recognized by philosopher and theologian as the first axiom in religion and philosophy— a truth to be admitted at the outset, and to deny which is to deny the existence of the universe. Assuming that there was a time when nothing existed, they jump to the conclusion that whatever began to exist thereafter, must have been spoken into being from absolute nothing by the fiat of the Almighty, not heeding the enormous absurdity and palpable contradiction which they are forced to swallow. They have adopted the convenient, and as it seemed to them, necessary conclusion, without ever placing before the mind's eye the glaring inconsistency which the very terms involve. Of nothing we can simply say that it is *nothing,* or *not any thing,* neither can anything be manufactured from it. No idea can be formed of it. Nothing but nothing can be predicated of nothing.

The following from Swedenborg casts some definite rays into this hitherto dark region, where philosopher and divine have groped their way together.

" It is commonly said, that the world in its complex was created out of nothing, of which nothing an idea is entertained as of absolute nothing ; but out of absolute nothing, nothing is made, or can be made. This is a manifest truth. Wherefore the universe, which is an image of God, could not be created but in God from God : for God is esse itself, and that which is, must exist from an esse : to create what does exist, from nothing, which does not exist, is an absolute contradiction." (*D. L. & W.* 55.)

And again he says—" *That the Lord from eternity, who is Jehovah, created the universe and all things therein from Himself, and not from nothing.*"

" Every one who thinks from clear reason, sees that the universe is not created from nothing, because he sees that it is impossible for anything to be made out of nothing ; for nothing is nothing, and to make anything out of nothing is a contradiction, and a contradiction is contrary to the light of truth, which is from the divine wisdom ; and whatever is not from the divine wisdom is not from the divine omnipotence. Every one who thinks from clear reason, sees also that all things were created out of a SUBSTANCE which is *substance in itself*, for this is the real esse from which all things that are can exist : and as God alone is *substance in itself*, and thence the real esse, it is evident that the existence of things is from no other source." (*Ib.* 282, 283.)

Here we have some definite, tangible, and rational ideas as to the source and origin of all things. Instead of being put off with the incomprehensible and irrational proposition that God spoke the universe into existence from nothing, since which time it has kept on its way by the eternal laws then impressed upon it ; we learn that it was created *in God from God*, or rather is continually being created and proceeding from Him as the infinite esse, or universal substance, from which all things are and subsist.

God is called esse itself, meaning thereby that He is or has life in and of Himself, which is the fountain of all life, and that all things must thence have begun in Him and flowed from Him. And since we cannot conceive of anything originating from nothing, but from the nature and constitution of our minds, are compelled to refer the origin of everything to a *substance*, therefore, our author declares that God is the one universal substance, in which all things have their origin and from which they subsist.

"There is but one only substance, which is really substance, and all things besides are formations from it. That one only substance rules throughout the formations not only as form, but also as non-form, such as form is in its origin. Unless this were so, it would not be possible for anything formed to subsist and act." (*A. C.* 7270.)

"What!" methinks I hear philosopher and divine exclaim, startled from their slumbers amid dust and darkness, by this ray from the eternal Sun—"God a substance! God a form! God, whom we are to think of as a Being, '*without body, parts, or passions,*' whom Bishop Beveridge calls 'the most pure and simple act,' or 'a pure idea,' of whom ' we are not to form any picture or idea in our minds,' and whom Peter Charron tells us we are to think of as ' a *luminous abyss,* without bottom, without shore, without banks, without height, without depth, without laying hold of or attaching itself to anything that comes into the imagination.' Who calls such a God substance and form does but rave."

We might reply that our Bible has talked to us ever since we could read it, and does now talk to us of a God who has eyes, ears, nose, mouth, tongue, arms, hands, legs and feet ; in a word, it describes Him as possessing *all* the organs and functions which he has given his creature man. It tells us of those who looked upon the Lord as having no *form or comeliness,* but it does not sanction such ideas of Him ; while, at the same time, it is clear from the nature of the subject, that all those ideas of *form, corporeal attributes,* &c., which involve the conception of *space* or·*matter,* are to be carefully excluded from our thoughts.

But the shock which our old vague notions and prejudices experience at the suggestion of the tangible and practical idea that God is very form and substance, ceases to disturb us just in proportion as we gain a correct view of what form and substance are. Neither of these terms are used by our author in their ordinary sense, but in a sense wholly abstracted from space, and from all properties of bodies belonging to space. He elaborately demonstrates that God, such as He is in Himself, is neither in time nor space. Indeed the very idea of his infinity precludes such a notion of Him, for the essential elements of space and time imply limitation. In all our inquiries, therefore, into the nature of God, as well as of his spiritual world, we must elevate our minds above the conditions of time and space, if we would gain any adequate conceptions of either the one or the other.

How then can God be essential substance and form if we

cannot attach to him any idea of space, nor conceive of him as limited by any of those outlines, boundaries, and peripheries, which we have commonly regarded as essential conditions of form?   We answer that metaphysicians and philosophers have used the terms *substance* and *form* in altogether too low and material a sense. They have made one nearly synonymous with *matter*, and the other with *shape*. But surely when we speak of the *substance* of a discourse, we attach no idea of materiality to the term; nor when we talk of the *form* of the constitution or government, do we mean their shape as determined by boundaries addressed to the natural senses. In either case we convey an idea wholly devoid of space and materiality. Substance, as thus used, signifies the essential qualities or properties which characterize the discourse; and form, as applied to government or society, designates the adaptations and designs to accomplish certain ends and uses.

So Jehovah or Essential Divine Love, is Essential Universal Substance, not that He is objective to touch or any of the other senses, nor that He is the universal substratum of nature, but because, being the one only cause in whom all things originate, *He alone subsists*, or has life in Himself, and from Himself continually imparts life to all things, upholding and sustaining them in being by His omnipotence. This power of *self-subsistence* and of sustaining all things in being, which is perpetual creation, can belong only to God, and belongs to Him as the Divine Substance. In this sense, which is that put upon it by Swedenborg, the term substance, when applied to the essential Being of God, simply means the one *sustaining* life of all that is created.

Having spoken of the Divine Esse as the Universal Substance from whom all things are created and sustained in being, let us next consider that passage in which it is said that this one only substance rules in all things that are formed from it, not only as *form*, but also as *non-form*, such as form is in its origin.

This passage appears at first sight quite enigmatical; but it is only necessary to give a definition of form both in relation to mind and matter, to see that, considered in its essence, it is *non-form*, or is devoid of form.

The form of a natural body in space is the general boundary to its dimensions, which the senses perceive, and by which the object is presented as a whole, and distinguished from other natural objects. But *form*, in relation to the human mind, as it is not an object to be determined by sight, touch, or any of the other senses, must be conceived of aside from the conditions which belong to space. The form of the mind is the concurrent tendency, and adaptation of the mental faculties to specific ends, by which it is contemplated as a unity, and distinguished from other minds.

Natural forms are the limitations of matter; mental or spiritual forms are the limitations of mind in will and intellect, and the specific extent of its powers. The peculiar determination of the powers of the mind is its form, as the peculiar arrangement of the particles and their limitations determine the form of material objects.

All form, whether natural or spiritual, originates in the Divine Mind, and limitation is its essential property. But the Divine Mind is infinite and unlimited, both in its essence and in its operation, and hence, it is rightly said, that Form, in its origin, is devoid of Form, that is, devoid of the limitations and boundaries of natural Forms, and also of the limited powers and capacities of spiritual Forms. But still the Divine Esse is to be considered as Essential Form, because in Him are the initiaments of all forms, and the inherent tendency to produce them, whether spiritual or natural. That life, which is devoid of limitation and hence of form in Him, assumes a form in the very act flowing into, and being received by, finite beings, which form is determined by the extent of capacities in the recipient subject.

The sum of what we have remarked is, that the Lord Jehovah is *the Essential Substance,* as subsisting independently of all things which proceed from him by a perpetual efflux, as the stream from its fountain, and are sustained in being by His omnipresent life; and He is the *Essential Form,* because the determinations and tendencies to all forms, both spiritual and natural, originate in Him.

Now, according to the philosophy o f Swedenborg, the Lord, who is Essential Love and Wisdom, created all things from His Divine Love, or Essential Being, through His Divine Wisdom, thus from His own Substance or Self; and it is the Divine Wisdom which, as a medium, determines the Divine Love, or Essential Substance, to specific forms. "The truth is," says our author, "that love and wisdom are a real and actual substance and form, and constitute the subject itself."—*D. L. & W.* n. 10.

Taking these as the substance and source of creation, let us next inquire by what laws they become "the subject itself" in the recipient. Says Swedenborg, in his Angelic Wisdom concerning the Divine Love; "In consequence of the Divine Essence itself being love and wisdom, man has two faculties of life, from one of which he has his understanding, and from the other his will. The faculty from which he has his understanding, derives all it has from the influx of wisdom from God; and the faculty from which he has his will, derives all it has from the influx of love from God.—Wherefore if those faculties were taken away, *all that is human would perish*, which consists in thinking and in speaking from thought, and in willing and in acting from will. Hence it is evident that the Divine resides with men in these two faculties, which are the faculty of being wise, and the faculty of loving."—n. 30.

There is deep philosophy here,—so deep that the New Church reader has not always fathomed the depths of the fountain of truth here presented to him.

The main purport of the paragraph is, that man is man, that is, distinguished from all other existences by reason of the possession of the two faculties of loving and thinking, in consequence of his being receptive of the love and wisdom of God.

The will and the understanding, according to our author, are essential conditions to the reception of the Divine Love and Wisdom from which all things are created. Indeed, "if those faculties were taken away, all that is human would perish." They are therefore, the sole recipients of love and wisdom, that is, Life from the Divine. They are essential mediums of that life through which alone it can flow forth and create. Strike them out of being, and all creation would perish, for creation is but a continual influx of life from the Divine through these faculties, and these faculties are *humanity*. No other creature possesses these faculties but man ;—neither beast, bird, fish, nor insect, nor any form in the *animal kingdom ;*—neither tree, shrub, plant, flower, nor any form in the *vegetable kingdom ;*—nor yet any earth, mineral, or any form whatsoever in the *mineral kingdom.* "Beasts have no ideas nor thoughts," says our author.—*T. C. R.* n. 335. And again, "Beasts have no perception and appropriation of the Divine Being."—*A. C.* n. 5114. Man alone is a recipient of the love and wisdom of the Lord ; he alone was created in His image and likeness. "From the Lord with man there are created and formed two receptacles and habitations of himself, which are called the will and the understanding, the will for his divine love, and the understanding for his divine wisdom.--*D. L. & W.* n. 358.

But love and wisdom are the essential elements of all creation. Yet man alone possesses faculties receptive of them. The human mind, therefore, as being, by virtue of its two faculties, receptive of creative life, it is within *that*, that we must look for the principles which give birth to the seemingly extraneous objects both of the spiritual and natural world. In other words, if the human mind is alone receptive of the Divine Love and

Wisdom from which all things exist, there can be no such thing as an influx into nature extraneous to man; but the constituents of humanity, the will and the intellect, must be the medium of all creations, as well in the natural, as in the spiritual world. That the mind is the medium of spiritual creations, that is, that they are outbirths of the thoughts and affections of the spiritual mind, every one, at all conversant with the writings of Swedenborg, readily acknowledges. But that natural creations are equally outbirths of the thoughts and affections of the natural mind, taking their rise upon the natural plane or degree of the mind from the same influent Life which calls forth spiritual objects upon the spiritual or interior degree of the mind, is not so generally acknowledged. But this conclusion follows from all the principles of our author. THE LAW OF CREATION IS ONE AND UNIFORM. Nature is not receptive of life; it is dead. The stream of life is not divided. As it is first received by the human mind, so it flows through and is modified by that, and upon the spiritual and natural degrees of the aggregate human mind as a theatre, produces the spiritual and natural worlds. They both have an *internal origin.*

To state our position here in full: we say that man, not individual but universal man, as to his mind, which is the real man, is an inhabitant of both the spiritual and natural worlds; of the spiritual in the interior or spiritual degree of his mind, and of the natural in the sensuous or natural degree; that the creative life flowing into the higher or spiritual region of his mind, there calls forth, by a divine law, the varied objects of his spiritual world, which, really existing within, are projected, as it were, without, and there seen as if extraneous to the beholder; and that the same creative life, in its further progress into the natural and sensuous region of the mind, there, by the same law, gives rise to all the phenomena of the natural world, the only difference between which and the spiritual world is, that in the one case the objects are spiritually perceived, and in the other naturally or sensually. But I am impressed with the overwhelming magnitude of the subject I have dared to propound, and in vain should I, or any other unilluminated man, seek to convey anything like an adequate idea of it, had not Swedenborg gone before and pointed out the principles, and made the path so plain, that any reader of ordinary intelligence may follow him without difficulty. With him for our guide, let us first investigate the laws by which spiritual creations are effected, after which we shall be prepared to apply the same principles to the existence of the phenomena of the natural world.

The natural sun is known to be the proximate cause of all

natural productions from the earth, its heat and light being the essential agents concerned in these productions. Let us see if there is a *spiritual* sun whose heat and light fulfil the same offices in the creations of the spiritual world as do the heat and light of the natural sun in the natural world. In other words, what is the spiritual sun, by what law does it exist as an object of light to the angels, and what are the uses which it performs? Let us premise the remark that the same principles which apply to the existence of the spiritual sun *in* the ground of the angelic mind, but which is seen apparently as an object in extraneous space, will explain the phenomena of all spiritual existences in the other life. *The spiritual sun is the real presence of the Divine Love and Wisdom in the interiors of the angelic mind, which Divine Essence, in consequence of an imperfect receptivity, produces the appearance of space or distance, and all the sensuous phenomena of an external world.* This proposition will now be proved by extracts from Swedenborg, which will open to us the law of all internal realities and external appearances.

"The Lord is omnipresent, and is not in space; distance, therefore, is an appearance according to conjunction with Him, and conjunction is according to the reception of love and wisdom from Him; and as no one can be conjoined with him such as He is in Himself, therefore He appears to the angels at a distance as a Sun; and yet He is in fact in the whole angelic heaven as the soul in man, and so He is in every society of heaven, as well as in every angel there, for the soul of man is not only the soul of the whole, but of every part."—*D. P.* n. 162.

"The truth is, there is no actual distance between the Sun of the spiritual world, which is the first (effect) proceeding from the Lord's Divine Love and Divine Wisdom, and the angels, the distance being an appearance only, answering to their reception in its degree of the Divine Love and the Divine Wisdom. That distances in the spiritual world are appearances, follows from this, that the Divine Essence is not in space, and also that the Divine Essence, though it fills all spaces, is devoid of space, and if there be no space (in the spiritual world), there can be no distances; in other words if spaces are appearances, distances must be appearances also, for distances are distances of spaces."—*D. L. & W.* n. 109.

"It has been said that though in the spiritual world, spaces, and consequently distances, appear just as in the natural world, they are appearances agreeing with the spiritual affinities which belong to Love and Wisdom, or Goodness and Truth. Hence it is that the Lord, though He is everywhere in the heavens with the angels, appears on high as a Sun above them."—*D. L. & W.* n. 10.

"That the Lord appears in heaven as a Sun, is because he is Divine Love, from which all spiritual things exist, and, by means of the sun of the world, all natural things; it is that love which shines as a sun."—*H. & H.* n. 117.

It appears from all these extracts that the Divine Love and Wisdom of the Lord, which in themselves are infinite and hence incomprehensible by the finite mind, are yet imperfectly received into the interiors of the angelic mind; but in consequence of that imperfect receptivity, they give rise to the phenomenon of a sun, without and above them, which sun is the embodied image of the Divine Love and Wisdom of the Lord *within* their minds. The apparent distance between them and the Lord who appears as a sun, is an effect of their imperfect reception of his Love and Wisdom. There is no actual distance, and when they think of him interiorly, they think of Him no otherwise than as *in themselves.* As the recipient state of the subject determines the spiritual proximity of every one to the Lord, therefore those who are pre-eminently receptive of His divine love are nearest to Him, not in space but in state, and constitute what is called the celestial or inmost heaven; those whose minds are more receptive of His wisdom than His love, are not so near Him, because not so much imbued with His essence, and they constitute the spiritual heaven; while those who think more naturally and externally concerning Him, are at a still farther remove, and of such the natural or ultimate heaven is composed. There are not only three heavens thus determined by the spiritual capacities of reception on the part of the subjects of the Divine Essence, but there are innumerable societies in each heaven, all determined by the spiritual affinities, and congenial spheres of mind among the angels.

But this *en passant.* The principal fact in the preceding extract to which we wish to call attention is, that the Divine Love and Wisdom, in the very act of flowing into finite minds, produce the appearance of a sun at a distance like that of the earth, which, nevertheless, is *within* the minds of those who behold it. It is within, because the Divine Love and Wisdom, of which it is the first proceeding effect, are received into the interiors of their minds. If, therefore, the Sun of the spiritual world, though appearing without, really exists *within* the minds of the angels, we conclude, by parity of reasoning, that all the phenomena, or sensuous world, which they seem to look upon as extraneous to themselves, are really within their own minds, and this because they are spiritual creations from the Spiritual Sun, alike as natural creations are from the natural sun; and as this Spiritual Sun is the product of the Divine Love and Wisdom within the minds of the angels; so all the proceeding creations from that sun, are effected within the mind, though they are seen without.

We next proceed to show that the Divine Love and Wisdom constitute the heat and light of this Spiritual Sun, and that from the combined agencies of these two constituents of the Lord, or the Spiritual Sun, the seemingly outward world of the angels, with all its objects and phenomena, is produced, and thus, that every angel's heaven, and everything that appears *objective* to him, is really *subjective*, and dependent upon his state of affection and thought.

"The light of heaven is not natural, like the light of the world, but it is spiritual, for it is from the Lord as a Sun, and that Sun is divine love;—what proceeds from the Lord as a Sun, in the heavens, is called divine truth; yet it is in its essence divine good united to divine truth. Hence is light and heat to the angels; from divine truth the angels have light, and from divine good they have heat."—*H. & H.* n. 127.

"As to what concerns the origin of (spiritual) light, it was from eternity from the Lord alone, for divine good itself, and divine truth from which light comes, is the Lord."—*A. C.* n. 3195.

"It is perfectly known in heaven, but not so in the world of spirits, whence so great a light comes, viz. from the Lord; and, what is surprising, the Lord appears in the third heaven to the celestial angels as a sun, and to the spiritual angels as a moon. This is indeed the only true source and origin of light."—*A. C.* n. 1529.

"From the sun of heaven, or from the Lord, there is not only light, but also heat; but it is spiritual light and spiritual heat; the light in their eyes appears like light, but it has in it intelligence and wisdom, because it is thence; and the heat to their senses is perceived as heat, but there is in it love, because it is thence; wherefore also love is called spiritual heat, and likewise constitutes the heat of man's life, and intelligence is called spiritual light, and likewise constitutes the light of man's life.'—*A. C.* n. 3636.

"In another life these lights, and also these heats, appear to the life: the angels live in the light of heaven, and also in the heat above mentioned; from the light they have intelligence, and from the heat they have the affection of good; for the lights, which appear before their external sight, are in their origin from the divine wisdom of the Lord, and the heats which are also perceived by them, are from the divine love of the Lord, wherefore as much as spirits and angels are in the intelligence of truth, and in the affection of good, so much they are nearer to the Lord."—*A. C.* n. 3339.

Enough has now been cited to show us the constituents of the spiritual sun, that sun which is to the spiritual world what the natural sun is to the natural world. We have seen that the first effect of the influx of Love and Wisdom from the Divine into the minds of the angels, is the *appearance* of a sun without them. That sun, however, is only the effect of the combined love and wisdom operating upon the ground of their interior affection and thought. But further it is said in what has been cited, that the heat and light of this sun, flow into the minds of the angels and that from the heat they have affection, and from the light intelligence. That they flow into the angelic mind from without is, an appearance only. The reality of the matter is, divine love and wisdom, or goodness and truth which, flowing into their minds from the Lord, who is essential goodness and truth, and there giving rise to the phenomenon of an external sun, because of their imperfect receptivity, do actually operate *within* their minds, the divine goodness imparting to them life and love and affection, and the divine truth giving them intelligence, thought, and understanding. These are perceived by their sensuous faculties as heat and light, emanating from the Spiritual Sun, or the Lord. Hence in the Scriptures, as well as common speech, light is used in the sense of truth, or information, and heat, or warmth, in the sense of love or affection. That these terms are so used in common discourse ; for instance, that light when reference is had to the mind, signifies truth, instruction, or information ; we only need to instance some familiar expressions. After having a subject explained to us, we say, "I now see it clearly." The light by which we see in this case, is clearly mental light, that is, *truth,* and it is the mental eye, that is the *understanding*, that sees or perceives the fact. We also speak of *enlightening* the minds of people, of throwing *light* upon a subject, and more specifically the *light of truth.* This use of language shows clearly that truth is mental or spiritual light. Likewise that love or affection is no other than spiritual heat, is implied in such expressions as a *warm* heart, *ardent* affections, *inflamed* with anger, *heated* with zeal, &c., all which expressions show the inherent connection between *love*, or its opposite, anger, and heat as applied to the will. Because these correspond, the love which the angels receive from the Lord gives them the sensation of heat, and the wisdom or truth that of light. They are so used in Scripture, which is written wholly according to the law of correspondency, that is, of effects from causes. And as the Lord is the *truth*, He is called the *light.* Hence He said, "I am the light of the world," "I have come a light into the world," "I am the way, the *truth,* and the life," and He "was the true Light, which lighteneth every man that cometh into the world." These and hundreds of other passages, affirm the identity of the Lord who is Truth itself with spiritual or mental light.

We have now seen that the Spiritual Sun, which appears as an external object to the angels is the effect, therefore the correspondent, of divine love and wisdom acting upon the ground of their interior thought and affection, which love and wisdom are perceived by them as heat and light proceeding from that sun as an image of the Lord.

We have now to show that every object which appears to the sight in heaven, whether as animal, vegetable, or mineral,

—in fact, the whole apparently external world by which the angels are surrounded, is created by the combined agencies of the heat and light of the Spiritual Sun, which are the Divine Love and Wisdom operating and creating *within* the minds of the angels; and therefore, that all things there do really exist *within the mind*, though seen as external objects.

"The universe and all things therein were created from the Lord by the Sun of the spiritual world, because that Sun is the proximate proceeding of the Divine Love and Divine Wisdom, and from the Divine Love and the Divine Wisdom all things are."—*D. L. & W.* n. 154.

Since the Divine Love as heat, and the Divine Wisdom as light, operate *within* the mind, and through that call forth the universe and all things therein, therefore the whole external world is an image and representative of man through whose mind it proceeds. Hence our author says:

"That there is a relation to man in all things of the created universe, may indeed be known from what has been adduced, but can only be seen obscurely, whereas in the spiritual world it is seen clearly. In that world also there are all things of the three kingdoms, *in the midst of which is the angel, who sees them about him, and knows that they are representations of himself; yea, when the inmost principle of his understanding is open, he knows himself, and sees his image in them as in a glass.*"—*D. L. & W.* n. 63.

Because every thing which the angel sees is an effect *within* his mind of the creative life, but shadowed outwardly, he appears to be standing in the midst of the perpetual creations which are emanating from his mind; but he knows that they are representations of his affections and thoughts, because he perceives that they flow from within him, and when he thinks more interiorly he knows and sees *himself*, that is, his own states of life, *in them as in a glass*, because he perceives that they are effects of those states of life imaged to his view. But this introduces us directly to the psychological law by which the heavens, with all their objects and scenery, exist really within the minds of the angels, but are seen as if extraneous. Says Swedenborg:—

"The heavens are celestial and spiritual states (of the mind), and consequently the inmost states of the Lord's kingdom in the heavens, and of his kingdom upon earth, or in the church, and of every man also who is individually a kingdom of the Lord, or a church. The heavens are also those celestial and spiritual states considered in themselves, which are states of Love and of Charity, and of the Faith which is derived from them. Thus, they include all states of internal worship, as well as the whole internal sense of the Word, for these are the heavens, and are called the Lord's Throne. But all the lower states (of the mind) which correspond to these, such as lower rational and natural states, are the land, and of these celestial and spiritual states (of life) are also predicated in consequence of their corresponding to them."—*A. C.* n. 2162.

From this passage we learn that heaven is not, as is usually supposed, a place where those who were created angels reside, together with the just who have lived in this world; but it consists in a heavenly or well-ordered state of the mind, springing from the capacity which it has acquired in this world by the regeneration of its affections and thoughts, of receiving heavenly love and wisdom from the Lord. While these, in their operations upon the interior mind, call into being all the higher states of life, which are represented by the correspondential phenomena of the higher forms of life, animal and vegetable, the lower states of the mind, which suffer the creative life to flow out into its ultimate and natural spheres, constitute the ground or earth, which seems to uphold the angel, just as our ultimate and final generalizations and deductions constitute a basis or ground of mind upon which we rest.

"In another life," says Swedenborg, "representative objects are brought forth to view, in agreement with the state of the Interior Faculties, for they are correspondences. The most beautiful Forms, such as mansions and palaces, refulgent with gold and precious stones, and also gardens and paradises of ineffable beauty, appear around those spirits who are in states of Truth derived from goodness; all which Forms are from correspondences."—*A. C.* n. 10,194.

"All things in the spiritual world that appear before the eyes and other senses, are correspondences. Land animals of every kind appear there, and also birds of wing;—but these appearances are from Affections and Thoughts of Angels and Spirits, the animals from their Affections, and the birds from their Thoughts. All who are in that world know that they are correspondences, for they know to what Affections and Thoughts they correspond. That they are correspondences of Affections and Thoughts is clearly shown, for no sooner does a Spirit, or an Angel depart, or cease to think on those subjects (represented by them), than they are dispersed and gone in a moment."—*A. E.* n. 1100.

"All beasts whatever, which are mentioned in the Word, signify affections, evil and useless beasts, evil affections, but gentle and useful beasts good affections. The cause of such signification is from representations in the world of spirits, for when there is discourse in heaven concerning affections, then there are represented in the world of spirits the beasts which correspond to affections of the kind discoursed upon, which also it has frequently been given me to see; and I have sometimes wondered whence this was, but it was perceived that the lives of beasts are nothing else than affections, for they follow their affections from instinct, without reason, and are thus carried each to its own use. To those affections without reason no other bodily forms are suitable, than such as they appear in our earth; hence it is, when the discourse is about affections only, that their ultimate forms appear like to the forms of the bodies of such beasts, for those affections cannot be clothed with other forms than such as correspond."—*A. C.* n. 5198.

We have been liberal in our quotations for the sake of showing the law according to which all spiritual objects originate in the mind and are presented to the senses in corresponding forms. A few remarks will be sufficient to place the whole matter distinctly before the mind.

Starting with the observation that all correspondences sustain the relation to their prototypes of an effect to its cause, let us conceive of the human mind existing with two faculties, its will receptive of the divine love or goodness, and its understanding of the divine wisdom or truth : these, though received *within* the mind, are presented to its sensuous faculties as a Sun, whose light, which is the divine truth, enlightens the understanding, giving it intelligence and thought, and whose heat, which is divine love, vivifies the will, and calls into play all the affections. Conceive next of this spiritual heat and light acting upon the affections and thoughts, and within the mind producing all those infinite varieties, and changes, and states, which, by its laws of being, are presented upon its sensuous and natural plane in corresponding objects and forms; and thus the heat and light of the Spiritual Sun originate all spiritual products, as natural heat and light do all natural products, the two modes of accounting for their existence being the sole difference between the spiritual and the natural world.

We learn from the quotations which have been made, that every animal or object presented to the spiritual mind is the effect, and thus the correspondent of a state of interior affection or thought ; that the degree of spiritual life therein determines whether the object belongs to the animal, vegetable, or mineral kingdom ; while the limitations of thought and affection give its particular form and outlines, as well as determine its apparent distance from the beholder. Another prominent feature developed by the foregoing extracts, is the absence of fixity in spiritual objects and scenery, and the reason of this is that they are wholly the reflections or outbirths of the thoughts and affections of the mind in which they arise. Hence they continually change with the states of the mind, and give place to new objects, and thus the seemingly extraneous world by which angels are surrounded, is ever changing and ever springing into being in exact accordance with the ever varying and ever renewed states of their thoughts and affections. As their world really exists within them, and is a reflection of themselves, they are continually conscious of their own states of life, by the fresh objects springing into being on every hand. They read in the seemingly external objects around them their own internal conditions ; they see in the lovely forms presented to their view, the lovely nature of the states of mind to which they correspond, and in the ineffable variations of light and colors, they are made conscious of the exquisite purity and beauty of the truth of which their minds are at the time receptive. All these things appear in the sensuous sphere of their minds, and constitute a volume of inexhaustible and ever varying interest in which they perpetually study their own internal states and those around them, while in all they perceive and glory in that divine creative life which sustains them in being, and by its perpetual influx into their minds, perpetually creates the glorious imagery with which they are surrounded.

Such is the very faint and meagre sketch which our limits have permitted us to give, of the universal laws of spiritual life; but which, whoever will take the trouble to examine, will find beautifully and harmoniously developed in the incomparable productions of Swedenborg, who lays them open with all the circumstantial precision of an eye witness.

T. D. S.

Concluded in our next.

EXTRACT.

"Certain novitiate spirits in walking in the world of spirits first turned the face towards the East where they saw the Sun shining in his strength; and where they were under his direct rays. They then inquired of the angels respecting that Sun, whether it was the Sun which they beheld in the former world, since it equals it both in its altitude and magnitude, has a similar fiery glow, and emits heat and light in like manner; and 'if it is the same Sun,' they said, 'are we not in nature, for whence is nature but from its own Sun?' But the angels replied, 'This Sun is not the Sun of the natural world but it is the Sun of the spiritual world; from this Sun is our universe; from its light and heat angels and spirits live; from its light both we and they have intelligence, from its heat both we and they have will and love. The essence of this Sun is pure Love, and the Lord Jesus Christ. who is the God of heaven and earth, and one with God the Father, is in the centre of it. The Divine love proximately proceeding from Him and surrounding Him, appears as a Sun, wherefore by the light and heat thence proceeding he has omnipresence, omniscience, and omnipotence extending to the utmost limits of each world. But the Sun from which nature took its origin is pure fire, in the light and heat of which there is nothing of wisdom and love, consequently nothing of life, but it still ministers to life, that is, to wisdom and love, by supplying it with a containing investiture, so that its various forms may retain consistency, and enjoy the conditions of time and space, but still in appearance rather than in reality, for it is love and wisdom that affects those who are in times and spaces, and the effect is according to reception, and reception according to the affection of wisdom, and according to a life confirmed to wisdom.' Upon hearing this the novitiates exulted with joy, and said, 'We perceive our hearts to thrill with an emotion before unknown to us.' The angels replied, 'This joy itself comes to you from celestial and spiritual love and its accompanying delights which proceed from our Sun."—*Sp. Di.*, P. vii. p. 130.

ARTICLE III.

LETTERS TO A TRINITARIAN.

LETTER IV.

THE DIVINE HUMANITY.

DEAR SIR,

In the preceeding series of letters we have found ourselves conducted, by a course of independent reasoning, to substantially the same result with that which forms the grand theme of Swedenborg's disclosures respecting the nature of our Lord prior to the incarnation. We have seen that a Divine Human principle pertains essentially to Jehovah and is actually involved in every just conception of his nature.* We do not say, however, that this result, announced by Swedenborg, could ever have been attained so as to be set forth clearly and distinctly if his illumination had not led the way and put us upon the right track of inquiry. But it is important to hold the assurance that his discoveries of divine things do find a response in the oracles of our own mind, and that thus they may be, as it were, rationally verified. I shall, therefore, henceforward feel under no embarrassment in quoting his language whenever occasion shall render it expedient. The views advanced by such a man on such a subject cannot but be entitled to the gravest consideration.

Our position, be it recollected, is, that a Divine Humanity exists in Jehovah as the very condition of his being, and the only adequate idea we can form on this subject results from mentally transferring to Him the distinctive attributes of our own humanity, and supposing Him to possess them in an in-

---

* "All the angels who are in the heavens never perceive the Divine under any other form than the human; and what is wonderful, those who are in the superior heavens cannot think otherwise concerning the Divine. They are brought into that necessity of thinking, from the Divine itself which flows in, and also from the form of heaven, according to which their thoughts extend themselves around: for every thought which the angels have, has extension into heaven, and according to that extension they have intelligence and wisdom. Hence it is, that all there acknowledge the Lord, because the Divine Human is given only in Him. These things have not only been told me by the angels, but it has also been given me to perceive them, when elevated into the interior sphere of heaven. Hence it is manifest, that the wiser the angels are, the more clearly they perceive this; and hence it is, that the Lord appears to them: for the Lord appears in a divine angelic form, which is the human, to those who acknowledge and believe in a visible Divine, but not to those who acknowledge and believe in an invisible Divine; for the former can see their Divine, but latter cannot."—*H. & H.* n. 79.

finite degree. If it be objected that our humanity exists in a
finite *form*, and that we cannot conceive of an infinite human
form, I would submit whether the same difficulty does not
press upon the conception of infinite Wisdom and infinite
Love, which being substance must necessarily have a form.
These attributes you admit are, in us, an image in miniature
of the same attributes in Jehovah. But in Him they exist in
infinite measure. How then can the finite be an image of the
infinite? Yet you do not whisper the least dissent from the
divine declaration that *such is the fact.* You will perceive,
therefore, that until this fact is in some way explained so as to
subvert our main position, we cannot be expected to recede
from our ground, simply from the urgency of an objection
which presses as heavily upon your argument as upon ours.
It is certain that man was created in the image of God—it is
certain that this image consists in the possession of wisdom
and love—it is certain that these principles in Jehovah are infinite and yet must inhere in a person, and that person must be
both a substance and a form, as a substance without a form, or
a form without a substance, is a nonentity. But an infinite substance must have an infinite form, and the conception labors no
more in regard to the one than to the other. Our difficulties
on this subject arise solely from our subjection, in this world,
to the influence of the ideas of time and space. Let these be
abstracted, and let us apprehend the real truth, that God has
no relation to space—that, as Swedenborg says, he is " in
all space without space, and in all time without time,"—and
we shall be enabled to rise to a higher and juster conception of
the divine nature.*
    You see then the conclusion to which we are brought, and
which we perceive no way of avoiding but by a direct denial
of the inspired declaration, that man was made in the image
of God, or by an equally direct assertion, that as to the constituents of that image we neither know nor can know any
thing. This, however, is itself no slight assumption—to be able

---

*" That God is Man, can hardly be comprehended by those who judge all things
from the sensual things of the external man : for the sensual man cannot think
otherwise of the Divine than from the world and from the things which are there;
thus not otherwise of the Divine and Spiritual Man, than as of a corporeal and
natural one. He concludes thence, that if God were man, He would be in size as
the universe: and if He ruled heaven and earth, it would be done by means of
many, according to the manner of kings in the world. If it should be said to him,
that in heaven there is not extension of space as there is in the world, he would
not at all comprehend it ; for he who thinks from nature and its light alone, never
thinks otherwise than from an extense, such as is before the eyes. But they are
exceedingly deceived, when they think in like manner concerning heaven ; the extense which is there is not as the extense in the world."—*H. & H.* n. 85.

to know how much or how little can be known—to define the exact limits of the human powers, and to prescribe the *ne plus ultra* of their attainments. As we have seen the futility of this claim in a thousand instances in the history of the past—as the boundaries once set to the human mind have been repeatedly broken through—so we have no distrust of its continued advances in time to come. By the ampler unfoldings of nature, we believe the Deity is for ever to be more and more fully disclosed to the intelligence of his creatures, and by the laws of interpretation a more distinct and definite conception gained of the import of the terms employed by revelation to set forth his being and perfections. If he addresses men in human language, we see no reason to doubt that that language is capable of an explication which shall incessantly bring it nearer and nearer to the grasp of our faculties, and that in proportion as this is done we shall see the God of the Universe becoming more perceptibly one with the God of the Bible, which is but to say that the highest Rationalism shall eventually harmonize with the highest Revelation-ism. That this result is even now actually realized in the system of Swedenborg, we are doubtless much more ready to assert than you are to admit; but our assertion is made upon the basis of a profound examination of the whole scheme, while the denials of our opponents are put forth upon a presumption that dispenses with inquiry. This we affirm, because we never meet with objections that take the least cognizance of the fundamental grounds of our belief. They invariably skim the surface without striking into the sub-soil of the *principles* of the system.

From the conclusion hitherto reached, that a Divine Humanity pertains to Jehovah, the mind is undoubtedly somewhat relieved on the score of the *theophanies* made to the patriarchs and prophets. We see an adequate ground for these appearances having been made under the human form, and we are naturally prompted to recognise in them, though spiritually perceived, a significant foreshadowing of that subsequent manifestation which was made in the *ultimates* of humanity, that is to say, in a body of flesh and blood.* Still I can easily conceive that you are not yet prepared to apprehend the precise mode in which the asserted angelic agency is involved in these manifestations of Jehovah. Why, you ask, was any medium

---

* " The Israelitish Church worshiped Jehovah, who in himself is the invisible God (Ex. xxiii. 18–23); but under a human form, which Jehovah God put on by means of an angel; and in which form he was seen by Abraham, Sarah, Moses, Hagar, Gideon, Joshua, and sometimes by the prophets, *which human form was representative of the Lord who was to come*, therefore all and every thing in that Church was made representative also."—*T. C. R.* 786.

of communication necessary? Why was it not competent to
omnipotence to bring down the requisite revelation *directly* to
the human faculties?—a question to which I acknowledge the
difficulty of offering a reply that shall be satisfactory to a state
of mind that is not at present in accordance with the vein of
Swedenborg's spiritual announcements. To one that is, the
difficulty is comparatively slight. In attempting, however, an
answer I must revert to the distinction above stated of Love
and Wisdom in the Divine nature, on which the true solution
entirely depends. This distinction must be regarded as extremely marked in itself, though the two principles, both in
God and man, really form *a one*. Love, constituting as it does
the *esse* of being, can never be directly manifested. Though
in reality the inmost element of the being of man and angel,
yet neither man nor angel can ever come even to the interior
sight of the love which constitutes their life, as they can in regard to their thought, which is the form or *existere* of love.
There is obviously a sense in which a man may be said to *see*
his thoughts. But love is made known only by *feeling*. It
reveals itself by the sense of itself. So also in regard to the
Divine Love. It is by influx *in* every thing that lives, but it
is in it latently, as heat is in the sun's light in the season of
spring, yet it is for ever incapable of *immediate* manifestation.
So far then as this element of the Divine nature is concerned,
it is utterly inaccessible to the vision of any created being,
and no language affirming visibility, in any sense, of Jehovah,
can by possibility be understood as relating to his essential
Love, or what may be termed the fundamental ground of his
being. "That," says our author, "which proceeds from His
Divine *Esse* without a medium reaches not man, for His Divine
Esse is invisible, and being invisible comes not within the reach
of thought." So far, therefore, as *manifestation* is predicated
of Him, it must always be conceived of as referring to his Wisdom or Truth alone, which is the appropriate *form* of his
Love, just as a man's intellect is the *form* of his affection.

I am well aware of the stone of stumbling which must necessarily lie in your way from the application of the term *form* to
subjects of a purely intellectual or spiritual nature. Yet how can
it be avoided when treating of *substance?* Are not the two inseparably united? Can there be a substance without a form?
and if a spiritual substance, must it not have a spiritual form?
Is there, in fact, any real impropriety or incongruity in saying
that a man's thought is the *form* of his affection?—for surely
we understand very easily what is meant when it is said that
a man's dominant affection controls and *moulds* his thoughts,
albeit this would be termed a metaphorical expression. We

cannot, therefore, dispense with the term, even in speaking of the Deity himself, in whom Wisdom or Truth is the *form* of Love, the two constituting in unison the basis of the similitude which renders man an image of God.

If, then, it be conceded that we may speak of the Divine Truth as the form of the Divine Love or Good, the question comes before us as to the relation which subsists between the Divine Truth and the Divine Humanity previously established; the determining of which will necessarily guide our researches as to the nature of the *theophanies* we are now considering.

The grand point of inquiry is to ascertain how the idea of God, as a personal being, can come to the human mind seeing that he is infinite and man is finite, and seeing too that the Divine *Esse* or Love cannot, in the nature of things, become a subject of *immediate* manifestation. Whatever of the Divine is made directly manifest to the perception of creatures, must pertain, not to his Love, but to his Wisdom or Truth. This is a fact of great moment in the discussion—that it is the Divine *Existere* and not the Divine *Esse* which becomes cognizable to the interior vision both of men and angels, just as a man in this world becomes visible to another by means of his body, which is his *existere*, though his soul, which is his *esse*, is *in* his body. But we do not *see* the soul; we see only the body, and the *man* is manifested in the body. Now apply this to the Lord himself, in whom the Divine Wisdom or Truth, which is his *existere*, is to the Divine Love, which is his *esse*, what the body is to the soul, or the form to the substance. How can this Divine Truth manifest itself, in its personality, to the mind of man, so as to concentrate upon it his affections and by an intelligent apprehension effect a saving conjunction with itself? Must it not come before him in a *form?* And yet this form must be finited to be brought within the reach of his finite faculties. He is incapable of perceiving an infinite form. Here then is the exigency—to conceive how the infinite Divine Truth can present itself in a form to the mental perception of a man. We have, however, the advantage of having previously established the fact that Jehovah is essentially Man, or that there is in Him a Divine Human from eternity. The only difficulty is in conceiving how this Humanity, which is infinite, can make itself cognizable to an intelligence which is finite.*

In the solution of this difficulty we must necessarily elevate

---

* " That Jehovah appearing denotes the appearing of the Lord's Divine in his Human, is evident from this, that his Divine cannot appear to any man, nor ever to any angel, except by the Divine Human: *and the Divine Human is nothing but the Divine Truth which proceeds from himself.*"—*A. C.* 6945.

our thoughts to a contemplation of Jehovah as the self-existent
and eternal fountain of the efflux of Love, Life, and Light to
the universe of angels and men.   In all ideas of communication to men from this boundless source of being we must conceive of him as *flowing down* through heaven into the minds
which are formed to be receptive of his Wisdom and Love.
But when we speak of the Lord's *descending by influx,* we are
carefully to exclude all ideas of mere *local transition.*   We are
dealing wholly with spiritual conceptions, from which time
and space are to be entirely banished.   So likewise as to
heaven—the true conception will be at once destroyed if we
think of it as *a place* spatially defined.   Heaven is the aggregate states of all heavenly minds, and these states are formed
by the pervading presence of the elements of Love and Wisdom.   It is the Divine of the Lord which constitutes heaven.
" The angels taken together, are called heaven, because they
constitute it ; but still it is the Divine proceeding from the
Lord which flows in with the angels, and which is received by
them, which makes heaven in general and in particular.   The
Divine proceeding from the Lord is the good of love and the
truth of faith ; as far, therefore, as they receive good and
truth from the Lord, so far they are angels, and so far they
are heaven."   " Heaven in general with all, and in particular
with each, is a reception of the influx which is from the
Divine Essence."   Thus teaches Swedenborg, and if revelation
does not expressly *say* as much, it must assuredly *mean* it, and
" the meaning of the Word *is* the Word."   The true sense of
the Scriptures can be no other than that sense which is according to truth.

For the Lord, therefore, to *descend* through heaven is for his
Divine Truth and Good to flow through the interiors of angelic
spirits downward to the natural plane of men on earth.   But
these angels are all men, and viewed collectively they are as
one Grand Man before the Lord, for the heavenly form is the
human form.*   This results from the plastic power of the
Lord's Divine Human principle which continually tends to
produce images of itself.   The Divine is in the Grand Man of
heaven as the soul is in the body ; and as the soul manifests

---

* " That heaven in the whole complex resembles one man, is an arcanum not yet
known in the world ; but in the heavens it is very well known."   " The angels indeed do not appear in the whole complex in such a form, for the whole heaven
does not fall into the view of any angel ; but they sometimes see remote societies,
which consist of many thousands of angels, as one in such a form ; and from a society, as from a part, they conclude as to the whole, which is heaven.   For in the
most perfect form, the wholes are as the parts, and the parts as the wholes ; the distinction is only as between similar things greater and less.   Hence they say the
whole heaven is such in the sight of the Lord, because the Divine forms the inmost and supreme of all things."—*H. & H.* n. 59, 62.

itself through the medium of the body, so the Lord, before he appeared in flesh, manifested himself through the medium of the angelic heaven.* He did this from necessity, for in no other way could he approach man so as to impart to him an intelligible idea of his personal mode of existence. "Before the Lord's advent into the world, whenever Jehovah appeared, it was in the form of an angel; for when he passed through heaven He clothed Himself with that form, which is the human form; the whole heaven from the Divine *Esse* there being as one man."—*A. C.* 10,579. The human mind might indeed have otherwise formed a vague *quasi* idea of Jehovah as a boundless, formless spirit—a kind of illimitable ether— but this is not the true conception of the true God, inasmuch as is it is one that is devoid of all conjunctive virtue. Of this, however, I shall have more to say hereafter.

It was then by an angelic medium that the Lord made himself known in the early ages to his people. He inflowed into an angel and filled him with his presence and in his form revealed his own form, as far it was possible to do it. The angel was his representative for the time being, and on this ground an identity of person is often predicated of the Lord and the angel in the sacred record. This is very clearly indicated in the following passage:

"The reason why the Divine Human is called the angel of Jehovah, is because Jehovah, before the coming of the Lord, when He passed through heaven, appeared in a human form as an angel: for the whole angelic heaven resembles one man, which is called the Grand Man: wherefore when the Divine itself passed through the angelic heaven, He appeared in a human form as an angel before those with whom He spake: this was the Divine Human of Jehovah before the coming of the Lord: the Lord's Human, when made Divine, is the same thing, for the Lord is Jehovah Himself in the Divine Human. That the Lord, as to the Divine Human, is called an angel, is further evident from several

---

* "The infinite *Existere*, in which is the infinite *Esse*, they (the most Ancient Church) perceived as a Divine Man, by reason that they knew that the infinite *Existere* was brought forth from the infinite *Esse* through heaven; and as heaven is the Grand Man, therefore they could not have any other idea or perception concerning the infinite *Existere* from the infinite *Esse*, than concerning a Divine Man, for whatever passes through heaven as through the Grand Man from the infinite *Esse*, this has with it an image thereof in all and single things."—*A. C.* n. 4687.

"The Lord spake with John through heaven, and through heaven he also spake with the prophets, and through heaven he speaks with every one to whom he does speak: and this by reason that the angelic heaven in common is as one man, whose life and soul the Lord is, wherefore all that the Lord speaks, he speaks through heaven, just as the soul and mind of man speaks through his body—for there is an influx of the Lord through heaven, just as there is an influx of the soul through the body; the body indeed speaks and acts, and also feels something from influx, but still the body does nothing from itself as of itself, but is acted upon; that such is the nature of speech, yea, of all influx of the Lord through heaven into men, has been given to me to know from much experience."—*A R.* n. 943.

passages in the New Testament, where the Lord says that He wa**s** *sent* by the Father; and *to be sent* signifies to *proceed*, and *sent*, in th**e** Hebrew tongue, signifies *an angel*. That the Lord calls Himself *th**e** Sent*, may be seen, Matt. x. 40; xv. 24; Mark ix. 37; Luke iv. 43 ; ix. 48; x. 16; John iii. 17, 34; iv. 34; v. 23, 24, 36, 37, 38; vi. 29, 39 , 40, 44, 57; vii. 16, 18, 28, 29; viii. 16, 18, 29, 42; ix. 4; x. 36; xi. 41 , 42; xii. 44, 45, 49; xiii. 20; xiv. 24; xvi. 5, 7; xvii. 3 to 8, 18, 21 to 23, 25."—*A. C.* n. 6831.

> "The Infinite itself, which is above all the heavens, and above the inmosts with man, cannot be manifested except by the Divine Human, which exists with the Lord alone. The communication of the infinite with the finite is not possible in any other way: which is also the reason that when Jehovah appeared to the men of the Most Ancient Church, and afterwards to those of the Ancient Church after the flood, and also in succeeding times to Abraham and the prophets, he was manifested to them *as a man*. Hence it may appear that the Infinite Esse never could have been manifested to man, except by the Human Essence, consequently by the Lord."—*A. C.* n. 1990.

It was in the finite person of the angel that his own infinite person was, as it were, reflected, and thus brought down to the perception of the finite faculties of man, and all this from the intrinsic necessity of the case. A divine manifestation to finite man was in no other way possible. This can by no means be deemed incredible when it is considered, that even in this world the human spirit, which pervades and animates the whole material man, may sometimes display itself, in its entire present *state*, by the medium of a single member of the body—by a cast of the countenance, a glance of the eye, a curl of the lip, or a wave of the hand. The face alone, we well know, will often mirror the whole actings of the soul under the predominance of a powerful emotion or passion, and even in its repose we see depicted the ruling character of the man. "The face," says Swedenborg, "is the external representation of the interiors, for the face is so formed that the interiors may appear in it, as in a representative mirror, and another may thence know what the person's mind is towards him, so that when he speaks he manifests the mind's meaning as well by the speech as by the face." Nothing more than this is necessary to afford a solution of the title מלאך פני, *malak panai, angel of the face* (or *faces*), usually rendered *angel of the presence*, because the affection of a being is made *present* in his face. The plural form *faces* occurs in the original to denote the varieties of affection which impress themselves upon the countenance. The divine *faces*, however, imply no *absolute* variation in the divine affections, but simply the effect produced by the state of reception in the beholder, which always modifies the manifestation made to him. That this should be Swedenborg's interpretation was of course to be expected. "The Divine Esse has never appeared in any visible form (*in facie*), although his Divine Human has so appeared, and by that, and, as it were, in that, the Divine Love has appeared." "The Lord in respect to the Divine Human is called the *Angel of the faces* of Jehovah, because the Divine Human is the Divine Esse in a visible appearance, that is, in a form."

I would here remark that I see nothing in the nature of the subject or in the exigencies of the Scriptural testimony to necessitate the idea of any *particular* angel—any one angel by *pre-eminence*—as having been uniformly employed on these occasions, notwithstanding the apparently specificating force of the article *the*—"*the* angel of the Lord." Considering the infinite interval which separates the highest conceivable creature from the Creator, it is plain that no angelic intelligence could possess in himself a dignity that should peculiarly entitle him to this honor; and as the end to be attained by the assumption of the angelic medium could, to human view, be as well secured by the intermediate agency of one of this class of beings as of another, we are at a loss to perceive the grounds of the supposition to which I am now adverting. The grand fact assumed is simply that of the presence of an angel-personator in the Divine *theophanies.* So far as I can see nothing depended upon the selection for the office of one being of this order rather than another.

We are now prepared for the presentation more *in extenso* of Swedenborg's grand announcement on this theme of the Lord's *theophany* through an angelic medium. In his explanation of Ex. xxiii. 23, "My Angel shall go before thee," he thus writes;—

"The reason why the Lord as to the Divine Human [principle] is meant by an angel is, because the several angels, who appeared before the Lord's coming into the world, were Jehovah Himself in a human form, or in the form of an angel; which is very manifest from this consideration, that the angels, who appeared were called Jehovah. Jehovah Himself in the human form, or what is the same thing, in the form of an angel, was the Lord. His Divine Human [principle] appeared at that time as angel, of whom the Lord Himself speaks in John, "Jesus said, Abraham exulted to see My day, and he saw, and rejoiced. Verily, verily, I say unto thee, before Abraham was, I am," viii. 56, 58. And again, "Glorify thou Me, O Father, with Thyself, with the glory which I had with Thee before the world was," xvii. 5. That Jehovah otherwise could not appear, is also manifest from the Lord's words in John, "Ye have not heard at any time the voice of the Father, nor seen His appearance," v. 37. And again, "Not that any one has seen the Father, except He who is with the Father, He hath seen the Father," vi. 46. From these passages it may be known what the Lord was from eternity. The reason why it pleased the Lord to be born a man was that He might actually put on the Human [princi—ple], and might make this Divine, to save the human race. Know therefore, that the Lord is Jehovah Himself, or the Father, in a human form; which also the Lord Himself teaches in John, "I and the Father are one," x. 30. Again, "Jesus said, henceforth ye have known and seen the Father. He who hath seen Me hath seen the Father. Believe Me that I am in the Father and the Father in Me," xiv. 7, 9, 11. And again, "All Mine are Thine, and all Thine Mine," xvii. 10. This great mystery is described in John in these words, "In the beginning was the Word, and the Word was with God, and God was the Word; the same that was in the beginning with God. All things were made by Him, and without Him was not any thing made which was made. And the Word was made flesh, and dwelt amongst us, and we have seen His glory, the glory as of the only-begotten of the Father. No one hath seen God at any time, the only-begotten Son, who is in the bosom of the Father, He hath brought Him forth to view," i. 1, 2, 3, 14, 18: The Word is the Divine Truth, which has been revealed to men, and since this could not be revealed except from Jehovah in a man, that is, except from Jehovah in the human form, thus from the Lord, therefore it is said, "In the beginning was the Word, and the Word was with God, and God was the Word." It is a known thing in the Church, that by the Word is meant the Lord, wherefore this is openly said, "The Word was made flesh, and dwelt amongst us, and we have seen His glory, the glory as of the only-begotten of the Father." That the Divine Truth could not be revealed to men, except from Jehovah in the human form, is also clearly said, "No one hath seen God at any time, the only-begotten Son, who is in the bosom of the Father, He hath brought Him forth to view." From these considerations it is evident, that the Lord from eternity was Jehovah or the Father in a human form, but not yet in the flesh, for an angel has not flesh. And whereas Jehovah or the Father willed to put on all the human [principle], for the sake of the salvation of the human race, therefore also He assumed flesh, wherefore it is "God was the Word, and the Word was made flesh." And in Luke, "See ye My hands and My feet, that it is I myself, handle Me and see, for a spirit hath not flesh and bones as ye see Me have," xxiv. 39. The Lord by these words taught, that He was no longer Jehovah under the form of an angel, but that He was Jehovah-Man; which also is meant by these words of the Lord, "I came forth from the Father, and am come into the world, again I leave the world, and go to the Father," John xvi. 28."—*A. C.* n. 9315.

From all this, taken in connection with the train of the foregoing remark, it would seem difficult to avoid the conclusion, not only that Christ is the supreme Jehovah, but that he is Jehovah in unity, to the entire and absolute exclusion of any such *hypostases* or *subsistents* in the Divine Nature as are usually understood by the term *persons.* What possible ground can there be for such *hypostases?* If the Divine Love and Divine Wisdom as already explained, together with the Divine *procedere,* i. e. act, energy, operation of the united two, comprise the totality of the Divine attributes, and form the complement of one Divine Person, what basis remains on which to build the theory of the three distinct persons of the Trinity? What is the idea which shall answer to the language of the popular creeds on this subject?* Is there any intelligible meaning to the words Father, Son, and Holy Ghost, so long as they are made the representatives of three distinct personalities in Jehovah? We have already found the Trinity complete in one person; why, then, seek for it in three? If you say that by persons is not meant persons, but unknown *somewhats*—certain mysterious *distinctions* in the Deity to which the word *persons* is applied for the want of a better—still I would beg you to task your intellect to the utmost, and see if you can conceive of any other distinctions than those which I have designated as the three *essentials* of the Godhead; yet these three constitute, of necessity, but one person.† I know, indeed, that it is common to speak of the Son of God as the second person of the holy Trinity, and also to refer the ancient *theophanies* before spoken of to him. But the Scriptures never speak of them in this manner. They give no warrant for this peculiar attribution. They recognize only the one, absolute, undivided Jehovah as the true subject of these manifestations. They never intimate that the Angel was Christ in any other sense than that in which the alone Jehovah was Christ, and even he could not properly be then so denominated, because the *anointing* on which the title is founded did not take place till after he was made flesh: nor was he, except prophetically, termed Son prior to that event. The *Son of God* was born in time, and not begotten from eternity, as I shall produce ample ground for asserting as I proceed. All such expressions, in such relations, are *proleptical*, and even the titles *Jesus* and *Christ*, strictly considered, are now retrospective, as the character indicated by them has merged itself, by reason of his glorification, in that of the alone Jehovah or Lord. Again, then, I ask, what are the grounds of the tripersonal theory of the Godhead? Where are its sanctions to be found? You surely will not refer me to those passages of Holy Writ which assert a triplicity in the Divine Nature; for the establishment and elucidation of this is the

---

* " What means this, That the Divine is distinguished into three persons? Where is this to be found in the Word? What means this, that the Divine was born from eternity? But that the Divine is one, or one person, or one man, this is intelligible, as also that the Divine should have been from eternity. But they are to be excused for thus teaching who have known nothing of the style of the Word, that a spiritual sense pertains to every expression."—*De Dom. et de Athan. Symb.* p. 1.

† " A trine or triune God is not one God, so long as this trine or triunity exists in three persons; but he in whom a trine or triunity exists in one person, is one person, is one God, and that God is the Lord; enter into whatever intricacies of thought you please, yet will you never be able to extricate yourself and make out that God is one, unless he is also one in person."—*A. R.* n. 490.

main feature of Swedenborg's doctrine, and what I have all along assumed as the primary truth of revelation. It amounts to nothing to tell me that you are taught by the Bible to acknowledge God under the threefold character of Father, Son, and Holy Ghost. I should be very sorry indeed if you were not ; but I am brought no nearer by this confession to an apprehension of three coequal and coeternal persons in the Godhead. And yet this is the very point to which, as an opponent of Swedenborg, you have put your faith, your logic, and your exegetic in pledge. If you make not this apparent on adequate grounds, you accomplish nothing to the purpose. The question is not concerning a revealed fact—in this we are both agreed —but concerning the manner in which this fact is to be understood. What is the absolute truth couched under the inspired words ? If you still insist upon a veritable Trinity of persons, are you not bound to show that your position can stand in entire consistency with the declaration of the Divine unity contained in the following passages : " Hear, O Israel, the Lord our God is ONE Lord." "There is none good but ONE, that is, God." "ONE is your Father, which is in heaven." "There is none other God but ONE." "God is ONE." "There is ONE God, and there is none other but He." "In that day Jehovah shall be King over all the earth : in that day there shall be ONE Jehovah, and his name ONE ;" this last passage plainly implying the advent of a period when the very views promulgated by the New Church on this head shall be universal.

You will not fail to perceive the central point of my position on the whole subject : that that Divine Essence which clothed itself with a material humanity in the person of Jesus of Nazareth, was no other than the one, exclusive, absolute, and eternal Jehovah. It is a position which utterly ignores, not only the fact, but the very possibility, of any such tripersonal mode of existence in the Deity as shall constitute a ground for ascribing the assumption of flesh and blood to the *second* of these persons in contradistinction from the other two. I hesitate not to affirm that such a view of the Divine nature is not only repugnant to the clearest voice of reason, but to the most explicit teaching of the Word. Where do you find anything to warrant it ? No passages can be cited from the Old Testament bearing more directly on the question than those which I have already adduced, and these, as we have seen, both admit and demand another mode of interpretation. In the Angel Jehovah we can recognize no manifestation but that of Jehovah himself in his indivisible unity. We see not the slightest intimation of any second *hypostasis* or person of whom the *theophany* is predicated. And if this be the purport of the

Old Testament, must not that of the New accord with it? If then the tripersonal theory be attempted to be sustained by Scripture, it must doubtless be on the ground of *inference.* It is to be *inferred* that, as a Trinity is expressly taught under the threefold appellation of Father, Son, and Holy Ghost, therefore these terms must imply the distinction of three persons. But this inference not only conflicts with the inspired declaration of the absolute unity of Jehovah, but is rendered useless by our previous ascertainment of the fact, that a distinction of three Essentials in the Godhead most perfectly consists with the idea of one person; thus answering all the demands of the acknowledged doctrine of the Trinity, without doing the least violence to the genuine conception of the Unity. The question then is as to the priority of claim between an interpretation which thus recognizes a Trinity entirely consistent with the Divine Unity, and one which is wholly at war with it: for this is clearly the alternative. I cannot doubt, indeed, that you will deny the existence of such a conflict, though you will confess to an utter inability to define the mode in which it is to be avoided. On this head you will resolutely fall back upon the buttress of the literal averments of Scripture and the devout acknowledgment of *mystery* which frowns rebuke upon the prying researches of the human mind. Such a posture of spirit the man of the New Church contemplates merely as a strange psychological curiosity. He finds no demand made upon him to give an implicit credence to inspired enunciations which he cannot receive without admitting both sides of a contradictory proposition. He cannot concede, in one breath, that Jesus Christ is the supreme and only Jehovah, and in the next grant that he is but the second *hypostasis* of a nature which the intuitions of his own mind, in response to the voice of revelation, declare can admit of but one. That there *are* inferences, and those too of transcendent moment, affecting the whole schéme of Christian doctrine, to be drawn from the scriptural language in regard to the true Trinity of Jehovah, it will be my object to evince in the sequel.

At present I must be permitted to adduce from Swedenborg another paragraph fraught with most important bearings upon the general subject:

" ' Behold I send an angel before thee'—that hereby is signified the Lord as to the Divine Human [principle], appears from the signification of sending, when concerning the Lord, as denoting to proceed; in this case, to cause to proceed; and from the signification of angel, as denoting Him who proceeds, for angel in the original tongue signifies sent. Hence is the derivation of that expression; and by sent is signified proceeding, as may be manifest from the passages quoted from the Word, n. 6831. Hence it is evident, that by the angel of Jehovah is meant the Lord, as to the Divine Human [principle], for this proceeds from Jehovah as a Father. Jehovah as a Father is the Divine Good of the Divine Love, which is the very Esse ; and the proceeding [principle] from the Father is the Divine Truth from that Divine Good, thus the Divine Existere from the Divine Esse ; this is here signified by angel. In like manner in Isaiah, ' *The angel of His faces* shall liberate them by reason of His love, and His indulgence ; *He redeemed* them, and took them, and carried them all the days of eternity,' lxiii. 9. And in Malachi, ' Behold the Lord, whom ye seek, shall suddenly come to His temple, and *the angel of the covenant* whom ye desire,' iii. 1, 2 ; to the temple of the Lord is to His Human [principle] ; that this is His temple, the Lord Himself teaches in Matthew, chap. xxvi. 61 ; and in John, chap. ii. 19, 21, 22. In the Church it is said, that out of three who are named, Father, Son, and Holy Spirit, there exists one Divine [being or principle], which is also called one God ; and that from the Father proceeds the Son, and from the Father by the Son proceeds the Holy Spirit ; but what it is to proceed or to go forth is as yet unknown. The ideas of the angels on this subject differ altogether from the ideas of the men of the Church who have thought about it ; the reason is, because the ideas of the men of the Church are founded upon three, but of the angels upon one. The reason why the ideas of the men of the Church are founded upon three is, because they distinguish the Divine [being or principle] into three persons, and attribute to each special and particular offices. Hence it is that they can indeed say, that God is One, but in no case think otherwise than that there are Three, who by union, which they call mystical, are One ; but thus indeed they may be able to think that there is one Divine [being or principle], but not that there is one God ; for in thought the Father is God, the Son God, and the Holy Spirit God ; one Divine [being or principle] is one by consent and is thus unanimous, but one God is altogether one. What is the quality of the idea, or what is the quality of the thought, which the man of the Church has concerning one God, appears manifestly in the other life, for every one brings along with him the ideas of his thought ; their idea or thought is, that there are three gods, but that they dare not say gods but God ; a few also make one of three by union, for they think in one way of the Father, in another way of the Son, and in another of the Holy Spirit ; hence it has been made evident, what is the quality of the faith which the Church has concerning the most essential of all things, which is the Divine [being or principle] Itself ; and whereas the thoughts which are of faith, and the affections which are of love, conjoin and separate all in the other life, therefore they who have been born out of the Church, and have believed in one God, fly away from those who are within the Church, saying that they do not believe in one God, but in three gods, and that they who do not believe in one God under a human form, believe in no God, inasmuch as their thought pours itself forth without determination into the universe, and thus sinks into nature, which they thereby acknowledge in the place of God. When it is asked what they mean by proceeding, when they say that the Son proceeds from the Father, and the Holy Spirit from the Father by the Son, they reply that proceeding is an expression of union, and that it involves that mystery ; but the idea of thought on the subject, when it was explored, was no other than of a mere expression, and not of any thing. But the ideas of the angels concerning the Divine [being or principle], concerning the trine [*trinum*], and concerning proceeding, differ altogether from the ideas of the men of the Church, by reason, as was said above, that the ideas of thought of the angels are founded upon one, whereas the ideas of the thought of the men of the Church are founded upon three ; the angels think, and what they think believe, that there is one God, and He the Lord, and that His Human [principle] is the Divine Itself in form, and that the Holy [principle] proceeding from Him is the Holy Spirit ; thus that there is a trine [*trinum*], but still one. This is presented to the apprehension by the idea concerning the angels in heaven ; an angel appears there in a human form ; but still there are three things appertaining to him, which make one—there is his internal, which does not appear before the eyes, there is the external which appears, and there is the sphere of the life of his affections and thoughts, which diffuses itself from him to a distance ; these three [things or principles] make one angel. But angels are finite and created, whereas the Lord is infinite and increate ; and inasmuch as no idea can be had concerning the infinite by any man, nor even by any angel, except from things finite, therefore it is allowed to present such an example, in order to illustrate that there is a trine in one, and that there is One God, and that He is the Lord, and no other."—*A. C.* 9303.

You may possibly have doubts as to what is said about the difference of angelic and human ideas on this profound subject, and say that you have no sufficient evidence of the fact ; but if the thing asserted is intrinsically true, the thoughts of the angels are undoubtedly in accordance with it, and the intrinsic truth of what they are said to think is certainly in itself some evidence that they do think it, and consequently that Swedenborg's assertion on the subject is also true.   But after all, the grand question is rather what you and I *ought* to think on this theme, than what the angels *do* think, although there is every likelihood that if we think as we ought, we shall think as they do.   If there is any truth of stupendous concern to mortal man, it is that which we are now considering.   The scriptural idea of God enters into the inmost vitalities of Christian faith, and it is vain to think of enjoying him in heaven so long as the idea of his nature and perfections does not conform to the essential verity, *for the true idea of God, with its appropriate affection, is the very medium of conjunction with him, and this conjunction is the essential element of heavenly bliss.**   "The

---

* Inasmuch as the church at this day does not know that conjunction with the Lord makes heaven, and that conjunction is effected by the acknowledgment that He is the God of heaven and earth, and at the same time by a life conformable to His commandments, therefore it may be expedient to say something on this subject : he who is utterly unacquainted with the subject may possibly ask, what signifies conjunction ? how can acknowledgment and life occasion conjunction ? what need is there of such acknowledgment and life ? may not every one be saved by a bare act of mercy ? what occasion then for any other medium of salvation but faith alone ? is not God merciful and omnipotent ? But let such an one know, that in the spiritual world all presence is occasioned by knowledge and acknowledgment, and all conjunction by affection which is of love ; for spaces there are noth-

reason," says Swedenborg, "why there is no appropriation of good with those who do not acknowledge the Lord is, because for man to acknowledge his God is the first principle of religion, and with Christians to acknowledge the Lord is the first principle of the Church, for without acknowledgment there is no communication given, consequently no faith, thus no love ; hence the primary tenet of doctrine in the Christian Church is, that without the Lord there is no salvation.   Hence it is manifestly evident, that those who do not acknowledge the Lord cannot have faith, thus neither can they have love to God, consequently neither can they be saved, which the Lord also teaches openly in John : ' He that believeth in the Son, hath eternal life ; but he that believeth not the Son shall not see life, but the wrath of God abideth in him.' " And again, " The reason why they who do not from faith acknowledge the Lord, have not eternal life, is because the whole heaven is in that acknowledgment ; for the Lord is the Lord of heaven and earth ; wherefore to those who do not acknowledge Him, heaven is closed ; and he who does not acknowledge in the world, that is, who is within the Church, does not acknowledge in the other life ; such is the state of man after death."   The acknowledgment here insisted on is not a bare verbal assent to a proposition which conveys no definite meaning to the mind. It is an acknowledgment founded on a distinct intellectual perception of the truth acknowledged.   Nothing short of this is entitled to the name.   You will understand, also, that in these passages, and in Swedenborg's writings generally, the title " Lord" is the equivalent of " Jehovah," and is the peculiar and distinctive appellation of Jesus Christ, than whom neither he nor his adherents know any other Jehovah or Lord in the universe.   Swedenborg has placed the following sentence at the very threshold of his great work, the *Arcana Cœlestia*, and the remark is of the utmost importance in the perusal of every part of his writings :—" In the following work, by the LORD is solely meant Jesus Christ, the Saviour of the world, who is

ing else but appearances according to similarity of minds, that is, of affections and their derivative thoughts ; wherefore when any one knows another, either from fame or report, or from intercourse with him, or from conversation, or from relationship, when he thinks of him from an idea of that knowledge, the other becomes present, although to all appearances he were a thousand furlongs distant ; and if any one also loves another whom he knows, he dwells with him in one society, and if he loves him intimately, in one house ; this is the state of all throughout the whole spiritual world, and this state of all derives its origin from hence, that the Lord is present to every one according to love ; faith and the consequent presence of the Lord is given by means of knowledges of truths derived from the Word, especially concerning the Lord himself there, but love and consequent conjunction is given by a life according to His commandments, for the Lord says, ' He that hath My commandments and keepeth them, he it is that loveth Me and I will love him, and make my abode with him,' John xiv. 21."—*A. E.* n. 1340.

called the LORD without other names. He is acknowledged and adored as the LORD in the universal heaven, because he has all power in heaven and earth. He also commanded his disciples so to call him when he said, ' Ye call me LORD, and ye say well, for so I am.' And after his resurrection his disciples called him LORD. Throughout all heaven they know no other Father but the LORD, because he and the Father are one." This term in Swedenborg's writings is always to be understood as the equivalent of *Jehovah.** In the New Church, therefore, is to be seen the incipient fulfilment of the prediction before advert-ed to : " In that day there shall be one LORD (Jehovah), and his name one." The propriety of this title in reference to Christ I shall consider more at length hereafter. The use of it in this relation is in fact bringing forward into the Christian Church, under its last form, the distinguishing appellation of Jehovah, the God of the Old Testament, the exclusive and supreme ob-ject of worship, who alone is to be recognized in the person of Jesus Christ the Saviour. The introduction of this name as the familiar title of Jesus, when apprehended in its full import, is the signal of a complete revolution in the entire scheme of Christian doctrine built upon the assumption of a threefold dis-tinction of persons, the second of whom makes an atonement to the first. No such theory of atonement can possibly stand when once it is seen that the Jehovah of the Jew is identically one with the Jesus of the Christian ; for one Divine Person cannot make an atonement to himself. This result, however, I do not ask you to receive, till you become convinced that it is inevitable. I announce it here that you may have a more vig-ilant eye on the successive evolutions of the argument whose ob-ject it is to establish it. And I may remark, also, by the way, that it is easy to perceive how insuperable is the obstacle in the way of the Jewish mind in general to the adoption of Christianity so long as it holds forth to them a view of the Di-vine Being so utterly at war with all the conceptions of the Deity which they have formed from their own Scriptures. I do not say that they would readily embrace even the true doc-trine of the incarnation of their own Jehovah, but they must necessarily be vastly more scandalized by the dogma which presents him under a threefold *hypostasis*. A Trinity of Es-sentials in one person they might possibly be led to concede ; but a Trinity of persons, I believe, never ; and who can blame them ? As to any special display of divine influence in their

---

* Without the above explanation the title of the first chapter of the treatise con-cerning Heaven and Hell would seem to announce a most obvious truism, viz " That the Lord is the God of Heaven." This assumes a new phase when it is understood as asserting that Jesus Christ is the God of heaven.

behalf, so far as this point is concerned, we can of course have
no hope of it, if the tenet itself is false, and that it is so we
have the same evidence that we have that the doctrine of the
Divine Unity is true; for the two we hold to be in diametrical
and everlasting antagonism with each other.　　　G. B.

(*To be Continued.*)

MISCELLANY.

DR. POND AND MR. CABELL.

WE have already made our readers acquainted with the fact that Dr. Pond had
published a long and recriminating letter in the Portland "Christian Mirror," in
respect to Mr. Cabell's "Reply," and upon which we passed some strictures in
our last. Since the inditing of that article, we have received a rejoinder from Mr.
C. himself, which we hasten to lay before our readers. In order, however, to present to them a fair view of the whole ground, we have determined to publish Dr.
P.'s letter entire, as it has doubtless been little read in the circles to which the Repository finds its way, while yet our readers cannot but be desirous of seeing for themselves what manner of man our opponent has shown himself in this new specimen
of "Swedenborgianism Reviewed." We are well aware that this is a courtesy
which would never be reciprocated in the "Mirror," nor any other journal that
gives place to assaults on our belief; but as we can *afford* to have the strongest
possible objections urged against our system through our own pages, we have no
hesitation to set an example, which, at the same time, we despair of seeing followed. We beg leave also, as our object is to elicit truth, to assure Dr. P. himself and
others, that our columns will be ever open to the propounding of any *fair* and *candid* objections to the system we have espoused, since if it has any weak or preg-
nable points, we have at least as deep an interest as others in seeing them exposed.
As we profess to have read and studied the *principles* on which the whole scheme
is built, we may moreover be enabled to solve some problems that would naturally stumble the novitiate reader.

PROF. POND'S NOTICE OF STRICTURES ON HIS REVIEW OF SWEDENBORG.

In the discharge of my official duties, I am called to examine, from time to
time—in presence of the members of the Seminary, and others who may please to
attend—the peculiarities of different religious denominations; as the Unitarians,
the Universalists, the Romanists, the Episcopalians, the Baptists, the Congregation-
alists, &c. In pursuance of this work I delivered, some two years ago, a course of
lectures on Swedenborgianism. No little interest was excited, during their delivery,
among the New Churchmen of Bangor. Several individuals attended, as they had
a right to do, and the lectures were severely animadverted on in one of our daily
papers. I was charged with ignorance, with misrepresentation, with being actuated by improper motives, and with making an unprovoked attack upon a quiet and
peaceable class of Christians. The matter was deemed of sufficient importance to

be brought to the notice of the General Convention of the New Jerusalem Church in the United States. In a letter to the Convention, Mr. David Worcester of this city speaks of "the unfair and jesuitical manner in which he (the lecturer) treated Swedenborg and his writings," and adds: "Few, except those who are incurably blind from bigotry and prejudice, will be so dim-sighted as to fail to discern *the motives* by which he has been actuated."*

I proceeded, however, with my work, and in July, 1846, my Review of Swedenborgianism was published. It was shortly after reviewed in the New Jerusalem Magazine, by Theophilus Parsons, Esq., of Boston. It has subsequently been attacked, in a separate pamphlet, by a Mr. Hayden, and in the New York Tribune by Rev. B. F. Barrett. Meanwhile, it has attracted notice on the other side of the water, and drawn down upon me the wrath of Mr. J. J. G. Wilkinson, a leading Swedenborgian in London.

It was publicly announced, in May last, that a full reply to my work was in progress, by Mr. R. K. Cralle, of Virginia, and might be expected in a few months. But Mr. Cralle, it seems, was unable to fulfil his undertaking, and so turned it over to another Virginian, Mr. N. F. Cabell. The gentleman will pardon me if I do not give him titles enough, as I am entirely ignorant of his profession, his standing, or his course of life. The Reply is just now published, in a closely-printed pamphlet of 194 pages—the joint production of Mr. Cralle and Mr. Cabell.

It will be seen that my Review has attracted a good deal of notice in the Swedenborgian community, and has drawn out opponents numerous and powerful. And yet they all profess to regard it as a very contemptible affair;—one not entitled, on its own account, to the least consideration. It is vast condescension in them to notice it at all.

Perhaps I ought to make a single exception. There is one Swedenborgian in the country—the most learned, and candid, and devoted of them all—who has had the magnanimity to acknowledge, that he regards my work as " the most formidable attack that has ever been made upon Swedenborgianism;" that it is written, "with some exceptions, in a good spirit;" and that it "cannot fail to produce a very decided effect upon the Christian community."

Most of the assaults which have been made upon me, have been before noticed; and in the few remarks that follow I shall confine attention to the joint production of Messrs. Cralle and Cabell.

In Mr. Cralle's " Preliminary Letter," extending through 38 pages, very little is said either of me or my Review. It is a series of remarks in explanation and defence of Swedenborgianism, which might have been put forth in any other connexion just as well. In what he says of me, however, he is sufficiently contemptuous and abusive. He charges me with " captiousness, illiberality, and cant;" with unfair statements, and gross misrepresentations; with "gross and unwarrantable imputations;" and with " errors of inference and mis-statements of facts, to all appearances deliberate." As there is no attempt, from first to last, to make good any of these charges, I can well afford to dismiss them without note or comment. If they do not injure the writer, they will not disturb or injure me.

The author of the " Reply" proper (so far as reply it can be called), is Mr. Cabell. In my remarks on his portion of the pamphlet, I propose, first, to notice some few things which he *has* done, and secondly, others which he *has not* done.

---

* N. J. Magazine, vol. 19, p. 440.

1. In the first place, then, he has entirely mistaken the *design* of my Review, as set forth in my preface. I said expressly : " This work is not to be regarded as strictly of a *controversial* character. My purpose has been rather to *exhibit* Swedenborg than to *refute* him. If the former of these objects can be well accomplished, the latter, I have supposed, would no longer be necessary." In pursuance of the purpose here expressed, I had no occasion to go into a consideration of the explanations and defences of Swedenborg which have been put forth by his followers; and if Mr. C. had understood the matter, his frequent and severe censures of what he deems my omissions in this respect might all have been spared.

2. Mr. C. has treated me, throughout his " Reply," with the most *wanton* and *outrageous abuse ;* such as has not been witnessed in any theological discussion in New England, probably, for half a century. I am " an incarnation of arrogance," p. 66. I " habitually violate the first principles of logic, and the usual courtesies of argument," and " deserve to be unfrocked," pp. 66, 76. I am a " profound, fastidious, magnanimous critic ;" a " redoubtable champion;" " the prudish, immaculate, fastidious Dr. Pond," pp. 142, 159, 170. My arguments are no better than " vaporing," and " twaddle," pp. 60, 66. I " resort to a species of trickery as paltry as any we can find in the columns of the unscrupulous political editor ;" and " make no pretensions to a sense of justice while writing on this subject," pp. 131, 180. " Here comes a learned pundit from Bangor, who says of himself, *I am Sir Oracle !*" p. 103. I " set up my factitious virtues as a standard for others to follow, and deal out my anathemas on all who deny my authority," p. 137. In the first part of my book " only a few drops of gall are infused ;" but " towards the close the venom is poured in without scruple, and almost without disguise," p. 50. After quoting a passage from my preface, which the Searcher of hearts knows was written with the utmost truth and sincerity, he exclaims, " Ma conscience ! can the writer have hoped to deceive the most prejudiced of his readers by this thin veil of Phariseeism ? Or blinded by the intensity of his theological hate, had he actually deceived himself ?" p. 50. Such is a specimen of the abuse which this champion of Swedenborgianism delights to employ, and with which he has interlarded his pages from beginning to end. I present it, that my readers may see with what kind of a spirit I am obliged to contend, and as my apology for closing with him in the fewest words possible. I have high authority for declining any needless intercourse with a " railer." See 1 Cor. v. 11.

3. But even this is not the worst of it. Mr. C. charges me, in several instances with *deliberate falsehood,* (1.) Because I expressed the opinion that Swedenborg's fit of sickness, of which Dr. Hartley, Mr. Wesley, and others speak, " occurred near the close of the year 1744, or early in the following year"—an opinion which, in view of all the testimony, I still entertain, regarding it as far more probable than any other. My reason for it was given at large in my reply to Mr. Barrett. (2.) Because I represented Swedenborg as teaching that the spirits of heaven " not only marry, but have children;" immediately subjoining, " *spiritual offspring*, of course." Here, says Mr. C., the Professor " states what he must have known at the time to be a *deliberate falsehood.* We use the term *of purpose,* because, although we are loth to attribute such conduct to any man of respectable social position—far less to a clergyman—yet, in this instance, the fraud and its motive are both palpable ; for Swedenborg asserts the very reverse, pronouncing such a result to be im-

possible," p. 79. And now, what will my readers think, when I assure them, that Swedenborg does actually teach the very thing I charge him with ? " The noviti-ates [in heaven] asked whether, from ultimate delights, any offspring were born there. The angelic spirits answered that there were not any natural offspring, but *spiritual offspring*." In another place, Swedenborg calls these spiritual offspring "*spiritual prolifications*," and adds, " If you are willing to believe it, *natural prolif-cations are also from that origin*."* It would seem from this, that those who are born *on earth* are first born, and have a kind of spiritual existence, in heaven. Thus much for my " second deliberate falsehood." (3.) My third known falsehood con-sists in the representation, that with Swedenborg " the obvious sense of Scripture is, *in comparison*, of small account, while the utmost importance is attached to certain hidden, spiritual, mystical senses," p. 126. The reader will observe, that I do not here say that the obvious sense of Scripture is, in the estimation of Sweden-borg, *of no* account, or of *actually* small account, but of small account *compara-tively*,—in *comparison* with the spiritual sense. And this every reader of Sweden-borg knows is the *exact truth.* I might quote whole pages from him and his fol-lowers in proof of it—not excepting Mr. Cabell. (4.) My fourth deliberate false-hood—and I shall take the trouble to nail but another—is, that I represent Swe-denborg as teaching that there are " mechanical *arts* and *trades* in heaven." " The pertinacious Doctor," says Mr. C., " *knew better all the time*," p. 144. Now the fact is, Swedenborg teaches *precisely as I had said.* In one of his relations, he speaks of three new comers from earth to heaven, who were much surprised to learn that heaven was not a world of rest. Whereupon their guide assures them that there are in heaven "administrations, ministers, judiciary proceedings, also *mechanical arts and trades*." In the course of the interview, there were exhibited " wonderful speci-mens of workmanship, which are made, in a spiritual manner, by the *artificers*." Also, " some virgins came with things *embroidered and spun* the work of their own hands, and presented them."†

I have dwelt the longer on these charges, that I might the more fully exhibit the character of the writer, and show the utter recklessness and groundlessness with which he hurls about him accusations of known and deliberate falsehood. In jus-tice to myself, I ought to have nothing more to say or do with him. He has for-feited all claim, I do not say to respectful notice, but to any further notice at all.

I do not forget, however, that I owe something to the cause of truth ; and for the *truth's* sake I will proceed.

4. In numerous instances, Mr. C. is chargeable with *misstating facts.* He has repeated with some variation, the erroneous statements of Mr. Parsons and Mr. Barrett, as to my putting down, as *two separate works*, in my list of books read, the different titles *of one and the same work* of Swedenborg; also as to the number of books which I read in a week. As I fully and publicly explained this matter, in two or three instances, I may be excused for not going into it again. Those who are *willing* to understand it may have the means of doing so, by consulting the N. York Tribune for April 16, 1847.

Mr. C. says " Swedenborg did not deny the doctrine of *future* or *general judg-ment*," p. 74. But this is a wrong statement. He taught that the *last* judgment

---

* Conj. Love, pp. 46, 104. † Conj. Love, pp. 173, 174.

which is ever to occur, took place in his presence, in the year 1757. Of course, there can be now no *future* judgment.

Again, Mr. C. says, "It is not true that Swedenborg denies *natural* theology, in the proper sense of the term, or as distinct from *revealed* theology," p. 78. But he expressly teaches "that *without the written word*, no one could know God," or "know any thing of the Lord;" and that what the old philosophers knew of God, they understood, "not from their own natural light, but from the religion of the ancients, among whom there had been a divine revelation."*

Mr. C. asserts, that Swedenborg does not represent Calvin as having yet entered on "his final destination," p. 94. But he does represent him as in a place, where they "are all enemies one to another," and "do evil to one another to the extent of their power, and this is the delight of their life," and is not hell, according to Swedenborg, the "final destination" of the wicked?

Mr. C. further denies, that Swedenborg represents men, before the fall, as having "no *oral* communication one with another," p. 107. Yet Swedenborg does say, that mankind at that period "had no *sonorous*, *articulate language*, such as took place afterwards, but communicated their ideas one to another by numberless changes of the countenance," &c. (A. C. §1118.)

Again, Mr. C. denies that Swedenborg teaches, "on any occasion, that there is no deception or hypocrisy in the other world," p. 116. With this assertion, let the reader compare the following quotation from Swedenborg: "In the other life, no one is allowed to assume a *semblance of affections* which are not properly his own; but all, of every description, are there reduced to such a state as to *speak as they think*, and to express the inclinations of the will by the countenance and gestures. Hence, therefore, it is that the faces of all are *the faces and effigies of their affections*." (Heaven and Hell, §§419, 422.)

According to Mr. C., Swedenborg believed those books of the Bible, which do *not* contain the spiritual sense to have been "written with a high degree of inspiration" as I ascribe to the whole Bible, p. 137. But I ascribe to the Bible, and to every part of it, *plenary* inspiration. I believe it all to be *the word of God.* Yet such is not the faith of Swedenborg and his followers. They regard almost half of the books—though in the main good and useful productions—as the word of *man*, and not of *God*. They are, as Mr. Hindmarsh says, "*human* and not *Divine* productions."

Mr. C. denies that Swedenborg enjoined it on his followers to search for "the most ancient Word" in China. "He enjoins no such duty," p. 151. But this again is a false statement. "*Seek for it* (the most ancient Word) *in China;* and peradventure you may find it there among the Tartars." (Apoc. Revealed, §11.). What is this but *a command—an enjoined duty?*

I will notice but another of the misstatements of Mr. C. He asks (p. 162), "Is it not true that the American Evangelical Missionaries in the East recently admitted a Mahometan convert to Christian communion, without requiring him to dismiss one of two wives which he had before? Such an outrage on all proper Christian feeling could not be perpetrated without question and remonstrance. The propriety of the step was accordingly discussed in a Missionary Convention, held at Bangor, under Dr. P.'s own nose." Now this whole statement, both Mr. C. and the public may rest assured, is without foundation. I never before heard of such a case as that propounded by Mr. C, nor do I think that such an one

---

* Sacred Scrip. §144, Swed. Library, No. 65, p. ?,

ever occurred. Certainly, nothing was said of any such case at the Missionary Convention at Bangor. There were some questions asked and answered about polygamy; but nothing resembling, I had almost said in the remotest degree, the statement before us.

5. In further showing what Mr. C. has done, it must be added, that he grossly and habitually *misrepresents* the friends of evangelical truth. Like Swedenborg himself, he makes them all *tritheists*, teaching that "God exists in three separate, distinct, individual beings," p. 74. He thus states the evangelical doctrines of *atonement* and *justification*. "A satisfaction has been made to the injured justice of Jehovah, by one who the same system declares was Jehovah himself; who paid the debt which mankind owed—its adherents do not very well agree to whom or to what;—but if sinners will only *believe* that *this* Divine person *was* actuated by love, and *another* Divine person by vengeance; and that the latter punished the former, though innocent, in the room and stead of sinners, though guilty, and *called* it *justice ;*—if he will only *believe* these and a few more such consistent, and probable, and honorable propositions; he will be *justified*, and (if there be time to do no more) will be saved," p. 71. Evangelical Christians believe, says our author, in "*arbitrary* rewards and punishments;" and represent God as "bestowing his favors *without reference to character*, and as delighting in vengeance," pp. 76, 81. With us, "a good life is not indispensable to salvation," p. 122. We "would give the veteran sinner, in the last hour of life, a passport to happiness, if he but *says* he repents, and believes a set of propositions, which contradict the clearest dictates of reason and the plainest declarations of holy writ," p. 166. Again, our system "damns the heathen; leaves the fate of infants uncertain ; and consigns the majority of men in Christian countries to eternal perdition, for not doing what they had no power to perform," p. 181.

These are but a few fragments of that tissue of misrepresentation which runs through the greater part of this long pamphlet. I have charity enough to believe that the most of them were put forth honestly. Owing to the palpable ignorance of the writer on points of theology, the probability is that he knew no better. As to his competency to engage discussions of this nature, and to write books, the public will judge.

I had designed to present some additional statements as to what Mr. C. *has done ;* and in particular to point out some of the more glaring of his *self-contradictions*. But I am not sure that the game would be worth the candle, and I desist.

Let us notice, in the second place, several things which he has *not* done.

1. He has not convicted me, nor so much as attempted to do it, of any error or inaccuracy in my *quotations*. My quotations from Swedenborg and his followers are very numerous,—some of them are long; for I preferred that, so far as possible, he should speak for himself. Mr. C. thinks I have quoted even more than was necessary. But there is no pretence that I have *misquoted*, or that I have failed to quote in every instance, errors of type excepted, with verbal accuracy.

2. Mr. C. has not invalidated any of my *statements*. He complains much of misstatements and misrepresentations; but I do not recollect a single instance in which I am convicted of error in this respect. My statements as to the teachings of Swedenborg, and the general features of his system and character, are all based on my quotations, which are fairly and truly made ; and as to the agreement of one with the other, my readers are competent to judge.*

---

* The only point on which Mr. C. has at all enlightened me, is that in which he speaks of

Mr. C. does not remove or obviate one of my numerous *objections* to the system of Swedenborg. Those who have read my Review will recollect that it consists, in great measure, of *objections* to this system. Now these objections Mr. C. disposes of in one of two ways: he either admits the facts on which my objections rest, and attempts to justify them ; or he denies the facts, and in so doing contradicts Swedenborg as flatly as he does me.* The most of my objections he encounters, and attempts to dispose of, by the former process. Thus my first objection is, that " Swedenborgianism professes to *supersede the gospel dispensation,* and to introduce a new dispensation, as distinct from it, and superior to it, as that is superior to the Jewish." This objection our author admits in full, and endeavors to prove that it is even so. My second objection is, that " the revelations of Swedenborg are not sufficiently *attested ;*" more especially as they were not attested by miracles. Mr. C. allows that they were not attested by miracles, and insists that miracles were not needed or to be expected. Indeed, he represents a miracle to be nothing more than a *strange,* an *unusual* occurrence, the attestation of which to any pretended revelation would, of course, be worthless, pp. 61, 62.

My third objection to the claims of Swedenborg is based on his treatment of *the Holy Scriptures.* " He rejects almost half the books of the Bible as constituting no part of *the Word of God ;*" and by his *spiritual, mystical interpretations,* he renders the remainder of comparatively little value. Now the facts on which this objection rests every Swedenborgian knows to be true ; and there is no evading or contradicting them, without contradicting Swedenborg himself. I further object to Swedenborg, that " he discards much important *Scripture truth,* and inculcates, on many points, *essential error.*" Under this head I show, that he rejects nearly all the great doctrines of evangelical religion. And Mr. C. admits that he does ; yes, more than admits it, he *glories in it.* " We are proud and happy to acknowledge, that we dissent not only from Calvin, but *from all the sects and parties who more or less symbolize with him, and appropriate to themselves the title of evangelical,*" p. 66. Let those who have been accustomed to think favorably of Swedenborgianism, then, remember, that by the confession of its most recent advocate, it rejects all the peculiar doctrines of evangelical religion.

I might, in this way, run over all my long list of objections ; but it is not necessary. Suffice it to say, that Mr. C. has not removed or obviated one of them. In most instances, as I said, he admits the facts, the statements, on which my objections rest, and attempts in vain to justify them ; and in the few cases where he denies the facts, he contradicts Swedenborg as flatly as he does me. He admits, for example, that " the planet Saturn is farthest distant from the sun ;" that "atmospheres, waters, and earths are the common or general principles by which and from which all and every thing exists ;" that love is the cause of the redness of the blood, and of animal heat ; that " the blood purifies itself in the lungs from things undigested," and " nourishes itself with" odors and exhalations ; that a vast multitude of animals, such as " tigers, wolves, foxes, and hogs," are not the creatures of God, but had their origin from hell ; that diseases are to be ascribed to the

---

Swedenborg as a *man of prayer.* There is more evidence—and I feel a pleasure in making the acknowledgment—that he valued prayer, and that he frequently practised it, than I had before discovered.

* Several instances of this nature I have noticed above. In speaking of Mr. C.'s erroneous statements. These errors of statement consist chiefly in misrepresentations of Swedenborg.

infestation of evil spirits; and he endeavors to show that, in the sense of Swedenborg, these assertions are strictly accordant with the facts of science.

Swedenborg states circumstances, in which it is not only permitted but recommended to the unmarried man to keep a ———. He also assigns some fifty causes (of the sufficiency of which the married man must be his own judge) which will justify him in deserting his lawful wife, and living in concubinage with another woman. Of course, Mr. C. was under the necessity of saying something on these painful, disgraceful subjects. And so, after much circumlocution and preparation, he puts forth the following statements : " When, therefore, Swedenborg pronounces it better, that those who will degrade themselves and stain their souls to some extent, should avoid all injury to maidenly purity, or matronly virtue, and without roaming at large, *content themselves with one*, preferring the state of marriage all the time, and only betaking themselves to this *as a refuge and an asylum, in the present necessity;* in such a question of casuistry, we ask, is not his judgment re-echoed by the common sense of the whole Christian world ?" p. 166. Again : " If he"—the married man, who feels constrained to desert his wife—" if he *cannot contain;* if he is the slave of sense generally, and in this respect of habit; then inasmuch as he is denied a resort to that preventive of sin which Paul himself prescribed to his Christian converts, his situation is manifestly similar to that of the unmarried man which has already been considered. It is perhaps one of greater hardship ; for the former can see no termination to his trials, during the life-time of his consort, whereas the latter may be, and often is, sustained by the hope of marriage at a future day. Such an one, then, *who feels that indulgence is to him in some sort a necessity, has some apology or exculpation* —for him a VALID EXCUSE, *for taking a substitute ;* provided there be but one, and she neither a virgin nor married woman, and the wife be not resorted to at the same time," p. 168.

On these admissions, these statements, I make no comment—I desire to make none. They do not come up to the full measure of Swedenborg's indulgence— far from it; but then they are *bad enough, in all conscience.* And how they can be written, and printed, and scattered abroad through this community, and that too by sensible men, I cannot understand.

After all that Swedenborgians have said and done to silence the objections relating to scortation and concubinage, and smooth them over, and cover them up, Mr. C. complains that they are not permitted to rest. " Ever and anon comes some resurrectionist of slander, to take up the carcase from the ditch, and again to galvanize it into life," p. 170. And so, Mr. C., rely upon it, *it will be in time to come.* Yourself and Prof. Bush (in his Reply to Dr. Woods) have treated the subject as plausibly, perhaps, as a Swedenborgian ever can do ; and yet, after all, it is not much relieved. It *cannot* be. Call it slander, if you will ; but the canons of your great teacher on these subjects never can be justified. They are a corroding ulcer upon your system, which cannot be healed. They are a mill stone about the neck of it which cannot be cast off, and which cannot be retained without sinking it to perdition. Depend upon it, this matter *will* be called up, and will be cast in the teeth of the men of the New Church, till the system has no longer an advocate, and has passed away as a thing of nought.

I repeat, in conclusion, that Mr. C. has not removed or obviated one of my many objections to the system of Swedenborg. They all remain with unabated force. When my work goes to a second edition (as it soon may) I shall be constrained to reiterate them *all.* And not only so, I shall be obliged to add *others.* There are other objections which have occurred to me since my Review was published, which must not be omitted.

In particular, I shall urge against the system of Swedenborg that it is a refined *materialism.* The present world is *material.* And yet it is an emanation, according to Swedenborg, from the very *substance of God.* It was made, in fact, from *his substance.* What then *is the substance of God?* And what, according to Swedenborg, is the *human soul?* It is no other than the *nervous* or *spirituous fluid.* "This fluid is the *spirit and soul* of its body." "We may take it for certain, that if this fluid and the soul agree with each other in their predicates, *the fluid must be accepted as the soul.*"* And what say the expounders of Swedenborg on this subject? "The distinction between mind and matter," says Mr. Clissold, "lies *not in essence,* but in form."† Mr. Dawson represents it as "one of the great uses of Swedenborg's writings, that they help to break down the mischievous, man-made distinction *between spirit and matter.*"‡ And Mr. Wilkinson says: "We regard body and soul together as *distinctly and inseparably one.*"§

But I cannot pursue this subject here; nor can I bestow any more attention upon the so-called reply of Mr. Cabell. My readers will be able to form some idea of it, and of the man, and of the manner in which he has treated me, and of the subject generally, from what I have written. If they desire to know more of it, let them read it for themselves   ENOCH POND.

Bangor, Feb. 23, 1849.

MR. CABELL TO DR. POND.

WARMINSTER, Nelson Co. Va. March 20th, 1848.

MR. EDITOR:—I can scarcely expect the Portland Mirror to be liberal enough to insert the following rejoinder to Dr. Pond's late "Notice." The age of miracles is last. May I ask of you a place for it in the Repository?

Respectfully yours,
N. F. C.

To Dr. Enoch Pond, Prof. of Theology in the Seminary at Bangor:

REV. SIR,—I received a few days since a No. of "The Christian Mirror" issued at Portland, Maine, on the 9th inst., containing your "Notice of Strictures on your Review on Swedenborgianism." From its angry tone, particularly when referring to the "Reply" to your Review, which was lately published, I should infer that the latter had done its work—at least in part. But from the pathetic ejaculations which were mingled therewith, it would appear that the Reply has also had an effect which was not originally intended.

No one questioned your right to deliver lectures to your pupils on this or any other subject which your fancy or polemic spirit might dictate; but when you committed those lectures to the press, they became public property, and, as such, fair subjects of criticism. That they should have proved so vulnerable was your fault, and not ours. You still protest that your object was "rather to *exhibit* Swedenborg than to *refute* him." Pity it is, that you should have so signally failed in both. Cer-

---

* Econ. of the Animal Kingdom, vol. ii. pp. 233, 238.   † Introduction to ditto. p. 64
‡ N. J. Mag. vol. 20, p 497.   § Tracts for New Times, No. 3, p. 25.

tainly, you have not refuted him, but you have " exhibited"—yourself, and in no very enviable light.

Your work was briefly reviewed in a magazine, criticised in a newspaper or two, and alluded to by a gentleman in a letter from London.   A small pamphlet was directed against it by *a* Mr. Hayden, who, with the weapons of truth, proved himself fully able to cope with *one* Dr. Pond.   In this writing and printing age, such things are common enough.   But your vanity has misled you, if you suppose that it was therefore regarded by New Churchmen as intrinsically formidable, or that it called for a reply, for any other reason than that it was addressed to public prejudice or ignorance of this subject.   For no other reason, I assure you, was it deemed worthy of special notice.

It was impossible, Sir, for any man of sense to have published such a book as yours, without making large calculations on popular credulity ; but it will be difficult to persuade the most blinded of your readers that you are not *the aggressor in this controversy.*   Wantonly and without provocation, you put forth a calumnious and shameless libel against the faith of a body of Christians who are not given to crusading against those who differ from them in belief, and who have proved themselves patient under the most long-continued and causeless injuries.   Because they did not think it worthy of a lengthened notice, until they had heard how industriously you and your satellites were circulating it through the broad length of the land, and that it was operating injuriously on the minds of the ignorant ; you therefore, if I am correctly informed, looked around in complacent triumph, and interpreted their comparative silence as a virtual acknowledgment of the truth of your charges. And now that your quasi refutation has been met and a merited rebuke bestowed upon its unfairness, you cry out as if you were a most injured man.

I dare say, Sir, it would have been more agreeable to you, if New Churchmen had borne your insults in silence (as they have done those of so many of your predecessors) and laid themselves down to be trampled on at your pleasure.   But you now find that not even your holy function which you have perverted from its original design, can shield you from the retort and exposure which you have drawn on yourself.   Sir, I never supposed that you could have reminded me of John Milton,—unless perhaps by the associating principle of contrast—but it is even so. The poet, we are told, complained that he had " fallen on evil days and evil *tongues.*" The days, says Dr. Johnson, were bad enough: "but of evil tongues for *Milton* to complain required impudence at least equal to his other powers.   Milton ! whose warmest advocates must allow, that he never spared any asperity of reproach or brutality of insolence."   And can any one doubt that you have an equal privilege of complaint in this case ? you, who have besprinkled your pages so liberally with such epithets as " absurd," " hideous," &c., and such compliments as charges of " slander" and " immoral principles."

In the " Advertisement to the Reader" you were informed that neither Professor Bush nor any body or member of the New Church was responsible for the Reply. The writer did not wish either his brethren, or the Truth of which he had undertaken the defence, to be compromised by any possible imprudence of his.   All others are equally guiltless of this rejoinder, and he fears not now, as then, to meet the responsibility alone.

If you had yourself observed the ordinary decencies—not say courtesies of literary combat, the ten or a dozen phrases which have so much ruffled your dignity would never have been employed ; or they would have been promptly withdrawn, if the writer could have even *doubted* the spirit which dictated your Review. Were they now entirely expunged, the *argument* of the pamphlet would remain unaffected. But doubt he could not; for though he is inclined to make large allowances for the force of prejudice and has seen much of its blinding influence on men otherwise commendable for their liberality and piety,—yet *there was your Preface* in which you vaunt the extent of your reading on this subject, and following it the long-drawn tissue of errors, both of fact and inference, which constitute the staple of your book, nine-tenths of which had been corrected long before in those very works. And so far from repairing the injury when an opportunity was afforded you by clearly pointing out your mistakes, you menace the renewal of the whole of them and in a more aggravated form. Be it so, Sir, your anathemas may *possibly* return on your own head; though we seek no agency in sending them there. But the annunciation of such a purpose, only confirms the original impression as to your motives.

Be it known to you then, Sir, that (with the exception of certain statements to be presently adverted to, and concerning which I may have been led into involuntary mistake), I retract not one word—for substance at least—of all I have written. If the opportunity of revision had been afforded me, respect for the public might have led me to modify certain expressions which, prompted by indignation, escaped me in the hurry of composition. But you, Sir, I am now persuaded, were treated *with all due respect*. I have no apology to make to you, nothing to retract, but now re-affirm all I have said. 'Tis true I am a Virginian, as is also the author of The Preliminary Letter. The public, I dare say, care nothing about me as an individual. I have not aspired to their notice—nor to yours—for notoriety's sake. Neither am I a volunteer in this behalf, nor yet shall I boast of my antagonist. But if you, Rev. Sir, feel any particular interest in knowing what is my " profession" or " standing" or " course of life," or whether I need your endorsement to prove my respectability in the community where I reside, you may send *one of your spies* to inquire into all these particulars for your own private satisfaction. You may instruct him to inquire farther, whether I have ever been in habits of rudeness to clergymen, who are entitled to public respect ? and whether from my position and circumstances I have any ostensible motive for contention with those whom you are pleased to call " Evangelical Christians ?—Virginia is moreover one of the United States, and her courts are open to all the world. If I have slandered you, appeal to them, and I will stamp every word I have written with the verdict of a Jury.

The man who proposes to argue a subject, and then assumes nearly every point in dispute *is* "arrogant." He who pretends that by the mere " exhibition"—though the fairest—of a system which has won the assent of intelligent minds, he has therefore refuted it, *does* "vapor." How much more, when he has misstated it throughout ? The repetition of arguments which have been surrendered as weak and irrelevant by judicious advocates of a cause, and which are farther weakened in the process, is " twaddle." One who affects to be *nicer* in his ideas and associations than all the professional men in his land—yea, than *the Word of God itself,* is " prudish and fastidious." To omit an essential part of a dogma while pretending to state if fairly, is a "paltry trick" in a clergyman, who should shun the very appearance of injustice. The Professor of Theology who, at this day, asserts that every sentence in the Bible must be interpreted in its merest literal sense *and no other*, does "deserve to be unfrocked." To take merit to one's self for refraining from that which God has not forbidden, is certainly a "factitious" virtue. And he who denounces others not under his jurisdiction for an opposite course deserves to meet a repulse. To garble quotations, or present statements so as to produce an effect different from that intended by the author, is "to poison" the minds of unwary readers. I spoke of you as a "redoubtable" champion, because I had understood you were one of those Indomitables who "even though vanquished could argue still;" and your "Notice" now under review proves that the epithet was not unmerited.

Once more.—(1.) He who bases a theory on the alleged *date* of a pretended fact, when his only witness who could know any thing personally of the matter, places it—if it ever occurred at all—at a period *eight years* subsequent to that alleged in the theory—does, in legal phrase—"falsify the record." And though I did not use the term in that connexion,—and never but once, when it was fully applicable, —I might have said he was guilty of ———. Pardon me, Sir, for using a blank. I have high authority, your own example. (2.) Under your general charge of "grossness," you designed to produce the impression that Swedenborg said "children were born in heaven." I know the fact that such impression was made on several minds. Now, when the declaration that *this could not be,* and the *reason therefor* were staring you in the face at the time the assertion dribbled from your pen, was I not warranted in saying that the ——— was "deliberate?" The passages your have now cited in your defence prove no such thing as your originial statement. (3.) Swedenborg no where enters into a comparison of the literal and spiritual sense of Scripture *with a view to depreciate either.* Both are important—both indispensable; the former especially so to men on earth. He has dwelt largely on the latter, because, as we suppose, it was a part of his mission to expound it. (4.) The very common idea that he taught "there are *mechanical* arts and *trades* in heaven," was founded on a *mistranslation* of certain terms in one of his works. This was corrected in one of the Apologies which you had read and the whole subject there set in a proper light,—*and you knew it.* The passage you now quote in justification when properly understood, does not sustain you. I leave the reader to draw his own inference.

But, Sir, I cannot consent that this matter shall degenerate into a personal contest between you and myself. In the pamphlet, I spoke of you as a Calvinistic Doctor of Divinity and Professor of Theology in the Theological Seminary at Bangor. In neither of those characters did I consider you as entitled to take the liberties you assumed, without rebuke. Of your more private relations I said nothing—knew nothing—and never inquired, feeling no particular interest therein. "If my readers," you say, "would form some idea of the Reply—of the man, and of *the manner in which he has treated me!* let them read it for themselves." And do you suppose, Sir, that the American Public, or so many of them as are interested in this discussion, care one groat "how I have treated *you?*" If your readers take you at your word, they will be more likely to inquire how we have respectively treated the subject. Those in your own immediate circle may endeavour to raise a little excitement—or perhaps get up an indignation meeting,—but the wave, I take it, would spend its force at a marvellously short distance from Bangor. For who are you, or who am I, that our readers should divert their attention to us as individuals, from this great controversy " whether a man shall worship one God or three ? and who is the one God ? and whether he whom we recognise as his messenger is to be accepted in that character ?—But a word or two as to certain minor matters.

(1.) Your explanation of how you came to speak of one book as two, and your denial of the incident at the Missionary Convention at Bangor, I had not seen. My statement as to the first was justified by your Preface. The other affair made considerable noise at the time. The account I first met with, appeared in an orthodox religious newspaper, nor had I ever seen it contradicted. And then as to the rapidity with which you read the works in your famous catalogue, whether your advance was swift or slow, you gathered but little true knowledge of the subject on which you undertook to write. If I was misled as to any of these particulars I do not regard them as material to the argument.

(2.) I must again remind you that Swedenborg does not deny " the *doctrine* of *future* or *general* judgment." The latter indeed, he tells us is already past, but he further assures his readers that now *a* judgment awaits every man, immediately or shortly after his departure. And is not a retribution so near at hand of far more immediate and stirring interest than one which is indefinitely postponed, as it is by your Creed? (3.) Neither is it true that he denies all *natural theology*" in the proper sense of the term. He says repeatedly that the light of reason reflected on Nature may lead to the conclusion that there is *a* God, but that without Revelation no one can know " *the true God*, or any thing of *the Lord*." Will you deny this position ? (4.) The destination of Calvin as described by him, may be " final" though he has not said so But as I know of no method by which you or I can determine this question, it need detain us no longer. (5.) It is true that Swedenborg represents men before the fall " as having no *sonorous, articulate* language such as took place afterwards," but among " the numberless changes of countenance" which he declares was their mode of communicating their thoughts, he includes " *motions of the lips*," and was this in no sense " oral ?" (6.) His statement that men in the other life are not permitted to indulge habitually in hypocrisy—whatever may be their internal disposition—and that " they are *reduced* to a state in which they must speak as they think," has reference to their " final destination." He often tells us, hypocrites have been permitted this indulgence for a time in *the intermediate state*, or until they are consigned to their own place. (7.) It is very easy for you to say in words that you regard every part of the Bible as *plenarily* inspired. But if by this you mean nothing more than that all the books that usually pass under that name *are true ;* and that none of them contain any other sense than that of the letter, and no profounder meaning than true words of man, I must still insist that you set no higher—nor so high a value on the Acts and Epistles, as does Swedenborg. (8.) If you do not wish to blanch the cheeks of your friends, I would seriously counsel you never again to refer to " Seek for it in China." So much for my misstatement of facts.—Now for the misrepresentations of the friends of evangelical truth.

And here we may remark in passing the continued exhibition of that arrogance which assumes a title as exclusively its own, to which others put in a claim on equal or better grounds, and which also begs the question in dispute. "What is *Gospel* Truth?" We know your answer to this inquiry, but that of other Christians is different.—My statements of your doctrines were fortified either by reference to your own Confession of Faith, or to the writings of approved Calvinistic divines. I had no occasion to enter at any great length into this subject, because it had so recently been done by Professor Bush. The view there given of your doctrines of *Vicarious* Atonement and Justification is such as was fairly deducible from those books and, as you very well know, was once held by the great body of Calvinists. If they no longer preach them, or are ashamed of them, or attempt to explain them away or give them a semblance of reason, why have they not the moral courage to expunge them from their standards?—You say something about "palpable ignorance" and "my incompetency to engage in such discussions,"—but how can you tell from the small expenditure of knowledge which was required for the refutation of your book, how much there was behind? Be it little or much I may readily grant that I have "none to speak of." I can also concede that you may be more profoundly versed in the mysteries of your own faith than I am or probably shall ever be,—although I have had *some* opportunity to learn what they are. For I am not the only one who has observed that the more of *that sort* of knowledge a man possesses, the worse it may be for him. If, however, you wish to know whether I have sufficient reasons for rejecting those dogmas, you are at liberty to test the matter whenever you please.

With respect to your "quotations," I said that it was an easy matter to cite the very words of an author and yet so to *garble* them, by suppressing certain portions essential to their being properly understood, and so to bring passages together which were separated in the original as to produce a false impression as to the author's meaning.—This you have often done, as proved in the Reply. And the same may be said of many of your "statements" of the system, both in general and particular.

With characteristic modesty you say that "I have not removed or obviated *one* of the numerous *objections* (of which your book is composed) to the system of Swedenborg" Do you not think, Rev. Sir, that it would be as well, perhaps more becoming in you, to leave the decision of that question to the judgment of our readers." I did not deny that you had raised abundance of objections. Any body can object to any system. The inquiry was, *whether your objections were valid?* I did not suppose that any thing I might say could convince *you:* and I was willing to let the Public decide whether every one of your objections was not completely set aside. You have certainly done nothing to strengthen them by their repetition here,—nor yet to prove your other assertion that "I have contradicted Swedenborg."

I must tell you further that I did *not* admit that "the planet Saturn was the farthest distant from the Sun,"—neither does Swedenborg say so. And if you think by dint of repetition to fasten it on him, it may provoke the reader to farther inferences as to your motives. With regard to the other particulars of that kind which you have again brought forward, I proved that some of them accorded with the views of the highest authorities in their several departments:—that others had been recently demonstrated:—and that concerning the remainder there were *conflicting opinions* among scientific men. In asserting their truth therefore, Swedenborg does *not* "contradict the plainest and *most universally* acknowledged principles of science."

In reiterating your abominable charges of immorality and appending thereto another scurrilous tirade, you have given a farther exhibition of your faculty of disingenuous statement. But as this renewed attack indicates rather a deepseated malice and a pertinacious spirit of misrepresentation, than any increase of power,—and as it has not in the least invalidated the explanation of this whole subject given in the Reply, I refer the reader to that exposition as containing the true views of Swedenborg on those questions of Casuistry. Some preliminary explanation was necessary to disperse the clouds which you and such as you have gathered around them, and this you call "circumlocution." The standard of Purity for the *Christian* is—Perfection. For him there must be no degrading compliances. But the *servant of sin* "who is holden of her cords" and who submits to her tyranny without resistance, is in danger of being bound and manacled with a sevenfold chain, in irretrievable slavery. If he sincerely desires to be free—but *cannot* immediately *burst* all his bonds, he may be tolerated in the effort to break them *separately;* though such a course necessarily protracts his struggle for that liberty which the free-man already enjoys. Such was the course of the Almighty with the Jews of old when "for the hardness of their hearts" "he gave them laws which were *not* good and statutes by which they should *not* live," (Ez. xx. 11, 24, 29 ; Matt. xix. 8 ; Gal. iii. 24), and though in denouncing Swedenborg for the presentation of such a principle, *you also indirectly censure your Maker,* yet it is by no means the first time you have done so. This *charitable judgment* of Swedenborg—for in effect it is nothing more—you pretend to think is "a millstone around the neck of his system which will sink it to perdition," and that "the time will come when it will not have an advocate left." The same prediction has been made, any time this fifty years, but we do not perceive that it is nearer fulfilment now than heretofore. That such is your desire I have no doubt; and the wish perhaps is father to the thought. In your effort to promote this object, it is clearly your purpose to frighten women and children —of every age and of either sex—and you may partially succeed with those without. But when the like suggestion is made to such as have embraced the system from intelligence—the inquiry immediately arises—" *To whom* shall we go, for *Thou only* hast the words of eternal life ?"

And so you have determined to pick up your old arrows which have fallen blunted at our feet and to point them anew; and not that alone,—for we are menaced with a new shower of darts. You have discovered that Swedenborg was a *materialist!* and that his system was a refined materialism ! ! Are we to understand from this that you have given up your endorsement of Messrs. Le Roy Sunderland, Ferriar, Knight and the like ? When you set about your task, we hope you will not forget that the "Economy of the Animal Kingdom" is not one of Swedenborg's *Theological* works: that Mr. Dawson is not an authorised expositor of his faith: that it is possible for what *flows from* a source to change in its properties when it has reached its boundaries and has become quiescent: that *two* things may be "*distinctly* and *inseparably* one" without being the *same.* When you have taken these things along with you and have told us also what *matter* is and what *spirit* is, and *where the former came from*, we can judge of your pretended discoveries in the writings of Swedenborg which his followers have never made. Commending you to the protection and enlightenment of the Searcher of hearts to whom you have appealed, I remain, Rev. Sir,

With all due respect, yours,

N. F. CABELL.

TRUST IN PROVIDENCE.

DEAR SIR,—I herewith send you an extract from a recent letter from a brother, on the subject of trust in the Divine Providence, which I *feel* has done me good, and thinking it might possibly be acceptable to the readers of the Repository, I have taken the liberty of sending it, and trust, if you deem it worthy, that you will give it a place therein.   Very truly, yours, &c.,   L. S. B.

* * * "Still, I am not ignorant of the unpleasant feature of merchandizing at the present day, arising mainly from the selfishness, want of veracity, and unreliability of many with whom one is obliged to deal. Nor am I unaware of the discomfort that may spring from *fear of failure* through various uncontrolable circumstances and violent fluctuations. How to get clear of the *unpleasant* feature I can hardly imagine: but for the *discomfort* I apprehend there is a "sovereign balm" in an *entire and loving trust* in the omnipotent Providence of our Heavenly Father—a providence which is the ever-present, all-embracing operative union of his boundless Love and Wisdom; and every merchant, every faithful, heaven-confiding, heaven-seeking merchant, may rest as assured of the constant, and full, and *entire* care of such a providence, as if *he* were the *only* creature receiving Divine Attention! In this mercy and this comprehension we can *assuredly trust;* and as they are constantly active in harmonious union, the rational eye can see a sufficient *reason* for trusting. When the heart, with this light in the eye, rightly trusts in this providence, the soul of the spiritually-minded business man will not become depressed, but be buoyant as air! since he *knows* and *feels* that every consequence of failure (should failure supervene) can, under the over-ruling of *such* providence, yield nothing but the sweetest fruits; for it can but prove one of the many propitious billows on the tide of his life, wafting him directly on toward that blessed haven in his Father's kingdom, where he is sure his every cherished aspiration will be crowned with the most complete and perennial fruition within the power of imagination to conceive. In relation to this, I have often thought that were any *one* of the collateral Christian graces sweet and adorning above the rest, it is (next to humility before God, which I always place *first*), this enlightened, heart-felt trust in the providence of our Lord.

"This trust we may not be, at first, capable of exercising uninterruptedly; still, it is the *true solace*, and it will strengthen as we advance, while its occasional apparent interruptions will become both fewer and shorter. What untold bliss in this *trust!* what grateful relief from the pangs of that disappointment incident to a self-confiding spirit!"

LETTER FROM REV. J. P. STUART, 20 MILE STAND, WARREN Co. OHIO, Feb. 26, 1848.

DEAR SIR,—Having been occupied as a missionary, since the first of October last, I have been requested to furnish you some account of the ground passed over.

I have visited 12 or 14 towns and villages and have lectured between 60 and 70 times, and have distributed about 200 tracts. Many are disposed to hear, and to read, and investigate. My audiences have varied from 40 or 50, to 400 or 500, and the indications of progress in the reception of the doctrines are decidedly cheering. Most generally some commodious house of worship is opened for my lectures in the villages where I have been. I have seldom met with any open opposition, although as the work goes on, this in the end is to be anticipated. In one place however, a village of 600 or 800 inhabitants, after my first lecture, which was on the Trinity, and at the close of which I distributed 20 or 30 tracts, the church was shut against me. The result however, was, that many indications of popular feeling in my favor were given. One man, a member of the church where I lectured declaring that the doctrines were good, and that he wished to hear more. Another who is a member of the Methodist connection, declaring that it was an outrage to shut the church, and that the tract which I had given him was worth five dollars. My own impression is that the day has come for us *to work*, that thousands are ready to receive the *new doctrines* whenever they are fairly presented to their view. Especially, do I think that this is true of this vast western country. We have here a more free and unfettered element of thought than perhaps you have further to the east. We need the literature of the church, and especially the smaller works of Swedenborg, and also the collateral works. I have found your pamphlet of " *Reasons*," a most excellent little work. I could have distributed thousands of tracts if they had been at my disposal, where I have only distributed hundreds, The converts to the New Church are necessarily *Readers*, and we need books and tracts, as well as missionaries. The *two* I think should be sent out together, neither can accomplish the work alone. I have seen the first No. of the New Church Repository and am much delighted with its appearance. I bid it a hearty welcome and wish it a brilliant success.

We are permitted to publish the following letter as descriptive of the workings of a very intelligent mind recently brought in contact with the doctrines of the New Church.

It is of little use for me to hide the fact that my sympathies are with the New Church. Though not able to solve all I read, yet the *vinculum* which binds all the writings of Swedenborg appears plainly to me to be A BAND OF TRUTH. In proportion as my heart accedes to this conclusion, a calm fixedness of purpose, a rest of spirit ensues, and inspires me with a steady resolution to honor the one Lord God, our Saviour, by shunning evil and doing good to all, as I have opportunity, knowing that every disposition and power to do so is inspired by the Lord alone.

It was very hard for me to adopt the sentiment that there was but one Lord. The doctrine of faith alone in the work of regeneration, was all in all to me. Also the Second Advent of the Lord, which I had viewed to have occurred at the destruction of Jerusalem. To this I held as with a death grasp.

Again and again did I reject the testimony of the Sage of Sweden. But the doctrines of co-operation, of a reconciling atonement, and progressive righteousness, would constantly demand my approval. I read the account of the Seeress of Prevorst in the Dublin University Magazine, and found her substantially confirmed by the memorable relations of Swedenborg. Your works on the Resurrection and the

Soul led me farther. I procured your pamphlet (Mesmer and Swedenborg), and was still more deeply influenced. Desiring to know more, I wrote to you. Refusing to be the sole expositor, you sent me to the illuminated author himself.

I have longed for a religion which was so simple that an unlettered child could practise its requirements, and at the same time so philosophical as to employ the profoundest intellect. I have found it. It is the faith of the city of our God, the heavenly doctrine of the New Jerusalem, which feeds alike the learned and the ignorant. Goodness is now wedded to truth. Science embraces religion. No more necessity of being charged with leaning toward carnal wisdom because we love to study the works of God.

In the faith of the one Lord—of a peaceful atonement—a progressive growth in righteousness, induced by co-operation with God working in us to will and do,— in short, with a hearty aspiration for the universal acknowledgment of the administration of the New Jerusalem—I remain truly and sincerely   Yours,   **

EDITORIAL ITEMS.

We shall soon commence the publication in our pages of a posthumous tract by Swedenborg, entitled *An Invitation to the New Church.* It is the outline of an argument rather than an argument itself, but the skeleton shows what the perfect body would have been. As it was written subsequently to " The True Christian Religion," which was finished the year before the author's death, it was probably among the last productions of his pen.——Mr. Hempell's work, announced in our last, entitled " Swedenborg and Fourier" has appeared. We shall probably have a thorough review of the book in a future number.——The late revolution in France reminds one of the following remarks of Swedenborg in relation to that people :—" ' The two horns which thou sawest are the kings who have received no kingdom as yet,' signifies the Word as to its power derived from divine truths among those who are in the Kingdom of France, and are not so much under the yoke of the popish dominion, with whom, nevertheless, there is not as yet a Church altogether separated from the Roman Catholic religion.— It is said that there is not as yet among those who are in the Kingdom of France a Church altogether separated from the Roman Catholic religion, because they adhere to that religion in its externals, but not so much in internals. Externals are formalities, and internals are essentials. The reason why they still adhere to it, is, because there are so many monasteries there, and because the priesthood there is under the pope's jurisdiction, and thus are guided in every formality according to papal edicts and statutes, from which circumstance many do still continue in the essentials of that religion, wherefore the church there is not yet separated. This is what is signified by their having received no Kingdom as yet."—*A. R.* 740. Their past history confirms this as a correct view of the genius of the French people, who have been far more in external than internal conjunction with the Church of Rome. Accordingly we cannot well doubt that in the recent movement there is a reach of the Divine Providence having for its end the more complete severance of the nation from the Roman Catholic body, in order to give freer scope to the operation of New Church principles, which will come in contact with many very favorable elements in the character of the

French as a people. We cannot but tender our felicitations to our devoted fellow-laborer in that country, Mons. Le Boys des Guays, the Editor of " La Nouvelle Jerusalem," and to the small band of his associates who have for years labored so assiduously in the good cause.———The Rev. Mr. Barrett of this city has received a very united call from the New Church brethren in Cincinnati to settle among them as pastor, and this call we understand he has determined to accept. His loss will be much regretted by the people of his former charge, who are only reconciled to it in view of the very important use he will be enabled to accomplish in that growing metropolis of the West. He leaves about the first of May.——— The "Letters to a Man of the World" are nearly all stereotyped and the work will be ready for delivery early in May.———We are happy to learn that those who have it in charge to procure books for the Congressional Library at Washton have ordered a complete set of Swedenborg's Scientific Works to be added to the collection of his Theological Writings which already have a place on the shelves of the Library. They are ordered from England, as they will come in for such a purpose duty free. We hear also that several of the gentlemen who have seats in Congress are far from indifferent to the doctrines and revelations of the herald of the New Church.———The associated movement in Boston, having for its object a *cheap postage* reform, similar to that which has wrought such wonderful effects in England, is one that we trust will meet with co-operation in every quarter of our country. The present rates of postage, though much reduced from the standard of former years, are still too onerous, and in view of the complete success of the British experiment even in a pecuniary respect, it must be a very short sighted policy that will still adhere to the exorbitancies of the present system. The measure proposed is to fix letter postage at two cents per half ounce, and newspapers at one cent each, for all distances, if pre-paid—and double postage if not pre-paid. Nothing is wanted to effect the change but the united will of the people, and the common will is made up of individual wills. Let every man favor the object and it is effected.———The April No. of the Southern Quarterly Review, published at Charleston, S. C. contains a most elaborate article, of more than forty pages, on the Philosophical Character and Works of Swedenborg. It is evidently from the same able pen that has before enriched the Southern Quarterly with masterly papers on Swedenborg, but with none better calculated to produce a favorable impression in regard to the man, as one of the great lights of the race, than the present. The prevalent idea of Swedenborg's *insanity* is very summarily and triumphantly disposed of.

THE

NEW CHURCH REPOSITORY

AND

MONTHLY REVIEW.

| Vol. 1. | MAY, 1848. | No. 5. |

ORIGINAL PAPERS.

ARTICLE I.

SUPERNATURALISM.*

THE publication of the Seeress of Prevorst—a work which doubtless has been read by many and heard of by most in the New Church—created a kind of epoch in Germany, from which dates a revival of belief in many things belonging to the class of the supernatural, which have long and generally passed as vulgar superstitions. Animal Magnetism had prepared the way, in some measure, for the book, and without such aid, it is not probable that it would have met with either the extended notice or the limited reception it has actually secured. The history of one who for several years passed her life more in the spiritual than in the natural world, with its detailed accounts of visits from persons deceased, and its unveilings of a world which is generally thought to be made inaccessible by some positive decree of the Almighty to all human inquisition, must otherwise have come too suddenly and

---

*BLATTER AUS PREVORST.—*Origininalien und Lesefruchte fur Freunde des Innern Lebens, &c.* (LEAVES FROM PREVORST.—*Articles original and selected, for the Friends of the Inner Life—communicated by the Editor of the Seeress of Prevorst.*)
MAGIKON.—*Archiv fur Beobachtungen aus dem Gebiete der Geisterkunde, &c* (MAGIKON.—*A Repository for Observations pertaining to Pneumatology and. Magic and the Magnetic Life—as a continuation of the Leaves from Prevorst.*)

violently upon men's minds and would have provoked only an incredulous hatred ; even as it is, it has by no means escaped the effects of such a spirit ; but, on the other hand, falling like seed upon minds in which a preparation for belief had been made by the wonders of Mesmerism, it did not remain without fruit. The respectable auspices under which the Seeress of Prevorst made its appearance helped to save it from present neglect and early oblivion. Kerner, under whose professional care the case of Mrs. Hauffe fell, and who observed and recorded its facts, was a physician of some celebrity, too well reputed for honesty to have his statements impeached on the score of truth and too intelligent to make it decorous in the unbelieving to dismiss them with a sneer. Besides, the case had attracted other witnesses even more respectable—Eschenmayer, one whose name stands high in German philosophy, had repaired to the spot to make his own observation on its remarkable phenomena, and give his attestation to them publicly. Claiming notice by its own wonderful character, by its keeping with the facts of the magnetic science, even while it went beyond them, and by the respectability of its vouchers, it received the notice of various newspapers, reviews, and magazines. By some of them it was assailed with wit and humor and Kerner cried down as a man of fantastic imagination. By others the facts were admitted with some degree of candor, and, thereupon, long and lumbering theories propounded, accounting for the case and for apparitions in general, on the ground of excited imagination, sensuous illusions, deception, exhalations from dead bodies, &c. The little handful of believers in the supernatural felt called upon, under these circumstances, to establish some public organ, in which they might present the rational grounds on which they rested their cause, support those grounds by well authenticated instances, and not only defend themselves against the ridicule of their opponents but retort in the same kind. Accordingly the first number of the " Blatter aus Prevorst" made its appearance in the February of 1831. It was succeeded by others, at irregular intervals, to the number of twelve when it was discontinued, and the " Magikon" took its place. This last publication was commenced in Sept. 1839, and has been continued to the present time.

The general nature of these two periodicals will appear by the following extract from the Prospectus to the " Magikon :"

" There is wanting to our literature some work which shall collect and preserve to coming times well authenticated facts from the night-realm of nature. The more one century gives itself up to unbelief in the invisible, the more are all occurrences connected with the unseen world passed by without regard or consigned speedily to oblivion. To remedy this want shall be the endeavor of this Repository. Its aim shall be to collect and hand down to posterity approved and authenticated observations going to show the inter-communion of a spiritual world with our own, instances of prophetic dreams, presentiments, visions, &c., and especially observations in the department of magic and magnetic healing. But along with these matters of fact, theoretical essays will by do means be excluded. Notices and critiques of writings that touch on the subjects to which the Repository is devoted will always find a place in it."

"It is designed that this Repository, with its proofs of a world of spirits and a personal continuance of being after death—proofs drawn from life and nature—shall march on by the side of that abstract world-wisdom of our days, which, turning itself away from life, God, and nature, negatives all that is most holy and is receptive of no internal revelation."

The contents of the "Blatter" as well as the "Magikon" appear, on examination, to answer very well to this Prospectus. They form a copious collection of instances purporting to be well authenticated, which may come under the general head of the "supernatural," as the term is commonly understood. We find there cases of witchcraft, divination, fortune-telling, second-sight, self-sight, trance, of dreams in which things were seen as transpiring or as they turned out subsequently, of castles, houses, and places haunted by a particular spirit—of compacts to return after death made and kept—of spirits either appearing or giving their presence to be understood by knocking—and finally of something approaching possession or obsession.

It will be asked, without doubt: are these accounts reliable? Are they well authenticated? Can it be seen that the editor and contributors have not imposed upon the world—or, at least is there any certainty that love of the marvellous has not swallowed up their discrimination and made them an easy prey to those who delight in putting off strange stories on the simple? For ourselves, having gone over the contents of these works with some care, we do not hesitate to say, that in our opinion, they are worthy of confidence. As regards the personal character of those engaged in the undertakng, the general standing of Kerner and Eschenmayer exempt them from all suspicion of voluntary fraud—a suspicion which a generous mind resorts to, it may be added, very reluctantly, even with regard to those who have not fairly won themselves an exemption from it by a blameless life. As for the other supposition, that they may have been imposed upon by mockers, it is not easy to imagine that men of some reputation to be preserved or lost with the public, would not guard themselves in their undertaking on this side—as well knowing that any instance in which they inserted any vulgar story open to contradiction would hurt their cause and confirm the existing prejudice against them as men of too easy a faith. This cautiousness actually expresses itself in the Preface to the "Blatter."

"The aid and active interest of all who wish well to the object will be gladly received—but no communications relating to internal vision, especially the apparition of spirits, can be admitted, except such as are authenticated or reported by credible persons."

There is every appearance about the communications themselves that they have proceeded from a truthful source. They are marked, for the most part, with what always passes for a note of truth, viz. a particular assignment of the time, place, and persons connected with the matters reported, and in general by *circumstantiality*.

But besides this species of evidence, there is another yet more interior to be drawn from the principles which belong to this whole department of knowledge. One conversant in any tolerable measure with this kind of lore soon seizes upon these principally and he thenceforward possesses in them a touchstone of what is false and true in any given account. Nay, we can make a pretty shrewd guess by their aid, as to what is false only by exaggeration. This will appear incredible to those whose only idea of discrimination is to reject in one huge lump every thing that rises above the senses and has not connection with every day life. Accustomed perpetually to dispute "*whether* the thing be so," they have no idea of the progress which can be made by those who have established it as a point of rational belief, "that it *is* so," and who advance from that point to an actual knowledge of particulars. But that discrimination is not monopolized, to say no more, by the deniers of the supernatural, let us hear Kerner.

"The learned Professors of that Philosophy, which, in explaining the phenomena of apparitions is perpetually uttering and writing the words 'hallucination,' 'monomania' and the like, may take my word for it, that to me, as a physician engaged in the active duties of his profession, much more than to them at their writing desks, there have occurred cases of morbid illusions of the senses, fever-phantasies, monomania, &c., and that I know tolerably well what judgment to pass on such

cases and how to distinguish them.   But had I ventured, either
from ignorance or from deference to a philosophy which admits no personal continuance of being after death, to explain
cases of the supernatural as only hallucinations and illusions
of the senses, I should have merited the name of one that tor-
tures nature, not interrogates her."

On such general grounds as are above indicated we do not
hesitate to avow the belief that in this large collection of documents there is very little purporting to be from immediate observation which is not reported with a sincere and honest purpose, and comparatively little which is not free from exaggeration.

This school, if such it can be called, numbering some men
of talent among its members—feeling its superiority above the
philosophy of the day by its recognition of the spiritual world,
animated with no little enthusiasm, and fighting its way by
the aid of *facts*—is doubtless destined to increase.   And every
one who looks with interest to every new movement in the
moral and religious sphere with the desire of appreciating its
bearing on the interests of the New Church in the world, must,
we think, rejoice that it is likely to do so—not that we can
perceive the adoption of any properly New Church truth.   Received into connection with the existing systems of faith, it
can be to all who are confirmed in those systems (which, however, we may hope is not the case with all), nothing better than
truth falsified.   It cannot fail, also, but that, relying in some
measure on the reports of clairvoyants, and having no spear
of Ithuriel, to touch them with, they will mix the false with
the true.   But with all these abatements, the movement cannot but be regarded as one, in its general nature, preparatory
for the ingress of pure truth.   It will perform the use of
unfixing and undermining the old systems, and producing a
recognition, with whatever false views of its detailed features
of the spiritual world, which is now openly denied or admitted only in word.   This must be considered again—inasmuch
as thereby there is preparation made of a general state of mind
more receptive of true and well grounded views.

It is easy to imagine one of this class taking up the " Heaven,
and Hell," and, struck with the many coincidences which it offers with his own conclusions, led on from that to the Arcana
Celestia, and finally allegorizing the internal sense of the
Word.   At least it is much easier to think this of him, than of
one of the disciples of Hegel, or of a confirmed adherent of the
Lutheran or Evangelical Church.   On the whole, though the
results which these men are likely to attain can be nothing
more than a mixture of the true and the false, we may yet

look to this movement, as one of those agencies, which, by
analogy with the regeneration of the individual, serve, by impure mediums, to introduce truth successively more pure.

We cannot but hail the rise of this school as a token for
good, not only in Germany, but every where. It is at once a
manifestation of the more spiritual tendencies which begin to
prevail in the human mind since the Last Judgment, and a
promise that the sensualism which has borne sway so long is
at length to sustain a check, on one side at least. An aversion
to the supernatural, to the discerning eye, coheres with the
vastuted state of the Church and interprets it. It might seem
a small matter, to a careless judgment, this general derision of
"vulgar superstitions ;" but, in fact, that which is mere mockery
on the surface, in the heart is hostility to what might draw
after it a spiritual inference. Men have a deep interest, which
they themselves are scarcely aware of, in denying the facts we
are considering. They wish that admission of a spiritual
world, to which their creed obliges them, to remain a formula
of mere words. Press them to make it real in any definite instance and their tone changes from raillery to angry contempt,
the spheres of the natural mind resisting, indignantly, the attempt to reverse their torsion. There is a sad interest, to one
who looks from this point of view, in seeing the endeavors
which are so frequently made to bring the facts of any supernatural tale within the range of merely natural causes. If it
concerns vision, it is divested of reality by aid of that potent word "imagination"—if it is sound, it is referred to the
wind, or to the rats and mice. Such efforts of ingenuity betray a
mind that makes its home only in the natural sphere, seeks its
companions among natural things and feels intruded upon
when any thing with a spiritual face presents itself at the
door. The New Church itself is not altogether exempt from
this spirit. Do we not hear, even at this late day, the
avowal from some, that though they can believe to a certain
extent "Animal Magnetism," they have strong doubts about
"Clairvoyance?" With how many others does a faith in these
marvels pass for a weakness carefully to be concealed from
those without, lest a recognition of such "vulgar superstions"
should be added in their minds to the reproach of laying plates
for the departed. Others, again, are willing that the whole
question should remain on the paradoxical footing, on which
the belief in witchcraft was placed by Addison, viz: a thing
credible in the general but to be resolutely disputed in all
particular instances. Now we cannot help thinking both
the scepticism and the caution which are thus manifested
matter of reproach, the one to the intelligence, the other to the

moral courage of the Church. It does not belong to her, with
the light which she has in those things from almost every page
of Swedenborg, to succumb to false opinion, but rather in the
exercise of that charity which delights in the propagation of
truth, to correct it. The time has come when the audacious
denial of supernatural facts which has been so long current is
to be declared *irreligious*, and the silly constructions put on
those which are not rejected is to be exposed—when the age
is to be told that its philosophy is unphilosophical, and its
proud elevation above supposed superstitions, is only as when
a serpent lifts its head awhile in the air—such towering as
may be done while the belly still cleaves to the ground. Such
representations will have their effect after a while, and that
effect, without doubt, will be a good. Any *real* recognition of
a spiritual world cannot but be useful to the mind that makes
it. For just as the prevailing denial betrays a disposition to
look outward, so confession indicates the probability, at least,
of the man's looking inward. That there is a religious value
to be attached to a belief in the supernatural was long ago seen
by Wesley. In introducing in his Journal (May 25, 1768) the
narrative of Elizabeth Hobson, he refers to the fact that the
English in general and most of the learned men in Europe had
surrendered all belief in tales of witches and apparitions,
and enters a solemn protest against the concession thus
made to the enemies of the Bible. He represents these last as
being very industrious in propagating the cry against all faith in
such things, as well knowing that to give up witchcraft was to
give up the Bible, and, on the other hand, that a single instance of intercourse between men and separate spirits must
be fatal to their own creed. "I know no reason," he adds,
"why we should suffer these weapons to be wrested from our
hands. There are, indeed, many proofs besides these, amply
sufficient to put their vain imaginations to shame, but we
need not suffer ourselves to be laughed out of any one ; neither
reason nor religion requires it." We cannot but think, in
agreement with the opinion of this Old Church worthy, that the
New will be fulfilling, in part, its mission of spiritual good in
the world, by taking a decided stand, and making its voice
heard on this subject.

In contemplating the mass of facts which are collected in
the "Blatter" and "Magikon," one feels as on looking at the
confused materials which the builder has brought together,
each stick and stone of which is to find its right place in the
beautiful structure that is shortly to be reared on the spot.
These facts will one day take order under some skilful hand
and rise before the admiring eyes of the world with all the

symmetry of a new *Science*—a science not unfruitful of good,
but capable of yielding most valuable hints for the cure of disease, both physical and mental. Let the whole subject then,
be with the Church for free and untrammeled discussion. It
is needful to bespeak liberality thus, because it is plainly to
be seen that caution, on this one subject, has degenerated into
something like straitness of spirit, and been indulged beyond
its proper functions. We would not deny that Animal Magnetism has its dangers and that therefore there was occasion for
the warning which has been given. But it has also its high
uses in the relief of suffering humanity, and in the confirmation which it lends, as a fact, to the disclosures of Swedenborg. Has this positive side been duly recognized among us?
We think not. On the contrary alarm has been sounded so
extensively that one who believes this agency to be the gift of
an all merciful Providence to suffering man—a blessing to the
body coming among the spiritual train of the new dispensation—cannot use it without risk of being thought to meddle
with forbidden arts, or attract the notice of the world to an actual case of clairvoyance, without imputation of running into
spiritual danger, and leading others after him. Away with
this narrow dread, and give us a caution which has an eye for
the positive in every subject and a heart for the uses which
may be drawn from any quarter whatsoever.   A. E. F.

ARTICLE II.

LETTERS TO A TRINITARIAN.

LETTER V.

JEHOVAH JESUS.

DEAR SIR,

If the tenor of my remarks in the preceding series of Letters shall have approved itself as resting upon a stable basis,
we have obtained an important clew, not only to the true character of the Saviour, as being no other than the one only Jehovah, but also to the correct interpretation of those numerous
passages in the Old Testament which speak of Him as having
been made *visible* to holy men of that dispensation. If I have
at all succeeded in my attempted solution of the *theophanies* of
the former economy, the conclusion reached cannot well be any

other than that they were really manifestations of the Supreme Jehovah in his undivided person, and made through the medium of an angel, because they could not possibly be made in any other way. " The Divine itself," says Swedenborg, " is far above the heavens, not only the Divine good itself, but also the Divine truth itself, which proceeds immediately from the Divine good ; the reason why those principles are far above heaven, is because the Divine itself is infinite, and the infinite cannot be conjoined with finites, thus not with the angels in the heavens, *except by the putting on of some finite first, and thus by accommodation to reception.*"

On the ground of what I have now advanced upon the general subject, you will see what we are taught by Swedenborg to believe concerning the relation which the ancient *theophanies* bear to the person of Christ. They were manifestations of Him only so far as he was identically one and the same with Jehovah himself, regarding this as the title of the Supreme Godhead. For ourselves, we are free to say that our minds utterly fail to grasp the idea of the *appearance* of any Divine personage termed the " Son of God" who made himself, by anticipation, visible to the patriarchs, prophets, and holy men of the early ages. We know of no " Son of God" but him who was born, as to his natural humanity, of the virgin mother, and who became a Son simply by being thus born.

But I may here be met by the position, that the Old Testament does in fact contain intimations respecting the " Son of God" which abundantly warrant the inference of such a distinction of persons as I am now endeavoring to show unfounded. Justice to the argument requires me to advert to these passages. The result, I think, will show that something far more decisive is demanded by the exigencies of the theory against which I contend. The first and most prominent text adduced by Trinitarians is Ps. ii. 7,—" Thou art my Son ; this day have I begotten thee." In regard to this we fully accord with Swedenborg's interpretation. "In this passage is not meant a Son born from eternity, but the Son that was born in time; for it is a prophetical Psalm, relating to the Lord who was to come, and therefore it is called the statute which Jehovah declared unto David; wherefore it is written before in the same Psalm, 'I have anointed my King over Zion' (v. 6); and it follows, 'I will give him the nations for an inheritance' (v. 8), and of consequence the expression, *this day,* does not mean from eternity, but in time; for with Jehovah the future is present. By the Son is meant the Lord as to his humanity." Are you prepared to deny this to be the true sense of the language of the Psalmist?

Another passage subsidized by theologians to the same

purpose is Prov. xxx. 4,—"Who hath ascended up into heaven or descended? Who hath gathered the wind in his fists? Who hath bound the waters in a garment? Who hath established the ends of the earth? What is his name, and what is his *Son's* name, if thou canst tell?" It is here supposed that these questions are affirmative of the wisdom and power of God, whose Son is here mentioned; but this is doubtless a mistake. The questions relate to man, and imply a strong denial that any man can do these things. In the foregoing verses Agur confesses his ignorance, and in this verse he declares that neither he nor any other man else can perform or explain the works of God. "What is his name or his son's name?" i. e. What is the man's name who hath done or can do these things? or what is the name of his son? Negative interrogations of this kind are frequent in the Scriptures.

Again, we are referred to Dan. iv. 25, where Nebuchadnezzar is said to have seen "one like THE SON OF GOD." This is adduced in evidence of Christ's being a Son abstract from humanity. But it would be strange if we were required to found our faith on the testimony of a heathen king, a polytheist, who was then compelling men to idolatry, and who a little while after was driven from among men for his pride and contempt of the true God. To suppose that he knew the Son of God—that he knew him to be such *abstract* from *humanity*, and yet called him a *man* whose form was *like* the Son of God—and farther, that he should afterwards call this same man an *angel* sent by God, as if he knew that this coequal Son of God was also his servant or messenger— all this is so unnatural and so unsupported by the whole history, as to be altogether incredible. Besides, you cannot be ignorant that it is generally conceded by the learned, that the proper reading is, "like *a son of the gods.*"[*] It is therefore, far more probable that by this expression he meant an *angel*, as he expressly terms him (v. 28), and if he intended a divine person, it was only according to the heathen mythology which abounded in begotten gods who were considered as subordinate divinities, and as coming down in the likeness of men, as the Lycaonians thought Paul and Barnabas were.

Besides the above I know of no other texts in the Old Testament which lend any support to the idea of the eternal Sonship of Christ. Nothing in fact can be adduced to prove him to have been a *Son* before he came in the flesh, but will, by the

---

[*] " It is greatly to be lamented, that so very an important mistranslation should remain in the English Bible to mislead the simple. Printed too, as it is, with the word " Son" commenced with a capital letter, none who are destitute of other means of information can avoid supposing, that there was a proper Son of God then existing; while no shadow of ground really exists for such an imagination."—*Noble's Appeal.* p. 367.

same course of argument, prove him also to have been *Jesus Christ* before that period, which is manifestly contrary to the tenor of the New Testament. Nothing can be more explicit than the announcement of Gabriel to Mary,—" Behold, thou shalt conceive and bear a Son, and shall call his name Jesus. He shall be great, and shall be called THE SON OF THE MOST HIGH. But Mary said to the angel, How shall this be since I know not man? And the angel answered and said to her, THE HOLY SPIRIT SHALL COME UPON THEE, AND THE POWER OF THE HIGHEST SHALL OVERSHADOW THEE; wherefore also THAT HOLY THING that is born, of thee, shall be called THE SON OF GOD."* As then we find no evidence of the existence of a Son of God from eternity, we see no ground for the opinion that such a Son was manifested in the ancient *theophanies,* which is the same as saying that they were not manifestations of what is termed the *second person* of the Trinity. They were manifestations of Jehovah, and if that term does not in itself convey the idea of such a threefold distinction, we must seek for the evidence of it elsewhere, and if you know where it is to be found, I should be grateful for having it pointed out.

Is it said that we are forced to recognize it in the peculiar use of the term " Word" (Logos) evidently applied to Christ in his ante-incarnate state, who was " in the beginning with God, and was God ?" Yet here, if I mistake not, it will be easy to show that the Scriptures are still conversant with the same Divine Personage, who has before been brought to our view under the appellation of Jehovah, and who was manifested in the earlier ages of the world, and to the Jews, under the form of an angel. As the subject is one of deep interest to the theologian I shall pursue it somewhat in detail.

You are well aware of the remarkable fact that the Chaldee Targumists or Paraphrasts, who were all Jews, wherever, in our version, there is any intimation of the visible display of the Divine glory or power, are accustomed to make use of the term " Shekinah," which signifies *dwelling* or *habitation,* from the Hebrew שכן, *shâkan, to dwell or inhabit.* The derivative *Shekinah* is used more particularly of the divine presence, glory, or

---

* " It is not known in the church, but that the Son of God is another person of the Godhead, distinct from the person of the Father. Thence is the faith concerning a Son of God born from eternity. Because this is universally received, and is concerning God, there is given no power or liberty of thinking about it, from any understanding, not even of thinking what it is to be born from eternity ; for whosoever thinks about it from the understanding, will surely say with himself, ' This is above my comprehension, but still I say it, because others say it, and I believe it, because others believe it.' But they may know, that there is no Son from eternity, but that the Lord is from eternity. When it is known what the Lord is, and what the Son is, one can also think from the understanding concerning the triune God, and not before."—*Doct. of the Lord,* 19.

majesty, or of the Divinity itself when said to be present to men, or to converse with them, or to vouchsafe to them his sensible and gracious aid. Accordingly the following, among hundreds of other passages, are rendered by the Chaldee Targums of Onkelos and Jonathan conformably to this import of the term ;—Ps. lxxiv. 2, " Remember thy congregation which thou hast purchased of old; this mount Zion wherein *thou hast dwelt.*" Chal. " Wherein thou hast made thy *Shekinah* to dwell." Num. x. 36, "Return, O Lord, unto the many thousands of Israel." Chal. "Return now, O Word of the Lord, to thy people ,Israel, make the glory of thy *Shekinah* to dwell among them, and have mercy on the thousands of Israel." Num. xi. 20, " Ye have despised the Lord which is among you." Chal. "Ye have despised the Word of the Lord whose *Shekinah* dwelleth among you." Hag. i. 8, "Go up to the mountain, and bring wood, and build the house, and I will take pleasure in it, and will be *glorified*, saith the Lord." Chal. " And I will make my *Shekinah* to dwell there in glory." Ps. lxxxv. 10, " His salvation is nigh them that fear him, that *glory* may dwell in our land."   This is distinctly explained by Aben Ezra as meaning that the *Shekinah* may be established in the land. It would be easy to multiply passages to the same effect ad libitum, for even the voluminous citations of Buxtorf do not embrace a tithe of the examples of the usage which may be drawn from the Pentateuch alone. It is the ordinary phraseology of the Chaldee Paraphrases wherever in our version we meet with any intimation of a visible display of the divine glory. Indeed the terms " Glory" and " Shekinah" are evidently recognized by the Targumists as convertible terms.

While this then is the current phraseology of these ancient Jewish paraphrases in regard to the visible manifestations of Jehovah, and to whom *as visible* (though not to the outward eye), and as dwelling or *Shekinizing* between the Cherubim, the whole worship of the Jewish Church was directed, it is a fact equally worthy of notice, that the Divine Personage thus manifested is termed by them *Mimra da-Yehovah, the Word of the Lord*, of which " Logos" is the Greek representative. As the Shekinah was the medium of the divine presence and of the declaration of the divine will, and as a voice inwardly audible frequently accompanied the manifestation, it was not unnatural that the title " Word of the Lord," or, by way of eminence, " The Word," should come to be habitually applied in this connexion. As words, either written or spoken, are the established vehicle for conveying the thoughts and feelings of one human being to another, so it is easy to conceive that the denomination " Word" should have been appropriated to what was deemed a medium of imparting the divine thoughts and counsels to men. The Shekinah and the Mimra, therefore, are in Jewish diction terms employed in most intimate connexion with those ancient divine manifestations which I have indicated by the term *theophanies.* I shall hope to show in the sequel that the ideas which, in their minds, were couched under these appellations were in all probability extremely inadequate when tried by the fundamental truth involved, yet as the usage itself is a fact of some moment in its relations to the general subject, I shall adduce, in tabellated form, a sufficient number of instances to illustrate it clearly.

HEBREW.	CHALDEE.
Gen. iii. 8. And they heard the voice of the Lord God walking in the midst of the garden.	And they heard the voice of *the Word of the Lord* walking in the garden.
Ch. xxviii. 20, 21. And Jacob vowed a vow, saying, If God will be with me, and keep me, &c., then shall the Lord be my God.	And Jacob vowed a vow to the *Word,* saying, If *the Word of the Lord* will be my help, &c., then shall the Lord be my God.
Ch. xxxv. 9. And God appeared unto Jacob again when he came out of Padan-aram; and blessed him.	And *the Word of the Lord* appeared to Jacob a second time, when he was coming from Padan-Aram; and blessed him.
Ex. xvi. 8. Your murmurings are not against us, but against the Lord.	Your murmurings are not against us, but against *the Word of the Lord.*
Ch. xix. 17. And Moses brought forth the people out of the camp to meet with God.	And Moses brought forth the people out of the camp to meet with *the Word of the Lord.*
Ch. xxx. 6. Where I will meet with thee.	Where I will appoint for thee *my Word.*
Lev. xxvi. 11, 12. And I will set my tabernacle among you; and my soul shall not abhor you. And I will walk among you and be your God.	And I will set my tabernacle among you; and *my Word* shall not reject you. And I will cause my *Shekinah* to dwell among you, and be to you a God.
Num. xi. 20. Because that ye have despised the Lord which is among you.	Because ye have contemptuously rejected *the Word of the Lord,* whose *Shekinah* dwelleth among you.
Ch. xiv. 9. Only rebel not ye against the Lord.	But rebel not ye against *the Word of the Lord.*

HEBREW.	CHALDEE.
Ch. xxiii. 4. And God met Balaam.	And *the Word from before the Lord* met Balaam.
Deut. i. 30. The Lord your God which goeth before you, he shall fight for you.	*The Word of the Lord thy God,* who is thy leader, shall fight for you.
Ch. i. 32, 33. Yet in this thing ye did not believe the Lord your God, who went in the way before you, to search you out a place to pitch your tents in, in fire by night, to show you the way ye should go, and in a cloud by day.	And in this thing ye did not believe in *the Word of the Lord your God,* who went as a leader before you, &c.
Ch. xiii. 18. When thou shalt hearken to the voice of the Lord thy God.	If thou shalt be obedient to *the Word of the Lord thy God.*

We have here, if we mistake not, indubitable evidence that the term " Logos" or " Word," which in Chaldee or Rabbinical usage is most intimately related to the " *Shekinah*," is in fact a designation of the very Personage whose recorded *theophanies* in the Old Testament were made through the medium of an angel, and on grounds which I have previously endeavored to explain. But I have utterly failed in my attempted elucidations of the subject, if I have not succeeded in showing that this Personage is indeed no other than the one only Jehovah, the Supreme God, the Creator of the universe, and the exclusive object of all religious worship. What can more unequivocally establish this than the title given to Christ by the Seer of Patmos ?—" And his name is called the WORD OF GOD.—And he hath on his vesture and on his thigh, a name written, KING OF KINGS AND LORD OF LORDS." Who is " King of Kings and Lord of Lords" but Jehovah himself? Consequently, if Christ is the Word, and the Word is Jehovah, the inference as to his sole and absolute Divinity is unquestionable, and all ground for recognizing any allusion to a tri-personal Trinity in this title vanishes from under our feet. As no such distinction is implied in the term Jehovah, so none is implied in the term Word.

Still I feel that, on the position which I assume, you are authorized to demand somewhat of a detailed explication of the language of the Evangelist in respect to the Divine Word. This I proceed to give, planting it, of course, on the basis of Swedenborg's theology. I have already remarked that the attributes of Love and Wisdom comprise the all of Deity. The Divine Love is the Divine *Esse,* the Divine Wisdom the Divine *Existere.* So far as manifestation is concerned, this is always predicated of the latter and never of the former, because the *Esse* is always *invisibly* latent in the *Existere*. When we speak, therefore, of the Divine Humanity we necessarily centre our thoughts upon the *Existere* of Jehovah, which is Wisdom or Truth, and from this the idea of the Human principle is inseparable. The "Word" is but another name for the Divine Truth, predicated especially of the Son, as Divine Good is predicated especially of the Father, and as the Divine Proceeding is predicated of the Holy Spirit. But I will here make Swedenborg the expounder of his own doctrine, the truth of which is to be determined by an appeal to Scripture, in its genuine sense, and not to alleged visions.

"From these words, 'In the beginning,' &c., it is manifest, that the *Lord* is from eternity *God*, and that He is that *Lord* who was born in the world; for it is said, The Word was with God, and God was the Word; as also, that without Him was nothing made that was made; and afterwards, that the Word became flesh, and they saw Him. That the Lord is called the Word, is little understood in the church; but He is called the Word, because the Word signifies divine truth, or divine wisdom'; and the Lord is divine Truth itself, or divine Wisdom itself; wherefore also He is called Light, concerning which also it is said, that it came into the world. Because divine wisdom and divine love make one, and in the Lord were one from eternity, therefore also it is said, 'In Him was life, and the life was the light of men.' Life is divine love, and light is divine wisdom. This one is what is meant by, 'In the beginning the Word was with God, and God was the Word.' *With* God is *in* God, for wisdom is in love, and love in wisdom. Likewise in another place in John; 'Glorify Thou Me, Father, with Thyself, with the glory which I had with Thee before the world was' (xviii. 5). *With* Thyself is *in* Thyself. Wherefore also it is said, that God was the Word; and elsewhere, that the Lord is in the Father, and the Father in Him; as also, that the Father and He are one. Now, because the Word is the divine Wisdom of divine Love, it follows that it is *Jehovah* himself, thus the Lord, by whom all things were made that are made; for all things were created by divine Wisdom, from divine Love."
—*Doct. of the Lord*, n. 1.

"How the Lord is the Word, is understood by few, for they think that the Lord can indeed enlighten and teach man by the Word, and yet that he cannot hence be called the Word: but let them know that every man is his own love, and thence his own good and his own truth, man not being a man from any other source, and nothing else appertaining to him being man. From this consideration that man is his own good and his own truth, angels and spirits are also men; for every good and truth proceeding from the Lord is in its form a man: but the Lord is divine good itself and divine truth itself; thus He is the man himself, from whom every man is a man."—*Swed. apud Clowes on John*, p. 11.

That by the Word in this relation is meant the Lord's Divine Humanity, is evident from its being said that "the Word became flesh and dwelt among us." This is a point which I venture to think, I have established in a former letter. The Divine

Humanity existing from eternity in" first principles," descended, in his incarnation, into " last principles," or " ultimates," or, as we may properly say, the Alpha descended into the Omega. He thus became an earthly man among earthly men, and became visible to the outward eye as he had been visible, in the angelic form, to the spiritual eye.   This is doubtless what is meant by the Apostle in saying that though he was " in the form of God, and thought it not robbery to be equal with God," yet " he made himself of no reputation, and took upon him the form of a servant," &c.   The " form of God" is the Divine Humanity in its first principles, as it exists in the Divine nature from eternity.   But nothing in the data on which our reasoning is founded requires the recognition of a triad of persons to make the Scriptural testimony intelligible or consistent., The Word is still the Lord, or Jehovah, in the indivisible unity of his nature, and he is the eternal Word, not because he is identical with an eternal Son, but because he is identical with the eternal Jehovah.

But has not the title " Word" some relation to the written Word? Undoubtedly it has. "Since truth is meant by the Word, by the Word is meant all revelation, thus likewise the Word itself or Holy Scripture." This relation I cannot better present than in the language of Swedenborg.   " He who understands these words, ' In the beginning,' &c., in their interior sense, may see that the Divine Truth itself in the Word which was formerly in this world, which likewise is in our Word at this day, is meant by the Word which was in the beginning with God and which was God; but not the Word regarded merely as to the words and letters of the languages in which it is written, but as seen in its essence and life, which is from within in the senses or meaning of its words and letters; from this life does the Word vivify the affections of that man's will who reads it devoutly; and from the light of its life it illuminates the thought of his understanding; therefore it is said in John, ' In him (the Word) was life, and the life was the light of man;' this constitutes the Word, because the Word is from the Lord, and concerning the Lord, and thus *is* the Lord.   *All thought, speech, and writing derives its essence and life from him who thinks, speaks, and writes; the man with all that he is being therein; but in the Word the Lord alone is.*"   You will probably find yourself compelled to demur to this explicit declaration of identity between the revealed Word and its Divine Author, but farther reflection will scarcely fail to bring you to the admission of the fact. The grounds of the position I have stated in a somewhat formal manner in a former production (" Statement of Reasons," &c.) and as the language suits my present purpose you will allow me to quote it: "He (Swedenborg) declares, that the Word is not only *from* the Lord, but *is* the Lord, just as any written or spoken communication of a man *is a form of the man himself.* A man's vocal speech is an emanation from the man himself; he is essentially *in* his utterance; and the case is not altered by its being embodied in written language. A letter addressed by one person to another, is as truly a going forth of his spirit, in the form of words, as if the communication were made by spirit coming in contact with spirit in the spiritual world. The Divine Word is the divine voice speaking to man, and the Divine voice is as much a form of the Divine being as a man's voice is a form of his being. But the human voice is effected by the medium of the undulations of the atmosphere, which of course cannot hold in respect to the Deity. The aerial sound, however, in man's case, is nothing more than a vehicle for conveying the thought and affection of the speaker's mind, and cannot be needed for the communication of spirits disembodied. They then communicate by impressing *themselves* upon each other. Now God is a spirit, and in our present corporeal state he comes into communion with our spirits through the medium of written speech, but this speech is *Himself*, in his essential Love and Truth, and whatever is in Himself is in his speech, that is, in his Word, just as Swedenborg remarks in a passage already quoted, that 'every thought, speech, and writing derives its essence and life from him who thinks, speaks, and writes, the whole man with his quality being in those things; but in the Word is the Lord alone.' The Word of God therefore is the *living* Divine Truth, and is at any one moment just as really the *present* utterance, expression, or emanation of the Divine Being, as when flowing into the minds of the sacred penmen by whom it was indited, as they were *moved* (φερομενοι, acted, borne, or carried away) by the Holy Ghost. But if the Divine Word *is* the Divine Lord, it is impossible to conceive that his inmost affections and thoughts—in a word, his essential Divinity—should not be in it, and consequently that there should not be a depth of import entirely transcending the sense of the outward letter."—P. 118.

In another paragraph of his writings, Swedenborg, in speaking of this passage in John, says: "Inasmuch as this has been understood in no other way than to mean, that God taught man by the Word; therefore it has been explained by an expression of elevation, which involves that the Lord is not the Word itself: the reason is, because it was not known, that by the Word is meant the divine truth of the divine good, or, what is the same thing, the divine wisdom of the divine love. In what manner the Lord is the divine truth of the divine good, shall here also be briefly shown : every man is not a man from his face and body, but from the good of his love, and from the truths of his wisdom ; and whereas man is a man from these principles, every man likewise is his own truth and his own good, or his own love and his own wisdom, and without these he is not a man ; but the Lord is good itself and truth itself, or, what is the same thing, love itself and wisdom itself ; and these are the Word, which 'in the beginning was with God, and which was God, and which was made flesh.' "—*Div. Prov.* n. 172. The evident intimation in this passage is, that as the most proper light in which to view man is in his *first principles* as constituted of love and wisdom, and apart from his bodily being, so also in regard to the Lord himself, we are to elevate our thoughts to what he is in his essential nature, that is, as infinite Love and infinite Wisdom ; and not only so, but we are always to conceive of him as *acting according to the principles of his nature.** Hence it is impossible to form any adequate idea of the process of creation, unless it be regarded as the normal operation of these two principles. But Love and Wisdom must necessarily operate by emanation or influx, so that when it is said, in the present connexion, that "all things were made by him, and without him was not any thing made that was made," we are to recognize the legitimate operation of the Divine Truth or Wisdom ultimating itself, by its own laws, in the material universe. Accordingly, Swedenborg says—

" Scarce any one knows at this day that there is any power in truth, for it is supposed that it is only a word spoken by some one who is in power, which on that account must be done, consequently the truth is only as breathing from the mouth, and as sound in the ear ; when yet truth

---

* The following extract from De Guay's " Letters to a Man of the World," presents a striking view of the analogy between the Word of God and the word of man considered as a creative agency.

" Man having been created in the image of God, every thing which exists in man, so far as he remains in the order of his creation, must be the image of something which exists in God ; so there must be a kind of analogy between the word of man and the Word of God. Let us see if this analogy confirms what has been said concerning the Word of God. We have said that the Word in its principle, or the Logos, created the universe, that is to say, all that God has made. Is it the same with the word of man relatively to all that man does ? By the Word or Logos creating we understand the Divine Wisdom of God acting from the Divine Love or Will of God. Man's word, analogous to the Logos, is, then, the understanding acting from the will, or what, is the same thing, thought acting from affection. Now it is evident that all that man does is done by his thought from his affection ; every work of man is, then, produced by his word. Thus considered, the word of man is not only that which he expresses, whether by sounds and articulations, or by the physiognomy of the countenance and gestures, but moreover, all that which is produced by him ; so that this word of man is the man himself, as the Word (Logos) is God Himself ; for will and thought are man, as Love Itself and Wisdom Itself are God."—*Letters, &c., 2d Series, Letter 3d.*

and good are the principles of all things in both worlds, the spiritual and the natural, by which principles the universe was created, and by which the universe is preserved; and likewise by which man was made; wherefore those two principles are all in all. That the universe was created by Divine Truth is plainly said in John, ' In the beginning was the Word, and the Word was with God; all things were made by Him.' And in David, ' By the Word of Jehovah were the heavens made,' Psalm xxxiii. 6; by the Word in both cases is meant the divine truth. Inasmuch as the universe was created by Divine Truth, therefore also the universe is preserved by it; for as subsistence is perpetual existence, so preservation is perpetual creation."—*T. C. R.* 224.

This is confirmed by the fact that the original word, *εγενετο, egeneto, were made,* does not properly signify *created* in its ordinary acceptation, but *became*—" all things *became* by him," —and I am fully prepared to accede to the views of Professor Lewis in his "Platonic Theology," where he clearly intimates, in his elaborate discussion of the distinctive sense of the verbs Ειμι, *to be,* and Γινομαι, *to become,* that the true sense of creation comes very near to that of *generation* (*γινεσις, genesis*), or *becoming.** We claim, therefore, to be occupying the soundest philosophical ground when we maintain that what is termed *creation* on the part of Jehovah is a process of *emanation* from himself, who is the first, absolute, only, self-existing substance. Matter is the elaboration of spirit, or, in other words, spirit has the potency of clothing itself in material forms. The most solid substances on our globe are the result of the combination of gases; the gases, therefore, must be conceived as of prior formation; but they are themselves the product of solar heat and light, and the heat and light of the natural sun are the effect of spiritual heat and light, and these are the Divine Love and Wisdom. To this then we come at last. We hold it to be impossible, on just grounds, to avoid the conclusion, that every thing created is from a spiritual origin, that is to say, *developed* from the Love and Wisdom of Jehovah; and this process never ceases, because these principles ever energize. The creation of the universe is as truly going on at this moment as it was millions of ages ago, for the Divine Love and Wisdom can never intermit their activities.† It

---

* This distinction is very clearly marked in our Lord's declaration, John viii. 58, " before Abraham *was* (γενεσθαι) *I am* (ειμι);" i. e. before Abraham *became.* The same word is applied to our Lord himself as the Son of God, Gal. iv. 4, " God sent forth his Son *made* (γενομενον) of a woman;" i. e. who *became* by a woman. It is in several cases thus translated in our version.

†" Were what is spiritual to be separated from what is natural, that which is natural would be annihilated. All things derive their origin in this mode. Every thing, both in general and in particular, is from the Lord. From Him is the celestial principle; by the celestial from Him exists the spiritual principle; by the spiritual, the natural; and by the natural, the corporeal and sensual principles; and as each thus exists from the Lord, so also does it subsist, for, as is acknow-

doubtless seems to our limited view, as if the work of *creation* were finished, and *preservation* alone could now be attributed to the Most High.   But subsistence is perpetual existence, and perpetual existence is perpetual creation.*   If we could suppose an individual of our race to have been introduced upon the globe myriads of centuries ago, in some of the immensely remote geological periods, and to have lived out the common measure of human life at the present day, he would doubtless have had as strong an impression of the *completed* state of the terrestrial creations as we now have.   Yet the work was then going on, as it is still going on, by incessant changes and new combinations.   Every thing is in the process of *becoming* by virtue of the same laws which were operative from the outset.   But the cycles are so vast—the sweep so boundless—the evolutions so slow—that the process to us seems to have become stationary.—But to return to the general subject.

The result of our investigations thus far has been, to establish the conclusion that all evidence is wanting which shall go to prove the existence of any such divided personality in the Godhead as is supposed on the tri-personal theory.   The Divine appearances under the old economy were appearances of the absolute Jehovah himself, under the form of angel.   That these appearances were preludes or anticipations of the Lord's advent in the flesh, is undoubtedly true, but not of his advent in any other character than that of the supreme and unipersonal Jehovah.   It becomes then a point of importance to establish the identity of Jesus of Nazareth with the Jehovah of the Old Testament, and the most obvious mode of doing this is to show that the title "Lord," so frequently bestowed upon Christ by the New Testament writers, is an express confirmation of this identity.   I would not imply by this that such a process of proof is absolutely indispensable to my argument, for it in fact follows by necessary consequence from all that I have hitherto said, if there is any reason to believe that such a personage as Christ is announced in the Old Testament.   Still, as the evidence is ample, I proceed to adduce it.   In assuming this position, however, I would not be understood to deny that the term "Lord" is often used even in reference to Christ, in a lower

---

lodged, subsistence is perpetual existence.   They who conceive otherwise of the existence and origin of all things, as do the worshippers of nature, who derive them all from her, have adopted such fatal principles, that the phantasies of the beasts of the forest may be said to possess more of truth; yet there are many such persons, who seem to themselves to excel the rest of mankind in wisdom."—*A. C.* 775.

* " The case is with influx, as with existence and subsistence ; nothing exists from itself, but from what is prior to itself, thus finally all things from the First, that is, from that which is, which is *Esse* and *Existere* from Itself; and also from the Same all things subsist, for the case is with subsistence as with existence, inas much as to subsist is perpetually to exist."—*A. C.* 6040.

sense, as an honorary compellation equivalent to "Sir" or
"Master,"—a usage for the most part easily determinable from
the context. But it is, in my view, equally beyond dispute,
that in a multitude of passages the title in question is most unequivocally bestowed upon the Saviour in such a way as to compel the inference that he can be no other than the Jehovah of
Moses and the Prophets. As the settlement of a *principle* is
the object aimed at, it will not be necessary to multiply instances to a great extent. What is proved of a few will probably be admited to be *proveable* of a great many more of the
same class. I present the examples in parallel columns.

OLD TESTAMENT.	NEW TESTAMENT.
Mal. iii. 1. Behold, I will send my messenger, and he shall prepare the way before me : and the Lord (Jehovah), whom ye seek, shall suddenly come to his temple, even the messenger of the covenant, whom ye delight in : behold, he shall come, saith the Lord of hosts.	Mark i. 1-3. As it is written in the prophets, Behold, I send my messenger before thy face, which shall prepare thy way before thee; The voice of one crying in the wilderness, Prepare ye the way of the Lord, make his paths straight.
Mal. iii. 1. Behold, I will send my messenger, and he shall prepare the way before me.	Luke i. 76. And thou, child, shalt be called the Prophet of the Highest, for thou shalt go before the face of the Lord to prepare his ways.
Is. xl. 3. The voice of him that crieth in the wilderness, Prepare ye the way of the Lord (Jehovah), make straight in the desert a highway for our God.	Mat. iii. 3. For this is he that was spoken of by the prophet Esaias, saying, The voice of one crying in the wilderness, Prepare ye the way of the Lord, make his paths straight.
Is. xliv. 6. Thus saith the Lord (Jehovah), the King of Israel, and his Redeemer the Lord (Jehovah), of hosts; I *am* the first, and I *am* the last; and besides me *there is* no God.	Rev. xxii. 13. I (Jesus) am Alpha and Omega, the beginning and the end, the first and the last.
Is. vi. 5. Then said I, Wo *is* me! for I am undone; because I *am* a man of unclean lips, and I dwell in the midst of a people of unclean lips; for mine eyes have seen the King, the Lord (Jehovah) of hosts.	John xii. 41. These things said Esaias. when he saw his (Christ's) glory, and spake of him.

OLD TESTAMENT.   NEW TESTAMENT.

Jer. xxiii. 6. In his days Judah shall be saved, and Israel shall dwell safely: and this *is* his name whereby he shall be called, the Lord (Jehovah), our Righteousness.

1 Cor. i. 30. But of him are ye in Christ Jesus, who of God is made unto us wisdom, and righteousness, and sanctification, and redemption:

Jer. ix. 24. But let him that glorieth, glory in this, that he understandeth and knoweth me, that I am the Lord (Jehovah), which exercise loving-kindness, judgment, and righteousness, in the earth: for in these things I delight, saith the Lord (Jehovah).

v. 31. That, according as it is written, He that glorieth, let him glory in the Lord.

Zech. xji. 4. In that day saith the LORD (Jehovah), v. 10, they shall look on me whom they have pierced.

John xiv. 37. "They shall look on him (Christ) whom they have pierced."

Is. xl. 10. Behold, the Lord (Jehovah) God will come—his reward is with him.

Rev. xii. 12. Behold, I (Jesus) come quickly, and my reward is with me. v. 20. Even so, come, Lord Jesus.

Is. xliii. 3, 11. For I am the LORD thy God, the Holy One of Israel, thy Saviour: I gave Egypt for thy ransom, Ethiopia and Seba for thee.

I, *even* I, *am* the LORD (Jehovah); and besides me *there* is no Saviour.
Is. xlv. 21. A just God and a Saviour; there is none beside me.

1 Pet. iii. 18. But grow in grace, and in the knowledge of our Lord and Saviour Jesus Christ.
Luke ii. 11. For unto you is born this day, in the city of David, a Saviour, which is Christ the Lord.

Ps. cii. 25. Of old hast thou laid the foundations of the earth: and the heavens are the work of thy hands.

Heb. i. 10. Thou, Lord, in the beginning hast laid the foundations of the earth; and the heavens are the works of thy hands.

Is. xlv. 23. I have sworn by myself, the word is gone out of my mouth in righteousness, and shall not return, That unto Me every knee shall bow, and every tongue shall swear.

Rom. xiv. 11, 12. For we shall all stand before the judgment seat of Christ. For it is written, As I live, saith the Lord, every knee shall bow to me.

Hos. i. 7. I will have mercy on the house of Judah, and will save them by the Lord (Jehovah) their God.

Luke ii. 11. For unto you is born this day in the city of David, a Saviour, which is Christ the Lord.

OLD TESTAMENT.	NEW TESTAMENT.
Ps. xxiv. 8. Who is this King of Glory? the Lord (Jehovah) strong and mighty, the Lord (Jehovah) mighty in battle.	1 Cor. ii. 8. Which none of the princes of this world know; for had they known it, they would not have crucified the Lord of glory.
Deut. x. 17. For the Lord (Jehovah) your God is God of Gods, and Lord of lords, a mighty and a terrible.	Rev. xvii. 14. These shall make war with the Lamb, and the Lamb shall overcome them; for he is Lord of lords and King of kings.

I am not aware that in the above citations there is any one as to which there can be any reasonable doubt that the reference is distinctly to Jesus Christ, "the only Lord God, and (i. e. *even*) our Lord Jesus Christ." Several of them are expressly explained of him by the sacred writers as the Personage to whom the title properly pertains, and by parity of reasoning numerous others obviously demand the same interpretation. If I am warranted in assigning to them this reference, the conclusion that naturally yields itself is, that in these passages, at least, the Saviour of men is distinguished by an appellation the highest that can be applied to the Supreme Deity, and which is, in fact, usually denominated his *incommunicable* name. The dignity of the Godhead knows no more august appellation than that of Jehovah, and yet nothing short of a torturing criticism can deny the attribution of this title to the Saviour of the world, or refuse to recognize in him the being justly denominated JEHOVAH JESUS. And to the present point of the discussion I have reserved the reference to a passage which is perhaps entitled to carry with it more weight than any of the preceding. I allude to Rev. i. 8, " I am Alpha and Omega, the beginning and the ending, saith the Lord, which is, and which was, and which is to come, the Almighty,"—evidently the language of Christ, as the same declaration occurs Rev. xxii. where there can be no doubt as to the speaker. The word Κυριος, *kurios, Lord,* here represents the Hebrew מהוה, *Yehovah* which is compounded of the *past, present,* and *future* tense of the verb היה, *hayah, to be,* of which the following words—" which is, and which was, and which is to come"—are plainly a definition, while the last epithet "Almighty" (παντοκρατωρ), answers obviously to צבאות, *tezbaoth, hosts,* of which it is the usual rendering in the Septuagint. The two terms are distinctly defined. There is the less doubt of this from the fact, that in the parallel passage, Is. xliv. 6, this title is expressly given;—" Thus saith the Lord the King of Israel, and his Redeemer, *the Lord of hosts;* I am the first, and I am the last; and besides me there is no God." Now if this is an assertion of the exclusive

Deity of the speaker, as is evident from the language, and yet the same character is expressly claimed for Jesus the Saviour, can more than one inference possibly be drawn? The entire clause, therefore, is an explanation, for the Greek reader, of the Hebrew צבאות יהוה, *Yehovah Tzebaoth*, or *Lord of hosts*, with the unequivocal intimation that this title belongs to Jesus Christ. By being *the Lord*, he is of necessity *the Lord of hosts*, as the titles are of equivalent import. It would seem difficult then to indicate any thing as wanting to establish completely the point which I am laboring, viz. the absolute identity of Jehovah and Jesus.

I will here adduce a passage from Swedenborg by way, not of simple authoritative declaration, but of confirmation, as I venture to regard the truth affirmed as sufficiently established from other sources.

"In the word of the New Testament, with the Evangelists and in the Apocalypse, Jehovah is nowhere named, but for Jehovah it is said Lord, and this from hidden causes, of which we shall speak presently. That in the Word of the New Testament it is said Lord instead of Jehovah, may appear evident with Mark: 'Jesus said, the first (primary) of all the commandments is, Hear O Israel, the *Lord* our God is one *Lord*, therefore thou shalt love the *Lord* thy God with all thy heart, and with all thy soul, and with all thy thought, and with all thy strength,' Mark xii. 29, 30; which is thus expressed in Moses; 'Hear O Israel, *Jehovah* our God is one *Jehovah*, and thou shalt love *Jehovah* thy God with all thy heart, and with all thy soul and with all thy strength,' Deut. vi. 4, 5; where it is manifest that it is said Lord for Jehovah. In like manner in John; 'Behold a throne was set in heaven, and one sat on the throne; and round about the throne were four animals full of eyes before and behind, each had for himself six wings round about, and within full of eyes: and they said Holy, holy, holy, *Lord* God Omnipotent,' Apoc. iv. 2, 6, 8; which is thus expressed in Isaiah: 'I saw the *Lord* sitting on a throne high and lifted up; the seraphim were standing above it, each had six wings; and one cried to another, Holy, holy, holy, *Jehovah Zebaoth*,' vi. 1, 3, 5, 8; there it is said *Lord* for *Jehovah*, or *Lord God Omnipotent* for *Jehovah Zebaoth;* that the four animals are seraphim or cherubim, is plain from Ezekiel, chap. i. 5, 13, 14, 15, 19; chap. x. 15. That in the New Testament the *Lord* is *Jehovah*, appears also from several other passages, as in Luke: 'The angel of the *Lord* appeared to Zacharias,' i. 11; the angel of the *Lord* for the angel of *Jehovah*. In the same evangelist, the angel said to Zacharias concerning his son: 'Many of the sons of Israel shall he turn to the *Lord* their God,' i. 16; to the *Lord* their God, for to *Jehovah* God. Again, the angel said to Mary concerning Jesus: 'He shall be great, and shall be called the Son of the Highest, and the *Lord God* shall give unto him the throne of David,' i. 32; the *Lord* God for *Jehovah* God. Again: 'Mary said, my soul doth magnify the *Lord*, and my spirit hath exalted itself on God my Saviour,' i. 46, 47; where the *Lord* also is for *Jehovah*. Again: 'Zacharias prophesied, saying, Blessed be the *Lord* God of Israel,' i. 68; where the *Lord* God is for *Jehovah* God. Again: 'The angel of the *Lord* stood near them (the shepherds), and the glory of the *Lord* shone round about them,' ii. 9; the angel of the *Lord* and the glory of the Lord, for the angel of *Jehovah* and the glory of *Jehovah*. In Matthew: 'Blessed is he that cometh in the name of the *Lord*,' xxi. 9; chap. xxiii. 39; Luke xiii. 34; John xii. 13; in the name of the *Lord*, for in the name of *Jehovah:* besides many other passages, as Luke i. 28; chap. ii. 15, 22, 23, 24, 29, 38, 39; chap. v. 17; Mark xii. 9, 11. Amongst the hidden causes that they called Jehovah Lord, were also, that if it had been declared at that time, that the Lord was the Jehovah so often mentioned in the Old Testament, it would not have been received, because it would not have been believed; and further, because the Lord was not made Jehovah as to his human also, until he had in every respect united the Divine Essence to the human, and the human to the Divine; the plenary unition was effected after in the last temptation, which was that of the cross, wherefore the disciples after the resurrection always called him *Lord*, John xx. 2, 13, 15, 18, 20, 25; chap. xxi. 7, 12, 15, 16, 17, 20; Mark xvi. 19, 20; and Thomas said, 'My *Lord* and my God,' John xx. 28; and inasmuch as the Lord was the *Jehovah*, who is so often mentioned in the Old Testament, therefore also he said to the disciples, 'Ye call me Master and *Lord*, and ye say right, for I am,' John xiii. 13, 14, 16; by which words is signified that he was *Jehovah* God. That the *Lord* was *Jehovah*, is understood also by the words of the angel to the shepherds, 'Unto you is born to-day a Saviour, who is Christ the *Lord*,' Luke ii. 11; where Christ is for the Messiah, the Anointed, the King, and *Lord* for *Jehovah*. They who examine the Word without much attention, cannot know this, believing that our Saviour, like others, was called *Lord* merely from respect and veneration, when yet he was so called from this, that he was *Jehovah*."—*A. C.* n. 2921.

From this it appears that the common rendering of *Jehovah* in the Old Testament is by *Lord* in the New, and this usage is obviously derived from the Septuagint where Κύριος, *kurios, Lord*, is employed in numberless instances for יהוה, *Yehovah*. Thus, for instance, as a sample of multitudes of similar cases, Ps. lxxiii. 18. "Thou, whose name alone is Jehovah, art the Most High in all the earth." Ex. vi. 9, "I appeared unto Abraham, unto Isaac, and unto Jacob, by the name of God Almighty (Shaddai); but by my name Jehovah was I not known to them." In these passages the original for *Jehovah* is rendered in the Septuagint by *Lord*, and as the New Testament writers followed this version, they undoubtedly by this title understood the proper name of God, *Jehovah*. Moreover, it is made very clear both by Pearson (*Creed*, p. 234), and Hengstenberg (*Christology*, vol. 1. p. 161–187), that the ancient Jews attributed the name *Jehovah* to their expected Messiah. Thus the former adduces the following remarkable testimony from Rabbinical sources;—"The Scripture calleth the name of Messias, *Jehovah our righteousness*." "God calleth the Messias by his own name, and his name is *Jehovah*." "What is the name of the Messias? R. Abba said, *Jehovah* is his name." But it is well known that the Jews worshiped but one God in one person, and if Jesus Christ was the true Messiah, they at least could never have regarded him as the second of a trinity of persons, for by the term *Jehovah* they could never have understood any other than the one Supreme Deity.

The result of the whole, if I am not mistaken, is that the title "Lord" (kurios), though like its Hebrew counterpart *Adon, Adonai,* often used as a mere term of civil respect, has in New Testament usage, when spoken of the Saviour, the dominant import of *supreme divinity.* The *Lord* Jesus Christ is Jesus Christ the true and only *Jehovah,* and as Jehovah is one without distinction of persons, so not the slightest trace of any such distinction can be properly recognised in any thing that is revealed of the character and offices of Christ.

As to the objections to this view founded upon his economical relations to the great scheme of redemption, in which he speaks of himself, and is represented by the sacred writers, as sent by the Father—as doing the Father's will and not his own—as inferior to the Father—as praying to him—as receiving glory and honor from him—all this will form the subject of future communications, in which I shall endeavor to show its entire consistency with every thing hitherto advanced in respect to the absolute unity and unapproached supremacy of his nature.

To one grand result of the whole discussion I cannot but here advert. You will readily perceive that the same train of evidence which makes the Jehovah of the Old Testament the Jesus of the New, makes, at the same time, the Jesus of the New the Jehovah of the Old. It therefore, establishes a perfect identity of Divine person and unity of worship, in the true Church, from Adam down to the present day. The very same Being, in his immutable grandeur, is presented to our contemplation in every period of the Divine dispensations, so that by christianizing the heathenism of Pope's—"Jehovah, Jove, or Lord," and reading it "Jehovah, Jesus, Lord," —we recognize under the triple denomination the one God whose worship hallowed the garden of Eden, and the temple of Jerusalem, and still consecrates the true churches of Christendom. We have at once a satisfactory clew to all such passages as the following;—"Esteeming the reproach of *Christ* greater riches than the treasures in Egypt."—"The rock that followed them was *Christ.*" "Neither let us tempt *Christ* as some of them tempted, and were destroyed by serpents." This title is indeed proleptically employed, but after the evidence above adduced there would seem to be no room to doubt the identity of the person. It was clearly he who was "to come forth from Judah, a Ruler of Israel ; *whose goings*

forth have been from of old, from everlasting ;" i. e. as we believe
is the true import of the words, whose *manifestations*—whose
prelusory *theophanies*—have been from of old, from the earliest
periods of recorded time. Our Lord and Saviour Jesus Christ
has been therefore the manifested God from the remotest ages
of human history. This one and immutable God, devoid of
all personal distinction, is the august I AM, or self-existent
Deity, who was before Abraham, and who revealed himself to
Moses at the burning bush, proclaiming the name of Jehovah
as his "memorial for ever." That this being is identically the
same with the Jesus of the New Testament, the predicted Messiah of the Jews, is the grand paramount truth of the inspired
oracles, the denial of which leaves those divine documents
shorn of their essential glory and the hopes of human redemption a very mockery. Who remains to accomplish it, when
the language affirming a God made flesh, though no more
expressive language ascertains the existence of a God at all,
is frittered away in forced and jejune explanations aiming to
obliterate the idea of *theanthropism* from the minds of men ?[*]
We can indeed find some apology for this extreme of the human-
tarian, in the equally gross error of the tripersonal, dogma,
revolting no less to Scripture than to reason, but we scruple
not to say that the reaction from that violent position has
transcended its legitimate limit, and that the mind of Unitarian Christendom must oscillate backward to the point where it
is met by the sublime annunciation of Unity and Trinity *in one
person,* and that Person "the Word made flesh and dwelling
among us." This, we are persuaded, is the common ground on
which the Unitarian and the Trinitarian must eventually
meet ; and as there must be mutual recession, so there must
be mutual concession. The Trinitarian now claims what the
Unitarian can never admit, and what he ought not to admit—
the doctrine of three persons. The Unitarian now denies what
the Trinitarian can never forego, and what he is entitled to insist
upon—the supreme and absolute divinity of Jesus Christ. *The
fatal error of Trinitarians has been to argue the Divinity of
Christ on grounds that supposed a Trinity of Persons ; that of
Unitarians, to maintain the Unity of the Godhead in the denial of
the Divinity of Jesus.* The word "persons" has wrought infinite mischiefs to the whole scheme of Christianity. Sweden-

---

[*] "The Divine itself, the Divine Human, and the Holy Proceeding, are the same as
the Lord, and the Lord the same as Jehovah. There are none who separate this
Trine which is in One, but they who say that they acknowledge One Supreme
Being (*Ens*), the Creator of the universe, which thing is forgiven those who are
without the Church ; but they who are within the Church and say thus, do not in
fact acknowledge any God, whatever they may profess or suppose ; still less do
they acknowledge the Lord."—*A. C.* 2156.

borg has shown how the two systems may harmonize their respective truths, and that in such a way as at the same time to secure, in the most eminent degree, all the practical interests of the *Christian life,* and it would be a weakness unworthy of both parties to suffer the mere force of prejudice against his name to neutralize the promptings to a union so devoutly to be wished.

I close my letter with an extract from this illuminated teacher of the last ages.

"Because the Lord, by the passion of the cross, fully glorified his Human, that is, united it to his Divine, and thus made his Human Divine, it follows, that He is Jehovah and God, also as to both. Wherefore in the Word, in many places, He is called Jehovah, God, and the Holy One of Israel, the Redeemer, Saviour, and Former, as in the following. 'Mary said, My soul doth magnify the Lord, and my spirit hath rejoiced in God my Saviour,' Luke i. 46, 47. 'The angel said to the shepherds, Behold, I bring you tidings of great joy, which shall be unto all people, that there is born this day, in the city of David, a Saviour, who is Christ the Lord,' Luke ii. 10, 11. 'They said, this is indeed the Christ, the Saviour of the world,' John iv. 42. 'I will help thee, saith Jehovah, and thy Redeemer, the Holy One of Israel,' Isaiah xli. 14. 'Thus saith Jehovah thy Creator, O Jacob, and thy former, O Israel; for I have redeemed thee. I am Jehovah thy God, the Holy One of Israel, thy Saviour,' xliii. 1, 3. 'Thus saith Jehovah your Redeemer, the Holy One of Israel: I am Jehovah your Holy One, the Creator of Israel, your King,' xlii. 14, 15. 'Thus saith Jehovah, the Holy One of Israel, and his Former,' xiv. 11. 'Thus saith Jehovah, thy Redeemer, the Holy One of Israel,' xlviii. 17. 'That all flesh may know that I Jehovah am thy Saviour and thy Redeemer, the Mighty One of Jacob,' lx. 26. 'Then he shall come to Zion a Redeemer,' lix. 20. 'That thou mayest know that I Jehovah am thy Saviour and thy Redeemer, the mighty one of Jacob,' lx. 16. 'Jehovah thy Former from the womb,' xlix. 5. 'Jehovah my Rock and my Redeemer,' Psalm xix. 14. 'They remembered that God was their rock, and the High God their Redeemer,' lxxxviii. 35. 'Thus saith Jehovah, thy Redeemer, and thy Former from the womb,' Isaiah xliv. 24. 'As for our Redeemer, Jehovah of hosts is his name, the Holy One of Israel,' xlvii. 4. 'With everlasting kindness will I have mercy on thee, saith Jehovah thy Redeemer,' liv. 8. 'Their Redeemer is strong, Jehovah of hosts is his name,' Jerem. l. 34. 'Let Israel hope in Jehovah, for with Jehovah there is mercy, and with Him plenteous redemption, He shall redeem Israel from all his iniquities,' Psalm cxxx. 7, 8. 'Jehovah my rock, my fortress, and the horn of my salvation, my Saviour,' 2 Samuel xxii. 2, 3. 'Thus saith Jehovah, the Redeemer of Israel, his Holy One; Kings shall see and arise because of the Lord, who is faithful, the Holy One of Israel, who hath chosen Thee,' Isaiah xlix. 'Surely God is in thee, and there is no other God besides. Verily thou art a God that hidest Thyself, O God of Israel the Saviour,' xlv. 14, 15. 'Thus saith Jehovah, the King of Israel, and his Redeemer, Jehovah of hosts, Beside Me there is no God,' xliv. 6. 'I am Jehovah, and beside Me there is no Saviour,' xliii. 11. 'Am not I Jehovah, and there is no other beside Me; and a Saviour, there is none beside Me,' xlv. 21. 'I am Jehovah thy God, thou shalt know no

God but Me, for there is no Saviour beside Me," Hosea xiii. 4. 'Look
unto Me, that ye may be saved, all ye ends of the earth; because I
am God, and there is none else,' Isaiah xlv. 22. 'Jehovah of Hosts
is his name, and thy Redeemer the Holy One of Israel, the God of the
whole earth shall He be called,' liv. 5.   From these it may be seen,
that the Divine of the Lord, which is called the Father, and here Jehovah and God, and the Divine Human which is called the Son, and
here Redeemer and Saviour, also Former, that is, Reformer and Regenerator, are not two but one; for not only is it said, Jehovah God
and the Holy One of Israel, the Redeemer and Saviour; but also it is
said, Jehovah the Redeemer and Saviour; yet also it is said, 'I am
Jehovah, and beside Me there is no Saviour.' From which it manifestly appears, that the Divine and Human in the Lord are one person,
and that the Human is also Divine; for the Redeemer and Saviour of
the world is no other than the Lord as to the Divine Human, which is
called the Son: for redemption and salvation constitute the proper attribute of his Human, which is called merit and righteousness; for his
Human endured temptations and the passion of the cross, and thus by
the Human He redeemed and saved. Now because, after the union of
the Human with the Divine in Himself, which was like that of the
soul and body in man, there were no longer two but one person, according to the doctrine of the Christian world, therefore the Lord, as to
both, is Jehovah and God; wherefore it is sometimes said, Jehovah
and the Holy One of Israel, the Redeemer and Saviour, at other times,
Jehovah the Redeemer and Saviour, as may be seen from the passages
above quoted.   It is said, the Saviour Christ; Luke ii. 10, 11; John iv.
42.   God and the God of Israel, the Saviour and Redeemer; Luke i.
47; Isaiah xlv. 14, 15; liv. 5; Psalm lxxviii. 45. Jehovah the Holy
One of Israel, the Saviour and Redeemer; Isaiah xli. 14; xliii. 3, 11,
14, 15; xlviii. 17; xlix. 7; liv. 5. Jehovah, the Saviour, Redeemer
and Former; xliv. 6; xlvii. 4; xlix. 26; liv. 8; lxiii. 16; Jeremiah l.
34; Psalm lxxviii. 35; cxxx. 7, 8; 2 Samuel xxii. 2, 3. Jehovah,
God, the Redeemer and Saviour, and besides Me there is no other;
Isaiah xliii. 11; xliv. 6; xlv. 14, 15, 21, 22; Hosea xiii. 4."—*Doct.
of the Lord*, 34.

"That God and Man in the Lord, according to the doctrine, are not
two, but one person, and altogether one, as the soul and body are one,
appears clearly from many things which He said; as, That the Father and He are one; that all things of the Father are his, and all his
the Father's; that He is in the Father, and the Father in Him; that all
things are given into his hand; that He has all power; that He is the
God of heaven and earth; that whosoever believes in Him has eternal life; and further, that the Divine and Human ascended into heaven, and that, as to both, He sits at the right hand of God, that is, that
He is Almighty; and many more things which were adduced above from
the Word, concerning his Divine Human, which all testify that *God is one
as well in person as in Essence, in whom is a Trinity, and that that God is
the Lord*.   The, reason why these things concerning the Lord are now
for the first time made publicly known, is, because it is foretold in the
Revelation, xxi. and xxii. that a new church should be instituted by
the Lord, at the end of the former, in which this should be the primary
thing.   This church is what is there meant by the New Jerusalem,
into which none can enter, but those who acknowledge the Lord alone
as God of heaven and earth.   And this I can aver, that the universal
heaven acknowledges the Lord alone; and that whosoever does not
acknowledge Him, is not admitted into heaven; for heaven is heaven

from the Lord. This acknowledgment itself from love and faith, causes all there to be in the Lord, and the Lord in them, as the Lord himself teaches in John; 'In that day ye shall know, that I am in my Father, and ye in Me, and I in you,' xiv. 20. And again; 'Abide in Me, and I in you. I am the vine, ye are the branches; he that abideth in Me and I in him, the same bringeth forth much fruit; for without Me ye cannot do any thing. If a man abide not in Me, he is cast out.' xv. 4–6; xvii. 22, 23. That this was not seen from the Word before, is, because, if it had been seen, still it would not have been received."
—*Ib.* 60, 61.   G. B.

(*To be continued.*)

ARTICLE III.

THE LAWS OF CREATION.

SPIRITUALLY AND NATURALLY CONSIDERED.

No. II.

It may be well to advert here to an objection which will not be unnaturally urged against the general view maintained. "How could our world be created through man, when man did not come into this world till long after it was created?"

The objection has all its ground and force in a misconception of the account of creation in the first chapter of Genesis. According to Swedenborg, that account does not in the remotest sense relate to natural creation, or the creation of this world, with man and the objects of nature. But it is asked, "Is not natural creation a type of the spiritual; and does not therefore the account in the first chapter of Genesis, in describing the creation of the spiritual man, or the church, indicate also the order of natural creation?" It is replied, that the account in Genesis does not set forth the creation of the spiritual man *originally*, but his re-creation, or regeneration from a mental state described as "without form and void." In the regeneration of man, or the creation of the church in him out of this chaotic state, the most ultimate kingdom or degree is first formed, which is represented by the earth, scientifically denominated the *mineral* kingdom; next is formed a higher degree, springing out of the natural, and this is represented by the *vegetable kingdom,* which succeeded the creation of the mineral kingdom; then the third and last degree of the church, or spiritual life, is formed in man, which is represented by the *animal kingdom,* or the highest order of natural life. After all these constituents of the church are provided by the Lord, and implanted in the various degrees of the human mind, then it is that the perfect spiritual man or the church exists, which spiritual man is represented by the formation of the physical man "of the dust of the ground," Gen. ii. 7.

The natural objection arising from the account of the creation in Genesis, being thus removed by the spiritual sense, we are thrown back entirely upon the principles developed by Swedenborg, by which to account for the *original* creation of the natural world. These principles, we trust, are set forth with sufficient clearness and fulness in this and the preceding articles.

We conceive Swedenborg as teaching that the Divine Life, influent primarily into the *inmost* of the human mind, elaborates its ultimates in the very act of proceeding, just as the soul elaborates the body from its interior or spiritual forces.

In n. 78 of the True Christian Religion, an angel is made to say that "God is Love itself and Wisdom itself; and the affections of his love are infinite, and the perceptions of his wisdom are infinite; and of these, all and everything that appears upon the earth are correspondences; * * * and because He is omnipresent, such correspondences of the affections of his love and wisdom are in the whole of the natural world; but in our world, which is called the spiritual world, there are similar correspondences with those who receive affections and perceptions from God ; *the difference is*, that such things, in our world, are created by God INSTANTANEOUSLY, *according to the affections of the angels*; but in your world (the natural) THEY WERE CREATED IN LIKE MANNER AT THE BEGINNING; but it was provided, that, by generations of one from another, they should be perpetually renewed, and thus that creation should be continued."

This is "the conclusion of the whole matter," and it is all that we contend for, namely, that natural creation *originally* was effected according to the same law by which spiritual creation is now effected.

We have seen that spiritual things " are created by God *instantaneously*, according to the affections of the angels;" that is, they are outbirths of their interior states, and are called into being spontaneously with the rise of the states of mind in the angels to which they correspond, and of which they are the effects. "But in your (natural) world, they were created *in like manner* at the beginning."

It may be necessary, before attempting to investigate the mental laws, according to which the natural world, with its spaces and times, its objects and phenomena, exists, to recapitulate briefly the results at which we have already arrived in regard to the like appearances in the spiritual world.

And first, with respect [to the *Sun* of the Spiritual World.

"Every angel as well as every man has an inmost or supreme degree. or a certain inmost or supreme state (of life), into which the Lord's Divine Essence is first of all proximately influent, and from which He arranges the other interior states (of life), which they have in succession according to degrees of order. This inmost or supreme state (of life) may be called the Lord's entrance to an angel, and to a man, and His veriest habitation with them. By this supreme state man is a man, and is distinguished from brute animals, which have it not. It is this which enables man—and in this respect too he differs. from animals—to be raised as to the whole of the interior states of his rational and natural mind, by the Lord to Himself, and also to believe in Him, to be affected with love towards Him, and in this way to see Him. From this source man derives his capacity for receiving intelligence and wisdom, and his power of discoursing from reason. It is the cause also of his living for ever."—N. 39.

Here Swedenborg defines what he calls the internal or spiritual man, or the inmost degree of the mind. It is that state of life which is most highly receptive of the inflowing divine Life. It is that sphere of the mind in which the Lord is more immediately present. Man alone has it. He is distinguished by it from all other animals ; it is that which constitutes humanity, and because it is the medium by which the divine and eternal life of God enters the soul, it is the only source of man's immortality,—of his intelligence, wisdom, and reasoning powers. The beasts have it not, therefore they are not immortal. Man alone has it, and it is his spiritual world, into which he permanently retires by the natural process called death.

We might appeal to individual consciousness in confirmation of this spiritual or heavenly region of the mind. Who has not at times left the world and retired within himself there to hold communion with his God, and drink in those divine influences which strengthen and arm the soul? Who does not know what it is to commune with one's self apart from the outward world, and to be wrapt in thought and elevated in feeling so that he seemed to dwell as it were in the presence of angels? How often does the devout and contemplative Christian retire into this inner sanctuary of the soul, this holy of holies within the temple of his mind, where he meets God face to face, and worships in His more immediate presence?

This may be described as the inmost degree or state of the mind, into which, when we retire, we are unconscious of space and time, of the outward and sensuous world, are absent from our outward selves, and present with our inner selves, and take note only of the mental or spiritual facts and phenomena which then present themselves to our view. This is man's spiritual world. He carries it within him. It is not afar off in space, nor does it endure in time; but it consists wholly *in* an abstract or internal state of mind, wherein the influent,

the objects themselves, aside from man, or is in the different degrees of the mind itself.

According to the philosophy of Swedenborg, the two worlds, natural and spiritual, are two subjective states of the mind itself, or the real man, and are discriminated only by the discriminated degrees of the mind in which they have their origin. Considered as to his mind, man is an inhabitant of both the spiritual and natural world. He has two minds, or two discriminated degrees of the same mind, called internal and external. The internal of his mind or spirit is his spiritual world, while the external, comprising actions and sensations, is his natural world.

In the work on Heaven and Hell, Swedenborg says, "men are as well in the spiritual world as in the natural world" (n. 135) ; and in the Divine Providence, " man, in respect to his mind or spirit, is either a heaven or a hell in its least form" (n. 299) ; and still more specifically :

"The spiritual world, in the universal acceptation of the term, is where spirits and angels are, and the natural world where men are ; but considered in their particular sense, *every man has his spiritual and natural worlds. His internal man is to him a spiritual world, but his external man, a natural world.* Those states (of mind) which inflow from his spiritual world, *and are exhibited in his natural world*, are in general representations, and, in so far as they agree together, correspondences." *A. C.* n. 2990.

This is definite and conclusive enough to those who can understand the terms employed by our author. Considered in their origin, both worlds are in the mind. "Every man has his spiritual and his natural worlds." He carries the essential elements of them within him. His internal mind is his spiritual world, and it depends wholly on the moral state of that mind, on its capacity or incapacity to receive the divine life, whether that world is to him a heaven or a hell. Man, in forming his moral character, or the real state of his interior self, makes his heaven or his hell, for they rest not on the arbitrary will of the Almighty, or the contingencies of circumstance and situation, but on the internal state or quality of the mind itself, and all the beautiful objects of the one, and the repulsive objects of the other, are alike the outbirths of the mind that beholds them. To use the expressive language of Milton,

> " The mind is its own place, and *in itself*
> Can make a heaven of hell, a hell of heaven."

But what this internal man, or inmost degree of the mind, which is man's spiritual world is, let Swedenborg give us a definite idea. He says, in the Heaven and Hell, that,

"Every angel as well as every man has an inmost or supreme degree, or a certain inmost or supreme state (of life), into which the Lord's Divine Essence is first of all proximately influent, and from which He arranges the other interior states (of life), which they have in succession according to degrees of order. This inmost or supreme state (of life) may be called the Lord's entrance to an angel, and to a man, and His veriest habitation with them. By this supreme state man is a man, and is distinguished from brute animals, which have it not. It is this which enables man—and in this respect too he differs from animals—to be raised as to the whole of the interior states of his rational and natural mind, by the Lord to Himself, and also to believe in Him, to be affected with love towards Him, and in this way to see Him. From this source man derives his capacity for receiving intelligence and wisdom, and his power of discoursing from reason. It is the cause also of his living for ever."—N. 39.

Here Swedenborg defines what he calls the internal or spiritual man, or the inmost degree of the mind. It is that state of life which is most highly receptive of the inflowing divine Life. It is that sphere of the mind in which the Lord is more immediately present. Man alone has it. He is distinguished by it from all other animals ; it is that which constitutes humanity, and because it is the medium by which the divine and eternal life of God enters the soul, it is the only source of man's immortality,—of his intelligence, wisdom, and reasoning powers. The beasts have it not, therefore they are not immortal. Man alone has it, and it is his spiritual world, into which he permanently retires by the natural process called death.

We might appeal to individual consciousness in confirmation of this spiritual or heavenly region of the mind. Who has not at times left the world and retired within himself there to hold communion with his God, and drink in those divine influences which strengthen and arm the soul ? Who does not know what it is to commune with one's self apart from the outward world, and to be wrapt in thought and elevated in feeling so that he seemed to dwell as it were in the presence of angels ? How often does the devout and contemplative Christian retire into this inner sanctuary of the soul, this holy of holies within the temple of his mind, where he meets God face to face, and worships in His more immediate presence ?

This may be described as the inmost degree or state of the mind, into which, when we retire, we are unconscious of space and time, of the outward and sensuous world, are absent from our outward selves, and present with our inner selves, and take note only of the mental or spiritual facts and phenomena which then present themselves to our view. This is man's spiritual world. He carries it within him. It is not afar off in space, nor does it endure in time ; but it consists wholly in an abstract or internal state of mind, wherein the influent, creative life is perceived as the immediate cause of all the phenomenal creations which are presented to view. " The kingdom of God is *within* you."

Man's interior mind, or that state of the mind in which he thinks abstractedly, and above the conditions of time, space, materiality, or anything addressed to the external faculties, being his spiritual world ; it no longer seems a strange thing how he may pass into it even without the change of death. It is simply a rapt or abstract state of mind, when all the external and sensuous faculties are at rest, and the individual is alone conscious of what is passing within. Into such a state the prophets and seers of old were introduced, when they saw visions and conversed with angels. In such a state much of the Bible was dictated to them. In such a state were the three disciples at the transfiguration, and the Revelator when the future destinies of the Church were symbolically represented to him. In such a state was Paul when he was caught up into the third heaven ; and finally, in such a state was Swedenborg himself when he heard and saw all those *memorabilia* which he has so minutely and philosophically described. His intromission into the spiritual world was merely the conscious opening of the interior region of the mind, in which the spiritual world, with every man, consists. Most who have passed into this state by trance, have retained little or no recollection, upon coming out of it, of what they saw or heard. The reason was that the connection between their rational and perceptive faculties, or external mind, was wholly cut off from the internal. When passing into the internal, or abstract degree of the mind, they passed into their spiritual world ; and on awakening from it they come again into the natural world, because into the external and natural faculties of the mind ; and when in the natural they retained no knowledge of what passed in the spiritual. But Swedenborg was able fully to describe and lay open the laws of the spiritual world, because he habitually and daily passed into the interior region of the mind, or into the spiritual world, in the full possession of all the rational and perceptive faculties which he enjoyed in his natural state. He, unlike other seers, was wholly *himself* when wrapt in the interiors of his mind. This is what he means by the opening of his spiritual sight, or his intromission into the spiritual world.

Having now seen what the internal man is : viz. that it is only the interior degree or region of the mind, in which the spiritual world with every man exists ; and that thus the spirit of man is his own spiritual world ; let us next inquire what constitutes the external or natural man; and whether this is not equally his sensuous and natural world.

Rightly defined, man's natural or sensuous world consists in those ultimate and sensuous states of his natural or external mind, in which the influent life terminates, and in which effects, that are from his interior or spiritual mind, are first perceived and become apparent.

"The external man," says Swedenborg, "is formed of things sensual; not such as belong to the body, but such as are derived from bodily things; and this is the case not only with men, but also with spirits."—*A. C.* 976.

Why is it said that the external man, by which is meant the external mind of man, is formed of things sensual? It is because our author, by such terms as the external man, the natural man, the external mind and the natural mind, all which are the same, invariably means the faculties of *sensation*, or that ultimate sphere of the mind which the *natural senses* affect, in contradistinction from that interior region which constitutes the spiritual world of every man. The natural or sensuous mind then, is simply those ultimate states or that ultimate degree in which the natural senses reside, in which man thinks and reasons sensuously, or according to appearances and laws, lives in, and is affected by the delights and sensations of the body. A man who is engrossed in such states we call a sensual man. His life and love are in that degree of his mind, are fed by the natural senses, instead of those higher and more spiritual states which constitute his inner and better self.

The distinction between these outer and inner, sensuous and spiritual degrees, states, or spheres of the mind, is the sole distinction between the natural and spiritual worlds. Man is an inhabitant both of the spiritual and natural world,—of the spiritual when he lives and thinks in his internal or spiritual mind, and of the natural when he lives and thinks in his natural mind. Thus his natural mind is his natural world, and his spiritual mind his spiritual world, as we have already shown that Swedenborg teaches. As his spiritual world, with all its objects and phenomena is the result of the influent, creative life operating upon the interior degree of his mind so his natural world, with all its objects and phenomena, is the result of the same creative life operating upon the external and natural degree of his mind. The outer world is simply the inner brought down into the sensuous region of thought.

In accordance with this position, Swedenborg remarks:

"Man, being a heaven, and also a world in its least form, after the image of the greatest, *has in himself both a spiritual world and a natural.* The interior states of his mind, which relate to his intellect and his will, are his spiritual world, but the exterior states of his body, which relate to his senses and his actions, are his natural world. Whatsoever then in his natural world, that is, in his body, its senses and its actions, exists from his spiritual world, that is, from his mind, its intellect and its will, is called a *correspondent.*"—*H. & H.* n. 90.

The same principle is asserted in various forms throughout these writings ; but this paragraph is sufficient for our purpose, both as to its distinctness and scope. The ground and origin of the two worlds, then, are inherently *within* man,— the natural alike as the spiritual. They are nothing but the display of creative Life upon the spiritual and natural degrees of his mind as a theatre. Hence he " *has in himself both a spiritual world and a natural.*"

Now with this distinct view of the difference between the internal or spiritual, and external or natural degrees in the human mind, as constituting the sole distinction between the spiritual and natural worlds, let us conceive, once for all, how the natural world exists as an EFFECT of the spiritual. And to this end we must again call to mind what has been said as to the laws of spiritual existence. Remembering that every seemingly external object of the spiritual world really exists within the minds of the angels ; that their sun, with its heat and light, is the first proceeding effect of the Divine Love and Wisdom flowing into their interior minds ; that the appearances of spaces and times are the results of the states of their affections and thoughts ; that all animals and objects which appear to view, are outbirths of their interior states under the combined agencies of goodness and truth as the heat and light of their sun ;—remembering this, and conceiving their world thus mirrored around them, but really and momentarily dependent upon the influx of divine life into the spiritual mind ; just view the whole as proceeding or brought down into the *natural and sensuous degree of the mind*, and it becomes a natural world or a world of effects, and everything is accounted for, by a uniform and direct influx of the divine life from the interior mind or spiritual world, into the exterior mind, or natural world.

Our sun is just as much the effect of the creative life inflowing into our natural and sensuous minds, as is the spiritual sun an effect of the same life flowing into the minds of angels. In no other way could the natural sun correspond to the spiritual ; and the same may be said of the natural world as a whole. Indeed there can be no such relation between the two worlds as that of *correspondency* except between the spiritual and natural degrees of the human mind, which are the basis of the two worlds, and the respective theatres upon which their phenomena are exhibited.

The natural sun, with its heat and light, *seems* to be the agent of natural creations from the earth altogether independent of man; and such is the appearance in regard to the spiritual sun. But as Swedenborg remarks, the natural sun is dead, and can create nothing. Its creative energy is clearly the creative life of goodness and truth (heat and light), operating upon the ultimate spheres of the human mind as a ground, and in and through that calling into being every production that springs from the earth. Thus it is God, the universal and Divine Life, acting by a uniform and undivided influx into and through the human mind, who creates, and not the vague thing called nature, nor the natural sun, as some have foolishly and absurdly imagined. The appearance is that the earth, and the sun both exist independently of man, and that natural productions are effected by the combined operation of the heat and light of the latter upon the former; but the reality is that they are both effects in different degrees of the divine influx into the sensuous region of the mind, as are the earth and the sun that appear in the spiritual world, of the same influx into the spiritual region of mind. In the spiritual mind, the sun, as an object of sight, is produced by influx into the highest faculties, while the earth there is the termination of that influx in the ultimate faculties of that degree of the mind. The same is the origin of the natural sun and earth, the sole difference being that they, as objects of sight, are presented in the sensuous faculties of the mind, and hence are objects of the natural senses. But as the spiritual sun is the first proceeding effect of influx from the Lord into the spiritual mind; so is the natural sun the first and highest effect of the same influx upon entering the natural mind. And as the earth which appears in the spiritual world, is the sphere of the spiritual mind where the Divine Order of the creative influx terminates, so also the natural earth is the ultimate proceeding of the same influx into the natural mind. And as all spiritual creations seem to result from the action of the spiritual sun upon the earth there; so also do the products which spring from the natural earth seem to result from the operation of the natural sun upon it, independently of man. But in both worlds the origin of both sun and earth is internal, and all creation is effected by the combined action of goodness and truth, as heat and light, in the highest plane of the mind upon the lowest as an ultimate ground or earth.

Thus the phenomena of the two worlds are not distinguished by a difference of origin, or of laws according to which they exist, but simply by their taking place, in the one case, within the spiritual mind, and in the other, in the natural. The two worlds are nothing but the two discriminated states of the mind of man. As Swedenborg distinctly affirms, "His internal man is to him a spiritual world, but his external man, a natural world." Thus man "has in himself both a spiritual world and a natural. The interior states of his mind, which relate to his intellect and his will, are his spiritual world, but the exterior states of his body, which relate to his senses and his actions, are his natural world."—*H. & H.* n. 92.

It is clear from this, that Swedenborg considers the two worlds as differing only as the two planes or degrees of the mind differ from which they are perceived. The one undeviating and undivided stream of influent life from God, creates the spiritual world within the spiritual mind, and the natural within the natural mind. They exist in nothing else than these two discriminated states of the will and the intellect, called the internal or spiritual, and the external or natural man, and they are the same in the externeity of their aspect. They are both alike representative worlds, for they are effects, corresponding, in all their variety of outward forms, to the states of the mind, either spiritual or natural, in which they originate. In both they are produced by the influx of the same divine life, terminating in the sentient faculties where they are presented as extraneous objects, with all the appearances of time and space. The angel knows how and where the phenomena exist; but the natural man sees nothing but an external world of effects, for he does not elevate his mind to causes.

The *Doctrine of Influx*, as developed in the writings of Swedenborg, is quite essential to a right understanding of the laws of creation, and of the relation which the spiritual world sustains to the natural. *Influx*, properly defined, is the *inflowing* of the Divine Love and wisdom, as the creative Life from God, into forms receptive of that life. God is one and indivisible, infinite and self-existent, by the finite and imperfect reception of whose life, every man becomes a conscious being, and his existence is momentarily dependent upon a continual influx of life from God. This influx of love and wisdom from God into the will and intellect of the regenerated or angelic mind, in whose sentient faculties it is perceived as heat and light, is the primary cause of all creation both spiritual and natural. It first flows into the human mind, which possessing a will and an understanding, is an image and likeness of God, and thus a form receptive of His love and wisdom. Now there is no other existence save the human mind, or man, that is endowed with these two faculties, and therefore nothing but man can be a medium capable of receiving and transmitting this influx of creative life to other subjects. This idea it is all-important to establish; for, if true, there can be but one channel of influx to give life to all things whether in heaven or earth, and that the human mind or *humanity.* There can be no such a thing as an influx from the spiritual world into the natural without, and independent of, the human mind, but that mind is the medium of all creations in the natural alike as in the spiritual world. The great idea is that *humanity* is the sole medium for transmitting the influx of divine life, whether spiritual or natural. As the Divine and Infinite Humanity is the medium of all life to man; as he could not be held in being without this link which connects him with the Eternal Jehovah; so finite humanity is the medium of life to all below it. Man is thus the lord of creation beneath him, as God is the Lord of man and all that is beneath Him.

We have seen that man is the medium of all spiritual creations; that the influx of divine life is into the interior or spiritual mind, and that the states of this mind, its affections and thoughts, its qualities and capacities, are the proximate causes of all the external phenomena of the spirit-world; and that that world considered as a whole, with all its representative animals and objects, is the out-birth of the mental states of the angels. The spiritual mind, then, which as Swedenborg affirms, is man's spiritual world, is the region of causes. The causes are the recipient states of that mind; but the natural mind, which as we have seen, is the natural world, is the region in which the divine influx terminates, and there all prior states of the mind co-exist as effects, and there too those prior states, which were causes, are lost sight of by him who thinks after a natural manner, and their effects are only perceived. This is the reason why Swedenborg invariably calls the spiritual world one of causes, and the natural, one of effects from those causes.

Just place the idea of influx distinctly before the mind, and see if you can gain any rational perception of an influx taking place from the spiritual world into dead matter aside from the human mind. What rational connexion can you discern between the spiritual world, which is purely an internal state of life, and the material world, unless they are both results of a uniform influx into the mind, creating these two worlds, the one from its spiritual, the other from its natural sphere, as a theatre? There can be, and there is, an influx of life from the spiritual into the natural region of the mind: and that is all the influx of which we can form any rational idea. That is the influx from the spiritual into the natural world; for these worlds consist in the distinctive states of the spiritual and natural mind. The same divine life, that calls into being the phenomena of the spiritual world through the spiritual mind, in its farther transflux into the natural mind, gives rise to the phenomena of the natural world, and *therefore* there is a correspondence between them as of cause and effect.

Now Swedenborg says;

" Man is so created, that the Divine things of the Lord may descend *through* him to the ultimate things of nature, and from the ultimates of nature may descend to Him; so that man might be a medium of union between the Divine and the world of nature, and thus by man, as by an uniting medium, the very ultimate of nature might live from the Divine, which would be the case, if man had lived according to Divine order. That man is so created, is manifest from this consideration, that as to his body he is a little world, since all the arcana of the world of nature are therein reposited."—*A. C.* n. 3702.

The fact is here explicitly affirmed that the influx of the creative life into nature is *through* man, and *hence* he is a little world, for the elements of the world of nature are in him, and all that constitutes nature has been ultimated from the Divine through men as " a medium of union." This influx descends through the human mind from the inmost spiritual region to the outmost natural,—from one discriminated degree to another, everywhere calling into being objects corresponding to the recipient state ; so that the ultimate sphere of the mind in which it terminates, and in which the previous *subjective* states of *causation* are perceived as *objective effects*, is the registry of the whole history of man. He is the prototype of the outward world, and nature is a faithful history of all the states through which universal man has passed,—of all the phases which the race has ever put on.

Swedenborg says that " creation all proceeds from first principles to ultimates" (*D. P.* 56) ; that " the divine truth proceeding from the Lord created all things" (*A. C.* 8200) : and that " Jehovah could not have created the universe, unless He had been a man" (*D. L. & W.* 285). Now if it is the divine truth that proceeds from first principles to ultimates, creating as it proceeds, how can it outflow except from one sphere of the mind to another? Truth can only operate upon and affect the intelligent recipient mind. But the divine truth proceeding from God, is that very influx which creates all things. How can truth act upon matter irrespective of mind? or in other words, how can there be an influx into nature except through man as a medium? Everything must originate in the human mind since that only is receptive of the divine truth, the creating influx. Hence in accordance with the affirmation of our author, "Jehovah could not have created the universe, unless He had been a Man;" for *humanity* is the sole medium for transmitting the creative life of God; and it can descend and create only in and through the discriminated degrees of that humanity as existing in the minds of human beings. The law of influx is uniform and undeviating. The creative life first descends into the will and the intellect of the human mind, and it never leaves it. Every sphere in that mind,—every degree of life, from the highest to the lowest,—from the celestial, called heaven, down to the natural, called earth, has its distinct phenomenal world; since the one Divine Life, that inflows into the interiors of the mind to produce its affections and thoughts in endless variety, inflows also into its ultimate recipient faculties, which correspond to the interior, and there creates those objects of sense, which, as a whole, constitute the sensuous world.

This opens to us some intelligible idea of *correspondences.* Swedenborg says that the natural world in general corresponds to the spiritual, and that correspondency is the relation of cause and effect. But how can the material world correspond to the spiritual except by the correspondency between the spiritual and natural degrees of the mind upon which these two worlds are respectively created? It is because the two worlds are alike the result of the states of the mind, that they correspond. If the spiritual world only were the result of mental states, and the natural existed independently of them, how could there be any correspondency between them? How can a cause wholly dependent upon the mind, produce an effect wholly independent of it? It is impossible. But if you conceive the cause to be located in the higher or spiritual sphere of the mind, and the effect in the lower or natural sphere, it all becomes plain and intelligible. For you can readily conceive how a particular state of thought or affection in the former, should act as a cause to produce a corresponding effect in the latter. The one is the sphere of causation, the other of sensation; hence a particular state of interior affection, when acting upon the sensuous or sentient sphere, there gives birth to, and is perceived as an animal which corresponds in its nature to that affection. In this view of the case the science of correspondences, as laid open by Swedenborg, becomes indeed a science, resting upon exact, rational, and universal laws, and is in truth the interpreter of the exhaustless and instructive volume of nature. But upon any other hypothesis it is a medley of unintelligible and arbitrary dicta which must be taken upon blind faith, and affords no food to the rational and spiritual mind. The reason which Swedenborg gives for the truth of correspondency is founded upon a perfect coincidence in the laws of influx and of creation in the two worlds. The reason that he gives, for instance, for the particular signification of a horse, or a camel, is, that whenever the thoughts of spiritual beings are intent upon those states of mind to which the horse or the camel corresponds, and of which they are the effects, these animals appear before them. This gives us a rational explanation of a creative process applicable to the spiritual life where there is neither space nor time, but only their appearances in the ultimate faculties of the mind. But how is it possible for this reason to be applied in proof of the spiritual meaning of such horses and camels as appear in nature, or those spoken of in Scripture? In order that the reason should here hold good, it must be granted that the appearances of camels and horses as objects of sense, are equally, in the natural as in the spiritual world, the effects of peculiar states of mind. Why does Swedenborg refer for the reason of the signification of these animals to the laws of the spiritual world, unless the natural world be created through the natural mind as the spiritual is through the spiritual mind, and thus the objects of the one correspond to the objects of the other, *because* the causative states correspond? This reason can hold only upon the ground that the two worlds are created by a similar influx of the Divine Life, the one through the states of the spiritual mind, the other through the corresponding states of the natural mind. So much for correspondency. That relation, as Swedenborg says, exists "between those things which appertain to the internal or spiritual man, and those which appertain to the external or natural man;" and such can be the case only upon the hypothesis that both worlds thus corresponding, with all their phenomenal aspects, are alike the outbirths of the states of man,—the one of the spiritual and the other of the natural mind. These subjective states of the mind do correspond, but that relation does not exist aside from the human mind. Says Swedenborg, "the natural mind is nothing else but a representation of the spiritual states from which it exists and subsists, and as it corresponds so it represents" (*A. C.* 4053). And again;—"The superior, or spiritual region of the human mind, is a heaven in its least effigy, and the lower or natural region is the world in its least effigy, on which account man was called by the ancients a microcosm or little world, and

he may also be called a microuranos or little heaven."—*T. C. R.* n. 604.

This idea that man is a microcosm or little world involves more than would appear at first sight. If he is such the whole of nature must be in its principles in him. He cannot be a type of nature unless it all proceeds through his mind and is an embodiment of everything that pertains to his being. If nature, together with the spiritual world, exists by a continual influx of life through man, so that preservation is no other than perpetual creation, and if it is the ultimation of the various thoughts, affections, and conditions of the human mind, then man indeed is the microcosm of which the universe is the macrocosm; then nature is the volume which contains the history of the whole human race, and when interpreted by the universal key of correspondency, every phenomenon will speak of an aspect of inner life in man from which it sprung. Geology, no longer the terror of the Christian and the sword of the sceptic, will utter an intelligible and significant language, recording in the strata of the earth and the various formations, the progress of universal man in all ages, and the peculiar states of the church which have characterized him in each.

"All created things in a certain image represent man," says Swedenborg. But all things can represent him and have relation to him only as having proceeded through him,—only as being embodiments of his affections and thoughts. Our author remarks that the lives of beasts are nothing else than affections, evil beasts being the forms of evil affections and gentle and useful beasts the forms of good affections, while fowls are the forms or images of the various states of the intellect. If this is so, all animals—every living thing, must be the outbirth of some subjective state of life in man. And hence we see the propriety of man being the appointed Lord of creation, —of his having "dominion over the fish of the sea, and over the fowl of the air, and over the cattle, and over all the earth, and over every creeping thing that creepeth upon the earth" (Gen. i. 26); for as man should be the lord and master of all his affections, passions, and interior states of life, so is he to have dominion over their embodied forms, and they are to be his servants, and to minister to his use according to the divine appointment (Gen. i. 29, 30).

Another conclusive proof of the internal origin of outward things, is furnished by Swedenborg where he represents that evil beasts, and birds, and poisonous productions of the vegetable kingdom, did not exist upon the earth, till after man became evil; that they are from hell; and that they were created only when the hells entered into the human mind, and were thus the outbirths of the evil and impure states of that mind. This position is so directly confirmed by Scripture, where we learn that the earth produced thorns and thistles only *after* the fall of man, and was ·cursed for *his* sake, that we need not dwell upon it. The fact is there recognized, that the sin of man did influence and alter the products of the earth ; but how could it unless they were the ultimate effects of his moral state, and proceeded through his mind as a medium? The hells are evil states of the human mind ; they are, as Swedenborg says, " in those who are wicked." But all noxious animals and products are, says he, from the hells ; *therefore* they are from those states of the human mind which constitute the hells, and are ultimate forms of them.

" That noxious things on earth," says our author, "*derive their origin from man*, and so from hell, may be proved by the state of the land of Canaan, as described in the Word ; for when the children of Israel lived according to the commandments, the earth gave forth her increase and in like manner the flocks and the herds : and that when they lived contrary to the commandments, the earth was barren, and, as it is said, accursed ; instead of harvest it produced thorns and briars, the flocks and herds miscarried, and wild beasts broke in. The same may be deduced from the locusts, frogs, and lice, in Egypt."—*D. L. & W.* n. 345.

Nothing can be more conclusive than this. The internal origin of things in nature is here affirmed, and amply proved by the testimony of Scripture. The human mind is the channel or medium of their creation, and they are the effigies, the ultimations of the states of that mind. It is said that man in this world is the medium of natural creation only so far as it regards the out-birth of the hells ; that forms of evil were indeed created from the hells in his mind, but that such was not the order of creation before the hells usurped his mind, and that the things which have a heavenly origin do not proceed through man, but independently of him. I reply in the words just quoted. "When the children of Israel *lived according to the commandments*, the earth gave forth her increase, and in like manner the flocks and the herds." Their heavenly or good states of life were ultimated as well as their evil states ; both equally affected the earth and the animals. And then, can there be two orders of creation—one for the evil, and another for the good ; one through the human mind in this life, and the other extraneous to and independent of it? The supposition is irrational and unphilosophical ; it is arbitrary and unnecessary. Influx is uniform and undivided from the highest to the lowest. It is *all through* man into nature, or none of it. The origin of all nature is one and the same, and its different objects determined only by the different mental states in which they originate.

But further, and in conclusion, let me say, that according to the principles of Swedenborg, *there is no such a thing as a physical influx, or an influx of the creative life from the spiritual world into nature aside from man; but that the creation of all things is through his internal states of mind, and thence into the external, natural, and sensuous degree of the mind, where influx terminates, and where all creations are perceived as objects of the senses.*

In the following brief extract the divine order of this creative influx is clearly and beautifully set forth.

"The divine truth which goes forth from the Lord, inflows into every man through the interior states (of his mind) into his exterior, and even into his outward sentient and bodily faculties, and every where calls forth corresponding objects in their order; in the sentient faculty such corresponding objects as appear in the world and upon earth. *It is a fallacy to suppose that external objects inflow into the interior faculties, for the truth is, the external state (of life)* does not flow into the internal, but the internal into the external."—*A. C.* 6948.

Here we leave the whole matter, resting in the grand conclusion, that this world, with its myriad objects and phenomena, is the effect of the continual proceeding of the creative life through universal man, and is the embodiment of his states of life in all times; that it is thus the history of the race, and that man will reunite himself to his Maker, by tracing out and appropriating for his spiritual perfection all those good qualities of the race in all ages, just as his physical man is perfected by the incorporation and use of their natural ultimates.

T. D. S.

EXTRACT.

"Every man is born natural from his parents, but becomes spiritual from the Lord, which is meant by being born again, or regenerated; and inasmuch as he is born natural, therefore the knowledges which he imbibes from infancy, before he becomes spiritual, are implanted in his natural memory; but as he advances in years, and begins to view rationally the knowledges of good and truth, which he has imbibed from the Word or from preaching, if he then lives an evil life, he seizes upon and imbibes the falsities which are opposite and contrary to these knowledges, and when this is the case, as he is then endued with the gift of reasoning, he reasons from falsities against the knowledges of his infancy and childhood, in consequence of which these are cast out, and falsities succeed in their place."—*A. E.* 403.

SELECTIONS.

—

SWEDENBORG'S INVITATION TO THE NEW CHURCH.

NOW FIRST TRANSLATED FROM THE ORIGINAL LATIN.

THE following Tract by Swedenborg, from the Spiritual Diary, Part VII. was wr.tten subsequent to the "True Christian Religion," and is evidently a rough first draught of a somewhat extended treatise which, if his life had been spared, he would doubtless have given to the world. The regret which is naturally experienced at his not having been permitted to execute the design is somewhat alleviated by the fact, that all the grand truths which it would have embodied are undoubtedly to be found in his published works, as will be evident from the imperfect sketch now presented. Still when it is considered with what a masterly hand he would have filled up the outline—what new lights he would have cast upon every point in the field of his vision—and with what urgency of motive he would have pressed the claims of the New Dispensation—it is with melancholy emotions, that we contemplate the grand desideratum before us.

The occasional breaks which occur are doubtless owing to some defects in the manuscript making it illegible. They are not numerous, nor do they materially mar the sense.

———

That there is not truly a Church, unless God be one, and that God Jehovah under a human form.—And thus that God is Man and Man God.

That the doctrinals which are contained in the "True Christian Religion" agree with the doctrinals of the Roman Catholics and Protestants, so far as the holders of each acknowledge a personal union (of the Divine and Human) in Christ, and go (directly) to Christ, and partake of the Eucharist in both kinds.

That the causes are various why these truths of the Church are now first announced, and not before, among which is this, that the New Church was not to be established but in connexion with the consummation of the former.

The Divine Providence on that head,—shown from the heresies propagated after the days of the Apostles.

Why the Roman Church arose—why there was a separation from it—causes—and why it was not worthy of its Mother (the primitive church). Why the separation took place of the Greek from the Roman Church.

Various things concerning miracles—that they have destroyed the Church, especially from the Lord's words, Matt. xxiv.

That everything has tended to the point of establishing the invocation of (dead) men, called saints.

That this Church is not to be set up and established by miracles, but by a revelation of the spiritual sense (of the Word), and by the introduction of my spirit and at the same time of my body into the spiritual world,* that I might there be instructed in the nature of heaven and hell, and might draw, in light and immediately from the Lord, those truths of faith by which man is to be led to eternal life.

Concerning the Advent of the Lord from the Word and from the Creeds.

An Invitation to the New Church, that there may be a going forth to meet the Lord, from Rev. xxi., xxii.; and from ch. i. etc. etc.

That hereafter the men of the church are not to be called Evangelical, Reformed, still less Lutherans and Calvinists, but Christians.

More concerning miracles.

———

1. That in Christ Jesus man is God and God man, appears evidently from the Lord's words to his Father, "All thine are mine, and all mine are thine;" from "all mine are thine," it appears that man is God, and from "all thine are mine," that God is man, John xvii. 10, 11.

2. That while man is regenerating the light of heaven is superadded to natural light, as also the heat of heaven, thus constituting, as it were, a new soul, by means of which 'man is formed by the Lord; that that light and heat are given in through the superior mind, which is called the spiritual mind; from which insition or insertion the man becomes a new creature, is illuminated and made more intelligent in the things of the church and in the understanding of the Word, and this is a new intellect and a new will; by this light and this heat man is afterwards led by the Lord, and from natural becomes spiritual.

3. There is given a still superior or interior light and heat, which is called celestial, and which is inserted or inwrought into the former: in this are the angels of the third heaven, who are called celestial.

4. The nature of this insertion may be illustrated by a comparison drawn from the grafting or inoculation of trees, when that which is inserted receives into itself the juices of the tree according to its own form, etc.

5. It is demonstrated beyond question, that without the advent of the Lord, no one could be regenerated and thence saved, and that this

———

* This will be intelligible to those who are aware that Swedenborg occasionally applies the term *body* to denote the functions of the bodily senses. He means nothing more than that in his preternatural state he enjoyed the use of the senses of sight, hearing, touch, &c., as perfectly as at any other time. This is the universal prerogative of man when translated into the spiritual world, and it clearly proves that these senses pertain to the spirit and not to the body.

is what is meant by the Lamb's taking away (i. e. bearing) the sins of the world. This is evident from the state of the spiritual world previous to the Lord's advent, which was such that no truth of faith nor any good of charity could proceed from the Lord to man—illustrated by the influx of truth and good into evil spirits, into the back side of their heads, etc.

6. That miracles close the internal man, and take away all free will, by which and in which man is regenerated, as free will is properly of the internal of man, which being closed the man becomes external and natural, and incapable of seeing any spiritual truth. Miracles are a kind of curtains and bars that preclude entrance from without, but this obstruction is gradually burst through and every thing true is dissipated.

7. It is said by the modern church that faith enters by hearing the Word, according to Paul, to which some add a certain meditation from the Word; but the thing to be understood is, that truths are to be drawn from the Word, and the life ordered according to them, and then the man goes directly to the Lord, who is the Word and the Truth, and thence receives faith, for all and singular truths are from the Word, which is spiritual light: thus faith is procured, because faith is of truth, and truth is of faith, and nothing else but truth is to be believed.·

8. That there are inwardly innumerable evils in man, yea, innumer-' able in each single concupiscence. Every concupiscence which comes to the knowledge of man is an agglommeration and heap of multiplied minor ones; these man does not see; he sees only their aggregate : wherefore while he by repentance puts away this, the Lord who sees the interiors and intimates of man, puts away those ; for which reason, unless man draws nigh to the Lord he labors in vain to purify himself. The case is similar to what is described in the *Memorable Relation concerning the Turtles.*

9. That the man who is fully confirmed in the faith and doctrine of the modern church makes nothing of repentance or of the law of the Decalogue, since he makes nothing of works and charity ; for when he says, "I can do no good of myself; those things are in faith, from which as a separate principle they flow in a way that I know nothing of ;" besides other things—when he says this, naturalism reigns, as it does at this day, triumphant.

10. That the fulness of time signifies consummation and desolation is because time signifies the state of the church, as in Rev. x. 6, and in Ezekiel, as also a time, times, and half a time. Times in the world are spring, summer, and autumn ; their fulness is winter ; times as to light are morning, midday, evening, their fulness night, &c. This is understood by the Lord's coming in the fulness of time or times, that is, when there should be no truth of faith or good of charity remaining. Con-

cerning the fulness of time, Rom. xi. 12, 25; Gal. iv. 4; especially Eph. i. 9, 10; Gen. xv. 16.

11. That the presence of the Lord's love is with those who are in faith in Him is evinced from the fact, that place cannot be predicated either of love or of faith, for they are both spiritual. That the Lord himself is present appears from this, that what is spiritual has no place. Place was never present with me when I was in the idea of it; in a word, presence in the spiritual world is according to love; wherefore He is omnipresent; He does not move in place; he is in place, but not through place; He is in space and extension, but not through space and extension.

12. The desolation of the truth of the Church may be compared to consummations on the earth, as when heat and all things pervaded by it are consummated by the winter, and then comes the spring; and as daylight is consummated by the night, when the morning comes; wherefore the Lord says in the Apocalypse to those under the altar, "Wait, &c." Rev. vi. 9, 10, 11. Adduce several things from the Apocalypse showing that the church was to be devastated to the last degree.

13. That at this day the union of the soul and body is unknown, on account of the hypotheses of the learned respecting the soul, especially of Des Cartes and others—as that the soul is a substance distinct from the body, in which it remains as long as the heart acts, when in fact it is the man himself, thus the most interior man, thus the man from head to heel, thence in the whole and every part, according to the ancients, and in whatever part the soul is not intimately present, there the life of the man is not. It is from their union that everything of the soul is of the body, and everything of the body is of the soul, as the Lord said of the Father that all of his own were His, and all His of his own. Hence it is that the Lord as to his flesh is also God, Rom. ix. 5; Col. ii. 9, as also that it is said, the Father in me, and I in the Father, and yet that they are one.

14. The human mind is of three degrees, the celestial, the spiritual, and the natural. In the first degree is the soul (*anima*), in the second the spirit or mind (*mens*), in the third the body. It is the same whether you say that the mind of man is of three degrees, or that the man himself is; for the mind is that element of the body which is in first principles, thus where its primitive is, from which the rest is propagated and continued. What is the mind if it is only in the head, unless as something separate or diverse, in which no continuous mind is given? This is evident from autopsy. The origins of the fibres are the little glands, so called, of the cortical substance; thence proceed the fibres, and these being confasciated together into nerves descend and permeate the whole body, and construct and adorn it. The celestial degree, in which is the soul (*anima*) or most interior man is in a special manner the degree of spiritual love; that in which is

the mind (*mens*) or spirit, which is the middle man, is especially the degree of wisdom from love; the third degree, in which is the body, which is the ultimate man, is the continent of both, without which the two former do not subsist. This matter may be further demonstrated from the three heavens, the celestial, the spiritual, and natural, which are within a man, whence it is that the angels of the superior heavens are invisible to those of the lower, while they approach them from their own heavens.

15. From these things it may clearly appear that the body exists by means of the soul, like a tree from its seed, from which also it derives its quality. Accordingly as the soul of Christ is from the Divine essence, it follows that his body is also thence.

16. That all theological preachers are in the profoundest ignorance concerning the falses of their religion; they preach that God is one, that the Saviour is to be worshiped, that man ought to believe the Word and preachings, that he ought to exercise charity and .repentance, that he should desist from evils; and when they do this they lose all recollection of three Gods, of their mystical faith, of man's impotence in spiritual things, and every thing else of the kind; but let them know that the falsity imbibed in the schools still adheres inwardly, and that these things are merely uttered with the lips, and that after death they will come into the interiors of their spirits. Wherefore those falsities are to be wholly eradicated, since what is merely external adheres like beard upon the chin, which is finally to be cut off and the man to become beardless.

17. That all that is declared by the priests in their preaching from the Word, concerning faith, or the belief in God, concerning charity towards the neighbor, concerning conversion, concerning penitence, and a life of piety and spirituality, falls, as it were, into a bucket of water, when orthodoxy enters and explains them; they are utterly overthrown by it, as by something which subverts a house or building, so that nothing but a heap of ruins remains; and yet they say that there is no truth if these are not believed, that charity, repentance, &c., are smitten down, that the Word itself must fall, &c. and thus it is that everything is overwhelmed in confusion, just as when a wall is tumbled down by ditches dug under it.

18. Let a single example be adduced of some pre-eminently pious doctrine on these subjects derived from the Word, and let one of these teachers apply his orthodoxy to the subject, and it will be seen from such an example what work is made of truly divine truths. Thus if orthodoxy is in the internal man they will affirm and then deny; and there will be very lofty preaching in the external man, while still this remaining external is mere froth and vanity; their eloquence is like a quaking of the earth, or the surging of the water in a shipwreck.

19. A fit example may be taken from true orthodoxy in its teaching concerning Faith, Charity, and Free Will, which will sufficiently disclose its absurdities.

20. That the spiritual things of Heaven flow into every man, and flow also through the world, thus carrying with them a luminous confirmation; that spiritual and natural things thus flow in conjointly, but the evil man inverts both, placing outwardly to his mind that which should be within, and within, that which should be outward, thus putting heaven not above, where it should be, but upon a par with hell. The good and pious man, on the contrary, receives each in the due order of influx, namely, spiritual things through heaven in the upper region of his mind, and natural things through the world in the lower; thus the one stands as a man erect upon his feet, the other as inverted.

21. That the universal Theology of the present day is solely the doctrine of the Divine Omnipotence; as (1) that it (omnipotence) confers faith when and where it will; (2) that it remits sins; (3) that it regenerates; (4) that it sanctifies; (5) that it imputes and saves; (6) that it will raise dead bodies from their graves, will quicken skeletons, and endow them with their former souls; (7) that it will destroy this world with the sun, stars, planets, earths, and create a new one. (8) Since omnipotence is thus every thing, and is made the same with that order which is God and from God in the universal world, on the ground of which the man of the Church can originate any fiction which he pleases, and lift himself above the sky, that is, above reason, and against reason, saying that reason is to be held captive to the obedience of faith, and demanding whether God is not omnipotent, and whether any one can or dare reason against omnipotence—since this is so, it is easy to see what is the character of the faith of the present day.

22. The reason why man cannot discover a single Divine Truth, unless he immediately sees the Lord, is that the Lord alone is the Word, and is Light and Truth itself, and man does not become spiritual except in the Lord, but remains natural, and the natural man sees everything spiritual inverted, as we learn from Paul. This is the reason that there is not a single genuine truth remaining in the Church, of which the consequence is consummation, desolation, decision, and filling up. But because the Lord himself is not dead, there remains " a root in the earth," according to Daniel, and because man " seeks death but cannot find it," according to the Apocalypse, there is thence a remaining faculty of understanding truth and willing good; this is the root that remains.

23. Those who are studious of the modern orthodoxy object that faith, charity, good works, repentance, remission of sins, &c., cannot be given with man before he has obtained the Holy Spirit; but the

fallacy of this appears when it is shown that the Holy Spirit, or the Divine Proceeding from the Lord, or the Lord himself, is perpetually present with every man, the evil as well as the good; that without His presence no one could live; and that the Lord continually acts, urges, and operates to effect reception—wherefore the Holy Spirit is a perpetual presence. In the spiritual world this was once put to the test, for the sake of confirmation, iu the case of a certain devil, from whom the Divine presence was, as it were, taken away, and he immediately fell prostrate as if dead, precisely like a corpse, and this was seen by thousands of spirits and among them the spirits of the clergy, who were astonished at the occurrence.—The presence of the Lord is that from which man has the faculty of thinking, understanding, and willing, which faculties result solely from the influx of life from the Lord. —Melancthon and Luther were present on the occasion referred to, and could not open their mouths in view of the fact.

24. The one single cause of the Reformation's being effected was, that the Word, which had lain buried, should again return into the world. It had been in the world for many ages before, but it was at length entombed by the Roman Catholics, in consequence of which no truth of the Church could be laid open; especially that respecting the Lord, for the Pope was worshiped as God in the place of the Lord. But when the Word was disinterred from its sepulchre, the Lord could be made known, truth could be thence derived, and conjunction effected with heaven. For this reason the Lord raised up at the same time so many men who assailed the church; he excited the Kingdoms of Sweden, Denmark, Holland, and England, to the reception of the Word, and that it might not be extinguished in Germany by the Pope, he raised up Gustavus Adolphus, who stood for the reformation, and rebelled against the Church.

25. Were not this little work to be added to the former, the church would not be healed; it would be merely a palliative cure; the festering wound would still remain, and eat into the neighboring parts. Orthodoxy is itself the gangrene; the doctrine of the New Church affords indeed a remedy, but only of an extrinsic kind.

26. The origin of all the errors in the Church has been that men have believed that they lived from themselves, or from their own life, and that this was increated in them; whereas man is internally only an organ of life, and placed in the midst between heaven and hell, and thus in equilibrium or free will.

27. That no one can see the desolation of truth in the Church before the truths from the Word come into light, as to which the heretic does not know but that these truths constitute all his faith. Every one will swear to the soundness of his own belief; especially as there will arise a new light from confirmations, a light in which the natural

man is while the spiritual man illuminates him; yea, even an atheistic naturalist will swear there is no God, that it is a mere empty conceit of the common herd, which the doctors of the Church ridicule in their hearts.

28. It is known in the Church that the Church is the Body of Christ, but it is as yet unknown how it is so; it is from this, that the universal heaven is as one man before the Lord, and this man is distinguished into societies of which each represents some one member or organ in man, in whom, or in this human body, the Lord is as the soul or life; when the Lord inspires men or is present with them, he is present through the heavens, as the soul through its own body. The case is similar with the church on the earth, for this is the external man, wherefore every one at death is gathered to his own in that body, &c.

29. That the things related concerning myself are not miracles, but testimonies to my having been introduced into the spiritual world for certain ends,——that miracles are not wrought at this day; the causes,——as also from the Lord's words, Matt. xxiv. Concerning the miracles of Anthony of Padua, and of others who are revered as Saints, of whose miracles the Monasteries are full; also concerning the miracles of (Father) Paris an account of which is published in 2 vols. 4to.

30. That the Lord was to come in the fulness of him and execute judgment, is indicated in his own words, Matt. xxv., "When the Son of Man shall come in his glory, and all his holy angels with Him, then shall he sit upon the throne of his glory, and all nations shall be gathered before him; and he shall separate them one from another, as a shepherd divided his sheep from the goats," &c. v. 31, 32. This advent of the Lord is understood by what is said in the Apostles' Creed concerning Jesus, that ''he ascended to the heavens, that he sits at the right hand of the Father Almighty, *whence he is to come to judge the quick and the dead,*'' as also in the Nicene Creed concerning the Lord Jesus Christ, that "he ascended to the heavens, that he sits at the right hand of the Father, and that he will come again in *glory to judge the quick and the dead, or* WHOSE KINGDOM THERE SHALL BE NO END."

31. So also in the Athanasian Creed: "He ascended to the heavens, and sits at the right hand of the Father Almighty, whence he is to come to judge the quick and the dead, who shall render an account of their deeds, and those that have done good shall go into life eternal, and those that have done evil into everlasting fire."—*F. C. pp.* 1, 2, 4. The Smalcaldic Articles moreover to the same effect: "Jesus Christ ascended to the heavens, sits at the right hand of God, and will come to judge the quick and the dead," in accordance with the Apostolic, Nicene, and Athanasian symbols on the same heads. Luther likewise in *Catechismo Minore,* p. 371, *Confess. Aug.* pp. 10, 14, and our *Catechism*

p. 303 teaches the same. From the Augsburg Catechism moreover we learn that " he ascended to the heavens, sits at the right hand of the Father, and will for ever rule and have dominion over all creatures: the same Christ will also openly return to judge the quick and the dead, &c." according to the Apostles' Creed, p. 10.

32. That this coming to judgment is not for the destruction of the heavens and the earth, appears from many things in the Word concerning it, and from his saying, " When the Son of Man cometh, shall he find faith on the earth ?" Luke xviii. 8 ; and from various other things adduced in the " The True Christian Religion," n. 765, as also that he does not come to destroy the visible heaven and the habitable earth, n. 768 seq., but to separate the evil from the good, n. 77 seq., where other · considerations are cited. The like is said in the Confession of Faith, which is inserted in every copy of the Book of Psalms circulated throughout the Christian world ; wherever the Apostles' Creed is uttered, the Psalms (from its being connected with them) declare the same thing. By the quick or living are to be understood those who are in charity and faith, and are called by the Lord sheep ; by the dead those who are not in charity and faith, and are called by the Lord goats. Add to these Apoc. xi. 13, and xx. 12.

33. *Title :* CONCERNING THE CONSUMMATION OF THE AGE, AND THE THEN ABOMINATION OF DESOLATION ; adduce what the Lord says, (1.) Concerning the abomination of desolation. (2.) What——————————— (3.) What he says concerning the tribulation. (4.) That no flesh could be saved. (5.) Concerning the darkening of the Sun and Moon. (6.) What is written, Apoc. ch. i. 18, "Behold, I am alive and was dead, and am alive for evermore ;" also, ch. ii. 8 ; ch. v. 6 ; also that the Lord says that " the night cometh wherein no man can work," John ix. 4 ; that in that night " there shall be two in one bed," Luke xvii. 34 ; also what the Lord says concerning Peter, John xxi. 18 ; also what Paul says concerning the last times, 1 Tim. iv. 1–3 ; 2 Tim. iii. 1–7 ; iv. 3, 4. Explain what the Lord says Matt. xxiv. 27, that it was fulfilled in the day of the last judgment, as likewise v. 30, 31 ; Vid. " True Christian Religion," n. 791.

(*To be continued.*)

———

EXTRACTS FROM SWEDENBORG'S SPIRITUAL DIARY.

NOW FIRST TRANSLATED FROM THE ORIGINAL LATIN.

Concerning Use.

4173. I conversed with spirits concerning use. They were indignant that I had so much to say on the subject, but it was said in reply that use is all in all—that in the world, in a kingdom, the main question is in regard to use ; and so in respect to a man, (we ask) what use does he subserve? If he is not useful he is rejected as worthless. How much more then in the Lord's kingdom, where use is everything. There was then represented, according to the ideas of angelic spirits, a sphere as an aura of uses, and it was said that in the Lord's kingdom there is nothing but uses. (One of the above mentioned class) being in such a sphere began to hurry away saying that he could not respire there.

Concerning the Beauty of Conjugial Love.

4175. There was presented to my view, though but in a very slight degree, a form of beauty veiled, as it were, by a kind of cloud, lest I should see it (entire), and at the same time a perception was given that it was the beauty of conjugial love. From the perception granted it was such as can scarcely be otherwise described than by saying it was beauty itself, because conjugial love is so formed—so (I say) as to be conjugial love itself, which is beauty itself, affecting the very inmost of the soul; and thence is all beauty. The quality of its representations was also seen, which were various cerulean rainbows and golden showers.

Concerning (certain) Acquaintances.

4179. During the whole night I was surrounded by numbers of those who were known to me, and I slept and was with them. I have also been present and spake in their presence in sleep when they appeared under the semblance of other persons. When I awoke they were detected in their true character, and I spake with them. I have twice dreamt of entering a ruined temple where nothing remained but the rubbish of altars, into one of which when I came I began to sink, wherefore I was seized with a dread (: hissua :*) of sinking into the abyss below, which caused me to awake.

Concerning the Word of the Lord from Angelic Speech.

4184. Angelic speech is such that every thing they think and say lives. They receive in each single particular a perception of life from the Lord ; yea, whatever pertains to life they thus exhibit to themselves in a kind of living way ; as, for instance, when (thinking or speaking) of any affection of the will or of the understanding, they have it as if alive (before them) with all that is involved in it, with its whole soul and body (as it were), comprising things innumerable and ineffable, of which there is with man barely a most general idea, and that too (one that might be termed) dead, from its being with him material and closed ; thus when any affection is described, innumerable things may be thought and written concerning it ; these are all simultaneously present with the angels, together with the interior things of which it

---

* A Swedish word signifying " horror."

is composed in order and series, just as the form of the body, or whatever belongs to the body, is known from the outer and inward structure of the fibres, vessels, and muscles, with their series and connexions, whence arises the form; all which are inexpressible, for these are alive with the angels. Such is their thought and speech.

4185. The Word of the Lord is such that when it is set forth by the Lord before the angels every particular of it is alive, so that the dead letter passes into life with the innumerable items which are in each single word and in the connexion of the words. Wherefore every thing in the letter is of the most general nature, and forms merely the vessels or receptacles of such living affections, and this with indefinite variety and in an ineffable manner.

4186. It was granted me to speak to some degree with angelic spirits, still to a very limited extent; yet sufficiently to know that the case is as I have mentioned.

That the Evil who deem themselves peculiarly subtle are grosser (and duller) than others.

4189. Certain evil spirits above the head, who, I think, had not been with me before, acted with peculiar subtlety, thinking themselves to be eminently possessed of this character. It was given to say to them that they were duller than others, as the evil are dull just in proportion to their subtlety. It was also said to them that they were evil in every particular of their being, and thus made up of evils, and that even their very subtleties were the evil of which they were composed. On the other hand, those who are not subtle may be evil outwardly, but not inwardly, wherefore they are not so dull.

What Marriage is and the Love thence derived.

4192. (The love of) marriage is a love of such a nature, that the parties so love each other that they mutually wish to become one. They each wish too to bestow upon the other what is respectively his own. From this mutual prompting to regard each one's self as the other's exists the love of marriage. Wherefore all other loves are thence derived, so far as reciprocity of sentiment is concerned, but yet without the possibility of such a complete interchange of being. Every other love consists in *velle* (*willing* or *wishing*), but not like this in *posse* (*being able*). It hence appears that the conjugial is the fundamental love, and is heaven itself.

4193. On the other hand, those who wish to appropriate all that which belongs to another, and thus are prompted to make it their own, esteeming the other as nothing—this is infernal, for it is contrary to the former. Such an one wishes to take away from another his life, and whatever he has, and make it his own.

Concerning Spheres, Instinct, and the Excitation of Ideas with Man.

4195. Every spirit, and still more every society of spirits, exhales a sphere from itself, which is from its principles or the life of principles or persuasions; with the evil genii from the life of cupidities. Thence flows their sphere which is a sphere, as it were, of instincts, arising from this source, and when this sphere exists, it is a certain operative general principle (*commune*), which, when it acts upon a man's memory, summons up thence whatever is in agreement with it, and thus the general principle of spirits excites all the concordant particulars from the man's memory; thence spirits speak, and think that it is from themselves, and they also persuade man that what he says is from himself. Where such a sphere predominates, there every thing which is excited, though in fact most false, appears as true, and is confirmed. The confirming things which flow forth are very numerous, and of such variety that I have wondered whence they could have procured them, as it were, extempore, when yet it is nothing else than this general sphere which excites them; for spirits, as they lack memory, are possessed of a certain instinctive something which acts in the manner described.

Concerning Dreams.

4200. I dreamt during the night and upon awaking spake with spirits who said that they had been watching around me, and that they had occasioned the dream, and had expressly induced every thing that I remembered and related. From this it is still more manifest to me that dreams are from the world of spirits.

Concerning the Providence of the Lord.

4201. I have heard and perceived spirits conversing together respecting the Lord's Providence in the minutest particulars, but what they said cannot be described, for their speech is at the same time representative involving things wholly indescribable. There are in one idea more things, combined with representations, than could be set forth in many pages, and many which could not be described at all. It was then perceived that the Lord's Providence extends to the most minute particulars, but not in such a series as man adopts and proposes to follow, for the reason, that all and singular things are disposed in their own order, and future events are previded and provided, which (at the same time) do not happen as man supposes.

MISCELLANY.

___

MINISTERS OF THE NEW CHURCH.

As it is doubtless an object of some interest to the New Church to preserve the record of its ministry, we have availed ourselves of such materials as we could command to make out the following list of living and deceased N. C. clergymen, both in England and in this country. We are not sure that the catalogue is complete, or the dates uniformly correct, though we believe there is no important omission or error. If any should hereafter be detected it will be rectified.

ENGLAND.

Samuel Noble, London	Ordained	May 21, 1820.
Thomas C. Shaw, do.	"	Aug. 30, 1840.
Thomas Chalklen, do.	"	Sept. 17, 1837.
Jonathan Bayley, Accrington	"	Oct. 3, 1836.
John W. Barnes, Bath	"	Aug. 19, 1833.
Richard Storry, Mirfield	"	Nov. 25, 1838.
William Mason, Melbourne	"	Sept. 8, 1825.
William Bruce, Edinburgh	"	July 21, 1829.
Woodville Woodman, Kersley	"	Jan. 7, 1838.
Richard Edleston, Leeds	"	Nov. 8, 1846.
John Cull, Liverpool	"	Aug. 12, 1838.
John H. Smithson, Manchester	"	Oct. 20, 1833.
Robert Abbott, Norwich	"	Aug. 9, 1846.
Elias D. Rendell, Preston	"	Aug. 13, 1830.
David Howarth, Salford	"	Aug. 12, 1824.
David T. Dyke, Salisbury	"	Aug. 18, 1844.
Thomas Goyder, Chalford	"	July 13, 1822.
David G. Goyder, Glasgow	"	Nov. 3, 1822.
James Bradley, Manchester	"	Aug. 16, 1818.
Edward Madely, Birmingham	"	May 8, 1825.
Joseph F. Wynn, Brightlingsea	"	Nov. 6, 1842.

ENGLISH N. C. MINISTERS DECEASED.

Rev. Arthur Munson	Ob.	Aug. 22, 1818.
" Joseph Proud	"	Aug. 3, 1826.
" Edward Madely	"	Nov. 25, 1827.
" John Clowes	"	May 29, 1831.
" Robert Hindmarsh	"	Jan. 2, 1835.
" Thomas Pilkington	"	April 7, 1837.
" Manoah Sibly	"	Dec. 16, 1840.
" Isaac Hawkins		not known.
" Richard Jones		not known.
" Joseph Enoch		not known.
" James Hodson		not known.
" William Faraday		not known.
" John Pownall		not known.

UNITED STATES.

*ORDAINING MINISTERS.

Maskell M. Carll, Riverhead, L. I.	Ordained	Dec. 31
†Lewis Beers, South Danby, N. Y.	"	Jan. 19
Thomas Worcester, Boston	"	Aug. 17
Richard De Charms, Baltimore	"	May 18
Benjamin F. Barrett, Cincinnati, O.	"	Nov. 14
James Seddon, Frankford, Pa.	"	June 17
David Powell, Ohio	"	May 29
Samuel F. Dike, Bath, Me.	"	Oct. 10
J. R. Hibbard, Peoria, Ill.	"	May 29
T. O. Prescott, Cincinnati, O.	"	May 29
Solyman Brown, South Danby, N. Y.	"	July 12

PASTORS AND TEACHING MINISTERS.

Isaac C. Worrell, Frankford, Pa.	Ordained	Dec
Samuel H. Wills, Abingdon, Va.	"	Aug. 29
Lemuel C. Belding, Wheeling, Va.	"	June 4
†Eleazer Smith, North Swanzey, Ms.	"	June 4
Joseph Pettee, Abington, Ms.	"	July 25
Warren Goddard, North Bridgewater, Ms.	"	Sept. 15
†Adonis Howard, Boston	"	Oct. 17
†N. C. Burnham, Columbus, Miss.	"	May 29
Horatio N. Strong, Edwardsburgh, Cass Co., Mich.	"	Aug. 25
Richard Hooper, Rockport, Cuyahoga Co., O.	"	Aug. 28
George Field, Detroit, Mich.	"	May 28
Thomas P. Rodman, Bridgewater, Ms.	"	May 6

MINISTERS AND LICENTIATES.

†Benjamin Essex, Lynchburg, Va.	Licensed about	
†Luther Bishop, Clayton, N. Y.	"	Dec. 30
†Edwin A. Atlee, Philadelphia	"	
†James Scott, Portland, Me.	Ordained	June 10
†John M. Hibbard, Athens, O.	"	May 29
†Joshua O. Colburn, Frankford, Pa.	Licensed	Nov. 19
T. B. Hayward, East Bridgewater, Ms.	"	May 6
Thomas D. Sturtevant, Providence, R. I.	"	May 6
†Rufus Dawes, Washington, D. C.	"	June 15
J. P. Stuart, Martinsville, O.	"	May 2
Elias Yulee, Cincinnati, O.	"	May 2
William H. Benade, Philadelphia	Ordained	June
Thomas Wilks, New York	"	June
Alfred E. Ford, Upper Darby, Pa.	"	June 2
Thomas H. Perry, St. Louis, Mo.		

AMERICAN N. C. MINISTERS DECEASED.

Rev. John Hargrove	Ob.	Dec.
" Adam Hurdus	"	Aug. 3
" Henry A. Worcester		
" Samuel Worcester	"	Dec. 2
" Charles J. Doughty	"	July 1
" Holland Weeks	"	July 2
" Alexander Kinmont		
" Elisha Hibbard,	"	Aug. 1

* The dates of ordinations in this class of Ministers designate the time they were ordained as Pastors, as most of them were introduced into two grades at the same time.

† Not constantly and regularly officiating.

For the N. C. Repository.

THE GUARDIAN ANGEL.

At night I slept at ease upon my couch,
And through the lattice came the evening wind,
Cooling my brow, while moonlight o'er me fell,
A dweller in the mystic land of dreams.
As maying zephyrs gently, lightly touch,
And wake to life the vernal buds, so touched
My spirit's eye a finger, gentle, light—
A voice unearthly fell upon my ear;
A thousand-stringed Æolian harp, each string
A thousand-toned, blending sweet harmonies,
Could breathe no sweeter sounds. My spirit roused:
Before me stood a nameless form—a form
Defined, yet all ethereal. A robe
Attenuated as the mountain mist,
And white as is the light the crescent moon
Pours from her vestal urn, fell o'er that form
Like folding clouds upon the sunset sky.
A turban fair of plumes and sunbeams wove
Sat lightly on the brow; and parting thence,
The hair about the neck in beauty flowed.
Such beaming eyes no earthly eyes e'er were!
Eternity in their blue depths I saw—
Knowledge of things past, things present, and of things
To come; in them I saw prophetic light,
And while I gazed, a thrill electric passed
Over my soul, while thus the vision spoke:
"I am thine angel, mortal once like thee—
Mortal no more : a willing ear awaits."
"My wish, sweet visitant, may much exceed
Desert. If angel, then inform me whence
Thy journeyings; thy mission what, and what
My angel's offices may be." I thus
My wish expressed; and expectation held
My eye, while thus my guest my wishes sung:

"I come, I come, from the spirit home;
I come, I come, thou hast sought me long
    By thy prayer and by thy song.
For ever I watch, for ever I roam,
Attendant on thy wish and care;
Thy th ught and mine, a wedded pair!

" My viewless wing did thee o'erbrood ;
Thy steps I watched with unsleeping eye
   When rushed the tempest by ;
When danger was near, as guardian should,
Thy shield was this, thine angel's arm,
Which kept thy infant years from harm.

" I turned thy thoughts to the buried past,
To learn the story of erring men—
   Of their weal and their ken.
The tomb of thy race, how darksome and vast !
The souls of men abide not there—
If good, with us still life they share !

" I walk with thee on the mountain height—
I sail with thee o'er the broad blue lake,
   And thy passions I wake
To visions of beauty and pageants of light,
Sublimely great, supremely fair—
Such, such thine angel's pleasing care.

" I am to thee a protecting power ;
I forecast give of the coming years,
   And lull all dark'ning fears ;
The beacon of hope I bear in the hour
When cloud and storm o'er thee portend ;
And thus thine angel doth defend !

" Then hope alway, nor distrust my aid ;
With right good cheer for ever pursue
   Both the good and the true ;
O, never complain, nor fortune upbraid,
Nor doubt as to who will provide :—
Behold thine angel and thy guide."

The angel ceased ; the spirit of the song
Imbued my heart with life afresh ; and hope
And faith revived, as drooping flowers revive,
Drinking the early rain ; and then, too soon,
With fleecy pinions spread, my visitant
Departed, with a smile.—My dream was sweet.

                        W. H. B
                        Lockport, N. .

EDITORIAL ITEMS.

WE are happy to announce that the republication of the "Apocalypse Explained" is at length completed. This, next to the reprint of the "Arcana," is the greatest publishing enterprize which has been undertaken in the New Church in this country. The work is now complete in five handsome volumes at $9,00 per set, instead of $12, the price of the English edition in six volumes. The thanks of all New Churchmen are due to Mr. Allen for putting this invaluable treasury of truth within their reach on terms so reasonable. The outlay on his part has of necessity been large, although an edition of only one thousand copies has been printed. Of these, however, several hundred have been disposed of by subscription, and an early application would doubtless be expedient on the part of those who would furnish themselves with the work. Like the Arcana, it is almost a library of itself, as the spiritual sense of thousands and thousands of texts is given in it, while its argumentative discussion of most of the great doctrines of the Word is unrivalled for its logical closeness and power. In no other work we believe in the whole compass of theology is the true rationale of Justification so luminously developed, and the distinct nature and offices of Charity and Faith, in the matter of salvation, set forth with such an irresistible force of demonstration. We agree fully with the remarks of a writer in the March number of the "Intellectual Repository" on this head :—" The power, simplicity, and clearness with which Swedenborg's principles of Truth are opened from the Word, and adapted to the mind, cannot be surpassed. I have also observed that these volumes are not so much read as the smaller works of the same author, and that consequently the great amount of spiritual instruction they contain is but little known. But in no part of his works has he exposed erroneous doctrines, and no where has he entered into the depths of the Word, and applied its truths to the soul, more clearly and powerfully than in these volumes." We cannot therefore but express our earnest hope that the right kind of response may be made to the present undertaking of Mr. Allen.——The New Jerusalem Magazine due on the first of March has been unavoidably delayed and now appears as a double number including March and April. Its contents, besides the Miscellaneous Intelligence, are, (1.) A Sermon from Rev. ii. 21-23. By Rev. Joseph Potter. (2.) The Law of Ultimates. (3.) Communication with Heaven by the Word. (4.) The Divine Providence. (5.) Servants and Servitude. (6.) Davis' Principles of Nature, &c. (7.) The Temptation. The Letter of the French correspondent is devoted principally to the political condition of France. The writer from London gives important information respecting the recently received Manuscripts of Swedenborg. "These manuscripts," the writer says, " are, 1. A Treatise on Human Generation, giving the author's theory of that subject. I have looked through a portion of this very elaborate and complete work, and am of opinion that in importance it is second to nothing in the author's published physiological writings. The treatment is orderly and detailed, and judging by appearances, that which I possess seems to be a fair copy, written out for the press. In English it will make a volume of some four hundred pages. It is proposed to translate it at once from the manuscript, since the New Church does not afford the means for continuing our Latin publications. In the same work on

Generation there are various other small treatises, which will perhaps some day furnish a fresh series of tracts; but respecting these nothing can be settled at present. The next manuscript is the Theory of the Affections of the Animal and Rational Minds, a work on the human faculties, states, endowments, passions, &c. It is cast into short and pithy chapters, something after the manner of Bacon's Essays, and, whenever published, will probably be *the favorite* among all the author's philosophical writings. This also will probably be translated from the manuscript without publishing the Latin,—a sad course to pursue, both for the author and the translator, yet one which circumstances appear to dictate with irresistible force. The third manuscript is *the Continuation of the Animal Kingdom*, a work written apparently just before the author's spiritual sight was opened, and which contains singular hints of strange things going on in him. In this manuscript we find several most valuable treatises, viz. (1.) The Theory of the Sense of Smell; (2.) Of the Ear and Hearing; (3.) Of the Eye and Sight; (4.) A Treatise or Epilogue on Sensation generally, with a copious Index. These will be indeed hailed as great additions by the students of Swedenborg's scientific views. The manuscript, however, is so obscure, that it must be transcribed by some skilful hand, and published in Latin, which it is proposed to have done by Dr. Tafel." In a subsequent letter from the same source we are happy to read the following. "I am glad, however, to be able to inform the public, that since I wrote you, 'a Friend,' who will remain *incognito*, has signified to me that he will subscribe in two instalments the sum of ONE HUNDRED POUNDS towards the publication, *in Latin*, of the three MSS. of Swedenborg, namely *the Essays on the Human Mind, the Treatise on Generation, and the Continuation of the Animal Kingdom*. Now, it is calculated that for £150 pounds the whole of the three works may be issued; and I therefore hope that those who are interested in England and America will join to subscribe the £50 still required for the purpose. It is greatly to be approved, that our munificent 'Friend' insists on the publication first of the Latin, which, by his assistance, will fall lightly on the New Church public; and which is so very requisite both for a good translation, and for doing justice to the Author's Works. Nor need the Latin edition cause any loss of time; for, if the translation is well subscribed for (say 500 copies), your correspondent may receive the proof sheets from Dr. Tafel (who is to be asked to edit these Works, on account of the superior cheapness of German printing), and issue the English version almost simultaneously with the original. The sooner therefore that some active measures are taken to collect names and moneys, and transmit them to the Swedenborg Association, the sooner may all these invaluable works take the position which they merit in Scientific and Philosophical Literature." If any of our readers should feel impelled to aid this work by their subscriptions, we will cheerfully charge ourselves with the transmission of their names to England.——One or two hundred pages are already printed of the forthcoming volume of Lectures on the Doctrines of the True Christian Religion, by the Rev. Mr. Noble. It will probably be out early in June.——The first N. C. Society in this city which has so long engaged the ministerial services of the Rev. Mr. Barrett, have extended an invitation to the Editor of the Repository to supply his pulpit for the present.——A new and stereotyped edition of the "Apocalypse Revealed," in one vol 8vo is just about being published by Mr. Allen of this city.

THE

NEW CHURCH REPOSITORY

AND

MONTHLY REVIEW.

| Vol. 1. | JUNE, 1848. | No. 6. |

ORIGINAL PAPERS.

ARTICLE I.

THE DRUIDISM OF ANCIENT BRITAIN:

ITS DOCTRINES, RITES, CORRESPONDENCES, ETC., AS DISCOVERED IN AN-
CIENT BRITISH MANUSCRIPTS, REVIEWED AND COMPARED WITH THOSE
OF THE ANCIENT CHURCH.

(Continued.)

Swedenborg informs us that the doctrinals of the Ancient Church were derived from the Most Ancient, these doctrinals being collected by the men of that church, called Cain
and Enoch, for the use of posterity. He thus speaks upon the
subject, " There were some at that time who framed doctrines
out of the things that had been objects of perception in the
Most Ancient and following Churches (Adam, Seth, and Enos),
that such doctrine might serve as a rule whereby to know
what was good and true; such persons were called Enoch.
This is what is signified by the word, and Enoch walked with
God: so also they called that doctrine; which is likewise signified by the name Enoch, meaning to instruct." "He was no
more for God took him, signifies that the doctrine was preserved
for the use of posterity. The case is thus respecting Enoch,
that, as was said, he reduced to doctrine what had been perceptive in the Most Ancient Church; which at that time was
not permitted; for to know from perception is entirely other
than to learn from doctrine: they who know from perception
have no need of the knowledge acquired in the way of system-

atized doctrines. But whereas it was foreseen that the perceptive faculty of the Most Ancient Church would perish, and that afterwards mankind would learn by doctrines what is good and true, or would come by darkness to the light, therefore it is here said that God took him, that is, preserved the doctrine for the use of posterity."—*A. C.* 519, 521. Again he says, "Because it was foreseen by the Lord that the state of man would become such, it was also provided that the doctrinals of faith should be preserved, in order that man might thereby know what the celestial was, and what the spiritual: those doctrinals, they who were called Cain, and they who were called Enoch, of whom mention was made above, collected from the man of the Most Ancient Church; wherefore it was said of Cain, that a mark was set upon him, lest any one should slay him, and of Enoch that he was taken of God. Representative worship was begun by the Ancient Church, and emanated thence to their posterity, and to all the nations round about." "By Noah is signified the Ancient Church, or the doctrine which remained from the Most Ancient Church. The few things which remained from the Most Ancient Church, were with those who constituted the church called Noah; but these were not remnants of perception but of integrity, and also of doctrine derived from the perceptions of the most ancient churches: wherefore a new church was now first raised up by the Lord, which being of a different character from the most ancient churches, was to be called the Ancient Church; ancient on this account, because it commenced at the end of the ages before the flood, and at the earliest time after the flood."—*A. C.* 530, 920.

What is here said by Swedenborg concerning the doctrines and origin of the Ancient Church, is in exact agreement with what is said by the Druids respecting their system. Taliesin, a chief Bard or Druid, in a poem descriptive of Druidism—the system being personified in him as the High Priest, as we learn was the case in the Ancient Church—speaks as follows,

> " I was happiness to the man
> Of wisdom in the primitive world,
> For I then had a being
> When the world was in dignity, and was beautiful;
> The glory of the Bard was I made.
> I incite the song of praise
> Which the tongue utters.

> " Truly I was in safety
> Amid the sea-like deluge,
> Encompassed and protected
> Between the royal knees,
> When from heaven came,
> With a dissolvent throe,
> The inundation to the great abyss."

In another passage of the same poem, the Bard says that the
system of Druidism was

> " The greatest of the three mental exertions
> That have disported in the world,
> And the one that was formed
> From the stores of the deluge."

From these verses we learn the following particulars respecting the Druids. They had a knowledge of the Most Ancient
Church ; they knew that that church was in a far more
elevated state than the Ancient which succeeded it, for they
represent that period as being *the time when the world was in
dignity, or magnificence, and was beautiful ;* the principles of
their religion, they say, was the happiness of the wise man of
that age—these principles, we have before shown, were love
and charity ; they say that these principles, or the knowledges
of them, were preserved in safety amid the deluge which
swept the evil to the great abyss, or hell—preserved between
the royal knees ; and that their system was afterwards formed
from the stores, or provisions which were thus preserved. The
expression, " *Between the royal knees,*" plainly proves that the
Druids' idea of the deluge was purely that derived from the
science of correspondence. A similar expression is used upon
another occasion in the Word, by which we may explain the
meaning of the Druids. " And Israel beheld Joseph's sons and
said, Who are these ? And Joseph said unto his father, They
are my sons whom God hath given me in this place. And
Israel said unto Joseph, I had not thought to see thy face ; and
lo, God hath showed me also thy seed. And Joseph brought
them out *from between his knees,* and he bowed himself with
his face to the earth" (Gen. xlviii. 8–12). "The sons of Joseph,
Ephraim and Manasseh, signify the intellectual and the will
principles of the spiritual church" (*A. C.* 3969) ; the principles
of the ancient church which were preserved in safety, when
the antediluvians perished in the inundation of their own falses
and evils which swept them to the great abyss. " And Joseph
took them away from his thighs ; thighs denote the affection
of love. By these things is signified, that the internal celestial
removed the good of the voluntary and the truth of the intellectual from spiritual good, that is, from the affection of the
love thereof, because Israel, by whom spiritual good is represented, caused that truth and good to come to himself, besides
that they were brought to him by Joseph, by whom is represented the internal celestial ; wherefore they were removed,
and afterwards brought by Joseph, as it follows. The reason
is, because hereby there is an influx of love from the internal
celestial good into them ; for this is according to order, and

hence this external ritual, when they were to be blessed was
strictly to be observed; for they were then presented before
the Lord, from whom is prediction, which is here signified by
blessing.   Hence then it is, that Joseph took his sons from the
thighs of his father, and himself afterwards brought them
thither."—*A. C.* 6265.

According to the explanation here given by Swedenborg,
the meaning of the language of the Druids is, that the remains
implanted in the man who was to form the new church, when
he was exposed to temptations, or the falses and evils of hell
which swept others away, were preserved unhurt in the affection of good in him; and after passing through temptation
they formed the church in him.   Mr. Davies, in his British
Mythology, states, with the design to show the superstition of
the Druids, that "The Druids represented the deluge under the
figure of a lake, called *Llyn Llion* (Lake of the floods), the
waters of which burst forth and overwhelmed the face of the
whole earth.   Hence they regarded the lake as the just symbol
of the deluge.   But the deluge itself was viewed, not merely
as an instrument of punishment to destroy the wicked inhabitants of the globe, but also as a divine lustration, which washed away the bane of corruption, and purified the earth for the
reception of the just ones, or of the deified patriarch and his
family."*—*Davies' Mythology, p.* 142.

We shall have occasion to speak concerning the deluge hereafter; all we wish to show here, is, that Druidism has some relation to the ancient church, and was derived from the same
source.   Lakes being representative, is in correspondence with
the Word.   The Red Sea through which Israel passed, and in
which the Egyptians were drowned, had a similar correspondence to the deluge of Noah.   The lake of Galilee also, agitated

---

* The deified patriarch and his family, is an unwarrantable expression of Mr.
Davies', for which there is no ground in the writings from which he professes to
derive his knowledge.   The Druids in their writings speak of principles, according to correspondence, represented under forms of men, beasts, birds, trees, &c.
which Mr. Davies understands only according to the literal sense.   Consequently
when the Druids speak of principles which he mistakes for persons, he substitutes
for the original word either the name of Noah, or the name of one of the gods or
goddesses of Greece, as it suits his purpose; it being Mr. Davies' object in his work
evidently, not to give a fair representation of the religion of the Druids, but to
show that the Mythology of Greece was derived from the Druidism of Britain.
Yet Mr. Davies in the same book repeatedly acknowledges that the Druids worshiped the one Supreme God.   In a note, on p. 502, he remarks, "The Bard
speaks of one Supreme God, as acknowledged by the Ancient Druids."   The Bard
alluded to is Taliesin, who begins a poem, quoted by Mr. D., with these words,
" I will adore the love-diffusing Lord of every kindred, the Sovereign of hosts and
powers round the universe."   Again, on p. 515, with reference to another poem,
Mr. D. remarks, " In the first stanza, we find the Bard acknowledging the existence of one Supreme God, and declaring his resolution to adore him.   This I conceive was a genuine principle of the patriarchal religion."

by the wind, was significative of temptation or influx from hell; hence the miracles of the Lord in quelling the storms upon that lake, are representative of his divine operations upon the mind when man has passed victoriously through temptations. Lakes. therefore, in the Jewish Church, as well as among the Druids, were representative of the deluge; that is, what is internally signified by the deluge; and that deluge, according to the doctrine of the Druids, not only destroyed the wicked, but also was the means by which evils were removed from the man of the church so that he might be regenerated.

The religion which, the British Bards inform us, was derived from the primitive world, the principles being preserved amid the deluge, and afterwards formed into a system, was from that time handed down among them from age, by memorial.

" The Druids and Bards of ancient Britain," observes Mr. James, " both one and the same people, are no where represented as Inventors. They were the jealous Conservators of early and primitive discipline, doctrines, customs, and opinions: and they studied the art of memory to an extent unknown in any other country of which we have any knowledge. Oral tradition was reduced into a systematic science." The Bards, in their compositions, simply clothed in language doctrines and sentiments well known, received in the church, and professedly derived from heaven.

We will here introduce a few triads which speak of the origin of Bardism, or Druidism, and of the manner in which the knowledge of it was preserved among its disciples; reminding the reader that in the language of the Druids, principles are frequently personified, as in the Ancient Church.

1. "The three primary Sages of the race of the Cymbry: Hu Gadarn (the mighty one who pervades, covers, inspects), who first collected the race of the Cymbry, and disposed them into tribes; Dyfnwal Moelmud (a deep laid rampart or defence), who first regulated the laws, privileges, and institutions of the country and nation; (this name is significative of the defence of truth or of the law: Dyfnwal, a deep laid rampart, and Moelmud, the removal of nakedness); and Tydain tad Awen (the central fire, the father of inspiration), who first introduced order and method into the memorials and preservation of the oral art and its properties; and from that order, the privileges and methodical usages of the Bards and Bardism of the Isle of Britian were first devised."

2. "The three primary Bards of the Isle of Britain: Plennydd (light or radiance), Alawn (harmony), and Gwron (energy or virtue); these were they who devised the privileges and usages which belong to Bards and Bardism."

3. " The three elementary masters of poetry and memorial, of the race of the Cymbry : Gwyddon Ganhebon (knowledge or wisdom with its language or utterance), the first in the world who composed poetry ; Hu Gadarn (the mighty one who pervades, covers, inspects), who first adapted poetry to the preservation of record and memorials : and Tydain tad Awen (the central fire, the father of inspiration), who first developed the art and structure of poetry, and the due disposition of thought."
—*Historical Triads.*

"The three memorials (or mediums of memory) of the Bards of the Isle of Britain : the memorial of song, the memorial of conventional recitation, and the memorial of established usage."
"There are three things without which no man can be a Bard : a poetical genius, a knowledge of the Bardic Institutes, and irreproachable manners."
" There are three indispensables of a Bardic Instructor : poetic genius from God, instruction by a master, and his office confirmed by the decision of the convention."—*Institutional Triads.*

The intelligent reader will at once perceive the perfect correspondence and beauty of the above historical triads; and from them learn that the Druids, or Bards, professed to have derived their religious system, with all that pertained to its origin and preservation, from God ; who, as to his divine principles, in his various relations to the church and his providence over her, is represented as the central fire, from whom is inspiration, the mighty one who pervades, overshadows, and inspects, and the strong defence : the primary constituents of the institution derived from him being light, harmony and virtue. The inspiration which in the historical triads is said to be the offspring of the central fire, is in the institutional triads called poetic genius from God, thus plainly showing that by the central fire was signified, according to correspondence, the divine love.
Poetry was used by the Druids as the best and most effectual method of imparting religious knowledge to the multitude, and of transmitting to posterity the wisdom of the ancients. It was therefore indispensably necessary for a Druid or priest to be a poet. Hence Bards and Druids are used as synonymous terms ; and Bardism is the word almost invariably employed in the ancient British records to designate the theology and maxims of the Druids. Consequently the aphorisms and triads from which we have so largely quoted, are included in the memorial of song mentioned above. The doctrinals of Druidism, thus reduced to a system, the disciples of the Bards committed

to memory, and made themselves perfect masters of them before they were admitted to order. They were twenty years under discipline. These, being committed to memory, were afterwards recited from time to time at the meetings or conventions of the Bards, so as to retain the knowledge of them perfect. Upon this subject Mr. E. Williams remarks, "The songs and aphorisms of the Bards were always laid before their grand meetings or conventions of the Solstices and Equinoxes : here they were discussed with the most scrutinizing severity : if admitted at the first, they were reconsidered at the second : if then approved of, they were referred to the third meeting ; and being approved of by that, they were ratified or confirmed ; otherwise they were referred to the triennial supreme convention for ultimate consideration ; at which all that had been confirmed at the provincial conventions were also recited ; and the disciples there attending from every province were enjoined to learn them, that thereby they might be as widely diffused as possible. These were recited for ever afterwards annually, at least at every convention in Britain. This being the practice it was impossible for perversion or interpolation to take place without being detected ; for all the Bardic traditions were thus to be recited annually at one or other of the four grand meetings of the year. This well-guarded tradition was a better guardian of truth than letters have ever been before the art of printing was discovered."

The *regular times* of holding a convention were the two solstices and equinoxes : subordinate meetings might also be held every new and full moon ; and also at the quarter days, which were chiefly for instructing disciples. The general meetings or conventions were always held in the open air, according to the motto, "*In the face of the sun, and in the eye of light ;*" their place of meeting being an open circular temple of huge stones, in the centre of which was a large flat stone, called the Altar of the Bards, and the Stone of Covenant. The ceremony used at the opening of the Convention was the sheathing of a sword on the central stone, at which all the presiding Bards assisted ; and this was accompanied with a short and suitable address, commencing and concluding with the motto, "*Truth in opposition to the world.*" The Bards always stood bareheaded and bare-footed, in their unicolored robes, at these general assemblies: thus representatively showing the necessity of putting off the external natural principle in order to appear in the Divine presence, or enter the sanctuary of God, and engage in his service.

It was our intention to describe at some length these circular temples, and the Druidical stones still remaining in various parts of Great Britain; but we must be content to notice a few of them only. There are frequent allusions to these in the works of the Bards, and the erection of them is mentioned in one of the historical triads as being the mighty labors of the Isle of Britian.

"The three mighty labors of the Isle of Britian; lifting the stone of Cetti, building the work of Emryss, and piling up the Mount of Assemblies.—*Triad* 88.

The stone of Cetti is, in the works of the Bards, called the Covering Stone, and the token of the supreme seat; and are evidently the huge blocks lifted by the Druids, which, to this day, are seen in various parts of the principality. One of these in Pembrokeshire is thus described in Camden's Britannia. "There are in this county several such circular stone monuments as that described in Carmarthenshire, by the name of Meineu Gwyr; and Kevn Llechart, in Glamorganshire. But the most remarkable is that which is called Y Gromlech, in Nevern parish, where are several rude stones pitched on one end in a circular order and in the midst of the circle, a vast rude stone placed on several pillars. The diameter of the area is about fifty feet. The stone supported in the midst of this circle is eighteen feet long, and nine in breadth; and at one end it is about three feet thick, but thinner at the other. There lies also by it a piece broken off, about ten feet in length and five in breadth, which seems more than twenty oxen could draw. It is supported by three large rude pillars, about eight feet high; but there are also five others, which are of no use at present, as not being high enough, or duly placed, to bear any weight of the top stone. Under this stone the ground is neatly flagged, considering the rudeness of monuments of this kind."

Another in Glamonshire is described as follows. "Another monument there is on a mountain called Kevn Bryn, the most noted hill in Gower, which may challenge a place among such unaccountable antiquities as are beyond the reach of history. The stones are to be seen upon a jutting, at the north-west of Kevn Bryn. Their fashion and posture is this. There is a vast unwrought stone, probably about twenty tons weight, supported by six or seven others that are not above four feet high; and these are set in a circle, some on one end and some edgewise, or sidelong to bear the great one up. The great one is much diminished of what it has been in bulk, as having five tons or more, by report, broke off it, to make millstones; so that I guess the stone originally to have been between twenty-five and thirty tons in weight. Under it is a well, which, as the neighborhood tell me, has a flux and re-flux with the sea."—*Gibson's Camden, p.* 620, 636.

Swedenborg informs us that altars of stone were common in the ancient church, and that they were representative of the Lord. "That by Noah's building an altar to the Jehovah, is signified a representative of the Lord, appears from what has been said. All the rites of the ancient church were representative of the Lord, as also were the rites of the Jewish church; but the principal representative in latter times was the altar, and also the burnt-offering. Nay, altars were built, before men knew to sacrifice oxen and sheep upon them, and that as a memorial."—*A. C.* 921. A passage before quoted from the writings of the Bards, evidently proves that the Druids viewed these stones as the representatives of the Supreme Being. "Before the covering stone, I tremble in the presence of the Sovereign of boundless dominion, lest I sink adhesive, to the quagmire of that multitude which people the depths of hell." These altars being of unwrought stones, is, according to correspondence, which correspondence we shall speak of in speaking of the temples. The well or spring of water being under the stone in Gower, reminds us of the passage in the Apocalypse. "And he showed me a pure river of water of life, clear as crystal, proceeding out of the throne of God and the Lamb."

"The doctrinals of the ancient church," says Swedenborg, "consisted of significatives, and thus as it were enigmatical terms, viz. what was signified by things on earth; as by mountains, that they signified things celestial and the Lord; by morning and the east, that they also signified things celestial and the Lord; by trees of different kinds and their fruits, that they signified man, and what is celestial in him; and so in other instances. Therefore their worship from such things was begun and permitted; hence this worship on mountains, and in groves, and in the midst of trees, and hence their statues in the open air; and at length their altars and burnt-offerings, which afterwards became the principal things in all worship. This worship was begun by the ancient church, and emanated thence to their posterity, and the nations round about."—*A. C.* 920. It is well known that the Druids worshiped in the open air, under trees, and in groves; and that they worshiped in open temples. on mountains and hills, is also evident from the allusions made by the Bards to the circular temples, which are found to be in such localities. There are many remains of such temples in Wales, noticed in Camden's Britannia: one of which is on Snowdon in the county of Caernarvon, the highest mountain in the Principality. But we must omit the detail of these provincial sanctuaries, and proceed to lay before the reader a description of the grand national temple, situated on a hill in the midst of an extended plain one hundred miles in circuit, in Wiltshire, England. It is thus noticed by Mr. Camden: "About six miles northward of Salisbury, on the plains, is to be seen a wild structure. For within a trench are placed huge unhewn stones in three circles, one within another, after the manner of a crown, some of which are twenty-eight feet in height, and seven in breadth, on which others, like architraves are borne up, so that it seems to be a hanging pile; from which we call it Stonehenge."—*Gibson's Camden, p.* 94. Dr. Stukely, after repeated and careful examinations of the structure, aided by several other gentlemen, gives a lengthy and full description of it. We select the following particulars from his work. " It is situated on a rising ground, anciently environed with a deep trench, still appearing about thirty feet broad; so that betwixt it and the work itself, a large and void space of ground was left. It had from the plain three open entrances, the most conspicuous of which lies north-east; at each of which were raised on the outside of the trench, two huge stones, gate-wise; parallel to which on the inside are two others of less proportion. After one has passed the ditch, he ascends thirty-five yards before he comes at the work itself. The whole work in general being of a circular form is one hundred and ten feet in diameter, and without a roof.

" The whole outer circle originally consisted of thirty stones; upon the top of these was placed an equal number of imposts in such a manner that the whole circle was linked together in a continued corona by the imposts being carried quite round. Two yards and a half within this great circle is a range of lesser stones, forty in number, forming with the outer circle, a very noble and delightful walk, three hundred feet in circuit. These stones are one half the height of the exterior uprights.

" The adytum or cell which presents itself next, is a most noble and beautiful ellipsis; nor is there any thing like it in all antiquity. It is an original invention of the Druids, an ingenious contrivance to relax the inner and more sacred part, where they performed their religious offices. The two outer circles were no disadvantage to the view from hence, but added much to the solemnity of the place and of the duties discharged in it by the frequency and variety of their intervals. They that were within would see a fine effect produced by this elliptical figure included in a circular corona, and having a large hemisphere of the heavens for its covering.

" The exterior oval is composed of certain compages of stones called Trilithons, being made each of two uprights with an impost at top. The uprights are ten in number, and the imposts five. The inner curve consists of nineteen upright stones in a pyramidal form. Their height is unequal like that of the trilithons, rising higher towards the upper end of the adytum.

"As you look from the grand entrance towards the altar, the jambs of the two hithermost trilithons present themselves with a magnificent opening twenty-five cubits wide. One remarkable particular in the construction of this oval is, that the two hitherto trilithons corresponding, that is on the right hand and left next the grand entrance, are exceeded in height by the two next in order, and those again by the trilithons behind the altar, this end of the choir. Their respective heights are thirteen, fourteen, and fifteen cubits (Hebrew measure).

"The altar is of a blue coarse and fine marble, placed a little above the focus of the upper end of the ellipsis, sixteen feet long, four feet broad, and twenty inches thick, leaving round it room sufficient for the ministrations of the Priests.

"The whole number of stones of which this most superb temple was composed, is one hundred and forty.

"The appearance of Stonehenge is stately, awful, and really august. When you enter the building, whether on foot or horseback, and cast your eyes around upon the yawning ruins, you are struck into an extatic reverie, which none can describe, and which they only can be sensible of that feel it. The dark part of the ponderous impost over our heads, the chasm of sky between the jambs of the cell, the odd construction of the whole, and the greatness of every part surprises. If you look upon the perfect part, you fancy entire quarries mounted up into the air; if upon the rude havoc below, you see as it were the bowels of a mountain turned inside outwards."—*Stukeley's Stonehenge*, p. 10–30. Mr. Maurice, in his "Indian Antiquities," speaking of Stonehenge, makes the following remarks.

"Whoever has read, or may be inclined to read, my history of Oriental Architecture, as connected with the astronomical, and mythological notions of the ancients, may see most of the assertions realised in the form and management of this old Druid temple. For, in the first place, it is circular, as it is there proved all ancient temples were. In the second place, the adytum, or sanctum sanctorum, is of an oval form representing the Mundane egg, after the manner that all those adyta in which the sacred fire perpetually blazed were constantly fabricated. In the third place, the situation is fixed astronomically, the grand entrances both of this temple and that of Abury, being placed exactly north-east, as all the gates or portals of the ancient caverns, and cavern temples were. In the fourth place, the number of stones and uprights in the outward circle, making together exactly sixty, plainly alludes to that peculiar and prominent feature of Asiatic Astronomy, the sexegenary cycle; while the number of stones forming the minor circles of the cove, being exactly nineteen, displays to us the famous Metonic, or rather Indian cycle; and that of thirty repeatedly occurring, the elevated age or generation of the Druids. Fifthly, the temple being uncovered, proves it to have been erected under impressions similar to those which animated the ancient Persians, who rejected the impious idea of confining the Deity within an enclosed shrine, however magnificent; and therefore, consequently, it must at all events have been erected before the age of Zoroaster, who flourished more than five hundred years before Christ, and who first covered in the Persian temples."—*Indian Antiq. Vol.* vi. p. 129.

The coincidences here mentioned by Mr. Maurice are an evidence of the truth of the statement so frequently made by Swedenborg in his writings, that the doctrines of the ancient church were spread far and wide, and that the systems of religion among the gentile nations, scattered through Europe and Asia, were all primarily derived from this one source; this religion, which was at first pure, gradually being corrupted, until at length man, losing the knowledge of the science of correspondence, substituted for the one true God, innumerable deities which they worshiped; these deities, however, being what to the ancients were representations of the principles or attributes of the one supreme God.

Let us now glance at the correspondence of this grand temple of the Druids, among whom was still retained the knowledge and worship of the one God of the ancient church.

The material of the temple was stone, representative of Divine truth. "The temples in the spiritual kingdom appear as of stone, because stone corresponds to truth, in which they are principled who are in the spiritual kingdom."—*H. & H.* 223.

These stones were all unwrought, signifying that nothing of self-derived intelligence should enter into the formation of that which was represented by the temple. "Hewn stones denote such things as are of self-intelligence: for stones denote truths, and to cut or fit them denotes to hatch or devise truths or such things as are like truths from the proprium, or from self-intelligence; for those things which are hatched or devised from the proprium have life from man, which life is no life; for the proprium of man is nothing but evil; whereas the things which are not from the proprium, but from the Divine, have life in them, for all life is from the Divine."—*A. C.* 8941.

The temple was of circular form, representative of the circle of life in the Lord and in the man of the church. " The process of the regeneration of man, and of the glorification of the Lord's human principle, is described and illustrated by the circle or life with man."—*A. C.* 10,057. The Druids in their writings speak of three circles of life ; first, *Cylch y Ceugant,* the circle of the infinite, which none but God alone can fill : second, *Cylch yr Abred,* the circle of courses, the state of life in which is a mixture of good and evil, and through which man passes in being regenerated : and third, *Cylch y Gwynfyd,* the circle of blessedness, which the regenerate ultimately attain.

The adytum in the interior of the temple, was of an oval form, representative of the principle of regeneration, in which the Lord is present in man, his presence being represented by the altar. " Awaking on a time out of sleep, I fell into a profound meditation about God ; and when I looked upwards, I saw in heaven above me a *very bright light of an oval form ;* as I fixed my eyes attentively upon that light it receded gradually from the centre towards the circumference, and, lo ! then heaven was open before me, and I beheld magnificent scenes, and saw angels standing in the form of a circle on the southern side of the opening, and in conversation with each other.— They conversed together concerning the one God, of conjunction with him, and salvation thereby."—*A. R.* 961. Again, this oval was the form of an egg, concerning which we read as follows, " Man when he is re-born, passes through the ages as he who is born ; and the preceding state is always as an egg in respect to the subsequent one, thus he is continually conceived and born : and this not only when he lives in the world, but also when he comes into another life to eternity: and still he cannot be further perfected, than to be as an egg to those things which remain to be manifested, which are indefinite."—*A. C.* 4379.

The temple was surrounded by a trench ; this trench being filled with water, was evidently intended to represent the sea ; for the Bards in their poetry generally represent their sanctuary as being surrounded and washed by the sea. The sea denotes the scientific principle, this sea, therefore, with the space of ground between it and the temple, itself was according to correspondence, representative of the natural man. The outer circle of the temple was composed of thirty upright stones, and thirty imposts : representative of the fulness of remains of goods and truths implanted in the natural principle of the man of the church ; for the upright stones were representative of truth, and the imposts, which joined the others together, the principle which conjoins, or the good of the spiritual church. " Thirty denotes a full state of remains, for that number results from three and ten multiplied into each other, and

by three is signified a full state, and by ten remains."—*A. C.*
7984.   The next circle is composed of forty stones, which number is significative of a state of temptation; hence the flood
was forty days on the earth (Gen. viii. 17).   The sons of Israel
were forty years in the wilderness, and the Saviour was tempted forty days of the devil.   Passing interiorly through that
state of temptation, the new or regenerated principle is represented by the stones of the adytum.   The outer ellipsis of this
was composed of five trilithons (the five three-stones), being
representative of the remains previously implanted being vivified, or brought into the life; for five, as well as ten and thirty,
signifies remains; and three denotes what is of the understanding, the will, and the life, or the celestial, spiritual and natural.
The number fifteen denotes the commencement of a new state
of life.—*A. C.* 8400.

Again, the inmost ellipsis was composed of nineteen stones,
which is seven and twelve added together; seven signifying
what is most holy or perfect, hence the Sabbath; and twelve
what is full or complete; hence, the twelve tribes of Israel
and the twelve apostles, representative of the church in every
complex.   This inmost ellipsis was representative of that which
immediately proceeds from the Lord—the Lord or the divine
principle being represented by the altar which was in the centre; and that which proceeds from him has perfect fulness and
is most holy.

The number of stones which composed the whole temple,
was one hundred and forty, a number significative of what is
perfect and full; for it is the product of seven multiplied into
twenty, and "twenty denotes what is full, in every measure,
and altogether" (*A. C.* 9641), and seven a state of rest, or the
Sabbath.

The grand entrance into this temple was on the north-east,
having in this particular, the same correspondence as the temples in heaven.   "The preacher stands in a pulpit on the east,
before his face sit those who are in the light of wisdom above
others, and on the right and left those who are in less light.
They sit in the form of a circus, so that all are in view of
the preacher.   The novitiates stand at the door, on the east of
the temple, and on the left of the pulpit."—*H. & H.* 223.   By
the left in heaven is signified the same as the north; consequently on the left of the pulpit in the east, is evidently north-
east.   It is said, in the same place, that no one is allowed to
stand behind the pulpit, nor on either side, so as to be out of
sight.   The north-east denotes a state of initiation, being a
state of comparative darkness, yet a state in which man is
drawn by the good of love.

(*To be concluded in our next.*)

ARTICLE II.

LETTERS TO A TRINITARIAN.

LETTER VI.

THE INCARNATION.

DEAR SIR,

THE results already reached in the foregoing discussion, though highly momentous in themselves, still leave many important phases of the subject unconsidered. The conclusion announced—I trust on legitimate and unimpeachable grounds—that Jesus of Nazareth is the Jehovah of the Old Testament, the Lord of the universe, the one only and true God, in whom is concentrated a Trinity of Essentials indicated by the terms Father, Son, and Holy Ghost, is doubtless, if sound, the fundamental fact of the revelations contained in the Bible; and yet it is a conclusion which must stand in perfect consistency with every other truth relating to his person and work, as the author and accomplisher of redemption. To this department of the subject, I now address myself, and I feel impelled to offer a general remark in regard to such a course of reasoning as that in which I have been thus far engaged, viz.: that if, on the whole, fairly and legitimately conducted, and the mind recognizes the truth of the result, we are authorized to abide by it. We are not required to forego our conclusions simply because we do not clearly perceive, at the present moment, how they may be made to consist with other results which seem to be of equal validity and yet of adverse bearing. Such an apparent conflict of issues ought doubtless to enforce the most rigid requisition of evidence in support of a conclusion that seems satisfactory, though, to our own minds, coming short of demonstration; but if upon the whole we see no way of avoiding it, and that if there be any yielding, it must be on the other side; then we say that the true course is to adhere firmly to what is firmly established, and to rest in the assurance that the seemingly opposite view may, when more fully apprehended, be seen entirely to harmonize with it. If, for instance, the process of proof in regard to the absolute identity of Jehovah and Jesus is fairly beyond question, then a moral compulsion rests upon us to interpret those passages of the Word, which seem to hold a different language, in a sense consistent with that unity of Divine essence and person which we have previously certified to our own minds. I am well aware of the difficulty that you will doubtless find, in the outset, in your attempts to solve the apparent problem which our main position sets before you.   The grand ideal which you have formed of the design and genius of the Christian system, involves, as an essential element, a certain *disjunction* and *duality* of the Father and the Son, which is virtually annulled in the view that I have now presented, so that you feel that its adoption would not be so much a modification, as a total subversion, of all your most cherished theories in regard to the redemption and salvation of men.   You perceive at a glance, that the established dogma of *vicarious atonement* sinks at once out of sight when the position is admitted, that Jesus Christ is as truly the Father as the Son, which of course he must be if he is the veritable Jehovah, and which, in the sequel, I shall show still more clearly that he is.   This result, if admitted, cannot fail to give a violent shock to your pre-conceptions, and it would not be strange, if under the first effects of the concussion, your faith should so "reel like a drunken man," that you should find yourself for a time *desperabund*, and ready to renounce the hope of *ever* attaining the truth on the most momentous of all themes. But cooler reflection will restore the equilibrium of reason and religion.   It is impossible for any honest mind to remain in an attitude of permanent rebellion against a clear and irresistible induction drawn from both the spirit and the letter of the Holy Oracles.   In the present case, I will venture to say that you will find every attempt abortive to array before yourself a *stronger* body of evidence in support of the common doctrine of atonement than I have above presented of the supreme and exclusive Godhead of Jesus Christ, and as surely as this is received as true, so surely will that doctrine be renounced as false, for the two cannot possibly stand together.   If the Deity exists in one person he cannot, in that person, as I have already remarked, make an atonement to himself.

What remains then but to attempt to show, that all the sublime ends of redemption may be more fully attained, and the Divine perfections be far more gloriously displayed, on the ground which I have' assumed than upon that which is made the basis of the current theology of the church?   This is what I have ventured to propose to myself in the sequel of these letters.   Whether I shall do justice to the theme, or even to my own imperfect views of it, I am not a little in doubt.   But that there is a great truth in relation to the subject, which is intrinsically *capable* of presentation, I am altogether satisfied, nor ought I perhaps to despair of exhibiting it in an intelligible form, if I have succeeded thus far in stating the preliminary argument out of which the ultimate results legitimately grow.

The aim of my preceding elucidations has been to evince
hat our adorable Lord and Saviour, being Jehovah in unity,
xists, in his very nature, in a Divine Humanity, the manifest-
ution of which, prior to the advent in the flesh, could only be
endered possible by the assumption of an angel as a medium.
The angel thus employed was not necessarily any particular
angel with whom the Divine Being was more permanently
onnected than with any other individual of the angelic order.
The Divine influx merely *infilled* the created angel, who thus
ecame, as it were, a body to that measure of the essence of
ehovah which for the time pervaded it as a soul, and appeared
and spake through it. The ontological grounds of this I have
already developed, and a secondary reason for renewing the
nention of it here, is, to introduce a remarkable passage from
Watts' "Glory of Christ as God-Man," which, with the abate-
nent of his idea respecting the angel as the *pre-existing human soul* of Jesus, and therefore *permanently* united with the
Supreme Divinity, and also with the understanding that by
he term angel is meant a real created angel temporarily as-
umed, exhibits a most striking approximation to the truth as
t regards the real relation subsisting between the visible angel
and the informing Deity. He is replying to an objection which
e thus states ;—"Though it should be allowed that God was
resent with this angel, and resided in him, and spake by him,
et is this sufficient to make a *personal union* between God and
he angel ? or is it ground enough to say that *God and the
angel were one complex person ?*" This objection he proceeds
o answer.

"The most common and most familiar idea that we have
f a *complex person* is human nature or man, who is
ade up of a soul and body. Let us now consider whether
ost of those mutual relations or communications between
oul and body which render man a *complex person* are not
ound in this glorious *person* composed of the great God and
his angel. Has the body of a man a *nearer relation* to his
oul than any other body in the world ? So had this angel a
earer relation to God than any other creature whatsoever. Is
he soul said to *inhabit* the body, or *reside* in it constantly dur-
ng the whole term of life ? So did God constantly reside in
his glorious angel. Does the soul *influence* the body to its
hief human actions ? So did God influence this angel. In the
ody the *constant and immediate instrument* of the soul, where-
y it speaks and acts and conveys its mind to men ? Such was
his angel to the Great God who dwelt in him. Is the body
bedient to the volitions of the indwelling soul ? Much more is
his angel to the indwelling God. Is the soul immediately

conscious of many of the motions of the body? Much more is God immediately conscious of every motion, action and occurrence that relates to this angel? Are the *properties* and *actions* of the body sometimes *attributed* to the soul, and the *properties* and *actions* of the soul sometimes to the body, in the common language of men? So in the language of Scripture the names, titles and properties of the great God are attributed to this angel; the appearances, speeches, voice, words, motions and actions of this angel are attributed to God. And if *man* upon these accounts be called a *complex person*, made up of *soul and body*, for the same reason we may suppose that the *Great God* and this *angel of his presence* make up a *complex person* also: and this is called a personal union."— *Watts on Glory of Christ*, p. 67, 68.

This, as I have remarked, is a wonderful approximation to the truth according to the New Church view of the subject, and the man of that church can hardly refrain from imaging to himself the cordial delight with which such a spirit would have welcomed revelations so well calculated to clear up the mysteries of the Divine nature with which his mind was evidently deeply oppressed. All that is necessary to bring this view into a very strict accordance with the truth, is to consider the angel as an angel, and to divest the relation set forth of the *permanency* which he attributes to it.

It was Jehovah, then, in his Divine Humanity, who appeared in the ancient *theophanies*, and these appearances were pre-intimations of his subsequent coming in the ultimates of our earthly humanity. The temporary intermediation of an angel, who was of course a man, gave a kind of sensible demonstration of the fact, but the procedure was all along in "first principles," and it was reserved for the "fulness of times," to realize the actual result of the Lord's advent in the flesh. In the consideration of this stupendous event, our attention is naturally drawn to two distinct branches of the subject; (1) The *mode* of its accomplishment; (2) The *ends* to be answered by it; on both which I shall be constrained to be somewhat full. I shall count also upon your indulgence for the rather copious extracts from Swedenborg.

In entering upon an attempted explanation of the *mode* of the incarnation, I would fain shield myself from the charge of rudely invading the region of mystery. The apostolic declaration, "Great is the mystery of godliness; God manifest in the flesh," will naturally rise up to your mind, and perhaps throw around it a sphere of repellency towards the least approach to a solution of the deep arcana which environ the subject. But I may plead as a sanction to the attempt, the fact, which *you* cordially admit, that such an incarnation has actually taken place. I am not arguing the antecedent possibility or probability of such an amazing occurrence. It has already passed into the category of things transpired. It stands emblazoned as the paramount fact of all human, if not of all Divine, history. Its occurrence is the glory of earth, and the wonder of heaven. The only question in regard to it, is, whether there be any presumption—any unlawful prying into the things hidden from mortal ken—in humbly endeavoring to bring our knowledge, such as it is, of the Divine nature, to bear on the nature of the great fact, with a view to learn how far the mode of it may be brought within the compass of our intelligence. I do not see that this is by any means forbidden, especially as after all our researches there will remain an immense residuum of absolute verity which will be for ever incomprehensible to our finite faculties. Yet we come, I think, to the inquiry with signal advantages if what we have already remarked as to the constitution of the Divine nature be conceded to be true. The cardinal tenet of the New Church, that Jesus is Jehovah, that Jehovah is one, and that a Divine Humanity is involved in the very essence of his being, prepares us to yield a more facile credence to the asserted fact of this eternal Humanity's having become incarnate in time, or, in other words, of its having "passed from first principles to last." Our conceptions of the subject are, moreover, somewhat aided by the views above advanced respecting emanation-theory of creation, according to which we learn that the Divine influx in its descent continually tends to clothe itself in material embodiments giving form and expression to the spiritual principle from which they are derived. Still, a measureless remove must for ever separate all other manifestations of the Divine agency from that which we are called to contemplate in the incarnation of Jehovah ; and we only refer to them as casting some collateral gleams of light upon a subject inevitably obscure to us, under whatever aspect it be viewed.

For myself, I am unable to perceive what advance can be made towards a correct apprehension of the theme before us, except by divesting ourselves entirely of the prevalent idea of a Trinity of persons. This idea is an effectual closure of the mind against all access to the light of truth. The inference—for, as I have shown, it is nothing more—that it was the *second person* of the Godhead who assumed our nature, completely vacates all just and Scriptural conceptions of the wondrous fact.* If there is any intelligible sense in the inspired decla-

---

* " It is believed that God, the Creator of the universe, begat a Son from eternity, and that this Son descended and assumed the Human, to redeem and save men;

rations as to what is to be believed on this subject, it is that Jehovah himself, in the unity of his person, condescended to become incarnate, and in so doing did not more assume our nature than *ultimate* his own, for our nature is human because his is infinitely so.*   But what is the true idea which is to be formed of Jehovah ?   Let our illumined author speak in reply.

"That by God and Jehovah in the Word was understood the Lord, was not known to the Jewish church, neither is it known at this day to the Christian church : that the Christian church has not known this, is because it has distinguished the Divine into three persons : whereas the ancient church, which was after the flood, and especially the most ancient church, which was before the flood, by Jehovah and God understood no other than the Lord, and indeed the Lord as to the Divine Human.   They had knowledge also concerning the Divine Itself which is the Lord, and which He calls his Father ; but concerning that Divine Itself which is in the Lord, they were not able to think, but concerning the Divine Human, consequently they could not be conjoined to another Divine, for conjunction is effected by thought which is of the understanding, and by affection which is of the will, thus by faith and by love : for when the Divine itself is thought of, the thought falls as into a boundless universe, and so is dissipated, whereby is no conjunction ; but it is otherwise when the Divine itself is thought of as the Divine Human.   They knew also, that unless they were conjoined with the Divine, they could not be saved : on this account the Divine Human was what the ancient churches adored, and Jehovah also manifested Himself with them in the Divine Human ; and the Divine Human was the Divine itself in heaven, for heaven constitutes one man, which is called the Grand Man, and which has been treated

---

but this is erroneous, and falls of itself to the ground, while it is considered that God is one, and that it is more than fabulous in the eye of reason, that the one God should have begotten a Son from eternity, and also that God the Father, together with the Son and the Holy Ghost, each of whom singly is God, should be one God. This fabulous representation is entirely dissipated, while it is demonstrated from the Word, that Jehovah God himself descended, and became MAN, and also Redeemer."—*T. C. R.* 82.

* " The reason that the Lord's internal man, which is Jehovah, is called a man, is, because no one is a man but Jehovah alone. · For ' man' signifies, in the genuine sense, that Esse from which man originates. The very Esse from which man originates is Divine, consequently, is celestial and spiritual ; without this Divine celestial and spiritual, there is nothing human in man, but only a sort of animal nature, such as the beasts have. It is from the Esse of Jehovah, or of the Lord, that every man is a man ; and it is hence also that he is called a man. The celestial which constitutes him a man, is that he should love the Lord, and love the neighbor : thus he is a man, because he is an image of the Lord, and because he has that celestial from the Lord ; otherwise he is a wild beast. The same may further appear from this, that Jehovah, or the Lord, appeared to the patriarchs of the most ancient church as a man ; as he did afterwards to Abraham, and likewise to the prophets ; wherefore also the Lord deigned, when there was no longer any man upon earth, or nothing celestial and spiritual remaining with man, to assume the human nature by being born as another man, and to make it Divine ; whereby also he is the only man. Moreover, the universal heaven presents before the Lord the image of a man, because it presents Him ; hence heaven is called the Grand Man, on this account especially, because the Lord is all in all therein."—*A. C.* 1994.

of heretofore at the close of the chapters. This Divine in heaven is no other than the Divine itself, but in heaven as a divine man; it is this man which the Lord took upon Him, and made Divine in Himself, and united to the Divine itself, as it had been united from eternity, for from eternity there was oneness; and this because the human race could not otherwise be saved; for it could no longer suffice that the Divine itself through heaven, thus through the Divine Human there, could flow into human minds; wherefore the Divine itself willed to unite to itself the Divine Human actually by the human assumed in the world; the latter and the former is the Lord."—*A. C.* 5663.

If this be well founded, the Divine nature does not present to our conceptions an *absolute simple*, but a *complex*, the elements of which are the Divine itself in its own super-celestial *esse*, or the infinite Love, and the Divine Wisdom or Truth, related to the former as Intellect ever is to Affection, which is the relation of the *existere* to the *esse*. The Divine Wisdom is the *form* of the Divine Love, and this *form* is what is more especially to be understood by the Divine Humanity existing in "first principles," or as the Alpha, which in the incarnation, assumed to itself the Omega; for when our Lord says of himself, "I am the Alpha and the Omega, the first and the last," it is obvious that he has no respect to time, as he is without beginning of days or end of years. In this character of the Divine Humanity from everlasting, our Lord was the Word, or the Truth, as I have already shown, and this "Word was made flesh," i. e., became incarnate.* The Word or Wisdom of Jehovah, indicated by the Son, could be made manifest, but not the Divine Love, answering to the Father. "That Jehovah's appearing denotes the Lord's Divine in his Human, is evident from this, that his Divine cannot appear to any man, nor even to any angel, except by the Divine Human; and the Divine Human is nothing but the Divine Truth which proceeds from Himself." This *proceeding* of the Divine Truth from the Divine Good or Love, is what is otherwise expressed by the word *sent*, and the idea of *sent* is intimately related to *angel*, which, as we have seen, denotes the medium of manifestation prior to the advent in the flesh. The bearing of this will appear

---

* "Who does not know that the Lord was conceived from God the Father, and who cannot thence understand, that God the Father who is Jehovah, took upon him Humanity in the world, and consequently that the Humanity is the Humanity of God the Father, and thus that God the Father and He are one, as the soul and the body are one? Can any one therefore approach the soul of a man, and descend from thence into the body? Is not his humanity to be approached? And is not his soul addressed hereby at the same time? I am aware it will be thought, How can Jehovah the Father, who is the Creator of the universe, come down and assume Humanity? But let these think also, How can the Son from eternity, who is equal to the Father, and also the Creator of the universe, do this? Does it not amount to the same thing? It is said the Father and the Son from eternity, but there is no Son from eternity; it is the Divine Humanity called the Son, that was sent unto the world."—*A. R.* 743.

more clearly in the sequel, when we shall show that the Father's sending the Son into the world implies, in a consistent sense, the *sending himself into the world.* But preliminary to this it is necessary to lay down the great law of generation which is perpetually involved in all Swedenborg's expositions of this profound subject.

" To the above I shall add this arcanum, that the soul, which is from the father, is the very man, and that the body, which is from the mother, is not man in itself, but from the soul; the body is only a covering of the soul, composed of such things as are of the natural world.—Since the soul of man is the very man, and is spiritual from its origin, it is manifest whence it is that the mind, soul, disposition, inclination and affection of the love of the father dwells in his offspring, and returns and renders itself conspicuous from generation to generation. Thence it is, that many families, yea, nations, are known from their first father ; there is a general image in the face of each descendant, which manifests itself; and this image is not changed, except by the spiritual things of the church. The reason that a general image of Jacob and Judah still remains in their posterity, by which they may be distinguished from others, is, because they have hitherto adhered firmly to their religious principles; for there is in the seed of every one from which he is conceived, a graft or offset of the father's soul, in its fulness, within a certain covering from the elements of nature, by which the body is formed in the womb of the mother; which may be made according to the likeness of the father, or according to the likeness of the mother, the image of the father still remaining within it, which continually endeavors to bring itself forth, and if it cannot do it in the first generation, it effects it the following. The reason that the image of the father is in its fulness in the seed is, because, as was said, the soul is spiritual from its origin, and what is spiritual has nothing in common with space ; wherefore it is similar to itself in a small, as well as in a large compass."—*T. C. R.* 103.

I have here given this law in full by reason of its vast importance in the present investigation, and though the principle involved comes fairly within the province of physiology, and may be said to demand proof, yet I scruple not to build upon it, not only because Swedenborg asserts it, after having given me reasons to warrant the most implicit reliance on his testimony, but because the presumptions in its favor amount very nearly, in my judgment, to positive proof. It cannot, I think, be doubted that there is, on the part of the father, a *descent* of the soul in its "first principles" to the ultimates of the body in the propagation of a human being, and that the office of the mother is to furnish the investment of the seminal principle or germ. Accordingly Swedenborg's remarks, in illustration of the asserted fact, " that the soul is from the father, and its clothing from the mother, may be illustrated by things analagous in the vegetable kingdom. In this kingdom the earth or ground is the common mother, which, in itself, as in a womb, receives and clothes seeds; yea, as it were, conceives, bears, brings forth, and educates them as a mother her offspring from the father."—*C. L.* 206. The position is at any rate boldly assumed by Swedenborg in the face of all physiological science, and may be considered as a virtual challenge to the schools to dispute its soundness. As the truth of the principle is so essential to a just view of the whole doctrine of the incarnation as given by him, we are perfectly sure he would never have hazarded the enunciation but upon the most ample assurance.*

But how does this law specifically apply in the case of our Lord? Here again we are furnished with an answer.

"That Jehovah himself descended and assumed the Human, is very evident in Luke, where are these words: 'Mary said to the angel, How shall this be done, since I know not a man? To whom the angel replied, The Holy Spirit shall come upon thee, and the virtue of the Most High shall overshadow thee: whence the Holy Thing that is born of thee, shall be called the Son of God,' i. 34, 35. And in Matthew: 'The angel said to Joseph, the bridegroom of Mary, in a dream, that which is born in her is of the Holy Spirit; and Joseph knew her not, until she brought forth a Son, and called his name Jesus,' i. 20, 25. That by the Holy Spirit is meant the Divine which proceeds from Jehovah, will be seen in the third chapter of this work. Who does not know, that the child has the soul and life from the father, and that the body is from the soul? What therefore, is said more plainly, than that the Lord had his soul and life from Jehovah God; and, because the Divine cannot be divided, that the Divine itself was his soul and life? Wherefore the Lord so often called Jehovah God his Father, and Jehovah God called Him his Son. What, then, can be heard more ludicrous, than that the soul of our Lord was from the mother Mary, as both the Roman Catholics and the Reformed at this day dream, not having as yet been awakened by the Word."—*T. C. R.* 82.

Elsewhere he remarks;

---

* Notwithstanding the general proclivity of Commentators to deny the reference of Jer. xxxi. 22; " The Lord hath created (i. e. shall create) a new thing in the earth, a woman shall compass a man," to the miraculous conception. I am for myself satisfied that no preferable explanation has ever been given. This original תסובב *tesobeb* properly signifies to *surround, environ, encompass, encircle,* and Michaelis renders and interprets it—*circumdabit,* i. e. *in utero habebit.* So also Pocock, Hulsius, Schmidt, and many others among the earlier Christian Commentators. This interpretation, like many others, seems to have been yielded out of a kind of complaisance to the objections of Jews and other Anti-Messianists of the school of Grotius, who have been followed by the mass of modern German critics. The import of the passage according to Pocock is, that the Lord would create a new thing in the unprecedented fact of a woman's *encompassing* a man—a man *par eminence*—contrary to the ordinary laws of generation. And what is this but a veiled announcement of the great fact of the miraculous conception.

"The Lord in the Word is called Jehovah as to Divine good, for Divine good is the very Divine, and the Lord is called the Son of God as to Divine truth, for Divine truth proceeds from Divine good, as a son from a father, and also is said to be born."—*A. C.* 7499.

This is according to the universal law, that all thought or intellect is the product of affection. In God, angel and man, the *genesis* of Truth is from Good. But we are called to advance farther in the direction upon which we have entered. The common doctrine of the incarnation, if subjected to a rigid analysis, will undoubtedly resolve itself into the teaching of no higher a fact than this, viz.: that the manhood of Jesus, both soul and body, was, as it were, externally *assumed* by God—was *appended* or *adjoined* to Deity—so that the union between the Divine and the human in our Lord, amounted to a mere *adjunction* of one nature to the other. This, however, as we conceive, comes very far short of the truth, for on this ground we are unable to perceive how the indwelling of Jehovah in Jesus differed, except in degree, from that which may be predicated of Moses, or David, or Daniel, or Paul, with each of whom there was doubtless a very special presence of the Divine Being endowing them for their work.* If Jesus Christ possessed a human soul, or *inmost*, from his mother, are you prepared to define in what sense he can be affirmed to have been essentially Divine? It will not, I conceive, avail to have recourse on this point to the convenient plea of mystery, for the proposition is a very plain one, and must be susceptible of a sense not difficult to be grasped, so far as the averment of the fact is concerned. We see, in regard to the ancient *theophanies*, that the assumption of an angel leaves the impression very distinct of the paramount presence and operation of Jehovah himself acting in and through him. The Divine person may be said to be translucent through the angelic humanity. In like manner, in the Lord's incarnation on earth, it is necessary that the Deity should be equally conspicuous, at least to the eye of the

---

* " The unition of the Divine Essence with the Human, is not to be understood as of two who are distinct from each other, and only conjoined by love as a father with a son, when the father loves the son, and the son the father, or when a brother loves a brother, or a friend a friend; but it is a real unition into one, so that they are not two but one, as the Lord also teaches in several places."—*A. C.* 3737.

" With respect to the union of the Lord's Divine essence with his Human, and of the Human with the Divine, this is infinitely transcendant; for the Lord's internal was Jehovah Himself, thus life itself; whereas man's internal is not the Lord: thus neither life, but a recipient of life. There was *union* of the Lord with Jehovah, but there is no *union* of man with the Lord, but *conjunction*. The Lord from his own proper power united himself with Jehovah, wherefore also he was made righteousness; but man's conjunction is never effected by his own power, but by the Lord's, so that the Lord joins man to himself."—*A. C.* 2005.

mind, in the terrestrial man with whom he is conjoined, for the natural body which he here assumed stands, in fact, in a very similar relation to the indwelling Divinity, as did the spiritual body of the mediating angel to the essential Godhead which temporarily informed it. But let it once be assumed that he received a human soul—understanding by that term an *inmost essence*—by nativity of the mother, and such a distinct Divine inhabitation becomes impossible, and nothing more than the bare *adjunction* of Deity can be recognized. Upon this ground, therefore, our Lord stands shorn of his essential glory, and his human principle will inevitably be thought of as the human principle of any other man, while his Divinity, though brought in contact with his humanity, will be viewed altogether apart from it, and ideally merged in that of the infinite Godhead, which is usually understood by the term Father. This is a virtual surrender of the great truth in question, and they to whom it is imputable have small cause to enter the lists with the Unitarians. Let once the humanity of our Lord be mentally *disjoined* from his Divinity, and "Ichabod" is written upon the pillars of the church. On this subject I will give place to higher authority.

"Another point which the Athanasian doctrine teaches, is, that in he Lord there are two essences, the Divine and the Human; and in hat doctrine the idea is clear that the Lord has a Divine principle and a Human, or that the Lord is God and man; but the idea is obscure hat the Divine principle of the Lord is in the Human, as the soul is in the body. Inasmuch as a clear idea prevails over an obscure idea, herefore most people, both simple and learned, think of the Lord as of a common man, like unto themselves, and in such case, they do not hink at the same time of his Divine principle; if they think of the Divine principle, then they separate it in their idea from the Human, and thereby also infringe the unity of person. If they are asked, where is His Divine principle? they reply, from their idea, In heaven with the Father; the reason why they so reply and so perceive, is, because they find a repugnance to think that the Human principle is Divine, and thus together with its Divine principle in heaven, not aware, that whilst in thought they thus separate the Divine principle of the Lord from his Human, they not only think contrary to their own loctrine, which teaches that the Divine principle of the Lord is in His Human, as the soul in the body, also, that there is unity of person, hat is, that they are one person, but also they charge that doctrine undeservedly with contradiction or fallacy, in supposing that the Human principle of the Lord, together with the rational soul, was from the mother alone, when yet every man is rational by virtue of the soul, which is from the father. But that such thought has place, and such a separation, follows also from the idea of three Gods, from which idea it results, that His Divine principle in the Human is from the Divine of the Father, who is the first person, when yet it is His own proper Divine principle, which descended from heaven and assumed the Human. If man does not rightly perceive this, he may possibly be led to suppose, that his begetting Father was not one Divine principle, but threefold, which yet cannot be received with any faith. In a word, they who separate the Divine principle from His Human, and do not think that the Divine is in His Human as the soul in the body, and that they are one person, may fall into erroneous ideas concerning the Lord, even into an idea as of a man separated from a soul; wherefore take heed to yourselves lest you think of the Lord as of a man like yourself, but rather think of the Lord as of a man who is God. Attend, my reader! when you are perusing these pages, you may be led to suppose, that you have never, in thought, separated the Divine principle of the Lord from His Human, thus neither the Human from the Divine; but, I beseech you, consult your thought, when you have determined it to the Lord, whether you have ever considered that the Divine principle of the Lord is in His Human as the soul in the body? Rather have you not thought, yea, if you are now willing to make the inquiry, do not you at present think of His Human principle separately, and of His Divine principle separately? And when you think of His Human principle, do not you conceive it to be like the human principle of another man, and when of His Divine principle, do not you conceive it, in your idea, to be with the Father? I have questioned great numbers on this subject, even the rulers of the church, and they have all replied that it is so; and when I have said, that yet it is a tenet taught in the Athanasian creed, which is the very doctrine of their church concerning God and concerning the Lord, that the Divine principle of the Lord is in His Human as the soul in the body, they have replied, that they did not know this: and when I have recited these words of the doctrine, "Our Lord Jesus Christ, the son of God, although He be God and man, yet they are not two but one Christ; one altogether by unity of person; since as the reasonable soul and body are one man, so God and man is one Christ;" they were then silent and confessed afterwards, that they had not noted these words, being indignant at themselves for having so hastily, and with so careless an eye, examined their own doctrine."—*A. E.* 1104.

To the same effect, he observes in another place, that "they who think of the Lord's Humanity and not at the same time of his Divinity, will on no account admit the phrase "Divine Humanity;" for they think separately of his Humanity, and separately of his Divinity, which is like thinking of a man separately from his soul or life, which, however, is not to think of a man at all; still less is it an adequate way of thinking of the Lord."

We have here, then, if we mistake not, the grand cardinal truth of all Divine revelation—"God (i. c. Jehovah) manifest in the flesh," not God merely *adjoined* to the soul and body of a human being like ourselves, but the true God truly *incarnated* in a tenement of flesh and blood received, not by ordinary generation, but by ordinary nativity, from the virgin womb of Mary. "That the Lord had Divinity and Humanity, Divinity from Jehovah the Father, and Humanity from the virgin Mary, is well known. Hence it is, that he was God and Man, and that he had a Divine Essence and a Human nature, the Divine Essence from the Father, and the Human nature from the Mother; and hence he was equal to the Father with respect to the Divinity, and less than the Father with respect to the Humanity. And further, *this Human Nature was not transmuted into the Divine Essence, neither commixed with it; for the Human Nature cannot be transmuted into the Divine Essence nor can it be commixed therewith.* Nevertheless, by our doctrine we maintain that the Divinity assumed a Humanity, that is, united itself to it, as the soul is united to its body, so that they are not two, but one person."

This we believe to be the true DOCTRINE OF THE LORD, or the doctrine *respecting* the Lord, and of such transcendant importance do we regard it, that we scruple not to subscribe with all our hearts to Swedenborg's declaration, that "the essential of all doctrines is to acknowedge the Divine Human of the Lord." Nay, we are expressly taught by him that the cordial recognition of this doctrine is that which really constitutes the Lord's Second Coming. "By the Lord's advent is not understood His advent in person, but that he will then reveal Himself in the Word, that He is Jehovah, the Lord of heaven and earth, and that He alone is to be adored by all who will be in His new church, which is meant by the New Jerusalem; for which end also He hath now opened the internal or spiritual sense of the Word, in which sense the Lord is everywhere treated of: this also is what is understood by His coming in the clouds of heaven with glory. Inasmuch as He Himself is the Word, as He is called in John, therefore the revelation of Himself in the Word is His advent." He comes in the revelation of His own essential glory as God-Man, Jehovah Jesus, Creator, Redeemer and Regenerator—a revelation made in connexion with the establishment of the Church of the New Jerusalem, as it is in this Church only that the doctrine in question is received in its genuine purport. "That there is in the Lord a threefold principle, namely, the Divinity Itself, the Divine Humanity, and the Divine Proceeding, is an arcanum from heaven and is revealed for the benefit of those who shall have a place in the Holy Jerusalem."—*H. D.* 997. For the inferential bearings of this averment upon the theological views or the moral state of others, we are not responsible, as we plant ourselves simply upon the intrinsic truth of the position, and if any truth has a train of just and inevitable consequences, we cannot reject the truth simply because we cannot dispose of the consequences entirely to our minds. In respect to the system, however, in which the present doctrine holds so prominent a place, we do not regard it as a harshly exclusive or denunciatory system, though very emphatic in its affirmations, and I propose, in the winding up of my discussion, to offer some remarks on the moral aspects of the subject, which may tend to correct certain unfavorable impressions on this score, that have probably arisen in the minds of some of my readers.

In the following paragraph, Swedenborg is relating the conversation of certain spirits in the other life. In the perusal I beg you will make as much or as little account as you please of his assertions, on the score of the reality of this intercourse with spirits. The grand question is rather what the Truth says on this subject, than what they are alleged to have said, yet, as I have before remarked, the evidence that they did say it, is undoubtedly enhanced in proportion to the evidence of its being intrinsically true.—The spirits were from some other earth in the universe.

"It is well to be observed, that the idea which any person entertains concerning any thing, in another world is presented to the life, and thereby every one is examined as to the nature of his thought and perception respecting the things of faith; and that the idea of the thought concerning God is the chief of all others, inasmuch as by that idea, if it be genuine, conjunction is effected with the Divine Being, and consequently with heaven. They were afterwards questioned concerning the nature of their idea respecting God. They replied, that they did not conceive God as invisible, but as visible under a human form; and that they knew him to be thus visible, not only from an interior perception, but also from this circumstance, that he has appeared to them as a man; they added, that if, according to the idea of some strangers, they should conceive God as invisible, consequently without form and quality, they should not be able in any wise to think about God, inasmuch as such an invisible principle falls not upon any idea of thought. On hearing this, it was given to tell them, that they do well to think of God under a human form, and that many on our earth think in like manner, especially when they think of the Lord; and that the ancients also thought according to this idea. I then told them concerning Abraham, Lot, Gideon, Manoah and his wife, and what is related of them in our Word, viz. that they saw God under a human form, and acknowledged him thus seen to be the Creator of the Universe, and called him Jehovah, and this also from an interior perception; but that at this day that interior perception was lost in the Christian world, and only remains with the simple who are principled in faith.

"Previous to this discourse, they believed that our company also consisted of those, who were desirous to confuse them in their thoughts of God by an idea of three; wherefore, on hearing what was said, they were affected with joy, and replied, that there were also sent from God (whom they then called the Lord) those who teach them concerning Him, and that they are not willing to admit strangers, who perplex them, especially by the idea of three persons in the Divinity, inasmuch as they know that God is One, consequently that the Divine Principle is One, and not consisting of three in unanimity, unless such threefold unanimity be conceived to exist in God as in an angel, in whom there is an inmost principle of life, which is invisible, and which is the ground of his thought and wisdom, and an external principle of life which is visible under a human form, whereby he sees and acts, and a proceeding principle of life which is the sphere of love and of faith issuing from him (for from every spirit and angel there proceeds a sphere of life whereby he is known at a distance); which proceeding principle of life, when considered as issuing from the Lord, is the essential Divine Principle which fills and constitutes the heavens, because it proceeds from the very Esse of the life of love and of faith; they said, that in this, and in no other manner, they can perceive and apprehend a threefold unity. When they had thus expressed themselves, it was given me to inform them, that such an idea concerning a threefold unity agrees with the idea of the angels concerning the Lord, and that it is grounded in the Lord's own doctrine respecting himself; for he teaches that the Father and himself are One; that the Father is in Him and He in the Father; that whoso seeth Him seeth the Father; and whoso believeth on Him believeth on the Father and knoweth the Father; also that the Comforter, whom he calls the Spirit of Truth, and likewise the Holy Ghost, proceeds from Him, and doth not speak from himself but from Him, by which Comforter is meant the Divine Proceeding Principle. It was given me further to tell them, that their idea concerning a threefold unity agrees with the Esse and Existere of the life of the Lord when in the world; the Esse of his life was the Essential Divine Principle, for he was conceived of Jehovah, and the Esse of every one's life is that whereof he is conceived; the Existere of life derived from that Esse is the Human Principle in form; the Esse of the life of every man, which he has from his father, is called soul, and the Existere of life thence derived is called body; soul and body constitute one man; the likeness between each resembles that which subsists between a principle which is in effort [conatus], and a principle which is in act derived from effort, for act is an effort acting, and thus two are one: effort in man is called will, and effort acting is called action: the body is the instrumental part, whereby the will, which is the principal, acts, and the instrumental and principal in acting are one; such is the case in regard to soul and body, and such is the idea which the angels in heaven have respecting soul and body; hence they know, that the Lord made his human principle divine by virtue of the divine principle in himself, which was to him a soul from the Father. This is agreeable also to the creed received throughout the Christian world, which teaches, that '*Although Christ is God and man, yet he is not two but one Christ; yea, he is altogether one and a single Person; for as body and soul are one man, so also God and man is one Christ.*'"—*E. U.* 158.

But the question which you will urge as paramount to all others is, whether the view now presented finds adequate warrant in the Scriptures fairly and legitimately interpreted. This question, of which I fully acknowledge the claims, I shall consider at length in my next.   G. B.

(*To be continued.*)

ARTICLE III.

THE PRESENT STATE OF THE CONTROVERSY

CABELL'S REPLY TO POND.[*]

IF there be one generalization more distinctly conspicuous than any other, which the last three-quarters of a century may be said to have contributed to the Philosophy of History, it is probably this:—that, as we gradually approach towards the present time, all the societary movements appear to have acquired an accelerated velocity.

We cast our eyes back over this period of time, and behold the roused spirit of our race bounding forward in its course of rapid invasion of the Unknown and the unapplied, pushing out its *feelers* in every possible direction, and asking all manner of questions, as if the knowledge of its high earthly destiny had become a fact of its *solidaritic* consciousness.

There are those, neither unlearned nor few in number, who regard these modern developments of the human activities, popularly called *progress*, as indications of the opposite of all true progress; as progress in error, and in evil, only; and believe that the race is rapidly leaving behind it everything of the good and the true. Without entering at this time into any debate with the advocates or the opposers of the doctrines of the progressionists, we may safely affirm, that there has been a vast development of materials, and an accumulation of instrumentalities, which may be used, as the race wills, either for good or for evil. That there has been, and now is, a great perversion of the means which Providence has thus placed in our hands, and that they have been caused to minister to an increased intensity of the evils of life and errors of doctrine with many, there can be no doubt.

That, on the other hand, they are capable of being applied to the accomplishment of nobler purposes; that, if any so will, they may be used to contribute to the more rapid advancement of the individual in a better life and truer thought, and that vast numbers have so applied, and are now so applying them, is equally undeniable. That the race as a unity

---

[*] " *Reply to Rev. Dr. Pond's ' Swedenborgianism Reviewed,' By N. F. Cabell, A.M., with a Preliminary Letter, by R. K. Cralle.*" 8vo. pp. 195.   New York: 1848.

will hereafter make a good use of its accumulations, we are unable to prove. Our trust is, that it will; and our hope is based upon Him who controls the causes which operate upon the minds of men. The proposition that it will make a bad use of them, has certainly not been proven: and before recording it in the affirmative, we prefer to wait for the result of the experiment.

For our present purpose it will suffice that we contemplate those developments under a single aspect. Inquisitive researches into numerous departments of Physical Science and Ethnological knowledge have brought to light facts, and given rise to inferences, which appear to many incompatible with, and in some cases, in direct contradiction to, the sacred scriptures, as these have been usually interpreted.

Philosophical theories, having for their object to account for the origin or the early history of nations, of languages, of different races, and of the earth, are boldly put forth in the face of Christendom, and defended by a large array of evidence, which leave out of view the divine authority of the Scriptures altogether. These have indeed been from time to time replied to by theological writers, but the replies have usually failed to convince any that the theorists were in error. Large schools of scientific men there are throughout Europe, numbering among their adherents names the most renowned for extensive acquisition, who, in the arrangement of their facts, and the organization of their systems of knowledge, leave the divine authority of Christianity and her documents entirely out of view. We see the enlightened portion of the world gradually sweeping away from its old theological moorings; and the clergy as a body progressively sliding from that pre-eminent station in the public esteem, and in the direction of the thought of this age, which, from their office, they ought, legitimately, to hold. We see the political, social, and intellectual destinies of nearly all the larger and more important communities of modern civilization, confessedly in the hands and under the proximate control of men to whom Christ and Christian principles are only secondary and subservient ideas. The influence of the church for the accomplishment of good, is brought almost to a stand-still, and we see it swaying convulsively to and fro, seeking to multiply counsel by "World Alliances" and "Unions"—Modern Theology, looking with jealous and supercilious eye upon the Speculative Philosophy and Physical Science of the age, and science in turn casting back its indignant frown on theology—theology on the one hand attempting to challenge, with its officious negation, many of the presumed advancements of profane knowledge, and, on the other, the scientific spirit, chafed, by what it conceives to be the narrow criticism of the cloister, redoubling its energies in the collation of obnoxious facts.

Thus there has at length become developed in the world of opinion two great schools of scepticism. First, a scientific scepticism, which is the growth of the facts collected, the inferences drawn, and the habits of mind induced by the pursuit of the modern sciences, and which calls in question, or regards lightly, the doctrines and the documents of Christianity. Secondly, an ecclesiastical scepticism, existing to a very considerable extent within the church; having its root primarily in that mental inertia natural to all masses of men, which more enjoys rest in old habits of thought, than the active pursuit of new, strengthened in its growth by the prevailing dogmatic teachings; and calling in question, talking lightly of, and striving to throw discouragement and discredit upon, presumed acquisitions of modern science.

Should we construct a correct chart of Religious Opinion, in which should be thrown together an exhibition of its leading phases—historically, in the past, geographically, in the present—into a single view, running back for three hundred years and including the present limits of Christendom; certain broad facts would stare out from the landscape. We should perceive that at the start, Christianity, having entire possession of the field and of all the avenues leading to the public mind, had, in proportion to the advancement of general knowledge, progressively lost larger and larger portions of it, until at length it has become divided as we now see it. Second, that within certain circles and around certain centres, in which the light of modern intelligence is supposed to burn brightest, a want of confidence in the received teachings of Christianity becomes most apparent. And, lastly, that in proportion as we recede from these circles and these centres, into those regions where the light of this intelligence is supposed to have penetrated least, we find the people more and more under the control of the ancient dogmas. Now it cannot fail to present itself as a serious question to every believing mind which carefully reflects upon it, why it is that a studious pursuit of the higher kinds of scientific knowledge has a tendency to lead men away from the prevailing religious tenets of Christendom? Why is it that an enlarged study of the Works of God has so marked a tendency to bring into discredit what is claimed to be the Word of God? Why has it become so nearly universal for those men who have lived up to the philosophical culture of the time, to graduate, so to speak, out of the trammels of the various theological teachings of the day, holding them in abeyance, if not arraying themselves in opposition to them? These observations point us to a series of effects, the proximate and exciting causes of which might be made the subject of an interesting inquiry. All have observed them, and they have been variously accounted for. The Dublin Review, Mr. Brownson, and the Catholic writers generally, charge them directly and solely to the protestant movement. High-Churchmen are disposed to attribute them to the rejection of the prelacy; and orthodox writers usually regard them as growing out of the rejection of the doctrine of the Trinity, and the prevalence of Unitarianism. Each system of church government manifests a disposition to charge them to the account of the system next below it, which has happened to have gone a little farther into liberalism than itself.

But all these are evidently only narrow empiricisms, which the future historian will have to reject. For the growth of the new opinions is not confined to one region, nor to any region where a particular form of ecclesiasticism is in the ascendant, but pervades the whole of Christendom. Moreover, protestantism is as much the result, historically, of catholicism, as rationalism is the product of protestantism. The *spirit* of rationalism is the natural growth of the human mind, marking its ascent to a higher plane of intelligence, and is as observable in Italy as in New-England or Germany. The New Churchman of course regards these indications as evidences, sown broadcast over the land, that the old church, protestant and catholic, has proved herself by experiment to be unequal to the task of Christianizing mankind. The promise to her was, "to the end of the dispensation," and that "end" we believe to have arrived. To us it appears that her prevailing teaching is insufficient to keep pace with the growing reason of the ages. The soul of the great humanity has ascended to the experience of spiritual wants which she is unable to provide for; and prospects are beginning to open upon its intellectual vision which she is unable to give an account of. Large classes of truth-seekers have sprung up around her, without her pale, and she has no territory on which to locate them. The spiritual interests of the race, which for so many centuries have been confided to her keeping, are in process of being taken from her by the Divine Master. The Spirit of Christ is gradually withdrawing itself from the body which was once His church.

In the present connection we trust we may be allowed to quote a single passage, which will be seen to have a bearing on this subject, from an article by the late Dr. Chalmers. It occurs in one of the last papers he penned for the public eye,[*] and may in some sense be said to record the departing testimony of this great and good man. Speaking of Mr. Carlyle, he says: " There lies an immense responsibility on professing Christians, if such men as he, with their importunate and most righteous demand for all the generous and god-like virtues of the Gospel, are not brought 'to the obedience of the faith.' There must be a deplorable want amongst us of the 'light shining before men,' when, instead of glorifying our cause, they can speak, and with a truth the most humiliating, of our inert and unproductive orthodoxy. These withering abjurations of Carlyle should be of use to our churches ; as things stand at present, our creeds and confessions have become effete, and the Bible a dead letter ; and that orthodoxy which was at one time our glory, by withering into the inert and the lifeless, is now the shame and the reproach of all our churches."

On our own authority had we presumed to say as much, we might have been charged with using defamatory language. It would not however be a difficult task to collate from the pages of the accredited organs of evangelical orthodoxy in our own country, and especially in New England, numerous and constant testimonials to the fact of a deplorable " absence of the Holy Spirit" in the churches. Articles in leading Theological Reviews begin with a reference to it, and columns of religious newspapers have it for a heading.

Suppose we should ask, what is the present attitude of the general mind in relation to certain beliefs which have hitherto been understood to constitute doctrinal Christianity ? The position of Germany is notorious. France and Italy still retain the name of " Catholic ;" but after making a due allowance for that large class which figures indeed in the statistics of population, but which can scarcely be posted into the rolls of opinion, is it not almost a misnomer to call the former so, and is there not confessedly enough of the new leaven in the latter to agitate violently the whole lump ? What account can prelacy in Great Britain give of that public which it has so long had in keeping ? To one asking within her pale, can she answer, "here are they ?" And what shall we say of New England, the home of the puritan fathers and the puritan faith ? She too has lived to have her Parkers, and her Emersons, her Brownsons, and her Anti-Sabbath Conventions. Is it requisite that we go into the statistics of the mind which

---

[*] North Br. Rev., Feb., 1847.

has risen up there in protest against the ancient faith? Is not "come-outism" largely on the "aggressive," and the received "orthodoxy" on the decline?

In this view of the matter, we would respectfully submit to the consideration of our opponents, whether, in their arguments with us, it be sufficient for them to show a discrepancy between our views and their own, in order to a condemnation of ours?—or whether the entire burden rests upon us, not only of establishing our own doctrines, but of first disproving theirs—whether they are after all so completely in possession of all the presumptions in the matter as they have been in the habit of assuming. After passing in rapid review before the mind's eye the various elements which go to make up an opinion on the subject, it would seem that the "presumptions" in the case were rapidly changing sides—that however the matter may formerly have stood, the indications now are that there is a certain *set* in the great current against the grounds of their own position. The more pressing questions of the time would seem to be, not so much, can the New Church succeed in introducing a belief in the spiritual sense of the Word, in the face of the received literal interpretation?—but rather, will the old church be able to sustain a belief in the inspiration of the letter, in the face of the developments of modern science? Not so much, will the New Church be able to introduce a belief in the Uni-personality of the Godhead, as, can the old church continue to retain the human mind in the belief of the Tri-personality? Not so much, can the New Church prove the elimination of the spiritual body from the material body at death, and the non-return of the spirit to its former tenement, as, can the old church give evidence which shall continue to be satisfactory to the mind of the present and the coming age, in the face of the philosophical presumptions to the contrary, that the spirit will hereafter return to the material body? Not so much, can the New Church prove, in opposition to the present teaching, that the future punishment of the wicked is not an arbitrary infliction, but only the natural and the necessary result of the fixed laws which govern the constitution of the universe, as, can the old church continue to hold men in the belief that any other kind of punishment is ever inflicted on the human spirit?

These, and considerations like these, we conceive will ere long succeed in attracting the attention of the surplus logical chivalry of the old church to the line of her own doctrinal defences; and we may now hope for a lengthened armistice with her. An attitude of opposition to each other, is an un-

natural position for both parties; for the new is only a continuation and a fulfilment of the old.

Notwithstanding the vantage ground which the aspects of
the time appear to have given to the New Church writers, they
have been contented not to avail themselves of them, but have
patiently descended into every detail in which the misconceptions of opponents have served to involve the controversy.
Of the truth of this remark the work on which we have predicated our observations furnishes a remarkable instance.
Those New Churchmen who may have looked over Dr. Pond's
book, will call to mind that it consists of an extraordinary
tissue of misconceptions, and unfair statements consequent
thereon. Many of his objections strike so wide of any mark
at all, that it becomes a work requiring considerable labor, so
to clear up the mist as to make the true point visible. To
follow in all their tortuous windings those who pursue their
course in apparent ignorance and in actual disregard of most
of the fundamental questions really at issue, is at best a dreary
task. But this unwelcome journey has been performed, and
every successive step of the way patiently toiled through, by
Mr. Cabell in the pages before us. So far as we have been
able to discover, not an objection stated or implied; not an
argument, not the semblance of an argument; not an hypothesis, nor an inuendo, nor a fling, in which the reverend Professor has seen fit to indulge, has escaped the searching
analysis of his reviewer. He has carefully considered all the
points advanced by him, set many false conceptions in a more
correct light, and made plain some issues which before seemed
dark. If there is one portion of the work with which our
feelings would impel us to express a greater degree of satisfaction than any other, it would undoubtedly be the tenth
chapter; in which the author has replied to the erroneous imputations which it has been attempted to fasten upon the New
Church, in relation to her doctrines of Marriage, Concubinage,
Polygamy, Scortation, &c. So general have misapprehensions on this subject become, that the current presentations
required "a prompt, unequivocal, and flat denial;" as well as
the doctrines themselves to be set forth in their true and proper light. And this has been accomplished by Mr. Cabell
within the limits of a compass so narrow, and in a manner so
lucid, as not to be likely to tire the patience of the most hasty
reader. We are glad to have some of the most obvious considerations in 'their favor so definitely and so compactly
brought out; and should be gratified to see these sixteen pages
issued by themselves, and sent to every clergyman of the old

church, that those who wish candidly to inquire may have their misapprehensions removed, and that those who are not seeking for the truth may be deprived of further excuse for circulating their calumnies against us.

The Preliminary Letter of Mr. Crallé is very happily conceived in its general scope; containing a well-digested summary of the various considerations which seem likely to exercise a counteractive influence upon the prevalent misapprehensions in regard to the New Church views; as well as a very convincing exposition of the doctrines in relation to the organization of the soul, its connection with the body, and the connection between the spiritual and the physical worlds. The more of such treatises we have, the better, for while they tend to multiply the aspects in which the views are capable of being presented, thus attracting the attention of a larger number from without, they also serve to generate new conceptions in the minds of her own children, of the undeveloped possibilities of the New Church IDEA.

Finally, New Churchmen, we think, have every reason to rest satisfied with the results of the controversy, of which this work of Mr. Cabell may be said to constitute the closing chapter. Every objection which the learning of our opponents has been able to suggest, has been promptly, and as we believe successfully, removed. At least, so plausible have been the replies that the argument must be counted to lie in our favor, until some satisfactory rejoinder is vouchsafed to them. It is true there are many prints, and among them no less a journal than the New Englander, which can still dispose of a something which they are pleased to call "Swedenborgianism" within the convenient compass of three or four pages; but, if we mistake not, the time is rapidly approaching in which it will be impossible for them to do this, without suffering in their reputation, both for candor and for intelligence. Ignorance is calculated to injure those most who are the subjects of it.

If our opponents are disposed to waive their right of rejoinder, and to let the case go by default, it will probably be far better for all the parties concerned; as it is exceedingly difficult to prolong, for any length of time, a discussion involving so many important issues, without getting its waters more or less discolored with the soil of personal feeling. And, as the New Englander is willing, we trust we shall hereafter be allowed to go on and "plant" our own "beans," and "hoe" our own "corn in peace and quietness."

We cannot better conclude what we had proposed to offer

on the present state of the controversy, than in the appropripriate language of Mr. Cabell:

"The warfare, as hitherto conducted against Swedenborg, persists in ignoring the *fundamental positions* involved in the system. Our adversaries refuse to deal with our premises, and incessantly urge their assault upon our conclusions. But on this ground what do all their 'arguings reprove?' What do all their earnest and voluminous diatribes amount to in the way of achieving a conviction of the falsity of our views? If they would reason to any purpose, let them show that the laws of the Divine and human nature are not what Swedenborg affirms them to be, or, failing this, let them evince that the great doctrines of Christianity, propounded by him, do not legitimately found themselves upon these underlying laws. When this is accomplished some progress is made towards our discomfiture in the field of debate; but until then we bestow only a tranquil smile upon the elaborate impotence of our opponents."
W. B. H.

ARTICLE IV.

BROTHERLY LOVE.

John xiii. 34. A new commandment I give unto you, That ye love one another as I have loved you, that ye also love one another.

"A NEW *commandment I give unto you.*" In the *internal* sense of the Old Testament, the command is constantly given *to love one another.* "The Jews were a people filled with the love of *self,* which is wholly opposed to the true love of the neighbor; and it was in accommodation to their degraded state, that the Old Testament was brought so low in its literal sense."

If the command, "Love your *enemies,* bless them that curse you, do *good to them* that hate you, and pray for them who despitefully use you and persecute you," had been plainly given to them, they would have utterly rejected it—and thus their state would have been rendered worse than before. The Jews considered the precept—"Thou shalt love thy neighbor as thyself," as merely a command to love those who loved them; thus with them the truth was wholly perverted; it was rendered merely selfish;—" even the publicans love those who love them."

The Lord could bring His Word no lower than it had been brought for the Jews. It had now been brought as low as it could be, and yet contain the Divine truth.

The most ancient church was instructed in spiritual things

by the Lord through His angels; the men of that church were of similar life with the angels; they enjoyed open intercourse with the angels, and learned of them, and with them from the Lord. But they fell from this high state: they ate of the tree of the knowledge of good and evil; they attributed all that they knew to themselves, and labored to acquire all knowledge by their own self-intelligence. When the church had reached this state, the Lord executed a great judgment upon it; this is meant by the *flood.* The church that received instruction by open intercourse with the spiritual world had now passed away; and a new form of revelation was adopted, suited to the condition of the class of persons who still had any ability to receive truth.

The character of this second or ancient church was more external; and therefore a more external form of revelation was used by the Lord. Books were now first written, and the Lord gave His *written* Word. His truth was in its external form brought down to the state of those to whom it was now revealed; but the written Word was still the *Word of the Lord,* and therefore contained within it *all truth.* In process of time, however, this ancient church profaned the truth, even in the accommodated form in which it was then revealed. It passed away, and the *Jewish* church was established.

This was from the first, merely a *representative* of a church; it did not contain within itself any principles of heavenly life. The Old Testament was now written. The Lord again brought this truth down to the fallen state of man. He still gave His Word; and it contained, in its internal senses, all truth; but in its literal sense it was composed of representatives, and appearances of truth; with these the internal senses were covered and protected, or man would for ever have been lost.

The Jews profaned even this. The Lord could bring His Word no lower; if brought lower it would have ceased to contain His Divine Truth. He therefore "bowed the heavens and came down;" He came into the world that He might restore all things in Himself. He took upon Himself all the sinful, evil nature of man; He was tempted to all sin, but He did no sin. He thus put off the gross material humanity, and in its place clothed Himself with a Divine Humanity. He thus fulfilled all the law, and made it *new* in Himself. He thus acquired power to descend and raise up all the bowed down—all that call upon Him in truth, how low soever their state may be; He became the *Last* as well as the *First.*

He thus showed His love for the good of the human race; He made this love *new* and *pure* in His own Divine Humanity and then said, " *A* NEW *commandment I give unto you, That ye*

*love one another ; as I have loved you, that ye also love one
another.*" The Lord is always giving this commandment new
from Himself, and it is our duty constantly to attend to His
instructions, and obey his voice. In this way only can we
abide in His tabernacle.

It is written, "Thou shalt love the Lord thy God, with all
thy heart, and with all thy soul, and with all thy mind. This
is the first and great commandment. And the second *is like
unto it,* Though shalt love thy neighbor as thyself." Let us
endeavor to see wherein this likeness consists. To love the Lord
our God, is to love the good and truth which He imparts to us
and others ; it is to love the good and truth which are the
Lord. He is called Lord in respect to good, and God in respect
to truth.

To love the neighbor, is to love to have him receive and exercise the Lord's good and truth or love and wisdom. Thus
the second commandment is like the first, and is derived from
it, for the love of having good and truth in the neighbor, or of
having good and truth his living principles, must be from love
of good and truth themselves, thus from love of the Lord who
in the supreme sense is our neighbor. The reason that the
Lord Himself should be regarded as our Neighbor in the highest sense, is, that all good is in and from Him ; and every person should be regarded as truly our neighbor in proportion to
the good which he has received and which he receives from
the Lord.

Charity consists of two parts ; one part is the love of the
good and truth in the neighbor, the other is the love of having
him receive good and truth ; these really make one love, for
they both are from the love of good and truth themselves, thus
they are from love of the Lord.

From what has been said, we may see that there can be no
true love of the neighbor where the Lord is not acknowledged
and loved ; love of the Lord, love of the good and truth which
are from the Lord, is the very essence of true love of the neighbor. Hence we may see that none are in a life of charity
who are not in a life of obedience to the Lord's commandments.
If we love the Lord we shall keep His commandments ; and
we shall also keep His commandments if we love the neighbor.

The works of charity consist in doing what is right ; in
doing our duty in every office, in obedience to the Lord's commandments. If we keep the commandments to love the Lord,
and to love the neighbor thus united, the Lord can constantly
impart from His Divine Humanity the true love of the neighbor ; He can impart it new and pure.

The general object in forming societies, should be to assist each other in more fully keeping the commandments: this should be the object of all our association with our brethren; none are truly brethren who come together without having this object in view.

The love of the Lord and the love of the neighbor, are the only loves which can enter the kingdom of heaven; they indeed are the kingdom of heaven; they are the very life of heaven. We must constantly strive to fill our hearts with these heavenly loves, for thus the kingdom of heaven will be within us; and we must do this by a life of obedience to the Lord's commandments. " Lay not up for yourselves treasures upon earth, where moth and rust corrupt, and where thieves break though and steal; but lay up for yourselves treasures in heaven, where neither moth nor rust doth corrupt, and where thieves do not break through and steal. For where your treasure is there will your heart be also."

Treasures upon earth are the chief objects of the labors of the present day. Before these can prove real blessings, they must like all Egyptian treasures be carried to the Holy land. They must be used to do good to the neighbor; and if so used, they will please the Lord better than sacrifice and burnt offering. Worldly knowledge and possessions ought not to be despised or disregarded, but ought to be raised up beyond the reach of moth and rust. If good is done to the neighbor with them, the good will remain for ever in heaven; treasures are laid up where no moth and rust can corrupt, where no thief can break through and steal.

It is only by imparting our treasures that we truly receive them; they are without life or use to us until we give them to the neighbor: but when we desire to impart them we shall gain them—when we become merchantmen, willing to sell all that we have for the pearl of great price, we shall surely find. Every blessing that we endeavor to impart to our neighbor, becomes truly a blessing to us: even if he refuse to receive a gift at our hand, we receive all that we desire to impart. But if we endeavor to do him any harm, in the same degree in which we desire to injure shall we be injured; in each case, with the measure with which we measure for others will it be measured to us.

True charity tends directly to unite those who exercise it. If there is no obstacle placed between those who love one another, they will hasten to unite, to be truly consociated as brethren and sisters of one family, with hearts warming towards each other; and they will so cohere that they cannot be separated without first being separated from the Lord; for it is love of the Lord and love from the Lord that draws them together, and which is the band of their consociation as brethren.

If we were as ready to see our wrongs to our neighbor as we are to see his to us, we should not stand so aloof from those who have done some wrong to ourselves or others. We should feel sorrow when our brother does wrong, sorrow that by his wrong conduct he more or less separates himself from his Heavenly Father; but "*He* maketh His sun to rise on the evil and on the good, and sendeth rain on the just and on the unjust;" and surely *we* have no right to condemn others, no right wholly to separate ourselves from those who should be our brethren. No one can sin against *us ;* all sin is against the Lord—against Him only; "Against Thee, Thee only, have I sinned, and done evil in thy sight." We of ourselves are wholly evil, and it is not becoming for us to raise our voices in judgment upon our brethren.

Most persons make a wide distinction between their treatment of evil which seems directed against themselves, and that which seems directed against others. This is entirely wrong; when an evil is manifested it should be plainly called evil, and condemned as such; it should be condemned as sin against the *Lord,* and not against any *man.* We have the right to call an act evil which is evidently contrary to the commandments of the Lord; we ought so to call it, but here our right ceases; we have no right absolutely to condemn any *individual* for evils of which he seems to be guilty. He only can judge who readeth the heart. "Judge not, that ye be not judged." When an evil seems directed against our neighbor, we ought to use all our power to protect him, and to do good to the person whose endeavor seems to be to do the wrong; we should bless those that curse us, and should pray for those who despitefully use us and persecute us. In this way only can we become the children of our Father who is in the heavens; in this way only can we receive and appropriate our measure of His Divine love of saving. And when the evils of others oppose *us,* we should do exactly the same as when they are directed against others; any other mode of treating them, any more violent opposition to them because they oppose *us,* cometh of evil, for it is grounded in our self-love. The combat then becomes the wrangling and quarrelling of devils and satans, and not the warfare between the evil and the false, and the good and true.

It is quite common for those who act from worldly prudence, to do great injustice by not calling evil evil, when it is not done to themselves or their personal friends. By not opposing the evil when it is manifested to them, they permit much harm to be done to the neighbor which they might prevent, were it not for their *non-committal* policy. This is not loving one's neighbor as himself. The Lord regards good or evil done to others as done to Himself. He says "so much as ye have done to the least of these, ye have done to me;" this shows that we should oppose evil in all its forms of manifestation as sin against the Lord—against Him alone—remembering that it is an evil, selfish feeling in us, which causes us to regard any thing as evil merely because it opposes us; and it also teaches that we should be ready to see and acknowledge all that is good, even in those who oppose us; and that we should acknowledge it as of and from the Lord; thus that we should acknowledge that the power to do good is not of ourselves, but is from the Lord; and that the glory also is His.

The greatest difficulty in exercising charity is in those cases in which our neighbor once walked with us, once lived in a similar manner with us from the same principles of action, and now has separated himself from us, and taken what seems to be another path. We are then too much disposed to shake him off, to feel unkindly towards him, and to keep up a state of opposition by thinking and speaking evil of him: we are too apt to undervalue the good and truth in him, and to magnify the evil and falsity. In this way we close the doors of the mind both against receiving and imparting the Lord's blessing.

It is quite incompatible with the true love of saving to indulge the habit of watching for each other's halting and talking of each other's faults, and indulging feelings of enmity. It should be our desire that our neighbor should receive and do good. We should watch his course in the hope that we shall find it good; we should say with a full heart of love, "O magnify the Lord with me, and let us exalt His name together."

We are all too much in the habit of dwelling upon the faults of others, and making them the subject of conversation. By often speaking of their faults, there is danger that we shall so confirm ourselves in our views of their state, that we shall become incapable of seeing and acknowledging any improvement. There is often in such a habit much of enmity towards others, and of willingness that they should remain in evil; thus there is a want of the true love of the neighbor which would save that which is lost.

When we impart anything to others which we regard as good and true, we should impart to them with the full desire that they may receive good from the *Lord,* through our agency; we must bear it constantly in mind that we are but stewards—that we of ourselves are nothing and have nothing. We must be in the constant endeavor not to impart any thing of *ourselves*, for self is wholly opposed to love of the Lord and of the neighbor. If we truly desire to be humble mediums of the Lord's good and truth to our neighbors, we shall not feel any degree of unkindness towards those who do not receive what we endeavor to impart; we shall feel sorrow that we are not more perfect mediums of the Lord's blessings, and shall pray that those persons may yet be found from whom they can receive good and truth more fully than they can from us. We shall earnestly desire to do them good, and shall rejoice when we can do good; we shall not feel anger when we are rejected, but hope that their rejection of us will not prove a rejection of the Lord.

A very great evil with many persons is their want of humility and sincerity in imparting to others. There is a manifest want of *humility* in us if we desire our neighbor to receive as truth what we say, because we say it; for we then wish the glory to be given to us; we make ourselves as Gods, to know good and evil, and are angry with all who will not bow down and worship us. If we impart in this spirit, there is also a great want of *sincerity* in our cause; we pretend to desire the good of our neighbor, but we really desire not his good, but our own advancement. We are willing to do him good in order to serve our own selfish purposes, but for nothing else. When we find that our own selfish inclinations are opposed, we are but too ready to regard those from whom the opposition proceeds as too far gone in evil to be helped by us—we are but too ready in our turn to oppose and destroy.

We must bear it in mind that not all the opposition which we meet with is opposition to good and truth; in many cases our evils and falsities are opposed and there is less real opposition to the Lord than there seems to be. It is written in the Gospel of Luke, that John said, "Master we saw one casting out devils in thy name, and we forbade him, because he followeth not with us." We are all much disposed to do as the disciples did in this case. We are not satisfied when others do good, when they cast out devils in the Lord's name, unless they do as we do, unless they follow with us; but this course is not right; so long as we remain in it we still retain some desire to cast out devils and to have others cast them out in our own name if at all. Jesus then said, and now says to us, "Forbid not; for he that is not against us is for us."

We have considered the duty and the dangers of those who *impart*; let us now see what is necessary that we may rightly *receive.*

All ought to be in the full desire to receive the Lord's good and truth, because they are the Lord's. We ought not to pre-fer truth received from one person, to truth received from another, but ought to be willing and desirous to receive from *all*, as well as to impart to all. There is need of watchfulness lest our feelings of opposition to the evils of any person should become opposition to the *individual*, and should make us un-willing to receive from him ; we must shut the mind against the evil, but we must open it to the good of every individual. It is our duty to hate and reject evil, but it is our duty to be willing to receive good and truth from all in whom we can find them ; and we must love to find them in all persons.

When a brother tells us of any fault, we should humbly ac-knowledge that the evil is in us—for we are wholly evil, and then should ask the assistance of the Lord and of the neighbor to examine ourselves, and find wherein the evil is operative; when we find it we must acknowledge it as evil, repent of it and remove it from our life. If we pursue this course we shall not feel offended with our brother when he tells us of a fault, but we shall feel thankful that through him we have been enabled to turn our attention to the removal of the evil.

Even if we cannot see that the evil is operative, we shall by the very act of self-examination remove it further from the mind. And if we cannot find the evil in ourselves, we must not be too confident that it is not in us, or even that it has not been manifested so that our brother really saw it in us; we must look to the Lord for help: we must say in deep humility, " Who can understand his errors? Cleanse thou me from secret faults." S. H. W.

EXTRACT.

" The reason why those who are in truths derived from good are understood by the ' servants of God,' is because, in the Word, they are called servants of God, who hearken to and obey God. Hearkening and obedience only exist in those who are in truths derived from good, but not with those who are in truths alone, or in truths without good : for these latter have truths only in the memory, but not in the life; whereas they who are in truths derived from good, have truths in the life, and they who have truths in the life do them from the heart, that is, from love. It is to be observed, that no truth ever enters into the life of man, unless he be in good, for good belongs to love, and love forms the whole man ; thus a man receives into his life all the truths which agree with his love. This may appear very manifest from this circumstance : that whatsoever a man loves, he appropriates to himself; whereas everything else he rejects from himself, yea, holds it in aversion. By good is here meant the good of love to the Lord, and the good of love towards our neighbor ; for this is the only spirit-ual good with which the truths of faith agree."—*A. E.* n. 6.

SELECTIONS.

SWEDENBORG'S INVITATION TO THE NEW CHURCH.

NOW FIRST TRANSLATED FROM THE ORIGINAL LATIN.

(Concluded.)

34. That the advent of the Lord is according to order, inasmuch as the spring does not come till after the winter, nor the morning till after the night, nor solace and joy to the woman with child till after her pain; that comforts succeed temptations; that life only flourishes after mortification, as the Lord says, and consequently that man does not live except he die. The Lord himself showed an example of this order, in that he suffered himself to be crucified and to die,—an example which signifies the state of the church. This is also involved (representatively) in the statue seen in the vision of Nebuchadnezzar. in which the Stone finally became a huge Rock; it is also implied in the vision of the four beasts, rising out of the sea, (one of them) shadowing forth that horrible power (the Roman)—all which to be explained. It is indicated also by the four ages known to the ancients, the golden, the silver, the copper, the iron; also by the successive periods of every man's life from infancy to old age, which is the end of the bodily life, but the beginning of the life of the spirit, which is the introduction into heaven of those who have lived well. Thus also it is with heaven, which previous to its renovation is to be done away. Apoc. xxi. 1, 2; and so likewise with the church.*

35. That the keys of the kingdom of heaven were given to Peter was because he represented the Lord as to Divine Truth, and this is understood by a Rock throughout the whole sacred scripture, wherefore we read, "upon this Rock (that is, upon this Divine Truth), will I build my church, viz. that the Lord is the Son of the living God. Show from the Word that Rock has this signification. Rock, in the Word, Exod. xvii. 6; xxxiii. 21, 22; Num. xx. 8–11; Deut. viii. 15; xxxii. 4-37; 1 Sam. ii. 2; 2 Sam. xxii. 2, 3, 32, 47; chap. xxiii. 3; Ps. xviii. 3, 32, 47; Ps. xxviii. 1; xxxi. 2, 3 [4]; xl. 2 [3]; xlii. 9 [10]; xlii. 2, 7 [3, 8]; lxxviii. 16, 20, 35; lxxxix. [27] 28; xcii. 16; xciv. 22; xcv. 1; cv. 41: Isai. ii. 10; xxii. 16; xlii. 11; li. 1; 1 Cor. x. 4. Fissures in a rock are falsified truths, Ap. vi. 15, 16; Isai. ii. 19; Jer. xvi. 16; Cant. ii. 14; Ez. xlvii. 21; Jer. xxiii. 29; xlix. 16; Obad. 3; besides in the Evangelists.

---

* A *lacuna* of a few words in the manuscript has here been supplied according to the conjectural reading of Dr. Tafel.

———So also some of the Fathers have explained this : vid. *Form. Conc.* p. 345.

36. Since the Son alone (according to the common doctrine) became man, and not the whole Trinity, is not the Divine Essence, which is one and indivisible in the three, separated, disunited, and divided ?

37. That the whole of the Lord's Prayer, from beginning to end, has respect to the present time, viz. that God the Father should be worshiped in human form; this will appear if the right explication be given.

38. The reason that the church, after the times of the apostles, fell into so many heresies, and that at this day there is nothing in it but falses, is, that they did not approach the Lord, when yet the Lord is the Word, and is the Light itself which enlightens the whole world ; and yet it is now as impossible to see one genuine Truth from the Word unless obscured and polluted by falses, and cohering with falses, as it is to sail to the Pleiades, or to dig gold from the centre of the earth; wherefore in order that the True Christian Religion might be laid open, it was absolutely requisite that some one should be introduced into the spiritual world, and derive from the mouth of the Lord the genuine Truths of the Word. The Lord cannot illustrate any one with his light unless He is immediately approached and is acknowledged as the God of heaven.

39. That miracles are not wrought at this day, for the reason mentioned in the *True Christian Religion*—wherefore God says, Matt. xxiv. 24, that they will be the means of seducing. What moreover is more common among the Roman Catholics than to fill the monuments of the saints and the walls of monasteries with miracles ? How many golden and silver plates are to be seen in the monument of Anthony of Padua ? What is there that is not exhibited where the three Wise Men are said to have been buried (at Cologne), at Prague, and other places ? And what is the result but gross delusions ? It is far more than all such miracles that I converse with angels and spirits, that I have described the states of heaven and hell, and the life after death ; and moreover that the spiritual sense of the Word is opened to me, besides many other things. This intercourse, so far as I know, has never been granted by the Lord to any one before—a sign that it is on account of the New Church, which is the crown of all churches, and to endure for ever.—That to be in the spiritual world, to see the wonderful things of heaven, and the miserable things of hell, and to be there in the light of the Lord, in which angels are—this surpasses all miracles. See the testimonies to the fact of my being there exhibited in great abundance in my writings.

40. The sole reason that the church has immersed itself in such falsities that not a single truth remains, and that it is like a shipwrecked

vessel, of which the top of the mast alone appears above the water, is, that it has not gone immediately to the Lord, and unless He is immediately approached, no Truth can appear in its own light; the reason is, that the Lord is the Word, that is, every Divine Truth in the Word, and He only is the light which enlightens all, as he Himself teaches, and every Truth of the Word shines from no other source than from the Lord alone. That is what is understood by spiritual Light; wherefore when that Light is not there, there is nothing spiritual in the understanding of man, but every thing is merely natural, and the natural man sees inversely every thing which contains spiritual things; he sees the false in the place of the true; wherefore when he reads the Word he bends every thing to his own falsity, and thus truths become falsities, in which he finds his delight; for the natural mind of man, when in the things of the world and of self, is delighted with them alone; and unless there is a spiritual light in such things he transfers them to worldly and selfish interests, which he puts in the first place, and thus not only shuns spiritual things, and holds them in abeyance, but afterwards ridicules them. Faith is no otherwise spiritual, nor can be called spiritual, except from the truths it contains being in light from the Lord; unless it be from this source, faith is merely natural, which neither conjoins nor is saving.

41. That in the spiritual world no one knows another from his name alone, but from an idea of his quality; this causes another to be present and to be known, so that in no other way are parents known by their children, children by their parents; neighbors, relations, and friends by their neighbors, relations, and friends; in like manner the learned are known by their writings and the fame of their erudition; great men and potentates by the fame of their exploits; in the same manner, kings, emperors, popes—all are known by their qualities alone. It has been given me to speak with those thus known, but not with others. The spirit itself is nothing else than its quality; wherefore with every one in that world no account is made of his baptismal name or the name of his family, but he is named according to his quality; hence it is that name in the Word does not signify name, but quality, as the Lord says in the Apocalypse. "I have many names in Sardis," and "I know my own by name." besides a thousand other places elsewhere, where name is mentioned. From all this it appears that no one has the Lord present to him unless he knows His quality; and this is unfolded by the Truths of the Word, for as many Truths as there are of the Word, so many mirrors and images are there of the Lord, for He is the Word and He is the Truth, as he Himself says. Qualities are of a twofold kind, one is that of knowledge concerning Him as being the God of Heaven, the Son of God the Father, one with the Father, as having all things in common with the Father, in a word,

as being the Human of God the Father; the other kind is that of
knowledges which proceed from Him, and those which proceed from
Him are Himself, as his teachings concerning Charity, Free Will, Repentance, Regeneration, the Sacraments, and many other things; these
also make the idea of the Lord, because they are from Him.

42. It is an arcanum from the spiritual world, that to him who has
not an idea concerning Him that is directly and immediately from Him
he is not made actually present, still less can such an one become a
recipient, but He is as if standing one side, and appears in obscurity;
nor can one (there) speak with another, unless he looks directly at him,
but communication is given when the inspection is reciprocal; thus
and not otherwise will ideas enter any one, and if there is love
there will be conjunction; if therefore one does not see the Father
immediately, He stands, as it were, one side, and cannot freely bestow
redemption, i. e. he cannot regenerate and afterwards save him.

43. That the manifestation of the Lord in person, and introduction
into the spiritual world, both as to sight and as to hearing and speech
from the Lord, excels all miracles, as it is no where read in history
that such intercourse with angels and spirits has been granted to any
since the creation of the world; for I am daily there with angels as
in the world with men, and so have continued to be for twenty-seven
years. The testimonies to this intercourse are the books published
by me concerning Heaven and Hell, and also the Memorable Relations
derived from that source and appended to the "True Christian Religion;" as also what is there related concerning Luther, Melancthon,
and Calvin, and concerning the inhabitants of various kingdoms; and
besides those numerous testimonies relating to the affairs of this world
—besides the things known and unknown spoken of—say, who has
ever before known any thing concerning Heaven and Hell, the state of
man after death, spirits and angels, etc. etc.?

44. Besides the preceding most evident testimonies, to whom before, since the Word was revealed in the Israelitish writings, was the
spiritual sense of that Word ever disclosed by the Lord as it has been
to me? And this is the very sanctuary of the Word, it is the Lord
Himself in it with his Divine, as he is in the natural sense with his
Human. Of all this not one iota could be opened except by the Lord
alone. This surpasses all the revelations that have been enjoyed
since the creation of the world; by means of it a communication has
been opened between men and the angels of heaven, and thus a conjunction of the two worlds, as man is in the natural sense and angels
in the spiritual sense. As to this spiritual sense, see what is written
in the chapter concerning the Sacred Scripture.

45. The correspondences, according to which the Word in all and
singular things is written, possess such power and efficacy that it may

be called the power and efficacy of the Divine Omnipotence, for by means of these the natural is conjoined with the spiritual, and the spiritual acts with the natural, thus the all of heaven with the all of the world; hence it is that the two sacraments are correspondences of spiritual things with natural, and hence too their virtue and potency.

46. As to miracles, on the other hand, they are not wrought at this day, because they seduce men, and make them natural, shutting up the interior of their minds, in which faith ought to be rooted, from whence proceed mere falsities. (See Matt. xxiv. 24). What else is to be said of the miracles of the saints and of the images of the Roman Catholics? They are made natural by them, and the natural man rejects and perverts every spiritual truth. What did the miracles among the children of Israel in Egypt effect? What, the miracles wrought before their eyes in the desert? What, the miracles that marked their entrance into the land of Canaan? What, the miracles performed by Elijah and Elisha? What, those wrought by the Lord himself! Was any one made spiritual by them? To what amount the miracles vaunted among the Roman Catholics, such as those of Anthony of Padua, those of the three Wise Men of Cologne, and innumerable others in their monasteries, which are filled with pictures, plates, and gifts? Have they been the means of making any one spiritual? Have they not rather been rendered thereby to such a degree natural, that there is scarcely any truth of the Word remaining among them, —anything, in fact, but a mere external worship, the product of men and of tradition?

47. That in Christ God is man and man God is confirmed three times in the *Formula Concordiæ*, as also where assumption into God is mentioned—proved from the Word, Rom. xiv. 11, Col. ii. 9, 1 John v. 20, 21, also from the Lord Himself, that He and the Father are one, that the Father is in Him, and He in the Father, that all things of the Father's are His, that He is life in Himself, and that He is the God of heaven and earth, etc.

48. That the soul is the intimate man, and thence, according to the ancients, in the whole and in every part of the body, is, because the principle of life resides in the soul; the part of the body in which the soul is not intimately present does not live, wherefore the union is reciprocal, and the body thence acts from the soul, and not the soul through the body. Whatever proceeds from God is in the human form, because God is Very Man, and thence especially the soul, which is the first principle of man.

49. Nothing is more common in the universal heaven and the universal world, than for one thing to be in another, thus that there should be an intimate, a middle, and an extreme, and that these three should communicate with each other, and that the power of the middle and the extreme, should be from the intimate; that then there are

those three, one within another, appears from all and single things in the human body. Around the brain there are three membranes, called the *dura mater*, the *pia mater*, and the *arachnoides*, and over these is the *cranium ;* around the whole body are membranes, one within another, which are called together the skin; around every artery and vein are three membranes, also around every muscle and fibre, and so around every thing else pertaining to the body ; the case is likewise the same in the vegetable kingdom. How these communicate with each other, and how the intimate enters into the middle, and the middle into the extreme, is demonstrated by anatomy, etc. Hence it appears that the case is similar with light; that spiritual light, which in its essence is truth, is inwardly within natural light; in like manner spiritual heat, which in its essence is love, is in natural heat; by natural heat is understood natural love, because that love warms, and this is enveloped (as it were) in the heat of the blood.

50. All that is said concerning the Holy Spirit falls to the ground when it is believed that man is not life, but only an organ of life, and that God is thus continually in man, working all things and urging to the reception of whatever pertains to religion and thence of the Church, of Heaven, and of Salvation. As to the idea that the Holy Spirit may be given or lost, it is an idle conceit ; for the Holy Spirit is nothing else than the Divine proceeding from the Lord, from the Father, and this Divine makes the life of man, and also his understanding and love, and its presence is perpetual ; man without the presence of the Lord or of the Holy Spirit, would scarcely be a beast; he would possess no more of life than a piece of salt, a stone, or the stump of a tree; the reason is that man is not born with an instinct like that of a beast, wherefore a chicken of a day old knows more of the order of its life than an infant.

51. That it is lawful to confirm, as much as one pleases, the truths of the church, by reason or by understanding, and also by various things in nature, and as far as they are confirmed they are rooted and also shine; it is also lawful to confirm truths by the Word, whenever it seems good, and thence to make the fullest application, in which case the Word is not falsified ; the sayings of Scripture, by which truths are confirmed, ascend to heaven, and are as smoke from incense; falses, on the other hand, if confirmed from the Word, do not ascend to heaven, but are rejected, and are rent on the way with a noise which I have heard a thousand times.

52. That the manifestation of the Lord and immission into the spiritual world surpasses all miracles ; this has not been granted to any since the creation as it has been to me. The men of the golden age spake indeed with angels, but it was not their privilege to be in any

other than natural light; but to me it has been granted to be at the same time in spiritual and in natural light; by this I have been enabled to see the wonderful things of heaven, to be present among the angels as one of them, and at the same time to receive truths in light, and thus to perceive and teach them; in a word, to be led by the Lord. As to what concerns miracles, they would be mere snares for seducing, as the Lord says, Matt. xxiv. 24; and thus it is related of Simon Magus, that he "bewitched the people of Samaria," who believed that these things were done by the great power of God. What else are the miracles among the Papists than snares and cheats? What else do they teach than that they themselves are to be worshiped as deities to the disparagement or abandonment of the worship of the Lord? What else is the effect produced by their wonder-working images? And so of the relics of the dead bodies of the saints throughout the whole of the papacy, such as Anthony of Padua, the three Wise Men of Cologne, and all the rest—what have they taught concerning Christ? What, concerning heaven and eternal life? Not one word.

53. That it is impossible that there should be any church, or any coherent system of religion, unless one God is believed in; consequently when the Divine Trinity is believed to be divided into three persons, how is it possible by means of the metaphysical term *Essence* to make One out of Three, while the properties of each person are different—so different in fact as to be said to be incommunicable; and when the equal persons properly subsist by themselves, and one has no part or quality in the other? But when it is believed that one God is not only Creator, but also Redeemer and Operator, then we have in truth one God, and then the church first exists and subsists, and religion lives. This union of three cannot be otherwise given than as the soul, the body, and the proceeding in every man; these three constitute one man. Why, then, does not this apply to God, who is Man Himself, Very Man, from first to last? All this is shown in the work on Love and Wisdom (which see) concerning God Man and that he is not ether, air, or wind.

That the soul of every man is the man himself; whence it follows that we have one God in the church, who is God Man and Man God; that church is called the crown of all churches.

54. That in Christ Man is God is shown from the *Formula Concordiæ* in three places; from Paul, Rom. xiv., Col. ii. 9, from 1 John v. 20, 21, from the Lord's words: (1) That God was the Word and the Word became flesh. (2) That all things of the Father are His. (3) That all things of the Father redound to Him. (4) That as the Father has life himself, so also has the Son; to have life in himself is to be God. (5) That the Father and He are one. (6) That he is in the Father and the Father in Him. (7) That he that sees Him sees the Father. (8) That

He is the God of heaven and earth. (9) That He rules the universe, according to the creed. (10) That He is called Jehovah the Redeemer. (11) That He is called Jehovah Righteousness. (12) That it is said that Jehovah was to come into the world. (13) In the Apocalypse, chap. i., that He is the First and the Last. (14) In a word that he is God the Father who is invisible, but who becomes visible before the mind in his Human.—That the Church is the Church, because there is thus one God in it, etc., etc. From the Athanasian Creed that God and Man are one person like soul and body; as also that the Human nature was assumed into God.

55. Concerning MIRACLES, from the case of the Sons of Israel; from the words of the Lord concerning Dives and Lazarus; from the words of the Lord, Matt. xxiv. 24. Concerning the popish miracles which are pompously cited—that they merely seduce, teaching nothing except the invocation of saints as divinities, and this with a view to the bestowment of gold and silver upon monasteries, or that they may rake together the wealth of the whole world. Their abundant miracles, their marvellous images, to which treasures are every where collected in their monasteries, where the walls are covered with the pictures of miracles performed by their saints and the relics of these saints, together with the books of the miraculous legends of Father Paris and others—what other end do they serve than to beget invocation and through that the heaping up of costly offerings? What one of their votaries has ever taught the way to heaven or the truths of the church from the Word? On this account it has pleased the Lord to prepare me, from my earliest youth, for a spiritual perception of the Word; he has introduced me into the spiritual world, and illustrated me by the mere light of his Word; from which it may be seen that this goes beyond all miracles.

Beelschebul wrought miracles superior to those of all the other Gentile gods, as appears from the Old Testament; so also did Simon Magus.

56. That the Lord made the natural man in himself Divine in order that he might be the first and the last, and thus could enter with men even into their natural man, and teach him and lead him from the Word; for He arose with his whole natural or external man, nor left any thing of it in the sepulchre, wherefore he said that he had bones and flesh, which spirits have not; and he also ate and drank with the disciples of natural food, and in their immediate presence. That he was still Divine was shown by his passing through doors and becoming invisible, which could not have been done unless the natural man itself had with Him been made Divine.

57. That all that is said at this day by the orthodox as to the mission of the Holy Spirit falls to the ground when it is known that the

Lord is continually present with every man and gives to him ———
——————, and that it remains with man that he go forth to meet
the Lord,·——————————; if the Lord should withdraw from man,
man would not be so much a beast as a dead carcass, which is dissipated; this is understood in Genesis by God's breathing into him the
breath of life.

. 58. That the Lord is the Kingdom, also Heaven and the Church—
show from the Word.

59. That the greatest power inheres in correspondences;———
show—because in them heaven and the world, the spiritual and the
natural, are conjoined, and therefore that the Word is written according to mere correspondences; wherefore it is the conjunction of man
with Heaven, thus with the Lord; the Lord by this means is in firsts
and at the same time in lasts; wherefore the sacraments are instituted
on the principle of correspondences, in which accordingly a Divine
potency resides.

SWEDENBORG ON A REPUBLIC.

The following is an extract from that portion of Swedenborg's "Itinerary"
which was written in Holland. It is vastly in advance of his time, and receives
additional interest from the current course of events in the old world.

" The Merchants' Hall is the finest building I saw, but it is less fre-
quented by merchants and other citizens than that at Amsterdam,
though a large concourse of men is the greatest ornament of such an
Exchange. It here occurred to me to inquire why it was that God had
blessed a people so barbarous and wild as the Hollanders (originally
were) with a soil of such surpassing fertility—why he had preserved
them for such a long course of years free from all disasters—and why
he had raised them above all other nations on the score of commercial
prosperity, and made their provinces a seat or centre into which the
riches of Europe and of other lands pour themselves. In reflecting
upon this the first and principal cause of that prosperity seemed to
be, that Holland was a Republic—a form of government better pleasing
in the sight of God than an absolute monarchy, as is evident from the
history of Rome. In a republic no undue veneration or homage is
paid to any man, but the highest and the lowest deems himself equal
to a king or an emperor, as is very manifest from the natural genius
and disposition of every person in Holland. The only being whom
they venerate is God. And when He alone is worshiped, and men
are not adored in His place, it is ever most acceptable to Him. Hence
in Holland there is the highest liberty. There are no slaves, but all
are governed, as so many masters, under the dominion of the Most

High God, for which reason they do not lower their elevation of soul under the influence of shame or fear, but always preserve a firm and sound mind in a sound body, and with a free spirit and an erect air commit themselves and their concerns to God, who alone claims to govern all things. It is otherwise in absolute governments, where men are trained to simulation and dissimulation; where they learn to have one thing shut up in the breast, and another ready on the tongue; and where the minds of men, by long custom, become so inured to what is fictitious and counterfeit, that even in divine worship they come to say one thing and think another, and so to palm off upon God their adulation and falsity. This, if I mistake not, is the main cause of the superior prosperity of the Hollanders above all other nations. Their excessive devotion to Mammon as a kind of divinity, and their comparative indifference to everything but gold, is indeed something which does not seem to be well compatible with a lasting prosperity; but perhaps there are ten among a thousand or ten thousand who are the means of averting the punishment, and of rendering the rest rich in the goods of this life and fortunate with themselves."—*Aug.* 21, 1736.

SWEDENBORG'S ACCOUNT OF DIPPEL.

Those who have perused the portions of Swedenborg's "Spiritual Diary," published in connexion with the Swedenborg Library will doubtless recollect the following account of a certain personage of the name of Dippel. He is introduced without any note of his character or profession while living, in an article headed simply—"Concerning Dippel." Having recently met with a sketch of his history in Jung Stilling's "Theobald, or The Fanatic," we here insert it, together with the article from the Diary, that the reader may judge of the points of coincidence between the character of the man in this world and his state in the next.

"*Concerning Dippel.*

"A certain one was for some time at my left side, who attempted wicked things; I did not know who he was, because he acted with much subtlety, so that I was scarcely aware of his influence, but yet it was given me to perceive it. He was also, as it were, within me on the left side, and I called him a most vile devil. He then receded to a station in front a little higher up, and spake, but he induced a common (or general) sphere of ideas, which cannot be described. It was however such that there was no idea of particulars, and yet he spake as if from particulars, for all discourse is of particulars. A similar sphere I do not recollect of having perceived before, that is, of one's speaking in such a general kind of sphere. His sphere therefore was the sphere of his nature, the nature of one who was bound to no principles, but was in general opposed to all, whoever they might be, of whatever principle or whatever faith. He therefore arrayed himself against all, and could ingeniously refute and vilify them, while he himself knew nothing of truth and good. I afterwards wondered that such a genius (or character) should exist—one that could refute others with so much dexterity, and sting them so keenly, when yet it was not from the knowledge of truth.

"He afterwards approached nearer, and appeared at first black in the face. At length advancing still nearer, and being in a certain light, he took an earthen flask, of a greyish white appearance, and came up to me with the flask in his hand, that he might offer it to me to drink from, at the same time insinuating that it (contained) excellent wine, so that I begun to be almost persuaded to comply, for I knew not who he was; but I was presently informed that it was Dippel, and that he displayed this flask of wine because he formerly practised the same stratagem, when in consequence of his becoming angry with any one for contradicting him, he would give him wine containing some poisonous mixture, that he might destroy his understanding, and cause him to know no more what he said than if he had been an infant. He was moreover of such a character in respect to those whom he deceived, from whom he took away, as it were, all understanding of truth and good; and even those who adhered to him (seemed to know nothing) except his own opinion. I had myself been among those who adhered to him, and had heard the various things collected from his writings, but could not retain in memory the least item, nor know what I thought, nor even help thinking things absurd. Such was his contrariety even to those who adhered to him, as to take away all their intelligence of truth and good, and leaving them in a kind of delirium, not knowing what they were about; yet still they adhered to him. Whether therefore he gave such a poisonous draught to any one, or whether by the flask and the wine was signified such a quality in himself which he imparted to others who adhered to him, I know not; it might be both.

"His quality was represented to me by a great hurdle (or crate) of teeth of a yellowish hue, like teeth indeed, but so large as to be monstrous, so that the entire face was apparently nothing but teeth."— *S. D.* 3485-3487.

Stilling having described the extremely depressed state of religion in Germany, and other countries of Europe, at about the middle of the last century, goes on to say:—"In this exceedingly low state of the church, two men made their appearance, essentially different in character, who proved a severe scourge to the clergy. The one was the well known Hochman, whose name was familiar throughout the Netherlands; and the other was the distinguished Dr. Dippel, or as he terms himself in his writings, Christian Democritus. These two men were the chief promoters of enthusiasm, pietism, separatism, and I may add of true religion, in Germany." After devoting several pages

to a graphic account of the life and labors of Hochman, he continues:
—"I have thus far endeavored to portray the character of one of the
founders of separatism; I now proceed to describe the other, the fore-
mentioned Dr. Dippel. This man, if I mistake not, was a Saxon by
birth; he studied at Strasburg, but having fallen in with the writings
of Paracelsus and Behmen, and other mystics, he fully adopted their
principles. His design was to become a professor of theology, but he
was disappointed in his hopes of promotion. He was a man of a
powerful mind, stern of purpose, haughty in demeanor, aspiring in
disposition, and withal possessed of a talent of most biting sarcasm,
that made him proof against every thing like fear. He would have
been a clergyman, and I fully believe that had he taken orders, he
would soon have risen from the lowest to the very highest degree of
promotion. The spirit of reform was deeply inlaid in his character;
and his perpetual efforts to reduce the power of the clergy, drew upon
him universal hatred. He thereby lost all hopes of promotion, and
accordingly betook himself to the study of medicine, in which he
made wonderful proficiency. During the celebrated visit of the Czar
Peter to Germany, Dippel was induced by some means to accompany
him to Russia, and was there soon promoted to the office of chief
physician. It is well known that the Czar with all his great talents,
was often disposed to exceed the bounds of moderation, and was at
times excessively severe in his treatment of those under him. We
ought not however to judge him by the same rules that we would a
ruler of a highly civilized people. He had a rude nation to govern,
which, as obstinate children, often needed the rod, when milder and
more rational methods were unavailing. Dippel could not endure the
perpetual hanging and knouting which he was caused to witness, and
proceeded to remonstrate with the emperor, but as that was useless,
he undertook to reprimand him, and the consequence was that he was
soon cashiered from his service. Dippel went from Moscow to Stockholm, in Sweden, where he remained for some time, and performed
many wonderful cures, for he was in fact a highly capable physician.

"There is one amusing instance of his ingenuity which I must here
undertake to describe, in order to illustrate the character of the man.
A certain distinguished citizen of Stockholm became hypochondriacal,
and was seized with the fancy that he must lie perpetually in bed.
He had no rest either day or night, from the apprehension that whenever he opened his eyes he saw a ghost before him. The wretched
man was reduced exceedingly low, and all the physicians who had
attempted to cure him, were baffled and gave him up in despair. A
number believed that he was bewitched. At length Dippel was consulted. He visited him, and without saying a word paced up and
down the room with the utmost gravity, and ever, now and then cast

a majestical glance toward the bed. He then sat down near the sick man: Dippel was a man of most dignified appearance, a certain majesty lay in his countenance that could be more easily seen than described; he also went very richly dressed. 'I understand,' said he, 'that you are vexed by a ghost?' 'Oh, yes, it has tormented me so long that I fear I shall die, and then God only knows what will become of me.' 'That is a most dreadful calamity—but where is it, I do not see it?' 'There it presses itself up close to the wall; oh, I wish somebody could once see it—look there at its horrible countenance—how it grins; it is dressed in a grey coat, and glides along there toward the corner.' Dippel pretended to look for it, and then said, 'Now I will open my eyes, and then I think I shall see it.' He accordingly anointed his eyes and went through certain ceremonies. Now he professed to see the ghost as well as the man himself. 'Yes,' said he, 'it is a monstrous fellow, but I will soon drive him to his own abode, that he shall never be permitted to set foot upon earth again.' He then described the ghost minutely to the man, and showed him where it moved so accurately that the sick man cried out with joy. 'There now am I not right; and you, sir, I believe, are the only man that can help me.' Dippel then returned home, and masked one of his servants in a form exactly corresponding to the ghost described to him by his patient. In the evening he went with his servant, and placed him near the foot of the bed behind the curtain, so that the sick man might not see him. He then commenced his conjurations, and the servant softly slipped out along the wall. When the sick man opened his eyes he saw the ghost more plainly than ever; and Dippel began to exorcise the ghost with a whip, and to conjure it, until he induced it to promise to take its departure, and never more trouble his patient. He then used tonic medicines, and restored the sick man to the perfect enjoyment of health.

"His rancor against the clergy found full nourishment in Sweden, where ignorance, stupidity and spiritual arrogance, flourished in a still greater degree than in Germany itself. He spoke and wrote against the clergy, and was so extremely caustic in his satires, that he was apprehended, and imprisoned in the isle of Bornholm. How long he remained there I am not able to state, nor indeed the mode of his release. Suffice it to say that he returned to Germany, and after many wonderful trials and persecutions, which he drew upon himself by his haughty and censorious disposition, he eventually took refuge at Berlinberg. In this and the neighboring regions, he acquired an astonishing influence, spreading far and wide the principles of the most rigid separatism. His writings all show an overbearing, imperious, and satirical character; and his admirers and followers were persons of the same unpleasant and unendurable disposition. Dippel's religious principles were a mixture of Socinianism, and Naturalism. Towards the end of life he viewed Christ as an indifferent being. He united the morality of the mystics with the doctrines of the later theologians, and with certain other fanatical sentiments. His whole system, if it may be termed such, was a singular hodge-podge. I can certify to the truth of what I say in relation to his character, for he resided in my own immediate vicinity, and all that I state is what I know personally, or have derived from undoubted authority."—*Stilling's Theobald*, p. 25–28.

POETRY.

THE EARLY CALLED.

" It was given me to see infants, * * with garlands of flowers around the breast, resplendent with the most beautiful and heavenly colors, and also around their tender arms."—*Swedenborg.*

Strew flowers o'er the tomb
   Of the first and only son;
Of the cherub child, whose earthly race
   Was, Oh! so quickly run;
Plant not the cypress here,
   Let not the willow wave
O'er dust that clad an angels form,
   Now covered by the grave.

What though the father's heart
   With agony is torn,
And the mother's silent grief bewails
   The loss of her first born;
What though a grandma's eyes
   Look for their darling pet,
We thank our Heavenly Father, God,
   There's comfort for us yet.

An angel now is he,
   A seraph babe in bliss,
Not for a crown would we call him back
   To a cold world like this.
The dawn breaks o'er our hearts,
   A light from the Throne above,
We shall meet again no more to part,
   Where the all of Life is Love.

Then strew with flowers the grave
        Of an angel's earthly form,
Though cold the little heart beneath,
        The soul above is warm.
The eyes that beamed on us,
        And lips we held so dear,
May look and whisper words of love
        From an angelic sphere.

J. K. H.

NOTICES OF BOOKS.

1.—THE LIFE OF JESUS CHRIST, *in its Historical Connexion and Historical Development.* By AUGUSTUS NEANDER. *Translated from the fourth German Edition, by John McClintock and Charles E. Blumenthal, Professors in Dickinson College.* NEW YORK, HARPER & BROTHERS, 1848, 8vo. pp. 450.

If this elaborate work fails to come up to the ideas of the New Church on the subject of the biography of our Lord, viewed in relation to his assumed Humanity, it is probably a nearer approximation to them than could have been anticipated from any other writer than a German, or from any other German than Neander. He has been long known as recognizing in Christianity the development of an *interior divine life,* and in his Church History he has aimed less to chronicle the external changes and fortunes of the Church, than to trace the evolutions of its germinal principle, in new moulding the *life* of Christendom. The same general view pervades the work before us. It is remarkable for the absence of any acknowledgment of a *vicarious* character in the Lord's life, sufferings, and death. He evidently *knows* no such atonement as is made the all in all in the great mass of the Creeds of Theology. In his idea Jesus Christ comes into the world as a great spiritual Quickener and Regenerator, by the immediate infusion of his own Divine life into the souls of men. This is the leading conception of the work, and our readers need scarcely to be informed how nearly this view symbolizes with that of the New Church, of which, indeed, the writer appears to have had all along a dim presentiment, as of something yet to be developed, not aware that it is already in being.

On the doctrine of the Lord's *person* we are frequently reminded how closely one may approximate the truth and not *quite* reach it. The following paragraph is perhaps the most explicit declaration on this point contained in the volume. It is headed, " *The Truth, that Christ is* GOD-MAN, *presupposed.*"

"What, then, is the special presupposition with which we must approach the contemplation of the Life of Christ? It is one on which hangs the very being of the Christian as such; the existence of the Christian Church, and the nature of Christian consciousness. It is one at whose touch of power the dry bones of the old world sprung up in all the vigor of a new creation. It gave birth to all that culture (the *modern* as distinguished from the *ancient*) from which the Germanic nations received their peculiar intellectual life, and from which the emancipation of the mind, grown too strong for its bonds, was developed in the Reformation.

It is the very root and ground of our modern civilization; and the latter, even in its attempts to separate from this root, must rest upon it: indeed, should such attempts succeed, it must dissolve into its original elements, and assume an entirely new form. It is, in a word, the belief that *Jesus Christ is the Son of God in a sense which cannot be predicated of any human being*—the perfect image of the personal GOD in the form of that humanity that was estranged from him; that in him the source of the Divine life itself in humanity appeared; that by him the idea of humanity was realized."

We may well be thankful even for this, as it doubtless contains a deeper truth on the subject than the author himself had grasped, or was free to announce, though the idea of tracing the main effects of the Lord's divinity in the superior civilization of modern times is a mighty derogation from the sanctity of the theme. The reader, however, may safely take this as an earnest of the spirit and genius of the book, which is rich in a spiritual vein of thought, and rich in the promise of a better day ere long to dawn upon the darkness of Christian theology. A main feature of the work is its elaborate refutation of the fallacies of Strauss's "Life of Jesus," which the author may be said to have completely demolished.

2.—POSTHUMOUS WORKS *of the Rev.* THOMAS CHALMERS, *D.D., L.L.D., Edited by the Rev. William Hanna, D.D.—Daily Scripture Readings, in Three Volumes; vols. I. and II.* NEW YORK: HARPER & BROTHERS. 1848 : *pp.* 442, 478.

Dr. Chalmers has left a high name in the roll of the theological worthies of the current century. A man of action as well as of thought, he held a foremost place in the movement that achieved the freedom of the Scottish church. His fame with after times will probably rest more upon his labors in the pulpit and in the synod than upon his closet elaborations. These, though ably wrought and distinguished by a flowing and affluent diction, are not marked by any peculiar richness or rareness of material. His was not a mind to extend the boundaries of human thought, although few were more capable of varying its phases. His great forte was in beating out the bullion of a single idea into laminæ covering an immense area. In after life he probably never surpassed his first work, "The Evidences of Christianity," in which, however, he discovers an inadequate appreciation of the internal evidence compared with the external. The "Daily Readings" is not a work of any great value, as the reflections are mostly of a common-place character, though indicating a close and careful study of the letter of the Scriptures. In the portion of the work entitled "Sabbath Exercises," which is a journal of his religious experience, we find a series of pious aspirations which bespeak a soul prompted to high attainments, but not expressive of any deep recognition of the principles which lie at the foundation of a true regenerative process. This, however, was doubtless rather the fault of the system he had embraced than of the man. His piety was perhaps of as high an order as his theology would admit. As it seemed to recognize Christ solely in his mediatorial relations, it lacked the virtue of those convictions which spring out of the assurance of his sole and undivided Godhead, than which the New Churchman can see no other sufficient basis for the complete development of a spiritual and heavenly life.

MISCELLANY.

Dr. W. Clay Wallace of this city has recently communicated, in several successive numbers, to the *Boston Medical and Surgical Journal*, a new scientific account of the physical phenomena which occur in the act of *vision*. He describes the surface of the retina as disposed in several distinct layers. 1. An exceedingly attenuated, and perfectly transparent membranous lining. 2. A very delicate series of nervous filaments. 3. A coating behind these exposing a finely granulated surface, upon which the picture to be seen is received. According to Dr. Draper, this granulated surface becomes oxydized by the action of light, in a manner similar to that which is effected in the daguerreo-type process. When the retina becomes excited to action by the presence of light, *the nervous structure rapidly passes its feelers over the surface of the picture*, thus conveying a report of it to the sensorium by touch. The readers of Swedenborg will call to mind what he says in relation to our senses; viz: that they are all finally resolvable into the *sense of touch.* Dr. W., we believe, has been the first to demonstrate the anatomical structure of the retina, as indicated above. He was ena-bled to accomplish this by employing a new and improved method of preparing and preserving the eye for this purpose; which is also de-tailed in the communications referred to. There is another feature in the result of these experiments which strikes us as of a very interest-ing character; viz: that, when, by placing a lamp before a lens in such a manner that a volume of confused light only is thrown upon the retina, so that no distinct picture is formed upon it, but only a strong sensation of light produced; the *feelers* being excited to action as before, and finding no picture to transmit, *report*, as it were, *upon the state of the granulated surface*, conveying a knowledge of it to the brain. The examination of it is thus entered upon by the *subject himself*. It is something new, we fancy, in physiology, for the study of the subtleties of our interior structure to become a *subjective process.*

MEETING OF GENERAL CONVENTION.

The Thirtieth General Convention of Societies and other associated bodies of the New Church in the United States, will assemble in the New Jerusalem Church in Boston, on the second Wednesday (the 14th day,) of June, at 9 o'clock, A. M.

T. B. HAYWARD, *Sec'y 29th Convention.*

Boston, April 1st, 1848.

SWEDENBORG ASSOCIATION.

There will be a special meeting of the Swedenborg Association held at Boston, in June next, during the session of the General Convention; and all members are requested to be present.

Per Order, OLIVER GERRISH, *Rec. Sec'y.*

Portland, April 20th, 1848.

EDITORIAL ITEMS.

The contents of the May No. of the N. J. Magazine are (1.) A Sermon on Ps. xxxvii. 34, by T. B. Hayward. (2.) The Scheme of Redemption. (3.) The Uses and Duties of a Church. (4.) Thoughts suggested by the late Revolution in France. The Letter of the London correspondent does not appear. That from France dwells upon the Providential aspects of the recent revolution in that country. In the Report of the Committee presented to the Michigan and Northern Indiana Association on Missionary Duties, we notice a somewhat labored discussion of the necessity of a duly authorized class of men to promulgate the doctrines of the New Church. In confirming this necessity by citations from Swedenborg we observe a very singular use of one or two extracts from the A. R. and the A. E. "It is not," he says, "lawful for any to teach from the Word, nor consequently to be inaugurated into the priesthood," &c., "unless he acknowledges that doctrine, and swears to the belief and love thereof." (A. R. 606.) But what doctrine? Of whom is Swedenborg here speaking? Not of the true Church, or of its doctrines or ordinances, but of the Beast and his institutes, which every adherent was compulsively forced to acknowledge on pain of being shut out from ecclesiastical dignities. The whole passage stands thus: "' *And that no man might buy or sell save he that had the mark, or name of the beast or the number of his name*,'" signifies, that it is not lawful for any one to teach from the Word, nor consequently to be inaugurated into the priesthood, honored with the magisterial laurel, invested with the doctor's cap, and called orthodox, unless he acknowledges that doctrine (the doctrine of faith alone), and swears to the belief and love thereof, or of that which is in agreement, or of that which is not at variance with it." Now we should hope that the committee did not mean to imply by this that the principles established in the Beast's kingdom were to be the rule of proceeding in the Lord's New Church, and yet what else is to be inferred from the quotation of the passage in this connexion? Is the mark of the Beast to identify the teachers of the New Jerusalem? Yet Swedenborg, in the context, is explaining the import of that mark. No one but he who has it is to be acknowledged as worthy of the honor of priesthood or magistracy unless he holds to the doctrine of faith alone. And thus the Report proceeds: "In explaining, in A. E. 840, the meaning of the words, 'that no one might buy or sell if he had not the mark of the beast,' he says, by it 'is signified prohibition lest any one learn and teach otherwise than what is acknowledged, thus also what is received in doctrine.'" This is undoubtedly a sound interpretation, but how does it bear upon the point in hand? Is there no way to prove the unlawfulness of lay-teaching but by an appeal to the statutes of the realm of Anti-Christ? If so, the position had better be abandoned, which perhaps it may be when the constitution of the Church is more thoroughly studied, the nature, origin, and use of the Christian ministry more clearly set forth, and the real distinction between clergy and laity definitively settled. If this is already done to the satisfaction of others, it is not to ours; and we are greatly at a loss to perceive how the New Church is to be spread or societies formed in many parts of our country, if men of zeal, wisdom, and ability are not considered as having competent authority from the Lord Himself to declare His truth as far as they are possessed of it and desirous of living according to it. That such a liberty may be abused and may generate various evils, is undoubtedly true; but are there no evils growing out of its being restrained? And on which side do the evils preponderate? This is a matter of grave consideration, and probably the time is not very distant when it will receive more attention than it has yet done.

——The " Advent Herald" thinks to have transfixed the theology of Swedenborg by an arrow feathered from the wing of his philosophy. That paper declares that the assertion that the sun is " pure fire" is so contrary to the *known facts* of science as effectually to undermine all confidence in the infallibility of his teachings on any subject. An anonymous writer shortly after called for his authority in opposition to Swedenborg. In his reply the editor says the evidence is not so strong of the correctness of his remark as he had supposed, but he still wonders how the sun, the density of which has been determined, is so much lighter than the substances which proceed from it, as if new chemical combinations did not often produce an increase of specific gravity. On the general subject a friend, well competent to judge, writes us as follows : " I noticed the article from the Advent Herald. The only reply, I suppose, is, that our ordinary word *fire* means a different thing from Swedenborg's *pure fire*—but a complete exposition of it should be coupled with an article on Swedenborg's 'Chemical' Philosophy, which would require some reading, as well as a knowledge of the original passages and of the use of his term ' pure fire.' There is no doubt but that the chemical philosophy of the day is nearing him very much, and it is getting to be a common opinion that our 'elements' are not made of matter having specific ' qualitative' differences. The sun, in *our* philosophy, consists of course of that material from which all those *forms* of matter, which we call *chemical elements* and their compounds, are educed. Consequently such material would, in a state of condensation, possess the *mean density* of all planetary matter. I shall keep my eye upon the subject."——Mr. Allen has now in press the admirable Tract by Swedenborg entitled " Canons, or the Entire Theology of the New Church." This work, which has never before appeared complete in English, contains in brief compass the pith of the New Church doctrines respecting the Divine Nature, God the Redeemer, the Holy Spirit, the Trinity, Creation, Redemption, Salvation, the Consummation of the Old Church, the Institution of the New, etc. etc. It will form a pamphlet of about 40 pages, and will be retailed at 12 1-2 cents the copy. It may be emphatically characterized as *multum in parvo*, and the New Churchman upon perusing it will be disposed to look back with regret upon his non-possession of it in years that are past. We hope that orders may be freely sent in for it, as the cost is trifling and every copy sold will do something towards disposing of one by gift where it promises to be useful.——De Guay's " Letters to a Man of the World" are now printed and the publisher is ready to respond to all applications. Owing to the increase of matter and the superior style of execution, the price will be put at 50 cents per copy.——Noble's Lectures are proceeding rapidly through the press. It will be accompanied by a new Preface by the editor of the Repository. ——A volume of Sermons by Mr. Noble has just been published in England. It has not yet been received in this country. We shall notice it immediately upon its reception.

THE

'EW CHURCH REPOSITORY

AND

MONTHLY REVIEW.

| l. 1. | JULY, 1848. | No. 7. |

ORIGINAL PAPERS.

ARTICLE I.

—

THE DRUIDISM OF ANCIENT BRITAIN:

I DOCTRINES, RITES, CORRESPONDENCES, ETC., AS DISCOVERED IN ANCIENT BRITISH MANUSCRIPTS, REVIEWED AND COMPARED WITH THOSE OF THE ANCIENT CHURCH.

(Concluded.)

THE Druids, being in the science of correspondence, under)od that the human soul exists in a substantial form, and that e life of all created beings is by influx from the Divine. ence Taliesin, in a poem called "Elements of Instruction," emingly reflecting upon the teachers of another system for eir lack of knowledge, says—

> "I marvel that, in their books,
> They know not, with certainty,
> What are the properties of the soul;
> Of what *form* are its *members*;
> What region is its abode;
> What breath, what flux sustains it."

These verses viewed in connection with the Triads in the [arch No. of the Repository which speak of the soul, and with e correspondence of the Druidical Temple in our last No, ake it evident that the system of psychology taught by the ruids was substantially the same as that now taught in the

writings of Swedenborg. In the Triads, the trine in the soul
is said to be, affection, understanding, and the act of the will;
and here the soul is represented as having a form and members, and as being sustained, or having life by a flux or stream
from a source higher than itself. This source the Druids believed to be the invisible God, whom they worshiped; and
who was represented to them by the Sun, the centre and secondary cause of life to the universe around it, and by the altar
in the centre of their temples. With reference to this Invisible
God, Taliesin, in the same poem, inquires—

> " Knowest thou
> Who is the Beatifier of the soul ?
> Who has seen him ? who knows him ?"

Not unlike the interrogation in the book of Job—a book of the
ancient church—"Canst thou by searching find out God ? Canst
thou find out the Almighty to perfection ?"—(Job xi. 7.) Also,
in the same book, the life is said to be wind, or breath : "O
remember that my life is wind: mine eye shall no more see
good."—(vii. 7.) Again, "All the while my breath is in me, and
the spirit of God is in my nostrils."—(xxvii. 3.) Thus rendered
by Swedenborg, "As long as my soul is in me, and the wind of
God is in my nose. By the wind of Jehovah, or his breath, is
signified the life which is of heaven, and which is of man who
is in heaven, that is, of a regenerate man."—(*A. C.* 8286.)

We shall now, according to promise, give some extracts from
works of the Bards, written purely in the language of correspondence. In a poem, entitled "The Seat, or Throne of Taliesin," the Bard speaks of the Druidic Church, and gives a
description of some of its internal qualities or principles. Taliesin was evidently a name common to the chief Druid in the
British Church, as Melchizedek was a name common to the
king and priest of the ancient church ; Taliesin, like Melchizedek, being representative of the Divine Principle which constitutes the church. The word is a compound of Tal (front,
forehead), and Iesin (radiant, glorious, fair); and therefore
literally means, the Radiant or Glorious Front; a name by no
means inappropriate to the high priest, who was representative
of the Divine, which was also represented by the sun. Aaron,
the high priest of the Jewish nation, signifies lofty, mountainous,
or mountain of strength (Cruden) ; for Aaron represented the
Lord as to the principle of divine good, to which the mountain
corresponds ; while Taliesin, like the Melchizedek of the ancient church, represented the Lord as to both principles, good
and truth. The throne of Taliesin, by correspondence, denotes
the spiritual church; which, also, in the Word, is called the

throne of God, the throne being predicated of Divine Truth by which the Lord governs the church. In the language of the Druids, this church is personified, and is represented as speaking of itself; and may be understood as speaking of itself either in its collective capacity, or in the individual man, the Druidical temple being representative of either, or of both. In speaking of this temple, in our last number, we said that the Bards generally represent it as being surrounded by the sea: this will be seen in the poem we now present to the reader.

THE THRONE OF TALIESIN.

Surrounded by the sea, I am
To the praise of God the Governor.
*   *   *   *   *   *
Profound is the all-sufficient source
Which fully supplies me,—the sacred circle,
In every evening festival,
When the calm dew descends,
With the blessing of wheat, and the suavity of bees,
And incense, and myrrh, and aloes, from beyond the sea;
And the gold pipes communicating,
And glad, precious silver, and the ruddy gem;
And berries, and the ocean wave;
And cresses,—the virtue watered by the gushing spring,
And a joint multitude of the herbs of the gentle flood,
And, borne by the effusive moon, placid, cheerful vervain;*
And stars of intelligence diffused around the moon,
And the wide spread aspect of the pure element;
And below, in the moving atmosphere,
The moisture, and the falling drops;
And the increase which succeeds;
And the vessel of glass in the hand of the pilgrim,
And the strong youth with the rosin of pine,
And the exalted one free from guile,
With the healing herbs where no delusion is,
And Bards with flowers.
*   *   *   *   *
Meet for a sovereign is the Druidic lore."

The above composition has but little merit viewed simply as a poem, its only value is in its correspondences; without the correspondences it really has no meaning.

In tracing these out, we refer the reader to the Dictionary of Correspondence for the correctness of our interpretation. The temple, representative of the church, has been fully described before. The evening festival denotes 1st, The worship of the Lord, hence the church is represented as saying, "I am to the praise of God the Governor:" it denotes secondly, conso-

---

* In the British Botanology the vervain has the following titles, expressive of its high esteem among the Ancient Britons; the Fiend's Aversion, the Blessed Tree, the Enchanting-Plant.

ciation, and the good of charity. The calm dew then descend-ing, denotes the truth of good, which is derived from a state of innocence and peace, and which is evidently received by the church when she is in the act of internal worship. The church is then supplied with the blessing of wheat, &c. Wheat denotes the things which are of love and charity; or respectively, those who are inwardly good. The suavity of bees, or honey, signifies the delight which is derived from good and truth, or from the affection thereof, and especially the external delight, thus the delight of the exterior natural principle: also the pleasantness and delight derived from the affections of knowing and learning goods and truths celestial and spiritual. Incense denotes worship and confession of the Lord from spiritual goods and truths. Myrrh signifies good of the first or ultimate degree, and aloes good of the second degree. Gold—the inmost good of the church, and pipes communicating—influx through the medium of that good. Glad, precious silver—spiritual truth; gladness is predicated of truth. The ruddy gem—truth grounded in good. The wave of the sea, scientifics. Berries, cresses, herbs, and placid cheerful vervain,—goods of various kinds and qualities. The vervain being borne by the moon, denotes the growth of that quality of good in the spiritual church. The moon denotes the light of that church, or the church as to its light, and the stars, as expressed by the Bard, the intelligence thence derived. The wide spread aspect of the pure element, the same as the brightness of the firmament, denotes the appearance of truth as it shines in the life, hence the garment of the ruling priest, was sky-blue. Air denotes perception and thought, consequently faith; rain, influx of spiritual truth which is appropriated to man; and the increase which succeeds—the fructifications and multiplications which take place by virtue of influx from the Lord. The vessel of glass in the hand of the pilgrim, signifies truth pellucid the receptacle of good, this truth in the hand denotes its power, and the pilgrim, the progress in the divine life where truth has power. The strong youth with the rosin of pine, signifies strong affection for the truth, and rosin, says Swedenborg, signifies truth derived from good, because it ranks amongst ointments, and also amongst aromatics. The exalted or dignified one, with healing herbs, denotes truth from a spiritual origin, efficacious to remove the falses and evils of the natural mind. The leaves of the tree are for the healing of the nations. The Bards with flowers, denote wisdom and regeneration. The budding and fructification of a tree, represents the re-birth of man; the leaves signify those things which are of intelligence, or the truths of faith, for these are the first things of regeneration, but the flowers are those things which are of wisdom, or the goods of faith, because these proximately precede the re-birth, and the fruits those things which are of life, or the works of charity, inasmuch as these are subsequent, and constitute the state itself of the regenerate.

The Druids being in possession of the science of correspon-dence, the Bard truly remarks at the close of his poem,

" Meet for a sovereign is the Druidic lore."

Swedenborg informs us that by Eber, in the Word, is signified a new church, which may be called the second ancient church; and that by Shem being the father of all the sons of Eber, is signified that this second ancient church, and the things apper-taining to it, had existence from the former ancient church.—(*A. C.* 1217.) The Druids had a knowledge of this church, knew it to be a reform of the ancient church which had preceded it, and speak of their own system as being the same as taught in the church Eber. In a poem, from which we have already quoted in our remarks upon the deluge, the church, or the high priest personifying the church, speaks as follows—

> " My afflictions have been related in Ebrew in Eber.*
> A second time have I been formed.
> I have been a blue salmon; I have been a dog;
> I have been a stag; and a roe-buck on the mountain;
> I have been the stook of a tree; a spade; an axe in the hand;
> I have been a pin in a forceps for eighteen months;
> I have been a variegated cock—* * * * *
> I have been a stud   *   *   *   *   *
> I have been a bull; I have been a buck
> Of yellow hue, yielding nourishment;
> I have been a grain concealed
> Which vegetated on a hill;
> And the reaper placed me in a smoky recess
> That by means of tribulation my virtue might be brought forth;
> A fowl with a divided crest and ruddy feet received me;
> Nine nights I remained in her womb—a male child;
> When I came forth from my entombment
> I was presented an offering to the Sovereign.
> I was dead, I have been vivified;
> And rich in my possession, I am made a medium of conveyance.
> In my prior state I was poor.
> For the heat-enkindling re-instruction
> Of the ruddy footed I received,
> Scarcely can be expressed the great praise which is due;
> I am Taliesin."

In the correspondence of the above poem, we trace the pro-cess of regeneration in the man of the ancient church; or the formation of the church itself, viewed collectively; the Bard

---

* In the Hebrew tongue, in the church Eber.

in his description, commencing with the scientific principle. The first thing mentioned is a species of fish; "Fishes in the Word, signify scientifics, which have their birth from things sensual: for there are scientifics of three kinds, intellectual, rational, and sensual, all of which are sown in the memory—or rather in the memories, and in the regenerate are thence called forth of the Lord by the internal man."—(*A. C.* 991.) The salmon consequently is a species of these scientifics appertaining to the sensual principle. Dog denotes the lowest things of the church, placed, as it were, between the good and the evil, as a guard to prevent the profanation of holy things.

This principle, though the lowest, is absolutely necessary for the safety of the church. "There was seen by me a great dog like Cerberus, and I asked what it signified, and was told, that by such a dog is signified a guard, lest in conjugial love any should pass from celestial delight to infernal delight, and the reverse; by a dog thus is represented, that those opposite delights should be prevented from communicating."—(*A. C.* 2743.) By a dog is also signified a desire of knowing truth from some natural affection.—(*Ap. Ex.* 455.) The stag, which is next mentioned, denotes the affection and perception of truth (Ibid); and the roe-buck on the mountain, the natural affection elevated. "That the hind (or female deer) signifies natural affection, is because it is among the beasts significative of the affections, as all those are which are for food and useful."—(*A. C.* 6413.) By the stock of a tree is signified the Word in the natural man, from which the church is afterwards formed. With reference to Nebuchadnezzar, King of Babylon, representative of the principle of the church profaned, it is said, "Hew down the tree, and cut off his branches, shake off his leaves, and scatter his fruit; and let the beasts get away from under it, and the fowls from his branches. Nevertheless leave the stump of his roots in the earth, even with a band of iron and brass, in the tender grass of the field."—(Dan. iv. 14, 15.) "By the stump of the roots which should be left in the earth, is signified the Word, which is understood as to the letter only, and the knowledge thereof is as somewhat residing in the memory only."—(*Ap. Ex.* 650.)

The spade is used to prepare the ground for the reception of seed, and therefore corresponds to truth in its operations upon the mind, preparatory to its reception of the divine seed of the Word.

The axe in the hand, has the same signification as the axe which was laid to the root of the tree, mentioned by John the Baptist, and the axe which was used by one of the sons of the prophets to cut down wood in order to erect a dwelling.—(2

Kings vi.) It denotes the Word moulding and preparing the mind, separating what is useless, for the indwelling of the divine principles, emanating from the Lord; for these principles, like the sons of the prophets, prepare for themselves a habitation in man, and afterwards dwell there. "To cut wood with an axe, signifies disputation concerning good from a religious principle; an iron axe denotes the truth of faith in the natural man, and a forest the church as to science."—(*A. C.* 9011.) The forceps is used in chirurgery to extract any thing out of wounds, and therefore corresponds to truth extracting what is false and evil in man. "Eighteen (the number of months during which it is said the principle of the church was a pin in a forceps,) denotes the holy things of combat, for this number is compounded of three and six; three signifies what is holy, and six, combat."—(*A. C.* 1709.) The pin in the forceps is that which conjoins the parts together, and therefore denotes the good of that truth, which gives it its power to combat. Fowls denote things intellectual, or thoughts and their affections; the horse, the understanding of the Word; the bull, or the ox, the good of the natural principle; and the buck of yellow hue giving nourishment,—celestial natural good, the food of the mind. The grain concealed, signifies remains implanted by the Lord in the inmost principles of the mind. This vegetating on a hill, denotes its growth in the principle of charity. "In regard to spiritual seed, what is implanted is never rooted, until the good of charity as it were warms it; then first it begins to strike root in itself, and afterwards to shoot it forth."—(*A. C.* 880.) The grain was placed by the reaper in a smoky recess, that by means of tribulation its virtue might be brought forth. Here is most obviously taught the doctrine, which Swedenborg teaches, that in the process of regeneration man passes through hell, and is subjected to its annoyances, that by means of temptations his natural evils may be removed, and the good implanted by the Lord be brought forth to life. This seed was received by a fowl with a divided crest and ruddy feet, and it remained nine nights in her womb, a male child. The fowl with a divided crest, denotes the rational principle, which distinguishes and divides the good from the evil,—the ruddy feet signifying the good of that principle in the natural. "The natural man is reduced to correspondence by the Lord through the rational, in that good is insinuated into the rational, and in this good as in ground, truths are implanted, and afterwards by rational truths the natural is reduced to obedience; and when it obeys then it corresponds; and as far as it corresponds, so far is man regenerated."—(*A. C.* 3286.) "Fowls signify things rational and intellectual."—(*A. C.* 745.) It lay in the womb of the rational, nine nights,—a male child. Nine nights denote a full state in obscurity through which man in being regenerated, or the principle of the church in man passes; and the male child signifies the good of the spiritual church, which is spiritual truth. The good, when brought forth from its entombment to life, was presented an offering to the Sovereign—to God, the King of the Church: and thus presented, it was, as the principle of the church, made the medium of communication from the Lord. The heat-enkindling re-instruction received by means of the rational, denotes the elevation of the mind from the natural into spiritual truths, and thus re-instruction in truths previously received into the natural mind; which re-instruction produces in the man of the church, the warmth of charity, and therefore truly is the heat-enkindling re-instruction. The praise due for this instruction, the Bard says, can scarcely be expressed; but the benefit derived from it is most beautifully represented in the last short sentence, "I am Taliesin," signifying that the church, in consequence of her regeneration by the Lord, is radiant in her countenance.

A large volume may be written upon the correspondences of the writings of the Druidical Bards; but we must leave them and devote the remainder of our article to the historical triads, which Mr. Davies, in his work, denominates " Mythological." The work from which we make the following selection is entitled,

" Triads of Memory, Record and Knowledge, respecting notable men and things which have been in the Isle of Prydain (Britain), and respecting the circumstances and misfortunes which have happened to the nation of the Cymbry from the remotest ages; (literally the age of ages)."

These triads, like other works of the Bards, are written in the language of correspondence, every name being a signification of internal things.

I. *Three names given to the Isle of Prydain.*
Before it was inhabited it was called Clas Merddin: After it was inhabited it was called Y Fel Ynys; and after the regular organization of government by Prydain the son of Aedd the Great, it was denominated the Isle of Prydain.

(No one has any right to it but the tribe of Cymbry, for they first settled in it; before that time no human being lived therein; but it was full of bears, wolves, crocodiles, and bisons.)

IV. *The three national pillars of the Isle of Prydain:*
1st. Hu Gadarn who brought the nation of the Cymbry to

the Isle of Prydain. They came from the land of Summer, which is called Deffrobani (Animative high-places); and they came through the Vapory Sea to the Isle of Prydain.

2d. Prydain the son of Aedd the Great, who first organized a social state and sovereignty in the Isle of Prydain; for before that time there was no justice but what was done from internal probity, nor was there any law but that of superior force.

3d. Dyfnwal Moelmud, who made the first orderly discrimination of laws, ordinances, customs, and privileges of country and tribe.

V. *The three benevolent tribes of the Isle of Prydian:*

1st. The tribe of the Cymbry, that came with Hu Gadarn into the Isle of Prydain, because he would not possess a country and lands by war and contest, but in equity and in peace.

2d. The tribe of the Sleogrians which came from the Land of Gwasgwyn (Gentle ascent), and they were descended from the primitive tribe of the Cymbry.

3d. The Brython, that came from the Land of Slydau (Flowing Breadth), and who were also descended from the primitive tribe of the Cymbry.

These three were called the three peaceful tribes, because they came by mutual consent and permission, in peace and tranquillity; these three tribes had sprung from the primitive race,—the Cymbry, and the three were of one language and of one speech.*

XIII. *The three awful events of the Isle of Prydain.*

1st. The bursting forth of Llyn Llion (the lake of the floods), and the overwhelming of the face of all lands, so that all mankind perished, except Dwyfan (the Divine principle), and Dwyfach (the offspring of the Divine), who were preserved in a ship without a mast, and of them the Isle of Prydain was repeopled.

2d. The consternation of the tempestuous fire, when the earth split asunder to Annwn (hell) and the greatest part of all living was consumed.

3d. The scorching summer, when the woods and plants were set on fire by the intense heat of the sun, and immense multitudes of men, and beasts, and kinds of birds, and reptiles and trees, and plants were irretrievably lost.

---

* Other tribes are mentioned in the triads which were of a different character, unjust and cruel, and whose religion was perverted and corrupt.

XCVII. *The three chief works of excellency of the Isle of Prydain:*

1st. The ship of Nefydd Naf Neifion (the Heavenly Lord of creating powers) which carried in it a male and female of every living thing, when the lake of the floods burst forth.

2d. The Branching oxen of Hu Gadarn, which drew the afanc (the amphibious) to land out of the waters, so that the lake burst no more.

3d. The stone of Gwyddon Ganhebon (knowledge with its utterance), on which are read all the arts and sciences of the world.

The last two triads precede the others in the order of time, but in our explanation we shall follow the order in which the triads are given, or rather commence with the second, as in so doing we shall have a better understanding of the terms used.

These triads inform us of the establishment of Druidism in Britain, and whence the nation emigrated to that country. The Cymbry came from the Land of Summer, denominated the Animative High Places, through the Vapory Sea, to Britain, which, before it was inhabited, was called Clas Merddin. The language of these triads, understood literally, has but little, or no meaning, and therefore must be understood according to correspondence, in which sense they are strikingly beautiful. The land of summer denotes the land of the church in the internal heat and light of heaven; and the animative high places, denote the spiritual things of the church, or the good of charity which gives life. "Summer and Winter, signify the state of the regenerate man as to the new things of the will, the changes whereof are like those of summer and winter. Because there is with him of himself nothing but evil, and all good is from the Lord alone, he must needs undergo changes, and now be as it were in summer, that is, in charity, and now in winter, that is, in no charity."—(*A. C.* 935.) "From the heat of the world conjoined with light, all things which grow on the earth revive and flourish: this conjunction takes place in the seasons of spring and summer: but from light separate from heat nothing revives and flourishes, but all things are torpid and die. This separation takes place in the time of winter, when heat is absent though light continues. From this correspondence, heaven is called paradise, because there truth is conjoined with good, or faith with love, as light is conjoined with heat in spring on earth."—(*H. & H.* 136.) "When times are predicated of the church, morning signifies its first state, noon its fulness, evening its decrease, and night its end: and the four seasons of the year, spring, summer, autumn, and winter, signify the same."—(*D. L. & W*

73.) Here then we are informed that the summer season denotes a state of charity,—that heaven is called paradise in consequence of its correspondence with the seasons of spring and summer,—and that when summer is predicated of the church, it denotes the church in its fulness. The British word Haf (summer) also denotes fulness; exactly corresponding with what Swedenborg says with reference to the church. This land of summer and fulness, say the Druids, is called the Animative High-places. "He made him to ride on the high places of the earth, and feedeth him with the produce of the field. These things are said concerning the ancient church, which was in truths from good: the intelligence of the spiritual man of the church is signified by making him to ride on the high places of the earth; to ride signifying to understand, and the high places of the earth the spiritual things of the church," the good in which he is, and of which are the truths.— (*Ap. Ex.* 411.) The high places mentioned by the Druids are animative, and therefore can be understood only of things which arouse to activity, or give life. The two other tribes mentioned in the triads with the Cymbry, came the one from the land of Gentle Ascent, and the other from the land of Flowing Breadth. By breadth is meant truth. The Psalmist says, "Thou hast caused my feet to stand in breadth. Here to stand in breadth signifies in the truth."—(*A. C.* 1613.) Also the truth is frequently represented in the Word as waters flowing. The gentle ascent may denote the elevation from truth to charity. Again, Cymbry, the name of the tribe who came from the animative high places, signifies the first, or highest; and Brython, the name of the tribe from the land of breath, signifies the warlike. We also read in Swedenborg, "Good is the first thing of order, and truth the last." "It is truth to which belongs the first of the combat, for the combat is supported from truth, since the knowledge of what is false and evil is of truth."—(*A. C.* 3726, 1685.)

From the land of Summer, the Cymbry, in their emigration, passed through the Vapory, or Misty Sea. The region occupied by the internal church mentioned in the Word, whose state corresponds to the summer season compared with the state of others of which we read, was the land of Canaan and the adjacent countries in Asia. Other churches mentioned in the Word, being in externals, were in comparative darkness. The locations of these eternal churches were portions of Europe, in the Word called the North, and also the West, and the islands of the sea because separated from the land of Canaan by the Mediterranean. Probably in regions of Europe, more remote from the internal church, than the regions occupied by

the corresponding external church, there were nations who
were in mere falses, in a similar state to some portions of the
heathen world in the present day.   In passing from the land
of the internal church to Britain, the Cymbry had necessarily
to pass through the countries of these various nations.   The
internal church is sometimes called the earth, and the external
church is called the ends of the earth, and the sea, and its doctrines are called vapors.   Also, those who are in falses, or who
are of the old church, we are informed, are in a state of inundation over the head, being encompassed about with a misty
cloud representative of their state.   "The sea signifies the
external of the church, consequently the church, as consisting
of those who are in its externals; and the earth signifies the
internal of the church, and consequently the church as consisting of those who are in its internals."—(*A. R.* 398.)   "By the
vapors which he causeth to ascend from the end of the earth,
are signified the ultimate truths of the church; vapors denote
these truths, and the end of the earth is the ultimate of the
church."—(*Ap. Ex.* 304.)   "They who are of the old church,
and are removed from heaven, are in a sort of inundation as to
the interiors, and indeed in an inundation over the head.   This
inundation is not apperceived by the man himself when he
lives in the body, but he comes into it after death; it appears
manifestly in another life, and indeed like a misty cloud with
which they are encompassed about."—(*A. C.* 4423.)   To pass
through the vapory, or misty sea, therefore, is, according to
correspondence, to pass through regions, where the church was
in the vapory atmosphere of mere external rituals, or through
nations who were enveloped in the mists of their own falses.
The British word *tawch* (vapor), conveys the idea of an exhala-
tion which is rather offensive to the nostrils, and thus evidently
expressive of evils, which were offensive to them, existing
among the nations through which they passed.   Through the
Vapory Sea, the Druids passed from the Land of Summer to
the Island which before it was inhabited they called "Clas
Merddin."   Clas, means a region or place; Merddin, is a compound from Merydd and In.   "Merydd, adj. moist, waterish,
slow, sluggish, lazy; it is sometimes used in connection with
the noun sin—Pechod meridd."—(*T. Richard's Dict.*)   "Merydd,
sub., that which is flaccid or sluggish, a plash, a sluggard."
"In, any thing pervading."—(*Dr. W. Richard's Dict.*)   Hence
it is obvious, that the compound word Merddin signifies the
pervading of sluggish or stagnant waters; and Clas Merddin,
a region pervaded by, or in stagnant waters.   But it is very
evident that there is nothing in the physical character of the
British Isle, which can make such a name in the least degree

appropriate to it; for it is naturally the very opposite of what it is here represented to be—a place most beautifully diversified with hill and dale, and silvery streams, perpetually clad in living verdure, and surrounded by a sea which is sometimes so boisterous as to make navigation on some parts of its coast extremely dangerous. It is therefore neither pervaded by sluggish water, nor surrounded by it. The name, viewed in connection with the vapory sea, through which the Druids passed, and the Land of Summer whence they came, denotes a region more remote from the animative internal principles of the church, than the regions through which they passed to it, according to correspondence, a region where nothing of the church existed, and therefore spiritually not reduced to order,—a region pervaded only by dead waters. After the Isle was inhabited, and consequently the principles of the church were implanted there, growing, and yielding their sweets, it was called "Y Fel Ynys" (the Honey Isle). "Honey denotes delight, because it is sweet, and every thing sweet in the natural world corresponds to what is delightful and pleasant in the spiritual world. It is said, the delight thereof, namely the delight of truth from good in the exterior natural, because every truth, and especially every truth of good has its delight, but a delight from the affection of good and truth, and from consequent use. Concerning Jerusalem, whereby is understood the spiritual church, the quality of which is described as it was with the ancients, it is said in Ezekiel, "So wast thou adorned with gold and silver; and thy garments were fine linen, and silk and needle-work; fine flour and honey, and oil, didst thou eat, whence thou becamest exceeding beautiful, and didst prosper even to a kingdom."—(Ezek. xvi.) Fine flour denotes the spiritual, honey its pleasantness, and oil its good. Honey also denotes the pleasantness and delight from the affections of knowing and learning goods and truths celestial and spiritual."—(*A. C.* 5620.)

After the organization of a social state and sovereignty by Prydain the son of Aedd the Great, it was denominated the Isle of Prydain, or the Isle Prydain. Prydain the son of Aedd, was not a person, but is the personification of a principle. The word is a compound of Pryd (beautiful), and ain (extension), and denotes, as we shall presently show, the order of truth. In the ancient church the priesthood and the royalty were in one person, hence Melchizedek was King of Salem and priest of the Most High God. We have before shown that this was the case in the Druidical church also. When, as the nation increased, the Druidical order of government was regularly established, the Druids gave the island (the home of their church, and which to them was representative of the church, as Canaan was to the church mentioned in the Word,) an appropriate name, and called it the Isle of Beautiful Extension ;— they called it beautiful from the order of its government. Here we see a striking instance of the correspondence mentioned in the above passage from Ezekiel : " Fine flour, and honey, and oil didst thou eat, whence thou becamest exceeding beautiful, and didst prosper even to a kingdom." " Form is the essence of a thing, but aspect is the existere thence : and whereas good is the very essence, and truth the existere thence, by beautiful in form, is signified the good of life, and by beautiful in aspect, the truth of faith."—(*A. C.* 4985.)   Beautiful extension may imply both form and aspect.

The ancient Britons came from the Land of Summer to their future home, under the guidance and protection of Hu Gadarn. Hu Gadarn signifies the mighty One, who pervades, overshadows, inspects.   Hu Gadarn is a personification of the Divine principle ; for his branching oxen drew the afanc to land at the time of the deluge.   This name therefore denotes the same Divine presence and guidance that were represented by the cloud which went before the Sons of Israel through the wilderness to Canaan.   Probably thousands of years before Israel passed through the wilderness, did the Divine Providence lead this ancient people from the regions of the church in Asia to their possession, where they instituted an internal church similar to that from which they had come forth, and, according to the instructions received from their forefathers, worshiped the true and living God.   Swedenborg informs us, that besides the churches which are mentioned in the Word, there have existed *very many* others, which are not so described, which in like manner (as those mentioned) decreased and destroyed themselves.—(*A. C.* 2910.)   One of these churches, it is abundantly proved, existed in Britain.   The government of this church was formed by Prydain, the son of Aedd the Great. Prydain signifies the beautiful extension or expansion, and is predicated of the order of truth, or of truth as to order.   Aedd (the father of Prydain) denotes din, clamor, confusion : and therefore denotes what is altogether contrary to order.   Nevertheless Prydain being called the son of Aedd, is in exact agreement with the correspondences of the Word, the very same idea being conveyed in similar language by the Lord himself.   " The father shall be divided against the son, and the son against the father, the mother against the daughter, and the daughter against the mother.   The father (says Swedenborg) denotes the evil which is of the proprium of man, and the son denotes the truth which man hath of the Lord ; and the mother denotes the cupidity of the false, and the daughter the affection of truth."—(*Ap. Ex.* 724.) We have already shown from the correspondences of the Druids, that they had correct views of the process of regeneration in man, and that they well knew the state of man before and after, and understood the principles of the human mind. The church in its collective capacity is in every particular the same, as it is in each individual of the church ; and the church and the state among the Druids formed but one government; consequently in speaking of their government they speak of their church, and truly, according to the correspondence of the Divine Word, represent truth in the order established by it, as being the son of the natural principle which is disorder, as the natural must necessarily exist before the spiritual, and as it were beget it. No truth can be received by man, or the church, but through the natural understanding.

Another name mentioned in the Triad, is Dyfnwal Moelmud, who made the first orderly discrimination of the laws, and ordinances, customs, and privileges of country and tribe. This name signifies a deep laid rampart, and the removal of nakedness, and therefore is significative of truth as a defence. He is said to be the son of Prydain, evidently signifying that the defence of truth is a consequence of the order of truth, or is derived from it. The correspondence of the name, and of the discrimination attributed to him is given in the following words of Swedenborg, "By a wall, a rampart, gates, and bars, are meant doctrinals."—(*A. C.* 402.) By doctrinals we discriminate truths and defend against the false, for without doctrine in the mind we have no understanding of truth, and therefore have no defence.

We must close our article with a few remarks upon the two remaining triads. The first speaks of three awful calamities of the Isle of Prydian. The island received its name from the church which it represented, as Canaan and the adjacent countries received their names from the church which they represented. Swedenborg informs us that this was invariably the case in the ancient church, and that every particular place, all, mountain, hill, river, lake, &c., were representative, and had names significative of spiritual things. That this was the case among the Druids is most certain, for many of the names of towns, mountains, rivers, and lakes in Wales, handed down from the Druidical age, are to this day significative of such things. Consequently, in their language, the Isle of Prydain, or the Isle of Beautiful Extension, signified the church; this being the name by which they designated the church. The term therefore conveyed to their minds an idea of the church generally wherever the church might have an existence. The church as to the principle of good, is called an *Island* in the Book of Job, which also is written according to correspondence, and is a book of the ancient church. "He shall deliver the Island of the Innocent, and it is delivered by the pureness of thine hands."—(Job xxii. 30.) In Psalm xxiv. we read, "The earth is the Lord's and the fulness thereof; the world, and they that dwell therein. For he hath founded it upon the seas, and established it upon the floods." "Earth denotes the church in a specific sense, world denotes the church in a universal sense." —(*A. C.* 6297.) Here the idea is conveyed that the church is on the seas, and is therefore necessarily surrounded by them; these seas signifying the scientifics of the church. The Isle of Beautiful Extension surrounded by the seas, also denotes the church founded upon scientifics, and in this sense may properly be understood of the church universally. The three awful events of the church, mentioned in the triad, are in exact agreement with the descriptions given by Swedenborg of the judgments which have befallen the church at its consummation. The deluge denotes the inundation of the false and the evil; the opening of the earth to Annwn, or Hell, the change by which the wicked are removed from false appearances of good to a state in which their externals are in agreement with their internals; and the scorching heat of the sun which consumed, men, beasts, birds, &c.; denotes the scorching concupiscences of the evil which destroy every good of the church, and reduce man to a state of moral death. Let the reader compare the triad with the description given by Swedenborg in his Treatise upon the "Last Judgment." The three chief works of excellency of the church. The ship of the Heavenly Lord of creating powers, is evidently the ark of God in which Noah and his family were preserved, the remains of the church then preserved being signified by the male and female of every living thing; or the Divine principle and the offspring of the divine, or that which proceeds from the divine, mentioned in the preceding triad. The branching oxen of Hu Gadarn, which drew the amphibious to land from out of the water, denotes good fructifying; the amphibious most evidently signifies the mere natural principle, delighting principally in mere scientifics, and living in them; the drawing of this to land, denotes the elevation of the natural by the fructification of good to the land or ground of the church, and consequently it denotes the reformation and regeneration of the natural principle, so that the floods overwhelmed it no more. The Stone of Knowledge with its utterance (Gwyddon Ganhebon), denotes truth, on which is written the all of science, and of every thing which pertains to

the life and uses of man; and on it therefore are read all the arts and sciences of the world. These three chief works of excellency, are evidently of the church, being the work of the Lord, by means of his church, in man.

We here leave the subject of Druidism, simply remarking at the close, that the system (as the reader now perceives,) has been most grossly and shamefully misrepresented by those who have undertaken to write upon the subject. Suffice it here to say, that these writers were men of a different religious persuasion; the reader therefore may expect the same truthfulness in their accounts of Druidism, as he finds in the writings of the same class of heathen authors and others of later date, respecting the christian religion; and the same that he now finds in the productions of modern orthodox divines respecting the doctrines revealed by the Lord through Emanuel Swedenborg to the world.   T. W.

ARTICLE II.

LETTERS TO A TRINITARIAN.

LETTER VII.

THE INCARNATION.

DEAR SIR,

It would not perhaps be possible to announce any proposition fraught with more momentous consequences to the interests of revealed truth, than that which I have thus far endeavored to establish, viz., that Jesus Christ is the true and only God, the Creator and Governor of the Universe, one with Jehovah, and comprising within his own Divine Person the three Essentials of the Godhead, denominated Father, Son, and Holy Spirit. How rich the discovery to the Christian, that that Being whom he had been taught to view simply as his Saviour, in some secondary character, is indeed no other than the Supreme Deity in the most absolute oneness of his nature, and not merely a proper, but the *only* proper, object of religious worship and adoration! With this view of our Lord's character firmly rooted and grounded in his mind, he knows no Father or Holy Ghost in the least degree separate from the person of

Christ, and offers no prayer to any other being. The sum
of all that he knows or acknowledges of God, is concentrated
in Jesus of Nazareth alone. This is "the true God and our
Saviour, whom to know aright is eternal life." Such an assurance is as the blaze of a fresh revelation pouring its beam
upon the dazzled eye-sight, and the soul awakes to the experience of a new-born joy in contemplating the full orbed glorie
of the Eternal Deity as dwelling in him who dwelt in huma
flesh and who accomplished his earthly sojourn in the land o
Judea. The "root out of thy ground," becomes the "plant o
renown," and he who was "without form and comeliness,
becomes "fairer than the sons of men," his ineffable huma
beauties fading away into the inconceivable splendors of th
Godhead. Discarded for ever from his mind is that chaos
confusion which had hitherto beset him in his attempts to p
an intelligible sense upon the language of the creeds whi
represent God as subsisting in three persons, and Christ v'
tually in two.* The day-dawn of truth has at length rise
upon the obscurities and mystifications of his faith, and h
has ceased to be perplexed by the subtleties of the Trinita
rian or the bald negations of the Unitarian dogma. H

---

* "The reason why the Lord is not acknowledged when His Divine principle is
not acknowledged in His Human is, because in such case He is not regarded as
God, but only as a man, who is not able to save: but whereas it is still believ
from the Athanasian creed, that the Lord is the Son of God born from eternity
and His Divinity equal to the Divinity of the Father, and yet they separate Hi.
Human principle from His Divine, it follows, that they distinguish the Lord as it
were into two persons, which they call natures, so that the Lord is one as the Son
of God from eternity, and another as the Son of Mary; and whereas they thus
distinguish the Lord, no one can approach Him, except he will approach him as
one person, when he approaches Him as God, and as another person, when he
approaches Him as man. Such an idea concerning the Lord has been entertained from the first foundation of the church, as may appear from the writings
of the fathers, and afterwards from those of their descendants. This division of
the Lord in the church from its beginning, arose from the Word not being understood, for where the Father is mentioned by the Lord. it was believed to be the
Divine principle distinct from His Human, when, nevertheless, it manifestly
appears in Matthew and in Luke, that the Lord was conceived of the Essential
Divine principle which is called the Father, and consequently that that Essential
Divine principle is in His Human as the soul is in its body, and the soul and body
are one person: and what is wonderful, the Athanasian creed, which is universally received in the Christian world, teaches this in express terms, and yet scarce
any one attends to it therein; that they do not attend to it has been made evident
to me from this circumstance, that many with whom I have conversed after death,
both learned and unlearned, have said that they did not know it, but that they
thought of the Son of God from eternity as of a divine person above His Human,
sitting at the right hand of God the Father: likewise also that they had not attended to the words of the Lord which declared that the Father and He are One,
likewise that the Father is in Him and He in the Father From these considerations it may appear that the church has not acknowledged the Divine principle of
the Lord in His Human, from its beginning; and that this is what is signified by
the Lamb being slain from the foundation of the world."—*A. E.* 807.

beholds the clear development of the Unity and Trinity of the Divine Nature, harmonizing all the discords of the established symbols of Christendom, and leaving intact the literal and spiritual integrity of the inspired Word. The perception of this glorious truth cannot fail to constitute an era in the experience of every soul that is visited by it, and from its inmost depths it must echo forth the response of the believing Thomas, "My LORD and my God. !"

The testimony in proof of this grand position I have adduced in copious measure in the preceding Letters. But I must have a very inadequate idea of the tenacity with which fixed opinions are held, were I to suppose that all objections would yield at once even to *any* amount of evidence that might be adduced upon the subject. So inveterate is the grasp laid upon our faith by the sermon, the catechism, and the hymn-book, which have always embodied our theology, so reluctantly is wrung from us the concession that the church of the past has failed to seize the most fundamental of all truths, and that such long lines of holy synods, erudite fathers, " angelical doctors," godly divines, learned laymen, the piously simple, and "devout women and children not a few," have disappeared from the earth with their spiritual vision filmed by an error so gross—that we must be under an equal delusion to imagine, that such a result will be acquiesced in without an internal renitency of the most vigorous kind. It is a strong man armed who keeps the house that is invaded by the doctrines of the New Church. There is much more than the pride of opinion at stake. There are multitudinous *interests* involved, around which every form of partisan weaponry will rally and bristle to ward off the menacing peril. The breaking down of sects, the making bonfires of libraries, the acknowledgment of the heavenly mission of Swedenborg, are not among the pleasing objects of contemplation, and truth finds but a heartless welcome when its entrance turns so many occupants out of doors. But apart from this, I do not doubt that there are those who will be deterred from a ready assent to my previous conclusions, from a lingering but honest fear that they grow rather out of a certain vein of theosophic speculation than from the fair and unforced interpretation of the Sacred text. Upon this head, I am conscious of deep anxiety, for as the Divine Word is all in all with the man of the New Church, as it is with Swedenborg himself, we cannot give ear for a moment to any doctrinal proposition which will not stand the test of the Word legitimately expounded. In pursuance, therefore, of the intimation in my last, I resume the thread of my discussion at the point where it connects itself more especially with the Scriptural testimony.

That a veritable Trinity, under the threefold designation of Father, Son, and Holy Ghost, is to be recognized in the Divine nature, is a point, on which you and I can of course have no debate. The only question between us is, whether this Trinity is a Trinity of *persons* in any proper use of language. For myself, I have no idea of distinct persons which does not involve that of distinct consciousness, nor can I conceive that three distinct Divine consciousnesses should not constitute three distinct Divine Beings, however conjoined by unanimity of counsel; in other words, that they should not constitute three Gods. There is something, in fact, so palpable in this— it presses down with so much weight upon the general *consensus* of the human mind—that it is no wonder that the word *persons* has occasioned such trouble to theologians, that, like Prof. Stuart and others, they should have been anxious to get rid of it. But as this could not be decently effected, nothing has remained but to refine upon it, till it has become evacuated of its genuine import, while the ruling *idea* still underlies the doctrine, and works out its legitimate measure of mischief in the conceptions of Christendom. The consequence is, that while in controversy the Trinitarian will not allow himself to be bound to the vindication of the term, in practical operation the tenet still retains its efficiency and closes the mind against the access of all higher views. My object thus far has been to propound a higher view, and I see not why it should fail to command assent, provided it can be shown to be in accordance with the fairest construction of the oracles of truth: Let us then bring it to the test.

The doctrine is that the Father became incarnate in the person of the Son. But the Father is the Divine *esse* or Love inseparably united with the Divine *existere* or Truth. Now although all truth is a proceeding or evolution from love, yet the generating love is necessarily *in* the truth as its life and soul; consequently the Divine Love or the Father must have been *in* the Divine Truth or the Son, however it were that the Son was the object visibly manifested to the eyes of men. Accordingly Swedenborg says that although Jehovah, the Creator of the universe, descended as the Divine Truth and assumed the Human, in order to our redemption, yet that in so doing *he did not separate the Divine Good or Love.* "That God, although he descended as the Divine Truth, still did not separate the Divine Good, is evident from the conception, concerning which it is read, that 'The virtue of the Most High overshadowed Mary;' and by the virtue of the Most High is meant the Divine Good. The same is evident from the passages where he says that the Father is in Him, and He is in the Father; that all things of the Father are His; and that the Father and He are one; besides many others: by the *Father* is meant the Divine Good." Now I feel wholly at liberty to put the question, whether, if what I have previously affirmed of the constitution of the Divine nature be in itself true, it does not necessarily follow that this statement is also true, or in other words, that the Father was essentially though invisibly present in the Son, as the *esse* is always present in the *existere?* And was he not thus most veritably *one* with Him as the true Jehovah incarnate?* Let this be a little farther explained by our author.

"There are two things which make the essence of God, the Divine Love and the Divine Wisdom; or, what is the same, the Divine Good and the Divine Truth. These two in the Word are meant also by Jehovah God; by Jehovah, the Divine Love or the Divine Good, and by God, the Divine Wisdom or the Divine Truth; thence it is, that, in the Word, they are distinguished in various ways, and sometimes only Jehovah is named, and sometimes only God; for where it is treated of the Divine Good, there it is said Jehovah; and where of the Divine Truth, there God; and where of both, there Jehovah God. That Jehovah God descended as the Divine Truth, which is the Word, is evident in John, where are these words; 'In the beginning was the Word, and the Word was with God, and the Word was God. All things were made by Him, and without Him was nothing made that was made. And the Word became flesh, and dwelt amongst us,' (i. 1, 3, 14.)"—*T. C. R.* 85.

We will now take a class of passages represented by the following,—"I *came forth* from the Father and *came* into the world." "I *proceeded forth* and *came* from God; neither came I of myself, but he *sent* me;" "The Father loveth you, because ye have believed that I *came out from God.*" How is this language to be fairly understood? It must surely have a meaning consistent with what we know to be the nature of God. If we fix our thoughts upon the simple material humanity of our Lord, he *came forth* from the womb of the virgin by a nativity similar to that of other men. Does this exhaust the meaning of the text? If understood solely in this sense, how did he proceed and come forth from the Father otherwise than do all other men? May we not all say in the words of Job, "Did not he that made me in the womb, make him? And did

---

* "All who belong to the Christian Church, and are under the influence of light from heaven, see and discern the Divine Nature in the Lord Jesus Christ; but such as are not under the influence of the light from heaven, see and discern in him only the Human Nature; when nevertheless, the Divinity and the Humanity are so united in him as to make one person; for so he himself declares, "Father, all mine are thine, and thine are mine."—*D. N. J.* 285.

not one fashion us in the womb?" Is it not clear that something higher than mere natural nativity is here intended? What is it? "Who shall declare his generation?" Do you say that as he had no human father, it is an allusion to the miraculous conception? Even granting this, still the question is not answered. *What was it* that came forth from the Father? The body indeed was generated from the maternal substance, but the soul which animated the body was not from her, as the soul is evermore from the father. The soul, or inmost principle of our Lord, was from Jehovah himself, and therefore essentially divine. But as the divine essence is not divisible, it is impossible, I think, to conceive that Divinity could proceed *from* Divinity, except as Truth proceeds from Good, or the *existere* from the *esse.* Is any other kind of *proceeding* consistent with a just view of the intrinsic nature of Deity? Can we hesitate to assent to the truth of Swedenborg's remark, that "from the Divine Good, which is the Father, nothing can *proceed* or *come forth,* but what is Divine, and this which *proceeds* or *comes forth,* is the Divine Truth, which is the Son." As to any idea of a *proceeding* by the Son, or a *sending* by the Father, which implies a *local removal,* as when in this world an embassador is sent abroad to a foreign court, you will at once unite with me in rejecting it altogether as wholly inconsistent with the nature of the subject. As God is a Spirit, and as whatever is predicated of Him must consist with spiritual attributes, so the *proceeding forth* of the Son from the Father must indicate something congruous to the properties of such a Being. I submit it then to your decision, what else can be gathered from this language than that our Lord, as the Divine Truth, *proceeded* from the Father as the Divine Good; consequently, as these principles cannot subsist apart from each other, that there is a consistent sense in which, as Swedenborg says, the Lord, by means of the assumed Human, *sent himself* into the world. If it was Jehovah who became incarnate, and if in Jehovah is the eternal Father, how can this inference be avoided? Nor in fact is the direct Scriptural testimony very remote from this. (Zech. ii. 10, 11), "Sing and rejoice, O daughter of Zion; for lo, *I come,* and I *will dwell in the midst of thee,* saith the Lord (Jehovah); and many nations shall be joined to the Lord (Jehovah) in that day, and shall be my people; and I *will dwell in the midst of thee,* and thou shalt know that the Lord of Hosts *hath sent me* unto thee." Here it is clear that Jehovah, the Lord of Hosts, is both *sender* and *sent.*

Thus too when Jehovah says to Moses, "Behold, I send an angel before thee, to keep thee in the way, and to bring thee into the place which I have prepared. Beware of him, and obey his voice, provoke him not; for he will not pardon your transgressions: for my name is in him. But if thou shalt indeed obey his voice, and do all that I speak; then I will be an enemy unto thine enemies, and an adversary unto thine adversaries. For mine Angel shall go before thee, and bring thee in unto the Amorites, and the Hittites, and the Perizzites, and the Canaanites, and the Hivites, and the Jebusites; and I will cut them off;" we are not to conceive of the angel as any divine person separate from Jehovah, but merely as a medium through whom Jehovah's presence was manifested, as I have already had occasion to explain it. His sending an angel, was therefore sending Himself, for that it was the supreme Jehovah, in His own person, who conducted the chosen people from Egypt, is again and again affirmed in the sacred record. Whatever, then, be the idea attached to the term *sending* in this connexion, it *must* be such as to consist entirely with the established unity and unipersonality of the Divine nature; and if this language may be properly employed in reference to the manifestation of Jehovah through an angelic medium, with the same propriety may it be employed in reference to his manifestation through the medium of the assumed Humanity. It must inevitably be a *sending of himself* in either case. So, on a smaller scale, when a man writes and publishes a book, he may be said to *send* his thoughts into the world; but he really sends himself, because his affection and thought, which are in his book, are in fact himself.

Again, the language of our Lord in Luke, xi. 13, is so peculiar, that without assuming it as an indubitable proof of the doctrine I am now advocating, I still feel at liberty to refer to it as worthy of special notice in the present connexion; "If ye then being evil know how to give good gifts to your children, how much more shall your Heavenly Father give the Holy Spirit to them that ask him?" The original exhibits the reading, πόσῳ μᾶλλον ὁ Πατὴρ ὁ ἐξ οὐρανοῦ, *how much more shall the Father that (is) from heaven give, &c.* This form of appellation in reference to the Father, occurs nowhere else in the New Testament. There the usual phraseology is, ἐν οὐρανοῖς, *in heaven*, instead of ἐξ οὐρανοῦ, *from heaven*. Why is not the inference fair that this expression really conveys an allusion to the assumed Humanity in the person of the Saviour, who with the utmost propriety might be called the *Father* (the Divine Good) *from heaven*, and from whom also proceeds the Holy Spirit (or Divine Truth) here adverted to? The intimation need not be any less valid for being somewhat veiled. I am aware that the commentators are here also ready with their

glosses and evasions by which to render pointless every form
of speech that enforces the recognition of a new aspect of truth.
They remark that *ἰξ οὐρανοῦ from heaven*, is here equivalent,
to *οὐρανιὸς heavenly*, " as often elsewhere." But this " elsewhere"
I have not been able to find; on the contrary, I am persuaded that not a single instance, apart from the present, can
be adduced from Matthew to the Revelation, where the phrase
ἰξ οὐρανοῦ, does not fairly imply some kind of *descent* or *proceeding* from heaven, as truly so as in Paul's expression—
" The second man is the *Lord from heaven* (*Κυριος ἰξ οὐρανοῦ*)"
which is undoubtedly tantamount to *Jehovah from heaven*, and
this is in effect the same with the *Father from heaven* in the
passage before us, for who is the *Father from heaven*, i. e.
who descended from heaven, but Jehovah God, incarnated and
manifested in the person of the Son? And what other inference
is forced upon us than that of the real and essential identity
of the Father and the Son all the while underlying the apparent divarication and duality of the two? If it be intrinsically
true that the Father descended in the person of the Son, why
should it be deemed incredible that the fact is alluded to in the
passage before us?

The dominant idea conveyed under the term *proceeding*, in
its reference to our Lord, is so clearly set forth and illustrated
in the following paragraph that I do not hesitate to insert it.

"That to *go forth* is to be of it, or its own, is evident from what goes
before and from what follows, and also from the spiritual sense of that
expression, for to *go forth* or *to proceed* in that sense, is to present oneself before another in a form accommodated to him, thus to present
oneself the same only in another form; in this sense, *going forth* is
said of the Lord in John; 'Jesus said of himself, I *proceeded forth* and
came from God,' viii. 42. 'The Father loveth you, because ye have
loved me, and have believed that I *came forth* from God: I came forth
from the Father, and came into the world; again I leave the world,
and go to the Father. The disciples said, we believe that thou camest
forth from God,' xvi. 27, 28, 30. 'They have known truly that I *came
forth* from God,' xxvii. 8. For illustrating what is meant by *going forth*
or *proceeding*, the following cases may serve. It is said of truth, that
it goes forth or proceeds from good. when truth is the form of good,
or when truth is good in a form which the understanding can apprehend. It may also be said of the understanding, that it goes forth or
proceeds from the will, when the understanding is the will- formed, or
when it is the will in a form apperceivable to the internal sight. In
like manner concerning the thought which is of the understanding, it
may be said to go forth or proceed when it becomès speech, and concerning the will when it becomes action. Thought clothes itself in
another form when it becomes speech, but still it is the thought which
so goes forth or proceeds, for the words and sounds, which are put on,
are nothing but adjuncts, which make the thought to be accommodately apperceived: in like manner the will becomes another form

when it becomes action, but still it is the will which is presented in such a form; the gestures and motions, which are put on, are nothing but adjuncts, which make the will to appear and affect accommodately. It may also be said of the external man, that it goes forth or proceeds from the internal, yea substantially, because the external man is nothing else than the internal so formed, that it may act suitably in the world wherein it is. From these things it may be manifest, what going forth or proceeding is in the spiritual sense, namely, that when it is predicated of the Lord, it is the Divine formed as a man, thus accommodated to the perception of the believing; nevertheless each is one."—*A. C.* 5337.

In like manner we infer, by parity of reasoning, that our Lord's going to the Father was in fact no local removing of himself from our globe to some distant part of the universe, called heaven, but a simple *recession*, or *returning*, into his own essential divinity, notwithstanding that it was *in appearance* an ascension in the clouds of heaven.

I could fain hope that the Scriptural testimony now adduced has not been *suborned* to the purpose of establishing a fallacious tenet of theology. As nothing can be clearer than the doctrine of the Divine Unity, and yet nothing in your view and mine more explicit than that of our Lord's divinity, I have attempted so to present the subject, as to make the Scriptures consistent with themselves.* This must be done upon some ground, or the argument yielded to the Unitarians. The mere establishment of a Trinity will go but little way towards it; for if the alleged Trinity is such as to subvert the Unity, it can never stand the ordeal to which, in this age, every doctrine of the Bible will be and ought to be subjected. That such is indeed the effect of the current doctrine of a *Trinity of persons* is, I think, beyond doubt. The mind left to the freedom of reason rejects it as a gross paralogism. The Scriptural Trinity must of necessity be such that the predicates of what are termed the *different persons* must be seen to be strictly applicable to *one person,* and to one only. The recognition of two or more persons discloses a state of mind in which the *appearances of truth* have gained an ascendancy over the *reality of truth,* no unusual result from making the simple *letter* of the Word the ultimate appeal, and building the strongest confirmations upon it. "In the sense of the letter," says Swedenborg, "it appears as if another who is

---

* On the ground of the common doctrine I believe it is impossible to assign any adequate reason why Joseph might not have been our Lord's father as well as Mary his mother. If he possessed a human soul from a human parent, why might not that soul have been propagated according to the ordinary law of generation? That doctrine makes his Divinity to be derived solely from the *adjunction* of the Divine nature to the Human, and how could this result have been affected by his having a human father?

superior is meant by Jehovah, but such is the sense of the letter, that it distinguishes what the internal sense unites. There are several (things or principles) in the Lord, and all are Jehovah; thence it is that the sense of the letter distinguishes, whereas heaven never distinguishes, but acknowledges one God with a simple idea, nor any other than the Lord."* Nothing therefore adverse to our view can be inferred from the use of terms so distinctive as the personal pronouns *I* and *Thou*, for as the indubitable doctrine of the Divine Unity absolutely precludes any such *real* distinction of person, so I trust it will appear from the following extract, that the solution set forth makes ample provision for the use of such language without at all weakening the ground of the main position.

"Inasmuch as all and single things in heaven, and all and single things with man. yea, in universal nature, have relation to good and truth, therefore also the Lord's Divine is distinguished into Divine Good and Divine Truth, and the Divine Good of the Lord is called Father, and the Divine Truth, Son; but the Lord's Divine is nothing else but good, yea, Good Itself, and the Divine Truth is the Lord's Divine Good so appearing in heaven, or before the angels. The case herein is like that of the sun; the sun itself in its essence is nothing else but fire, and the light which thence appears is not in the sun, but from the sun. This is the arcanum which lies hid in the circumstance, that the Lord so often speaks of His Father as if distinct, and as it were another from Himself, and yet in other places asserts that He is one with Himself. This being so, and it being so evident from the Word, it is surprising that they do not, in the Christian world, as in heaven, acknowledge and adore the Lord alone, and thus one God; for they know and teach, that the whole Trine is in the Lord. That the Holy Spirit, who also is worshiped as a God distinct from the Son and the Father. is the holy of the spirit, or the holy principle which by spirits or angels proceeds from the Lord, that is, from His Divine Good by Divine Truth, will be shown elsewhere by the Lord's Divine mercy."—*A. C.* 3704.

The last sentence of the above reminds me that in order to render the argument complete it is necessary to exhibit the evidence that the Holy Spirit is no more to be considered a Divine *person* than the Son, while yet the term as truly denotes an Essential of the Divine nature as either that of Father or Son. In this as in every other part of the discussion I shall avail myself of the light shed upon the subject by Swedenborg.

* "They who are not of that church (the New Jerusalem), who are such as do not acknowledge the Divine principle in the Lord's Human, cannot have the understanding illustrated so as by virtue thereof to see whether a thing be true or not, but they see appearances of truth as genuine truths, and confirm them as genuine from the literal sense of the Word, notwithstanding most things in that sense are appearances, which, if confirmed as genuine truths, are falsified, and falsified truths are falses: these (persons), inasmuch as they cannot see truths from the light of truth, and so apprehend them in the understanding, are in an obscure, yea, in a blind faith concerning things to be believed, and a blind faith is like an eye which can see little or nothing; yea, a blind faith is not faith, but persuasion."—*A. E.* 597.

And, first, I remark that the Holy Spirit is the Divine Truth proceeding from our Lord's Divine Human subsequent to his glorification, and that it is in effect the Lord himself. The general position is thus stated.

"That the Divine Truth is the Lord Himself, is evident from the consideration, that whatsoever proceeds from any one is himself, as, what proceeds from man, while he speaks or acts, is from his will-principle and intellectual; and the will-principle and intellectual constitutes the life of man, thus the man himself; for man is not a man from the form of the face and body, but from the understanding of truth, and the will of good. Hence it may be manifest that what proceeds from the Lord is the Lord."—*A. C.* 9407.

"That the Comforter (*Paracletos*), or Holy Spirit, is Divine Truth proceeding from the Lord, manifestly appears, for it is said the Lord himself spake to them 'the truth,' and declared that, when he should go away, he would send the Comforter, 'the Spirit of Truth,' who should guide them 'into all truth,' and that he would not speak from himself, but from the Lord. And because Divine Truth proceeds from the human principle of the Lord glorified, and not immediately from his Divine itself, inasmuch as this was glorified in itself from eternity, it is therefore here said, 'The Holy Spirit was not yet, because that Jesus was not yet glorified.' It is greatly wondered at in heaven that they who compose the church do not know that the Holy Spirit, which is Divine Truth, proceeds from the human principle of the Lord, and not immediately from his Divine, when notwithstanding the doctrine received in the whole Christian world teaches that,—'As is the Father, so also is the Son, uncreate, infinite, eternal, omnipotent, God, Lord, neither of them is first or last, nor greatest or least. Christ is God and man: God from the nature of the Father, and man from the nature of the mother; but although he is God and man, yet nevertheless they are not two, but one Christ; he is one, not by changing the divinity into the humanity, but by the divinity receiving to itself the humanity. He is altogether one, not by a commixtion of two natures, but one person alone, because as the body and soul are one man, so God and man is one Christ.' This is from the creed of Athanasius. Now forasmuch as the divinity and humanity of the Lord are not two, but one person alone, and are united as the soul and body, it may be known that the Divine Proceeding which is called the Holy Spirit, goes forth and proceeds from his Divine principle by the Human, thus from the Divine Human, for nothing whatsoever can proceed from the body, unless as from the soul by the body, inasmuch as all the life of the body is from its soul. And because, as is the Father so is the Son, uncreate, infinite, eternal, omnipotent, God and Lord, and neither of them is first or last, nor greatest or least, it follows that the Divine Proceeding, which is called the Holy Spirit, proceeds from the Divinity itself of the Lord by his Humanity, and not from another Divinity, which is called the Father, for the Lord teaches that he and the Father are one, and that the Father is in him, and he in the Father. But the reason why most in the Christian world think otherwise in their hearts, and hence believe otherwise, the angels have said is grounded in this circumstance, that they think of the Human principle of the Lord as separate from his Divine, which nevertheless is contrary to the doctrine which teaches that the Divinity and Humanity of the Lord are not two persons, but one person alone, and united as soul and body. Inasmuch as the Divine Proceeding, which is Divine Truth, flows into man, both immediately and mediately, by angels and spirits, it is therefore believed that the Holy Spirit is a third person, distinct from the two who are called Father and Son; but I can assert, that no one in heaven knows any other Holy Divine Spirit, than the Divine Truth proceeding from the Lord."—*A. E.* 183.

At the risk of trespassing a little on your patience, I give another extract which has come before me since penning the foregoing.

"In the Doctrine of the New Jerusalem concerning the Lord, it has been shown, that God is one in person and in essence, that there is a trinity in Him, and that that God is the Lord; also, that His trinity is called Father, Son, and Holy Spirit, and that the Divine from whom all things are, is called the Father, the Divine Human, the Son, and the Divine proceeding, the Holy Spirit. Although the latter is called the Divine proceeding, yet no one knows why it is called proceeding: this is unknown, because it is also unknown that the Lord appears before the angels as a sun, and that heat, which in its essence is divine love, and light, which in its essence is divine wisdom, proceeds from that sun. These truths being unknown, it was impossible to know that the Divine proceeding was not divine by itself, and thus the Athanasian doctrine of the trinity declares, that there is one person of the Father, another of the Son, and another of the Holy Spirit: but when it is known that the Lord appears as a sun, a just idea may be had of the Divine proceeding, or the Holy Spirit, as being one with the Lord, yet proceeding from Him, as heat and light from the sun; which is the reason why the angels are in divine heat and divine light in the same proportion as they are in love and wisdom. No one who is ignorant that the Lord appears in the spiritual world as a sun, and that His Divine Spirit proceeds from Him in this manner, could ever know what is meant by proceeding, whether it only means communicating those things which are of the Father and the Son, or illuminating and teaching. Still, even in this case, there is no ground for enlightened reason to acknowledge the Divine proceeding as separately divine, and to call it God, and make a distinction, when it is known that God is one, and that He is omnipresent."—*D. L. & W.* 146.

This will doubtless suffice on this head, as it is less necessary to dwell upon the identity of the Holy Spirit with Jehovah, inasmuch as there will be comparatively little difficulty in admitting it, when once the identity of the Son with the Father is conceded. That the prevailing idea, in the Church, of the Holy Spirit is that of a *person* in some way proceeding from the Father rather than from the Son, is beyond question. This is conclusively met in one of Swedenborg's Memorable Relations where he was auditor to a discussion on this subject. One of the speakers says, " ' What then is the Holy Ghost mentioned in the writings of the evangelists and Paul, by whom so many learned men of the clergy, and particularly of our church,

rofess themselves to be guided? Who at this day in the Chris-
an world denies the Holy Ghost and his operation?' Upon
iis, one who sat on the second row of seats, turned himself,
nd said, 'The Holy Spirit is the divinity proceeding from
ehovah the Lord; you insist that the Holy Spirit is a person
y himself and a God by himself, but what is a person going
orth and proceeding from a person except it be operation going
orth and proceeding? One person cannot go forth and proceed
:om another through a third, but operation can. Or what is a
iod going forth and proceeding from a God, but divinity going
orth and proceeding? One God cannot go forth and proceed
rom another, and by another, but divinity can go forth and
roceed from one God. Is not the Divine Essence one and
ndivisible, and since the Divine Essence or the Divine Esse is
iod, is not God one and indivisible?' After hearing these
hings, they that sat on the seats came to this unanimous con-
lusion, that the Holy Ghost is not a person by itself, nor a God
y itself, but that it is the holy divine going forth and proceed-
ag from the one only omnipresent God, who is the Lord. To
his the angel who stood at the golden table, on which was the
Vord, said, 'It is well; we do not read in any part of the Old
'estament that the prophets spake the Word from the Holy
ipirit, but from Jehovah the Lord; and wherever the Holy
ipirit is mentioned in the New Testament, it signifies the pro-
eeding divinity, which is the divine that illustrates, teaches,
ivifies, reforms, and regenerates."—*A. R.* 962.

On the whole, I see not but that I am entitled to propose the
uestion, whether the view above presented of the *Divine Trin-
!y in Unity*, is not one that fairly meets the demands of the
aost rigid exegesis of the Scriptures, and, at the same time, of
he most enlightened reason? Does it not adequately har-
nonize all the discordant theories which have been offered on
he subject, and propose a common ground on which all can
aeet who receive the Old and New Testament as embodying
he inspired counsels of heaven, and constituting the infallible
ule of faith? While it dissolves in rational light the alleged
iystery hanging over the *manner* in which the Trinity exists,
; still leaves, without the attempt to penetrate it, the mystery
f the Divine Essence, of which we can only say that it *is*,
rhile it must for ever be incompetent to created beings to com-
rehend *what* it is. That the expose which I have attempted,
ests in great measure upon the asserted illumination of Swe-
enborg, cannot vacate the intrinsic evidence of truth accruing
o it from its obvious agreement with the genuine import of
icripture. You can never show that the claim which he pre-
ars is a mere nullity. There is nothing in the laws of the

human mind—nothing in the known order of the Divine Providential government of the world—which absolutely forbids the expectancy of such a mission as that with which he declares himself to have been invested. Nor can you say with any justice, that his advocates are following a mere *ignis fatuus* in embracing the doctrines he has announced. It is impossible for a fair mind to charge with absurdity a single extract that I have given, or to say that the credence yielded to their truth implies a mental weakness in their recipients. " These are not the words of him that hath a devil or is mad." Our calmest reason assents to his propositions from their self-evidencing power, nor have we the least fear that their soundness can be soundly impugned ; and it is upon internal testimony equally strong, that we receive all parts of his amazing disclosures. In regard to no feature of the system do we find the evidence less luminous or convincing. That it often contravenes established dogmas—that it brings against them the most emphatic charges of fallacy and falsity—is with us no argument of error, but rather the reverse. We should believe him less if he respected them more. We perceive that in all cases his principles and premises necessitate his conclusions, and we find too that his *principles,* as they are unassailable, never are assailed by opponents, but always the conclusions. In the present case the fundamental principle laid down is that of a necessary and eternal distinction between the *Esse* and *Existere* of the Divine nature. Is not this true ? What is the import of the sublime declaration, " I AM THAT I AM !" Is not this a synonim of JEHOVAH, and does it not imply the absolute and underived *Esseity* of the Most High ? What can be more pertinent to this point than the striking elucidations of Prof. Lewis in his chapter on the " Philosophy of the verb *To Be ?*" where he contends that ειμι, *I am,* " expresses *essential, eternal, necessary, self-existent, independent, uncaused essence or being ;*" and where too he says that it denotes " a general and most important proposition, namely, that the idea of *goodness* is not merely relative or accidental, or the result of the mind's generalization from outward facts, but an absolute and eternal verity ; that it has an absolute existence in the Divine Mind, and that there is a fixed foundation for the absolute, and not merely relative, nature of moral distinctions."—(*Plat. Theol.*, p. 171, 173). This is by no means remote from Swedenborg's incessant inculcation, that the Divine *esse* is the Divine Good, of which the Divine Truth is the *existere* in form. And what is the distinction in effect between the two, but that between ειμι, *to be,* and γινομαι *to become,* which Prof. Lewis has so clearly developed, and to which he justly attaches so much importance ?

But having already transcended the proper limits of a single letter, I forbear to enlarge upon the various aspects of the subject which invite discussion. Several points of interest to which I have hitherto barely alluded, will come before us here-after for fuller consideration, especially the grounds on which the idea of *disjunction* between the Father and the Son has established itself in the minds of most Christians. For the present, I conclude by presenting from Swedenborg, a kind of *resume* of the whole subject.

"That by the Father, when he is mentioned by the Lord, is under-stood the Divine Good which is in the Lord and from the Lord, is, because the Lord called the Divine principle which was in him from conception, his Father, and which was the *esse* of his life, to which Divine principle He united His Human, when he was in the world. That the Lord called this principle his Father, appears manifest from this circumstance, that he taught that he himself was one with the Father; as in John: 'I and my Father are one.' Again: 'Believe that the Father is in me, and I in Him.' Again: 'He that seeth me seeth him that sent me.' Again: 'If ye had known me, ye should have known my Father also; and from henceforth ye know him, and have seen him. Philip saith unto him, Lord, show us the Father. Jesus saith unto him, Have I been so long time with you, and yet hast thou not known me, Philip? he that hath seen me hath seen the Father; and how sayest thou then, show us the Father? Believest thou not that I am in the Father, and the Father in me? The Father that dwell-eth in me he doeth the works. Believe me, that I am in the Father, and the Father in me.' Again: 'If ye had known me, ye should have known my Father also.' Again: 'I am not alone, because the Father is with me.' Inasmuch as the Lord is one with the Father, therefore he also declares, that all things of the Father are his, and his are the Father's; that all things that the Father hath are his; that the Father hath given all things into the hand of the Son; and that all things are delivered to him by the Father; that no one knoweth the Son but the Father, nor any the Father except the Son; also, that no one hath seen the Father except the Son, who is in the bosom of the Father; that the Word was with God, that the Word was God, and that the Word was made flesh. From this latter passage it is also manifest that they are one, for it is said, that 'the Word was with God, and the Word was God.' It is plain, too, that the Human principle of the Lord was God, for it is said, 'and the Word was made flesh.' Inasmuch then as all things of the Father are also the Lord's, and inasmuch as he and the Father are one, therefore the Lord, when he ascended into heaven, said to his disciples, 'All power is given to me, in heaven and in earth;' by which he taught his disciples that they should approach him alone, because he alone can do all things; as he also said to them before, 'Without me ye can do nothing.' Hence it appears how these words are to be understood: 'I am the way, the truth, and the life; no man cometh unto the Father but by me;' namely, that the Father is approached when the Lord is approached. Amongst many other reasons why the Lord so often named the Father as another, was this, that by Father, in the internal or spiritual sense, is understood the Divine Good, and by Son, the Divine Truth, each in the Lord and from the Lord; for the Word is written by correspondences, and is thus adapted both for men and angels. The Father therefore is mentioned, that the Divine Good of the Lord may be perceived by the angels, who are principled in the spiritual sense of the Word; and the Son of God and the Son of Man are mentioned, that the Divine Truth in like manner may be perceived.

"To what has been said above, it is here to be added, as an appendix, that if it be assumed as doctrine, and acknowledged, that the Lord is one with the Father, and that his Human principle is Divine from the Divinity in himself, light will be seen in every particular of the Word; for what is assumed as doctrine, and acknowledged from doctrine, appears in light when the Word is read. The Lord also, from whom all light proceeds, and who has all power, enlightens those who are in this acknowledgment. But, on the other hand, if it be assumed and acknowledged as doctrine, that the Divine principle of the Father is another principle separate from that of the Lord, nothing will be seen in light in the Word; inasmuch as the man who is in that doctrine turns himself from one Divine being to another, and from the Divinity of the Lord, which he may see, which is effected by thought and faith, to a Divinity which he cannot see, for the Lord says: ' Ye have never heard his (the Father's) voice at any time, nor seen his form ;' and to believe in and love a Divine being, which cannot be thought of under any form, is impossible."—*A. E.* 200.   G. B.

(*To be Continued.*)

ARTICLE III.

THE CHARGES OF MISREPRESENTATION CONSIDERED.

There is one element which has hitherto mingled somewhat largely in our controversy with the Old Church, which all good men must necessarily deplore ;—We mean, the charges and counter-charges of mutual misrepresentation. Our object here will be to exhibit briefly some of the grounds on which our writers have charged our opponents with misrepresenting some of the New Church doctrines, and also the grounds by which, in rejoinder, they claim not to have misrepresented them. And we would premise, that in conducting any inquiry involving truths like the present, it is not only requisite that we put forth our views in a distinct and intelligible form, but our opponents must not overlook the fact, that it is equally important for them to bring to the subject minds possessing the proper moral and intellectual qualifications for carrying on such an inquiry. It is utterly impossible for any mind to possess itself of elevated moral truths, which comes to their primary consideration with a fixed determination against them. A man will never attain to the knowledge of divine truth, if he always persists in averting his eyes from it. On the contrary, it is absolutely necessary that he not only have no indisposition, but he must heartily strive to enter into the temple. He may rest assured that he can very easily fail to see correctly, and so remain outside, if he is thus disposed: No man will be convinced against his will. If he would apprehend the doctrines he must *strive* to do so, and come to the subject with a determination to seek as for hid treasures. He must endeavor to elevate his mind into the region in which these subjects, from their own nature, necessarily lie, and not try to drag down the truths to a level with himself. We do not at all subscribe to the current doctrine, that all abstruse, moral, and metaphysical subjects can be brought down to the comprehension of the common mind: that all transcendentalism is merely another set of names for very common objects. We do indeed hold that all minds may come fully to the apprehension of all such ideas; but it must be accomplished by bringing the mind, through the necessary culture, *up* to the region of the truths; and not by attempting to degrade the truths to a lower level. Such traduction in fact cannot be effected; for every time you translate it to a lower level, and clothe it in a less apt terminology, you abate somewhat of its original force; you dilute, and reduce it. Therefore the higher the fountain at which a man can fit himself to drink, the purer will be the waters he will imbibe; and this is not to be accomplished by mulishly *sagging back* in the harness, and refusing to go any further or faster than you are forced, but, on the contrary, is far more likely to be compassed by an *agonizing* effort to reach the goal. The Alpine valleys cannot be reached by attempting to bend the suns rays around the lofty peaks, but must wait for the earth itself to change its position before they can be faced up to the great luminary. What progress would ever have been made in any of the sciences, if every philosopher should resolutely set himself to discover as little, and to see as short a distance before him as possible? Instead of thirstingly grasping the hint, and making it yield him far more than would its mere literal import, had he banished it from his mind and thought no more of it, would Newton have deduced gravitation from the fall of an apple? Therefore we are willing to be understood in the outset, that the truths are of such a nature that, if a man *wishes*, he can continue to misapprehend, and to misrepresent, and still sustain himself apparently by literal quotations: just as it has been said that almost any doctrine could be sustained by quotations taken literally from the Bible. The system of New Church doctrines is a revelation which in these latter days has been vouchsafed to the sincere lovers of, and earnest searchers after, *more* of God's Truth. For those who have a sufficient supply already, and do not *want* any more, it is not intended; to them it is not addressed; it cannot enter into their comprehension. The promise, "*ye shall find,*" is coupled with the condition "*seek.*" For the *seekers*, then, after "more light" do we write, and for none else. We have the highest authority for affirming that the light *may* shine in the darkness, and the darkness comprehend it not.

We proceed to adduce some of the instances to which we have referred. Rev. Dr. Pond in his "Swedenborgianism Reviewed," says, "he (Swedenborg) teaches that the angels not only marry, but have children; *spiritual offspring*, of course." After the reader has gathered the impression likely to be received from the above language, let him read the following from Swedenborg. "The reason why marriages in the heavens are *without prolification*, and that in the place thereof there is experienced spiritual prolification, *which is that of love and wisdom*," &c., (or, *goods* and *truths.—C. L.* n. 52.) Again, when he refers to the subject in the work on *Heaven and Hell*, he says (n. 382), "Marriages in the heavens differ from marriages upon earth in this, that marriages on earth are also for the procreation of offspring, *but not in the heavens;* instead of that procreation, there is in the heavens a procreation of *good* and *truth*," &c. While considering this whole subject of spiritual marriages, and in all that both Swedenborg and our opponents say concerning Conjugial Love, &c., it should be borne in mind what is the definition we apply to the *term*, viz., that love truly conjugial originates in the marriage, so to speak, of *good* and *truth*, and refers to the union of two *minds*, joined together by a mutual conjunctive inclination; and not merely the external conjunction indicated by the marriage relation. This is a distinction which we fear some of those who have undertaken to "exhibit" our views have not taken much pains to make their readers acquainted with. The passage from Dr. Pond, is undoubtedly calculated to convey the impression that the offspring of the heavenly marriages were separate conscious existences. From this inference the apparently saving clause, "*spiritual offspring*, of course," does not redeem it in the minds of nine tenths of the unwary readers. Whereas it is evident from Swedenborg's language, that *he* was trying to convey directly the *opposite* impression. That such perverted views should get into the minds of those who merely run over his writings, in a hurried manner, for the express purpose of finding something to object to, is not perhaps to be wondered at: but that they should be gravely reiterated, after an explanation, by those whom we are bound to suppose are trying to do us justice, we confess does somewhat surprise us.

Again, Dr. Pond says, page 64, " The obvious sense of Scripture, that which strikes the eye and affects the heart of the common reader, is, in comparison, of small account, while the utmost importance is attached to certain hidden, spiritual, mystical senses ;" and in reply to Mr. Cabell's representation that this was not the case, he reiterates in his " Letter" that " this every reader of Swedenborg knows is the *exact* truth." We confess ourselves very much surprised that such a manner of treating such a subject should emanate from such a source. We subjoin some extracts from Swedenborg in relation to this subject.

" The reason why all strength, and all power are in the ultimates of divine truth, thus in the natural sense of the Word, which is the sense of the letter, is, because this sense is the continent of all the interior senses, namely, of the spiritual and celestial, spoken of above ; and since it is the continent, it is also the basis, and in the basis lies all strength ; for if things superior do not rest upon their basis, they fall down and are dissolved, as would be the case with the spiritual and celestial things of the Word if they did not rest upon the natural and literal sense, for this not only sustains the interior senses, but also contains them, wherefore the Word or divine truth, in this sense, is not only in its power, but also in its fulness."—*A. E.* 593.

" He who does not know how the case is, may conjecture, that the Word as to the literal sense is thus annihilated, that by reason that sense is not attended to in heaven. It is however to be noted, that the literal sense of the Word is in no ways annihilated thereby, but is rather confirmed, and that singular the words derive weight, and are holy, from the spiritual sense which is in them, inasmuch as the literal sense is the basis and fulcrum on which the spiritual sense leans, and to which it coheres in the closest conjunction, insomuch that there is not even an iota or apex, or little twirl in the letter of the Word, which does not contain in it a holy Divine principle, according to the words of the Lord in Matthew, ' Verily I say unto you, until heaven and earth pass, one iota shall not pass from the law, until all things be done.' "—*A. C.* 9349.

Numerous other passages might be quoted, from various portions of his writings where similar views are set forth, but sufficient has been adduced to show that one who would studiously do complete justice to the views of Swedenborg on this head, should word his expressions with more care.

The next charge we shall notice is, that we "reject nearly one half of the Bible as not having been written by inspiration ;" and in reply to Mr. Cabell's denial of it, Dr. Pond remarks, " I ascribe to the Bible, and to every part of it, *plenary* inspiration. I believe it to be the word of God." Now this last proposition has very much the appearance of asserting something which bears on the question ; such however is not the case, for the governing term in the proposition, needs a *definition.* What does Dr. P. mean by "*plenary inspiration?*" It is very well known that we use it in a very different sense from what he does. *We* call that *plenarily inspired,* which has the *internal sense* and none other. Now it would be precisely as proper for us to charge Dr. Pond with denying the "plenary inspiration" of the whole Bible, because he denies the existence of an internal sense, as for him to charge us with denying it to one portion. He does indeed deny the plenary inspiration of the whole Bible, as we understand that term.

So again as to a denial of "*future* or *general judgment,*" and nearly all the other charges, which our space will not at present allow us to specify, they are a mere *play upon words,* to which a negative or an affirmative may be true, as they shall be explained. The astronomer who teaches that the sun is in the centre of our system, and that day and night are caused by a revolution of the earth on its axis may, in some sense, a *literal* sense, be said to deny that the sun rises and sets, but in a higher and better sense, he does not deny it, but affirms it from a higher and more scientific point, and this is precisely what the New Church does in respect to the entire Christian scheme. Its denial is only apparent. It affirms all the truths from a higher point of view. It *turns the position* of all the old terminology, and necessitates a new set of definitions. The old words and phrases do not meet the exigencies of the new cases, and those who continue to use them as though they were *things,* will always find themselves at fault.

The question which we have endeavored to present, is not whether, by a dexterous use, or *mis*-use of words, our opponents can escape the charge of *falsehood* in the representation of our opinions; with *that* we do not intend to charge them; but whether, after all their fairness, they have succeeded in giving such an "exhibition" of our views, as they would be willing in return that we should put forth of theirs. We trust that every lover of truth will not decide hastily, but will particularly inquire; that he will not take the words of opponents, nor our own, in so important a matter as the "second coming," but that he will betake himself to the writings themselves to see what they *do* teach, and search diligently to see if what they teach be true.

W. B. H.

ARTICLE IV.

LETTERS TO A PERFECTIONIST.

LETTER I.

DEAR SIR,

You ask why I hold no longer to the doctrine of *sinless perfection;* my answer shall not be withheld. The sentiment that we become perfectly holy, and free from sin by the simple exercise of faith, and that too long before the birth of any genuine spirit of charity, is not philosophical; and when a little more closely canvassed, it will be found unscriptural. The deep seated depravity of the human race is such, that a process of reformation and regeneration must be equally as profound. Evil so firmly rooted needs a corresponding and long-enduring course of discipline, in order to its removal. Nor has it ever been, in the providence of God, that any one should undergo an instantaneous change, which should accomplish all the work.

A man's life is his ruling love. Hence the eradication at once of that love, would also destroy the life itself. It is seen therefore, that *progress* is the true mode of developing the good and the true in the human soul. We learn the truths of science by degrees. Our physical and mental vigor increase gradually. We come into existence by an extended course of development. Analogy then leads us to infer that we also are born into the heavenly life in like manner. Regeneration is progressive.

I am aware how you sustain the above mentioned doctrine. It is an offshoot from the commonly received dogma that we are justified by faith alone: which faith is generally referred to one simple exercise of mind. By being justified, you regard yourself freed from sin—insomuch that you "cannot sin."

You will doubtless admit that man by nature is in evil, and must be withdrawn from it in order to reformation. This renders necessary that each type of corruption with which a person is tainted, should be made manifest to him—so that he can discard it. So long as any species of evil does not appear, so long it will be held to and practised. Evils are therefore removed from us when we perceive them to be such, and reject them with our whole heart. Yet are they never wholly separated from us. Though ejected from the core of the being, they still remain—so to speak—in the shade of our life.

In noticing this part of the subject, I am forcibly reminded of the words of Swedenborg. "There are some men after

Ancient Church was lifeless, did the Ancient begin. Nor till
this second had ceased its ministry, did Moses give the Law.
And it was only when Judaism and the world had sunk to the
lowest abyss of apostacy, and the law proved utterly powerless to direct men into the way of life—and they could no more
hear the voices of angels—only then that Jehovah assumed our
humanity; and by effecting a judgment (John iii. 17–21; xii.
31, and xvi. 11), established the Christian Church. Would
you insist upon your Perfectionist notion that the consummation transpired when literal Jerusalem met its downfall? I
answer—Not so. The Lord announced when on earth, "Now
IS THE JUDGMENT." As was proclaimed by the prophet (Isaiah
xl. 3–11), "The voice of him that crieth in the wilderness,
Prepare ye the way of Jehovah, make strait in the desert a
highway for our God. Every valley shall be exalted, and
every mountain shall be made low; and the crooked shall be
made strait, and the rough places plain. And the glory of
Jehovah shall be revealed and all flesh shall see it together.
* * * * Oh, Zion! that bringest good tidings, get thee
up into the high mountain. Oh, Jerusalem! that bringest
good tidings, lift up thy voice with strength! lift it up! be not
afraid! say to the cities of Judah—Behold your God! Behold
the Lord Jehovah will come with strong hand, and his arms
shall rule for him! behold—his reward is with him, and his
work before him. He shall feed his flock like a shepherd," etc.

Will you point us to the text—"Verily, I say to you, This
generation shall not pass away till all these things be fulfil-
ed?" This hold is weaker than a reed. "*This generation,*"
evidently means the Jewish nation. And indeed they have
not passed away. But now that these things are in the ultimate stage of fulfilment, we behold the Jews adopting by
degrees Christian institutions, and merging their identity into
that of Christian nations. *It is so.* Analogy, consistency,
external evidence must compel you to admit this interpretation. The destruction of Jerusalem so far from being the precursor of the Second Advent, was the token to mankind that a
crisis had past in the interior world. So now the French and
other Revolutions which have shaken and are now agitating
all the world, are tokens of a catastrophe of similar character.
Your question, I anticipate, will be, when are we to expect it?
The laws of life require that the internal essence shall always
precede, and never follow the external manifestation. The
moral, scientific, and political revolutions in this outer sphere,
show conclusively that the end of the Christian Church—the
consummation and Last Judgment—have already past. A
skeleton of the old order remains to assure us of its former

in promoting morality. The constant doctrine of the Word is —*obedience from the heart.* A theology which neglects this important item, must necessarily gravitate into Antinomianism and immorality. And now, my dear sir, do you not think that the irreligion, the disorder, and licentiousness of Perfectionists, is directly attributable to their pertinacious adherence to the dogma of Justification by Faith alone? Standing in all the pride of self-intelligence, they refuse to be taught except in their own manner; and thus exclude a nobler, higher light. Can we expect otherwise than that they should sport with their own deceivings? I think not. Hence their abrogation of the moral law, and their characteristic practice of unwarrantably assailing the present regulations and institutions of society.

Bound up in the same bundle is the doctrine that the Devil is a self-existent being, uncreated by God, and of course not reasonably subject to his law. I shall not go at length into the examination of this notion. It was originated by the author's perusal of the theology of Zoroaster, and is Magian in its most important features. But the theory is immoral. It inculcates that a portion of the human race are by birth children of Satan, and legitimate enemies of God, the constant subjects of divine hatred. Thus is the character of the Lord made to appear odious, and the same hateful disposition becomes a necessary element in the character of your saints. Does not this account for the brutal ferocity of certain Perfectionist leaders? And while such ferocity is styled holy and Christian, does not the standard vary far, very far, from that of the Lord Jesus? Be candid, and you will admit it.

Reflect but for a moment, and you will see that the doctrine is irrational; I need not say unscriptural; for the Sacred Word nowhere ascribes eternity to the devil. Our standard of goodness must be that of our Divine Father, for he is independently good; but if the devil be co-equal in existence, he too must have his moral standard, and that must be proved evil, by adjudication from before a superior tribunal. No principle in ethics could admit God to possess that superiority. All would be summed up in these words: God is strongest, therefore he and his works are called good: were Satan stronger, goodness would have been ascribed to him.

Do you not see that Byron's Doge, would be amply sustained when he imputes an unforgiving temper to Heaven.

"Heaven says, forgive your enemies; does Heaven forgive its own? Is Satan yet restored from wrath eternal?"

Can you not readily perceive that evil in all its forms is self-destructive. Good is one, and always one with itself. While evil is often as antagonistical to evil as to good. This shows

not so much a *Diabolus Magnus* as it does, a host of discordant malicious spirits, which spoken of collectively are called
the Devil.

In concluding this epistle, let me entreat you utterly to put
away from your mind such degrading sentiments. Not only
do they give you dishonoring views of the Lord, but they tend
to injure your usefulness. It is impossible to love God and be
of service to your brethren, if bolstered up in a self-sufficient
unpractical holiness, founded on an unphilosophical theology,
and interwoven with a lawless theory of spiritual morality.
Such is Perfectionism.

LETTER II.

DEAR SIR,

I now propose to examine the other stronghold of Perfectionism—*the Second Coming of Christ.* I am well aware that
your brethren are not agreed upon the exact manner of that
Advent, and therefore I will endeavor to state the more prevalent opinion—using for authority a pamphlet published at
Putney, Vt., in 1840.

The Perfectionist doctrine is that the Lord made his second
appearance at the period when Jerusalem was overthrown.
At this time was consummated the judgment of this world.
Some hold that as the American Constitution is obligatory
upon all in this country who are born after its adoption, so
the adjudication referred to extended over all who come into
existence thereafter. But the tract just mentioned is the
advocate of a different interpretation. It teaches that the
Judgment consists of two acts—the first taking place at the
time when the Jews were dispersed—the other to occur within our own time. Each judgment to be attended with a
resurrection of righteous and wicked. In accordance with the
doctrine of Prof. Bush on the Millennium—he teaches that it
is a celestial period and has already past.

It is claimed that the Lord distinctly affirmed that he would
come while some of his auditors were yet alive; and that in
Matt. xxiv. 29–36, he distinctly set the time of his Advent.
Gibbon and the apostles are all cited as evidence that the
early Christian church expected the crisis at that time. The
premonitory signs are all said to have been given.

Nor is any New Churchman specially disposed to assert
that the apparent sense of the word unfolds a doctrine greatly
different. Although if we make the meaning too literal we

shall find the utter destruction of our universe as plainly asserted. (See the iii. ch. of 2 Peter.)

The real question at issue between Perfectionism and the New Church in this matter is the Internal Sense of the Word. Without going into an explicit argument, it is necessary to say something in proof of the existence and correctness of our mode of interpretation. "The natural Word such as it is in the world with Christians, inwardly in itself contains both the spiritual and celestial Word." Hence the Lord says, "The words that I speak unto you, they are *spirit*, and they are *life*." Paul also speaks of Jewish ceremonies as possessing an interior meaning, and styles portions of their Scripture, "types," and "allegory." The body of Jewish and Christian commentators, in consistency with this sentiment, settled their expositions by their views of the Internal Sense. The charge so often made against us of using a fanciful system of interpretation, falls to the ground. It would tell as forcibly against Jesus Christ, Paul, Barnabas, Origen and the ancient church, as against Swedenborg.

Indeed, sir, you admit yourself the same doctrine. When the prophet sings the glories of Zion and Jerusalem, you at once perceive that the church is meant by those epithets. For example read the account of the New Covenant, in the xxxi. ch. of Jeremiah. That alliance you understand to be made with the Church, whereas the language is, "I will make a new covenant with the house of Israel, and the house of Judah." And so Paul also construed the same scripture. The prophet goes on in the same connection to show the manner of the rebuilding of Jerusalem, and the account is carefully worded so as to be topographically correct. All this does not stumble you ; you adhere firmly to the inner sense. And if I were to assert that the literal construction would be more plausible, you would triumphantly refer me to the fact, that the city of Jerusalem was not rebuilt ; insisting that I must adopt the spiritual signification or discard the text.

Very well, I will now meet you upon your own ground. Turn over to your proof chapter, the xxiv. of Matthew. There you will find a form of speech similar to that of Isaiah. See the xiii. and xxxiv. ch. of that prophet ; also Ezekiel xxxii. and the ii. of Joel. To all this imagery let us apply the internal sense. The Son of Man is to come in the clouds of heaven. The clouds are the Word in its literal signification. Jerusalem must first be overthrown : i. e. the Church must be consummated and become barren, void of power and life. For no new dispensation of Truth can be introduced while the preceding one retains vitality and energy. Not till the Most

Ancient Church was lifeless, did the Ancient begin. Nor till
this second had ceased its ministry, did Moses give the Law.
And it was only when Judaism and the world had sunk to the
lowest abyss of apostacy, and the law proved utterly powerless to direct men into the way of life—and they could no more
hear the voices of angels—only then that Jehovah assumed our
humanity; and by effecting a judgment (John iii. 17–21 ; xii.
31, and xvi. 11), established the Christian Church. Would
you insist upon your Perfectionist notion that the consummation transpired when literal Jerusalem met its downfall? I
answer—Not so. The Lord announced when on earth, " Now
IS THE JUDGMENT." As was proclaimed by the prophet (Isaiah
xl. 3–11), " The voice of him that crieth in the wilderness,
Prepare ye the way of Jehovah, make strait in the desert a
highway for our God. Every valley shall be exalted, and
every mountain shall be made low ; and the crooked shall be
made strait, and the rough places plain. And the glory of
Jehovah shall be revealed and all flesh shall see it together.
    *   *   *   * Oh, Zion ! that bringest good tidings, get thee
up into the high mountain. Oh, Jerusalem ! that bringest
good tidings, lift up thy voice with strength ! lift it up ! be not
afraid ! say to the cities of Judah—Behold your God ! Behold
the Lord Jehovah will come with strong hand, and his arms
shall rule for him ! behold—his reward is with him, and his
work before him. He shall feed his flock like a shepherd," etc.
    Will you point us to the text—" Verily, I say to you, This
generation shall not pass away till all these things be fulfil-
ed ?" This hold is weaker than a reed. " *This generation*,"
evidently means the Jewish nation. And indeed they have
not passed away. But now that these things are in the ultimate stage of fulfilment, we behold the Jews adopting by
degrees Christian institutions, and merging their identity into
that of Christian nations. *It is so.* Analogy, consistency,
external evidence must compel you to admit this interpretation. The destruction of Jerusalem so far from being the precursor of the Second Advent, was the token to mankind that a
crisis had past in the interior world. So now the French and
other Revolutions which have shaken and are now agitating
all the world, are tokens of a catastrophe of similar character.
Your question, I anticipate, will be, when are we to expect it ?
The laws of life require that the internal essence shall always
precede, and never follow the external manifestation. The
moral, scientific, and political revolutions in this outer sphere,
show conclusively that the end of the Christian Church—the
consummation and Last Judgment—have already past. A
skeleton of the old order remains to assure us of its former

existence, but the *vita*, the *animus*, the glory have departed. A New Church is now in the earth. The kingdom of the Lord is set up. New Jerusalem descendeth from God out of heaven. The glory and crown of the ages. And now for a date to all these transactions. You must fix your mind upon that very period when the event took place in the unseen world. I mean the time when the Last Judgment was beheld and recorded by heaven's chosen Witness—the illustrious Harbinger of the New Era—Emanuel Swedenborg!

The Day-spring from on high hath indeed visited us! Behold! the Lord hath come in the clouds, the letter of his Word; and every eye, spiritually open, seeth him; and they also, who pierced him by falsifying his teachings; and the kindreds of the earth—the sensible ones in the churches around us—are wailing their spiritual death, because of Him. Wilt you not abandon your self-derived wisdom and pride of opinion, and in a spirit of true humbleness of soul cry out—*"Even so, Amen ?"* A home is ready for all who will enter through the gates into the heavenly city. Come, and take the water of life freely.

LETTER III.

DEAR SIR,

I will now review the subject of the Resurrection; related as it is to the doctrine of the Second Advent, and justification, it needs a correct understanding. And no body of people are in greater need of correct views of that subject, than our modern Perfectionists. Their peculiar doctrine of holiness teaches that the impulses of a sanctified will are to be obeyed. They therefore assume that they are themselves so completely regenerated, as to be empowered to follow their "spiritual instincts." These instincts have in many instances, impelled them to live in practice of the sentiment proclaimed eleven years since by one of their leaders; "When the will of God is done in earth as it is in heaven, there will be no marriage. God has placed a wall of partition between the male and female during the apostacy for good reasons, which will be broken down in the resurrection, for equally good reasons."

Far be it from me to slander your sect. I know many of you to be men of pure lives, and high moral sentiments. Still the looseness of your views concerning regeneration and discipline, the grossness of those sentiments touching the resurrection state, and the anarchical spirit so prevalent among you, must naturally induce a tendency toward subverting social

order. Your theology is impeached. Were I so disposed, I could
mention names, beginning from the commencement of your
denomination till the present time, forming a succession of
leaders and abettors of lewdness. As the last of that number,
common fame gives us the example of the self-styled leader of
New Haven Perfectionists. And you, as well as myself, have
very strong, unquestionable, reliable evidence that the report
is true. If this is the exterior, what is the *spirit* of your creed!
Avowing unbridled license to be the resurrection order, making
that resurrection a resuscitation of flesh and blood, and then
anticipating its approach by the practise of " cross-fellowship,"
or sanctified debauchery. I upbraid you not, but here is your
theology, *gone to seed*. In the example of the man who two
years since held up Swedenborg to odium and scorn for teaching pellicacy and concubinage in certain cases—behold the fruit!
 Now turn your attention to the belief of the New Church.
We adhere to the doctrine of our Illuminated Teacher, that the
spiritual body is a substance enveloping the spirit; not gross
and corporeal, but of an ethereal and electric nature.   Hence
like thought, it moves at will, over all space.   We thus agree
with Paul—"Flesh and blood cannot inherit the kingdom of
God—nor doth corruption inherit incorruption."
  We do not agree with Perfectionists in calling marriage the
" law of the apostasy." It is as old as God, for in him it exists;
the union of love and wisdom. It was in the earth before man
fell from purity. And we believe still farther, that it will exist
to all eternity.
  Again, do we agree with Paul—" Neither is the man (husband), without the woman (wife), nor the woman (wife), without the man (husband), in the Lord."   Here you will urge the
affirmation of the Lord—" In the resurrection they marry not."
The advocates of *Battle-Axism*, all use these texts to sanction
their unbridled obscene sports.   The Old Church too insist
upon these texts, to urge a loose conjugal fellowship, as they
believe that the relation is not indissoluble.   But we avow that
the meaning is wholly perverted.   The Lord only referred to
marriage in the gross libidinous sense in which the Jews regarded it. In the resurrection, the exterior, with its crassitude,
is laid aside, and the interior only holds sway.   Man is man,
and woman is woman, as completely from spiritual formation,
as from physical.   The primal law of being is that the two
shall form a nuptial pair.   In the male is the constitutional
predominance of the intellectual element, while affection cha-
racterizes the female.   These must of necessity each attract
its correspondent, and thus unison will be formed.   Thus is
the principle firmly fixed—" they are no more twain, but one.

What God hath joined together, let no one put asunder." God's work progresses, and needs no doing over again. If you call for a living witness, I refer you to the pages of "the Delights of Wisdom, concerning Conjugial Love," by Swedenborg.

But you object to summoning him as evidence. Why? His piety and high moral rectitude are proof that he would not willingly deceive us; his philosophy and theology are on a strictly Scriptural ground-work, and if we are to steer clear of vulgar hallucination, the extraordinary mental attainments of the gifted Swede are proof positive against such danger. The exigences of the times, the great crisis in the spiritual world which must lead to revolution in the natural, the dearth of sound doctrine and life in the Old Church, all called for the ministry of a human agent. Do you ask me for proof of this assumption? I refer you to the testimony of John Wesley. Such an agent was wanted to herald forth the New Dispensation. A man who was at home in all departments of genuine science, whose sanctity was proof against demoniacal attack, and who was adapted to the work. Such a man was EMANUEL SWEDENBORG.

In conclusion, I ask you to compare Perfectionism with the spiritual system of the New Church. The former bases itself upon the old dogmas of Calvinism, while in the latter, "all things are become new." The Father and the Son composing your Godhead, give place in our theology, to "one Lord," even Jesus Christ. Your Eternal Devil is out of our sight altogether. We know of no evil, but perverted goodness. We know no Father whose justice riots in the agony and death of his Son. To us God is Love, and he forgives all their trespasses. If any perish, it is their own choosing, not an arbitrary decree, nor the necessary result of a diabolical parentage. Man's moral agency, as free for good as for evil, is the constituent element of our whole system. You hold to a faith which is presumed to remove sin at once—and so virtually and actually covers the vilest enormities with the garb of holiness. In the New Church we know of no supreme principle but charity. Our moral code is to shun all evils because they are sins against God, and to do all good in our power as though holiness were our inherent nature, while we acknowledge that every good wish is from the Lord. Our highest good is always to co-operate with the one Jehovah.

I now close this correspondence. My object has not been to lay before you the body of the New Church Doctrine—abler pens have done that already—but to notice the distinctive tenets of your own system, and refute them by a fair presentation of the truth in a form adapted to the case. If I have succeeded, my end is gained. "Blessed are they that keep his commandments, that they may have a right to the tree of life, and enter in through the gates into the city. Make no war with the Lamb, he is the Lord of lords, and King of kings."

A. W.

SELECTIONS.

EXTRACTS FROM THE "CANONS, OR THE ENTIRE THEOLOGY OF THE NEW CHURCH."

A TRACT BY SWEDENBORG.

[A notice of the translation and speedy publication of this work, has already appeared in our pages. It is now nearly ready to be issued in a pamphlet of forty-eight pages. To a portion of our readers, some parts of it will not be new, as they have been re-printed in the New Jerusalem Magazine from the London Intellectual Repository. The ensuing pages, however, now appear in English for the first time. They will give the reader a fair idea of the character of the whole work, which is scarcely to be paralleled for the clear enunciation of principles and condensed vigor of style.]

Concerning the Divine Trinity.

1. That the idea of the common people concerning the Divine Trinity, is, that God the Father sits on high, and His Son at His right hand, and that they (together) send the Holy Spirit to men.

2. That the idea of the clergy in respect to the Trinity, is, that there are three persons, each of which is God and Lord, and that to the three there is one and the same essence.

3. That the idea of the wiser among the clergy, is, that there are three communicable properties or qualities, but, by three persons are understood such as are incommunicable.

4. That there is a Divine Trinity is clear from the Sacred Scripture and from reason.

5. That from a trinity of persons there inevitably follows a trinity of gods.

6. That if God is one, the Trinity of God becomes necessary, and thus the Trinity of person (not persons).

7. That the Trinity of God, which is also a Trinity of person, is from God incarnate, or Jesus Christ.

8. This is confirmed from the Sacred Scripture.

9. And also from reason, inasmuch as there is a trinity in every man.

10. That the Apostolic Church never thought of a trinity of persons, as appears from their Creed.

11. That a trinity of persons was first invented by the Nicene Council.

12. That it was admitted into the churches that arose after that time, and has been continued to the present day.

13. That the errors of that doctrine could not be corrected at any time previous to the present.

14. That a trinity of persons has inverted the whole church and falsified all and singular things pertaining to it.

15. That all say that it is beyond comprehension, and that the understanding is to be held captive under the obedience of faith. What is a son born from eternity ?

16. That in the Lord there is a Trinity, and in Trinity is Unity.

CHAPTER I.

That there is a Divine Trinity, to wit : the Father, the Son, and the Holy Spirit.

1. That the Unity of God is received and acknowledged throughout the whole world wherever there is religion and sound reason.

2. That therefore the Trinity of God could not have been known, for if it had been known, yea, if only declared, man would have thought that the Trinity of God implied a plurality of Gods, which both religion and sound reason abhor.

3. That therefore the Trinity of God could not have been known except from revelation, thus not except from the Word, nor could it have been received unless the Trinity of God were also the Unity of God, for otherwise it would be a contradiction which begets a nonentity.

4. That the Trinity of God did not actually exist before the Son of God, the Saviour of the world, was born, and that previously there was neither Unity in Trinity nor Trinity in Unity.

5. That the salvation of the human race depends upon the Trinity of God, which is at the same time Unity.

6. That by the Trinity of God, which is at the same time Unity, is understood the Divine Trinity in one person.

7. That the Lord, the Saviour of the world, taught that there was a
Divine Trinity, to wit: the Father, the Son, and the Spirit; for he
commanded the disciples to baptize in the name of the Father, of
the Son, and of the Holy Spirit; he said also that he would send to
them the Holy Spirit from the Father; he spake moreover very often
of the Father, and of himself as his Son, and breathed upon the disciples, saying, "Receive ye the Holy Spirit." Add to this, that when
Jesus was baptized in Jordan a voice came forth from the Father,
saying, "This is my beloved Son," and the Spirit appeared over him
in the form of a dove. The angel Gabriel said also to Mary, "The
Holy Spirit shall come upon thee, and the virtue of the Most High shall
overshadow thee, and the Holy which shall be born of thee shall be
called the Son of God." The Most High is God the Father. The
Apostles likewise in their epistles often name the Father, Son, and
Holy Spirit; and John in his first epistle says, "There are three that
bear record in heaven, the Father, the Word, and the Holy Spirit," etc.

CHAPTER II.

That those three, Father, Son, and Holy Spirit, are three Essentials
of one God, since they are one as Soul, Body, and
Operation with man are one.

1. That the Divine Trinity, which at the same time is Unity, can
by no means be comprehended by any one, unless (it be viewed) as
the Soul, Body, and proceeding Operation with man; consequently
unless the Divine Itself, which is called the Father, be considered as
the Soul, the Human, which is called the Son, as the Body of the Soul,
and the Holy Spirit as the proceeding Operation from both.

2. That therefore in the Christian Church it is every where acknowledged that in Christ, God and Man, that is, the Divine and Human,
are one person, as the soul and body in man. This is thus acknowledged from the Athanasian Creed.

3. Therefore he that apprehends the union of the soul and body
and the resulting operation, apprehends the Trinity, and at the same
time the Unity, of God in a kind of shadow.

4. That the rational man knows, or may know, that the soul of the
son is from the father, and that the soul clothes itself with a body in
the womb of the mother, and that afterwards all operation proceeds
from both.

5. That he who knows the union of the soul and body, knows or may

know, that the life of the soul is in the body, and thus that the life of the body is the life of the soul.

6. Consequently that the soul lives, and therefore feels and operates in the body and from the body, and that the body lives, feels, and operates from itself while still from the soul.

7. That the reason of this is, that all things of the soul are of the body, and all things of the body of the soul; from this and nothing else is their union.

8. That it is only an appearance that the soul operates separately, from itself through the body, while yet it operates in the body and from the body.

9. That from all this the rational man who knows the intercourse of the soul and the body may comprehend these words of the Lord, that the Father and He are one—that all things of the Father redound to Him—that the Father hath given all things into his hand—that as the Father works, so the Son also works—that he that sees and knows the Son, sees and knows the Father also—that they who are one in the Son are one in the Father—that no one hath seen the Father except the Son, who is in the bosom of the Father, and who hath brought him forth to view—that the Father is in the Son and the Son in the Father—that no one cometh to the Father except through the Son— that as the Father hath life in Himself, so he has given to the Son to have life in himself—that in Jesus Christ all the fulness the Divinity dwells bodily—besides many more. By the Son, in these passages, is meant the Human of the Father.

10. That from these things it follows, that the Divinity and the soul of the Son of God are not distinctly two, but one and the same. That the Son of God is the Human of God the Father, is fully shown above; for what else did Mary, the mother, bring forth than the Human in which was the Divine from the Father? Hence He was called from nativity the Son of God; for the angel Gabriel says to Mary, the Holy thing which shall be born of thee shall be called the Son of God, and the Holy which was born of Mary was the human in which was the Divine from the Father.

CHAPTER III.

That before the world was created there was no Trinity of God.

1. That God is one the Sacred Scripture teaches, and reason illustrated by the Lord sees it there and thence; but that God was triune before the world was created the Sacred Scripture does not teach, nor

does reason thence illustrated see. That it is said in David, "This day have I begotten thee," does not imply that it is from eternity, but in the fulness of time, for the future is present in God, thus also "to-day;" in like manner with that of Isaiah, "A child is born to us, a Son is given, whose name is God, Hero, the Father of eternity."

2. What rational mind, when it hears that before the creation of the world there were three Divine persons called Father, Son, and Holy Spirit, does not say within itself when thinking on the subject, What is meant by a Son's being born from God the Father from eternity? How could he be born? And what is the Holy Spirit proceeding from God the Father through the Son from eternity? And how could he proceed and become God by himself? Or how could a person beget a person from eternity, and both produce a person? Is not a person a person? How can three persons, of which each is God, be con-joined in one God, otherwise than in one person? And yet this is con-trary to theology, and that to this. How can the Divinity be distin-guished into three persons, and yet not into three Gods, when yet each person is God? How can the Divine essence, which is one, the same, and indivisible, fall into number, and consequently be divided or mul-tiplied? And how can three divine persons be together and take counsel with each other in the non-extense of space, such as was be-fore the world was created? How could three equalities themselves be produced from Jehovah God, who is One, and thence Sole, Infinite, Immense, Increate, Eternal, and Omnipotent? How can a trinity of persons be conceived of in the unity of God, and the unity of God in a trinity of persons?—besides that the idea of plurality destroys that of unity, and *vice versa*. It might perhaps have been possible for the Greeks and Romans to conceive of all their Gods, which were many, as being compacted solely by identity of essence into one God.

3. The rational mind, in revolving and investigating a Trinity of persons in the Godhead from eternity, might also ponder upon the question, of what use it could be for a Son to be born before the world was created, and for the Holy Spirit to go forth from the Father through the Son? Was there a use for three to consult how the universe should be created?—and thus that three should create it, when yet the universe was created by one God? Neither was there any occa-sion for the Son to redeem, since redemption was accomplished after the world was created in the fulness of time; nor for the Holy Spirit to sanctify, when as yet there were no men to be sanctified. If then there were those uses in the idea of God, still they were not realized before the creation of the world, but after it actually came into exist-ence; from which it follows, that a Trinity from eternity was not a

real Trinity, but an ideal (or potential) one, and still more so a Trinity of persons.

4. Who in the church, while reading the Athanasian Creed, can understand this, that it is of the Christian verity, that each person by himself is God, and yet that it is not lawful from the Catholic religion to name them Gods? Is not religion to such a man something else than truth, (when he holds) that three persons are from truth three Gods, but that from religion they are one God?

5. That a Trinity of persons in the Godhead before the world was created, never came into the mind of any one from the time of Adam down to the advent of the Lord, appears from the Word of the Old Testament and from the histories of the religion of the ancients. That neither did it come into the minds of the Apostles, as is evident from their writings in the Word. That it moreover came into the mind of no one in the Apostolic Church prior to the Council of Nice, as appears from the Apostles' Creed, in which no Son from eternity, but a Son born of the Virgin Mary, is mentioned. That a Trinity of persons is not only above reason, but against it; it is against reason that three persons should have created the universe; that there should have been three persons, and each person God, and yet not three Gods but one, and then three persons and not one person. Will not the future new church call this age of the old church benighted and barbarous, as worshiping three Gods? Equally irrational are the various inferences deduced from that Trinitarian dogma.

6. That a Trinity of persons existing in the Godhead from eternity, was first taught by the Nicene Council, as appears from the two Creeds, the Nicene and the Athanasian, and that it was afterwards received by the churches from that time onward to the present day, as the principal dogma—the head indeed of all doctrines. That there were two causes why this doctrine of the Trinity was propounded by the council of Nice; the first, that they knew not how otherwise to dissipate the scandals of Arius who denied the Divinity of the Lord; the other, that they did not understand what is said by the evangelist John, ch. i. 1, 2, 10, 14; ch. xvi. 22; ch. xvii. 5. How these things are to be understood may be seen above.

7. That the Divinity before the world was created was believed to consist, according to the Nicene council and the churches afterwards, of three persons of which each was God, and the second born from the first, and the third proceeding from the other two, is not only above comprehension, but contrary to it, and the faith of a paradox which does violence to the rational understanding. It is a faith in which there is not any thing of the church, but is rather a persuasive of the false, such as obtains among those who are insane in matters of

religion. Still we do not here affirm this religious insanity of those who fail to perceive things so contradictory and contrary to Sacred Scripture, and therefore yield their credence to them; consequently we do not affirm it of the council of Nice, and the subsequent churches, because they did not see (the repugnancy).

———

CHAPTER IV.

That the Trinity of God came into being after the world was created, and actually in the fulness of time, and then in God incarnate, who is the Lord, the Saviour Jesus Christ.

1. That the Trinity of God neither did nor could exist before the creation of the world, as also that there are three essentials of one person in God Man, from which the Trinity is predicated of God, has been shown above.

2. That God as the Word was to come into the world and to assume the human in the Virgin Mary, and that the Holy thence born was to be called the Son of the Most High, the Son of God, the Only Begotten, is known from the Old Word where it is predicted, and from the New where it is described.

3. Since therefore the Most High God, who is the Father, begot, through his Divine proceeding, which is the Holy Spirit, the human in the Virgin Mary, it follows that the human born from that conception is the Son, and the begetting Divine the Father, and that both are together the Lord, God, Saviour, Jesus Christ, God and Man.

4. It follows also that the Divine Truth, which is the Word, and in which is the Divine Good, was the seed from the Father from which the human was conceived; the soul is from the seed, and by the soul is the body.

5. For confirmation let this arcanum be related, that the spiritual origin of all human seed is Truth from Good, yet not Divine Truth from Divine Good in its own infinite and uncreated essence, but in its own finite and created form. See the "Delights of Wisdom concerning Conjugial Love," n. 220, 245.

6. It is known that the soul adjoins to itself a body which may serve it for operating uses, and that it afterwards conjoins itself to the body as it serves, and that too while yet the soul is of the body, and the body of the soul, and this is what is in effect implied in the Lord's words, that He is in the Father, and the Father in Him.

7. From these things it follows, that the Trinity of God came into being after the world was created, and then in God who is the Lord, the Saviour, Jesus Christ.

POETRY.

HUMILITY.

LINES SUGGESTED BY A PERSIAN FABLE.

‘ . . . High o'er the earth it hung,
A murky canopy, impending drear,
Till denser grown by gathering mists upraised,
And irretentive of its watery load,
The cloud, from out its treasury of rain,
A shining drop lets fall.　Downward amain,
Its height empyreal forsaking swift, ·
The tiny globe descends.　No drooping flower,
Sweet suppliant of the clouds, receives
Upon its leaves or petals parched, the drop;
But lo! self-rendered to its primal source,
The ocean's boundless bosom drinks it in.
And now commingling with the mighty waves,
And lost amid the grandeur of the scene,
The drop, not senseless, lay entranced in awe.
Diminutive at best, it now itself
Confessed of no dimensions or account,
Amidst the wastes unfathomed of the deep.
" How vast,"—to give its voiceless musings speech
How vast and limitless the sea!　How dread
The elemental roar!　What depths profound,
That mock the sounding plummet's scanty throw,
And yawn capacious of a continent!
What then am I, great parent Ocean, I,
Amidst the wide extension of thy dark domain!
An atom only, when aloft in air
Distinct and pendulous I hung, and now,
Upon thine awful mass of waters cast,
Minuter still, I'm dwindled to a mote.
Stupendous Ocean! on thy bosom broad,
Ten thousand thousand kindred atoms fall,
Untold when added, and unmissed when gone!
How sink I then to insignificance!
How less than nothing, when compared with thine,
My puny bulk, thou venerable main!
Fitly I feel—amidst the waste immense
Of waters circumfused—myself I feel

A viewless point amidst infinity.
In the wider range of being, then,
And in the vastness of thy handy-work,
Creation's Architect! Almighty Lord!
Who pour'dst the ocean from thy hollow hand,
And set yon azure vault the billows' bound,
Oh, I am nothing! All abashed, I shrink
Deep into conscious nothingness! My thoughts
Within the compass of my atom size
Retire, and find a sphere commensurate
And fit for one, just on the verge of things,
Whom scarce annihilation could make less."

Soliloquizing thus in humble strain,
The drop, meek offspring of the mighty deep,
Sunk gently downward—as the place is low
Humility still seeks—when all at once,
Conducted near by impulse not its own,
A shelly tenant of the ocean's realms,
Well deemed a strange artificer of gems,
Its craving jaws extending wide, absorbs
The musing particle. And now fast locked,
As in a casket rude but rich, the drop
Much loved of meekness-recompensing Heaven,
And precious as the tear of penitence,
Imbedded lies, reserved for other rest.
Long time imprisoned thus 'tis held secure
Within its living tenement, now borne,
A richer freight than sails the upper wave,
Among the coral caverns, Ocean's halls,
And now descending, undefiled itself,
Into the ooze and slimy bottom of the sea;
Till quickening Nature's magic powers at length,
And chemic virtues, unattained by man,
Begin to change the aqueous particles,
And by the secret process slow transformed,
The little cloud-drop ripens to a pearl!
Nor is it long ere man, rapacious man,
Whom thirst of gold doth make amphibious,
And tempt to rifle ocean, earth, and heaven,
Into the sea's abysses finds his way
And spoils its briny chambers of the gem!
An eastern diver, plunging deep, lays hold
Tenacious of the pearl's receptacle,

And brings the hidden treasure to the day.
No longer now a minion of the main,
But disenthralled and ushered to the light,
Through traffic's mazy course it takes its way.
Long, long the sport of fortune made, yet still
The care and favorite of the skies, it roams,
Till lodged at last in Persia's royal court,
Its wanderings end.

See meekness honored—on the kingly crown
Of Persia's monarch, glittering like a star,
Shines the resplendent Drop, the beauteous Pearl!

G. B.

MISCELLANY.

TO THE EDITOR OF THE NEW CHURCH REPOSITORY.

DEAR SIR,

Under the head of "Editorial Items," in your last number, you say, speaking of the Abstract of the Report of the Mich. & N. Ia. Association on Missionary duties, "we observe a very singular use of one or two extracts from the A. R. & A. E. 'It is not,' he says, 'lawful for any one to teach from the Word, nor consequently to be inaugurated into the Priesthood,' &c., 'unless he acknowledges that Doctrine, and swears to the belief and love thereof.'—(*A. R.* 606). But what Doctrine? Of whom is Swedenborg here speaking? Not of the true church, or of its doctrines or ordinances, but of the beast and his institutes which every adherent was compulsively forced to acknowledge on pain of being shut out from ecclesiastical dignities." Then after saying "The whole passage stands thus: 'And that no man might buy or sell save he that had the mark, or name of the beast or the number of his name,'" and giving a brief quotation of its meaning from Swedenborg, you remark, "Now we should hope that the Committee did not mean to imply by this, that the principles established in the Beast's Kingdom were to be the rule of proceeding in the Lord's New Church, and yet what else is to be inferred from the quotation of the passage in this connection?" &c. After which you make similar remarks on the quotation from A. E. 840, passing over the argument itself, together with its reasons and other corroborations, and ask, "Is there no way to prove the unlawfulness of Lay teaching but by an appeal to the statutes of the realm of Anti-Christ?" So happy a turn as this gives to the subject may be very convincing to some, but it does not seem to us that the objection meets the case. Is the mode of initiation or inauguration into an office, the same thing as the office itself, or the "principles" of the office ? *Forms* and *ceremonies* are much less likely to be changed than *opinions, or modes of belief.*

The first Christian Church, though of a lower order than the second, was not in its commencement in faith alone, or in false doctrines, and it does not appear that its ceremonial worship, or ecclesiastical government is ever rebuked or censured by Swedenborg—but he speaks of it not only as the orderly method which prevailed in the best states of the Church (as fixed in Correspondences), but also as remaining even unto this day. It does not follow therefore that because a Church is consummated as to every thing that is internally good and true that its *external* or *ceremonial forms* are all to be rejected as wrong. The argument might rather be, that the *Old Church* should itself discard these forms which no longer are the proper clothings of *its* internal state, and that the New Church should as necessarily put on either the same, or a very similar kind of external or outward observances. Thus the New Church does not reject the observances of the *Sabbath*, by *meetings for worship*, and *preaching ;* by *kneeling* in prayer ; by *standing* in singing, and by *sitting* in receiving instruction : nor does it reject the ordinances of *Baptism* and the *Holy Supper, because they continue to be practised in the Beast's Church.* Neither has it been thought necessary to depart from a similar mode of determining who are properly qualified for the office of its ministers, and the method of their "inauguration" to that which is practised in the realm of "Anti-Christ."

If the Doctrines of the Old Church were *true*, the mode of admission into its ministry as stated by E. S., we suppose would not be questioned ; why then should it be questioned for Doctrines that *are true ?* Though in the explication of the passage before us the doctrines were obviously false, yet, says Swedenborg, "the acknowledgment of them however *for truths and goods* is signified by giving and receiving a mark upon their right hand and upon their forehead. A mark signifies the sign of *acknowledgment*," *A. E.* 838—(whether true or false).

It may doubtless be a question *to what extent* the New Church may adopt these ceremonial forms, but surely it cannot be a question whether there should be *any form at all.* Because the New Church is a Spiritual Church, must it have no government, no laws, or rules of obedience ? If so, there must be more than an internal dictate of what is right, or we shall be continually exposed to the infestations of deceiving spirits ; and, subject as we are to such influences, we rather need legitimate restraints to prevent us from acting under their suggestions.

Surely others can tell as accurately as we can ourselves, whether we have that genuine light which we are seldom at a loss to believe we possess, and whether its diffusion will be for the good of others or not. Is it not better therefore modestly to wait (however full of light we may be), till the recognized authorities in the church to which we belong shall see it also, before we let it shine in the public assembly,—the solemn meeting,—or the House of God ?—See Rom. x. 15.

But you further say "we are greatly at a loss to perceive how the New Church is to be spread. or societies formed in many parts of our country, if men of zeal, wisdom, and ability are not considered as having competent authority from the Lord himself to declare His Truth as far as they are possessed of it, and desirous of living according to it."

Certainly we could not object to this, as it is the very highest ground we could assume, viz., "authority from the Lord Himself," but does not every Quaker spirit, every enthusiastic and fanatic preacher, de-dare this! He believes himself moved by the Holy Ghost, even in his wildest ravings. Surely then such an impression is not to be relied on alone, but the spirits should be tried to see whether they *are of God;* and in the absence of more immediate authority for this purpose, we might be well content to abide by such mediate instrumentality as is afforded us in this lower world; which is in the organized forms already provided, or which may hereafter be provided, for Church government.

And of what avail to us is our Convention and Association, if (whilst on the most republican principles laws are instituted and rules of action adopted), every protecting wall is to be thrown down and we yield to the promptings of our wills, fanned into ardor by congenial spirits?

Certainly within our Association, there need be no "loss to perceive how the New Church is to be spread" consistently with the mode recommended in the above Report.

Respectfully and sincerely, yours,
GEORGE FIELD.

—

REMARKS.

We insert the above with pleasure, and freely accord to our brother all the benefit which his position can claim from the considerations proposed. To us they are not conclusive, because we do not gather from Swedenborg that in his interpretation of the Apocalyptic oracles respecting the Beast, he has peculiar reference to the earlier and purer states of the Christian Church, but rather to its later periods subsequently to the Reformation, which indeed he expressly affirms. Moreover, the remarks fail to convince us, for the reason that the question is not merely a question of *form*, but of *institution* and *office*. The ground taken by the committee is of such importance in its bearings on the whole subject of the ministry, and the very nature and authority of the function itself, that it really needed the support of quotations direct, unequivocal, and emphatic. This demand is hardly answered by paragraphs that relate to a system whose evils and corruptions grew up in great measure out of an abuse and prostitution to the love of dominion of that very office which is the subject of debate.

As to the other points touched upon in the communication of Mr. F., it is difficult to say enough to satisfy one's self without saying too much to be agreeable to our readers. It does not, however, follow, to our minds, that the rejection of all order and government in the Church ensues as a necessary consequence of dissenting from the popular notions of the distinction between clergy and laity. The grand question is, whether the established order is truly divine order or human. This we do not regard as yet put beyond the bounds of debate, nor do the delusions of "Quaker spirits," &c. conclusively prove that every man's inalienable right to declare the truth which he esteems infinitely important to his fellow-creatures, is nullified by his coming into the

Christian Church, or that the judgment of others respecting his qualifications, is *necessarily* more correct than his own. We are no friends to disorder, but we deprecate such a stringency in the application of rules, as shall fetter the freedom of a love that would fain be governed by wisdom.

MEETING OF THE GENERAL CONVENTION.

The recent meeting of the Convention in Boston, is spoken of by those who were present, as one of great interest, distinguished by a spirit of fervent brotherly love, and an effort at conciliation and harmony in regard to all important measures. Among these, was a proposition for the union of the Ohio Association (late Western Convention), with the General Convention, on such conditions as should still leave in their own hands the management of all affairs strictly ecclesiastical. This was discussed at some length in an amicable manner, and the following resolution finally adopted : "Resolved, That the application of the Ohio Association and the report thereon of the committee to which the same was referred, together with the resolution just passed, be now referred to a committee of three clergymen and four laymen, who shall take into consideration our Rules and Recommendations, and correspond with the Ohio Association, or with individuals in their behalf, and with other bodies of the church in this country, with the view of arranging the reception of that Association into this Convention on grounds satisfactory to that Association, and as far as may be found proper, common to all the Associations and other bodies of the New Church which are, or shall become, members of this Convention ; And that this committee may sit during the recess, and report to the Convention at its next annual meeting." This resolution contemplates, we understand, the possibility that very important changes may be proposed in respect to the entire frame-work and economy of the Convention, as at present constituted.

ERRONEOUS TRANSLATION IN THE ARCANA.

In a recent reading of A. C. 10,135, we noticed the following passage,—"From these considerations it may now be manifest what is signified by morning, and what by evening ; but, let it be observed, that this morning involves also mid-day, and that evening involves also the *earliest dawn (diluculum).*" This should evidently be rendered *twilight,* as it is in the sentence immediately following ; "For when mention is made in the Word of morning and evening, in such case the whole day is meant, thus by morning also mid-day, and by evening also night or *twilight (diluculum).*" The error is so obvious, that we trust it may be corrected in future editions.

NOTICES OF BOOKS.

1.—THE DIVINE LAW OF THE TEN COMMANDMENTS EXPLAINED, *according to both its Literal and its Spiritual Sense, in a Series of Sermons; intended to show that they include the Chief Essentials of the True Christian Religion. To which are added Sermons on the Lord's Discourse with the Rich Man, whom he referred to the Commandments of the Decalogue: and on his subsequent Discourse with the Disciples.* By the REV. S. NOBLE, London, 1848, 8vo. pp.

The name attached to this volume as author, will at once stamp it in the estimation of most of our readers, as an extremely able and invaluable exposition of the doctrines which it proposes to elucidate and defend. Nor will the perusal disappoint the favorable pre-impressions with which it will be opened by every New Churchman. It takes up and discusses at length every one of the precepts of the Decalogue, first in the literal, and then in the spiritual sense; showing their application to life, and how far we may count upon the Divine assistance to enable us to keep them. In the exposition of the first, the reader will find an elaborate train of remark on the unity of the Divine Person, by whom the commandments are uttered, and the results on this head are confirmed by an able philological essay on the plural form of the Hebrew word for GOD (Elohim), which evinces the author's profound acquaintance with the literature of the subject. The same excellent vein discloses itself, in that portion of the volume which treats of our Lord's discourse with the rich young man of the Gospel, where he considers at large whether riches disqualify for Heaven, what kind of riches is meant, how what is impossible with man is possible with God, and how man is to forsake all his kindred and possessions and follow the Lord. We should be glad to hope there was encouragement enough for the sale of the work to warrant a reprint in this country, but we fear the time is not yet come when it can be considered a safe enterprize. Meantime the English edition may be ordered of Mr. Allen of this city, and of Mr. Clapp of Boston.

2.—A SERIES OF POSTHUMOUS PHILOSOPHICAL TRACTS *on the following subjects:* 1. *The Way to a Knowledge of the Soul.* 2. *The Red Blood.* 3. *The Animal Spirits.* 4. *Sensation, or the Passion of the Body.* 5. *The Origin and Propagation of the Soul.* 6. *Action.* 7. *Fragment on the Soul, and the Harmony between it and the Body, written in Latin before his Illumination, by* EMANUEL SWEDENBORG, *and translated by* J. J. G. WILKINSON; *Copied from the London Edition;* Boston, Otis Clapp, 1848. 8vo. pp. 40., price 12 1-2 cts.

It gives us great pleasure to announce the above as the commencement of a series of reprints, from the London editions, of the minor Scientific and Philosophical Works of Swedenborg. It would doubtless be more agreeable to the publisher, if the patronage were adequate, to be an agent of the London Society, and by a large sale, to be the means of increasing its funds so that we could promise ourselves still further issues from the mine of manuscripts which Swedenborg has left behind him. But it is useless to disguise the fact that the splendid style of printing, and the consequent high prices of the English editions, offers an insuperable obstacle in the way of the wide circulation of the works in this country. Yet there is a growing demand for them, and they ought, by some means, to be made generally accessible. Urged by this conviction, Mr. Clapp has been induced to supply the desideratum by reprinting these works at a reduced price, and yet in a very handsome style. The present work is even beautifully executed, and yet is sold at the extremely low price of 12 1-2 cts., less than one third the price of the English. So with the next contemplated issue, " The Philosophy of the Infinite, &c." The price we see is announced at 25 cts. a copy, whereas the English price of the same work, is $1,87, a vast reduction indeed. As nothing more could be desired on this score by purchasers, we earnestly hope that Mr. C. may find ample encouragement for prosecuting his begun enterprise. To give the reader a fuller idea of this, we subjoin his advertisement.

"It is in contemplation to publish, in this style, most, if not all of these great Works, written before his ILLUMINATION, or, *Opening of his Spiritual Sight.* In the writings of this great and good man, may be found the SEEDS, or PRINCIPLES, of much that is known in Science and Philosophy ; involving the Mineral, Vegetable, Animal, and Human kingdoms ; all of which are commended to the operation of our two essential powers, LIBERTY and RATIONALITY : hence, all are invited to become investigators, discoverers and improvers, of the extraordinary natural truths developed by Swedenborg.

"In the history of literature, there is probably no one, who has left behind him so complete a transcript of his external and internal experience as this Author; for nearly every state and process, from the beginning to the end of his long life, appear to be recorded. In his numerous works, we see various subjects in all stages of development, from nebula to system; from the commencement of incubation to the day of exclusion ; from the influent image of chaos, to the mature and conservative formality of creation. When all his Works are published, his *literary biography* will be one of the most perfect extant, reaching from his twentieth to his eighty-fourth year, and fraught with one continuous purpose, deeply interesting to every friend of human progress.

"NOTE. ' *The Philosophy of the Infinite,* or Outlines of a Philosophical Argument on the INFINITE, and the Final Cause of Creation, &c.,' is in progress, in a similar style, and will probably be ready for publication in a few weeks. PRICE, 25 CENTS: 5 COPIES FOR $1 : $15 PER HUNDRED."

3.—THE THEOLOGICAL AND LITERARY JOURNAL. *Edited by* DAVID N. LORD. *No.* 1. NEW-YORK : F. KNIGHT. Price $3 per annum.

This is a quarterly journal to be devoted mainly to the discussion of Prophecy. We have already made our readers somewhat acquainted with the peculiar views of Mr. Lord on the laws of symbolic interpretation. Though not attaining to the point of full accordance with the principles laid down by Swedenborg as a key for deciphering the literal enigmas of the prophetic Word, they are yet far in advance of those which have hitherto been propounded by other writers, and we shall watch with much interest the developments of a new school in Biblical interpretation. The principal articles in the present No. are—1. Introduction— Importance of a just understanding of the Prophetic Scriptures. 2. False methods that have prevailed of interpreting the Apocalypse. 3. Professor Stuart's Commentary on the Apocalypse. 4. The late Revolutions in Europe. These articles are all by the Editor, and are each of them distinguished by great ability and the most outspoken freedom of animadversion. His review of Prof. Stuart is fearfully scathing. He leaves neither root nor branch of the exegetical Upas which the Professor has planted and watered with so much care according to the best rules of German critical arboriculture. From the showing of Mr. L. there could not easily be a greater desecration of the sacred book than such a *quasi* commentary as that of Prof. S. The reviewer has in this department performed a work supplementary to that of Mr. Clissold in exposing the crudities and absurdities of the great mass of Apocalyptic interpreters, and thus evincing the indispensable need of a new and divinely endowed expounder of these dark oracles.

4.—Sermons, *Doctrinal, Miscellaneous, and Occasional.* By Thomas O. Prescott, Glasgow, 1848, 12mo. pp. 358. Price $1.

This is a beautiful volume just received from Glasgow, and for sale by O. Clapp of Boston, and J. Allen of this city. It will be a very acceptable memento to the friends of the author, and a very suitable work for reading in worshiping societies destitute of a pastor. The Doctrinal portion consists of ten sermons on the following subjects: 1. Doctrine concerning the Lord: His Assumption of the Humanity, His Work of Redemption, His Glorification. 2. Doctrine of the Trinity. 3. The Spiritual Sense of Scripture. 4. The Peculiar Character of the Literal Sense of Scripture. 5. The Nature of Heaven and Hell; with the origin of Evil. 6. The Nature of Spirit, and of the Spiritual Body. 7. The Resurrection. 8. The Necessity of Regeneration. 9. The Nature of Regeneration. 10. The Second Coming of the Lord. From the hasty glances which only we have thus far been enabled to bestow upon the Sermons, we are satisfied that the subjects are admirably treated, and we rejoice to think that so many able expositions of the Doctrines of the New Church are now being given to the world, as every new attempt of this kind will do something towards dissipating that dense cloud of delusion which has so long brooded over the mind of Christendom in regard to the real character of Swedenborg's theology. The time surely cannot be far distant when the prevailing church will awake to the conviction that it has something else to do in its controversy with New Churchmen, than to launch the shafts of ridicule at their faith in a crazy farrago of visions and dreams. The problem has yet to be solved how these wild reveries, as they are termed, should form part and parcel of a system of religious doctrines which constantly appeal to the Scriptures, fairly interpreted, as their standard of authority, and which have as much the air of sobriety as the systems of Calvin, Edwards, Wesley, or Dwight. But in this department there is doubtless much more coming. We have scarcely seen "the commencement of the beginning." A self-complacent theology may, for the present, look down with supercilious eye upon the assumptions of the New Church on the score of doctrine and interpretation, and class them with the ravings of Mormonism and the wildest heretical crudities, but it is impossible that a system presenting such a show of fair argument, and enlisting in its support such a number of calm, deliberate, and assured minds, can always remain under a cloud.

EDITORIAL ITEMS.

THE N. J. Magazine for June contains a caustic review of the work mentioned in a former No. of the Repository, entitled "The True Organization of the New Church, as indicated in the Writings of Emanuel Swedenborg, and demonstrated by Charles Fourier." With the general tone of the article, so far as it relates to the work in question, we have little fault to find. It points out very clearly what every New Churchman must regard as a huge falsification of the teachings of Swedenborg, in several most important particulars. But we have been grieved to see that the writer has not been content to confine his castigation to the prime offender. In the following paragraph he has seen fit to couple another enormity with that which he mainly feels himself called upon to denounce. "The book which we propose now to notice, is quite a systematic attempt to show an agreement or harmony between the doctrines of Swedenborg and those of Fourier. This is perhaps no more surprising than the efforts which have been made to show the connection between Mesmerism, and even the blasphemies of Andrew Jackson Davis, and the truths of the New Church. But whether more surprising or not, the present attempt is no less a signal failure than either of the others already alluded to. (By the "other" failure hinted at, allusion is had to "Tracts for the New Times, No. I," and to some articles that have appeared in the Harbinger.) Now on reading the above paragraph we have felt in nearly as much need as the King of Babylon, of some "shewer of hard sentences and dissolver of doubts," to interpret the purport of the insinuation conveyed so as to make it consistent at once with known facts and Christian motives. Our own powers are hardly adequate to the task. The intimation in respect to the "efforts made to show a connection between Mesmerism, &c. and the truths of the New Church" is too plain to be mistaken, but the *justice* of it, and especially the truth of the charge of "signal failure," is not quite so obvious. The reader will see that the question is simply a question of *facts*. We have written a work to show that the phenomena of Mesmerism, in certain of its forms,—phenomena which are widely admitted to be real both out of the New Church and in it—are capable of a satisfactory solution on the principles of psychology laid down by Swedenborg and confirmed by his experience in the spiritual world. If this be so, we have undoubtedly done what we aimed to do—shown that there is a connection between Mesmerism and the truths of the New Church, so far at least as those truths are identical with Swedenborg's disclosures. And we would ask if there is anything wrong in this? Is there any compromising or desecrating the doctrines of the Church in the attempt to show that those who receive them have a key which enables them to solve a very remarkable and astounding class of facts? Is there anything in such an attempt which *ought* to subject it to the stigma of being placed in the same category with the attempt to identify the revolting dogmas of the book in question with the pure and heavenly doctrines of the New Jerusalem? If not, why does the reviewer seek to involve it in the same odium? And what does he mean by speaking of the attempt adverted to as a "signal failure." Are not the Mesmeric phenomena facts? And is it not equally a fact that Swedenborg explains them? And is it not the whole drift of our work to establish this? Where then is the "failure?" Is this dealing fairly with the truth, to intimate a charge without adducing the grounds to sustain it? —to throw disparagement upon blameless efforts and yet withhold every consideration which can justify it?—But our offence has a still deeper dye. We have even presumed to attempt to show a connection between the blasphemies of A. J. Davis, and the truths of the New Church. Here also we plead guilty. We have had our share in the preparation and publication of a work expressly designed to show how those blasphemies, outrageous as they are, could be fully accounted for, on the ground of the revelations which Swedenborg has made to the world. We have thus, beyond all question, if our solution is sound, established a "connection" between the two. But assuredly the thought never entered our minds that our success in this matter would be a sin, or that we were likely to subject ourselves thereby either to the open or the covert censure of our brethren of the Church. We had not once imagined that a principle or a truth was virtually blasphemed by simply showing that it explained blasphemy. We should as soon have supposed that any one established an unhallowed connection between the doctrines of Christ and the blasphemies of demoniacs by barely asserting that His doctrines respecting the agency of evil spirits would account for their utterances. But the absurdity as well as the illiberality of these *hinted* charges is too palpable to be dwelt upon. Our friends of the Magazine must allow us to say, that this is a very weak and unworthy crusade in which they are engaged against the harmless aim of disclosing the laws of Mesmerism by applying to it the principles of the New Church philosophy. It is utterly impossible at this day to suppress the evidence of just such a *connection* between them as we have proposed to establish, and as no truth can injure any other truth, the members of the New Church have much more reason for gratitude than for grief that such a stupendous phenomenon as Mesmerism has been permitted at this crisis to make its appearance in the world. The tendencies to naturalism and sensualism are so immensely strong—the resisting power of New Church truths so relatively (not intrinsically) feeble—and all counteraction from any other source so well nigh a nonentity—that we cannot but admire the wisdom of the Divine Providence in the development of an order of facts so well calculated to serve as a useful ally in breaking up the despotism of the senses, and proclaiming through unconscious but eloquent organs a spiritual world and a deathless destiny. That evils, perversions, and abuses may attend the manifestations of this strange power is true and much to be deplored, but they cannot stifle the inferences which reflecting men will still draw from the facts, and those inferences are in the main favorable to the claims of our doctrines. They procure for them a hearing from many an ear that would otherwise be turned away in inexorable aversion. They prompt inquiry in quarters never reached by the voice of the preacher or the visitation of the tract. And we should probably be not a little surprised could we know how large a portion of the present receivers of the doctrines of Swedenborg would be compelled to recognize the facts of Mesmerism as among the first occasions of their attention being turned to the subject. But the evidence of the truth drawn from this source has gradually given way in their minds to that which is higher and brighter, and like the Samaritans who first believed in the Lord from the report of the women who met Him at the well, but afterwards from what they themselves saw and heard, so with these persons, the assurance begotten by this kind of testimony dies away before that arising from a deeper knowledge of the system. The Mesmeric torch was of service in guiding their gropings through under-ground passages, but it may be thrown away as they emerge into sunlight. Our task in the above explanation, so far as it has put us in an attitude of protest against the tone of the reviewer's remark, has been an unpleasant one. But if the Magazine persists in making a false issue in this matter, we must persist in making a true one, and a true issue is simply an issue of *facts.*

A recent number of the Boston "Christian World" (a Unitarian paper) has an editorial article which breathes the anticipation of new movemen in the sectarian circles. " It would not surprise us if there should be a coaliti on the part of the seceders from the extreme liberality of Unitarianism and extreme liberality of Orthodoxy. Present tendencies are all in favor of such amalgamation. There is another movement under way, which is an earne we think, of a better day to the church. We refer to a manifest revival of t doctrine of the *pre-existence of Christ.* Let this doctrine be once preached in t fulness of gospel revelation, and a new life and light and joy would be sh abroad over the land. Notwithstanding this sublime doctrine has been kept ou of sight by Unitarian ministers, it has been gradually working its way into th minds and hearts of the people of that faith, and will ultimately prevail through out all the churches. We have written in no spirit of boasting; but merely t express the convictions of one, who has been for years anxiously watching th phases of the religious community, and hoping for the deliverance of the churc from all sectarian uncharitableness. It will not be possible to go back to the da of the Westminster Catechism, or to the platforms of later formularies of beli The march is onward. Progress is the watchword; and no earthly power, conclave of bishops, or presbyters, or councils, ot conferences, can stem the curren of conscientious investigation now going on." The New Churchman will of course look with interest upon any such developments as the editor of the " World" sees to be " casting their shadows before." When the Unitarians shall begin in earnest to consider the doctrine of the " pre-existence of Christ," we shall encourage ourselves in the hope that the question will soon assume in their minds its proper form—" the pre-existence of God"—and in this form it can be a question no longer. What idea can the mind attach to the words " pre-existence of Christ?" In what nature, state, or character did he exist before he was born of the virgin, except that of the Divine Humanity which was from everlasting, or of the Word which was made flesh? But was not this Word the absolute and eternal Jehovah? Are not our arguments on that score in the " Letters to a Trinitarian" entitled to attention? We venture on the whole to suggest that if our Unitarian friends are firmly fixed in their rejection of the doctrine of the supreme and exclusive Divinity of our Lord Jesus Christ, they had better retain their present position and not advance to the perilous ground of the " pre-existence," for once upon this ground they will find it impossible to arrest their steps. Meantime we humbly submit it to their consideration whether a view of the Divine nature which asserts a Trinity, while utterly discarding the tri-personal dogma, does not in fact vacate the force of their chief objection against the orthodox theology on this head.

THE

NEW CHURCH REPOSITORY

AND

MONTHLY REVIEW.

| Vol. 1. | AUGUST, 1848. | No. 8. |

ORIGINAL PAPERS.

ARTICLE I.

THE DOCTRINE OF FORMS.

In Part Third of the Economy of the Animal Kingdom, Swedenborg has given an exposition of the Doctrine of Forms, which, we believe, as yet remains untranslated into English. We had hoped to see a translation by some one well qualified to give a precise and elegant version worthy of the original.

We shall not attempt what we deem ourselves incapable of performing sufficiently well. The work of translation we leave to others. We shall, however, attempt to give an exposition of the Doctrine as we have learned it, following the original more or less closely as we may deem proper; and at the same time illustrating and confirming it by such examples and suggestions as may present themselves to our mind.

In the first place it may be well to understand what is the signification of the term "form" and the term "figure."

Form is the essential determination, or the determinate fluxion, of parts, points, substances and forces. Thus we have a form of motion, a form of modification, and a form of substances. We cannot conceive of form without at the same time having the idea of a fluxion.

Figure is the limit of extension, or the boundary of such fluxion, that is, the termination of such essential determination. Or figure may be otherwise denominated external form.

Figure or external form is an image or likeness of internal
form. Yet the converse does not hold true; for we may cut
away the angles, and shape the planes of a cube into the
figure of a sphere; yet the internal form or essential determinations, as well as the interior qualities, remain unchanged.
Yet from unchanged figure we may learn the quality of the
form: as from the countenance we may recognize the character of the soul.

THE ANGULAR FORM.

The Angular is the most imperfect, as well as the ultimate.
of forms. It consists of angles and interjacent planes, is composed of lines merely rectilinear, which are otherwise determined than uniformly to a common centre; as may be seen
in triangles, quadrangles and all other forms known to plane
geometry. If from assumed points in the planes of such forms
we demit lines perpendicularly, then such lines will not converge to a fixed centre, but will be parallel to, or continually
intersect each other. In the circle or sphere all the lines falling from the periphery or superficies are concentrated in one
point; and if we desire by external force or pressure to reduce it permanently to an angular form, all its determinations
must undergo a mutation, so that the lines converging to its
centre must remove themselves therefrom, to other points out
of the centre, and intersect others falling perpendicularly from
other rectilinear planes; otherwise the circle or sphere will
resume its own form.

Thus it appears that in these forms, the determinations are
opposite, or more or less contrary, falling upon and intersecting each other more or less obliquely or directly, and since in
each intersection and coming together, there is a cessation of
progression, a termination of fluxion, and an extinguishment
of forces; it follows that such forms are in their very nature
unsuited to continued motion: but are on the contrary the
very forms of rest and inertia. Yet not from the concourse of
perpendicular lines alone arises a high degree of rest within
the internal compages of a body, but also within many forms
where they mutually oppose each other; for in external appearance they are similarly angular: that is, constructed of
planes and angles, since such as is the essential determination
such is the limit, or what amounts to the same thing; such as
is the form such is the figure which is the limit of extension.
Also as many as are the angles so many are the causes of
obstruction; and as many the planes, so many the causes of
coherence.

The angular forms cannot be rotated upon an axis, much less about a centre, which they do not possess. Angles and points hinder, delay; and planes, if conformable, unite and conjoin. Thus every angular form is to be conceived as intrinsically consisting of mere trigons, or cubes; altogether as in effigy in the larger mass into which they coalesce when many of them are mutually applied to each other, for then they cannot be moved about unless all contiguous ones yield their places.

Therefore these forms are the most imperfect, and subject to the force of inertia; wherefore they are properly earthy and identical with those termed saline, acid, alkaline, urinous, sulphurous, nitrous and vitriolic.

The plane triangle, among planes; or the trigon or tetraedron among solids, is the first and simple of angular forms—to which the compound forms refer themselves, and to which they reduce themselves, when resolved into their simplest elements. The equiangular, or equilateral triangle is the most perfect, and the scalene triangle the most imperfect. The quadrangular plane, and the solid octohaedron are the second, in order, of angular forms, being immediately composed of the former. The equiangular and equilateral quadrangle is the most perfect of such forms. The more imperfect are parallelograms, rhomboides, trapeziums, with unequal angles and sides. To these succeed polygons and multilaterals, which are similarly regular and irregular; and hence more perfect and imperfect; the latter of which exceed all computation. Thus we have genera and species of angular forms.

From all which it follows, that the first angular forms are exceedingly minute tetraedrons and octohaedrons, and may be deemed the elements, primitive entities, or principles, of saline, acid and sulphurous substances. All these with their compounds are so many hard and inert corpuscles, immoveable among themselves without the assistance of fluids; properly heavy, material, extended, and figured; of themselves fixed and fixing; inexpansible and unelastic, cold, tempering the fluidity and heat of active forms in various modes; but best fitted for forming various compositions. Without these neither the earth, the vegetable or animal kingdom, in a word, the world, such as it is, could exist. These minute forms affect with so great variety the senses of taste and smell, and properly constitute that part of animals, which we call the body; and they are such as fall within the province of the sciences of Geometry, Trigonometry, Physics, and Chemistry.

The Circular or Spherical Form is proximately superior to the angular, divested of the angles and planes of the latter. It may be termed a form infinitely angular, with a perpetual plane. It is a likeness of what is perpetual and infinite, relatively to what, in the angular, is finite. What is perpetual, is also a One—thus there are not many angles, nor many planes, for in the circular form there is one common angle, and one common plane. This is also a natural consequence, when a volume of angular forms are forced to rotate about their axis, and similarly when they are exposed to the action of surrounding flames, then, the angles being cut off, the forms become round, and adapted to a rotary motion among themselves; and the longer the motion continues, and greater the velocity and force with which they are carried round, the more do they assume the extrinsic form of the perfect sphere and are liberated from the form of inertia.

Yet there still remains something rectilinear in the circular form, for there are as many right lines demitted perpendicularly from the periphery, as there are semi-diameters or radii.

Hence it follows that this form is the veriest of motion itself, and that it possesses the greatest power of resisting, and in its nature is most constantly permanent and unchanging; and likewise when consociated with angular forms is most aptly accommodated to all kinds of compositions.

That the spherical is the very form of motion itself follows, from the consideration that it is devoid of angles and planes, for resistance is in proportion to the angles; and the coherence, to the planes. Many spheres or globes in one volume and confined in a given space are most freely and easily rotated upon their axes: one does not move another from its place, neither touch the other except in the least and similar point, and instantly after contact it returns to and revolves in its own plane.

Therefore angular forms, moved and turned among themselves, are turned by the force of motion alone, are rounded by the abscission of angles, and are adapted to an axillary motion among their associates.

The spherical forms most readily gyrate upon any axis whatever, for there are as many axes as diameters; but gyrate not about a centre, unless the rectilinear directions are changed into circular, and a spiral determination exist; for in the more perfect forms of motion there is both an axillary and central motion, upon which depends the nature of fluidity, undulation and modification. The smoother the superficies, the better fitted for continued motion ; and the rougher, the less suited ; so that there may be forms of motion more perfect and imperfect. The determination of the lines, also within the circle or sphere conspires to the same thing, for this is the genuine form of motion ; since the semi-diameters fall perpendicularly from every point of the periphery together into one and a common centre ; nor at any other point of their course do they mutually fall upon each other, as in the angular forms, wherein the oppositions are in proportion to the points ; and the causes of inertia, which are perpetual and infinite, to the oppositions. From the concourse of the determinations in one centre, it follows that axillary gyration is suited to the very form of motion itself; for without the centre nothing impedes, so that it may not revolve and each diameter represent an axis. That the diameter represents an axis not only follows because one diameter may differ from another, and that one, always in its place, represents an axis; but also because the spherical form may be considered as consisting purely of concentric circles from its ultimate periphery to its centre.

That the spherical form affords the greatest power of resistance against every impetus and external assault whatever appears from this; that all lines, as so many radii, run together in one common point, in which is singular and all absolute opposition, so that one cannot be moved from its place unless others are moved at the same time ; the forces are thus conjoined, one regarding the safety of the other lest it be destroyed. This is the cause of resistance in the sperical form which escapes less than those having more centres, between which the determinations are divided—as in the ellipse, having two centres, and in other curves in which there are more ; for the relation of centres to periphery from which perpendiculars fall, is what measures the degree of resistance. In the circle the relation of all the lines, or if for lines we substitute forces, then of all the forces, is to one centre in which all concur to every given kind of opposition; for in this centre every line respects another as diametrically opposite, others obliquely, and others at every conceivable obliquity. Wherefore it is said that nothing is more inert, hard, resisting and cold than the centre of this form. Hence it follows generally, that the spherical forms in their essence are most constantly permanent, however their modes are varied, for the determination of one line is most similar to that of the others ; neither can it be changed unless all are simultaneously changed, and lest that should occur one regards the safety of all, and all of each ; for each one respects the universal state of its form, from a centre, and in a manner contemplates it, so that it is sensible of whatever happens to other of its associates.

If it be supposed that the essential determinations in the circle or sphere do not consist of lines or radii, or hard corpuscles, but of innumerable lesser spherules; and that in these are those still smaller; and that the more interior they are, the more perfect the forms; then it will follow that the whole sphere composed thus in order of smaller ones included, will possess the highest elasticity, that its superficies will yield to every assault and impetus. For if the lesser sphericles are most yielding, then the larger complex or totality of the smaller must possess a similar power of yielding, or an elastic virtue. Now suppose that the spherical forms are most constant in their essential determinations, it will follow that from no accidental cause, as pressure from without, can possibly reduce it from its own proper form into another; much less change it into an angular form; but in proportion as they are urged or pressed upon they will be compressed to a less diameter, or dimensions, and when the compressing force is removed, they will relapse into their primitive expansion. Thus the variation of their modes consists in this, that they suffer themselves to be forced into a lesser spherical sphere, but not into an oval form. Thus they correspond to every ratio of the assailing forces; and under the least impulse react as they are acted upon: for in proportion as the sphericles are constricted, do they become hard and resisting, even until they produce a resistance corresponding to the action of the extrinsic forms; which is a consequence of the law, that nowhere is there anything more inert, hard, and resisting than in the centre of the spherical form, and this in proportion to the distance from the centre. That the atmospheric particles are such forms appears from experiments upon air.

The spherical forms associated with the angular are exactly accommodated to all kinds of compositions, as appears from this; that the primitive parts of salts, sulphurs, and minerals, are not simply angular forms, but are mediate between angular and circular; for there are as many minute trigons and octohedrons, with their sides excavated exactly in conformity with the convexity of spherical particles, as there are particles of water, to which they can thus be mutually applied, and conveniently united into a larger corpuscle. This would be otherwise if their sides were unexcavated planes.

For a full development of this theory, see the Author's "Principles of Chemistry," where this, and his theory of Chrystalization are tested on geometrical principles.

Moreover, the circular or spherical form is the measure, and

form of all angular forms and thus in sort their universal
type and complex, for angular forms and figures cannot be
measured without the aid of the circle, and much less subjected to calculation.

It follows from this that the spherical form is a perpetual
angle and infinite plane ; and that it gives a perpetual and
infinite law to the changeable and finite ; and thus it adjudicates upon its quantities and qualities.

There are genera and species of circular and spherical
forms, varying in perfection ; thus there are elliptical, cycloidal, parobolic, and hyperbolic forms besides others, as well
geometrical as arithmetical.   Their determinations are not to
one, but to more or less fixed centres; and their directions are
not wholly opposite but flow together upon a certain line or
plane, so that they are less perfect than the simply circular,
but more perfect than the angular forms.

We suppose that all curves and surfaces whose co-ordinates
are rectilinear, and are referable to rectangular axes, primarily—whose element lies in one plane or is a single curvalim,
and whose equation is, in its degree, limited by the conditions
of the curve—belong properly to this class of forms.   Perhaps
this class should not be limited by the latter two conditions ;
if we refer its co-ordinates and determinations necessarily to
rectangular axes.

THE SPIRAL FORM.

The Spiral Form is the next in degree above the circular,
and is anterior and more perfect than it.   Its determinations
do not flow in continuous concentric circles ; nor through
right lines to a common centre ; but through continuous spires
to and upon a certain circular form, holding the place of a
centre ; with associated endeavor they flow ; around such
circular superficies they continue or endeavor to continue their
fluxions ; and from which superficies they respect the centre
of its sphere by radii, as in the perfect circle..

Thus in this form there is again something perpetual and
infinite compared with the circular ; as in the latter compared
with the angular form ; for the spire is a sort of perpetual
circular fluxion ; from any part of the superficies which is the
limit of its fluxion ; by perpetual winding spirals unto some
lesser sphere holding the place of a centre : so that each spire
is as well a circle as a semi-diameter ; or it represents both

inued around a medium, or a certain central globe, it follows
hat as a necessary consequence, there will arise a spiral
yration, but it will be otherwise if the fluxions are terminated
n a centre.

It also follows that the spiral form is in its essence more
onstantly permanent than the circular : for the more perfect
he forms the greater their constancy, since they approach to
he perfection of primitive nature ; wherefore also with the
reater difficulty do they undergo essential mutation, but the
ore easily accidental mutations ; for the faculty of under-
oing the latter is the perfection of their nature.   That these
orms may undergo essential mutations appears from this, that
here are genera and species of these forms; but when they
ave once suffered such mutation with increased difficulty are
hey restored to their primitive perfection ; for the more diffi-
ult the reduction ; likewise the more difficult the return, so
hat into forms still superior they are incapable of being re-
tored or elevated.   There are, of these forms, genera and
pecies perfect and imperfect, to express which, terms and
ymbols are wanting, for this form rises above the common
pprehension, because above the common geometry ; its lines
nd circles, in the fastnesses of which it is placed.

The spires of this form may be termed circular, elliptical,
arabolic, &c.; according to the nature of the spire, for its
entral globe or nucleus assumes one of the forms just named
ccording to the nature of the spires of this form.

In the mean time, this form is very obvious and conspicu-
us in nature and her kingdoms, for whatever has a circular
orm owes it to this form.   In this spiral form flow the parts
nd volumes of the ether, and by it they represent their modi-
cations.   In such manner also flow and are represented the
uxions and modifications of the parts and volumes of the
urer blood, as well as the medullary and nervous fibres in
he living body.   They also conspicuously occur in the vege-
able and animal kingdoms.

We have thus followed our Author through three degrees
f forms, the angular, the circular, and the spiral ; these suc-
eeding and arising from each other, as offspring and parents,
s effects and causes.   Before proceeding to the higher forms,
olding their places so much above the ken of the senses, we
ill for a while contemplate those to which we have already
een introduced and unravel if possible some of their latent

qualities, for if we mistake not we shall find many hidden secrets among the graceful sinuosities of the spiral form.

In order to represent to ourselves these forms, and the relations they really sustain to each other, let us in the first place suppose a body, our Earth for instance, at rest, its axillary and orbital motions having ceased ; then a body falling to its centre, or towards its surface in the direction of the centre, under the action of one force, or as many forces as can be reduced to one resultant, will flow or move along a right line : and several bodies falling under the same conditions will likewise describe right lines, and their determinations will be such as properly belong to the angular form.

Let us again suppose that a body, instead of moving towards the centre in a right line, moves around the axis at an equal distance from it.

Then such a body describes a form simply circular.

All parts of the earth situate out of the axis of rotation and revolving around it describe such a form, when we contemplate the axillary motion without reference to the orbital motion.

Two forces are necessary in such a case ; and however many the forces, if their resultant is a circular motion, they may be reduced to two.

The equation of the curve is referable to rectangular axes : and the curve being of single curvature may be deemed to lie in one plane.

In the simple circle the forces act at right angles to each other, with constant intensities.

If we now suppose the direction and intensities of the two forces to vary according to a given law or conditions, there will result curves of other genera or species as the case may be, yet properly belohging to the degree of circular forms provided the co-ordinates of those curves are right lines, and are referred most appropriately to rectangular axes.

All the conic sections find their place here. No person we suppose will have any difficulty in forming a correct idea of the angular and circular forms ; for we are busied with them in all our occupations, but in approaching the spiral form we must fix our attention, for here we approach unexplored labyrynths.

Let us again contemplate the earth as having an axillary motion only, and at the same time suppose a body is falling conformably towards its centre ; that is, falling in such a manner that, to a person moving with the earth, it will *appear to fall in a right line*, as a body does falling under the action of the force of gravity.

The body thus falling, although it *appears to fall in a right line, yet in truth, instead thereof, describes a spiral line.* So we affirm that all bodies so falling to the earth, or to other revolving bodies, actually move along spiral paths, although the appearance is otherwise ; except when the body falls in the line of the axis of rotation.

The spiral will vary in kind according to the relations of the central and rotary forces, and according to the direction of the motions in reference to the centre of gravity or of force.

If the body move in a plane passing through the centre of force and perpendicular to the axis of rotation, then the spiral path described by the body will lie in one plane, and if the central velocity be in arithmetical proportion to the velocity of rotation, then the curve will be simply spiral.

If the central velocity vary as the square of the velocity of rotation, the latter being uniform ; then the moving body will describe a *parabolic spiral.*

If the direction of the central force lie between the equator and the axis, the moving body will describe a curve of double curvature, and may be conceived as moving spirally upon the surface of a cone, whose apex is at the centre of force, and whose semi-base subtends an angle equal to the complement of latitude of the moving body.

Such then, are the motions of all bodies falling conformably to another rotating body, according to a law founded upon the relation of the central and rotating velocities.

The motion of the body moving between the equator and the pole or axis, as above instanced, describes a spiral cone and is similar to the fluxion of the ether in the polar cones of the earth's vortex. The curvature is double and is the result of at least three forces.

If instead of referring the spiral curve to axes simply circular, we refer them to any curve belonging to the degree of circulars, or what is the same thing, if the rotating surface be elliptical, parabolic, &c. we shall obtain various genera and species of spiral curves.

Since then bodies falling to the earth in apparent right lines, really move in spiral curves ; do not likewise rays of light, the undulations of the ethereal medium, when coming from without, or from the heavenly bodies, move in similar curves ? Is it not necessary they should so move in order to act harmoniously with the earth's rotation ?

And further, may not all the phenomena of the polarization of light be due to spiral motions of the etheral medium? We have no doubt, that all such phenomena can be explained on such an hypothesis. The facts stated in the following paragraph taken from Somerville's "Connection of the Physical Sciences," sec. 22, go very far in our opinion to establish such an hypothesis.

"Professor Airy in a very profound and able paper published in the Cambridge Transactions, has proved that all the different kinds of polarized light are obtained from rock crystal. When polarized light is transmitted through the axis of a crystal of quartz, in the emergent ray the *particles of ether move in a circular helix,* and when it is transmitted obliquely, so as to form an angle with the axis of the prism. *the particles of ether move in an elliptical helix;* the ellipticity increasing with the obliquity of the incident ray, so that when the incident ray falls perpendicularly to the axis the particles of ether move in straight lines. Thus the quartz exhibits every variety of elliptical polarization."

From these facts it seems to be entirely clear that the forces active in the formation of quartz crystals, and those active during the passage of light through the crystal, act in spiral curves.

Space will not permit us to pursue this interesting subject further. We will only inquire how far the *magnetic power of the solar beam* may be due to the action of spiral forces.

In order to obtain a clear idea of the three degrees of forms already discussed, and of their mutual relations let us briefly recapitulate.

The angular form has one force,—right lines, properly referable to a point.

The circular form has two forces, curved lines, single curvature, properly referable to rectangular axis, or angular forms.

The spiral form has three forces—lines double curvature, in general—properly referable to circular axis or curves.

The angular may be considered as possessing one dimension —length; the circular two dimensions, length and breadth; and the spiral curve, three dimensions, length, breadth and thickness.

Thus the forces, dimensions and powers increase, *pari passu,* with the ascent of the degrees. The passage from one degree to another is not as from more to less, or an arithmetical progression, but is as cause to effect; the simple to the compound; the prior to the posterior. The degrees are discrete. When we compare the circular to the angular and the spiral to the circular forms, we consider the circle as consisting of an infinite number of angles, and the spiral as consisting of an infinite number of circular elements or axes. Thus these degrees, considered mathematically, are to each other in the

ratio of infinity ; and their relations fall under the province of
the calculus of infinites.

W. H. B.

(To be Continued.)

ARTICLE II.

LETTERS TO A TRINITARIAN.

LETTER VIII.

THE GLORIFICATION.

DEAR SIR,

THE course of the present discussion up to this point has
been mainly devoted to the attempt to unfold the true constitution of our Lord's person, both before and after the advent,
and to develope the grounds on which the New Church holds
to a Trinity in the Divine nature, while at the same time most
strenuously rejecting the Tripersonality which that doctrine
has been supposed to involve. I have endeavored to show
that a Divine Humanity pertains essentially to Jehovah, and
that in the Incarnation this Divine Humanity "passed from
first principles to last." On no other grounds do we hold such
an incarnation to be possible, and that, consequently, the prevalent doctrine of Christendom, by ignoring the fact of such a
Divine Humanity, does in effect deny the fundamental verity
of the incarnation, and substitute for it the fallacy of the simple
adjunction of the Divine to the Human nature. This is the
inevitable issue of ascribing to our Lord a human soul as well
as a human body derived from the virgin mother. Let it be
understood, on the other hand, that the inmost element of our
Lord's being was, by conception, from the Father, and therefore, as the Divine essence is indivisible, was the Father Himself, and we have a clear and consistent enunciation of the
doctrine of Christ's Divinity, without the least invasion of the
great truth of the absolute Unity of the Godhead. We behold
God and man united in Him in one person, and the key afforded us, on this view, for a rational explication of the various and
sometimes apparently conflicting texts of Scripture bearing
upon the subject.

With such a presentation of the grand theme before us, it is at least sufficiently curious to contemplate in juxtaposition with it the following extract from Professor Norton's "Statement of Reasons," in which he unequivocally denies the possibility of the truth of such a doctrine as Swedenborg has proposed.

"With the doctrine of the Trinity, is connected that of the HYPOSTATIC UNION, as it is called, or *the doctrine of the union of the divine and human natures in Christ, in such a manner that these two natures constitute but one person.* But this doctrine may be almost said to have pre-eminence in incredibility above that of the Trinity itself. The latter can be no object of belief when regarded in connexion with that of the Divine Unity ; for these two doctrines directly contradict each other. But the former, without reference to any other doctrine, does in itself involve propositions as clearly self-contradictory, as any which it is in the power of language to express. It teaches, that Christ is both God and man. The proposition is very plain and intelligible. The words, *God* and *man*, are among those which are in most common use, and the meaning of which is best defined and understood. There cannot (as with regard to the terms employed in stating the doctrine of the Trinity) be any controversy about the sense in which they are used in this proposition, or, in other words, about the ideas which they are intended to express. And we perceive that these ideas are wholly incompatible with each oher. Our idea of God is of an infinite being ; our idea of man is of a finite being ; and we perceive that the same being cannot be both infinite and finite. There is nothing clear in language, no proposition of any sort can be affirmed to be true, if we cannot affirm this to be true,—that it is impossible that the same being should be finite and infinite ; or, in other words, that it is impossible that the same being should be man and God. If the doctrine were not familiar to us, we should revolt from it, as shocking every feeling of reverence toward God ;—and it would appear to us, at the same time, as mere an absurdity as can be presented to the understanding. No words can be more destitute of meaning, *so far as they are intended to convey a proposition which the mind is capable of admitting*, than such language as we sometimes find used, in which Christ is declared to be at once the Creator of the universe, and a man of sorrows ; God omniscient and omnipotent, and a feeble man of imperfect knowledge.

"The doctrine of the Trinity, then, and that of the union of two natures in Christ, are doctrines, which, when fairly understood, it is impossible, from the nature of the human mind, should be believed. They involve manifest contradictions, and no man can believe what he perceives to be a contradiction. In what has been already said, I have not been bringing arguments to disprove these doctrines ; I have merely been showing that they are intrinsically incapable of any proof whatever ; for a contradiction cannot be proved ;—that they are of such a character, that it is impossible to bring arguments in their support, and unnecessary to adduce arguments against them."—*Norton's Statement of Reasons*, p. 17–19, 22.

You will see from this that it is not possible to array two distinct exhibitions of Christian doctrine in more direct antagonism with each other than is done by the citation of this passage in connexion with the scope of my previous reasonings. To what extent the author will be admitted as an accredited expounder of Unitarian sentiments, I know not; but yourself and my other readers must judge on which side the truth lies, if the inspired oracles are to be the standard of faith; and also whether there is any intermediate ground on which the Lord's essential Divinity can be safely made to rest. For myself, I see none. If the doctrine of Swedenborg on that head is not the true doctrine, I despair of finding it either in the Bible or out of it, and I should despair too of successfully refuting the above argument on the basis of the common Trinitarian theory. If you feel competent to the task, I hope you will undertake it.

According to the plan proposed, having treated at some length the *mode* of the incarnation, I am now brought to the consideration of the *ends* to be accomplished by it. This would, perhaps, most naturally enforce upon me the direct and formal discussion of the doctrine of the Atonement, which is commonly regarded as embodying or concentrating within itself the ends of the Divine Benevolence in ordaining the assumption of human nature on the part of the Son of God. That doctrine I shall submit to examination as I proceed, but my purpose is to anticipate what would perhaps appear to be the regular course of the argument, and to devote the present letter to the subject of our Lord's Glorification. I do this because, in the views of the New Church, the process of glorification stands in most intimate connexion with the incarnation, as it commenced with the assumption of the natural humanity and reached its acme simultaneously with the laying it aside. As the design, in fact, of his becoming incarnate was that he might be glorified, and by being glorified might become the Saviour of men, this fact prescribes the more orderly mode of discussion, and the subject thus treated will virtually cover the ground of the Atonement, as it will evince that nothing of a *vicarious*-character is involved in the economy of redemption. By showing what the Atonement *is*, we show at the same time what it *is not*, and if there be any basis of truth to what I shall now advance, it will at least be made clear that the essence of our Lord's atonement was *not* concentrated in his death on the cross or in what is termed the *sacrifice* there offered up to Divine Justice. But of this you will be able to judge better hereafter.

That the Lord was appointed to pass through a process termed *glorification* is abundantly evident from the following among other passages;—" After Judas had gone out, Jesus

Figure or external form is an image or likeness of internal form. Yet the converse does not hold true; for we may cut away the angles, and shape the planes of a cube into the figure of a sphere; yet the internal form or essential determinations, as well as the interior qualities, remain unchanged. Yet from unchanged figure we may learn the quality of the form: as from the countenance we may recognize the character of the soul.

THE ANGULAR FORM.

The Angular is the most imperfect, as well as the ultimate, of forms. It consists of angles and interjacent planes, is composed of lines merely rectilinear, which are otherwise determined than uniformly to a common centre; as may be seen in triangles, quadrangles and all other forms known to plane geometry. If from assumed points in the planes of such forms we demit lines perpendicularly, then such lines will not converge to a fixed centre, but will be parallel to, or continually intersect each other. In the circle or sphere all the lines falling from the periphery or superficies are concentrated in one point; and if we desire by external force or pressure to reduce it permanently to an angular form, all its determinations must undergo a mutation, so that the lines converging to its centre must remove themselves therefrom, to other points out of the centre, and intersect others falling perpendicularly from other rectilinear planes; otherwise the circle or sphere will resume its own form.

Thus it appears that in these forms, the determinations are opposite, or more or less contrary, falling upon and intersecting each other more or less obliquely or directly, and since in each intersection and coming together, there is a cessation of progression, a termination of fluxion, and an extinguishment of forces; it follows that such forms are in their very nature unsuited to continued motion: but are on the contrary the very forms of rest and inertia. Yet not from the concourse of perpendicular lines alone arises a high degree of rest within the internal compages of a body, but also within many forms where they mutually oppose each other; for in external appearance they are similarly angular: that is, constructed of planes and angles, since such as is the essential determination such is the limit, or what amounts to the same thing; such as is the form such is the figure which is the limit of extension. Also as many as are the angles so many are the causes of obstruction; and as many the planes, so many the causes of coherence.

The angular forms cannot be rotated upon an axis, much less about a centre, which they do not possess. Angles and points hinder, delay; and planes, if conformable, unite and conjoin. Thus every angular form is to be conceived as intrinsically consisting of mere trigons, or cubes; altogether as in effigy in the larger mass into which they coalesce when many of them are mutually applied to each other, for then they cannot be moved about unless all contiguous ones yield their places.

Therefore these forms are the most imperfect, and subject to the force of inertia; wherefore they are properly earthy and identical with those termed saline, acid, alkaline, urinous, sulphurous, nitrous and vitriolic.

The plane triangle, among planes; or the trigon or tetraedron among solids, is the first and simple of angular forms—to which the compound forms refer themselves, and to which they reduce themselves, when resolved into their simplest elements. The equiangular, or equilateral triangle is the most perfect, and the scalene triangle the most imperfect. The quadrangular plane, and the solid octohaedron are the second, in order, of angular forms, being immediately composed of the former. The equiangular and equilateral quadrangle is the most perfect of such forms. The more imperfect are parallelograms, rhomboides, trapeziums, with unequal angles and sides. To these succeed polygons and multilaterals, which are similarly regular and irregular; and hence more perfect and imperfect; the latter of which exceed all computation. Thus we have genera and species of angular forms.

From all which it follows, that the first angular forms are exceedingly minute tetraedrons and octohaedrons, and may be deemed the elements, primitive entities, or principles, of saline, acid and sulphurous substances. All these with their compounds are so many hard and inert corpuscles, immoveable among themselves without the assistance of fluids; properly heavy, material, extended, and figured; of themselves fixed and fixing; inexpansible and unelastic, cold, tempering the fluidity and heat of active forms in various modes; but best fitted for forming various compositions. Without these neither the earth, the vegetable or animal kingdom, in a word, the world, such as it is, could exist. These minute forms affect with so great variety the senses of taste and smell, and properly constitute that part of animals, which we call the body; and they are such as fall within the province of the sciences of Geometry, Trigonometry, Physics, and Chemistry.

THE CIRCULAR FORM.

The Circular or Spherical Form is proximately superior to the angular, divested of the angles and planes of the latter. It may be termed a form infinitely angular, with a perpetual plane. It is a likeness of what is perpetual and infinite, relatively to what, in the angular, is finite. What is perpetual, is also a One—thus there are not many angles, nor many planes, for in the circular form there is one common angle, and one common plane. This is also a natural consequence, when a volume of angular forms are forced to rotate about their axis, and similarly when they are exposed to the action of surrounding flames, then, the angles being cut off, the forms become round, and adapted to a rotary motion among themselves; and the longer the motion continues, and greater the velocity and force with which they are carried round, the more do they assume the extrinsic form of the perfect sphere and are liberated from the form of inertia.

Yet there still remains something rectilinear in the circular form, for there are as many right lines demitted perpendicularly from the periphery, as there are semi-diameters or radii.

Hence it follows that this form is the veriest of motion itself, and that it possesses the greatest power of resisting, and in its nature is most constantly permanent and unchanging; and likewise when consociated with angular forms is most aptly accommodated to all kinds of compositions.

That the spherical is the very form of motion itself follows, from the consideration that it is devoid of angles and planes, for resistance is in proportion to the angles; and the coherence, to the planes. Many spheres or globes in one volume and confined in a given space are most freely and easily rotated upon their axes: one does not move another from its place, neither touch the other except in the least and similar point, and instantly after contact it returns to and revolves in its own plane.

Therefore angular forms, moved and turned among themselves, are turned by the force of motion alone, are rounded by the abscission of angles, and are adapted to an axillary motion among their associates.

The spherical forms most readily gyrate upon any axis whatever, for there are as many axes as diameters; but gyrate not about a centre, unless the rectilinear directions are changed into circular, and a spiral determination exist; for in the more perfect forms of motion there is both an axillary and central motion, upon which depends the nature of fluidity, undulation and modification. The smoother the superficies, the better fitted for continued motion; and the rougher, the less suited; so that there may be forms of motion more perfect and imperfect. The determination of the lines, also within the circle or sphere conspires to the same thing, for this is the genuine form of motion; since the semi-diameters fall perpendicularly from every point of the periphery together into one and a common centre; nor at any other point of their course do they mutually fall upon each other, as in the angular forms, wherein the oppositions are in proportion to the points; and the causes of inertia, which are perpetual and infinite, to the oppositions. From the concourse of the determinations in one centre, it follows that axillary gyration is suited to the very form of motion itself; for without the centre nothing impedes, so that it may not revolve and each diameter represent an axis. That the diameter represents an axis not only follows because one diameter may differ from another, and that one, always in its place, represents an axis; but also because the spherical form may be considered as consisting purely of concentric circles from its ultimate periphery to its centre.

That the spherical form affords the greatest power of resistance against every impetus and external assault whatever appears from this; that all lines, as so many radii, run together in one common point, in which is singular and all absolute opposition, so that one cannot be moved from its place unless others are moved at the same time; the forces are thus conjoined, one regarding the safety of the other lest it be destroyed. This is the cause of resistance in the sperical form which escapes less than those having more centres, between which the determinations are divided—as in the ellipse, having two centres, and in other curves in which there are more; for the relation of centres to periphery from which perpendiculars fall, is what measures the degree of resistance. In the circle the relation of all the lines, or if for lines we substitute forces, then of all the forces, is to one centre in which all concur to every given kind of opposition; for in this centre every line respects another as diametrically opposite, others obliquely, and others at every conceivable obliquity. Wherefore it is said that nothing is more inert, hard, resisting and cold than the centre of this form. Hence it follows generally, that the spherical forms in their essence are most constantly permanent, however their modes are varied, for the determination of one line is most similar to that of the others; neither can it be changed unless all are simultaneously changed, and lest that should occur one regards the safety of all, and all of each; for each one respects the universal state of its form, from a centre, and in a manner contemplates it, so that it is sensible of whatever happens to other of its associates.

If it be supposed that the essential determinations in the circle or sphere do not consist of lines or radii, or hard corpuscles, but of innumerable lesser spherules; and that in these are those still smaller; and that the more interior they are, the more perfect the forms; then it will follow that the whole sphere composed thus in order of smaller ones included, will possess the highest elasticity, that its superficies will yield to every assault and impetus. For if the lesser sphericles are most yielding, then the larger complex or totality of the smaller must possess a similar power of yielding, or an elastic virtue. Now suppose that the spherical forms are most constant in their essential determinations, it will follow that from no accidental cause, as pressure from without, can possibly reduce it from its own proper form into another; much less change it into an angular form; but in proportion as they are urged or pressed upon they will be compressed to a less diameter, or dimensions, and when the compressing force is removed, they will relapse into their primitive expansion. Thus the variation of their modes consists in this, that they suffer themselves to be forced into a lesser spherical sphere, but not into an oval form. Thus they correspond to every ratio of the assailing forces; and under the least impulse react as they are acted upon: for in proportion as the sphericles are constricted, do they become hard and resisting, even until they produce a resistance corresponding to the action of the extrinsic forms; which is a consequence of the law, that nowhere is there anything more inert, hard, and resisting than in the centre of the spherical form, and this in proportion to the distance from the centre. That the atmospheric particles are such forms appears from experiments upon air.

The spherical forms associated with the angular are exactly accommodated to all kinds of compositions, as appears from this; that the primitive parts of salts, sulphurs, and minerals, are not simply angular forms, but are mediate between angular and circular; for there are as many minute trigons and octohedrons, with their sides excavated exactly in conformity with the convexity of spherical particles, as there are particles of water, to which they can thus be mutually applied, and conveniently united into a larger corpuscle. This would be otherwise if their sides were unexcavated planes.

For a full development of this theory, see the Author's "Principles of Chemistry," where this, and his theory of Chrystalization are tested on geometrical principles.

Moreover, the circular or spherical form is the measure, and form of all angular forms and thus in sort their universal type and complex, for angular forms and figures cannot be measured without the aid of the circle, and much less subjected to calculation.

It follows from this that the spherical form is a perpetual angle and infinite plane; and that it gives a perpetual and infinite law to the changeable and finite; and thus it adjudicates upon its quantities and qualities.

There are genera and species of circular and spherical forms, varying in perfection; thus there are elliptical, cycloidal, parobolic, and hyperbolic forms besides others, as well geometrical as arithmetical. Their determinations are not to one, but to more or less fixed centres; and their directions are not wholly opposite but flow together upon a certain line or plane, so that they are less perfect than the simply circular, but more perfect than the angular forms.

We suppose that all curves and surfaces whose co-ordinates are rectilinear, and are referable to rectangular axes, primarily—whose element lies in one plane or is a single curvalim, and whose equation is, in its degree, limited by the conditions of the curve—belong properly to this class of forms. Perhaps this class should not be limited by the latter two conditions; if we refer its co-ordinates and determinations necessarily to rectangular axes.

THE SPIRAL FORM.

The Spiral Form is the next in degree above the circular, and is anterior and more perfect than it. Its determinations do not flow in continuous concentric circles; nor through right lines to a common centre; but through continuous spires to and upon a certain circular form, holding the place of a centre; with associated endeavor they flow; around such circular superficies they continue or endeavor to continue their fluxions; and from which superficies they respect the centre of its sphere by radii, as in the perfect circle.

Thus in this form there is again something perpetual and infinite compared with the circular; as in the latter compared with the angular form; for the spire is a sort of perpetual circular fluxion; from any part of the superficies which is the limit of its fluxion; by perpetual winding spirals unto some lesser sphere holding the place of a centre: so that each spire is as well a circle as a semi-diameter; or it represents both determinations at the same time; thus it is everywhere a circle and everywhere a semi-diameter; that is, perpetually circular.

This fluxion, as was said, is terminated in the superficies of a central sphere: but the determinations never mutually oppose each other, but unanimously fall upon all points of this superficies at a certain obliquity; and thus they continue their gyre. When all the spires fall or terminate upon such a superficies, the central sphere, if it consist of angular forms, will move about its axis; or if it consists of spherical forms, these will flow around circularly. This central sphere is not dissimilar to our Earth floating in its atmosphere, revolving upon its axis, and upon whose superficies the continual spires of the ether are in a certain manner determined.

The spiral form enters and forms the circular and through it respects the angular, not as *actually* existing, but *potentially*, or as what is possible to exist; according to the proposition above stated that the angular form is produced by the circular, wherefore this is its measure and form also, but not immediately; for this would be contrary to the law of derivations; for each singular thing cannot be otherwise than unfolded or developed successively. Since whatever is the cause of a cause, is the cause of the causate, or thing caused; the spiral form is the measure of the circular and thus the form of all succeeding forms.

This spiral form is superior to, more present, or still more perfect than the circular; or is the form of active forces; for in it there is no concentration of determinations, but where the spires are terminated, they are still continued through circles, wherefore there arises therefrom something naturally spontaneous. For so great is the power in this form, that the fluxion once begun is continued almost spontaneously;—which faculty, power, and force, nature transcribes into the spiral fluxion, as clearly appears from the mechanism of the helix and screw.

The circular form revolves and rotates upon its axes or diameters; but the spiral form gyrates about a centre, which central gyration is the same as the perpetually axillary, or properly spiral. Since the circular forms cannot gyrate about a centre, or cannot possess a central gyration, but a kind of axillary motion as above described, therefore, that a central gyration may exist a more perfect form is required.

The mode in which these central gyrations are performed, is not easily expressed in words, or by figures, for when we ascend above the circular forms, our mental vision becomes, as it were, veiled with a cloud. Yet if the fluxions are continued around a medium, or a certain central globe, it follows that as a necessary consequence, there will arise a spiral gyration, but it will be otherwise if the fluxions are terminated in a centre.

It also follows that the spiral form is in its essence more constantly permanent than the circular: for the more perfect the forms the greater their constancy, since they approach to the perfection of primitive nature; wherefore also with the greater difficulty do they undergo essential mutation, but the more easily accidental mutations; for the faculty of under-going the latter is the perfection of their nature. That these forms may undergo essential mutations appears from this, that there are genera and species of these forms; but when they have once suffered such mutation with increased difficulty are they restored to their primitive perfection; for the more diffi-cult the reduction; likewise the more difficult the return, so that into forms still superior they are incapable of being re-stored or elevated. There are, of these forms, genera and species perfect and imperfect, to express which, terms and symbols are wanting, for this form rises above the common apprehension, because above the common geometry; its lines and circles, in the fastnesses of which it is placed.

The spires of this form may be termed circular, elliptical, parabolic, &c.; according to the nature of the spire, for its central globe or nucleus assumes one of the forms just named according to the nature of the spires of this form.

In the mean time, this form is very obvious and conspicu-ous in nature and her kingdoms, for whatever has a circular form owes it to this form. In this spiral form flow the parts and volumes of the ether, and by it they represent their modi-fications. In such manner also flow and are represented the fluxions and modifications of the parts and volumes of the purer blood, as well as the medullary and nervous fibres in the living body. They also conspicuously occur in the vege-table and animal kingdoms.

We have thus followed our Author through three degrees of forms, the angular, the circular, and the spiral; these suc-ceeding and arising from each other, as offspring and parents, as effects and causes. Before proceeding to the higher forms, holding their places so much above the ken of the senses, we will for a while contemplate those to which we have already been introduced and unravel if possible some of their latent qualities, for if we mistake not we shall find many hidden secrets among the graceful sinuosities of the spiral form.

In order to represent to ourselves these forms, and the relations they really sustain to each other, let us in the first place suppose a body, our Earth for instance, at rest, its axillary and orbital motions having ceased; then a body falling to its centre, or towards its surface in the direction of the centre, under the action of one force, or as many forces as can be reduced to one resultant, will flow or move along a right line: and several bodies falling under the same conditions will likewise describe right lines, and their determinations will be such as properly belong to the angular form.

Let us again suppose that a body, instead of moving towards the centre in a right line, moves around the axis at an equal distance from it.

Then such a body describes a form simply circular.

All parts of the earth situate out of the axis of rotation and revolving around it describe such a form, when we contemplate the axillary motion without reference to the orbital motion.

Two forces are necessary in such a case; and however many the forces, if their resultant is a circular motion, they may be reduced to two.

The equation of the curve is referable to rectangular axes: and the curve being of single curvature may be deemed to lie in one plane.

In the simple circle the forces act at right angles to each other, with constant intensities.

If we now suppose the direction and intensities of the two forces to vary according to a given law or conditions, there will result curves of other genera or species as the case may be, yet properly belonging to the degree of circular forms provided the co-ordinates of those curves are right lines, and are referred most appropriately to rectangular axes.

All the conic sections find their place here. No person we suppose will have any difficulty in forming a correct idea of the angular and circular forms; for we are busied with them in all our occupations, but in approaching the spiral form we must fix our attention, for here we approach unexplored labyrinths.

Let us again contemplate the earth as having an axillary motion only, and at the same time suppose a body is falling conformably towards its centre; that is, falling in such a manner that, to a person moving with the earth, it will *appear to fall in a right line*, as a body does falling under the action of the force of gravity.

The body thus falling, although it *appears to fall in a right line, yet in truth, instead thereof, describes a spiral line.* So we affirm that all bodies so falling to the earth, or to other revolving bodies, actually move along spiral paths, although the appearance is otherwise ; except when the body falls in the line of the axis of rotation.

The spiral will vary in kind according to the relations of the central and rotary forces, and according to the direction of the motions in reference to the centre of gravity or of force.

If the body move in a plane passing through the centre of force and perpendicular to the axis of rotation, then the spiral path described by the body will lie in one plane, and if the central velocity be in arithmetical proportion to the velocity of rotation, then the curve will be simply spiral.

If the central velocity vary as the square of the velocity of rotation, the latter being uniform ; then the moving body will describe a *parabolic spiral.*

If the direction of the central force lie between the equator and the axis, the moving body will describe a curve of double curvature, and may be conceived as moving spirally upon the surface of a cone, whose apex is at the centre of force, and whose semi-base subtends an angle equal to the complement of latitude of the moving body.

Such then, are the motions of all bodies falling conformably to another rotating body, according to a law founded upon the relation of the central and rotating velocities.

The motion of the body moving between the equator and the pole or axis, as above instanced, describes a spiral cone and is similar to the fluxion of the ether in the polar cones of the earth's vortex. The curvature is double and is the result of at least three forces.

If instead of referring the spiral curve to axes simply circular, we refer them to any curve belonging to the degree of circulars, or what is the same thing, if the rotating surface be elliptical, parabolic, &c. we shall obtain various genera and species of spiral curves.

Since then bodies falling to the earth in apparent right lines, really move in spiral curves; do not likewise rays of light, the undulations of the ethereal medium, when coming from without, or from the heavenly bodies, move in similar curves ? Is it not necessary they should so move in order to act harmoniously with the earth's rotation ?

And further, may not all the phenomena of the polarization of light be due to spiral motions of the etheral medium ? We have no doubt, that all such phenomena can be explained on such an hypothesis. The facts stated in the following paragraph taken from Somerville's "Connection of the Physical Sciences," sec. 22, go very far in our opinion to establish such an hypothesis.

" Professor Airy in a very profound and able paper published in the Cambridge Transactions, has proved that all the different kinds of polarized light are obtained from rock crystal. When polarized light is transmitted through the axis of a crystal of quartz, in the emergent ray the *particles of ether move in a circular helix*, and when it is transmitted obliquely, so as to form an angle with the axis of the prism, *the particles of ether move in an elliptical helix;* the ellipticity increasing with the obliquity of the incident ray, so that when the incident ray falls perpendicularly to the axis the particles of ether move in straight lines. Thus the quartz exhibits every variety of elliptical polarization."

From these facts it seems to be entirely clear that the forces, active in the formation of quartz crystals, and those active during the passage of light through the crystal, act in spiral curves.

Space will not permit us to pursue this interesting subject further. We will only inquire how far the *magnetic power of the solar beam* may be due to the action of spiral forces.

In order to obtain a clear idea of the three degrees of forms already discussed, and of their mutual relations let us briefly recapitulate.

The angular form has one force,—right lines, properly referable to a point.

The circular form has two forces, curved lines, single curvature, properly referable to rectangular axis, or angular forms.

The spiral form has three forces—lines double curvature, in general—properly referable to circular axis or curves.

The angular may be considered as possessing one dimension —length ; the circular two dimensions, length and breadth; and the spiral curve, three dimensions, length, breadth and thickness.

Thus the forces, dimensions and powers increase, *pari passu,* with the ascent of the degrees. The passage from one degree to another is not as from more to less, or an arithmetical progression, but is as cause to effect ; the simple to the compound ; the prior to the posterior. The degrees are discrete. When we compare the circular to the angular and the spiral to the circular forms, we consider the circle as consisting of an infinite number of angles, and the spiral as consisting of an infinite number of circular elements or axes. Thus these degrees, considered mathematically, are to each other in the ratio of infinity ; and their relations fall under the province of the calculus of infinites.

W. H. B.

(*To be Continued.*)

ARTICLE II.

LETTERS TO A TRINITARIAN.

LETTER VIII.

THE GLORIFICATION.

DEAR SIR,

THE course of the present discussion up to this point has been mainly devoted to the attempt to unfold the true constitution of our Lord's person, both before and after the advent, and to develope the grounds on which the New Church holds to a Trinity in the Divine nature, while at the same time most strenuously rejecting the Tripersonality which that doctrine has been supposed to involve. I have endeavored to show that a Divine Humanity pertains essentially to Jehovah, and that in the Incarnation this Divine Humanity " passed from first principles to last." On no other grounds do we hold such an incarnation to be possible, and that, consequently, the prevalent doctrine of Christendom, by ignoring the fact of such a Divine Humanity, does in effect deny the fundamental verity of the incarnation, and substitute for it the fallacy of the simple *adjunction* of the Divine to the Human nature. This is the inevitable issue of ascribing to our Lord a human soul as well as a human body derived from the virgin mother. Let it be understood, on the other hand, that the inmost element of our Lord's being was, by conception, from the Father, and therefore, as the Divine essence is indivisible, was the Father Himself, and we have a clear and consistent enunciation of the doctrine of Christ's Divinity, without the least invasion of the great truth of the absolute Unity of the Godhead. We behold God and man united in Him in one person, and the key afforded us, on this view, for a rational explication of the various and sometimes apparently conflicting texts of Scripture bearing upon the subject.

With such a presentation of the grand theme before us, it is at least sufficiently curious to contemplate in juxtaposition with it the following extract from Professor Norton's "Statement of Reasons," in which he unequivocally denies the possibility of the truth of such a doctrine as Swedenborg has proposed.

"With the doctrine of the Trinity, is connected that of the HYPOSTATIC UNION, as it is called, or *the doctrine of the union of the divine and human natures in Christ, in such a manner that these two natures constitute but one person.* But this doctrine may be almost said to have pre-eminence in incredibility above that of the Trinity itself. The latter can be no object of belief when regarded in connexion with that of the Divine Unity ; for these two doctrines directly contradict each other. But the former, without reference to any other doctrine, does in itself involve propositions as clearly self-contradictory, as any which it is in the power of language to express. It teaches, that Christ is both God and man. The proposition is very plain and intelligible. The words, *God* and *man*, are among those which are in most common use, and the meaning of which is best defined and understood. There cannot (as with regard to the terms employed in stating the doctrine of the Trinity) be any controversy about the sense in which they are used in this proposition, or, in other words, about the ideas which they are intended to express. And we perceive that these ideas are wholly incompatible with each oher. Our idea of God is of an infinite being ; our idea of man is of a finite being ; and we perceive that the same being cannot be both infinite and finite. There is nothing clear in language, no proposition of any sort can be affirmed to be true, if we cannot affirm this to be true,—that it is impossible that the same being should be finite and infinite ; or, in other words, that it is impossible that the same being should be man and God. If the doctrine were not familiar to us, we should revolt from it, as shocking every feeling of reverence toward God ;—and it would appear to us, at the same time, as mere an absurdity as can be presented to the understanding. No words can be more destitute of meaning, *so far as they are intended to convey a proposition which the mind is capable of admitting*, than such language as we sometimes find used, in which Christ is declared to be at once the Creator of the universe, and a man of sorrows ; God omniscient and omnipotent, and a feeble man of imperfect knowledge.

"The doctrine of the Trinity, then, and that of the union of two natures in Christ, are doctrines, which, when fairly understood, it is impossible, from the nature of the human mind, should be believed. They involve manifest contradictions, and no man can believe what he perceives to be a contradiction. In what has been already said. I have not been bringing arguments to disprove these doctrines ; I have merely been showing that they are intrinsically incapable of any proof whatever ; for a contradiction cannot be proved ;—that they are of such a character, that it is impossible to bring arguments in their support, and unnecessary to adduce arguments against them."—*Norton's Statement of Reasons*, p. 17–19, 22.

You will see from this that it is not possible to array two distinct exhibitions of Christian doctrine in more direct antagonism with each other than is done by the citation of this passage in connexion with the scope of my previous reasonings. To what extent the author will be admitted as an accredited expounder of Unitarian sentiments, I know not; but yourself and my other readers must judge on which side the truth lies, if the inspired oracles are to be the standard of faith; and also whether there is any intermediate ground on which the Lord's essential Divinity can be safely made to rest. For myself, I see none. If the doctrine of Swedenborg on that head is not the true doctrine, I despair of finding it either in the Bible or out of it, and I should despair too of successfully refuting the above argument on the basis of the common Trinitarian theory. If you feel competent to the task, I hope you will undertake it.

According to the plan proposed, having treated at some length the *mode* of the incarnation, I am now brought to the consideration of the *ends* to be accomplished by it. This would, perhaps, most naturally enforce upon me the direct and formal discussion of the doctrine of the Atonement, which is commonly regarded as embodying or concentrating within itself the ends of the Divine Benevolence in ordaining the assumption of human nature on the part of the Son of God. That doctrine I shall submit to examination as I proceed, but my purpose is to anticipate what would perhaps appear to be the regular course of the argument, and to devote the present letter to the subject of our Lord's Glorification. I do this because, in the views of the New Church, the process of glorification stands in most intimate connexion with the incarnation, as it commenced with the assumption of the natural humanity and reached its acme simultaneously with the laying it aside. As the design, in fact, of his becoming incarnate was that he might be glorified, and by being glorified might become the Saviour of men, this fact prescribes the more orderly mode of discussion, and the subject thus treated will virtually cover the ground of the Atonement, as it will evince that nothing of a *vicarious* character is involved in the economy of redemption. By showing what the Atonement *is*, we show at the same time what it *is not*, and if there be any basis of truth to what I shall now advance, it will at least be made clear that the essence of our Lord's atonement was *not* concentrated in his death on the cross or in what is termed the *sacrifice* there offered up to Divine Justice. But of this you will be able to judge better hereafter.

That the Lord was appointed to pass through a process termed *glorification* is abundantly evident from the following among other passages;—" After Judas had gone out, Jesus

proper ability"—it is all in Himself and from Himself. It is thus but another term for "glorified." This is very clearly anounced in the following passage. "That the Lord might make the human divine, by an ordinary way, he came into the world, that is, was willing to be born as another man, and to be instructed as another, and as another to be re-born, but with the difference, that man is re-born of the Lord, but that the Lord not only regenerated himself, but also glorified himself, that is, made himself divine; further, that man is made new by an influx of charity and faith, but the Lord by love divine, which was in him, and which was his; hence it may be seen, that the regeneration of man is an image of the glorification of the Lord; or what is the same, that in the process of the regeneration of man, as in an image, may be seen, although remotely, the process of the Lord's glorification."—(*A. C.* 3138.

I have thus endeavored to exhibit somewhat of a correct view of the doctrine of our Lord's glorification as taught in the illuminated theology of the New Church. It is the doctrine of the gradual deposition of the natural humanity received from the mother, and of the gradual assumption of a Divine humanity received from the Father. That our Lord, viewed as to his essential nature, had a Divine Human from eternity, is undoubtedly true, but in coming into the world he *superinduced*, says Swedenborg, a natural Humanity upon the Divine, and this natural Humanity he successively glorified by victories over temptation, which continually tended to *bring down* the Divine influx into its forms, and thus eventually fill them with its own plenitude.—But upon this and several other phases of the subject I shall dwell at greater length in another letter.   G. B.

(*To be Continued.*)

EXTRACT.

"In order that a more distinct idea may be had of the union or the Lord's Divine Essence with the Human, and of the Lord's conjunction with mankind by the faith of charity, it may be expedient both here, and in other places, to call the former 'union,' and the latter '*conjunction*.' Between the Divine and Human Essence of the Lord there was a union; whereas between the Lord and mankind, by the faith of charity, there is a conjunction. This appears from the consideration that Jehovah, or the Lord, is Life, whose Human Essence was also made life, as has been shown above; and there is union of life with life: but man is not life, but a recipient of life, as has also been shown above; and when life flows into a recipient of life, there is conjunction; for it is adapted to it as an active to a passive, or as what in itself is alive to what in itself is dead, which thence obtains life."—*A. C.* 2021.

is heaven,.because when heaven is analysed it resolves itself into the very being of God. So he says also that a spirit *is* his own love, because his love is his essence. It is on this ground, moreover, that he informs us that everything in the Word has an ultimate reference to the Lord. The natural, the spiritual, the celestial senses are, as it were, unrolled, as so many swathings, and then the Divine appears. Hence Abraham, Isaac, and Jacob interiorly represent the Lord, each in some one of the aspects in which he is to be viewed. And who can doubt this when it is said of the people of Israel as representing the church, " My servant David shall rule over them." Is not the Lord ultimately indicated under the title David? And was not Abraham, for instance, as fit a representative of the Lord as David?

You will perceive from this that the idea conveyed by the term *glorification* as applied to our Lord, is far different from that of a mere *splendid* or *glorious state* resulting from the exercise of kingly dominion or from the bare *display* of the most exalted prerogatives whether in the midst of angels or men. It is a term applicable to an internal or subjective condition which in the case of our Lord viewed in his Humanity brought him into the capacity of saving the human race. On the common theory of Redemption the glorification of Christ was a mere resulting effect, in the Divine economy, from the previous state of humiliation and suffering to which he condescended to stoop, and could not be said even to have commenced so long as that state continued. Indeed it is for the most part spoken of as a *reward* for the voluntary endurance of the pains and afflictions which he underwent on our behalf, and our ideas of it are governed by the letter of such texts as the following ;—" Who for the joy that was set before him endured the cross, despising the shame, and is now set down on the right hand of God." But on the higher and truer view, as I conceive it to be, of the New Church, the glorification commenced from the outset of the earthly humanity of Jesus and ran paralel with it to the termination of his career in the flesh, when it reached its culminating and consummating point in the complete deposition of everything that bore the taint of the maternal infirmity. So far from being a mere result and sequence of the atoning work of the Saviour it was the very essence of the atonement itself, apart from which the term loses entirely its genuine force. Instead of indicating a state into which a transition was first made upon his emergence from the depth of his humiliation into the height of his exaltation, it denotes an interior process which was going on through the whole course of his earthly pilgrimage, and which

embrace, in one complete and harmonious system, the whole range of Science, Philosophy, Theology, and Religion? We believe that that day is at hand, and that it is our bounden duty to hail its approach and to lend our aid to usher it in.

But however inseparable, according to a true system, are religion and philosophy, yet as things are, they are in a state of most woful alienation and antagonism, so that no hope can be entertained of an ultimate harmony. The result of their continued antagonism must be disastrous to one or the other, and perhaps fatal to both. For where philosophy and religion are separate in their bearing on the mind, both claim the entire dominion, even to the utter exclusion or subordination of the other. Consequently when they meet in the same mind they wage a war for the mastery there, and one or the other must be driven from the plain, or both must die together. But little observation is necessary in order to convince any one that there is a conflict now going on in the public mind which threatens the present forms both of the current philosophy and religion, and that they are often thrown into the most earnest conflict with each other. A few observations of a very general nature will aid to place this subject in its true light.

The present age is characterized by a series of discoveries and improvements in the arts and sciences that are brilliant beyond measure, and without a parallel in the past. The human mind, at large, has become most deeply engrossed in these astonishing movements, and every step is noted with the utmost interest, still there are but few who can divine to what these changes are tending, or what will be the final result. All are, however, agreed that the man of science and philosophy is pursuing his work without the slightest reference to the man of the church ; while on the other hand, the minister of religion is equally regardless of the deductions of science ; that the philosopher gives no aid to the theologian, nor the theologian to the philosopher : furthermore it is believed that devotion to the church, and reverence to its doctrines do not rise with the dawn of the *new era* in the arts and sciences, but, on the contrary, that there is a most lamentable tendency to the opposite result.

It often happens that while the philosophy of the day is above the horizon, the light and the love of religion grow cold and dark, the fervor of devotion ceases, and the dreary demonstrations of scepticism fill the firmament of the mind. So that it is not until philosophy, so called, is under the horizon, that religion of the day, in its lively and enchanting forms, rises full in the dominion of the soul. It may be that there is no open conflict between the two, while still, there is a deplo-

He became God in human flesh. The human nature, however, received from the mother was a *fallen* nature, as she could impart no other.* It was consequently *liable* to temptation, to suffering, and to sin, though "he knew no sin," nor was "iniquity found in his lips." But it was in the economy of redemption that this fallen, infirm, and peccable humanity, hereditarily received from the mother, should be gradually put off, and a perfectly Divine humanity received from the Father, gradually put on. "He put off the human," says Swedenborg, "taken from the mother, which in itself was like the human of another man, and thus natural, and put on a Human from the Father, which was in itself like his Divine, and thus substantial, from which the Human also was made Divine." The process by which this was effected was our Lord's *glorification.* This is thus explained.

"The Lord by the most grievous temptation-combats, reduced all things in himself into divine order, insomuch that there remained nothing at all of the human which he had derived from the mother; so that he was not made new as another man, but altogether divine; for man, who is made new by regeneration, still retains in himself an inclination to evil, yea evil itself, but is withheld from evil by an influx of the life of the Lord's love, and this by exceedingly strong power; whereas the Lord entirely cast out every evil which was hereditary to him from the mother, and made himself divine, even as to the vessels, that is, as to truths; this is what in the Word is called glorification."—*A. C.* 3318.

But in order to a clearer discovery of this great truth, it is important to advert to certain principles in the constitution of our nature which rendered such a process necessary. Among the remarkable developments made by Swedenborg is that of a clear distinction between the *external* and the *internal* man.† This is not a distinction simply between the body and the spirit. It is rather a distinction between the *animal* or *sensitive,* and the *spiritual* and *heavenly* nature, thought pertaining to each. Still it is one which recognizes the animal or *psychical* affec-

---

* "The Lord's divine good natural, is what was Divine to Him from nativity, for He was conceived from Jehovah, hence He had a Divine esse from nativity, which was to Him for a soul, and consequently the inmost of his life. This was exteriorly clothed by those things which He assumed from the mother, and because this from the mother was not good, but in itself evil, therefore He expelled it of his own proper power, chiefly by temptation-combats, and afterwards conjoined this human, which he made new in Himself, with the divine good which He had from nativity."—*A. C.* 4641.

† Thought is evidently inseparable from sensation. Brute beasts have sensations and thoughts, and therefore an external man, but no internal. See A. C. 978, where the distinction is fully explained.

tions and appetencies as bearing a very close relation to the body and as manifesting their power and predominance chiefly through it. These two principles are opposed to each other, the internal man inclining to heaven and heavenly things, and the external to earth and earthly things, and the end of regeneration is to bring them into harmony. The external is thus to be made not only a fit instrument, but a living image, of the internal, and to incline, like it, to heavenly things, and only to earthly in subordination to heavenly. Now in order that our Lord might be truly a man it was necessary that he should be possessed of both these principles and in order that he might be a Saviour, competently endowed, that they should both be brought to act in unison. But in His case that which answers to *our* internal man was Jehovah, or the Essential Divinity itself, whereas his external, being derived from a human parent, was subject to human infirmity, and therefore before He could enter into perfect oneness with the Father his external man was to be formed anew, so as to become the exact image of his internal; in other words, his Human was to become Divine. In this process consisted his glorification, and this process was gradual. It is thus more fully explained by one of the ablest expounders of Swedenborg.

" The Lord Jesus Christ while in the world, *so far* as he had anything appertaining to him from the mother, or *so far* as He was the Son of Mary, was not strictly One with the Father: but in proportion as what He received from her was *put off*, and a Divine Human Nature, received or brought forth from the Father, *put* on in its place, He advanced towards perfect union: till at length, all the life of the maternal nature being extinguished at the passion of the cross, and the Divine life from the Father being brought down into the lowest natural principal in lieu of it, at the resurrection, He thenceforward, and for ever, was, and is, One with the Father,—One God in One Divine person; his Divine Soul being the very Father or what is called God in his inmost essence, and his Divine Body being the Son of God, or a clothing of the Divine Essence, brought forth solely from that Essence itself, to be the medium of its manifestation to mankind."—*Noble's Lectures*, p. 118, 119.

*   *   *   *   *

" Even the natural body, it is to be remembered, was conceived of Jehovah, and was, as to its inmost principles, divine from conception, having for its inmost soul the whole Divine Essence. The Divine Essence, while the Lord Jesus Christ was living as a man in the world, was in the continual effort to assimilate the assumed Humanity to itself. In the interior forms of that human nature a glorifying process was going on, from the first to the last moment of his life. The Divine Principle within kept descending lower and lower, imparting its own divine nature to the interior forms of the human essence in succession; extirpating everything that partook of infirmity,—everything, in fact, that was derived from the mother; but yet retaining every human principle entire, though rendered infinitely perfect and truly divine. When all that belongs to man beyond or above the mere shell of clay had been submitted to this wonderful process, the crucifixion took place: and then, the merely human life being altogether extinct, the divine life descending to the extremes of the bodily frame, renewing the whole by its descent. This fully accomplished, He arose again with his human form complete, nothing being lost or left behind,—a truly Divine Man, having in his Glorious Person every thing, and every principle, which is found in the constitution of man, but all perfectly assimilated in nature to the pure Divinity Itself. In this Divine Humanity, therefore, He is truly the Alpha and the Omega, the First and the Last,—the very immediate *Esse* or Source of being to everything that exists, the immediate Upholder and Supporter of all things, both in heaven and earth. Thus the child once born, the son once given. is of a truth the Mighty God, the Everlasting Father, upon whose shoulders, of right, the government rests, and to whom belong glory and dominion for ever."—*Ibid.* 140, 141.

I could fain hope that the main position has been so stated as to be exempt from the charge of disparaging in any degree the pure and perfect character of the Saviour, but in order to guard still further against any misapprehension, I insert the following paragraph, unfolding the sense in which alone evil is predicable of his nature.

"It may be a matter of surprise to many, to hear it said that hereditary evil from the mother was with the Lord; but . . . it cannot be doubted that it was so. It is altogether impossible for any man to be born of a human parent, but he must thence derive evil. But there is a difference between hereditary evil which is derived from the father, and that which is derived from the mother. Hereditary evil from the father is more interior, and remains to eternity, for it can never be eradicated: the Lord had no such evil, since he was born of Jehovah as his Father, and thus, as to internals, was Divine, or Jehovah. But hereditary evil from the mother appertains to the external man: this was attached to the Lord. Thus the Lord was born as another man, and had infirmities as another man. That he derived hereditary evil from the mother, appears evidently from the circumstance of his enduring temptations; for it is impossible that any one should be tempted who has no evil, evil being that in man which tempts, and by which he is tempted. That the Lord was tempted, and that he endured temptations a thousand times more grievous than any man can possibly sustain, and that he endured them alone, and by his own proper power overcame evil, or the devil and all hell, is also manifest. It is not possible for any angel to be tempted by the devil, because, being in the Lord, the evil spirits cannot approach him even distantly, as they would be instantly seized with horror and fright; much less could hell approach to the Lord, if he had been born Divine, that is, without an adherence of evil from the mother. That the Lord also bore the iniquities and evils of mankind, is a form of speaking common with preachers; but for him to take upon himself iniquities and evils, except in an hereditary way, was impossible. The Divine Nature is not susceptible of evil: wherefore, that he might overcome evil by his own proper strength, which no man ever could, or can do, and might thus alone become righteousness, he was willing to be born as another man. There otherwise would have been no need that he should be born; for he might have assumed the Human Essence without nativity, as he had formerly done occasionally, when he appeared to those of the Most Ancient Church, and likewise to the prophets. But in order that he might also put on evil, to fight against and conquer it, and might thus at the same time join together in himself the Divine Essence and the Human Essence, he came into the world. The Lord, however, had no actual evil, or evil that was his own; as he himself declares in John: 'Which of you convicteth me of sin?' viii. 46."—*A. C.* 1573.

Our Lord's external man, then, was to be brought into a state of complete and harmonious union with the internal, which is otherwise expressed by saying that his Human was to be, as it were, merged in his Divine, and when this was fully effected he was fully glorified, of which the passion of the cross was the last and consummating step. The rationale of the process is thus strikingly unfolded in the Arcana.

"It is known that the Lord was born as another man, and that when an infant He learnt to speak as another infant, and that He next grew in science, also in intelligence and wisdom; hence it is evident, that his human was not Divine from nativity, but that He made it Divine by his own proper ability. That it was done by his own proper ability was because He was conceived by Jehovah, and hence the inmost of his life was Jehovah Himself; for the inmost of the life of every man, which is called soul, is from the father, but what that inmost puts on, which is called body, is from the mother. That the inmost of life, which is from the father, is continually flowing in and operating upon the external, which is from the mother, and endeavoring to make this like to itself, even in the womb, may be manifest from sons, in that they are born to the natural inclination of the father, and in some cases grandsons and great-grandsons to the natural inclinations of the grandfather and great-grandfather: the ground and reason of this is, because the soul, which is from the father, continually wills to make the external, which is from the mother, like to itself. Since this is the case with man, it may be manifest that it was especially the case with the Lord. His inmost was the Divine Itself, because Jehovah Himself, for He was his only-begotten Son; and inasmuch as the inmost was the Divine Itself, could not this, more than in the case of any man, make the external, which was from the mother, an image of itself, that is, like to itself, thus make the human, which was external, and from the mother, Divine? and this by his own proper ability, because the Divine, which was inmost, from which He operated into the human, was his, as the soul of man, which is the inmost, is his. And whereas the Lord advanced according to divine order, He made his human when He was in the world, to be divine truth; but afterwards, when He was fully glorified, He made it to be divine good, thus one with Jehovah."—*A. C.* 6716.

The drift of these remarks affords us a clue to the solution of the apparent paradox of our Lord's praying to the Father as to another person, when in fact, as I have endeavored to show, He was one with the Father, as the Divine Truth is ever really one with the Divine Good. It is doubtless this circumstance more than any other which has tended to beget and confirm that idea of *disjunction* and *duality*, in relation to the Father and the Son, which has become so deeply inwrought in the mind of Christendom, and which is at the same time so utterly at war with all consistent views of the Divine Unity. The general impression on this score derived from the literal import of the Scriptures, in a multitude of passages, is in fact so strong as to have produced a virtual denial of one only God manifested in the person of Jesus of Nazareth, and the virtual assertion of three Gods in three persons. I do not say that this belief is formally avowed, but I say that the prevalent doctrine constructively amounts to this, and that every attempted explanation which would render the alleged Trinity consistent with the admitted Unity avoids a logical contradiction only by running on the fog-banks of mystery— a mystery inscrutable, unapproachable, defiant alike of angelic and human inquisition. To the view of the New Church all mystery *on this score* is completely banished. We see an entire consistency between these apparently repugnant aspects of our Lord's character. The solution given in the ensuing paragraphs of the seeming inconsistency is to us perfectly satisfactory.

" So long as the Lord was in a state of temptation, he spake with Jehovah as with another ; but so far as his Human Essence was united to his Divine, he spake with Jehovah as with himself. This is evident from many passages in the evangelists, and also from many in the prophets, and in David. The reason is plain from what has been said above concerning the hereditary from the mother ; in proportion as any thing of this remained, he was as it were absent from Jehovah, but in proportion as this was extirpated, he was present and was Jehovah himself."—*A. C.* 1745.

" So far as the Lord was in the human not yet made Divine. so far He was in humiliation ; but so far as He was in the human made Divine, so far He could not be in humiliation, for so far He was God and Jehovah. That He was in humiliation when in the human not yet made Divine, was because the human which He derived from the mother was hereditarily evil, and this could not approximate to the Divine without humiliation : for man in genuine humiliation divests himself of all ability to think and do anything from himself, and leaves himself altogether to the Divine, and thus accedes to the Divine. The Divine was indeed in the Lord, because he was conceived of Jehovah, but this appeared remote, so far as his human was in the maternal hereditary ; for in spiritual and celestial things, dissimilitude of state is what causes removal and absence, and similitude of state is what causes approach and presence ; and it is love which makes similitude and dissimilitude. From these things now it may be manifest, whence was the state of humiliation with the Lord when he was in the world; but afterwards when he put off all the human which he derived from the mother, insomuch that he was no longer her son, and put on the Divine, then the state of humiliation ceased, for then he was one with Jehovah."—*A. C.* 6866.

"Whereas the Lord had from the beginning a humanity from the mother, and successively put off the same; therefore during his abode in the world, he passed through two states, one a state of humiliation, or emptying himself, and the other a state of glorification, or union with the divinity which is called the Father: the state of humiliation was at the time and in the degree that he was in the humanity from the mother; and the state of glorification, at the time and in the degree that he was in the humanity from the Father. In the state of humiliation he prayed unto the Father, as to one different from himself; but in the state of glorification he spoke with the Father as with himself: in this latter state he said, that the Father was in him, and he in the Father, and that the Father and he were one; but in the state of humiliation he underwent temptations, and suffered the cross, and prayed unto the Father not to forsake him; for the divinity could not be tempted, much less could it suffer the cross. Hence then it appears, that by temptations, and continual victories therein, and by the passion of the cross, which was the last of those temptations, he entirely conquered the hells, and fully glorified the humanity, as was shown above. That the Lord put off the humanity from the mother, and put on the humanity from the divinity himself, which is called the Father, appears also from this consideration, that so often as the Lord spoke by his own mouth unto the mother, he did not call her mother, but woman."—*Doct. of the Lord*, 35.

Is there anything in this calculated to stumble one who appreciates what may be termed the twofold personality of the old and new man in the regenerating Christian. Is anything more palpable than the conflict which is continually going on in the bosom of such an individual, and which is so graphically described by Paul in the record of his own experience? "For that which I do I allow not: for what I would, that do I not; but what I hate, that do I. If then I do that which I would not, I consent unto the law that it is good. Now then it is no more I that do it, but sin that dwelleth in me. For I know that in me (that is, in my flesh,) dwelleth no good thing: for to will is present with me; but how to perform that which is good I find not. For the good that I would I do not: but the evil which I would not, that I do. Now if I do that I would not, it is no more I that do it, but sin that dwelleth in me. I find then a law, that, when I would do good, evil is present with me. For I delight in the law of God after the inward man: but I see another law in my members, warring against the law of my mind, and bringing me into captivity to the law of sin which is in my members. O wretched man that I am! who shall deliver me from the body of this death? I thank God through Jesus Christ our Lord. So then with the mind I myself serve the law of God; but with the flesh the law of sin." Rom. vii. 15–25.

Here is the "law of the mind" and the "law of the flesh" in direct antagonism with each other, each striving for the mastery, and each alternately claiming to be the real *ipseity* or self-hood of the man. Now is it not evident that so long as this contest continues the man is internally divided in himself, and that just in proportion as the opposition is strong the external man is remote from the internal, and as it grows weaker that they come into conjunction? The end of regeneration is that they may both be brought *at one*, and this, in respect to our Lord, was the very essence of *atonement* (*at-onement*), as will perhaps be made more obvious in the sequel. But at present I would exhibit, in a still clearer manner, the analogy between regeneration and glorification, which I do in the words of our author.

"The state of the Lord's glorification may in some manner be conceived from the state of the regeneration of man, for the regeneration of man is an image of the Lord's glorification; when man is regenerated, he then becomes altogether another, and is made new, therefore also when he is regenerated, he is called born again, and created anew; then, although he has a similar face, and a similar speech, yet his mind is not similar; his mind, when he is regenerated, is open towards heaven, and there dwells therein love to the Lord, and charity towards his neighbor with faith; it is the mind which makes another and a new man; change of state cannot be perceived in the body of man, but in his spirit, the body being only the covering of his spirit and when it is put off, then his spirit appears, and this in altogether another form when he is regenerated, for it has then the form of love and charity in beauty inexpressible instead of its pristine form, which was that of hatred and cruelty with a deformity also inexpressible; hence it may appear what a regenerate person is, or one that is born again, or created anew, viz., that he is altogether another and a new man. From this image it may in some measure be conceived what the glorification of the Lord is; he was not regenerated as a man, but was made divine, and this from the veriest divine love, for he was made divine love itself; what his form then was, was made apparent to Peter, James, and John, when it was given them to see him, not with the eyes of the body, but with the eyes of the spirit, viz., that his countenance shone like the sun, Matt. xvii. 2; and that this was his divine human, appears from the voice which then came out of the cloud, saying, 'This is my beloved son,' verse 5."—*A. C.* 3212.

In all this it is carefully to be noted that although Swedenborg occasionally applies the term "regenerated" to the Lord, he would yet be understood to mean that the process, unlike what takes place with man, is not effected by any influence or agency foreign to Himself, but it is due solely to his "own proper ability"—it is all in Himself and from Himself. It is thus but another term for "glorified." This is very clearly anounced in the following passage. "That the Lord might make the human divine, by an ordinary way, he came into the world, that is, was willing to be born as another man, and to be instructed as another, and as another to be re-born, but with the difference, that man is re-born of the Lord, but that the Lord not only regenerated himself, but also glorified himself, that is, made himself divine; further, that man is made new by an influx of charity and faith, but the Lord by love divine, which was in him, and which was his; hence it may be seen, that the regeneration of man is an image of the glorification of the Lord; or what is the same, that in the process of the regeneration of man, as in an image, may be seen, although remotely, the process of the Lord's glorification."—(*A. C.* 3138.

I have thus endeavored to exhibit somewhat of a correct view of the doctrine of our Lord's glorification as taught in the illuminated theology of the New Church. It is the doctrine of the gradual deposition of the natural humanity received from the mother, and of the gradual assumption of a Divine humanity received from the Father. That our Lord, viewed as to his essential nature, had a Divine Human from eternity, is undoubtedly true, but in coming into the world he *superinduced,* says Swedenborg, a natural Humanity upon the Divine, and this natural Humanity he successively glorified by victories over temptation, which continually tended to *bring down* the Divine influx into its forms, and thus eventually fill them with its own plenitude.—But upon this and several other phases of the subject I shall dwell at greater length in another letter.   G. B.

(*To be Continued.*)

EXTRACT.

" In order that a more distinct idea may be had of the union or the Lord's Divine Essence with the Human, and of the Lord's conjunction with mankind by the faith of charity, it may be expedient both here, and in other places, to call the former ' *union,*' and the latter ' *conjunction.*' Between the Divine and Human Essence of the Lord there was a union; whereas between the Lord and mankind, by the faith of charity, there is a conjunction. This appears from the consideration that Jehovah, or the Lord, is Life, whose Human Essence was also made life, as has been shown above; and there is union of life with life: but man is not life, but a recipient of life, as has also been shown above; and when life flows into a recipient of life, there is conjunction; for it is adapted to it as an active to a passive, or as what in itself is alive to what in itself is dead, which thence obtains life."—*A. C.* 2021.

ARTICLE III.

PHILOSOPHY AND RELIGION.

The importance of cultivating a true and lofty Philosophy, in connexion with the high and holy Theology of the New Dispensation, cannot be overrated. It is a familiar thought, and yet most deeply significant, that natural and scientific truth are the orderly basis of spiritual and divine truth; and that therefore true philosophy and true theology are essentially harmonious, and indeed utterly inseparable. Religion and philosophy which are true are never at war, but, on the contrary, true religion may always rest in the broad field of natural science, and there lead the steps of the philosopher, and cast light upon his path, and inspire him with hope, and encourage him in his weary way, while he is attempting to trace the arcana of nature, and disclose their laws in their most comprehensive bearings, and in their profoundest entanglements. True philosophy, moreover, may be and ought to be embued with the deepest emotions of the devout worshiper, and with the sincere acknowledgment of the spirituality and truth of the holy word itself. This will appear from the nature of the case:

Philosophy, unfolding the forms, affinities and powers of Nature and of Man, as manifested in the *phenomena,* and as demonstrated by science, experience and reason, can never be hostile to true religion—a religion which unfolds the *invisible* things of the Divine Nature, and his holy law, together with the nature of man, the nature of angels and of spirits, of heaven and of hell, and the laws of spiritual life. Things *invisible,* "principalities and powers," are necessarily in harmony with things *visible :* the Creator is in harmony with the creation. That system, therefore, which truthfully sets forth the natural world—the world of effects—and which we call Philosophy, should, in all good faith harmonize with our holy religion—a religion which unfolds the interior world of causes, and of ends—that vast spiritual orb which sustains this natural sphere, and fills it with life. Nor is it merely true that religion and philosophy harmonize, for in truth, they are so inseparable that either is, in a measure, defective and fragmental without the other; and in a true system, they would thus be held, and studied, and taught. May we not hope that the day is at hand when a comprehensive Theosophy will

"After the publication of this first work, termed the 'Arcana Cœlestia,' Swedenborg published another on the Book of Revelations in the New Testament—'a Book,' said the lecturer, 'which all commentators agree to be the most mysterious and difficult to be understood of all the books of the Bible. But Swedenborg, applying his key of the spiritual sense, opens this closed casket, and brings forth its treasures, makes the meaning simple, clear, connected, and intelligible to all. After this he published a work, entitled a " Treatise on Heaven and Hell," in which,' said the lecturer, 'Swedenborg has presented a rational and plain, as well as striking view of those two states of existence. It is a book,' said the speaker, 'the truth of which, to the reflecting and unprejudiced mind, carries its own testimony with it.'

" Having thus presented a view of some of the chief of Swedenborg's theological works, the lecturer came to the question, 'What could be the origin of the discoveries there exhibited?' He argued that they could not be considered as inventions of Swedenborg, both from the fact of his entirely disclaiming them as such, and from the fact, moreover, that had they been inventions, their nature was such that their falsity could instantly be detected. He then quoted distinguished authorities to show both the strict integrity of Swedenborg's character and perfect soundness of his intellect, that he could neither have been himself deceived, nor could have wilfully deceived others. The conclusion, then, and which was to be drawn as the most probable and most fair, was, that he was, as he fully believed himself to be, a chosen medium, under Providence, for making known important spiritual truths to mankind. It was certainly not impossible, argued the speaker, for a Paul to rise up now, as one had risen up before—for a man to be called now, as one had been called in former times—to teach the doctrines of what was *then* the new church. This was certainly possible. It was then only a question of probability, and that was a question that could be decided by no one, till after a candid and fair examination of the doctrines taught in this writer's works. Was it not evident, continued the speaker, that the world was demanding more light,—that such a new revelation of truth was needed—when, on looking round us in the Christian world, we see doubt and disputation on the first and most vital points of theology and religion ; the nature of God, whether trinity or unity ; the nature of the future state ; the right interpretation of Scripture itself? The lecturer concluded by inviting persons of candid and reflecting minds to examine these new and important doctrines."

rable want of that positive harmony, sympathy, and co-operation which the nature of the case demands : sure we are, that there is no absolute alliance either open or occult : science does not help religion ; nor does theology help philosophy. They seem, for aught that appears in the current schools of either, to belong to different minds, and to be work for different hands, and to be tending to different results. It is often said that they *belong* together, but their relation is not clearly seen, and they are left to *find out* each other the best way they can—for they are not *brought* together. Our young men must go to the university or the college to be instructed in natural and scientific truth, they must go to the church or the conference room to be impressed with religion, and they must go into the world to learn practical wisdom. Thus to all intents and purposes, religion and philosophy, and philosophy and practical wisdom are held in a state of utter separation and divorce ; instead of being *one*, like the emotions, the thoughts, and the actions of man : for evidently what is wanted is that philosophy should be religious, and religion philosophical, and that both should be one in being practical and useful.

Nor do we suppose that this doctrine is new, for it is not merely the exact doctrine of the New Church, but it is also believed to be the doctrine of a large number of the best minds in every quarter. Still it is notorious that there is scarcely the slightest reference to this vital idea in the institutions of society at large, nor in the investigations of the scientific, nor in the teachings of the learned. But on the contrary the clashing of philosophy and religion is daily becoming more and more manifest. Especially is this true, between what may be called the *high philosophy* and the *high theology* of the day ;—between those who are exploring the deepest arcana of nature, and those who are endeavoring to enter the sanctum sanctorum of revealed religion. The *marines* may not know where the breakers run, and whither the fatal currents tend, but the *sailors* do ! The day has gone by when the rigid demonstrations of science, or the conclusions of reason, can be cancelled by the mystic wand of implicit faith : wherefore when the teachings of science contradict the dogmas of the popular theologian, he is apt to regard them as the forerunners of an unknown and an unwelcome system from a hostile region, and to shrink from these demonstrations, as the king of Babylon did from the hand-writing upon the wall.

When the theologian and philosopher are united in the same individual, the conflict is often most intense, producing contradictory and mingled states of mind, and courses of conduct, comprehended by none but the individual himself : being perhaps, at one time borne down with intolerable misery and utter despair, and at another, lifted up into the most ineffable states of fantastic delight and self-aggrandizement. It is thus that many an unfortunate individual in the present age, is pressed, and tossed, and dashed, and broken, in the deep currents of emotion and thought and theory, which are far away from the praise or the blame of the more unthinking multitude. " I would that my mind were settled," said one who had devoted his life to the study of philosophy and theology. "I would that my mind were settled, and that I could find a resting place of thought," said another, and another. Yes, truly my brother, I would that your mind were settled, for I know that light is pleasant to the eye, and that truth is pleasant to the mind, and that the condition of that individual is dreary and desolate, whose eye is lifted up upon an expanse of utter darkness—whose mind is shrouded in the clouds of error and doubt. Who can recount the blessings of living from the very dawn of being in the element of truth ? Who can estimate the calamity to a youth of *relying*, from the dawn of life, upon instruction which is utterly inadequate and fallacious ? Who can measure the evil, which it may be to an individual to be obliged in the meridian of life, to unlearn what he has learned, to unsay what he has said, and to undo what he has done? *Fully* to undo the past is impossible ; but a desire to do this often exists, and this indicates, that a state has been passed through, deplorable in the extreme. In the golden age, religion treated of love to God, and of charity to the neighbor, and philosophy, of the relation of the spiritual to the natural world ; and of the representatives of spiritual and celestial principles which are given in natural and terrestrial objects. The religion and philosophy of that age were consequently *one*, being occupied in that which is useful and that alone.— (*A. C.* 4964.)

Seeking then, as we do, the union of theology and philosophy, how shall this end be gained? Shall we look to the sceptical Naturalist to give an adequate system? But how can he who discards theology, give the union of Theology and Philosophy ? Shall we look to the old Christian Church ? If so, to which branch of it ? But if this could be determined,— we are met with the fact that these churches have not the elements of harmony either in their philosophy, or their theology ; much less, the *unity* and *harmony* of the *two*. Shall we look to the New Jerusalem Church, for a harmonious and universal system ? We believe that we are left to this alternative ; for we think that it may be shown that this is the only system of religion whose doctrines are in constant harmony with science in its widest range, and with philosophy in its deepest, and purest reasonings. But we do not propose a discussion of this point at present. For we must now for a moment look at the condition and prospects of the old church: and here some very general considerations will show us that the current churches have passed the day of their power, that their influence is on the wane, and that nothing very hopeful, by way of a *new* and *universal system*, is to be expected at their hand.

A view of the present condition of the christian world, must fill the mind of the devout believer with mingled emotions of hope and melancholy forebodings. Since the dawn of the Christian religion, there never was a time when such unparalelled efforts were made for its propagation throughout the various nations of the earth. At home and abroad, from Lapland to Patagonia, from Greenland to Australia, from the rivers to the ends of the earth, everywhere, the heralds of this religion are at work; and with Bibles, tracts and Sunday-school books; in classes and conferences; with preaching, harangues, and exhortations, the majestic work is urged onward. In our own land the voice of its ministers is lifted up in almost every city, and town, and village, and hamlet, from Maine to the Mexican Gulf. And besides this aggressive warfare upon the impenitence and unbelief of the natural man, every means has been used to fortify the assailable points, and to wrest from the man of the world the munitions of power. To this end, throughout Europe and America, the *institutions* of *learning*, from the university down to the village academy, have been *manned* by the church. And notwithstanding the discrepancies which are everywhere becoming manifest between philosophy and religion, still the prayers of those churches are daily offered up in these public institutions, and their doctrines are distilled into the minds of the youth, by men of uncommon learning and skill and assiduity. Furthermore, that great engine of power, THE PRESS, with very few exceptions, is everywhere in harmony with the general movement. Also, the *civil government*, in all civilized lands, is either in open and avowed union with the Christian church, or in tacit obedience to its wishes; yielding to it every necessary protection and assistance.

Situated thus, what was to be expected at the hands of the extant churches? With such engines of aggression, and with munitions of power, was it not to be expected that christianity would reign triumphant, and that every institution of society would be imbued with its hallowed influences, to its very centre: that every man, woman and child, would be won over

should be accompanied with the proviso, that this Association be left in perfect freedom to adopt such rules and regulations in regard to its ministry, and such a form of ecclesiastical government, as may seem to us consistent with the doctrines of the New Church, and best adapted to our wants, and to the uses we have to perform."

We must insist upon these conditions, brethren; 1st, because we believe there must be variety in the forms of church government on earth, as we are taught there is variety in heaven; and 2d, because we think each section of the Church understands its own wants best; and is, therefore, able to legislate best for itself. We think it right that the Ohio Association, and every other state association of the New Church, should be left free to make laws for itself; because we think it knows better than the General Convention, or any other body can tell it, how to govern itself, and what rules are best suited to its wants.

You will see by the 8th Article of our Constitution, that we say nothing about three grades in the Ministry. We have made provision for granting licenses. and for introducing candidates into the ministry; and it is left with the Association itself to determine when, where, how, and by whom, each ordination shall be performed. But it is understood by us, that when a minister is ordained, he is ordained into all the functions of the priesthood. We see not the use, we feel not the need at present, of three degrees in the ministry, as these degrees are commonly understood. Yet our Association, by providing for a class of teaching ministers or licentiates, and by reserving to itself the final action upon all applications for license and ordination. does, as you will perceive, practically recognize a trinal distinction of ministerial uses. But if the Association of Massachusetts, Pennsylvania, Maine, or any other state, can clearly see, as we cannot, the propriety and necessity of a personal trine in the ministry—if they can see, as we cannot, why there should be three separate ordinations,—a second to qualify the candidate to officiate at weddings and in receiving members into societies, and to administer the Holy Supper, after having been, by his first ordination. authorized to administer the rite of baptism,—and a third, to qualify him to institute societies, to preside at meetings of the Convention and of Associations, and administer the Holy Supper to these larger bodies,—if any state Association. we say, see clearly the importance and use of such a trine in the ministry, and feel it to be adapted to their immediate wants, as we do not, we have not the slightest objection to their incorporating these views into a constitution, *for their own* government. We are quite willing, on our part, to leave every section of the Church free to organize itself, and to establish its ministry, in the manner most agreeable to its own views of order, and of adaptation to its own wants. We believe it ought to do so. And all we ask, is, that the same freedom, in these particulars, may be granted to us.

But we do not think that a difference of opinion between you and us in relation to the grades in the ministry, need be any obstacle to our acting together in the same organization, and mutually strengthening and aiding each other in advancing those great and permanent interests of the Church, which we presume it is the primary object of your Convention to promote. We believe that our ends are one and the same; and if this be the case, variety in externals need not separate us; it will help to make us more perfectly one. We are taught that there was great variety in the external order, and in the form of worship of the First Ancient Church; and yet that church was one,

the *revival* and *camp-ground* is broken up,—for if this were all no evil would be the result,—but more than this, religion in its more rational form, is falling into disrepute, and its legitimate power is sinking down under the horizon. *Things being thus,* we leave it to others, to divine the causes, if they be not what we have already declared them to be.

J. P. S.

SELECTIONS.

EXTRACTS FROM SWEDENBORG'S SPIRITUAL DIARY.

NOW FIRST TRANSLATED FROM THE ORIGINAL LATIN.

Concerning Spirits who think (much) of the Future.

4150. There are spirits who ponder upon the future, which they do from a habit and nature contracted in the world. They appear with a broad face, but it is not properly a face, but barely the broad area of a face, which becomes narrow in proportion as the area is narrow, nor is there aught of life in it ; it is, as it were, simply a certain wooden something; neither do they speak, but only think. By their means the sense of a man becomes so general that he thinks of nothing distinctly, and thus the mind remains indeterminate. Such is the state of those who give way to prevailing thoughts of the future, and thence become (mentally) emaciated, and void of understanding.

Concerning Societies.

4154. There exist in the other life societies corresponding to everything which can ever enter into the thoughts of man and into his concupiscences. As to the thoughts, let an example be taken from this, viz. that when I thought concerning any subject that was not clearly ascertained, but was hidden (as it were) in the Word, as concerning Noah's ark, then there were societies, (1) of those who thought of nothing else than whether it was to be ascertained at all : (2) of those whose concern it was whether it was true ; (3) of those who inquired whether it might be divulged. Those were most numerous who sought to know *whether it was,* and then those who inquired *whether it was so,* of which last there were very many societies. As soon as the question came up *whether it was so*, they wandered into innumerable conjectures, yet still in such a way that they roved about in externals only; upon the *quality* they did not enter. There were very many societies of these which were dissipated for they hindered the seeing what the thing *was;* they inhered every where in this, viz. *whether it was*, and while thus engaged turned to, *whether it was so*, yet still (back again to) *whether it was*, and (then once more) whether *it was so;* wherefore these last mentioned wandered about on the surface of the skin. (4) There were a great many societies which conjectured from their proprium, one in this way, another in that, in a long series. (5) There are societies which do not wish the truth to be detected, some from resentment that they cannot be supreme, some from unmercifulness, some from indolence, some from a desire that others should make the investigation by their own efforts, as they themselves do theirs. Others again desire that one should be kept in trying, with no other end than that simply of trying, in order that the man or spirit may despair, become enraged, and precipitate himself into every evil and insanity. With these I spake, saying, that such an end was diabolical, since mere trials determine nothing to any useful purpose; besides various other things concerning ends. But others had wholly different views. (6) The good, on the other hand, desire to know the truth, desire to teach, desire to have the truth open to all, being mainly anxious to unbosom themselves of all that they know, and to free others from trial and its consequent evil. Thus there are innumerable societies.

Conjugial Love.

4156. Conjugial love was represented near the scene of Paradisaical joys, by adamantine (or diamond-like) auras, sparkling as from rubies or carbuncles. There were certain ones present who were but little known to me during their bodily life, and to whom when conjugial love was thus represented, they said, under the influence of the admiration prompted by the delicious sweetness of their sensations that by no idea could such exquisite delight, such a diamond life, be conceived of, or its many unutterable accompaniments which thrilled the soul to its centre with bliss. Such was there the representation of conjugial love. I afterwards conversed with one that was present, saying, that conjugial love flowing from the heavenly marriage, thus from the Lord and from his compassion towards the human race, was the principal and fundamental of all the loves by which the celestial societies are distinguished, and he could not but wonder that the human race is ignorant of it, and cares scarcely at all about it.

Concerning the Sight of Spirits.

4159. It has been evinced to me from a multitude of proofs, that the sight of spirits among themselves is so exquisite that they have no other idea than that they clearly perceive others, and also themselves, and that they even have the sense of touch. Examples are numerous ; as that while I was myself in that state I really saw and touched spirits, just as if I had been awake, with all the sensation of sight, hearing, and touch. Spirits indeed oftentimes affirmed that they clearly saw themselves, their garments, their body, their hands. They frequently said also that they saw representations as in the brightest light, when I was permitted to make them, and that too so distinctly that they perceived every item ; yea, even those who were in an interior sphere saw in like manner from barely a general kind of thought, which included many other things that they perceived ; not to mention that I have seen spirits themselves more, I presume, than a thousand times, their faces, their bodies, and their representative creations, as in the light of day, besides (seeing them) in their habitations, etc. etc,

Concerning a certain good Spirit.

4160. A certain female known to me in the life (of the body) was, in the other life enabled to be among the blessed after the short space of a few weeks. She was in the society of the blessed, and it was perceived that her interiors were open, and that she then felt and perceived everything justly, to say nothing of other particulars. She was in the midst of paradisaical scenes and on beholding them said, that this was not to be happy, but that true happiness was something more interior, at which the spirits wondered, as they did still more at perceiving that she acknowledged the Lord from an interior principle. She was from among those on earth who lived in riches, splendor, and rank.

Concerning the proprium of Spirits.

4161. There were spirits with me who, from their proprium, wished to direct what I should write. They were of a quality scarcely to be described. They limit the ideas in such a way that I seemed to know nothing of what would be of advantage and what would not. They take away all extension of thought, narrowing it in such a manner that scarcely anything (general) can be known. They take away from other spirits all freedom, and all the delight thence arising. In a word, they are closed (as to their minds), so that there is scarcely anything of life in them ; they know nothing, and yet desire to know everything, being, as it were, a kind of wooden entities. They bring a man into bondage, nor leave him any freedom; they wish to occupy and possess him, when yet so long as man is in consort with the angels everything is free, and he has extension of thought, and is enabled to know what is good and true; but with these every thing is the reverse.

Concerning Evil and the Proprium.

4162. I perceived that man is the cause of evil, which appears from this, that it is an eternal law, that man should seem to himself to enjoy freedom, so that nothing should be done (by him) contrary to his will, as otherwise faith could never be implanted. Faith is implanted in the full exercise of freedom, never by force, compulsion, fear, or miracles. It hence appears that since, by an eternal law, it shall seem to man that he enjoys (entire) freedom, he is himself the cause of his evil.

REV. MR. PRESCOTT'S LECTURE.

We extract from the "Liverpool Mercury" the following interesting sketch of a Lecture by the Rev. T. O. Prescott.

"The Rev. Thos. O. Prescott, from America, delivered, on Monday evening, the 19th instant, a lecture on the life and character of Emanuel Swedenborg, in the New Jerusalem Church, Russell street.

"The lecturer began by stating, that the New Church did not regard itself merely as a sect of the present church, but as a new and distinct dispensation;—that, as the Lord Jesus Christ, at his first coming, established a new church, the Christian, which was to succeed the former, or Jewish dispensation—so, at his second coming, he again establishes a new church, or new dispensation of truth;—that, according to the doctrine of the new church, *now* is the time of the Lord's second coming,—not a coming in person, but in spirit, as Divine truth,—by a manifestation of the Divine truth that is contained in the *spiritual sense of the Scriptures*. Now, such manifestation of truth needs a medium through which it may be revealed and published to the world, which medium must be some human mind, prepared and enlightened for the purpose; that such a chosen medium was Emanuel Swedenborg, whose naturally great intellect, purity of character, and enlarged and thorough education, fitted him peculiarly for being, in the hand of Providence, a medium for performing this service to mankind.

"The lecturer proceeded then to give an account of Swedenborg's life and writings, giving a rapid sketch of his course,—first, as a philosopher and man of science, and taking a hasty review of some of his chief scientific works, the 'Principia,' the 'Animal Kingdom,' the 'Mineral Kingdom,' &c., and describing the high reputation which these works procured for the author among his contemporaries throughout Europe.

" The publication of these works occupied the author until his fifty-second year. Up to that time he had written nothing on theology. Here the lecturer paused, and put the question, ' What, supposing we knew nothing more of this philosopher's history than had already been related, what we should naturally conclude would be his course for the remainder of his life ?' Certainly, it would be natural to suppose that he would go on in the course he had hitherto pursued—that, namely, of the philosopher and man of science, continuing to prepare and give to the world valuable works on natural science, connected with those already published. This would be the reasonable proba-bility, had he been permitted to follow the bent of his own mind,—had he not been influenced by a direct interference, as it would seem, of Divine Providence, to turn his thoughts in another direction —his talents to other and still higher uses.

" The Lecturer proceeded then with his account. ' In the year 1749, or about eight years after the publication of the " Animal Kingdom," we find,' he said, ' this philosopher, Swedenborg, publishing, in the city of London, a work of remarkable character—a work professing to disclose discoveries far more important than his scientific discove-ries—laying open and describing, in detail, a new and hidden sense in the word of God, or Holy Scripture—a sense heretofore unknown, or of which the Church had had only occasional glimpses, such as are seen in the works of Origen and other early writers. This is called the *spiritual sense* of Scripture. This spiritual sense, as explained by Swedenborg,' continued the speaker, ' is not merely a general, indefi-nite, allegorical sense, such as is sometimes imagined or supposed by commentators, but is exceedingly exact and accurate, a kind of translation of the literal sense of scripture, word by word, into a high-er or deeper sense, each word retaining everywhere its own definite signification. The author begins with the first chapter of Genesis, and goes on, verse by verse, word by word, showing the internal sense as he proceeds, and connecting the various spiritual significations of the words together into a general meaning; so that, in this way, each verse is shown to have, as it were, two distinct senses, the literal and the spiritual. Thus, according to the view of Swedenborg, the word of God has two distinct senses—the one higher, more interior, more of a celestial character than the other, and capable of throwing great light on the lower or literal sense. And this,' argued the speaker, ' is the true key to the mysteries contained in the letter of God's word,' the only power that can reconcile the declarations contained in that letter with the well-attested facts of geological science, in regard to the creation of the world, &c.

number on commission. The third volume (I., 3) could, if the Lord will enable me, appear in the next summer, and, in the next year, the remaining parts. At present, I let them be copied by my amanuensis, and continue to translate the Arcana Cœlestia, of which at present the twelfth sheet (chapter 9) of the second volume is in print, although the sale is very small, and brings back very little of the expences. In Germany, the natural foundation of the spiritual truths must be restored; and this foundation consists in the rational or philosophical truths, by which the existence of God, of the spirituality and immortality of the soul, of the freedom of our will, and of the value and sanction of the moral law, are proved out of the depths of rational light; for sensualism, as prevailing in other countries, and the extreme of idealism, as prevailing in Germany, unite themselves in denying and destroying these great truths; wherefore, a new foundation must be laid, in the light of the New Church, in a catholic or all-assuming way, so that the proceedings of all times are taken together and concentrated, reasons and reasons put *vis-a-vis*, and justice given to every one. This spirit of universal inquiry, will increase in every country, together with its civilization, as has been well shown in Morell's Historical and Critical View of the Speculative Philosophy of Europe in the 19th Century, 2 vols., 2d ed., London, 1847; of which work, I gave, according to Professor Fichte's desire, a censure in Fichte's Philosophical Periodical. The said aim was that of my fundamental philosophy, and I hope to prepare the way by it to the New Church. Many important truths, for instance, the personality of God; the creation of the world, not from nothing, but out of him, by emission of substances; the non-materiality of the soul, and its independence from the body, etc., could already be shown in it, and Professor Fichte here (Professor of Philosophy) joins me fully in these general truths, whilst the Hegelians are denying them. I received also a kind and acknowledging letter from M. Eichhorn, at Berlin, the minister of the ecclesiastical affairs of the king of Prussia, in which he wishes that I might apply my method to the whole system of philosophy, for which, however, I need time, and it is not my custom to deprive our library of any hour which I owe to the state. There is very much to do, not only in the field of philosophy, but still more in that of theology, in order that ways may be from Israel to Assyria and to Egypt. The importance of the Adversaria has already been acknowledged in the New Universal Literary Gazette of Jena (Eine Jenaer Allgemeine Literaturzeitung) of December, 1847, in a proper article, it was said, that they are the uniting chain of Swedenborg's former and later works, and most important to see his mental development.

I take the liberty to join here two letters; one to our dear friend Zina Hyde, and another to Mr. Chauvenet, at Philadelphia, which I beg you to read first, and to send them afterwards, under covers, to their addresses. It will be good to inform orally the Receivers, concerning Dr. Ostenhold's letter, inserted in the Magazine of October last, p. 48.

I beg to greet the members of the General Convention from my heart's part, and to express to them my best thanks for their assistance. My wife joins me in kindest regards to yourself, to Mrs. Dike, and to all brethren and sisters, especially Mrs. Parker.

I remain, my dear brother in the New Church,

Yours, very affectionately,

EMANUEL TAFEL.

REMARKABLE LETTER OF ST. AUGUSTINE.

(Epistola 159, Antwerp Ed.)

" ' I will relate to you a circumstance,' he writes, ' which will furnish you matter for reflection. Our brother Sennadius, well known to us all as an eminent physician, and whom we especially love, who is now at Carthage, after having distinguished himself at Rome, and with whose piety and active benevolence you are well acquainted, could not yet, nevertheless, as he has lately narrated to us, by any means bring himself to believe in a life after death. Now God, doubtless not willing that his soul should perish, there appeared to him, one night in a dream, a radiant youth of noble aspect, who bade him follow him; and as Sennadius obeyed, they came to a city where, on the right side, he heard a chorus of the most heavenly voices. As he desired to know whence this divine harmony proceeded, the youth told him that what he heard were the songs of the blessed; whereupon he awoke, and thought no more of his dream than people usually do. On another night, however, behold, the youth appears to him again, and asks if he knows him; and Sennadius related to him all the particulars of his former dream, which he then remembered. "Then," said the youth, "was it whilst sleeping or waking that you saw these things ?" "I was sleeping," answered Sannadius. "You are right," returned the youth, "it was in your sleep that you saw these things; and now, oh, Sennadius, that which you see now is also in your sleep. But if this be so, tell me where, then, is your body ?" "In my bed-chamber," answered Sennadius. "But know you not," continued the stranger, "that your eyes, which form a part of your body, are closed and inactive ?" "I know it," answered he. "Then," said the youth, "with what eyes see you these things ?" And Sennadius could not answer him; and as he hesitated, the youth spoke again, and explained to him the motive of his questions. "As the eyes of your body," said he, "which lies now on your bed and sleeps, are inactive and useless, and yet you have eyes wherewith you see me, and these things I have shown unto you, so after death, when those bodily organs fail you, you will have a vital power, whereby you will live; and a sensitive faculty, whereby you will perceive. Doubt, therefore, no longer that there is a life after death." And thus,' said this excellent man, ' was I convinced, and all doubts removed.' "—*Mrs. Crowe's* " *Night Side of Nature.*"

DR. CHANNING'S VIEW OF HEAVEN.

"The true view of heaven, that which the Scriptures give, that which reason sanctions, and that which we can most powerfully realize, is, that it will not essentially change, but rather improve, our nature. We shall be the same beings as on earth; we shall retain our present faculties, our present affections, our love of knowledge, love of beauty, love of action, love of approbation, our sympathy, gratitude, and pleasure in success. We shall probably, too, have bodies not very different from what we now have,—the eye to behold creation and receive its beauties, the ear to hear the voice of friendship and to receive the pleasures of harmony, and even sense refined and purified. This we know, that Jesus in a form like ours ascended into heaven, and when Moses and Elijah conversed with him on the Mount, they appeared in the human form, differing from ours only in its splendor; and from these facts it would seem that our future bodies will bear a general resemblance to the present."—*Memoirs of Channing, Vol. II.* .p 22.

MISCELLANY.

PROCEEDINGS OF THE GENERAL CONVENTION.

(For the benefit of such of our readers as may not have access to the N. J. Magazine, we select from the journal recently published the most important Resolutions and Reports presented at the late sitting of the Convention.)

Communication from the Ohio Association.

To the General Convention of Societies and other Associated Bodies of the New Church in the United States.

Dear Brethren,—At the last meeting of the New Church Western Convention, held in Cincinnati the present month, the following resolutions, appended to a report of considerable length, on the subjects herein referred to, were adopted with great unanimity:

"*Resolved*, 1. That this body now change its name, and adopt, instead of the 'New Church Western Convention,' the name of the 'Ohio Association of the New Church,' as being more appropriate, and more expressive of the truth.

"*Resolved*, 2. That a committee of five persons be appointed, to propose such alterations in our Constitution, as the contemplated change of name may seem to require, and to report thereon to this Convention.

"*Resolved*, 3. That, as the Ohio Association of the New Church, we connect ourselves with the General Convention of Societies, and other associated bodies of the New Church in the United States, on the conditions specified in this Report; and that a communication, expressive of this our wish, accompanied by a copy of our Constitution, be forwarded to that body, at its approaching session in June next."

By the passage of another resolution, it was made the duty of the
undersigned, to prepare and forward to your body, an address, accompanied by a copy of our Constitution, which you will receive along
with this, and to express to you the desire of our Association to connect itself with the General Convention. And this duty is the more
pleasing to us, brethren, on account of the very great unanimity with
which the above resolutions were adopted—there being *but one* dissenting voice on the first two, and *not one* on the last.

We deem it quite unnecessary to express any opinion here, as to
the sufficiency or insufficiency of the reasons for a Western Convention, at the time it was organized, or as to the extent or importance
of the uses which this Convention has performed. But from a careful
examination of the journals of proceedings of the Western Convention,
from its commencement up to the present time, it is manifest, that it
has never been what it was intended it should be, and what the name,
under which it was constituted in 1832, would seem to import. It
has never been a ' *General* Convention of the Receivers of the Doctrines
of the New Jerusalem, west of the Alleghany Mountains ;' which is
the name, as printed on the cover of its first journal of proceedings.
For, out of the state of Ohio, no considerable portion of the Church
west of the Alleghanies, has ever been represented in the Western
Convention. An examination of our journals shows, that, taking one
year with another, not more than five individuals out of the state of
Ohio, have been present at each of our annual meetings.

Recorded facts, therefore, abundantly testify, that the Western
Convention has been little more than a Convention of the Receivers
of the Heavenly Doctrines in our own state, and has never, we believe,
embraced *all* of them. And from information lately received from the
Michigan and Northern Indiana Association, and also from Illinois, as
well as from other facts that came before us at our late session, it is
evident that the Receivers west of the Alleghanies are not at this time
generally desirous of a Western Convention.

But we need not trouble you at present, brethren, with the various
reasons which induced us to change our name, and to adopt the
course proposed in the above resolutions. Our reasons will appear
in detail in the Report of our Committee on that subject, which will
shortly be published in our journal of proceedings. It is sufficient to
say here, that a General Convention of the Receivers west of the Alleghanies, has proved impracticable. Yielding, therefore, to the clear
indications of the Divine Providence, which manifestly do not favor
such a Convention, we have agreed henceforward to be known by
what we ourselves, as well as our Michigan, Indiana, and Illinois
brethren, regard as the more appropriate name, of the Ohio Association of the New Church; and we hereby express the desire of our
Association to become connected with the General Convention.

But, in asking admission into your body, we must not forget to
mention. and would not have you overlook, the *conditions* of admission,
.referred to in our resolution upon that subject. The conditions alluded to are expressed in the following language, which we copy from
the Committee's Report. They say :

" But it is the unanimous and decided opinion of your Committee,
that, in asking admission into the General Convention, our application

should be accompanied with the proviso, that this Association be left in perfect freedom to adopt such rules and regulations in regard to its ministry, and such a form of ecclesiastical government, as may seem to us consistent with the doctrines of the New Church, and best adapted to our wants, and to the uses we have to perform."

We must insist upon these conditions, brethren ; 1st, because we believe there must be variety in the forms of church government on earth, as we are taught there is variety in heaven ; and 2d, because we think each section of the Church understands its own wants best ; and is, therefore, able to legislate best for itself. We think it right that the Ohio Association, and every other state association of the New Church, should be left free to make laws for itself ; because we think it knows better than the General Convention, or any other body can tell it, how to govern itself, and what rules are best suited to its wants.

You will see by the 8th Article of our Constitution, that we say nothing about three grades in the Ministry. We have made provision for granting licenses. and for introducing candidates into the ministry ; and it is left with the Association itself to determine when, where, how, and by whom, each ordination shall be performed. But it is understood by us, that when a minister is ordained, he is ordained into all the functions of the priesthood. *We* see not the use, *we* feel not the need at present, of three degrees in the ministry, as these degrees are commonly understood. Yet our Association, by providing for a class of teaching ministers or licentiates, and by reserving to itself the final action upon all applications for license and ordination. does, as you will perceive, practically recognize a trinal distinction of ministerial uses. But if the Association of Massachusetts, Pennsylvania, Maine, or any other state, can clearly see, as we cannot, the propriety and necessity of a personal trine in the ministry—if they can see, as we cannot, why there should be three separate ordinations,— a second to qualify the candidate to officiate at weddings and in receiving members into societies, and to administer the Holy Supper, after having been, by his first ordination. authorized to administer the rite of baptism,—and a third, to qualify him to institute societies, to preside at meetings of the Convention and of Associations, and administer the Holy Supper to these larger bodies,—if any state Association, we say, see clearly the importance and *use* of such a trine in the ministry, and feel it to be adapted to their immediate wants, as we do not, we have not the slightest objection to their incorporating these views into a constitution, *for their own* government. We are quite willing, on our part, to leave every section of the Church free to organize itself, and to establish its ministry, in the manner most agreeable to its own views of order, and of adaptation to its own wants. We believe it ought to do so. And all we ask, is, that the same freedom, in these particulars, may be granted to us.

But we do not think that a difference of opinion between you and us in relation to the grades in the ministry, need be any obstacle to our acting together in the same organization, and mutually strengthening and aiding each other in advancing those great and permanent interests of the Church, which we presume it is the primary object of your Convention to promote. We believe that our ends are one and the same ; and if this be the case, variety in externals need not separate us ; it will help to make us more perfectly one. We are taught that there was great variety in the external order, and in the form of worship of the First Ancient Church ; and yet that church was one, by virtue of the principle of charity. They were all "of one lip, and their words were one." We are also taught that there is great variety among the societies of heaven; and yet these societies are all so united in respect to *ends* or *uses*, that they appear before the Lord as one man. And how various in form, organization and function, are the different organs in the human body! Yet all being pervaded and animated by one life, they act together in one and the same general organization, in the most beautiful harmony. The Human system is the most perfect of all created forms, because it consists of the greatest number and *variety* of parts acting together in perfect concert. And herein is imaged forth the true form of Heaven and the Church. "In heaven," says our illumined author, "there are innumerable societies, *and all various*, but still they form a one, for they are all under the Lord's guiding and governance as one. In this respect heaven is like any individual man, in whom, although there are so many viscera, and so many smaller viscera within the larger, so many organs and so many members. each of which has a different operation from the rest, yet they are all and each of them governed as one by one soul." *A. C.* 1285.

Moreover, brethren, we think that a *General* Convention in these United States ought to embrace every associated body of well disposed Receivers—every *variety* of the New Church in our country. Otherwise there would not be a propriety in calling it a *General* Convention. And the Ohio Assocation. with whatever peculiarities belong to it, is certainly one among the existing varieties. If only there be a sufficiency of that heavenly cement, charity, to bind in one these various parts, these varieties will serve but to render more perfect the General Body. "Mutual love and charity," says Swedenborg, "are effective of unity, or oneness, even amongst varieties, uniting varieties into one; for let numbers be multiplied ever so much, even to thousands and ten thousands, if they are all principled in charity or mutual love, they have all one end, viz. the common good, the kingdom of the Lord, and the Lord himself; in which case the *varieties* in matters of doctrine and worship, are like the varieties of the senses and viscera in man, which contribute to the perfection of the whole." *A. C.* 1285.

We say, therefore, in conclusion, brethren, that we desire to be united with your body, if you can receive us on the terms here proposed; because we believe that such union will tend to promote the interests of the whole church; because we wish to see the New Church in this country organically united as one man, and desire to do all we can to effect such a union; because we believe that in union there is strength, and would gladly do all in our power to increase the strength and extend the influence of the New Jerusalem.

Praying that the Lord Jesus Christ may be in your midst at your approaching session, that He may reign and rule in all your deliberations, and direct them to wise and healthful issues, we remain,

On behalf of the Ohio Association of the New Church,

Truly and affectionately your brethren,

B. F. BARRETT,	
OLIVER LOVELL,	*For the*
S. HOLMES,	*Acting Committee.*
E. HINMAN.	

Cincinnati, May, 30, 1848.

Report of the Committee on the Application of the Ohio Association.

The Committee to whom was referred the communication from the Ohio Association, together with so much of Rev. Mr. Barrett's communication as relates to the same, have considered the subject as fully as the short time allowed would permit, and as they trust in a spirit of conciliation and kindness, and with every disposition to meet and accommodate the wishes of our Western brethren, which they feel assured is the earnest desire of the convention. But they have found difficulties in the case, by which they have been not a little embarrassed. This of course has been a subject of serious regret; and after considerable discussion, they have adopted the course which on the whole seemed the best under all the circumstances of the case. The Committee cannot doubt but it is the wish of the Convention to receive the Ohio Association with open arms; and without conditions or restrictions to give them a cordial welcome; and this the Committee would certainly have recommended, if the application had been in the usual form and they had themselves proposed to unite with us in full. But this they have not seen proper to do; and we doubt not they have reasons which are satisfactory to themselves; and, for anything we know, reasons which are sound and sufficient. And as to going to the extreme, and declining entirely the proposal, the Committee could not bring themselves to such a conclusion. In this condition, a middle ground was suggested, which it was thought would meet the peculiarities of the case; and though it is not all we should be glad to grant, it yet seems to be all that is asked, and perhaps we ought to suppose, all that would be freely received; for, from the abundant expressions of good will, and the most earnest desire for free and full intercourse and co-operation, with which the communication abounds, we feel constrained to suppose that a full union with the Conveotion would have been as great a pleasure to the Association, as we are sure it would be to the Convention, if circumstances had not made it expedient in their opinion to guard their application by a reservation of powers to their own exclusive exercise. But while they have so explicitly made this reservation an express condition of their application, we cannot of course suppose, that they would think of acting in the Convention in relation to the same subjects as applied to the other parts of the Convention. For it would not be equal and just, that they should have the exclusive management of a certain portion of their own affairs and at the same time have a share in the management of the same affairs, so far as the rest of the Convention is concerned. We repeat then, that the reservation which we propose on the part of the Convention is one which we feel bound to provide, for the sake of equality and right in reference to the question considered in itself, and in justice to the Convention as a body, and to the other Associations which have joined the Convention without conditions or reservations.

However reluctant therefore we may feel to recommend any partial or restricted action, justice to all parties seems to require it; and the Committee have felt constrained to reply, by inserting in the Resolutions of admission a condition corresponding as nearly as possible with that of the request,—a condition which we doubt not the Convention would be most happy to abolish. as soon as the Ohio Association shall be disposed and prepared to take such a step as will tend to a fuller union of duties and responsibilities.

The Committee conclude by offering the following Resolution:

. " *Resolved*, That this Convention cordially receives the Ohio Association agreeably to the terms of their request; it being understood that they shall have no vote in the Convention in the regulation of its Ministry, or the form of its ecclesiastical government.

The following resolution was also adopted without dissent :

" *Resolved*, That the application of the Ohio Association, and the report thereon of the Committee to which the same was referred, together with the resolution just passed, be now referred to a Committee of three clergymen and four laymen who shall take into consideration our Rules and Recommendations, and correspond with the Ohio Association, or with individuals on their behalf and with other bodies of the Church in this country, with the view of arranging the reception of that Association into this Convention on grounds satisfactory to that Association, and, as far as may be found proper, common to all the Associations and other bodies of the New Church, which are or shall become members of this Convention. And that this Committee may sit during the recess, and report to the Convention at its next annual meeting.

Rev. Mr. Carll's Resolution.

Mr. Carll offered the following, which were adopted :

" *Resolved*, 1. That the following suggestions be communicated to the different Associations and Societies in the United States :

" 1. That the title of this Convention be altered to that of the ' General Conference of the New Jerusalem Church in the United States.'

" 2. That immediate steps be taken to form a Triennial Conference.

" 3. That this Conference, based upon charity and neighborly love, shall be of an advisory character.

" 4. That each Association be left in freedom to regulate its own concerns.

" *Resolved*, 2. That the above suggestions be referred to the Committee already raised, relative to the report and resolution on the application of the Ohio Association."

Communication of the New York Delegates.

Whereas the first Society of the New Jerusalem of the City of New York has engaged the ministerial services of the Rev. George Bush, a member of said Society, who declines being ordained on the ground of the authority claimed for that purpose by the Convention, and in accordance with the views of the nature and constitution of the Christian Ministry as put forth by that body, the undersigned, in behalf of the Society, respectfully submit to the Convention, the inquiry, whether the employment of Prof. Bush under these circumstances, is to be considered as inconsistent with, or in any manner affecting, the relations of said Society to this Convention ; and if so, in what way, and on what specific grounds.

SAMUEL L. WALDO, ⎫
SAMUEL HUNT, ⎬ *Delegates of the N. Y. Soc.*
L. S. BURNHAM, ⎭

Report of the Committee on the Communication of the N. Y. Delegates.

The Committee to whom was referred the communication of the Delegates from the New York Society, ask leave to report that they have considered the subject. and are of opinion that the employment of Professor Bush, in the manner stated, is irregular, but does not affect the relations subsisting between said Society and this body, in such a manner as to require action on the part of the Convention.

M. M. CARLL, *Chairman.*

Report of the Committee on the Turner Legacy.

The Committee to whom was referred the application of the Hon. Josiah Turner for a portion of his brother's legacy, and instructed to consider and Report what disposition should be made of the legacy of the late O. P. Turner, and whether any steps should be taken to facilitate the reception of the same, have attended to their duties, and ask leave to Report.

On the supposition that the statement of Mr. Josiah Turner is true, of which there appears to be no reason to doubt, the Committee think his request a reasonable one, and recommend that it should be granted.

On the supposition that Mr. O. P. Turner has bequeathed for the use of his only child the sum of $2500 only (which has been reported to be the amount), the Committee are of the opinion that the Convention ought not so to dispose of the amount bequeathed to itself, as to deprive itself of the ability to add to the means of said child's support and education, if circumstances at a future day should seem to render it expedient.

The Committee do not know of any measures that will be likely to facilitate the receipt of the legacy.

The Committee offer the following Resolutions.

" *Resolved,* 1. That the Treasurer is authorized to receive the same in behalf of this body, and give full receipts and acquittances therefor.

" *Resolved,* 2. That when said legacy shall be received, the Treasurer be authorized, in concurrence with the advisory Committee hereafter provided for, to pay the sum of one thousand dollars to Hon. Josiah Turner, of Michigan ; and to invest the remainder in some safe manner, until farther order be taken by the Convention on the same.

" *Resolved,* 3. That out of the first interest accruing from said investment, the Treasurer be instructed to pay over to the Book Committee a sum sufficient to purchase 25 copies of the Apocalypse Explained, to be purchased and distributed according to resolutions No. 48 and 49 of the journal of 1847.

" Whereas important questions may arise in obtaining and disposing of this legacy, in deciding which the Treasurer may wish advice; therefore,

" *Resolved,* 4. That Messrs. T. Parsons, J. M. Marsh, Sampson Reed, and John G. Davis, be a Committee to advise with the Treasurer in all such cases.

" And whereas, owing to unavoidable circumstances, the original statement and application of Judge Turner has not been laid before the Convention, but only an oral statement of its contents, and it is deemed right and proper that such statement and application, and such corroborative document as may be reasonably asked, should be on the files of the Convention, before the request of Judge Turner be finally granted ; therefore,

" *Resolved,* 5. That Judge Turner be requested to furnish the Treasurer and advising Committee with a full statement of his case, and such other facts and documents as they may require, and to them may be satisfactory."

Report of the Committee on the Observance of Christmas Day.

(An extended and able Report is offered on this subject, but our space allows us to present only the general conclusion.)

Your Committee are of the opinion, that the instruction which we have received, and the feelings which we have been taught to cherish would lead us to celebrate the event under consideration upon the Sabbath, rather than upon any other day in the week.

Report of the Committee of Foreign Correspondence.

The Committee of Foreign Corespondence report that during the past year, considerable intercourse has taken place between the receivers of the Church in this country and those in Europe ; and much intelligence has been received from time to time. Most of this, and all of it which has come within our reach, and been deemed valuable, has been published in the New Jerusalem Magazine, and is probably familiar to the members of the Convention.

We have, however, one letter of much interest from Dr. Tafel, which has not been published ; and we annex it to this Report, and place it at the disposal of the Convention.

THEOPHILUS PARSONS, *Chairman.*

Letter from Dr. Tafel, to the Rev. Samuel F. Dike.

TUBINGEN, 13 February, 1848.

My very dear Brother in the New Church,—Accept my heartfelt thanks for your dear letter of 4th October, 1847, which I sent in the mean time to my brother at Schorndorf, whose two sons have long ago reached the United States, and will probably be followed in this year by their eldest brother, an able apothecary, to whom favorable offers were made from thence. I am very glad to hear from you, that each of the Conventions in your country are now coming upon very friendly terms with each other, and that you, on your part, have established a correspondence with the Central and the Western Conventions. Unity is what we need. You give me some hope to be visited by Mr. Prescott, of Cincinnati, and afterwards perhaps by yourself, which would afford to myself great joy. You ask, if I have heard of the king of Prussia of late ; if he has given any particular attention to the writings of E. S. ? I answer, that I have nothing heard of it ; what has been said of him, respecting this, was a mistake. I sent him some of my books,—the Supplement to Kant's Biography, and the Twelve Proofs for the Immortality of the Human Soul (4th Part of the Documents concerning the life and character of E. Sw.), for which he thanked me friendly. This is the fact. The same did our crown prince and our king, who also accepted, with "pleasure and interest," my Fundamental Philosophy, Part 1. ; and, upon the favorable sentence of our philosophical faculty here, the king gave me, by decree of 8 December last, the title and rank of Professor of Philosophy, in spite of the opposition of our theological and philosophical adversaries in the Academical Senate, who feared an increase of my influence in ecclesiastical matters everywhere, and consider now the doing of the king as a kind of acknowledgment. You ask, how long it will take me to get out the rest of the Adversaria ? Of Part I., I sent, the 25th August last, 30 copies to Mr. J. H. Wilkins, of Boston ; and now the second volume (I., 2) is finished, of which he will receive the same

"To suppose that any idea of the Divine of the Lord exist, which is above the human, is irrational. Examine this idea, which is the deepest subject of human thought, and compare it with the angels in heaven, for with them the Humanity is altogether Divine. To separate the Divine of the Father from the Humanity in heaven, is to make the Lord not one, but two. Such an idea of the Lord is rejected, and it can gain no admission there.

"To speak of one substance, or of one essence, and yet with some specific distinction or difference, as of a Divine attribute of Deity, is to destroy the Unity. Think very carefully within yourself, whether it is possible to speak of the Father as Creator, or of the Son as Redeemer, or of the Holy Spirit as Illustrator. Can you think of a Divine attribute, separately or distinctly, without it being in communion or common to each other? Examine the ground of thought? Can you think of one God, or of one substance, or of one essence, and then proceed to consider how the work of Creation is to be effected from the Father in the Son, and from the Son through the Holy Spirit; and whether by this order any idea is elicted of such a reciprocal and proceeding operation? Can such an idea be entertained? Is it not contrary to the laws of a Divine order if viewed in relation to one substance, or to a reciprocal progression together? Surely, such an idea cannot be entertained by any well constituted mind.

"Let us attempt to ascertain the quality of the idea which those possess, whether in speech or in thought, when they beseech the Father to have mercy for the sake of the Son; and let them inquire, whether the idea perceived is not contrary to the doctrine of faith as taught in the Word? By the separation of Father and Son, whether the Lord is not considered only as a common man,—in which they look in vain for any perception,—in which nothing remains, although admitted to be one with the Father. Still, a union, or oneness, is professed to be understood. Why is the Humanity or the Son preferred, while the thought is elevated to the Divine above it? And why is the Humanity placed below separately? In one word, is not the contradiction in the Athanasian doctrine here made apparent? that the Divine and the Human are together one person, so that the Human is also in the Father and one with the Father. Surely, no thought can admit this unless the Humanity is also Divine. For the Father is infinite, uncreate, and omnipotent God; and the Humanity cannot be less truly so, if together they are one substance, or one essence with the Father; and consequently no less equally Divine! Contradictions like these equally appear from the consideration of Christ as a rational and perfect man, when derived solely from the mother. Equally absurd is the supposition, that the Lord, as a mere man, could be in the Father, or one with the Father, or in the Divine, while it is said that they together are one person, and consequently, Divine. The contradiction appears from the supposition, that, as God and man, they could be together one person, if the Humanity is not admitted to be Divine."

He speaks thus of Athanasius himself in the spiritual world.

"I have been permitted to speak with Athanasius upon the subject-matter of this Creed, because he had confirmed himself in the faith of three Gods, so that his mind continually vacillated between the three, that he could not acknowledge one God. He was in error almost in everything, as he had not any clear ideas of the truths of faith. Such is the case and state of others, who have confirmed themselves in the faith of three Gods. But those, however, who have not such confirmation, having only heard of that faith, and retained it in their remembrance, and are yet established in the faith of one God, when they come into heaven, reject the idea of three Gods, and preserve only a correct idea of the Divine personality of one God.

"Some persons who have never permitted their understandings to entertain any correct idea concerning the Trinity, being so strongly impressed with the literal and external sense of the Word, are unable to elevate the thoughts above it. For while this faith rules, and is confirmed with delight, there is no ground in the understanding that will admit of illustration from the spiritual sense. For such a faith closes the understanding, and prevents the reception of light, and it gives a false tinge or coloring to every passage in relation to its spiritual meaning. But let the sole Divinity of the Lord be once clearly perceived, and then

Letter from Mr. W. H. Butterfield of Lockport, N. Y.

Rev. Thomas Worcester, *Lockport, June* 1, 1848.

Dear Sir,—Knowing that all information relating to the progress and prospects of the New Church is solicited for the benefit of all whose feet are within or approaching the precincts of the New Jerusalem, I communicate what little I have. In the latter part of the year 1845, being deeply absorbed in questions relating to the social and spiritual destiny of man, having followed the thoughts and speculations of the celebrated authors, so far as they were within reach, hoping to find the solution of certain problems, on which seemed to depend a successful issue to the questions raised, the writer, when on the point of yielding up a fruitless effort to plant his feet on a solid philosophical basis, and his hopes upon an unwavering spiritual faith, accidentally fell in with a Medical periodical, containing in part Mr. Wilkinson's exposition of the Scientific Doctrines of Swedenborg as contained in the Animal Kingdom. His attention was at once arrested; he read again and again the fragment, endeavoring to grasp those new and absorbing doctrines. During some three weeks, every leisure moment was occupied upon that fragment: every sentence was measured, every word was weighed; and every moment new light, yet obscure, was breaking upon his mind. Just at that time he saw a notice of the Swedenborg Library, indicating the subject of the second No. "The Nature of the Soul." It was immediately ordered; after a delay of three or four weeks it came to hand; yet how forbidding at the first sight, without cover, pages soiled, its leaves ruffled and marred. An unfavorable impression was made; yet a perusal was commenced. What a strange air pervaded it—what strangeness of style—what a truthful sincerity—what thoughts—how they light up the mind!—how they sink to the very depths of the soul! Assuredly these thoughts are true—they are attested by an intuition too clear, too deep, to be false! An impression was made never to be effaced. The remaining part of the work was ordered. The works, "Heaven and Hell," "Divine Providence," and others of Swedenborg's theological works were soon procured and read. The Animal Kingdom, and all of his scientific and philosophical works which have appeared in an English translation, have been read at the same time with the former. All leisure time, to the present, has been occupied in studying these works. The results of such a study can be duly appreciated by those who have had a similar experience; who clearly perceive that the word and works of our Lord are in perfect harmony; and who are watching with intense interest the descent of the New Jerusalem, affecting all worldly interests; and who hope to ascend to its higher courts. The works of Swedenborg have from time to time been placed in the hands of such persons as have expressed any desire to peruse them; and the writer is happy to be assured that five or six persons have become receivers, and several others more or less interested in the New Church doctrines. Two of the receivers, a sister and nephew of the writer, have removed to Illinois. Several individuals had during the last winter, expressed a wish that public lectures should be delivered upon the scientific and theological writings of Swedenborg; and the writer had, to some extent, prepared himself to comply with their wishes; but it has been hitherto deemed inexpedient so to do; yet it may hereafter be thought best to meet those wishes.

I regret very much that I cannot attend the Convention; nothing could give me more pleasure. Sincerely, yours, W. H. Butterfield.

to issue anything upon their own responsibility for which there is not the certainty of an immediate demand that shall preclude any pecuniary risk, and
there is unhappily an apathy on this score among the body of New Churchmen
that gives no assurance of such a demand. This is a fact much to be regretted,
and for which we hope a remedy may be found in the waking up of better impulses towards the promotion of a great and good cause.

3.—EUREKA: *A Prose Poem.* By EDGER A. POE. NEW YORK: J. WILEY.
1848; pp. 143.

A poet here enters upon profound speculations, shooting ahead of the New-
tons, Laplaces, Herschells, and Nicholses, in the solution of the great problems
of the Universe. He calls his work a poem, perhaps because, with Madame
De Stael, he regards the Universe itself as more like a poem than a machine, and
therefore to be treated *poematically*. Others might say it was because he had
invested the subject with all a poet's imagination. But this would be, we think,
to withhold its due meed of praise from the vein of real philosophic thought which
runs through it. It is a book devoted indeed to a theory, but a theory by no
means to be despised nor lacking in some of the higher elements of scientific
probability. We might perhaps feel the want of a certain property termed
demonstration as a buttress to his reasonings, but that the author has effectually
estopped any such inconvenient demand in his case by the peremptory position
that " in this world, at least, there is *no such thing* as demonstration"—that such
affairs as axioms or self-evident truths are " all in my eye," mere figments and
phantasies. Waving, however, the application of this sweeping *negatur* to his
own speculations, we refuse not to concede that the work before us does offer
some hints towards solving no less a problem than that of the *cause of gravitation*,
before which the grandest geniuses have shrank abashed. Of this we can
scarcely make the barest *statement* in a manner which shall do full justice to
the propounder's thought, but we may afford an inkling of it by saying that he
assumes a created unitary and irrelative particle as the first principle or germ of
the Universe, and supposes an internal force, identical with the Divine volition,
to have radiated or projected all but an infinity of minimal atoms from this parent
particle into the regions of space, and that the attraction of gravitation is nothing
else than a *conatus* on the part of these atoms to return to the central unity. It
would doubtless be easy to suggest a multitude of difficulties that weigh upon
this theory in the form in which it is proposed by the poet-philosopher, but we
may take the main position apart from all the accessories by which it is surrounded and give it the credit of at least a very plausible and sagacious guess. The
hypothesis of the generation of the Universe from a *simple monad*—not however the
monad of Leibnitz—plainly approximates, in several of its features, to the view
given by Swedenborg in his philosophical works, of the evolution of all things
from " the first natural point," and Mr. Poe will recognize a striking analogy
between his own theory and that presented in the following paragraph from
the " Outlines on the Infinite:"

" Let us confine our attention still to the first and smallest natural principle, so
that we may not disturb the worshipers of nature in their circles and spheres, but

DEATH NOT ALWAYS PAINFUL.

We think that most persons have been led to regard dying as a much more painful change than it generally is; first, because they have found by what they experienced in themselves and observed in others, that sentient beings often struggle when in distress; hence struggling to them is a sign, an invariable sign, of distress. But we may remark, that struggles are very far from being invariable signs of distress; muscular action and consciousness are two distinct things, often existing separately; and we have abundant reason to believe that in a great portion of cases, those struggles of dying men which are so distressing to behold, are as entirely independent of consciousness as the struggles of a recently decapitated fowl. A second reason why men are led to regard dying as a very painful change, is, because men often endure great pain without dying, and forgetting that like causes produce like effects only under similar circumstances, they infer that life cannot be destroyed without still greater pain. But the pains of death are much less than most persons have been led to believe, and we doubt not that many persons who live to the age of puberty, undergo tenfold more misery than they would, did they understand correct views concerning the change. In all cases of dying, the individual suffers no pain after the sensibility of his nervous system is destroyed, which is often without any previous pain.

Those who are struck dead by a stroke of lightning, those who are decapitated with one blow of the axe, and those who are instantly destroyed by a crush of the brain, experience no pain at all in passing from a state of life to a dead state. One moment's expectation of being thus destroyed far exceeds in misery the pain during the act. Those who faint in having a little blood taken from the arm, or on any other occasion, have already endured all the misery they ever would did they not again revive. Those who die of fevers and most other diseases, suffer their greatest pain, as a general thing, hours, or even days, before they expire. The sensibility of the nervous system becomes gradually diminished; their pain becomes less acute under the same existing cause; and at the moment when their friends think them in the greatest distress, they are more at ease than they have been for many days previous; their disease, as far as it respects their feelings, begins to act upon them like an opiate. Indeed, many are already dead as it respects themselves, when ignorant by-standers are much the most to be pitied, not for the loss of their friends, but their sympathizing anguish. Those diseases which destroy life without immediately affecting the nervous system, give rise to more pain than those that do affect the system so as to impair its sensibility. The most painful deaths which human beings inflict upon each other, are pro-

enters to reunite the world to the Eternal. God was in Christ reconciling the world, not reconciling God, but the world to God. * * * Irenæus opened the dogmatic history of atonement by teaching that it was a ransom to the devil. Since then, it has been a ransom paid to God, sometimes vindictive, sometimes expiatory. Sometimes the criminal law afforded the illustration, sometimes the civil law, sometimes the ceremonial. The most modern orthodoxy is, that Christ's suffering expresses the same love of right as if we were punished, and so God's character is cleared. It is remarkable that so powerful a doctrine dissolves away at the touch ; that it offers *such marvellous fecundity of self-refutation!* If Christ suffered unwillingly, it was the direst cruelty ; if willingly, the character of the government was impeached. If Christ was God and Ruler, in suffering the penalties of his own law, his government would suffer. Again, if all guilt is satisfied for, there can be no farther suffering for guilt. There are no limits to the objections this old theory provokes, while it *fails to answer any theological purpose.*"

This is a direct and palpable repudiation of the doctrine of Atonement as held at present, and for two centuries past, by the great mass of Protestant churches, and no where with greater tenacity than in New England. The theory adopted by the preacher, so far as we can glean from a meagre abstract, is *substantially* that of the New Church. We hope Dr. C. may not recoil from it when he becomes aware of this fact. That he should have remained for so long a time in doubt on this point is probably owing to his association during that period with a system under the influence of which doubt, on this head, is seldom permitted to arise ; and that he has at length emerged from it, is because he has ventured to think for himself in disregard of the prescribed *pattern.* We honor the manly independence which has prompted this bold avowal of opinion, while we tremble for the preacher's repute with his school. What will the N. E. Puritan say to this new outbreak of heresy? What reprisals will it not now make for the Dr.'s hardihood in writing of that paper that it was " not only behind the age, but behind all ages ?" and so of all the papers, pulpits, and reviews which charge themselves with the especial conservation of the Calvinistic creed in its purity. Will they not with one accord deem the " crack of doom" to be at hand when the doctrine of *vicarious atonement* is offered up, bound with fillets, upon a Unitarian altar, and that too upon the very chief of the high places of sacrifice of that priesthood—the soil of Cambridge University ? We can easily picture to ourselves the horror which such a sacrilegious surrender, cannot but excite in many a bosom laden with anxious concern for the great dogma of evangelism—the grand palladium of the orthodox faith. And how will this horror be increased when it comes to be known that the doctrine espoused is substantially that of the New Church, to wit, that the Lord assumed the Human, not to make an expiation to Divine justice, but to impart a new spiritual *life* to a fallen race ? That Dr. B. himself had any thought or intention of advocating the views of Swedenborg on the subject in question, we have no authority for asserting, but a friend who was present on the occasion, and who is verging to a full reception of Swedenborg, writes us as follows ;—" It did much to give completeness to my own views of the doctrines discussed. It increased my love for Swedenborg. Perhaps he did me quite as much good as anything that could have been said by a New

and the character of Christ we cannot but consider him as having swerved widely from the truth. But we can easily account for his error on this head when we look at the opposite error against which he felt called to contend. The Trinity which he opposed was a Trinity of three co-equal persons, and as the Divinity of Christ was taught in inseparable connection with this Trinity, it is no matter of wonder, at least to a New Churchman, that in rejecting the one he should reject the other. Yet it is evident from the whole course of his writings, and especially from his private letters, that his mind was never perfectly settled as to the light in which the Saviour was to be viewed. Though assured that he was not God on the Trinitarian scheme, still there was a mystery about Him, which he knew not how to solve, and by which he was incessantly oppressed. If he was not the true God, yet neither was a mere man, and between these two negations Dr. C.'s mind was to the last in a state of painful vacillation. Would that his eyes could have been opened to the light shed upon this sublime doctrine by the disclosures of the New Church. Can we doubt that his eager aspirations after truth, prompted by its kindred love of good, and coupled with his inflexible fidelity to evidence, would have conducted him to a conclusion fraught with that "peace in believing" for which he so earnestly panted? Here he would have found repose in a faith which, discarding the tripersonal Trinity, contemplates in Jesus the incarnate God instead of a "miraculous man," whose very being confounds all ideas of divine order and clusters around it more problems than he sought to avoid. He would here also have found a doctrine of regenerate life, that is, of salvation, most strikingly in accordance with the grand tenor of his pulpit teachings and answering all his demands for a religion founded upon Love, the true parent of Faith. But in his day the writings of Swedenborg were buried under the obloquy attached to his name, and though none was ever freer from the narrowness of prejudice, yet it is not at all surprising that he should have imbibed so much of the general sphere of incredulity on the score of his claims as to prevent his bestowing upon the subject that examination which multitudes of enlightened minds are now satisfied is due to the system.

We have been struck in the perusal of the Memoirs by scores of passages redolent of the spirit of the New Church, and impressing us deeply with the conviction of their issuing from a mind and heart intrinsically receptive of its truths, and inspiring a grateful confidence that the *good* of such a life will not remain separate from the *form of faith* which constitutes its proper receptacle.

The work as a biography is admirable, and as we cannot well say more in its praise, so neither can we less, than that our estimate of the author has risen somewhat in the same proportion with that of the subject.

2.—The Divine Personality, Incarnation, and Glorification of the Lord; *with a Critical Analysis of the Athanasian Creed.* By Emanuel Swedenborg. *A Posthumous Work, first printed in London, in* 1840, *but now translated. Dedicated to the Right Honorable the Lord Archbishop of Canterbury; with the Translator's Apology for Swedenborg.* London, 1848; 8vo. pp. 67.

We are happy to find ourselves anticipated in the translation of this Tract by Swedenborg, which has remained so long locked up in the bureau of its Latin surdity. Creation physically viewed is the clothing of spiritual things with material forms. These spiritual things originate from the Lord as a spiritual sun, and the natural sun, by his light and heat, invests them with their outward coverings. Our earth, as science clearly teaches, was not instantaneously created. It is the result of long processes of chemical combinations, the materials of which are all finally resolvable into the light and heat of the natural sun, and these again into the Divine Love and Wisdom, which produce their effects by influx or emanation through discrete degrees. Created substances must necessarily flow from the first and only uncreated self-existing substance. This is an idea much more adequate to the comprehension of children than that of absolute creation out of nothing, which the ripened intellect will inevitably reject when it becomes master of the facts of geology. Where then is the wisdom of storing the infant mind with falsities which must be eventually eradicated before genuine truth can find its way to their understandings? And if the writer is so sedulous to explain creation as a mere *fiat* of omnipotence, why does he not bestow some measure of comment upon the Lord's "speaking?" "He only spoke and it was made." How did he speak? Did he utter vocal sounds? This would evidently be the impression of the unsophisticated child. And this impression he is left to cherish without a word by way of correction, while the mystical notion of creation out of nothing is carefully fastened upon his mind. We do not of course expect children to be made philosophers, or that they shall be taught *all* truth, but we would still insist that what they *are* taught should be intrinsically true. With all our efforts to the contrary there will be error enough to be discarded in subsequent years. Let it not be systematically inculcated.

From our estimate of the work in question we read with regret the following announcement on the cover of the "Intellectual Repository" for June:— "To the various inquiries respecting the appearance of the second volume of the 'Spiritual Diary,' we beg to state, that there is at present no prospect of its being put to press." We have better hopes for the work in this country. The third and fourth volumes are now in process of translation, with the assurance from a private source of their being published when completed. Some few years may elapse, but we believe the means will be furnished for the whole, including the Index in two vols. by the time the translation is ready for the press.

The reprint of the "Edinburgh Phrenological Journal" for July, issued by the Messrs. Fowlers, contains an article on "The Right of Religious Freedom" by Judge Hurlbut, of this city. The object of the writer is to show that the civil law ought to take no cognizance whatever of religious opinions—that no form of belief or disbelief in regard to a God, to immortality, to a heaven and hell, &c., ought to come under the supervision of the legal statutes adopted by communities and states, or to constitute any kind of civil disability, whether in respect to holding office or giving testimony in courts of justice. Without entering upon the discussion of this question in the abstract, we are still prompted to advert to some of the positions of the writer as a remarkable specimen of the fallacies which may sometimes be enlisted in support of a favorite thesis. How far the pernicious sentiments embodied in this article are the genuine outbirth of Phrenology we presume not to say. Our impression is that there may be and is a grand fundamental truth in the Science itself, and that the truth, when soundly

would afterwards be assumed as the essential article of the Church which can never be reconciled with the doctrine of the Lord as God alone.

" To make three persons in the Trinity out of the words, Father, Son, and Holy Spirit, is to falsify the Word In the Word there are some apparent truths, which, if taken as real and actual truths, are false and erroneous. And some truths are used in both senses, literal and spiritual. The spiritual is acquired from the Lord, through the medium of the rational by illustration, and similar to what appears in the progressions of light from the Sun. See ' Apocalypse Revealed.' No. 720. Passages, also, may be adduced, in which both Father and Son are named, and true in both senses, and if viewed only in the literal sense, are falsified. Ib. 673 and 714·

" The chief and primary element of a church, is the acknowledgment of God— and of the Lord as the only God, and so the one God—for all other doctrines and views of a church are based on this fundamental principle. In no other way can a man understand the Word ; which is evident from the testimony of ancient nations, who had similar rites and ceremonies, of altars and sacrifices, with many other things in accordance with the outward forms of a church, but yet they did not worship Jehovah, but some Shaddai, or attribute of Deity, and which had no relation to true doctrine and to that worship which is acceptable in heaven. 'It was from this cause that the Lord so often referred to those among whom He performed His miracles, to the absence of their faith, in their acknowledgment of Him as the Son of God, and therefore the Omnipotent God, who had come down from heaven. For this is the primary doctrine of the conjunction of Deity with man, and which is now the first article of the Church which is to be named the New Jerusalem.

" The quality of the idea, entertained among those who admit of the tri-personal doctrine of the Trinity, is to place the Divine Himself above, which is the same as without, the Lord. And the reason is, because they think only of the Lord as a common man, so that they separate the Divine of the Father, which is conjoined within Him. For to speak of the conjunction of the Lord with the Father, without including the idea of the Divine in the Humanity, is to remove the Divine from within Him,—the Father is thus approached, and mercy is implored for the sake of the Son. Thoughts of this kind ascend above the Lord, and escape as in the Athanasian faith. They have nothing in common with the supreme Divinity of the Lord, and are contrary to the genuine faith of the Church, which maintains that the conjunction of the Divine Humanity in the Lord is like soul and body.

" It is true that many Christians find a difficulty in obtaining a correct idea of the Divine of the Father within the Lord, because they suppose it impossible, that the Divine of the Father, as the creator of the Universe, could be said to exist within the Humanity. But the imperfection of this idea originates in the weakness of the analogy, as drawn from the extension of time and space in the Universe, or from the human body, while it is thought of solely from the outward appearances in nature. Such thoughts do not ascend beyond the aspects of the visible world ; they are merely the ideas of the natural mind ; they are of an atheistical tendency, and lead to the worship of nature instead of the Creator. Such ideas are not permitted to enter the spiritual world, without being immediately rejected For no ideas are received into that state, but what have relation to the Lord as a Divine man ; nor even of the creation of the Universe, except from the laws of analogy derived from a Son—the offspring of a Divine Love and of the Divine proceeding operation—from which all the effects in outward nature have originated. It is from the same almighty power they continue to subsist and are upheld.

" The things which are now recited, are a few angelic ideas and expressions concerning the Lord ; they are such only as are most familiar and common. There are innumerable others, which are far beyond the knowledge and thought of finite men in this world—even the thousandth part of which it is impossible to express in human language—nor can they be pronounced by human voices. They are things ineffable and incomprehensible—such as the Lord spake of Himself, and are treated of in the inmost sense of the Word, and which have relation to the Lord alone.

" To suppose that any idea of the Divine of the Lord exist, which is above the human, is irrational. Examine this idea, which is the deepest subject of human thought, and compare it with the angels in heaven, for with them the Humanity is altogether Divine. To separate the Divine of the Father from the Humanity in heaven, is to make the Lord not one, but two. Such an idea of the Lord is rejected, and it can gain no admission there.

" To speak of one substance, or of one essence, and yet with some specific distinction or difference, as of a Divine attribute of Deity, is to destroy the Unity. Think very carefully within yourself, whether it is possible to speak of the Father as Creator, or of the Son as Redeemer, or of the Holy Spirit as Illustrator. Can you think of a Divine attribute, separately or distinctly, without it being in communion or common to each other ? Examine the ground of thought? Can you think of one God, or of one substance, or of one essence, and then proceed to consider how the work of Creation is to be effected from the Father in the Son, and from the Son through the Holy Spirit ; and whether by this order any idea is elicted of such a reciprocal and proceeding operation ? Can such an idea be entertained ? Is it not contrary to the laws of a Divine order if viewed in relation to one substance, or to a reciprocal progression together? Surely, such an idea cannot be entertained by any well constituted mind.

" Let us attempt to ascertain the quality of the idea which those possess, whether in speech or in thought, when they beseech the Father to have mercy for the sake of the Son ; and let them inquire, whether the idea perceived is not contrary to the doctrine of faith as taught in the Word ? By the separation of Father and Son, whether the Lord is not considered only as a common man,—in which they look in vain for any perception,—in which nothing remains, although admitted to be one with the Father. Still, a union, or oneness, is professed to be understood. Why is the Humanity or the Son preferred, while the thought is elevated to the Divine above it ? And why is the Humanity placed below separately? In one word, is not the contradiction in the Athanasian doctrine here made apparent? that the Divine and the Human are together one person, so that the Human is also in the Father and one with the Father. Surely, no thought can admit this unless the Humanity is also Divine. For the Father is infinite, uncreate, and omnipotent God ; and the Humanity cannot be less truly so, if together they are one substance, or one essence with the Father ; and consequently no less equally Divine ! Contradictions like these equally appear from the consideration of Christ as a rational and perfect man, when derived solely from the mother. Equally absurd is the supposition, that the Lord, as a mere man, could be in the Father, or one with the Father, or in the Divine, while it is said that they together are one person, and consequently, Divine. The contradiction appears from the supposition, that, as God and man, they could be together one person, if the Humanity is not admitted to be Divine. "

He speaks thus of Athanasius himself in the spiritual world.

" I have been permitted to speak with Athanasius upon the subject-matter of this Creed, because he had confirmed himself in the faith of three Gods, so that his mind continually vacillated between the three, that he could not acknowledge one God. He was in error almost in everything, as he had not any clear ideas of the truths of faith. Such is the case and state of others, who have confirmed themselves in the faith of three Gods. But those, however, who have not such confirmation, having only heard of that faith, and retained it in their remembrance, and are yet established in the faith of one God, when they come into heaven, reject the idea of three Gods, and preserve only a correct idea of the Divine personality of one God.

" Some persons who have never permitted their understandings to entertain any correct idea concerning the Trinity, being so strongly impressed with the literal and external sense of the Word, are unable to elevate the thoughts above it For while this faith rules, and is confirmed with delight, there is no ground in the understanding that will admit of illustration from the spiritual sense. For such a faith closes the understanding, and prevents the reception of light, and it gives a false tinge or coloring to every passage in relation to its spiritual meaning. But let the sole Divinity of the Lord be once clearly perceived, and then how many parts of the Word can be distinctly seen and rationally understood, more especially in relation to the union of the Lord with the Father.

" I have heard certain spirits, among the departed, in the spiritual world, reasoning together concerning three Divine persons in one God, and arguing from the words of the Creed, that they together are one in substance or essence—a Trinity in Unity, and a Unity in Trinity—and yet believing it to be one Divine, but this belief was merely oral, for they were informed, that they listened only to the sound of words. From which it was evident, that each thought only of three persons, as three Gods. For such is the vacillated state of mind acquired by a confirmation of the words of this Creed, to which they adhered, that the one idea could not be connected with the other. So strong is the impression of the Divine Unity in opposition to the doctrine of the Tripersonality, or to that illustration which arises from the interior knowledge of the Word—that God is one in essence and in person one.

" That the Lord did redeem and liberate, and will continue to deliver from the hells, all those who are in truths derived from good, as being thus made receptive of the Divine Humanity of the Lord. Concerning the subjugation of the hells and the glorification of the Divine Humanity of the Lord, many points receive illustration in the ' Apocalypse Revealed,' which the reader may trace in the Index, under the heads—' To Redeem, and Redemption'—as confirmed by the Evangelists, and chiefly in Luke i. ii., and Matt. i. 21 to the end.

" In the Athanasian Creed, the Humanity is made to consist of a rational soul and body, as the soul of every man is supposed to be taken from the mother. But the soul of every man is derived from the father, and the covering only from the mother. Therefore, in the words of the Athanasian Creed, there is a fallacy which should be detected. The soul of the Lord was from the Divine within Himself, which is stated in Matthew and Luke. The soul was therefore the Divine Himself, and in effect the Divine Operation. The body is not the man without the soul. Each particle, even in the body, derives its life from the soul, which as a form is a receptacle of life, and the body or covering is the effigy of the soul. As the chicken in the egg, which, as a key to this mystery, is well known.

" Three distinct parts are assigned to the Lord, while yet there are only two— the Divine and the Human. But these two are one person, the soul and body are one man, so the Divine Humanity is one Christ. The contradictions, therefore, in this Creed, are rendered self-evident."

The Translator has prefixed to the work an " Apology" of 22 pages, written with considerable vigor, and insisting upon some of the leading points of the New Church theology. Taken as a whole the tract must be considered as a valuable accession to our previous stores of the Swedenborgian relics, of which there is still an immense mass to be presented to the English reader, and the thanks of the church are due to the anonymous author of the translation before us, who seems to have executed the work as a private enterprise on his own responsibility. We should perhaps for ourselves have preferred a version somewhat closer to the original, mainly in the style of Mr. Smithson's translation of the "Spiritual Diary," which we regard as an excellent model, though well aware of the difficulties on this score, in the present work, arising from its fragmentary character, as constituting rather a programme than a complete work itself. In this respect it differs from the " Canons," which, though not remaining entire, is yet much more compact and coherent in its structure. We trust the essay may be speedily re-printed in this country, as it is desirable to have those accommodated who may wish Swedenborg's works *entire*, and as we doubt not the time will come when every vestige of his pen will be accounted precious. But we see at present no prospect of any such enterprise being undertaken except by private means. New Church publishers are not in a situation

then refer themselves to a circular periphery, or superficies of a sphere by and through spiral radii, as in the perfect spiral form; and from the latter they again refer themselves to the centre of the circle or sphere itself. Whether it continue thus to flow, or endeavors so to do, amounts to the same thing; for the reason, that conatus or endeavor is the very essential of all motions and is the first and the last thereof, wherefore it is the inmost existence and continuation of motion.

Since there is a similar ground and ratio between this form and the spiral, as between the spiral and circular, the same terms may, by a certain transposition, be applied to the vortical form.

Thus the vortical form determines and enters the spiral, and through the medium of this the circular, and again through this the angular, which is not actually, but potentially, in the vortical form. Hence it appears how much the angular differs in degree from the vortical, and how this beholds it afar off, as existing in itself, not actually but potentially; thus passing into the angular or ultimate only through successive derivations.

Hence it appears how great an immunity from injury the superior prior and more perfect forms possess over the inferior forms, or those which in their nature and in themselves are more imperfect. Relatively to this form, the circular begins to be considered imperfect; because in its centre is the beginning of inertia and rest, and is the continent of gravity, but not so with the vortical and still less with higher forms.

Hence also the vortical form is the measure of the spiral form, and of all succeeding forms. In each form there is a certain representation, or kind of exemplar, as the ancients expressed it—or image or idea, as the moderns express it—of the succeeding forms; for nothing can be derived from the prior into the posterior, unless there is something of its image within it—one thing cannot impart to another what itself does not possess. It is contrary to nature, to produce something from nothing. But that which is given so remotely in the parent differs much in the progeny when unfolded through successive derivations.

The vortical form is a still superior and more perfect form of motion than the spiral; which is rather a superior form of active force or conatus itself, which is incident within active forces; for within the vortical form there is no point of opposition, but a something which is naturally spontaneous. The reason is because its radii or determinations tend to the superficies of a most active, or of the spiral form; and from this to the circular form, thus its force of acting is increased in a triplicate ratio.

may keep them constantly attentive to their own principles, and allow no foreign considerations to interfere between their minds and the conclusion. It is granted then that the least natural entity derived its origin from the infinite, for we have already seen that no other origin of it was possible: the question now is, What are the distinctive qualities of this least natural or primitive entity? Is it the first seed of nature? Does it involve any natural predicate, like what we find in nature? Or is it only an analogue or simile of the substances, essentials, attributes, modes, &c., that we observe in nature? Here I will answer agreeably and in conformity to the principles of those I am reasoning with, that it has in it every primitive quality that there is in nature, and every simple also; that consequently it is the seed of all natural things; that it is their principle; that it is that out of which, by degrees and moments, ultimate nature is unfolded: in a word, that there is in it, as primitive entity, everything whatever that we can possibly conceive as existing in nature; and that thus in this prime, or in an indefinite number of these primes or leasts, nature exists in her very seed; out of which, whether considered as one or many, she ultimately issues forth in her diversity, in all her manifoldness, with all her distinct and abundant series, mighty in the heavens, in the worlds, in the planets, in the kingdoms of each peculiar planet, elemental, mineral, vegetable, in the parts of all these kingdoms, and in the parts, of the parts; in short, with whatever can be predicated of her as nature, in her least or her greatest sphere. But as to what the *Simple* seems to have been, we have treated of this subject at some length in our *Principia*, in the Chapter on the Elements."

Indeed, we have no doubt that Mr. Poe would be vastly surprised, upon reading Swedenborg's "Outlines on the Infinite" to see to what extent many of the prominent ideas of his own work had been anticipated in that masterly dissertation on the origin of the Universe and "the final cause of creation." We trust too that if he should ever turn his attention to this work, he may feel the force of Swedenborg's reasoning in regard to the being and agency of a God distinct from nature, in which, if we understand Mr. P. he is disposed to sink the Universal Cause. Its pantheistic tendency is the worst feature of his book, and it is felt the more from the contrast between the passages where this is broadly avowed, and those in which he speaks of the Divine volition as if he regarded the subject from a Christian stand-point. With all abatements, however, the book will repay perusal.

EDITORIAL ITEMS.

The Rev. Dr. Bushnell of Hartford, Conn. lately preached a sermon to the graduating class at the Theological Seminary, Cambridge, Mass., on the subject of the *Atonement*. From a brief report of the discourse we learn that "he began by saying that he had just emerged from doubt of fifteen years' standing, when the invitation to address the Cambridge Theological School was laid on his table. Now, at last, the question seemed to open itself. He hoped his view might lead to re-examination, if not re-construction. 'Twould be a public shame for him to feel imprisoned to any neutral subject. A just compliment to his invitors was to speak in a spirit as liberal as their invitation. * * *. All souls have their proper life in God. Sin separates from God, is selfhood, or life in sense. Christ enters to reunite the world to the Eternal. God was in Christ reconciling the world, not reconciling God, but the world to God. * * * Irenæus opened the dogmatic history of atonement by teaching that it was a ransom to the devil. Since then, it has been a ransom paid to God, sometimes vindictive, sometimes expiatory. Sometimes the criminal law afforded the illustration, sometimes the civil law, sometimes the ceremonial. The most modern orthodoxy is, that Christ's suffering expresses the same love of right as if we were punished, and so God's character is cleared. It is remarkable that so powerful a doctrine dissolves away at the touch ; that it offers *such marvellous fecundity of self-refutation !* If Christ suffered unwillingly, it was the direst cruelty; if willingly, the character of the government was impeached. If Christ was God and Ruler, in suffering the penalties of his own law, his government would suffer. Again, if all guilt is satisfied for, there can be no farther suffering for guilt. There are no limits to the objections this old theory provokes, while it *fails to answer any theological purpose.*"

This is a direct and palpable repudiation of the doctrine of Atonement as held at present, and for two centuries past, by the great mass of Protestant churches, and no where with greater tenacity than in New England. The theory adopted by the preacher, so far as we can glean from a meagre abstract, is *substantially* that of the New Church. We hope Dr. C. may not recoil from it when he becomes aware of this fact. That he should have remained for so long a time in doubt on this point is probably owing to his association during that period with a system under the influence of which doubt, on this head, is seldom permitted to arise ; and that he has at length emerged from it, is because he has ventured to think for himself in disregard of the prescribed *pattern.* We honor the manly independence which has prompted this bold avowal of opinion, while we tremble for the preacher's repute with his school. What will the N. E. Puritan say to this new outbreak of heresy ? What reprisals will it not now make for the Dr.'s hardihood in writing of that paper that it was " not only behind the age, but behind all ages ?" and so of all the papers, pulpits, and reviews which charge themselves with the especial conservation of the Calvinistic creed in its purity. Will they not with one accord deem the " crack of doom" to be at hand when the doctrine of *vicarious atonement* is offered up, bound with fillets, upon a Unitarian altar, and that too upon the very chief of the high places of sacrifice of that priesthood—the soil of Cambridge University ? We can easily picture to ourselves the horror which such a sacrilegious surrender, cannot but excite in many a bosom laden with anxious concern for the great dogma of evangelism—the grand palladium of the orthodox faith. And how will this horror be increased when it comes to be known that the doctrine espoused is substantially that of the New Church, to wit, that the Lord assumed the Human, not to make an expiation to Divine justice, but to impart a new spiritual *life* to a fallen race? That Dr. B. himself had any thought or intention of advocating the views of Swedenborg on the subject in question, we have no authority for asserting, but a friend who was present on the occasion, and who is verging to a full reception of Swedenborg, writes us as follows ;—" It did much to give completeness to my own views of the doctrines discussed. It increased my love for Swedenborg. Perhaps he did me quite as much good as anything that could have been said by a New

Churchman. I think there could not have been more done in two hours to strengthen my confidence in Swedenborg." But the discourse is ere long to be published, and we shall have an opportunity to judge more accurately for ourselves of its bearings. Meantime one of the Boston religious papers concludes its notice of the discourse as follows :—" We hope that we have succeeded in this extremely synoptic sketch, to convey to our readers some faint idea, at least, of a discourse, which is destined, we think, like many other productions of the author, to make much noise in the theological world. That it will perfectly suit any party, we do not anticipate. Unitarians will stand in greater doubt of the soundness of a brother, whom they love, whose talents they respect, but whose idiosyncracy gives such an unusual cast to his opinions, that they find it difficult to assign him a place anywhere in the ranks of strict Orthodoxy." The New York Observer also in a notice headed, *Dr. Bushnell's Atonement*, speaks thus of the discourse :—" As the sermon is not yet printed, it is deemed prudent to abstain from confident expressions of opinion as to his position. But it is obvious that what is commonly called the *orthodox* view of the atonement, he rejects, and that he proposes a scheme not half way between this and the Unitarian, but three quarters of the way from the former to the latter. The orthodox repudiate his theory, the Unitarians hail it as an approximation to theirs. We are informed that some time ago at a meeting of Unitarian ministers in Boston it was proposed to establish a Unitarian church at Hartford, when one gentleman rose and said that he had recently listened to Dr. Bushnell's preaching there, and thought there was no necessity of a Unitarian church. The anticipations thus awakened have been greatly strengthened by the views which he has now set forth on a cardinal doctrine of grace."

We notice in a little work entitled " Line upon Line," designed for " the earliest instruction the infant mind is capable of receiving," the following enlightened comment upon the Scripture history of the creation.

" My dear children,—I know that you have heard that God made the world. Could a man have made the world ? No; a man could not make such a world as this. Men can make many things, such as boxes and baskets. Perhaps you know a man who can make a box. Suppose you were to shut him up in a room, which was quite empty, and you were to say to him, ' You shall not come out till you have made a box,'—would the man ever come out ? No —never. A man could not make a box, except he had something to make it of. He must have some wood, or some tin, or some pasteboard, or some other thing. But God had nothing to make the world of. He only spoke, and it was made. Making things of nothing, is called ' creating.' No one can create anything, but God. Do you know why God is called the Creator ? It is because he created all things. There is only one Creator. Angels cannot create things, nor can men. They could not create one drop of water, or one little fly. You know that God was six days in creating the world. I will tell you what he did on each day."

Why do sensible people of the old Church persist in furnishing as " milk for babes" such groundless dogmatisms as the above? Where does the writer learn that " making things of nothing is called ' creating ?'" This idea is not conveyed by the import of the original term, and the reason left to itself sees that it is an absurdity. Creation physically viewed is the clothing of spiritual things with material forms. These spiritual things originate from the Lord as a spiritual sun, and the natural sun, by his light and heat, invests them with their outward coverings. Our earth, as science clearly teaches, was not instantaneously created. It is the result of long processes of chemical combinations, the materials of which are all finally resolvable into the light and heat of the natural sun, and these again into the Divine Love and Wisdom, which produce their effects by influx or emanation through discrete degrees. Created substances must necessarily flow from the first and only uncreated self-existing substance. This is an idea much more adequate to the comprehension of children than that of absolute creation out of nothing, which the ripened intellect will inevitably reject when it becomes master of the facts of geology. Where then is the wisdom of storing the infant mind with falsities which must be eventually eradicated before genuine truth can find its way to their understandings? And if the writer is so sedulous to explain creation as a mere *fiat* of omnipotence, why does he not bestow some measure of comment upon the Lord's "speaking?" " He only spoke and it was made." How did he speak? Did he utter vocal sounds? This would evidently be the impression of the unsophisticated child. And this impression he is left to cherish without a word by way of correction, while the mystical notion of creation out of nothing is carefully fastened upon his mind. We do not of course expect children to be made philosophers, or that they shall be taught *all* truth, but we would still insist that what they *are* taught should be intrinsically true. With all our efforts to the contrary there will be error enough to be discarded in subsequent years. Let it not be systematically inculcated.

From our estimate of the work in question we read with regret the following announcement on the cover of the " Intellectual Repository" for June:— "To the various inquiries respecting the appearance of the second volume of the 'Spiritual Diary,' we beg to state, that there is at present no prospect of its being put to press." We have better hopes for the work in this country. The third and fourth volumes are now in process of translation, with the assurance from a private source of their being published when completed. Some few years may elapse, but we believe the means will be furnished for the whole, including the Index in two vols. by the time the translation is ready for the press.

The reprint of the " Edinburgh Phrenological Journal" for July, issued by the Messrs. Fowlers, contains an article on " The Right of Religious Freedom" by Judge Hurlbut, of this city. The object of the writer is to show that the civil law ought to take no cognizance whatever of religious opinions—that no form of belief or disbelief in regard to a God, to immortality, to a heaven and hell, &c., ought to come under the supervision of the legal statutes adopted by communities and states, or to constitute any kind of civil disability, whether in respect to holding office or giving testimony in courts of justice. Without entering upon the discussion of this question in the abstract, we are still prompted to advert to some of the positions of the writer as a remarkable specimen of the fallacies which may sometimes be enlisted in support of a favorite thesis. How far the pernicious sentiments embodied in this article are the genuine outbirth of Phrenology we presume not to say. Our impression is that there may be and is a grand fundamental truth in the Science itself, and that the truth, when soundly developed, will be found to accord with the leading revelations of the New Church respecting the mental and physical constitution of man. We trust therefore that the principles asserted by Judge |Hurlbut in the extracts that follow are not to be regarded as a fair exposition of the teachings of Phrenology. Placing the religious sentiment in the organ of Veneration, the degree in which it is possessed by any individual he makes to be dependent upon his peculiar organization in this respect. Faith and Hope, according to him, constitute the two grand elements of the religious instinct (though we should put in a plea for Love), and as he considers these as having reference the one to infinity, and the other to the future, he therefore draws the inference that "the religious feelings proper have little concern with the affairs of our present existence." As little concern have they, on this ground, with the Word of God which treats of them, for if that be admitted as a standard, the love of the neighbor has something to do with the "religious feelings," and this it would not be very easy to exclude from "the affairs of our present existence." Again he says that "reverence for the Divine Being, faith in the infinite mystery which shrouds his existence, and his power, and an expectation of a blessed immortality, refer rather to the Deity and man's relations to him in a future world, than to those humble practical relations in which man stands to his fellow in the social state." The assumption that man, as to the higher principles of his nature, will ever stand in closer relation to the Deity than he does in this world is of course entirely gratuitous, as he is, in respect to his spirit, even now in the spiritual world; nor is it possible that he should sustain right relations to the Divine Being without their governing, at the same time, his relations with his fellow man. Another choice morsel of this writer's theology is to be found in the following;—"Although faith and hope abide in the human mind, yet greater than these is charity, and greater far than this favorite sentiment of the apostle, is justice." Where did our author learn this? Charity is but a modification of love, the very element of all others by which we are most assimilated to the Divine, and how any principle can be "greater" than this it baffles our efforts to conceive. "The religious as well as the moral sentiments are of themselves blind; they produce mere feelings or emotions, which are altogether crude and ignorant until reformed and directed by the intellectual faculties." The true basis of the religious sentiments is love, and in the affection of love is the germ of all wisdom and intelligence. The intellect is governed by the affection instead of the reverse. But the acme of these paradoxes is reached in the following sentiment;—"The exclusion of a witness for this cause (religious opinion) is based upon the notion that religious faith is necessary to ensure a proper regard for truth. This is unphilosophical and opposed to the experience of practical men. *The religious sentiments are independent of that faculty of the mind which respects the truth.*" (!) This is about as correct as to say that the power of vision is independent of that function of the eye which has respect to light. It is well matched by what succeeds in the connexion. "They may exist to a striking degree, and the possessor may, nevertheless, commit perjury with great facility. I have known religious perjurors and infidel perjurors; and as many of one as of the other." A "religious perjuror!"—an odd species of "religious sentiment" that must surely be which allows its possessor to "commit perjury with great facility." It will scarcely be believed that we have correctly given the above quotations, yet we have transcribed them verbatim. And upon what are we to rely for assurance that any man will utter the truth in testimony or in any thing else ? " It is to the sentiment (organ ?) of conscientiousness that we owe the regard for truth ; and we have seen that that may exist independent of the religious feelings." A conscientiousness that knows no alliance with the religious principle, if it were not a nonentity, would be as little to be trusted as the pious perjury principle of a devout man.—But enough of Judge Hurlbut's philosophy. The evident drift of the whole is to divorce religion from all the practical relations of life, and reduce it to a mere empty abstraction that has to do with man as a spirit in the other world, of which the consequence would be that he would be found to have as little of it there as here. If such doctrines are the legitimate fruit of Phrenology, it must look for advocates in other quarters than the New Church.

The Princeton (Presbyterian) Repository for July contains an article on Swedenborg and the N. C. doctrines, evidently penned under the impression that the Christian community needs to be put on its guard against the insidious advances of this pernicious heresy. The writer says Swedenborg himself predicted that in eighty years from his death the system would have acquired a wide extension, and as only three or four years remain to the expiration of that period, the reviewer sagely remarks that the zeal of his disciples is prompting them to redoubled efforts in order that their master may not turn out a false prophet. Upon this and other points of the attack we shall probably have something to say in a future No. The writer condescends not to bestow the least argument upon the subject ; his avowed object is not to *confute* but to *expose ;* and with this view he harps upon the old string of the rejected books of Scripture, with ominous hints of horrid immoralities, the bare mention of which is too odious for print, embodied in the doctrines, and the *positive assertion* of the supernumerary plates upon Swedenborgian dinner tables. The article, on the whole, is a curious document. It is evidently intended as a kind of theological *ukase* promulgated from the head quarters of Presbyterianism to deter the faithful from looking with the least tolerance upon the portentous dogmas which are silently finding their way, like " a worm in the bud," into the bosom of many churches and acting the canker to many creeds. Probably both their people and ours will hear more of the matter.

We are gratified with the announcement that Theophilus Parsons, Esq. of Boston has been elected to the Dane Professorship of Law in the University, made vacant by the resignation of Prof. Greenleaf. It seems that in the estimation of the Trustees of that institution a man's being an avowed *Swedenborgian* does not necessarily vacate his claims to the character of an enlightened civilian, or his qualifications to occupy one of the most respectable stations in the country. The notice is thus given in a Boston paper ;—" We understand that Theophilus Parsons, Esq. son of the late Chief Justice Theophilus Parsons, has been unanimously elected, on the part of the Corporation, Dane Professor in the Law School at Cambridge, in place of Professor Greenleaf, resigned. Mr. Parsons, it is understood, will enter upon the discharge of his duties at the commencement of the next academical term. The distinguished talents, professional accomplishments, and amiable personal qualities of the professor elect, authorise the most confident anticipations of his success."

THE

NEW CHURCH REPOSITORY

AND

MONTHLY REVIEW.

| Vol. 1. | SEPTEMBER, 1848. | No. 9. |

ORIGINAL PAPERS.

ARTICLE I.

THE DOCTRINE OF FORMS.

THE VORTICAL FORM.

THE form proximately superior and prior to the spiral, and at the same time more perfect than it, is the Perpetual Spiral, properly called the Vortical. The ground of the denomination lies in the fact, that such forms are properly those of the higher ether, which constitutes the great vortex about our earth, within which the moon accomplishes her orbits and periods. Its determinations are not through spires, such as in the spiral forms tend to the surface of a circle or of a certain sphere, but they tend to direct themselves, after the manner of a perpetual spire, which we call the vortical, to a certain globe or gyre of the spiral form occupying the place of a centre, and mainly towards its surface. The quality of the spire or the vortical fluxion of spires, is with difficulty comprehended unless the idea be had of a line composed of the circle and spiral, for as the spiral line is a mediate between the circular and rectilinear, so the vortical line and fluxion may be deemed a mediate between the circular and spiral; it cannot well be otherwise explained. Perhaps we may consider the vortical force as resolvable into a circular and spiral force; or in a certain sense their resultant.

The vortical spires continue, or endeavor to continue, their fluxion through that spiral superficies, from which latter they then refer themselves to a circular periphery, or superficies of a sphere by and through spiral radii, as in the perfect spiral form; and from the latter they again refer themselves to the centre of the circle or sphere itself. Whether it continue thus to flow, or endeavors so to do, amounts to the same thing; for the reason, that conatus or endeavor is the very essential of all motions and is the first and the last thereof, wherefore it is the inmost existence and continuation of motion.

Since there is a similar ground and ratio between this form and the spiral, as between the spiral and circular, the same terms may, by a certain transposition, be applied to the vortical form.

Thus the vortical form determines and enters the spiral, and through the medium of this the circular, and again through this the angular, which is not actually, but potentially, in the vortical form. Hence it appears how much the angular differs in degree from the vortical, and how this beholds it afar off, as existing in itself, not actually but potentially; thus passing into the angular or ultimate only through successive derivations.

Hence it appears how great an immunity from injury the superior prior and more perfect forms possess over the inferior forms, or those which in their nature and in themselves are more imperfect. Relatively to this form, the circular begins to be considered imperfect; because in its centre is the beginning of inertia and rest, and is the continent of gravity, but not so with the vortical and still less with higher forms.

Hence also the vortical form is the measure of the spiral form, and of all succeeding forms. In each form there is a certain representation, or kind of exemplar, as the ancients expressed it—or image or idea, as the moderns express it—of the succeeding forms; for nothing can be derived from the prior into the posterior, unless there is something of its image within it—one thing cannot impart to another what itself does not possess. It is contrary to nature, to produce something from nothing. But that which is given so remotely in the parent differs much in the progeny when unfolded through successive derivations.

The vortical form is a still superior and more perfect form of motion than the spiral; which is rather a superior form of active force or conatus itself, which is incident within active forces; for within the vortical form there is no point of opposition, but a something which is naturally spontaneous. The reason is because its radii or determinations tend to the superficies of a most active, or of the spiral form; and from this to the circular form, thus its force of acting is increased in a triplicate ratio.

The spiral form gyrates around its one centre, but the vortical around as many centres as there are points in the central periphery or superficies, which it respects; wherefore this form of gyration is the perpetually central, or it may rather be termed the simply vortical. Hence it also follows that this form is still more constantly permanent and enduring in its essence than the spiral. Nevertheless these forms may undergo essential mutations like the inferior forms, but with greater difficulty, and likewise the greater the difficulty with which they suffer such mutation, the greater the difficulty with which they return to their pristine perfection.

If we assume a substance, abiding most constantly in such a form, there will be many causes of such mutation, so that every state may be essentially changed or perverted; that is, not only into the spiral form, to which the vortical tends as its centre, thus into another genus and species of form, but also into the circular, to which the spiral looks as its centre;—so that the centre of the vortical should be moved and transposed from its place, before its entire disposition is changed; for one form cannot succeed another unless there occur an essential mutation, and if it occur, this mutation should necessarily itself be similarly permanent, and indeed as constantly enduring as it was in its own prior form.

There are likewise genera and species of this form, perfect and imperfect, as in other forms; but to express the varieties and differences thereof, as they occur among themselves, terms and expression are likewise wanting. Consult what was said above concerning the spiral form and make a simple application here; and because this form nearly transcends the head, we may in unfolding and contemplating it enter the shade of ignorance; yet because we cannot understand it, we do not admit that in the nature of things, or as to the things alleged of it, we shall fall into paradoxes and conjectures. Nothing denies it; while there are innumerable phenomena actually confirming the existence of this form and its fluxions. There are in nature infinite things which can never be reduced to geometrical or analytical calculation, so as to be clearly intelligible, yet we are not the less persuaded that they exist, for we are confident that many things actually are, although we are ignorant what they are. The quality of this form cannot be comprehended otherwise than in the manner of other forms, which fall under the calculus of infinites; and are thereby raised to higher powers, resolvable neither by right lines nor by spheres.

The vortical form is obviously everywhere in nature; and is conspicuous in phenomena, for to it should be attributed

brute animal, or the soul of brutes, in itself may be most perfect, although it cannot attain to the perfection of man, or his
soul. The circle is perfect in itself, although the spiral may
be more perfect than it, for that is necessarily relatively imperfect, which comes after, in the order of derivation.

But the forms which, in their own degree, are most perfect
can be rendered or made more imperfect, that is, be essentially
changed. We do not herein include the world-forms, wanting
life; but the forms of the animal kingdom, or souls, and also
angelic souls, which are gifted with liberty of action; from the
change of whose state from the more perfect to the most imperfect follows also a change of the elements; and even of the
Earth itself, which may be confirmed by many things and which
the sacred Scriptures themselves teach.

This change occurs from causes without and below, and indeed within themselves, but not from causes above themselves.
For if a form, in itself, and in its own nature, more imperfect
than a superior, and more perfect than an inferior form, strives
and endeavors to become such as is the superior, or the inferior,
then (in case it changes), it must undergo necessarily, an essential mutation.

Afterwards the forms which descend and are generated from
the same form, induce a similar or a greater imperfection according as they are removed from their origin.

That we may represent to ourselves an idea of the generation and derivation of such forms, one from another, we must
cultivate the idea the *in*-existence of supreme forms within
singular the inferior forms; and also at the same time the idea
of accidental mutation; for the perfection of superior forms
consists in their capability of undergoing accidental mutations.

When many superior forms unanimously consociate themselves, and form, determine, and constitute a one (a unit), which
should be regarded as a substance in itself; then there exists a
proximately inferior form, and when these (ones or units) in
like manner consociate themselves and form a one (or unit),
there exists a form still inferior; and so on in order. Wherefore also when a compound form is resolved, it returns to a prior
form. Thus one flows-in into another, and what is prior is always interior, and what is posterior is always exterior, and
thence more remote: thus the first differs (distat) from the last
toto cœlo; although most intimately resident within it. From
which it follows that nothing substantial is given in the composite, except the first, and that *one* (unit), which is called a
simple substance; and likewise that force itself, which is perpetually impressed, is incident within. In order to illustrate
how a number, quantity, or volume of such superior unities,

so that it will continually retrograde or advance, until these points of intersection or nodes have traced out an orbit upon the equatorial plane. On this supposition the orbit of the revolving body never returns into itself; but winds into a perpetual spiral, and weaves, as it were, a zodiacal superficies from one unbroken thread.

Again, let us suppose that while the body is thus tracing out these zodiacal superficies it has receded from or approached to the central body so that the superficies will not return into itself, but the body continue to trace out such superficies receding from or approaching to the central body, and thus wind into continual spiral surfaces—and thus duplicating them, weaves as it were, a solid, or a form of triple dimensions.

Now if we suppose that the revolving body alternately recedes from and approaches the centre through given periods or according to a given law, we shall have what may be called the perpetually spiral or vortical motion; and it will vary in genera and species according to that law and according to the form of its centre or spiral superficies to which it relates.

Now it is a well established fact in astronomy, that our Earth, around the sun, and the moon, around the earth, in performing their circuits, move in just such continual spiral circuits as we have above described; for the Earth by the precession of the Equinoxes, and the moon by the precession of her nodes, weave just such zodiacal surfaces as above described; and by their motions in Erection describe such surfaces continually, or by continual duplication weave, as it were, zodiacal solids. If we contemplate the moon as performing such spiral circuits around the Earth, as a centre, which at the same time traces out a spiral surface to which the moon continually refers as her centre; then every point of this surface is a centre to the moon, and around this surface the moon performs circuits perpetually spiral; and weaves a form simply vortical.

All moons about their planets, and all planets about their suns, and suns doubtless too, through their spheres, perform such vortical circuits, or circuits of a higher degree of form. When we contemplate the heavenly bodies thus performing their perpetual circuses, from centre to centre, and from sphere to sphere, who can say that our earth, or any other planet, or even sun, will ever twice occupy the same absolute point of space!

Astronomers ascribe these motions to the force of gravitation; but, pray, what is the cause of gravitation? That question will find a solution only, when the vortical form shall have opened its bosom, and yielded to human research the key to its celestial geometry and mechanism.

We have thus in a very general manner compassed the Doctrine of Forms. Its application can be learned by consulting the works of our Author, especially the part of the present work immediately succeeding the part under consideration; where it is applied to the organization of the living fabrics of the Human Body.

It will have been seen, that there are six degrees of forms from the angular to the spiritual, both inclusive—that these degrees are discrete, holding to each other the relation of cause and effect—that there is no passage from one degree to another by a simple ratio—that such ratio is, mathematically considered, one of infinity, thus there is no simple relation between the right line and the circle, for we consider the circle as consisting of an infinite number of right lines; only on such an hypothesis does one measure the other. From this, the distinction between discrete and ordinary degrees will be readily comprehended. Without a knowledge of discrete degrees all the works of the Divine Hand will remain a problem unsolved, a labyrinth unexplored.

A quantity of units or simples of a higher and prior degree or form, flow-in and compose one unit or simple of a lower degree or form; so that the form of the parts, units, individuals or simple substances are in themselves always of a superior form to that of a volume of such parts or units, organized into a new unit; and that the units or individuals of a lower form can only attain to a higher by a division or dissolution of the units or individuals of such lower form; and that the units of a higher form can descend to a lower form only by a congregation, unition, or composition of its units or parts. This rule is universal, holding true not only in the microcosm or world, but also in the microcosm, or human organization.

The higher the degree of form, the higher its substances, forces, powers, qualities and attributes, and vice versa; and as the degrees of form descend, in each degree thereof, a force becomes latent, a power absorbed, an energy sinks to repose, a life becomes extinct, until in the lower and lowest forms substances become so compounded, forces by mutual opposition become so equilibrated; motion seems to have ceased, life to have become extinct; and rest, inertia, and gravity appear to be at once cause and effect. Yet nothing has perished —the supreme form has only clothed itself in lower forms, and thus induced new qualities—living and incessant forces have only embraced each other in friendly arms, balanced each other no new pivots—and in the degree they seem to repose, seem to have perished, in that degree have they renovated their energies and recruited their latent forces—and when they shall

Those which we cannot penetrate, we cannot express adequately by words, or sufficiently represent by figures.

Wherefore if we may express mere paradoxes in reference to this form, we may say, that its form or substance is simple; and respectively to all lower forms and natural substantial unities, it is wanting in figure, extension, magnitude, gravity or levity; therefore not material. That within it nothing can be said to be carried either up or down, or to a centre, to a superficies or according to a diameter; but one and the same point by its fluxion will seem to constitute and occupy every centre, radius and periphery, and a thousand thereof simultaneously and successively.

If we unfold the nature of the modifications of the ether by which the sensation of sights exist we shall perceive a likeness of such a fluxion, or similar phenomena and paradoxes, for, from all points of an object, each emits rays, and passing through streams and myriads of rays flowing from other objects diametrically, obliquely, or rectilinearly in all directions, so that this one and the same thing (or point) represents a centre, somewhere else a periphery, and otherwheres a diameter; and indeed many simultaneously and successively.

Into this form flows the universe, which we call heaven, or each solar or stellar vortex; likewise its volumes greater and lesser, and also its individual entities; we say volumes and individual entities just as if they were composed, properly speaking, of parts; it so happens because otherwise we are not supplied with words by which its fluxion and determinations, so far as it is a form, can be expressed; therefore it is speaking infranaturally, but it is to be understood, as said above, analogically or supereminently.

Every such individual is an exemplar representative of its universe. Such is the internal form of each individual of the purest blood, or the first essential animal essence, which runs through the simplest fibre; so that its form deserves to be called celestial, deriving its essence from the celestial ether, or primitive nature.

But very few phenomena from this aura or form approach and energe to our senses, for they are deeply hid in nature. Notwithstanding it is not doubtful whether this form really exists, for without it, neither the vortical, or lower forms, or the world could exist; neither the simplest fibre in the animal kingdom, neither those infinite wonders of nature which arise from her deepest bosom and from the simplest fibre and its most pure essence, both mediately and immediately.

In the spiral form we found that its lines proceeded circularly in all directions, through each dimension; that is, they were perpetually circular; properly spiral. So also in the spiral form, its lines wound around spirally in all directions, through each dimension, that is, they were perpetually spiral; properly vortical; so likewise, in this celestial form, we must contemplate its lines and forces, as performing their circuits in all directions, through each dimension, by and through perpetually winding gyres.

We can form no idea of the fluxions of this form, until we possess something of a distinct idea of the winding paths of the vortical form, to which this refers itself as its centre, and around which it performs circuits perpetually vortical, or properly celestial.

Moons and Planets perform their circuits through limited vortical forms, but Suns, the progenitors of these, holding in perpetuity the qualities of their offspring, perform their circuits through flaming gyres, perpetually vortical or, properly, celestial, during periods of time wholly incomprehensible to the human mind. The Zodiacal period of our Earth is about 25,000 years, and this is but one of its vortical days! What then must be the duration of the highest solar period, the celestial Cycle!—This form must be considered the highest and first of natural forms, powers and substances. The next higher form passes into the spiritual world, and opens the way to higher spheres—for suns are the highest and first of the forms, powers, and substances, which affect the senses of the natural man, and the first that dawn upon his vision.

THE SPIRITUAL FORM.

The form next above, prior and more perfect than the celestial is the perpetually celestial, or as it is properly called, the spiritual, from the last or the terrene most remote.

By philosophers, ancient and modern, also by theologians those essential forms, which inhabit the heavens, as well as ourselves of the Earth, are called spiritual; others instead of forms substitute substances or powers, and call them spiritual substances or celestial powers—therefore we do not forsake the usual mode of speaking when we term, by figure of speech, the divine spirit, a spiritual form; wherein substance and form are one and the same thing, as will be seen in the sequel. Relatively to this, the forms of angels are called angelic forms; and even our mind (mens) is called by the philosopher an immortal and eternal form of forms, and by this, he understands this spiritual form—but the forms of angels, and the forms of our minds (animæ) cannot be properly called spiritual, but rather. more perfect celestial forms, created and accommodated to the reception and influx of the spiritual form—such are not the forms above discussed. But the forms of our minds and of angels, rather than the celestial forms of which the star-teeming heaven consists, deserve to be called spiritual; for they are images of spiritual forms, and their operations are immediately due to the spiritual form, for in themselves they are inferior and posterior, and likewise subject to the spiritual.

Therefore this spiritual form is above every created thing, and therefore incomprehensible, undefinable, and inexpressible by the most sublime analysis of the human mind,—it is form in the abstract, contemplating others, in order, out of itself; and at the same time within itself, so far as they are perfect.

If we proceed through a series, similar to the one above instituted, it will follow that this form refers itself to the celestial as this does itself to the vortical and so on to the angular, which is the last in order of the relations and representatives; so that it may be said that this form contemplates the others as well out of itself, as in itself, so far as they are most perfect in their own degree, for nothing imperfect can proceed from what is most perfect.

To the spiritual, nothing material, extended, fluid, neither anything of natural expression, wherefore neither accidents or modes, are suited; thus no terms by which material things are signified, except by way of supereminence; for it is above all predicates. Thus abstractly speaking or in more sublime thought, what is spiritual and angelic, is used in determining and expressing the powers and essences of this form. Unless this form flowed-in into the inferior they could not exist, nor subsist, nor be moved, much less could they live, understand, be wise; so that it is the beginning (principium) of existing, subsisting, acting, living, understanding, and of being wise.

The Spiritual Form, truly perpetual, is the DIVINE itself, not properly form, but pure essence, life, intelligence, wisdom, wholly abstracted from space, time, matter, figure, motion, change and perishability—the Creator, beginning and end of all things; far above nature, without or below which are all things. Thus it is incomprehensible; in it is whatever is perpetual, infinite, eternal, unlimited, holy, and is the order, law and idea of the universe. This Form flows-in into the celestial and angelic forms, and into our souls (animos) by the medium of the spiritual form, and by the medium of the Word. But so many are here the hidden things, that it is sufficient to be silent, to be humble; to worship and to adore that concerning which, it is unholy to speak naturally.

CONCERNING FORMS GENERALLY.

Besides the natural and universal or world-forms above treated of, among the first of which is the celestial form, there are others, which are living forms, and may be called spiritual, as the angelic, and the forms of the human soul and mind, and also the souls of brutes.

These forms are in themselves posterior, inferior and more imperfect than the spiritual, and therefore without and below it, and subject to it. They are not only created and accommodated to the *beginning of motion ;* but also to the *reception of life and intelligence* by influx from the spiritual form. Wherefore they are images and likenesses thereof and may be termed spiritual forms. Those forms descend and ascend in the ultimate world by a similar scale, and by a similar series as the above forms, which are purely natural, and consequently respectively dead, because partakers of no life and no sensation, much less of intelligence ; neither are they capacitated therefor. But as to their essential determinations and fluxions, these forms altogether emulate the universal or world-forms: and to them they so correspond that the one most conveniently flows-in into the other, as, for example the angular forms correspond to, and flow-in into the sensories of taste and smell; the circular or the modifications of air into the sensory of hearing, the spiral, or the modifications of ether, into the sensory of sight, or the eye; and so on. Thus likewise the spiritual form into the soul itself, which is formed to the reception of its Divine (divinarum) operations, and hence the principle (principium) of its life and intelligence.

Thus we may learn from the forms of nature, what are the forms of life, the series of which is not otherwise represented in the animal kingdom than as in its own microcosm.

Besides the universal or world-forms, and the forms of life, there are also forms of the vegetable kingdom as well as of the mineral kingdom, of all which thers are genera and species more perfect and imperfect. Besides the world-forms, the forms of the animal kingdom, the forms of the vegetable kingdom, and the forms of the mineral kingdom, there are no others given.

The forms of the three kingdoms depend upon the world-forms ; and to them they correspond. Thus we may learn from the world-forms the forms of its three kingdoms ; and in what manner the spiritual form immediately and mediately flows-in so that all things, in a provided order, constantly flow from an end, by ends, to an end.

(On the subjects of the preceding paragraphs see the "Economy of the Animal Kingdom," Second Part, n. 241 to 292.)

Such is the ascent of forms from inferior to superior, but not only of forms, but also of substances, forces, modes, qualities and accidents, which cannot exist without forms. Thus when we rise from inferior to superior forms we may be said to rise and ascend into a superior, prior, more universal, simpler, purer and more perfect nature, sphere, power, world, aura or ether, indeed even to the supreme heavens. But within each sphere there is given a higher and lower region. We speak of a superior and supreme, as well as inferior and lowest region of the atmosphere or air, so also of other spheres, yet such region cannot be said to be prior or more universal.

When the forms are raised through the scale or series, there is in each degree thereof something earthly, material, and finite thrown off, eliminated, and laid aside ; and something celestial, perpetual and infinite superadded and induced, even until nothing, except what is perpetual, infinite, eternal, pure and holy, that is, divine, remains. The perpetual or infinite in the circular form is the circle or periphery itself; because it is without beginning or end ; the remaining lines, the semidiameters or radii, because they are terminated in a centre, are finite. This finiteness is, in the spiral form, laid aside, the radii of which are terminated in the superficies of some circle whose fluxion is infinite, and because no finiteness remains in it, this spire in this superficies is determined into another form of motion : and even this is laid aside in the superior forms, and the relations of centre, or rest, always recede farther off in proportion to the extent of the progression.

We have arrived at these principles by way of analysis ; and now from these, thus investigated, we must descend from first principles to the last or lowest, by way of synthesis. For in order to attain to principles which are so many verities, it is necessary to approach, *a posteriorily*, that is from the experience of effects.

In the same order then it follows that the spiritual proceeds from the Divine ; the celestial is created from the spiritual ; the vortical is produced by, and flows from, the celestial ; the spiral from the vortical ; the circular from the spiral ; and the angular from the circular form. Thus by a long series of succession and derivation, or through six degrees, from what is most perfect is derived what in itself and in its own nature is more imperfect ; yet in its own sphere or degree there is nothing more perfect. It is not therefore imperfect in itself because it does not approach the perfection of a prior degree ; but may be most perfect in its own degree. For example, the brute animal, or the soul of brutes, in itself may be most perfect, although it cannot attain to the perfection of man, or his soul. The circle is perfect in itself, although the spiral may be more perfect than it, for that is necessarily relatively imperfect, which comes after, in the order of derivation.

But the forms which, in their own degree, are most perfect can be rendered or made more imperfect, that is, be essentially changed. We do not herein include the world-forms, wanting life; but the forms of the animal kingdom, or souls, and also angelic souls, which are gifted with liberty of action; from the change of whose state from the more perfect to the most imperfect follows also a change of the elements; and even of the Earth itself, which may be confirmed by many things and which the sacred Scriptures themselves teach.

This change occurs from causes without and below, and indeed within themselves, but not from causes above themselves. For if a form, in itself, and in its own nature, more imperfect than a superior, and more perfect than an inferior form, strives and endeavors to become such as is the superior, or the inferior, then (in case it changes), it must undergo necessarily, an essential mutation.

Afterwards the forms which descend and are generated from the same form, induce a similar or a greater imperfection according as they are removed from their origin.

That we may represent to ourselves an idea of the generation and derivation of such forms, one from another, we must cultivate the idea the *in*-existence of supreme forms within singular the inferior forms; and also at the same time the idea of accidental mutation; for the perfection of superior forms consists in their capability of undergoing accidental mutations.

When many superior forms unanimously consociate themselves, and form, determine, and constitute a one (a unit), which should be regarded as a substance in itself; then there exists a proximately inferior form, and when these (ones or units) in like manner consociate themselves and form a one (or unit), there exists a form still inferior; and so on in order. Wherefore also when a compound form is resolved, it returns to a prior form. Thus one flows-in into another, and what is prior is always interior, and what is posterior is always exterior, and thence more remote: thus the first differs (distat) from the last *toto cælo;* although most intimately resident within it. From which it follows that nothing substantial is given in the composite, except the first, and that *one* (unit), which is called a simple substance; and likewise that force itself, which is perpetually impressed, is incident within. In order to illustrate how a number, quantity, or volume of such superior unities, or so called simples, consociate and constitute themselves into a single composite unity of a lower degree, let us suppose, that one particle of the vapor of water is distended by a little volume of air particles, and then again that such particle of air is in like manner distended by a little volume of ether, and this ether again by a superior ether or aura thus from so many simple forms in order; then it follows that one form may be generated from another and that this aqueous vapor or bulla is a complex of all and that all forms from the first natural to the ultimate exist within it.   It also follows that, if the fluxion of the superior (magnetic) ether is vortical in its fluxion, the fluxion of the ether is spiral, and of the air circular.   Such is the in-generation, and such the creation of composite forms or substances from their simples; but that inferior forms may not be destroyed, but may subsist and the superior forms flow-in into them, it is necessary that they should be distinct and each one should form and occupy its own sphere, that is, the more perfect forms, the superior, and the more imperfect, the inferior spheres; so that the superior may always be within the inferior, but not conversely.   On such grounds a vacuum is impossible.   Hence likewise it follows that the posterior forms may undergo essential mutation while the prior forms remain in their integrity; besides that these undergo accidental mutation in the same manner as if they were absent, although most intimately present, as first; but not with a similar power and virtue.

If the generation of forms is such as has been described, it follows that the most interior forms can remain entirely in their essential integrity, although the external or exterior determinations are changed.   As in the air bulla or vesicle, above spoken of; whose form is circular, if its form should be changed into the elliptical form, it would not prevent the interior bullas from retaining the determinations of their fluxions; for the change of the composite does not extend so far towards the simple forms as to change them in a similar manner.   They may not indeed flow forth according to the fulness of their nature, because in the ellipse, two centres are to be respected, but in the circle, one; therefore by their accidental mutations they accommodate themselves, that is, mutually respect each other, by the variations of expansions and contractions; and thus they consociate themselves: thus certainly it changes nothing of their essence, though the force of operating is diminished according to their whole power.   Thus in the triangle there exists perpetual opposition of determinations, and it may be said to be deprived of its fluxion; but not therefore of its conatus or endeavor of acting.

We have thus in a very general manner compassed the Doctrine of Forms. Its application can be learned by consulting the works of our Author, especially the part of the present work immediately succeeding the part under consideration; where it is applied to the organization of the living fabrics of the Human Body.

It will have been seen, that there are six degrees of forms from the angular to the spiritual, both inclusive—that these degrees are discrete, holding to each other the relation of cause and effect—that there is no passage from one degree to another by a simple ratio—that such ratio is, mathematically considered, one of infinity, thus there is no simple relation between the right line and the circle, for we consider the circle as consisting of an infinite number of right lines; only on such an hypothesis does one measure the other. From this, the distinction between discrete and ordinary degrees will be readily comprehended. Without a knowledge of discrete degrees all the works of the Divine Hand will remain a problem unsolved, a labyrinth unexplored.

A quantity of units or simples of a higher and prior degree or form, flow-in and compose one unit or simple of a lower degree or form ; so that the form of the parts, units, individuals, or simple substances are in themselves always of a superior form to that of a volume of such parts or units, organized into a new unit ; and that the units or individuals of a lower form can only attain to a higher by a division or dissolution of the units or individuals of such lower form ; and that the units of a higher form can descend to a lower form only by a congregation, unition, or composition of its units or parts. This rule is universal, holding true not only in the microcosm or world, but also in the microcosm. or human organization.

The higher the degree of form, the higher its substances, forces, powers, qualities and attributes, and vice versa ; and as the degrees of form descend, in each degree thereof, a force becomes latent, a power absorbed, an energy sinks to repose, a life becomes extinct, until in the lower and lowest forms substances become so compounded, forces by mutual opposition become so equilibrated ; motion seems to have ceased, life to have become extinct ; and rest, inertia, and gravity appear to be at once cause and effect. Yet nothing has perished —the supreme form has only clothed itself in lower forms, and thus induced new qualities—living and incessant forces have only embraced each other in friendly arms, balanced each other no new pivots—and in the degree they seem to repose, seem to have perished, in that degree have they renovated their energies and recruited their latent forces—and when they shall have unfolded their arms, unlocked the barred doors, they will return and again expatiate in higher forms. Thus the highest descends to the lowest; and in the lowest, clothed with its form, exist the higher and the highest simultaneously—activity is latent in repose, life slumbers in death, generation and birth are a descent to a lower, but regeneration and dissolution, a return to a higher sphere.

The world-forms and the forms of the human, animal, vegetable and mineral kingdoms, mutually, unanimously, and harmoneously act and react, impart and respond, correspond and represent, image and typify each other; otherwise there could possibly be no harmony, concord, affinity, assimilation or correlation between them—otherwise the air world not respond harmoniously to the ear; the ether vibrate concordantly with the eye, or the higher auras bear sympathetic messages from soul to soul.

W. H. B.
Lockport, N. Y.

ARTICLE II.

—

FOURIERISM AND THE NEW CHURCH.*

It is understood that the writer of this book is Dr. Charles Julius Hempel, a German by birth and education, and now a resident of the city of New York. For several years past he has been much interested in the system of Social Science propounded by Charles Fourier, as the work before us evinces. And undoubtedly he saw, or *imagined* that he saw, sufficient reasons for coupling the names of Swedenborg and Fourier together, as he has in the title page of his book. And of this no one has a right to complain, any more than he would have to complain of a farmer, who, to gratify a fancy of his own, should harness a horse and goose together. We would not be understood to mean that the absurdity in the one case was as great as that in the other; neither are we prepared to say that there exists no connection between the teachings of Swedenborg and Fourier. But *if* any such connection exists as the

---

* *The True* Organization of the New Church as indicated in the Writings of EMANUEL SWEDENBORG, and demonstrated by CHARLES FOURIER. New York: William Radde, 322 Broadway. London: H. Ballière, 219 Regent Street. 1848.

title of this book would naturally lead one to infer, we have only to say that, in our humble opinion, Dr. Hempel's attempt to exhibit it is a signal failure.

We are not of the number of those who feel that the social problem is one to be ignored, despised, or treated with indifference by New Churchmen. On the contrary we have long believed, and still believe, it to be a problem whose importance is equalled only by its depth; a problem which deserves the attention of the profoundest and best minds, and to the solution of which the highest wisdom of this age may scarcely be equal. Upon the general subject of Industrial Association, or the Reorganization of Society, we may have some thoughts to offer in a future number of the Repository. At present we shall only attempt a review of Dr. Hempel's book.

We have read this work with great care, and with mingled feelings of disappointment, sorrow, and disgust. We do not remember ever to have met with so strange a medley in the shape of a book—or in any other shape. Along with some brilliant and beautiful passages, some lofty and noble thoughts, some clear and just views of our existing social order, some tolerably conclusive reasoning, and some signs of a tender sympathy for the wants, weaknesses, and woes of our degraded humanity, which are to be found in the book, we meet with much bombast, vanity, and self-conceit; much weakness and puerility; much extravagance and falsehood; much miserable logic; many bold assumptions and unauthorized conclusions; and many signs of a mind infected with a virulent and unrelenting misanthropy. But the worst, among the many bad features of this book, is the author's gross and repeated perversions of the teachings of Swedenborg. These are so numerous, that the instances in which he has interpreted him fairly form the exceptions. Some of his perversions appear to have been deliberate and wilful: but we have the charity to believe that in most cases they arose from his misunderstanding of Swedenborg. And yet it is a very severe reflection upon the author's state of mind, to suppose that the truths of the New Jerusalem really *appear* to his mental vision in the shape in which he has presented them in his book. If this be so, it affords a striking illustration of a fact mentioned by Swedenborg as often occurring in the other world, viz., that heavenly truth in its *descent* takes on an appearance corresponding to the state of mind of those into whom it flows; and when it has descended low enough, it is changed into that which is opposite to the truth. (See Ath. Creed, 46.)

The author, without announcing himself as a New Churchman, professes the highest regard for Swedenborg, speaks of

his revelations as "sublime truths," as "true universal principles"—of "treasures of Truth deposited, in the philosophical and
theological writings of Swedenborg," &c., and says that he is
one of the deepest and truest psychologists that has ever blessed
Humanity with good and useful doctrines about the constitutive principles of the mind and soul of man" (p. 306) ; and his
numerous quotations from his writings, together with the ob-
sequious manner in which he defers to him on all occasions,
exhibit quite as much "man-worship of Swedenborg" as we
have ever witnessed in any of "the members of the New
Church."

The author's idea appears to be, that the new social order
propounded by Fourier is the proper and necessary ultimate of
the psychological and heavenly principles revealed by Swedenborg. In other words, that the social science of the former and
the spiritual doctrines of the latter are the true counterparts
of each other, related like body and soul. And his aim is to
exhibit this relation to the minds of the members of the New
Church, and impress upon them the importance of forthwith
organizing Phalansteries after the plan proposed by Fourier.
His appeal, therefore, seems to be mainly to the receivers of
Swedenborg's theological system. The book appears to have
been written for their especial benefit. This may be inferred
from the following, among other passages.

"The revelations of Swedenborg, by which I mean his grand cos-
nogonic psychological generalizations, all point to that Social Order
which Fourier has described as the true Social Code, pre-established
or Humanity by its maker.

"This work, then, especially commends itself to those who receive
he doctrines of Swedenborg, either partially or in their totality," p.
2, 23.

Again he says:

"I pray God that this present attempt to introduce the doctrines of
Fourier to the followers of Swedenborg as the foundation of their
Church, may throw a firebrand amongst them that will kindle their
ouls with the love of charity, and with the holy desire of giving to
heir New Jerusalem that unitary organization which alone can command the attention and ultimately secure the conquest of the world,"
. 19.

This announces the author's design in writing the book,
and in our opinion a book *worse* adapted to the end aimed at
was never been written. If the author's desire be *really* what
is language would lead us to infer, we should advise him by
ll means to withdraw his book from circulation and commit
t to the flames as soon as possible. We fully believe that
his would best promote the end for which he professes to have

written. For sure are we that none of the receivers of Swedenborg's doctrines can read this book with much attention, without feeling greater repugnance to the whole subject of Association, and especially to the doctrines of Fourier, than he ever felt before.

Our readers will bear in mind that our author professes to take Swedenborg as his teacher in theology and psychology. He perpetually refers to him as *authority* in these matters. He will not, therefore, be likely to complain of us for testing some of his positions by the standard which we both acknowledge to be correct.

Notwithstanding his professed regard for, and faith in, the teachings of Swedenborg, Dr. Hempel denies the fallen state of man (i. e. the individual man) and the existence of hereditary evil—doctrines so perpetually proclaimed by Swedenborg, and which lie at the foundation of his whole system. He says:

"Man is a conflux of every order of heavenly power: he is a type of heavenly Goodness and Wisdom," p. 169.

"Every rational soul is a conflux of *good affections*, each of which has a tendency to be united with an external object, that is agreeable to it, upon which it may rest as a basis, and into which it may expand as its natural and true receptacle. The realization of that union is the fulfilment of human destiny," p. 124.

That our author is not here speaking of the spiritual or regenerate man, but of every individual in his unregenerate or natural state, is plain from many other parts of his book. Thus he says:

"Heretofore we have legislated upon the principle that man is naturally depraved: let us now legislate upon the principle that he is naturally good," p. 250.

"Let it be decreed that man is incapable of wilful deception, of wilful violation of his engagements, and that if he does violate his engagements, it is from some *uncontrolable necessity*," p. 251.

"Man is born honest; man desires to be honest; he *cannot* commit an act of wilful dishonesty," p. 252.

"Our legislators should assume the ground that man is instinctively inclined to goodness, to honesty," p. 381.

The doctrine of man's natural innate goodness, so emphatically announced in these extracts, is no new doctrine. Nor shall we now find fault with it, or attempt to refute it. But the question is, how does it tally with the teachings of Swedenborg on the same subject? Is it possible that Dr. Hempel can be ignorant of the fact that it is the very opposite? How

can he ?   For in an extract on page 256 of his book, Sweden-.
borg says :

"Man, when he is born, as to hereditary evils is a hell in the least
form, and also becomes a hell so far as he takes from hereditary evils,
and superadds to them his own; hence it is that the order of his life
from nativity and from actual life is opposite to the order of heaven."
—*A. C.* 9336.

Again in the True Christian Religion he says :

"That man is born in all kinds of evils, and unless he remove
them in part, by repentance, he remains in them ; and whosoever remains in them cannot be saved."—520.

"Man from nativity loves nothing except himself and the world,—
and this love is corporeal natural, and may be called material."—
D. L. & W. 419.

"It must appear plain to every one, both from the Word and from
doctrine thence derived, that the proprium or self-hood of man is evil
from his birth, and that it is in consequence of this that he loves evils
from an innate concupiscence, and is hurried on to the very commission of them, from a desire to revenge, to defraud, to defame, and to
commit adultery ; and in case he does not think that they are sins,
and resist them on that account, he commits them as often as opportunity offers, and when his interest and reputation are not endangered.
"Inasmuch as this proprium or self-hood of man constitutes the
first root of his life, it is evident what sort of a tree man would become, if that root were not to be extirpated, and a new one implanted ;
he would be a rotten tree, of which it is said that it is to be cut down
and cast into the fire.   Matt. iii. 10; vii. 19.   This root is not removed,
and a new one implanted in its stead, unless man regards the evils
which constitute the root, as destructive to his soul, and is on that
account desirous of removing them : but inasmuch as they appertain
to his proprium, and are consequently delightful to him, he cannot
effect their removal but with a degree of unwillingness, and of struggle
against them, and thus combat."—*Doct. of Life*, 92, 93.

Such is the doctrine on this subject taught by Swedenborg
in every volume of his writings, and clearly implied on every
page.   His statement of it is so clear and explicit that it is
not possible to misunderstand him.   And do not the Word of
God, the experience and observation of men, and the past
history and present condition of our race, bear their united
testimony to its truth ?

Now Dr. Hempel professes to believe that this, like the other
doctrines taught by Swedenborg, came from heaven ; that it
is a doctrine which the angels themselves see to be true.
Whence then could have come *his* doctrine on the same subject, which the reader sees and knows to be the exact opposite ?   Surely not from the Word,—not from the writings of
the Church,—not from heaven.   We must therefore pronounce
it the offspring of self-derived intelligence.

"This cheating and falsifying is the *unavoidable* result of that system of individual buying and selling which is *necessarily* established in civilization," p. 200. (See also pp. 46, 50, 52, 53, 66, 89, 121, 138).

Our Saviour taught that the things which defile men— "murders, adulteries, fornications, thefts, false-witness, blasphemies"—have their origin within and "come forth from the heart" (Matt. xv. 18, 19). But this, Dr. Hempel regards as quite a mistake. He says they come from without, and are the unavoidable result of a mal-organization of Society. No individual, therefore, can justly be held accountable for crimes which *he could not avoid* committing. A man who is driven by an uncontrollable *necessity*, is not to blame for what he does. There is, then, no such thing as individual accountability. Civilization alone is guilty. Civilization is accountable for all the crimes that men commit. (How moral guilt or accountability can attach to a soulless thing, as civilization is, our author does not tell us.) This doctrine, we see, of no individual accountability, flows as a logical sequence from the foregoing. And our author does not shrink from the conclusion, but stoutly maintains its truth. He asserts " that we are *collectively* [not individually] responsible for the evil which each of us commits," p. 120. Again : " The evils which man commits are mere accidents, originating not in man's essence, but in his accidental ignorance and in the circumstances of society," p. 119. Once more : " Man can no more be responsible for the actions done in the world, than he can be made responsible for the bad dreams which may trouble him in his sleeping hours," p. 135. And on the same page he speaks of man's regeneration being " the *necessary* result of his position in society."

"The doctrine of individual responsibility is one of the illusions of infant Humanity," p. 123.

And not only does Dr. H. maintain the impossibility of keeping the commandments as Society is at present constituted— the *absolute necessity* of all the crimes that are committed, but he goes farther, and insists that these crimes and all existing evils, entered into, and made a part of, the original design of the Creator ; that they were not only *foreseen*, but *foreordained* and *provided* by the Lord. Thus he says:

"God must have both wished, and known how, to avoid Evil; and if nevertheless, Evil exists, it must be, because *He* deems it *essentially* necessary to the accomplishment of His providential ends," p. 53.

Again : "Responsibility can only attach to the creating Cause. How can man be responsible in the place of the Cause which *created* him ?" p. 122.

iism is not ADAPTED to the nature of man and to his passions; that
its laws are in flagrant opposition to those which regulate or govern
their action; that it perverts, misdirects, and develops them subver-
sively, and that the selfishness, oppression, fraud. injustice, and crime,
which mark the course of his societies, are attributable to that artificial or social misdirection and perversion, and not to any inborn, inherent depravity in the human being himself."

Thus Dr. Hempel, in common with many of the school to
which he belongs, fails to recognize the most important fact in
man's spiritual history and condition, and substitutes, instead
of it, the opposite error. How can we look upon any class of
men as true reformers, who have not yet learned what it is,
which, *first of all*, and *most of all*, needs reforming, viz. the
individual human heart? And what are we to think of a
system by which it is proposed to reform existing political and
social evils, which utterly ignores or mistakes the seat and
source of those evils?—which denies anything like a hereditary evil taint in human hearts, and assumes, as its grand
starting point, the native "inborn goodness" of men—their
natural love of all that is good and true, and their hatred
of the opposite? Are not the political and social evils of
which we complain, *effects*? And if so, must they not have a
cause? And must not that cause be spiritual? Where, then,
shall we seek for the cause, with any hope of success, but in
the depraved hearts of men? In their inborn tendencies, to
evil—their supremely selfish and worldly loves? And how can
existing social evils be removed, without first removing or sub-
duing their cause? And how can their cause be removed,
unless it be understood, or recognized *as* the cause? The
physician who attempts to heal our bodily maladies, seeks
first of all to know the cause of the pains we suffer. And if
he should mistake the cause, we should not expect him to treat
our case successfully. How, then, can we expect successful
treatment of our social and political ills, by those who overlook or utterly mistake the true cause of these maladies?
Let us look at some of the logical consequences that flow
from our author's fundamental error respecting man's natural
or hereditary state. If it be true that each individual is born
" good"—that his moral nature is untainted—that his inclinations are all right—that his " attractions" are in the proper
direction, or, what is the same, that his ruling loves are good,
then man has only to yield to his attractions—only to act freely
as his inclinations prompt, and he will live just as he ought
to live. No change in the strength or quality of his ruling
love can be necessary. The declaration of our Saviour, that
a man " must be born again" before he can enter the kingdom

ARTICLE III.

THE QUESTION OF BAPTISM CONSIDERED.

IT will be the object of this paper to examine the question, whether baptism should be administered again to one who has received it among Christians external to our New Church organization, when he presents himself for admission into any one of its societies. Before entering on the merits of the question itself, we shall bestow a few remarks upon the propositions laid down in the Report of the Massachusetts Association on this subject, printed in the Journal of 1847.

1. An argument against the necessity of re-baptism may be maintained on the very grounds which the Report itself takes. It is there contended, that the former church is the external of the New Church, and in connection with the external of the new Heaven—the new *Christian* Heaven, and that, therefore, its baptism (to use its own words) "must connect them (its members) with the external Christian Heaven, and that when any one is baptized in that church, angels from the external Christian Heaven are appointed to attend upon him, to take care of him, to keep him in a state for receiving the faith of their heaven, to give him an inclination for their religion and a disinclination for all other religions." What is thus in connexion with Christian angels must, clearly, be a church, and, as the Report terms it (p. 475), "a Christian Church." Baptism into it, therefore, is baptism into the New Church, as to its external. Now, when it has once been admitted that one is fully and properly baptized into the New Church, as to its external, how can it be contended that he must be baptised again? If, by virtue of his baptism in some sect of what is called by some "the old Church," he really was introduced into the *external* of the New Church, he was introduced into the New Church *absolutely*. The distinction of internal and external is nothing, in this point of view. For baptism was not designed to give admission into one or another division of the Christian Church, but into the Church as a whole; and, therefore, one admitted into its external, is, so far as introduction is concerned, as much in the church as a whole, as if he had been admitted into its internal; just as one who enters by a door into an outer apartment is as much *in* the house as he who is in one of its inner chambers.

2. But again; if the question be asked, Why should baptism,

vocabulary, or will be placed among obsolete terms. No self-denial, self-sacrifice, or self-compulsion, is necessary to our growth in virtue, or to our progress in the heavenly life. These duties, so much insisted on and lauded heretofore, are "by no means conducive to salvation." For he declares it to be a "great truth, that nothing is more opposed to Heavenly Order or Harmony, than the denial or sacrifice of any one portion of our innate tastes, appetites, faculties, or 'goods,' to use the New Church appellation." *Goods*, according to our author's understanding of the term, are all man's inborn tendencies or "attractions," all his natural inclinations. But man, our readers will say, is naturally inclined to love himself supremely. So Swedenborg teaches; and so teach the Bible and all human experience. Very well. Our author admits it; and maintains that this is right, this is heavenly. It was intended that man should love himself supremely. Then only is he in a state of true order. Thus he says: "Self-love in the Phalanx, is the pivotal or fundamental love of every individual man;" "Self-love in the Phalanx enjoys unrestrained development," p. 386. And after quoting a passage from Swedenborg (*C. L.* 269) in which self-love is said to be *as the feet* of man, in a state of heavenly order, he remarks:

"This does not mean that self-love is the lowest in order; but from the correspondence of feet to the *Ultimate* or *Fundamental* Principle, the above distinctly means that, in True Order, self-love is for every individual man the most immediate, the fundamental love; he cannot be in heaven as long as he is not permitted to love himself above all things."—*Ib.*

This language is too plain to be misunderstood. And the construction which our author has here put upon one of the plainest passages in Swedenborg, argues either great dishonesty, or most unaccountable stupidity. *How could* he believe the meaning of the passage he quotes to be what he says it is? For in the same article of Conjugial Love, and in the lines *immediately preceding* those extracted by our author, Swedenborg says:

"There are three universal loves, which form the constituent principles of every man by creation; neighborly love, which also is the love of doing uses; the love of the world, which also is the love of possessing wealth; and the love of self, which also is the love of bearing rule over others. Neighborly love, or the love of doing uses, is a spiritual love; but the love of the world, or the love of possessing wealth, is a material love; whereas the love of self, or the love of bearing rule over others, is a corporeal love. A man is a man while neighborly love, or the love of doing uses, constitutes the head, the love of the world the body, and the love of self the feet; whereas if

the love of the world constitutes the head, a man is not a man otherwise than as hunch -backed; but when the love of self constitutes
the head, he is not a man standing on his feet, but on the palms of
his hands with his head downwards and his haunches upwards."—
C. L. 269.

How is it possible for an honest and sensible man to conclude from this, that self-love, in true order, is the pivotal or
fundamental love?   This word *pivotal* has a well-defined
meaning among Phalansterians, which Dr. Hempel must be
supposed to understand.   It is predicated of what is primary—
what rules or predominates in any system.   Thus the sun " is
the *pivot* of the solar system, because it governs or directs the
movements of that system."   "The general and his staff, are
the *pivot* of an army," because they direct and govern it, and
upon them the movements of the army depend.   It is plain,
therefore, what our author's meaning must be when he says
that self-love, in the Phalanx, and "in true order," "is the
pivotal or fundamental love of every individual man."   It is
plain that his meaning is the exact *opposite* of what Swedenborg teaches in the number from which he quotes, as well as
everywhere else in his writings.   Does Dr. Hempel need to
be told that, "to love himself above all things," is, according to Swedenborg, a characteristic not of heavenly but of
hellish life?—That self-love is the fundamental, ruling, or
pivotal love of all in the hells?   We had supposed that this
was one of the first lessons that every student of Swedenborg
learns from him.   And our author must indeed have learned
little from his works, if he has not learned this.

" An additional reason, which also in heaven is the primary one, why
the angels can receive so great wisdom, is because they are without
self-love ; for as far as any one is without that love, so far he can grow
wise in divine things : it is that love which closes the interiors to the
Lord and to heaven, and opens the exteriors and turns them to self;
wherefore all those with whom that love rules, are in thick darkness
as to the things which are of heaven, howsoever they are in light as to
the things which are of the world.   But the angels, on the other hand,
because they are without that love, are in the light of wisdom; for the
heavenly loves in which they are, which are love to the Lord and
love towards the neighbor, open the interiors, because those loves
are from the Lord, and the Lord Himself is in them."—*H. & H.* 272.

And where in Swedenborg will our author find anything to
favor his idea of the needlessness or impropriety of self-denial
and self-compulsion, both of which imply not only a sense of
duty, but the actual *doing* of our duty, when natural inclination would lead us to do differently.   How will he interpret
all that is taught in the Heavenly Doctrines concerning tempt-

ation-combats, and their *necessity* to every man's regeneration? What does he understand Swedenborg to mean when he says, "that man ought *to force himself* to do good, and to speak truth."—*A. C.* 1937. "Man ought to *compel himself* to do good, to obey the things which the Lord has commanded," &c. *ib.* "Whilst man compels himself to resist the evil and the falsity, which are infused and suggested by wicked spirits, there is more of freedom than ever exists in any state out of temptations, although man cannot conceive it at the time; it is an interior freedom, by virtue whereof he is desirous to subdue the evil," *ib.* Does not all *self-compulsion* imply something more than yielding to "the attractions of our nature?" Does it not imply acting from a sense of duty, and doing something which we are naturally disinclined to do, and which it requires some self-denial to do? How unauthorized, then, is Dr. Hempel's assertion, that, "whatever man does from a mere external necessity [or from a sense of duty and not from love] is a dead work *and kills the soul*," p. 184.

Our readers having learned what, according to Dr. Hempel's idea, is the ruling or *pivotal* love of all in the heavens— having seen that he believes no one can be *in* heaven unless he "love himself above all things,"—will not perhaps be surprised, however they may be shocked, at a remark like the following.

"Christ and the Devil are the fundamental constituents of the Divine Principle, and will ultimately coalesce into ONE COMPOUND UNIT" (!!) p. 52.

And he would have his readers believe that this too is the doctrine of Swedenborg, although he does not refer us to the passage where it is taught. And we verily believe that the doctrine might be drawn from Swedenborg without doing any more violence to the plain dictates of reason, the principles of common honesty, and the established rules of interpretation, than our author has been guilty of doing repeatedly.

But the Bible insists on *regeneration* as necessary to man's entrance into the kingdom of heaven. And the importance and necessity of this, together with the nature of the change itself, and the means and manner of its accomplishment, forms the burden of Swedenborg's teachings. Our readers may feel some curiosity to know what Dr. H. understands by *regeneration*. If man is "born good," if his native "attractions" are all in the right direction, then surely he needs only to follow the strong and innate tendencies of his nature, and he will live right. The phrase "born again," therefore, can have no application or reference to the individual man. The hearts of

individuals are right—just what they should be ; what need,
then, is there of any change of heart? What need of any reformation or re-creation of our inward man? Any renewal
of the spirit and temper of our minds? Any casting off of
the old man, and putting on of the new man, which, " after
God, is created in righteousness and true holiness ?" There is
not the least need of this, says our author—and for this we
give him credit for consistency. Regeneration, to his mind.
means nothing of this sort. It implies a radical change or
remodelling of the Social man ;—a reorganization of Society
upon the principles of Charles Fourier. We have only to alter
the external condition of men—place them in true relations
to each other externally—bring them together into the Phalanx and arrange them in groups and series, and man is regenerated : The kingdom of heaven is come upon earth. This
is our author's idea of regeneration, clearly and repeatedly set
forth in his book. Thus he says :

" At present we are all in *false positions*, that is, our positions have
not been fully and truly worked out," p. 85.

" It remains with us not only to facilitate the fulfilment of duty, but
to make it a source of heavenly bliss, *by establishing such relations between man and man*, and man and nature, as will make the desires of
passion identical with the requirements of order," p. 113.

"In this vast combination of industrial elements [i. e. in Associa-
tion], every faculty manifests itself in truthfulness and freedom ; *there
is a complete regeneration of man ;* there is the accomplishment of his
Destiny! This *integral regeneration* or rebirth of the soul Fourier in
his technical language expresses by the phrase, ' elevation from the
simple to the *compound* mode.'
" *Such an organization* of men and things constitutes the True Church."
p. 264.

Again, quoting the text " Seek ye first the Kingdom of God
and his righteousness," he says concerning this Kingdom, "if
it mean anything, it must mean *an arrangement of Men and
Things* which God himself has designed ; an arrangement
which will do away with all causes of envy and strife, which
will conciliate our interests, harmonize our passions, and make
of every human being a living form of Goodness and Wisdom,"
p. 242. (See also pp. 71, 112, 119, 135, 247, 264, 271, 283, 297.
448.)
The proposed new external "arrangement of men and
things," then, is what our author understands by "the kingdom
of God." He does not tell us how he understands those words
of our Saviour, " The kingdom of God cometh not with observation: Neither shall they say Lo ! here, or Lo ! there ; for,
behold the kingdom of God *is within you*." And since this

radical change in the form of society—this remodelling of our existing social fabric, is what is to be understood by *regeneration*, of course there can be no such thing as regeneration in Civilization, or in Society *under its present* form. This is a legitimate deduction from the foregoing ; and this our author very consistently maintains. Thus he says : "There cannot be any Christian Church without a Serial Organization," p. 265. And he complains of "the disciples of Swedenborg," because they "do not consider such an arrangement as *a necessary* condition of man's regeneration," p. 170.

Again: "Without a collective arrangement around man, of all those things of Nature [which can be provided only in Association], according to the laws of Divine Order, there is no Church, no Society, no Heaven, and consequently spiritual death"—no regenerate men of course, p. 172.

And speaking of the command "Love your enemies," &c., he says it is "a commandment for all men to do that which it is absolutely impossible to do" in Society as now organized : "that commandment is impossible in Civilization," p. 447. And he goes on to say that "the means by the application of which the fulfilment of the law will be rendered not only possible, but certain—are the Phalanx of Fourier," *ib*.

And not only is it impossible for men in civilized society to obey this commandment, but they cannot, according to Dr. H., always obey the commandments of the Decalogue. Men, in Civilization, are *obliged* to commit fraud, theft, murder, adultery, and the like. These and other like crimes result necessarily from the existing bad organization of society. The passions which lead to them are good, and ought not, cannot be restrained. All the evils, therefore, with which society is at present afflicted, are *necessary* results, not of anything evil in men's hearts, but of our present social arrangements. Not the hearts of men, therefore, but our social mechanism needs to be reformed. Thus he says :

"It is irrational to contend that the perpetrator of that deed [murder] might have controlled his passions, for the simple reason that it remains yet to be proved whether the passions *can at all be controlled* by a mere determination of the will under any circumstances," p. 44.

"That *all* our acts are providentially necessary, and that all of them are preparatory to our ultimate salvation, has first been scientifically expressed by Charles Fourier," p. 49.

"The *transgression* of God's commandments is a condition of salvation," p. 51.

"Every action which man performs, is a result of his Passional Organization, and, whether the action be good or bad, it is a *necessary*, though a subversive manifestation of his Passional principle," p. 137.

"This cheating and falsifying is the *unavoidable* result of that system of individual buying and selling which is *necessarily* established in civilization," p. 200. (See also pp. 46, 50, 52, 53, 66, 89, 121, 138).

Our Saviour taught that the things which defile men— "murders, adulteries, fornications, thefts, false-witness, blasphemies"—have their origin within and "come forth from the heart" (Matt. xv. 18, 19). But this, Dr. Hempel regards as quite a mistake. He says they come from without, and are the unavoidable result of a mal-organization of Society. No individual, therefore, can justly be held accountable for crimes which *he could not avoid* committing. A man who is driven by an uncontrollable *necessity*, is not to blame for what he does. There is, then, no such thing as individual accountability. Civilization alone is guilty. Civilization is accountable for all the crimes that men commit. (How moral guilt or accountability can attach to a soulless thing, as civilization is, our author does not tell us.) This doctrine, we see, of no individual accountability, flows as a logical sequence from the foregoing. And our author does not shrink from the conclusion, but stoutly maintains its truth. He asserts "that we are *collectively* [not individually] responsible for the evil which each of us commits," p. 120. Again: "The evils which man commits are mere accidents, originating not in man's essence, but in his accidental ignorance and in the circumstances of society," p. 119. Once more: "Man can no more · be responsible for the actions done in the world, than he can be made responsible for the bad dreams which may trouble him in his sleeping hours," p. 135. And on the same page he speaks of man's regeneration being "the *necessary* result of his position in society."

"The doctrine of individual responsibility is one of the illusions of infant Humanity," p. 123.

And not only does Dr. H. maintain the impossibility of keeping the commandments as Society is at present constituted— the *absolute necessity* of all the crimes that are committed, but he goes farther, and insists that these crimes and all existing evils, entered into, and made a part of, the original design of the Creator ; that they were not only *foreseen*, but *foreordained* and *provided* by the Lord. Thus he says:

"God must have both wished, and known how, to avoid Evil ; and if nevertheless, Evil exists, it must be, because *He* deems it *essentially* necessary to the accomplishment of His providential ends," p. 53.

Again : "Responsibility can only attach to the creating Cause. How can man be responsible in the place of the Cause which *created* him ?" p. 122.

"God must have foreseen, *and therefore have provided*, the present wretchedness of mankind—He foresaw, and therefore *provided* its sufferings,"—i. e. the sufferings of Humanity, p. 91.

"There must be those through whose instrumentality evil must be planned and committed, and we cannot suppose, without an insult to the Deity, that He should have created men for the execution *of his designs*, and cursed them with eternal reprobation after *they had fulfilled the destinies of their existence*," p. 141.

A charming code of ethics, this! Then, according to our author, the men who have committed the most nefarious crimes that ever disgraced Humanity, were, at the very moment of committing them, doing the will of our Father in the heavens —"executing His designs," as truly as the men whose noble and philanthropic deeds have shed showers of blessings on the world. They have alike "fulfilled the destinies of their existence." Nero was as much the servant of God as Moses or John ; and those who have most wronged and enslaved mankind deserve our love and gratitude not less than the greatest benefactor of our race. Both classes were created for the very deeds which they performed—deeds which they *could not help* performing, and in the execution of which they were merely carrying out " *God's designs*"—"fulfilling their destiny." After this, our readers will not be surprised at the following passage, where, addressing himself to the murderer on the gallows, the author says :

"The day of judgment will come, not for thee, O man, to be judged; God does not judge his creatures ; the day of judgment will come, but it is God who will suffer himself to be judged by his creatures. . . . [And] on that glorious day of universal Restoration, of universal Union of the Father and his children, will even thy errors and thy crimes stand justified *as necessary elements* in that Divine Concert of Love and Adoration," p. 138.

Now that Dr. Hempel himself should entertain such notions as these, and should present them to the American public as great and important truths, is nothing remarkable. The same doctrines, and others equally false and foolish, have been believed and published before. But that he should perpetually refer *to Swedenborg* as authority for what he says (we shall notice hereafter his *manner* of quoting him), and should seriously attempt to make him stand god-father to this beautiful system of moral philosophy, "excites our special wonder." We must say that it argues a degree of intellectual imbecility or moral obliquity, which is as extreme as it is rare.

B. F. B.

(*To be Continued.*)

ARTICLE III.

THE QUESTION OF BAPTISM CONSIDERED.

It will be the object of this paper to examine the question, whether baptism should be administered again to one who has received it among Christians external to our New Church organization, when he presents himself for admission into any one of its societies. Before entering on the merits of the question itself, we shall bestow a few remarks upon the propositions laid down in the Report of the Massachusetts Association on this subject, printed in the Journal of 1847.

1. An argument against the necessity of re-baptism may be maintained on the very grounds which the Report itself takes. It is there contended, that the former church is the external of the New Church, and in connection with the external of the new Heaven—the new *Christian* Heaven, and that, therefore, its baptism (to use its own words) " must connect them (its members) with the external Christian Heaven, and that when any one is baptized in that church, angels from the external Christian Heaven are appointed to attend upon him, to take care of him, to keep him in a state for receiving the faith of their heaven, to give him an inclination for their religion and a disinclination for all other religions." What is thus in connexion with Christian angels must, clearly, be a church, and, as the Report terms it (p. 475), " a Christian Church." Baptism into it, therefore, is baptism into the New Church, as to its external. Now, when it has once been admitted that one is fully and properly baptized into the New Church, as to its external, how can it be contended that he must be baptised again? If, by virtue of his baptism in some sect of what is called by some " the old Church," he really was introduced into the *external* of the New Church, he was introduced into the New Church *absolutely*. The distinction of internal and external is nothing, in this point of view. For baptism was not designed to give admission into one or another division of the Christian Church, but into the Church as a whole; and, therefore, one admitted into its external, is, so far as introduction is concerned, as much in the church as a whole, as if he had been admitted into its internal; just as one who enters by a door into an outer apartment is as much *in* the house as he who is in one of its inner chambers.

2. But again; if the question be asked, Why should baptism,

after it has been administered by the former church be administered again? it would be answered, on the grounds of the Report: Because other angels will then be appointed to attend upon the man and take care of him, and they will give him an inclination for *their* faith and religion—which the angels under whose care he was before, could not do. This answer supposes that the "faith" and the "religion" of the internal and the external heavens is not one and the same. Now Swedenborg uniformly applies "religion" to Pagan and Mahometan beliefs, never to any form of Christianity, except that of the Roman Catholics to mark its great corruption. Surely, in all the Christian Heavens with which those who draw their creeds from the Word can be in connection, it is the *Christian* "religion" the angels are in. Nor is there any difference of "faith" among them. They are in absolutely one and the same faith, only some are more interiorly in it than others. Accordingly Swedenborg says generally of all infants baptized into the Christian church, that "they are kept in a state of receiving faith *in the Lord*." Now, if the angels under whose care one comes by baptism in the former church are always endeavoring to lead him into this faith, that is, to lead him *away* from his tripersonal faith, what benefit, as to this particular, will arise to him from another baptism? The Report obviously goes on the supposition, that the angels with whom his first baptism associated him, endeavor to keep him in *the faith of his church*, instead of *their heaven*.

3. Again; according to the views of the Report, angels of the external Christian heaven, are assigned to infants baptized in the former church. But, with *all* infants, at first, angels of the inmost heaven are present. "They (certain angelic spirits) discoursed moreover concerning infants on earth, declaring that immediately after their nativity there are angels with them from the heaven of innocence."—*A. C.* 2303. Again. "It has been told me from Heaven that infants are particularly under the auspices of the Lord, and that their influx is from the inmost heaven, where there is a state of innocence."—*H. & H.* 277. It cannot be answered to these citations that the external Heavens meant in the Report are themselves divided into internal and external, and angels of the former division are meant. For, the term used by Swedenborg is "inmost" making it clear that he speaks of angels of the highest or third heaven, which is further manifest from its being called "the Heaven of innocence." Thus the foundation on which the whole doctrine of the Report is built is removed.

4. There are three further objections which might be expanded, but which shall only be mentioned. The first is, that

the angels associated with the person at baptism are supposed,
by the Report, to continue with him until they are changed
at his second baptism; whereas, they leave him, as he grows
up and comes to the exercise of his own right and reason.—
T. C. R. 677.   Again; the Report makes the kind of angels
associated with any given person to depend upon the faith of
the church in which he is baptized; whereas, what angels
are associated with a man, must depend on the exigencies of
his life.   Again.   It supposes that Christians of the former
church, are, uniformly or generally, of the external church,
and those of New Church organizations of the internal; whereas, it *may* be, in some cases, that the former are of the internal,
and the *probability* is, that all of the latter are of the external,
at this day.   The distinction between those who are internal
and external being so uncertain, how can we undertake to
signalize a transition from one to the other by a second baptism?   Again; the external and internal in the church with
which the external and internal of the new Heavens correspond,
are made by differences of *life*, and not of faith except as connected with life, much less are they made by differences of the
faith *merely professed* in the outward body with which individuals are connected.   Again; there is an internal and an
external appertaining to each of the three heavens; what is
there in the church on earth, where the Word is, which answers
to these differences—and if we could point them out, would
not the grounds taken in the Report oblige us to administer not
.two only but many baptisms?

But leaving the Report and proceeding to the question proper—the true position, it is thought, is not merely a negative
or defensive one, that Old Church baptism, so called, *may* be
considered sufficient, but a positive one, that such a baptism
is good New Church baptism, and that it is forbidden by right
order to repeat it.   The arguments which go to sustain this
position are as follows.

1. Whenever an old Church is set aside, a new Church is,
on the instant, constituted by the Lord out of its remains, that
is to say, out of all, externally connected with the consummated church, who are in charity and some faith from the Word.
Such persons there must be in every church about to expire,
to keep up the conjunction between Heaven and the human
race.   When the New Church begins, it begins with them.
It takes them just *where* and *as* the era of the last judgment
finds them.   The first influx of the new Heavens, so far as it
is received in charity and faith on earth, is into their minds.
Now, who, it is asked, in the light of this principle, constituted
the New Jerusalem, at its first setting up?   Certainly not

merely the little handful, who had read and embraced the latter volumes in theology which Swedenborg had published before the year 1757, but, together with them, *all* the remains of the Old Church.   The very hour of its establishment, therefore, it had its members in every country where the Word was read, and among all sects who held it sacred and did not deny the Lord's divinity.   These members were not known to others, they did not even know themselves in their new capacity ; yet had they, in reality, been translated from the Old to the New Church.   That union of charity and faith which made them living members of the old dispensation, now made them living members of the new.   Let us hold fast this thought, the New Church is to be found, at its origin, almost entirely with those who are, in all their outward connections, of Old Church sects, though dissentients internally from the doctrines professed among those sects, and, in some imperfect manner no doubt, in the internal acknowledgment of the Lord.   This is the rudimental New Church—the New Church, in that " evening"—*A. C.* which makes its first state.   The point to be distinctly marked here, is, that persons thus intermixed and blended with the various denominations of Christendom, constitute, with very few exceptions, the Lord's New Church at its first setting up, or that else, with those exceptions, He had no Church on earth for all the time that elapsed between the era of the last judgment and the formation of the first New Church Society.   Now, what we have to observe concerning this rudimental Church, is, that it continued to grow from that time, and has its existence *now,* by the side of the societies composed of those who are in the acknowledgment of doctrines drawn from the internal sense of the Word.   For, that which made the original members of the New Church, will make members of it at any time, viz. a state of charity from the Word.   For one in charity from the Word must be in corresponding truth or faith from it, thus in the union of both. This will make him a Church in particular; and being a Church, he must be *of* that Church, which the Lord, at the time being, has in the world.   The number of such is no doubt continually swelling among the Old Church sects.

Let us now, to advance in the argument, ask, whether that branch of the New Church whose existence has been demonstrated, has always been, and is now, without either of the sacraments.   Howsoever some may answer this question, others feel constrained to reply, that this is not to be supposed. Surely the Lord does not allow those whom he has conjoined with Himself by means of the Word to go without the highest acts of worship.   Do we not see, with our outward eye, that

Christians in the spiritual world.   It gives insertion, says the
argument, among Christians *of a particular kind*—those in
truths, if it is New Church baptism, those in falses, if Old.
There is a wide difference between these two propositions.
Swedenborg himself explains the first.   He says, there are
different religions in the spiritual world, as Mahometans and
Christians.   An infant just born has no determinate place.
How shall he be assigned to one or the other division?   The
answer is, the Lord makes use of baptism, to determine its
place away from Mahometans, Jews and idolaters among
Christians.   The other view says baptism does more than this.
It determines the place of the child not only among Christians,
but among divisions of Christians—among those who believe
the tripersonal doctrines, or salvation by faith alone, rather
than among those who believe in the Lord, and salvation by a
life of uses.   Now this is carrying the words not only beyond
their first meaning—for that is plain—but further than the
end to be answered requires.   That end is, that those belonging to the *grand* religious divisions of the natural world, shall
have spirits of their respective religions, not different ones
associated with them, "without the Christian sign which is
baptism, some *Mahommedan* spirit, or some one of the *idolaters*
might apply himself to Christian infants newly born," &c.   All
the contrasts in this passage are relative to "religions" not to
modifications of any particular religion.   Baptism is called
the *Christian* sign.   It is to distinguish Christians *in general*.   It is to distinguish them from Mahommedans and others
not among themselves.   It is to guard them from being drawn
off, not from one of their own divisions to another, but from
among Christians altogether.

This last mistake has arisen from the fact that Swedenborg
does not confine himself in the passage to these grand divisions,
but does speak repeatedly of societies, and of their distinctness.   What more natural, since, at the same time, he says
each society has its sign, and he is speaking of baptism *as a*
sign, than to take that for the sign he intended.   Does he not
say, it might be asked, first, that societies are distinctly arranged, next, that this arrangement is essential to the preservation of the universe and then, "that this distinction" to use
his own words "cannot be effected without baptism?"   Does
not baptism then insert every one who receives it into particular societies?   The answer is, by no means—the words
do not require this construction.   For, to say that the distinction into societies *cannot be effected without* baptism and to
say that baptism *effects* that distinction, are statements of
widely different import.   The former, which is Swedenborg's,

It is not said, explicitly, whether this change will work its way through the sects of the former Church, while they retain their present organization ; or, whether the New Church will be generally diffused by the transition of individuals, as they adopt New Church doctrines, from those sects to New Church organizations. Without denying that very many cases of this latter kind will happen, it is highly probable that the former supposition will prove correct also. We see such a process actually beginning. Old Church falses begin to be stated, in some parts, with less sharpness and urgency. The more odious of them are kept out of sight. Isolated portions of New Church truth are put forth by independent thinkers in various quarters. Do we not know personally those who are, to some extent, in an acknowledgment of the Heavenly doctrines, and in their spirit also, who hung to the Old Church sects as by a thread, yet still hang to them ? All these instances are indications of what will be. The Old Church organizations, by a series of changes like those by which a vicious and thoughtless youth lays aside his profligate sentiments and ways, will be found, at the end of many generations, to have become New Church bodies. Let us take them in this state in the full and open profession of New Church doctrine. No one can doubt, *now*, that the baptism given among them is New Church baptism. But, *when* did it first become good, if it was not so at the outset ? Or was it all along of a quality perpetually varying, according to the purity of the doctrine professed among them, and making hair-breadth advances to a full validity ? We can hardly think, that the question of rebaptizing unhapily commenced among us will be continued, until the last shade of doctrinal discrepancy shall have ceased to separate these approximating bodies from us.

2. That must be held New Church baptism which fulfils the *three uses* of baptism, so far as they can be fulfilled at the time of administration. Let us take these uses in their order, and see whether what is called Old Church baptism does not answer them all. The first is, " introduction into the Christian Church, and, at the same time, insertion among Christians in the spiritual world." It can easily be seen that this use, in the true sense of the word, is fulfilled by what is called " Old Church baptism." It is said, *the true sense*, because many reason on this subject from the mere phrase, " introduction into the Church." But baptism is not really an introduction into the Church, for the Church is a *state* of charity and faith. It only *signifies* to the infant, that he must cultivate these two things as he grows up. It introduces him to the Church only so far as it teaches him these things, and he learns them—and it in-

teaching with a power it otherwise would not possess; this presents a proposition altogether to be dissented from, as being indeed full of horror, when once fully realized. Is an infant so at the mercy of our human agency, that by a ceremony of our own (for surely, it is not in this case the Lord's), we can subject it to the dire influences of hell? No rite, the most abominable and infernal which could be contrived by human ingenuity, could have this effect. It would pass over an infant harmless. That which gives advantage to false spirits must be *internal*, something embraced by the child or man from his own native or acquired *tendencies*, and a rite performed over an infant cannot effect either. Let the passage in Swedenborg, in which baptism, which he often declares useless except in conjunction with a good life, is declared to be hurtful in any case, be produced. If by possibility, baptism could be a vantage ground for the assaults of the infernal legions independent of being first misconstrued and perverted, it would be a sacrament of Satan and an introduction into hell.

But to urge another objection—how can the one sign of baptism be a distinctive sign for each one of innumerable societies? That it should distinguish Christians in general is easily understood, for it is a different sign in its external form from the signs of other religions, e. g. from circumcision. But if the distinction of these societies depended on a sign which is always like itself, it would effect such a distinction, as would result among the different companies of a regiment, when each one carries for its ensign an exact copy of the standard of the regiment itself. To this we know it is answered, that the external is, indeed, the same, but that it becomes a different baptism, and is so read by attendant spirits and angels, in consequence of its internal, which internal is the doctrine of the Church when it is administered. According to this, the falses of the Old Church are, as it were, wrapped up in the sacrament, at the time of giving, and take immediate effect upon the infant, causing it to come into relation with false spirits, or with angels of one heaven rather than another. But the answer is not a satisfactory one. The internal in baptism is the meaning which was in the representative act, and the words used from the Sacred Scripture, and with that meaning the administrator and the Church he is baptized in have nothing to do. Since the external is always the same and the angels who are present understand from the act purification, and from the words obligation to acknowledge and follow the Lord, how can it effect distinctions among many societies? It cannot even effect a distinction between the former and the latter Church, for (it cannot be repeated too often,) the falses of the

lses of that doctrine (which it cannot rationally mean), must
) understood as implying an idea that the child is bound to
:lieve them, *because* of his baptism. In this case that bap-
sm might well be looked on with suspicion. But nothing
in really bend one to believe what is false in religion. On
le contrary nothing more effectually signifies to the child
nd tells him, that he is to shun the falses of his Church, than
le words once pronounced over his head. Would not any
ne be thought to argue very justly who should say to him,
Come where the Lord Jesus Christ is acknowledged as the
od of heaven and earth, and doctrines are professed which
ow from that belief. You were baptized into His single
ame, as being Father, Son and Holy Ghost?" And would
e well answer such an appeal by saying, "my minister, my
arents, my sponsers, my church, believe that three persons
'ere meant, and I have learned to believe so too." No: the
ply would be, " the question is about the real meaning of the
'ords themselves, not what others think they mean—follow
leir real meaning."

But that Old Church baptism, so called, fulfils the second
se, is manifest from Swedenborg's own authority. After
iting from the Word some passages in which the name of
le Lord occurs, he says (*T. C. R.* 682), " Who cannot see,
1at by the name of the Lord, in those passages, is not meant
1at name only, but the acknowledgment of Him, that He is
le Redeemer and Saviour, and, at the same time, obedience,
nd at length, faith in Him. For, at baptism, an infant *re-
eives the sign of the cross upon the forehead and breast, which
1 a sign of inauguration into the acknowledgment and worship
f the Lord.*" He desires to show that baptism really signifies
his second use, and he does it by pleading a certain ceremony
onnected with baptism, which ceremony, it turns out, was
ppended to the baptism of the Old Churches of that day.

That he attributes the third use to so called Old Church
aptism is yet more manifest in the following passage: " That
aptism involves purification from evils and thus regeneration,
nay be very well known to every Christian; for, when the
riest, as an infant is baptized, makes with his finger a sign of
he cross on the forehead and on the breast, as a memorial of
he Lord, he afterwards *turns himself to the sponsors and asks
vhether he renounces the devil and all his works, and whether he
'eceives faith, to which, instead of the infant, it is answered by
he sponsors:* Yes. Renunciation of the devil, that is, of the
vils which are from hell, and faith in the Lord perfect regen-
ration." *T. C. R.* 685. Now, what kind of baptism does Swe-
lenborg here appeal to to show that it signifies regeneration

being, the various Christian denominations external to our New Church organizations being supposed to constitute it. When these bodies have once been called "the Old Church," the argument appears irresistible. Is not that "Old Church" baptism it is asked, which was given in an "Old Church" denomination, by an "Old Church" minister, who, at the same time lectured and prayed according to the doctrines of the Old Church? And if it was, did it not introduce into the Old Church, and into the doctrines of the Old Church? The answer to all this is—here is a troop of fallacies and fallacious phrases, their captain of fifty being this, that the Christian denominations about us are the Old Church. There is no particular objection we will grant to *calling* them the Old Church ; it is an easy and compendious phrase by which to describe them; but the name must not be made a basis to argue upon. If it is, we must steadily deny, that a man belongs to the Old Church because he belongs to an Episcopal or Presbyterian body of Christians, and that the baptism he received was an Old Church baptism from that circumstance.

Here may fitly come in for consideration the argument from the analogy of the ministry. If one may claim to belong to the New Church by an Old Church baptism, why not to the New Church ministry by an Old Church ordination? The answer to this will be, that the sacraments of the Church and the ministry are so different, that there is no just analogy between them. Besides, an ordination confers privileges, jurisdictions, power of legislating in the affairs of the Church, and it would manifestly be destruction to the Church as an outward organization, if such powers could be conferred by the acts of bodies external to itself.

It is argued for re-baptism on some other grounds, which cannot here be noticed, as well because this paper has already been extended too far, and because they are involved in others which have already been passed under review.

It is to be observed, that the Report of the Massachusetts Association, rests re-baptism upon a ground, not only new, but quite contradictory to that hitherto assumed, viz. that the first baptism was Old Church baptism, and associated the person receiving it with false spirits. It assumes, we suppose true ground, in so far as it contends that the baptism brought in question is *New Church* baptism, and brings the person receiving it under the guardianship of New Church angels. With those who have heretofore advocated re-baptism, this would have been considered a surrender of the whole question.

When one is invited to do over again an act, which, by its very nature, is to be done but once, he is invited to look upon

Such a repetition is contrary to its very nature. Baptism is
the badge given to each one *at his first entrance* into the Church,
and, therefore, is no more to be given again, than a student
matriculates twice in the same University, or a soldier, while
he yet remains in the army, enlists in it over again. If this
is not explicitly stated in the writings of the Church, it is because there are certain things which no writer ever thinks of
asserting because they are always supposed to be understood.
It is alleged, however, that we have a precedent for a second
baptism, in the nineteenth chapter of the Acts of the Apostles,
where it is stated that Paul found certain disciples of John at
Ephesus and baptized them in the name of the Lord Jesus.
But the answer here is conclusive. John's baptism was not
the baptism of the first Christian Church, was not *Christian*
baptism. The weight both of authority and of argument has
always been against the identity of the two, nor is there any
room left for doubt on this point in the writings themselves.
Observe how Swedenborg, in the article on baptism, in *T. C. R.*,
treats separately of each, and how the use and effect of the
one, viz. preparing a way for Jehovah, that He might come
down to perform redemption, was different from the other.
The one supposed redemption not yet accomplished, the other
supposes it finished. Consider also the following passage :
" As to what concerns the baptism of John, it represented the
cleansing of the external man, but the baptism which is *at
this day with Christians* represents the cleansing of the internal
man, which is regeneration, wherefore it is read, that John
baptized with water, but that the Lord baptizes with the Holy
Spirit and fire, and therefore the baptism of John is called the
baptism of repentance. The Jews who were baptized were
merely external men and the external man cannot become internal without faith in Christ. That those who were baptized
with the baptism of John became internal men when they received faith in Christ, and then were baptized in the name of
Jesus, may be seen in the Acts of the Apostles," xix. 6. We
gather from this passage the following points. 1. " John's
baptism" is contrasted with " the baptism which is at this day
with Christians," implying that John's baptism was not with
Christians, consequently was not Christian baptism. 2. It did
not imply " faith in Christ"—how then could it be Christian ?
3. These disciples were baptized in the name of Jesus in consequence of receiving faith in Christ, plainly implying that
they were not baptized in that name before. 4. John's baptism was different from Christian baptism as to what it represented. 5. John's baptism is called by a *distinctive* name,
the baptism of repentance, because of a difference of effect, or

rather of *signified* effects, between it and the Lord's baptism. How can it be said, that rites between which such differences exist are identical ? If the men whom Paul found at Ephesus were baptized a second time with the *same kind* of baptism they had before, these men who had " received faith in Christ" were baptized back again " to repentance," that is, the cleansing of the external man, and " by means of that were introduced into the future (not their present) Church of the Lord, and in Heaven were inserted among those who expected and desired the Messiah" (*T. C. R.*), not among those who have acknowledged and believed he had come. Christian baptism was designed to introduce into the Christian Church. No such effect could attend John's baptism, for that Church was not yet formed. The Holy Ghost by which alone those of the Lord's spiritual kingdom who were in the lower earth could be liberated, and formed into a new Heaven, " was not yet, because Jesus was not yet glorified"—and there can be no introduction save by that into the Christian Church. In a word, the Christian Church had a date—John's baptism was *before* that date, and could no more introduce into that Church than one can be introduced into a house from which he is separated by the space of a hundred miles. Consequently it was not Christian baptism, and the case under consideration is therefore appealed to in vain, as a precedent to authorize a second baptism.

That the discussion of the subject may be more complete, it is proposed now to take up the positive arguments commonly adduced and examine them.

The main authority adduced for rebaptism is found in *T. C. R.* Nos. 677–680. Those numbers are an expansion and elucidation of the canon : That the first use of baptism is introduction into the Christian Church, and at the same time insertion among Christians in the spiritual world. The following is the passages most directly applicable to the point.

"Baptism is an introduction into the Christian Church as is plain from the following circumstances : 1. Baptism was instituted in the place of circumcision ; and as circumcision was a sign that the persons circumcised were of the Israelitish Church, so baptism is a sign that the persons baptized are of the Christian Church, as was proven in the preceding article ; and a sign answers no other purpose than a mark of distinction like swaddling-clothes of different colors put on infants belonging to different mothers, in order that they may be distinguished from each other, and not be changed. 2. It is only a sign of introduction into the Church, as is evident from the baptizing of infants before they come to the use of reason, and while they are as incapable of receiving anything relative to faith, as the young shoots of a tree. 3. Not only infants are baptized, but likewise proselytes converted to the Christian Religion, whether they be young or old, and others before they have been instructed, if they do but confess themselves desirous of embracing Christianity, into which they are inaugurated by baptism; and this also was the practice of the apostles, according to the Lord's words, 'Go ye and teach all nations, baptizing them,' Matt. xxviii. 19. 4. John baptised all that come to him from Judea and Jerusalem in the river Jordon, iii. 6; Mark i. 8. The reason why he baptized in Jordon was because the entrance into the land of Canaan was through that river, and this land signified the Church, because the Church was there; in consequence of which Jordon signified introduction into the Church. That land signified the Church, and Jordon signified introduction into it as may be seen in the Apocalypse Revealed, n. 285."

The argument constructed from this passage runs somewhat in this wise. Baptism, according to the writings of the Church, gives insertion into some society in the world of spirits, and is the sign to all in that world that the recipient is of that society and of its faith. What society he is inserted in, is determined by the Church in which he receives that baptism, for though the external is the same both in the New Church and the Old yet the internal is different—the internal being the doctrine of the Church in which it is administered. This doctrine together with the sphere of the administrator, the parents and assistants who are in it makes present similar spirits, who recognize the sign for that of their faith and thenceforth claim the person as their own and exercise an influence upon him in favor of that faith. Since this is the effect of Old Church baptism, it is further argued, it is matter of order, that on coming into a New Church society on earth, one should receive its baptism. Otherwise he is without the distinctive sign of the New Church faith, and will be infested by spirits of that faith, who recognize in him their proper sign. On the contrary he will be protected from them by another baptism.

Such an interpretation has against it the following considerations,

1. It takes " the spiritual world" in the passage cited, to mean the world of spirits, whereas it means "heaven" "This is done on earth, but, in *the heavens,* infants are introduced into the Christian Heaven." Again. "In the spiritual world, *by which we mean both heaven and hell,* all things are most distinctly arranged." It is not necessary to say that there are no societies in Old Church falses in Heaven into which any kind of baptism can give insertion.

2. For "among Christians" this interpretation substitutes "among a particular society or class of Christians." The first use of baptism, says Swedenborg, is to give insertion among

peated in this Princeton essay. Still, we have great confidence in the intended candor of the reviewer, and suppose that no one would be more ready than he, to do us in future complete justice in regard to any of the points on which he should become convinced he had misreported us. Therefore we hope that should occasion again call him to speak of our doctrines, he will not persevere in putting upon the language in which they are conveyed the worst construction "which to others it might possibly bear," but on the other hand, that he will interpret it "precisely according to our explanations."

Near the commencement of the paper we have undertaken to notice, occurs the following passage.

"We must however premise that we have no idea of attempting to tell our readers all or half that is involved in Swedenborg's views. No man can read his writings and those of his followers without thinking of the Chaos, described by Ovid as *rudis indigestaque moles*. We do not remember in our lives to have seen so many incoherent, strange and wild opinions brought together. We do not, like one of our countrymen, profess to have read the whole of Swedenborg's works. *Twenty-seven* pretty large volumes of such writings far transcend our powers of endurance, although we are not esteemed by our intimate friends very impatient of labor, if any reward is to follow."

The writer, it must be remembered, does not set out with the intention of refuting Swedenborgianism, but only with a view of giving a faithful exposition of it. This every New Churchman will allow is in itself a very laudable undertaking; and one in which, as will be seen by a reference to the cover, this very journal is engaged. So far therefore as his exposition of our views should appear correct, he would carry with him our best wishes for the success of his enterprise. Of his qualifications for such an office some conception may perhaps be gathered from the words we have just quoted. He does not pretend to have read all of Swedenborg's works, or to be able to tell the half his opinions involve. This we should have been abundantly able to infer, even in the absence of any such acknowledgment. We can assure him there are many living, who, for the sake of learning the truth, would not readily be frightened from the search for it, even by so imposing a force as twenty-seven volumes; but who would esteem the perusal of a much larger number rather a pleasure than a labor. In regard to the *rudis indigestaque moles*, it is entirely a *subjective phenomenon*, inhering in the circle of the writer's own hastily formed conceptions, and having no corresponding *objective reality* in the writings of Swedenborg.

"As views of a material object may be taken from points so remote or so distinct that they seem at first sight incompatible, and especially as

only imports that baptism is an indispensable *preliminary*, the latter, that it *effects* the thing *by itself*. The one affirms that baptism effects the distinction, *mediately* and *eventually*—the latter that it does it *immediately* and *at once*. The scope of the whole passage therefore may be exhibited thus: All hell and all heaven consist, finally, of societies; this is a fundamental principle of order. To secure that this order shall be for ever upheld, the Lord provides that every child, wheresoever born in our earth, shall be known, by some mark, to what most general religion he belongs. The Mahommedan child has his mark. Every idolater has his. The Jewish child has his. To the *Christian* child this mark is baptism. Hereby each child is kept under the influences of the religion he belongs to by birth. This is the *remote* commencement of that final order spoken of. Because, hereby, no one is distracted between the teaching he receives in the natural sphere, and the influences that bear upon him from the spiritual. He remains with one general division of the spiritual world, and, as he grows up, *his ruling love,* formed according to his doctrine, determines him *to a particular society* either of heaven or of hell. Baptism, therefore, " is the sign indicating to what religious *assembly*" (not society) the child "belongs." *T. C. R.*

It is one thing in the way to another. It distinguishes men first as Christians, and the *laws* of Christians in the end arrange them into societies. The point intended appears very plainly in the concluding sentence. " By these things is illustrated this first use of baptism, which is a sign in the spiritual world, that he is of Christians where every one is inserted among societies and congregations there according to the *quality of the Christianity* in him or out of him" according to his state of charity and faith or their opposites.

If, however, any one still insists upon the interpretation of the passage, which makes baptism a distinctive mark among different societies, let him reflect, that the societies spoken of are expressly said to be societies of heaven and of hell, and ask himself whether he can subscribe to the idea that Old Church baptism gives insertion among the latter.

It may be said, perhaps, that Old Church baptism, though it does not give immediate insertion into spiritual societies, yet is a mark to the spirits of the dragon, by which they may approach the child as he grows up, and incline him to falses. Not, is the reply, unless the child is falsely instructed about the meaning of his baptism and then *that teaching* is solely in fault, and his baptism not at all. If it be maintained, that the baptism, in itself considered, enables them to approach the opening mind of the child more closely, and to clothe this false

other is arrested by them, and never forgets them. Such is the difference between reading the Apostolical Father with or without a
knowledge of theological language."

Whatever of justness may be contained in the above considerations as pertaining to the writings of the *fathers*, we
suppose both the receivers and rejectors of Swedenborg will
agree that they apply with increased weight and particular
aptness to his system : consisting as it does, of so many "wild,"
"strange," and apparently "incoherent" doctrines ; coming to
us as it does, fenced round and wrapped up in a new and peculiar phraseology, clothed often in terms before unknown,
and making extensive use of ordinary words in some new and
unparalleled sense.   Now it is certainly probable that those
who believe these writings to contain a vast system of truth
and who by a long and patient study of them, in many instances including the larger portion of a lifetime, have arrived, as
they believe, at some sober views of what that system is, will
be better able to put a correct construction on some isolated
passage, than would one, knowing nothing of this system, and
who, immersed for the most part in other and to him more
congenial occupations, should hastily turn the leaves of these
volumes, here and there taking a note, for the express purpose
of finding matter for ridicule or for objection.   As first and
crude impressions shall gradually give place to more deliberate
thought, we trust, after a while it will come to be very generally conceived by those worthy logicians who attempt to write
against us, that *Swedenborgians are* the best qualified of any
class of persons to be the interpreters of Swedenborg's opinions, and that they are entitled to be the *sole* authoritative
expounders of their own.   This point once gained, all the
questions involved in the controversy will in order at once
begin to emerge into sunlight.   We are now prepared to proceed in company with the reviewer.   On page 334 he remarks,
"Our readers will perhaps be much surprised at hearing that
Swedenborg and his followers reject from the canon of scripture a large number of the books received by the Christian
world as divinely inspired.   This is their language: 'The
books of the Word are all those which have the internal sense,
but those which have not the internal sense are not the Word.'"
Here follows a list of the books we are said to "reject," and a
list of those we are said to "retain."   We think his readers
will " be very much surprised at hearing" this ; and his *Swedenborgian* readers no less than his Presbyterian.   We reply, we
do not reject the books referred to from the sacred Scriptures.
We allow them to have been written under a kind and degree
of inspiration equal to that which you claim for the entire

Church have nothing to do with baptism as it comes to the infant.

It is frequently urged as an argument, that re-baptism by some New Church body, is necessary to escape the infestation of Old Church falses. As often as one who has come into the doctrines of the New Jerusalem, it is said, finds himself doubting between them and his former doctrines, it is proof that the false spirits, with whom he was in consociation before, are with him, and they are with him because they perceive in him an Old Church baptism. It is their badge, and sign of fellowship; it both authorizes and facilitates their approach to him. If he will take a New Church baptism, he renounces, it is said, that sign and receives one which will warn them away. Thus he will get rid of infestation. This representation has more weight, perhaps, than all the other arguments used on this question. But what confidence can we repose upon such a remedy for doubt and internal conflict? A false spirit by the laws of the world where he and we reside together is drawn towards, and flows into, the falses which he finds towards the centre of any mind, and not even a sacrament can hinder him from exciting them. These falses are ingrained in the soul—they have been wrought by the thoughts of many years into its very texture, and it is as foolish to think they will be rejected to the sides by re-baptism, as it would be to suppose that the internal causes of jaundice could be removed by remedies applied to the skin to extract its yellow hue. And, after all, what is this infestation which it is sought to remove in this summary mode? It is one of the mercies of the Lord's permissive Providence. If one could lead away infesting spirits by such an expedient, he would lose his opportunity of resisting them, rationally, by truth, and his falses would stay with him. The peace that comes in this way is liable to a strong suspicion of fantasy.

Various arguments are used against the validity of " Old Church" baptism from the consideration, that the Old Church was set aside by the Lord at the time of the Last Judgment. But the conclusion from this principle is adverse to re-baptism. If the Old Church really went for ever out of existence at that era, how can there be such a thing as an Old Church baptism? How can one be introduced into the Old Church? Is not all fear of this kind as if one should dread that his child should be introduced into the garden of the Hesperides, and be devoured by the dragon there, while he asserted at the same time, that there was no such garden? By a fallacy of the senses, it is no sooner said in this way of thinking that the Old Church has ceased, than it is revived in the mind and treated as if yet in

that *we* find no warrant in Scripture or from any other source,
for classing the kind of inspiration here indicated in the same
category or on the same level with that which we find exhibited in the Book of the Apocalypse ; where at the commencement it is expressly stated that it is neither Paul, nor Peter, nor
Saint John, but the LORD JESUS CHRIST who speaks. The
Apostle is wholly withdrawn "from earth and earth-born
scenes," and rapt away in the Spirit, consecrated for the
time to the sole office of merely uttering not his own words,
but the Lord's. Entirely dead to all the influences of, and
of his relations to, a material state of existence. Paul
sometimes wrote so fully under the recollection of his own
personal and worldly relations as to request Timothy to bring
with him the cloak he had left at Troas, as well as some
parchments. How utterly unlike is this to anything which
obtains in the Word which was issued from "Patmos." We
have thus briefly alluded to these two prominent cases of inspiration, for the purpose of showing that we have the very strongest grounds in the "obvious sense" of the Scriptures themselves, for the very kind of distinction which we make. We
trust we have now made the precise point of difference between us sufficiently plain to all those who *wish* to understand it. In fact as candid men more and more examine our
doctrines, they will more and more be found to bear a genuine
scriptural type, and it will finally be acknowledged that we
really place a *higher estimate* on the Word of God than do any
other class of Christians in the world.

Again, the reviewer says, page 336, "Every scholar knows
that by the terms *Law, Prophets,* and *Psalms,* every Jew in
the days of our Saviour understood every book of the Old Testament as contained in the Hebrew Bible, the Septuagint, or
our English version of the Old Testament."

We wish that for the sake of being explicit the writer had
left out "*the Septuagint,*" otherwise he leaves us in doubt
whether he does not intend to include the *Apocrapha* in the
Canon. Abating this, however, what he says is very correct.
But "every scholar" also knows that between the different
books included under these terms, the Jews made this very
distinction for which we have been contending. In the
Hebrew Bible, certain of the books which are arranged together at the beginning, were claimed by the Jews to have
been written under the *highest degree* of inspiration. Certain
other books termed *Ketubim,* or *Hagiographa,* were held to
have been written under a *lower degree* of inspiration, and
were thrown together at the end, thus constituting as it were,
the second part of the *Law, Prophets, and Psalms,* or of our

it, either as a nullity or as positively hurtful. If one who meditates an accession to a New Church society is counselled to look at his baptism in this light, he is counselled by parity of reasoning, to view all his past *communions* in the same manner. But if he were pressed in explicit terms to do this, he would revolt at the idea, for he knows that his Old Church communions served to mature in his mind, that state which enabled him to receive the New Church doctrines, when they came to him. He acknowledges in them rather the Lord's goodness. Now he would do,the same by his baptism, if specious reasoning did not come between. He would perceive, that by recurring often in thought to that ordinance, by meditating on its pledges, by consequent endeavors to fulfil them, it had been made the instrument in the Lord's hand for furthering him to his present enlightenment. He would then be far from regarding it as a nullity—much farther, from casting it away as a thing defiled with falses in its very doing. He would see, that it had bound him, from the pivot to the utmost points of life, and to the acknowledgement of the Lord. He would repent of the falses, which had holden his eyes from seeing this, and set about fulfilling those uses which it signifies to have now, and which it signified all along. And if, at any time, one should approach him with the mere *persuasion*, that, at any rate, as the question was debated, it would be *safe* for him to be re-baptized, he would more than balance it, by asking himself, whether it was not a thing to be passed over, in the face of all Christian principle and practice hitherto, after having entered the Christian Church once by baptism, go out of it, as it were, and take a *second* introduction.

A. E. F.

ARTICLE IV.

THE PRINCETON REVIEW* ON SWEDENBORGIANISM.

BANGOR, Andover, New Haven, Princeton, all have at length spoken, in the exact order of their geographical distribution. That species of " incipient insanity," or of a " peculiar mania," popularly denominated " *Swedenborgianism*," constitutes a pha-

---

* The first article in the number for July, 1848.

SELECTONS.

EXTRACTS FROM SWEDENBORG'S SPIRITUAL DIARY.

(NOW FIRST TRANSLATED FROM THE ORIGINAL LATIN.)

Concerning the Influx of the Grand Man.

3972. It is a general rule that nothing can exist or subsist from itself, but only from something else, that is, by or through something else; so also that nothing can be held in form except from something else, or by something else; and this appears from all and singular things in nature. The human body cannot be retained in its form except by the pressure of the atmosphere on every side, since it is well known that on the recession of the atmospheric pressure the form perishes. And as these are truths, it manifestly follows, that nothing can be held in its form in man, in his body, in his brain, in his organs of sense, both exterior and interior, unless it exist and subsist, and be retained in forms from other things, and indeed from something general and universal, thus from the grand man; in like manner, neither the grand man himself except from the Divine, that is, from the Lord alone.—1748, 13th Nov. this was perceived.

Concerning the Eternal.

3973. As the Divine Infinite is not of space, so neither is the eternal of time. That a kind of idea of the infinite, and an idea of the Divine Eternal is insinuated into the angels by the Lord, appears from this, that they know not what space is, for those who are in the extreme of the universe are present in a moment: and as to the eternal, that they have no idea of things past and future, but the past and future are in their present, concerning which, many more things might be said: neither is there in their idea anything of old age or of death, but only of life; wherefore they have no notice of time, but in all their present every thing is as eternal.

What it is to be nothing.

4067. It was perceived that when the most deceitful spirits above the head spake among themselves, wishing even to destroy me, they said they could not do it, because there was nothing of me to be found, but if there had been anything, they could have done it. It was then perceived, and so represented, that for one to be anything so as to have a proprium, was to present something which they could assault and destroy, as the most deceitful would then have it in their power. But when it was represented that I was, as it were, nothing, then they

have had reason to complain of the incorrectness of some Orthodox writers, who have undertaken to make a statement of your views. It is with manifest propriety that you have now claimed the right, and through him who acts as your organ of communication, have exercised the right, of declaring your own opinions. If you are just to yourselves, you will not stop here. Whenever others impute to you opinions which you do not entertain, or deny to you those which you do entertain; and whenever they are doubtful as to your faith, or in any way misrepresent it; you will feel that it belongs to you to interpose, and do yourselves justice. And you would think it a gross violation of the rules of christian candor, for any man to declare your opinions to be different from your own serious declaration. Grant me, and those with whom I have the happiness to be united in opinion, the right which you so justly claim for yourselves, *the right of forming and declaring our own opinions, and of being believed, when we declare them.* We have a claim to the latter as well as to the former, unless there are substantial reasons for questioning our veracity.

" By the diligent application of our rational powers to the study of the Scriptures, with the best helps afforded us, we have arrived at some sober, settled views on religious subjects. These views we wish, for various reasons, to declare. And if we would declare them justly, we must declare them in *our own language,* and do what is in our power to make that language intelligible. Where the meaning of the terms employed is doubtful, or obscure; it belongs to us to give the necessary explanations. Where the terms are liable to be understood with greater latitude, than comports with our views; it belongs to us to give the necessary limitations. And where our positions, in any respect whatever, need modifying; it belongs to us to modify them. Further. It is certainly reasonable to expect, when dealing with men of candid, liberal minds, that the language which, in any case, we use to express our faith, will be understood, not in the sense which, taken by itself, it would possibly bear, nor in the sense which men of another party might be inclined to put upon it,—but *precisely according to our explanations.* These explanations, you will understand, do as really make a part of the proper enunciation of our faith, as the words which form the general proposition. Nothing can be more obviously just than all this, especially in relation to a subject which is of a complex nature, or of difficult illustration."

We request our readers to ponder well the canons laid down in the above extract. The sentiments contained in it are so obviously just as to command the immediate assent of every rational mind. Their truth will not pass away with the occasion which called them forth. We felt compelled to give the entire paragraph, as we despaired of being able to set forth in anything like so clear and forcible a manner what we desired to express. We are impelled to advance such considerations on the present occasion, because it has been a common custom among our opponents to give a false exhibition of our views on certain important points: and this practice has been continued in the face of our repeated and constant asseverations that they are untrue; and in total disregard of our explanations. Several of these misrepresentations are resuch, when they first came into anxiety in view of death, could be in a state for receiving this instruction and of thinking precisely concerning it. But it was said in reply, that this might occur in sickness and anxiety, when such an effect may take place, but if they return again to life they would be as they were before, for (in the prospect of death) the *propria* of man cease to act, being thus removed from his voluntary principle; and in such a state, and in similar ones, the Lord (temporarily) operates. But this does not last; although while such a state of anxiety remains confession and devotion agree with it, yet it immediately recedes when the man returns into his life; just as in the other life, such persons may be held in a similar confession, but in such a state, or a state of anxiety, the confession is from a sinful fear.

4262. It was moreover said, that there may be a certain devout affection, as with preachers, which may produce something similar, something pious and devout, as if it were a confession of the heart, but this confession is exterior, more of the lip than of the heart, and which, as appears from examples in the other life, can be made to assume various aspects. As to the taking away sins, they know not what it means, and are filled with the conceit of their being free from evil and having eternal life.

MISCELLANY.

THE CORRESPONDENCE OF BREAD IN THE HOLY SUPPER.

It is customary with some of the Societies of the New Church to use bread at the Communion of the Holy Supper *cut* with a *knife*. That those in this practice may see the correspondence of the bread by them used upon this solemn occasion, we give the following extract from Swedenborg's Spiritual Diary.

Concerning Broken Bread.

" 2626. In a vision there was offered to me a small dishful of bread cut into square pieces, like cubes, which I thought signified the communication of bread, namely, of celestial things, and I was rejoiced. The dish was placed to my mouth that I might eat, and there it was held some time; but it was not eaten whilst I was in that opinion that that bread signified celestial things. I was told that *broken* bread, not *cut*, signified celestial things; for as bread is broken by the lips and the teeth before it is eaten, so it is first broken by the hand (before it is put into the mouth); and since this is according to nature, therefore celestial things are signified by bread broken by the hand,* by

---

* Hence we see the reason why bread is uniformly said to be broken in the Word, as—" Break thy bread to the hungry," &c.—(Isaiah viii. 7); and the Lord when he fed the multitude and instituted the Holy Supper, brake the bread;

their shadows will be disproportionate or even monstrous, and yet all these will be harmonized together by taking account of the point of vision or the surface of projection, so also all the representations of an idea, even all the misrepresentations, are capable of a mutual reconciliation and adjustment, and of a resolution into the subject to which they belong, and their contrariety when explained, is an argument for its substantiveness and integrity, and their variety for its originality and power."—*Newman on Development.*

There is no system to which the above remarks apply with greater force or truthfulness than to that of Swedenborg's. As it is oftener seen and more closely inspected it will gradually round itself out upon the mental vision as a compact, harmonious, and unitary whole. It requires to be *studied*, and not merely glanced at. We do not expect that the public are going to take our word altogether in regard to its character and value; but we hope that neither will they take that of our opponents. All that we wish to do is to attract candid and patient inquiry to the system. The more minds there are brought to bear upon the subjects treated of in it, the clearer and truer will be the ideas evolved; and we trust that none will take their opinions of it second hand, but will have the patience or the curiosity to examine for themselves.

We trust we shall be pardoned for still another quotation as somewhat preliminary to our remarks. In the "British Critic," the organ of the Oxford school, for January, 1839, in an article on St. Ignatius' Epistles, occurs the following passage.

"Men fancy, that though they have never seen Clement or Ignatius, or any other Father before, they are quite as well qualified to interpret the words λειτουργία or προσθορά as if they knew them and their brethren well. How different is their judgment in other matters ! Who will not grant, except in the case of theology, that an experienced eye is an important qualification for understanding the distinction of things or detecting their force and tendency ? In politics, the sagacious statesman puts his finger on some apparently small or not confessedly great event, promptly declares it to be ' no little matter,' and is believed. Why ? because he is conceived to have scholarship in the language of political history, and to be well read in the world's events. In the same way the comparative anatomist falls in with a little bone, and confidently declares, from it, the make, habits, and the age of the animal to which it belonged. What should we say to the unscientific hearer who disputed his accuracy and attempted to argue against him ? Yet, is not this just the case of sciolists, or less than sciolists in theology, who, when persons have given time to the Fathers recognize in some phrase or word in Clement or Ignatius a Catholic Doctrine, object that the connection between the phrase and the doctrine is not clear *to them*, and allow nothing to the judgment of the experienced, over that of ordinary men ? Or again, surely it needs not be formally proved that sympathy and congeniality of mind are concerned in enabling us to enter into another's meaning. His single words or tones are nothing to one man, they tell a story to another: the one man passes them over; the other is arrested by them, and never forgets them. Such is the difference between reading the Apostolical Father with or without a knowledge of theological language."

Whatever of justness may be contained in the above considerations as pertaining to the writings of the *fathers*, we suppose both the receivers and rejectors of Swedenborg will agree that they apply with increased weight and particular aptness to his system: consisting as it does, of so many "wild," "strange," and apparently "incoherent" doctrines; coming to us as it does, fenced round and wrapped up in a new and peculiar phraseology, clothed often in terms before unknown, and making extensive use of ordinary words in some new and unparalleled sense. Now it is certainly probable that those who believe these writings to contain a vast system of truth and who by a long and patient study of them, in many instances including the larger portion of a lifetime, have arrived, as they believe, at some sober views of what that system is, will be better able to put a correct construction on some isolated passage, than would one, knowing nothing of this system, and who, immersed for the most part in other and to him more congenial occupations, should hastily turn the leaves of these volumes, here and there taking a note, for the express purpose of finding matter for ridicule or for objection. As first and crude impressions shall gradually give place to more deliberate thought, we trust, after a while it will come to be very generally conceived by those worthy logicians who attempt to write against us, that *Swedenborgians are* the best qualified of any class of persons to be the interpreters of Swedenborg's opinions, and that they are entitled to be the *sole* authoritative expounders of their own. This point once gained, all the questions involved in the controversy will in order at once begin to emerge into sunlight. We are now prepared to proceed in company with the reviewer. On page 334 he remarks, "Our readers will perhaps be much surprised at hearing that Swedenborg and his followers reject from the canon of scripture a large number of the books received by the Christian world as divinely inspired. This is their language: 'The books of the Word are all those which have the internal sense, but those which have not the internal sense are not the Word.'" Here follows a list of the books we are said to "reject," and a list of those we are said to "retain." We think his readers *will* "be very much surprised at hearing" this; and his *Swedenborgian* readers no less than his Presbyterian. We reply, we do not reject the books referred to from the sacred Scriptures. We allow them to have been written under a kind and degree of inspiration equal to that which you claim for the entire

Scriptures. We simply *discriminate* between the two *kinds* of inspiration, viz : between that which is generally believed in the Christian world as pertaining to the whole Bible, and called by you "*plenary inspiration*," and that other kind of inspiration, which in your system you have no word to express, because you have not the *idea* which possesses the peculiarity of containing a superior or angelic sense behind the sense of the letter. In other words, we claim for the "retained" books a kind of inspiration *higher* than that which you allow to pertain to any. We do not *lower* those which you say are rejected ; we only *elevate* those which you say are retained. "But," you will say, "here are Swedenborg's *words*, in which he says that the rejected books are no part of the Word." "Now we believe the *whole Bible* to be the Word of God." We reply : you use your phrase *Word of God* to indicate a very different set of conceptions from that for which *we* use it. We employ the term *Word* in a *restricted*, and, as it may be called, *technical* sense ; as referring only to that particular portion of what in more general language we call the Word of God, in which, as we believe, resides an *internal sense*. We should suppose the true statement of this question to be a matter not very difficult of comprehension. You will probably claim that "Saint Paul, as well as the Prophets, wrote while under the immediate influence of the Holy Spirit, and that by It he was guarded from teaching any error." This we claim also. Nevertheless, we hold further, that although the Holy Spirit rested upon him, and that his ideas were set in motion by Its influence, yet, according to his own uniform testimony, it was, "I Paul" who chose the language, and retained the full consciousness of the utterances being his. In short that there was not in his case that total absorption of his own personality as there was in the case of the Prophets ; who, instead of uttering their own words, were constrained to utter " the Word of the Lord." In his Epistles it is always " I Paul," who addresses the churches ; he does not in any instance give way to any other impression than that it is his own distinctive self who is holding forth. Moreover, his writings prove that at different times he was in different subjective states in regard to the degree of the divine afflatus with which he was favored. On one occasion when strongly impressed he says, " Now the Spirit speaketh expressly ;" and on another when less strongly impressed, he says : " And I think I have the Holy Spirit ;" thereby implying somewhat of doubt in regard to the presence of a full measure of the divine influence ; and in one or two instances we find him plainly declaring that he has " no command from the Lord," but writes " his own judgment." We must confess

rison with that spiritual creation of which it was a figure. But as the difference between things natural and spiritual is very great, so this comparison is but as a shadow compared with the substance."

"To the spiritually minded the comparison between natural and spiritual things is plain and obvious. The light of the sun, being the source or fountain of light in the natural creation, is a most striking figure of the Fountain of spiritual light, the bright Source of everlasting life, the glorious Light of Heaven, of which all souls who shall be found faithful to improve the light which God has given them, will be made partakers. The darkness of the night evidently prefigures the shades of spiritual darkness, and the gloomy mansions of hell, where all souls who choose darkness rather than light must sink at last. The beautiful and harmonious songsters of the grove are so many emblems of happy spirits, whose blessed influences communicate happiness to all around them. The voracious raven, the midnight screech-owl, and the like, are emblematical of those destructive and tormenting spirits which haunt the infernal regions, and torment the wicked."

⌁ "The fact that sheep and lambs, as well as a variety of other creatures, were given to be slain, both for food and for sacrifice, did not prevent their being used as figures to typify the sacrifice to be made for sin, and to represent the meek and innocent character of the Saviour, who was 'brought as a lamb to the slaughter.' Nor were they, on that account, less typical of the meek and innocent character of his people, whom he calls his sheep and his lambs. So also the best fruits of the earth, which were evidently created for the immediate use of man, and expressly given for his subsistence, are no less figurative on that account; but even the very circumstance of their being given for food, was intended to show that they are figurative of that spiritual fruit with which the righteous will be fed in the Kingdom of Heaven. Jesus Christ had reference to this, when he said to his disciples, 'I will not drink henceforth of the fruit of the vine, until that day when I drink it new with you in my Father's Kingdom.'"

"It is well known that those who are born into this world, must be nourished with temporal food, or they would soon perish. And it is as certain that the new-born soul, who has been begotten in the regeneration and brought forth in the new creation, by the renovating power of Christ, as really requires spiritual food, as the natural man requires that which is natural. Even the pure waters of the fountain, so refreshing to a thirsty man, are figurative of those spiritual waters which flow from the fountain of everlasting life, and without which souls in the spiritual world must suffer, and be constrained to cry out, like the rich man in the parable, for a drop of *the water of life* to cool their tongues."

As might be readily inferred, the recognition by them of such important truths as we have indicated, has a tendency to throw a gleam of light over their entire scheme of Christian theology. Their general position in relation to the current doctrines of the Old Church being on many points essentially the same as that which the New Church occupies, they are naturally lead into a similar manner of handling many subjects to that which prevails generally among our own writers. This may be more clearly shown by adducing two or three instances. They believe that "The second coming of Christ is not the appearance of the same personal Being, but a manifestation of the same Spirit;" and

present Bible. The whole of the *Hagiographa* were very often indicated by the general term *Psalms*, probably because, according to their arrangement, the Book of Psalms was the first book of the *Hagiographa*. Now if the reviewer will take the pains to refer to his list of Old Testament books which he charges us with "rejecting," he will find that the Jewish Church have always "rejected" them in the same manner; that is, have placed them among the *Ketubim*, or books of the lower degree of inspiration.* The truth is, the *consensus* of Jewish authorities is decidedly *Swedenborgian* on this point. But we cannot enlarge, and so pass on. As we proceed the *locale* of the *rudis indigestaque moles* becomes more and more apparent. The writer is very much puzzled to understand the meaning of the term "internal sense," and to discover what our doctrines of the *Trinity, atonement, justification, regeneration,* and *correspondences* really are. In regard to a doctrine of *regeneration,* he seems to be in great doubt whether we have one at all: on the whole, perhaps the inference would remain that we had none. Finally, in seeming despair, he cries out that " the writings of Swedenborg and his followers constitute a labyrinth, the like of which he never before attempted to thread." Strange undertaking, we should think, to conduct his readers through a labyrinth, himself not being in possession of any clue to unravel its windings; to offer himself for a pilot where he is unable to point out the shoals and the quicksands. It gives us pleasure to state that on the subject of the *Resurrection,* his success was more happy; and by dint of pretty lengthy quotations from our writers he has exhibited the difference between us with very tolerable fairness. This is not the place to go into a defence of the New Church scheme of doctrines; but they have not been generally charged by men of good understanding, with being either indefinite or obscure. One thing we are gratified to learn from the reviewer—that there has been great zeal and activity of late displayed in the propagation of these "tenets." We have been afraid that New Churchmen were falling into a state of greater apathy in this respect than accorded with their urgent duty. At such a time as this, when the world is in motion, and men are more than ever inquiring into the *grounds* of old opinions, it behoves us that we spare no proper pains in spreading the truth before them.

---

* See Kitto, Hengstenberg, Stuart, or O. T. Cannon, &c.

(*To be continued.*)

SELECTONS.

EXTRACTS FROM SWEDENBORG'S SPIRITUAL DIARY.

(NOW FIRST TRANSLATED FROM THE ORIGINAL LATIN.)

Concerning the Influx of the Grand Man.

3972. It is a general rule that nothing can exist or subsist from itself, but only from something else, that is, by or through something else; so also that nothing can be held in form except from something else, or by something else; and this appears from all and singular things in nature. The human body cannot be retained in its form except by the pressure of the atmosphere on every side, since it is well known that on the recession of the atmospheric pressure the form perishes. And as these are truths, it manifestly follows, that nothing can be held in its form in man, in his body, in his brain, in his organs of sense, both exterior and interior, unless it exist and subsist, and be retained in forms from other things, and indeed from something general and universal, thus from the grand man; in like manner, neither the grand man himself except from the Divine, that is, from the Lord alone.—1748, 13th Nov. this was perceived.

Concerning the Eternal.

3973. As the Divine Infinite is not of space, so neither is the eternal of time. That a kind of idea of the infinite, and an idea of the Divine Eternal is insinuated into the angels by the Lord, appears from this, that they know not what space is, for those who are in the extreme of the universe are present in a moment: and as to the eternal, that they have no idea of things past and future, but the past and future are in their present, concerning which, many more things might be said: neither is there in their idea anything of old age or of death, but only of life; wherefore they have no notice of time, but in all their present every thing is as eternal.

What it is to be nothing.

4067. It was perceived that when the most deceitful spirits above the head spake among themselves, wishing even to destroy me, they said they could not do it, because there was nothing of me to be found, but if there had been anything, they could have done it. It was then perceived, and so represented, that for one to be anything so as to have a proprium, was to present something which they could assault and destroy, as the most deceitful would then have it in their power. But when it was represented that I was, as it were, nothing, then they seemed to themselves to have no power over that which thus appeared as nothing, for they would then have nothing to assault. Thus he is safe who, in the truth of faith, believes himself to be nothing.

Concerning the Love of Faith.

4077. When thinking of faith, it was manifestly perceived, that faith alone cannot save, since faith is of thought. What (I would ask,) is faith? No one denies that those things are of faith which are in the articles of faith, in the doctrine of faith, since abstractedly from doctrine there is no faith. The doctrine of faith plainly declares that the love of the neighbor is the principal law; and since this is the principal law, it is the principal point in the doctrine of faith; wherefore unless one loves his neighbor, he is destitute of faith. Thus they cannot but rave who would separate faith from the life of love and good works, and say that faith alone is saving, apart from loving one's neighbor as himself, and thus apart from the life of love.

4078. Faith is life, and to live according to the principles of faith is not (merely) to think, for the tree is known by its fruit.

Concerning Heaven and heavenly Joy, that some supposed it could be bestowed on every one.

4260. There was a spirit with me who said he had supposed that every one could be made a possessor of heavenly joy, however he had lived, if it seemed good to the Lord. But it was given to reply that the thing is not possible, because the evil have acquired to themselves another life which does not accord with the heavenly life. If this kind of joy were given them their life would be destroyed; or would come so near it that they could scarcely be said to live. But he said that certain of the evil in the world could, upon occasion, lay aside corporeal and wordly things, and he therefore could not see why they might not, after the life of the body, forego and forget every thing of this kind, and come into the heavenly life. But it was again replied that this could not be except by the previous destruction of the life which one has acquired to himself. As to what may occur in certain states, it was shown that even the wicked may have transient good impressions, but when their states are changed, they return again to their own life.

Concerning Faith Alone.

4261. I spake with those who held that faith alone was saving; their confession was that they would be saved if they believed; that the Lord had redeemed them, had delivered them from hell, and taken away all their sins, saying, that they thus consoled the sick who were at the point of death, and thus taught, to which they added that some

trines correctly. Being on a different *plane* from the world around them, they are almost always misunderstood, and consequently almost always misrepresented. They are by very common report charged with denying the Word, or with holding it in very low esteem: this we feel assured has arisen from misconception. So far from this being the case, we think it would be difficult to point to a class of Christians who regard it with more veneration, or who make more constant use of it both for daily reading and for the confirmation of doctrine. The great point on which they will no doubt be regarded as differing most widely from the New Church is in their doctrine of *celibacy*. At first sight this does indeed appear to stand directly opposed to Swedenborg's doctrine of *Conjugial Love*. But here also, strange as it may seem, the antagonism is more apparent than real, as may be gathered from the following paragraph:—

" The natural creation, and the things therein contained, are figurative representations of the spiritual creation which is to supercede it, as we have already shown. The first parents of the natural world were created male and female. The man was first in his creation, and the woman was afterwards taken from his substance, and placed in her proper order to be the second in the government and dominion of the natural world; and the order of man's creation was not complete till this was done. For it must be acknowledged by all, that without male and female, the perfection of man, in his natural creation, must have been less complete than that of the inferior part of the creation, which was evidently created male and female. Hence it must appear obvious, that in the spiritual creation, man and woman, when raised from a natural to a spiritual state, must still be male and female: for the spiritual state of man, which is substantial and eternal, cannot be less perfect in its order, than his natural state, which is but temporal, and figurative of the spiritual."

Consequently, in accordance with the spirit of the above, they hold that the distinction of sex is eternal, that a union of the two is necessary to the formation of a complete man-angel; but that the true spiritual marriage pertains only to a spiritual state of existence, and they therefore regard the celibate life as a purer preparation for the true conjugial relation which is to be entered into in the other life. They allow that Swedenborg was divinely illuminated; that he taught truly the general doctrines of the New Dispensation; that in truth he was the " John the Baptist" of this Dispensation, the harbinger of the second coming. In relation to their peculiarity of dress, it is not a principle with them, but only a matter of convenience: it happened to be the style of the times in which the early believers were gathered together, and has therefore been retained. Their views appear to have some show of plausibility in them even on New Church grounds, and for many reasons present us with a remarkably interesting object of study. We are of the opinion expressed by some of their members, that they and the New Church will be gradually led into a closer intimacy with each other, and that a thorough discussion of the points of variance, and a final settlement of the differences will be the result. A single peculiarity of theirs remains to be noticed, namely, that of *dancing*, as being an act of public worship. This they also found on the doctrine of correspondences, and affirm that it is the orderly and appropriate outward expression of the joys of their particular spiritual state. Those who wish to examine the grounds of this, can consult A. C. 8339, 10,416.

W. B. H.

the lips and the teeth; and it is moreover broken into the smallest pieces by the muscles and fibres, as it were by the minutest hands, lips and mouths, of the recipient vessels.

"2627. But bread cut with a knife is that which counterfeits what is celestial, and which is, nevertheless, not celestial, like all that which is effected by art, or which is artificial; wherefore the bread which was offered to me, because it was cut with a knife into cubic pieces, signified filthy delights, concerning which I have spoken above, which delights are thought by those who are in them to be heavenly, whereas they are infernal.—1748, July 16."

—*Intellectual Repository, Sept.* 1845.

A FEW WORDS ABOUT SHAKERISM AND THE SHAKERS.*

NOT a little has of late been written in various books of travel and periodical publications concerning this singular people. The economical arrangements of their industrial processes have especially been the theme of many a societary reformer and humanity philosopher. In the few remarks here purposed, it will be our object chiefly to confine ourselves to an exhibition of some of those views held by them and advocated in their writings, which bear the most striking resemblance to those of the New Church. Many of our readers are no doubt already acquainted with these coincidences, but there are others, we are persuaded, who have not become aware of the extent of this similarity on some of the most fundamental points of belief. In the first place, they claim that the old Christian Dispensation has come to an end, and that a new one commenced *about the year* 1747. They believe that this was communicated directly from the spiritual world, and that the manifestations from that source have continued to increase up to this time, and that they will be multiplied in the future. Their ideas of the spiritual body, of the resurrection, of the nature of the life after death, of the laws of the spiritual world, &c., are very nearly identical with those of the New church. In a chapter in one of the above named works, entitled "The Natural World a Figure of the Spiritual," the general doctrine of correspondences is very plainly set forth. We subjoin a few extracts, that the reader may form some idea of *their* mode of presenting it.

"The natural world, and the things therein contained, were, from the beginning, wisely designed as figurative representations of spiritual things to come. As this earth was created for a temporary use, and was never intended to be the abiding place of man, but only a place of preparation for a more substantial, durable, and glorious state, in the spiritual world; it was therefore highly proper and necessary that, in its creation and order, it should bear a suitable compa-

---

and he was known of his disciples after his resurrection in the breaking of bread.— (Luke xxiv. 35.)

* " 1. A Summary view of the Millennial Church, or United Society of Believers, commonly called Shakers. Published with the approbation of the Ministry. 12mo. pp. 348."

" 2. The Nature and Character of the True Church of Christ proved by plain Evidences, and showing whereby it may be known and distinguished from all others. Being extracts from the writings of John Dunlevy.—1847, pp. 93."

rison with that spiritual creation of which it was a figure. But as the difference between things natural and spiritual is very great, so this comparison is but as a shadow compared with the substance."

"To the spiritually minded the comparison between natural and spiritual things is plain and obvious. The light of the sun, being the source or fountain of light in the natural creation, is a most striking figure of the Fountain of spiritual light, the bright Source of everlasting life, the glorious Light of Heaven, of which all souls who shall be found faithful to improve the light which God has given them, will be made partakers. The darkness of the night evidently prefigures the shades of spiritual darkness, and the gloomy mansions of hell, where all souls who choose darkness rather than light must sink at last. The beautiful and harmonious songsters of the grove are so many emblems of happy spirits, whose blessed influences communicate happiness to all around them. The voracious raven, the midnight screech-owl, and the like, are emblematical of those destructive and tormenting spirits which haunt the infernal regions, and torment the wicked."

↲ "The fact that sheep and lambs, as well as a variety of other creatures, were given to be slain, both for food and for sacrifice, did not prevent their being used as figures to typify the sacrifice to be made for sin, and to represent the meek and innocent character of the Saviour, who was 'brought as a lamb to the slaughter.' Nor were they, on that account, less typical of the meek and innocent character of his people, whom he calls his sheep and his lambs. So also the best fruits of the earth, which were evidently created for the immediate use of man, and expressly given for his subsistence, are no less figurative on that account; but even the very circumstance of their being given for food, was intended to show that they are figurative of that spiritual fruit with which the righteous will be fed in the Kingdom of Heaven. Jesus Christ had reference to this, when he said to his disciples, 'I will not drink henceforth of the fruit of the vine, until that day when I drink it new with you in my Father's Kingdom.'"

"It is well known that those who are born into this world, must be nourished with temporal food, or they would soon perish. And it is as certain that the new-born soul, who has been begotten in the regeneration and brought forth in the new creation, by the renovating power of Christ, as really requires spiritual food, as the natural man requires that which is natural. Even the pure waters of the fountain, so refreshing to a thirsty man, are figurative of those spiritual waters which flow from the fountain of everlasting life, and without which souls in the spiritual world must suffer, and be constrained to cry out, like the rich man in the parable, for a drop of *the water of life* to cool their tongues."

As might be readily inferred, the recognition by them of such important truths as we have indicated, has a tendency to throw a gleam of light over their entire scheme of Christian theology. Their general position in relation to the current doctrines of the Old Church being on many points essentially the same as that which the New Church occupies, they are naturally lead into a similar manner of handling many subjects to that which prevails generally among our own writers. This may be more clearly shown by adducing two or three instances. They believe that "The second coming of Christ is not the appearance of the same personal Being, but a manifestation of the same Spirit;" and that " the second manifestation of Christ is not instantly universal, but gradual and progressive, like the rising of the sun." In speaking of the almost universal unbelief prevailing in the churches of the present day, in regard to the character and time of Christ's second appearing, they make use of the following language :—

" The Jews believed that God would send them a *Deliverer*, according to his promise. But when he came they rejected him, because he did not come in the manner which they expected, nor do the work which they expected. So in the present day, the professors of Christianity are living in the full belief that Christ will come the second time, according to his promise. And why are they not as likely to be disappointed in the manner of his coming, and the nature of his work, as the Jews were ? Do they profess to be favored with the Word of God ? So did the Jews. Do they profess faith in the promises of God ? So did the Jews. Do they profess to enjoy the blessings of divine light, and to worship the only living and true God, while the heathen nations walk in darkness and bow down to dumb idols ? So did the Jews. Do they profess to be a people highly distinguished and chosen of God to support and maintain the only true religion ? So did the Jews. Is their claim to that distinction greater than that of the Jews ? By no means, as will readily appear by a little examination."

"Considering all these circumstances, are they not likely to be more full of unbelief concerning the testimony of his second coming, than the Jews were concerning that of his first coming ? The unbelief of the Jews is proverbial. And it is a truth which is confirmed by the experience of all ages, that every renewed manifestation of divine light to a lost world, which has been attended with an increasing degree of the power and testimony of God against the nature of sin, has never failed to meet with opposition from the great body of the high standing professors of religion, who have lived in the day in which the light was given. Is it not then a matter of importance to all who profess the Christian religion, and expect to be saved by it, but who do not believe that Christ has made his second appearance, to beware of rejecting the testimony of those who do believe it, lest they be found fighting against God."

And again,

" In short, they seem not to know what is meant by the ' new heavens and new earth ;' nor what is to be understood by the passing away of the first heavens and earth. For such is the force of natural ideas on the mind of ' the natural man,' who ' receiveth not the things of the Spirit of God,' that he always inclines to put a natural construction on those prophetic descriptions in the sacred writings, which relate to the second coming of Christ, and to the day of judgment. Hence the idea of personality and locality in contemplating the coming of Christ; and hence the opinion of his coming in the natural clouds of the atmosphere, and operating upon the natural elements."

"The same ideas concerning an instantaneously universal display of the coming of Christ, in the clouds of the sky, which so generally prevail at the present day, were doubtless entertained by the translators of the Bible. Hence it is easy to account for the translation of so many passages in a manner most favorable to their pre-conceived notions ; and especially where the words in the original would admit of such a translation."

They profess, as we have seen, to belong to the new Dispensation, and to receive their impressions directly from the spiritual world. They hold that since the year 1747, or thereabouts, the new doctrines have been taught in the world of spirits, and from thence are continually pressing themselves down upon the minds of men in the natural world. Accordingly, their scheme of doctrines bear upon them a general New Church type, viz :—those in relation to the Trinity, Atonement, Election and Reprobation, Predestination, Imputation, Regeneration, Justification. &c. Their testimony against those forms of current belief in which the New Church joins them with her protest, is remarkably plain and pointed. In the chapter on the progressive falsification of the true doctrines, or " The rise of Antichrist," occur the following passages :—

" Thus Antichrist, which implies a spirit against Christ, under the Christian name and profession, first began his work in the primitive Church, even in the days of the apostles, as is evident by their zealous labors and warnings against his works. 'For many walk, of whom I have often told you, even weeping, that they are the enemies of the cross of Christ.' 'Know ye not that the unrighteous shall not inherit the Kingdom of God? Be not deceived!' Such deceivers are ministers of Satan, assuming to be ministers of righteousness; whose end shall be according to their works."

" Yet these deceivers of the kingdom of Antichrist, teach that the unrighteous *can* inherit the Kingdom of God, *through the merits of Christ.* And this is the doctrine which has been taught ever since the Christian profession has become popular in the world ; and this doctrine has been handed down through all the branches of those popular establishments called *orthodox churches,* to this day.

" They generally and confidently teach that no soul can, by any grace or power which they could receive by the gospel, ever be able to live free from sin in this life; but that they can be saved by their faith and profession, through the righteousness and atonement of Jesus Christ. This is the complete doctrine of Antichrist; and to all such, however high their profession, the testimony of Christ is, and ever will be, ' Depart from me ye workers of iniquity, for I know ye not.' "

" Many of the Gentiles embraced Christianity by profession. Among these were men eminent for natural wisdom, literary talents, and even learned philosophers. These obtained great influence in the church, and thereby brought in various mysteries pertaining to the religions of the Gentile nations, particularly those in high repute for their wisdom and learning. These were mysteriously blended with the doctrines of Christ and the apostles."

" From this source originated the doctrine of the *Trinity,* or three persons in one God, all in the masculine gender."

The above language certainly cannot be justly charged with equivocation, and we think for apparent severity very far exceeds the usual tone of New Church writers on the same subjects. We have no doubt that our opponents who are in the habit of complaining that their doctrines receive unmeritedly harsh treatment at our hands, would be willing to pronounce it mild in comparison with that which is dealt to them in the writings before us.

The following we suppose would be received as inculcating very good New Church doctrine :—

" The want of just conceptions concerning the character of God, as manifested in his attributes, has been the cause of the many different opinions which prevail among mankind, respecting divine things. Hence it is that people in the pursuit of religion, are so often led to adopt false principles, and establish themselves upon a wrong foundation. And false principles, when once adopted as divine truths, have a delusive tendency; and however inconsistent with the plain dictates of right reason, they are very apt to obtain a strong hold in the mind, and, like an inveterate disease, are very difficult to eradicate, especially when supported by the authority of great names, and confirmed by length of time."

" All doctrines which represent God as making any difference in the future state of his rational creatures, respecting their salvation or damnation, without a special regard to their works, and all the reasons advanced in support of such doctrines, are fallacious and unfounded, and ought to be rejected as inconsistent with the attribute of *righteousness* and *justice*. Such doctrines, being fraught with the greatest possible evil to the creature, are equally inconsistent with *goodness*. They also operate against the attribute of *lights;* for no doctrine ever produced a more darkening and discouraging effect upon the mind of man."

Their teaching in regard to the essential nature and progressive character of the work of Regeneration, and the typical analogy which it bears, as carried on in the individual, to that work which the Lord accomplished in himself while in the flesh, is also remarkably coincident with ours. The limited amount of space we are enabled to devote to this subject, will debar us from making more than a single extract on this point.

" Though Jesus Christ had a miraculous birth, yet ' he took not on him the nature of angels; but he took on him the seed of Abraham. Wherefore in all things it behoved him to be made like unto his brethren.' Hence it appears that nothing was excepted, not even the death of the fall. It is therefore evident that he was born into a fallen nature, with all its propensities. This nature he received, through the medium of his natural birth, of the Virgin Mary, who was but a natural woman; therefore he necessarily had a progressive travel out of it. And by yielding obedience to the will of his heavenly Parents, he overcame the power of that death which reigned in the fallen nature of man, and rose triumphant out of it; and was thus formed into the very nature of eternal life, the elements of which he had received from his Eternal Parents. Thus he was the ' first begotten from the dead, and the first-born among many brethren.' "

Their doctrine of life is pre-eminently the doctrine of charity as exhibited in the will. The whole professed direction of their efforts is towards freeing themselves entirely from evils or sins in act and in thought, and to arrive at that state where temptation ceases and the regenerated soul is at rest. And we must confess that so far as we have been able to judge from a short visit among them, they appear to have succeeded in reducing the true doctrine of Charity to practice more fully than any other class of people with whom we are acquainted. If the external order exhibited around them be an outbirth of the spiritual order which reigns within (as they claim it is), then must their internal order far exceed that which obtains in most of the religious bodies of the day. One thing we think will become perfectly obvious to any New Churchman who takes the trouble to visit them, namely, that no one who has not received the New Church truths can'report their doctrines correctly. Being on a different *plane* from the world around them, they are almost always misunderstood, and consequently almost always misrepresented. They are by very common report charged with denying the Word, or with holding it in very low esteem: this we feel assured has arisen from misconception. So far from this being the case, we think it would be difficult to point to a class of Christians who regard it with more veneration, or who make more constant use of it both for daily reading and for the confirmation of doctrine. The great point on which they will no doubt be regarded as differing most widely from the New Church is in their doctrine of *celibacy*. At first sight this does indeed appear to stand directly opposed to Swedenborg's doctrine of *Conjugial Love*. But here also, strange as it may seem, the antagonism is more apparent than real, as may be gathered from the following paragraph:—

" The natural creation, and the things therein contained, are figurative representations of the spiritual creation which is to supercede it, as we have already shown. The first parents of the natural world were created male and female. The man was first in his creation, and the woman was afterwards taken from his substance, and placed in her proper order to be the second in the government and dominion of the natural world; and the order of man's creation was not complete till this was done. For it must be acknowledged by all, that without male and female, the perfection of man, in his natural creation, must have been less complete than that of the inferior part of the creation, which was evidently created male and female. Hence it must appear obvious, that in the spiritual creation, man and woman, when raised from a natural to a spiritual state, must still be male and female: for the spiritual state of man, which is substantial and eternal, cannot be less perfect in its order, than his natural state, which is but temporal, and figurative of the spiritual."

Consequently, in accordance with the spirit of the above, they hold that the distinction of sex is eternal, that a union of the two is necessary to the formation of a complete man-angel; but that the true spiritual marriage pertains only to a spiritual state of existence, and they therefore regard the celibate life as a purer preparation for the true conjugial relation which is to be entered into in the other life. They allow that Swedenborg was divinely illuminated; that he taught truly the general doctrines of the New Dispensation; that in truth he was the " John the Baptist" of this Dispensation, the harbinger of the second coming. In relation to their peculiarity of dress, it is not a principle with them, but only a matter of convenience: it happened to be the style of the times in which the early believers were gathered together, and has therefore been retained. Their views appear to have some show of plausibility in them even on New Church grounds, and for many reasons present us with a remarkably interesting object of study. We are of the opinion expressed by some of their members, that they and the New Church will be gradually led into a closer intimacy with each other, and that a thorough discussion of the points of variance, and a final settlement of the differences will be the result. A single peculiarity of theirs remains to be noticed, namely, that of *dancing*, as being an act of public worship. This they also found on the doctrine of correspondences, and affirm that it is the orderly and appropriate outward expression of the joys of their particular spiritual state. Those who wish to examine the grounds of this, can consult A. C. *8339, 10,416.*

W. B. H.

THE

NEW CHURCH REPOSITORY

AND

MONTHLY REVIEW.

Vol. 1.   OCTOBER, 1848.   **No. 10.**

ORIGINAL PAPERS.

ARTICLE I.

THE INFLUENCES OF PLATONISM AND GNOSTICISM UPON
THE EARLY CHRISTIAN CHURCH, IN MOULDING ITS VIEWS
OF THE DOCTRINE OF THE TRINITY.

"He that hath seen me, hath seen the Father."--John xiv. 7.

THE condition of the apostles prior to the crucifixion, was
analogous to that of an unregenerate but awakened man,
seriously occupied about the accomplishment of his eternal
salvation. That it should be such was necessary in order to
the future instruction and comfort of the church; for the human mind to this day is tortured by doubts and anxieties
which would be doubly distressing unless precedents for them
were to be found in the experience of those who literally sat
at the feet of Jesus, both hearing him and asking him questions. Nor could these common doubts and anxieties ever
have been dispelled, unless the apostles themselves, being
afflicted in the same way, had been permitted to inquire fa-
miliarly of the Lord concerning them, and to record his divine
answers for the solution of like questions in all time to come.
The desire to see the Father is the natural instinct of humanity, and without its gratification the most painful doubts
must beset even those who have the least reason to question
either his goodness or his majesty—much less the fact of his
existence. This is remarkably exemplified in the history of
Moses. In vain had he heard the voice of the Lord from the

burning bush; in vain had he confronted Pharaoh at the instance of Jehovah and desolated Egypt by his consecrated rod; in vain had the Red Sea opened on either side for his passage with the children of Israel and then buried his pursuers beneath its returning flood; in vain had Moses stood with the Lord amid the seven-fold thunders and lightnings and quakings of mount Sinai, and received orally the commandments and institutes which were set for the government of the Jewish nation; in vain did the Lord speak unto Moses, "face to face as a man speaketh unto his friend" even in that very interview, which was subsequent to all the foregoing stupendous displays of the Divine Majesty, and at the very door of the tabernacle where the miraculous conversation was held. Moses virtually confessed himself tortured by a scepticism which he could not control, and demanded ocular demonstration of the existence of the Almighty—"*Show me now thy way, that I may know thee.*"—(Ex. xxiii. 13.)

After a lapse of more than fifteen hundred years, we find the same request urged under very different and far more affecting circumstances. The little band who had staked every thing upon the apparently doubtful fortunes of our Lord and Master; who upon his simple behest, "Follow me!" had left all and followed him, were assembled to receive his distressing valedictory. They "trusted that it had been he which should have redeemed Israel," and in that simple faith they had hung about his holy teachings. Their hearts had been strengthened by his various consolations; been purified by his few but well-timed rebukes, and been confirmed in the reality of his mission by the *wonders of works* which he had done. The dead had been brought to life by him in their presence; they themselves had cast out devils in his name; and, conscious of his mighty power, their untutored hearts had refused full credence to those mysterious intimations of his approaching crucifixion which seemed so much at variance with what they had reason to expect. But alas! in whom could they then trust? Could they even trust themselves? For the feast of the passover with them had ended. The integrity of their little band had been ominously questioned by their Lord and Master. One of them should betray him! and that one had been designated, and had slunken from their midst. Another, the boldest of them all, had been warned to his face that the cock should not crow until he had thrice denied the Being for whose sake he had just professed himself willing to sacrifice his life. In addition to all this, they were stunned by the intelligence that their Master was about to leave them! It was true he was going to prepare a place for them, but *whither*

was he going and how could they know the way? His answer was apparently enigmatical and did not dispel their
anxieties or even prepare them for the worst by giving some
definite shape to their apprehensions. Thus fluttering upon
the confines of despair, their feeble hopes trembled towards
the unknown Father in whose house there were so many mansions, and they had but a single, humble, doubting request to
make, upon the verge of the fearful separation with which
they were, as it seemed, so cruelly threatened—"Show us
the Father, and it sufficeth us!" Their very souls melted into
the soft entreaty, and all their hopes, temporal and eternal,
were concentred upon the expected answer. And more than
that; the agonizing wail of embryo Christendom burst forth
there, from the womb of the Future, and echoed the cry,
"Show us the Father." In that stupendous moment, when to
have hesitated would have overthrown the tottering faith of
his affectionate followers; when to have been less clear and
explicit would have been to treat the devotion of future martyrs and saints with a mockery of which the bare imputation
would be blasphemous; in that solemn moment upon which
the creeds and the destinies of a universe were dependent, our
Lord, with a humility suitable to his not yet glorified Humanity and in terms wonderfully adapted to the unilluminated
minds of his devoted followers, proclaimed the vital, the fundamental truth, that in him God was conjoined with man,
and man was conjoined with God: that the Father whom they
sought was present before them and identical with Himself.
"He that hath seen me hath seen the Father."

Such an explicit allegation of our Lord's identity with Jehovah satisfied the simple faith of those to whom it was addressed; carrying them joyfully through the trials of persecution and martyrdom at a time when Christianity, just loosed
from the ark of the old covenant, found scarcely a place for
the sole of her foot; and when martyrdoms were so common
as to be considered rather the badges of discipleship than tests
of constancy. And here it may be remarked that martyrdoms
are most valuable to the cause of Truth when they constitute
the natural penalty of its vindication. At the close of the
second century, when they were sought after as the cancel-
ling of all sins, as the equivalents of baptism, as the keys of
Paradise, and when in point of actual fame the posthumous
celebrity of a mere martyr out-rivalled that of a secular hero
slain in battle, even a Simon Magus would probably have died
for the cause in order to be placed upon the Calendar with
Stephen and the Apostles.

The faith of the Apostles was superior to that of the later

clergy, because, among other peculiarities, it was an unquestioning faith, and it was unquestioning because based on love. They admitted the mystery of Godliness, but disposed of it by the simple announcement that God was manifest in the flesh. That in Jesus Christ dwelleth all the fulness of the Godhead bodily, was enough for them to know, without making Revelation darker by holding up to it the rushlights of cotemporary science and philosophy. They confessedly saw "as through a glass, darkly," and were content so to see until the dawn of that effulgent day of which they were the chosen heralds. Flesh and blood had not revealed to them the ineffable truths upon which they reposed in the fulness of faith nor did they permit that faith to be disturbed by questions of science and philosophy, "falsely so called." It was reserved for the church in succeeding ages to foster the countless heresies which were the spawn of unbelief, and in the periodical reconciliation of which Truth was so often compromised nearly out of existence.

If there was one article of Apostolic Christianity which above all others was to the Jews a stumbling block and to the Greeks foolishness, it was that very article which had been singled out by our Lord as the Rock of the Church, against which all the gates of hell were to be opened without being able to prevail. The gates of hell would, indeed, have been opened against it to little purpose, if the infernal cohorts could have found allies among the heathen only. But the wily serpent, repeating the experiment of Eden, found in the bowers of the new Paradise many who were willing to pluck rashly from the tree of forbidden knowledge—a tree that stands in the midst of the garden of every Revelation. Love, which is the life of faith, had waxed cold in the church before the death of the last of the apostles. The simple facts of the gospel soon began to be too often treated with less reverence than the *ipse dixit* of the old philosopher had commanded from his followers. The water of life must needs be re-distilled in the laboratories of heathen science, and truth was stabbed in her own house for the purposes of amateur dissection. The countless throng of idle subtleties that exercised the brains, pointed the paragraphs, and crowded out the charity, of the early controversialists would doubly astonish us, if we did not know with what facility evil spirits (who were more powerful against the church then than now,) "frame various shadowy things which do not truly relate to the subject in hand, and these they connect with numerous other phantasies and shadows of the subject, and which can only be taken as the *imagery* of dreams."

At the risk of being a little tedious, we feel compelled to fortify our allusions to the state of Christian Theology during the interval between the death of John and the convocation of the council of Nice, by copious references to a work of the highest authority. We allude to Gieseler's Text Book of Ecclesiastical History, the superior value of which needs no higher voucher, than its recommendation by Professor Stuart, which is given at length in the note below.*

Speaking with reference to the close of the period, A. D. 1—117, our author says; "As Paul had foreseen (Acts xx. 29; 2 Tim. iii. 1 seq.), the faith of the Christians came now more than ever into peril from the influence of the sophistical religious 'speculations of the time; and the germs of Christian gnosticism, allusions to which may be traced in his epistles, became more and more evident."

We find a tolerably full detail of the Gnostic heresies in that part of Gieseler's work which treats of the period A. D. 117—193. The Gnostics, assuming matter to contain the origin of evil, were at loss to perceive how the Supreme Deity, being infinitely pure and holy, could have had contact with matter for the purpose of impregnating it with vitality. Their minds had already been led perhaps by a literal understanding of the Old Testament, to attribute a higher character to the God of the Christians than to the Jehovah of the Jews; they therefore considered the latter as Demiurgus (Artizan, Creator), and supposed him to be descended from the

---

* " The undersigned has frequently consulted Gieseler's Church History, as published by the author in German: and he has no hesitation in saying, that on the whole he prefers it, for purposes such as he has had in view, to any other church history within his knowledge. His particular reason for this is, the uncommon diligence, judgment, and accuracy, with which the writer has given the essence of the sources on which he relies for important facts and documents: by virtue of which one is enabled in a good measure to judge for himself what the state of the original testimony is. This is a privilege which must often be abandoned, for the most part, in reading many writers in this department of history, inasmuch as they only give their own judgment and estimation of facts, without enabling the reader to form his.

" With some of the *theological* opinions of Gieseler, the writer of this supposes himself to disagree; but these are seldom admitted to be the guide of his historical statements. In general, I think great candor, accuracy, and thorough search, are developed in Gieseler's work, although its studied brevity cuts off detail which now and then would be grateful to the reader.

"I fully admit the learning and ability of Neander, as a Church historian; but Gieseler places one in a better condition to judge for himself than Neander does, who gives his sources very meagerly, and seems to expect that you will always take his own views as well grounded and correct. Gieseler places his reader in a condition, in which he is enabled to pursue his investigations to any extent that he pleases. On this account, I use him as my most common manual, when I have occasion to pursue a topic which belongs to his department, and as a *manual* for consultation, I think this work can hardly fail of the patronage of our American community."   MOSES STUART.

Supreme God, through a long succession of Æons. They regarded Christ as one of the highest Æons, whose mission was
to free the soul from the fetters of matter and the Demiurgus,
and to enable it to know the Supreme God, in order that it
might return to him.   According to the Alexandrian Gnostics,
as taught by *Basilides* (A. D. 125), there emanated from the
great first cause, seven Æons, the highest of which (νοὺς)
united itself with the man Jesus at his baptism, in order to
bring about the restoration of the human soul to the world of
light.   The other two sects of Alexandrian Gnostics, the followers of *Valentine* and the *Ophites*, regarded Christ as an
Æon, subordinate to the great first principle or cause, though
they differed from each other respecting the actual character
of the Messiah.

The most remarkable Gnosis, was that of *Marcion*, who
supposed three sources of all things, a good Deity, a just
Deity, and the Hyle, or matter.   " To free mankind from the
yoke of the just Deity, from whom they had only to expect
either damnation, or at best a limited happiness, according to
the strictest measure of justice, Christ (was) supposed to have
descended and appeared at Capernaum, proclaiming to men
the good Deity, whom as yet they had never known."   Salvation, under this system, was accorded to those who believed
on Christ and out of free love to the good Deity led a holy
life; whilst the rest were left to the strict justice of the Demiurgus or just Deity.

Gieseler mentions as a very important circumstance, the
conversion during this period (A. D. 117—193) of several Platonic philosophers to Christianity, "and, through their influence, the growing popularity of Platonism amongst the
Christians." He adds (Vol. I. 100, 101), "The Platonic-eclectic
philosophers, many of whom were now converted to Christianity, retained with their philosopher's cloak, their philosophical turn of mind also, and many of their philosophical
opinions.   Instead of making any essential change in Christianity, as other philosophers had done, their aim seems to have
been to give form, order, and connexion to the received Christian doctrines, *and keep a middle course between the various
heresies ; though they could not avoid some mixture of their philosophy.   * * *   Their Platonism displayed itself chiefly in
developing the theory of the Logos, in which they followed
Philo,* making a distinction between the λόγος ἐνδιάθετος (dwelling in the thought of God), and λογος προφορικος (brought forth,
emitted)."   A note to the same page observes, " Thus Christianity became in their hands a complete system of philosophy;" and another note; "The Platonism of the church fathers

is acknowledged by Dion. Petavius (Dogm. Theol. T. II. lib. I. c. 3). To this some have traced the doctrine of the Trinity;" and justly, we think, as this doctrine is held by the old church.

In connection with the acknowledged fact that during the succeeding period (A. D. 193—324), "the doctrines of the church were developed chiefly at Alexandria, at that time the seat of the sciences" (p. 134), the influence which Gnosticism and Platonism exerted over the Alexandrian school, becomes a question of paramount importance; for if those systems materially affected the doctrines of that school, and it, in its turn, chiefly developed the doctrines of the church down to A. D. 325, the year of the Nicene Council, it would seem to follow, as a matter of course, that the Athanasian Creed, which was the after-birth of that council, was at least *leavened* with the philosophy of Plato and the Gnostics.

The opening of the period referred to found the Alexandrian school at the height of its prosperity. Numbering among its teachers, Clemens Alexandrinus, Origen, Dionysius, and others hardly less distinguished, it "was the source of all the advances made in Christian Theology during this period."—(1 Gies. 135). In this school, continues our author, "Philosophy was held in high esteem, not only as having been to the Heathen what the Law was to the Jews, a preparation for Christianity, *but as the only means of penetrating the hidden spirit of its doctrines* (γνῶσις, γνωστικοί). This Gnosis was certainly different from that of the heretics, since it took for its foundation the received doctrines of the church (πιστις) which had been modified in express opposition to the Gnostics. Still however, these *orthodox Gnostics were led, by the attempt to combine Christianity with general philosophical principles, into some speculations not wholly unlike those of their heretical brethren.* Like them, too, they believed that their Gnosis had been handed down to them as a mystery, and was only to be communicated to the initiated" (p. 137, seq.).

The opinions of the Alexandrian school are summarily detailed by Gieseler (pp. 137—142), supported by notes containing ample quotations from their writings. For our purposes it is sufficient to say that, apparently following the Gnostics, they rejected all notions of God borrowed from human nature, considering it his peculiar attribute to be (unlike angels and men) without a body. They "speak of the Logos as a highly exalted being, though their expressions are not always distinct. Evidently however, *they make him inferior to the supreme God.*" Here we see, again, the Æon of the Gnostics. "The wish to remove every thing that could be unworthy of God from the notion of the generation of the Son, led at last to the doctrine taught by Origen, that the Logos did not proceed from the essence of the Father, but was produced by the will of God, generated from all eternity. He taught also that the Holy Ghost was created by the Son." In this view of the Logos we can readily perceive the adulterated Platonism of the Alexandrian eclectics.

We find ourselves strongly supported in this connection by a passage relating to the same subject, which we take from Enfield's History of Philosophy, Book VI. chap. 2.* " There can be no doubt that a strong predilection for Platonic tenets prevailed among those Alexandrian philosophers who became converts to the Christian Faith. These philosophers, who, whilst they corrupted the system, had been accustomed to entertain the highest reverence for the name of Plato, easily credited the report, that the doctrine of Plato concerning the Divine Nature had been derived from Revelation, *and hence thought themselves justified in attempting a coalition between Plato and Jesus Christ.* A union of Platonic and Christian doctrines was certainly attempted in the second century, by Justin Martyr, Athenagoras, and Clemens Alexandrinus, in whose writings we frequently meet with Platonic sentiments and language: and it is not improbable that this corruption took its rise still earlier. * * * * From the time that Ammonius Sacca, in order to recommend his Eclectic system to the attention of Christians, accommodated his language to the opinions which were then received among them, the mischief rapidly increased. *Origen* and other Christians *who studied in his school*, were so far duped by this artifice, as to imagine that they discovered in the system of the Platonists, traces of a pure doctrine concerning the Divine Nature, which, on the ground above mentioned, *they judged themselves at liberty to incorporate into the Christian faith.* Entering upon the office of Christian teachers under the bias of a strong partiality for Plato and his doctrine, they tinctured the minds of their disciples with the same prejudice, *and thus disseminated Platonic notions as Christian truths;* doubtless, little aware how far this practice would corrupt the purity of the Christian faith, and how much confusion and dissension it would occasion in the Christian church."

In the passage preceding the last, the doctrine of the Alexandrian school respecting the Logos is referred to as the doctrine of Origen, yet we are not to close our eyes upon the notorious contradictions on this subject with which the writings of that father abound. In one place (*contra Celsum*, p.

---

257) he calls the Son πρἰσβύτατον πάντων τῶν δημιουργηημάτων (the most ancient of created things), and Justinian (l. c.) accuses Origen of calling the Son κτίσμα (a creature or created being), *de Princip. lib.* IV. It must be observed also that the Septuagint was then in universal use, and that its version of Prov. viii. 22, which was a chief passage on the subject of the Logos, rendered the Hebrew word which is now translated *possessed,* ἐκτισε (*created*), which made wisdom, or the Logos, say, The Lord *created* me in the beginning of his way; thus it would seem apparent that such expressions as Origen was accused of using, were general at that time.—(Gies. Vol. I. p. 140, n. 13.) The same writer remarks (p. 192), "Throughout the third century theologians had been speculating on the relation of the Son to the Father, but had never attained to clear and uniform views on the subject. The followers of Origen in particular had been led, in their various investigations, to results entirely irreconcilable with each other, as they must themselves have perceived, but for the obscure nature of the subject. This was the state of things (A. D. 325), when Arius, a presbyter of Alexandria, &c. took up the one side of Origen's theory, namely, that the Son is a subordinate being, created by the Father, and carried it out in all its particulars—rejecting entirely Origen's other position, *which is in fact contradictory to this,* that the Son was begotten from all eternity."

Having traced the Arian side of Origen's theory to the heretical Gnostics, it now remains to show that the orthodox side of it is an adulteration of Platonism. We have already proved this *prima facie* by the numerous citations we have made from Gieseler, and the passage taken from Enfield, but the veritable fact of the adulteration can only be made apparent by a brief comparison of Origen's orthodoxy with Plato's paganism.

Plato considered God to be the principle opposite to matter; the intelligent, incorporeal, eternal, unchangeable first cause of all things spiritual and material. Distinct both from matter and this Efficient Cause, he imagined to himself the Divine Reason, in which, as in their original and eternal region, there subsisted ideas, which he conceived to be the intelligible forms or patterns of all things; deriving a real existence from the fountain of the divine essence, and, in the formation of the visible world, united to matter by the energy of the Efficient Cause, so as to produce sensible bodies. This Divine Reason he styled the Logos, not being as we have seen a separate subsistence in one divine essence, but a subsistence distinct from the Efficient Cause, or God. Plato taught the unity of the Divine Nature, and based this doctrine upon the unity of the material system. The notion of generation, in its present theological acceptation, was entirely foreign from his theory of the Logos.

The Alexandrian Platonists, however, seem, according to Enfield, to have conceived of the Logos as a being neither separate in nature and essence from God, nor merely as a simple attribute, but as a substantial virtue or power, radically united in the Divine Essence, and distinct from the First Principle only in its peculiar mode of existing and acting. This was the doctrine of Philo, at least, whose Platonism, Enfield remarks (p. 401), " was of that adulterated kind which at this time prevailed in Alexandria."

But Philo, whose distinctions in regard to the Logos were afterwards adopted by the Christian philosophers, commended himself to their notice more particularly in this, that being a Jew, he forced a coalition between Plato and Moses, boldly asserting that the former was a disciple of the latter, and passing off the Platonic dogmas as Mosaic teachings. His development of the Logos is thus summed up by Enfield (p. 400); " Philo supposed a quaternion of principles in the Divine Nature ; the first fountain of divinity, and three emanations from this fountain, each possessing a distinct, substantial existence, *but all united in essence with the First Principle. The first of these emanations, which he called the Logos,* he conceived to have been the divine intellect, the seat of those ideas which form the intelligible world ; and the second and third, to have been the substantial principles or powers by which the sensible world was created and governed."

It appears then that according to Philo, the Logos was merely the Divine Intellect ; not an integral constituent of the Divinity as the human intellect is an integral constituent of the human soul, without which the soul would cease to be, (or rather could never be,) but a distinct, substantive emanation from the Divine fountain ; of the same essence, yet acting a part as the instrumental agent of the First Principle in the work of Creation. Substitute now the term generation for emanation, begotten for emanated, and the candid reader will have before him the Logos of Origen. The result is the Pseudo-Platonic absurdity that God the Father begat his own Intellect (or Wisdom) ; that this Intellect was a substantial existence, distinct from himself, though of the same essence; and that through the distinct, substantive, though co-essential Intellect, He, by communcation of his original Divine Energy, carried on the work of Creation.

We have thus given Origen credit for the Logos assumed for him by the orthodox, thinking at the same time, in our own mind, that his real theory was of the Gnostic order, and that he was a better authority for Arius than for Athanasius. But since both these controversialists relied upon him in support of their respective opinions, and since those of the latter prevailed with the Council of Nice, and were afterwards incorporated in the Athanasian Creed, it would have been unfair to avoid that version of Origen's theory which has been adopted by the Orthodox, and upon which hinges the controversy between the New Church and the Old. How appropriate in this connection is the solemn language of Enfield, in the Preface to his History of Philosophy: "When it is clearly understood (as from the present free discussion of these subjects it is likely soon to be) that many of the doctrines commonly received as of Divine authority, originated in Pagan schools, and were thence transplanted *at a very early period* into the Christian Church; more particularly, when it is generally known (and it is impossible it can be long concealed even from the lowest classes of the people) that the fundamental doctrine of the UNITY OF THE DIVINE NATURE has undergone corruptions, from which no established Church in Christendom has even yet been purged; it cannot fail to become an object of general attention to produce such a reform in religion, as shall free its public institutions from the incumbrance of scholastic subtleties, and to render religion itself more interesting and efficacious, by making its forms more simple and intelligible." Thus, in the year 1791, writes a distinguished Christian Philosopher, who yet awards Swedenborg no panel in the Portrait Gallery of Philosophy nor makes mention of his name either as an enemy or a friend of Christianity.

It is impossible for us to dwell longer upon the sojourn of the Church in Alexandria, which was literally its bondage in Egypt; nor does time permit as to follow its journey through the wilderness of the Dark Ages to the final Canaan of its temporal dominion. Its various sectarian tribes, who date their dispersion from the period of its consummation, still wage an internecine warfare upon the old Gnostic and Platonic issues; one party virtually contending that our Lord was a mere man, into whom the νους entered at his baptism; while the mother of all orthodoxy puts down opposition with a plain tale like the following: "We must not therefore so far endeavor to involve ourselves in the darkness of this mystery, as to deny that glory which is clearly due unto the Father; whose preeminence undeniably consisteth in this, that he is God not of any other, but of himself, and that there is no other person who is God, but is God of him. It is no diminution of the Son, to say, he is from another, for his very name imports as much; but it were a diminution of the Father to speak so of him;

and there must be some pre-eminence where there is place for derogation. What the Father is, he is from none; what the Son is, he is from him: what the first is, he giveth; what the second is, he receiveth. The first is a Father indeed by reason of his Son, but he is not God by reason of him: whereas the Son is not so only in regard of the Father, but also God by reason of the same."*

We now ask the candid and serious of all denominations, whether they can read the above passage, reflecting at the same time that it has reference to a Son of God begotten from all eternity, without having in their minds the idea that God is not one, or else that being one, there is another. But as if to make the idea of duality more manifest, and to exclude the idea of unity more completely, there is assigned to the Father a pre-eminence which would be derogated from or diminished if he were placed in the same rank of Divinity as the Son. So, likewise, if it would be a derogation from the Father to speak of Him as we do of the Son, it would be an equal derogation to speak of the Son as we do of the Father; and if God is Father by reason of his having begotten the Son from all eternity, whence is the Son himself the Everlasting Father, as he is styled in the sixth verse of the ninth chapter of Isaiah? Moreover, if it be the Father Almighty, who says (Ex. xx. 2), "*I am* THE LORD THY GOD, *which have brought thee out of the land of Egypt, out of the house of bondage*", who is it who says (Isaiah xliii. 3), "*For I am* THE LORD THY GOD, *the Holy One of Israel, thy* SAVIOUR?"

But while we thus allude to the passage upon which we are commenting, we must be understood as excepting to its doctrine, not to its logic. For if the premise be admitted that there is a Son of God, begotten of the Father from all eternity, the conclusion is irresistible that there is a pre-eminence of the Father as being God of Himself, whereas the Son is God only by reason of the Father. But another conclusion equally follows. This Bishop Pearson also draws for us and we state it in his own language, with his own italics: "Again, we say, that *God the Father is Almighty*; but then we cannot say that the *Father only* is *Almighty*; for the reason why we say the *Father* is *Almighty* is because he is *God*; and therefore we cannot say that *he only* is *Almighty* because it is not true that *he only* is *God*." (Art. VI. p. 408.) Compare this with the following; "*I, even I, am the Lord, and besides me there is no Saviour; Therefore ye are witnesses, saith the Lord, that I am*

---

* Pearson on the Creed, Art. I. pp. 49, 50. 21st Lon. Ed.

God" (Isaiah xliii. 11, 12), *"and there is no God else besides me;
a just God and a* SAVIOUR ; *and there is none besides me"* (*ib.*
xlvi. 21).

The phrase, The Son of God begotten from all eternity, as
used by the Old Church, is confessedly synonymous with the
Wisdom of God, or Logos, begotten from all eternity. Thus
God is represented as having begotten his own wisdom from
all eternity and thereby his wisdom is represented as being
from all eternity, his Son. If it were predicated of a man that
his wisdom was his Son, it would be a flat absurdity, yet not
more absurd than the idea of a man's begetting his own wisdom. We can understand and readily admit the propriety of
the word " begotten," when used with reference to our Lord's
humanity; but when used with reference to the eternity of the
Logos (which eternity we also admit, for the Word or Wisdom
was God), we cannot understand it, nor can we consider it as
otherwise than " more than fabulous in the eye of reason."
Bishop Pearson himself, in order to avoid the obvious difficulty,
is compelled (p. 193) to ascribe fecundity to God (which certainly is not a scriptural attribute), and which at least bears
no analogy to the act of begetting. Indeed, while the whole of
Christendom most justly regards Bishop Pearson's work as a model of Aristotelian logic, his reasoning on this head has only its
parallel in the following, which occurs in another part of the
same volume ; " Thus our Redeemer, the man *Christ Jesus,* was
born of a woman, that he might redeem both men (and) women ;
that both sexes might rely upon him, who was of the one, and
from the other."—(Art. iii. p. 256.) This, by the way, is the only
reason he gives for the fact.

Without dwelling upon the Bishop's amusing distinction between Divine and human generation, we come at once to the
sum of his argument, which, in order to avoid mistake, we
give in his own language ; " We must not look upon the Divine
Nature as sterile, but rather admire the fecundity and com-
municability of itself upon which the creation of the world
dependeth : God making all things by his Word to whom he
first communicated that omnipotency which is the cause of all
things. And this may suffice for the illustration of our third
proposition, that the Father communicated the Divine essence
to the Word, who is that *Jesus* who is the *Christ.* The fourth
assertion followeth, that the communication of the Divine essence
by the Father is the generation of the Son ; and Christ, who
was eternally God, not from himself but from the Father, is
the eternal Son of God. That God always had a Son, appeareth by Agur's question in the Proverbs of Solomon ; " Who

hath established the ends of the earth; what is his name, and
what is his Son's name, if thou canst tell?"*

The distinction between Plato and the Old Church (at the
head of whom is the one we have quoted) on this subject is,
that while Plato assigned the communication of the Divine
Essence to the ideas, or patterns, dwelling in the Logos, as the
institution of the work of creation, the Old Church writers
teach that the Divine Essence was communicated directly to
the Logos, and that two results followed; namely, the generation of the Son and the creation of the world, through the
Son. But the Son is the Logos; hence a vital objection
opposes itself to the whole theory. The theory involves, 1st,
an agent; 2d, an action; 3d, an object. In a thought of
the mind, the Agent must precede the Object and each must
precede the Action. The Agent is God; the Object is the
Word; the Action is the communication of the Divine Essence. But the communication of the Divine Essence is the
generation of the Son, who is the Word; and hence the act
of generation is predicated and made the cause of a consequence, which, by the hypothesis, already existed.

Nor is this difficulty avoided by the assumption that the
Logos is not the eternal Son of God, except by the communication of the Divine Essence; for such an assumption pre-
supposes an eternal Logos, distinct in essence from God the Father, which would be nothing more nor less than the Logos or
Reason of God, assumed by Plato. Certainly it would not be
the Logos of the Apostle John, for that Word was God; and
if the Old Church should make it a distinct Logos, they would
make it a distinct God. We are willing to have it said, in
answer to the same difficulty, that God, the Communication,
and the Word—the Agent, the Action, and the Object,—are
each from all eternity; but if the Word be from all eternity,
the communication of the Divine Essence can never have
generated it; and if never generated, it can never have been
begotten; and if never begotten, the Father has no pre-eminence by reason of a supposed eternal paternity. It was in order to reconcile, so far as possible, these conflicting difficulties,
that the Old Church Fathers were compelled to compensate
Plato for their departure from his distinction of essence by en-
grafting on his theory their distinction of persons. But when
errors breed in and in, the stock must at length die out by a law
of moral physiology; and this is the great difference between
the propagation of Error and that of Truth.

We have already protracted this article to an unreasonable

---

* See Dr. Clarke's Commentary on this passage from Proverbs, chap. xxx. 4.

length, but we beg the indulgence of our readers upon the ground, that we have not been detaining them so much by the obtrusion of our own lucubrations, as by extracts from authors of high authority, whose works are of general interest. We are far from having done justice to the subject, nor could we exhaust it in a volume. But if our feeble manner of presenting it, shall prompt other minds to its investigation, our main object will be accomplished. We think none can examine it without feeling that from the early influence of Platonism and Gnosticism, "the fundamental doctrine of the unity of the Divine Nature has undergone corruptions" from which no branch of the Old Church has ever yet been purged: that although with the mouth it is professed that God is one, yet, in the secret of the soul, the idea of three Gods is so radically fixed, that the distinctive personalities of each either paint themselves separately to the imagination, or else that the spirit groans in laboring to individualize, portray, and define them ; also that Faith, in her fruitless efforts to consolidate three persons into one God, either sinks in the sea of doubt, or else, shutting her eyes upon Reason, challenges merit to herself, because she believes in that which is impossible. Witness the following striking illustration from the Diary of the late lamented Chalmers : " *October* 18.—It is in my attempts to realize by an effort of conception, the unseen God, or any of His characteristics, that I feel oppressed by the impotency of nature's deadness and nature's blindness—though perhaps even in the greatest stupor of my spiritual faculties there is the fittest opportunity for the exercise of a greater than ordinary faith. Certain it is that in the philosophical arrangement of the mental powers, conception and belief are distinct from each other ; and when the belief is not helped by the conception, then it is more like belief in the absence of sense—and all the stronger, therefore, if without the aid of any manifestation it can bring its confidence without another foundation to rest upon the bare testimony of God. Let me believe in the midst of heaviness. Let me believe in the dark. We read of faith in the *name* of Christ—and a name might awaken as dull and feeble an idea of an archetype as a symbol in algebra does of the thing represented by it. To that name I will nevertheless adhere. On that name I will depend ; and, O God, may I find at all times that it is an anchor of the soul, both sure and steadfast."

What is this but a repetition of the old question that followed the Feast of the Passover and which has been authoritatively answered for more than eighteen hundred years ? What is it but the exaltation of faith, because, refusing to repose in child-like confidence upon that answer, she erects to herself a greater mystery and compensates for unbelief in one particular, by supererogatory belief in another? Nay, it is the galvanising of faith beside the corpse of charity, and mistaking spasmodic convulsions for the energy of true life. In vain has light come into the world if the probationary state of the children of God, through the alleged defects of revelation, is for ever to be clouded with thick darkness; and in vain was the Comforter promised if heaviness of soul be the consummation of faith. Availing ourselves of the philosophical distinction between conception and belief, we can form to ourselves an idea of the Presbyterian heaven. We can imagine a Chalmers there reposing upon the bosom of that fancied second person in the Trinity, whose name in this life, afforded him as dull and feeble an idea of its supposed archetype, as does an algebraic symbol of a mathematical quantity. This communion having been sufficiently enjoyed, we can imagine him to request the additional manifestation so necessary to the plenitude of his bliss; "Show us the Father, and it sufficeth us." But conception and belief can sustain their divorce no longer. We can only see the angels bow and the archangels veil their faces; we can only hear that heavenly voice reiterate its mild response, —" Have I been so long time with thee, and yet hast thou not known me, *Thomas?* He that hath seen me hath seen the Father; and how sayest thou then, Show us the Father?"

In conclusion of this article, already too long, we can only say that, in yielding to the argument that the doctrine of the tripersonality of the Godhead is drawn from the Pagan schools, the reader need not surrender himself to be tossed upon a sea of speculation, without the prospect of chart or compass whereby to attain the haven of truth. In the writings of Swedenborg he will find explained, that in Jehovah, the One God, there exists infinitely that Trinity in Unity which is the Father, Son, and Holy Spirit; that the Father is infinite Love manifested through infinite Wisdom, which two infinites, being inseparable even in thought, are in form the Divine Humanity in the image of which man was originally created; and that, as from this terrestrial image there proceeds a certain finite sphere or influence which operates upon all within its range, so, from the infinite Archetype there proceeds an infinite Efflux, universal in its operation and presence, and which is the Holy Spirit: that the advent of our Lord Jesus Christ was the descent of Jehovah as to the Divine Truth, and that the phrase " *The Son of God,*" is predicable only of the human form by which the Divine Truth was manifested to the eye of sense; of which form, the Divine Good was the inmost soul; that thus the Divine Humanity ultimated itself by assuming the form of a man among men for the redemption of the human family and the subjugation of the hells; that this terrestrial body was ineffably glorified after its resurrection from the bondage of temporal death, but can be spiritually discerned as the medium through which the indwelling Father communicates with his creatures; that thus faith, no longer stretching a vacant and ever unsatisfied gaze after a Deity hyper-spiritualized by the process of orthodox rarefaction, may at length follow her risen Jehovah from the sepulchre towards the throne, and, assuming his terrestrial body as the basis of her contemplations, find that body progressively transfigured before her, as she herself shall ascend from glory to glory. But lest these truths, which are as an anchor to the soul of the New Churchman, should fail to commend themselves to the mind of the novitiate reader, by reason of their apparent (not real) opposition to the abstract letter of a few passages in the Bible, which are actually no more repugnant to them than they are to our Lord's reply to Philip, and which beautifully harmonize with each when rightly understood, we beg the conscientious inquirer to avail himself of that assistance which enlightened commentary and interpretation so abundantly afford. If it were proper for us to single out a body of information, within the reach of all who have access to this work, we might particularize the series of " Letters to a Trinitarian," running through the pages of this Repository, as amply elucidating the whole subject and presenting in connection with it a line of new, cogent, and (may we say?) unanswerable argument. But the world is full of truth. Even within the depths of error it is often to be found, imbedded like the pearl, waiting only for some successful diver to detach it from its protecting shell and set it sparkling in the coronet of a progressive and beautified humanity. The world is full of truth!—written indeed, originally, as with sympathetic ink, yet we may at length rejoice that the genial warmth of a new dispensation is daily developing its hidden characters and bringing its glorious letters into view. The world is full of truth as it is of light: but truth like the light SHINETH IN DARKNESS AND THE DARKNESS COMPREHENDETH IT NOT.

B. W. H!

ARTICLE II.

FOURIERISM AND THE NEW CHURCH.

(*Concluded.*)

WE have not yet reached the end of that chain of errors which link themselves by inevitable sequence to our author's fundamental falsity respecting the "inborn goodness" of man, or his freedom from any hereditary moral taint. From his false and unauthorized assumption on this point, we think we are able to trace the principal errors of his book, as well as his many and strange perversions of Swedenborg.

If the evil deeds that men commit flow not from their evil loves, not "from the heart," not from any thing *in the individual* which needs rectifying, but from the constitution or form of Society;—if, as our author maintains, the internal of every man is good, and that this innate goodness *must* sooner or later be developed, then the eternity of the hells is impossible. All who enter the other world as devils, (how can they *be* devils unless their ruling loves be evil or devilish?) will finally become angels. And here we are prompted to inquire how it happens, that, since all evil as well as good spirits in the other world are arranged *by the Lord* into societies, this social arrangement does not at once make them all good and happy? Strange indeed, if the Lord does not know how to organize societies of spirits in such a manner that "Passional Harmony" shall at once result from each one's following his "Passional Attractions!"—*if* such harmony depends entirely on the social arrangements. But Dr. Hempel does not attempt to enlighten us on this point. He is, however, quite consistent in denying the permanence or eternity of the hells. He says they are "states of society not yet reduced under the laws of Divine Order" (p. 246). And "that Swedenborg understands by Hells, young Humanities going through the process of regeneration" (p. 65). He occupies about fourteen pages in attempting to prove from Swedenborg that "eternal punishment does not exist," or that the state of the wicked in the other world is only temporary. He goes quite a round-about way, of course, and gives us as proofs merely his own inferences, of the value of which our readers may by this time form a pretty correct estimate.

But Swedenborg himself is very explicit on this point; and uniformly teaches that the life or ruling love of every individual remains for ever what it is when he leaves this world; hence that evil spirits always remain such. He says:

" The life of man cannot be changed after death, but remains then such as it had been in the world ; for the whole spirit of man is such as his love is, and infernal love cannot be transcribed into heavenly love, because they are opposite."—*N. J. D.* 239.

" If the natural man be not prepared to receive the truths and goods of faith in the life of the body, *he cannot receive* them in the other life, thus he cannot be saved."—*A. C.* 4588.

" Man after death remains to eternity of the same quality as his will or ruling love."—*H. & H.* 480.

" The angels say, that the life of the ruling love remains unchanged to eternity, because every one is his own love, and therefore to change the ruling love of a spirit would be to deprive him of his life, or to annihilate him."—*Ib.* (*See also C. L.* 524 ; *A. C.* 3762, 8206, 3993, 4464, *et passim.*)

Our readers may feel some curiosity to know how Dr. H. gets over Swedenborg's repeated and explicit announcements on this point.   He does it in a very easy way, thus : " Whatever Swedenborg may have said of the future of existing spirits, *he has not said from revelation, but from reason*" (p. 131); and then quotes the passage in *Divine Providence,* No. 179, in which Swedenborg says "it is not given to any one to know the future," from which he infers that Swedenborg himself could not have known that the hells would be eternal, or that all whose ruling loves are evil when they depart this world, will for ever remain evil.

But Swedenborg, in all such passages as this that our author has referred to, is speaking of what is the case with man *generally* in regard to a knowledge of things future, and has no reference to exceptional cases like his own.   This is so obvious that an honest and sensible critic, we should think, could not fail to see it.   For in the article of the Divine Providence, cited by the Dr., Swedenborg says, "Every one is allowed to conclude concerning things to come, from reason ; and hence reason, with all that appertains to it, is in its life ; it is on this account that man does not know his lot after death, or know any event before he is in it."

Swedenborg repeatedly declares that open intercourse with the spiritual world, i. e. seeing and conversing with spirits and angels, is a very dangerous thing; and that it was not permitted to men in this day.   Now if the Dr. would be consistent with himself, he ought, and if it were necessary to the maintenance of any of his favorite notions, no doubt *would*, insist that therefore Swedenborg himself never had his spiritual senses opened—never actually saw or conversed with spirits. This conclusion would be of precisely the same nature, and just as legitimate as the one he draws from the passage in the Divine Providence concerning man's knowledge of the future.

Besides, Dr. Hempel knows full well that the *whole* of the New Church theology comes to us professedly by revelation, and none of it from the writer's own reason. He knows that Swedenborg repeatedly declares that he has never given any explication of his own, nor that of any angel, but simply that which has been communicated to him from the Lord alone. "Since the first day of my call," he says, "I have not received anything which pertains to the doctrines of that Church [the New Church] from any angel but from the Lord alone, while I read the Word."—(*T. C. R.* 779 ; *also Pref. to A. R.*) Will Dr. Hempel say that Swedenborg was mistaken here, or that he spake " not from revelation, but from reason ?" Perchance we may force him to confess, what we apprehend to be the real truth, that he has small faith in Swedenborg's extraordinary divine illumination ; that he does not really believe him to have been especially authorized and " sent to teach the things relating to the New Church," nor that all the doctrines he has taught were received "from the Lord alone." His unbelief, spite of his professed deference to the teachings of Swedenborg, and his copious quotations from his writings leaks out here and there. Thus knowing how confidently the disciples of Swedenborg usually rely upon their illumined author's disclosures concerning the spiritual world, and as if to weaken their confidence somewhat, or to turn their thoughts away from his plain and oft repeated assertions respecting the future condition of the wicked, he says :

" It is by no means important to speculate about man's condition in the spiritual world. Speculative inquiries into man's future life, are indeed interesting and necessary, but they often spring from a childish and weak intellect, and are apt to engender fanaticism and bitterness of heart. This speculative spirit has taken hold, to a great extent, of some of the best minds among Swedenborg's disciples"—(*p.* 134).

But who are the *speculators,* Dr. Hempel? Those who receive Swedenborg's revelations as true, as coming from the Lord out of heaven, or those who, professing to receive them like yourself, array the doctrines of self-derived intelligence against such parts of them as happen not to agree with their pre-conceived notions? There certainly is not much room for *speculation* upon a subject concerning which the truth has been clearly revealed, *among those who accept the revelation as from heaven,* and therefore true.

But Dr. Hempel concedes that there are hells—evil spirits—in the other world ; and we presume he means *such* evil spirits as Swedenborg has told us of—spirits opposed to all that is good and inclined to all that is evil. He only insists " that their evil state cannot last for ever." And at the same time that he believes all will finally become angels, even those who have passed into the other world in an evil state, and before their regeneration *has commenced,* he admits with Swedenborg "that no regeneration *can begin* in the spiritual world." This looks like a flat contradiction. Not so, however, in our author's estimation. And as the solution of the difficulty may reveal at least *one* gift which seems to have been pretty liberally bestowed upon the Dr., and at the same time amuse our readers somewhat, we make room for the substance of it.

" Fourier," he says, " solves this difficulty in a highly interesting manner, by a doctrine of Compound Immortality (!) or of the Periodical Migration of the soul from the spiritual to the natural, and from the natural to the spiritual world.

" The only way in which the doctrine of the periodical migration of the soul could be explained consistently with the numerical development of mankind upon this earth, would be to suppose that the souls, after returning to the spiritual world, produce new souls out of themselves from the Universal Life.

" According to Swedenborg's doctrine, the material man is an ultimate of the spiritual ; hence the materialization of the body must have taken place once, and may, therefore, take place again. In this transformation itself, there is nothing absurd or improbable.

" Fourier thinks that the soul *re-enters* the body at the period of dentition, and that, up to that period, the body is sustained *by the soul of the earth.* Fourier asserts that the soul of the earth is similar to the soul of man, except that it is *of a higher order*"—(*pp.* 132, 133, 134).

" A highly interesting " solution of the difficulty this, indeed ! No *speculation* here, we presume—none at all. All sound philosophy. To the mind of our author it may be so; but to our mind, it is as arrant nonsense as ever fell from the brain of a bedlamite. It matches well enough, however, with the religious doctrines of the book and its folly is equalled by the remarks concerning the " *Boreal Crown,*" on pp. 233, 234, 235.

Our author not unfrequently assumes quite a didactic tone and manner towards " his friends of the New Church," as in his remarks upon the marriage of the Good and the True as " a law of life," p. 258. (See p. 185.) This tone and manner would be offensive enough, even if Dr. Hempel were as much superior to all the disciples of Swedenborg in his ability to understand and interpret his teachings aright, as he vainly imagines himself to be. But how supremely ridiculous do they appear in one who seems so incapable of understanding the great Swede, and who misinterprets some of his plainest teachings, as the Dr. does.   The doctrine concerning the Heavenly Marriage, or the marriage of the Good and the True, is one so clearly set forth in the writings of Swedenborg, that it seems impossible for any one to misunderstand it.   Yet see what pitiful work our author makes of this plain and beautiful doctrine!

" In proportion as man is permitted to act out his affections [be they good or bad] he lives in goodness and truth"—(*p.* 157).

" Now the conjunction of Good with Truth in the Natural Principle simply means this, that the present results of industry shall be so arranged around man that he may be enabled to choose from among their totality those which correspond to his affections"—(*p.* 177).

"When the action of the Intellectual principle typifies or represents an inborn passion or love of the soul [good or bad] then there is a marriage of the Good and the True."

"If I am fond of cultivating grapes, and am permitted to indulge that taste as often as it is felt, and in such a manner as suits my understanding, I am in the marriage of the Good and the True"—(*p.* 257).

" Liberty, bliss or salvation, is to live in correspondence.   Every work which man performs, must correspond to an affection ; then only is the work a Good in the divine sense"—(*p.* 184).

Does Dr. Hempel need to be told that all he has here said will apply to those in the hells? They all "live in correspondence ;" and every work which they perform "corresponds to an affection." So also the works of thieves, adulterers, and murderers here on earth, correspond to their affections.   But none of these are *good* works.

Swedenborg says that "the delights of every one's life are changed after death, to things *corresponding* thereto ;" and those who are under the influence of self-love, do not know it, "because they take delight in it, and call their evil good, and the false, wherewith they confirm themselves in their delusion, they call truth ; and yet, were they but willing to take advice from men wiser than themselves, they might be set right in this matter ; but such willingness is wanting in them.   So great is the infatuation of self-love, as to shut the ear to the voice of wisdom."—(*H. H.* 487.)   Thus he tells us that "all who are in the principle of evil, and have confirmed themselves in opposition to the truths of religion, and more especially by their disbelief of the Scriptures, all such avoid the light of heaven, and hide themselves in dark caverns and the clefts of rocks, and that because they hated the truth, and loved the false which *corresponds* to darkness, as represented by such hiding places wherein

they take pleasure. . . . They who had applied themselves to the study of the sciences, merely for the sake of being
accounted men of learning, priding themselves in what they
know from their memory relating thereto, whilst at the same
time they have neglected to cultivate their minds with knowledge useful for life, such take delight in sandy places which
they prefer to the most pleasant fields and gardens, as the former *correspond* to the use they had made of such studies."—
(*H. H.* 488.) And so with every other class of evil spirits. They
all " live in correspondence." They are "permitted to act out
their affections" too, as far as is compatible with their own
good and the good of the race. They choose from the things
around them "those which correspond to their affections." All
" the actions of their intellectual principle" are representative
or typical of the "inborn passions or loves of their souls."
And whatever tastes they have they are permitted to indulge
" in such a manner as suits *their* understanding." Yet none of
these spirits have any love of what is really good and true.
Therefore they are none of them in the heavenly marriage of
the Good and the True, but all in the infernal marriage of the
Evil and the False.—(*See the New Jerusalem and its Heavenly
Doctrine, Nos.* 11—19; 230—245.)

So little does Dr. Hempel understand of the true nature of
the Heavenly Marriage, concerning which he nevertheless so
confidently presumes to instruct "his friends of the New
Church!" A far wiser course for him would be, to come and
learn of them, before he sets himself up as a teacher. For
however competent he may be to teach on other subjects, his
book affords abundant evidence that few are so ill qualified as
himself to instruct others in the things of heaven, or to expound
for them the doctrines of the New Jerusalem.

We have seen how closely linked together our author's theological errors are and how naturally they all flow from the
fundamental error assumed by him in regard to the natural or
hereditary state of man. " He who confirms false principles,"
says Swedenborg, "first assumes some principle of his own,
from which he will not depart, nor in the least remit, but col-
lects and accumulates corroborating proofs from every quarter, thus also from the Word, till he is so thoroughly self-per-
suaded that he can no longer see the truth."—(*A. C.* 589.) " All
things of every doctrine have a mutual respect to each other
as in a kind of society, and are joined together as in consan-
guinity and affinity, which acknowledge the common principle
as a father."—(*A. C.* 4720.)

Dr. Hempel's manner of referring to and quoting from Swedenborg, is very remarkable, though quite in keeping with

other things in this most remarkable book. Thus he wishes to
prove from Swedenborg that the existing social order upon our
globe is infernal and an ultimate of hell. How does he go to
work ? He quotes *Divine Love and Wisdom*, Nos. 340—343,
in which Swedenborg asserts the connection between the natural and the spiritual world, and the influx of the latter into
the former, and says, "that the hells are not remote from men,
but that they are about them, yea in them who are evil ;" and
that "the influx from hell operates those things which are evil
uses, in places where there are things which correspond to
them." The things which Swedenborg mentions as evil uses,
or correspondences thereof, are poisonous herbs, noxious animals, cadaverous, putrid, and stercoraceous matters. And as
Dr. Hempel finds all such things on our earth, *therefore* it is
proved from Swedenborg and existing facts "that the present
order of things upon this globe is an ultimate of Hell " (*p.* 85
et. seq). The author seems to have not the remotest idea, that,
by the same mode of argumentation, he could have proved just
as easily that the present order of things upon this globe is an
ultimate of heaven, for there is an influx into this natural
world from Heaven as well as from Hell ; and there are all
around us forms of *good* uses corresponding to heavenly things,
as well as of *evil* uses corresponding to hellish things.

Pursuing the same mode of reasoning, the author quotes
A. C. 7773, 8232, 9188, in which Swedenborg gives an account
of the imperiousness, tyranny, love of dominion, &c., which
prevail in hell, and which originate in the evil of self love.
And because the Dr. sees the same dispositions manifested here
on earth, his conclusion is, that therefore our present social
order is devilish. He forgets here, as before, that it might just
as easily and in the same way, be proved that our social order
is heavenly ; for we find in society, as it now is, numerous instances in which are exhibited feelings, dispositions, and actions, the very opposite of those in Hell, as described by Swedenborg.

Then see what profound ignorance this author betrays of
the importance of the domestic or family institution, as well as
of all that Swedenborg has so beautifully said on that subject.
To the mind of Dr. Hempel the isolated household is a type of
hell. Thus he says : "The individual household typifies man's
'selfish or infernal proprium'" (*p.* 200). And hereupon quotes
several passages from the *Arcana* to show that man's proprium is all evil and the false, thus altogether infernal. He then
adds :

"And yet it is upon the individual household that our whole social
system revolves. It is time that the real friends of Humanity should

dare to lay bare the insidious falsity and the hidden selfishness of the isolated family, which has for thousands of years been enveloped with the drapery of sanctity, goodness, and love. . . Spiritual relationship, sympathy springing up from similarity of taste, inclination, affection, is the highest form of Love; but it is completely choked by the narrow exclusiveism of the family"—*(p. 202).*

" The *real* friends of Humanity " never speak of the family institution in this manner : No, *never.* Nor would any man speak thus of it, who had *begun* to comprehend the doctrines of heaven. Yet immediately after the above language, this author says (and his book abounds with just such inconsistencies) : " Still let no one cry out that I wish to see the family-tie loosened or perhaps destroyed." But why not, if the family be *of necessity* the nursery of a mean selfishness, a " narrow exclusiveism ?"—if the individual household be a type of hell ? —if " all spiritual relationship," as he says, " remains unregarded and undeveloped in the family ?"—why not invade its sanctity, loosen its ties, and utterly destroy it as soon as possible ?

This author, notwithstanding his pretended familiarity with the writings of Swedenborg, and his fancied superiority to all others in expounding them, appears to be totally ignorant of the fact that the " individual household" *exists in heaven,* and therefore may with more propriety be regarded as a type of heaven than of hell. As he needs enlightening on this as on other points, we will cite a few passages from the treatise on *Heaven and Hell.*

" All are consociated in heaven according to their spiritual affinities for good and truth, in their several ranks and degrees, whether in the universal heaven, in the several societies, or *in particular families*" (205)—which looks as if there were " individual households" there.

In another part of the same treatise certain angels are spoken of as living " in single houses and families," more solitary, or widely dispersed than others ; and it is there said that " these are under the Lord's more particular care and direction, *and are the best of the angels*" (50, 189).

" As the angels live in societies, *as men do on earth,* so in like manner they have *their particular dwellings,* and these different according to their states of life respectively, magnificent for those who are worthy of greater honor, and less so for those of inferior degree" (183).

" As often as I have conversed with the angels face to face, it was in their habitations, which are *like to our houses on earth,* but far more beautiful and magnificent, having rooms, chambers, and apartments in great variety, as also spacious courts belonging to them, together with gardens, parterres of flowers, fields, &c. Where the angels are formed into societies, they dwell *in contiguous habitations,* disposed of after the manner of our cities, in streets, walks, and squares" (184).

Swedenborg also informs us that there are in every family in heaven "a master and servants, and the master loves his servants, and servants their master, and so serve each other from love" (219).

Our readers will bear in mind that it is no part of our business now to inquire into the *truth* of Swedenborg's disclosures concerning heaven. Dr. Hempel all along concedes this. We wish only to see how far the doctrines of heaven support this author's positions. And from the passages just cited we learn that there are in heaven isolated households, private dwellings, and cities formed somewhat like ours with houses contiguous. Such things then are not, *per se,* what the Dr. pronounces them to be, types of hell, and his attempt to prove them such from the writings of Swedenborg, only proves his ignorance of, or his utter incompetency to expound, the doctrines of heaven.

Let us pursue a step farther this author's manner of proving his social science from Swedenborg, that we may get a full view of his most remarkable logical skill and accuracy. He says :

" Labor in the Phalanx is a constant materialization of the affections; it is the eternal rest or peace of the angels" (p. 383).

He then quotes some passages from Swedenborg in which it is said that the peace and rest of heaven consist not in idleness, but in the active performance of good uses. *Therefore* the Phalanx is a heaven on earth.

Again :

" In the Phalanx every group is clad in an uniform representation of the uses or functions, which the group performs" (p. 384).

Then, to show the connection between Heaven and the Phalanx, he quotes from *A. C.* 9158, in which Swedenborg says that all in heaven appear clothed in garments according to the truths of faith appertaining to them.

Again :

" The Phalanx being a heaven of pleasure, it is in the Phalanx alone that man really and truly LIVES" (p. 385).

He then quotes from the *Heavenly Arcana,* Nos. 678, 1016, to show that, according to Swedenborg, "nothing grows and multiplies with man unless there be some affection;" and that " no scientific and rational which man acquires, from infancy to old age, is ever insinuated into him except by what is good and delightsome."

Again :

" In the Phalanx no union exists except from similitude of character or taste" (p. 386).

Whereupon the author quotes such passages as the following from the *Arcana.*

" In the angelic societies they love each other, acknowledge each other, and consociate with each other according to the similitudes and proximities of goods" (9079).

Again :

" The laws, to which the conjunction of the heavenly societies into one heaven has reference, are fully obeyed in the Phalanx" (p. 387).

And then the author quotes *A. C.* 9613, which states five laws, to which the conjunction of angelic societies has reference ; one of which laws is, " that the universal bond [that binds the heavenly societies together] is the Lord, thus love from Him, and hence to Him."   But the love of self, which Swedenborg declares to be the opposite of love to the Lord, is the bond that binds Dr. Hempel's Phalanx together.   For this is the *pivotal* or ruling love. "Self-love in the Phalanx," he says, " is the pivotal or fundamental love of every individual man" (p. 386).

And so on to the end of the chapter.

We very much doubt whether our readers ever before saw such a display of logic as this. It needs no comment. Following the example of our author, we might just as easily prove that a state-prison or a galley-ship were a heaven on earth. For we have only to commence with asserting that in the state-prison or galley-ship they are all clad in a uniform, all labor, that the serial arrangement exists there, &c. &c. and then quote from Swedenborg where such things are predicated of angelic societies, and the work is done, the proof is complete.

Among the glaring defects of this book, are the numerous inconsistencies of its author, some of which we cannot refrain from noticing. Thus on page 89, where he is speaking of the social order which exists in civilized countries at the present day, and which he regards as a " type" and " ultimate of hell," he says, " our whole social mechanism pivots upon self-love."

And on page 386, where he is speaking of the new order of things which will exist in the Phalanx, which he regards as the type and ultimate of heaven, he says: "Self-love in the Phalanx is the *pivotal* or fundamental love of every individual man." And again, "A man cannot be in heaven as long as he is not permitted to love himself above all things." Thus it appears that our present *hellish*, and Dr. Hempel's future *heavenly* form of society, *pivot* upon one and the same principle, viz. the love of self. How is this, Dr. Hempel?

Again our author says: "And we have every reason to believe, from the evidence of actual facts, that the *sudden* transition of Humanity from Civilization to Compound Association is, in the nature of things, impossible" (p. 57). But in another place he says: "Fourier·is confident that the grand social transformation of the Globe from Social Incoherence to Social Harmony, will take place *suddenly* over the whole surface of the Globe" (p. 449). And the Dr. immediately intimates his belief of this, and cites "*an actual fact*" in the life of each individual, viz. his birth, in support of it.

Again: on page 81, he speaks of "visible forms of constraint" being "able to exercise an efficient restraint of the passions; and then *it is the soul*," he says, "*that restrains itself.*" But on a previous page (44) he says "it is irrational to contend that the perpetrator of that deed [murder] might have controlled his passions, for the simple reason that it remains yet to be proved whether the passions can at all be controlled by a mere determination of the will under any circumstances."

In such palpable contradictions does this work abound. So that, if one were to assert what the author believes on any particular subject, and prove his assertion from his book, another might assert that he believes the opposite, and prove it from the same authority.

But among the gravest offences of this writer, are his strange and repeated perversions of Swedenborg. In this particular he transgresses almost as often as he quotes him. We have already referred to his attempt to make Swedenborg teach, or to appear to teach, that self-love is the pivotal or fundamental love of all in the heavens (p. 386). We will refer to only three or four more things of this sort, though we have marked nearly a score of them.

Wherever Swedenborg speaks of the external or natural man, Dr. Hempel persists in understanding him to mean the *social man*, i. e. the external form or organization of society, and interprets him accordingly. (See pp. 17, 18, 77, 181, &c.) Consequently, whatever Swedenborg says about the external or natural man being full of all kinds of evils, has reference to

our existing Social order, and not to any thing appertaining to
the mind of the individual.   Now every one at all familiar with
the writings of Swedenborg knows that this is a gross perversion.   And if Dr. Hempel himself does not know it, we would
refer him to one or two passages where Swedenborg himself
has defined what he means by the " natural man."

" The mind makes the man, for the mind of man consists of understanding and will ; hence it is the same thing whether we use the expression mind or man, or whether we say the spiritual and natural
mind, or the spiritual and natural man."—*Ap. Ex.* 406.

" Every man has an inferior or exterior mind, and a mind superior
or interior, the inferior or exterior mind is the natural mind, *which is
called the natural man*, but the superior or interior is the natural mind,
which mind is called the spiritual man."—*Ib.* 527.

In view of passages like these, how is it possible for Dr.
Hempel or any one else to maintain that the "natural man"
as used by Swedenborg means "the organization or form of
Society and the Church," without rendering himself justly
amenable to the charge of wilful perversion ?   We do not assert, however, that the perversion was wilful.   We would
rather believe it was not.

Again: on p. 204, our author says: "Regeneration is impossible, so long as man is not furnished with an abundance of
material and spiritual riches."   And then he quotes *A. C.* 677,
in which Swedenborg speaks of the necessity of man's being
"furnished with all those things which serve as means, with
the good and delightful things of the affections, as means for
the will ; and with truths from the Word of the Lord, and also
with confirming things from other sources, as means for the
understanding :" all of which things he calls "meats or food."
Now that by "meats" Swedenborg has not reference here to
"an abundance of *material* riches," is plain from the following
sentence which occurs on the same page of the Arcana : " The
meats with which his soul [i. e. the soul of a wicked man] is
fed, when he is dead, are the delights arising from evils, and
the pleasantnesses arising from falses, which are the meats of
death."

Again, on page 433, this author quotes Divine Providence
No. 73, where it is said, " All liberty is of love, insomuch that
love and liberty are one ; whereas love is the life of man, liberty also is of his life."   And he adds : " By love is here meant
the love-principle, which Fourier designates by the term 'Passion'"—i. e. love of any kind, no matter how selfish or worldly
it may be ; than which, scarcely a greater perversion of Swedenborg's meaning can be conceived.

An equally perverse construction of Swedenborg's language, "that the natural principle ought altogether to become as nothing in respect to the will-faculty," may be seen on page 180, and in fifty other places.

Then on page 193 we find something still worse. In the middle of a quotation from *Divine Love and Wisdom*, Nos. 419, 420, we find the following sentence *interpolated*, without any sign to indicate that it is the author's own language. "And it is again evident from correspondence, that this purification takes place first, by the Intellectual principle arraying the external world or the Social Form in such a manner as to remove from it all those influences which might disturb the harmonious action of the Love principle ; and, secondly, by the Social Form being so arranged by the Intellectual principle, that Society will hold out to the Love-principle no other motives for development except such as will make true and beautiful manifestations of the Love-principle the necessary results of its movement."

Now Dr. Hempel's readers are left to suppose that all this is to found in Swedenborg's treatise on the *Divine Love and Wisdom*, when not one word of it is to be found there. The whole is an interpolation by the author. And not only so, but there is not a sentence in the *Divine Love and Wisdom*, or in any other of Swedenborg's works, to warrant such language as is here put into his mouth by Dr. H. *How* the Love-principle is purified by the Intellectual principle, is, indeed, plainly taught by Swedenborg in the very article with which our author commences the quotation wherein occurs the above interpolation. It is there said that " by the understanding, the love, that is the man, sees those evils that pollute and defile the love ; and he also sees, that if he shuns and turns away from those evils as sins, he loves the things that are opposite to them, which are all heavenly ; then also he sees the means whereby those evils may be shunned and turned from as sins ; this the love, that is, the man, sees, by the use of the faculty of elevating his understanding into the light of heaven, whence comes wisdom."—(*D. L. W.* 419.) And by way of illustrating his meaning, and precluding the possibility of being misunderstood by any sincere inquirer of ordinary intellect, Swedenborg immediately tells us that it is the understanding which enables every one to see rationally, and then to turn away from, thefts and fraudulent acts, hatreds, revenges, adulteries, and the like; and *thus* it is that the purification of the love by means of the understanding, takes place, and not " by the intellectual principle arranging the external world or the Social Form" after the manner stated by Dr. Hempel. So that our author in this instance has been guilty of a double transgression. He has, in the first place, foisted in eight or ten lines of his own in the middle of an extract from Swedenborg; and in the next place he teaches in this *interpolated* passage a doctrine altogether different from anything taught by Swedenborg in the article from which he quotes.

Now without saying a word here unfavorable to the general subject of Social Science—for we have a very friendly feeling towards that subject—we cannot refrain from giving it as our opinion that the manner in which the subject has been treated by Dr. Hempel in the work before us, the author's unsatisfactory effort to show the agreement alleged between Swedenborg and Fourier, the artifices resorted to, the errors of doctrine and of reasoning, and the perverse construction of the great Swede—and indeed of the Word also—in which this book abounds, are little calculated to win for the Association movement the favorable regard of any intelligent or honest New Churchman. Such a book as this is rather calculated to fill our minds with a thorough disgust, if not contempt, for the whole subject. And if the Association School acknowledge Dr. Hempel as a proper exponent of their principles, and his book as a fair exposé of the doctrines and views of Fourier, we can assure them that their appeal to Swedenborgians will be all in vain. Swedenborgians, before they can adopt the doctrines of this book, must renounce some of the plainest and most important truths taught by Swedenborg himself.

But we strongly suspect—and we have our reasons for the suspicion—that this author has misconceived and misinterpreted Fourier as well as Swedenborg. We cannot speak positively on this point, because of our imperfect knowledge of the works of Fourier, with which we hope ere long to be better acquainted.

There are several other things which we had intended to notice in the work before us, but which we must content ourselves with merely referring to. Such as its *extravagant* expressions, so extravagant as to render them utterly untrue, for which see pp. 158, 196, 204, 205, 219, 223, 224, 226, 264, 299; its *superficiality* and *great weakness* on certain points, for which see pp. 162, 392, 395, 409; its *false views of education*, for which see pp. 220, 221, 297; *its false views of liberty*, when judged by the teachings of Swedenborg, for which see pp. 414, 415, 421, 432; its false idea respecting *Distributive Justice* or the *Law of Compensation*, for which see pp. 139, 393; its low and contracted views of *use*, and consequent mistake in regard to the *productive* and *non-productive* classes in society, for which see pp. 236, 238; its *mistakes* and *false assertions*, arising no doubt from the author's imperfect knowledge of the things whereof he affirms, for which see pp. 20, 203, 208, 226, 368; and its *different expositions of the Word* from those given by Swedenborg, whom the writer professes to follow, for which p. 447, 448, and elsewhere.

Now with such errors as we have here pointed out, and with which almost every page of this book absolutely bristles, the author's opinion of his own superior ability in interpreting the doctrines of heaven, his repeated advice to New Church-men, and occasional remarks upon what he considers their mistakes or errors, appear laughable indeed—scarcely less than supremely ridiculous.

We have given a more extended review of this book than we at first intended, and much more extended than is needed by any of the members of the New Church into whose hands the work may fall. But we trust the article may be of some service to others, who, for lack of a thorough knowledge of the writings of Swedenborg, may need some such aid to show them how signally this author has failed in the work which he undertook, and how little respect for Association this book is likely to win from intelligent New Churchmen. Had the Editor of the New York Harbinger examined this book critically, or had he been as familiar with the teachings of Swedenborg as some others, he would never have used this language in reference to the work, which we find in the number of that Journal, for February 26, 1848 : "The appeal," says this editor, " which the writer makes to the reason is in our opinion as irresistible as that made to the heart, and his book will prove as satisfactory, therefore, to the mere logician as to the man. It will do an immense service, if we mistake not, to both the classes of readers to whom it is more especially addressed, Swedenborgians and Associationists, by exhibiting to one the scientific basis of their faith, and to the other the spiritual grounds of their science."

An immense service to Associationists this book may do, by commending to their notice the theological works of Sweden-borg, and inducing them to read them. And it may do this even more effectually on account of some of the very errors with which its pages abound. It may thereby be better suited to the states of these persons. But that it will prove at all useful to "Swedenborgians" in the way the Editor of the Har-binger expects, we have no ground whatever to hope."

B. F. B.

AMONG the many proofs, that the general mind, in our day, is sunk down into a state in which it reasons from the senses, and what is derived from them, the disbelief in witchcraft and magic is one. This subject is treated, almost universally, after the manner of the sensual mind. The course with those who are under its dominion is, to observe what is called the order of nature, to deduce from it certain principles, and to attribute to them the energy of certain causes. For example, a man labors under mental alienation, and his brain, after death, is discovered to have undergone certain structural changes, and, thereupon the cause of his madness is supposed to have been detected; it flowed from a diseased state of the cerebrum; this was the origin of all its phenomena. Having gathered a vast store of these causes, they inquire as often as new or strange facts are brought to their notice, whether they will admit of being derived from them; if not, the facts are rejected, or perverted into a form in which they will. To those who proceed after this manner witchcraft is necessarily incredible. A child falls into a pining condition of body, and exhibits strange symptoms, such as do not, in their complex, belong to any known disease; and it is alleged that they proceed from some person who operates at a distance in some inscrutable manner known by the designation of witchcraft. Against this statement the man of the senses reasons, as seems to himself, irresistibly, thus: "How can the supposed witch operate where she is not? This is as absurd as to suppose that she conveys herself, in spite of the laws of gravitation, through the air, and becomes present invisibly with her victim." *Therefore*, the facts, so far as they will not be accounted for by natural causes, hysteria, imagination or the like, are exaggerated or otherwise misrepresented. Thus testimony is set aside, because it leads to the acknowledgment of a supernatural or spiritual operation. The absolute repugnance of such men to step out of the circle of what they call natural causes, but which are really nothing but effects, appears by the immense sum of the facts they thus deny or pervert, and the resistance they oppose to the authority of great names, though ready enough generally to be swayed by an argument of this latter kind. If one of their natural causes is in the way their minds can no more *move* under the impulse of facts and just reasonin from them towards a recognition of truth, than the wheels of a watch can revolve with a hair wound in among them.

The testimony of the Word to the existence of witchcraft and magic, is quite explicit. First, we have narratives in which its practice is mentioned, as where the magicians of Egypt imitated the miracles of Moses and Aaron, and the witch of Endor called up the spirit of Samuel. Then there is a long list of passages speaking of magic, enchantments, sorceries, witchcrafts, &c. as things in use among the children of Israel and the heathen by whom they were surrounded. Finally, we have a statute with a penalty annexed; "Thou shalt not suffer a witch to live." All this proof can be *turned*, in adroit ways known to sensual reasoners, but still it stands in the sacred volume to teach all who are willing to be taught.

The legislation of almost every land bears testimony to the reality of witchcraft. Legislators are generally shrewd men of the world, and their laws therefore are good evidence that there has been observed a class of phenomena, bearing a distinctive character, that could not be referred to merely "natural causes." They are generally men of sagacity also, and it is fairly presumable that they did not refer these phenomena to human agency without other grounds than those of mere opinion. That these laws should have been repealed or fallen into desuetude is no proof on the other side, as this may have been owing to the cessation of the phenomena, and the gradual encroachment of the sensuous tendency on just conclusions from facts and reason.

There have not been wanting men of celebrity and in late times—those further back might come under the suspicion of living in the "dark ages" or near them—who have felt constrained to avow their belief in the supernatural. Not to mention Bacon, we have Addison, Dr. Johnson, and Robert Hall. Blackstone's opinion on the subject is well known. "To deny the possibility, nay, actual existence of witchcraft and sorcery is at once flatly to contradict the revealed laws of God in various passages both of the Old and New Testament; and the thing itself is a truth to which every nation in the world hath in its turn borne testimony, either by examples seemingly well attested, or by prohibitory laws, which, at least, suppose the possibility of a commerce with evil spirits." Here we have sentence given in the disputed matter with a deliberation and gravity little short of judicial, and doubtless after evidence and argument heard on both sides. Sir Walter Scott, also, there is reason for thinking, had more belief in the supernatural than he was willing to avow.

But why is the opinion of the common people treated, in

this matter, with so much scorn? Thousands and tens of
thousands of them are found affirming facts and adopting an
unavoidable conclusion from them, if they are facts. May it not
be, after the age of scoffing at vulgar superstitions has gone
by, that *they* shall be adjudged in the right, and reasoners from
the senses be convicted of blindness? Instances might be pointed out, in the domain of natural science, where philosophers
long contradicted common opinions, because they seemed irrational, and at least had to concede that they were well founded.
To give one example: The common people of Germany, give
the name of " ground-ice" to the floating cakes which are seen
in rivers at the beginning of frost, supposing that they are
formed at the bottom of the stream. The philosophers long
pronounced this an impossibity, but, of late, it has been ascertained by one of their own number, that the fact is so.
May not something like this yet take place here?

As for the facts themselves, few persons probably are aware
of their number and extent and the respectability of the witnesses. To speak of those nearest home—the evidence that
witchcraft was really practised in New England, is, by all the
usual rules of estimating evidence, perfectly overwhelming;
but all close reasoning upon the character of the reporters,
the number of the cases, the confessions of the parties, upon
coincidences, &c. is shunned, while the facts are impugned on
the ground of their extraordinary and incredible character,
and of the power of a delusion shared by multitudes while the
intellectual feebleness of such arguments is helped out by exciting pity for the victims of a blind superstition. The testimony is in effect scoffed out of court; but it is yet to have a
hearing before a more impartial tribunal.

The root of this unbelief is taken away in every mind that
has imbibed the truths of the New Church. The view of such
a mind is not limited to the circle of effects. It recognizes a
spiritual sphere, and places causes properly so called exclusively there. There is therefore to it no antecedent improbability
in the idea that men should enter into a compact with evil
spirits, and that they should with their help operate effects
seemingly miraculous. It has no secret interest leading it to
control and distort facts, and it is not unwilling to let those
facts lead it towards the recognition of a spiritual, though
perverted agency. One of such a mind, when he comes
to examine the subject by the light of the New Church,
discovers that there is a positive internal evidence of genuineness about these rejected tales of witchcraft. That very consent between causes and effects which sensualists desiderate
in them he finds, because his causes are other than theirs, and

this becomes to him an argument in their favor. We shall append an example as illustrating this position, after first citing a passage or two, bearing on the subject from Swedenborg.

"That by the Egyptians are signified scientifics contrary to the truths of the Church, is because the representatives and significatives of the Ancient Church, which Church has also been with them, were there turned into magic; for by the representatives, and significatives of the Church at that time there was communication with Heaven, which communication was with those who lived in the good of charity, and with some of them was open; but with those who did not live in the good of charity, but in things contrary to charity, *open communication was sometimes given with evil spirits, who perverted all the truths of the Church, and therewith destroyed goods, whence came magic:* this may likewise be manifest from the hieroglyphics of the Egyptians, which they also employed in sacred things, for by them they signified spiritual things and perverted divine order. Magic is nothing else but the perversion of order, and especially is the abuse of correspondence."—*A. C.* 6692.

From various passages in the Spiritual Diary it appears that the world of spirits as well as hell abounds with magical arts.

The case alluded to, is that of the celebrated Pascal when an infant. We take it from his biography through the German. It is given in the words of Margaret Perier the niece of Pascal, and is as follows.

"When my uncle was a year old there befel him something extraordinary. My grandmother, among her other virtues, was very pious and charitable, and had a large number of poor families to whom she gave a small sum of money every month. Among the poor women to whom she thus distributed alms was one who passed for a witch; all the world called her so. But my grandmother, who was a woman of considerable understanding, and did not belong to the number of these credulous people, laughed at their warnings, and continued to give her alms. It happened at this time that Pascal, then an infant, fell into a sort of decline which is expressed in Paris by the term *tomber en chartre*, which, however, in his case was accompanied by two unusual circumstances. One was, that he could not see water without falling into great agitation. The other was yet more surprising; for he could not endure the sight of his father and mother close together. He would readily suffer himself to be caressed by either of them separately, but as soon as they approached him together, he cried and resisted with the utmost violence. All this lasted for a year, the disease all the while increasing, until he fell into so desperate a state, that they thought he must surely die. Every body told my grand parents that this came without doubt from arts which this witch had practised on the child. They both laughed at the idea, and regarding these speeches as fancies which people are apt to take up when they see things out of the usual course, and therefore observed no precautions against the woman, but allowed her free access to the house to receive her alms. At length my grandfather, out of patience at all that was said to him on the subject, bade the old woman, one day, come into his cabinet; he thought that the way in which he intended to speak to her would give him an opportunity of putting an end to this foolish talk. He was much surprised, to find that, at the first mention of the thing, she answered quietly, that it was not the case, and that people said it of her 'from mere envy at the alms she was receiving. Wishing however to try the effect of fear, he pretended himself, fully satisfied that she had bewitched his child, and threatened her with the gallows, unless she confessed the truth. At this she was much alarmed, and cast herself on her knees before him, declaring she would confess all, if he would promise that her life should be spared.

"My grandfather, greatly astonished at this, asked her what she had done, and what had induced her to do it. She thereupon told him, that she had once applied to him to bring an, action at law for her, and that he had refused, believing that she had not the right on her side; that, seeing how'much he loved his child, she had bewitched him, to avenge herself for this refusal; and that she was sorry to say it was likely to prove fatal. My grandfather exclaimed—'What! I must lose my son then!'—'There is one way to prevent it,' she replied, 'some one on whom the charm can be transferred must die for him.' My grandfather saying, that he would rather have his son die, than any one in his place, she replied, that the spell might be transferred to an animal. My grandfather offered her a horse, but she said it was not necessary to part with any thing so valuable, and that a cat would be enough for her. Thereupon she threw the cat out of the window, and it died, though the fall was only six feet. She asked for another cat, and my grandfather had one brought for her.

"His strong affection for his child made him forget, that before the spell could be transferred the Devil must be invoked anew. This thought, which did not suggest itself until long after, made him regret that he had given any occasion for such a thing.

"The next day the old woman applied to the abdomen of the child a poultice of three different kinds of herbs which a child not yet seven years old had gathered for her. When my grandfather came home from court at noon, he found the whole house and his wife in tears, and was told that the child was dead; he was actually lying apparently so in his cradle. He met the old woman on the stair-case, and gave her such a blow under the ear, that she tumbled over the balustrade to the bottom. When she got up she said that she had forgotten to tell them in the morning, that the child would be apparently dead till midnight, but would then come to again. Although there were all the signs of death about him, his father gave orders to wait the event, though his friends mocked at his credulity in a sort of people so different from his usual habits.

"My grandparents watched by the child's side themselves, not being willing to trust any one else; they heard one hour strike after another, and at length the hour of midnight without discovering any signs of life. At length between twelve and one o'clock, but nearer to one, the child began to gape. All astonished they took him up, and warmed him, and gave him wine and sugar which he swallowed; afterwards he took the breast, but without giving any signs of consciousness, and without opening his eyes; this lasted till six in the morning. As soon as he saw his father and mother together, he began to cry, as usual. They saw from this that he was not yet restored from the effects of the spell, but they comforted themselves by thinking that he was yet alive. Some six or seven days afterwards, he began to bear the sight of water, and as my grandfather returned one day from high mass, he found him amusing himself in his mothers lap with pouring water from one glass into another. He endeavored to approach, but the child could not yet endure him. This came about in a few days more, and in three weeks he was fully recovered and regained his former healthy and plump appearance."

The facts in this case rest upon evidence altogether unexceptionable, and they certainly go to prove that some mischievous power was exerted by the old woman of the kind generally understood by witchcraft. They would have this effect upon any mind not barred against the admission of spiritual principles. But to those who look at the subject in the light of Swedenborg's disclosures, there are circumstances in the account itself which vouch for its genuineness. We may infer the general nature of witchcraft, from those disclosures to be somewhat as follows.

Every man is connected with spirits, and has his life from them. He receives it by the influx of their sphere in the midst of which he is always placed. According to the laws of order this influx of particular spirits does not reach to the body and its senses, that influx being continued into these last according to the general laws of correspondence. The consequence is that though spirits are so closely associated with man that they are in the very affections that he is in, and in thoughts that correspond with his, they have no *sensations* in common with him. This when the connection between them is normal or regular. In cases of witchcraft the influx is into the mind, and also into the things of the body. An influx into the body takes place in all cases of disease, but in ordinary cases, this is from a general sphere of some one of the hells, not from particular spirits with the individual. In these latter cases, the spirits must be to some degree consociated with man in the senses of the body and thereby capable of taking cognizance, with more or less distinctness, of things that transpire in the natural sphere, and of being affected by them according to their correspondences. It is easily understood, on this view of Pascal's state, why he was so affected at the sight of water. Its correspondence being with truth, it was intolerable to the evil spirit or spirits with him, who communicated their feelings to him, and through his cries sought to have it removed. This is illustrated by something parallel in the experience of Swedenborg.

"When I ate butter upon bread, then certain spirits or a society of spirits were so indignant that they threatened evil to my tongue, saying that they could not endure it, for the reason that butter signifies the celestial, whence arises the sphere of the good which the evil cannot bear; wherefore I ought (they said) for a long time to abstain from butter; likewise that one vessel was more agreeable than another, for the sole reason that they thence contracted a sphere which was less spiritual.   So also in regard to many other things which I ate and drank, as milk and the like."—(*S. D.* 3894.)

For a similar reason the child could not bear the sight of his parents together.   It brought upon the spirits with him the sphere of conjugial love which was contrary to their life.   On this point we have the following passage.

"In order that it may be still more distinctly manifest that they [scortatory love and conjugial love] are opposites, it is permitted to relate what I have frequently seen in the spiritual world: when those who in the natural world have been adulterers from what is confirmed, perceive the sphere of conjugial love flowing down out of Heaven immediately they either flee away into caverns and hide themselves, or, if they make themselves obstinate against it, are enraged with fury, and become as furies."—(*D. C. L.* 425.)

To the same effect in the Diary, 6096.

"That, as it were, a fury fires the infernals when they feel the sphere of conjugial love, *I know* from much experience."

Thus it is that an account incredible to those who judge from natural *lumen*, carries its own confirmation with it, when examined according to spiritual principles.

We propose to lay before our readers, at some future time, a remarkable *self-authenticating* case of witchcraft from the judicial records of Germany.

A. E. F.

ARTICLE IV.

AUTHORITY IN MATTERS OF FAITH.

A GREAT deal of unprofitable discussion has existed, and still exists, in Christendom upon the nature and exercise of authority in matters of religious opinion. It has been commonly supposed that we must have some authoritative standard by which to bring all matters of opinion to a test; and for this purpose it has been supposed that some individual, or collection of individuals, must be clothed with authority to determine questions relating to matters of opinion. It has so happened, in nearly all ages of the world, that there has been no want of persons who were ready, either in an individual or collective capacity, to assume and to exercise these functions. The consequence is that *ipse dixits* and dogmatism have been the order of the day, while reason has been nearly banished from the earth. Ecclesiastical history teaches us that nearly all the efforts of ecclesiastical bodies have been for power in this direction. And yet how fruitless in good, if not prolific in evil, have these efforts usually been ! In the attempt to raise a standard of authority to dictate and control opinions, the result has been the opposite of that proposed, as might have been foreseen. One extreme usually begets another, and it is not therefore surprising that a general aversion to authority of all kinds should exist.

Under the influence of the New Dispensation a new order of things is developed. Every thing in the shape of authority or dogmatism in matters of faith, recedes into the back ground, to prepare the way for rational demonstration and perception.

Thus Swedenborg teaches us that man ought to *compel himself* to do good, and to obey the things which the Lord has commanded. Also that "there is a difference between a man's compelling himself, and his being compelled ; for no good can possibly come from being compelled, as when one man is compelled by another to do good : but for a man to compel himself, is to act from a certain free principle unknown to himself: for nothing that is compulsive comes from the Lord. Hence it is a universal law, that all good and truth should be inseminated in freedom, otherwise the ground is not at all recipient and nutritive of good ; nay there is not any ground in which the seed can possibly grow."—(*A. C.* 1937.) He says also that "all reformation is effected by freedom," and that "all worship must be from freedom."

Hence we find that Swedenborg never sets himself up as authority, but goes patiently and quietly at work to set forth his positions, and to illustrate them so that they may be seen in rational light, with the assurance that all who read his works, in a right spirit, will be convinced.

Thus, he says in his work on " Conjugial Love," the things "which are written in this book, have for an end, that the reader may *see truths from his rational*, and thus consent, for thus is his spirit convinced; and the things in which the spirit is convinced, have their place allotted *above those which enter from authority* and its faith without the reason being consulted ; for these do not enter the head more deeply than into the memory, and there commix themselves with fallacies and falses, thus beneath the rational things which are of the understanding; every man can speak from these as it were rationally but preposterously, for he then thinks as a crab walks, the sight follows the tail; it is otherwise if from the understanding; when he speaks from this, then the rational sight selects from the memory things congruous, by means of which it confirms the truth seen in itself."—(*No.* 295.)

Here we see that every thing like authority or dictation in matters relating to reason and the understanding, is repudiated.

In the Word also we are taught thus; "Ye know that the princes of the Gentiles exercise *dominion* over them, and they that are great exercise *authority* upon them. But it shall *not be so among you;* but whosoever will be great among you, let him be your minister; and whosoever will be chief among you, let him be your servant." "To minister," says Swedenborg, "denotes to instruct;" and ministering, as being "to subserve in supplying what another is in want of," &c. By the ministry of Aaron was signified worship and evangelization, "because by evangelization are meant all things which in the Word treat of the Lord, and all things in worship which represented Him; for evangelization is annunciation concerning the Lord, concerning his coming, and concerning those things which are from Him, which relate to salvation and eternal life."—(*A. C.* 9925.) "To serve," says Swedenborg, "denotes study;" and "in the heavens they who are greatest are more servants than others."

It thus appears that mere authoritative or dogmatic expositions of faith form no part of the New Dispensation, and that whoever assumes this course, with that supposition, entirely mistakes its character.

Our Lord says, "be ye not called Rabbi, for one is your Master, even Christ; and *all ye are brethren.*" "And call no man Father upon the earth, for one is your Father which is in heaven. Neither be ye called masters; for one is your master, even Christ."

Hence the true minister never approaches any one in the character of a master, claiming authority, but as a brother who is travelling the same road in the way of regeneration. His efforts are to teach truths, and thereby lead to the good of life. All idea of authority beyond what consists in the rational demonstration of truth is lost sight of; and to this end his suggestions are always ready, where they can be given and received in freedom.   C.

THE PRINCETON REVIEW ON SWEDENBORGIANISM.

(Concluded.)

OUR reviewer has given to his readers another specimen of that peculiar style of controversy which seems to have obtained, as by universal consent, among the assailants of Swedenborg and the New Church, viz., the utter ignoring of all replies previously made to the same objections previously urged; for we never hear of *new* objections. A little novelty of reproach would go a good way towards reconciling us to its malignity. Instead of this, everlasting iteration of the same charges, as if they had never been met and answered, is the *role* of our revilers. Thus it would by no means do to let the reader go unedified by the following stale and sterrotyped slander.

" Some of Swedenborg's writings are worse than wild. The tendency of all of them as we think is to relax the bonds of moral obligation. But some of them sunder every bond of purity, and introduce the wanton and lewd to the paradise of the vile. We do not choose to defile our pages with extracts. But we have never seen or heard of any work more likely to familiarize the mind with the lowest forms of vice than one of Swedenborg's. Those who have read his writings, know to which work we refer. Those who do not know, would not have their useful knowledge increased by our telling them."

We do not altogether feel the force of the logic in this last sentence, for surely if there be any work of Swedenborg's so exceedingly pernicious as this is said to be, the knowledge of its title would at least be " useful," and highly so, in putting men on their guard against it, especially at a time when his works are beginning to be inquired for and read with an avidity hitherto unknown. But passing this, we cannot refrain from pressing our censor with the interrogation, whether he knew, or did not know, that the adherents of Swedenborg universally deny the justice of the charge here constructively brought against his scortatory doctrine, and that they have given at great length their reasons for the denial. The character of these reasons —their soundness or unsoundness—their sufficiency or insufficiency—is not now the question. Did the reviewer know of their existence ? Was he aware that Mr. Bayley and Mr. Smithson in England, Mr. Worcester, Mr. Parsons, Prof. Bush, and Mr. Cabell in this country, had expressly and elaborately expounded the true doctrine of Swedenborg on this head and claimed, at least, *to* have confuted the cavils of opponents ? If he knew not the

fact, he *should* have known it, or devolved the task assumed
upon those who had some knowledge of what had been done by
predecessors in the same line of debate.   If he did know it,
then we should be pleased to learn the kind of casuistry by
which he justifies an entire disregard of our arguments.   We
trust he does not impute to us the stupidity of believing either
Swedenborg or Paul without reasons which we deem adequate
to sustain our faith.   It is with these *reasons* that we request
our adversaries to deal.   Even if they deem them utterly worthless and contemptible, still we hold it a demand of equity, or at
least of courtesy, that they should say so, and give us some inkling of a ground for their judgment.   But our stern reviewer
obstinately refuses to concede to us even the slight boon that
formed the burden of the lamentation of honest Dogberry in
the play; "O that I had been writ down an ass!"   This were
too great a stretch of Princetonian grace towards such an unmitigated heresy.   Accordingly neither here nor elsewhere
throughout the critique do we meet with the least intimation
that a sentence had ever been penned by an apologist in vindication of Swedenborg's doctrine.   Yet this is the man who
coolly takes it upon him to say, that the tendency of all Swedenborg's writings is, in his opinion, to relax the bonds of moral
obligation!   We shall heed his sentence more when we see
more evidence that he is entitled to pronounce it.   We recognize but a very weak sense of "moral obligation" in one who
can hold up to ridicule or contempt the features of a religious
system which thousands of sensible men regard as coming directly from God out of heaven, without even adverting, in the
remotest way, to the various pleas which its advocates have put
forth in its behalf.   Nor is it very easy for us to perceive how
a system that is not worthy of being *argued with* is of sufficient
importance to be worthy of being *exposed.*

But although we can have no hope that our reply will reach
a hundredth or a thousandth part of the readers of his aspersions,
yet from courtesy to our opponent, we will put forth in debate
what would be an *opus operatum* in morals.   Even at the risk
of "thrice slaying the slain," we will encounter his cavil hand
to hand, and not only name the baleful book, but reaffirm its
most pointed positions.

The work, then, about which such dark and horrible things
are hinted is a treatise concerning "Conjugial Love," to which
is appended at the close another minor work entitled "The
Pleasures of Insanity concerning Scortatory Love."   In this
latter tractate he has given a virtual commentary on the precept of the Decalogue,—"Thou shalt not commit adultery."
His object is to do what no Protestant theologian has ever done,

to lay open from its inmost grounds the entire *morale* of the seventh commandment. In accomplishing this object he has, with a masterly power of analysis, *discriminated* between the different degrees of guilt which attach to the greater or less departure from the strict rules of chastity. " The head and front of his offending hath this extent, no more." Viewed in the light of Criminal Jurisprudence, it bears the same relation to the command " Thou shalt not commit adultery," as the statute law on the different degrees of manslaughter does to the command " Thou shalt not kill." The statute laws wisely discriminate between murder and manslaughter in the first, second and third degrees, awarding a different degree of penalty to each. But who, for that reason, would think of charging the laws with "laxity of morals," or with encouraging murder? Yet the charge of encouraging vice has as little foundation in truth when applied to Swedenborg as it would have if applied to the laws. He discriminates the sins under this head into eight degrees, and teaches that the greater the departure from the right, the greater the sin and consequent penalty, and, of course, the slighter the departure from strict rectitude, the less grievous the sin and consequent penalty. He shows how, when a man's heart appears to be fully set in him to do evil in this respect, he may be restrained from plunging into still greater evils than he is already in the practice of, and how he may be led into a state of comparatively less evil, and finally back into the paths of true virtue. In all this there is no intimation that *any* such practices are anything else than grievous sins, which are to be even more strenuously striven against than other sins : which is a reason for his being more minute. His constant language in regard to them is, that they are " vile," " detestable to christians," and " lead to hell."

Now in reference to this whole subject, the real question at issue, and with which the reviewer is called to grapple, is whether the propositions of Swedenborg are not in themselves *strictly true*. When he shall have shown, or attempted to show, that they are not, his essays on this head will begin to acquire some logical value. As to saying that he "does not choose to defile his pages with extracts," we would submit whether his pages are not morally much more defiled by ominous inuendos which excite prejudice without specifying its grounds, then by an open exposure of the offensive doctrines, from which *we* never shrink when they are *fully* and *fairly* declared with all the author's distinctions, qualifications, and caveats. It is the distorted and garbled presentation of the views advanced of which we complain, and of the fact, that *our* explanations and vindications never receive the slightest attention.

To the insinuated charge on the score of offensive language, we oppose a direct *negatur*. We affirm, on the contrary, that, considering the nature of the subject discussed, it would scarcely be possible to manage the diction with more tact, with a nicer sense of delicacy and decorum, then Swedenborg has done. There is no ground for the critic's charge, provided the theme is proper to be treated *at all* by the Christian moralist, and this we presume he will hardly deny. The effect of delicate allusions depends very much upon the relations in which they are introduced, and our reviewer, who is so chary of his pages, might feel just as sensitive as to extracts from the various works which treat of Physiology, Anatomy, and Medical Jurisprudence. Even the Bible itself affords specimens of phraseology which he would probably be very backward to parade in quotations when dislocated from their connexion, and having no view to a palpable *use*. In fact, the method of treating this department of Swedenborg's writings (which, by the way, is a very small department), exhibits a species of warfare to which no mind of a generous and philosophical cast would ever descend. Such a mind would not fail to see that there are grand moral *principles* involved in this, as there are in every part of the controversy relating to Swedenborg, which frown upon the petty cavilings and invidious tirades so often resorted to by our opponents. But what face does the discussion for the most part present? Grave and reverend Clergymen and Professors of Theology in our Seminaries are seen almost invariably to hurry slightingly over the great body of Swedenborg's works, reaching to twenty or thirty volumes, and covering the whole field of Theology with a force of argument and illustration of which it is impossible for a candid mind to speak lightly, and throughout which not an immodest word would be noticed, and heedless of all the profound philosophy and spiritual wisdom which they encounter on the way, they light upon, or rather pounce upon, a little tract of 80 or 90 pages, forming a sequel to another volume, and this they seem *to know all about*; giving room to the suspicion that this is the only one of Swedenborg's works which they have really *had the endurance to read*. We could wish, for their own sakes, that they would consent to pause over other portions—that they would open their minds to the teachings of the "Arcana," for instance, and ponder those developments of the working of the interior life in the process of regeneration; and then see how much heart they would have to dwell, in the way of reproach, upon the scortatory doctrines. They would soon feel the forceful pressure of another question;— "Whence hath this man this wisdom?" Every thing else would comparatively die out of sight till the problem was solved whether they were listening to a message from God or to the lucubrations of a mortal. If the writer speaks as he is moved by a higher power, then dissentients have a controversy to settle before another tribunal. This is an issue which is yet assuredly to be made.

In conclusion on this head, we have only to say that while yielding a cordial credence to the divine mission of Swedenborg we hold no doctrines which go in the slightest degree to loosen the bonds of moral obligation. We claim, on the other hand, that rightly construed they have a direct tendency to strengthen the bonds and elevate the tone of a sound and scriptural morality. In proof of this we appeal, first, to the great body of Swedenborg's theological works, and, secondly, to the uniform tenor of our own publications. Let us be brought as religious teachers to this ordeal, and by this accordingly let us be condemned or acquitted.

A few miscellaneous paragraphs occurring here and there through the article demand a passing notice.

" Until we read for ourselves, we had no conception of the extent of Swedenborg's assaults upon fundamental truths and principles."

We are forced to precisely the same acknowledgment in regard to John Calvin, and the Presbyterian Confession of Faith. The avowal on the one side has just as much logical weight, and just as little, as it has on the other. Meantime the intelligent reader would probably suggest the propriety of some attempt to determine on which side it is that the aforesaid "fundamental truths and principles" are held. For this we are ready whenever called upon.

" This rejection of *thirty two* books is an open and arbitrary act of infidelity; and no reason can be given why we may not, upon like grounds, renounce the whole word of God. We are therefore constrained to admit that Swedenborgianism is strongly tinctured with the spirit of infidelity."

As we are furnished with no data by which to judge how strong was the constraint under which this admission was wrung from the critic, or of the heartfelt sorrow and grief that attended it, we may perhaps properly hold our sympathy at bay until further enlightened on that head. In the mean while we trust the reviewer will allow us to extract a little gleam of hope and comfort under his sentence from the fact, that we are unable to recognize *any rejection at all* in the case. Our reasons we have given above. To much of the same stamp in this connection we make the same reply.

"It is as much an act of infidelity to add to the word of God as to take from it. The theological writings of Swedenborg claim, not to be conjectures, nor philosophical reasonings, nor uninspired interpretations, but to be revelations, and in one sense of a higher order than the writings of the prophets themselves."

It is one thing for man unauthorized to add to the word of God, and another for God himself to add to it, not in the form of new canonical scripture, but in the form of supplemental disclosure designed to elucidate what he had already revealed. This we affirm that he has done through Swedenborg as an instrument, and though we are not in the habit of making comparisons between his revelations and those of the prophets, yet we do not hesitate to regard them as *revelations*, and we have waited long, but thus far in vain, for an answer to the *reasons* which determine our faith in this particular.

"His biographer claims for him that he understood all he wrote, but that the prophets did not understand what they wrote. Thus we suppose he intends to prefer him in the matter of inspiration."

What he intends is comparatively a matter of little moment. The question is, whether Swedenborg understood what he wrote, and whether, *in this respect*, his state was higher than that of the prophets. But as this question involves the real merits of the whole controversy, it will of course be declined.

"There is no doubt that his followers do claim for him the very highest character that a servant of God could have. Practically they put his writings before those of the prophets. They do 'take Swedenborg's disclosures as the standard of every thing' which has a relation to the unseen world."

And right glad should we be to be informed why we should *not* take them as such a standard. If the critic will condescend to enlighten us on this head, and show wherein lies the fallacy of the confidence we repose in these disclosures, he will perform a service which we shall gratefully acknowledge. But we warn him it must be something more than a mere asserted *a priori* objection against the idea of any new revelations from heaven. We see no argument in such an objection, because we see no logical or scriptural ground on which it rests. As at present advised we see every authentication of Swedenborg's disclosures which we could reasonably desire, and therefore receive them and rest in them with the utmost strength of assurance.

"Swedenborgians also deny the doctrine of the Trinity as understood and received in the Christian world."

And so, on the other hand, the Christian world denies the doctrine of the Trinity as understood and received by Swedenborgians. It is as broad as it is long. When the writer will clearly define the doctrine of the Trinity as held by the Christian world, we shall be better able to judge of the enormity of our offence on this score. He seems to be astonished that we can acknowledge a Trinity at all consistently with our denial of three persons in the Godhead, and New Churchmen will perceive from the following extract what reason they have to tremble in view of their sentiments on this head.

"We have strenuously endeavored to understand the Swedenborgian doctrine concerning the Trinity. In brief it seems to be this, that Jesus Christ is the Father, Son, and Holy Ghost."

How it has happened that this sentence is not followed by some half a score of exclamation points, is to us somewhat of a wonder, as the writer evidently regards the doctrine as the height of absurdity, if not of impiety. Yet probably most of us will go to our graves with this grand lie, *if it be one*, in our right hand; and not only so, it will be the staff in that hand to sustain us in walking through the dark valley.

In denouncing Swedenborg's teachings on the subject of Atonement, Justification, Regeneration, &c. he has done the system the favor of adducing a number of confirmatory extracts for which we are profoundly grateful, as we are very willing to let them stand by the side of his disclaimer. The doctrines thus gain a partial hearing in quarters where they would otherwise be little likely to obtain any, and inquiry will occasionally be promoted by the very means taken to stifle it. In what follows we forbear comment, except in regard to one or two of the paragraphs cited.

"We have called it above 'a system' but we used the term for the want of a better. It is a maze, a howling wilderness, a dreary waste of confusion and impiety."

"There is little in these doctrines offensive to the pride or lust of the natural mind."

"Our readers will ere this have gathered that we do not regard the New Church doctrines as innocent or inoffensive."

"In other words Swedenborgianism is essential to salvation. Let not the friends of truth fear to oppose this bold and impudent error."

"As to the mode of treating this delusion; * * *" &c.

"The recent attempts to propagate Swedenborgian doctrines in some parts of our country have been anything but candid and fair. Indeed in reading the books and tracts sent out by the New Church, hardly anything has struck us more forcibly than the attempt to inveigle and deceive the unwary. Especially is this true of the smaller publications. They contain the less exceptionable opinions of Swedenborg and his followers, and are circulated with great industry in order to prepare the way for other things, which will come in due time. We are not surprised at this. Paul and Christ and the prophets long since told us that guile would mark the course of errorists. It has ever been so. It will be so to the end of the world. The world has never yet seen and will never see a zealous propagator of dangerous doctrines, who has been or shall be candid and fair and open in his avowals."

Upon this we have something to say, as in this department we have had something to do. The charge of unfairness and want of candor here brought against New Churchmen in disseminating their views, receives its point from the imputed design of inveigling and deceiving the unwary. The intimation is very express of a Jesuitical style of propagandism. The choicer and less exceptionable portions of the works are culled out and sent abroad as *avant-couriers* of the deadly missives which are to follow in their train. Having had ourselves some humble agency in this sphere of effort, and knowing well the views of others, our co-laborers in the same field, we take it upon us, in our name and theirs, utterly and unequivocally to deny the fact of any such sinister intention as that here gravely charged by the reviewer. That we have dispersed somewhat freely several of the minor tracts and treatises both of Swedenborg and his adherents is undoubtedly true; but that we have any *corps de reserve* of publications of a different character with which to follow them up, is as far from the truth as such a policy would be from the morality of the New Church. The object aimed at in our tract distribution is, by means of certain striking views of truth therein presented, to create such an interest in the system, from the specimens afforded, as shall lead the reader to form an acquaintance with the larger works, and thus to judge for himself of their character and claims. It is a proceeding very similar to what might be, and we believe has been, adopted by missionaries among the heathen, viz., to select and publish and circulate certain portions of the Sacred Scriptures, before the whole were printed, in order if possible to awaken a desire in the minds of the readers to become possessed of the treasure of the entire volume. Is there anything unfair or uncandid in this, even though the missionary should see fit, in his selections, to fix upon such parts of the Word as would not uselessly shock the prejudices of his heathen readers? Would it be either "fair" or "candid" for a Brahmin priest, for instance, to come out in a flaming protest against the measure, and accuse the missionary of endeavoring to "inveigle and de-

illustrate the manner in which the Lord's servants were received, at his Second Coming, by some of that body which professed to be his Church, just as we now refer to the opprobious epithets applied to the early Christians contained in the writings of Suetonius, Tacitus, and Pliny.

[The engagements of the writer of the first part of this article being such as to prevent him from furnishing the matter in season for our present number, the responsibility of continuing the reply has been assumed by the Editor.]

SELECTIONS.

EXTRACTS FROM SWEDENBORG'S SPIRITUAL DIARY.

(NOW FIRST TRANSLATED FROM THE ORIGINAL LATIN.)

That Spirits are bound to speak as they think.

3976. When a spirit speaks otherwise then he thinks, the fact is immediately perceived, wherefore he is compelled to a truthful mode of speaking; otherwise he cannot be conjoined with any society, but all such are instantly cast out and maimed. Such a thing disturbs and disjoins societies; wherefore in the other life it is not allowable for one to speak otherwise than as he thinks. If he is bad or thinks badly, it is permitted him also to speak badly, because he thus thinks; for in this case he speaks truth, inasmuch as it is not lawful for him to utter any thing but truth, that is, what is true to him; and this principle extends so far that one who thinks evil, speaks evil, thus what is true, since he is evil; and so on.

Concerning the Lord.

3990. Evil spirits, according to their wont, are continually in falsities and negations concerning the Lord, and when they infused something respecting the angels, it was given to demand of them that they should show me, if they could, one single angel, or point to one heaven where they are in all wisdom, in intelligence, in mutual love, in truth, in light,—that they should point (I say) to any angels or any heaven except those which acknowledge the Lord as the life of all, and that from Him they derive every thing which they are taught, and their happiness also. But they were not able, whereas, if there were any

" intercourse with spirits," which is evidently intended as an opprobrium, we should be less at a loss for a reply if we knew whether the writer would himself be understood as denying the fact of any such intercourse at all.   He is doubtless a *professed* believer in the divine revelations of the Bible, and they surely are not lacking in the most explicit affirmations on this head. We hope he will not charge our faith, in this matter, as a crime, if he is himself in the same condemnation.   If his meaning be that, not of *real*, but of *open* and *sensible* intercourse with spirits, then we have only to admonish him that an excellent preliminary to a round assertion of a fact is a competent knowledge of the grounds on which it is made.   This preliminary is very palpably wanting in the present case.

It would be an easy matter to adduce a still longer string of just such pearls of truth and charity as we have shown to hang around the neck of the tenant of one of the niches in the pagoda of the Princeton Review.   But the parade is as useless as it would be tedious.   Our refutation of the falsities continually uttered against the New Church could only be important in quarters where it will be sure not to be read.   It is a one-sided warfare that is waged against us.   The vehicle of the assault is never the vehicle of the defence.   The assault itself, moreover, is never against the fundamental principles of the system, but always against its salient points of detail.   No pen is wielded against its positions *viewed in themselves*, but only as arrayed by the side of the acknowledged formulas of the Church.   These are infallible of course, and every intimation to the contrary too contemptible to be met by argument. Of no form of " heretical pravity" does this hold more pre-eminently than of that known as *Swedenborgianism.*   Nearly every other phasis of error will stand some little chance of being argumentatively debated, but not this.   It is too low a condescension for orthodoxy to bestow upon Swedenborg or his adherents aught but *exposure.*   This, however, is a policy perhaps best adapted to promote the good, and eventually the growth, of the New Church.   Shut out from the field of honorable controversy we are prompted to turn more inwardly upon ourselves, and to make it a study so to regulate our lives as to falsify whatever of evil may be spoken against us.   The time, however, of mere vilification, we are persuaded, will not be of very long duration.   The system of Swedenborg will inevitably ere long loom up to the eye of Christendom in all its colossal dimensions and its irresistible claims, nor will the time fail to come when such passages as those cited above from our reviewer will be cited again, not to be confuted, of which they will then be seen to be too trivial to be worthy, but to illustrate the manner in which the Lord's servants were received, at his Second Coming, by some of that body which professed to be his Church, just as we now refer to the opprobious epithets applied to the early Christians contained in the writings of Suetonius, Tacitus, and Pliny.

[The engagements of the writer of the first part of this article being such as to prevent him from furnishing the matter in season for our present number, the responsibility of continuing the reply has been assumed by the Editor.]

SELECTIONS.

EXTRACTS FROM SWEDENBORG'S SPIRITUAL DIARY.

(NOW FIRST TRANSLATED FROM THE ORIGINAL LATIN.)

That Spirits are bound to speak as they think.

3976. When a spirit speaks otherwise then he thinks, the fact is immediately perceived, wherefore he is compelled to a truthful mode of speaking; otherwise he cannot be conjoined with any society, but all such are instantly cast out and maimed. Such a thing disturbs and disjoins societies; wherefore in the other life it is not allowable for one to speak otherwise than as he thinks. If he is bad or thinks badly, it is permitted him also to speak badly, because he thus thinks; for in this case he speaks truth, inasmuch as it is not lawful for him to utter any thing but truth, that is, what is true to him; and this principle extends so far that one who thinks evil, speaks evil, thus what is true, since he is evil; and so on.

Concerning the Lord.

3990. Evil spirits, according to their wont, are continually in falsities and negations concerning the Lord, and when they infused something respecting the angels, it was given to demand of them that they should show me, if they could, one single angel, or point to one heaven where they are in all wisdom, in intelligence, in mutual love, in truth, in light,—that they should point (I say) to any angels or any heaven except those which acknowledge the Lord as the life of all, and that from Him they derive every thing which they are taught, and their happiness also. But they were not able, whereas, if there were any such they certainly could have done it within so long a space as three years and a half, but they were never able.

3991. It was perceived that all the reflections which a man exercises, as in regard to seeing and looking out for himself while he walks, besides others elsewhere spoken of; in a word, that he enjoys the use of his senses—this he has solely from the Lord, from whose influx it is that he exercises a general reflection enabling him to avoid injury from the persons and things that he meets with. All this arises from a certain general reflection or advertence which flows in from the Lord's care towards every one, and without which reflection is never enjoyed; and so in other things.

Concerning Sirens.

4019. It was shown how the sirens hold those bound whom they endeavor to obsess, viz. that (they pervert) all the influx from the angels, which is continual, whenever evil spirits induce evil; the angels then avert it, and react against it. But whenever permission is granted to sirens, they would enter into the interior of thoughts, and by perverting, turn away every thing which flowed from heaven. Thus whithersoever my own thought was directed, still it was turned to evil, and that to such a degree that I was at length so wearied by it as to be induced to desist from writing, for it was then especially that they flowed in, and, as was also perceived, into interior things with which it had not then been given me to become so well acquainted. They have the eyes, as it were, of serpents, which seem to possess sight or ideas on every side, giving them a kind of ubiquity of presence.

4020. It was perceived and heard that both the deceitful and most deceitful above the head adjoined themselves to them, and flowed through them, whom I also heard and learned their machinations; and when it was said to them that they should desist, or they would be reduced to a miserable state if they persevered, they said they could not by any possibility desist.

Concerning the Memory of Spirits.

4313. I heard a certain spirit speaking with another. I was acquainted with both in the life of the body. He described the genius and character of the other, and what opinion he had of him, and then (recited) a letter which he had written and many other things in a series. The other acknowledged the whole and was silent. Hence it may manifestly appear that spirits have a memory of material things (*particularium*,) but it is not allowed them to draw upon it except when the

Lord permits. He afterwards said that he knew a great many other particulars and was desirous to produce them, but he was not permitted.

Concerning the State of Fear.

4314. There was a spirit who wished to frighten infants that were seen. He was concealed with me at the lower quarter behind, but he was manifested by a knife which he put into the hand of another, by whom however it was rejected and thus fell back into his own, in consequence of which he was disclosed. He then began to supplicate with the greatest earnestness, for he was one who wished to appear good in the other life. He made use of such humble terms that the spirits could scarcely believe that he was any other than he seemed to be. Conversation was then had on the state of fear, as to which it was said, that when such persons are in a state of fear it cannot be known but that they are good, or can become good. The spirit in this case would fain have been suppliant towards the Lord, and said he was willing to dwell in the lowest hell, and that he knew that he deserved it; but it was all the effect of fear; being inspected by the angels they said that he was infernal, wherefore he was cast down thither.

Concerning Comedians in the other Life.

4315. Conversing with comedians in the other life, I found that they were such as could simulate everything, or seize upon and represent it in such a dexterous manner that it could scarcely be distinguished from the original. For this reason they serve societies as mediums of lively representation. They were not evil, nor were they easily excited to anger. When any one inveighed against them, they seemed to take no notice of it at the time, though they spake of it afterwards. They can be led both by the evil and the good. They represent the teeth, which was also shown by their being made to appear as injured and aching teeth. Although they speak tolerably well, yet they have but little life of their own.

Concerning Speech.

4316. There was an evil spirit who when he said anything good could only do it in so low a voice that it scarcely seemed to be speaking at all. The cause was stated to me, viz. that he thought concerning good, and said that he wished to be good, but because such was not his quality, he could not speak distinctly. When one thinks concerning anything that does not agree with his nature, he has not the power of clear utterance. If he speaks at all it is as if he were absent, or at a distance, and the angels perceive just how far distant. Wherefore speech is of the mind or nature. But if they do not think, then they can speak so as to be plainly heard; in that case, however, it is not from the heart or the nature, but only from the mouth.

Concerning the End and the Life of Spirits thence, (and concerning) Memory.

4324. It is not permitted to spirits to be such towards each other as they were in their social relations in the body, namely in externals, as, for instance, in well-seeming but fictitious externals, for all externals are abolished in the other life, as also actions merely external, whether good or evil, so that nothing then acts from the external, as in the world, but the quality of each one's thought and affection (is then discovered) from internals, thus from the end and the love, and by this is their conversation and intercourse with each other governed. They are sometimes remitted into externals, but only for a short time, and then they speak otherwise than as they think, and act otherwise than as they will, as is the case with many preachers; but as soon as their externals are taken away they are no more known; they become different persons; and their ends and loves are laid open. Thus all their (external) acts are abolished. Some say, while in externals, that they have never injured any one, that they have been upright, that they have preached, that they have done many good things for the Church; but when their external substances are removed, the quality of their ends, and the quality of their loves is laid open, and some are found to be such as to have done evil from ignorance with a good end; these are of the better sort; for the same reason, neither is the memory of material things granted.

That in the other Life there are no such external Things as there were in the Body, but of internal Things there are.

4325. I conversed with spirits respecting the external things pertaining to man during his life in the body, that they all have respect to human society, to wit, to functions and honors. riches, houses, clothing, subsistence for themselves and theirs, and distinction on these accounts. These are the ends of external life in the world. But in the other life they do not think of honors, riches, houses, clothing, or food; wherefore they have no need of those external things that minister to decorum and respectability, and of various other things, which men are prone to affect. Externals ought to cease with the cessation of such uses, wherefore a man, when he comes into the other life, is separated from them, especially because they are assumed and disagree with internals. He is therefore left to his internals such as distinguished him during his life-time, and in which his life must be supposed to have consisted. Spirits however are indignant that it is not permitted them to live in external show, in which while they remained they appeared respectable notwithstanding they were interiorly in evil, which was the case with some preachers, who said they had preached, instructed, and done good, while they were in externals. They thus spoke well, as they did while in the world, by applying the things of the Word, but as soon as they were remitted into internals they were seen to be diabolical, for then their former ends appeared, which were of self-honor, wealth, hatreds and malignities, and the like. It is wonderful that they do not know this while they are in such externals, for their thoughts are engrossed by them; but it is all laid open when their externals are removed.

MISCELLANY.

The following extract of a recent letter from Dr. Tafel contains some items of information which will be interesting to most of our readers.

TUBINGEN, Aug. 10th, 1848.

—— The parcel will contain P. IV. of the "Regnum Animale" published the first time from E. Swedenborg's own hand-writing, sent me by the "Swedenborg Association" of London (together with that on the Mind and that on Generation), and the said P. IV. will not leave the press before two months. * * * * * * * * You wish an account of my present labors, and when you may expect the forth-coming "Adversaria." I answer that I have already sent the second vol. of P. I. to Mr. Wilkins of Boston, but only 30 copies. This work was principally supported and its publication made possible by the London Printing Society, but this Society wrote me by Mr. Bateman, formerly their Treasurer (June 2, 1848), "Being present when the propriety of taking more of the Diarium and Adversaria was discussed, I offered to write to you for the purpose of acquainting you with their determination on that point. I have therefore to inform you that the state of the Society's funds absolutely compels them to forego the prospect of taking any more of these works at all, and I am directed to acquaint you with this lamentable fact lest you should be going on with the printing of any more in the expectation that they will be taken by the Printing Society at some future period. Of this there is no probability whatever, for even if the Society should recover itself in a few years, the impolicy of locking up its funds in those works is so thoroughly felt, that it is utterly improbable they would, even at the expiration of 8 or 10 years, be disposed to take more than twenty-five copies of each."—Now as there remains still vol. 3—5, together with the "Analekta," from the very originals to such parts of the Diary and Adversaria which were not published from the originals themselves, but from vicious copies, I do not know at present by what other means the Lord will enable me to publish them. I am sure that if I will be in the necessity to send back the manuscripts to the Academy of Stockholm, this Royal Society will not give them out of her rooms a second time. Therefore either now or never they will be preserved by publication. On account of want of means I cannot publish all parts also of the scientific manuscripts at present in hands, but some parts must be reserved to Analekta for the case that afterwards there will be means for them according to the determination of the Swedenborg Association. At present also I am preparing "Hours of Devotion and Meditation on the Doctrines of Christianity," which shall contain our system with its reasons, but without the learned apparatus. As we have the permission of full religious liberty, we thought also that the time is come to invite a General Conference of the receivers and friends of the New Church for Oct. 1, 1848, to Constatt near Stuttgard, for which purpose I wrote a short confession or sketch of our belief with its reasons, of which I send you here inclosed the correction-sheet (for it is not yet printed): short advertisements in reference to it shall appear in some newspapers. In November last I published also my "Fundamental Philosophy in its Genetical Development," with the history of every problem, P. I. On a favorable sentence upon it given by the philosophical faculty of this University, our King gave me by Decree of 8 Dec. 1847, the title and rank of "Professor of Philosophy."

* * * * * I fear only that a great part of our people will confound liberty with anarchy, and we shall have a civil war, especially as there are in many parts of Germany, principally in Prussia, many people who have peculiar or separate interests and no feeling of the absolute necessity of German unity. They oppose their Prussia to an united Germany, whilst only by our unity we are mighty and can resist the barbarism from the East, which could only overcome for some time in consequence of such separations. Your United States on the contrary is our natural friend. Every sound mind with us however wishes no violent change, as our states are different from yours, the majority of the Germans will retain or conserve the monarchy, but with a republican foundation, so that all legislative power lies nevertheless in the people and we have all liberties as the republicans, with all sureties.

A principal point of our General Conference, if it will be held, would be convenient institutions for the education and convenient instruction of our children. But I must conclude. In hope to be soon rejoiced by an answer, I beg to salute heartly all friends and brethren, and remain with much esteem and fraternal regard, Yours,

EMAN. TAFEL.

It will be seen from the foregoing that mention is made of a proposed Convention in October of the friends of the New Church in Germany and of an Address prepared by Dr. Tafel for the occasion. We have received a copy of the original, a translation of which by the Editor of the Intellectual Repository we here insert.

"It has been truly observed, that the time has certainly come, when not only the constitution of states but also the doctrines of a renovated Christianity, purified from the traditions of men, shall be brought under solemn consideration. This, however, cannot be done in mixed ecclesiastical assemblies, where the parties are not yet agreed as to the primary and leading points; but in smaller circles in which the persons assembled have the same foundation of faith, and who thus prepared, come together in a greater assembly, in order that they may build upon the common foundation, and unite their energies and co-operate together for the sake of the Church, and its establishment amongst men. Such circles have already long been formed in most countries of the cultivated world, and also in Germany and Switzerland, and in these meetings or conventions the parties agree in the following declaration of faith : —

"God is love, wisdom, and life itself, and this Trinity has existed not only from all eternity in one Person, but also, when the fulness of time had come, it came forth into the world, by the assumption of human nature, and was manifest in the incarnate God, in whom, as the apostle observes, "all the fulness of the Godhead dwelleth bodily" (Col. ii. 9), and who, as he declares, "has all power in heaven and on earth," and who is "the judge of the living and the dead." This incarnation, or this God-becoming-Man, was a necessity not only for this earth, but for all other earths in the universe upon which human beings exist, and not only for man on this side the tomb, but for angels and spirits on the other side, or in the spiritual world, who are in close connection with mankind here. For the thought of God as an impersonal being, who is the Infinite and Invisible, is, without being able to find a resting place, dissipated and falls to nothing ; and because God, who should be loved above all things, must necessarily have made himself accessible to the thought and the heart, and in his Humanity have drawn near to man, and exhibited his perfections in his acts. But this incarnation of God happened once for all, and according to the eternal laws of divine order grounded in his own nature, upon our earth in consequence of the relation which it bears to the universal system of worlds. Inasmuch as God is pure, disinterested, unselfish love, the end of his creation, (which is not a creation out of nothing, but, as the Scripture says, out of Himself,) can only contemplate free beings, to whom he can communicate himself, and thereby bless them and form them into a heavenly kingdom. For if men were mere instruments, and not free rational beings, God, contrary to his inmost nature, in communicating himself to them, would have only loved himself, nor could he have formed a heavenly kingdom of the human race. Men, therefore, must needs have been created free and with the possibility of falling, that is, constituted with a two-fold organization, with which a spiritual and unselfish tendency, and also an earthly and selfish tendency, are connected, this latter tendency, if not duly subordinate, being opposed to the former. so that man is placed in the middle, free to allow either the one tendency or the other to prevail within him. All evil arises from the prevalence of the earthly and selfish over the spiritual and unselfish tendency. The earthly and selfish tendency is, however, in itself not evil, but evil arises when this tendency prevails over the other. This fall and its natural consequences, God could not prevent, without changing his nature and the laws of his being, which we know is impossible. What God, in such a case, according to the established order of his unchangeable nature and operations, could do in order to help and restore his fallen creature, was to preserve the possibility of being restored, and to provide the necessary means and institutions for that purpose. No *guilt* was inherited by the posterity of the fallen race,—that is, no evils for which they were responsible,—they did, however, inherit an hereditary tendency to evil, which when unrestrained and indulged, must necessarily unfit them for happiness in that spiritual world which is inseperably connected with their spiritual organization ; because every man after he lays down his material body, takes himself, that is, his very being and nature, which he in freedom, has contracted and made his own, into that world; and it is only the unselfish tendency of the love of God operating in the soul, which makes a man capable of true and lasting happiness. That hereditary tendency to evil must, by the actual sins of succeeding generations, have been increased, and at length have become so strong, that regeneration or preparation for heaven would have been impossible, had not God in his infinite love and pity, by the assumption of our nature, have become our Redeemer, and accomplished universal redemption by subjugating the hells, and by glorifying his Humanity. This divine work He accomplished according to the laws of his own divine order. So infinitely important was this work, that had it not been performed, both the natural and the spiritual worlds must have perished; for evil spirits would, by the departure of wicked men from the world, have so much increased in the world of spirits, as to have rendered the operation of God through heaven of none effect upon the minds of men; Hence no flesh could have been saved if "God had not been manifest in the flesh," to work out redemption by destroying these works of the devil, and delivering mankind from their infernal bondage. The Humanity which he assumed could on the one side reach into the deepest depths of human degradation, and hence " save to the uttermost," by drawing them to himself; —thus his Humanity, on the one side, partook of our nature and its hereditary tendencies to evil; and on the other, that is, in its inmost ground, was united with the Father himself, and thus he had the power of overcoming the hereditary tendency to every thing evil and false, and of subjugating the powers of darkness connected therewith. In this manner he gradually put off everything inherited from the mother, and thus glorified his Humanity and made it divine. By this means he also restored and established the spiritual equilibrium between heaven and hell, and secured freedom to the human mind, that it might freely love and choose what is good and true, and thus be saved. In this way he also established order in both worlds, which, by the Spirit proceeding from his glorified Humanity, he can constantly and eternally uphold and preserve. He thus really took upon himself and bore the sins of the world, not by imputation, but by inheritance from a mother, whose nature was sunk in the common depravity; and by means of this human nature he made himself accessible to temptations, which he in all cases overcame by the Father, or essential Divinity dwelling within him. Hence he became, as the apostle says, " perfect through sufferings," or temptations, the last of which was the passion of the cross, by which he completed the work of redemption and of glorification, and finally ascended above the heavens, that he might enter into his glory, and exercise all power in heaven and on earth.

"Now if the spiritual freedom and power by which mankind could thus be saved, were again restored, it is evident that the divine justice, that is, the divine order, was satisfied, and a universal forgiveness of sins could be proclaimed. But it was not God who was reconciled,— and by no means through the shedding of the blood, and the death of an innocent victim,—for God had never ceased to love mankind, and his *justice* is not *injustice*,—nor Asiatic despotism,—but mankind who were his enemies were reconciled, that is, by redemption they were placed in a friendly relation to God. Hence the apostle nowhere says, that " *God was reconciled to the world*," but the contrary, that " *God was in Christ reconciling the world to himself*." But individual reconciliation with God, and consequent salvation, can only be realized in man in proportion as he avails himself of the divine power procured by redemption, and performs actual repentance by turning away from evil because it is a sin against God, and by allowing the Lord's Spirit to prevail within him, and in this manner to feed on his Flesh and Blood, (of which bread and wine in the Holy Supper are the corresponding symbols,) and to appropriate them in faith and love by keeping the divine commandments. Men, therefore, are by no means saved (as is sometimes stated by objectors against the New Church) by their own merit ; it is, however, most true, that we are saved by the reception and appropriation of the Lord's gifts of love and faith, and of the fruits which proceed from the heavenly marriage or union of those two divine principles ; so that faith can by no means be placed in opposition to love or charity and good works, for as the Apostle says, the only thing that availeth is '*the faith which worketh by love ;*' and again, ' *If I have all faith, so that I could remove mountains, and have not love or charity, I am nothing.*' Again says the apostle, ' *Every one will be judged according to his works, according to what he hath done in the body.*' He therefore who '*hath the faith¶working by love,*' is, as the¶Lord says, not condemned, but he who has not this faith is already condemned, for he thereby manifests his preverse state and disposition, which is incapable of salvation, and is consequently of his own accord separated from heaven,—'*he shuns the light because his deeds are evil.*'

"Every man, after the death of his material body, continues to live in a spiritual body, with all his senses and mental powers far more acute, and his ' works do follow him.' These departed souls, however, who had left the world in a mixed state of good and evil, and who, in consequence, were not decided in their character, remained in the world of spirits, or the intermediate world between heaven and hell, until the time of the harvest, when a general judgment would be performed, by which the wicked would be removed into hell, and the good raised from the intermediate world into heaven. The Scriptures no where say that this judgment is to take place at the end of the world, or that the human race will perish ; but the Scriptures declare that such a judgment is to take place at ' *the consummation of the age ;*' that is, at the period when the church should come to its end ; for the *aion*, in Scripture, does not mean the world, but a period of time, or an age, especially that period or age through which a dispensation, or a church. such as the Jewish, and also the first Christian church, lasted. (See Hebrews, ix. 26.) Thus, at the end of this age, a judgment is executed upon spirits in the world of spirits. This judgment, and the consequent removal of the wicked, and the resurrection or the elevation of the good, are, as the Scripture says, acts of redemption, and have also correspondent effects in the natural world, at which time a new age, or *aion*, or a new church, commences, for the Lord Himself says, in reference to this new age or period,—' *Behold I make all things new.*'

" If these doctrines of the New Church were generally received and practised ; if the unity and true worship of God were not destroyed ; and if His divine commandments were not rendered of non effect, and even set at nought, by prevailing false doctrines, which destroy, even in the tender minds of children, the very germs of vital religion and of genuine morality,—if all this were not actually the case, we should certainly have better times, and should be more established in order, harmony, and peace. The best civil constitution is of no use to us whatever, if the states of our people are not so improved and elevated as properly to enjoy the superior privileges and liberties it confers. But the doctrines of the New Church, which, like a compact and beautiful city, cohere together, are eminently calculated to improve and elevate the minds of men, and to promote and accomplish the regeneration of the church, and to make it so universal as that one flock and one Shepshall be acknowledged."

After this follows an enumeration of the various works in which the doctrines of the New Church can be read and known. Amongst these works the following tracts, translated from the English, are especially mentioned, viz :—" *The True Object of Christian Worship*," &c. ; " *The Apostolic Doctrine of the Atonement*," &c. ; " *Is it true that we cannot keep the Commandments ? &c. ;* and also the " *Catechism*" prepared by the General Conference.

" We have translated and inserted this address," says the Editor of the Intellectual Repository, " not because it contains anything new for our readers, but in order that our brethren in England may see that efforts are now made in Germany to collect the scattered receivers of the doctrine of the New Church in that country and in Switzerland, that they may organize themselves into an association for extensive usefulness in promoting the Lord's New Kingdom upon earth."

REV. T. O. PRESCOTT'S VISIT TO IRELAND.

The following extracts from Mr. Prescott's visit to Ireland, spoken of in our Editorial Items, will give the reader an idea of the whole.

" It was on Saturday morning, the 29th April, that I landed at Belfast, It was a charming morning, and Green Erin appeared in its verdant, beauty. I was delighted with the scenery. I knew of only one receiver of the New Church doctrines in Ireland—this was a widow lady, Mrs. Stuart, residing near Belfast. I soon found her, and was received with great cordiality, as a brother in the Church. The family with whom she was residing were Unitarians, and, having no other place of worship, she was in the habit of attending, in company with them, the Unitarian Church in Belfast. They invited me to accompany them, the next day, Sunday, to church. I accepted the invitation, and was introduced to the pastor of the society, who received me with much kindness, as a stranger and minister from America. It was Communion day. The next day, Monday, there was also service, as is customary in the north of Ireland, on the day of after Communion. Having again accompanied my friends, and again meeting the minister, I was at once,—with the usual liberality of clergymen of that denomination,—invited to preach. I at first declined, on the ground of being totally unprepared at the moment, either by having with me a manuscript sermon, or by previous meditation,—and it was now time for the service to begin. Instantly reflecting, however, that here was an opportunity presented such as might never occur again, I determined to accept the invitation, and trust in Divine Providence for light and strength to go through the duty. I was not disappointed. A passage of Scripture presented itself to my mind, and at once it seemed fully illustrated, and I saw at a glance the general divisions of the subject of which it treated ; and when I opened the Word, and began, I felt myself manifestly enlightened and sustained, even to the close. I felt peculiarly grateful for this Divine aid, at such a moment —a critical one, as I felt it to be, in my course in Ireland. When I descended from the pulpit, the clergyman came warmly forward, and congratulating and thanking me, kindly expressed the hope that I would remain and preach for him the following Sunday. Though I had had no thought of staying so long in Belfast, I felt it my duty to accept the invitation. I accordingly preached both morning and afternoon on the Sabbath following, setting forth the New Church doctrines of regeneration, and of the internal sense of the Word. All the discourses seemed to be received with much attention and favor by the audience, and some little spirit of inquiry appeared to be excited. I cannot conclude the account of my visit to Belfast, without an expression of the grateful feelings I entertain for the universal kindness and hospitality I met with on all sides. I was honored with the calls and invitations of ministers of various denominations. Unitarian and Trinitarian, and of several of the professors in the college, as well as of many private individuals,—all of whom, though entertaining theological views so far removed from my own, yet suffered that distinc tion to make no difference in their kind regard and attentions, but seemed to take a pleasure in meeting me cordially on the broad ground of gentlemanly intercourse and literary taste, and, yet more, of Christian kindliness and friendship. I had heard much, even in my own distant land, of Irish hospitality, and I found these reports fully confirmed by my own experience of it. I shall ever retain a grateful remembrance of the kind reception I met with at Belfast.

"One opportunity improved leads to another; it seemed as if Divine Providence was opening the way before me. At the church on Sunday afternoon, there was a lady present from Strabane, a considerable town near Londonderry. Having been introduced to her a day or two after, at the house of a friend, she inquired whether I could not make it convenient to be at Strabane on the next Sunday, for if I could do so, I might be useful there. I readily assented to the arrangement, and after visiting the Giant's Causeway, I reached the house of my Strabane friend on Saturday evening. I was received with the most hearty cordiality—not only by the family of the friend who had invited me, but also by the minister of the society to which they belonged (Unitarian, also,)—a young clergyman who had lately been ordained. It was soon arranged that I should preach on the morrow, morning and evening, which I did, to a small but attentive audience. I had much conversation afterwards with the young minister, whom I found exceedingly intelligent and well-educated, and disposed to listen without prejudice to any views which could be shown to be the truth. At parting, I presented him with a copy of the Four Leading Doctrines, which I happened to have with me.

"At Cork resides the celebrated Father Mathew, the 'Apostle of Temperance.' I paid him my respects, and on announcing myself as a clergyman from America, was received by him with marked attention and regard. He took me out in his carriage to his brother's country-seat, a short distance from Cork, where I dined and spent the evening with him. I regard him as a truly good man,—his countenance shows it. And when at parting, he uttered the words, 'God bless you,' in an affectionate manner, I valued the benediction not the less that it was from the lips of one nominally a Roman Catholic. 'The Lord knows his own :' names are of small consideration in His sight. As a memento of my agreeable visit, I promised to send him a copy of my volume of sermons, lately published, which he said he should be most happy to receive."

TESTIMONY TO SWEDENBORG AS A MAN OF SCIENCE.

The following paragraph we have recently noticed in a valuable work on Geology, by G. F. Richardson, published in London in 1846. The abatements which he makes on the score of mysticism, &c. adds to the value of the testimony in other respects.

" The celebrated Emanuel Swedenborg (1720), in the early part of his career, acquired considerable proficiency in the physical sciences, traces of which are discernable in his latter and more mystical writings. His publication entitled, *Opera Philosophica et Mineralogica*, in three volumes folio, with numerous engravings, was justly regarded as a most extraordinary performance. On its appearance, various learned bodies vied with each other in electing him a member of their respective societies ; and the Academy of Sciences of Paris translated into the French language, for their *Histoire des Arts et Métiers*, his Treatise on Iron from this work, as affording the most valuable authority on the subject then extant. His scientific observations, though alloyed with the mysticism and extravagance which pervade his writings, contain some sound principles and instructive facts ; and the nebular theory of the solar system, the original fluidity of our planet, the various preparatory changes of the earth, as opposed to the prevailing idea of its instantaneous creation in its present matured condition ; the succession of various tribes of animals ; these, with other assertions the truth and accuracy of which have been demonstrated by modern science, are the lights which shine through the misty maze of superstition and absurdity of which his productions so largely consist. It may incidentally be noticed, that the writings of this extraordinary man evince that he was also acquainted with phrenology."

EDITORIAL ITEMS.

The Intell. Repository for July contains a long and interesting letter from Rev. T. O. Prescott giving an account of a recent tour made by him in Ireland—a kind of exploring tour in which his object seemed to be to ascertain what progress the New Church had made or was likely to make in that ill-fated country, and at the same time to scatter as far as possible the seeds of heavenly truth as he passed along. It is remarkable that with the exception of Dublin, Mr. P. found only a *single* receiver in the places previously indicated to him as containing one or more representatives of the New Church. In Dublin he found two. The whole number of receivers in Ireland does not seem to exceed eight or ten. He found, however, that the writings of Swedenborg were to be met with in several public libraries in the large towns, and Mr. P.'s visit promises to operate as a stimulus to many individuals with whom he conversed to become acquainted with them——The Forty-first General Conference of the New Church in England was recently held at Leeds, and the Annual Assembly of the New Church in Scotland at Edinburgh, July 14. Both meetings are said to have been largely attended, and a very pleasing and hopeful impression produced by the various exercises. Our brother, Rev. T. O. Prescott seems to have entered upon a field of very active and acceptable service among the N. C. friends in Great Britain. The newly erected Temple at Glasgow, in which he has been called to officiate, was opened and dedicated with appropriate ceremonies, July 2d. A new place of worship has also been opened at Paisley.——We learn from a letter from Rev. J. H. Smithson of Manchester, Eng. that he does not find sufficient encouragement to warrant him in going on with the translation of vol. 2d. of the "Spiritual Diary" of Swedenborg. He is therefore obliged for the present to abandon the idea. Meantime he expresses an earnest hope that the work may be accomplished in this country. We have good reason to believe that this will be the case. We know, at any rate, of three competent individuals who are at present more or less engaged in translating the different portions of the series. Having nearly completed ourselves the third volume we shall ere long be prepared to enter upon the second.——From the same source we learn that the Manchester Printing Society contemplate publishing a new and revised edition of "Clowes on the Four Gospels" in one volume, 8vo. This will be a great accession to our present apparatus on the Word. The separate vols. of this work have become scarce, while at the same time they are none the less indispensable as a manual of convenient reference. We trust the enterprise may be rewarded by an adequate demand.——The volume of Lectures by Mr. Noble, on the principal doctrines of the Christian Religion, and recently republished by Mr. Allen, is achieving, as we hear, a vast amount of good in various circles of readers to which it finds its way. It is beyond question one of the most eminently valuable works ever issued from the bosom of the New Church, and we would that we could impress upon our brethren of that Church the immense service they would perform to the cause of truth by aiding to give it circulation. The price ($1,50) is reduced almost one half from that of the London edition, and still the volume is well got up. Hundreds who do not need it for their own confirmation would still find it a most powerful instrument in dispelling from the minds of others the theological fallacies of the old system.——The October No. of the "Journal of Insanity," published at the Utica Asylum under the care of the superintendent, Dr. Brigham, contains an extract of two or three pages from Swedenborg's Spiritual Diary, where he treats of the causes of Monomonia and other forms of diseased mental action. The extract is very respectfully introduced by the Editor.——The first edition of the "Canons of the New Church" is very nearly exhausted; single copies or quantities of the second edition may be ordered of the Editor of the Repository, who is also Translator.

THE

NEW CHURCH REPOSITORY

AND

MONTHLY REVIEW.

| Vol. 1. | NOVEMBER, 1848. | No. 11. |

ORIGINAL PAPERS.

ARTICLE I.

THE DUTY OF NEW CHURCHMEN TO ATTEND PUBLIC WORSHIP.

When a church becomes corrupted, and approaches the period of its consummation, the men of that church invariably substitute for the internal worship of the Lord, or the life of charity, the mere external forms of worship, and make the whole of religion to consist in the observance of a certain course of religious duties, which are in no ways connected with the everyday life of man, and his transactions with the world,—religion and the common affairs of life being, in their minds, altogether distinct and separate things. Such was the case in the Jewish Church when the Lord made his appearance in the world. The Scribes and Pharisees, and the common people taught by them, attended simply to the external things of the law, according to the interpretation given of the law by the traditions received from the fathers. In their observance of these externals they were remarkably zealous, and left nothing undone that their traditions required them to perform. But while they were so zealous and strict in their attendance upon the outward forms of religion, they were entire strangers to the internal principle of heavenly life; and, consequently, altogether omitted the weightier matters of the law—the spirit of love and charity without which all religion is dead, and all outward forms but a mere vain show. With reference to the course of life pursued by them therefore, the Lord said to them, "Woe unto you, Scribes and Pharisees, hypocrites! for ye pay tithe of mint and anise and cummin, and have omitted the weightier matters of the law, judgment, mercy, and faith: these ought ye to have done, and not to leave the other undone." (Matt. xxiii. 23.) These words of the Lord, though condemnatory of the course of life pursued by this people, do not condemn them for attending to the external duties of religion, but they rather commend the performance of these external acts, and, indeed, show that it is necessary for man to pay proper attention to them. "These ought ye to have done, and not to leave the other undone." The Lord's words condemn, not for what they did, but for what they omitted to do. They were condemned for attending to externals only, while the internal was never thought of, and was entirely lost sight of by them. Therefore, the Lord further said to them, "Woe unto you, Scribes and Pharisees, hypocrites! for ye make clean the outside of the cup and of the platter, but within they are full of extortion and excess. Thou blind Pharisee, cleanse first that which is within the cup and platter, that the outside of them may be clean also. Woe unto you, Scribes and Pharisees, hypocrites! for ye are like unto whited sepulchres, which indeed appear beautiful outward, but are within full of dead men's bones, and of all uncleanness. Even so ye also outwardly appear righteous unto men, but within ye are full of hypocrisy and iniquity."

The state of the consummated Christian church is similar to that of the Jewish; the religion of that church being merely the performance of certain religious exercises at stated periods, in a devotional frame of mind, and efforts for the support and wider spread of their particular faith at home and abroad. To the internal, animative, all pervading spirit, which is characteristic of the true Christian church, its members, in general, are entire strangers, mistaking for this internal principle of heavenly life, a certain feeling of infatuation, which they call the love of God, that leads them to the performance of those religious exercises which they consider the only true worship of God.

But while the men of the old church attend mainly to the externals of worship, to the neglect of the weightier matters of the law; believing that to meet together at stated periods to read and hear the word of God, to pray in the sanctuary, to sing the praises of the Most High, and to give and receive religious instruction, and to be regular in their devotional exercises in the family, and other similar duties, constitute the whole of religion; there are some in the New Church who go to the other extreme, and think that inasmuch as true religion is an internal principle, having relation to the spirit and life of man ; that therefore, external acts of worship are of no importance whatever, and may be easily dispensed with ; and that we need pay no attention to them, unless we can do so without any inconvenience to ourselves, or interference with other affairs.

It is perfectly proper that every man should enjoy his own opinion upon this as well as upon every other subject ; but before we come to a final decision with reference to the right and wrong of our opinions and doings, we should certainly learn what are the teachings of *Divine Truth* in relation to them ; for our own thoughts and opinions are no proper guide to us in our duty either to God, or man, or ourselves, unless we are positively certain that they are in strict accordance with the teachings of the Word of the Lord.

True religion is, indeed, an internal principle, pertaining to the mind, and is the inmost life of man. It is, as expressed by the prophet, " To do justly, to love mercy, and to walk humbly with God ;" or, as defined by the Lord, " To love the Lord our God with all our heart, and with all our soul, and with all our mind, and with all our strength : and to love our neighbor as ourselves ;" that is, so to love the neighbor, as it is elsewhere expressed, as to do unto others as we would that others would do unto us. The simple meaning of this language is, that we are to love supremely, or solely, the good exhibited in the Lord Jesus Christ, and practice it according to the teachings of the divine truth of the Word.

But can we truly and properly perform these spiritual duties, while we live in the neglect of those external means, which the Lord has appointed as auxiliaries to our spiritual life? Can we love the Lord supremely, while we take no interest in the public worship of God, and absent ourselves, sabbath after sabbath, from the sanctuary, simply on account of some trifling inconvenience, or because we feel no disposition to go there? We think not. Be it remembered, that it was with reference to the external acts of worship, which the Pharisees performed, that the Lord said unto them, " These ought ye to have done." These words being Divine, and spoken by the Lord in his gospel, must be viewed by Christians as having reference to the duties of man under the gospel dispensation ; so that the duties here spoken of are most emphatically binding upon all who profess to be the disciples of the Lord Jesus Christ. They are virtually a positive command, and disobedience to them, as well as to every other divine commandment, is an evil. The Lord imposes no duty upon us that is not necessary to our good and the promotion of his kingdom among men : in neglecting our duty therefore, we pursue a course which is detrimental to our own spiritual interest, and which tends, as far as we have any influence, to injure the church.

But it is believed that Swedenborg in his writings teaches that external acts of worship are of no importance, provided man, by being in the good of life, is in internal worship: and that therefore the receivers of the Heavenly Doctrines can spend their time on the sabbath as profitably at home, or among their friends, as they can in the house of God in the act of public worship.

Swedenborg, indeed, teaches that the essential of worship is the internal life of charity, but he no where teaches, as far as we can learn, that the men of the New Church who are to profess the essential internal principle, may dispense with the external acts of worship; but he teaches a very different doctrine,—a doctrine which is in strict accordance with the teachings of the Lord himself upon the same subject. We will give his words.

"Where there is a church, there must of necessity be both an internal and an external; for man, who is the church, is internal and external: before he becomes a church, that is, before he is regenerated he is in externals, and when he is regenerating, he is led from externals, yea, by externals, to internals, as was said and shown above, and afterwards when he is made regenerate, then all things which are of the internal man terminate in things external: thus of necessity every church must be internal and external. This was the case with the Ancient Church, and at this day with the Christian Church; the internals of the Ancient Church, were all things of charity and faith, thence, all humiliation, all adoration of the Lord from charity, all good affection toward the neighbor and other things of like nature; the externals of that church were sacrifices, libations and several other things, all which by representation had reference to the Lord, and regarded him; hence things internal were in things external and formed one church: the internals of the Christian Church were altogether similar to the internals of the Ancient Church, but other externals took place, viz. symbolical rites or ordinances instead of sacrifices and such things, which had a like reference to the Lord; thus also things internal and external form one. The Ancient Church did not differ in the least from the Christian Church as to internals, but only as to externals; for the worship of the Lord from charity can never vary, whatever variation may be made in things external. And since, as was said, no church can exist, unless there be an internal and an external, *the internal without the external would be something indeterminate, unless it were terminated in somewhat external:* for mankind are, and indeed mostly, such, that they know not what the internal man is, and what belongs to the internal man; wherefore *unless there were external worship, what is holy would be altogether unknown:* nevertheless where there is charity, and thence conscience, there is internal worship in the external, for the Lord operates with them in charity, and in conscience, and causes all their worship to partake of what is internal." —(*A. C.* 1083.)

Here, then, we are taught that the external of worship is essential to the internal, and that the latter cannot exist in men without the former. Again, Swedenborg, in the *Heavenly Doctrines*, speaking of piety, says:

"Many believe that the spiritual life, or the life which leads to hea-ven, consists in piety, in external sanctity, and the renunciation of the world: yet piety without charity, external without internal sanctity, and a renunciation of the world without a life in the world, do not constitute spiritual life. Life truly spiritual consists in *piety from charity:* in *external sanctity from internal sanctity;* and in a renunciation of the world during a life in the world."

Let the reader mark the expressions. Life truly spiritual consists in *piety from charity;* in *external sanctity from inter-nal sanctity.* And lest we should make a mistake in regard to the meaning of the terms "piety" and "external sanctity," he thus proceeds to explain them.

"Piety consists in thinking and speaking piously; in devoting much time to prayer; in behaving with becoming humility during that time; in frequenting places of public worship, and attending devoutly to the discourses delivered there; in receiving the sacrament of the Holy Supper frequently every year; and in due observance of the various other parts of divine worship, according to the appointments of the church."

Such is the piety, described by the Lord's messenger to us, which is to be the external of charity, and derived from it, in the man of the church. He proceeds:

"But the life of charity consists in cultivating good will towards the neighbor, and endeavoring to promote his interest; in being guided in all our actions by justice and equity, good and truth, and in this manner discharging every duty; in one word, the life of charity con-sists in the performance of uses. Divine worship primarily consists in the life of charity, and secondarily in that of piety; he, therefore, who separates the one from the other, that is, who lives in the practice of piety, and not at the same time in the exercise of charity, does not worship God." "External sanctity is like external piety, and is not holy with man, unless his internal be holy; for the quality of man's internal determines that of his external, since the latter proceeds from the former, as action from its cause. External worship, without inter-nal, may be compared to the life of the respiration without the life of the heart; but external worship arising from internal, may be com-pared to the life of the respiration conjoined to the life of the heart." "From these particulars it may be clearly seen, *that a life of piety is valuable, and is acceptable to the Lord, so far as a life of charity is conjoined with it;* for this is the primary, and such as the quality of this is, such is that of the former. *Also, that external sanctity is of value, and is accepta-ble to the Lord, so far as it proceeds from internal sanctity;* for such as the quality of this is, such is that of the former."—(H. D. 123–128.)

Again, in speaking of the doctrine of charity, he says :

"In the man of the church there must be the life of piety, and there must be the life of charity; the two lives must be conjoined : the life of piety without the life of charity conduces to nothing, but the former united with the latter to all things. The life of piety consists in thinking piously and speaking piously, in giving much time to prayer, in behaving then with due humility, in frequenting temples and then devoutly attending to the preachings, and frequently every year receiving the sacrament of the Supper, and in a right observance of other parts of worship according to the ordinances of the church."—(*A. C.* 8252, 8253.)

Now it is most obvious, according to the teachings of the Herald of the New Dispensation, that a faithful and punctual attendance upon the public worship and ordinances of the church, is an important duty, and may not be neglected by the man of the church: for we are taught that the life of piety, which consists in these external acts of worship, must be conjoined with the internal principal of charity in him, and that piety is derived from charity, it being the external with which charity is clothed. Consequently, if this piety does not manifest itself in us, who are in possession of the truth, by our regard to, and attendance upon, the public worship and ordinances of the Lord's sanctuary, there is great reason to fear that we are destitute of that internal charity, which is the church and the life of heaven in man.

To suppose that we can, in our present imperfect state, worship God internally, without corresponding external acts of devotion, and a due regard to the outward ordinances of worship instituted by the Lord, is altogether a mistake; for the piety which is of charity, is indispensable to the life of charity, and is the natural upon which rests, as its foundation, the spiritual of our worship. "Where there is a church," says Swedenborg, "there must of necessity be both an internal and external." To suppose, therefore, that we are in internal worship, without the corresponding external, or the piety above described, is to suppose that we have a spiritual superstructure within, which has no foundation to rest upon. The foundation must necessarily exist in the natural as the ground work of the interior temple, otherwise the temple can never be erected within us.

But the external acts of worship, which we are taught are necessary to the existence of the church on earth, also exist in the heavens, and are means by which the angels ever perfect themselves in love and wisdom, thus in the life of heaven. Concerning the worship of angels, we read as follows, in the Treatise on Heaven and Hell.

" Divine worship in the heavens, is not unlike that on earth in externals, but it differs as to internals. In the heavens, as on earth, there are doctrines, preachings, and temples. The *doctrines* agree as to essentials, but are of more interior wisdom in the superior than in the inferior heavens. The *preaching* is according to doctrines : and as they have houses and palaces, so also they have *temples*, in which preaching is performed. Such things exist in heaven, because the angels are continually perfected in wisdom and love ; for they have understanding and will like men, and are capable of advancing for ever towards perfection. The understanding.is perfected by the truths which are of intelligence, and the will by the goods which are of love.

" But real divine worship in the heavens does not consist in frequenting temples and hearing sermons, but in a life of love, charity, and faith, according to doctrine. Sermons in the temples serve only as means of instruction in the conduct of life. I have conversed with angels on this subject, and have told them, that it is believed in the world that divine worship consists merely in going to church, hearing sermons, attending the sacrament of the holy supper three or four times a year, and in other forms of worship prescribed by the church : to which may be added, the setting apart of particular times for prayer, and a devout manner while engaged in it. The angels replied, *that these are external forms which ought to be observed, but that they are of no avail unless there be an internal principle from which they proceed*, and that this internal principle is a life according to the precepts of doctrine.

" I have conversed with one of the preachers concerning the holy state in which they are who hear the sermons in their temples, and he said, that every one has a pious, devout, and holy state according to his interiors which are of love and faith, because love and faith are the essentials of holiness from the Divine of the Lord within them ; and that he had no conception of external holiness separate from love and faith."—(*H. & H.* 221, 222, 224.)

Angels then, according to Swedenborg, have external worship in heaven, they assemble together in their temples, and hear preaching ;—they attend to these externals for the sake of the internal worship, life according to the precepts of doctrine being the end ;—and the angels, by means of preaching, are for ever perfected in love and wisdom. Therefore, since the angels of heaven have these external means, and are in the use of them, and through them perfected in the divine life to eternity, how much more are such means necessary to our regeneration and elevation to the life of charity and love, in our present imperfect and external state on the earth, where we are exposed to so many temptations, and are so liable to be led astray from the internal worship of the Lord?

But it is said, that we have the writings of the church, revealed to us by the Lord, and the Word itself, from which we may learn all the truths and doctrines of life necessary for us to know. True, we have them, and they are given to us, that we may learn them, and practice according to them. But have not the angels of heaven, upon whom the Lord perpetually shines and sheds his light divine, and into whom the influx of celestial love and wisdom flows freely and uninterruptedly from him, equal facilities with men on the earth to arrive at the possession of heavenly truths? And yet they meet in temples, engage in the external acts of worship, and hear sermons, in order thereby to be advanced and perfected in the internal life of their respective heavens. Therefore, to think that we can do as well without the public worship of the sanctuary as with it, because we have the writings of the church, and the Word, which we may read and study at home, is virtually to think ourselves in a more elevated state than the angels, who, according to divine order, meet in their temples to worship the Lord and learn his truths. Were we better acquainted with ourselves and the Divine Word, and felt more of its power, we should never absent ourselves from the house of God otherwise than by necessity, but, hungering and thirsting for righteousness, we should always feel desirous to meet with those who assemble for divine worship, to take our part therein, and receive from the Lord the blessing which he delights to communicate to those, who, in his own appointed way, wait upon him in his sacred courts.

The public services of the sanctuary, and the preaching of the Word, are the means which the Lord has specially appointed by which to communicate his blessings to mankind. And it is according to divine order, that we should receive far more abundantly and freely the divine influx, which enlightens, elevates, and fills with heavenly beatitudes the mind, when in charity assembled for divine worship, than we could otherwise receive. That this is, and must of necessity be, the case is obvious. The angels of heaven are formed into societies, like being consociated with like, that they may unitedly receive influx from the Lord. The influx received by one of the society, is from that one communicated to all, while the influx received by all unitedly, is communicated to each individual according to his state of reception. The divine law by which this is effected is universal, and operates in like manner with reference to the societies of heaven; so that the influx received by one society is communicated to all in that heaven, and the influx received by all is communicated to each in the degree it is capable of receiving. The happiness of each therefore, is the happiness of all, and the happiness of all is the happiness of each. Then how immeasurably greater the reception and enjoyment of each and all in heaven, than it possibly could

be if each angel were an isolated receiver from the Lord!
The same law of divine order operates upon the minds of men
in the church upon earth ; for the same law, in the degree it
is permitted to operate upon our minds, governs the church
both in heaven and upon earth.   Collected together as a society, christians here meet for divine worship in the sanctuary ;
and in the degree that their minds are internally assimilated
to each in the order of worship they receive influx from the
Lord in common through the appointed means, each individual
in the general assembly, in the spirit of christian charity,
willing, and thereby communicating to all, and all communicating to each ; and thus all receive more abundantly, and are
mutually and progressively fitted for the consociations of heaven.   It is very different with him who voluntarily absents
himself from the house of God, and pleases himself with the
idea that he can receive greater benefit by reading for his own
instruction.   Such an one is isolated from others in his
thoughts and feelings, and may be termed in the course he is
pursuing, purely selfish.   Indeed, the fact that he cares only
for himself, and seeks only his own good, clearly evinces the
absence from his mind of that charity which seeketh not her
own.   The influx he receives, therefore, cannot be the pure
divine emanation, which proceeds from the Lord through the
heavens into the minds of those, who as brethren meet and
unitedly engage in divine worship agreeably to the order instituted by the Lord ; but it must be that which is in agreement
with his own mind in his reception of it.   He consequently,
does not, and cannot, receive the blessing received by him,
who in the true Christian spirit worships in the sanctuary.

But Christians meet in public, not merely for their own mutual benefit, but also for the advancement of the Lord's kingdom, and the good of mankind.   The Lord wills the salvation
of all, and he has instituted his church on earth that the world
might be regenerated and saved by its means.   This can be
accomplished only by the stated and public ministry of the
Word, sustained by the co-operation of the men of the church,
according to the instruction given us by the Lord.   Our attendance upon, and our support of, the public worship pro-
motes this end, while our absence from the house of God, and
the indifference manifested by us, in the same degree, militates
against it.   Therefore, the love of the Lord and the neighbor,
where this love is felt, will most assuredly lead us to the public sanctuary, sabbath after sabbath, even were it for no other
purpose than simply to give our countenance and support to
that institution, which we know is from the Lord out of hea

freedom and independence. Our great duty,—the high mission to which we are called,—is to furnish it with wholesome food, so that it may be nourished, sustained, and strengthened, until it shall have attained the full stature and vigor of manhood. We waste time and expend labor to no purpose in reciprocating the saw of controversy with these men. He who has a day's journey before him must not halt on his way to mark every trivial or strange object that may present itself on the road side. The publication and dissemination of the works of the Church, present, in my humble judgment, the most orderly and the most effectual means, of correcting the misrepresentations, exposing the calumnies, and dispelling the thick clouds of delusion, ignorance and error which (to use the strong language of Bishop Warburton,) have contributed to make this Earth " *the great madhouse of the Universe.*"

There is another consideration, too, which seems to me to be entitled to great weight. The Old Church, awfully perverted as it is, is still permitted by the Divine Providence to maintain its outward, external form ; just as are the Jewish, the Mahomedan, and others of like character. This is doubtless for wise and good ends. The truth is, in the present state of our fallen race, such systems of faith and worship seem to me as necessary as artificial scare-crows in a field of springing corn. Men must have some religion suited to their states of life, or they would rush into the most dangerous excesses. Though obviously in a course of preparation, they are not generally prepared to receive the high dispensation of Truth as revealed to the New Church: nor is it consistent with the order of the Divine Providence, by any sudden jerk of arbitrary power, to elevate them at once. He acts not in such modes, or by such means, but orderly and progressively, and we may rest assured that when the world shall be prepared *to do the truths* of the church, it will *receive* them: and that neither men nor devils shall arrest its progress. In the meantime the Old Church is unwittingly performing important uses. Its members, for the most part, can, as yet, conceive of no more powerful principle of action than the fear of punishment. Hence they are wisely permitted to contemplate the horrors of Hades, as being *without* themselves, and not *within ;* and hence the eloquence of their pulpits is so often garnished with terrific descriptions of Hell. Without the restraints imposed by such a faith, the organism of civil society would itself be dissolved, and we should plunge at once into chaos. To them the trite old Scottish proverb, " *Tak' awa' the De'il, and gude bye to the Lord,*" is eminently applicable. The good men who attended the famous politico-religious Assembly at Dort in 1618,

to those whom it especially contemplates it may savor of a tone of too caustic
severity, while it is blandness itself compared with the terms of vituperation so
often showered by its opponents upon the Swedenborgian heresy. We would remark, moreover, that we have reason to know that the writer did not design to
convey the impression that all controversy, under all circumstances, was to be
peremptorily eschewed by the friends of the New Church. His dissuasives apply
not to such a calm and argumentative discussion of the points at issue, as we
may *conceive* as occurring between candid disputants, although it has never yet
been the lot of the New Church to *realize* such an ideal of doctrinal debate. In
recommending a dignified silence, the writer has especially in view that style of
ribald reproach and vilification, without the least show of *reasoning*—that
avowed policy of invidious *exposure*—which has heretofore seemed so congenial
to the spirit of our impugners. On this head we think the suggestions of our correspondent well-timed and weighty, and deserving the most serious consideration
of New Churchmen ; and as to the somewhat stringent tone of his remarks upon
the doctrinal tenets of our opponents, it is to be borne in mind that *if* they are
indeed erroneous and false, they are enormously so, and their appearing as truths
to their advocates does not remove them from this category, though it prescribes
a charitable discrimination between the *doctrines* and the *doctors*.

L————, Va., *July 5th*, 1847.

MY DEAR SIR :
    * * * As to Dr. P—— himself, I cheerfully admit that he
may have been induced to write his book from praiseworthy
motives. I infer this from the general tone of his reflections,—
without any personal knowledge of his character ; for, until
his book was laid on my table, I had never either heard of him,
or of the sectarian institution to which it seems he belongs.
But this, be it as it may, is of little import. The time is past
when sectarian denunciations can avail anything. Men
whose religious education and discipline allow them to think
only in harness, can no longer stamp their moral impressions
or mental habitudes on the minds of others, and thus enslave
their fellows. This power has passed away with the church
to which it appertained ;—and which is indebted to it for most
of that external influence which it has exercised in the world.
I feel persuaded the book in question will be productive of
good ;—though in a very different way than was intended and
anticipated by the author. All that we desire is, that men
may inquire and examine for themselves ; and the very extravagance of our views, as caricatured by Dr. P—— and
others,—when viewed in connection with the known character of the individuals who are members of the church,—will
contribute no little to advance this object. The age in which
we live takes nothing upon trust ; and I am confident that the
statements and opinions of Dr. P—— will not weigh a feather's avoirdupois with any sincere inquirer after truth ;—and

grossly absurd, and of evil tendency, yet it by no means follows, that the merciful Creator cannot educe some good out of them. I feel assured they have contributed no little to keep men in a state of external order. To be assured of one's special, individual election, without the hard condition of *"good works,"* is, indeed, quite comfortable, especially when we add to it the all-quieting conviction that being *in grace* to-day is full and perfect security that we *cannot* be *out of* it to-morrow. These special and partial favors make those who enjoy them *"love God,"* as they say ;—not, indeed, because he is kind and merciful to *all their brethren* in the flesh, but because he is so *to them* —a distinction not less flattering to our pride than agreeable to our feelings. True, they may induce us to shut up our bowels of compasion and withhold our sympathies from the vast majority of our fellow-men ; but then it must be remembered, by way of extenuation, that God himself has been *"pleased to pass by, and ordain them to dishonor and wrath in praise of his vindictive justice."* They may, too, stimulate our zeal in *His cause* so far as to imprison the bodies and shed the blood of our brothers ; as Michael Servetus and James Arminius can testify ; but it must not be forgotten that the one was incarcerated for the good of *the church*, and the other burnt for the good of *his soul*. By the bye, it may be asserted on the authority of ecclesiastical records, that no man until the last century has been ever successful in founding religious sects, who has not shed blood in support of his mission, and in proof of his zeal. This seems to have been an excellent substitute for miracles ; and as Swedenborg brought neither the one nor the other, it is not wonderful that his views should be regarded as the ravings of a madman.   •

Further ; men, in what may be called their *religious actions*, are operated upon by considerations having reference immediately or remotely, to Heaven or to Hell. The influence of these must, of course, depend upon the estimates they may form either of the joys of the one, or the torments of the other; and these estimates, in their turn, must depend on their *states of life* respectively. The Heaven of the Old Church, which is situated in some determinate, yet undetermined portion of space, has, I confess, but very few positive charms, and offers very inadequate inducements to the mortification of our natural appetites. Passing by its promise of negative bliss in a life of idleness, the only active employment of the evangelicals and others who may assemble there, will be psalm-singing ; with occasional interludes when they will be called upon, with crowns on their heads and wings folded, to adjudge their unfortunate fellow-beings to their pre-ordained destination (by

time to read but one of them ; and you may infer the tone, temper, taste (and one other essential of useful history) in which it is written when I inform you that he belongs to the *evangelical* subdivision of the Old Church ; and, as such, enjoys the comfortable assurance of a " *vessel of honor,*" not liable to fracture from a *fall.*

I mention these instances in order to show how useless the effort, how endless the labor must be of correcting the misrepresentations of such assailants. If the Lord, in his infinite goodness and mercy, be, as we believe, now establishing on the earth the New Church spoken of in the Apocalypse, these things must needs be ; these signs must follow ;—and we have the highest assurance that, though the enemy be amongst us, " *having great wrath,*"—truth, divine in essence and omnipotent in operation, will ultimately prevail.

In short, I am persuaded that but little good is effected by what is commonly called religious controversy. There is so much of self-love mixed up with our opinions, especially in Religion and Politics, that it is next to impossible for one man to correct the errors of another. The pride of self-derived intelligence is far stronger than the love of truth ; and the experience of Mr. Jefferson,—who once remarked that he had never known an individual convinced, by argument, of error of opinion on either of these subjects,—is the experience of every observing man. In the existing state of the Old Church this fact is eminently striking. Each sect has its own particular idol ; and reason, science, truth and orthodoxy are determined, in a summary way, by the voice which issues from it. The followers of John Calvin, Joanna Southcote and Joe Smith, however differing amongst themselves, concur, with great readiness, in denouncing us as *Heretics,* because we do not believe that the voice of their idols is the voice of God. The disciples of Luther, Fox, Muggleton and John Wesley have the same ready *postulates, ergos,* and *conclusions,* while the Pope and the Archbishop of Canterbury deliver us over quickly to the evil one, because we are unable to settle a mere question of genealogy, and to determine which of the two is the legitimate, and which the bastard, descendant of the Apostles.

Now, in all seriousness, it appears to me the course of true wisdom to let these railing assailants vent their sectarian spleen in peace. The world but little regards the clamor of fanatics. Since the last Judgment the human mind has become more free in matters of religious faith. The *fact,* and its *effects,* are stamping themselves on every day's history. Hour by hour the mind of man is casting off the manacles by which it has been so long enslaved, and asserting its native

grossly absurd, and of evil tendency, yet it by no means follows, that the merciful Creator cannot educe some good out of them. I feel assured they have contributed no little to keep men in a state of external order.   To be assured of one's special, individual election, without the hard condition of "*good works*," is, indeed, quite comfortable, especially when we add to it the all-quieting conviction that being *in grace* to-day is full and perfect security that we *cannot* be *out of* it to-morrow.   These special and partial favors make those who enjoy them "*love God*," as they say ;—not, indeed, because he is kind and merciful to *all their brethren* in the flesh, but because he is so *to them* —a distinction not less flattering to our pride than agreeable to our feelings.   True, they may induce us to shut up our bowels of compasion and withhold our sympathies from the vast majority of our fellow-men; but then it must be remembered, by way of extenuation, that God himself has been "*pleased to pass by, and ordain them to dishonor and wrath in praise of his vindictive justice.*"   They may, too, stimulate our zeal in *His cause* so far as to imprison the bodies and shed the blood of our brothers; as Michael Servetus and James Arminius can testify; but it must not be forgotten that the one was incarcerated for the good of *the church*, and the other burnt for the good of *his soul*.   By the bye, it may be asserted on the authority of ecclesiastical records, that no man until the last century has been ever successful in founding religious sects, who has not shed blood in support of his mission, and in proof of his zeal.   This seems to have been an excellent substitute for miracles; and as Swedenborg brought neither the one nor the other, it is not wonderful that his views should be regarded as the ravings of a madman.   •

Further; men, in what may be called their *religious actions*, are operated upon by considerations having reference immediately or remotely, to Heaven or to Hell.   The influence of these must, of course, depend upon the estimates they may form either of the joys of the one, or the torments of the other; and these estimates, in their turn, must depend on their *states of life* respectively.   The Heaven of the Old Church, which is situated in some determinate, yet undetermined portion of space, has, I confess, but very few positive charms, and offers very inadequate inducements to the mortification of our natural appetites.   Passing by its promise of negative bliss in a life of idleness, the only active employment of the evangelicals and others who may assemble there, will be psalm-singing; with occasional interludes when they will be called upon, with crowns on their heads and wings folded, to adjudge their unfortunate fellow-beings to their pre-ordained destination (by

were fully sensible of this ; and, indifferent alike to the schemes
of the Prince of Orange, and of Barnevelt and his pensionaries,
settled the *Quinqueticulat Controversy* in a very sensible way,
by compounding a Deity, after the model of John Calvin, of
such contradictious elements, that in naming his attributes,
Wesley characteristically observed—" *I defy you to say as hard
a thing of the Devil himself.*" The " *Five points,*" you will
remember, which were *settled* in this *evangelical* conventicle
were :—

First. That God has chosen a certain number in Christ to
everlasting glory, before the foundation of the world, according
to his immutable purpose, and of his *free grace* and *love ;* without the *foresight of faith, good works,* or *any conditions performed by the creature ;* and that the *rest of mankind* he was
pleased to *pass by,* and *ordain* them to *dishonor* and *wrath* for
their sins, in *praise* of his *vindictive justice.*

Second. That Christ, by his death and sufferings made an
atonement *only* for the sins of *the elect.*

Third. That mankind are totally depraved in consequence
of the fall.

Fourth. That all whom God has *predestinated to life* he is
pleased in his appointed time effectually *to call* by his Word
and Spirit out of that state of sin and death, in which they are
by nature, to grace and salvation by Jesus Christ.

Fifth. That those whom God has effectually called and
sanctified by his spirit shall never finally fall from a state of
grace.

These are the famous " *five points,*" which, I presume, Dr.
P—— and the Evangelicals generally believe to contain a true
statement of *the faith once delivered to the saints,*—the " *godly
consideration of which*" (to use the language of another sect)
" *is full of sweet, pleasant and unspeakable comfort to godly persons ;*" while, on the other hand, "*for curious and carnal persons, lacking the spirit of Christ, to have continually before their
eyes the sentence of God's predestination, is a most dangerous
downfall, whereby the Devil doth thrust them either into desperation, or into wretchedness of most unclean*?*living, no less perilous than desperation.*"

Now, my dear sir, with men who have so abused their
rational faculties as to make them confirm these extravagan-
ces as sober truths, all argument founded in reason or revelation is utterly lost. You had as well attempt to convince them
that three distinct *persons,* discharging three distinct *offices,* cannot make *one God.* But though these paradoxes be obviously inconsistent with the dictates of common sense, and the
clear declarations of the Divine Word ; though they be most

ing assurances of the "*elect*" principle, the potent promises of "*justification by faith alone,*" and the labor-saving machinery of "*imputed righteousness,*" can account for such a prodigy. But although it be admitted that this view of a future state may present but slight positive inducements to a good life, it cannot be denied that it imposes strong negative restraints on evil actions: and this is great gain, at least in a civil and social point of view. When one ceases to do evil he *may* learn to do well, but not before. And until men are prepared to acknowledge and act upon higher motives to a virtuous life, a life of inward and outward obedience to the Divine commandments, this frightful picture must be held up before their eyes as the only preventive of a vicious one. I therefore take no exceptions; but, on the contrary, occasionally go to Methodist *camp,* or Presbyterian "*anxious meetings*" for the express purpose of studying the terrible topography of the place; for some of those preachers commonly called "*revival preachers,*" have the most vivid conceptions of it and its minutest instruments of torture, and can, withal, describe them with such graphic and frightful fidelity, that I have known the avaricious member to suspend his shaving operations, the ambitious to forget his schemes of power, and the dissolute to look grave for a week afterwards. In brief, without the terrors of this theology, I am persuaded that men, in the present state of the Old Church, would rush headlong into the most lawless excesses. Our province is gradually to substitute for these terrors higher and holier motives of action; to inform the understanding, to elevate the thoughts, and to purify the affections in freedom; to teach men that if they would know what is *true,* they must do what is *good,* not from the fear of punishment, nor from the hope of reward, but from a pure uncalculating love of truth and goodness themselves. This is not the work of a day; it is the labor of centuries: and in its performance difficulties meet us at every step. Stereotyped systems of mental and moral education, long cherished opinions that whisper to our pride, and menacing dogmas that speak to our fears, ancient fanaticisms with one eye, and time honored bigotries with empty sockets, and venerable fooleries of every sort, start up wrathfully around us and cry aloud against the invasion of their prescriptive prerogatives. As the younger candidates for medical honors are represented, in the bitter satire of Le Sage, swearing to the evil one to practise their profession only according to the formulas of the day, by which nine tenths found the doctor more to be dreaded than the disease— so these ancient worshipers of Chaos and of night have settled all questions of science, reason and revelation, prescribed fixed

no means, I should suppose, an agreeable duty), and then back
to their singing again. These are the chief, if not the only
employments of Heaven, so far as I have been able to ascertain from the perusal of (I design no equivoque,) many *ponderous* tomes of popular Theology. I beg pardon; Dr. Dick, I
believe, puts them on the study of Astronomy, Physiology, and
some other of the natural sciences; an idea probably suggested by reading some such work as Dr. P——'s Review; and
without expressing either concurrence or dissent, so far as the
theory applies to the other world, I can, after reading the work
referred to, readily admit its expediency in this.

But whatever may be thought of Heaven, and the rewards
which it holds out as inducements to a good life, it cannot be
denied that the Hell of the Old Church is pretty well supplied
with punishments, as securities against an evil one (I speak,
of course, in both cases, of an outward and external life). I
need not enter into details. Homer, Virgil, Dante and Milton
have saved the world any further trouble on this head. Suffice
it to say, that all accounts represent it as at a *great distance
from us;* whether in the comets, as the Whistonian theory will
have it,—or in the Sun, as Mr. Swinden maintains,—or in the
centre of the Earth, as the Heathen Poets teach,—or on the
other side of the globe, considered as an extended plain, as the
primitive Christian Fathers believed,—a sulphurous lake, lying
broad, deep and dark, and bubbling with eternal fires, created
expressly for the purpose of exhibiting the *wrath* and *vindictive*
justice of God towards "*the passed by,*" to wit: nine tenths of
the human species, created, prepared and fore-ordained to this
terrific destiny!

Now, men may think as they please about the reasonable-
ness and orthodoxy of all this; yet I am persuaded that the
world is indebted to these conceptions for much of that external
morality which is still to be found in Christendom. The idea
of being raised again in the flesh, after having lain in the cool,
damp grave for so many centuries, having bodies fresh and tender as a new-born babe's, with scarcely a cuticle to cover the
epidermis, and to be suddenly merged into such a scalding flood
as this, is, to most men's minds, inexpressibly terrible. And
then, according to Mr. Whiston, to be whirled as suddenly out
of their fiery bath, and, with a comet's velocity, cast beyond
the orbits of Saturn and Herschel, and plunged into "thrilling
regions of thicked ribbed ice," presents to contemplation a see-
saw of horrors to which imagination can add nothing! *And
to be thus, eternally but thus, having been otherwise!* Amazing
that man should believe all this, aye, in the *ipsissima verba* of
the account, and yet live as they live! Nothing but the quiet-

majority of mankind. *This must needs be*, for it results as a necessary consequence of the unchanging laws of the Divine Providence. Ignorance is permitted for the wisest and most merciful ends, when knowledge would only lead to profanation. He who is not *morally* prepared (I use the word in its popular sense,) to receive the truths of the New Church, he who has *confirmed* himself in the faith of his sect, and is, therefore, no longer *inquiring after truth*, had better be left to his idols; for though you should offer to him the most precious of spiritual pearls, he would but trample them under foot, and turn and rend you. On the other hand there are many, and will yet be more, who are seeking and will seek *truth* as the very jewel of their souls. These will not be without a Heavenly guide to lead them to the fountains of living waters. These are the Gentiles of our time to whom the Gospel will be sent, and of whom the Church must be formed. As to the Doctors, Rulers, Scribes and Pharisees of the Old Church, they must be left where the Lord, at his first advent, left their predecessors. Their looks of scorn, of mocking and derision, why should we heed them, even for a moment? *They* have made the *Word of God* of no effect by *their* traditions, as the past and present state of Christendom, distinguished and disfigured by every imaginable form of vice, too fully, too fearfully, attests. But the day of their pride and power is passing away, and they *feel* it, yet they know not the cause. Day by day some fragment of the vast fabric of superstition, fraud, and force, which has cast its dark shadow over the world for so many ages, is tumbling to the earth with a crash, startling its roused inmates. Its dungeons shall no more echo with the clank of manacles; nor resound with the cries of tortured victims expiring in agony. Its towers shall no more be garnished with human skeletons bleaching in the rains and creaking in the winds of heaven. Its courts shall never again be lit up with midnight fires, presenting to high Heaven the horrid spectacle of men and women, the old and the young, the strong and the weak, the innocent and the unoffending, quenching the blazing faggots with their blood; while around them shall stand a circle of merciless priests and their bigotted myrmidons, gloating on the scene, and drowning their last death shrieks with loud hosannas of praise and thanksgiving to the MOST HIGH GOD, for the blessed privilege of perpetrating such crimes and witnessing such orgies. It may, indeed, in the providence of the Lord, still retain some of its stern outward features, like the bat-tenanted ruins of Palmyra of the desert. It may still point to its bent towers, its broken arches, its rent curtains, its tottering columns and crumbling capitals; and hollow voices

limits to the progress, of the human mind, and proclaimed the penalties of treason and rebellion against all who shall dare to transcend them. We see this in every day's history; Dr. P——'s book will furnish you with many examples. Look at his ancient canons of theology, his *ex-cathedras* in geology, metaphysics, physiology, archæology, &c. &c., and you will see in what manner, and how easily he settles all controverted points in questions of scientific and religious truth. Observe his arguments and conclusions in relation to Conjugial Love, in which, ignorant of the degrees of life, and the grades of good and evil, he preposterously confounds the natural appetites of a goat with the spiritual affections of an angel. With him the sexual propensities of all animals, men and brutes, are the same. He has no conception whatever of the conjugial princi- ple, neither as respects its foundation in the spiritual and physi- cal structure of the sexes, nor its final use in the temporal and eternal concerns of men. His idea sinks down and ter- minates in simple, naked, natural copulation. And thus that holy principle, proceeding from the very nature and essence of God himself, stamped in lasting and living characters on all living things, that principle which, in its development, gives men to earth and angels to heaven, and happiness and joy to both, is degraded down to the low, lewd, and lecherous concu- piscence of mere brute beasts ! And how shall you, by reason- ing, teach him otherwise? His mind is *filed* against you; and you had as well discuss the subject of colors with a man born blind; for he might, at least, show that some impression can be made, though he should conceive that *red* was "like the sound of a trumpet." The very language,—the words which you must needs use to convey information would, of themselves, defeat your object; for though it might be lawful for you to mention the head, heart, hand or foot, and to discuss their respective functions; yet the moment you venture to name the peculiar organs which appertain to the sexes, or even refer to their uses (which, unabused and according to the Divine order, are the highest, the noblest and the best), so delicate are the sensibilities of Dr. P——, that he instantly falls into convul- sions and dies the death of the soft Sybarite, whose nerves can- not bear the rustling of a rose-leaf. There are many men of this peculiar artificial structure; men who are much more easily shocked at *words* than *ideas;* and of whom Dean Swift ventures a theory, the truth of which I am much more ready to admit, than, in this case, to apply.

Such are some of the impediments to the progress of truth which induce me to believe that the Philosophy and Theology of the New Church must long remain sealed up to the large majority of mankind. *This must needs be,* for it results as a necessary consequence of the unchanging laws of the Divine Providence. Ignorance is permitted for the wisest and most merciful ends, when knowledge would only lead to profanation. He who is not *morally* prepared (I use the word in its popular sense,) to receive the truths of the New Church, he who has *confirmed* himself in the faith of his sect, and is, therefore, no longer *inquiring after truth,* had better be left to his idols; for though you should offer to him the most precious of spiritual pearls, he would but trample them under foot, and turn and rend you. On the other hand there are many, and will yet be more, who are seeking and will seek *truth* as the very jewel of their souls. These will not be without a Heavenly guide to lead them to the fountains of living waters. These are the Gentiles of our time to whom the Gospel will be sent, and of whom the Church must be formed. As to the Doctors, Rulers, Scribes and Pharisees of the Old Church, they must be left where the Lord, at his first advent, left their predecessors. Their looks of scorn, of mocking and derision, why should we heed them, even for a moment? *They* have made the *Word of God* of no effect by *their* traditions, as the past and present state of Christendom, distinguished and disfigured by every imaginable form of vice, too fully, too fearfully, attests. But the day of their pride and power is passing away, and they *feel* it, yet they know not the cause. Day by day some fragment of the vast fabric of superstition, fraud, and force, which has cast its dark shadow over the world for so many ages, is tumbling to the earth with a crash, startling its roused inmates. Its dungeons shall no more echo with the clank of manacles; nor resound with the cries of tortured victims expiring in agony. Its towers shall no more be garnished with human skeletons bleaching in the rains and creaking in the winds of heaven. Its courts shall never again be lit up with midnight fires, presenting to high Heaven the horrid spectacle of men and women, the old and the young, the strong and the weak, the innocent and the unoffending, quenching the blazing faggots with their blood; while around them shall stand a circle of merciless priests and their bigotted myrmidons, gloating on the scene, and drowning their last death shrieks with loud hosannas of praise and thanksgiving to the MOST HIGH GOD, for the blessed privilege of perpetrating such crimes and witnessing such orgies. It may, indeed, in the providence of the Lord, still retain some of its stern outward features, like the bat-tenanted ruins of Palmyra of the desert. It may still point to its bent towers, its broken arches, its rent curtains, its tottering columns and crumbling capitals; and hollow voices may still issue from beneath its fallen and bloody altars, saying, "This is the House of the Lord Jesus Christ;" but other tongues from amidst its trophied pyramids of human bones shall exclaim—"It is the House of Death!"—*Babylon is fallen, is fallen.* In the meantime the truths of the New Church are steadily advancing, and with a rapidity far beyond my most sanguine anticipations eighteen years ago. Its growth, like that of the cedar of Lebanon, is imperceptible yet constant —*occulto velut arbor ævo*—and I, for one, am content to wait quietly on the Divine Providence. I see, daily, incontestable proofs that a high-way is opening from Egypt to Assyria, and I doubt not, in the least, that Israel will yet be a blessing in the midst of them.

R. K. C.

ARTICLE III.

LETTERS TO A TRINITARIAN.

LETTER IX.

THE GLORIFICATION.

DEAR SIR,

I may perhaps presume that the tenor of my two last letters has conveyed to you somewhat of a correct general idea of the doctrine of the Lord's Glorification as held by the New Church. You will have seen that it is something altogether different from that state of post-resurrection glory and grandeur which is usually understood by the term. It is the designation of an internal process which was continually going on in the Lord's human nature, as the result of that series of temptation-combats by which alone the hereditary evils of the maternal principle could be expelled and a Divine humanity be substituted in its stead.* It is in this view of the

---

* " With respect to the Lord's essential life, it was a continual progression from the human to the Divine, even to absolute union; for that he might fight with the hells and overcome them, it was needful that he should fight from the human, inasmuch as there can be no combat with the hells from the Divine; therefore he was pleased to put on the human as another man, to be an infant as another, and to grow up into sciences and knowledges. That the Lord's progression from the human to the Divine was such can be doubted by no one, who only considers that he was an infant, and learned to speak as an infant, and so forth; but there was this difference, that the essential Divine was in him, as being conceived of Jehovah."—(*A. C.* 2523.)

subject that we see the ground of the analogy between the glorification of our Lord and the regeneration of his people, to which I have already adverted. Swedenborg has in fact given to the world what may be termed a *philosophy of temptation* which constitutes one of the most remarkable features of his system, and as it lies at the very foundation of the doctrine of glorified and regenerate life, I shall dwell at some length upon it as essential to a right apprehension of the grand scope of my argument. And first, as to the *fact* of a continued series of temptations endured by the Lord throughout the whole period of his earthly sojourn.

" That the life of the Lord, from his earliest childhood even to the last hour of his life in the world, was a continual temptation and continual victory, appears from several passages in the Word of the Old Testament: and that it did not cease with the temptation in the wilderness, is evident from these words in Luke: ' After that the devil had finished all the temptation, he departed from him for a season,' iv. 13: also from this, that he was tempted even to the death of the cross, thus to the last hour of his life in the world. Hence it appears that the Lord's whole life in the world, from his earliest childhood, was a continual temptation and continual victory; the last was, when he prayed on the cross for his enemies; thus for all on the face of the whole earth. In the Word of the life of the Lord with the Evangelists, no mention is made, except the last, of any other than his temptation in the wilderness: others were not disclosed to the disciples: those which were disclosed, appear, according to the literal sense, so light, as scarcely to be anything; for so to speak and so to answer is not any temptation; when yet, it was more grievous than any human mind can conceive or believe. No one can know what temptation is unless he has been in it. The temptation which is related in Matt. iv. 1–11, Mark i. 12, 13, Luke iv. 1–13, contains in a summary to Lord's temptations, namely, that, out of love towards the whole human race, he fought against the loves of self and of the world, with which the hells were replete. All temptation is made against the love in which man is, and the degree of the temptation is according to the degree of the love. If it is not against the love, there is no temptation. To destroy any one's love, is to destroy his very life; for love is life. The life of the Lord was love towards the whole human race; which was so great and of such a nature, as to be nothing but pure love. Against this his life were admitted continual temptations, as already stated, from his earliest childhood to his last hour in the world. During all this time the Lord was assaulted by all the hells, which were continually overcome, subjugated, and conquered by him; and this solely out of love towards the human race. And because this love was not human but divine, and all temptation is great in proportion as the love is great; it may be seen how grievous were his combats, and how great the ferocity with which the hells assailed him. That these things were so, I know of a certainty."—(*A. C.* 1690.)

" That the Lord, more than all in the universe, underwent and sustained most grievous temptations, is not so fully known from the

Word, where it is only mentioned that he was in the wilderness forty days, and was tempted of the devil. The temptations themselves which he then had, are not described except in a few words; nevertheless these few involve all ; as what is mentioned in Mark, chap. i. 12, 13, that he was with the beasts, by which are signified the worst of the infernal crew ; and what is elsewhere related, that he was led by the devil upon a pinnacle of the temple, and upon a high mountain ; which are nothing else but representatives of most grievous temptations which he suffered in the wilderness.—(*A. C.* 1663.)

The end to be attained by this indispensable process of temptation-combats, accompanied always by victory, was the gradual reduction of the external man to conformity or correspondence with the internal, and the final union of the Human Essence with the Divine in the Lord, which is but another name for his glorification.* The general principle is thus stated by our author.

"Temptations have for their end the subjugation of what is external in man, that they may thereby be rendered obedient to what is internal ; as may appear to any one who reflects, that so soon as man's loves are assaulted and broken, as during misfortunes, sickness, and grief of mind, his lusts begin to subside, and he at the same time begins to talk piously ; but as soon as he returns to his former state, the external man gets the dominion, and he scarcely thinks at all on such subjects. The like happens at the hour of death, when corporeal things begin to be extinguished ; and hence every one may see what the internal man is, and what the external ; and the mode in which lusts and pleasures, which are of the external man, hinder the Lord's operation by the internal."—(*A. C.* 857.)

In the following extract the same view is expanded from a deeper ground and a strong light shed upon the rationale of the whole subject. The theology of the schools sounds no such depths as those that are reached by Swedenborg's plummet. The intimation of organic and recipient *vessels* in the soul of man into which the influx of life from the Lord is received may, at first blush, outrage your psychology, but I have no hesitation to adduce it, as it is a very natural sequence from the

---

* "Temptation is the means of the conjunction of the internal man with the external, inasmuch as they are at disagreement with each other, but are reduced to agreement and correspondence by temptations."—(*A. C.* 3928.)

"The external things that are discordant, which were spoken of above, are the only things that hinder the internal man, when it acts upon the external, from making it one with itself. The external man is nothing else but an instrumental or organical something, having no life in itself, but receiving life from the internal man, and then it appears as if the external man had life from itself. With the Lord, however, after he had expelled hereditary evil, and thus had purified the organicals of the Human Essence, these also receive life ; so that the Lord, as he was life with respect to the internal man, became life also with respect to the external man. This is what is signified by glorification."—(*A. C.* 1603.)

admission which even you yourself would probably make, that the *soul is a substance*, and a substance, too, receptive of life from a Divine source, which it must be unless it have life in itself independent of the uncreated and self-subsisting life that pertains to the Lord alone. But if the soul be a substance adapted to the reception of influent life, we see no reason to doubt, what Swedenborg has affirmed, that this substance is *organized* for that purpose, as we find throughout the whole domain of vegetable and animal existence that *organized forms* are the fixed receptacles of vital influx. And if this holds in the lower departments of the universe, why not in the higher? What is the difficulty of conceiving that there may be spiritual substances duly organized as well as material? Assuming then as a postulate, what every intelligent receiver of Swedenborg is prepared argumentatively to maintain, that the human mind is as truly distinguished by recipient vessels as the body is by a cellular tissue, I transfer the paragraph in question.

" Good cannot be conjoined with truth in the natural man without combats, or, what is the same, without temptations: that it may be known how this case is, in respect to man, it may be briefly told; man is nothing else but an organ, or vessel which receives life from the Lord, for man does not live from himself; the life, which flows in with man from the Lord, is from his divine love; this love or the life thence, flows in and applies itself to the vessels which are in man's rational and which are in his natural; these vessels with man are in a contrary situation in respect to the influent life in consequence of the hereditary evil into which man is born, and of the actual evil which he procures to himself; but as far as the influent life can dispose the vessels to receive it so far it does dispose them: these vessels in the rational man, and in the natural thereof, are those things which are called truths, and in themselves are nothing but perceptions of the variations of the form of those vessels, and of the changes of state, according to which, in divers manners, the variations exist, which are effected in the most subtile substances, by methods inexpressible. * * Good' itself, which has life from the Lord, or which is life, is what flows in and disposes; when therefore these vessels, which are variable as to forms, are in a contrary position and direction in respect to the life, as was said, it may be evident that they must be reduced to a position according to the life, or in compliance with the life; this can in nowise be effected, so long as man is in that state into which he is born, and into which he has reduced himself, for the vessels are not obedient, being obstinately repugnant, and opposing with all their might the heavenly order, according to which the life acts; for the good which moves them, and with which they comply, is of the love of self and the world, which good, from the crass heat which is in it, causes them to be of such quality; wherefore, before they can be rendered compliant, and be made fit to receive any thing of the life of the Lord's love, they must be softened; this softening is effected by no other means than by temptations: for temptations remove those things which pertain to self-love, and to contempt of others in comparison with self, consequently things which pertain to self-glory, and also to hatred and revenge thence arising; when therefore the vessels are somewhat tempered and subdued by temptations, then they begin to become yielding to, and compliant with the life of the Lord's love, which continually flows in with man; hence then it is, that good begins to be conjoined to truths, first in the rational man, and afterwards in the natural; for truths, as was said, are nothing else than perceptions of the variations of the form according to states which are continually changed, and perceptions are from the life which flows in; hence is the reason why man is regenerated, that is, is made new, by temptations, or what is the same, by spirtual combats, and that he is afterwards gifted with another temper or disposition, being made mild, humble, simple, and contrite in heart: from these considerations it may now appear what use temptations promote, viz., this, that good from the Lord may not only flow in but may also dispose the vessels to obedience and thus conjoin itself with them. * * * * But as to what respects the Lord ,he, by the most grievous temptation-combats, reduced all things in himself into divine order, insomuch that there remained nothing at all of the human which he had derived from the mother, so that he was not made new as another man, but altogether divine; for man who is made new by regeneration, still retains in himself an inclination to evil, yea evil itself, but is withheld from evil by an influx of the life of the Lord's love, and this by exceedingly strong power; whereas the Lord entirely cast out every evil which was hereditary to him from the mother, and made himself divine even as to the vessels, that is, as to truths; that is what in the Word is called glorification."—(*A. C.* 3318.)

The bearing of this upon the case of the Lord will not be of difficult apprehension. Receiving, as he did, a humanity from the mother tainted from the necessity of its nature with hereditary evil, this element of evil was to be gradually put away and a Divine humanity assumed according to the purport of our author's language in what follows: "The human with the Lord was from the mother, thus infirm, having with it thence an hereditary, which he overcame by temptation-combats, and entirely expelled, insomuch that nothing remained of the infirm and hereditary from the mother; yea, at last not anything from the mother remained. Thus he totally put off the maternal, to such a degree as to be no longer her son, as also he himself says in Mark; 'They said unto Jesus, Behold, thy mother and thy brethren without seek thee! and he answered them, saying, Who is my mother or my brethren? and looking round upon them who sat about him, he said, Behold my mother and my brethren, for whosoever shall do the will of God, he is my brother, and my sister, and my mother' (iii. 32, 33, 34, 35; Matt. xii. 46, 47, 48, 49; Luke viii. 20, 21). And when he put off this human, he put on the Divine human, by virtue whereof he called himself *the Son of Man*, as he frequently does in the Word of the New Testament, and also *the*

Son of God ; and by the Son of Man he signified the truth itself, and by the Son of God the good itself, which appertained to his human essence when it was made Divine : the former state was that of the Lord's humiliation, but the latter of his glorification. In the former state, viz. that of humiliation, when he had yet with himself an infirm human, he adored Jehovah as one distinct from himself, and indeed as a servant, for the human is respectively nothing else."—(*A. C.* 2159.)

That the prevailing theology of Christendom involves no such view of a progressive glorification in the Lord is beyond debate. That theology maintains that whatever may have been the change in circumstances and state, still the *nature* of Jesus Christ was the same before and after the event termed his glorification. Accordingly all those passages in which the letter represents the Lord as distinct from the Father, and in which he prays to Him in the hour of his agony, appear to the mass of Christians as equally applicable to the Lord sojourning on earth and to the Lord reigning in heaven.· They do not recognize the fact of his having undergone an inward change of nature still more marked than anything that occurred in the vicissitudes of his outward lot. Thus, the dogma of Catholicism has established that Mary is still the mother of our Lord, and the result has been a glorification of her little short of that ascribed to her son. Protestantism, though rejecting the Mariolatry of the Romanist, is still equally explicit in recognizing the complete separation between Jehovah and Jesus. The Son offers himself a sacrifice to propitiate the Father ; as, otherwise they must hold that God died to propitiate himself, which is of course absurd. It holds, moreover, that the Son in virtue of his atoning sacrifice perpetually intercedes in behalf of his elect. He is, therefore, practically regarded as distinct from the Being with or before whom he intercedes. How exceedingly diverse from all this is the view presented by Swedenborg may be seen from his statement of the true Scriptural doctrine of Intercession.*

"The Lord's intercession for the human race was during his abode in the world, and indeed during his state of humiliation, for in that state he spake with Jehovah as with another; but in the state of glorification, when the human essence became united to the Divine, and was also made Jehovah, he does not then intercede, but shows mercy, and from his Divine (principle) administers help and saves; it is mercy itself, which is intercession, for such is its essence."—(*A. C.* 2250.)

---

* See the subject of our Lord's Intercession treated with consummate ability by Mr. Noble, in his "Lectures on the Important Doctrines of the True Christian Religion."—*Lectures* XVII. *and* XVIII.

This view of intercession we hold to result necessarily from the doctrine of the Divine unity. As there is but one God, and Jesus Christ is himself that God, we find it as impossible to conceive of his interceding with himself as of his making an atonement to himself; and we can admit no requisition upon our faith to acknowledge any doctrine as divine which clearly conflicts with the fundamental tenet of the supreme Deity and absolute Unipersonality of Jehovah-Jesus.

Still objections suggest themselves. If the inmost soul of Jesus was Jehovah, then the Lord in praying to the Father prayed to his own soul. Unquestionably he did, on the principle before alluded to, and which is clearly developed in the two following paragraphs, which I give at length from the very great importance of the subject-matter as throwing light upon one of the profoundest arcana of revelation, to wit, the manner in which the duality of the letter is to be reconciled with the unity of the sense in what is related of our Lord's intercourse with the Father.

"The internal of the Lord, that is, whatever the Lord received from the Father, was Jehovah in him, because he was conceived of Jehovah. There is a difference between what man receives from his father, and what he receives from his mother. Man receives from his father all that is internal, that is, his very soul or life; but he receives from his mother all that is external: in a word, the interior man, or the spirit, is from the father, but the exterior man, or the body, is from the mother. This every one may comprehend merely from this; that the soul itself is implanted from the father, which begins to clothe itself with a bodily form in the ovary, and whatsoever is afterwards added, whether in the ovary or in the womb, is of the mother, for it receives no addition from elsewhere. Hence it may appear, that the Lord, as to his internals, was Jehovah; but as the external, which he received from the mother, was to be united to the Divine or Jehovah, and this by temptations and victories, as was said, it must needs appear to him in those states, when he spake with Jehovah, as if he was speaking with another, when, nevertheless, he was speaking with himself; so far, that is, as conjunction was effected."—(*A. C.* 1815.)

"That the Lord adored and prayed to Jehovah his Father, is known from the Word in the Evangelists, and this as if to a Being different from himself, although Jehovah was in him. But the state in which the Lord then was, was his state of humiliation, the quality of which was described in the First Part, namely, that he was then in the infirm human derived from the mother. But so far as he put off that human, and put on the Divine, he was in a different state, which is called his state of glorification. In the former state he adored Jehovah as a Person different from himself, although he was in himself; for, as stated above, his internal was Jehovah: but in the latter, namely, the state of glorification, he spake with Jehovah as with himself, for he was Jehovah himself. But how these things are cannot be conceived, unless it be known what the internal is, and how the internal acts upon the external; and, further, how the internal and external are distinct from each other, and yet joined together. This, however, may be illustrated by its like, namely, by the internal in man, and its influx into, and operation upon, his external. The internal of man is that by which man is man, and by which he is distinguished from brute animals. By this internal he lives after death, and to eternity; and by this he is capable of being elevated by the Lord amongst angels: it is the very first form by virtue of which he becomes, and is, a man. By this internal the Lord is united to man. The heaven nearest to the Lord consists of these human internals; this, however, is above the inmost angelic heaven; wherefore these internals are of the Lord himself. Those internals of men have not life in themselves, but are forms recipient of the life of the Lord. In proportion, then, as man is in evil, whether actual or hereditary, he is as it were separated from this internal, which is of the Lord and with the Lord, consequently, is separated from the Lord: for although this internal be adjoined to man, and inseparable from him, still, as far as man recedes from the Lord, so far he as it were separates himself from it. This separation, however, is not an evulsion from it, for man would then be no longer capable of living after death; but it is a dissent and disagreement of those faculties of man which are beneath it, that is, of the rational and external man. In proportion to this dissent and disagreement, there is a disjunction; but in proportion as there is no dissent and disagreement, man is conjoined by the internal to the Lord; and this is effected in proportion as he is in love and charity, for love and charity conjoin. Thus it is in respect to man. But the internal of the Lord was Jehovah Himself, inasmuch as he was conceived of Jehovah, who cannot be divided and become another's, as the internal of a son who is conceived of a human father; for the divine is not capable of division, like the human, but is one and the same, and is permanent. With this internal the Lord united the Human Essence; and because the internal of the Lord was Jehovah, it was not a form recipient of life, as the internal of man is, but was life itself. His Human Essence also, by union, was in like manner made life; wherefore the Lord so often says that he is life: as in John: 'As the Father hath life in himself, so hath he given to the Son to have life in himself,' chap. v. 26; besides other passages in the same Evangelist, as chap. i. 4; v. 21; vi. 33, 35, 48; xi. 25. In proportion, therefore, as the Lord was in the human which he received hereditarily from the mother, he appeared distinct from Jehovah, and adored Jehovah as one different from himself; but in proportion as he put off this human, the Lord was not distinct from Jehovah, but one with him. The former state, as remarked above, was the Lord's state of humiliation, but the latter was his state of glorification."—(*A. C.* 1999.)

The same mystery, then, if we may so term it, is to be recognized in its degree in every man who becomes a subject of regeneration. This work is carried on by a process of temptation, or, in other words, of conflict between the flesh and the spirit, equivalent to the external and internal man. Just in proportion to the disagreement between these two principles, the man feels himself possessed, as it were, of a double personality, the one yielding, the other resisting.

In this state of inward self-divulsion it is not difficult to conceive of one department of the man's being addressing the other, as we find in the case of David;—"Why art thou cast down, O my soul, and why art thou disquieted within me? Hope thou in God, for I shall yet praise Him." The case of Paul, as exhibited in the epistle to the Romans (Ch. vii.) I have already cited as strikingly illustrative of the grand position. This conscious antagonism of the two natures becomes less and less as the victories are multiplied over temptation, for the effect of this is evermore to bring the soul into harmony and unity with itself, and this is in truth an image in miniature of the sublime conjunction of the Human and the Divine, which constituted the glorification of the Lord. As this, however, was a result accomplished by degrees, as it was the issue of a process extending through the whole term of the Lord's terrestrial life, and was brought to a consummation by the passion of the cross, which was the last stage of his temptations, at once his sorest trial and his crowning triumph, so the conclusion presses upon us, that the regeneration of man, which is conformed to this exemplar, is not an instantaneous act but a gradual process.

That the plenary glorification of the Lord was accomplished by the death on the cross, he himself teaches in John xiii. 31, 32; "Therefore when he was gone out Jesus said, Now is the Son of man glorified, and God is glorified in him. If God be glorified in him (ἐν αὐτῷ), God shall also glorify him in himself (ἐν ἑαυτῷ), and shall straightway glorify him." Here the glorification is predicated both of God the Father and of God the Son, since God is glorified *in him*, and if so, he will glorify him *in himself*, clearly evincing that the glorification was an act of union and identification between the Father and the Son, in consequence of which the Son was henceforth to be so merged in the Father that they could no longer be viewed as in a state of even apparent separation. This was effected at the crisis of the crucifixion when the mysterious process reached its acme; "Father, the hour is come; glorify thy Son that thy Son also may glorify thee." The son of Mary is nailed to the cross and suffers the agony of dissolution, and in the article of death the union of the Divine and Human becomes completed; the man Christ Jesus is fully identified with the one only God, Jehovah, and hence is he now known in the New Church by the distinguishing and appropriate title of THE LORD. At this eventful moment the bonds of his terrestial relationships were severed, the Lord rejected whatever he held in common with the *fallen* race of men, and Mary ceased to be his mother: " *Woman*, behold

ARTICLE IV.

THE QUESTION OF RE-BAPTISM RE-CONSIDERED.

An attempt has been made in Article III. of the Sept. No. of the Repository, entitled the "Question of Baptism Considered," and signed "A. E. F.," to show that there is not only no necessity for re-baptism on entering the N. C. from the old, but that it is positively wrong ; and the reasoning and authority adduced by the writer, so far from resolving the question satisfactorily in this way, tends to clear and confirm the true New Church-man in the opposite. The premises we regard as erroneous, the arguments as fallacious, and the conclusions false. This being in our humble opinion the truth, we look upon the appearance of the article, and the harm that it is likely to do with a melancholy regret. Emanating from so respectable a source and on a subject treating of so important an ordinance of the new dispensation, unsatisfactory as the article is, yet it is calculated to have a great influence on the minds of persons passing from the Old Church to the New, and not yet fully in-doctrinated in or clearly understanding the faith of our New Church. It becomes, then the imperative duty of a conscientious receiver of those doctrines, to counteract, if possible, this effect by a faithful and candid exposition of the fallacies, contained in the article in question. This shall be done by the authoritative teachings of the New Church.

The writer contends, first, that an argument against the necessity of re-baptism may be maintained on "the grounds of the Report of the Massachusetts Association on this subject," printed in the Journal of 1847, where it is contended that the former Church is the *External* of the New Church, and is in connexion with the External of the New Heavens, and that therefore its Baptism must connect them (its members) with the External Christian Heaven, and that when any one is baptized in that church, the angels of the External Heaven are appointed to attend upon him, to take care of him, to keep him in a state for receiving the faith of their Heaven, to give him an inclination for their religion, and a disinclination for all other religions. "What is thus in connexion with christian angels must clearly be a church and, as the Report terms it, a christian church. Baptism into it therefore is baptism into the New Church as its external."

The other reasons which the writer draws from this Report in favor of his proposition are all predicated on this assumption.

out in the process which takes place in ourselves. The soul during its sojourn in the body makes use of it as a vestment and an instrument. Every day and every hour it is laying aside the old and assuming new substances. The life on earth is an incessant death and an incessant resurrection. The body of the child is not, as to substance, identically one with that of the adult man, nor that of the adult man with that of the old man. How then can we maintain that precisely the same material body will arise, when the same flesh is not, for a single day, subject to the same soul? By this analogy we may comprehend the sublime process of our Lord's glorification, as far as it is given to the finite of man to grasp the infinite of God.*

The Lord however successively laid aside the substances received from the virgin mother, not to borrow and substitute for them new *material* substances, but to put on in their stead the spiritual substances of his Divine Humanity, such as it appeared, by anticipation, to Peter, James, and John, on the hallowed mount of transfiguration. The completion of this process was the consummated union or unition of the Human with the Divine Essence, in virtue of which the Lord is now able to put forth a redeeming and saving power towards our lost race which would otherwise have been for ever impossible consistently with those laws of order from which the Most High cannot depart without denying his own nature. But upon this point I propose to dwell more at length in another letter.

G. B.

(*To be Continued.*)

---

* The following extract from the Lectures of Rev. B. F. Barrett presents a pertinent but still inadequate view of the subject, by means of a striking illustration. As our argumentative scope is substantially the same, it serves both our purposes equally well.

"Our conception of this divine operation may perhaps be somewhat aided if we reflect upon how the case is in that natural phenomenon which is called petrifaction—a process by which wood or any other organic substance is changed to stone. As often as a particle of the organized substance which undergoes this operation, is removed, a particle of mineral or silicious matter comes in and takes its place. And thus when the process is completed, the substance of the wood has all been removed and replaced by mineral matter; yet so gradual has this process been that the form and organic structure of the wood has been completely preserved. And so perfectly is this the case that it appears as if the wood had been *changed* to stone Something similar to this is also taking place continually in our bodies. Particles are constantly passing off, and their place is supplied by new ones; yet the form and organic structure of our bodies is still preserved.— (*Barrett's Lectures, p.* 307.)

Son of God; and by the Son of Man he signified the truth itself, and by the Son of God the good itself, which appertained to his human essence when it was made Divine : the former state was that of the Lord's humiliation, but the latter of his glorification.   In the former state, viz. that of humiliation, when he had yet with himself an infirm human, he adored Jehovah as one distinct from himself, and indeed as a servant, for the human is respectively nothing else."—(*A. C.* 2159.)

That the prevailing theology of Christendom involves no such view of a progressive glorification in the Lord is beyond debate.   That theology maintains that whatever may have been the change in circumstances and state, still the *nature* of Jesus Christ was the same before and after the event termed his glorification.   Accordingly all those passages in which the letter represents the Lord as distinct from the Father, and in which he prays to Him in the hour of his agony, appear to the mass of Christians as equally applicable to the Lord sojourning on earth and to the Lord reigning in heaven.· They do not recognize the fact of his having undergone an inward change of nature still more marked than anything that occurred in the vicissitudes of his outward lot.   Thus, the dogma of Catholicism has established that Mary is still the mother of our Lord, and the result has been a glorification of her little short of that ascribed to her son.   Protestantism, though rejecting the Mariolatry of the Romanist, is still equally explicit in recognizing the complete separation between Jehovah and Jesus.   The Son offers himself a sacrifice to propitiate the Father ; as, otherwise they must hold that God died to propitiate himself, which is of course absurd.   It holds, moreover, that the Son in virtue of his atoning sacrifice perpetually intercedes in behalf of his elect.   He is, therefore, practically regarded as distinct from the Being with or before whom he intercedes.   How exceedingly diverse from all this is the view presented by Swedenborg may be seen from his statement of the true Scriptural doctrine of Intercession.*

"The Lord's intercession for the human race was during his abode in the world, and indeed during his state of humiliation, for in that state he spake with Jehovah as with another ; but in the state of glorification, when the human essence became united to the Divine, and was also made Jehovah, he does not then intercede, but shows mercy, and from his Divine (principle) administers help and saves ; it is mercy itself, which is intercession, for such is its essence."—(*A. C.* 2250.)

---

* See the subject of our Lord's Intercession treated with consummate ability by Mr. Noble, in his " Lectures on the Important Doctrines of the True Christian Religion."—*Lectures* XVII. *and* XVIII.

Now the truth is, there is no more unwarrantable assumption to be found in all New Church theology than this, that the Old Church is the External of the New, and in connexion with the External of the New Heavens. It is no where to be found in the writings of Swedenborg, and is palpably contradicted by the whole tenor of his theology and philosophy. Such an assumption, if it were true, would lead directly and unequivocally to the establishment of the fact that the New Church might have been contained in the Old, like the soul within the body, or the life within the form, or to the revolting absurdity that Heaven might have been contained in the bosom of Hell! For if that which is purely good, can be contained within that which is entirely evil, as we hold the Old Church to be, and pledge ourselves to show from the writings of the New Church, what is the alternative? But the truth is, the External is the *ultimate* of the internal, and such as is the *internal* such will be the *external*, for such as a man is, in his will and understanding, such is the true quality of his External, and such he is, in every point thereof. Hence if the Old Church is the External of the New, then the Old Church would still be the True Church and the mission of Emanuel Swedenborg would be superfluous and a mistake, and there would be no necessity for a new dispensation.

But the writings of the New Church teach in almost every page that the Old Church was entirely vastated, that all spiritual life had departed from it; that it was at an end, "the abomination of desolation, and a cage of every unclean and hateful bird;" that the spirits from it had filled the world of spirits so as to endanger the equilibrium of the Heavens by the powers of evil. Hence the necessity for the last Judgment in 1757, the formation of a New Heaven and the institution of a New Church on Earth to make *One* with the New Heavens. In proof of the foregoing the following are adduced.

"That there is nothing spiritual remaining in the Old Church but that it is full of blasphemy against the Lord."—(*T. C. R.* 132, 133 and *A. R.* 692–715.)

"That it is a Trinity of Gods which is acknowledged. and worshiped in the Old Church, and from the faith of every church is derived not only all its worship, but also all its doctrine; wherefore it may be said that such as its faith is, such is its doctrine, that *that* faith which is a faith in three Gods has perverted every thing of the Church follows thence. If *any one examines* the doctrines, one by one, as that which is concerning God, concerning the person of Christ, Charity, Repentance, Regeneration, Free Will, Election, the *Use of the Sacraments*, BAPTISM and the HOLY SUPPER, he will clearly see that a *Trinity of Gods* is in every one of them; and if it does not actually appear to be in them, still they flow from it as from their fountain. If the faith be false, it commits whoredom with every truth there and perverts and falsifies it, and causes man to be insane in spiritual things. That the faith of the present time, which in the internal form is that of three Gods but in the external form that of One God, has extinguished the light in the Word. and removed the Lord from the Church and thus precipitated its morning into night."—(*T. C. R.* 177–179, 180, 758.)

"That so long as men adhere to and are influenced by the faith of the Old Church, so long the New Heaven cannot descend to them and consequently so long the New Church cannot be *established* among them." —(*T. C. R.* 182, 380. "That the Lord is departed from the Old Church." —(*A. C.* 4231.) "That the Old Church is rejected and the New Church adopted."—(*A. C.* 4332, 4333, 4334, 4422, 4638.)

"That the internals and EXTERNALS of the Old Church shall perish, and that this is what is meant in the Word by Heaven and Earth passing away."—(*A. C.* 4231.)

"That the Old Church is a DEAD CARCASS or a CORPSE: and that *reasonings in favor* of the Old Church are what are signified in Matthew (xxiv. 28,) by the eagles gathered together about the carcass."—(*A. C.* 3900.) *A. E. F.* will please mark that! "That at this day there is no Church in the Christian world, neither among the Roman Catholics nor among the REFORMED."—(*A. R.* 263.)

"That the Old Church is spiritual Sodom and Egypt where our Lord was crucified."—(*A. R.* 502–504; *T. C. R.* 634, 635.)

"That the faith that prevails at this day contains nothing of the Church. That it is not anything but only an idea or shadow of something, and therefore it is DESERVEDLY TO BE REJECTED: yea, it rejects itself as a thing that bears no relation to a Church."—(*B. E.* 96.)

"That the faith and imputation of the New Church cannot abide together with the faith and imputation of the Old Church, and in case they abide together such a collision and conflict will ensue as will prove fatal to every thing that relates to the Church in man."—(*T. C. R.* 647–649; *B. E.* 106.)

"That the doctrines of the Old and New Church do not agree together, no not in one single point or instance, however minute."—(*B. E.* 96, 103; *T. C. R.* 648.)

"That the destruction of the Old Church is foretold by the Lord in the Evangelists, and by John in the Revelation, and is what is called the Last Judgment, not that Heaven and Earth were then to perish, but that a New Church will be raised up in some region of the Earth. though the former still continues in its EXTERNAL worship as the Jews do in theirs."—(*A. C.* 1850.)

"Hence it is that when any New Church is established by the Lord, it is not established amongst those who are *within the Church* (old), but amongst them who are *without*, that is the Gentiles."—(*A. C.* 4747.)

"But when the Church is consummated and perishes, then the Lord always raises up a New Church elsewhere, yet seldom if ever from the men of the former Church, but from the Gentiles who have been in ignorance."—(*A. C.* 2910, 3898.)

"That the Gentiles being in ignorance and without grounds of offence and are in a better state for receiving truths than those who are of the Church, and those amongst them in the good of life easily receive truths."—(*A. C.* 2986.)

"That the Christian Church at this day is so completely vastated that there is no longer any faith in it."—(*A. C.* 407.)

"That the Christian Church, such as it is, in itself, is now *first commencing*; the former church was Christian only in name, but not in essence and reality."—(*T. R.* 668.)

It is clearly evident from the foregoing extracts, that the position of " A. E. F.," that the Old Church is the external of the New, adopted by him from the Massachusetts Report, is palpably false.   A. E. F. should have carefully examined the grounds of this Report before he constituted it the basis of his argument against the necessity of rebaptism.*   We shall find in the further examination of his article the same assumption contained in some of his further reasons.

Leaving the reasons drawn from this Report, the writer comes to the question proper, and affirms that " the true position is not merely a negative, or defensive one; that Old Baptism, so called, *may* be considered sufficient, but a positive one, that such baptism *is* good New Church baptism, and that it is forbidden by right order to repeat it."   In support of which he says, first, " whenever an Old Church is set aside, a New Church is on the instant constituted by the Lord *out of its remains,* i. e. out of all externally connected with the consummated church, who are in charity, and some faith from the Word.   Such persons there must be in every church about to expire, to keep up the conjunction between heaven and the human race, where the New Church begins with them.   It takes them just *when* and *as* the Era of the Last Judgment finds them.   The first influx of the New Heaven, so far as it is received in charity and faith on Earth, is into their minds."

These are his promises.   We will examine them in order. It is obvious, that this involves the same gratuitous assumption of the New Church being contained within the Old.   Before an old church is set aside it must become entirely vastated, every principle of spiritual good must have departed from it.   It must have become the " abomination of desolation" and a " cage of every unclean and hateful bird," and such was the fact with the Old Church, as Swedenborg expressly says, at the time of the Last Judgment, in 1757.   All its forms were evil from the greatest to the least.   The extracts given above will show the utter fallaciousness of this opinion.

If the remains, of which A. E. F. speaks, were to receive the influx of the New Heavens as he supposes, would it not be

---

* We doubt if our correspondent takes the right view of " A. E. F.'s" argument on this score.   We do not understand him as adopting the truth of the position taken in the M. A. Report, but that simply assuming for the present, and by way of argument, the soundness of that position, he was still prepared to show that the inference drawn by the writer in regard to Baptism could not be fairly sustained. It would be a hard case, in argumentative debate, if a disputant were to be considered responsible for the defence of ground which he merely assumes hypothetically.—*Ed. Repos.*

simply the resuscitation of the Old Church and the inspiration of life into its dead carcass ?

The great mistake of A. E. F. is in supposing, that the remains of the Old Church, or "those who are in some goodness and truth from the Word," and out of which the Lord is said to constitute a New Church, remain good New Churchmen in the Old Church, in external communion with it, in the participation of its ordinances and sacraments, conforming to its ceremonies and observances, subject to its jurisdiction and control, and acquiescing in all its external manifestations, yet being interiorly of the true New Christian Church,—that therefore the sacraments of which they partake and particularly that of Baptism, receiving it according to New Church doctrine and life, is in their case *efficacious* New Church baptism. It matters not, according to his view, that the Old Church belief and forms are totally vitiated and vastated, and that there is not a spark of spiritual life remaining in it —that it is a *dead carcass*—that the idea of three Gods is in all the most minute particle of their belief and sacraments— that it is the spiritual whoredom of the evil and the false— that it is the spiritual Sodom and Egypt.

At first view, this appears repugnant to all our ideas of the fitness of things, to our conceptions of Heavenly order and even the natural man's sense of propriety. But yet, when closely examined, we see that the fallacy of the Old Church being thus the external of the New, grows out of one still, if possible, more dangerous, because not so obvious. This parent fallacy is, that a church does not consist of a society of *persons* as subjects, as recipients of the true doctrines of the church, and thus of those who are in similar life and doctrine internally and externally, but that it is merely a *system of abstract principles*—that it is *not* the *principles* in *persons*, but that it is what they *think* and *do*. Hence, that there is no necessity for organizing societies of persons in New Church doctrines and life as subjects for those principles, for he assumes the church to be those principles without the persons! This is trifling and absurd. How can a principle exist out of, or independent of, its subjects? How can the sight exist without the eye? How can a Heaven from the Lord exist without the subjects, angels? and how can a church exist on earth without men as its subjects? Yet the direct *a posteriori* relation of "A. E. F.'s" views above stated lead back to this conclusion.

The New Church does not therefore consist of the few persons remaining in the Old Church, as "A. E. F." says, but the truth is that it is a separate and independent organization of *persons* as *subjects*, in New Church doctrines and life, apart from Old Church organizations, doctrines and life ; and that this separate organization is composed of good Gentile minds, and the very few *remains* of the Old Church drawn forth from it, its order, jurisdiction, government and communion, who are " collected, initiated and instructed"—(*Ap. Rev.* 813), and that it is into these Gentile minds and remains thus drawn forth, "collected, initiated and instructed," and organized apart, that the influx of the New Heavens flow.   Hence it is not plain that this New Church must have its own ordinances and sacraments, which are indispensable to its being a church, so that it is with this church among men, that the New Heaven is *conjoined*, and thus with the Lord, whilst "those who are in some goodness and truth from the Word," as the pious of the Old Church, are only *adjoined* to the New Heavens, as taught by Swedenborg in the following extract :

"The Lord is *con*joined to his New Church, but is only *ad*joined to the pious in the Old Church."—(*A. C.* 8901.)

If the Old Church is then entirely vastated, and *all* its ordinances and sacraments corrupt ; its offices and administrations having no spiritual life ; how can the sacrament of Baptism performed by its functionaries be efficacious New Church baptism ?   So far as the New Church is concerned, is not the act void and of none effect ?   How can it give insertion into the New Heaven to which it is not *conjoined ?*   The act has no positive good in it, and from the disjunction and non-communication of the Old Church with the New Heavens it falls far short of any spiritual efficacy by its *pretended* insertion of the subject into the societies of the New Heaven.   If it was efficacious for this purpose why may not the baptism of a Mahomedan be sufficient for the same purpose ? why may not the baptism of a Brahmin or a Hindoo be sufficient ?   But it is said the "passive infant" may receive it, and afterwards, as his mind matures, be instructed in its true New Church meaning, and thus it may be regarded by the infant in its true character, and of course be efficacious, and if it is not so regarded by the matured mind of the infant his "*teaching* is solely at fault."

But if Old Church baptism is thus efficacious where the infant is properly instructed *afterwards*, it is a matter of entire indifference who and under what circumstances the ordinance was performed, or whether it was performed at all, provided that the infant was properly instructed afterwards and *believed* that it *was* done and *in order*.   He may have been baptized in mockery in the midst of all manner of profanity, yet if he is afterwards led to believe that it is efficacious it will pass. It matters not how hellish the external circumstances were, the innocent "passive infant" cannot be affected by it. Hence, if the false and corrupt external of baptism works no evil to the "passive infant," neither does it work any good ; that for spiritual good or evil the rite thus performed "passes over the infant harmless," and of course would be a nullity.

If we were more astonished in the perusal of "A. E. F.'s" article, at one paragraph than another, it was at the following, the mere statement of which is itself almost sufficient condemnation. He says,

> "If the old church really went for ever out of existence at the era of the last judgment, how can there be such a thing as an Old Church Baptism? How can one be introduced into the Old Church? Is not all fear of this kind as if one should dread that his child should be introduced into the garden of the Hesperides and be devoured by the dragon there, while he asserted at the same time that there were no such garden? By a fallacy of the senses it is no sooner said in this way of thinking, that the Old Church has ceased than it is revived in the mind and treated as if yet in being; the various christian denominations external to our New Church organization *being supposed to constitute it.* When these bodies have once been called the 'Old Church' the argument appears irresistible. Is not that 'Old Church' baptism it is asked, which was given in an 'Old Church' denomination, by an Old Church minister who at the same time lectured and prayed according to the doctrines of the 'Old Church?' And if it was, did it not introduce into the 'Old Church' and into the doctrines of the 'Old Church?' The answer to all this is—Here is a troop of fallacies and fallacious phrases, their captain of fifty being this, that the *Christian denominations about us are the Old Church.* There is no particular objection, we will grant, to *calling* them the 'Old Church;' it is an easy and compendious phrase by which to describe them; but the name must not be made the basis of an argument. If it is, we must steadily deny that a man belongs to the Old Church because he belongs to an *Episcopal* or *Presbyterian* body of Christians and that the Baptism he received was an Old Church baptism from that circumstance."

If the "christian denominations about us are not the Old Church" who is? If a "man belonging to an Episcopalian or Presbyterian body of Christians" does not belong to the Old Church, to what church does he belong? Are Episcopalians and Presbyterians New Churchmen? "A. E. F." avers they are. But does Swedenborg so teach in his writings as may be seen in the extracts above? Does not a New Churchman mean by the "Old Church" the "*dead carcass*" in which there is no spiritual life mentioned in the extracts already given? Again, "A. E. F." continues :

" Here may fitly come in for consideration the argument from the analogy of the ministry. If one may claim to belong to the New Church by an Old Church baptism, why not to the New Church ministry by an Old Church ordination ? The answer to this will be that the sacraments of the church and the ministry are so different that there is no just analogy between them. Besides, an ordination confers privileges, jurisdictions, power of legislating in the affairs of the church, and it would manifestly be destruction to the church as an outward organization, if such powers could be conferred by the acts of bodies external to itself.

From this extract it appears that " A. E. F." has but an inadequate idea of what New Church ordination is.—(Vide *T. C. R.* 146, 155; *H. D.* 311–325.)

We see no reason why, if Old Church baptism is considered good for the New Church, all other Old Church sacraments and acts should not also be so considered. The same arguments apply to each with equal force, and the argument of "A. E. F." followed out leads to this conclusion, for the distinctions insisted upon by him are not true, and are mere assumptions, there being in truth and in fact no adequate ground for the discrimination. We will merely glance at one difficulty, if they should still be insisted upon as not being determined by the same arguments, namely ; If it be the province of regularly ordained ministers to administer the rite of baptism, in order to render it effectual, then it inevitably follows that an Old Church minister is to all intents and purposes a regularly ordained New Church minister to make the baptism good New Church baptism, and yet "A. E. F." admits that Old Church ordinations are not valid ordinations for the New Church. How then can they be ministers competent to perform any ordinance for the New Church ? But that ALL the rites, ordinances, and sacraments of the Old Church are sufficient for the New, is inculcated by " A. E. F." in the concluding paragraph of his article. " If one who meditates an accession to a New Church society is counselled to look at his baptism in this light, he is counselled by parity of reasoning to view all his past *communions* in the same manner. But if he were pressed in explicit terms to do this he would revolt at the idea, for he knows that his old church communions served to mature in his mind, that state which enabled him to receive the New Church doctrines when they came to him. He acknowledges in them the Lord's goodness. * * * * * He would then be far from regarding it as a nullity—much farther from casting it away as a thing defiled with falses in its very doing, &c."

This might warrant the conclusion that ' A. F. F." either does not understand truly the teachings of E. S. or that from a strong Old Church proprium he wilfully perverts them. If his

ARTICLE V.

A SERMON PREACHED AT THE CENTRAL CONVENTION IN NEW YORK, OCT. 1848.

BY THOS. WILKS.

" Seek ye first the Kingdom of God, and his righteousness ; and all these things shall be added unto you."—(Matt. vi. 33.)

THE end which the Lord has in view in all that is done by him, is to form an angelic heaven out of the human race. This is the end for which he has created man, and all things else for the sake of man. This is the sole end for which the human race are sustained in being, and for which Divine Providence perpetually operates, both generally and particularly, with reference to nations, families, and the individual man. And it is for the accomplishment of this end that the Holy Word has been revealed from the Lord out of heaven ; and that the Lord himself, who is the Word, descended to the earth, and as a man appeared among men, glorified his assumed humanity, and made it divine. He therefore said, "For their sakes I sanctify myself, that they also may be sanctified through the truth. Thy Word is truth."

The Lord effects his purposes of mercy towards us in our elevation to heaven, by our submission of ourselves to his divine will, and our co-operation with him according to the instructions of his Word, he working in us to will and to do of his good pleasure. But in our submission to the Lord and co-operation with him, it is necessary to the effectual accomplishment of his divine purpose, that we, in the highest degree we are capable, should have the same end in view in all we do as he has,—that is, the spiritual and eternal good of all mankind. Nor are we to permit any selfish cares, or personal ends to draw us aside from the grand object which we should ever have before us ; but we are to confide in the Lord's mercy, that, while we submit to the divine will and obey the divine Word, he will provide for us, and will supply us with all things that can in any degree be conducive to our good, and that will promote our happiness, and that he will withhold from us that only which if received would injure rather than benefit us. His Word declares, "The Lord God is a sun and shield ; the Lord will give grace and glory : no good will be withheld from them who walk uprightly." He has, therefore, given us, as his disciples, his divine command, annexing thereto his gracious promise, "Seek ye first the Kingdom of God, and his righteousness; and all these things shall be added unto you."

We have met here, as the Lord's disciples, to consult with reference to the promotion of his Kingdom on earth, and the words of the Lord in our text, rightly understood, teach us how this end is to be accomplished by our means. We should seek to know the true character of the Lord's instructions to us upon this subject, and in all we do, endeavor to act according to them, that in our efforts for the advancement of his Church he may approve of our doings, and bless the labor of our hands.

Our text is interpreted in the A. E. as follows, "By the Kingdom of the heavens, in the spiritual sense, is understood the divine truth, and by justice the divine good; wherefore it is said, Seek first the Kingdom of the heavens, and the justice thereof; and, in the supreme sense, by the Kingdom of the heavens is understood the Lord, inasmuch as he is the all of his Kingdom, and by justice, in the same sense, is signified the merit of the Lord: and whereas man, who is ruled by the Lord, wills and loves only such things as are of the Lord, he is led unknown to himself to the felicities of eternity, therefore it is said that all things shall be added unto him, whereby is understood, that all things shall happen for salvation according to his wishes. Inasmuch as heaven is heaven from the reception of divine truth from the Lord, and in like manner the church, therefore heaven and the church are understood in the general sense by the kingdom of the heavens."—(*A. E.* 688.)

We will give another passage illustrative of our text from the Arcana Cœlestia: "Truths which are of faith enter by hearing, thus by the external man, and the internal man (before regeneration) relishes only those things which are of the world and of self, and these are delights arising from gain and from honors: but when the internal man is opened by regeneration, then good from the Lord flows in through that man, and adopts and conjoins to itself the truths of faith which have entered through the external man; and according to conjunction the order is inverted, that is, that which had been in the first place is put in the last: in this case the Lord attracts to himself all things which are of the life of man, that they may look upwards: then man regards as ends those things which are of the Lord and heaven, and the Lord himself as the end in which all things centre, and the former things, namely, the delights of gain and of honors, as means conducive to that end. It is known that means have no life from any other source but from the end; thus the delights of gain and of honors, when they are made means, then have life from the life out of heaven, that is, through heaven from the Lord, for the Lord is the end in which they centre.   When man is in such an order of life, then gains and honors are blessings to him : but if he be in an inverted order, gains and honors are curses to him.   That all things are blessings where man is in the order of heaven, the Lord teaches in Matthew, "Seek ye first the Kingdom of the heavens, and the justice thereof'; and all things shall be added unto you."—(*A. E.* 9184.)   In another passage in the same work we read, "The truths of the church, without conjunction by good with the interior man, have nothing else for an end but gain, with whomsoever they are : but when they are conjoined by good with the interior man, they then have for an end good and truth itself, thus the church, the Lord's Kingdom, and the Lord himself; and when they have these things for an end, then also accrues to them gain as much as is needed, according to the Lord's words in Matthew, Seek ye first the Kingdom of God, and the justice thereof; and all things shall be added unto you."—(*Ibid.* 5449.)

. From the above extracts, it is most obvious that our sole end, in all the plans we adopt, and in all the acts we perform, is to be the Lord and his Kingdom, or his church, that is, the internal government of truth and justice from the Lord, and that while we seek this end according to the leadings of Divine Providence, all things necessary thereto, both temporal and spiritual, will be provided for us by the Lord: for it is said with reference to those who thus seek,

1st. "That man is led by the Lord unknown to himself to the felicities of eternity, and that all things shall happen for salvation according to his wishes ;" consequently that all spiritual good, signified by food, drink, and clothing, and all things else necessary to the life and happiness of heaven, are provided for him by the Lord without his care.   It is said,

2d. "That all things are blessings when man is in the order of heaven," and,

3d. "That gain," that is, temporal good, "will accrue to him as much as is needed ;" consequently that the external things of this life, as far as they can be beneficial to him, he will receive as blessings from the Lord, without any unnecessary care on his part to provide himself with them.   Therefore with reference to all these provisions, both temporal and spiritual, necessary to man, the Lord says, "Take no thought for your life, what ye shall eat, or what ye shall drink ; nor yet for your body, what ye shall put on.   Is not the life more than meat, and the body than raiment ?   Behold the fowls of the air ; for they sow not, neither do they reap, nor gather into

barns : yet your heavenly Father feedeth them. Are ye not
much better than they? And why take ye thought for raiment ?   Consider the lilies of the field, how they grow ; they
toil not, neither do they spin ; and yet I say unto you, that
even Solomon in all his glory was not arrayed like one of
them.   Therefore take no thought, saying, what shall we eat!
or, what shall we drink? or, wherewithal shall we be clothed?
for your heavenly Father knoweth that ye have need of all
these things."   These words of the Lord are explained by
Swedenborg as follows, "These words, although they are
spoken of the life of the body, still signify such things as are
of the life of the spirit, for all things of the literal sense of the
Word, which is natural, contain within them an internal sense,
which is spiritual: in this sense by eating, drinking, and by
meat, is signified spiritual nourishment, which is the nourishment of faith and therewith of the understanding, whence
comes intelligence in things spiritual: hence it is said, be ye
not solicitous for your soul what ye shall eat, and what ye
shall drink, is not the soul more than meat ? to eat denoting to
perceive good intellectually, thus spiritually, to drink denoting
to perceive truth in the same manner, and meat denoting the good
and truth from which is spiritual nourishment : by clothing
the body, and by raiment, is signified truth investing the good
of love and of the will, raiment denoting that truth, and the
body the good of love which is the good of the will."—(*A. E.*
750.)   The meaning conveyed in the language of the Lord,
therefore, obviously is, that we are to have no other care, or
solicitude, than merely the performance of present duty according to the instructions of his Word and the leadings of his
providence, and that while we thus perform our duty, confiding in him, he will make all necessary provisions for the
church, or the spiritual life within us, and will supply it with
all spiritual nourishment, will give it form according to his
own divine order, and will invest it with the external clothing
in which his divine Wisdom thinks it best it should be clad.
These are the things which will be added unto us, while we,
confiding in the Lord, seek first the Kingdom of God, and the
justice thereof.

    What is true with reference to the church in the individual
man, is also true with reference to the church in its collective
capacity ; for every truth of the Word is of universal application, and the church in man is, in every particular, the exact
correspondence of the church in a larger form; for the church,
both in man and in a collective body of men or angels, is the
image and likeness of the divine human of the Lord. It is
therefore true with reference to us in our collective capacity

as a Convention, that if we seek first the Kingdom of God,
and the justice thereof; all the things spoken of by the Lord
will be added unto us, without any solicitude on our part with
reference to them.

Now, inasmuch as the external clothing of the church, or
the external form which the church assumes in its descent to
ultimates, is a thing the provision for which is entirely of the
Lord, and the care of which belongs exclusively to him, it is
most obvious, that it is no part of our duty, in our efforts for
the good of the church, to study and aim at the formation of
an external order of government, which, according to our idea,
is representative of the Lord and his Kingdom; or even to
study that the external form of the church should be according
to divine order; for the form which the church is to assume, is
not to be in any respect our care, this care for the church being that which pertains exclusively to the Lord. Our duty is
simply to aim at the performance of uses, according to the
instructions of the Word and the leadings of divine providence:
or in other words, we are, from the love of good, in all things
to aim only at the spiritual and eternal good of our fellow-men,
by the proper use of the means which the Lord has placed in
our hands for the establishment of his heavenly reign of righteousness and peace on earth. Nevertheless, in our efforts for
the advancement of the church, it is necessary that we assume
some external form of government, this being necessary in
order that we, being many, may co-operate, and act together
as one; for union of purpose and effort on the part of the men
of the church, is indispensable to the accomplishment of the
good contemplated. But as the end of order established by
us for our government, is simply the performance of use to the
church, nothing more is necessary in that order than its
adaptation to the end for which it is designed.

When the church was representative, there were other uses
to be performed by its rituals and external forms of order,
than are effected by these means in the present day. Before
the coming of the Lord, communication with heaven was effected by means of these external rituals, which were representative of heavenly things: and the Lord accordingly
made the necessary provisions for his church. Upon this subject we read as follows: " All these things are representative,
such as continually appear before the angels in the heavens,
and present in a visible form the divine celestial things which
are of the good of love, and the divine spiritual things which
are of the good of faith: such things in the sum were represented by the tabernacle, and by those things which were in the
tabernacle, as by the ark itself, by the table on which was

bread, by the altar of incense, by the candlestick, and by the
rest of the things; which, inasmuch as they were forms of
divine celestial and spiritual things, therefore when they were
seen by the people, at the time they were engaged in holy
worship, then were presented in heaven such things as were
represented, which, as was said above, were the divine celestial things which are of the good of love to the Lord, and the
divine spiritual things which are of good of faith in the Lord:
such an effect in heaven had all the representatives of that
church. It is to be known, that spirits and angels are always
with man, and that man cannot live without them; in like
manner, that by them man has connection with the Lord, and
that so the human race subsists, and also heaven. Hence it
may be manifest, for what end the representatives, and also
the rituals of the church, with the Israelitish nation, were instituted: also for what end the Word is given, wherein all things
which are in the sense of the letter, correspond to the divine
things which are in heaven, thus wherein all things represent,
and all expressions signify: hence man has connection with
heaven, and by heaven with the Lord; without which connection he would have no life at all, for without connection
with the very Esse of life, from whom is all the existere of life,
no one has life."—(*A. C.* 9481.) Concerning communication
with the angels of heaven by means of the external rituals of
the Israelitish church, we are further informed in these words,
"Communication with the angels in heaven by representatives
was effected at that time in this manner: their external worship was communicated with angelic spirits, who are simple,
and do not reflect on things internal, but still are interiorly
good; such are they who in the Grand Man correspond to the
skins; these do not at all attend to the internal of man,
but only to his external; if this latter appears holy, they also
think holily concerning it: the interior angels of heaven saw
in those spirits the things that were represented, consequently
the celestial and divine things which corresponded; for with
these spirits they could be present, and see those things, but
not with man, except by them; for angels dwell with men in
interiors, but where there are no interiors, they dwell in the
interior of simple spirits, for the angels have no relish except
for things spiritual and celestial, which are the interiors contained in representatives."—(*Ibid.* 8588.) The men of the
Ancient Church, we are informed, were in internal worship
which was represented by their external, and were therefore.
by means of their external representatives, in which they saw
heavenly and divine things, consociated with the angels of
heaven. But all consociation with angels, and conjunction

with the Lord, in the representative church, were effected by means of these external representatives; consequently, external representatives were in those days indispensable to the existence of the church on earth and in the heavens: for without them no conjunction could be effected, and the human race would necessarily have perished.

But after the coming of the Lord, an entire change was effected as to the medium of conjunction between heaven and earth, and men are now consociated with angels and conjoined to the Lord altogether otherwise than they were before his advent. Concerning the medium of conjunction before and after the coming of the Lord, we read as follows; "A representative church, when the ancient church ceased, was instituted with the Israelitish people, that by such things there might be conjunction of heaven, thus of the Lord with the human race, for without conjunction of the Lord through heaven, man would perish; for man has his life from that conjunction. But those representatives were only external mediums of conjunction, with which the Lord miraculously conjoined heaven: but when conjunction by those things also perished, then the Lord come into the world, and opened the internal things themselves which were represented, which are the things of love and of faith in him: these things now conjoin: nevertheless *the only medium of conjunction at this day is the Word,* inasmuch as it is so written, that all and single things therein correspond, and hence represent and signify the divine things which are in the heavens."—(*A. C.* 9457.) Concerning the change effected as to the reception of intelligence and wisdom by man, we read "Before the Lord came into the world, the Divine Itself flowed into the universal heaven, and as heaven at that time consisted for the most part of celestial angels, that is, of those who were in the good of love, though that influx, from the Divine Omnipotence, was produced by the light which is in the heavens, and thence the wisdom and intelligence. But after mankind removed themselves from the good of love and charity, then that light could no longer be produced through heaven, consequently, neither could intelligence and wisdom, so as to penetrate to the human race; therefore, it was of necessity, in order to their salvation, that the Lord came into the world, and made the human in himself Divine, that he himself as to the Divine Human might become Divine light, and thus might illuminate the universal heaven, and the universal world."—(*Ibid.* 4180.) Again, concerning the order of heaven, before and after the coming of the Lord, we read; "By order is meant that order which was in heaven from the time when the Lord from his Divine Human began to arrange all things in heaven and in earth, which was immediately after the resurrection. According to that order, they who were of the spiritual church could then be elevated into heaven, and enjoy eternal blessedness, but not according to the former order: for the Lord heretofore arranged all things by or through heaven, but afterwards by or through his Human, which he glorified and made Divine in the world, by which there was such an accession of strength, that they were elevated into heaven who before could not be elevated ; also that the evil from on all sides receded, and were shut up in their hells: this is the order which is meant."—(*Ibid.* 7931.) From the preceding extracts we deduce the following most obvious truths :

First. Before the coming of the Lord, representative worship was necessary as the medium of conjunction between heaven and earth, or between the Lord and man ; hence representative worship was instituted, that through this medium the divine from the Lord might flow through the heavens to man on earth.

Secondly. In consequence of man's being immersed in evil, this medium by degrees became altogether inefficient, so that the divine through it could not flow to man; consequently mankind by its means could not be saved, nor could the heavens be preserved in order.

Thirdly. When this medium failed, the Lord assumed the human, and made it Divine, and thus ultimated in himself all things of the Word, and all the representatives of the ancient churches, and made his own Divine Human, or the Word ultimated in himself, the only medium of conjunction between heaven and earth, or between his own essential Divine and man.

Fourthly. The divine order, according to which the Lord now governs the heavens and the church, and according to which angels and men receive intelligence and wisdom from him, is altogether different from that which existed previous to his advent, the inefficiency of which made it necessary that he should come into the world to institute a new order for the preservation of the heavens and the salvation of man. Therefore,

Fifthly. Since the order of the heavens and the church is changed, and since the Divine Human, or the Word is the only medium of conjunction, the external order and representative worship which were once essential to the conjunction of man with the Lord, have now necessarily ceased to be of any importance to the church.

This truth is most expressly and clearly taught in the following words of Swedenborg, "At that time (that is, the time of the representative church) all things which existed with the man of the church, were changed, according to the signification of things in their internal sense, into spiritual correspondent representations with the angels? "All things that were done in that church were turned in heaven into corresponding representatives. But after the coming of the Lord, when external rites were abolished, and thus representatives ceased, then such things were no longer changed in heaven into corresponding representatives: for when man becomes internal, and is instructed concerning things internal, *then external things are as nothing to him,* for he then knows what is holy, viz. that charity is so, and faith thence : from these his externals are then viewed, namely, as to how much of charity and faith towards the Lord there is in the externals: "Wherefore, *since the Lord's coming,* MAN IS NOT CONSIDERED IN HEAVEN WITH RESPECT TO THINGS EXTERNAL, *but to things internal:* if any one be considered in respect to things external, *it is hence, that he has* SIMPLICITY, *and in simplicity has* INNOCENCE AND CHARITY, *which are in things external, or in his external worship, from the Lord,* whilst the man himself is ignorant of it."—(*A. C.* 1001, 1003.) Language cannot express more clearly and forcibly, than it does here, that the externals of the church are nothing, only so far as they are means for the exercise of charity; and that consequently, no importance whatever is to be attached to any particular order of ecclesiastical government, or form of worship, in the present day, as being the essential order of the church, into which only the divine influx can flow, and in which the Lord can be present; internal worship, or the life of charity in man, being the only essential of the church. For it is said,

First. That the externals of worship are not now, as they were formerly, changed into corresponding representatives in heaven :

Secondly. That man being in internals, and instructed concerning them, external things are as nothing to him : and,

Thirdly. That since the coming of the Lord, man is not considered in heaven with respect to things external, but to things internal ; and that his externals are viewed only as to how much of charity and faith towards the Lord there is in them ; or, as again expressed, if any one be considered in respect to things external, it is hence, that he has simplicity, and in simplicity has innocence and charity from the Lord in his external worship.

Now, since the men of the church are not considered in heaven with respect to things external, except only as to how

much of charity and faith towards the Lord there is in their
externals; and since things external are as nothing to the
.men of the church, otherwise than simply as means for the
exercise of charity in the performance of uses; it is most obvious that these external things should be regarded by us only
in their relation to our external duties, or the uses to be performed by us to the church; and that in our adoption of any
form of worship, or ecclesiastical government, all that is necessary, and all we should aim at, is, that it be properly adapted to the use for which it is intended; for we are regarded in
heaven, not as to our externals, consequently not as to our external form of government, but only as to our internal charity
and faith thence, in the performance of our duties under the
government which may be appointed over us, whatever it be,
or which we may adopt for ourselves.

The end of order is use; therefore, the end which we are to
have in view in the government of the church, is the use to be
performed thereby to the church; and the order of its government should be such only as its uses make necessary it should
possess, the form in every instance originating from, and suited to, the use which it is to perform. Such, according to Swedenborg, is Divine order. Speaking of the form and government of the Grand Man, that is, of heaven and the church, he
says, "It is use which rules in forms. Hence it is manifest,
*that before the organic forms of the body existed, use was, and
that use produced and adapted them to itself, but not vice versa;*
but when the forms were produced, or the organs adapted,
uses then proceed, and in this case it appears as if the forms
or organs are prior to the use, *when yet it is not so;* for use
flows in from the Lord, and this through heaven, according to
the order and according to the form in which heaven is arranged by the Lord, thus according to correspondence (the
correspondence of the form to the use). Thus man exists, and
thus he subsists."—(*A. C.* 4223.)

Now since every form, according to Divine order, is produced by the use of which it is the instrument, exists and
subsists from that use, and is for the sake of that use only, it
would be extremely unwise in us as a Convention, and contrary to the order of heaven, to adopt an ecclesiastical form of
government, for which at present we can see no use whatever.
It is enough, and all that the law of divine order requires, that
we adopt a form, demanded by and suited to the uses which
the church has now to perform; and the less complicated,
consequently the more simple this form, provided it answer the
end for which it is intended, the better and more efficient will
it be in the performance of its uses.

The uses, and nothing but the uses to be performed to men on earth, is the end to which we are to look in the government of the church, as well as in our efforts under that government, according to the words of the Lord in our text, "Seek ye first the Kingdom of God, and the justice thereof; and all these things shall be added unto you." The formation of the ultimates of the church according to heavenly order, is the care of the Lord's divine providence, and not ours : for the things which are added unto us, while in the performance of our duty, we look only to the internal principles of the church as our end, or seek to advance the reign of truth and righteousness among men, include, among other things, the ultimate truths which clothe the church, or the external form which the church assumes in its descent from heaven to earth. Therefore it does not belong to us to aim at the establishment of an ultimate form of the church on earth which will correspond to the form of the church in heaven ;—nay, we are most explicitly taught in the Word not to concern ourselves about the particular form which the church may assume, but in all we do, to seek only the internal reign of truth and justice, having the assurance from the Lord that the life, the body, and the clothing of the church, are cared for, and will be provided for by him, without any care or anxiety on our part with reference to them. His words to us are these, "Take no thought for your life, what ye shall eat, or what ye shall drink ; nor yet for your body, what ye shall put on. Is not the life more than meat, and the body than raiment ? Therefore take no thought, saying, What shall we eat ? or, What shall we drink ? or, Wherewithal shall we be clothed ? For after these things do the Gentiles seek : for your heavenly Father knoweth that ye have need of all these things. But seek ye first the Kingdom of God, and the justice thereof; and all these things shall be added unto you."

All we should aim at therefore, by and in the form of government which we may assume, if we act according to the Lord's instruction to us, is, simply the performance of duties, in the uses of charity for the advancement of the Lord's kingdom of righteousness and peace on earth. With anything beyond this, it is not our prerogative to interfere, nor is it right for us to attempt it ; for to provide for, and give to the church the form which is according to divine order, both as to internals and externals, and from first principles to last, is the work of the Lord alone. It is therefore most evident, that we, in our order, should only look to the present use to be performed by us ; and this use, as far as ecclesiastical order is concerned, is simply the preaching of the Word, no other duty being assigned to the minister of the gospel, either in the Word, or the writings of the church. "With respect to priests, their duty is to teach men the way to heaven, and likewise to lead them therein. They are to teach them according to the doctrine of the church, which is derived from the Word of God: and to lead them to live according to that doctrine. Priests, or ministers, who teach the doctrine of truth, and lead their flocks thereby to goodness of life, and so to the Lord, are the good shepherds spoken of in the Word; but they who only teach, and do not lead to goodness of life, and so to the Lord, are the bad shepherds.

"Ministers ought to instruct the people, and to lead them, by truths, to the good of life; but in matters of faith, they ought not to use compulsion, since no one can be compelled to believe contrary to what he thinks in his heart to be true. He who differs in opinion from the minister ought to be left in the peaceable enjoyment of his own sentiments, provided he make no disturbance: but when such a person disturbs the peace of the church, he must be separated; for this also is agreeable to order, for the sake of which the priesthood or ministry is established."—(*H. D.* 315, 318.)

SELECTIONS.

EXTRACTS FROM SWEDENBORG'S SPIRITUAL DIARY.

NOW FIRST TRANSLATED FROM THE ORIGINAL LATIN.

Concerning each Kind of Life of a Spirit.

4114 1-2. There are with a spirit two lives which he takes with him from the body, and which remain, as it is not given him to use the corporeal memory; namely, the life of persuasion and the life of cupidities. As respects the life of persuasions, I wondered that spirits could converse with each other as they do, and that whatever they think and speak they are able to confirm by so many reasons or reasonings as no man could scarcely believe; for they adduce so many and so various confirmations, which they have at hand, that I have often been filled with wonder (at witnessing it). I was given to understand, that confirmations so various and manifold, which are ever in readiness and, as it were, present to them, are from the life of persuasions; for when a spirit is in persuasion, he immediately excites or suggests confirmations from a man's memory, that is, from the things stored up in his memory; for the persuasion of a thing excites, as any one may be aware (who reflects). Hence proceed their discourses replete with such multiplied confirmations.

But with men whose interiors are not opened so that one can speak with spirits, the case is different; for to him such spirits apply themselves as are of a nearly similar persuasion; for if two contrary persuasions were present, there would be a discord. With me it is otherwise, in order that I may know the qualities of spirits. When a man changes his persuasions then other spirits apply themselves to him; wherefore, whatever be the man's persuasion, such is the persuasion of the spirit, and the spirit continually excites confirmations. Moreover the spirit that is with a man is led into his persuasion, and adopts a similar, as I have learnt by experience.

The life of cupidities is distinct from this, but wherever cupidity has induced a persuasion, then each life acts. Wherefore it is good for a man not to be persuaded concerning falsities, but to be confirmed in truths; for he is not easily brought to renounce a pre-assumed persuasion.

Concerning the Life of Persuasion.

4115. The life which remains after death is the life of persuasion and the life of cupidity. When a spirit is in the life of his persuasion he excites every thing in the memory of a man that is in conformity with the persuasion, just as the man himself knows it. This it was given to know by experience when spirits were present in their persuasion, as they then excited whatever was conformable to the persuasion, so that I sometimes wondered whence flowed such prudence, astuteness, cunning, and keenness of discovery in regard to things which they had never known. I supposed it to be taken from the corporeal memory (of spirits), but the fact is not so; it comes from the memory of the man which is made subservient to them; the spirit merely comes into his persuasion, when immediately whatever is conformable is excited. That there are such lives with spirits, that they are a kind of remaining instinct from the confirming and persuading things of the bodily life, that by means of this instinct the spirit excites other confirmations, with many things besides, and that much more acutely than in the life of the body, things too which were previously unknown—all this was made evident by much experience.

4116. There is also a life of cupidity which is altogether a different kind of life; for the life of persuasion has respect to the true and the false, and the confirmation of the true, being contracted from the knowledges of things, and many other sources, but the life of cupidity has respect to evil and good, thus to whatever is called love.

4117. It may be manifest that persuasion, in the life of the body, is able to subdue cupidities, as, for example, when any one persuades himself that a particular kind of food is more wholesome than another, although it may be of no taste at all, or of a disagreeable taste, so that previous to the persuasion he may have actually nauseated it; still he gives it the preference, and in process of time it becomes palatable to him, and even agreeable, so that he is able to prefer the nauseous and the bitter to the sweet. Thus he subdues cupidity; and similar is the case in other things. The life of cupidities, however, acts in a great measure to induce persuasion; for that which is loved perniciously is confirmed on many grounds, even until the man is persuaded, which might be illustrated and established by innumerable proofs.

4118. The life of cupidities remains to spirits, and excites various cupidities with man, and thus also confirmations, as was made manifest in many ways.

4119. There are spirits with a man who are in a like persuasion and a like cupidity, and who may be called the subjects of many; for the persuasion and the cupidity of the man immediately excite those who are (in this respect) like him. Every single idea represents the whole man, thus the whole spirit, whose idea or image being presented, he is immediately present himself. Such is the order (of things) in the other life, as was evinced to me by a multitude of proofs. Yet there still remains a common persuasion, or a ruling persuasion, thus also a ruling cupidity. Thus spirits of a like kind are with man, and they remain with him until his persuasion and his cupidity are changed, or till he is reformed and becomes regenerate, when, as a consequence, other spirits succeed (and take their place).

4120. I spake with spirits on these points, and they could not but acknowledge that the fact was so, for all experience agrees with it; only spirits suppose that they produce, from the corporeal memory, the things which they utter, and the fact of this impression was sometimes clearly evinced to me.

Concerning (my) Revelations.

4123. There are spirits who are averse to any thing being said concerning the things revealed (to me), but it was replied that they are instead of miracles, and that without them men would not know the character of the book, nor would they buy it, or read it, or understand it, or be affected by it, or believe it—in a word, they would remain in ignorance (of the whole subject), none would wish to hear any thing respecting the interiors of the Word, which they regard as mere phan tasies. Such as are simply men of learning will for the most reject them.

Concerning the Memory of Spirits.

4125. If it were permitted to spirits to be in corporeal memory, they could not possibly be among other spirits, for then evil spirits would immediately know whatever of evil any one thought or did; for all ideas are communicated in the other life. Thus they would bring forth from his memory nothing else than evil and falses, and thus rush upon him and continually infest and torment him. Wherefore the Lord alone knows what man thinks and does prior to his becoming a spirit.

Concerning the Pulsation of the Heart.

4136. It was given me to feel, with the utmost distinctness, the pulsations of the heart in the occiput. The pulse of the heart of the spirituals is rapid, vibratory, and strong; that of the celestials is slow, tacit, and non-vibratory, almost like the pulse of the human heart. The momentum of the spiritual pulse is to that of the celestial as 2 1-2 to 1. The reason is, that the celestial pulse may be continued through the spirituals, and thus issue from a celestial source.

MISCELLANY.

We yield the remainder of our space in the present No. to the ensuing documents, forwarded us by Rev. Mr. Barrett, containing the minutes of the proceedings of the Ohio Association at their late meeting at Dayton. The very interesting Missionary narrative presented at the meeting by Rev. J. P. Stuart we shall be obliged to defer to our next.

PROCEEDINGS

OF THE SEMI-ANNUAL MEETING OF THE OHIO ASSOCIATION,

Held in Dayton, October 13–15, 1848.

At the Beneficial Hall,
Dayton, Ohio, Oct. 13, 1848.
9 o'clock, A. M.

1. The Ohio Association of the New Church met agreeable to adjourment, and was called to order, John Murdock presiding.

2. Religious worship was conducted by Rev. B. F Barrett, by reading from the Word and prayer; after which the Association united in chanting a selection from the Word.

3. A list of the ministers and delegates present was then made out, and the roll called.

4. Reports of the Standing Committees were then called for, and the following were presented, read, accepted and laid on the table:

Report of the Acting Committee.

Report of the Missionary Committee.

5. The communication of Rev. R. De Charms, mentioned in the Journal of our last meeting, Min. No. 438, was called up and referred to a Special Committee, consisting of M. G. Williams and John Murdock.

6. John Murdock and B. F. Barrett were appointed a committee to report an answer to the question,—"What relation do isolated receivers stand in to this Association?"

7. The Association adjourned till to-morrow morning at 9 o'clock.

8. There were public religious services in the evening, and a discourse preached by Rev. B. F. Barrett from Matt. v. 4.

SATURDAY, OCT. 14, 1848,
9 *o'clock,* A. M.

9. The Association met, and being called to order, was opened with prayer by Rev. J. P. Stuart.

10. The committee on the communication of Rev. Mr. De Charms presented their report which was excepted and adopted. The report is as follows:

" Whereas, the memorial of the Rev. R. De Charms, relating to the Education Fund, which was read and laid on the table in order that it might be afterwards taken up and disposed of by the Association, was in the press of business overlooked;—Therefore *Resolved,* That the said memorial be now referred to a special committee to examine and report fully, at our next annual meeting, the origin, objects, and present condition of the Education Fund, and to present some definite plan of action for the Association."

M. G. Williams, Oliver Lovell and E. Hinman were appointed a committee, in accordance with the above resolution.

11. The committee on the relation of isolated receivers to this body, reported the following resolution, which was adopted as a standing rule of the Association:

Resolved, That isolated, and other receivers who may be present at the meetings of the Association, shall be entitled to sit as consulting members.

12. The reading of communications was made the order of the day for this afternoon at 3 o'clock.

13. The Association adjourned till 2 o'clock, P. M.

SATURDAY, 2 *o'clock,* P. M.

14. The report of the Acting Committee and of the Committee on Missions were taken up, and after some discussion, and some modifications of the Reports, they were adopted, together with the resolutions appended thereto, and ordered to be printed with the Journal.

15. On motion of Mr. M. G. Williams, it was

Resolved, That the further consideration of the case of Mr. E. Yulee, mentioned in the Report of the Acting Committee, touching the validity of his ordination, be referred to the next meeting of the Association.

16. The order of the day for 3 o'clock was called up, and several communications, together with the Missionary Narrative of Rev. J. P. Stuart, were then presented and read.

17. The Acting Committee were instructed to publish the Missionary narrative in full, and such parts of the communications as they may deem expedient.

18. J. H. Miller and Thomas Newport being called upon reported such missionary labors as they had performed since the meeting of the Association in May last.

19. On motion of B. F. Barrett, it was resolved that the most holy ordinance of the Lord's Supper be administered to-morrow, immediately after the morning service, and that after the supper the Association stand adjourned, until our annual meeting.

20. J. P. Stuart, J. Holmes and John Cook were appointed a committee on the subject of Church Music.

21. J. P. Stuart stated that David Espy, of the 20 Mile Stand, is desirous of donating a lot of land to this Association for educational purposes;—whereupon, by motion of B. F. Barrett, it was *Resolved* that the thanks of this body be presented to Mr. Espy for his generous proposition and that Mr. M. G. Williams be a committee to confer with him in regard to it, and to report at our next meeting.

22. The Association adjourned, and was closed with prayer by Rev. B. F. Barrett.

23. There was religious service in the evening and a discourse by J. P. Stuart from Matt. xxiv. 1, 2.

SABBATH, Oct. 15, 10 *o'clock*, A. M.

24. Rev. B. F. Barrett conducted public worship and delivered a discourse from Luke xxii. 19, after which the Holy Supper was administered to about 40 communicants. Mr. Barrett also delivered a lecture in the evening to a full and attentive house.

25. The Association now stands adjourned to meet in Cincinnati on the 3d Friday of May, 1849, at 8 o'clock, A. M.

By order of the Association.

J. P. STUART,   JOHN MURDOCK,
Recording Secretary.   *President.*

[The meeting of the Association, though not large, was very pleasant. All its deliberations were marked by a kind, conciliatory, and free spirit; and every one went away feeling that it had been good for him to be there. Much of the time and attention of the Association was taken up with the plan of Missionary operations, as suggested in the Report of the Acting Committee. And we would here call the particular attention of receivers throughout the State of Ohio to the resolutions on this subject, appended to the Report of said Committee; and would urge upon them the speedy formation of auxiliary missionary societies to aid this cause throughout this and the neighboring States.]

Intelligence.

In the communications received, there was but little that was new and of general interest in regard to the progress of the Doctrines; therefore we omit publishing them entire. The course pursued at our last annual meeting in changing the name of our body, and applying as an association for admission into the General Convention, seems to have meet with the cordial approbation of our brethren throughout the State. All who have alluded to the subject in their

well-disposed, the dissatisfaction with the Old Church dogmas has grown from alienation to disgust.

" As an evidence of the necessity of inquiring in respect to the New Church truth, I would state, that a gentleman of my acquaintance (who is still a member of the Presbyterian Church), and who is engaged in the sale of Law, Professional and other books, and whose business leads him to visit very frequently the principal towns in this part of the State, told me early in the summer that he not unfrequently heard inquiries for the works of Swedenborg, and that if he had a supply he thought he would find sale for them to some extent. Accordingly, at his suggestion, I wrote to Otis Clapp, the New Church Bookseller at Boston, and he sent him on a pile of books to the amount of about $30,00. I saw the gentleman some three weeks since, and he told me he had disposed of all except one copy of Clissold's Letter and a few tracts, and should send on for more. Into what hands they have generally fallen, I do not know."

Mr. F. Ecstein, of Louisville, Ky. writes: "Our zealous brother Mr. Fulton, has imported, at his own expense, a tolerably complete assortment of our author's theological and scientific works, with a good collection of all the smaller works, and tracts which he keeps for sale, and liberally lends whenever called on: his principal object being to invite reading, and the enterprise has already been productive of much good. I daily discover more and more, that where there is plane of the good of life with simplicity of mind, the truth is at once seen and acknowledged, when reading can be induced. Several instances of this kind I have recently witnessed; and what multitudes of human beings may there be in this state, though outwardly belonging to sectarian institutions!"

Report of the Acting Committee.

Since the last meeting of this Association, no business of any considerable importance has engaged the attention of the Acting Committee. Immediately after the adjournment of our last meeting, the Committee attended to the printing and distributing of the Journal of Proceedings. 500 copies were printed. Of this number, 50 copies were sent to the English New Church Conference, 50 copies to the General Convention of New Church Societies, &c. in the United States, 25 copies to the Central Convention, 15 to the Massachusetts Association, and the same number to the Maine, Pennsylvania, Michigan and Illinois Associations, and one to every New Church minister in the country: and the remainder to individuals and Societies within the limits of this Association.

It will be seen by reference to the list of New Church ministers in Western States, as published in the last Journal, that the name of E. Yulee, does not occur there. The Acting Committee assumed the responsibility of omitting this name for the following reasons.

A few days before the last meeting of the late Western Convention, Mr. Yulee went to Louisville, Ky., and was there ordained by the Rev. S. H. Wills. But the ordination did not, as we have been able to learn, take place at the request of any regular Society or other associated body of the New Church. And by reference to the "Report on the case of the Rev. S. H. Wills," published in the Journal of 1847, the committee found that Mr. Wills was " ordained a priest and teaching minister of the Lord's New Church"—" with authority, at the request, or with the approbation of any regularly organized society of the New Jerusalem, to license or ordain other priests and ministers into the said Church."

It would appear from this, that the Rev. Mr. Wills had authority conferred on him by his ordination to ordain any one into the ministry of the New Church, when he should be requested to do so by some regular New Church Society, who may have enjoyed a sufficient opportunity of judging of the qualifications of the candidate—or when the ordination should be approved by some formal act of such a Society, but in no other case. And this seems a wise and judicious provision. The obvious intention of it was, to guard the pulpit of the New Church as far as possible against incompetent and unworthy men, by making it necessary that a candidate for the ministry be approved and his ordination be requested by some regularly organized body of receivers, whose personal knowledge of his character and qualifications might be such as to enable them to judge of his fitness for the office,—as in the cases of Messrs. Hough and Stuart.

Now the Acting Committee, conceiving that the Rev. Mr. Wills, in ordaining Mr. Yulee *without* the formal request or approbation of any such organized body of receivers, transcended the powers conferred upon him—felt some embarrassment upon the question of placing Mr. Yulee's name in the list of our ministers. To have placed it there would have been an acknowledgment on their part of the validity of his ordination. But this they were not prepared to do. And as the term for which Mr. Yulee was *licensed* had expired (a fact unknown to the Committee when they commenced printing the Journal), they therefore, omitted to insert his name in the list of Ministers and Licentiates. But in doing this, the Committee acted conscientiously according to their own views of the case merely, and did not expect or wish their decision to be final. They have deemed it proper, therefore, to state the case here and their reasons for doing as they did, and they now leave it with the Association either to correct or confirm their judgment.

Although no official communication has been received from the General Convention of New Church Societies, &c. in the U. States relative to the application of this Association for admission into that body, yet it appears from their Journal of Proceedings that we were "cordially received" by the Convention on the condition that we are to be allowed "no vote in the Convention in the regulation of its ministry, or the form of its ecclesiastical government." Now if the Convention had really intended all that the language of the Resolution by which our Association was received would seem to imply, the terms of admission must be pronounced alike ungenerous and unusual. and are such as we ought not and could not accept. For in case we did accept them, we should exhibit the singular anomaly of being in connection with a larger ecclesiastical body, with our hands tied and our mouths sealed in regard to the various questions relating to the constitution and government of that body. We should not be allowed to vote upon any of the following questions, and others like them :

Who shall be received into the General Convention, and upon what terms ?

How many delegates shall Societies or Associations be entitled to ?

Shall the presiding officer of the Convention be an Ordaining Minister in all cases ?

How shall the President be chosen, and how long shall he be continued in office ?

What special duties may be assigned to the President? Shall all committees be nominated by him? &c.

All these and many more similar matters are clearly involved in, and make a part of, the *Convention's* "form of ecclesiastical government;" and therefore our Association could have no vote upon them. Neither could any of our ministers be allowed to sit and act with the Committee on the Education of Ministers, the Committee on Missions, the Pasotral Committee, or the Ecclesiastical Committee; for these Committees also enter into, and make a part of, the Convention's form of government.

Now such a connection as this which the General Convention, by a fair construction of its language, proposes to our Association, is one of which we know no example either among the members of the human body, among the societies in heaven, or among orderly associations of men on earth.

But we are convinced that the Convention did not mean all that its language seems to us to imply. And in this conviction we are sustained by the declarations of some of its own members, as well as by the statements of our delegate to that body, Mr. Glascoe. One member of the Convention, in a private letter to one of your Committee, states in substance that the Convention intended only to deny us the privilege and right of voting upon questions touching the ecclesiastical government of other associated bodies belonging to it. In other words, that the privilege of voting in Convention should be denied us only when our vote would obviously be interfering with matters which concerned other sections of the Church, or which might be of a nature kindred to those which we would not allow others to interfere with in our own Association, and this is the way our delegate to the Convention understood the terms of our admission. Believing this to have been the meaning of our Eastern brethren in the Resolution referred to, the Acting Committee are of the opinion that the action of the General Convention on this subject ought to be quite satisfactory to this Association. It grants us all the rights and privileges in that body which we asked for, or could reasonably expect; for in our application we disclaimed all right or disposition on our part to interfere in any way with the ecclesiastical government of other Societies or associated bodies of the Church.

Our application led to another step on the part of the General Convention, which must be highly gratifying not only to this association, but to the members of the New Church every where throughout our country—a step which promises to result in the organic union of the different sections of the New Church in the U. States—a consummation which the lovers of unity, peace, and concord, cannot but devoutly wish. For it led to the appointment of a committee to take into consideration the Rules and Recommendations of the Convention, with the view of arranging the reception into that body not only of this Association, but of all the Associations and other bodies of the New Church in this country, upon satisfactory grounds. The cheering prospect, therefore, is thus opened to us, of having a Convention ere long which shall embrace all varieties of the New Church in our country, and which shall therefore be general in *reality* and not merely *in name*. The good which will undoubtedly result to the whole church from this, can hardly be estimated beforehand.

The principal objects which, in the opinion of the Acting Committee, claim the immediate attention and the united and persevering efforts of this Association, are the Missionary, the Book and the Tract enterprises. And upon these subjects we desire to make a few remarks, and to offer some suggestions in regard to a plan of efficient operations.

The first inquiry which suggests itself in relation to these subjects, is : What needs to be done ? And the second inquiry is : How shall we do it ?

As to the first inquiry : The living voice—the public speaker, seems needed to call the attention of the public to the Heavenly Doctrines in the first instance, and to awaken a desire to know more of them. Hence the importance and need of the Missionary and missionary labor.

But in order that the labors of a Missionary may prove permanently useful, they need to be followed by New Church Books and Tracts. The Missionary goes into some town or village that has never before been visited, and delivers some discourses on the doctrines of the Church. The public curiosity is awakened, and many are induced to go and hear, prompted by the desire to know "what this new doctrine is." Of this number it will generally be found that *some,* by the time the lectures are finished, will have been sufficiently interested to desire to know more of our doctrines. They will be glad to receive and read tracts if given to them, or even to purchase some books if they can obtain them. And if the Missionary is able to furnish them with books and tracts when a spirit of inquiry is awakened, their interest in what they have heard will not subside when he departs. It will go on increasing. The lectures will often be a theme of conversation among the people for some time after ; and if books and tracts have been left behind, they will often be borrowed and read by others, and in this way all the free minds in the village or neighborhood will stand a fair chance of becoming more or less familiar with our doctrines. And thus the way will be prepared, on the return of the Missionary to that place, for a larger audience, for the distribution of more tracts, and for the sale of more books.

In order, therefore, that our missionaries may be in the highest degree useful, it seems important that they should be kept well supplied with tracts to give away to such as may desire to read, and with the best pioneer books to sell to such as are willing to purchase. The books should be furnished to the missionaries at the lowest possible wholesale prices ; so that, by selling them at the ordinary retail prices, something may be realized in this way towards the support of the mission. But the greatest benefit anticipated from this course, will result to the purchasers. A man when he has purchased a book, is generally desirous of obtaining the worth of his money from it, and therefore will often read it more attentively than he would if it had cost him nothing.

It is impossible to estimate the amount of good which may be done in our State in the course of a few years by keeping our missionaries well supplied with books and tracts. We firmly believe that, with such aids, a single missionary may accomplish more in five years in the way of disseminating the Heavenly Doctrines, than ten, without these aids, could accomplish in twice that time.

Now to accomplish the work which seems so desirable, we require some means—means to support missionaries and to furnish them with books and tracts. How shall the requisite amount of means be raised, and how, or by whom shall they be disbursed ?

It is well known that things are generally done best, when they are done in some orderly or systematic manner. There is method everywhere in creation, and all God's works are done systematically, or according to some fixed plan. Should not men endeavor to imitate their Creator in this as in other things, and try to do all their works systematically?

The Acting Committee would venture to suggest a plan, which, if adopted generally, will undoubtedly effect all that is desired. Its general features may be stated thus:

Let the missionary enterprise be understood to embrace the book and tract enterprises also; and let it be under the direction of this Association. Let the Missionaries be employed and paid by the Association, and be required to render a full account of their doings at each of our regular meetings. Let the Association see to providing the Missionaries with tracts for distribution and suitable books for sale. Let the receivers in every town and village within the limits of our association unite to form auxiliary missionary societies. Let them organize, (each society in its own way) perhaps by the appointment of a President, Secretary, Treasurer, and Collector—for little or nothing can be accomplished without organization. Let each member subscribe such an amount as he feels able to pay monthly, or quarterly, or at any other stated time. Let the Treasurer of each of these Auxiliary Societies make a remittance to the Treasurer of the Association, once a quarter, of the amount received by him; and let the several sums received from the several auxiliaries be inserted in our Treasurer's report at each meeting of the association. Let each auxiliary society, for the purpose of keeping up and increasing an interest in the cause, hold regular meetings, perhaps once a month, for conversation on the doctrines of the church, for imparting to each other any information they may have concerning the spread of the doctrines,—reading letters from the Missionary or other persons, and by these means keeping the missionary cause before their minds, and deepening their sense of its importance. Each Society contributing $20,00 or $50,00, or more, per annum, should be entitled to a proportional share of the labors of the missionary.

Now if the receivers in every town, village, and city, within the limits of our Association, would adopt and pursue some such plan as the one here suggested, and if each individual would contribute 25 cents a month, or even half that sum—and some could doubtless contribute several times that amount without difficulty—there is no doubt but we should obtain funds sufficient to accomplish all that seems desirable to be done. An incalculable amount of good might be done in this way in the course of a few years, even by a single Missionary. The principles of the New Theology would thus be sown broadcast throughout our State, and ere long they would be found germinating in many a town and hamlet,—in many a humble truth-loving heart, and shedding their fragrance all around. Light would soon be in the dwellings of many who have hitherto dwelt only in darkness. The waters of heavenly life would be seen breaking out in the wilderness, and streams in the desert; and many a moral waste—many a spot now barren, parched and cheerless, would ere long be converted into a well-watered, fertile and blooming Eden.

Brethren, shall we not, one and all, relying on the Lord for needed wisdom and strength, gird ourselves for this good work, and try what we can do?

Already we have one missionary (Rev. J. P. Stuart) constantly employed; recently a horse and carriage have been purchased for the use of Mr. Stuart by the united contributions of some of the brethren in Cincinnati and Lebanon. This is a good step towards the accomplishment of our grand object. Mr. Stuart will now be able to meet his appointments promptly—to pass easily and with little expense from place to place, and, what is especially desirable, will be able to take with him to all the towns he may visit a good supply of our books and tracts. A systematic plan of operations, steadily adhered to, seems all that is now wanting to accomplish the great object we have in view.

The Acting Committee would close their Report by offering the following resolutions:

Resolved, 1st. That, if the meaning of the General Convention in the Resolution by which the Ohio Association was admitted into that body be what the Acting Committee in this Report have supposed it was. this Association cordially accepts the terms, and is happy to consider itself in formal connection with that Convention.

Resolved, 2d. That this Association rejoices at the appointment by the General Convention, of a committee to take into consideration the Rules and Recommendations of that body, with the view of forming a platform sufficiently broad, if possible, to allow all the associated bodies of the New Church in this country to stand and act upon together, in their labors to promote the great and permanent interests of the Church.

Resolved, 3d. That the cause of Missions within the limits embraced by this body, be determined upon as a leading use to be performed by our Association.

Resolved, 4th. That it be the duty of the Acting Committee to execute the plan of missionary operations by appointing one or more missionaries, defining their routes, &c., and that they present a report of their doings to the next annual meeting of the Association.

Resolved, 5th. That this Association earnestly recommends to the receivers within its limits the immediate formation of auxiliary missionary societies, or the adoption of some systematic plan similar to the one suggested in the following report, by which they may most effectually aid the Association in its efforts to disseminate the doctrines of Heaven throughout this and the neighboring States.

Resolved, 6th. That the auxiliary societies as soon as formed, or before the 1st of Jan. 1849, be requested to transmit to the Treasurer of this Association, Mr. E. Hinman of Cincinnati, the amount of their quarterly subscriptions to the missionary and book fund, to be by him disbursed under the direction of the Acting Committee of the Association.

All of which is respectfully submitted.

B. F. BARRETT. ⎫
O. LOVELL.   ⎪ *For*
E. HINMAN.   ⎬ *the Acting* ·
S. HOLMES.   ⎭ *Committee.*

THE

NEW CHURCH REPOSITORY

AND

MONTHLY REVIEW.

| Vol. 1. | DECEMBER, 1848. | No. 12. |

ORIGINAL PAPERS.

ARTICLE I.

CONCERNING THE DIVINE WORD.

(Translated from the " Nouvelle Jerusalem.")

Every believer holds that the Word is inspired, that the Word is holy; but he often repeats it from having heard others say so, without being able to assure himself of the grounds of the assertion. Nevertheless, if we do not form a just idea upon this subject, we run the risk of having our convictions shaken, and of saying, with the opposers of the Word, that the Sacred Scripture is no more than a human work full of incoherences and contradictions.

Another reason why we ought to form a just idea upon this subject is, because, in the age in which we live, when men are happily awakened from their mental stupidity, the faith of our ancestors is no longer relied upon or considered as a sufficient basis for our own belief. The habit of conceding to others the right to think and believe for us has gradually been removed, and would now appear as absurd as it would be to require another to eat, to drink, to sleep for us. He who seeks truth wants to see and comprehend for himself; he wishes to make use of the faculties which he has received from the Creator, to understand the present, to explain the future, and from this to regulate his existence. What privilege could be more legitimate, more sacred, and more susceptible of elevating mankind!

It is then to you, my thinking friends, that this treatise is addressed; not to those who put human tradition in the place of the Lord's commandments, and who, by antiquated arguments and obsolete prejudices, have closed up to themselves all entrance to truth; nor is this treatise addressed to those who do not believe in the Divine Word;—blinded by their own reasoning, they are confirmed in error; truth, alas! is not accessible to such conditions.

Affirming that the *Word is divinely inspired*, let us consider in what this inspiration consists. But for the better understanding of this, it ought first to be seen that *the Gospel is not precisely a historical book;* else, how could it contain such dissimilar relations of one and the same event, as can be easily proven to any one the least acquainted with this Divine Record? Yet, there is certainly much history in the general exposition of the life, actions, and doctrine of God manifested in the flesh; but in the particulars it may be easily seen that the history is not the principal subject of the Gospels; the numerous differences which exist between them clearly prove this. We proceed to quote some passages in support of our position.

1. In the Gospel according to Matthew, i. 6–16, it is said that *David begat Solomon, that Solomon begat Roboam,* and so on to *Joseph the husband of Mary.* In the Gospel according to Luke iii. 23–31, the genealogy is described in an ascending order, and it is said that Joseph decends from Matthat, from Nathan, from David, and at the same time the persons which are found between Joseph and David are entirely different. There is then no history *there;* and whatever pains theologians have taken to make these proper names agree, saying that *Heli,* the father of Joseph, is only an abbreviation of Heliakim, and that *Heliakim* and *Joakim* are used indifferently, and that consequently *Heli* named in the 23d verse as the father of Joseph, is *Joakim,* the father of Mary, and that then the genealogy described in Luke is not the genealogy of Joseph but of Mary, still this explication is completely in contradiction with the simple and clear testimony of the Word of God, the forced interpretations still remaining in a state of hypothesis and doubt.

2. In Matthew xvii. 1, 2, and Mark ix. 2, it is said: *After six days Jesus was transfigured;* whilst in Luke ix. 28, 29, the Lord was transfigured *after about eight days.* Which then of these chronologies is the most correct? Yet it would be impossible to consider as insignificant and of little value any thing which belongs to the Word of God, as might be allowable with the word of man!

3. In Matthew xxvi. *There came unto him a woman having an alabaster box of very precious ointment, and poured it on his head, as he sat at meat.* In Mark xvi. 3, the fact is related in the same words. In John xii. 3, this same circumstance is described quite differently ; it is there said that *she anointed the feet of Jesus and dried them with her hair.* Where then is the history ?

4. In Mark xv. 25, it was the third hour when they crucified Him, whilst in John xix. 14, we read *that it was only on the sixth hour that Pilate delivered Jesus to the Jews.* And if we must attribute these contradictions to some errors in the manuscripts, as many theologians affirm, what limit can be fixed to these mistakes of the copyists ?

5. In Matthew xxvii. 44, the *thieves also, which were crucified with him, cast the same in his teeth ;* in Luke xxiii. 39, 40, 41, 42, *one of the malefactors which were hanged, railed on him, saying, If thou be Christ save thyself and us also. But the other answering rebuked him, saying, Dost thou not fear God * * * and he said unto Jesus, Lord, remember me when thou comest into thy kingdom.* Can any one say which of these two facts should be considered as true ? Here there cannot have been an error in the copies.

Besides these examples, there are many other particulars quite as much at variance, and which equally prove that the Gospel was not entirely designed to be an historical exposition relative to the terrestial life of Jesus Christ, but that it has another end—an end much more elevated as *should* be that of a Divine Work ! For this reason the contradictions, which we meet with in many places in this Sacred Book, are but apparent contradictions, and permitted in the letter only, because of the correspondence which necessarily exists between the spiritual and the natural ; for it is impossible to admit any contradiction in the Divine idea, otherwise it would be necessary to suppose also that God Himself is contradiction. But we will recur to this again ; for the present let us examine the contradictions which are met with in the doctrinal part :

1. The law of love, this sublime basis upon which all christianity is founded, commands us to love even our enemies ; in another passage, Matthew xix. 5, 6, Mark x. 7, 8, 9, the Lord himself teaches that *a man shall leave his father and mother and cleave unto his wife, and they two shall be one.flesh, that man should not put asunder what God has joined together.* In the decalogue he is commanded to honor his father and mother, a commandment which the Lord has confirmed with his own mouth in Matthew xix. 19 ; Mark x. 19 ; Luke xviii. 20 : but in Mark x. 29, 30, he says Himself that a man must leave

his father, mother, wife, brothers and sisters, children, lands, to receive a hundred fold as much in this time and in the life to come ; and, what is still more surprising, in Luke xiv. 26, he says, *If any man come unto me and hate not his father, and mother, and wife, and children, and brethren and sisters, yea, and his own life also, he cannot be my disciple.*　How reconcile these contradictions ?　What arguments then, according to this, would be sufficiently persuasive or strong, to calm the conscience of married partners, prompted by an ardent love, of children honoring their parents, of parents animated with solicitude for their children and loving them with that ineffable sentiment which has been put in the heart by the Lord Himself ?　And, on the other hand, what will be the state of the unhappy fanatic, who, acting solely according to the literal sense of the passages quoted above, having left his father, his mother, his wife, his children, shall have come at last to hate them ?　What will become of him, when he shall read in the word of the Lord that the law of love forbids the sundering of those cherished ties with his parents, his children, his deserted wife ?　All the arbitrary interpretations of men, not based upon sure and revealed data from on high, with a view to make intelligible these passages in their true or interior sense, would always remain insufficient, these interpretations not proceeding in fact from the domain of human comprehension and intelligence.

2. In Luke xiv. 12, 13, 14, The Lord says to him who had come to invite him : *When thou makest a dinner or a supper, call not thy friends, nor thy brethren, neither thy kinsmen, nor thy rich neighbors ; lest they also bid thee again, and a recompense be made thee.　But when thou makest a feast call the poor, the maimed, the lame, the blind : and thou shalt be blessed ; for they cannot recompense thee : for thou shalt be recompensed at the resurrection of the just.*　Is not this passage, taken literally, in direct contradiction with the usual custom now prevalent not only among men of the world, but also among the just ? and can it be a fact, that a feast given to relations and friends and reciprocated by them would deprive them of the recompenses of the heavenly kingdom ?　It is then very evident that this is an allegory ; but who will undertake the difficult task to explain this allegory, in such a way, that the explanation shall not savor of what is arbitrary, and lead into error those who would confide in it ?　Revelation alone can explain revelation.

3. In Matthew xix. 24, Mark x. 25, and Luke xvii. 25, it is said, *that it is easier for a camel to pass through the eye of a needle, than for a rich man to enter into the Kingdom of God.*

Cruel decree, and one which taken in the letter, condemns all the social institutions of governments tending to enrich the public and individuals; a decree which finds a contradiction in the sacred scripture itself, for it is known that Abraham, Isaac, and Jacob were very rich, and the Lord in Matthew xxii. 32, Mark xii. 26, 27, and Luke xx. 37, 38, calls Himself *their God, the God of the living.* Thus in comparing these passages with the real facts, we meet again contradictions in the literal sense, contradictions which, like all others, cannot be reconciled together, but by the positive and only true means of the interior sense. But what but revelation can give us this key?

4. It is said in Matthew v. 28, 29, xviii. 8, 9, Mark ix. 43, 45, 47, *If thy right eye offend thee, pluck it out, and cast it from thee: And if thy right hand offend thee, cut it off, and cast it from thee.* Here the question presents itself, is it reasonable to pluck out one's eyes and cut off the hands, and in general, to mutilate oneself, when the members of themselves cannot offend or tempt; but the sensations and the thoughts? Thus then we have here again an allegory,—an allegory which it is hardly possible for human wisdom to explain. Many celebrated men have commented upon this passage in a way more or less satisfactory, according to the degree of their perception and illumination, but not conformably to the true knowledge of the interior sense, thus we meet with incoherences in their explanation, and not one presents that fulness and power of conviction, which must necessarily be the infallible attribute of an inspiration from on high,—the attribute of revelation itself.

5. In the Apocalypse, xix. 17, 18, it is said, *I saw an angel standing in the sun; and he cried with a loud voice, saying to all the fowls that fly in the midst of heaven, come and gather yourselves together unto the supper of the Great God, that ye may eat the flesh of kings, and the flesh of captains, and the flesh of mighty men, and of the flesh of horses and them that sit on them, and the flesh of all men, both free and bond, both small and great.* What does this signify? Can it be possible that the supper of the Great God should consist in the assembling together of all the birds which fly in the midst of heaven, to devour the flesh of all who are named in this passage? Is it not then clear that it is an allegory, as well as the whole of the Apocalypse, and that without a particular key this allegory could not be understood? But where shall we seek for this key, if the Lord Himself does not give it to us?

From all these examples, whose number could be greatly increased, we should naturally conclude:

1st. That the contradictions found in the literal sense of the

Word of God, a book revealed by God Himself, and the relations which it contains differing upon one and the same historical fact, are not the effect of chance, and do not proceed from mistakes of the writers employed on so grave a subject : but that they are the product of the connection of the Divine idea with the natural ideas manifested in human language; and, 2nd, that if this same book contains in many places contradictory doctrines, doctrines little conformable to the spirit of those for whom they were promulgated, and to the spirit of the institutions based upon the word of God itself, institutions which the book itself justifies ; that if it contains also, dogmas in contradiction with the laws of nature drawn from the same Divine source ; this is but the result of the graduated manifestation of the Divine idea expressed in the letter or envelope, an idea necessarily full of exactness and spiritual order, God Himself being the principle of order.   Omnipotence itself cannot act contrary to order, for this would be to act contrary to itself—a contradiction incompatible with the Divinity.

If the Sacred Scriptures were not inspired; if they were only a human contrivance, there would be many passages which would always remain in a state of inexplicable doubt, and would become the source of the most dangerous controversies and errors ; if, on the contrary, they are inspired and holy, it naturally follows that the contradictions which their literal sense presents, are but appearances, such as are so many of the phenomena in nature ; for example, the diurnal rotation of the sun and stars, which seem to turn round the earth, and yet we very well know that it is the earth which turns, whilst the sun and stars are immovable.   In like manner the literal sense does not constitute all the Divine word; it is by its signification the smallest part of it, the whole being the indispensable continent of the more elevated sense, of the hidden and spiritual sense, whose existence was confirmed by the Lord Himself, when he said in the synagogue of Capernaum: *My words are spirit and life* (John vi. 63) ; and when he so often cries out in his discourse: *He that hath ears to hear, let him hear.*

Though such is the literal sense of the Word, and though at the first examination it presents so many stumbling blocks, we nevertheless repeat that the *Gospel is divinely inspired*, and we will soon demonstrate that the contradictions of the sense of the letter testify to its divine revelation.   Many, notwithstanding, will be offended and re-enact the words of the Jews: *This is a hard saying ; who can hear it?   They walked no more with Him* (John vi. 60, 66).   Others perceiving, though in a vague manner, and without being able to give an account of it, that the exterior and gross envelope must conceal "the *words of eternal life* (John vi. 68), set about inquiring, and being aided by some Divine inspirations, but ordinarily resting on their own intellectual power to find this other sense, this more elevated sense, succeed at last in discovering that it existed; but what it is in reality, the celebrated Clement of Alexandria, nor Origen himself, who has done so much for the Sacred Scriptures, nor any other has wholly understood it, because the science of correspondences, lost in the most ancient times, was not known to them, and because the laws according to which the Word of God was written, were not revealed to them. This precious gift of the Divine mercy was reserved for the epoch of the *coming of the Son of Man, coming in the clouds with power and great glory* (Matthew xxiv. 30); it was reserved for the time when the *branches of the fig tree should begin to grow tender and put forth leaves* (ibid. 33); the epoch when natural good should begin to develope itself in the christian world and manifest itself in its acts (rejecting the morbid system of intolerance and violence, as well in matters of religion as in civil and moral institutions); this gift was reserved, I say, for the epoch when natural truths were beginning to revive humanity, supinely slumbering under the dark yoke of ignorance; for that epoch, in fine, when the spirit of man should have attained the degree of desired maturity, and his heart those affections which render us capable of acknowledging, receiving and applying to our life the sublime and spiritual truths concealed under the veil of the letter. It was not then until this present age that the laws of inspiration began to be disengaged from their mysterious envelopes, those laws which presided at the creation of the universe, and at the promulgation of the Word of God, those laws of the correspondence of the natural with the spiritual, of the correspondence of the interior sense with that of the letter; it is now then, in our own age, that the glory of the Lord illuminates with a brilliant lustre the hieroglyphics of the letter, and explains all the contradictions which it presents.

We know that two distinct parts compose every rational discourse: *The sense* and the expression; the expression is only the form or receptacle of the sense, this being clothed with the expression which is identical with or correspondent to it, and in this manner vivified by it. It is the same with the Divine Word; if then the *letter* or the *expression* in the Divine Word differs completely from its spirit or its sense, though they are connected together, like the *thing containing* with the *thing contained;* if there is a concealed harmony between the expression or the letter of the Word, and the sense or spirit enclosed in the Word and expressed by the letter, and if this harmony is always constant and invariable, as it should be in the Divine order, it follows that there can be one only true way to interpret the Sacred Scriptures, and this way must be based upon the knowledge of the connection and exact correspondence between the *expression* and the *sense*, the same as in explaining a man's discourse we must know the signification and extent of the words which compose it, or rather precisely the idea which it contains.

The knowledge of this harmony between the *letter* of the Sacred Scriptures and its *sense* or *spirit* as the only true means of interpreting the Word of God, will receive an incontestable confirmation when in applying it, we will be able to prove:

1st, That more than twenty writers of the Word of God, living in ages and countries very remote, nevertheless coincide in the expression subject to these same laws and these same rules, which, when they are applied, discover every where one and the same connection between the *letter* and *spirit*, or between the *expression* and the *sense*, when it is altogether impossible that these writers could have communicated to each other these laws or these rules.

2d. That these laws or rules are derived from the very works themselves of these writers of the Word of God.

3d. That these laws or rules contain the most profound wisdom, bear the seal of the Divinity, and are of the highest importance and edification to man.

4th. That without the knowledge of these laws and rules, and without their application to the inspired writings, no one can discover the sublime, ineffable, and infinite truths contained in these writings.

5th, And lastly, that, if with the knowledge of these laws and rules applied to the Holy Scriptures, we have the sincere desire to know and comply with the will of the Most High. these laws, like a key, open the inexhaustible treasures of Wisdom, Mercy and heavenly Truth, every where present in the Holy Word.

And, in fact, when this key opens the letter, all the contradictions, all the anachronisms, all the incoherences disappear, and are transformed into an admirable and harmonious agreement of sublime Divine truths And it is only the secret union of the letter with the sense which proves the inspiration of the Sacred Scriptures.

By means of this key every thing in the Scriptures can be explained, its mysteries penetrated, and all religious doubts resolved. It discovers to us in the Bible all that which is from man, and all that is not from him. All that bears not the character of Divinity fails to stand this test, and not being vivified by contact with this key, remains a work merely human in the state of an inanimate corpse : on the other hand, that which is of God, though it should be apparently lifeless and shapeless, immediately, through the help of this precious key, receives *spirit* and *life*, and is completely transformed into *love* and *light*, so that there remains nothing obscure, nothing incoherent. And this it is which convinces us of the inspiration of the Word.

To those who have read without prejudice the "*Doctrines concerning the Sacred Scriptures*," written by that illustrious man, whom it has pleased the Lord to choose to communicate this key, all this is already proven; they have acknowledged the Sacred Scriptures to be an inspired book, containing striking and irrefutable proofs of its Divine Origin; they have acknowledged that the key, of which we have just spoken, discovers its mysteries; they have acknowledged also, that the discovery of a combination, as sublime as it is wonderful, and which embraces all particularities, could not be possible but by the intermediacy of the Divinity. But for those who have not read the Doctrine concerning the Sacred Scriptures, what has been said will be sufficient to put them in the way, and if they are guided by a sincere love for truth, they will find in this work what will fully satisfy them.

To identify ourselves further with the subject of what is necessary here to give an idea, and to explain what revelation is, let us turn our attention to the analogy which exists between the spiritual and the natural. The Scripture says, that *man is created in the image and likeness of God.* We cannot comprehend this truth but by regarding man as a being endowed with the capacity of receiving, in a finite degree and measure, the qualities and faculties belonging to the Divinity in their infinite fulness. In this way the qualities with which the spirit of man is endowed must, in their normal state, be derived images, types, and impressions of primordial and uncreated prototypes existing in God. The whole body of man also is but a compound of similitudes, types and impressions of that which exists in his mind; the physiology of man proves it clearly, and that to the degree that very often, even in conversation, we borrow from the organs of the body images and comparisons to explain the different dispositions and various qualities of the mind. In poetry also how often are similitudes, taken in a lower sphere, substituted for objects which correspond to them in a higher sphere, and even for prototypes existing in the Deity. An attentive and profound study of nature discovers that as *man is the image and likeness of God,* so also all the creatures in the lower sphere of creation are, to a certain degree, the image of man, and that each separately, in a less elevated order, is the impress or image of a type identical to it, existing in man. It is then easy to see and prove that every thing in nature being the exterior product of an interior essence, all these objects become natural, sensual, and material images of moral, intellectual, and spiritual forms identical to those images, which are all identical to the prototypes of the Deity.

This is not the place to prove the existence of all these similitudes and images; there are books which treat of them at length and clearly; I will only say that there is not a single atom in the whole visible universe which has not its proper type in the superior and spiritual orders of creation, and which consequently has not its prototype in God, the sole source of every thing, without which this atom could neither *be* nor exist, for *all things were made by Him; and without him was not any thing made that was made.*

The knowledge of all these similitudes of the spiritual with the natural, and of the relations of the images produced, as well with that which produces, as with the prototypes themselves, constitutes a science, called the *science of correspondences,* which flourished in remote antiquity, and served as a basis to the language of the ancients and the language of hieroglyphics so well known in Egypt, and among the ancient Eastern nations. This science teaches such a method of interpretation, that that which is superior is rendered, by analogy, by that which is inferior, and that objects of a less elevated order are employed in the place of ideas which correspond to them in a higher sphere. Some traces of this language, as we have before said, still remain in poetry; and the key, which is the subject of the present discussion, and which is founded upon the great and universal science of correspondences, discovers to us that the whole Word of God, the Old as well as the New-Testament, is written in this language, while a sound and impartial judgment, proves that the Word could not have been written in any other manner, precisely because it is Divine and not human.

Many, while conceding inspiration to the Sacred Scriptures, yet believe that each of the words, taken separately, does not contain any other idea than that expressed by said word, according to its commonly received sense; whence it follows that the Deity could not have had, in the inspiration, any other idea than that which is expressed in the letter; but such a conclusion tends to the rejection of the whole of the internal sense, or to the adoption of arbitrary commentaries. Is it not in this way, that, up to the time of this *new dispensation of grace and truth*, the doctors and preachers of the Church have interpreted the word of God, interpretations which have caused many to lose all confidence in the Word, and sown in others the tares of infidelity by suggesting this altogether natural reasoning. How could God express himself in many places in a manner so incomprehensible, so contradictory, and even so vulgar? Whilst the Lord Himself by the mouth of the prophet Isaiah says, *My thoughts are not your thoughts, and my ways are not your ways, saith Jehovah, for as far as the heavens are above the earth, so far are my ways above your ways, and my thoughts above your thoughts* (ch. lv. 8, 9). Applying this prophecy to the Sacred Scripture, we see that the Divine Word, clothed with the letter, differs entirely from the idea expressed by the letter which serves it only for an envelope.

From these words of Jehovah we recur to what was said above concerning the language in which the supreme Divine prototypes are expressed, by correspondence, by means of images and types produced by them in a lower order. This language unrols the mystic scale of Divine truth proceeding from the very bosom of the Deity, and passing gradually into the spheres of creation, from the highest, through the lower, even to the last limits of the intelligent creation—human rationality; it shows us, in fine, its manifestation in natural forms, that is to say, in that form under which the Divine truth presents itself in the sense of the letter, where it is said: *The Word was made flesh.*

I beg the reader, however, not to think that I apply the text above quoted (John i. 14), only to the efflux of the Divine truth from the bosom of the Deity, and to its expression in the Sacred Scriptures; no, this passage refers directly to the incarnation of the Saviour of the world; but in either case it testifies to the manifestation of the Divine truth, as well in the Word of God as in the human form, it is equally to be referred to the whole order of creation; for all these acts of the love and wisdom of the Lord are performed only according to the laws of his own order.

When the Divine truth proceeds from God to enlighten the minds of intellectual beings, it communicates to them, as in spiritual light, ideas conformable to their qualities, to their faculties, and conformable also to the degree of their receptibility, just as natural light, corresponding to spiritual light, affects the physical organ of sight with sensations indefinitely diverse and shaded, conformably to the construction of this organ and to the quality of the object which receives it; as the eagle soaring on high rejoices in the splendor of the brilliant sun, whilst the owl is paralyzed, blinded by it, and finds its true existence only in the profound darkness of night. And yet neither spiritual nor natural light are the property of these organs which receive them—each is communicated to them by causes existing without; that is to say, no action appertaining to light operates in the eye, unless this light flows into it from without; in like manner, in the human understanding, no comprehension of truth is formed, unless this truth be me-diately or immediately communicated to it.

This reasoning unfolds a remarkable fact. It proves that all beings the nearest to the Throne of the Most High, or the Spiritual Sun, as well as those who are more remote, are enlightened not by a light which is proper to them as their own, but by a spiritual light, flowing from the source of eter-nal wisdom, and that consequently the comprehension of truth, received by a finite and limited spirit, must differ entirely from the truth, such as it is in its source or infinite principle. In proceeding to a lower sphere, it must necessarily limit and modify itself conformably to the limited faculties of the spirit who receives it, but it is modified according to the exact and strict analogy existing between the prototypes and images derived from them. Thus then the sublime Divine truth clothes itself with the transparent essence of the angelic nature, when it communicates itself to the angel, and if it should express itself in words, it would then be necessary that these words be drawn up in angelic ideas, and in objects be-longing to the angelic world, and yet the supreme Divine ideas would not cease to be found continually present in these words. For the better understanding of this, let us compare this action to that of natural light; natural light exists really in all its integrity only in the sun, for in the objects which reflect it even the most faithfully, it already loses something of its splendor, and clothes itself with a diverse infinity of colors and shadowings, produced by the quality of the bodies upon which it falls, and through which it shines, and nevertheless it is always the same light which is found in all the innumera-ble modifications. If then the purely Divine light or truth itself continuing its progression according to these laws, even to the lowest sphere of creation, in which man occupies the same place as the angel in *his* sphere *does his*, if it descends there to be rendered into natural language, what, I ask, will be the language of that truth? will it not be composed of images and similitudes taken in the correspondences and analogies of all the visible objects of nature, and of the mode of thinking and acting habitual to the beings whom the truth shall have met in the boundary of its course? And notwith-

standing this, truth, which changes only in its forms and representatives, remains nevertheless immutable in its essence
under the envelope of our letter. It is thus that the Word of
God is written, because, as we said before, it could not possibly
have been otherwise, for *as the heavens are higher than the
earth, so are my ways higher than your ways, and my thoughts
than your thoughts, saith Jehovah.*—(Isaiah lv. 9.)

Behold the proper and essential origin of the allegory of the
Sacred Books, an allegory not conventional nor arbitrary, but
positive, exact, immutable, corresponding to the letter just as
the soul of man corresponds to his body, first, because every
soul at the moment of conception forms a body to itself according to its quality, and secondly, because no soul can inhabit a body which is not proper to it, or which should not be
identical to it.

Having in this way proved the indubitable existence of
another sense, interior, contained in that of the letter as the
soul is contained in the body of man, as the thought in the discourse, as motion in action, and differing nevertheless from
this sense, just as the soul differs from the body, I will quote
here the words of the sage who published that *Doctrine concerning the Sacred Scriptures* which I have once before mentioned. Really thinking men will be confirmed in the truths
here uttered. He says in the Apocalypse Revealed, No. 959 :
"The Word which was dictated from the Lord, passed through
the heavens of his celestial kingdom, and the heavens of
his spiritual kingdom, and thus came to man by whom it
was written ; wherefore the Word in its first origin is purely
divine : this Word as it passed through the heavens of the
Lord's celestial kingdom, was divine-celestial, and as it passed through the heavens of the Lord's spiritual kingdom, was
divine-spiritual, and when it came to man it became divine-
natural, hence it is that the natural sense of the Word contains
in itself the spiritual sense, and this the celestial sense, and
both a sense purely divine, which is not discernible by any
man, nor indeed by any angel."

There are two general modes according to which Divine
truth communicates itself to man. The *first*, when the writer
is enlightened by the Divine Spirit, as a man who is enlightened by the light of the sun, sees the objects which he describes ;
he examines them according to the clearness of the light
which surrounds them, and according to the penetration of his
sight, enjoying at the same time the liberty of making his conclusions, of choosing, or creating even, expressions which he
supposes most suitable to express more clearly the subject
treated of by him ; this is called being under the illumination

of the Divine Spirit. The other mode is that in which the writer is *transported* in *ecstacy*, in *exaltation*, or, in other words, when he is *in the Spirit :* in this state he has not even the consciousness of the natural objects which surround him; he is wholly absorbed in the Divine Spirit which fills him. The Divine Spirit then causing to descend, through the sphere of the angelic world, the rays of its wisdom and its love, even to the lowest sphere composing the last limit of creation, clothes them with the natural forms of thought and sensation which it finds corresponding to them in the understanding and will of the subject chosen for this mission. In this way the same Divine truth puts on, in Isaiah, natural forms quite different from those which it invests itself with in Hosea, though both of these natural forms may be equally divine, equally holy, because, as it was said above, the ineffable and supreme truth of God does not cease to dwell interiorly in these forms, and because these two organs, Isaiah and Hosea, being under this mode of inspiration, could not freely choose either expression, or conclusion, or action, but were only passive instruments acting without even the knowledge of that which they did. In this state more than ever, man is *nothing* and the Divinity *all;* this is the reason why what man produces in this moment is called the Word of God, for in it there is nothing human. The Divine Spirit assuming then the natural forms which it finds in the writer, causes to follow, in these forms, absolutely the same progression and the same order which the Divine thought has followed in the communication of a similar influx, and the natural or literal expression of these forms being arranged by the immutable law of analogy and correspondence, this expression becomes the most suitable to serve for a correspondent receptacle and envelope of the prototype-thought of the Divinity, while at the same time it is exactly and essentially the representative of the Divine idea which produced the expression. This is called writing under the immediate influx (or inspiration) of the Holy Spirit. It is thus that the whole Word was written; it is thus that Moses, David, the Prophets, the Evangelists wrote; it is thus that John wrote the Apocalypse, and because it is thus, he also said; *And if any man shall take away the words of the book of this prophecy, God shall take away his part out of the book of life, and out of the holy city, and from the things which are written in this book* (Apoc. xxii. 19). It is for this that the Lord said, *it is easier for heaven and earth to pass, than one tittle of the law to fail* (Luke xvi. 17). *Verily I say unto you, Till heaven and earth pass one jot or one tittle shall in no wise pass from the law, till all be fulfilled* (Matthew v. 18).

It is only upon this mode of writing the Word of God that is based the conjunction which is effected between the Lord and man by the aid of the Word, and no conjunction with the Lord could have been possible, if it had been written in any other way, and if man had been left free to express the Divine thought or truth in such or such a manner, according to the degree of his intelligence and civilization, according to the conventional principles of art.

From what has been said it may be clearly seen that they are not historical facts nor merely natural notions which constitute the principal subject of the Word of God, but that it is the communication of the Divine Truth and the Divine Good to man, to elevate and lead him, as by a ladder, from the visible to the invisible, from the exterior to the interior, and bring him into complete conjunction with the Lord. If then, in certain parallel passages, the Divine ideas put on natural forms differing apparently from each other in the exposition, it arises from the fact that in the internal sense the same idea is expressed by means of different subjects, with other shadowings, taken under different points of view; and from the fact that the union and harmony of that inspiration in natural forms exact a like exposition; and because, moreover, any other exposition, would not satisfy all the laws of the strict analogy and correspondence of the natural with the spiritual. I will go further, I will even say that the contradictions, the anachronisms, the incoherences of the literal sense of the Word of God may serve to develope our spiritual view, by causing us to have a preception of something more elevated, and awakening in us a desire to comprehend that which is interior, the desire of knowing this inmost treasure where are contained all the means of regeneration and salvation. Woe to him who, knowing this truth, has no desire to profit by it, and prefers adhering only to the envelope, without seeking for spiritual illumination.

But to confirm what has been said concerning the *Influx of the Spirit* in inspiration, and of the completely passive state of the subject chosen to record the words of the Divine Spirit, we remark, that when man is in Spirit and in vision, the eyes of his body are closed, and those of the soul open, so that many writers of the Word, in this state, believed themselves to be transported from one place to another, while in fact their body remained in the same place (Ezekiel iii. 12, 14; viii. 3; xi. 1, 2, 4; xliii. 5; Apoc. i. 10; xvii. 3; xxi. 10). This proves to what degree they were deprived of the knowledge of objects with which they were surrounded, and how the laws of inspiration are the same for all, differing only in the manifestation always analagous to the receptibility of forms. It is then in a like state that the Evangelists wrote *their annunciation of glad tidings ;* consequently on meeting, in the New Testament, quotations from the Prophets of the Old, we may be sure that the Evangelists have not copied them from the Bible, but that they have recorded them by the same inspiration under which they were influenced at the moment. It is for this reason that the same Divine thought, expressed by the Prophet under the envelope of natural forms assumed in *his* memory, had to be expressed by the Evangelist in other terms conformably to *his* natural ideas, because there are no two beings perfectly identical to each other, and because the natural forms which exist in the memory of the one, whatever resemblance they may have with the natural forms which exist in the memory of the other, nevertheless always present shadowings proper to the individuality of each. Thus scarcely any of the passages from the Old Testament, quoted in the New, are rendered exactly with the same words which compose the text, and it is to be supposed also that the Divine thought could, by permission of Jehovah, be communicated with some modification in itself which would necessarily be reflected in the letter.

From what has been said, many questions which present themselves, when we read the Gospel attentively, and when we compare it with the Old Testament, are found to be satisfactorily explained. It is known that the greater part of the quotations from the Old Testament are more conformable to the Greek translation than to the inspired Word of the original Hebrew, which is given as a reason, by the Doctors of the Eastern Church, for preferring the Greek Bible to the original Hebrew, though it is evident that the inspired original must be more exact than a translation, made especially at a time when there was no clear idea of an internal sense. To support their opinion, they assert that the Hebrews had falsified the literal sense of the Hebrew Bible. Notwithstanding this we know that Providence, in order to secure its Divine ends, and always observe faithfully the universal law of its order, which consists *in never violating the free will of man,* has again here preserved its work from the mutilation of the ill-disposed, yet without in the least impairing the free action of the copyists in their involuntary faults, which has occasioned some discordances in the editions of Bibles, as has happened also to the New Testament, discordances which however do not hurt the interior sense. But a single reflection based upon the laws of inspiration as they have been here explained, decides this question; the universal use of the Greek language in the time of the Evangelists, and the almost total forgetfulness of the Hebrew, which was then only known to the learned, made the Greek translation of the Bible more familiar than the original Hebrew, just as in our day, excepting the learned, scarcely any one reads the New Testament in Greek, but they read it translated into all the other languages. Conformably then to this historical fact, the Evangelists, as well as all the faithful of that time, made use of the Greek translation and retained in their memory the expressions and phaseology of the Greek Bible, and this is the reason why the Divine Inspiration itself, meeting in their memory forms of the Greek translation, manifested itself in the letter in forms rather Greek than Hebrew, and so much the more as the Evangelists were then meditating and writing the Gospels in Greek.

If what has been said concerning inspiration is true, by applying it to the four Gospels we again decide this other question: Why in the relation of one and the same fact do we meet with discordances in them? Precisely because the principal subject of their writings, as we have already frequently repeated, was not history, but the expression of Divine Truth in natural forms; and as the Divine Truth could communicate varied influences conformably to the faculty of each of them, each Evangelist must necessarily express the same inspiration in forms proper and identical to his ideas. It is from this that apparent contradictions have place in the sense of the letter which cannot possibly exist in any manner in the spiritual sense.

The interior state of each Evangelist stamps a seal upon the whole Gospel written by him, and establishes the means made use of by him to express himself, as well as the whole series of truths uttered by him. Let us elucidate this by an example: let us examine the state of the Lord entering upon his final sufferings and nailed to the cross: Matthew and Mark relate this event chiefly in its external part, for they speak much, and particularly Matthew, of the outrages endured by the Saviour, of the grievousness of his temptations which, increasing to the last limit of despair, force from him this heart rending exclamation, " My God ! My God ! why hast thou forsaken me !" (Matt. xxvii. 46; Mark xv. 34.) Luke dwells less upon the grief and sufferings endured by the Lord; he speaks more of the constant solicitude which the Lord manifests for the well-being and salvation of humanity; when ascending Golgotha he addresses these words of compassion to the weeping women: *Daughters of Jerusalem, weep not for me, but weep for yourselves and your children* (Luke xxii. 28); and when upon the cross he prays for his executioners : *Father, forgive them, for they know not what they do.*"—(*Ibid.* 43.)

We see clearly that Luke relates this fact with sentiments and thoughts more elevated than those of Matthew and Mark, and that each of them relates it conformably to the impression which this fact produced in him by the force of inspiration. But this difference is still more striking in John, who, speaking also of the state of Christ, as a martyr, exalts him to the point of having become completely insensible to the temptations and pains endured. It is thus that inspiration is manifested in John. He makes no mention of the outrages inflicted upon the Lord on the cross ; in this Evangelist the Lord at this last hour thinks not at all of himself, his concern is only for the church, assigning to it a place in the midst of those whom the disciple whom he loved represents, in the midst of those who do good from the love of good, saying to his mother who represents the Church : *Woman, behold thy son,* and to the disciple : *Behold thy mother* (John xix. 26–27). The desire that man may be saved and the Scripture be fulfilled he expresses in his incommensurable love, by saying, "I thirst," betraying not the least tinge of despair, not invoking the aid of a superior Being, strong in the consciousness of his Divinity, convinced of his triumphant victory ; as God Omniscient, He cries out, *It is finished.*

It is then evident that all these relations of one and the same fact are divinely animated impressions, altogether different, and each bearing the seal of the interior state of the writer. Resting upon the same law of inspiration, we can now explain a very serious fact which can in no other way be satisfactorily explained. In Matthew xxvii. 9, 10, it is said : *Then was fulfilled that which was spoken by Jeremy the prophet, saying, And they took the thirty pieces of silver, the price of him that was valued whom they of the children of Israel did value ; and gave them for the potter's field, as the Lord appointed me.* and yet this passage is nowhere found in *Jeremiah,* but occurs in *Zechariah,* xi. 12, 13. To call this a mistake would be impossible, since it is the word of God ; to attribute it to the carelessness of the copyists of the Gospel, in the first ages of christianity would again be impossible, for the error is too palpable, too gross, to have been left without correction for eighteen hundred years! Thus we cannot seek for the cause of this transposition of the Prophet but in Inspiration itself. Those who have read the *Doctrine concerning the Sacred Scriptures* well know that names in the interior sense of the Word signify the *spirit* and quality of the individuals who bear them. Jeremiah describes principally the dissolution and fall of the Jewish church, and the manner in which it rejected and falsified the

Divine Word; this is the characteristic trait of this Prophet.[*]
Thus, then, when in the supreme region of inspiration, the
Divine Truth concenters in a single idea all the qualities and
all the spirit of a like description; in its descending progression,
into the sense of the letter, that idea must necessarily express
itself by a name which corresponds to it, and it is expressed
by that of Jeremiah, because this name properly expresses the
spirit of this Prophet; but as the text quoted above comes
truly into the category of the *Lamentations of Jeremiah*, thus it
is Jeremiah who is named, and not Zechariah, the prophet, who
recorded these words. To suppose that the name of Jeremiah
was pronounced by the Holy Spirit itself would be a contradiction of that which has just been proved, that is to say, that
it is not the words themselves of the literal sense which are uttered by the mouth of the Lord, but the ideas or Divine
thoughts which produced them—thoughts which, according to
the testimony of the prophet, taken under the aspect under which
they flow from their supreme source, *are above our thoughts
as far as the heaven is above the earth.* All these examples
clearly demonstrate the truth of the laws of inspiration which
have just been deduced, and dissipate all doubt concerning the
Inspiration of the Word of God. The key of which we have
spoken is based upon these same laws, and initiates into all
the mysteries of the Word. This Doctrine is then solid
and true, its foundation is of *precious stones* (Apoc. xxi. 19), and
the angel placed at the *gate of pearls* from the transparent
stones of Jerusalem invites us to enter into the city to com-
template the Divine Glory!

And it is by this light of the luminous Glory that he who
has his eyes open will see that all the Holy Word, in its
supreme sense, treats but of the Lord alone, of the church
which He was to establish, of his combats against the hells, of
his Glorification, of the Redemption effected by Him, of the
Heavens existing from him alone, and of all that is contrary to
these sublime works; and all this because the Lord is the
Word. He will comprehend that as God, from eternity, was
man in firsts (premieres) or in the prototype, so also, by means
of the incarnation, he made himself *man in lasts* (derniere),
and in his substantial conjunction with the most ultimate
limits of creation; as He Himself has said: *I am the Alpha
and the Omega, the First and the Last* (Apoc i. 8, 11); he will
comprehend that among the reasons for which the Lord came
upon the earth and assumed the human form, one of the principal, relates to the Word of the New Testament; it was
that this Word might be communicated by means of inspira-

---

[*] This trait is vividly represented in the Hebrew signification of his name, the
casting away of, or by the Lord.

claims of inspiration to govern our views of religious doctrine, it cannot be necessary to construct a formal argument to prove, that if the conclusions already announced do in fact accord with the genuine teachings of scripture, they are of transcendent moment to every Christian man. The only question which you and I can debate is, whether the *doctrine of the Lord*, as taught by Swedenborg, is really the doctrine of the Lord as taught by Himself and his Apostles. This question I, on my part, have largely discussed in the foregoing series of Letters. The ground already traversed it will be needless again to go over. I would simply reaffirm my previous positions, and close this branch of the argument by adverting to some results which seem to grow naturally out of it.

You will of course have seen that, throughout the discussion, I have claimed to present the true, and the *only* true, view of the scriptural doctrine of our Lord's nature as conjointly divine and human, and becoming known to us as Jehovah-Jesus, God-man in one person, in which person subsists the Trinity of Father, Son, and Holy Spirit. For the correctness of this view, I have adduced a long array of evidences, which may or may not have carried weight to your mind. The light however in which you regard them does not affect their intrinsic character. They are as valid after rejection as before. In my own estimate, the ground assumed is impregnable, but you are of course at liberty to demonstrate the contrary if you feel competent to do it, and deem it expedient to be done. Assuming, meantime, the validity of my conclusions, I proceed to exhibit, from the sources from which I have hitherto drawn, certain practical issues that will be seen to be important just in proportion to the soundness of the data on which they rest. These issues bear equally upon the prevalent Trinitarian and the prevalent Unitarian tenet on this head. Viewed in the light of Swedenborg's exposé of the doctrine, they both involve an essential denial of the cardinal truth of the Incarnation of Jehovah, the true basis of the divine work of Redemption. They therefore necessarily lay themselves open to the consequences which it is my present purpose to unfold—consequences, as you will see, far, very far, from being of slight concern to those who are chargeable with them, while at the same time they leave the system inaccessible to the stigma of uncharitableness, intolerance, or bigotry, to which at first blush it might seem to render itself liable.

Nothing, you are well aware, is more frequent in our Lord's discourses, than the solemn affirmation of the absolute necessity of a true knowledge of, and a true faith in, Him, in order to eternal life. The grounds of this necessity is the point to which you will allow me to call your attention, and if I draw freely upon Swedenborg in support of my remarks, it will be simply because I regard him as having drawn largely and directly upon the fountain of eternal truth. However it might appear to a superficial view that the demand of a cordial belief in the divine testimony was an arbitrary demand, and to be obeyed simply from a religious respect and reverence for the Divine will, yet, upon deeper reflection, it will be seen to result from the very nature and necessity of things. It is evident that all saving truth, communicated by God to man, must not only be intellectually apprehended, but cordially acknowledged. It must be received not merely with *cognition*, but also with *agnition*, as otherwise it barely floats through the understanding, and lodges itself in the memory, the outer court of the mind, where it is as far from being practically received and incorporated into the mind, as is a sparrow from becoming a worshiper, merely because she builds her nest near the altar of the Lord's house. But even acknowledgment, unless prompted by the affection of the heart, comes short of being the proper entertainment of divine truth, as it comes short of genuine faith. "It is one thing," says Swedenborg, "to know truths, another to acknowledge them, and yet another to have faith in them. Merely to know what relates to faith, is an act of the memory, without the consent of the rational principle, to acknowledge what is of faith is the assent of the rational principle, influenced by certain causes, and with a view to certain ends; but to have faith is an act of the conscience, or of the Lord operating by means of conscience."— (*A. C.* 896.)

We may safely affirm then that in order to the adequate reception of all Divine truth, and especially of that which is of the highest import, there must be in the recipient a certain subjective state of adaptation, congruity, or accordance with the truth which is to be believed. As I endeavored to show in my last letter, truth divine comes into the mind by influx from its Author, somewhat as light comes to the eye from the sun, and unless it finds the fitting vessels in the spiritual organization of the soul, an adapted or orderly reception is impossible.

We can scarcely gain an adequate conception on this head without mentally divesting man of his body and resolving him into his last analysis, which is that of understanding and will, or intellect and affection. Suppose him in this condition of elementary being to be brought into contact with the Deity as the source of his happiness, is it not obvious that there must of necessity be a reciprocal congruity or inter-adaptation between the great truth of the Divine nature and character, and the intellectual and moral state of the recipient spirit? This mutual relation may be illustrated by that which subsists between the atmosphere and the human lungs in the matter of respiration. Unless the lungs were so formed as to be receptive of the aerial influx, the respiratory function could never be performed. In like manner, unless the intrinsic *status* of the human mind be in accordant relation with those attributes and aspects of the Divine nature in which it is presented, it is plainly impossible that a saving *conjunction* between the soul and God can ever take place.

The use which I have now made of the word *conjunction* defines, in fact, what I conceive, and what you will perhaps grant, to be the true and fundamental idea of salvation. For a created, intelligent being like man, there is no such thing as salvation, but in interior vital union with the Lord as the self-subsisting and infinite fountain of life and bliss. But as the very ground-elements of the Divine nature are Goodness and Truth, or Love and Wisdom, so it is requisite that there should be a deep laid conformity to that nature in the spiritual state of the creature, and such a spiritual state is in fact *a spiritual organism*. It is only in such a state that Divine truth can be cordially *acknowledged*, for as truth is the *actuality* or *verity of things*, the state of the soul must be in unison with the state of the things with which it is to be united, in order that the heartfelt acknowledgement of the truth may ensue. Let the soul be once in that moral posture which quadrates with the reality of things, and the profoundest and sincerest acknowledgement will be the result, an acknowledgement not so much of the lips as of the heart.

Abiding then in the soundness of the principle thus far maintained, the great question of questions which is at the foundation of the whole debate is, what is the precise idea of the Lord which corresponds with the truth?—for it is by that idea, with its appropriate affection, that the soul is conjoined to the Lord and in that conjunction, and in that only, is salvation. To this question there is, I conceive, but one answer. The only correct idea of the Lord as revealed in the Word is that which answers to the following formula: "That Jehovah God, the Creator and Preserver of heaven and earth, is Love Itself and Wisdom Itself, or Good Itself and Truth Itself. That He is one, both in essence and in person, in whom, nevertheless, is the Divine Trinity of Father, Son, and Holy Spirit, which are the Essential Divinity, the Divine Humanity, and the Divine Proceeding, answering to the soul, the body, and the operative energy in man: and that the Lord and Saviour Jesus Christ is that God."

This then is the paramount asserted and constitutive truth of

tion; that it might be written in the sense of the letter; that it might be spread abroad every where; that it might be preserved and transmitted to posterity, to prove to all men, as well in this life as in the other, that God Himself became man, that He accomplished the work of salvation, and that by means of the Word he effects the conjunction of Humanity with Himself. And, in conclusion, the men whose eyes are opened must decide with a full conviction that without the coming of the Lord upon the earth, the Word of the New Testament could never have been written, because the one necessarily establishes the other, to the degree that the one cannot exist without the other; and, penetrated with a profound adoration, man, convinced and renewed by this Divine Light, will prostrate himself before the *Inspired Word*, before that Word proclaiming to the whole universe the Incarnate Word.

J. M.

ARTICLE II.

LETTERS TO A TRINITARIAN.

LETTER X.

PRACTICAL RESULTS.

"Upon a just idea of God, the universal heaven, and the church universal on earth, are founded, and in general the whole of religion; for by that idea there is conjunction, and by conjunction, light, wisdom, and eternal happiness."—(*Sweden-borg—Preface to A. R.*)

MY DEAR SIR:

The earnest advocate who attempts to plead the cause of Scriptural truth has not unfrequently a double task to perform; first, to vindicate the apprehended or alleged truth from error; secondly, to show that it is a truth eminently worthy of vindication,—the latter not seldom the most difficult task of the two. It is, however, a requisition that will hardly hold in the present case. You cannot fail to agree with me in assigning the highest possible estimate to the importance of the doctrine of our Lord's essential Divinity, however you may refuse to concede the soundness and the *scripturalness* of the view which I have thus far aimed to present. With one who maintains so strenuously as you do the supremacy of the claims of inspiration to govern our views of religious doctrine, it cannot be necessary to construct a formal argument to prove, that if the conclusions already announced do in fact accord with the genuine teachings of scripture, they are of transcendent moment to every Christian man. The only question which you and I can debate is, whether the *doctrine of the Lord*, as taught by Swedenborg, is really the doctrine of the Lord as taught by Himself and his Apostles. This question I, on my part, have largely discussed in the foregoing series of Letters. The ground already traversed it will be needless again to go over. I would simply reaffirm my previous positions, and close this branch of the argument by adverting to some results which seem to grow naturally out of it.

You will of course have seen that, throughout the discussion, I have claimed to present the true, and the *only* true, view of the scriptural doctrine of our Lord's nature as conjointly divine and human, and becoming known to us as Jehovah-Jesus, God-man in one person, in which person subsists the Trinity of Father, Son, and Holy Spirit. For the correctness of this view, I have adduced a long array of evidences, which may or may not have carried weight to your mind. The light however in which you regard them does not affect their intrinsic character. They are as valid after rejection as before. In my own estimate, the ground assumed is impregnable, but you are of course at liberty to demonstrate the contrary if you feel competent to do it, and deem it expedient to be done. Assuming, meantime, the validity of my conclusions, I proceed to exhibit, from the sources from which I have hitherto drawn, certain practical issues that will be seen to be important just in proportion to the soundness of the data on which they rest. These issues bear equally upon the prevalent Trinitarian and the prevalent Unitarian tenet on this head. Viewed in the light of Swedenborg's exposé of the doctrine, they both involve an essential denial of the cardinal truth of the Incarnation of Jehovah, the true basis of the divine work of Redemption. They therefore necessarily lay themselves open to the consequences which it is my present purpose to unfold—consequences, as you will see, far, very far, from being of slight concern to those who are chargeable with them, while at the same time they leave the system inaccessible to the stigma of uncharitableness, intolerance, or bigotry, to which at first blush it might seem to render itself liable.

Nothing, you are well aware, is more frequent in our Lord's discourses, than the solemn affirmation of the absolute necessity of a true knowledge of, and a true faith in, Him, in order to eternal life. The grounds of this necessity is the point to which you will allow me to call your attention, and if I draw freely upon Swedenborg in support of my remarks, it will be simply because I regard him as having drawn largely and directly upon the fountain of eternal truth. However it might appear to a superficial view that the demand of a cordial belief in the divine testimony was an arbitrary demand, and to be obeyed simply from a religious respect and reverence for the Divine will, yet, upon deeper reflection, it will be seen to result from the very nature and necessity of things. It is evident that all saving truth, communicated by God to man, must not only be intellectually apprehended, but cordially acknowledged. It must be received not merely with *cognition*, but also with *agnition*, as otherwise it barely floats through the understanding, and lodges itself in the memory, the outer court of the mind, where it is as far from being practically received and incorporated into the mind, as is a sparrow from becoming a worshiper, merely because she builds her nest near the altar of the Lord's house. But even acknowledgment, unless prompted by the affection of the heart, comes short of being the proper entertainment of divine truth, as it comes short of genuine faith. "It is one thing," says Swedenborg, "to know truths, another to acknowledge them, and yet another to have faith in them. Merely to know what relates to faith, is an act of the memory, without the consent of the rational principle, to acknowledge what is of faith is the assent of the rational principle, influenced by certain causes, and with a view to certain ends; but to have faith is an act of the conscience, or of the Lord operating by means of conscience."— (*A. C.* 896.)

We may safely affirm then that in order to the adequate reception of all Divine truth, and especially of that which is of the highest import, there must be in the recipient a certain subjective state of adaptation, congruity, or accordance with the truth which is to be believed. As I endeavored to show in my last letter, truth divine comes into the mind by influx from its Author, somewhat as light comes to the eye from the sun, and unless it finds the fitting vessels in the spiritual organization of the soul, an adapted or orderly reception is impossible.

We can scarcely gain an adequate conception on this head without mentally divesting man of his body and resolving him into his last analysis, which is that of understanding and will, or intellect and affection. Suppose him in this condition of elementary being to be brought into contact with the Deity as the source of his happiness, is it not obvious that there must of necessity be a reciprocal congruity or inter-adaptation between the great truth of the Divine nature and character, and the intellectual and moral state of the recipient spirit? This mutual relation may be illustrated by that which subsists between the atmosphere and the human lungs in the matter of respiration. Unless the lungs were so formed as to be receptive of the aerial influx, the respiratory function could never be performed. In like manner, unless the intrinsic *status* of the human mind be in accordant relation with those attributes and aspects of the Divine nature in which it is presented, it is plainly impossible that a saving *conjunction* between the soul and God can ever take place.

The use which I have now made of the word *conjunction* defines, in fact, what I conceive, and what you will perhaps grant, to be the true and fundamental idea of salvation. For a created, intelligent being like man, there is no such thing as salvation, but in interior vital union with the Lord as the self-subsisting and infinite fountain of life and bliss. But as the very ground-elements of the Divine nature are Goodness and Truth, or Love and Wisdom, so it is requisite that there should be a deep laid conformity to that nature in the spiritual state of the creature, and such a spiritual state is in fact *a spiritual organism*. It is only in such a state that Divine truth can be cordially *acknowledged*, for as truth is the *actuality* or *verity of things*, the state of the soul must be in unison with the state of the things with which it is to be united, in order that the heartfelt acknowledgement of the truth may ensue. Let the soul be once in that moral posture which quadrates with the reality of things, and the profoundest and sincerest acknowledgement will be the result, an acknowledgement not so much of the lips as of the heart.

Abiding then in the soundness of the principle thus far maintained, the great question of questions which is at the foundation of the whole debate is, what is the precise idea of the Lord which corresponds with the truth?—for it is by that idea, with its appropriate affection, that the soul is conjoined to the Lord and in that conjunction, and in that only, is salvation. To this question there is, I conceive, but one answer. The only correct idea of the Lord as revealed in the Word is that which answers to the following formula: "That Jehovah God, the Creator and Preserver of heaven and earth, is Love Itself and Wisdom Itself, or Good Itself and Truth Itself. That He is one, both in essence and in person, in whom, nevertheless, is the Divine Trinity of Father, Son, and Holy Spirit, which are the Essential Divinity, the Divine Humanity, and the Divine Proceeding, answering to the soul, the body, and the operative energy in man: and that the Lord and Saviour Jesus Christ is that God."

This then is the paramount asserted and constitutive truth of the New Jerusalem—the essential Divinity and the assumed but now glorified Humanity, co-existing in the one person of the Lord the Saviour, in whom also is the divine trinity of Father, Son and Holy Spirit, equivalent to the three distinct principles of Love, Wisdom, and Operation in the Divine nature, and shadowed out in soul, body, and act, as pertaining to man and angel. The true conception, therefore, will be that of One and not of Three, except as three combined in one, so that the idea of unity shall still be predominant. This august verity, as we are informed by Swedenborg, is expressly revealed "for the comfort and instruction of those who shall be admitted into the New Jerusalem." It is the very badge of discipleship and fellowship in that divine dispensation. No one who receives this grand truth in heart and life is really *without* the New Church; no one who rejects it *ex animo* is *within* it. The declarations on this head are very explicit, as will appear from the following extracts, which I give without reserve, because I am not at liberty to disguise from myself or others a doctrine upon which such momentous consequences depend.

" They who live within the pale of the Church, and do not acknowledge the Lord Jesus Christ and his Divinity, can have no union with God ; and of consequence can have no place with the angels in heaven; for no one can be united with God but by the Lord and in the Lord."*— (*H. D.* 283.)

" All who belong to the church and are under the influence of light from heaven, see and discern the Divine nature in the Lord Jesus Christ; but such as are not under the influence of light from heaven see and discern in Him only the human nature ; when nevertheless the Divinity and the Humanity are so united together in Him as to make one

---

* " By the Lord the Redeemer we mean Jehovah in the Human ; for that Jehovah himself descended and assumed the human, for the purpose of accomplishing redemption, will be demonstrated in what follows. The reason why it is said the *Lord*, and not *Jehovah*, is because *Jehovah*, in the Old Testament, is called the *Lord* in the New, as is evident from these passages : it is said in Moses, ' Hear, O Israel, *Jehovah* your God is one *Jehovah;* and thou shalt love *Jehovah* thy God with all thy heart and with all thy soul' (Deut. vi. 4, 5); but in Mark ; ' The *Lord* your God is one *Lord*, and thou shalt love the *Lord* thy God with all thy heart and with all thy soul' (xii. 29, 30). Also in Isaiah ; ' Prepare a way for *Jehovah* ; make smooth in the desert a path for our God' (xl. 3); but in Luke; ' Thou shalt go before the face of the *Lord*, to prepare a way for him' (i. 76); besides in other passages. And also the *Lord* commanded his disciples to call Him *Lord*, and therefore He was so called by the apostles, in their Epistles, and afterwards by the apostolic church, as appears from their creed, which is called the ' Apostle's Creed.' The reason was, because the Jews durst not use the name *Jehovah*, on account of its sanctity; and also, by *Jehovah* is meant the Divine Esse, which was from eternity, and the Human, which he assumed in time, was not that Esse. For this reason, here, and in what follows, by the *Lord*, we mean *Jehovah in his Human*,"— (*T. C. R.* 81.)

person: for so he Himself declares; 'Father, all mine are thine and thine are mine.'"—(*Ib.* 285.)

"They who entertain an idea of three persons in their conceptions of the Godhead, cannot possibly have an idea of one God; for though they say with their lips there is but one God, yet in their minds they conceive three. But they who in their conceptions of the Godhead entertain an idea of a Trinity in one person may have an idea of one God, and both with their lips and with their hearts confess that there is but one."—(*Ib.* 289.)

"The first and grand fundamental of the Church is to know and acknowledge its God; for without such acknowledgment there can be no conjunction with Him."—(*Ib.* 296.)

"All who come into heaven have their place allotted them there, and thence everlasting joy, according to their idea of God, because this idea reigns universally in every particular of worship; the idea of an invisible God is not determined to any God, nor does it terminate in any, therefore it ceases and perishes; the idea of God as a spirit, when a spirit is thought of as ether or air, is an empty idea; but the idea of God as a man, is a just idea, for God is divine love and divine wisdom, with every quality belonging thereto, and the subject of these is man, and not ether or wind. The idea of God in heaven is the idea of the Lord, he being the God of heaven and earth, as he himself taught; of how great importance it is to have a just idea of God may appear from this consideration, that the idea of God constitutes the inmost thought of all those who have any religion, for all things of religion and divine worship have respect unto God: and inasmuch as God is universally and particularly in all things of religion and worship, therefore unless it be a just idea of God, no communication can be given with the heavens. Hence it is that in the spiritual world every nation has its place according to its idea of God as a man, for in this and in no other is the idea of the Lord."

As the view of the subject I am now endeavoring to present is obviously one of the most urgent and imperative claims upon the church, if true, you will pardon the insertion of a somewhat extended paragraph from Swedenborg. He is speaking of interior rejection of the Lord.

"The Lord is said to be rejected, when he is not approached and worshiped, and also when he is approached and worshiped only as to his human principle, and not at the same time as to his divine; wherefore at this day he is rejected by those within the church who do not approach and worship him, but pray to the Father to have compassion on them for the sake of the Son, when notwithstanding no man, or angel, can even approach the Father, and immediately worship him, for the divinity is invisible, with which no one can be conjoined in faith and love; for that which is invisible does not fall into the idea of thought, nor, consequently, into the affection of the will; and what does not fall into the idea of thought, does not fall into the faith, for what pertains to the faith must be an object of thought. So likewise what does not enter into the affection of the will, does not enter into the love, for the things which pertain to the love, must affect the will of man, as all the love which man has resides in the will. But the Divine Human Principle of the Lord falls into the idea of the thought, and thus into faith, and thence into the affection of the will, or into the love; hence it is evident, that there is no conjunction with the Father unless from the Lord, and in the Lord. This the Lord himself teaches very clearly in the Evangelists: as in John: 'No one hath seen God at any time; the only begotten Son, who is in the bosom of the Father, he hath declared him' (i. 18). Again: 'Ye have neither heard his voice at any time, nor seen his shape' (v. 37). And in Matthew, 'Neither knoweth any man the Father save the Son, and he whomsoever the Son will reveal him' (xi. 27). And in John: 'I am the Way, and the Truth, and the Life, no man cometh unto the Father but by me' (xiv. 6). Again: 'If ye had known me, ye should have known my Father also; he that hath seen me hath seen the Father; believest thou not that I am in the Father, and the Father in me? believe me, that I am in the Father, and the Father in me' (xiv. 7-11). 'I and my Father are one,' (x. 30, 38). Again: 'I am the vine, ye are the branches; without me ye can do nothing' (xv. 5). Hence it is plain, that the Lord is rejected by those within the church, who immediately approach the Father, and pray to him to have compassion for the sake of the Son; for these cannot do otherwise than think of the humanity of the Lord as of the humanity of another man, not at the same time of his Divinity in the humanity, and still less of his Divinity conjoined with his humanity, as the soul is conjoined with the body, according to the doctrine universally received in the Christian world. Who, in the Christian world, that acknowledges the Divinity of the Lord, is willing that this acknowledgment should be such as to place his divine principle out of his human; when nevertheless to think of the human principle alone, and not at the same time of the divine in the human, is to view them separate, which is not to view the Lord, nor both as one person, when yet the doctrine received in the Christian world is, that the Divinity and Humanity of the Lord make not two persons but one person? They who constitute the church at this day do, indeed, think concerning the divine principle of the Lord in his human, when they speak from the doctrine of the church, but altogether otherwise when they think and speak with themselves without that doctrine: but let it be known, that man is in one state when he thinks and speaks from doctrine, and in another when he thinks and speaks without it. Whilst man thinks and speaks from doctrine, his thought and speech are from the memory of his natural man; but when he thinks and speaks out of doctrine, his thought and speech are then from his spirit; for to think and speak from the spirit, is to think and speak from the interiors of his mind, wherefore what he thence speaks is his real faith. From these considerations it also appears how it is to be understood, that the Lord is rejected at this day by those who are within the church, namely, that from doctrine indeed it is allowed that the Divinity of the Lord is to be acknowledged and believed in the same degree as the Divinity of the Father, for the doctrine of the church teaches, "that as is the Father, so also is the Son, uncreate, infinite, eternal, omnipotent, God, Lord, neither of them greater or less, before or after the other." Notwithstanding this, however, they do not worship the Lord as divine, but worship the Divinity of the Father, as is the case when they pray to the Father that he may have compassion on them for the sake of his Son, and when they use these words, they do not at all think of the divine principle of the Lord, but of his human separate from the divine, thus of his humanity, as similar to that of another man. On such occasions, they think not of one God, but of two, or three. To think thus concerning the Lord, is to reject him; for not to think of his divine principle in conjunction with his human, is by separation to exclude the divine, which nevertheless are not two persons but one person, and make a one as soul and body."—(*A. E.* 114.)

From all this, the inference is very clear that a conception of the Lord, according to the absolute truth of his being and attributes, is all important in order to salvation; and the ground of this is, that in no other way can that conjunction take place which is the very essence of eternal life. I am well aware, however, that in speaking of conjunction with the Lord as salvation, I am using a term that is for the most part extremely unwelcome and unpalatable to those whose theological system is run in the moulds of Wittemberg, Geneva, and Westminster. Having formed to themselves the idea of a salvation founded on vicarious atonement and made available by means of forensic imputation, they inevitably cherish a latent aversion to a term which involves, by implication, a virtual denial of the whole scheme, and resolves the very element of religious principle into harmonious and vital union with the Lord. They cannot well refrain from charging it as *mystical*, to say nothing of the disparagement thrown upon it as really subversive of the work of Christ viewed as a satisfaction for sin, and as confounding justification with sanctification. But all this passes with the man of the New Church unheeded as objection, though awakening sad sentiments as evidence of moral state. With such a ground work for our position as we find laid in the following extract we should be strangely wanting to ourselves to abate an iota of the strength of our confidence in its impregnability.

"Inasmuch as the church at this day does not know that conjunction with the Lord constitutes heaven, and that conjunction is effected by the acknowledgment that he is the God of heaven and earth, and at the same time by a life according to his commandments, therefore it may be expedient to say something on this subject. A person altogether ignorant of these matters may possibly say, What signifies conjunction? how can acknowledgment and life occasion conjunction? what need is there of these things? may not every one be saved from mercy alone? what need is there then for any other medium of salvation but faith alone? is not God merciful and omnipotent? But let him know, that in the spiritual world all presence is effected by knowledge and acknowledgment, and that all conjunction is effected by affection which is of love; for spaces there are nothing else but appearances according to similarity of minds, that is, affections and consequent thoughts; wherefore, when any one knows another, either by fame or report, or by intercourse with him, or by conversation, or by relationship, when he thinks of him from an idea of that knowledge, the other becomes present, although to all appearance he were a thousand miles distant; and if any one also loves another whom he knows, he dwells with him in one society, and, if he loves him intimately, in one house. This is the state of all throughout the whole spiritual world, and this state of all derives its origin from the circumstance of the Lord being present with every one according to faith, and conjoined according to love. Faith and the consequent presence of the Lord is given by the knowledges of truths derived from the Word, especially by those concerning the Lord himself there, but love and consequent conjunction is given by a life according to his commandments, for the Lord saith, ' He that hath my *commandments and keepeth them,* he it is that loveth me, and I will love him, and will manifest myself to him.' John. xiv. 21."— (*A. R.* 913.)

If then the idea of God in heaven be the idea of the Lord Jesus Christ in his Divine Humanity, and saving conjunction with him can ensue only from this view of his nature, surely the idea of a tri-personal Deity is not only false in itself, but, if confirmed, absolutely destructive of genuine truth and fatal to the possibility of that conjunction in which salvation is enwrapped.[*] Equally disastrous to the interests of the soul is the Unitarian tenet when fully inwrought into the deepest convictions of the holder, because it is equally at war with that essential truth with which the spirit of man must be in what we may term *organical accordance* in order to be saved. It is one of the prominent positions of Swedenborg that "every man *is* his own will and his own understanding; because the will is the receptacle of love and thus of all the goods which are of that love, and the understanding is the receptacle of wisdom, and thus of all the things of truth which are of that wisdom, it follows, that every man is his own love and his own wisdom; or, what is the same, his own good and his truth. Man is not man from any thing else, and not any thing else with him is man. He who thinks, and speaks nothing but truth, becomes that truth; and he who wills and does nothing but good, becomes that good." If this be so—and I see not how it can be denied—the same principle must hold good as to what one holds and believes to be truth, though in reality it be falsity, consequently as a man's apprehension of truth becomes the very form of his being, as its good does its essence, how can this being be to him a source of happiness unless the belief within him corresponds to the truth without him?

That the positions above assumed should be at one time of more urgent and imperative character than at another might seem at first blush incredible, but the following passage implies that causes are operating at the present day to give ad-

---

[*] " They who are in falsities, and yet in the good of life, according to their religion, cannot be saved until their falsities are removed, so that truths may be implanted in their place."—(*A. E.* 478.)

ditional solemnity and sanction to the conclusions already announced.

> "To confirm this further, I will relate what I know, because I have seen, and therefore I can testify what follows; that the Lord, at this day, is forming a new angelic heaven, and that it is formed of those who believe in the Lord God the Saviour, and go immediately to Him; and that the rest are rejected. Wherefore, if any hereafter comes from Christendom into the spiritual world, into which every man does come after death, and does not believe in the Lord, and go to Him alone, and then is not able to receive this, because he has lived wickedly, or has confirmed himself in falses, he is repelled at his first approach towards heaven. Every man also in Christian countries, who does not believe in the Lord, is not hereafter heard with acceptance; his prayers, in heaven, are like ill-scented odors, and like eructations from ulcerated lungs; and if he thinks that his prayer is like the perfume of incense, still it does not ascend to the angelic heaven, otherwise than as the smoke of a fire, which is driven back by a violent tempest, into his eyes, or as the perfume from a censer under a monk's cloak : thus, after this time it is with all piety which is determined to a divided trinity, and not to one conjoined."—(*T. C. R.* 108.)

But here I am prepared to encounter the objection which will scarcely fail to be urged, if not by yourself, at least by others ;—to wit, that of uncharitableness, intolerance, and bigotry in the system. As the New Church claims to be preeminently, a dispensation of love—as its doctrines are frequently termed *heavenly* doctrines—as its genius is often avowed to be angelic, which at the least implies mild, gentle, benignant—how can such a severe and exclusive spirit consist with such professions? Are there not multitudes of good men who sincerely embrace, some the Trinitarian and some the Unitarian dogma? And if they are good will they not be saved? I have hinted a doubt whether you yourself would urge this objection, for my impression is, that with you the great question is the intrinsic truth of the doctrine advanced, and that when once satisfied on that head you are prepared for the most stern and stringent issues that may legitimately ensue. Your profound reverence for the divine oracles in all the length and breadth of their genuine purport would rather lead you to exclaim—"Purity before peace—let God be true, but every man a liar—let the truth stand though the heavens should fall." But this is not the mood of many. There is a certain sentiment of *soi-disant* liberality and charity which frowns upon and denounces any thing in the shape of an asserted fundamental doctrine of faith. In the system of the New Church we have such a doctrine, and that is the *doctrine of the Lord* upon which I have thus far descanted. We are taught to regard this doctrine as vital to salvation, and yet I shall hope to show that notwithstanding the rigor of demand on this score, nothing of

undue severity or revolting exclusiveness is, on that account,
really chargeable upon the system. It will be the height of
injustice to impute an intolerant or anathematizing spirit to
Swedenborg if he gives an adequate reason for his sentence,
founded in the very nature of things. Let the question first
be settled whether the principles above stated, respecting acknowledgement and conjunction, be *true*, and then let it be determined whether he is justly open to the reproach of a bigotted intolerance. The fact is, the decision of this point is suspended upon that of another, viz., whether Swedenborg speaks
on this subject in his private personal capacity, or as a divinely commissioned messenger of heaven to men. If the latter,
then his enunciations are to be referred to a higher source
than his own spirit, and are merged in the dictates of eternal
truth. Since, however, we have no hope that this question will
be entertained by the mass of the Christian world, we are
happy to be able to rest his vindication on another basis, and
one of a character so truly philosophical that it can hardly
fail, when rightly understood, to win back the confidence and
esteem which may have been chillingly repulsed by the literal
assertions above adduced.

A fundamental principle of the New Church theology, as expounded by Swedenborg, is that the closest and most indissoluble relation exists between Goodness and Truth, as there does
also between Evil and Falsity. Truth in the understanding is
the normal and legitimate product of goodness in the will
(*voluntas*) which, with Swedenborg, is but another name for
love or affection, as a man wills what he loves. The *voluntary* principle is accordingly thus distinguished from the *intellectual*. In saying that truth is the legitimate outbirth of good,
I do not of course mean to imply that no degree of the false is
found in conjunction with good, and no degree of truth in conjunction with evil. I only mean that when such conjunctions
do exist they are abnormal and illicit. The true relation
is that which I have stated above, and we learn, that, in
virtue of this relation, truth and falsity virtually change their
nature accordingly as they are severally in alliance with good
or with evil. Genuine truth is not truth to him who is in evil,
and absolute is only apparent falsity to him who is in the good
of life. The teachings of Swedenborg on this subject are so
immeasurably in advance of any thing before given to the
world and are so instinct with a wisdom that savors of the superhuman, that I shall presume upon your indulgence in offering somewhat copious extracts. You will see from these that
it is *confirmation* which determines the effect of a man's intellectual errors upon his destiny.

" From the contrariety existing between good and evil, the true and
the false, it is plain that truth cannot be joined with evil, nor good with
the false that originates in evil ; for if truth be joined with evil, it is no
longer truth, but becomes false, inasmuch as it is falsified : and if good
be joined with the false of evil, it is no longer good, but becomes evil,
inasmuch as it is adulterated.   Nevertheless the false, which has not
its ground in evil, is capable of being joined with goodness."—
(*T. C. R.* 398.)

" Because the Word was written by mere correspondences, many
things there are appearances of truth, and not naked truths ; and many
things are written according to the capacity of the merely natural man,
and yet so that the simple may understand them in simplicity, the intelligent in intelligence, and the wise in wisdom.   Now, because the
Word is such, appearances of truth, which are truths clothed, may be
taken for naked truths, which, when they are confirmed, become fallacies, which in themselves are falses.   From this, that appearances
of truth may be taken for naked truths, and confirmed, have sprung all
the heresies which have been and still are in the Christian world.
Heresies themselves do not condemn men ; but confirmations of the
falsities, which are in a heresy, from the Word and by reasonings from
the natural man and an evil life, do condemn.   For every one is born
into the religion of his country or of his parents, is initiated into it from
infancy, and afterwards retains it ; nor can he extricate himself from its
falses, both on account of business in the world, and on account of the
weakness of the understanding in perceiving truths of that sort ; but to
live wickedly and confirm falses, even to the destruction of genuine
truth, this does condemn.   For he who continues in his religion, and
believes in God, and in Christendom, believes in the Lord, and esteems
the Word holy, and from religion lives according to the commandments
of the decalogue, he does not swear to falses ; wherefore, when he
hears truths, and in his own way perceives them, he can embrace them,
and thus be led out of falses ; but not he who had confirmed the falses
of his religion, for the false, when confirmed, remains, and cannot be extirpated ; for a false, after confirmation, is as if one had sworn to it, particularly if it coheres with the love of himself, or with the pride of his
own intelligence.
I have spoken with some in the spiritual world, who lived many
ages ago, and confirmed themselves in the falses of their own religion,
and I have found that they still remained firmly in the same ; and I
have also spoken with some there, who were in the same religion,
and thought like those, but had not confirmed its falses in themselves,
and I have found, that, when instructed by the angels, they have rejected falses and received truths ; and that these were saved, but not those.
Every man is instructed by the angels after death, and those are received who see truths, and from truth, falses ; but those only see truths
who have not confirmed themselves in falses ; but those who have confirmed themselves are not willing to see truths : and if they do see, they
turn themselves back, and then either laugh at them or falsify them ;
the genuine cause is, that confirmation enters the will, and the will is
the man himself, and it disposes the understanding according to its
pleasure ; but bare knowledge only enters the understanding, and this
has not any authority over the will, and so is not in man, otherwise
than as one who stands in the entry, or at the door, and not as yet in
the house."—(*T. C. R.* 254, 255.)

" From evil exist all falses; but the falses which are not from evil, in the external form indeed are falses, but not in the internal; for there are falses given with those who are in the good of life, but interiorly in those falses there is good, which causes the evil of the false to be removed; hence that false before the angels does not appear as the false, but as a species of truth; for the angels look at the interior things of faith and not at its exterior: hence it is that every one, of whatsoever religion he be, may be saved, even the Gentiles who have no truths from the Word, if so be they have respected the good of life as an end."
—(*A. C.* 10, 648.)

" All are saved who are in the good of life according to the dogmas of their religion which they believed to be truths, although they were not truths, for what is false is not imputed to any who lives well according to the dogmas of his religion, for the good of life according to religion contains within itself the affection of knowing truths, which such persons also learn and receive when they come into another life, for every affection remains with man after death, and especially the affection of knowing truths, because this is a spiritual affection, and every man when he becomes a spirit is his own affection; of consequence the truths which they desire they imbibe, and so receive them deeply in their hearts."—(*A. E.* 455.)

As this subject is treated at great length in various parts of Swedenborg's works I will content myself with transcribing the following references, to the *Arcana*, which contain an argument in themselves.

" That there are falses of religion which agree with good, and falses which disagree, n. 9259; that falses of religion, if they do not disagree with good, do not produce evil except with those who are in evil, n. 8318; that falses of religion are not imputed to those who are in good, but to those who are in evil, n. 8051, 8149; that truths not genuine, and also falses, may be consociated with genuine truths with those who are in good, but not with those who are in evil, n. 3470, 3471, 4551, 4552, 7344, 8149, 9298; that falses and truths are consociated by appearances from the literal sense of the Word, n. 7344; that falses are verified and softened by good, because they are applied and made conducive to good, and to the removal of evil, n. 8148; that the falses of religion with those who are in good, and received by the Lord as truths, n. 4736, 8149; that the good whose quality is from a false principle of religion, is accepted by the Lord if there be ignorance, and if there be in it innocence and a good end, n. 7887; that the truths which are with man are appearances of truth and good, tinctured with fallacies, but the Lord nevertheless adapts them to genuine truths with the man who liveth in good, n. 2053; that falses in which there is good exist with those who are out of the church, and thence in ignorance of the truth, also with those within the church where there are falses of doctrine, n. 2589-2604, 2861, 2863, 3263, 3778, 4189, 4190, 4197, 6700, 9256."—(*A. E.* 452.)

You will hardly fail to draw from all this the inference that one may be internally in such a state of good, as it concerns the affections, as to counterbalance and neutralise the errors of the intellect. Consequently as this good has a powerful elective affinity for truth, the presumption is, that in the other life, if not in this, the good will come into conjunction with its appropriate truth, and when this result takes place, salvation cannot but ensue ; for it is in this that salvation consists. The imputation of narrowness and denunciation grows legitimately out of the current views of human destiny in the other life. It is taught in all the popular theologies, that man goes at death either to heaven or to hell, and that anything like *instruction* is superseded by the full blaze of truth, which flashes at once upon the translated spirit, revealing to it an eternal inheritance of bliss or woe, according to its moral state. From Swedenborg we learn an entirely different doctrine of the future, and by his own revelations are his decisions as to character and state to be judged. He teaches from direct illumination that there is an intermediate state into which man enters upon leaving the present world, and that in that state a process takes place by which his interior loves and thoughts shall be developed in freedom, and his lot finally determined according as goodness and truth shall predominate over evil and falsity, or the reverse. It is a state in which every spirit is instructed by angels, and if he be found to have been interiorly principled in good, the truths which he may, from various causes, have refused to receive in this life are then seen to be truths and as such cordially embraced. When this result is fully accomplished the spirit is prepared for heaven, for the conjunction of good and truth is heaven. " It is not permitted," says Swedenborg, " to any one in heaven nor in hell to have a divided mind, that is, to understand one thing and to will another ; but what he wills he must also understand, and what he understands he must also will. Wherefore, in heaven, he who wills good must understand truth, and in hell he who wills evil must understand what is false ; therefore with the good falses are then removed and truths are given agreeable and conformable to their good, and with the evil truths are removed, and falses are given agreeable and conformable to their evil."—(*H. & H.* 425.)

With these fundamental principles before us we can see how it is that two such apparently conflicting classes of declarations as are represented in the following extracts may still be perfectly consistent with each other.

" The reason why there is no appropriation of good with those who do not acknowledge the Lord is, because for man to acknowledge his God is the first principle of religion, and with Christians to acknowledge the Lord is the first principle of the Church, for without acknowledgment there is no communication given, consequently no faith,

ing of Swedenborg in the passages he has cited; and, what is still more unfortunate, he has *mis*-quoted him in almost every instance. Besides being dishonest, it is unjust, alike to Swedenborg and the readers of the Repository, for a writer to *pretend* to give us the very words of our author, when he does not, but changes them and substitutes some of his own. It is what no writer ought ever to allow himself to do, because it unavoidably deceives and misleads his readers. Swedenborg, when speaking of the Christian Church which in his day was consummated, calls it "the present church," "the present christian church," "the church at this day," "the men of this age," &c. Now in all such cases our friend W. S. C. has substituted for Swedenborg's language the phrase "Old Church." And when he defines what *he means* by "Old Church" it becomes plain that this change of Swedenborg's phraseology is a manifest perversion of his meaning. For our brother understands by "Old Church" all those "*persons*" in Christendom at this time who belong to any other church organization than the New, who are "in external communion with it, in the participation of its ordinances and sacraments, conforming to its ceremonies and observances," &c.

But is there no difference between the state of the christian world now, and when Swedenborg wrote? Are the interiors of these so-called Old Church societies or organizations the

---

in his day, that it was consummated and utterly destroyed; that it was without charity, and consequently without faith; that it had no spiritual life; was a mere dead carcass; that its doctrines were altogether false, and did not agree in a single point with the doctrines of the New Christian Church. But we commit a great mistake if we conclude from such language that there were *no individuals* in the church at that time who were in any charity or faith, or who had any spiritual life. We could cite scores of passages in proof that such is not our author's meaning; that, so far from it, he admits that there were a great many, especially among the simpleminded laity, who were in the good of life, and whose good, therefore, must have been interiorly conjoined to truth (*See A. E.* 233; *A. R.* 426) What then *are* we to understand by this language of E S.? Simply, as we conceive, that the great system of doctrinal theology upheld and taught by the learned of his day—expressed in the various Christian creeds and formularies of faith, expounded from pulpits and chairs of theology—was utterly false, and as such destitute of the spirit and life of the Gospel. He sometimes says that a church is a church from doctrine and according to it (*A. R.* 923), "and whereas doctrine from the Word constitutes the church, therefore when doctrine disagrees with the Word, it is no longer a church (*A. E.* 786). It is in this sense that he uses the word *Church* when he says " that at this day there is *no church* in the christian world, neither among the Roman Catholics, nor among the reformed;" that is, there was no true system of doctrinal theology. (*See A. R.* 263, 923). The whole fabric was rotten; the system was false and corrupt throughout. Hence it was foretold that the Temple should be entirely demolished, and not one stone (*falsity*) be left upon another. That the simple among the laity of his time were not only in good, but in some truths also, and wiser than the learned. (*See A. C.* 5059, 4760, 3677, 3747; *A. R.* 500, 426.) In the last article here referred to, Swedenborg says " that faith alone, as being competent to justification, is the faith of the clergy, and *not of the laity*, save such of them as live unconcernedly," &c.

"But we are pressed by the consequences. If the doctrines held and taught by such men as Leighton, Baxter, Scott, Edwards, Brainerd, Payson, and others of similar stamp, really involved grand and essential errors, do we not, by the very force of the allegation, pronounce sentence upon the men, and cut them off from all hope of heaven? Do we not consign them over to a fatal fellowship with "the dragon and his crew?" No other inference could well be drawn from the above presentation of the subject, and yet no inference could be more unjust and injurious to our author and to the true character of his system. Not the least striking among its wonderful features is that of the enlarged and catholic charity which it breathes towards every degree of real *good*, with whatever error of understanding it is found in conjunction. The fundamental distinction upon which it every where insists between the *love* or *life principle* and the mere intellectual conviction of *truth*, upon the former of which and not upon the latter salvation is suspended, enables him to recognize the heirs of eternal life in multitudes of those whose doctrinal belief is widely at variance with that which he inculcates. Indeed I have often been deeply and admiringly impressed by the *tender solicitude* he evinces so to discriminate between the falsities of the head and the heart as to embrace as many as possible within the range of the Lord's saving goodness. Nothing approaching to a spirit of stern and gloomy denunciation is to be found in his writings. It is only when falsities are intelligently *confirmed* and thence wrought into the texture of the *life*, that he despairs of a happy result. And it would certainly be strange if one who assures us that even the well-disposed heathen, who lives up to the light of his convictions, is saved as far as his goodness and truth will admit, should still exclude from the prospect of heaven such men as the pious worthies whose names you have recited. That their *faith* was at fault so far as it coincided with the leading popular dogmas upon which I have dwelt, is undoubtedly true, but you will see from the extracts which follow, that their errors might still consist with a salvable state, though they must necessarily detract from that completeness and symmetry of character, which results from the fair and full conjunction of Goodness and Truth"—(*p.* 165).

G. B.

EXTRACT.

"If this divine truth is not received, that the Lord's Human is Divine, it necessarily hence follows that there is a trine which is to be adored, but not a one, and also that half of the Lord is to be adored, namely his Divine but not his Human; for who adores what is not divine? And is the church anything where a trine is adored, one separately from the other, or what is the same, where three are equally worshiped? For although three are called one, still the thought distinguishes and makes three, and only the discourse of the mouth says one. Let every one weigh this with himself, when he says that he acknowledges and believes one God, whether he does not think of three; and when he says that the Father is God, the Son is God, and the Holy Spirit is God, and they also distinguished into persons, and distinguished as to offices, whether he can think that there is one God, except so that three distinct among themselves make one by concordance, and also by condescension so far as one proceeds from another; when therefore three Gods are adored, where is then the church? But if the Lord alone be adored, in whom there is a perfect trine, and who is in the Father and the Father in Him, as He himself says; then there is a Christian church."—(A. C. 4766.)

ing of Swedenborg in the passages he has cited; and, what is still more unfortunate, he has *mis*-quoted him in almost every instance. Besides being dishonest, it is unjust, alike to Swedenborg and the readers of the Repository, for a writer to *pretend* to give us the very words of our author, when he does not, but changes them and substitutes some of his own. It is what no writer ought ever to allow himself to do, because it unavoidably deceives and misleads his readers. Swedenborg, when speaking of the Christian Church which in his day was consummated, calls it "the present church," "the present christian church," "the church at this day," "the men of this age," &c. Now in all such cases our friend W. S. C. has substituted for Swedenborg's language the phrase "Old Church." And when he defines what *he means* by "Old Church" it becomes plain that this change of Swedenborg's phraseology is a manifest perversion of his meaning. For our brother understands by "Old Church" all those "*persons*" in Christendom at this time who belong to any other church organization than the New, who are "in external communion with it, in the participation of its ordinances and sacraments, conforming to its ceremonies and observances," &c.

But is there no difference between the state of the christian world now, and when Swedenborg wrote? Are the interiors of these so-called Old Church societies or organizations the

---

in his day, that it was consummated and utterly destroyed; that it was without charity, and consequently without faith; that it had no spiritual life; was a mere dead carcass; that its doctrines were altogether false, and did not agree in a single point with the doctrines of the New Christian Church. But we commit a great mistake if we conclude from such language that there were *no individuals* in the church at that time who were in any charity or faith, or who had any spiritual life. We could cite scores of passages in proof that such is not our author's meaning; that, so far from it, he admits that there were a great many, especially among the simple-minded laity, who were in the good of life, and whose good, therefore, must have been interiorly conjoined to truth (*See A. E.* 233; *A. R.* 426.) What then *are* we to understand by this language of E. S.? Simply, as we conceive, that the great system of doctrinal theology upheld and taught by the learned of his day—expressed in the various Christian creeds and formularies of faith, expounded from pulpits and chairs of theology—was utterly false, and as such destitute of the spirit and life of the Gospel. He sometimes says that a church is a church from doctrine and according to it (*A. R.* 923), "and whereas doctrine from the Word constitutes the church, therefore when doctrine disagrees with the Word, it is no longer a church (*A. E.* 786). It is in this sense that he uses the word *Church* when he says "that at this day there is *no church* in the christian world, neither among the Roman Catholics, nor among the reformed;" that is, there was no true system of doctrinal theology. (*See A. R.* 263, 923). The whole fabric was rotten; the system was false and corrupt throughout. Hence it was foretold that the Temple should be entirely demolished, and not one stone (*falsity*) be left upon another. That the simple among the laity of his time were not only in good, but in some truths also, and wiser than the learned. (*See A. C.* 5039, 4760, 3677, 3747; *A. R.* 500, 426.) In the last article here referred to, Swedenborg says "that faith alone, as being competent to justification, is the faith of the clergy, *and not of the laity*, save such of them as live unconcernedly," &c.

Church being "contained in the Old, like the soul within the body, or the life within the form," he declares that "such an assumption, if it were true, would lead directly "to the revolting absurdity that Heaven might have been contained in the. bosom of Hell ! For if that which is *purely good*, can be contained within that which is *entirely evil*, as we hold the Old Church to be, and pledge ourselves to show from the writings of the New Church, what is the alternative ?"

Now *is this* the doctrine taught by our illumined scribe? Are all who compose our New Church organization "purely good," and all who belong to the so-called Old Church organizations "entirely evil?" Is the influx of the New Heavens entirely into these New Church organizations? ·And is there not one speck of genuine good and truth to be found elsewhere? The idea is preposterous. And how a reader of the writings of Swedenborg, or any man in his senses, can harbor it for a moment, is something which we confess ourselves quite unable to comprehend. We commonly speak of the New Jerusalem as a *rational* dispensation; but among all the dogmas of Romanism, and of the Reformed Protestant Churches together, we know of *not one* more palpably false and absurd, or more revolting to every man of generous and charitable feelings, than the idea advanced by W. S. C. that all who compose our New Church organizations are "purely good," and all belonging to other organizations "entirely evil." Our friend may think us "no *true New Churchman*," but we are free to acknowledge that we should, without the least hesitation, reject such an idea if it were put forth by Swedenborg himself. So far from this being true, we think that the nominal members of the New Church (and we speak from a pretty extensive and intimate acquaintance with them) are generally *not so good* in proportion to the light they have, as the members of other church organizations. This is rather a humiliating fact; but we believe it would do us all good to see and acknowledge it.

And not only is this position of our Pittsburg brother unreasonable, and to our mind preposterous in the superlative degree, but we know of nothing in all the writings of E. S. to sustain or favor it, notwithstanding "he pledges himself to show [its truth] from the writings of the New Church." And how does our brother redeem his pledge? He immediately proceeds to quote from Swedenborg some fifteen or twenty passages, in which the utter perversion, consummation, and spiritual death of the First Christian Church is declared; and then he would have his readers think that his promise has been. fulfilled.* But it is plain that he does not understand the mean-:

---
* We are well aware that Swedenborg often says of the Christian Church

ing of Swedenborg in the passages he has cited; and, what is still more unfortunate, he has *mis*-quoted him in almost every instance. Besides being dishonest, it is unjust, alike to Swedenborg and the readers of the Repository, for a writer to *pretend* to give us the very words of our author, when he does not, but changes them and substitutes some of his own. It is what no writer ought ever to allow himself to do, because it unavoidably deceives and misleads his readers. Swedenborg, when speaking of the Christian Church which in his day was consummated, calls it "the present church," "the present christian church," "the church at this day," "the men of this age," &c. Now in all such cases our friend W. S. C. has substituted for Swedenborg's language the phrase "Old Church." And when he defines what *he means* by "Old Church" it becomes plain that this change of Swedenborg's phraseology is a manifest perversion of his meaning. For our brother understands by "Old Church" all those "*persons*" in Christendom at this time who belong to any other church organization than the New, who are "in external communion with it, in the participation of its ordinances and sacraments, conforming to its ceremonies and observances," &c.

But is there no difference between the state of the christian world now, and when Swedenborg wrote? Are the interiors of these so-called Old Church societies or organizations the

---

in his day, that it was consummated and utterly destroyed; that it was without charity, and consequently without faith; that it had no spiritual life; was a mere dead carcass; that its doctrines were altogether false, and did not agree in a single point with the doctrines of the New Christian Church. But we commit a great mistake if we conclude from such language that there were *no individuals* in the church at that time who were in any charity or faith, or who had any spiritual life. We could cite scores of passages in proof that such is not our author's meaning; that, so far from it, he admits that there were a great many, especially among the simpleminded laity, who were in the good of life, and whose good, therefore, must have been interiorly conjoined to truth (*See A. E.* 233; *A. R.* 426) What then *are* we to understand by this language of E S.? Simply, as we conceive, that the great system of doctrinal theology upheld and taught by the learned of his day—expressed in the various Christian creeds and formularies of faith, expounded from pulpits and chairs of theology—was utterly false, and as such destitute of the spirit and life of the Gospel. He sometimes says that a church is a church from doctrine and according to it (*A. R.* 923), "and whereas doctrine from the Word constitutes the church, therefore when doctrine disagrees with the Word, it is no longer a church (*A. E.* 786). It is in this sense that he uses the word *Church* when he says "that at this day there is *no church* in the christian world, neither among the Roman Catholics, nor among the reformed;" that is, there was no true system of doctrinal theology. (*See A. R.* 263, 923). The whole fabric was rotten; the system was false and corrupt throughout. Hence it was foretold that the Temple should be entirely demolished, and not one stone (*falsity*) be left upon another. That the simple among the laity of his time were not only in good, but in some truths also, and wiser than the learned. (*See A. C.* 5099, 4760, 3677, 3747; *A. R.* 500, 426.) In the last article here referred to, Swedenborg says "that faith alone, as being competent to justification, is the faith of the clergy, and *not of the laity*, save such of them as live unconcernedly,". &c.

same now that they were then? If not, then the phrase "Old Church," as used and defined by our friend, means something different from "the christian church" as it was in Swedenborg's time; and the substitution of the former for the latter phraseology is clearly a perversion of the teachings of E. S.

Now we have Swedenborg's own authority for saying that the interiors of the various church organizations in Christendom are *not* the same now that they were in his day; consequently that what is commonly called the "Old Church" now, is not identically the same as "the Christian Church" when Swendenborg wrote. For, in the Treatise on the Last Judgment, speaking of the state of the world and of the church *after* that event, our author says: "But as for the state of the church, this it is which will be *dissimilar* hereafter; it will be similar indeed *in the outward form,* but *dissimilar in the inward,* To outward appearance divided churches will exist as heretofore, their doctrines will be taught as heretofore; and the same religions as now will exist among the Gentiles. But henceforth the man of the church will be in a more free state of thinking on matters of faith, that is, on spiritual things which relate to heaven, because spiritual liberty has been restored to him."— (*L. J.* 73.)

Nothing could be plainer, or more to the purpose than this. We are here taught that the various christian sects, commonly called "Old Church," divided, as they were in Swedenborg's time, and still teaching different doctrines, are internally in quite a *dissimilar state* from what they were then. They are in greater "spiritual liberty," and therefore they must be less under the dominion of hell—more disengaged from the thraldom of evil spirits. And whence is the influx into their minds of this greater freedom to think "on spiritual things which relate to heaven," but from the Lord through the New Heavens? And how, in view of this, and a great deal more of the same sort in the writings of E. S., can our brother think that it is exclusively into minds "*drawn forth*" from Old Church organizations, "and *organized apart,* that the influx of the New Heavens flows?"

But in substituting "Old Church" for other phraseology used by Swedenborg, our brother has been betrayed into still greater errors. He has quoted *A. C.* 4221 thus: "That the internals and EXTERNALS of the Old Church shall perish, and that this is what is meant in the Word by heaven and earth passing away." From this he argues "that the Old [christian] Church belief and *forms* are totally vitiated and vastated," that their sacraments, "particularly that of Baptism," are inefficacious, good for nothing, dead. He is led to this conclusion, we presume, by his own misquotation of the above passage, and from considering that the sacraments of Baptism and the Holy Supper are among the most important *externals* of the Christian Church. But on referring to the passage in the Arcana, we find that what the writer here calls the "Old Church," leading his readers to suppose that it is the Old *Christian* Church that is meant, is the *Jewish* Church, whose *externals* as well as internals were to perish. The passage correctly quoted, reads thus : " *Heaven and earth shall pass away, but my words shall not pass away,*" signifies the internals and externals of the *former church*, that they should perish, but that the Word of the Lord should abide." Now that by "the former church" here mentioned, Swedenborg meant the Jewish nation or church, is obvious from what immediately precedes in the same article, as well as from the words which follow it, which are : "These words were spoken immediately after what was said concerning the Jewish nation, because the Jewish nation was preserved for the sake of the Word." The "*externals* of the former church," therefore, which E. S. refers to in this passage, are the externals of the *Jewish* church, which were to perish along with its internals. And what were these externals ? "The altars and sacrifices offered thereon, which, it is well known, were external things ; in like manner the bread of proposition, also the candlestick with its lights, and likewise the perpetual fire, which it may also be known to every one, represented things internal : the case was the same in regard to other rituals" (*A. C.* 4292). They were all "external things," which "resemble the body." And the Jewish church being merely "the representative of a church, its internals being altogether corrupt and filthy and not in *correspondence* with these external things" (*A. C.* 4288), therefore, both the internals and the externals of *that* church were to perish ; and not as W. S. C. imagines and has made our author say, the internals and externals of the Old or first Christian Church.

We beg our friend then to re-examine and re-consider this subject. We know of nothing in all the writings of Swedenborg to sustain him in his position in regard to the Old Church as he has defined it, that "all its forms are evil from the greatest to the least," and "all its ordinances and sacraments corrupt —its offices and administrations having no spiritual life." On the contrary, his writings abound with things that are utterly opposed to such an idea.

We are aware that many New Churchmen (and our Pittsburg brother is among the number) are accustomed to speak of New Church Baptism and Old Church Baptism, New Church ordinances and Old Church ordinances, &c., but we know of no sufficient warrant for the use of such language. There is certainly nothing in Swedenborg to justify it, any more than there is to justify such expressions as New Church Word and Old Church Word. It is true that a New Churchman's *understanding* of the Word is quite different from that of one who has no knowledge or belief of its internal senses—so different as to make it almost a new Word; but is the Word itself any the less divine and holy, any the less *the Word*, when read by the latter than when read by the former? Suppose we listen to the reading of the Word by a minister who is principled in falses, or who understands it only in its most external sense, does *his* understanding of it affect *us*? Do *his* false views of what is read flow into *our* minds? Is it not the same Word to us, and equally a divine medium of conjunction with the Lord and consociation with the angels, as if read by one who understood it better? And if so, then we would ask whether the sacraments, which the Word enjoins upon christians, are any the less holy, any the less *sacraments*, and consequently any the less efficacious, when administered by a bad than when administered by a good priest? How can the character of the administrator affect the holiness or efficacy of an ordinance enjoined by the Lord (provided it be performed in sincerity and not in mockery) any more than the character of a religious teacher can affect the holiness of the Word itself, or its power to open a communication with heaven? But there need be no dispute on this point among those who are willing to be taught by Swedenborg; for he settles it beyond controversy in the following passage.

" All kings whosoever they are, and of whatsoever quality, by virtue of the principle of royalty appertaining to them, represent the Lord ; in like manner *all priests*, whosoever or of whatsoever quality they are, by virtue of the priestly principle ; the principle of royalty (*regium*) and the priestly principle (*sacerdotale*) is holy, whatsoever be the nature and quality of the person who ministers therein ; hence it is that the Word taught by a wicked person is alike holy as when taught by a good person, *and also the sacraments of Baptism and the Holy Supper, and the like.*"—(*A. C.* 3670.)

What can be more explicit or conclusive on the subject than this? Our author here tells us that " *all priests*," whatever be their character or quality, "represent the Lord." And we presume that our friend W. S. C. will not deny, that the clergy of the various Christian denominations around us are recognized by Swedenborg as *priests*, however great and grievous may be the falses in which many of them no doubt are. For, speaking of the descent of the New Church from heaven, and its reception among men, he says (*T. C. R.* 784): " Wherefore this cannot be done in a moment, but it is done as the falses of the former church are removed; for what is new cannot enter where falses have been ingenerated, unless these are eradicated, *which will be done among the clergy, and thus among the laity.*" Are these the clergy of the Old or of the New Church, of whom Swedenborg here speaks? Evidently of the former; for they are those by whom, he tells us, the doctrines of the New Jerusalem would be first received and communicated to others. Then Old Church clergymen, as we call them, are clearly recognized by our author as clergy or priests: therefore, whatever he says of the office or duties of priests must be understood as applicable alike to Old and New Church ministers—to all who exercise the priestly function.

Now if the clergy of the so-called Old Church congregations be *priests* (they may be in great falses, but no matter), and if, as our author so plainly teaches, the character of the administrator does not in anywise affect the holiness of the Sacraments adminstered by him, neither can it affect their efficacy or validity.

Let us then abandon the use of such expressions as Old · Church Baptism and New Church Baptism, Old Church Sacraments and New Church Sacraments. There is not, that we are aware of, any where in the writings of E. S. the slightest authority for the distinction herein implied. The idea is one which we are constrained to regard as purely the offspring of self-derived intelligence. Let us say rather that Baptism is Baptism, and the Holy Supper is the Holy Supper, wherever reverently administered, and in obedience to the command of Him by whom these ordinances were enjoined. They are *Christian* ordinances and as such are to be received by all who are in possession of the Word, who profess the Christian faith (however imperfectly they may comprehend it) and who desire to live a christian life. The meaning and use of these ordinances may be but little comprehended, and their internal sense be but little understood by those who administer or those who receive them; still, if they are regarded as holy, and administered and received with devout feelings, they are useful, efficacious, valid. The act is then a good religious act, and, as such, effects for the time a more intimate communion of the recipients with the Lord and the angels.

In this belief we find ourselves amply sustained by our illumined scribe. He says:

"Unless the internal of the Word flows in with those who read the Word, and abide in the literal sense, there is not effected conjunction of truth from the Word with good; and the internal of the Word then flows in, and is conjoined with good, when man *accounts the Word holy*, and he then accounts it holy when he is in good. The same may be illustrated also by the Holy Supper; scarcely any know that bread in the Holy Supper signifies the Lord's love towards the universal human race, and the reciprocal love of man, and that wine represents charity; nevertheless with those who receive the bread and wine *holily*, there is effected conjunction with heaven and with the Lord thereby, and the goods of love and charity flow in by (or through) the angels, who then do not think of bread and wine, but of love and charity. Hence it is · evident that external truth is conjoined with internal truth, when man is in good, *he himself being ignorant of it*."—(*A. C.* 6789.)

Again our author says concerning the most holy Sacrament;

" But if any one is so simple that he cannot think any thing else from the understanding, than what he sees with the eye, I advise him to think with himself concerning the Holy Supper, when he takes the bread and wine, and hears them then called the flesh and blood of the Lord, that it is the most holy thing of worship, and to remember the passion of Christ, and his love for the salvation of man."—(*T. C. R.* 709; *A. C.* 9410, 3464, 3735.)

Now in these passages Swedenborg recognizes the propriety and *use* of administering the Holy Supper to those who regard it as a divine ordinance, but who do not understand its spiritual meaning—who do not know that bread signifies the good of the Lord's love, and wine the truths of His wisdom—who, in short, think concerning it precisely as many in the so-called Old Church congregations around us think. We presume our Pittsburg brother would not maintain that the persons of whom Swedenborg here speaks, as being in such an external state— not understanding the internal sense of the bread and wine used in the Holy Supper—are members of the New Church as he understands it, "drawn forth" from Old Church organizations. Then there is a propriety and a use in this ordinance being administered to those belonging to other religious organizations than our own, who think naturally concerning it, but who yet receive it "*holily.*" "There is effected conjunction with heaven and with the Lord thereby, and the goods of love and charity flow in by (or through) the angels, who then do not think of bread and wine, but of love and charity." Then there is *validity* and *efficacy* in the ordinance when administered *by* others than New Church clergymen, and *to* others than those who understand and receive our doctrines; for it effects conjunction with the Lord and consociation with the angels.

And if the ordinance of the Holy Supper be valid and efficacious when administered by others than professedly New Church ministers, then surely must that of baptism, which is less holy, be equally valid; and we have no difficulty in answering the question of W. S. C., "How can the sacrament of Baptism performed by its [the Old Church] functionaries be efficacious New Church Baptism?" Abandon the use of this unauthorized language, brother—throw away your fancied distinction between the nature and efficacy of this rite as performed by one or another of the ministers of Christ—settle it in your mind that it is a *Christian* ordinance, or "the *Christian* sign," and that such a thing as *New Church* Baptism or *Old Church* Baptism has no real existence save in your own or in others' imagination, and your question is speedily resolved.

But our friend, in common with many others, seems to mistake the design and use of Baptism, and attributes to the ordinance an efficacy which we feel warranted in saying does not really belong to it. He thinks that, when administered in the New Church, it " inserts the subject into the societies of the New Heaven;" and asks, " How can it [Old Church Baptism] give insertion into the New Heaven to which it is not *conjoined?*" We have often been surprised to hear receivers of the Heavenly Doctrines speak in this manner; as if Baptism inserted one into the New Heaven, if it be performed by a New Church minister, and into Hell, or among the Methodists, Episcopalians, Presbyterians, &c., in the other world, if performed by a minister belonging to one of these communions. We conceive that a greater mistake than this could not possibly be committed. If this were so, not only would Baptism give faith and salvation when performed by those who are in true doctrine, or by the Ministers of the New Church, but it would be equally efficacious in causing infidelity and damnation when performed by those who are in false doctrine, or by the so-called ministers of the Old Church. And what can be more absurd, or more revolting to the feelings of every true christian, than such an idea? And were it true that baptism, when administered to a little infant or to an adult, by one who is principled in a false doctrine, has power to insert the subject of it among spirits of darkness in the other world, can we believe that Swedenborg would have been silent in regard to a matter of such infinite moment? Besides, we call the New Jerusalem a *rational* dispensation. And what is there, we would ask, that addresses the rational mind, in the idea that an external rite has power to insert the subjects of it among the angels in heaven or the devils in hell, according as it happens to be performed by one or another individual, or in one or another christian congregation? Can you find among all the dogmas of Calvinism and Romanism together any thing more irrational than such a belief? And must not all our ideas both of heaven and of hell as derived from the writings of E. S., be entirely reversed, before we can seriously entertain such a view of the power and efficacy of an outward rite?

And not only is this idea most unreasonable, but it derives not a shadow of support from the writings of our illumined author. It is *not*, according to his teachings, a Baptist, a Methodist, a Lutheran, or a Presbyterian rite, having power to insert the subject of it among similar societies of spirits in the other world, according as it happens to be administered in one or the other of these communions. No more is it a *New Church* or an *Old Church* rite, according to the profession of faith of the administrator, having power to bind the subject of it to New or Old Church spirits in the other world. Our author teaches nothing of this kind. On the contrary he every where speaks of it as a *christian* and not as a *sectarian* rite—as a *sign* to distinguish christians from those of other religions in the spiritual world—and as possessing its full validity as a discriminating sign, when solemnly performed by any minister professing the christian faith. He tells us that one of its first uses is "insertion *among christians* in the spiritual world." By this he means, as he elsewhere says, that it is " *the christian sign*,"—" a sign of introduction into the [christian] church"— " a sign in the spiritual world that he [the subject of it] *is of christians*," as distinguished from Jews, Mahometans or Pagans —and *not*, as many seem to think, that he is of this or that christian society or congregation—a New-Churchman or an Old-Churchman—according to the faith of the administrator, for "every one is inserted among *societies* and *congregations* there [in the spiritual world], *according to the quality of the Christianity in him or out of him*,"—not according as he chanced ed to be *baptized* in this or that congregation.—(*T. C. R.* 680, 677, 678.)

Now we should remember—and it is a point of some importance in this discussion—that there are in the spiritual world, the same as in this world, *bad* christians as well as good ones. There are christian *devils* as well as christian *angels*—christian *hells* as well as christian *heavens*. And we are also taught that some of the hells which are formed of the spirits of those who have been born and educated in christian countries, are the very worst of all. Now these bad christians, or christian hells, are discriminated from the Mahometan and other hells, by the same "*sign*" by which the christian heavens are discriminated from the Mahometan and other heavens, i. e. *Baptism*. It deserves therefore to be well remembered, that our author, in teaching that Baptism is " a sign in the spiritual world that the person is of christians," that all are inserted by it "among christians in the spiritual world," &c., no where intimates that it inserts him among *good* rather than *bad* christians there, or into one or another christian society. He no where intimates that it signifies any thing in regard to the present or future character of the subject of it—whether he is, or will be, a good or a bad christian, or that it necessarily makes him the recipient of any purer spiritual influences. Nor does he any where favor the opinion of our Pittsburg brother (which seems to be the opinion of many other receivers of the Heavenly Doctrines) that, when performed by a New Church minister, "it gives insertion into the New Heaven." This would be to attribute a *saving* efficacy to the ordinance, which our illumined scribe declares *it does not* possess. For he says (and the form of expression is worthy of note), " *Let it be known,* therefore, to those who are baptized, that baptism itself *gives neither faith nor salvation,* but that it testifies that they will receive faith, and that they will be saved, *if they are regenerated*" (*N. J. D.* 207). And still more explicit and conclusive is the teaching of the following passages.

" No one can come into heaven unless he hath received spiritual life by regeneration. * * * *No one enters by Baptism,* but baptism is significative of regeneration, which the man of the church ought to remember."—(*A. C.* 5342.)

" Baptism is a *symbol* of regeneration, and thereby of introduction into the Church, that is, into good by truths from the Word."—(*A. C.* 9032.)

" It is evident how falsely they think, who believe that evils or sins appertaining to man are wiped away, as filth is washed from the body by waters; and that they were cleansed as to the interiors who were formerly washed by waters according to the statutes of the Church : and also *that they are saved at this day by being baptized ;* when yet washings formerly only represented the cleansing of the interiors, and baptism signifies regeneration, waters denoting the truths of faith by which man is cleansed and regenerated, for by them evils are removed ; baptism is for those who are within the Church, *because these have the Word* containing *the* truths of faith by which man is regenerated."—(*A. C.* 9088.)

" The Holy Supper and Baptism are for them alone, who are in possession of the Word, and to whom the Lord is known from the Word; for they are symbols of that church [the Christian] and are testifications and certifications that they are saved who believe and live according to the Lord's precepts in the Word."—(*A. E.* 1180.)

The whole of the article from which this last extract is taken is interesting and valuable, and we invite particular attention to it. The reader will there see that Swedenborg calls all those " *Christians,*" who have the Word, and who learn from it and believe such plain truths as nineteen-twentieths of the so-called Old Church congregations have learned and profess to believe. And he declares that Baptism and the Holy Supper are for all such, and for "*those alone* ;"—i. e. they are not for "Mahometans," or "Gentiles," being symbols of the Christian Church.

From the above extracts we gather,

1. That baptism, viewed as an outward ceremony, is a symbolical rite, and *nothing more* than a symbol.

2. That it is significative of regeneration ; but that it *does not* insert the subject of it into heaven, nor give salvation to any one; and that this ought to be well remembered.

8. That it does not even introduce one into the Church, much less into Heaven; for it is only " a *symbol* of introduction into the Church," because a symbol of regeneration.

4. That those think very *falsely* "who believe that they are saved by being baptized;" for baptism in itself possesses no saving efficacy.

5. That it is a symbol of the *Christian Church*, and to be received as such by all who are in possession of the Word, and who profess the Christian faith.

These things are gathered not by logical *inference* merely, but they are taught in the most explicit and positive manner. Regarding this rite then, as merely symbolical and significative, we would ask if its signification be not always the same to the eye of Him who enjoined it, or to the eyes of angels? Does the meaning of the symbol absolutely change with the faith of the admistrator or of the recepient? Does it not really signify the same thing, viz. that the subject of it "*is of Christians*" and not of Jews or Mahometans, and that " he will be saved if he be regenerated," whether it be administered in a Methodist, Baptist, or Church of England communion? And does it signify *any thing more* than this, if administered in a New Church Temple, and by the hands of a professed New Church minister? We wish that our brethren everywhere might so far divest their minds of early prejudices and prepossessions on this subject, as to give these questions a calm, dispassionate, and mature consideration.

We could afford to dismiss the subject here ; but there are several other things in the article of W. S. C. which it was our intention to notice. We will however remark only upon one or two of them, and with as much brevity as possible.

A. E. F. had said, that " when ever an Old Church is set aside, a New Church is on the instant constituted by the Lord out of its remains, that is to say, out of all, externally connected with the consummated church, who are in charity and some faith from the Word. Such persons there must be in every church about to expire, &c. The first influx of the New Heavens, so far as it is received in charity and faith on earth, is into their minds." He then goes on to say that " the very hour of its [the New Church] establishment, therefore, it had its members in every country where the Word was read, and among all sects who held it sacred, and did not deny the Lord's divinity. [These] persons thus intermixed and blended with the various denominations of Christendom, constitute, with very few exceptions, the Lord's New Church at its first setting up. [And] it continued to grow from that time, and has its existence *now*, by the side of the societies composed of those who are in the acknowledgment of doctrines drawn from the internal sense of the Word. For, that which made the original members of the New Church, will make members of it at any time, viz. a state of charity from the Word."

Now we understand our Pittsburg brother to object most decidedly to all this. For he says it "involves the same gratuitous assumption of the New Church being contained within the Old;" and adds, "If the remains, of which A. E. F. speaks, were to receive the influx of the New Heavens as he supposes, would it not be simply the resuscitation of the.Old Church and the inspiration of life into its dead carcass?"

But let us see what our illumined author says on the subject. In *A. C.* 407, from which our friend has made a brief quotation, he says: "So also with the primitive church, or that after the coming of the Lord, which at this day is so vastated, that there is not any faith; nevertheless there always remains *some kernel* of the church, which they who are vastated as to faith do not acknowledge." Now where do we expect to find the *kernel*? Is it not *within* the shell?

Our author again: "that *they within the church* may be regenerated by means of any doctrine whatsoever, but they especially who are in genuine truths" (*A. C.* 6765), "That there are evils and falses, to which goods and truths can be adjoined, may appear from this consideration, that there are so many diverse dogmas and doctrinals, several of which are altogether heretical, and yet in every one of them salvation is attainable" (*A. C.* 3993).

Now the point to which we would here direct the reader's attention, is the breadth of meaning which our author attaches to the word *Church*. He embraces in his idea of the *Christian Church* (for he speaks of Gentiles and others as " out of the Church," *A. C.* 3993) some who are not in genuine truths, some in all the "diverse dogmas and doctrinals" of christendom and he recognizes these as "*within* the Church" and surely he cannot be understood to mean that these persons, whose dogmas and doctrinals are so "*diverse*," are such as have been "drawn forth from the Old Church, its order, jurisdiction, government and communion," according to the idea of W. S. C., and composing "a separate and distinct organization." He must mean persons still in connection with the various so-called Old Church communions, or, in the language of A. E. F "persons intermixed and blended with the various denominations of christendom."

But that our author leaves us in no doubt as to his meaning on this point, nor as to how those who are in diverse and false doctrinals may be saved, the following extract will clearly show.

"They *within the Church* are in falses and at the same time in good. who are in heresies and in the life of good. But falses with these do not damn, unless they be such falses as are contrary to good, and destroy the very life of good; but the falses which are not contrary to good, in themselves indeed are falses, but in respect to the good of life which they are not contrary to, they almost put off the quality of the false, which is effected by application to good. To illustrate this by example: It is said that faith alone saves, which in itself is false, especially with the evil, who thereby exclude the good of charity, as if it contributed nothing at all to salvation; but this false grows mild mith those who are in the good of life, for they apply it to good, saying, "that faith alone saves, but that it is not faith unless together with its fruit, consequently unless where good is: so in other cases."—(*A. C.* 8311.)

We presume our brother would not maintain that these persons, spoken of as "within the Church," who are in the doctrine of salvation by faith alone, belong to what he calls New Church societies, "organized apart." Our author elsewhere represents them, together with all who belong to the Lord's kingdom, as belonging to societies that "are scattered through the whole world," yet forming "a communion;"—these scattered elements being "collected by the Lord, that they may also represent one man, as the societies in heaven" (*A. C.* 7396). *Collected*, not in the sense of forming "a separate and independent organization of persons," on earth—by no means; but collected and arranged into a heavenly form, as He alone, before whom Heaven is as one man, knows how to collect and arrange human spirits. Again:

"It is generally believed that the Church exists wherever the Word is, and where the Lord is known; whereas the Church consists only of those who from the heart acknowledge the Divinity of the Lord, and who learn truths from Him by the Word, and do them; *no others form any part of the church whatever.*"—(*A. E.* 388.)

Not a word here about the necessity of being "drawn forth" from one organization, and "organized apart" in a separate communion, in order to the reception of influx from heaven.

And we would ask W. S. C., and all who hold to his opinion,
whether they seriously believe and are prepared to maintain,
that there are *none* in the various christian denominations
around us, who are of the character of those of whom E. S. here
says "the church consists." And whether these persons are
really any the less of the church, or *in* the church, because of
the society with which they happen to be connected? And
whether they believe that *none* are to be found in our New
Church societies, who, according to the definition here given,
" form *no part* of the church whatever ?"

Where, then, is the New Church? Can we point to the societies and associations organized under this name, and say,
"Lo! here, or lo! there?" No. This New Dispensation—it
"cometh not with observation"—not in any such observable,
tangible, definite, numerical form; but rather as a new dawn
breaking forth in the east, for the illumination of all eyes and
the rejoicing of all hearts. " For as the lightning cometh out
of the east, and shineth even unto the west, *so shall also the
coming of the Son of Man be.*"

The Report of the Committee of Ministers of the Massachusetts Association of the New Church, referred to by A. E. F.,
takes the ground that the Former Church (i. e. the present so-
called Old Church organizations) is the *external* of the New
Church; and that baptism into that church is orderly and useful, being "the means of connecting them [the subjects] with
the external Christian heavens." Our Pittsburg brother considers this a great error, and declares that "there is no more
unwarrantable assumption to be found in all (the) New Church
theology than this."

But where, then, will our brother find that vast multitude
which E. S. says are in an external state, " who have qualified
their good by exterior truths, such as are those of the literal
sense of the Word," and who therefore are "of the external
church ?" Will he find them in our New Church organizations?
He may find *some* of them there, just as he may find some who
are of the *internal* church in other organizations. But those
who are technically called New Churchmen have the spiritual sense of the Word, and most of them are presumed to qualify their good by it ; and so far as they do this, they are " of the
internal church" (*A. C.* 7840). But the New Church must
have an external as well as an internal ; and this external, as
consisting of persons, must exceed the internal in numbers as
much as the other parts of the human body exceed in size the
heart and lungs. Thus our author says:

" A church, in order to be a church, must be internal and external ;

for there are who are in the internal of the church, and there are who are in its external ; the former are *few*, but the latter are *numerous ;* nevertheless where the internal church is, the external must be also, for the internal of the church cannot be separated from its external."—(*A. C.* 6587, 9276.)

Swedenborg also tells us that *even in his day*, " the greater part" of the lay members of the church, who professed the doctrine of faith alone, "did not know what faith alone is," but "thought that a life according to the precepts of God in the Word is thereby understood." And when they were instructed concerning faith alone and justification thereby, they " believed no otherwise than that faith alone is to think concerning God and salvation, and *how they ought to live :* and that justification is *to live* before God" (*A. E.* 233). These persons were providentially preserved in this simple state of thought and faith. And if the greater part of the laity in Christendom were of this character when Swedenborg wrote, may we not reasonably conclude that a still greater number of such are to be found in the various christian congregations of the present day ? For the persons composing the external of the church must be "*numerous.*"

If any doubt should still exist as to who compose the external and who the internal of the church that now is, or in what organizations they are likely to be found as a general thing, we would invite careful attention to the following extract from our author.

" Internal good appertains to those who are called men of the internal church, but external good appertains to those who are men of the external church. Men of the internal church are they who have qualified their good by interior truths, such as are those of the internal sense of the Word : but men of the external church are they who have qualified their good by exterior truths, such as are those of the literal sense of the Word : men of the internal church are they who from the affection of charity do good to their neighbor, but men of the external church are they who do good from obedience. Every man when he is regenerating, first becomes a man of the external church, but afterwards a man of the internal church : they who are of the internal church are in superior intelligence and wisdom to those who are of the external church, and on that account also more interiorly in heaven."—(*A. C.* 7840. *See also* 6775.)

The great error of the Massachusetts Report, then, consists not so much, as we conceive, in regarding those of the various christian sects around us as constituting the external of the New Church, as in teaching that, when one has been introduced by baptism into this external church, he ought again to receive that ordinance in passing from the external into the in-

ternal church. We know of nothing in the Word or in the
writings of the Lord's chosen servant for expounding the Word,
to sustain such an opinion. And if anything more were needed
after the able article of A. E. F. to prove this opinion erroneous, we think the above extract ought to be sufficient. For
Baptism is a sign of *introduction* into the church—is *the first
gate* of entrance. Where else, then, but into the *external* church
can this gate open? For our author here teaches that *every*
regenerating man comes first into the external and afterwards
into the internal church. And is not the external a *part* of the
church? And are not those, therefore, who compose it, really
in the church? Then why should the ordinance, which we are
taught to regard as the *introductory* rite, be repeated after one
has entered within the walls of the city? Besides, if repeated
in one instance, why should it not be in every other? Why
should not *every* person who has been baptized in infancy by a
New Church minister, again be baptized as the interiors of his
mind open, and he comes into the interior goods and truths of
the church? For *every* one—no matter where or by whom
baptized—comes *first* into the external church, and afterwards
into the internal.

Moreover, Swedenborg tells us that this ordinance, as administered by Christian ministers when he wrote the "True
Christian Religion," which was some twelve years after the
former church was consummated, and when there were *no* professed New Church ministers, had all the significance, and
consequently all the validity and efficacy, that it ever did or
ever can have. "The Baptism," he says, "*which is at this day*
with Christians, represents the cleansing of the internal man,
which is regeneration."—(*T. C. R.* 690.)

Under every aspect of the subject, therefore, we must be allowed to say—and we say it with all deference to the Committee who drafted the "Report" referred to—that we think their
opinion erroneous and their position untenable. We know of
nothing either in the Word or in the writings of the Church, to
favor the idea that the ordinance of Baptism should be *repeated
when* a person passes, by an orderly process of regeneration,
from the external into the internal church.

Let us, then, abandon the idea that the little handful of New
Church ministers now on the earth have the *exclusive* right to
administer the Christian ordinances, and that, out of their
hands, these ordinances have no—or at most but a *partial*—
vitality, efficacy or use. Let us remove ourselves as soon and
as far as possible from a position, which is not only unsupported by the teachings of our illumined author, but which savors
too much of something like ecclesiastical arrogance and pre-

sumption. Let us be willing to acknowledge that there is some real good and truth in all the various religious societies or church organizations around us ; and that, where there is any good and truth—any thing of the Church—there, and in that degree the Lord is; and that from Him they have authority to teach, and baptize, and do all things that He enjoins.

Swedenborg teaches us to expect, as one necessary consequence of the Last Judgment, that there would thenceforward be a freer influx of heavenly light and warmth, not merely into a few *Swedenborgian* minds, " organized apart," but into the general intellect and heart of humanity. He teaches us to regard this New Dispensation of truth, as the coming of a new day to the children of men—a day that is to shine upon all and for all—as " a new light shining forth, which in the Word is called morning" (*A. C.* 408). Now when a new day breaks and the morning comes, it sheds its light merely not on a few favored districts here and there, leaving the rest in midnight darkness. No. It lights up the whole hemisphere. The loftiest summits, it is true, catch the first beams of the rising sun ; but instantly these are reflected into the valleys, and the deepest ravines and obscurest nooks are in some measure illumined thereby. So with the coming of the Son of righteousness in this new morning of the church. He comes, agreeably to divine promise, not for a few but for all; for it is written, " and every eye shall see Him, even they that pierced Him." His heavenly beams may fall earlier or more directly on some minds than on others ; but they can no more remain there to the exclusion of other minds, than the beams of the morning sun can remain exclusively on the lofty mountain tops that first receive them. The entire spiritual horizon is filled with a blaze of light.

Let us, then, not be so weak and presumptuous as to claim for our New Church ministers and New Church societies any exclusive rights or privileges, as if we alone were the elect of God, and in possession of all the good and truth there is in the world. Let us discard, as untrue and utterly unworthy the receivers of the doctrines of heaven, the idea that we alone have authority from the Lord to administer the Christian ordinances; and that these ordinances are without validity, without efficacy, and altogether corrupt, when administered by others than ourselves.

We trust that our Pittsburg brother will pardon us, if, in imitation of his example, we close our remarks at this time with an extract from the Heavenly Arcana, to which we invite his particular attention, and that of all who think with him on this subject.

" There are also societies of interior friendship [in the other life]. They were such in the life of the body, that they loved from the heart those who were within their common consociation, and also mutually embraced them as united in brotherhood.   They believed that *they themselves alone were alive and in the light, and that they who were out of their society were respectively not alive and not in the light.*   And this being the quality and character they also thought that the Lord's heaven *consisted solely of those few.*   But it was given to tell them that the Lord's heaven is immense, and that it consists of every people and tongue, and that all are therein who have been principled in the good of love and of faith ; and it was shown that there are in heaven they who have relation to all the provinces of the body as to its exteriors and interiors; but that if they aspired further than to those things which correspond to their life, they could not have heaven; *especially if they condemned others who were out of their society;* and that, in such a case, their society is a society of interior friendship, the quality whereof is such, that they deprive others of the blessed principle of spiritual affection when they approach them, for they regard them *as not the elect, and as not alive;* which thought, when communicated, induces what is sad, and yet this sadness, according to the Laws of Order in the other life, returns to them."—(*A. C.* 4805.)

Cincinnati, *Dec.* 4, 1848.   B. F. B.

SELECTIONS.

EXTRACTS FROM SWEDENBORG'S SPIRITUAL DIARY.

(NOW FIRST TRANSLATED FROM THE ORIGINAL LATIN.)

That all and Singular Things of the Word are Vessels.

4121. The contents of the Word, viewed in the literal sense, are most general vessels, indeed so general, and some parts so extremely general, that celestial and spiritual things, or goods and truths innumerable, may be insinuated thereby.   Externally viewed (these vessels) are unsightly, because so very general, but inasmuch as men are of such a quality that they gather their wisdom solely from sensual things, and have no disposition to know aught else than things corporeal and most general, therefore it is that there are such vessels; such, for instance, is the proposition that all evil is from the Lord, when in fact no evil, not the very least (is from him); but because man would fain be wise from corporeals and from darkness (itself), therefore it is thus confirmed that the Lord governs and forsees all things, and in this way he who simply believes, without any restriction, that there is nothing which is not of the Lord, thus that it is He alone who

does all things, may (safely) remain in such an opinion, as also that
the Lord tempts man, and many other things of the like kind.

4122. At the same time, truths may be applied to those vessels, as
that the Lord does and foresees every thing, and is omnipotent, but that
evils accrue mediately through evil spirits; as also that He so orders
and disposes, that all and singular evils are converted into good. In
this way one and the same vessel receives contrary senses, and thus
applies itself to every kind of truth, for it is a truth that no evil can exist without the Lord's permission; it is a truth also that whatever he
permits takes place through the agency of evil spirits, and that he
would not permit it, were not man so evil that without evil he cannot
be reformed. It is moreover a truth, that there is no evil from the
Lord. In order therefore that the words of the Word may be applicable to every one (according to his state), they are of the most general
character, in consequence of which they become available to each
individual. Upon these points I conversed with spirits.

Concerning Evil Spirits.

4130. That evil spirits should continually and for a long course of
years, by cunning and malice, by deceits, threats, and innumerable
machinations, labor to destroy the interior things of the Word, which
machinations, from their long continuance, I am unable to describe in
detail, (may well excite astonishment).

4131. I thence observed, that spirits and angels are never able to
discover or utter any thing of truth from themselves; as often as they
were left to themselves, with a view to such discovery, they were
wholly incompetent to it. Whatever they lay hold of, it is not truth, as,
for instance, in respect to the interior sense of the Word, they were
never able to discover it of themselves, and when spirits were sometimes indignant, I perceived that it was in consequence of this inability.
The case is the same with a man, who is never able of himself to do
any thing good or to think any thing true, though it seems to himself
that he does, but the impression is false; as when one trusts to his own
prudence, he thinks the result to be due to himself, and yet it tends to
evil, if not in the life of the body, as it seems to him, yet still in the
other life. It hence appears evident that all good and truth is from
the Lord.

4132. The state of spirits and angels is, in general, a state of comparative sleep, for since they are in the present (instead of the past or
future), they distinctly perceive things as present (like one asleep), but
he who sees all things from eternity, and the series of all results, is in
a state of wakefulness, which fully holds of the Lord alone. That it
is a sleep was shown me from the circumstance of my falling into a
sleep with them, in which state I supposed that things were really so

and so, when yet it was afterwards given to know that such was not the case. Thus spirits and angels can of themselves do nothing which is good and true.

MISCELLANY.

MISSIONARY NARRATIVE.

To the Committee of Missions of the Ohio Association of the New Church.

DEAR BRETHREN ;— ·

Having been engaged as a missionary in the New Church, for about a year, and having made no formal report hitherto, I now present to you, in as brief a form as possible, an account of my year's work.

Last Sept. while at Jeffersonville, Ind. where I had been employed as the teacher of an Academy, I was invited by Bro. Hough, and several of the brethren in Cincinnati, to enter upon this field as a missionary. To this I agreed, on the supposition that the work which I might do would meet the sympathy and co-operation of the church in this region. The work thus far has seemed to be productive of good fruits, and has met with a most cordial sympathy and co-operation on part of the brethren ; and has been the means of awakening in some an apparently permanent interest in the doctrines of the New Church. There has most generally been an encouraging if not a flattering attention paid to the doctrines wherever they were offered. In most cases I have had full and sometimes crowded houses and always attentive and well-disposed audiences. There has been but little open opposition offered on the part of the clergy of the Old Church, but on the contrary several of them have warmly co-operated with me in getting places of meeting, inviting me into their own pulpits, asking themselves to be instructed in the New Doctrines, and attending, when they could, my public lectures. Some of the clergy, however, have made opposition in a private way to the spread of what they call the *worst of heresies*. The people, however, are far more ready to learn than their ministers, and have not, as I remember, offered any open opposition to· my lectures during the year. In fact many of the church members take hold of the tracts and read them gladly, and some of them purchase the works of the church. A general state of receptivity is manifest, entirely unparalleled in the past; and proof enough is given that a vast interior change has taken place in the states of affection and modes of thought of the man of the church. Whenever an occasion has served I have entered into a free conversation with members and ministers of the Old Church, and I am confident in the declaration, that there is every where indicated a vastated condition of the various denominations, which is at once terrible to the votaries of the Old systems and highly encouraging to the New Jerusalem. In every branch of the Old Church there is a state of disquietude, perplexity, and doubt, both in regard to faith and practice. The existing doubts and actual changes in modes of thought give rise among ministers to experiments in the use of the *New Phraseology*. These new forms of expression, arising with the dawn of the New Dispensation, tend to increase the doubts of church members, at large, and to break up the rigor of party lines, and to produce what may be called a state of *universal mixedness*, or *chaos*. To minds immersed in this, who are still in the simple love of truth, the clear and distinctive doctrines and phraseologies of the New Church are vastly welcome and enchaining. There is a fact here rather of an external nature of which I would speak, indicating in a still more striking light that the religion of the denominations is fading away for the want of a true interior life. It is this.

In many of the villages where I have been, there are houses of worship which are standing idle on the sabbath; some being used only once a month, some twice, and some only when a stranger passes along. These houses are generally under such a guardianship that they are freely opened to ministers of the New Church. In some of them they have invited and even importuned me to preach. When I have done so the people have come in large bodies to hear me, and inasmuch as the people who have built these chapels gladly resort to them when anything is offered which promises to gratify or to instruct them, they certainly furnish a most admirable platform for the propagation of New Jerusalem. From sources of information which are reliable, I conclude that there are within the bounds of this Association not less than 100 well built and comfortably furnished houses of this kind. which are standing unoccupied a majority of the sabbaths of the year.

A field thus prepared, people thus waiting to be instructed, labors of others thus standing to be entered upon, I believe has never been found since the dawn of the Church.

In order that the present state of that portion of this field may be better understood I will add the following particulars :—

I commenced the mission at Carthage on the 29th of September, 1847, where I lectured at the Disciples Church, on the Doctrine of Regeneration. There were present about 50 persons.

Oct. 2. I lectured again at the same place on the Trinity; present about 70.

Oct. 3. At 2 o'clock, P. M. I lectured at the New Light Church at Finney Town, on the Nature and Design of Religion, and in the evening at the same place, on the Nature and Immortality of the Soul : at each meeting there were 60 or 70 present. There are in Carthage, Finney Town and vicinity several families of the New Jerusalem, enough to form a small society ; and among those not of the church there are many who are willing to learn and investigate.

Oct. 6. Lectured at Yankee-town, a village about 24 miles from Cincinnati, settled by people from the State of Maine. Here we obtained the Methodist Church and I presented on two consecutive evenings the Doctrines of the Trinity and the Atonement. Present at the first meeting about 50, and at the last about 20 persons. The weather was stormy.

Oct. 9. Lectured at the Liberty Chapel near the 20 Mile Stand, on the subject of Regeneration : present about 30.

Oct. 10. (Sabbath.) Preached twice to-day at the same place, once on the Trinity and once on the Atonement : present about 100.

There are at the 20 Mile Stand three families of the New Church, including my own, and some few who are readers of the works. When at home I have sometimes during the year preached at the house of

Mr. Espy and sometimes at my own house—at which times generally as many of the neighbors as we have notified have attended. They have accepted of the tracts when offered to them, but none have reported themselves as receivers of the Doctrines.

Oct. 11. This evening I lectured at Harveysburg at the church of the United Brethren, on the Immortality of the Soul. About 150 were present and much anxiety manifested to hear. I found several readers of Swedenborg here.

Oct. 12. Lectured again in the same place, on the Trinity: present about 20; the weather was very stormy.

I have preached and lectured at the Harrison school house, near Sweeny's, 26 times during the year, to audiences varying from 20 to 200. There are four New Church families in this neighborhood, and a great interest is felt in the Church. Many of the books and tracts are in circulation here, and the most of the young people of the vicinity are turning their attention to the Doctrines. A Methodist minister lately, in a discourse in this part of his circuit, complained bitterly of the prevalence of the New Church influence, saying that the people are led away with it and that he found it impossible, as heretofore, to get up revivals and to convert the young people to Methodism. He repeated the calumnies of John Wesley against Swedenborg, and attempted in every way to bring down a storm on our feeble efforts in the vicinity. On my first return to the place, after his demonstration, by special request I delivered a lecture, which was numerously attended, on the claims of Swedenborg and the calumnies of Wesley, and which has had a very happy effect; the interest felt in the New Doctrines being thereby sensibly increased. At this place by the well-timed advice. and cordial co-operation of the Sweenys' and their relatives in the vicinity, we have endeavored to make a regular and systematic effort for the dissemination of the New Doctrines. I have generally preached there once a month; and have distributed the tracts to all who would receive them, have lectured on scientific subjects to the young men, and have conversed much on the Doctrines from house to house.

Others also of our brethren have preached here. One discourse was delivered by our brother Thomas Newport, a licentiate in the New Church. Our Bro. J. H. Miller has also lectured three or four times in this place. Mr. Barrett also has recently visited this neighborhood and preached once. These systematic and repeated efforts in this place have had the desired effect, and the result seems to be a permanent interest on the part of many in the Truths of the New Jerusalem. At Lebanon I have lectured and preached fifteen times during the year, to audiences which have varied from 100 to 400, with the exception of several meetings which were failures on account of stormy weather and other accidental causes. For these meetings we have generally obtained the use of the Protestant Methodist Church, a very fine and commodious building. Several of the leading and most intelligent citizens of the village have attended these meetings, and are much pleased with the doctrines. In Lebanon there are two New Church families, and also we have here some new readers and receivers of the Heavenly Doctrines. A society of the New Jerusalem had been formed at Lebanon as early as 1812, and a small library of the works established. But owing to the removal of some of the members and of the decease of others this society has been extinct for near 20 years. The records and papers of the old society also were not to be found, having been taken out of the vicinity since the death of the late Rev. Thos. Newport, by one of his sons. On the 26th of Dec. last a new society was formed, to which several members have since been added, and it now consists of 20 members.

During the year two persons have been baptized in this society, one adult and one infant: the Holy Supper has been administered three times, to about 20 communicants: one marriage has been solemnized: the marriage of Mr. Thomas Newport and Miss Elizabeth Sweeny; and one death has occurred, the death of Mr. William Sweeny—for many years an ardent receiver of the Heavenly Doctrine. This father in the church departed into the spiritual world on the 22nd of Feb. last. His last words were in relation to the New Jerusalem, expressing his own firm reliance on the truth of the New Doctrines, and on the Lord alone as his God and Saviour.

In Lebanon, and also at Sweeny's neighborhood, I think we may safely say that the interest, every way, in the church has quadrupled during the year: this is decidedly encouraging, and shows the importance of persevering and systematic efforts.

I ought also to mention here that Mr. Barrett, in his visit into the country, spent an evening at Lebanon, and preached at the Methodist Protestant Church, to a very intelligent and attentive audience of about one hundred persons.

In several places in the vicinity of Lebanon and Sweeny's, I have frequently preached and lectured during the year. At the Red Lion, a small village, I lectured once on the Trinity in October last, to about twenty persons. No good result seemed to be gained. I have preached twice at Mr. Coffeens, near this. Mr. C. and his wife are an old couple, unable to leave their homestead for religious service of any kind; wherefore at their request I have preached there to them and to such of the neighbors as they invited in. In this manner our doctrines may have reached some who otherwise would never have heard them. At Utica, about three miles from Lebanon, I have lectured twice. First, on Tuesday evening, September 5, and second on Wednesday evening following. At the first lecture there were about thirty persons present, and at the second about one hundred. Here I sold a copy of H. & H., and distributed several dozen of Tracts.

At Fox's Meeting House, about five miles from Lebanon, I preached twice on Sunday, the twentieth of August. There were present about one hundred and fifty each time, and a strong spirit of inquiry seemed to be manifest. Several dozen of the tracts were gladly received; and five of the smaller treatises sold. Here is a meeting house in the midst of a dense population, which is used only once a month; and would be free to us the most of the remaining time; people also resort here who are of an inquiring mind, and are mainly untrammelled.

Mason, about eight miles south of Lebanon, is a village of three or four hundred inhabitants. Here I have lectured four times, to audiences varying from one hundred and fifty to two hundred persons. There is a handsome little chapel here, which is offered to us whenever we want it, excepting the first Sunday of each month. There is here an intelligent and pleasant population. I have presented to them some of the leading doctrines of the Church, have distributed upwards of one hundred tracts and have sold about a dozen of the small treatises, all of which appear to be well received and to be doing good.

At Springboro, a village seven miles North of Lebanon, of about five or six hundred inhabitants, I have lectured twice, once last fall and once this. I had a full house each time, there being present at the first lecture about one hundred, and at the last two hundred, and there is indicated an encouraging state of inquiry in many minds. When last there, I distributed about four dozen tracts, and sold six or eight of the small treatises. There is a very commodious house here which is used only once a month, and is free to us when not in use.

I have lectured during the past summer twice at Rochester, once at Zoar, once at Montgomery, twice at Oakland, four times at Cortsville, and twice at Mechanicsburg. At Oakland the doctrines had never been preached, and I visited the place at the request of Judge Dakin who resides there, and has recently embraced the doctrines. The Judge is a well read and hospitable old gentleman of about fifty-five, who for many years has stood aloof from all participation in the Old Church, and who with his wife seems to have been waiting in hopes of something better. Last winter we sent him Bush's Reasons, &c., which was the first thing he read; and since which time he has been a constant reader of the Doctrines. When I was with him he was much pleased with the system as far as he had seen it. He subscribed for the Magazine, and purchased some of the works. He has in his house at present, several of the leading works of the Church, and cannot fail, I think, in the end to embrace the system fully. My lectures at Oakland were well attended, and I distributed five or six dozen of the tracts. The people of the neighborhood are thoroughly rid of any partiality for the Old Church. They are extensive readers of Davis and many kindred infidel works, and seem quite ready to admit the inspiration of any body who will announce to them, as if from a spiritual sphere, what they already believe. They declared themselves better pleased with the New Jerusalem than with any other form of Christianity. At Cortsville I found a very receptive state. I sold here two copies of H. & H., and a dozen or more of the smaller treatises, and distributed six or seven dozen of the tracts.

At Mechanicsburg, a village fourteen miles east of Urbanna, I sold one copy of the T. C. R., and one copy of the Four Leading Doctrines; also several of the smaller works, besides distributing about three dozen of the tracts. It was in the midst of summer when I was at these places, and the time inconvenient for evening lectures, but still the attendance was good, and a cordial invitation was given me to return in the fall season. I have paid three visits to Richmond, Indiana: one in November, one in January, and one in May last. At the first visit I lectured nine times; at the second, four times, and at the last, three times. The audiences varied from twenty to sixty persons. Richmond is a beautiful place, with a wealthy and intelligent population of four or five thousand. There are here at present five or six New Church families, and in all, about twelve or fourteen receivers of the Doctrines. They hold regular meetings on Sunday for reading the Doctrines and social worship; confined chiefly to the receivers and their families.

At my last visit there, I baptized one adult, and administered the Holy Supper, at the house of our Brother Dr. Hawells, and solemnized the marriage of Mr. Daniel H. Roberts, and Miss Elizabeth P. Austin.

I have visited Milford once, and lectured there to a very attentive audience of three or four hundred. I happened to have with me neither tracts nor books at the time, which I much regretted, inasmuch as there might have been a large number disposed of. At Milford the doctrines had not been preached before, at which I was led to wonder. The Old Church has but a very feeble hold in this place, there being no Church of any bearing but a Methodist Church. There was to be an attempt the week after I was there to form a Presbyterian Church, but I was told by one of that order that only three members had yet presented themselves in the place. The Masonic Hall in a central position, is an excellent place for meeting, and is accessible to us, at least two Sabbaths in the month. I was strongly urged to return and lecture there again, which I promised to do, during the fall. Our Brother, William Tingly and his family, receivers of the Doctrines, reside in the vicinity of Milford. It was by his advice and assistance that the way was opened for me at this place; and he has secured the use of the hall for a course of lectures, whenever they can be delivered. While at this place I fell in with a young man of good talents, a recent graduate of Lane Seminary, and just entering the Presbyterian Ministry, who made the startling acknowledgment that he was entirely unsettled as to the truth of the Presbyterian doctrines, that he had no expectation of preaching them as they had been taught to him, that he had served his time and spent his money to be instructed in doctrines which were now falling away from him, and promising no consolation whatever. He told me that he was reading Swedenborg, but could not understand him; he asked for information on several points—he wished to know what we mean by the term " THE LORD" —whether we teach " that there is no *other* God but the Lord Jesus ?" &c.

Although it often happens that such questions are put, and such a state of mind manifested, yet it is a rare occurrence to find a young man fresh from the Seminary, with the brightness of the polishing wheel still on him, giving such lamentable proof that the silver is tarnished, and the fine gold become dim.

On Sunday, the 18th of June, I preached to the little Society in Springfield; we had a pleasant meeting at the house of our Brother Richards there. This Society numbers about fourteen or fifteen members, and meets regularly on the Sabbath for worship.

On Sunday, September 24, I preached in Dayton; in the forenoon at the Beneficial Hall, where the Society generally meets, to an audience of about twenty: and in the evening by the request of the Universalist minister of the place at his church, to a full house of three to four hundred.

During the two months of March and April, I was occupied preaching at the temple in Cincinnati, and while there I did not attempt to hold evening meetings elsewhere through the week. While there I baptized one infant; solemnized the marriage our Brother Smith, and Miss Jane Ross, and officiated at two funerals.

I have made also one visit during the year to Columbus; and on the 1st day of November last, in that place officiated at the funeral of our worthy and venerable brother in the Church, Josiah Espy.

In all during the year I have delivered about one hundred and twenty discourses; have baptized four persons, have administered the Holy Supper on four occasions, have solemnized three marriages, and have preached seven funeral discourses.

At the time of the Convention in the Spring, I obtained a supply of the works of the Church from our Brother J. H. Williams, and have since been authorized by some of the brethren in the city to distribute the tracts gratuitously. Since then I have distributed about one thousand tracts, five hundred and fifty-two of which were furnished me by Mr. John Murdock, and the rest have been paid for by the brethren in the city. I have also sold about twenty-five dollars worth of the books. Since I have had access to the books and tracts, I have never offered the books without selling, at the very least, one or more of the smaller treatises, and I have never offered the tracts, but that some persons received them gladly. But since I have had the works, my operations have been very much hindered in three ways :—*first*, it has been the summer season, which is by no means a favorable season for operations : *second*, I have had no direct means of conveyance, from place to place, being entirely dependent on our friends to convey me to my appointments : and, *third*, I have been hindered from an actual lack of the necessary funds.

But the fall season has now come, and the winter is at hand which are the seasons to work. In the second place, by the joint contributions of our friends in the city and country, a convenient horse and buggy have been purchased, at an outlay of one hundred dollars, for the use of the mission, thus giving the means of conveyance from place to place without much delay or expense.

And in the third place, it is believed that the funds necessary for the support of the mission will be forth-coming, when the work is properly entered upon. In fact, I have no complaints to offer as to the contributions already made—for in whatever part of the field I have been, where there were receivers of the Doctrines, they have been prompt and liberal in their contributions. But many of my appointments have been where there were no receivers residing, and consequently nothing was expected in the way of funds in such places. I have also had to encounter expenses in moving and arranging my family the past year, which may not require to be encountered again.

My receipts during the year, have been about as follows :
I have received from the 1st N. J. Society in Cincinnati, about
$100 00

From other sources about as follows:

From	John Murdock,	45 00
"	William E. White,	20 00
"	James Sweeny,	25 00
"	Ely Sweeny,	15 00
"	William Sweeny,	7 00
"	Robert Sweeny,	6 00
"	Mrs. Robinson,	5 00
"	William Frost,	10 00
"	Dr. Hawels,	20 00
"	Sidney Smith,	2 00
"	David Espy,	5 00
"	Dr. Murdock,	5 00
"	Horace Wells,	5 00
"	The Gwyns, at Urbanna,	5 00
"	Abel Sherman,	3 00
"	Ogden Ross,	2 00
"	Dayton Society,	5 00
"	Various brethren through Mr. Hough,	25 00
"	Ministerial Land Fund about	15 00

$325 00

Besides this I have had my house rent presented free by our brother David Espy; this is equivalent to about forty dollars. Mr. Espy has also during the summer carried me to the most of my appointments and has thus very materially diminished my expenses. His family have also furnished many articles of daily consumption, equivalent in every way to cash and thus preventing an actual outlay. Our friends also, the Sweenys, have furnished us many of the luxuries and necessaries of life, curtailing thus very sensibly our expenses. From which sources we may estimate an equivalent to forty or fifty dollars : additional to the above amount we have realized, making in all during the year, as follows :

Cash,	.	.	.	.	$325 00
Rent,	.	.	.	.	40 00
Sundries,	.	.	.	.	45 00

$410 00

Hoping sincerely that the mission if continued will be far more use-future than hitherto, I am dear brother,

Truly and affectionately your
Obedient Servant,
J. P. STUART.

20 MILE STAND, *Oct.* 10, 1848.

REPORT OF THE COMMITTEE ON MISSIONS.

(Submitted at the Meeting of the Ohio Association, Oct. 13, 1848.)

NOTHING has come officially before this committee since the meeting of the Association in May. Some missionary labor has been performed by different individuals, but nothing has been done under the supervision of this committee. Wherefore it only remains for your committee to present some suggestions touching the subject of missions in general.

In the first place, we are of opinion that the missionary operations within the bounds of the Association, ought to be under its patronage and direction.

At present it is not known by whom our missionaries are employed, to whom they are responsible, nor how they are to be directed and advised ; either as to their field of labor, their routes, or their operations in general and particular. Nor is it known how much or how little they receive for their labor ; whether they are over-supplied or famished.

Wherefore your committee are of opinion that a specific plan of missions ought to be devised by this body, and that the whole arrangement of missionary operations ought to come under its general supervision, and that missionaries within our limits ought to be employed and directed by the Association.

From the many considerations in favor of this proposition your committee would submit the following :

1. We know of nothing within the power of the Association which is a more important use than this. This body, we believe, is designed as a bond of union, a medium of intelligence, and an organ of active use. These ends refer themselves mainly to the propagation of the Doctrines in every laudable and orderly manner. Moreover it is known that the voice of the living ministry must lead the way in every successful effort in disseminating the Heavenly Doctrines.

2. But if the cause of missions is to be sustained, the work, we think, ought to be equalized and distributed among the receivers of the Heavenly Doctrines, as far as possible in accordance with the conditions of ability and willingness. But if the work requires to be done, and if it demands a co-operation among the receivers of the church, we

know no way the result can be gained so w
of the Association.

While this body was nominally "the We
ties were in the way to a movement of this
For example, the funds in the hands of tha
designed for a more general use than accorc
sionaries laboring in a circumscribed field.
but little money contributed to the Conver
missions were left to isolated individual eff
acting without concert, and without any g
Association, as the name indicates, has a mo
ed boundary; and hence it may properl
missionary operations within definite limit
aside all division of purpose, and apply
work which is before us.

3. Your committee are of opinion that 1
be far more likely to be available to the *Asso*
merely. It is believed that the societies c
receivers would be more likely to mingle
to lay to a helping hand in a systematic mii
the guidance of the Association, than to an
missionary, who should come to their vicin

4. Again, by the measure proposed, the
would be protected from becoming a dt
There is danger of this, as things have been
is not changed, the *necessities* of the missions
measure of the charity; and the charity, the
ry's obligations to personal benefactors, un
idea of giving a just and equitable compe
doing a useful and arduous work; and the
may become as the return of the beggar c
would be thrown into such a votex. Nor
means necessary. Let the work to be do
let the way be marked out, so that funds c
regular channel, and let the missionaries em
supervision;—and it is believed that soo
church within our limits, available for this pa
compacted together in a movement of great

In the second place, your committee wou
in the church ought, in every instance, if po
the works of the Church for sale, and tracts
without this we believe that the labors of
well directed, will, in the end, be in a great m
this,—with the avowal of the living minister, t
prepare the way, accompanied and followec
Church, great good, we believe and devoutl
ble result.

All of which is respectfully submitted,

J. P. S

Dayton, *Ohio, Oct.* 13, 1848.   J. H. N

Lightning Source UK Ltd.
Milton Keynes UK
UKHW02n1253120218
317657UK00008B/1398/P